# In Memory of Lawrence Revsine

We are indeed fortunate to have co-authored this book with Larry. He was passionate about changing the way financial accounting is taught and he was always the driving force behind the book. Larry believed, as we do, that traditional upper level financial reporting textbooks adopt a misguided approach to accounting education. He understood the important role that accounting numbers play in bonus plans and debt contracts, and the incentives this creates for management to "bend" the reported numbers in ways that often fail to reflect the underlying economics of the firm.

So, together we set about writing a financial reporting textbook that explained not only how accounting works and why, but also how the flexibility in generally accepted accounting principles (GAAP) sometimes is used to conceal rather than reveal a company's true performance. This approach, coupled with a relentless stream of financial press stories about accounting shenanigans and fraud, has revitalized accounting education. It has introduced an element of intrigue into this otherwise dry subject, and made accounting fun for faculty to teach and fun for students to learn.

Larry was a master at making accounting come alive in the classroom. He had an uncommon knack for creating a sense of mystery and excitement about seemingly mundane accounting topics. Each class had a clear message that Larry delivered with great energy and enthusiasm. And each class was sprinkled with anecdotes and stories delivered with an element of wit that only Larry could pull off. It was his deep understanding of the subject matter and his dynamic delivery that endeared him to so many Kellogg students over the years. As we both can attest from personal experience, it was a joy to watch the master at work.

As you read this book, listen carefully and you will hear his voice on every page.

*Dan Collins and Bruce Johnson*
*May 2008*

| (in millions) | 6.0 | $22,011.9 |
| --- | --- | --- |
| Sales | | |
| Costs, Expenses and Other | | |
| Materials and production | 001.1 | 5,149.6 |
| Marketing and administrative | 65.4 | 7,155.5 |
| Research and development | 82.9 | 3,848.0 |
| Restructuring costs | | |
| Equity income from | 42.3 | 322.2 |

# FINANCIAL REPORTING AND ANALYSIS

**4**th EDITION

**Lawrence Revsine**
*Late of Northwestern University*

**Daniel W. Collins**
*Henry B. Tippie Research Chair in Accounting*
*Tippie College of Business*
*The University of Iowa*

**W. Bruce Johnson**
*Sidney G. Winter Professor of Accounting*
*Tippie College of Business*
*The University of Iowa*

**H. Fred Mittelstaedt**
*PricewaterhouseCoopers Faculty Fellow*
*Mendoza College of Business*
*University of Notre Dame*

Boston    Burr Ridge, IL    Dubuque, IA    New York    San Francisco    St. Louis
Bangkok    Bogotá    Caracas    Kuala Lumpur    Lisbon    London    Madrid    Mexico City
Milan    Montreal    New Delhi    Santiago    Seoul    Singapore    Sydney    Taipei    Toronto

FINANCIAL REPORTING AND ANALYSIS

Published by McGraw-Hill/Irwin, a business unit of The McGraw-Hill Companies, Inc., 1221 Avenue of the Americas, New York, NY, 10020. Copyright © 2009 by The McGraw-Hill Companies, Inc. All rights reserved. No part of this publication may be reproduced or distributed in any form or by any means, or stored in a database or retrieval system, without the prior written consent of The McGraw-Hill Companies, Inc., including, but not limited to, in any network or other electronic storage or transmission, or broadcast for distance learning.

Some ancillaries, including electronic and print components, may not be available to customers outside the United States.

This book was previously published by Pearson Education, Inc.

This book is printed on acid-free paper.

2 3 4 5 6 7 8 9 0 QPD/QPD 0 9 8

ISBN    978-0-07-352709-3
MHID    0-07-352709-2

Editorial director: *Stewart Mattson*
Executive editor: *Tim Vertovec*
Senior developmental editor: *Christina A. Sanders*
Editorial assistants: *Christina Lane* and *Christa Selig*
Marketing manager: *Scott S. Bishop*
Managing editor: *Lori Koetters*
Lead production supervisor: *Carol A. Bielski*
Lead designer: *Matthew Baldwin*
Lead media project manager: *Cathy L. Tepper*
Cover design: *Laurie Entringer*
Interior design: *Laurie Entringer*
Typeface: *10/13.5 Minion*
Compositor: *Aptara®, Inc.*
Printer: *Quebecor World Dubuque Inc.*

**Library of Congress Cataloging-in-Publication Data**

Financial reporting and analysis/Lawrence Revsine . . . [et al.].—4th ed.
    p.cm.
    Rev. ed. of: Financial reporting and analysis/Lawrence Revsine, Daniel W.
Collins, W. Bruce Johnson. 3rd. ed.
    Includes index.
    ISBN-13: 978-0-07-352709-3 (alk. paper)
    ISBN-10: 0-07-352709-2 (alk. paper)
    1. Financial statements. 2. Financial statements—Case studies. 3. Corporations—
Accounting. I. Revsine, Lawrence. Financial reporting and analysis.
HF5681.B2R398 2009
657'.3—dc22
                                                                    2008015737

# About the Authors

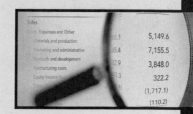

## Lawrence Revsine

*Lawrence Revsine passed away in May 2007. Larry was an incredible leader in the field of accounting education and his contributions to the discipline will be greatly missed.*

Lawrence Revsine joined the Northwestern University faculty in 1971 and served as chair of the Accounting Information and Management Department for eight years. He is the author of books on various financial reporting issues, and leading academic journals have published approximately 50 of his articles.

His academic recognitions included participation in three American Accounting Association Doctoral Consortia. He received both Ford Foundation and Peat Marwick Mitchell Foundation research grants. The American Accounting Association selected him as Distinguished Overseas Lecturer and named him the 1992 Outstanding Educator. The Illinois CPA Society designated Revsine its 1993 Outstanding Educator. Professor Revsine received the Alumni Choice Faculty Award from the 1995 Reunion Class; this award is given to the Kellogg faculty member who has had the greatest impact on their professional and personal lives.

Professor Revsine was a consultant to the American Institute of Certified Public Accountants, the Securities and Exchange Commission, and the Financial Accounting Standards Board and served on the Financial Accounting Standards Advisory Council.

He was a consultant to industry on external reporting issues and regulatory cases and taught extensively in management development and continuing executive education programs in the United States and abroad. Professor Revsine received numerous commendations for teaching excellence, including Teacher of the Year from the Kellogg Graduate Management Association student group and the Sidney J. Levy Teaching Award presented by the Kellogg Dean's Office.

## Daniel W. Collins

*Henry B. Tippie Research Chair in Accounting, Tippie College of Business, The University of Iowa; BBA 1968, Ph.D. 1973, The University of Iowa*

Professor Collins was the recipient of the University of Iowa Board of Regents Award for Faculty Excellence in 2000 and the American Accounting Association (AAA) Outstanding Educator Award in 2001. His research focuses on the role of accounting numbers in equity valuation, earnings management, and the relation between firms' corporate governance mechanisms and cost of equity and debt financing. A prolific writer and frequent contributor to the top academic accounting journals, he has been recognized as one of the top 10 most highly cited authors in the accounting literature over the past 20 years.

Professor Collins has served on the editorial review boards of the *Journal of Accounting Research* and the *Journal of Accounting and Economics.* He has also served as associate editor of

*The Accounting Review* and as director of publications for the AAA. Professor Collins has served on numerous AAA committees including the Financial Accounting Standards Committee and has chaired the Publicantions Committee, the National Program Committee, and the Doctoral Consortium Committee. He also served on the Financial Accounting Standards Advisory Council.

A member of the American Accounting Association and an invited member of Accounting Researchers International Association, Professor Collins is a frequent presenter at research colloquia, conferences, and doctoral consortia. He has also received outstanding teaching awards at both Michigan State University and The University of Iowa.

## W. Bruce Johnson

*Sidney G. Winter Professor of Accounting, Tippie College of Business, The University of Iowa; BS 1970, University of Oregon, MS 1973, Ph.D. 1975, The Ohio State University*

W. Bruce Johnson joined the University of Iowa faculty in 1988 and has served as director of its McGladrey Institute for Accounting Education and Research, accounting group chairman, and associate dean for graduate programs. In the latter position, he was responsible for Iowa's MBA and Executive MBA programs.

Professor Johnson previously held faculty appointments at the University of Wisconsin, Northwestern University, the University of Chicago, and the China European International Business School (CEIBS).

His teaching and research interests include corporate financial reporting, financial analysis, value-driven management systems and investment strategies, executive compensation practices, and forensic accounting. He received the Gilbert P. Maynard Award for Excellence in Accounting Instruction and the Chester A. Phillips Outstanding Professor Award.

A well-respected author, Professor Johnson's articles have appeared in numerous scholarly publications and in academic and professional journals. He has served on the editorial boards of several academic journals and as a litigation consultant on financial reporting matters. Professor Johnson is past president of the Financial Reporting and Accounting Section (FARS) of the American Accounting Association (AAA). He has also served as a research consultant to the Financial Accounting Standards Board and on the Research Advisory, Professional Practice Quality, and Outstanding Educator committees of the AAA. He is a member of the AAA, the Financial Executives International, and Academic Advisory Council for Grant Thornton LLP. He was formerly senior vice president for Equity Strategy at SCI Capital Management, a money management firm.

## H. Fred Mittelstaedt

*PricewaterhouseCoopers Faculty Fellow, Mendoza College of Business, University of Notre Dame; BS 1979, MS 1982, Illinois State University, Ph.D. 1987, University of Illinois*

Fred Mittelstaedt joined the University of Notre Dame faculty in 1992. He has served as the faculty director of the M.S. in Accountancy Program since 2003 and as the Accountancy chairman since 2007. Prior to coming to Notre Dame, he held a faculty appointment at Arizona State University. He worked as an auditor for Price Waterhouse from 1980 to 1981.

Professor Mittelstaedt has taught financial reporting courses to undergraduates, masters in accountancy students, MBAs, and Executive MBAs. While at Notre Dame, he has received the Kaneb Undergraduate Teaching Award and the Arnie Ludwig Executive MBA Outstanding Teacher Award.

His research focuses on financial reporting and retirement benefit issues and has been published in the *Journal of Accounting and Economics, The Accounting Review, Review of Accounting Studies,* the *Journal of Pension Economics and Finance,* and several other accounting and finance journals. He is a reviewer for numerous academic journals and has served on the Editorial Advisory and Review Board for *The Accounting Review.* In 2002, he testified on retiree health benefit issues before the U.S. House of Representatives Committee on Education and the Workforce.

Professor Mittelstaedt is a member of the American Accounting Association and the American Institute of Certified Public Accountants.

# Preface

Consistent with the mandates of the Accounting Education Change Commission (AECC), our objective in writing *Financial Reporting and Analysis* is to change the way the second-level course in financial accounting is taught both to graduate and undergraduate students. Typically this course—often called *intermediate accounting*—focuses on the details of GAAP with little emphasis on understanding the economics of business transactions or how statement readers use the resulting numbers for decision making. Traditional intermediate texts can be encyclopedic in nature and approach, emphasizing the accounting process and the myriad of arcane accounting rules and procedures that comprise GAAP.

In contrast, the goal of our book is to develop a "critical thinking" approach to financial accounting and reporting. We seek to develop students' understanding of the environment in which financial reporting choices are made, what the options are, how these data are used for various types of decisions, and—most important—how to avoid misusing financial statement data. We convey the exciting nature of financial reporting in two stages. First, we provide a framework for understanding management's accounting choices and how the accounting affects reported financial numbers. Business contracts—such as loan agreements and management compensation agreements—are usually linked to accounting numbers. We show how this often creates incentives for managers to exploit the flexibility in GAAP to "manage" reported accounting numbers to benefit themselves at stakeholders' expense. Second, we use real-world financial reports and events to illustrate vividly how GAAP alternatives and subjective accounting estimates give managers discretion in the timing of earnings and in reporting the components of financial position.

The approach adopted in this book integrates the perspectives of accounting, corporate finance, economics, and critical analysis to help students grasp how business transactions are reported and understand their decision implications. In this approach, we cover all of the core topics of intermediate accounting by first describing the business transactions that affect various accounts, the technical details of GAAP, how these rules are applied in practice, and what the financial statements look like. Then we go a step further and ask these questions: What do the reported numbers mean? Does the accounting process yield numbers that accurately reflect the company's underlying economic situation? If not, what can statement users do to overcome this limitation to make more informed decisions?

Our book is aimed not only at those charged with the responsibility for preparing financial statements but also those who will use financial statements for making decisions. Our definition of "users" is broad and includes lenders, equity analysts, investment bankers, boards of directors, and others charged with monitoring corporate performance and the behavior of management. As such, it includes auditors who establish audit scope and conduct analytical review procedures to spot problem areas in external financial statements. *Statement on Auditing Standards (SAS) 99*, "Consideration of Fraud in Financial Statement Audit," stresses that auditors must act as "financial detectives" to uncover financial reporting irregularities. It further states that "the auditor should conduct the engagement with a mind-set that recognizes the possibility that a material misstatement due to fraud could be present . . ." (p. 10). To do this effectively requires an understanding of managers' incentives, how the flexibility of GAAP can sometimes be exploited to conceal rather than reveal financial truth, and the potential danger signals that should be investigated. Our intent is to help readers learn how to perform better audits, improve cash flow forecasts, undertake realistic valuations, conduct better comparative analyses, and make more informed judgments about management performance.

*Financial Reporting and Analysis* provides instructors a teaching/learning approach for achieving many of the goals stressed by the AECC. Specifically, our book is designed to instill capacities for (1) thinking in an abstract, logical manner, (2) solving unstructured problems, (3) understanding the determining forces behind management's accounting choices, and (4) encouraging an integrated, cross-disciplinary view of financial reporting. Text discussions were written—and exercises, problems, and cases were carefully chosen—to help achieve these objectives. The book achieves these AECC goals without sacrificing technical underpinnings. Throughout we explain in detail where the numbers come from, what measurement rules are used, and how they are entered into the accounting records. We have strived to provide a comprehensive user-oriented focus while helping students build a strong technical foundation.

## Key Changes from the Third Edition

The first three editions of our book have been widely adopted in accounting departments of business schools throughout the United States, Canada, Europe, and the Pacific Rim. The book has been used successfully at both the graduate and undergraduate levels as well as in investment banking, commercial lending, and other corporate training programs. Many of our colleagues who used the first three editions have provided us valuable feedback. Based on their input, we have made a number of changes in this edition of the book to achieve more effectively the objectives previously outlined. Key changes include the following:

- Expanded coverage of international issues throughout the text.
- Updated end-of-chapter material.
- Real world companies and events "ripped from the headlines."
- Comprehensive coverage of current and pending GAAP rule changes.

### Chapter Highlights

#### Chapter 1: The Economic and Institutional Setting for Financial Reporting

- Expanded coverage of the PCAOB's central roles.
- New discussion of the GAAP hierarchy.
- Timely coverage of U.S. GAAP and IFRS convergence.

#### Chapter 2: Accrual Accounting and Income Determination

- The material in the Reporting Accounting Changes section has been rewritten to highlight the reporting requirements for the retrospective approach to reporting changes in accounting principles under *SFAS No. 154*.
- New and updated examples from real company reports.
- New end-of-chapter problem material on accounting changes.

#### Chapter 3: Additional Topics in Income Determination

- New material on a CFO survey citing important financial reporting benchmarks.
- New illustration and discussion of accounting restatement using Apple Computer Inc.
- New end-of-chapter material on restatements.

### Chapter 4: Structure of the Balance Sheet and Statement of Cash Flows

- Updated exhibits on balance sheet disclosures.
- Updated coverage within the section International Difference in Balance Sheet Presentation, now featuring Burberry PLC.
- Updated exhibits on footnotes for accounting policies, subsequent events, and related party transactions.
- New exhibits on cash flow statement presentation.
- New end-of-chapter material on financial reporting research—related party matters and balance sheet presentation for an international (British) company.

### Chapter 5: Essentials of Financial Statement Analysis

- Improved organization of material coupled with inclusion of cash flow analysis (formerly in Chapter 7).
- Comprehensive illustration based on Whole Foods Market woven throughout.
- New end-of-chapter material on financial ratio interpretation and cash flow analysis.

### Chapter 6: The Role of Financial Information in Valuation and Credit Risk Assessment

- New section on Fair Value Accounting and *SFAS No. 157*.
- Expanded coverage of credit risk assessment from the perspective of credit-rating agencies.
- New end-of-chapter material on financial ratios and credit ratings.

### Chapter 7: The Role of Financial Information in Contracting

- Expanded discussion of accounting-based debt covenants including how mandated accounting changes can sometimes trigger covenant violation.
- Incorporation of recent trends in executive compensation practices.
- New section Catering to Wall Street added.
- New problem and case material that includes EVA-based compensation at Whole Foods Market.

### Chapter 8: Receivables

- Updated material on relevant International Financial Reporting Standards (IFRS).
- Expanded coverage of the securitization process and the role of guarantors and rating agencies.
- New section Securitization and the Subprime Mess of 2007 (subprime loans) including News Clip "Market Shock: AAA Rating May Be Junk."
- New section on the fair value option permitted under *SFAS No. 159*.
- Updated and expanded end-of-chapter material.

### Chapter 9: Inventories

- Additional coverage of mitigating the absorption costing effect.
- New section on Vendor Allowances.
- Coverage added within the FIFO, LIFO, and Inventory Holding Gains section.
- Updated and expanded end-of-chapter material.

### Chapter 10: Long-Lived Assets and Depreciation

- New section on computing avoidable interest.
- Updates to the section Intangibles Accounting under U.S. GAAP and IFRS: Similarities and Differences—FASB definition of fair value.

- New material on IFRS intangibles.
- New material on *SFAS No. 121*.
- Updated data on depreciation choices.
- Updated coverage within the International Perspective section on *IAS No. 16*.
- New section on investment property—difference between GAAP and IFRS.
- New end-of-chapter material on financial statement effects of capitalized interest, capitalizing versus expensing of R&D, and financial statement effects of depreciation policy changes.

### Chapter 11: Financial Instruments as Liabilities

- New section on financial instruments with characteristics of both debt and equity.
- New section on the Fair Value Option permitted under *SFAS No. 159*.
- New problem and case material, including Groupe Casino's perpetual debt.

### Chapter 12: Financial Reporting for Leases

- Updated lessee example in chapter and appendix now features Safeway.
- Updated comparison of operating and capital lease obligations by industry.
- New material on "rent holidays."
- Expanded coverage of *FIN No. 46* related to synthetic leasing.
- New section on reconsidering GAAP for leases.
- Updated and expanded end-of-chapter material.

### Chapter 13: Income Tax Reporting

- New learning objective covers *FIN No. 48* disclosures on uncertain tax positions.
- Updated material on tax footnote disclosures.
- New section on Measurement and Reporting of Uncertain Tax Positions—FASB *FIN No. 48* (features Merck as example).
- New end-of-chapter material on uncertain tax positions (*FIN No. 48*).

### Chapter 14: Pensions and Postretirement Benefits

- Completely new chapter and end-of-chapter materials that reflect *SFAS No. 158*.
- Expanded coverage of pension contract types.
- New discussion of the Pension Protection Act of 2006.
- New GE pension and postretirement benefit examples for accounting under *SFAS No. 158*.
- New discussion of pension-related accumulated other comprehensive income items and deferred income taxes.
- Revised sections on Extracting Additional Analytic Insights from footnote disclosures and OPEB liability disclosures.
- Expanded discussion of IFRS on pensions and postretirement benefit plans.

### Chapter 15: Financial Reporting for Owners' Equity

- Updated coverage of stock option accounting and political debates surrounding *SFAS No. 123R*.
- New section on the Options Backdating Scandal.
- Expanded problem and case material including how *SFAS No. 150* tripped up X-Rite.

### Chapter 16: Intercorporate Equity Investments

- New coverage of fair value option for equity investments under *SFAS No. 159.*
- New discussion of the acquisition method for reporting business combinations under *SFAS No. 141R.*
- New discussion of reporting noncontrolling interests under *SFAS No. 160.*
- New appendix describing accounting requirements for held-to-maturity debt investments under *SFAS No. 115.*
- Expanded EOC material on using the fair value option for equity investments and the acquisition method of accounting for business combinations, and reporting of noncontrolling interests.

### Chapter 17: Statement of Cash Flows

- Updated exhibits and discussion of direct method of presenting the operating cash flow section.
- Updated discussion of complexities in reconciling changes in working capital accounts on the balance sheet with accruals reported on the cash flows statement.
- New section on Ways Operating Cash Flows Can Be Distorted or Manipulated.
- New end-of-chapter material on reconciling balance sheet and cash flow statements information and ways operating cash flows can be distorted.

### Chapter 18: Overview of International Financial Reporting Differences and Inflation

- Updated chapter introduction on cross-border transactions.
- Expanded discussion of IASB activities and convergence with those of the FASB.
- New discussion of SEC regulations for foreign firms including the elimination of the reconciliation requirement for foreign registrants using IFRS as issued by the IASB.
- Updated discussions of specific IFRS and related end-of-chapter materials for revisions to the standards.
- Fresh discussion of inflation accounting.

## Acknowledgments

Colleagues at Iowa, Northwestern, and Notre Dame as well other universities have served as sounding boards on a wide range of issues over the past years, shared insights, and provided many helpful comments. Their input helped us improve this book. In particular we thank: Jim Boatsman, Arizona State University; Tom Frecka, University of Notre Dame; Bill Nichols, University of Notre Dame; Cristi Gleason, University of Iowa; Ryan Wilson, University of Iowa; Tom Linsmeier, Michigan State University and the Financial Accounting Standards Board; Robert Lipe, University of Oklahoma; Don Nichols, Texas Christian University; Paul Zarowin, New York University; and Stephen Zeff, Rice University.

We are grateful to many users of prior editions of our book and reviewers of this edition's manuscript whose constructive comments and suggestions have contributed to an improved and expanded fourth edition. In particular, we wish to thank the following for their valuable input: Brandt Allen, University of Virginia; Mark P. Bauman, University of Illinois–Chicago; Frank J. Beil, University of Minnesota; Brent Bertrand, University of Toronto–St. George; Earl R. Brownlee, University of Virginia; Stephen J. Bukowy, University of North Carolina-Pembroke; David M. Cottrell, Brigham Young University-Provo; Marthanne Edwards, University of Minnesota;

David Fricke, University of North Carolina at Pembroke; Mike Gallagher, Defiance College; Pat Griffin, Lewis University; Paul Griffin, University of California–Davis; Bill Hamby, Lincoln Memorial University; Robert Hartman, University of Iowa; Rachel Hayes, University of Utah; Ole-Kristian Hope, University of Toronto; Elizabeth Keating, Harvard University; Andrew J. Leone, Penn State University; Brian Leventhal, University of Illinois–Chicago; Kin Lo, University of British Columbia; Troy Luh, Webster University; Robert Magee, Northwestern University; Mike McLain, Hampton University; Syed Moiz, University of Wisconsin–Platteville; Milo Peck, Fairfield University; Eric Press, Temple University; Kurt Schulzke, Kennesaw State University; Praveen Sinha, Chapman University; Doug Smith, Samford University; Thomas L. Stober, University of Notre Dame; Ron Stunda, Birmingham Southern College; Gary Taylor, University of Alabama; Walter Teets, Gonzaga University; John Twombley, Illinois Institute of Technology; Suneel Udpa, University of California–Berkeley; Flora Zhou, Chapman University.

A special thanks to Steve Willits, Bucknell University; John Phillips, University of Connecticut; Ryan Wilson, University of Iowa; James Boatsman, Arizona State University, who helped with problem development for the fourth edition, as well as to our graduate assistants Ciao-Wei (Theo) Chen, University of Iowa, and Courtney Bishop, Notre Dame University, and supplement authors Steve Willits, Bucknell University, and Randy Johnston, Michigan State University, who prepared the Test Bank, Charles Fazzi, St. Vincent College, who prepared the Instructor's Resource Manual, L. Kevin McNelis, New Mexico State University, who prepared the PowerPoint Presentations, and David Baglia, Grove City College for preparation of the online quizzes.

We gratefully acknowledge the McGraw-Hill/Irwin editorial team for their encouragement and support throughout the development of the fourth edition of this book: Stewart Mattson, Editorial Director; Tim Vertovec, Executive Editor; Christina Sanders, Sr. Developmental Editor; Lori Koetters, Managing Editor; Christina Lane, Editorial Assistant; Christa Selig, Editorial Assistant; Scott Bishop, Marketing Manager; Matthew Baldwin, Lead Designer; Carol Bielski, Lead Production Supervisor; and Cathy Tepper, Lead Media Project Manager.

Our goal in writing this book was to improve the way financial reporting is taught and mastered. We would appreciate receiving your comments and suggestions.

*—Daniel W. Collins*

*—W. Bruce Johnson*

*—H. Fred Mittelstaedt*

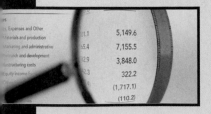

# Walkthrough

## Chapter Objectives

Each chapter opens with a brief introduction and summary of learning objectives to set the stage for the goal of each chapter and prepare students for the key concepts and practices.

## Boxed Readings

**Sidebar margin boxes** call out key concepts in each chapter and provide additional information to reinforce concepts.

---

**Structure of the Balance Sheet | 4
and Statement of Cash Flows**

The **balance sheet**—sometimes called the *statement of financial position*—contains a summation of the assets owned by the firm, the liabilities incurred to finance these assets, and the shareholders' equity representing the amount of financing provided by owners at a specific date.

The Financial Accounting Standards Board (FASB) defines the three basic elements of the balance sheet:[1]

1. **Assets:** Probable future economic benefits obtained or controlled by an entity as a result of past transactions or events.
2. **Liabilities:** Probable future sacrifices of economic benefits arising from an entity's *present* obligations to transfer assets or provide services to other entities in the *future* as a result of *past* transactions or events.
3. **Equity:** The residual interest in an entity's assets that remains after deducting its liabilities. For a corporate form of organization, this interest is referred to as *shareholders'* or *stockholders' equity.*

The balance sheet tells us how management has invested the firm's money and where the money came from. It provides information for assessing rates of return, capital structure, liquidity, solvency, and financial flexibility of an enterprise.

Two **rate of return** measures for evaluating operating efficiency and profitability of an enterprise are return on assets (ROA) and return on common equity (ROCE). (The precise calculation of these two performance measures is detailed in Chapter 5.) By comparing ROA to ROCE, statement users can see whether debt financing is being used to enhance the return earned by shareholders.

The balance sheet provides critical information for understanding an entity's **capital structure**, which refers to how much of an entity's assets are financed from debt versus equity sources. An important decision in corporate finance is determining the proper mix of debt and equity financing. Management must weigh the benefits of using debt financing (with tax-deductible interest) against the dangers of becoming overleveraged

**LEARNING OBJECTIVES**

After studying this chapter, you will understand:

1. How the various asset, liability, and stockholders' equity accounts on a typical corporate balance sheet are measured and classified.
2. How to use balance sheet information to understand key differences in the nature of firms' operations and how those operations are financed.
3. Differences in balance sheet terminology and presentation format in countries outside the United States.
4. The information provided in footnotes on significant accounting policies, subsequent events, and related party transactions.
5. How successive balance sheets and the income statement can be used to determine cash inflows and outflows for a period.
6. How information provided in the cash flow statement can be used to explain changes in noncash accounts on the balance sheet.
7. The distinction between operating, investing, and financing sources and uses of cash.
8. How changes in current asset and current liability accounts can be used to adjust accrual earnings to obtain

---

*Revenue Recognition Prior to Sale* **131**

**Market Price (Production) Method** There is another way for measuring income in the previous example. This alternative recognizes that well-organized markets exist for most agricultural and many mining commodities. In addition, the quantities offered for sale by any individual producer are usually very small in relation to the total size of the market. Producers face an established price for as many units as they choose to sell. These factors mean that a readily determinable market price at which output *could be sold* is continuously available. In this view, revenue recognition Condition 2 ("measurability") is satisfied prior to the actual sale of actively traded commodities.

Because revenue recognition Condition 1 ("critical event") occurs at harvest, both conditions necessary to recognize revenue are satisfied as soon as the crop is safely out of the field (that is, at the point of production or harvest). Thus, farming income on all 110,000 bushels is recognized under this approach on September 30 (when grain is harvested):

The International Accounting Standards Board (IASB) requires agricultural produce harvested by an enterprise to be measured at its fair value at time of harvest less estimated cost to transport the grain to the local elevator. The difference is referred to as **net realizable value.** Any gain or loss arising from initial recognition of harvested assets and from the change in fair value less estimated transportation costs of harvested assets are to be included in net profit or loss for the period in which it arises. See "Agriculture," *IAS 41* (London: International Accounting Standards Board [IASB], 2002).

**2008 Income Statement**
*Market price (production) method*

---

*Why Financial Statements Are Important* **5**

### NEWS CLIP

**ACCOUNTING'S PERFECT STORM**

WorldCom's revelation in June 2002 that it improperly hid $3.8 billion in expenses during the previous five quarters, or longer, set a low-water mark in a tide of accounting scandals among many firms. One of every 10 companies listed on the stock exchanges (or 845 companies in total) found flaws in past financial statements and restated earnings between 1997 and June 2002. Investors in those companies lost more than $100 billion when the restatements were announced. By comparison, only three companies restated earnings in 1981.

According to some observers, a confluence of events during the late 1990s created a climate in which accounting fraud wasn't just possible but was likely! This was accounting's perfect storm: the conjunction of unprecedented economic growth with inordinate incentive compensation, an extremely aggressive management culture, investors preoccupied with quarterly profits, and lax auditors. At companies that didn't make the Wall Street earnings number by even as little as a penny, the stock price tanked and put top management jobs at risk. Individually, some of these forces may have been good news. But when they all came together, it was a disaster waiting to happen.

Congress responded to the almost daily onslaught of accounting scandals by passing the **Sarbanes-Oxley Act** (SOX) in late July 2002. This legislation was hailed as the most groundbreaking corporate reform since the 1934 Securities Act that, among other things, had established the Securities and Exchange Commission. Key provisions of SOX are intended to

- Requiring the CEO and CFO to certify in writing that the numbers in their company's financial reports are correct. Executives face potential civil charges of fraud or criminal charges of lying to the government if their company's numbers turn out to be bogus.
- Requiring each annual report of a public company to include a report by management on the company's internal control over financial reporting. Among other things, this report must disclose any material internal control weaknesses (i.e., deficiencies that result in more than a remote likelihood that a material accounting misstatement will not be prevented or detected).
- Banning outside auditors from providing certain nonaudit services—bookkeeping, financial system work, appraisals, actuarial work, internal audits, management and human resource consulting, investment-advisory work, and the audit client's other advocacy-related services—to their audit clients so that independence is not compromised. Fees paid to auditors for services must now be disclosed in the client's annual report.
- Requiring public companies to disclose whether the audit committee—comprising outside directors and charged with oversight of the annual audit—has a financial expert and if not, why not. Companies must also now reveal their off-balance-sheet arrangements (see Chapter 11) and reconcile "pro forma" earnings (see Chapter 5) with the audited earnings number.

In the words of one observer, "Our free market system does not depend on executives being saintly or altruistic. But markets

---

**News Clip boxes** provide engaging news articles that capture real world financial reporting issues and controversies.

---

**Recap boxes** provide students a summary of each section, reminding them of the key points of what they just covered in small doses to reinforce what they just learned.

To be categorized as extraordinary and to appear below the Income from continuing operations line, an item must be unusual in nature *and* occur infrequently. Special or unusual items that do not meet both criteria, but are considered material, must be disclosed separately as part of pre-tax income from continuing operations.           RECAP

# Icons

Special "Getting Behind the Numbers" icons appear throughout the text to highlight and link discussions in chapters to the analysis, valuation, and contracting framework. Icons in the end-of-chapter materials signify a variety of exercises or direct students to the text Web site for materials such as Excel Templates.

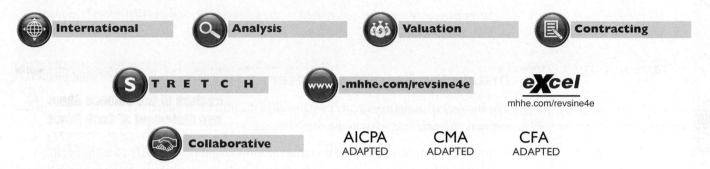

# End-of-Chapter Elements

The text provides a variety of end-of-chapter materials to reinforce concepts.

**Summary**

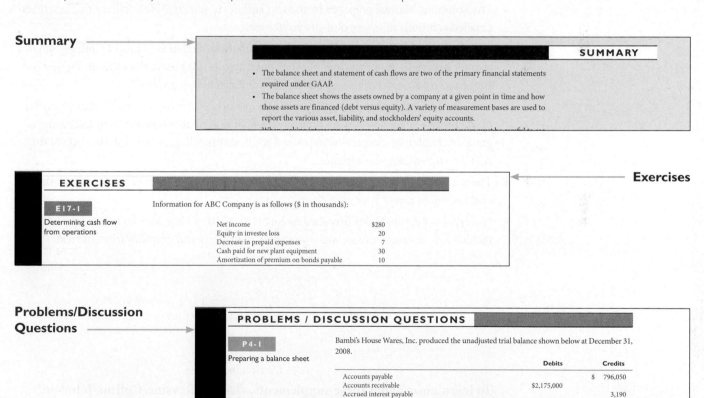

**SUMMARY**

- The balance sheet and statement of cash flows are two of the primary financial statements required under GAAP.
- The balance sheet shows the assets owned by a company at a given point in time and how those assets are financed (debt versus equity). A variety of measurement bases are used to report the various asset, liability, and stockholders' equity accounts.

**Exercises**

**EXERCISES**

**E17-1**

Determining cash flow from operations

Information for ABC Company is as follows ($ in thousands):

| | |
|---|---|
| Net income | $280 |
| Equity in investee loss | 20 |
| Decrease in prepaid expenses | 7 |
| Cash paid for new plant equipment | 30 |
| Amortization of premium on bonds payable | 10 |

**Problems/Discussion Questions**

**PROBLEMS / DISCUSSION QUESTIONS**

**P4-1**

Preparing a balance sheet

Bambi's House Wares, Inc. produced the unadjusted trial balance shown below at December 31, 2008.

| | Debits | Credits |
|---|---|---|
| Accounts payable | | $ 796,050 |
| Accounts receivable | $2,175,000 | |
| Accrued interest payable | | 3,190 |

**Cases**

**CASES**

Robinson Company's statement of financial position on January 1, 2008, follows:

**Statement of Financial Position**
**January 1, 2008**

**C18-1**

Robinson Company: Making general price level and current cost adjustments

| Assets | | Equities |
|---|---|---|
| Cash | $ 5,000 | |
| Inventory | 8,000 | |
| Fixed asset—cost | $10,000 | |

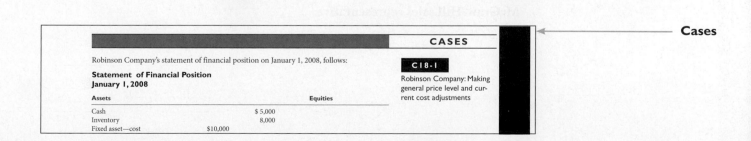

## Student Center

The text Online Learning Center at www.mhhe.com/revsine4e contains a variety of student study materials including:

Online interactive quizzes written by David Baglia of Grove City College that include multiple-choice questions so students can quiz themselves. Grading occurs on the spot!

Spreadsheet transparencies prepared by the authors are templates that provide students text data in Excel format.

## Instructor Resource Center

The Instructor's Resource Center contains all of the instructor materials for your course in one convenient location at www.mhhe.com/revsine4e.

- Additional problem and case material for most chapters is provided for Instructors in PDF form. This material is available to provide alternative questions to those appearing in the text. Solutions for these additional questions are provided in the text solutions manual.

- The Solutions Manual prepared by the text authors is an extensive ancillary that provides detailed solutions for every end-of-chapter assignment.

- The Instructor's Resource Manual written by Charles Fazzi of St. Vincent College contains chapter overviews, outlines, and questions and answers. It also includes teaching tips and suggested readings to enhance your lectures and discussion groups.

- The new Test Bank prepared by Steve Willits of Bucknell University and Randy Johnston of Michigan State University includes a variety of examination questions to test students' grasp of chapter-by-chapter concepts and applications. All questions are also tagged for AACSB and AICPA accreditation.

- The EZ Test Computerized Test Bank is the computerized version of the Test Bank that enables you to create your own exams.

- Powerpoint Lecture Slides prepared by Kevin McNelis of New Mexico State University include key lecture points as well as a variety of exhibits and graphics from the text.

**To learn more about these supplements, visit the Revsine/Collins/Johnson/ Mittelstaedt text Web site at www.mhhe.com/revsine4e or contact your McGraw-Hill sales representative.**

# Brief Contents

# Contents

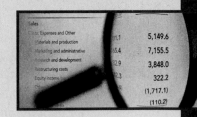

# The Economic and Institutional Setting for Financial Reporting | 1

*"No one ever said accounting was an exact science."*

I n late June 2002, WorldCom stunned investors by announcing that it intended to restate its financial statements for 2001 and the first quarter of 2002.[1] According to the company's press release, an internal audit of capital expenditures had uncovered $3.8 billion in improper transfers from line cost expense to the balance sheet. Without those transfers, the company would have reported a loss for 2001 and the first quarter of 2002. The company's chief financial officer was fired, and its controller resigned. Its board of directors formed a special committee to look further into the matter. Trading in the company's stock was immediately halted on the exchange. When trading resumed a few days later, the stock was worth only 6 cents per share, having lost more than 90% of its value.

To understand what happened at WorldCom and why financial statements are so very important to investors, let's step back in time to May 2002.

## WorldCom in May 2002

According to a report on the company from a highly regarded Wall Street analyst, World-Com is doing surprisingly well despite tough times throughout the industry. The company is a global leader in the telecommunications industry, providing a complete package of communications services (voice, data, and Internet) to businesses and consumers. WorldCom grew very fast—an average of 58% each year from 1996 through 2000—as a result of a robust economy and a nearly insatiable demand for wireless communications and high-speed Internet access. Then, in March 2001, the dot-com bubble burst, and Internet spending came to a screeching halt. Telecommunications companies such as WorldCom suddenly faced excess capacity and shrinking demand for their services.

Despite the industry downturn, WorldCom's 2002 first quarter results are quite robust: sales of $8,120 million and pretax profits of $240 million. That's a 16% decline in sales

## LEARNING OBJECTIVES

**After studying this chapter, you will understand:**

1. Why financial statements are valuable sources of information about companies, their current health, and their prospects for the future.

2. How investors, creditors, securities analysts, and auditors use financial statements.

3. How accounting rules are established, and why management can shape the financial information communicated to outsiders and still be within those rules.

4. How the demand for financial information comes from its ability to improve decision making and monitor managers' activities.

5. How the supply of financial information is influenced by the costs of producing and disseminating it and by the benefits it provides.

*Chapter*

---

[1] This publication is designed to provide accurate and authoritative information in regard to the subject matter. It is sold with the understanding that the publishers and the authors are not engaged in rendering legal, accounting, investment, or other professional services. If legal advice or other expert assistance is required, the services of a competent professional person should be sought.

and a 40% decline in profits, but other firms in the industry, including giants such as AT&T, are reporting even steeper sales and earnings decreases. WorldCom shares look incredibly cheap at the current price of $2 per share. As the stock analyst points out, "The company has $2.3 billion in cash, which translates into a $20.50 book value per share. And you have to pay only $2 a share for this gem! You cannot find a more attractive investment opportunity in the market."

The analyst's enthusiasm for WorldCom makes you think about investing in the company. After all, WorldCom still dominates its segment of the telecommunications industry, and it continues to report solid sales and profits. Perhaps other investors have overreacted to the slump in wireless and Internet spending by penalizing WorldCom's stock too much. If so, now may be the ideal time to buy.

A closer look at WorldCom's financial statements confirms what the analyst is saying. Sales and earnings outpace the competition by a wide margin. Operating cash flows are positive and exceed the cash being spent for capacity expansion, and the balance sheet remains healthy. Overall, the company seems to be on a solid footing.

But what's this? An article in this morning's newspaper raises a new concern. The article says that WorldCom's "line costs," the rent WorldCom pays other companies for the use of their telecommunications networks, are holding steady at about 42% of sales. That's odd because line costs as a percentage of sales are rising at AT&T and other companies in the industry. WorldCom decided several years ago to lease large amounts of network capacity instead of building its own global communications network. These leases call for fixed rental payments each month without regard to message volume ("traffic"). This means that WorldCom must still pay the same amount of rent even though its customers are not sending much traffic through the network these days. What seems odd to the news reporter is that the same rental payment each month combined with lower traffic revenue should produce an increase in line costs as a percent of sales. Higher line costs per dollar of revenue should translate into lower profits. That appears to be what's happening at other companies in the industry, but at WorldCom, line costs haven't increased. Perhaps WorldCom is particularly adept at managing this aspect of its business.

You call your broker, who confirms that WorldCom's stock is available at $1.75 per share in early trading. Should you take advantage of this investment opportunity and buy 10,000 shares? Should you avoid the stock because WorldCom's income statement may contain a line cost accounting torpedo that could potentially sink the share price? Should you take a closer look at company fundamentals—traffic volume, line costs, and other business aspects—before deciding whether to buy or avoid WorldCom shares? The unusual trend in line costs could indicate that WorldCom is successfully managing its excess capacity problems during a period of slack demand, or it could be a cautionary yellow flag warning of problems at the company.

What do you do?

## WHY FINANCIAL STATEMENTS ARE IMPORTANT

This dilemma illustrates a fundamental point: Without adequate information, investors cannot properly judge the opportunities and risks of investment alternatives. To make informed decisions, investors use information about the economy, various industries, specific companies, and the products or services those companies sell. Complete information provided by reliable sources enhances the probability that the best decisions will be made. Of course, only later will you be able to tell whether your investment decision was a good one. What we can tell you now is that *if you want to know more about a company, its past performance, current health, and prospects for the future, the best source of information is the company's own financial statements.*

Why? Because the economic events and activities that affect a company and that can be translated into accounting numbers are reflected in the company's financial statements. Some financial statements provide a picture of the company at a moment in time; others describe changes that took place over a period of time. Both provide a basis for *evaluating* what happened in the past and for *projecting* what might occur in the future. For example, what is the annual rate of sales growth? Are accounts receivable increasing at an even greater rate than sales? How do sales and receivable growth rates compare to those of competitors? Are expenses holding steady? What rates of growth can be expected next year? These trends and relationships provide insights into a company's economic opportunities and risks including growth and market acceptance, costs, productivity, profitability, and liquidity. Consequently, *a company's financial statements can be used for various purposes:*

- *As an analytical tool.*
- *As a management report card.*
- *As an early warning signal.*
- *As a basis for prediction.*
- *As a measure of accountability.*

As our prospective WorldCom stockholder knows, financial statements contain information that investors need to know to decide whether to invest in the company. Others need financial statement information to decide whether to extend credit, negotiate contract terms, or do business with the company. Financial statements serve a crucial role in allocating capital to the most productive and deserving firms. Doing so promotes the efficient use of resources, encourages innovation, and provides a liquid market for buying and selling securities and for obtaining and granting credit.

However, published financial statements do not always contain the most up-to-date information about a company's changing economic fortunes. To ensure that important financial news reaches interested parties as soon as possible, companies send out press releases or hold meetings with analysts. Press releases typically announce things such as contract awards, new product introductions, capital spending plans, or anticipated acquisitions or divestitures.

Although not as timely as press releases, periodic financial statements do provide an economic history that is comprehensive and quantitative, and therefore can be used to gauge company performance. *For this reason, financial statements are indispensable for developing an accurate profile of ongoing performance and prospects.* Financial reports also help in assessing the company's viability as changes occur in input and output markets, in production technologies, among competitors, or in general economic conditions.

WorldCom stockholders learned an even more important lesson: Financial statements sometimes conceal more than they reveal.

## Untangling the Web at WorldCom

In late May 2002, Cynthia Cooper, the vice president of internal audit for WorldCom, and two of her employees discovered a number of questionable accounting entries made during 2001 and the first quarter of 2002. To Cooper's dismay, she realized that WorldCom had probably shifted $3.8 billion of line cost expense from the income statement to the balance sheet, a deceptive practice that made the company look far more profitable than it actually was. In early June, she and a coworker contacted a member of the audit committee of the company's board of directors and discussed the line cost transfers. The audit committee then launched its own investigation. By late June, following a report by the audit committee, WorldCom's board decided to restate the company's financial statements and to terminate the employment of two

## Figure 1.1

WORLDCOM'S
DISAPPEARING PROFITS

WorldCom transferred a total
of $3.8 billion in line cost ex-
penses from the income statement to the balance sheet.
This chart shows the company's profits (in millions) by
quarter as reported originally
and as later restated.

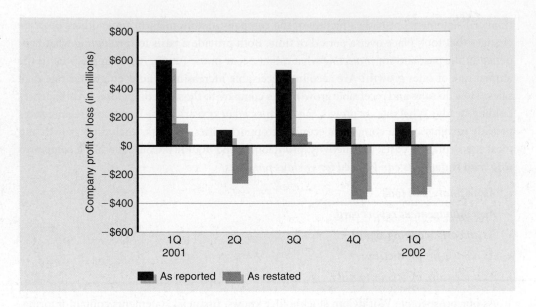

top executives. See Figure 1.1 for the way the company's profit picture for 2001 and early 2002
changed after restating the reported numbers.

The accounting rule that WorldCom violated is easy to understand. It says that when expenditures (think "money spent") provide a future benefit to the company, then and only then can the
expenditures be recorded as balance sheet assets (Chapters 2 and 10 provide the details). This
means that if the company spends a dollar today buying equipment that will be used for the next
five years (the "future benefit"), the dollar spent should be shown as a balance sheet asset. But what
if the dollar spent doesn't buy a *future* benefit? Then it cannot be shown as a balance sheet asset but
instead must be shown on the income statement as a current period expense. That's the rule!

What did this accounting rule mean for the money WorldCom spent on line costs? Recall
that these line costs were just the monthly rent WorldCom paid to other companies for the use
of their communications networks and systems. Because the rent had to be paid each month,
the money WorldCom spent wasn't buying a *future* benefit. So, all line costs should have been
shown on the income statement as a current expense. Instead, WorldCom improperly "transferred" $3.8 billion of these costs from the income statement back to the balance sheet where
they were shown as an asset. This transfer violated the accounting rule and allowed WorldCom
to appear more profitable than was actually the case. The improper transfer also inflated
WorldCom's operating cash flows.

Over the next few weeks, the situation at WorldCom grew far worse:

- Shareholder class action lawsuits were filed against the company and its management.
- The Securities and Exchange Commission (SEC) sued the company for accounting fraud
  and launched its own investigation.
- Five former company executives were indicted on criminal charges, and four of them
  pleaded guilty.
- The company defaulted on a $4.25 billion credit line and was negotiating new payment
  terms with more than 30 banks.
- In mid-July 2002, WorldCom filed for bankruptcy. The company was saddled with more
  than $40 billion in debt and had less than $10 billion in assets that could be readily
  converted into cash.
- In August, the company acknowledged more than $7 billion in accounting errors over the
  previous several years.

# NEWS CLIP

## ACCOUNTING'S PERFECT STORM

WorldCom's revelation in June 2002 that it improperly hid $3.8 billion in expenses during the previous five quarters, or longer, set a low-water mark in a tide of accounting scandals among many firms. One of every 10 companies listed on the stock exchanges (or 845 companies in total) found flaws in past financial statements and restated earnings between 1997 and June 2002. Investors in those companies lost more than $100 billion when the restatements were announced. By comparison, only three companies restated earnings in 1981.

According to some observers, a confluence of events during the late 1990s created a climate in which accounting fraud wasn't just possible but was likely! This was accounting's perfect storm: the conjunction of unprecedented economic growth with inordinate incentive compensation, an extremely aggressive management culture, investors preoccupied with quarterly profits, and lax auditors. At companies that didn't make the Wall Street earnings number by even as little as a penny, the stock price tanked and put top management jobs at risk. Individually, some of these forces may have been good news. But when they all came together, it was a disaster waiting to happen.

Congress responded to the almost daily onslaught of accounting scandals by passing the **Sarbanes-Oxley Act** (SOX) in late July 2002. This legislation was hailed as the most groundbreaking corporate reform since the 1934 Securities Act that, among other things, had established the Securities and Exchange Commission. Key provisions of SOX are intended to strengthen auditor independence and improve financial statement transparency by:

- Creating the Public Companies Accounting Oversight Board (PCAOB) charged with establishing audit, independence, and ethical standards for auditors; investigating auditor conduct; and imposing penalties.

- Requiring the CEO and CFO to certify in writing that the numbers in their company's financial reports are correct. Executives face potential civil charges of fraud or criminal charges of lying to the government if their company's numbers turn out to be bogus.

- Requiring each annual report of a public company to include a report by management on the company's internal control over financial reporting. Among other things, this report must disclose any material internal control weaknesses (i.e., deficiencies that result in more than a remote likelihood that a material accounting misstatement will not be prevented or detected).

- Banning outside auditors from providing certain nonaudit services—bookkeeping, financial system work, appraisals, actuarial work, internal audits, management and human resource consulting, investment-advisory work, and the auditors' other advocacy-related services—to their audit clients so that independence is not compromised. Fees paid to auditors for services must now be disclosed in the client's annual report.

- Requiring public companies to disclose whether the audit committee—comprising outside directors and charged with oversight of the annual audit—has a financial expert and if not, why not. Companies must also now reveal their off-balance-sheet arrangements (see Chapter 11) and reconcile "pro forma" earnings (see Chapter 5) with the audited earnings number.

In the words of one observer, "Our free market system does not depend on executives being saintly or altruistic. But markets do rely on institutional mechanisms, such as auditing and independent boards, to offset opportunistic, not to mention illegal, behavior."* The Sarbanes-Oxley Act strengthens those important institutional mechanisms and, in so doing, calms the accounting storm.

* Robert Simmons as quoted in *CFO Magazine* (August 2002).

The investigation would eventually uncover more than $11 billion in improper transfers and other accounting improprieties at the company. At least two dozen WorldCom employees were dismissed or resigned over the fraud. WorldCom—which now calls itself MCI—reached a settlement with the SEC to pay $750 million in penalties, the largest fine ever levied against one company by the SEC. The company's former chief executive officer (CEO) and chief financial officer (CFO) were both sentenced to lengthy prison terms. In March 2004, after correcting hundreds of thousands of accounting entries, WorldCom restated profits by $74.4 billion for revenues, expenses, asset write-downs, and adjustments to liabilities including the $11 billion of fraudulent transactions first uncovered in 2002. Most experts agree that WorldCom's accounting improprieties were designed to meet the financial targets of Wall Street analysts.

Financial statement fraud is rare.[2] Most managers are honest and responsible, and their financial statements are free from the type of distortions that occurred at WorldCom. However, this example underscores the fact that investors and others should not simply accept the numbers in financial statements at face value. Instead, they must analyze the numbers in sufficient detail to assess the degree to which the financial statements faithfully represent the economic events and activities of the company.

Company data used by investors and analysts come primarily from published financial statements and from the company's willingness to provide additional financial and operating data voluntarily. Management has some latitude in deciding what financial information will be made available and when it will be released. For example, although financial statements must conform to accepted guidelines and standards, management has considerable discretion over the particular accounting procedures used in the statements and the details contained in supplemental footnotes and related disclosures. To further complicate matters, *accounting is not an exact science.* Some financial statement items, such as the amount of cash on deposit in a company bank account, are measured with a high degree of precision and reliability. Other items are more judgmental and uncertain in their measurement because they are derived from estimates of future events, such as product warranty liabilities.

Statement readers must:

- Understand current financial reporting standards and guidelines.
- Recognize that management can shape the financial information communicated to outside parties.
- Distinguish between financial statement information that is highly reliable and information that is judgmental.

All three considerations weigh heavily in determining the quality of the information in financial statements—and thus the extent to which it should be relied on for decision-making purposes. By **quality of information,** we mean the degree to which the financial statements are grounded in facts and sound judgments and thus are free from distortion. The analytical tools and perspectives in this and later chapters will enable you to understand and better interpret the information in financial statements and accompanying disclosures as well as to appreciate fully the limitations of that information.

## ECONOMICS OF ACCOUNTING INFORMATION

The role of financial accounting information is to facilitate economic transactions and to foster the efficient allocation of resources among businesses and individuals.[3] Perhaps the most familiar transactions involve raising financial capital; in these cases, a company seeks to attract additional financial resources by issuing common stock or debt securities. Here financial reports provide information that can reduce investors' uncertainty about the company's opportunities and risks,

---

[2] See *Fraudulent Financial Reporting 1987–1997* (Washington, DC: Committee of Sponsoring Organizations of the Treadway Commission, 1999) and *2006 Fraud Survey* (New York: KPMG LLP, 2007).

[3] The company may participate directly in the transaction as, for example, when it issues debt or equity securities, or when it negotiates a loan or acquires equipment on credit. However, financial statement information also facilitates transactions in secondary markets, such as the New York Stock Exchange (NYSE), where the company's debt and equity securities are subsequently traded.

thereby lowering the company's cost of capital. If you think about this, you can see demand and supply at work. Investors **demand** information regarding the company's opportunities and risks. Because companies need to raise capital at the lowest possible cost, they have an economic incentive to **supply** the information investors want. In this section, you will see that the amount and type of financial accounting information provided by companies depend on demand and supply forces much like the demand and supply forces affecting any economic commodity.

*Financial statements are demanded because of their value as a source of information about the company's performance, financial condition, and stewardship of its resources.* People demand financial statements because the data reported in them improve decision making.

*The supply of financial information is guided by the costs of producing and disseminating it and the benefits it will provide to the company.* Firms weigh the benefits they may gain from financial disclosures against the costs they incur in making those disclosures.

Of course, regulatory groups such as the SEC, the Financial Accounting Standards Board (FASB), and the International Accounting Standards Board (IASB) influence the amount and type of financial information companies disclose as well as when and how it is disclosed.

> Managers have a **stewardship** responsibility to investors and creditors. The company's resources belong to investors and creditors, but managers are "stewards" of those resources and thus responsible for their efficient use and protecting them from adversity.

## Demand for Financial Statements

A company's financial statements are demanded by:

1. Shareholders and investors.
2. Managers and employees.
3. Lenders and suppliers.
4. Customers.
5. Government and regulatory agencies.

### Shareholders and Investors

Shareholders and investors, including investment advisors and securities analysts, use financial information to help decide on a portfolio of securities that meets their preferences for risk, return, dividend yield, and liquidity.

Financial statements are crucial in investment decisions that use **fundamental analysis** to identify mispriced securities: stocks or bonds selling for substantially more or less than they seem to be worth. Fundamental analysis uses financial statement information—including footnotes in those statements—along with industry and macroeconomic data to find companies that are built to last but are undervalued in the short run. Investors who use this approach consider past sales, earnings, cash flow, product acceptance, and management performance to predict future trends in these financial drivers of a company's economic success or failure. Then they assess whether a particular stock or group of stocks is undervalued or overvalued at the current market price. Fundamental investors buy undervalued stocks and avoid overvalued stocks.

Investors who believe in the **efficient markets hypothesis**—and who thus presume they have no insights about company value beyond the current security price—also find financial statement data useful. To efficient markets investors, financial statement data provide a basis for assessing risk, dividend yield, or other firm attributes that are important to portfolio selection decisions.

Of course, shareholders and investors themselves can perform investment analysis as can professional securities analysts who may possess specialized expertise or some comparative advantage in acquiring, interpreting, and analyzing financial statements.

> The **efficient markets hypothesis** says a stock's current market price reflects the knowledge and expectations of all investors. Those who adhere to this theory consider it futile to search for undervalued or overvalued stocks or to forecast stock price movements using financial statements or other public data because any new development is quickly reflected in a firm's stock price. This perspective does not entirely preclude the use of financial statements for investment decisions, however, because financial information about a firm can still have value for predicting the stock's systematic risk (or Beta). Systematic risk—the degree to which a company's stock price moves up or down with marketwide stock price movements—remains important to the investment decision even if markets are efficient. One commercial service, BARRA, provides fundamental estimates of systematic risk to investment professionals worldwide. See T. D. Coqqin and F. J. Fabozzi, *Applied Equity Valuation* (New Hope, PA: Frank J. Fabozzi Associates, 1999).

Shareholders and investors also use financial statement information when evaluating the performance of the company's top executives. This use is referred to as the **stewardship** function of financial reports. When earnings and share price performance fall below acceptable levels, disgruntled shareholders voice their complaints in letters and phone calls to management and outside directors. If this approach doesn't work, dissident shareholders may launch a campaign, referred to as a **proxy contest,** to elect their own slate of directors at the next annual meeting. New investors often see this as a buying opportunity. By purchasing shares of the underperforming company at a bargain price, these investors hope to gain by joining forces with existing shareholders, replacing top management, and "turning the company around."

Such a company's performance as described in its recent financial statements often becomes the focal point of the proxy contest. Management defends its record of past accomplishments while perhaps acknowledging a need for improvement in some areas of the business. Dissident shareholders point to management's past failures and the need to hire a new executive team. Of course, both sides are pointing to the same financial statements. Where one side sees success, the other sees only failure, and undecided shareholders must be capable of forming their own opinion on the matter.

### Managers and Employees

Although managers regularly make operating and financing decisions based on information that is much more detailed and timely than the information found in financial statements, they also need—and therefore demand—financial statement data. Their demand arises from contracts (such as executive compensation agreements) that are linked to financial statement variables.

Executive compensation contracts usually contain annual bonus and longer term pay components tied to financial statement results. Using accounting data in this manner increases the efficiency of executive compensation contracts. Rather than trying to determine first-hand whether a manager has performed capably during the year (and whether the manager deserves a bonus), the board of directors' compensation committee needs to look only at reported profitability or some other accounting measure that functions as a summary of the company's (and thus the manager's) performance.

Employees demand financial statement information for several reasons:

- To learn about the company's performance as a result of the increasing popularity of employee profit sharing and employee stock ownership plans (ESOPs, discussed in Chapter 15).
- To monitor the health of company-sponsored pension plans and to gauge the likelihood that promised benefits will be provided on retirement.
- To know about union contracts that may link negotiated wage increases to the company's financial performance.
- More generally, to help employees gauge their company's current and potential future profitability and solvency.

### Lenders and Suppliers

Financial statements play several roles in the relationship between the company and those who supply financial capital. Commercial lenders (banks, insurance companies, and pension funds) use financial statement information to help decide the loan amount, the interest rate, and the security (called **collateral**) needed for a business loan. Loan agreements contain contractual provisions (called **covenants**) that require the borrower to maintain minimum levels of working capital, debt to assets, or other key accounting variables that provide the lender a safety net. Violation of these loan provisions can result in technical default and allow the lender to accelerate repayment, request additional security, or raise interest rates. So, lenders monitor financial statement data to ascertain whether the covenants are being adhered to or violated.

Suppliers demand financial statements for many reasons. A steel company may sell millions of dollars of rolled steel to an appliance manufacturer on credit. Before extending credit, careful suppliers scrutinize the buyer's financial position in much the same way that a commercial bank does—and for essentially the same reason. That is, suppliers assess the financial strength of their customers to determine whether they will pay for goods shipped. Suppliers continuously monitor the financial health of companies with which they have a significant business relationship.

**Customers**   Repeat purchases and product guarantees or warranties create continuing relationships between a company and its customers. A customer needs to know whether the seller has the financial strength to deliver a high-quality product on an agreed-upon schedule and whether the seller will be able to provide replacement parts and technical support after the sale. You wouldn't buy a personal computer from a door-to-door vendor without first checking out the product and the company that stands behind it. Financial statement information can help current and potential customers monitor a supplier's financial health and thus decide whether to purchase that supplier's goods and services.

**Government and Regulatory Agencies**   Government and regulatory agencies demand financial statement information for various reasons. For example, the SEC requires publicly traded companies to compile annual financial reports (called *10-Ks*) and quarterly financial reports (called *10-Qs*). These reports are filed with the SEC and then made available to investors and other interested parties. This process of **mandatory reporting** allows the SEC to monitor compliance with the securities laws and to ensure that investors have a "level playing field" with timely access to financial statement information.

Taxing authorities sometimes use financial statement information as a basis for establishing tax policies designed to enhance social welfare. For example, the U.S. Congress could point to widespread financial statement losses as justification for instituting a tax reduction during economic downturns.

Government agencies are often customers of businesses. For example, the U.S. Army purchases weapons from suppliers whose contracts guarantee that they are reimbursed for costs and that they get an agreed-upon profit margin. So, financial statement information is essential to resolving contractual disputes between the Army and its suppliers and for monitoring whether companies engaged in government business are earning profits beyond what the contracts allow.

Financial statement information is used to regulate businesses—especially banks, insurance companies, and public utilities such as gas and electric companies. To achieve economies of scale in the production and distribution of natural gas and electricity, local governments have historically granted exclusive franchises to individual gas and electric companies serving a specified geographical area. In exchange for this monopoly privilege, the rates these companies are permitted to charge consumers are closely regulated. Accounting measures of profit and of asset value are essential because the accounting **rate of return**—reported profit divided by asset book value—is a key factor that regulators use in setting allowable charges.[4] If a utility

> In the United States and most other industrialized countries, the accounting rules that businesses use for external financial reporting purposes differ from the accounting rules required for taxation purposes. As a consequence, corporate financial reporting choices in the United States are seldom influenced by the U.S. Internal Revenue Code. See Chapter 13 for details.

---

[4] This regulation process is intended to enhance economic efficiency by precluding the construction of duplicate facilities that might otherwise occur in a competitive environment. Eliminating redundancies presumably lowers the ultimate service cost to consumers. Regulatory agencies specify the accounting practices and disclosure policies that must be followed by companies under their jurisdiction. As a consequence, the accounting practices that utility companies use in preparing financial statements for regulatory agencies sometimes differ from those used in their shareholder reports.

company earns a rate of return that seems too high, regulators can decrease the allowable charge to consumers and thereby reduce the company's profitability.

As noted, banks, insurance companies, and savings and loan associations are also subject to regulation aimed at protecting individual customers and society from insolvency losses—for example, a bank's inability to honor deposit withdrawal requests or an insurance company's failure to provide compensation for covered damages as promised. Financial statements aid regulators in monitoring the health of these companies so that corrective action can be taken when needed.

Regulatory intervention (in the form of antitrust litigation, protection from foreign imports, government loan guarantees, price controls, etc.) by government agencies and legislators constitutes another source of demand for financial statement information.

RECAP

**Financial statement information has value either because it reduces uncertainty about a company's future profitability or economic health or because it provides evidence about the quality of its management, about its ability to fulfill its obligations under supply agreements or labor contracts, or about other facets of the company's business activities. Financial statements are demanded because they provide information that helps improve decision making or makes it possible to monitor managers' activities.**

## Disclosure Incentives and the Supply of Financial Information

Investment bankers and commercial lenders sometimes possess enough bargaining power to allow them to compel companies to deliver the financial information they need for analysis. For example, a cash-starved company applying for a bank loan has a strong incentive to provide all of the data the lender requests. Most financial statement users are less fortunate, however. They must rely on mandated reporting (for example, SEC 10-K filings), voluntary company disclosures that go beyond the minimum required reporting (for example, corporate "fact" books), and sources outside the company (for example, analysts and reporters) for the financial information needed to make decisions.

What forces induce managers to supply information? Browse through several corporate financial reports and you will notice substantial differences across companies—and perhaps over time—in the quality and quantity of the information provided.

Some companies routinely disclose operating profits, production levels, and order backlogs by major product category so analysts and investors can quickly spot changes in product costs and market acceptance. Other companies provide detailed descriptions of their outstanding debt and their efforts to hedge interest rate risk or foreign currency risk. Still other companies seem to disclose only the bare minimum required. What explains this diversity in the quality and quantity of financial information?

If the financial reporting environment were unregulated, disclosure would occur *voluntarily* as long as the incremental benefits to the company and its management from supplying financial information exceeded the incremental costs of providing that information. In other words, management's decisions about the scope, timing, and content of the company's financial statements and notes would be guided solely by the same cost and benefit considerations that influence the supply of any commodity. Managers would assess the benefits created by voluntary disclosures and weigh those benefits against the costs of making the information available. Any differences in financial disclosures across companies and over time would then be due to differences in the benefits or costs of voluntarily supplying financial information.

In fact, however, financial reporting in the United States and in many other developed countries is regulated by public agencies such as the SEC and by private agencies such as the FASB. The various public and private sector regulatory agencies establish and enforce financial reporting requirements *designed to ensure that companies meet certain minimum levels of financial disclosure.*[5] Nevertheless, companies frequently communicate financial information that exceeds these minimum levels. They apparently believe that the benefits of the "extra" disclosures outweigh the costs. What are the potential benefits from voluntary disclosures that exceed minimum requirements?

> The SEC passed Regulation Fair Disclosure, known as "Reg FD," in 1999 in an effort to prevent selective disclosure by companies to market professionals and certain shareholders. In the past, many companies released important information in meetings and conference calls that excluded shareholders and the general public. Reg FD helps to level the playing field between individual investors and institutional investors.

**Disclosure Benefits**   Companies compete with one another in capital, labor, and product markets. This competition creates incentives for management to reveal "good news" financial information about the firm. The news itself may be about a successful new product introduction, increased consumer demand for an existing product, an effective quality improvement, or other matters favorable to the financial perception of the company. By voluntarily disclosing otherwise unknown good news, the company may be able to obtain capital more cheaply or get better terms from suppliers.

To see how these incentives work, consider the market for raising financial capital. Companies seek capital at the lowest possible cost. They compete with one another in terms of both the return they promise to capital suppliers and the characteristics of the financial instrument they offer. The capital market has two important features:

1. Investors are uncertain about the quality (that is, the riskiness) of each company's debt or equity offerings because the ultimate return from the security depends on future events.
2. It is costly for a company to be mistakenly perceived as offering investors a low-quality ("high-risk") stock or debt instrument—a "lemon."[6]

This lemon cost has various forms. It could be lower proceeds received from issuing stock, a higher interest rate that will have to be paid on a commercial loan, or more stringent conditions, such as borrowing restrictions, placed on that loan.

*These market forces mean that owners and managers have an economic incentive to supply the amount and type of financial information that will enable them to raise capital at the lowest cost.* A company offering attractive, low-risk securities can avoid the lemon penalty by voluntarily supplying financial information that enables investors and lenders to gauge the risk and expected return of each instrument accurately. Of course, companies offering higher risk securities have incentives to mask their true condition by supplying overly optimistic financial information. However, other forces partially offset this tendency. Examples include requirements for audited financial statements and legal penalties associated with issuing false or misleading financial statements. Managers also want to maintain access to capital markets and establish a reputation for supplying credible financial information to investors and analysts.

---

[5] Corporate financial reporting in the United States has been regulated by the SEC since its creation by an act of Congress in 1934. The SEC has historically relied on private sector organizations such as the American Institute of Certified Public Accountants (AICPA) and FASB to formulate financial accounting and reporting standards. Another example involves the financial accounting and disclosure standards in Germany; before 1998, those standards were prescribed by law in the Commercial Code (*Handelsgesetz*), the Corporation Act (*Aktiengesetz*), the Cooperatives Act (*Genossenschaftsgesetz*), and other laws related to specific types of business. Now publicly traded German companies must use International Financial Reporting Standards (IFRS) as prescribed by the IASB.

[6] "Lemon," a term commonly associated with automobiles, refers to an auto with hidden defects. In financial capital markets, "lemon" refers to a financial instrument (for example, stock or debt) with hidden risks. See, G. Akerlof, "The Market for 'Lemons': Quality Uncertainty and the Market Mechanism," *Quarterly Journal of Economics*, August 1970, pp. 488–500.

*Financial statement disclosures can convey economic benefits to firms—and thus to their owners and managers. However, firms cannot obtain these benefits at zero cost.*

**Disclosure Costs** Four costs can arise from informative financial disclosures:

1. Information collection, processing, and dissemination costs.
2. Competitive disadvantage costs.
3. Litigation costs.
4. Political costs.

The costs associated with **financial information collection, processing, and dissemination** can be high. Determining the company's obligation for postretirement employee health care benefits provides an example. This disclosure requires numerous complicated actuarial computations as well as future health care cost projections for existing or anticipated medical treatments. Whether companies compile the data themselves or hire outside consultants to do it, the cost of generating a reasonable estimate of the company's postretirement obligation can be considerable. The costs of developing and presenting financial information also include the cost incurred to audit the accounting statement item (if the information is audited). Owners— who are the shareholders—ultimately pay all of these costs, just as they ultimately bear all other company costs.

> Many firms promise to pay some of the health care costs employees incur after retirement. See Chapter 14 for details.

Another financial disclosure cost is the possibility that competitors may use the information to harm the company providing the disclosure. Several disclosures—financial and nonfinancial—might create a **competitive disadvantage:**

- Details about the company's strategies, plans, and tactics, such as new products, pricing strategies, or new customer markets.
- Information about the company's technological and managerial innovations, such as new manufacturing and distribution systems, successful process redesign and continuous quality improvement methods, or uniquely effective marketing approaches.
- Detailed information about company operations, such as sales and cost figures for individual product lines or narrow geographical markets.[7]

Disclosing sales and profits by product line or geographical area may highlight opportunities previously unknown to competitors, thereby undermining a company's competitive advantage. For example, Uniroyal Inc., an automobile tire manufacturer, objected to disclosing its financial data by geographical area because:

> this type of data would be more beneficial to our competition than to the general users of financial data. This is especially true in those countries or geographical areas where we might not be as diversified as we are in the United States. In these cases, the data disclosed could be quite specific, thereby jeopardizing our competitive situation.[8]

Labor unions or suppliers may also use the company's financial information to improve their bargaining power, which would increase the company's costs and possibly weaken its competitive advantage.

**Litigation costs** result when shareholders, creditors, and other financial statement users initiate court actions against the company and its management for alleged financial

---

[7] R. B. Stevenson, Jr., *Corporations and Information: Secrecy, Access, and Disclosure* (Baltimore, MD: Johns Hopkins University Press, 1980), pp. 9–11.

[8] Uniroyal Inc. correspondence as reported in G. Foster, *Financial Statement Analysis* (Upper Saddle River, NJ: Prentice Hall, 1986), p. 185.

misrepresentations. For example, it's common for shareholders to initiate litigation when there's a sudden drop in stock price. If the price falls soon after the company has released new financial information, shareholders may sue the company and claim damages based on the disclosure. These shareholders argue they would not have purchased shares in the company if they had known then (back when they bought the stock) what they know now (after the company's disclosure).

The costs of defending against suits, even those without merit, can be substantial. Beyond legal fees and settlement costs is the damage to corporate and personal reputations and the distraction of executives from productive activities that would otherwise add value to the company.

There are potential **political costs** of financial reporting, especially for companies in highly visible industries such as oil and pharmaceuticals. Politically vulnerable firms with high earnings are often attacked in the financial and popular press, which alleges that those earnings constitute evidence of anticompetitive business practices. Politicians sometimes respond to (or exploit) heightened public opinion. They propose solutions to the "crisis" that is causing high earnings, thereby gaining media exposure for themselves and improving their chances for re-election or reappointment. These "solutions" are often political initiatives designed to impose taxes on unpopular companies or industries. The windfall profits tax levied on U.S. oil companies in the early 1980s is one example. This tax was prompted, in part, by the large profit increases that oil companies reported during several years prior to enactment of the legislation.

Antitrust litigation, environmental regulations, and the elimination of protective import quotas are other examples of the costs politicians and government bureaucrats can impose on unpopular companies and industries. Financial reports are one source of information that politicians and bureaucrats can use to identify target firms or industries. For this reason, astute managers carefully weigh political considerations when choosing what financial information to report and how best to report it. As a result, some highly profitable—but politically vulnerable—firms may make themselves appear less profitable than they really are.[9]

---

**RE**CAP

**A company's financial reporting decisions are driven by economic considerations and thus by cost-benefit trade-offs. Companies that confront distinctly different competitive pressures in the marketplace and that face different financial reporting costs and benefits are likely to choose different accounting and reporting practices. A clear understanding of the economic factors that influence a company's financial reporting choices can help you to assess more keenly the quality of the provided information. That's what we'll help you do in this textbook.**

## A CLOSER LOOK AT PROFESSIONAL ANALYSTS

Financial statements that help users make informed decisions also help allocate capital efficiently. Different types of users—investors, lenders, customers, suppliers, managers, employees, and so on—find corporate financial statements helpful in making decisions. *Financial statement users have diverse information needs because they face different decisions or may use different approaches to making the same kind of decision.* For example, a retail customer deciding which brand of automobile to purchase needs far less financial information about each automotive manufacturer than does a long-term equity investor who is planning to

---

[9] There is another side to this "excessive profits" story. Politicians sometimes respond to public concern over record losses at highly visible companies by providing subsidies in the form of government loan guarantees (for example, Chrysler Corporation), import tariffs (for example, Harley-Davidson), and restrictions on the activities of competitors.

> "To perform good audits, we need more skills than just forensic accounting . . . general accounting skills, tax planning, risk management, and securities analysis are all vital competencies for auditors to possess." Samuel DiPiazza, Jr., global CEO of PricewaterhouseCoopers.

purchase stock in one of those companies. Similarly, a commercial banker engaged in asset-based lending—meaning the borrower's inventory or receivables are pledged to repay the loan—needs far different financial information about the business than does a banker who lends solely on the basis of the borrower's projected future cash flows.

It would be difficult (maybe impossible!) to frame our examination of corporate financial reporting and analysis around the diverse information needs of all potential users and the varied decisions they might possibly confront. Instead, we focus attention on professional analysts. But we define **analyst** broadly to include investors, creditors, financial advisors, and auditors—anyone who uses financial statements to make decisions as part of their job. Let's see what professional analysts do.

## Analysts' Decisions

The task confronting **equity investors** is first to form an educated opinion about the value of the company and its equity securities—common and preferred stock—and then to make investment decisions based on that opinion. Investors who follow a *fundamental analysis approach* estimate the value of a stock by assessing the amount, timing, and uncertainty of future cash flows that will accrue to the company issuing the stock (Chapter 6 shows how). The company's financial statements and other data are used to develop projections of its future cash flows. These cash flow estimates are then discounted for risk and the time value of money. The discounted cash flow estimate or **fundamental value** (say, $25 per share) is then compared to the current price of the company's stock (say, $18 per share). This comparison allows the investor to make decisions about whether to buy, hold, or sell the stock.

Investors use other valuation approaches. One is to estimate a company's **liquidation value.** Here the investor tries to determine the value the company's assets would yield if sold individually and then subtracts any debt the company owes. Another is to compute the price-to-earnings (or price-to-cash flow) ratio for other companies in the industry and then to apply that ratio to the company's current or projected earnings. Still other approaches rely on projections of the company's quarterly earnings, changes in earnings, and changes in trends of earnings to identify possible short-term changes in share prices.

*Financial statement information is essential, in one way or another, to all these equity investment strategies.*

**Creditors'** decisions require an assessment of the company's ability to meet its debt-related financial obligations through the timely payment of interest and principal or through asset liquidation in the event interest and principal cannot be repaid. Creditors include commercial banks, insurance companies and other lenders, suppliers who sell to the company on credit, and those who invest in the company's publicly traded debt securities. Creditors form educated opinions about the company's **credit risk** by comparing required principal and interest payments to estimates of the company's current and future cash flows (Chapter 5 explains how). Companies that are good credit risks have projected operating cash flows that are more than sufficient to meet these debt payments. Credit risk assessments are also influenced by the company's **financial flexibility:** the ability to raise additional cash by selling assets, issuing stock, or borrowing more.

Companies judged to be high credit risks are charged higher rates of interest and may have more stringent conditions—referred to as **covenants**—placed on their loan agreements. These loan covenants may restrict the company from paying dividends, selling assets, buying other companies, forming joint ventures, or borrowing additional funds without the lender's prior approval. Other types of covenants, particularly those based on reported accounting figures, protect the lender from deterioration in the borrower's credit risk. This is why creditors must monitor the company's ongoing ability to comply with lending agreement covenants.

**Financial advisors** include securities analysts, brokers, credit rating agencies, portfolio managers, industry consultants, and others who provide information and advice to investors and creditors. They are often able to gather, process, and evaluate financial information more economically and accurately than individual investors and creditors can because they possess specialized skills or knowledge (for example, industry expertise) or because they have access to specialized resources provided by their organizations. As a consequence, financial advisors can play a crucial role in the decision-making process of investors and creditors. Securities analysts, in particular, are among the most important and influential users of financial statements.

**Independent auditors** carefully examine financial statements prepared by the company prior to conducting an audit of those statements. An understanding of management's reporting incentives coupled with detailed knowledge of reporting rules enables auditors to recognize vulnerable areas where financial reporting abuses are likely to occur. Astute auditors choose audit procedures designed to ensure that major improprieties can be detected.

But the Treadway Commission believes that independent auditors can (and should) do more:

> The potential of analytical review procedures for detecting fraudulent financial reporting has not been realized fully. Unusual year-end transactions, deliberate manipulations of estimates or reserves, and misstatements of revenues and assets often introduce aberrations in otherwise predictable amounts, ratios, or trends that will stand out to a skeptical auditor.[10]

Current auditing standards require independent auditors to use analytical review procedures on each engagement. Why? Because they can help auditors avoid the embarrassment and economic loss from accounting "surprises," such as the one that occurred at WorldCom.

Independent auditors need to be well versed in the techniques of financial analysis to design effective audits. That's why auditors are included among those people we call "analysts." Current auditing standards echo the lessons of past audit failures: ***You can't build a bulletproof audit unless you know how the game is played.*** That means understanding the incentives of managers and being a skilled financial analyst.

> "Consideration of Fraud in a Financial Statement Audit," *Statement of Auditing Standards No. 99* (New York: AICPA, 2002) provides examples of **fraud risk factors** that auditors must be aware of in designing audit procedures. These examples include rapid growth or unusual profitability compared to other firms in the same industry, unduly aggressive financial targets, a significant portion of management pay tied to accounting numbers, an excessive interest by management in maintaining or increasing the firm's stock price or earnings trend, and ineffective board of directors or audit committee oversight of the financial reporting process. These fraud risk factors identify possible motives for managers to engage in fraudulent financial reporting.

> **Analytical review procedures** are the tools auditors use to illuminate relationships among the data. These procedures range from simple ratio and trend analysis to complex statistical techniques—a tool kit not unlike that used by any financial analyst. The auditor's goal is to assess the general reasonableness of the reported numbers in relation to the company's activities, industry conditions, and business climate. Astute auditors are careful to "look behind the numbers" when the reported figures seem unusual.

## Analysts' Information Needs

What specific information about a company do professional analysts want? What types of information are most useful in predicting a company's earnings and cash flows when valuing its equity securities, assessing its debt repayment prospects, and evaluating audit vulnerabilities? Professional analysts say three types of financial information are needed:

1. Quarterly and annual financial statements along with nonfinancial operating and performance data such as order backlogs and customer retention rates.

---

[10] *Report of the National Commission of Fraudulent Financial Reporting* (Washington, DC: 1987), p. 48. The "Treadway Commission"—officially the National Commission on Fraudulent Financial Reporting—was formed in 1985 to study the causal factors that can lead to fraudulent financial reporting and to develop recommendations for public companies and their independent auditors, for the SEC and other regulators, and for educational institutions.

2. Management's analysis of financial and nonfinancial data (including reasons for changes) along with key trends and a discussion of the past effect of those trends.

3. Information that makes it possible both to identify the future opportunities and risks confronting each of the company's businesses and to evaluate management's plans for the future.[11]

The Securities Exchange Act of 1934 requires that public companies solicit shareholders' votes because many shareholders will not be physically present at annual meetings to vote on corporate matters. This solicitation is called a **proxy,** and the information that accompanies it is called the **proxy statement.** Annual meetings are required by state corporation laws.

A company's financial statements provide professional investors, creditors, financial advisors, and auditors with information that heavily influences their decisions. Published financial statements of public companies also contain a **management's discussion and analysis (MD&A)** section. This section describes in considerable detail the company's business risks, its financial condition, the results of its operations, its contractual obligations, and critical accounting estimates that affect the financial statement numbers.

MD&A is one way management communicates the reasons for changes in financial condition and performance. Because management presumably understands the business, MD&A disclosures are an important information source for analysts. MD&A is the starting point professional analysts use in forming their own assessment of the company's profitability and health, and the reasons for changes in financial condition or performance. This is especially true when the MD&A also contains forward-looking information about changing business opportunities and risks and about management's plans for the company.

Some of the information needed by professional analysts is contained in documents other than the financial statements. For example, annual proxy statements furnished to shareholders contain information about the credentials of senior corporate executives and directors, management compensation and ownership, and the identity of major stockholders. Trade journals, industry surveys, and various other sources contain information about current and potential competitors, changing technologies and markets, threats from substitute products or services, and customers' and suppliers' bargaining power. Such information is essential to those who want to form a complete picture of a company's opportunities and risks—and its prospects for the future.

## RECAP

**Financial statement information helps investors assess the value of a firm's debt and equity securities, creditors assess the company's ability both to meet its debt payments and to abide by loan terms, financial advisors and securities analysts to do their job of providing information and advice to investors and creditors, and auditors both to recognize potential financial reporting abuses and to choose audit procedures to detect them.**

## THE RULES OF THE FINANCIAL REPORTING GAME

*"There's virtually no standard that the FASB has ever written that is free from judgment in its application."*

—D. R. Beresford, chairman of the FASB (1987–1997)[12]

Professional analysts are forward looking. Their goal is to predict what will happen in the future to the value of a company and its ability to repay debt. Financial statements and footnotes

---

[11] These findings are based on a comprehensive study of professional analysts' information needs conducted by the American Institute of Certified Public Accountants (AICPA). Further details can be found in *Improving Business Reporting—A Customer Focus: Meeting the Information Needs of Investors and Creditors* (New York: AICPA, 1994). Another perspective is provided in *A Comprehensive Business Reporting Model: Financial Reporting for Investors* (CFA Institute, October 24, 2005). Formerly known as the Association for Investment Management and Research (AIMR), the CFA Institute is a global professional organization for individuals who hold the chartered financial analyst (CFA) designation. See also C. Graziano, "What Do Users of Private Company Financial Statements Want?" *Financial Executive,* May 2006.

[12] As quoted by F. Norris, "From the Chief Accountant, a Farewell Ledger," *New York Times,* June 1, 1997.

depict the past: an economic history of transactions and other events that affected the company. These past data provide analysts a jumping-off point for forecasting future events, especially future earnings and cash flows.

To extrapolate into the future from financial statement data, investors, creditors, and their financial advisors must first understand the accounting measurement rules, estimates, and judgments used to produce the data. Financial statements present a picture of the company at a point in time, a picture that translates many (but not all) of the economic events affecting the business into financial terms. For example, the company's accounting system translates the act of providing goods and services to customers in exchange for promised future cash payments into financial statement amounts known as "sales revenue" and "accounts receivable." This linkage between economic events and how those events are depicted in a financial statement can sometimes seem mysterious or confusing to the analyst. For example, some companies record sales revenue *before* goods are actually delivered to customers. Other companies record revenue at the date of delivery to customers. And still others record revenue only when payment for the goods is received from the customer, which can be long *after* delivery. We'll now look more closely at the rules that govern accounting and financial reporting practices.

> Revenue recognition alternatives are explained in Chapter 3.

## Generally Accepted Accounting Principles

Over time, the accounting profession has developed a network of conventions, rules, guidelines, and procedures, collectively referred to as **generally accepted accounting principles** (**GAAP**). The principles and rules that govern financial reporting continue to develop and evolve in response to changing business conditions. Consider, for example, the lease of retail store space at a shopping mall. As people moved from the city to the suburbs, shopping malls emerged as convenient and accessible alternatives to traditional urban retail stores. Leasing became a popular alternative to ownership because it enabled retailing companies to gain access to store space without having to bear the burden of the large dollar outlay necessary to buy or build the store. Leasing was also attractive because it shared risks—such as the risk of competition from a new mall opening nearby—between the retailer and shopping mall owner. As leasing increased in popularity, the accounting profession developed guidelines, some complex, that are followed when accounting for leases. The guidelines that evolved are now part of GAAP and are discussed in detail in Chapter 12.

The goal of GAAP is to ensure that financial statements clearly represent the company's economic condition and performance. To achieve this goal, financial statements should possess certain qualitative characteristics (summarized in Figure 1.2) that are important to the needs of professional analysts:[13]

- **Relevance:** Financial information that is capable of making a difference in a decision. Relevant information helps users form more accurate predictions about the future, or it allows them to better understand how past economic events have affected the business. Relevant information is timely and has both predictive and feedback value.

    *Timeliness:* Information that is available to decision makers while it is "fresh" and capable of influencing their decisions. An example is sales to customers made during the current quarter as opposed to sales made several quarters ago.

    *Predictive value:* Information that improves the decision maker's ability to forecast the future outcome of past or present events. For example, suppose a company's balance sheet lists accounts receivable of $200,000 and an allowance for uncollectible accounts

> This "reflect economic condition and performance" philosophy of financial reporting describes GAAP in Canada, Mexico, the United States, and many other countries. But GAAP financial reports in a few other countries are required to conform to tax law and/or commercial law. Chapter 18 provides details.

---

[13] A detailed discussion of these qualitative characteristics and related issues is contained in "Qualitative Characteristics of Accounting Information," *Statement of Financial Accounting Concepts No. 2* (Stamford, CT: FASB, 1980).

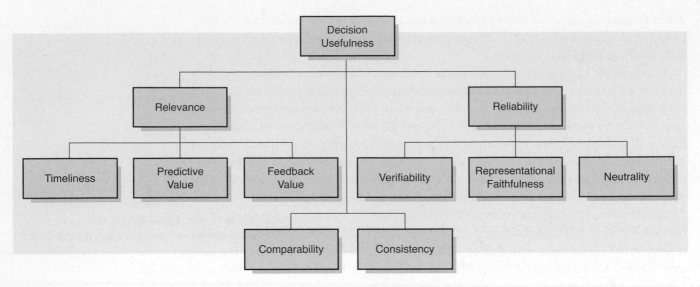

**Figure 1.2** DESIRABLE CHARACTERISTICS OF ACCOUNTING INFORMATION

*SOURCE:* "Qualitative Characteristics of Accounting Information," *Statement of Financial Concepts No. 2* (Stamford, CT: FASB, 1980).

of $15,000. The information has predictive value with regard to future cash collections; that is, management is saying that only $185,000 ($200,000 − $15,000) of the receivables will be collected.

*Feedback value:* Information that confirms or alters the decision maker's earlier expectations. For example, suppose we learn next year that the company mentioned above collected $190,000 of its accounts receivable instead of the $185,000 originally forecasted. This information has feedback value and indicates that management's earlier estimate of uncollectible accounts was too high.

- *Reliability:* Financial information that is reasonably free of error and bias and faithfully represents what it purports to represent. Reliable financial information is factual, truthful, and unbiased. Reliability can be further described using three characteristics:

    *Verifiability:* Independent measurers should get similar results when using the same accounting measurement method. For example, the 2006 net sales of $5,607 million reported by Whole Foods Market is verifiable to the extent that knowledgeable accountants and auditors would agree on this amount after examining the company's sales transactions for the year. So, verifiability refers to the degree of consensus among measurers.

    *Representational faithfulness:* The degree to which the accounting actually represents the underlying economic event. If a company's balance sheet reports trade accounts payable of $254.3 million when the company actually owes suppliers $266.2 million, then the reported figure is not a faithful representation.

    *Neutrality:* Information cannot be selected to favor one set of interested parties over another. For example, accountants cannot allow a company to reduce an estimated expense just so the company can evade a bank loan covenant.

- *Comparability:* Financial information must be measured and reported in a similar manner across companies. Comparability allows analysts to identify real economic similarities and differences among diverse companies because those differences and similarities are not obscured by accounting methods or disclosure practices.

- **Consistency:** The same accounting methods are used to describe similar events from period to period. Consistency allows analysts to identify trends—and turning points—in the economic condition and performance of a company over time because the trends are not obscured by changes in accounting methods or disclosure practices.

No single accounting method has all of these characteristics all of the time. In fact, GAAP frequently requires financial statement users to accept a compromise that favors some qualitative characteristics over others. For example, GAAP financial statements would show a real estate company's office building investment at its historical cost (original purchase price) minus accumulated depreciation. The most *relevant* measure of the office building is often the discounted present value of its expected future rental revenues, but this measure is not as *reliable* or *verifiable* as historical cost because future vacancy rates are unpredictable. GAAP's use of historical cost trades off increased reliability and verifiability for decreased relevance. Qualitative trade-offs such as this arise frequently and make it difficult to identify what are the "best" accounting methods and disclosure practices.

> Companies can voluntarily change accounting methods, but the changes are restricted to situations for which it can be persuasively argued that the newly adopted accounting method is "preferable" to the old one. Companies that change accounting methods must disclose the nature and effect of the accounting change, as well as the justification for it, in the financial statements for the period in which the change is made. Common justifications include "to conform to industry practice" (that is, improved comparability) and "to more accurately represent the company's activities" (that is, greater representational faithfulness).

In evaluating whether financial reports are complete, understandable, and helpful to readers, accounting professionals use two additional conventions: **materiality** and **conservatism.**

Materiality plays a critical role, first in management's judgments in preparing the financial statements, and then in the judgments of independent accountants who audit the statements. Suppose management unintentionally fails to record a $100,000 expense and the bookkeeping error is discovered shortly after the end of the quarter. Unless this error is corrected, quarterly earnings will be overstated by, say, 2.4%, but the overstatement will reverse out next quarter when the expense is eventually recorded. Is the misstatement material? Should the quarterly financial statements be corrected now? Or is the self-correcting misstatement immaterial and unimportant?

According to both the FASB and the SEC, the answer depends on both *quantitative* (the amount of the misstatement) and *qualitative* (the possible impact of the misstatement) considerations. Financial statements are materially misstated when they contain omissions or misstatements that would alter the judgment of a reasonable person.[14] Quantitative materiality thresholds, such as "an item is material if it exceeds 5% of pre-tax income," are inadequate because they fail to recognize how even small misstatements can impact users' perceptions. For example, a small percentage misstatement can be material if it allows the company to avoid a loan covenant violation, reverses an earnings trend, or transforms a loss into a profit.

Conservatism in accounting strives to ensure that business risks and uncertainties are adequately reflected in the financial reports. For example, it is prudent to record possible losses from product liability litigation as soon as those losses become probable and measurable. Doing so helps statement readers assess the potential cash flow implications of the litigation even though an exact dollar amount has not yet been determined. Unfortunately, conservatism is sometimes used to defend poor accounting judgments such as overstated provisions for "big bath" restructuring costs or "cookie-jar" reserves described in Chapter 3.

---

[14] Material misstatements can result either from errors, which are unintentional, or fraud, which is intentional and meant to deceive financial statement users. See "Materiality," *SEC Staff Accounting Bulletin No. 99* (Washington, DC: SEC, August 12, 1999).

## Who Determines the Rules?

GAAP comes from two main sources:

1. Written pronouncements by designated organizations such as the FASB for U.S. companies or the International Accounting Standards Board (IASB) for many non-U.S. companies.

2. Accounting practices that have evolved over time.

The U.S. federal government, through the SEC, has the ultimate authority to determine the rules to be followed in preparing financial statements by companies whose securities are sold to the general public in the United States. This authority was given to the SEC when it was established in 1934 by Congress in response to the severe stock market decline of 1929. The SEC requires companies to file both annual *and* quarterly financial statements as well as other types of reports. The SEC's Electronic Data Gathering and Retrieval (EDGAR) system receives, processes, and disseminates more than 500,000 financial statements every year.

> Statements of Financial Accounting *Standards* establish new standards, such as how to value convertible debt securities, or amend standards previously issued by the FASB and its predecessors. Statements of Financial Accounting *Concepts* establish the fundamentals, such as what qualitative characteristics accounting reports should possess. Financial accounting and reporting standards are based on the concepts. The FASB also issues *Interpretations* that clarify existing GAAP, as well as rules for emerging accounting issues.

Although the SEC has the ultimate legal authority to set accounting principles, it has looked to private-sector organizations to establish these principles. The FASB, or simply "the Board," is the organization that currently sets accounting standards in the United States. The SEC monitors the FASB's activities and works closely with the FASB in formulating reporting rules. Although the FASB is funded through accounting support fees levied against issuers (as provided for by the Sarbanes-Oxley Act of 2002), it exists as an independent group with seven full-time members and a large staff. Board members are appointed to five-year terms and are required to sever all ties with the companies and institutions they served prior to joining the Board. The FASB has issued more than 159 financial accounting standards since it was created in the early 1970s. The Board has also issued seven statements of financial accounting concepts, which serve to guide the Board in setting accounting standards.

Prior to the establishment of the FASB, the **American Institute of Certified Public Accountants** (**AICPA**) had the primary responsibility for setting accounting standards in the United States through its Accounting Principles Board.[15] The AICPA continues to take an active role in establishing GAAP through its participation in the FASB's deliberation process. Until recently, the AICPA has set *auditing* standards for public companies.

Now auditing standards for public companies are set by the **Public Company Accounting Oversight Board** (**PCAOB**), a private-sector, nonprofit corporation created by the Sarbanes-Oxley Act of 2002. (The AICPA's Auditing Standards Board still sets standards for private companies.) The PCAOB has two central roles: (1) to establish standards for auditing and ethics at public accounting firms under its jurisdiction and (2) to inspect and investigate the auditing practices of public accounting firms. The PCAOB can bar a person from participating in audits of public companies in the United States. The Sarbanes-Oxley Act (SOX) prohibits accounting firms that are not registered with the PCAOB from auditing public companies in the United States. The SOX act also requires foreign accounting firms that audit U.S. companies to comply with PCAOB rules. Currently, about 1,670 U.S. and foreign accounting firms are registered with the PCAOB.

 Chapter 18 describes how financial reporting standards are determined outside the United States. In some countries, it's by professional accounting organizations akin to the FASB, and in other countries, it's by commercial law and/or tax law requirements. The growth of global

---

[15] Before the Accounting Principles Board was formed in 1959, accounting rules were issued by a predecessor organization, the Committee on Accounting Procedure. The evolution of U.S. GAAP is discussed in more detail in the appendix to this chapter.

investing has spurred the development of worldwide accounting standards. These standards are written by the **International Accounting Standards Board (IASB)**, an organization formed in 1973 following an agreement by professional accounting organizations in Australia, Canada, France, West Germany, Japan, Mexico, the Netherlands, the United Kingdom, and the United States. The IASB works to formulate accounting standards, promote their worldwide acceptance, and achieve greater convergence of financial reporting regulations, standards, and procedures across countries. The IASB has issued 49 International Financial Reporting Standards, including 5 standards issued by the IASB's predecessor body, the International Accounting Standards Committee (IASC).

## The Hierarchy of GAAP

Over the years, accounting regulatory groups in the United States have published a seemingly endless stream of documents—concept statements, standards, opinions, interpretations, bulletins, and so on—that collectively comprise GAAP. Because these pronouncements are not equally authoritative, eventually the need arose to establish a pecking order among them. Responding to this need, the AICPA defined the phrase *generally accepted accounting principles* and established a **GAAP hierarchy** in 1975 in *Statement on Auditing Standards No. 69.*[16] According to the AICPA, GAAP is:

> . . . a technical accounting term that encompasses the conventions, rules, and procedures necessary to define accepted accounting practice at a particular time. It includes not only broad guidelines of general application, but also detailed practices and procedures. (para. 2.02)

The GAAP hierarchy provides accountants and auditors guidance about where to look for answers to financial reporting questions such as how to value convertible debt securities or when to record asset impairment charges. The hierarchy also provides guidance on how to resolve matters in cases in which the different accounting approaches suggested in the professional literature conflict.

*SAS No. 69* creates four distinct categories of GAAP, each corresponding to different types of accounting standards, and a fifth category denoting "Other" sources. Figure 1.3 shows each category in descending order of authority. Category A of the hierarchy is limited to formal statements of accounting principles issued by the FASB and its predecessor organizations. Category B is other pronouncements issued by a recognized group of accounting experts (e.g., the FASB or the AICPA) after having been exposed for public comment. These pronouncements—FASB Technical Bulletins, AICPA Industry Accounting Guides, and so on—often provide technical guidance for implementing Category A principles. In Category C are pronouncements by these same groups of accounting experts that have not been exposed for public comment. Category D consists of practices that are widely recognized as being generally accepted simply because they represent how things are currently done in a particular industry or for a specific set of circumstances. At the bottom of the hierarchy sits "Other accounting literature," which includes FASB concept statements, international accounting standards, and accounting textbooks such as the one you're now reading. *SAS No. 69* says these sources should be considered only when the higher categories of the hierarchy fail to provide guidance on the accounting issue.

It seems odd that the GAAP hierarchy is found in an auditing standard, not in an accounting standard. The SEC agrees.[17] The SEC objects to the current status of the hierarchy largely because it is aimed at the company's outside auditor when the responsibility for selecting and applying appropriate GAAP lies instead with company management. Additional objections are

---

[16] "The Meaning of Present Fairly in Conformity with Generally Accepted Accounting Principles," *Statement of Auditing Standards No. 69* (New York: AICPA, 1975).

[17] *Study Pursuant to Section 108(d) of the Sarbanes-Oxley Act of 2002 on the Adoption by the Unlisted States Financial Reporting System of a Principles-Based Accounting System* (Washington, DC: SEC, 2003).

| | **Where to Look for Answers to Financial Reporting Questions** | |
|---|---|---|
| | *SAS No. 69* hierarchy | **FASB proposed interim hierarchy** |
| **Category A** | • FASB Statements and Interpretations<br>• Accounting Principles Board Opinions<br>• AICPA Accounting Research Bulletins<br>• SEC rules and interpretative releases | • FASB Statements and Interpretations<br>• Accounting Principles Board Opinions<br>• AICPA Accounting Research Bulletins<br>• SEC rules and interpretative releases<br>• FASB Staff Positions<br>• FASB Derivatives Implementation Group Issues |
| **Category B** | • FASB Technical Bulletins<br>• AICPA Industry Audit and Accounting Guides*<br>• AICPA Statement of Position* | • FASB Technical Bulletins<br>• AICPA Industry Audit and Accounting Guides*<br>• AICPA Statements of Position* |
| **Category C** | • AICPA Practice Bulletins*<br>• Consensus positions of the FASB Emerging<br>  Issues Task Force (EITF) | • AICPA Practice Bulletins*<br>• Consensus positions of the FASB Emerging<br>  Issues Task Force (EITF) |
| **Category D** | • AICPA accounting interpretations<br>• FASB Staff Implementation Guides<br>• Widely recognized and prevalent practices | • AICPA accounting interpretations<br>• FASB Staff Implementation Guides<br>• Widely recognized and prevalent practices |
| **Other** | • FASB Statements of Financial Accounting Concepts<br>• AICPA Issues Papers<br>• International Accounting Standards<br>• Other accounting literature including textbooks | • FASB Statements of Financial Accounting Concepts<br>• AICPA Issues Papers<br>• International Accounting Standards<br>• Other accounting literature including textbooks |

*If cleared by the FASB.

**Figure 1.3**  THE GAAP HIERARCHY

Categories are listed in descending order of authority.

that the hierarchy is overly complex and that it ranks FASB concept statements at the bottom (in "Other") and below industry practices (in Category D) that are not subjected to the lengthy due process required for the issuance of a Statement of Financial Accounting Concepts.

In April 2005, the FASB responded to these concerns by issuing an exposure draft that proposed moving the GAAP hierarchy to an accounting standard, simplifying the hierarchy into two broad categories—authoritative and nonauthoritative—and elevating FASB concept statements to the highest level in the hierarchy.[18] Some of these changes lie down the road. So, as an interim solution, the exposure draft updates and carries forward the GAAP hierarchy established in *SAS No. 69* (see Figure 1.3). The FASB's proposed interim GAAP hierarchy includes two types of accounting standards—FASB Staff Positions and FASB Derivatives Implementation Group Issues—that came into being after *SAS No. 69* was issued. In doing so, the FASB decided that its due process approach to establishing accounting principles is an essential characteristic of the documents in Category A.

The exposure draft clarifies that companies may not represent that their financial statements comply with GAAP if their selection of accounting principles materially departs from the GAAP hierarchy. This differs from the language in *SAS No. 69,* which contained an "escape clause" that allowed companies to depart from strict adherence to the hierarchy.

## Adversarial Nature of Financial Reporting

GAAP permits alternatives (such as LIFO versus FIFO for inventory valuation), requires estimates (for example, the useful life of depreciable assets), and incorporates management judgments (are

---

[18] "The Hierarchy of Generally Accepted Accounting Principles," *Exposure Draft* (Norwalk, CT: FASB, 2005).

assets impaired?). Managers have a degree of flexibility in choosing specific accounting techniques and reporting procedures, and the resulting financial statements are sometimes open to interpretation.

Managers have reasons to exploit this flexibility. Their interests may conflict with the interests of shareholders, lenders, and others who rely on financial statement information. Some companies adopt exemplary reporting standards while others tend to be less forthright. Analysts who understand these conflicting incentives as well as the flexibility available under GAAP will see that a decision based on uncritical acceptance of financial statement data may turn out to be naïve—and financially dangerous.

The flexibility of GAAP financial reporting standards provides opportunities to use accounting tricks that make the company seem less risky than it really is. For instance, some real liabilities such as equipment leases can be transformed into off-balance-sheet (and thus less visible) items. The company would then appear, from the balance sheet data alone, to have less debt and more borrowing capacity than is really the case. Commercial lenders who fail to spot off-balance-sheet liabilities of this sort can understimate the credit risk lurking in their loan portfolios.

Companies can also **smooth** reported earnings by strategically timing the recognition of revenues and expenses to dampen the normal ups and downs of business activity. This strategy projects an image of a stable company that can easily service its debt even in a severe business downturn. The benefits of such deceptions can be large if lenders are fooled.[19] Furthermore, once the loan is granted, the company has additional incentives to report its financial results in ways that avoid default on loan covenants tied to accounting numbers.

Self-interest sometimes drives managers to manipulate the reported financial statement numbers to earn bonuses linked to sales or earnings targets. For example, if earnings are down late in the fiscal year, product deliveries may be accelerated to increase recognized revenues and income before year-end. Managers could also delay until next year discretionary expenses such as building repairs and maintenance if earnings this year are expected to be too low. On the other hand, if earnings are comfortably above the bonus goal, managers may write off obsolete equipment and inventory or increase allowances for uncollectible trade receivables, whereas those same accounting adjustments may be postponed if earnings are inadequate.

> Manville Corporation's 1982 bankruptcy changed the way analysts view legal contingencies. Although some people had been asking questions about the company's exposure to asbestos-related litigation for quite some time, Manville's bankruptcy announcement on August 26, 1982, caught most analysts and investors by surprise. That's because the company's last quarterly report prior to bankruptcy estimated the total cost of settling asbestos-related claims at about $350 million, less than half of Manville's $830 million of shareholders' equity. On August 26, Manville put the potential damages at no less than $2 billion, and the company's stock plunged by 35% the next day.

Another way in which financial reporting practices can be molded to suit management's interests is to downplay the significance of contingent liabilities, such as unresolved product liability lawsuits, that may affect the firm's value. For many reasons, management is likely to understate the true significance of a major legal contingency. In a lawsuit, candid disclosure could compromise the company's case. Similarly, public disclosure of impending financial hardships may harm the company if creditors respond by accelerating loan repayment schedules, curtailing trade credit, or seeking to liquidate the business.

This discussion states the case boldly and may portray the motives underlying financial reporting practices in an unflattering light. In reality, most companies strive to provide fair and reasonable disclosure of their financial affairs. Some of these companies are undoubtedly motivated as much by honor and integrity as by the knowledge that they will be rewarded for being forthright. Nevertheless, companies take full advantage of the leeway available under GAAP.

---

[19] Lenders are fooled when they mistakenly assign too little risk (thus charging too low an interest rate) to the borrowing. An interest cost savings of one-half of a percentage point on $1 billion of borrowings equates to $5 million (pre-tax) per year. If the company is in a 34% tax bracket and its stock trades at 15 times earnings, the payoff for concealing risk on financial statements is $49.5 million in share value. This value increase represents a wealth transfer to shareholders from creditors.

The SEC and the FASB provide constraints that limit the range of financial statement discretion. Auditors and the courts further counterbalance opportunistic financial reporting practices. Nevertheless, the analyst should recognize the adversarial nature of financial reporting, maintain a healthy skepticism, and understand that financial disclosures sometimes conceal more than they reveal. The flexibility inherent in GAAP can have dire consequences for those caught unaware.

## Aggressive Financial Reporting: A Case Study

*"We're not saying they're cooking the books, but there's ample evidence to wonder if everything is on the up-and-up."*

—Arthur Russell, equity analyst at the investment firm of Edward Jones[20]

As the information technology sector ballooned during the 1990s, Computer Associates International Inc. (CA) emerged as the world's third-largest software company. In the business of software for managing mainframes and computer networks, CA was king. It offered business customers more than 1,200 software products that operated and connected large computers, storage technology, wireless products, and high-tech security systems. Annual revenues hit nearly $7 billion by fiscal 2000, net profits approached $700 million, and the company's 40% operating margin rivaled that of Microsoft Corporation.

Investors were well rewarded for the company's success. An investor who bought CA stock for $5 a share in January 1990 could have sold the stock for $75 in January 2000 when the tech bubble peaked. That's a whopping 1,400% investment return, or about 31% each year for 10 straight years. As for CA's management team, in 1998, the company's top three officers took home stock grants collectively worth $1.1 billion, the largest award of this sort ever paid to U.S. executives. Outraged by the sheer size of the awards, investors sued the company and a judge later reduced the awards by almost half, but even $500 million is a princely sum.

Concerns about aggressive financial reporting at the company surfaced in 2000. CA and other software companies faced a vicious downturn in customer sales once the dot-com bubble burst. As customers cut back their software spending, CA's stock price tumbled (see Figure 1.4). CA changed its revenue accounting policies in May 2000 and sliced a hefty $2.56 billion off the total for the previous five years. Then in July 2000, CA said that quarterly revenues would fall short of analysts' estimates. Investors ran for cover, and the stock plunged 42% that day.

Starting in October 2000, CA revamped its software license contracts and began offering customers more flexible payment terms. Rather than making a single upfront payment, customers could opt for a "subscription" plan and pay the multiyear license fee in equal installments over time. CA also radically changed the way it reported its financial results. In addition to the required GAAP financial statements where all contract revenue was booked immediately, CA provided "pro forma" results that recalculated past revenue and earnings as if they were based on the new subscriptions approach. The difference between the two sets of numbers, GAAP and "pro forma," was often quite startling. For example, in the first quarter after adopting the new approach, CA reported pro forma profits of $247 million while under GAAP it suffered a $342 million loss. Analysts didn't entirely trust the pro formas numbers, in part because revenue was being double counted.

Aggressive accounting concerns continued to dog CA for several years. In February 2002, the company announced that the SEC had launched an investigation into CA's accounting practices. The announcement followed on the heels of an investment rating downgrade of CA

---

[20] As quoted in S. Hamm, "Getting to the Bottom of Computer Associates," *BusinessWeek*, September 30, 2002.

**Figure 1.4**

COMPUTER ASSOCIATES
INTERNATIONAL

Daily Stock Price from
January 4, 1999, through
December 31, 2002

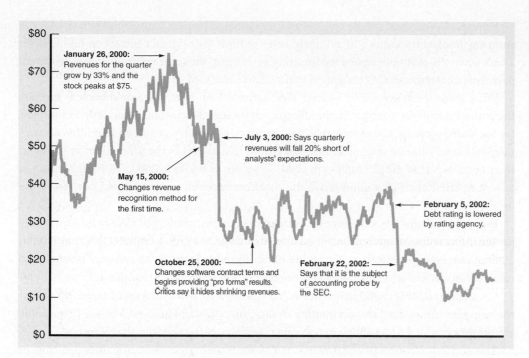

debt. News articles in the financial press described the company's accounting woes and questioned whether there was anything illegal about the way CA kept its books.

## The Accounting Issues at Computer Associates

The first accounting controversy surfaced in May 2000 when CA changed how it booked revenues from software licenses that were renegotiated during the licensing period. Here's an example to illustrate the issue. Suppose that CA sells a one-year software license on July 1, 1999 for $20 million to a business customer who pays the full amount in cash upfront. On January 2, 2000, the customer renegotiates the license, adding several more software products and extending the licensing period for another six months. The new license bundle is priced at $25 million, but the customer pays only $15 million cash after deducting a $10 million credit for the unused portion of the original license. The following diagram shows the licensing period and payment associated with the original and renegotiated contract.

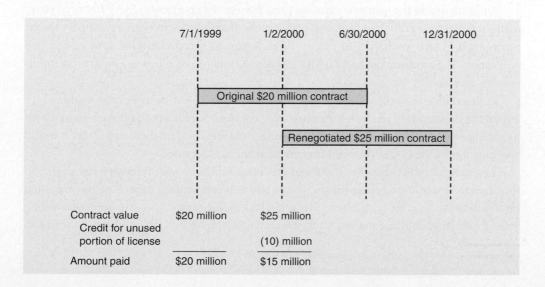

How did CA account for the original and renegotiated license? Consistent with GAAP, the company booked the entire $20 million of revenue from the original contract on July 1, 1999. That's when the customer signed the licensing agreement, the software product was delivered, payment occurred, and CA's obligation to the customer ended.

You'll learn more about the GAAP rules for recognizing revenue in Chapters 2 and 3.

What about the renegotiated license? Well, prior to May 2000, CA would book as revenue the entire value of the contract ($25 million) even though the customer paid only $15 million for the added software and extended license. In effect, CA double counted $10 million of revenue associated with the original license agreement, first as part of the $20 million in 1999 and then again as part of the $25 million in 2000. To square its books in 2000, CA would deduct as a "cost of sales" the $10 million credit the customer received for the unused portion of the original license.

Investors and analysts who were unaware of the double counting at CA would mistakenly presume that software revenue increased over time, from $20 million in 1999 to $25 million in 2000 in our example. However, the reality of our example is that both software revenue and cash receipts from customers instead declined from $20 million to $15 million.

CA stopped double counting revenue on renegotiated software licenses in May 2000. When the company announced this accounting change, investors and analysts learned that double counting had added $2.56 billion to software revenue over the previous five years.

The second accounting controversy at CA stemmed from the company's decision in October 2000 to roll out a new subscriptions-based business model and begin reporting results using nonstandard pro forma accounting in its press releases. Here's an excerpt from the quarterly earnings press release issued just after CA launched the new business model and revamped accounting:

> Reaping the benefits of an innovative business model designed to provide greater flexibility to customers, to improve revenue predictability, and to unlock shareholder value, Computer Associates International, Inc. (NYSE: CA) today reported financial results for its third fiscal quarter. The results, reported on a ***pro forma pro rata basis,*** beat analysts' consensus earnings per share estimates of $0.40 by $0.02.[21] [Emphasis added]

The press release also stated that software revenue increased 13% to $1.284 billion compared to the same quarter the previous year and that operating income increased 28% to $247 million. CA touted the pro forma numbers as providing more clarity to investors and analysts because they presented sales as if all revenues, past, present, and future, were based on the company's new subscription business model.

Also disclosed in the quarterly earnings press release, the company's GAAP financial statements painted a very different picture of performance that quarter. Software revenue measured according to GAAP was only $783 million, down almost 53 percent from the same quarter one year earlier. The company also had a GAAP loss of $342 million compared to a profit of $401 million one year earlier.

CA urged investors and analysts to ignore the traditional GAAP numbers and to instead focus on the nonstandard pro forma numbers. The company said it would offer guidance about its anticipated sales and earnings results only under the nonstandard method but that it would continue to provide GAAP financial statements as the SEC required.

The discrepancy between the GAAP and pro forma numbers made it tough for analysts and investors to determine whether the company's business was actually improving or worsening on a quarter-to-quarter basis. Some just scratched their heads. "They are definitely selling software for sure," said one analyst, "[but] it is hard to tell how much and to whom. . . ."[22] Critics

---

[21] Computer Associates International Inc. press release issued January 22, 2001.

[22] A. Berenson, "Computer Associates Stock Drops Sharply Once Again," *New York Times,* February 22, 2002.

# NEWS CLIP

## GETTING TO THE BOTTOM OF COMPUTER ASSOCIATES' BOOKS

There might be a company in the world with more baffling accounting than Computer Associates International Inc.—but, then again, maybe not. The Long Island software company has made two major shifts in the way it presents its financials over the past three years. And ongoing probes of CA's finances by the Securities & Exchange Commission and the Justice Dept. only add to the bewilderment. The feds have subpoenaed CA's auditors and are zeroing in on how it recognized revenues, say former CA executives interviewed by investigators.

All this makes it hard for investors to tell how CA is performing. "We're not saying they're cooking the books, but there's ample evidence to wonder if everything is on the up-and-up," says Edward Jones analyst Arthur Russell, who recently suspended coverage of CA because of the accounting issues.

CA says it has not violated accounting rules. And Walter P. Schuetze, former chief accountant for the SEC who joined CA's board this summer [2002], says he has reviewed the company's past and current accounting practices and has confidence in them. He says that today, "CA's financial statements are very simple. It's like looking at a Rand McNally atlas. There's no hidden road."

But there have been plenty of twists and turns. The company's first major accounting shift came in 2000. Since the early 1980s, CA had double-counted revenues when it renegotiated multiyear contracts with corporations before they expired. After the new contract went into effect, CA would book the entire amount, even though that included revenues from the overlap period. The practice added $663 million to revenues in fiscal 2000, inflating the total by 9.7% and helping drive the stock to an all-time high of $75 per share in January, 2000. Because CA also took a $663 million expense to balance out the double-counting, though, the accounting treatment didn't affect its earnings. In May 2000, following a recommendation by its new auditor, KPMG LLP, CA began subtracting previously counted revenues from its new tallies when it booked renegotiated contracts—the way competitors had always handled things. CA's change retroactively chopped $2.56 billion off revenues it had reported over a five-year period.

Is there anything illegal about the old way of accounting? The feds aren't talking. But some stock analysts who have studied CA's books wonder what the fuss is about. "If this is what they're looking at, I don't know that they'll find anything wrong with it," says Morgan Stanley analyst Joe Farley.

When you drill down deeper, though, the way CA's sales force handled these contracts raises questions about whether it artificially boosted its numbers. According to several former CA sales people, managers pressured them to reopen multiyear maintenance contracts with customers and craft new agreements that included lots of new software. The former employees say CA sometimes essentially threw software in for free. But in the resulting contracts, software made up a significant piece of the total price, and since software license revenues were largely recognized up front, this practice jacked up revenues and profits in the short term. A "gray area," according to Prudential Securities Inc. analyst John McPeake, is whether CA's practices inflated short-term revenues and profits at the expense of future performance without reflecting that in the financial reports. "I'm concerned that they were too aggressive," says McPeake.

CA denies it pressured employees to do anything improper to boost revenues. It says, though, that there may have been cases where salespeople, acting on their own, structured deals to boost commissions.

The company made an even more drastic change in accounting shortly after CEO Sanjay Kumar took over. Starting in December 2000, CA began to recognize most software-license revenues in equal annual increments over the life of multiyear contracts. The stated purpose: to smooth out earnings from quarter to quarter. Critics, however, say it was intended to obscure the fact that CA's business was in decline.

No matter what the motivation, the effect was dramatic. The company's revenue declined from $6.09 billion in fiscal year 2000 to $2.96 billion in fiscal year 2002. Net profit of $696 million in fiscal year 2000 dropped to a net loss of $1.1 billion in fiscal year 2002. And Kumar compounded the confusion. Initially, for communicating with investors, he adopted pro forma accounting that recalculated past revenues and earnings as if they were based on the new accounting system. Some analysts complained, saying they didn't trust the pro forma numbers. Ultimately, CA backed off.

The company's finances remain murky. Because many of CA's long-term contracts have yet to be renewed under the new accounting principles, it could be two to three years before investors can tell for sure what the company's longer-term growth rate and profit margins will be.

With all of its accounting changes, CA has chased investors away. And if the feds file charges, the numbers at CA could be stirred up yet again.

*Source:* S. Hamm, "Getting to the Bottom of Computer Associates' Books," *BusinessWeek,* September 30, 2002.

complained that the pro forma numbers allowed CA to hide the fact that it had previously stretched accounting rules to inflate its sales. While analysts seemed perplexed, investors were decisive in their reaction, sending the stock up 5.8% the day quarterly earnings were released.

**Questions to Consider**   This scenario raises several intriguing questions about corporate financial reporting practices, managerial behavior, and the influence of accounting information on the decisions of investors, creditors, and others:

- How flexible is GAAP, and how much latitude is available to managers in the choice of "acceptable" accounting practices?
- What factors influence the accounting methods managers use? Why do firms change accounting methods? Does a change in accounting imply that previously reported figures (that is, those produced using the old method) were incorrect?
- Do company disclosures make clear what accounting methods are used? Do those disclosures enable analysts to adjust reported figures when a company's accounting method either deviates from industry norms or changes through time?
- Can firms use one accounting method in their GAAP financial statements and some other pro forma method when reporting results in press releases?
- How do analysts and investors use reported earnings and balance sheet numbers when valuing a firm's common stock?
- How does an accounting change alter creditors' opinions about a company's future cash flows and credit risk?

Perhaps the most provocative question, however, centers on the allegations raised by an SEC investigation launched in 2002. Did the company violate GAAP and mislead investors by using accounting procedures that failed to provide an accurate and timely portrayal of the company's historical profit performance, current financial condition, and future prospects? Subsequent chapters of this book help you formulate answers to these and related questions about financial reporting practices in the United States and other countries.

**Epilog**   Computer Associates admitted in October 2003 that some software license contracts had been backdated, a practice known internally as "the 35-day month," to mask declining performance and meet Wall Street forecasts for quarterly sales and profits. An internal investigation was launched, and CA restated $2.2 billion in sales that had been improperly booked during 1999 and 2000. The company spent $30 million on the investigation and reviewed tens of thousands of internal e-mail messages and 1,000 license agreements with customers. Employees who did not cooperate with the investigation were fired.

The Justice Department and the SEC sued CA and several top executives. CA agreed in 2004 to pay $225 million in restitution to shareholders and submit its accounting to an independent monitor. Seven former executives pleaded guilty to civil charges of securities fraud and obstruction of justice in connection with the company's accounting scandal. Two other top executives, the company's former chief executive and the former top salesman, confessed to a wide-ranging conspiracy to inflate sales and interfere with the subsequent federal inquiry. They face maximum prison sentences of up to 30 years each.

## AN INTERNATIONAL PERSPECTIVE

Because financial reporting practices vary widely in countries outside the United States and because international business transactions are now more frequent and complex, the professional life of an analyst—in any country—has become more difficult. Multinational companies

> *Backdating* occurs when someone intentionally alters the contract signing date so that revenue can be booked in an earlier period. For example, suppose a customer and seller sign a $20 million software license agreement on January 3, 2000, but then backdate it to December 30, 1999. Unless the backdating is discovered, the seller would mistakenly record the $20 million as revenue in 1999 rather than in 2000.

**EXHIBIT 1.1**  Coca-Cola Company

**Operating Revenue and Income by Geographical Area**

| | 2005 (%) | | 2004 (%) | | 2003 (%) | |
|---|---|---|---|---|---|---|
| | Revenue | Income | Revenue | Income | Revenue | Income |
| North America | 28.9% | 25.5% | 29.5% | 28.2% | 29.5% | 24.6% |
| Africa | 5.5 | 6.8 | 4.9 | 6.0 | 4.0 | 4.8 |
| East, South Asia, and Pacific Rim | 5.4 | 3.3 | 5.9 | 6.0 | 6.4 | 7.0 |
| European Union | 29.4 | 36.9 | 30.2 | 31.8 | 29.2 | 36.3 |
| Latin America | 10.9 | 19.8 | 9.8 | 18.8 | 9.8 | 18.6 |
| North Asia, Eurasia, and Middle East | 19.5 | 28.1 | 19.2 | 28.6 | 20.7 | 28.5 |
| Corporate | 0.4 | (20.5) | 0.5 | (19.3) | 0.4 | (19.7) |
| Consolidated | 100.0% | 100.0% | 100.0% | 100.0% | 100.0% | 100.0% |

*Source:* Coca-Cola Company 2005 Annual Report.

are regularly shifting resources throughout the world. These shifts cannot be accomplished efficiently without reliable financial information that permits careful analysis of investment opportunities and continuous control over how resources are deployed. Multinational companies must also resolve differences in national currencies and accounting rules when combining the financial statements of all their foreign and domestic businesses into consolidated reports.

The Coca-Cola Company, for example, conducts business in more than 200 countries, hedges foreign currency cash flows, and uses foreign loans to finance investments outside the United States. Exhibit 1.1 indicates the scope of Coca-Cola's worldwide operating activities from 2003 through 2005. Sales in North America (Canada and United States) represented 28.9% of 2005 worldwide revenues and generated 25.5% of worldwide operating income. By contrast, Latin America sales were only 10.9% of 2005 operating revenues, but this region produced 19.8% of Coca-Cola's worldwide operating income.

Understanding the economic, political, and cultural factors that contribute to regional differences in operating performance is daunting even for the most experienced financial analyst. Yet assessing a multinational company's current performance and future prospects requires experience, knowledge, and skill with these factors.

Global competition is prevalent in most industries today as companies facing mature domestic markets look outside their home borders for new customers and growth. Exhibit 1.2 presents 2005 sales, net income, and assets for three automobile manufacturers that compete on a worldwide basis: Ford Motor Company, Fiat S.A., and Honda Motor Company. Honda, a Japanese firm, reports financial statements in Japanese yen, Ford uses U.S. dollars, and Fiat, an Italian company, uses the euro for financial reporting purposes. Which company was the most profitable in 2005?

In the upper part of Exhibit 1.2, the financial statement amounts reported by these three companies are not directly comparable because each firm uses a different currency. For example, Honda had sales of 9,907,996 million yen and net income of 597,033 million yen for 2005, but the yen/dollar exchange rate averaged 117.47 for the year. This means that each U.S. dollar was worth about 117.47 yen during 2005. In the case of Fiat, the euro/dollar exchange rate averaged about 0.84 for the year. The lower part of the exhibit shows each company's sales, net income, and assets expressed in U.S. dollars. Here, you can see that Ford has the largest sales ($177,089 million), but Honda is the most profitable ($5,082 million). Fiat is the smallest of the three companies in terms of sales, net income, and assets.

**EXHIBIT 1.2**     Ford, Fiat, and Honda

### Revenue, Net Income, and Assets for 2005 (in millions)

|                               | Ford Motor Co. (United States) | Fiat S.A. (Italy) | Honda Motor Co. (Japan) |
| ----------------------------- | ------------------------------ | ----------------- | ----------------------- |
| **As reported in local currency** |                           |                   |                         |
| Revenue                       | 177,089                        | 46,544            | 9,907,996               |
| Net income                    | 2,024                          | 1,311             | 597,033                 |
| Assets                        | 269,476                        | 62,454            | 10,571,681              |
|                               |                                |                   |                         |
| **U.S. dollar equivalents**   |                                |                   |                         |
| Revenue                       | 177,089                        | 55,117            | 84,345                  |
| Net income                    | 2,024                          | 1,576             | 5,082                   |
| Assets                        | 269,476                        | 73,958            | 89,995                  |
|                               |                                |                   |                         |
| Local currency                | U.S. dollar                    | Euro              | Yen                     |
| Accounting methods            | U.S. GAAP                      | IFRS              | U.S. GAAP               |
| Fiscal year-end               | December 31                    | December 31       | June 30                 |

*Note:* Sales and net income in the lower part of the table are restated into U.S. dollars using the average exchange rate for the fiscal year because the flows occur throughout the year. Year-end assets are restated into U.S. dollars using the exchange rate as of the end of fiscal year.

*Source:* Company financial statements.

Another factor complicates our analysis. Financial statement comparisons of this type become less meaningful when accounting standards and measurement rules vary from one country to another. Both Ford and Honda use U.S. GAAP, but Fiat prepares its financial statements using IFRS. As a result, Fiat's lower reported sales and net income might not be attributable to economic factors if IFRS income recognition rules are more conservative than U.S. rules.

In some countries, there must be conformity between the accounting methods used in shareholder financial statements and the rules used in computing taxable income. So, the legislative branch of the government sets acceptable accounting principles for shareholder reporting purposes. In other countries, the accounting profession, through its various committees, sets accounting principles. These financial reporting rules differ from taxation rules.

The differing objectives of these standard-setting organizations (for example, taxation versus fair reporting to investors) result in diverse sets of accounting principles across countries. Analysts must be aware of this diversity and guard against the tendency to assume that financial statements are readily comparable across national borders. These issues are examined in Chapter 18.

In the United States, the SEC permits foreign businesses to list their securities on a U.S. stock exchange as long as certain procedures are followed. Foreign businesses that do not use U.S. GAAP to prepare financial statements must file a Form 20-F each year with the SEC. This form transforms (in part or in whole) the foreign GAAP financial statements into U.S. GAAP. Form 20-F filings are public information, and thus they can be of considerable value to the analyst.

The financial reporting requirements for foreign companies listed on the London Stock Exchange permit greater flexibility than those that currently exist in the United States. Foreign businesses listed there can file financial statements that conform to the accounting principles of

> In November 2007, the SEC dropped its Form 20-F reconciliation requirement for foreign companies that use IFRS accounting rules.

the IASB or their own national GAAP. Certain extra information is required if the specific GAAP used does not give a "true and fair view" according to IAS. Beginning in 2007, all foreign firms on the Exchange are required to use IFRS.

## The March toward Convergence

Consider the financial reporting choice faced by Toyota Motor Company, the Japanese automobile manufacturer. The company's stock is traded on the Tokyo Stock Exchange and on the New York Stock Exchange. Investors worldwide can buy or sell Toyota shares on either exchange. Which set of presently available accounting standards—Japanese GAAP, U.S. GAAP, or IFRS—should Toyota use to prepare its financial statements?

Perhaps the best answer is none of the above. Suppose there is a fourth choice, a single set of accounting standards accepted worldwide and superior to the three choices presently available. This is the goal of the growing movement toward international convergence of accounting standards.

The arguments favoring convergence are both clear and compelling. Differences in accounting practices and reporting systems make cross-border comparisons difficult and costly and impose an increasing burden on economic efficiency. Without convergence, some countries might be tempted to reduce the quality of their accounting standards in a short-sighted attempt to attract foreign firms to list on their local stock exchanges. As a first step toward achieving convergence, more and more countries outside the United States are requiring their listed companies to adopt IFRS rather than domestic GAAP. Foreign companies listed on stock exchanges in the United States must use U.S. GAAP or IFRS.

The FASB and IASB are also working toward eliminating differences between U.S. GAAP and IFRS. The process for doing so is stated in a memorandum of understanding signed February 2006 by the IASB and FASB and blessed by the U.S. SEC and the European Commission. According to the memorandum, the IASB and FASB will begin work on substantial improvements in areas where IFRS and U.S. GAAP are judged deficient. Working together, the two boards are expected to develop a single set of high-quality, compatible accounting standards that can be used for both domestic and cross-border financial reporting.

---

**Diversity is a fact of life in international accounting practice. Readers of financial statements must never lose sight of this diversity.**

RECAP

## CHALLENGES CONFRONTING THE ANALYST

During the last three decades, financial statements have become increasingly complex and more accessible.

Corporate financial reports are more complicated today simply because the business world has become more dynamic and complex. Global competition and the spread of free enterprise throughout the world prompted firms to rely increasingly on foreign countries as a market for products and services and as a source of capital and customers. Competitive pressures have also contributed to a fundamental change in the way firms organize and finance their activities. Corporate restructurings abound. Companies now use new types of financial instruments to raise capital and manage risk. Service firms and e-commerce companies now comprise a major portion of business activity. These and other features of the changing business landscape pose difficult challenges for contemporary financial reporting practices and for an accounting model originally developed to fit companies engaged in local manufacturing and merchandising.

The use of electronic means to assemble and examine financial information has had explosive growth in the last three decades. The accessibility of computers and analytical software continues to rise as their costs fall. Quantitative methods for analyzing financial data have become increasingly popular, which in turn has meant increasing demand for and use of electronic databases containing financial information. Corporate press releases, analysts' research reports, historical financial data, and complete annual and quarterly financial reports are now readily available in electronic form through commercial vendors. Documents filed with the SEC can now be obtained from the agency's EDGAR system (available at www.sec.gov).

These developments place new burdens on analysts. On the one hand, a wealth of financial statement data and related information is available to the analyst at relatively low cost. On the other hand, firms today operate in a dynamic environment that has made the task of analyzing financial statements even more complex. The financial reporting practices of business firms are continually challenged on many fronts, and the astute analyst must remain vigilant to the possibility that financial reports sometimes do not capture underlying economic realities.

## SUMMARY

Financial statements are an extremely important source of information about a company, its economic health, and its prospects. They help improve decision making and make it possible to monitor managers' activities.

- Equity investors use financial statements to form opinions about the value of a company and its stock.
- Creditors use statement information to gauge a company's ability to repay its debt and to check whether the company is complying with loan covenants.
- Stock analysts, brokers, and portfolio managers use financial statements as the basis for their recommendations to investors and creditors.
- Auditors use financial statements to help design more effective audits by spotting areas of potential reporting abuses.

But what governs the supply of financial information?

- Mandatory reporting is a partial answer. Most companies in the United States and other developed countries are required to compile and distribute financial statements to shareholders and to file a copy with a government agency (in the United States, that agency is the SEC). This requirement allows all interested parties to view the statements.
- The advantages of voluntary disclosure are the rest of the answer. Financial information that goes beyond the minimum requirements can benefit the company, its managers, and its owners. For example, voluntary financial disclosures can help the company obtain capital more cheaply or negotiate better terms from suppliers. But benefits like these come with potential costs: information collection, processing, and dissemination costs; competitive disadvantage costs; litigation costs; and political costs. This means that two companies with different financial reporting benefits and costs are likely to choose different accounting policies and reporting strategies.

Different companies choose different accounting policies and reporting strategies because financial reporting standards are often imprecise and open to interpretation. This imprecision gives managers an opportunity to shape financial statements in ways that allow them to achieve specific reporting goals.

- Most managers use their accounting flexibility to paint a truthful economic picture of the company.
- Other managers mold the financial statements to mask weaknesses and to hide problems.
- Analysts who understand financial reporting, managers' incentives, and the accounting flexibility available to managers will maintain a healthy skepticism about the numbers and recognize that financial statements sometimes conceal more than they reveal.

**APPENDIX**

# GAAP IN THE UNITED STATES

This is a brief, historical overview of the public and private sector organizations that have influenced the development of financial accounting practices in the United States. As you shall see, some organizations have explicit legal authority to decide what constitutes U.S. GAAP. Other organizations lack that authority but remain influential.[23]

## Early Developments

Corporate financial reporting practices in the United States prior to 1900 were primarily intended to provide accounting information for management's use. Financial statements were made available to shareholders, creditors, or other interested external parties on a limited basis. The **New York Stock Exchange** (**NYSE**), established in 1792, was the primary mechanism for trading ownership in corporations. As such, it could establish specific requirements for the disclosure of financial information and thereby dictate accounting standards for corporations whose shares it listed. Beginning in 1869, the NYSE attempted to persuade listed companies to make their financial statements public. Few companies complied. The prevailing view of corporate management was that financial information was a private concern of the company and that public disclosure would harm the company's competitive advantage.

Passage of the Sixteenth Amendment to the U.S. Constitution in 1913 and subsequent legislation allowing the federal government to tax corporate profits set the stage for expanded corporate financial disclosure. This legislation required companies to maintain accurate financial recordkeeping systems; the goal of this legislation was to ensure proper tax accounting and to facilitate collection. However, corporate financial disclosures to outsiders were still limited.

> The library archive at the University of California at Berkeley contains examples of public company annual reports dating back to the 1850s. The archive includes General Electric (1892), National Biscuit Company (Nabisco, 1898), and Procter & Gamble (1891).

The stock market crash of 1929 and the Great Depression that followed provoked widespread concern about financial disclosure. Some observers alleged that the collapse of the stock market was due largely to the lack of meaningful requirements for reporting corporate financial information to investors and creditors.[24] Many also believed that economic conditions would not improve until investors regained confidence in the financial markets. Responding to this concern in January 1933, the NYSE began requiring all companies seeking exchange listing to submit independently audited financial statements and to agree to audits of all future reports.

---

[23] We gratefully acknowledge the substantial contributions of Professor Stephen A. Zeff to the material in this appendix.

[24] See E. R. Willet, *Fundamentals of Securities Markets* (New York: Appleton-Century-Crofts, 1968), pp. 208–14.

When Franklin D. Roosevelt was sworn in as president in March 1933, the economy was paralyzed, unemployment was rampant, and the nation's banking system was on the verge of collapse. In the Senate, public hearings exposed a pattern of financial abuse by such distinguished banking institutions as J.P. Morgan, National City Bank, and Chase National Bank that included insider trading, market manipulation, reckless speculation, and special favors to influential friends.

In an effort to bolster public confidence and restore order to the securities market, Congress enacted the Securities Act of 1933, which required companies selling capital stock or debt in interstate commerce to provide financial information pertinent to establishing the value and risk associated with those securities. One year later, the Act was amended to establish the SEC as an independent agency of the government, an agency whose function was to regulate both the securities sold to the public and the exchanges where those securities were traded. Companies issuing stock or debt listed on organized exchanges were required to file annual audited reports with the SEC.[25] The SEC was also empowered to establish and enforce the accounting policies and practices followed by registered companies.

These powers are given to the SEC in Section 19(a) of the Securities Act of 1933 as amended:

> the Commission shall have authority, for the purposes of this title, to prescribe the form or forms in which required information shall be set forth, the items or details to be shown in the balance sheet and earning statement, and the methods to be followed in the preparation of accounts, in the appraisal or valuation of assets and liabilities, in the determination of depreciation and depletion, in the differentiation of recurring and nonrecurring income, in the differentiation of investment and operating income, and in the preparation, where the Commission deems it necessary or desirable, of consolidated balance sheets or income accounts of any person directly or indirectly controlling or controlled by the issuer, or any person under direct or indirect common control with the issuer. The rules and regulations of the Commission shall be effective upon publication in the manner which the Commission shall prescribe.

In addition to its primary pronouncement—*Regulation S-X,* which describes the principal formal financial disclosure requirements for companies—the SEC issues *Financial Reporting Releases, Staff Accounting Bulletins,* and other publications stating its position on accounting and auditing matters.

The SEC's Division of Corporation Finance (DCF) reviews the financial statements in both periodic filings and prospectuses to ensure compliance with SEC requirements. The DCF writes deficiency letters to companies when it has questions about their accounting and disclosure practices. If a company cannot satisfy the DCF's concerns, it must revise and reissue its financial statements accordingly. Companies that fail to do so risk an SEC-imposed trading suspension or offering curtailment. No other securities commission in the world has such extensive authority to regulate financial reporting practices.

*Accounting Series Release No. 4,* issued in April 1938, first expressed the SEC's position that generally accepted accounting principles for which there is "substantial authoritative support" constitute the SEC standard for financial reporting and disclosure. The release further indicated that a company filing financial statements reflecting an accounting principle that had been formally disapproved by the SEC or for which there was no substantial authoritative support would be presumed to be filing misleading financial statements even though

---

[25] Security registration statements and other reports filed under the 1934 amendments to the Securities Act are public information and are available for inspection at the SEC and at the securities exchange where the company's securities are listed.

there was full disclosure of the accounting principles applied. However, the release did not provide guidance as to what the SEC meant by *substantial authoritative support*. This void was later filled.

## Emergence of GAAP

The Securities Exchange Act of 1934 required the financial statements of all publicly traded firms to be audited by independent accountants but only if so stipulated by the SEC, which soon did so. This requirement elevated the role of the independent accountants' professional organizations. These organizations were active in influencing accounting policy prior to the 1930s, but the securities acts accentuated the need for more formal accounting standards and for systematic public announcement of those standards.

> In 1938 and 1939, Congress permitted companies to use a new inventory method—LIFO or last-in, first-out described in Chapter 9—for income tax purposes, but only if LIFO is also used in corporate annual reports to shareholders. This is one of the very few instances in which tax policy has influenced GAAP.

During the years immediately following passage of the 1933 and 1934 securities acts, the SEC relied primarily on the American Institute of Certified Public Accountants (AICPA), the national professional organization of certified public accountants, to develop and enforce accounting standards.[26] In response to the SEC and to the growing need to report reliable financial information, the AICPA created the Committee on Accounting Procedure in 1939 to establish, review, and evaluate accepted accounting procedures. This committee began the practice of developing U.S. financial accounting and reporting standards in the private sector. The SEC, by a narrow vote, expressed its support for this private-sector approach to establishing U.S. accounting standards. The SEC did not delegate its standard-setting authority to the committee—by law, it cannot delegate that authority.

Until its demise in 1959, the AICPA's Committee on Accounting Procedure was responsible for narrowing the differences and inconsistencies in accounting practice. The committee issued 51 Accounting Research Bulletins (ARBs) and four Accounting Terminology Bulletins that set forth what the committee believed GAAP should be. These pronouncements were not binding on companies or their auditors.

In 1959, the AICPA established the Accounting Principles Board (APB) to replace the Committee on Accounting Procedure. The APB's basic charge was to develop a statement of accounting concepts—that is, a conceptual foundation for accounting—and to issue pronouncements resolving current accounting controversies. During its existence from 1959 to 1973, the APB issued 31 Opinions and four Statements designed to improve external financial accounting and disclosure. At the outset, the force of these pronouncements, as with earlier ARBs, depended on general acceptance and persuasion. The APB sought compliance with financial reporting standards by attempting to persuade corporations and independent auditors that the standards improved the quality of financial reporting. By 1964, many accounting professionals and business leaders were convinced that persuasion alone could neither reduce the tremendous latitude available under then-existing accounting and reporting practices nor eliminate inconsistencies in the application of those practices. Critics cited instances in which identical transactions could be accounted for by any one of several different methods and net income could be manipulated by selecting a particular accounting approach from among several considered to be "generally accepted."

---

[26] The American Association of Public Accountants was established in 1887 and represented the core of the accounting profession in the United States. The name of the organization was changed to the American Institute of Accountants in 1917, and it became the AICPA in 1957.

A turning point in the development of corporate financial reporting standards occurred in October 1964 when the Council (or governing body) of the AICPA adopted a requirement that was later incorporated into the rules of ethics for independent CPAs:

**Rule 203—Accounting Principles:**
A member shall not (1) express an opinion or state affirmatively that the financial statements or other financial data of any entity are presented in conformity with generally accepted accounting principles or (2) state that he or she is not aware of any material modifications that should be made to such statements or data in order for them to be in conformity with generally accepted accounting principles, if such statements or data contain any departure from an accounting principle promulgated by bodies designated by Council to establish such principles that has a material effect on the statements or data taken as a whole. If, however, the statements or data contain such a departure and the member can demonstrate that due to unusual circumstances the financial statements or data would otherwise have been misleading, the member can comply with the rule by describing the departure, its approximate effects, if practicable, and the reasons why compliance with the principle would result in a misleading statement. [As amended.][27]

This requirement provided further impetus to corporations and their auditors to implement the accounting standards prescribed in APB opinions and in earlier pronouncements not superseded by these opinions (of course, the SEC's DCF is responsible for ensuring GAAP compliance). This in turn caused greater attention to be focused on the APB's activities.

Complaints about the process used to develop financial reporting and accounting standards surfaced in the 1960s and early 1970s. Corporate management, government regulators, and other interested external parties voiced concern about the lack of participation by organizations other than the AICPA, the quality of the opinions issued, the failure of the APB to develop a coherent conceptual foundation for external financial reporting, the insufficient output by the APB, and the APB's failure to act promptly to correct alleged accounting and reporting abuses.

> In 1968, the SEC required companies to include a Management's Discussion and Analysis of Operations (MD&A) narrative along with the financial statements. The MD&A describes the risks and uncertainties facing a company and their implications for future liquidity and solvency.

The APB was not immune to criticism from politicians, government regulators, and the business community. One example occurred in the early 1960s when the APB attempted to resolve the question of accounting for the **investment tax credit.** The APB initially required the tax credit to be treated as a balance sheet item, a reduction in the asset's purchase cost, rather than as an immediate increase to earnings. This decision met with strong resistance from government, business, and several major accounting firms who argued that the APB's approach would impede economic growth. After the SEC said it would allow both methods in filings with the Commission, the APB had no alternative but to rescind its earlier pronouncement (*Opinion No. 2*) and to permit the earnings increase (*Opinion No. 4*).[28] This change in the accounting standard enabled firms to use the accounting methods they preferred for the investment tax credit. This disagreement over the accounting treatment for the investment tax credit epitomized the political interference inherent in the establishment of GAAP.

The 1971 Study Group on Establishment of Accounting Principles (or "Wheat Committee") was formed by the AICPA to review and evaluate the private-sector standard-setting process as well as to recommend improvements where possible. This committee was created because of

---

[27] The special bulletin approved by the Council in 1964 referred to departures from APB Opinions, not GAAP, and did not mention the term *misleading*. In 1973, the Council approved the inclusion of language from the Special Bulletin as Rule 203. The GAAP "override" provision described in the last sentence of Rule 203 is rarely seen these days in the financial statements of companies subject to SEC oversight, and most observers believe the SEC will not accept departures from GAAP.

[28] In fact, Congress passed legislation in December 1971 permitting the investment tax credit to "flow through" to reported earnings in the year the credit was taken against the company's federal tax obligation. This situation illustrates the ultimate power of the Congress over the establishment of financial reporting and accounting standards in the United States. See "Accounting for the Investment Credit," *APB Opinion No. 2* (New York: AICPA, 1962); "Accounting for the Investment Credit," *APB Opinion No. 4* (New York: AICPA, 1964).

growing concern among accounting professionals over the APB's ability to withstand pressure from the business community. The committee recommended that a new and independent, full-time standard-setting organization be established in the private sector to replace the APB. This recommendation, which the AICPA approved and which became effective in July 1973, created the FASB. The FASB was the first full-time accounting standards-setting body in the world.

The FASB differed from its predecessors in several ways:

1. Board membership consisted of 7 voting members, in contrast to the 18 members on the APB.
2. Autonomy and independence were enhanced by requiring members to sever all ties with their prior employers and by dictating that the FASB directly pay member salaries.
3. Broader representation was achieved by not requiring board members to hold a CPA license.
4. Staff and advisory support was increased substantially.

> During the transition period between the APB and FASB, the SEC took a more active and aggressive role in policy making. During its last nine months of operation (October 1972 through June 1973), the APB issued seven opinions in an attempt to complete its agenda of in-process accounting policy considerations. The SEC issued eight releases on accounting matters during this same period and another nine during the first year of the FASB.

*Accounting Series Release No. 150,* issued by the SEC in December 1973, formally acknowledged that financial accounting pronouncements of the FASB (and its predecessor organizations) are ordinarily considered by the SEC as having "substantial authoritative support" and thus are the SEC standards for financial reporting and disclosure. Accounting practices that are contrary to FASB pronouncements are considered to not have such support. This release also reaffirmed the SEC's private-sector approach to standard setting. It said,

> the Commission intends to continue its policy of looking to the private sector for leadership in establishing and improving accounting principles and standards through the FASB with the expectation that the body's conclusions will promote the interests of investors.

## Current Institutional Structure in the United States

The SEC still retains broad statutory powers to define accounting terms, prescribe the methods to be followed in preparing financial reports, and specify the details to be presented in financial statements. Under the Securities Act of 1933, companies wanting to issue securities interstate must file a **prospectus** with the SEC. The prospectus is a public document prepared for each new security offering containing information about the company, its officers, and its financial affairs. The financial section of the prospectus must be audited by an independent CPA who is registered to practice before the SEC. Once securities have been sold to the public, the company is required to file publicly accessible, audited financial statements with the SEC each year. These annual statements are known as the *10-K filing*. In addition, unaudited quarterly financial reports (called *10-Q filings*) are required. The annual 10-K disclosure requirements closely overlap the information in the company's published financial statements but are more extensive.[29]

Although the SEC has wide statutory authority to impose financial reporting rules, it continues to rely on the accounting profession to set and enforce accounting standards and to regulate the

---

[29] The financial reporting and accounting requirements pertaining to SEC registrants are described in the following publications: Regulation S-X, the original and comprehensive document issued by the commission that prescribes financial reporting rules and the forms to be filed with the SEC; Accounting Series Releases, which are amendments, extensions, and additions to Regulation S-X; Special SEC Releases that relate to current issues as they arise; Accounting and Auditing Enforcement Releases (AAERs), which document the SEC response to accounting and auditing irregularities; and Financial Reporting Releases (FRRs). The FRRs and AAERs are the successors to Accounting Series Releases. Staff Accounting Bulletins are issued by Office of the Chief Accountant and DCF and serve as interpretations of Regulation S-X and its amendments, extensions, and additions; they do not carry the legal weight of SEC releases.

profession. The SEC has occasionally forced the accounting profession to tackle critical problems, and it once rejected an accounting standard issued by the FASB.[30] Such situations occur rarely.

Since July 1973, the FASB has been responsible for establishing accounting standards in the United States. The FASB has issued more than 155 Statements of Financial Accounting Standards, seven Statements of Financial Accounting Concepts, and numerous interpretations. FASB Technical Bulletins, Staff Implementation Guides, Staff Announcements, and Staff Positions provide clarification and interpretation guidance, but they represent the views of staff, not the Board. The FASB has neither the authority nor the responsibility to enforce compliance with GAAP. That responsibility rests with company management, the accounting profession, the SEC, and the courts. Some observers believe that compliance is the weak link in the private-sector standard-setting chain. These critics point to frequent litigation on financial reporting matters in the courts, the escalating cost of liability insurance premiums paid by audit firms, and criticism by the SEC's chief accountant regarding the independence of external auditors.[31]

The FASB follows a "due process" procedure in developing accounting standards. This process is designed to ensure public input in the decision process. Most accounting standards issued by the FASB go through three steps:

1. *Discussion-memorandum stage:* After the Board and its staff have considered a topic on its agenda and perhaps consulted with experts and other interested parties, it issues a discussion memorandum. This memorandum outlines the key issues involved and the Board's preliminary views on those issues. The public is invited to comment in writing on the memorandum, and public hearings are sometimes held to permit interested individuals to express their views in person.

2. *Exposure-draft stage:* After further deliberation and modification by the Board and its staff, an exposure draft of the standard is issued. During this stage, a period of not less than 30 days, further public comment is requested and evaluated.

3. *Voting stage:* Finally, the Board votes on whether to issue the standard as contained in the exposure draft or to revise it and reissue a new exposure draft. For a proposed standard to become official and a part of GAAP, five of the seven Board members must approve it.

Influential groups and organizations use the FASB's due process to plead for alternative solutions. The arguments often include cost-benefit considerations, claims that the proposed accounting treatment is not theoretically sound or will not be understood by users, implementation issues, and concerns that the proposed standard will be economically harmful to specific companies, industries, or the country.[32] Government agencies, preparer organizations such as the Business Roundtable, and industry trade organizations such as Financial Executives International create substantial pressures on the Board. Some contend that the interests of investors, creditors, and other financial statement users are not always well represented in this political forum. Others disagree.

---

[30] "Financial Accounting and Reporting by Oil and Gas Producing Companies," *Statement of Financial Accounting Standards (SFAS) No. 19* (Stamford, CT: FASB, 1977). This statement was issued after protracted deliberation, and it identified a single method of accounting that was to be followed by all affected companies. In August 1978, the SEC ruled that a new method of accounting for oil and gas reserves needed to be developed and that in the meantime, companies could use any method that had been generally accepted prior to *SFAS No. 19*. This directly contradicted the FASB and required the issuance of both a statement suspending *SFAS No. 19* and a second FASB statement finally bringing the SEC and FASB into conformity with one another. SEC involvement was, in part, due to enactment of a public law requiring an investigation into and action on the state of oil and gas accounting rules by December 25, 1977. Such legal deadlines in connection with the accounting standard setting process are rare. Aspects of this controversy are discussed in Chapter 10.

[31] W. P. Schuetze, "A Mountain or a Molehill?" *Accounting Horizons,* March 1994, pp. 69–75.

[32] For example, SEC reversal of *SFAS No. 19* was justified on the grounds that implementation of the proposed accounting standard would sharply inhibit petroleum exploration and development activities.

What does the future hold? According to one keen observer of the process by which accounting principles are established in the United States, history is destined to repeat itself:

> When a highly prescriptive standards setter is coupled with a rigorous enforcement process used by a government regulator to secure compliance with accounting standards, especially in a confrontational society such as the United States, companies and even branches of government will lobby the standards setter not to approve standards that interfere with their business plans and strategies. This is what has happened increasingly in the United States since the 1970s, and there is no sign that, on sensitive and controversial issues, it will diminish in intensity or frequency.[33]

**Public Company Accounting Oversight Board**   When Congress gave the task of setting accounting standards to the newly created SEC in 1934, it left the job of overseeing auditing standards and individual audit firms to the accounting profession. For nearly seven decades, the AICPA and its predecessor organization have performed the job. In the late 1970s, the AICPA formed the Public Oversight Board to monitor the conduct of auditors. The Board was funded by industry, but it had little power to enforce auditing standards or discipline wayward audit firms.

The successor to the old Board, the Public Company Accounting Oversight Board (PCAOB), is funded by mandatory fees from public companies and operates under the SEC's oversight. The new Board was created by the Sarbanes-Oxley Act (SOX) of 2002. The PCAOB is empowered to establish auditing standards, including standards for independence and ethics, and to conduct periodic quality reviews ("inspections") of auditors' work. It can also investigate alleged audit failures and impose penalties on auditors and their firms. The PCAOB can fine, censure, suspend, or bar from practice auditors and audit firms for wrongdoing.

**SOX Compliance**   The groundbreaking SOX was enacted to reign in earlier accounting abuses by strengthening auditor independence and improving financial reporting transparency. In addition to establishing the PCAOB, SOX requires company compliance in a number of areas. For most companies, Sections 302 and 404 represent the bulk of SOX compliance work. The following is a brief overview of each section.

> **Section 302: Corporate Responsibility for Financial Reports.** This section requires CEOs and CFOs to personally certify the accuracy of financial statements and related disclosures in the annual and quarterly reports. CEOs and CFOs must certify that those statements fairly present in all material aspects the results of operations and financial condition of the company.

> **Section 404: Management Assessment of Internal Controls.** This section requires an annual evaluation of internal controls and procedures for financial reporting. CEOs and CFOs must periodically assess and certify the effectiveness of internal controls and procedures. Companies are obliged to include an internal control report in their annual report. Among other things, this report:

> - Acknowledges management's responsibility for establishing and maintaining internal control over financial reporting.
> - Contains an assessment of the effectiveness of the company's internal control over financial reporting as of the end of the most recent fiscal year.
> - Discloses any material weaknesses uncovered in the company's internal controls.

Section 404 also requires a company's external auditor to examine and report on management's assessment of internal controls as well as the effectiveness of the controls themselves.

---

[33] S. A. Zeff, "The Evolution of U.S. GAAP: The Political Forces Behind Professional Standards," *The CPA Journal,* February 2005.

In addition to these provisions, SOX **Section 906** requires CEOs and CFOs to sign and certify that the company's financial statements comply with SEC reporting requirements and fairly represent the company's financial condition and results. Willful failure to comply with this requirement can result in fines of up to $5 million and imprisonment for up to 20 years.

The accounting profession and SEC have long recognized that sound internal controls are essential to ensure financial statement credibility. For example, in December 1977, after hundreds of public companies disclosed bribes, kickbacks, and political payoffs, Congress amended the Securities Exchange Act of 1934 to require issuers to have reasonable internal controls. In 1981, the U.S. Senate attempted to delete this section of the law but failed. Over the years, several professional groups have urged the SEC to require management reporting to shareholders on the effectiveness of internal control. Among these are the *Report of the National Commission on Fraudulent Financial Reporting* (the Treadway Commission) in 1987, the Public Accounting Oversight Board in 1993, and the General Accounting Office in 1996. In the end, a crisis of confidence and congressional action rather than a proactive SEC resulted in legislation requiring that corporations have adequate internal controls to ensure complete and accurate financial reporting.

## International Accounting Standards

When looking to register securities in U.S. markets, a major impediment that foreign companies encounter involves the significant differences that exist between U.S. and foreign accounting standards. Several groups have long worked to achieve "convergence" of worldwide accounting and reporting standards. At the center of this effort are the International Accounting Standards Board (IASB), which sets international accounting rules, and the International Organization of Securities Commissions (IOSCO), of which the SEC is a member. The International Accounting Standards Committee (IASC) was the predecessor body of the IASB. As part of an agreement with IOSCO, the IASC developed a core set of International Accounting Standards (IAS), completed in 1998. IOSCO endorsed these accounting standards for cross-border capital raising and stock exchange listing purposes in May 2000.

Formed in 1973, the IASC was the result of an agreement by accountancy bodies in Australia, Canada, France, West Germany, Japan, Mexico, the Netherlands, the United Kingdom, and the United States. The IASC was restructured in 2001 and the IASB assumed its duties. At that time, the IASC membership included 153 professional accounting organizations from more than 112 countries around the world. The standard-setting function is now performed by the IASB, made up of 14 people with broad technical expertise and substantial practical experience. The IASB has issued 46 standards and 33 interpretations of existing standards. Existing IASB standards typically allow firms greater latitude in their accounting and reporting practices than does U.S. GAAP.

Founded in 1974, IOSCO seeks member cooperation to improve domestic and international financial markets, promote the development of domestic markets through information exchange, establish standards and effective surveillance of international securities transactions, and ensure the integrity of markets by rigorous application of standards and enforcement. In 1998, IOSCO adopted disclosure standards that enable multinational companies to prepare a single nonfinancial statement disclosure document (including, for example, a description of the company's history, business, risks, and ownership) for cross-border securities offerings and stock exchange listings. In addition to greatly simplifying preparation, investors benefit from the comprehensive required disclosures and enhanced comparability of information. The SEC adopted these IOSCO disclosure standards in 1999.

The SEC has made it clear that U.S. financial reporting standards will not be lowered for domestic public companies. The SEC previously said it will consider international accounting standards for use by foreign companies, without reconciliation to U.S. GAAP, but only when the standards meet certain criteria:

- They include a core set of accounting pronouncements constituting a comprehensive, generally accepted basis of accounting.
- They are high quality; that is, they result in comparability and transparency and provide for full disclosure.
- They can and will be rigorously interpreted and applied.

These criteria seem to have been met in November 2007—or perhaps the SEC softened its view—because that is when the SEC eliminated the U.S. GAAP reconciliation requirement for foreign companies using IFRS. The inevitable march toward global convergence of financial reporting standards continues.

# PROBLEMS / DISCUSSION QUESTIONS

**P1-1**

**Demand for accounting information**

**Required:**
1. Explain why each of the following groups might want financial accounting information. What type of financial information would each group find most useful?
   a. The company's existing shareholders.
   b. Prospective investors.
   c. Financial analysts who follow the company.
   d. Company managers.
   e. Current employees.
   f. Commercial lenders who have loaned money to the company.
   g. Current suppliers.
   h. Debt-rating agencies such as Moody's or Standard and Poor's.
   i. Regulatory agencies such as the Federal Trade Commission.
2. Identify at least one other group that might want financial accounting information about the company, and describe how it would use the information.

**P1-2**

**Incentives for voluntary disclosure**

**Required:**
1. Describe how the following market forces influence the supply of financial accounting information:
   a. Debt and equity financial markets.
   b. Managerial labor markets.
   c. The market for corporate control (for example, mergers, takeovers, and divestitures).
2. What other forces might cause managers to voluntarily release financial information about the company?
3. Identify five ways managers can voluntarily provide information about the company to outsiders. What advantages do these voluntary approaches have over the required financial disclosures contained in annual and quarterly reports to shareholders?

**P1-3**

Costs of disclosure

**Required:**

1. Define each of the following disclosure costs associated with financial accounting information, and provide an example of each cost:

    a. Information collection, processing, dissemination costs.

    b. Competitive disadvantage costs.

    c. Litigation costs.

    d. Political costs.

2. Identify at least one other potential disclosure cost.

---

**P1-4**

Proxy statement disclosures

A company's proxy statement contains information about major shareholders, management compensation (salary, bonus, stock options, etc.), composition of the board of directors, and shares owned by top managers and members of the board of directors.

**Required:**

Explain why this information might be useful to a financial analyst following the firm.

---

**P1-5**

Relevant and reliable information

You have decided to buy a new automobile and have been gathering information about the purchase price. The manufacturer's Web site shows a "list price" of $24,500, which includes your preferred options: leather trim and CD player. You have also consulted the "Blue Book" guide to car prices and found that the average price paid for a similar vehicle is $19,500. However, the guide also indicates that recent selling prices have ranged from $18,000 up to $22,000.

**Required:**

1. Which price quote, the "list price" or the "Blue Book" average price, is the more relevant for your decision? Why?

2. Which price quote is the more reliable? Why?

---

**P1-6**

Relevant and reliable accounting information

Farmers State Bank is considering a $500,000 loan to Willard Manufacturing. Three items appearing on Willard's balance sheet are:

a. Cash on hand and in the bank, $20,000.

b. Accounts receivable of $60,000, less an allowance for uncollectibles of $15,000.

c. Accumulated depreciation of $36,000.

**Required:**

1. Which of the balance sheet items—cash, net accounts receivable, or accumulated depreciation—is the most relevant for the bank's loan decision? Why?

2. Which of the balance sheet items is the most reliable? Why?

---

**P1-7**

Accounting conservatism

Suppose your company purchased land and a warehouse for $5 million. The price was steep, but you were told that a new interstate highway was going to be built nearby. Two months later, the highway project is canceled and your property is now worth only $3 million.

**Required:**

1. How does the concept of accounting conservatism apply to this situation?

2. Suppose instead that you paid $3 million and later learned that the property is worth $5 million because a new highway is going to be built nearby. How does the conservatism concept apply to this new situation? Why?

**Required:**

Provide a two- or three-sentence response that argues for or against (indicate which) each of these statements:

**P1-8**

Your position on the issues

1. Accounting is an exact science.
2. Managers choose accounting procedures that produce the most accurate picture of the company's operating performance and financial condition.
3. U.S. accounting standards are influenced more by politics than by science or economics.
4. If the FASB and SEC were not around to require and enforce minimum levels of financial disclosure, most companies would provide little (if any) information to outsiders.
5. When managers possess good news about the company (that is, information that will increase the stock price), they have an incentive to disclose the information as soon as possible.
6. When managers possess bad news about the company (that is, information that will decrease the stock price), they have an incentive to delay disclosure as long as possible.
7. An investor who uses fundamental analysis for investment decisions has little need for financial statement information.
8. An investor who believes that capital markets are efficient has little need for financial statement information.
9. Managers who disclose only the minimum information required to meet FASB and SEC requirements may be doing a disservice to shareholders.
10. Financial statements are the only source of information analysts use when forecasting the company's future profitability and financial condition.

A wide variety of financial and nonfinancial information is used in managing a company and in making decisions about whether or not to invest in a company. A survey of senior corporate managers and professional investors asked each group to rank the following items according to their relative importance ("1" being the most important and "14" being the least important). How do you think each item was ranked?

**P1-9**

How managers and professional investors rate information

| | Importance Ranking | |
|---|---|---|
| | **Corporate Managers** | **Professional Investors** |
| Business segment results | | |
| Capital expenditures | | |
| Cash flow | | |
| Cost control | | |
| Customer satisfaction | | |
| Earnings | | |
| Market growth | | |
| Market share | | |
| Measures of strategic achievement | | |
| New product development | | |
| Product and process quality | | |
| Research and development (R&D) | | |
| R&D productivity | | |
| Strategic goals | | |

<table>
<tr><td>

**P1-10**

Economic consequences of accounting standards
</td><td>

In the early 1990s, the FASB issued new rules that dramatically altered the way in which many companies recorded their obligations for postretirement health care benefits. The Board found that most companies used "cash basis" accounting and waited until expenditures for benefits were actually made before recording any expense. This meant that no liability to pay future benefits appeared on the companies' balance sheets even though an obligation to pay future health care benefits clearly existed. The FASB concluded that this approach was inappropriate and instead required companies to record the cost of future health care benefits as incurred.

The affected companies and their trade organizations argued that having to record a liability and an expense equal to the extremely large dollar amounts of these health care benefit commitments would cause employers to substantially reduce their promised benefits to employees and perhaps curtail the benefits entirely.

**Required:**

1. Why were companies concerned about suddenly reporting a large liability (and corresponding expense) for postretirement health care benefits? What economic consequences might this accounting change have on the affected companies?

2. Some affected companies said they would reduce or eliminate promised benefits to avoid recording the liability and expense. This action harms employees who will then have to bear the burden of future health care costs. Should the FASB consider economic consequences of this sort when setting accounting standards? Why or why not?
</td></tr>
<tr><td>

**P1-11**

Two sets of books
</td><td>

"It's time for the government to stop enabling accounting fraud. The Internal Revenue Service and the SEC let companies keep two sets of books, one for tax reporting and the other for financial reporting. There should be no difference in the figures corporations report to the IRS and the SEC. The combined surveillance and enforcement by these agencies of one set of books and identical tax and financial reports should give the investing public a clearer picture of corporate performance." Letter to the Editor, *BusinessWeek,* August 12, 2002.

**Required:**

1. Why do companies keep two sets of accounting books, one for tax reporting and the other for shareholder financial reports?

2. Why might it *not* be a good idea to force companies to issue the same financial statements for both IRS and SEC purposes?
</td></tr>
<tr><td>

**P1-12**

Accounting quality and the audit committee
</td><td>

The New York Stock Exchange (NYSE), the National Association of Securities Dealers (NASD), and the American Stock Exchange (AMEX) require that listed firms have audit committees of independent (that is, outside) company directors. Audit committees review the firm's audited financial statements with management and with the outside auditor and recommend to the full board of directors that the statements be included in the company's annual report. As a committee member, you might ask management about the following:

1. What are the key business and financial risks the company has to deal with in its financial reporting?

2. What financial reporting areas involved subjective judgments or estimates?

3. Are there significant areas where the company's accounting policies were difficult to determine?

4. How do the company's accounting practices compare with those of others in the industry?

5. How are significant accounting judgments made and estimates determined?
</td></tr>
</table>

6. Are the financial statements and underlying accounting methods consistent with those used last year?

7. What major business transactions or events required significant accounting or disclosure judgments?

8. Are alternative accounting practices being proposed or considered that should be brought to the committee's attention?

9. Were there serious problems in preparing the financial statements?

10. Have outside parties including the SEC, major investors, analysts, and the news media voiced concern about the company's accounting practices?

11. Were there disagreements between management and the auditor regarding accounting practices and, if so, how were they resolved?

*Source:* Audit Committee Update 2000, PricewaterhouseCoopers LLP.

**Required:**

Explain for each question why the audit committee and investors might be interested in the answer.

---

The IASB and its predecessor organization have as a stated objective to narrow worldwide differences in accounting practices and the presentation of financial information. In February 2006 at a ceremony in Beijing, People's Republic of China, the Chinese Ministry of Finance announced the adoption of new Chinese accounting standards that bring about substantial convergence between them and the IASB's IFRS. These are excerpts from a statement made during the ceremony by Sir David Tweedie, chairman of the IASB:

> I am honoured to be here today to mark what I believe is an important step for the development of the Chinese economy and its place in the world's increasingly integrated capital markets. The adoption of the new Chinese accounting standards system brings about substantial convergence between Chinese standards and International Financial Reporting Standards (IFRSs), as set by the International Accounting Standards Board (IASB). Like the United States and Japan, China is committed to convergence with IFRS. . . .
>
> The benefits of these accounting reforms for China are clear. The new Chinese standards that incorporate accounting principles familiar to investors worldwide will encourage investor confidence in China's capital markets and financial reporting and will be an additional spur for investment from both domestic and foreign sources of capital. For Chinese companies that are increasingly playing a global role, the acceptance of the new standards should also reduce the cost of complying with the accounting regimes of the different jurisdictions in which they operate. . . .

**P1-13**

**Worldwide convergence of accounting standards**

**Required:**

1. Why might it be beneficial to narrow worldwide differences in accounting practices? Are there any disadvantages associated with convergence?

2. Explain how the convergence of Chinese accounting standards and IFRS can benefit the Chinese investor who invests only in Chinese companies.

3. Explain how the convergence of Chinese accounting standards and IFRS can benefit the U.S. investor who sometimes invests in Chinese companies.

---

Friedman's Inc. is a leading fine jewelry retailer. In November 2004, the company said that it might default on certain of the financial covenants contained in one of the company loan agreements. Here is an excerpt from the company's press release:

> In particular, Friedman's expects that it will fail to meet cumulative EBITDA requirements for the period ending October 30, 2004, constituting a default under its term loan, and it will fail to meet a minimum ratio of Accounts Payable to Inventory as of October 30, 2004, constituting a default under both its term loan and its revolving loan. Friedman's is currently in discussions with its senior lenders under the credit facility regarding the amendment of its covenants to eliminate the default.

**P1-14**

**Debt covenants and aggressive accounting practices**

EBITDA stands for earnings before interest, taxes, depreciation, and amortization. Apparently, Friedman's term loan contained a provision that required the company to maintain a minimum level of profitability (measured using EBITDA) over several periods (hence, the use of "cumulative," meaning summed over the periods in question).

**Required:**

1. What will happen to the company if it violates these two covenants and is unsuccessful in obtaining a waiver or amendment from senior lenders?

2. Explain how the EBITDA covenant creates an incentive for Friedman's to engage in aggressive accounting practices. Provide one or more examples of aggressive accounting that Friedman's might use to avoid violating the EBITDA covenant.

3. Explain how the accounts payable to inventory covenant also creates an incentive for Friedman's to engage in aggressive accounting practices.

---

**PI-15**

Proxy contests and aggressive accounting practices

### HEINZ PROFIT, SALES TOP ESTIMATES

New York (Dow Jones)—H.J. Heinz Co. on Thursday said fiscal first quarter net income rose 23%, helped by strong sales of Weight Watchers Smart One meals and Classico pasta sauces.

Heinz (HNZ), which is awaiting the results of a proxy fight with the Trian Group hedge fund, said profit increased to $194.1 million, or 58 cents a share, from $157.3 million, or 45 cents, a year ago. Excluding charges in the year-ago quarter, income would have grown 18.6%.

Sales for the three months ended Aug. 2 increased 8.4% to $2.06 billion from $1.9 billion, helped by higher selling prices

and foreign currency exchange. Volume advanced 5.1%, driven by higher consumption and new products. . . .

Shares in Heinz fell as much as 19 cents to $41.79 in early trading.

"Heinz's impressive first-quarter performance demonstrates that the company is delivering results with a clear focus on growing its key brands and enhancing shareholder value," said spokesman Michael Mullen in an e-mail. . . .

**Required:**

Why might investors have been skeptical about the source and sustainability of the quarterly earnings increase reported by Heinz?

---

## CASES

**CI-I**

AST Research: Restating quarter results

AST Research Inc., a personal computer manufacturer, announced a change in its accounting for acquisition-related expenditures. Costs previously deferred were to be expensed immediately. The change had no direct impact on current or future cash flows. A copy of the *The Wall Street Journal* article announcing AST's accounting change follows:

## AST RESEARCH

AST Research said it is restating results for its fiscal 1994 fourth quarter as a result of a disagreement with the Securities and Exchange Commission over accounting rules.

The restatement will cause AST to report a loss of $8.1 million, or 25 cents a share, for the fourth quarter ended July 2, instead of the previously reported net income of $14.1 million, or 41 cents a share. The dispute arose out of an SEC review of AST's proxy statement for a $377.5 million investment in the company by Samsung Electronics Company.

The SEC staff concluded that $33.6 million of the expenses related to AST's 1993 acquisition of the computer manufacturing operations of Tandy Corporation should be charged to sales during the fourth quarter, rather than amortized over future quarters as goodwill.

AST said that the SEC didn't force it to restate the results, and that AST had agreed to the restatement to avoid delays in approval of the proxy and the Samsung investment. The redesignation of income has no material effect on AST. It's a noncash loss and will be offset by increases in net income in subsequent quarters, because of the lack of goodwill amortization.

In Nasdaq Stock Market trading yesterday, AST closed at $17.625, up 25 cents.

"They [the SEC] had a different interpretation on a piece of the accounting for the acquisition," said Bruce Edwards, AST's chief financial officer. "We decided to do the restatement to move forward on the transaction" with Samsung.

An SEC official acknowledged that the agency's corporation finance division had been in talks with AST about its fourth-quarter earnings report but wouldn't say whether the SEC pressured AST to revise the report.

It isn't unusual for the agency to question a company's account of its own earnings, the official said. Only in rare cases does such a review spell bigger problems for the company, such as when the SEC thinks executives intentionally misstated earnings to hype a stock price. But there isn't any indication that AST did that in this case, the official added.

AST also agreed to issue additional shares to Samsung if AST incurs any uninsured losses, in excess of a certain threshold, as a result of being sued by shareholders. AST said it has now received all necessary approvals for Samsung's investment.

The company scheduled a special meeting of shareholders for June 30 to vote on the transaction.

**Required:**

Why was the stock market so forgiving in evaluating the accounting method change made by AST Research?

---

As your first week at Henley Manufacturing Inc. draws to a close, you find a memorandum on your desk from the company's CEO. The memo outlines sales and earnings goals for next year: Sales are expected to increase 15% with net income growing by 20%.

The memo says that these goals are ambitious in light of the company's performance over the past two years—ambitious but attainable if "everyone remains focused and committed to our business strategy."

As you finish the memo, your boss, the vice president of finance, steps into your office. She asks you what you think about the memo. You reply that it is important to have clear financial goals but that you would need to know more before making any comments on whether the goals will be easy or difficult to achieve. As she leaves your office, you ask if the CEO will be announcing these goals at next week's annual shareholders' meeting. Your boss answers, "We've never disclosed our sales and earning goals in the past." When you ask why, she says, "We aren't required to under U.S. securities regulations."

Two days later, your boss stops by again and tells you that she raised the issue of disclosing to shareholders the firm's net income and sales goals at this morning's executive committee meeting. The CEO was intrigued but requested that someone identify the costs and benefits of doing so. As she leaves your office, your boss asks you to prepare a briefing document for presentation at the next executive committee meeting.

**C1-2**

Henley Manufacturing Inc.: Announcing sales and earnings goals

**Required A:**

1. What are the potential costs and benefits to Henley Manufacturing of announcing its sales and earnings goals at the shareholders' meeting?

2. Would you recommend that the CEO announce both, one, or neither goal? Why?

3. If the company's sales and earnings goals covered three years rather than just next year, would your recommendation change? Why or why not?

**Required B:**

Suppose the memo was more detailed and described the following financial goals for next year: annual sales growth of 15%; annual earnings growth of 20%; a return on net tangible assets of 16%; a return on common equity of 20%; a minimum current ratio of 2.4; a minimum interest coverage ratio of 7.0; a minimum profit margin of 5%; a dividend payout ratio (dividends/net income) of 35% to 40%; a maximum long-term debt to common equity ratio of 40% to 45%; a minimum increase of 15% in annual capital expenditures; and a minimum inventory turnover ratio of 4.5.

Would you recommend that the CEO disclose all, some, or none of these goals at the shareholders' meeting? Which ones and why?

---

### C1-3

**Whirlpool: Disclosing major customers**

The following excerpt is from Whirlpool Corporation's 2005 10-K report filed with the SEC and is a required disclosure:

> The company is a major supplier to Sears of laundry, refrigerator, dishwasher, and trash compactor home appliances. Some products that the company supplies to Sears are marketed by Sears under the Sears Kenmore brand name. Sears is also a major outlet for the company's Whirlpool and KitchenAid brand products. In 2005 approximately 16% of the company's net sales were attributable to sales to Sears.

**Required:**

1. Why does the SEC require companies like Whirlpool to alert financial statement readers to the existence of major customers?

2. How might this information be of use to a financial analyst?

3. Why might Sears want to monitor the financial performance and health of Whirlpool? What specific information about Whirlpool would be of most interest to Sears?

4. Why might Whirlpool want to monitor the financial performance and health of Sears? What information about Sears would be of most interest to Whirlpool?

---

### C1-4

**The gap in GAAP**

It is often alleged that the value of financial statement information is compromised by the latitude that GAAP gives to management. Companies can use different accounting methods to summarize and report the outcome of otherwise similar transactions. Inventory valuation and depreciation are examples in which GAAP allows several alternative accounting methods.

At one extreme the FASB and the SEC could limit accounting flexibility by establishing a single set of accounting methods and procedures that all companies would apply. At the other extreme, the FASB and the SEC could simply require companies to provide relevant and reliable financial information to outsiders without placing any restrictions on the accounting methods used.

**Required:**

1. Why should managers be allowed some flexibility in their financial accounting and reporting choices?

2. Of the two approaches to accounting standard setting that are mentioned, which better describes the current financial reporting environment in the United States?

3. Describe the advantages and disadvantages of these two approaches to accounting standard setting, and tell how these advantages and disadvantages vary across different groups of financial statement users.

---

In early 1996, IES Industries signed a definitive merger agreement with two other neighboring utilities, Wisconsin Power and Light (WPL) and Interstate Power Company (IPC). This was the first "three-way" merger in the rapidly consolidating electrical utility industry.

**C1-5**
IES Industries: Voting on a merger

The merger seemed to make good economic sense. Predictions indicated that industry deregulation would create intense price competition. All three companies had low-cost generating capacity when compared to other utilities in the Midwest. By forming a single company, the merger partners could become even more price competitive by eliminating redundancies in energy distribution, maintenance, customer service, and corporate staffs. They could then expand their combined geographical reach to lucrative metropolitan markets in the region.

Wall Street was ambivalent about the merger. The merger announcement resulted in a 10% share price increase for IPC, but IES and WPL share prices remained flat. Part of the market's ambivalence was due to the fact that the merger required state and federal regulatory approval. Analysts predicted a lengthy approval process and voiced uncertainty about the eventual outcome.

In July 1996, MidAmerican Energy launched a hostile takeover of IES Industries. MidAmerican offered to pay $35 per share for IES stock, a $5 per-share premium over the closing price that prevailed before the takeover announcement. The IES board of directors rejected the buyout offer and told shareholders that the company was worth more than $35 per share when combined with WPL and IPC. Shares of IES common stock closed at $33.50 following MidAmerican Energy's hostile offer, and this price was unchanged after the IES rejection.

MidAmerican's tender offer could not have been better timed. IES shareholders were scheduled to vote on the three-way merger agreement in mid-August. With MidAmerican's offer on the table, IES shareholders could vote either to approve the WPL and IPC merger or to reject it in favor of MidAmerican's cash bid. IES and MidAmerican launched intense advertising and public relations campaigns to sway IES shareholders. This contest for proxies (shareholder votes) cost the two companies in excess of $10 million.

**Required:**

1. As an employee of IES Industries and the owner of 100 shares of the company's common stock, what questions would you like answered at the August shareholders' meeting just prior to submitting your vote? How might the company's financial reports help answer those questions?

2. As an institutional investor with 5% of your portfolio invested in IES shares, what questions would you like answered at the August shareholders' meeting just prior to submitting your vote? How might the company's financial reports help answer those questions?

---

Returning home from your job as a financial analyst covering the airline industry, you find a message from your father, a veteran pilot for TWA. He will be in town this evening and would like you to join him for dinner. He needs your investment advice. Having been with TWA during the company's two trips to bankruptcy court, he is ecstatic over an article in today's issue of *The Wall Street Journal*.

**C1-6**
Trans World Airlines (TWA): Making sense of an earnings announcement

TWA announced net income of $623.8 million for the year, compared to a loss of $317.7 million in the prior year. At last the company seems to have recovered from its financial difficulty.

As a TWA stockholder, your father is wondering whether he should purchase more of the company's stock and whether TWA might start paying dividends again now that it is profitable. He thinks the pilots' union might recover some of the wage concessions that it made during the bankruptcy process. Given the age of TWA's fleet (about 18 years), he hopes that some of the profits might be used to buy new airliners.

As you finish reading the news article, you realize that dinner is less than two hours away. What advice do you have for your father?

## TRANS WORLD AIRLINES

St. Louis—Trans World Airlines, helped by a big gain from retiring debt, posted 1993 net income of $623.8 million compared with a year-earlier loss of $317.7 million.

Before the $1.08 billion gain, TWA's 1993 loss widened to $451.8 million from $317.7 million in 1992. TWA, which emerged from bankruptcy-law proceedings last November, said the gain reflected a debt-for-equity swap that was part of its reorganization plan. Creditors received a 55% stake in TWA for forgiving about $1 billion in debt.

The airline's operating losses, before taxes and credits and charges, were $281.3 million in 1993 and $404.6 million in 1992. TWA's revenue fell 13% to $3.16 billion from $3.63 billion, as the company reduced its airline operations about 15% beginning in the fall of 1992.

The carrier didn't break out fourth-quarter results, saying there is "no meaningful comparison" with the year-earlier figures. Because of its emergence from Chapter 11 protection from creditors, TWA said its financial statements were prepared on both a pre- and post-reorganization basis for different parts of the fourth quarter.

The company's load factor, or percentage of seats filled, slipped to 63.5% during 1993 from 64.7%. TWA's yield, or revenue per passenger mile, increased to 11.35 cents in 1993 from 10.22 cents the year before.

*Source:* "Trans World Airlines," *The Wall Street Journal,* April 1, 1994. Copyright © 1994 Dow Jones & Company, Inc. All rights reserved worldwide. Reprinted with permission.

## COLLABORATIVE LEARNING CASES

**C1-7**

Landfil's accounting change

You have been asked to attend a hastily called meeting of Landfil's senior executives. The meeting was called to formulate a strategy for responding to questions from shareholders, analysts, and the media about Landfil's accounting for site development costs. A major competitor, Chambers Development, announced yesterday that it would no longer capitalize site development costs but instead would expense those costs as they were incurred. Stock market reaction to the Chambers announcement was swift and negative, with the stock down 57% at this morning's opening of the NYSE.

Landfil Inc. acquires, operates, and develops nonhazardous solid waste disposal facilities. Landfil is the third largest waste management company of its type in the United States with 37 disposal sites. Sales have been growing at the rate of 30% annually for the last five years, and the company has established a solid record of earnings and operating cash flow performance.

**Accounting Policy**

Landfil capitalizes site development costs in much the same way that Chambers Development did prior to its announcement yesterday. Under the old accounting method at Chambers Development, when the firm spent $20 million on landfill site development, it would book the entire amount as a deferred asset. Then Chambers would spread the cost over 10 years by charging $2 million to earnings each year. Under the new accounting method, all $20 million is expensed in the first year.

Landfil has included the following description of its site development accounting in all annual reports issued during the last five years:

> The Company capitalizes landfill acquisition costs, including out-of-pocket incremental expenses incurred in connection with the preacquisition phase of a specific project (for example, engineering, legal, and accounting due-diligence fees); the acquisition purchase price, including future guaranteed payments to sellers; and commissions. If an acquisition is not consummated, or a development project is abandoned, all of such costs are expensed. Salaries, office expenses, and similar administrative costs are not capitalized. Landfill development and permitting costs, including the cost of property, engineering, legal, and other professional fees, and interest are capitalized and amortized over the estimated useful life of the property upon commencement of operations.

**The Meeting**

Discussion at the meeting became rather heated as several different points of view emerged. Some members of the executive team argued that Landfil should do nothing but reaffirm its capitalization policy, informing shareholders and others who contacted the company that this policy was consistent with GAAP and disclosed fully in the annual report. Other members of the team argued for a more proactive response involving both direct communication with shareholders and analysts as well as press releases to the media. These communications would also reaffirm the company's capitalization policy but in a more strident manner. Still other members of the executive team argued that Landfil should immediately announce that it too was discontinuing capitalization in favor of immediate expensing. No clear consensus emerged as the meeting progressed, and the group decided to take a 10-minute break before resuming discussion.

As the meeting was about to reconvene, the CEO stopped by your chair and said, "I've been handed a phone message indicating that our largest shareholder has just called. She wants to know our reaction to the events at Chambers Development. I have to call her back in 15 minutes with an answer. When the meeting starts, I'd like you to summarize the major issues we face and to state how you think we should proceed."

**Required:**

Prepare your summary.

---

Yesterday, AstroText announced its friendly acquisition of TextTools Inc. AstroText intends to pay $20 per share for all of the outstanding common stock of TextTools. At this price, TextTools stockholders will be receiving a per share premium of $7 over the company's closing stock price just two days ago. There are 3 million shares outstanding, so the $7 per share premium represents $21 million in total.

AstroText and TextTools are both relatively young software development companies with similar product lines. Both companies have developed leading edge document creation software for the Internet. AstroText has focused its product line on individuals, small businesses, and academic markets. TextTools has targeted the corporate market where security and encryption are extremely important. To maintain their technological edge, both companies must continue to invest heavily in software research and development. Frequent product updates are the norm for companies such as AstroText and TextTools. In addition, both companies have historically spent considerable resources on product marketing and advertising.

AstroText is hosting a stockholders' meeting later today to discuss details of the acquisition. So far, the company has said very little about why it's willing to pay a $7 per share premium for TextTools, how the all-cash deal will be financed, or why the two companies will be worth more together than they are separately.

**C1-8**

AstroText Company: Questions for the stockholders' meeting

**Required:**

1. Suppose you are an AstroText employee who owns 100 shares of the company's stock. You have also received a substantial number of long-term stock options as part of your compensation package. What questions do you want answered at the stockholders' meeting? What information (if any) in the company's financial reports might help answer those questions?

2. Assume that you are the lead banker for AstroText. You were quite surprised to learn of the TextTools acquisition, in part because your loan to AstroText contains a provision that prohibits the company from making cash acquisitions without your approval. What questions do you want answered at the stockholders' meeting? What information (if any) in the company's financial reports might help answer those questions?

**Remember to check the book's companion Web site
for additional study material.**

# Accrual Accounting and Income Determination | 2

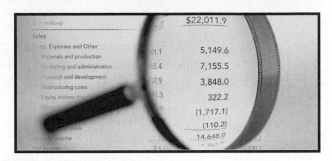

| ($ in millions) | | $22,011.9 |
| --- | --- | --- |
| Sales | | |
| Costs, Expenses and Other | .01.1 | 5,149.6 |
| Materials and production | 65.4 | 7,155.5 |
| Marketing and administrative | 2.9 | 3,848.0 |
| Research and development | 2.3 | 322.2 |
| Restructuring costs | 4) | (1,717.1) |
| Equity income fr... | | (110.2) |
| Other income | | 14,648.0 |
| Net income | 44.3 | 7,365... 830.1 |

T his chapter describes the key concepts and practices that govern the measurement of annual or quarterly income (or earnings) for financial reporting purposes. Income is the difference between **revenues** and **expenses**. The cornerstone of income measurement is **accrual accounting.** Under accrual accounting, *revenues are recorded in the period when they are "earned" and become "measurable"*—that is, when the seller has performed a service or conveyed an asset to a buyer and the value to be received for that service or asset is reasonably assured and can be measured with a high degree of reliability.[1] *Expenses are the expired costs or assets "used up" in producing those revenues, and they are recorded in the same accounting period in which the revenues are recognized using the "matching principle."*

A natural consequence of accrual accounting is the decoupling of measured earnings from operating cash inflows and outflows. Reported revenues under accrual accounting generally do not correspond to cash receipts for the period; also, reported expenses do not always correspond to cash outlays of the period. In fact, *accrual accounting can produce large discrepancies between the firm's reported profit performance and the amount of cash generated from operations. Frequently, however, accrual accounting earnings provide a more accurate measure of the economic value added during the period than do operating cash flows.*[2]

The following example illustrates this point; it highlights the basic distinction between cash and accrual accounting measures of performance.

## EXAMPLE: CASH VERSUS ACCRUAL INCOME MEASUREMENT

In January 2008, Canterbury Publishing sells a three-year subscription to its quarterly publication, *Windy City Living*, to 1,000 subscribers. The subscription plan requires

---

[1] In "Elements of Financial Statements," *Statement of Financial Accounting Concepts (SFAC) No. 6,* the Financial Accounting Standards Board (FASB) defines revenues as "inflows or other enhancements of assets of an entity or settlements of its liabilities (or a combination of both) from delivering or producing goods, rendering services, or other activities that constitute the entity's ongoing major or central operations" (para. 78). Expenses are defined as "outflows or other using up of assets or incurrences of liabilities (or a combination of both) from delivering or producing goods, rendering services, or carrying out other activities that constitute the entity's ongoing major or central operations" (para. 80).

[2] *Economic value added* represents the increase in the value of a product or service as a consequence of operating activities. To illustrate, the value of an assembled automobile far exceeds the value of its separate steel, glass, plastic, rubber, and electronics components. The difference between the aggregate cost of the various parts utilized in manufacturing the automobile and the price at which the car is sold to the dealer represents economic value added (or lost) by production.

The entries to record the initial borrowing and repayment of the loan principal are ignored because they are financing activities that do not affect the determination of cash-basis income.

prepayment by the customers, so Canterbury received the full subscription price of $300 (12 issues × $25 per issue) from each of the subscribers ($300 × 1,000 = $300,000) at the beginning of 2008. To help finance the purchase of newsprint and other printing supplies, Canterbury takes out a $100,000 three-year loan from a local bank on January 1, 2008. The loan calls for interest of 10% of the face amount of the loan each year (10% × $100,000 = $10,000), but the interest is not payable until the loan matures on December 31, 2010. The cost of publishing and distributing the magazine amounts to $60,000 each year ($60 per subscriber), which is paid in cash at the time of publication. The entries to record the **cash-basis** revenues and expenses for each year follow:

Throughout this book, **DR** represents the debit side and **CR** represents the credit side of the accounting entry to record the transaction being discussed. See the appendix to this chapter for a review of how these transactions are recorded.

**Cash-basis entries for 2008**

| | | |
|---|---|---|
| **DR** Cash | $300,000 | |
|     **CR** Subscriptions revenue | | $300,000 |

To record collection of 1,000 three-year subscriptions at $300 each for *Windy City Living*.

| | | |
|---|---|---|
| **DR** Publishing and distribution expense | $ 60,000 | |
|     **CR** Cash | | $ 60,000 |

To record publishing and distribution expenses paid in cash.

**Cash-basis entries for 2009**

| | | |
|---|---|---|
| **DR** Publishing and distribution expense | $ 60,000 | |
|     **CR** Cash | | $ 60,000 |

To record publishing and distribution expenses paid in cash.

**Cash-basis entries for 2010**

| | | |
|---|---|---|
| **DR** Publishing and distribution expense | $ 60,000 | |
|     **CR** Cash | | $ 60,000 |

To record publishing and distribution expenses paid in cash.

| | | |
|---|---|---|
| **DR** Interest expense | $ 30,000 | |
|     **CR** Cash | | $ 30,000 |

To record interest expense paid on the three-year loan ($100,000 × 0.10 × 3 years = $30,000).

A schedule of operating cash inflows and outflows and cash-basis income would look as follows:

**Cash-Basis Income Determination**

| ($000 omitted) | 2008 | 2009 | 2010 |
|---|---|---|---|
| Cash inflows | $300 | $ — | $ — |
| Cash outflows for production and distribution | (60) | (60) | (60) |
| Cash outflow for interest on loan | — | — | (30) |
| Net income (loss)—cash basis | $240 | $(60) | $(90) |

Publishing the magazine and servicing the subscriptions require economic effort in each of the years 2008 through 2010, as indicated by the $60,000 of operating cash outflows each period. However, under cash-basis accounting, the entire $300,000 of cash inflow from subscription receipts would be treated as revenue in 2008, the year in which the subscriptions are sold and cash is collected with no revenue recognized in the remaining two years of the subscription period. Likewise, the $30,000 of interest ($10,000 per year × 3 years) paid on December 31, 2010, would be recorded as an expense in year 2010 under the cash basis of accounting with no interest expense recognized in the first two years. Consequently, on a cash basis, Canterbury Publishing would report a relatively high "profit" of $240,000 in 2008 when the subscriptions are sold and collected, and this 2008 profit would be followed by operating "losses" of $60,000 in 2009 and $90,000 in 2010 when the costs associated with publishing the remaining issues and financing the operations are paid.

Clearly, cash-basis accounting distorts our view of Canterbury's operating performance on a year-by-year basis. Moreover, none of the annual cash-basis profit figures provide a reliable benchmark for predicting future operating results. This distortion is due to differences in the timing of when cash inflows and outflows occur. Recognizing cash inflows as revenue and cash outflows as expenses results in a cash-basis income number that fails to properly match effort and accomplishment.

> Revenues are "earned" as a consequence of publishing magazines and servicing subscriptions—economic activities that span a three-year period. Canterbury's obligation to subscribers is fulfilled gradually over these three years as each issue is delivered, not just in 2008 when cash is collected.

*The principles that govern revenue and expense recognition under accrual accounting are designed to alleviate the mismatching problems that exist under cash-basis accounting, making accrual earnings a more useful measure of a firm's performance.* Accrual accounting allocates $100,000 of subscription revenue to each of the years 2008, 2009, and 2010 as the magazine is delivered to subscribers and the revenues are "earned." Likewise, accrual accounting recognizes $10,000 of interest expense in each year the bank loan is outstanding, not just in year 2010 when the interest is paid. These modifications to the cash-basis results to obtain accrual earnings are accomplished by means of the following series of "deferral" and "accrual" **adjusting entries,** which are made at the end of each year under accrual accounting (see the appendix for details).

---

**Adjusting entries on December 31, 2008**

| | | | |
|---|---|---|---|
| **DR** | Subscriptions revenue | $200,000 | |
| | **CR** Deferred subscriptions revenue | | $200,000 |

To adjust the Subscriptions revenue account for subscriptions received but not yet earned. ($300,000 was initially credited to Subscriptions revenue. Only $100,000 was earned in 2008. Therefore, Subscriptions revenue must be debited for $200,000.) Deferred subscriptions revenue is a liability account reflecting Canterbury's obligation to provide subscribers with future issues of *Windy City Living.*

| | | | |
|---|---|---|---|
| **DR** | Interest expense | $ 10,000 | |
| | **CR** Accrued interest payable | | $ 10,000 |

To adjust for interest expense incurred, but not yet paid, and to set up a liability for interest accrued during the period that will be paid on December 31, 2010.

**Adjusting entries on December 31, 2009**

| | | | |
|---|---|---|---|
| **DR** | Deferred subscriptions revenue | $100,000 | |
| | **CR** Subscriptions revenue | | $100,000 |

To adjust deferred subscriptions revenue and recognize revenue for subscriptions earned during the year by providing customers four issues of *Windy City Living.*

| | | | |
|---|---|---|---|
| **DR** | Interest expense | $ 10,000 | |
| | **CR** Accrued interest payable | | $ 10,000 |

To adjust for interest expense incurred, but not yet paid, and to set up a liability for interest accrued during the period that will be paid on December 31, 2010.

On December 31, 2010, the accrued interest is paid and the following entry made:
**DR** Accrued interest
payable ... $30,000
    **CR** Cash ... $30,000

---

**Adjusting entries on December 31, 2010**

| | | |
|---|---|---|
| **DR** Deferred subscriptions revenue ..................... | $100,000 | |
|     **CR** Subscriptions revenue ........................ | | $100,000 |

To adjust Deferred subscriptions revenue and recognize revenue for subscriptions earned during the year by providing customers with four issues of *Windy City Living*.

| | | |
|---|---|---|
| **DR** Interest expense ..................................... | $ 10,000 | |
|     **CR** Accrued interest payable ...................... | | $ 10,000 |

To adjust for interest expense incurred during the year. After this adjusting entry, the Accrued interest payable account will have a balance of $30,000.

---

After these adjustments, the diagram of accrual-basis income looks like this:

**Accrual-Basis Income Determination**

| ($000 omitted) | 2008 | 2009 | 2010 | |
|---|---|---|---|---|
| Cash received | $300 | | | |
| | | | | |
| Deferred to future years | –$200 | | | |
| Revenues recognized as earned each year | $100 | $100 | $100 | |
| Expenses | | | | |
|   Publication and distribution (paid in cash) | (60) | (60) | (60) | |
| | | | (30) | Interest paid in cash |
| Interest accrued | (10) | (10) | 20 | Add: Amounts accrued in prior years |
|   Net income—accrual basis | $ 30 | $ 30 | $ 30 | |

From this example, note that accrual accounting revenues for a period do not correspond to cash receipts for the same period ($100,000 of accrual-basis revenue in 2008 does not correspond to the $300,000 of cash received in that year, nor does the $100,000 of recorded accrual revenue in 2009 and 2010 correspond to $0 cash received in those years). Likewise, the reported accrual-basis expenses in a period do not correspond to cash outflows in that period ($10,000 of interest expense recorded under accrual accounting in 2008 and 2009 does not correspond to the $0 of interest paid in those periods, and the $10,000 of interest expense in 2010 does not correspond to the $30,000 of interest paid in cash in that year). As you can see, ***accrual accounting decouples earnings measurement from operating cash flows.*** Indeed, accrual accounting can result in large discrepancies between the firm's reported accrual-basis earnings and the amount of cash generated from operations (cash-basis earnings) year by year, as shown in Figure 2.1.

As this example illustrates, ***accrual accounting better matches economic benefit*** (revenues from subscriptions) ***with economic effort*** (magazine publication and distribution expenses and interest costs), ***thereby producing a measure of operating performance—accrual earnings—that provides a more realistic picture of past economic activities.*** Many believe that accrual accounting numbers also provide a better basis for predicting future performance of an enterprise.

The view that accrual earnings dominate cash flow measures of performance is asserted in *Statement of Financial Accounting Concepts No. 1* issued by the Financial Accounting Standards Board (FASB) in 1978. It stated:

> Information about enterprise earnings and its components measured by accrual accounting generally provides a better indication of enterprise performance than does information about current cash receipts and payments.[3]

---

[3] "Objectives of Financial Reporting by Business Enterprises," *Statement of Financial Accounting Concepts No. 1* (Stamford, CT: FASB, 1978), para. 44.

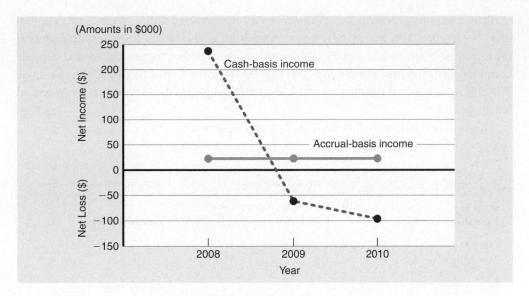

**Figure 2.1**

CANTERBURY PUBLISHING

Comparison of Accrual- and Cash-Basis Income

Despite the assertions of the FASB and others regarding the superiority of accrual earnings relative to net cash flows as a measure of a firm's performance, it is important to recognize that reported accrual accounting income for a given period may not always provide an accurate picture of underlying economic performance for that period. One of our objectives is to help you, as a user of accounting information, understand not only the benefits of accrual accounting numbers but also their limitations. Throughout the book, we contrast accounting measurements and their earnings impact with the underlying economic circumstances, highlighting those situations in which the two may diverge.

## MEASUREMENT OF PROFIT PERFORMANCE: REVENUES AND EXPENSES

We have introduced the concept of accrual accounting income and contrasted it with cash-basis earnings in a simplified setting. Now, in more realistic (and complex) settings, we review some of the mechanics associated with measuring accrual accounting revenues and expenses.

For virtually all firms, income is not earned as a result of just one activity. A manufacturing firm, for example, earns income as a result of these separate and diverse activities:

1. Marketing the product.

2. Receiving customers' orders.

3. Negotiating and signing production contracts.

4. Ordering materials.

5. Manufacturing the product.

6. Delivering the product.

7. Collecting the cash from customers.

> The sequence of activities comprising the **operating cycle** that is presented here is only one of several possible sequences. The activities comprising the operating cycle can vary across firms or even across products for a given firm. Some companies manufacture the product for inventory prior to identifying a particular purchaser and perhaps even in advance of launching a marketing campaign intended to stimulate product demand (for example, Apple manufacturing a new model of laptop computer). In other cases, the product is manufactured to customer order (for example, Boeing manufacturing a new airplane for one of the airlines).

Because income is earned as a result of complex, multiple-stage processes, some guidelines are needed to determine at which stage income is to be recognized in the financial statements. The key issue is the *timing* of income recognition: *When*, under generally accepted accounting principles (GAAP), are revenues and expenses—and thus income—to be recognized?

The accounting process of recognizing income comprises two distinct steps. First, revenues must be recorded. This process of **revenue recognition** establishes the numbers that appear at the top of the income statement. The recognition of revenue then triggers the second step: the **matching** against revenue of the costs that expired (were used up) in generating the revenue. The difference between revenues and expired costs (expenses) is the **income** that is recognized for the period.

This two-step process is illustrated in the following journal entries:

|  | Accounting Entry | Effect on Income (+ or −) |
|---|---|---|
| (*Step* 1) **Revenue recognition** | **DR** Cash or accounts receivable<br>**CR** Sales revenues | Sales revenues (+) |
| (*Step* 2) **Matching of expense** | **DR** Cost of goods sold<br>**CR** Inventory | Cost of goods sold (−) |
| **Income recognition** |  | Net Income |

Income recognition is a by-product of revenue recognition and expense matching. It is not a separate step that is independent of the other two steps. Once revenues have been recognized and expenses have been matched against the revenue, net income is simply the net difference that results.

The process of revenue recognition and matching expenses against revenue has an obvious effect on the income statement: The excess of recognized revenues over expired costs increases the bottom-line net income number. But accrual accounting affects more than income statement accounts. Due to the double-entry, self-balancing nature of accounting, important changes also occur in **net assets** (that is, assets minus liabilities) on the balance sheet. To understand the effect that accrual accounting has on net assets, consider the following example.

ABC Company has only one asset, inventory, with a $100 cost. Its balance sheet appears as:

## ABC Company

### INITIAL BALANCE SHEET

| Assets | | Liabilities + Owners' Equity | |
|---|---|---|---|
| Inventory | $100 | Initial equity | $100 |

Assume that all of the inventory is sold for $130, which is immediately received in cash. Clearly, income should be recognized as a result of this transaction. We focus on the balance sheet effects and analyze the transaction using the basic accounting equation:

| Assets | = | Liabilities | + | Owners' equity |
|---|---|---|---|---|

First, we record the inflow of the asset (cash) and the source of the inflow (sales revenues):

### Step 1: Revenue recognition

| Assets | = | Liabilities | + | Owners' equity |
|---|---|---|---|---|
| +$130 Cash | | | | +$130 Sales revenue |

Next, we record the outflow of the asset (inventory) and match this expired cost against recognized revenues:

### Step 2: Expense matching

| Assets | = | Liabilities | + | Owners' equity |
|---|---|---|---|---|
| −$100 Inventory | | | | −$100 Cost of goods sold |

After recording these transactions, the balance sheet shows:

## ABC Company

### SUBSEQUENT BALANCE SHEET

| Assets | | Liabilities + Owners' Equity | |
|---|---|---|---|
| Cash | $130 | Liabilities | $ — |
| Inventory | — | Initial equity | $100 |
| | | + increase in equity: | |
| | | Income (+$130 − $100) | 30 |
| | $130 | | $130 |

Comparing the initial and subsequent balance sheets shows that equity has increased by $30, the amount of income recognized from the transaction. Equally important, net assets have also increased by $30 (that is, $130 of cash inflow minus $100 of inventory outflow = net asset increase of $30). The point of this example is that when income is recognized in the financial statements, two things happen:

1. Owners' equity increases by the amount of the income.
2. Net assets (that is, gross assets minus gross liabilities) increase by an identical amount.

Thus, there are two equivalent ways of thinking about the financial statement effects of income recognition. One perspective is that when income is recognized, the bottom-line income number (and thus, owners' equity) increases. The other is that when income is recognized, net assets are increased.

The two approaches to thinking about income recognition merely focus on different aspects of the same transaction. The approach that focuses on the net asset effect on the balance sheet provides a means for understanding the *total* financial statement effects of income recognition. This approach reminds us that income recognition simultaneously triggers an increase in the book value (carrying value) of net assets; *that is, net asset valuation and income determination are inextricably intertwined.* When income is recognized in the financial statements, the accountant is acknowledging that the company's net assets have increased in value.[4] The real issue in income recognition is this: At what point in the cycle of operating activities is it appropriate to recognize that a firm's net assets have increased in value? The next section addresses this.

As noted, income recognition has two separate steps:

1. Revenue recognition
2. Expense matching

Let's consider each step separately.

> **Book value** or **carrying value** refers to the amount at which an account (or set of related accounts) is reported on a company's financial statements. For example, the cost of Property, plant and equipment may be reported at $1,000,000 with accumulated depreciation of $300,000. The net book value or carrying value of Property, plant and equipment is the cost minus accumulated depreciation, or $700,000.

---

[4] Notice that the accounting concept of income recognition is really a specific application of the economic concept of value added.

# Criteria for Revenue Recognition

According to GAAP, revenue is recognized at the *earliest* moment in time that *both* of the following conditions are satisfied:

**Condition 1:** The **critical event** in the process of earning the revenue has taken place.

**Condition 2:** The amount of revenue that will be collected is reasonably assured and is **measurable** with a reasonable degree of reliability.

---

**U.S. GAAP Revenue Recognition Criteria**

U.S. GAAP uses different words to describe these two revenue recognition conditions. Condition 1, rephrased using the FASB's terminology, says revenues are not recognized until **earned.** The Board defines *earned* as:

". . . [R]evenues are considered to have been earned when the entity has substantially accomplished what it must do to be entitled to the benefits represented by the revenues."*

The FASB's terminology for Condition 2 says revenues must also be **realizable.** The Board defines *realizable* as (para. 83):

Revenues and gains are realizable when related assets received or held are readily convertible to known amounts of cash or claims to cash. Readily convertible assets have (i) interchangeable (fungible) units and (ii) quoted prices available in an active market that can rapidly absorb the quantity held by the entity without significantly affecting the price.

While the concepts embodied in "earned" and "realizable" are identical to "critical event" and "measurable," we believe that the latter terms are more easily understood and accordingly use them throughout this book.

* "Recognition and Measurement in Financial Statements of Business Enterprises," *Statement of Financial Accounting Concepts No. 5* (Stamford, CT: FASB, 1984), para. 83.

---

**IASB Revenue Recognition Criteria**

The International Accounting Standards Board (IASB), formerly called the International Accounting Standards Committee (IASC), uses the following criteria to determine when an entity should recognize revenue.

1. Significant risks and rewards of ownership have been transferred from the seller to the buyer.

2. Managerial involvement and control over the asset being transferred has passed from the seller to the buyer.

3. The seller can reliably measure the amount of revenue or consideration received in the exchange.

4. It is probable that the seller will receive economic benefits.

5. The seller can reliably measure the costs (both past and future) of the transaction.*

* "Revenue," *IASC Statement No. 18,* 1984, Revised and Reissued 1995 (London: International Accounting Standards Committee [IASC], 1995).

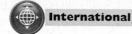 **International**

---

**Condition 1: The Critical Event** While the earnings process is the result of many separate activities, it is generally acknowledged that there is usually one critical event or key stage considered to be absolutely essential to the ultimate increase in the firm's net asset value. The exact nature of this critical event varies from industry to industry, as we show in subsequent examples. Unless the critical event takes place, no increase in value is added to the firm's net assets. Thus, the occurrence of the critical event is a first step that must be satisfied before revenue can be recognized. It is a necessary, but not sufficient, condition for revenue to be recognized.

**Condition 2: Measurability** Accountants do not immediately recognize revenue just because the critical event has taken place. There must be something else: It must be possible to measure the amount of revenue that has been earned with a reasonable degree of assurance. Condition 2 indicates that revenue cannot be recognized merely on the basis of an intuitive "feel" that certain events have added value to the firm's assets. Objective, verifiable evidence as to the amount of value that has been added must exist. Unless the amount of value added can be reliably quantified, GAAP does not allow an increase in asset values to be recorded. Generally, this translates into having a readily determinable price for the goods or service, a price established in the marketplace where buyers and sellers are free to negotiate the terms of trade. So-called "list prices" assigned to the good or service by the seller often do not satisfy the measurability condition because they can deviate from the market-clearing price paid by the buyer.

Only after Conditions 1 and 2 are *both* met can revenue be recognized under GAAP. To illustrate how these revenue recognition conditions are applied, let's return to the example of the three-year subscriptions sold by Canterbury Publishing in January 2008. Recall that accrual accounting would not recognize the $300,000 as revenue when the cash is received because the subscriptions revenue will be earned only as each magazine issue is published and delivered to the customers. If the publisher were to discontinue the magazine before all 12 issues were published, a refund would be owed to the subscribers. ***In this magazine example, the critical event in earning subscription revenue is actually providing the product to the customers.*** Thus, $100,000 of revenue will be recorded in each of the three years as the magazine is published and sent to subscribers. Stated somewhat differently, while revenue recognition Condition 2 is met in this example on initial receipt of the subscription order (that is, the amount of ultimate revenue, $300,000, is measurable with a high degree of assurance and reliability), Condition 1 is not met at that time and, therefore, no revenue is recognized because the critical event has not yet occurred. Canterbury has not *earned* the revenue that has been collected because the company has not delivered the magazines promised to the customer.

To further illustrate how the revenue recognition conditions are applied, let's consider another example. On January 2, 2008, Gigantic Motors Corporation assembles 1,000 automobiles, each with a sticker price of $18,000. These cars have not yet been sold to dealers, so they are parked in a lot adjacent to the plant. Let's examine how revenue recognition Conditions 1 and 2 operate in this setting.

Most observers would agree that the critical event in adding value in automobile manufacturing is production itself.[5] Accordingly, the critical event occurred as the automobiles rolled off the production line. However, no revenue would be recognized at that time. Although revenue recognition Condition 1 is satisfied, Condition 2 is *not* satisfied merely on completion of production. ***This revenue recognition condition is not satisfied because the ultimate sale price of the automobiles is still unknown.*** While Gigantic Motors has established a suggested list price of $18,000 per vehicle, the ultimate amount of cash to actually be received in the future depends on general economic conditions, consumer tastes and preferences, and the availability and asking price of competing automobile models. Thus, the specific amount of value that has been added by production is not yet measurable with a reasonable degree of assurance. Revenue is recognized only when the cars are sold to dealers at a known price. Only then is revenue recognition Condition 2 satisfied.

The magazine subscription and automobile production examples illustrate that revenue recognition takes place only when revenue recognition Conditions 1 and 2 are *both* met. When Canterbury Publishing receives the cash subscriptions to the magazine, Condition 2 (measurability) is satisfied but not Condition 1: No revenue is recognized until Canterbury provides the magazines to the customers and earns the revenue. When automobile production takes place at Gigantic Motors, Condition 1 (critical event) is satisfied but not Condition 2: No revenue is recognized until the sale takes place, which determines with reasonable assurance the amount that Gigantic will receive from the customer.

The financial reporting rules governing revenue recognition are often misunderstood. Because revenue is usually recognized at the time of sale in most industries, some observers erroneously conclude that the sale is itself the sole criterion for recognizing revenue, but this is not correct. The financial reporting rule for recognizing revenue is more complicated and subtle. Specifically, revenue is recognized as soon as Condition 1 (critical event) *and* Condition 2 (measurability) are *both* satisfied. ***In most instances the time of sale turns out to be the earliest***

---

[5] Automobile manufacturers eventually sell all units produced, although not always immediately following production or always at the sticker price.

*moment at which both Conditions 1 and 2 are satisfied, which is why revenue is most fre-
quently recognized at the time of sale of the product or service.*

However, Conditions 1 and 2 are occasionally satisfied even before a legal sale (that is,
transfer of title) occurs. The following example illustrates when revenue can be recognized
prior to sale:

---

Weld Shipyards has been building ocean-going oil tankers since 1981. In January 2008, Weld
signs a contract to build a standard-design tanker for Humco Oil. The contract price is $60
million, and construction costs are estimated to total approximately $45 million. The tanker
is expected to be completed by December 31, 2009. Weld intends to account for the project using the **percentage-of-completion** method.

---

Under the percentage-of-completion method (discussed in Chapter 3), revenues and expenses
are recognized as production takes place rather than at the time of completion (the sale). For example, if the tanker is 40% complete at the end of 2008 and finished in 2009, revenues and
expenses would be recognized according to the following percentage-of-completion schedule:

| ($ in millions) | 2008 | 2009 | Two-Year Total |
|---|---|---|---|
| Percentage | 40% | 60% | 100% |
| Revenue | $24 | $36 | $60 |
| Expense | (18) | (27) | (45) |
| Income | $ 6 | $ 9 | $15 |

GAAP permits this method when certain conditions—as in the Weld Shipyards example—
are met. Condition 1 (critical event) is satisfied over time as the tanker is built, just as it was in
the Gigantic automotive production example. Unlike the Gigantic Motors example, however,
*revenue recognition Condition 2 is satisfied* for Weld Shipyards because a firm contract with a
known buyer at a set price of $60 million exists. Thus, the tanker example satisfies *both* of the
two conditions necessary for revenue to be recognized. Additionally, expenses are measurable
with a reasonable degree of assurance because the tanker is of a standard design that Weld has
built repeatedly in past years. This example provides an overview of why the percentage-of-
completion method, when used properly, meets revenue recognition Conditions 1 and 2.

In other circumstances, Conditions 1 and 2 may not both be satisfied until *after* the time of
sale—for instance, until the cash is collected. In these cases, it would be inappropriate to recognize income when the sale is made; instead, income recognition is deferred and is ultimately
recognized in proportion to cash collections. Chapter 3 discusses the **installment-sales
method,** an example in which revenue and expense are recognized at the time of cash collection rather than at the time of sale.

Figure 2.2 is a time-line diagram depicting the activities comprising the revenue recognition process for some selected industries.

To justify recognizing revenue during the **production phase,** the following conditions must
be met:

1. A specific customer must be identified and an exchange price agreed on. In most cases, a
   formal contract must be signed.

2. A significant portion of the services to be performed has been performed, and the expected
   costs of future services can be reliably estimated.

3. An assessment of the customer's credit standing permits a reasonably accurate estimate of
   the amount of cash that will be collected.

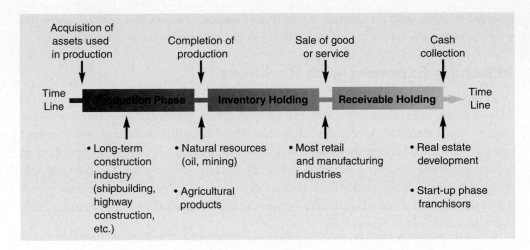

**Figure 2.2**

THE REVENUE
RECOGNITION PROCESS

Industries Recognizing
Revenue at Indicated Phases

Situations in which these conditions may be satisfied include long-term contracts for the construction of ships, bridges, and office buildings as well as, for example, special-order government contracts for the production of military equipment.

As depicted in Figure 2.2, in some industries revenue may be recognized on **completion of production.** This is justified under the following conditions:

1. The product is immediately saleable at quoted market prices.

2. Units are homogeneous.

3. No significant uncertainty exists regarding the costs of distributing the product.

Examples where these circumstances exist include mining of natural resources and harvesting agricultural crops. These commodities are traded in active, organized markets, and thus a reliable market price can be determined at production even though the eventual buyer's identity is unknown at that time. Although GAAP permits mining and other natural resource companies to recognize revenue at completion of production, few actually do so. Instead, most delay revenue recognition until the time of sale.

Revenue recognition *at the time of sale* is the dominant practice in most retail and manufacturing industries. Occasionally, revenue is not recognized until *after the time of sale.* To justify postponing recognition of revenues, one or more of the following conditions must generally be present:

1. Extreme uncertainty exists regarding the amount of cash to be collected from customers. This uncertainty may be attributable to various factors:

   • The customer's precarious financial condition.

   • Contingencies in the sales agreement that allow the buyer or seller to terminate the exchange.

   • Customers have the right to return the product and this right is frequently exercised.

2. Future services to be provided are substantial, and their costs cannot be estimated with reasonable precision.

These conditions exist in circumstances such as real estate sales, when collection of the sale price occurs in protracted installments, and in sales of franchises for new or unproved concepts or products.

*Regardless of which basis of revenue recognition is used, the recognition of expenses must always adhere to the matching principle: All costs incurred in generating the revenue must be recorded as expenses in the same period the related revenue is recognized.* Matching expenses with revenues is the second step of the income recognition process and is discussed next.

## Matching Expenses with Revenues

Once gross revenues for the period have been determined, the next step in determining income is to accumulate and record the costs associated with generating those revenues. Some costs are easily traced to the revenues themselves. These **traceable costs,** also called **product costs,** are described as being **matched** with revenues. Other costs are also clearly important in generating revenue, but their contribution to a specific sale or to revenues of a particular period is more difficult to quantify. Such costs are expensed in the *time periods benefited,* which is why they are called **period costs.** Let's see how the matching principle is applied to traceable or product costs and to period costs.

**Traceable or Product Costs**   This next example illustrates how product costs are matched with revenue under GAAP income measurement rules.

> Cory TV and Appliance, a retailer, sells one 24-inch color television set on the last day of February for $500 cash. The TV set was purchased from the manufacturer for $240 cash in January of that same year. Cory provides a 60-day parts and labor warranty to the customer. A typical 24-inch color TV requires $10 of warranty service during the first month following the sale and another $15 of service in the second month.

The expected (as well as the actually experienced) cash flows associated with this single transaction are depicted in Figure 2.3.

GAAP revenue recognition criteria are satisfied by the cash sale in February, so $500 of revenue is recorded in that month. The current and expected future costs of generating that revenue are $265 ($240 + $10 + $15), and these costs are recorded as expenses in the same month (February) that the revenue is recognized. Thus, accrual accounting transforms the cash flow diagram of Figure 2.3 into the revenue recognition and expense matching diagram shown in Figure 2.4.

## Figure 2.3

CASH FLOW DIAGRAM

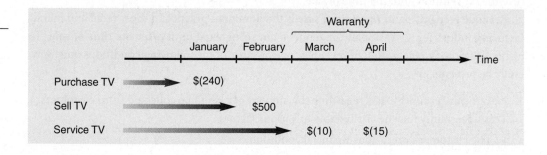

## Figure 2.4

REVENUE RECOGNITION AND EXPENSE MATCHING

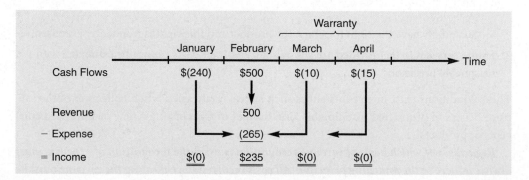

**Period Costs**   Cory TV and Appliance incurs other types of costs that also are crucial in generating revenues. However, the linkage between these costs and individual sales is difficult to establish. One example of costs of this nature is advertising expenditure.

Assume that Cory TV buys five minutes of advertising time on a local radio station each month for a cost of $700. Obviously, the purpose of advertising is to generate sales. However, it is virtually impossible to associate any month's advertising expenditure with any specific sale because consumer behavior is the result of diverse influences and repeated advertising exposure. Consequently, GAAP does not try to match advertising expenditures with specific sales. Instead, the cost of advertising is charged as an expense in the period in which the ads run. Such costs are called *period costs*. No effort is made to link any particular advertising campaign with particular sales, because no objective means for establishing this linkage exists.

The distinction between traceable (product) costs and period costs is discussed further in Chapter 9. At this point, it is important to understand that in applying the matching concept, some costs are directly matched against revenues while others are associated with time periods.

---

**RECAP**

**Revenue is recognized at the point when it is (1) earned, and (2) realized or realizable. These two conditions can be satisfied at different points in time in different industries. Matching associates expired costs (expenses) with the revenues recognized in a period or with the passage of time. Costs directly matched against revenues are called *product costs;* costs matched with the passage of time are called *period costs.***

## INCOME STATEMENT FORMAT AND CLASSIFICATION

Virtually all decision models in modern corporate finance are based on future cash flows. Recognizing this, the FASB stated:

> Thus, financial reporting should provide information to help investors, creditors, and others assess the amounts, timing, and uncertainty of prospective net cash inflows to the related enterprise.[6]

One way to provide users with information regarding prospective future cash flows is to present them with cash flow forecasts prepared by management. Traditional financial reporting rejects presenting *forecasted* cash flow information because such numbers are considered to be too "soft"—that is, too speculative or manipulable.

Another way to satisfy users' needs for assessing future cash flows is to provide financial information based on past and current events in a format that gives statement users reliable and representative baseline numbers for generating *their own* forecasts of future cash flows. To accomplish this, an income statement format that segregates components of income has evolved. The intent of this format is to classify separately income components that are "transitory" and to clearly differentiate them from income components believed to be "sustainable" or likely to be repeated in future reporting periods.

As we survey the existing format and classification rules, you will see that the rationale behind the rules for multiple-step income statements is intended to subdivide income in a manner that facilitates forecasting. Most of the disclosure formats reviewed in this section

> In a joint effort with the IASB, the FASB is currently working on a Conceptual Framework project designed to provide a sound foundation for developing future accounting standards. One element of this project involves financial statement presentation. As part of these deliberations, the Board is considering requiring firms to provide a new statement of Financial Performance broken down into three sections: (1) Operating, (2) Financing and treasury, and (3) Other gains and losses. Further details on proposed changes to financial Statement format can be found on the FASB Web site at www.fasb.org under Project Updates—Financial Statement Presentation.

 **Valuation**

---

[6] *Statement of Financial Accounting Concepts No. 1,* op. cit., para. 37.

---

**EXHIBIT 2.1** **Mythical Corporation**

### Income Statements For the Years Ended December 31, 2006–2008

| ($ in millions) | 2008 | 2007 | 2006 |
|---|---|---|---|
| Net sales | $3,957 | $3,478 | $3,241 |
| Costs of goods sold | (1,364) | (1,189) | (1,096) |
| Gross profit | $2,593 | $2,289 | $2,145 |
| Selling, general and administrative | (1,093) | (949) | (922) |
| ② **Special or unusual charges (Note 1)** | (251) | — | — |
| Income from continuing operations before income taxes | 1,249 | 1,340 | 1,223 |
| Income tax expense | (406) | (436) | (411) |
| ① **Income from continuing operations** | $ 843 | $ 904 | $ 812 |
| ③ **Discontinued operations (Note 2)** | | | |
| Income from operation of discontinued business division, net of tax | 203 | 393 | 528 |
| Gain on disposal of discontinued business division, net of tax | 98 | — | — |
| Income before extraordinary item | $1,144 | $1,297 | $1,340 |
| ④ **Extraordinary loss, net of income tax effect (Note 3)** | — | (170) | — |
| Net income | $1,144 | $1,127 | $1,340 |

*Note 1: Special or Unusual Charges*—A strike closed operations in the Pleasant Grove manufacturing facility for five months in mid-2008. The fixed costs incurred at the idle plant totaled $251,000,000.

*Note 2: Discontinued Operations*—The Company discontinued a business segment in 2008. The 2008 operating income and gain on disposal of this segment, net of tax, were $203 million and $98 million, respectively.

*Note 3: Extraordinary Loss*—The extraordinary loss arose as a consequence of a fire that partially destroyed the chemical plant in River City. The Company had no insurance coverage for such losses due to its long-standing policy of self-insurance.

---

were written into GAAP by the standard-setting organization that preceded the FASB, the current private sector standard-setting group.[7] Our discussion is based on the comparative income statements of Mythical Corporation for 2006–2008, presented in Exhibit 2.1. This exhibit illustrates how existing disclosure rules are designed to help users predict future events.

The income statement isolates a key figure called **Income from continuing operations.** (See ① in Exhibit 2.1.) This component of income should include only *the normal, recurring, (presumably) more sustainable, ongoing operating activities* of the organization. As we discuss shortly, this intermediate income number can sometimes include gains and losses that occur infrequently—called **Special or unusual items** (item ② in Exhibit 2.1)—but nevertheless arise from a firm's ongoing, continuing operations. With the possible exception of some of these special or unusual items, "Income from continuing operations" summarizes the wealth

---

[7] The opinions of the predecessor group—the Accounting Principles Board (APB)—continue in effect until they are either rescinded or altered by the FASB. The disclosure formats discussed in this section were developed in three separate APB opinions: "Reporting the Results of Operations," *APB Opinion No. 9* (New York: AICPA, 1966); "Accounting Changes," *APB Opinion No. 20* (New York: AICPA, 1971); and "Reporting the Results of Operations—Reporting the Effects of Disposal of a Segment of a Business, and Extraordinary, Unusual and Infrequently Occurring Events and Transactions," *APB Opinion No. 30* (New York: AICPA, 1973). More recently, the FASB issued two statements that amend or supersede certain provisions of *APB Opinion No 30*: "Accounting for the Impairment or Disposal of Long-Lived Assets," *Statement of Financial Accounting Standards No. 144* (Norwalk, CT: FASB, 2001), and "Rescission of FASB Statements No. 4, 44, and 64, Amendment of FASB Statement No. 13, and Technical Corrections," *Statement of Financial Accounting Standards No. 145* (Norwalk, CT: FASB, 2002).

effects of recurring transactions or activities that are expected to continue into the future. Therefore, this figure is intended to serve as the anchor or jumping-off point for forecasting future profits.

There are other components of income that are not recurring and, hence, do not form a good basis for projecting future income. These other, more transitory components of income are isolated and disclosed separately so that statement users can place less weight on these earnings components when forecasting the future profitability of an enterprise (see discussion in Chapter 6). These transitory earnings components fall into three categories:

- Special or unusual items (item ②).
- Discontinued operations (item ③).
- Extraordinary items (item ④).[8]

The rules governing the classification and placement of these three categories of transitory items within the income statement are discussed in the following sections. These classification rules provide detailed guidance regarding what qualifies for inclusion in each statement category. As you will see, the rules standardize the format of disclosures as well as prevent certain abuses or distortions that might occur if firms were allowed to commingle these nonrecurring components of earnings with more sustainable, recurring revenue and expense items.

## Special or Unusual Items (Item ②)

Material events that arise from a firm's ongoing, continuing activities but that are either unusual in nature or infrequent in occurrence, but not both, must be disclosed as a separate line item as part of income from continuing operations (or in footnotes to the financial statements). For example, the Mythical Corporation income statement presented in Exhibit 2.1 includes special or unusual charges for losses incurred in conjunction with a labor strike, which is disclosed as a separate line item and discussed in a statement note (see item ② and Note 1 in Exhibit 2.1).

> As used in the authoritative accounting literature, an item is considered material if it is of sufficient magnitude or importance to make a difference in a statement user's decision.

Other examples of special or unusual items include:

1. Write-downs or write-offs of receivables, inventories, equipment leased to others, and intangibles.
2. Gains or losses from the exchange or translation of foreign currencies.
3. Gains or losses from the sale or abandonment of property, plant or equipment.
4. Special one-time charges resulting from corporate restructurings.
5. Gains or losses from the sale of investments.[9]

Including special or unusual items as a component of income from continuing operations complicates financial forecasting and analysis. These special items are treated as a part of

---

[8] Prior to the issuance of *SFAS No. 154,* which became effective in 2005, a fourth transitory earnings component called a **cumulative effect of an accounting change** was reported on the income statement when a firm made a voluntary change in accounting principle. The cumulative effect was measured as the after-tax difference between prior periods' income that was reported under the old accounting method and what the prior periods' income would have been if the new method had been used in those prior years. *SFAS No. 154* calls for **retrospective application** of a change in accounting principle (described more fully later in this chapter), which effectively eliminates the reporting of cumulative effect adjustments on the income statement. For further details on the retrospective application approach, see "Accounting Changes and Error Corrections—A Replacement of APB Opinion No. 20 and FASB Statement No. 3," *Statement of Financial Accounting Standards No. 154* (Norwalk, CT: FASB, 2005).

[9] *APB Opinion No. 30,* para. 23.

income from continuing operations because collectively they represent events that arise repeatedly as a normal part of ongoing business activities.[10] However, some special items occur often while others recur sporadically. For example, some firms are continuously selling or disposing of obsolete manufacturing assets as well as taking write-downs on inventory or selling investment securities. However, other special items such as strikes and reorganizations occur less frequently. Consequently, the persistence of special or unusual items is likely to vary from period to period and from item to item. As a result, separate disclosure is provided for these items to assist users in forecasting future results. Because these items are included as part of income from continuing operations before tax (sometimes referred to as being reported "above the line"), they are not disclosed net of tax effects.

## Discontinued Operations (Item ③)

Because a primary objective of financial reporting is to assist users in generating estimates of future cash flows, transactions related to operations that the firm intends to discontinue or has already discontinued must be separated from other income items.[11] The reason is straightforward because, by definition, discontinued operations will not generate *future* operating cash flows.

In Exhibit 2.1, Mythical Corporation discontinued a component of its business in 2008 (item ③). Notice that the operating results of this recently discontinued business component are not included in income from continuing operations in the current period (2008) when the decision to discontinue was made; nor are they included in any of the prior years (2007 and 2006) for which comparative data are provided.[12] That is, the revenues and expenses of this component of Mythical Corporation that was disposed of in 2008 are removed from the corresponding numbers reflecting 2007 and 2006 results (highlighted). This makes the Income from continuing operations number of $843 million in 2008, the year of the discontinued operations, truly comparable with the Income from continuing operations numbers of $904 million and $812 million in 2007 and 2006, respectively. Restating the 2007 and 2006 results to make them comparable to the 2008 results means that all the numbers from the Net sales line through the Income from continuing operations line reported in the 2007 and 2006 columns of the 2008 annual report will be different from the corresponding numbers originally reported in the 2007 and 2006 statements. While initially confusing to analysts who wish to review the past sequence of earnings numbers to detect trends in a company's financial performance (often referred to as **time-series analysis**), this adjustment to the numbers is essential for valid year-to-year comparisons.

Prior to 2001, the authoritative guidance for reporting discontinued operations was provided by *APB Opinion No. 30.*[13] This standard defined a discontinued operation as a separate line of business or a separate class of customer. *SFAS No. 144,* issued in August 2001, broadened the scope of operations that qualify for separate disclosure as discontinued operations by introducing the notion of a **component of an entity,**[14] which comprises operations and cash

Some companies tend to report special or unusual items on a regular basis, perhaps hoping that investors will discount or ignore what are frequently large charges to earnings. For example, Motorola was recently cited for reporting special, nonrecurring items for *fifteen* consecutive quarters.*

* J. Drucker, "Motorola's Profit: 'Special' Again?" *The Wall Street Journal,* October 15, 2002.

---

[10] Evidence that special items are likely to recur in the aggregate is provided by P. M. Fairfield, R. J. Sweeney, and T. L. Yohn, "Accounting Classification and the Predictive Content of Earnings," *The Accounting Review,* July 1996, pp. 337–55.

[11] *SFAS No. 144,* op. cit., para. 43.

[12] Securities and Exchange Commission (SEC) rules (Regulation S-X, Article 3) require that comparative income statement data for at least three years and comparative balance sheet data for two years be provided in filings with the Commission. For this reason, most publicly held corporations provide these comparative income statement and balance sheet data in their annual report to shareholders.

[13] *APB Opinion No. 30,* op. cit.

[14] *SFAS No. 144,* op. cit., para. 41.

flows that can be clearly distinguished, operationally and for financial reporting purposes, from the rest of the entity.[15] A component of an entity may be a reportable segment or operating segment, a reporting unit, a subsidiary, or an asset group. An asset group represents the lowest level for which identifiable cash flows are largely independent of the cash flows of other groups of assets and liabilities within the entity.

To illustrate the broadened scope of operations that qualify for discontinued operations treatment under *SFAS No. 144* versus *APB Opinion No. 30,* consider Quaker Oats' 1997 sale of its Snapple beverage business to Triarc Companies. Under *APB Opinion No. 30* guidance, Quaker reported the $1.4 billion loss on the Snapple sale *above the line* as a special item adjustment to income from continuing operations. This treatment was deemed appropriate because Quaker continued in the beverage business by producing and marketing Gatorade. Therefore, it did not sell its entire beverage drink product line. Under *SFAS No. 144* guidelines, the Snapple sale would likely qualify for separate disclosure as a discontinued operation (with associated restatement of prior year sales and expense figures as illustrated for Mythical Corporation) because the operations and cash flows from Snapple, a wholly owned subsidiary of Quaker, were clearly distinguishable from those of Gatorade.

> *SFAS No. 144,* para. 30, sets forth six conditions for an asset group to be considered "held for sale." The most important of these are:
>
> - Management has adopted a formal plan to sell the asset group.
> - An active program to locate a buyer has been initiated.
> - The sale of the asset group is probable and the sale is expected to be completed within one year.

If a component of an entity has either been sold during the period or is classified as **held for sale,** its results of operations are to be reported as discontinued operations ("below the line") if the following two conditions are met:

- The operations and cash flows of the component have been (or will be) eliminated from the firm's ongoing operations.
- The firm will not have any significant continuing involvement in the operations of the component after the disposal transaction.

If either of these two conditions is not met, then the component's operating results are reported as part of income from continuing operations and prior years' results will not be restated for comparative purposes.

## Amounts Reported When Assets (Disposal Group) Have Been Sold
When the discontinued component is sold before the end of the reporting period, companies are required to report two elements as part of discontinued operations:

1. Operating income or loss (that is, revenues minus expenses) from operating the component from the beginning of the reporting period to the disposal date, net of related tax effects.
2. Gain or loss on disposal computed as the net sale price minus book value of net assets disposed of, net of related tax effects.

Panel (a) of Exhibit 2.2 illustrates a typical income statement disclosure for this situation whose disposal date is September 5, 2008.

## Amounts Reported When Assets (Disposal Group) Are Considered "Held for Sale"
If a company has decided to discontinue a component of its business

---

[15] *IAS 35:* "Discontinuing Operations" provides authoritative accounting and disclosure guidance for those firms following international accounting standards for operations that are to be discontinued. The standard defines "discontinuing operations" as a business or geographical segment that an enterprise either is disposing of entirely or is terminating through abandonment or piecemeal sale. Among other things, entities are required to disclose (1) the amounts of revenues, expenses, and pre-tax profit or loss attributable to the discontinuing operation and related tax expense (benefit) and (2) the amount of any gain or loss that is recognized on the disposal of the discontinuing operation, net of related tax effects. [See "Discontinuing Operations," *IAS 35* (London, UK: International Accounting Standards Committee [IASC], 1998.)]

 **International**

**EXHIBIT 2.2**     Alternative Disclosure for Discontinued Operations

### Partial Income Statement Format for Discontinued Operations

**Panel (a): When Assets Have Been Sold on September 5, 2008**

| | |
|---|---:|
| Income from continuing operations | $800,000 |
| Income tax expense | (280,000) |
| Income from continuing operations after tax | 520,000 |
| Discontinued operations | |
|     Operating income (net of taxes of $35,000) from | |
|         January 1, 2008 through September 5, 2008 | 65,000 |
|     Loss on disposal of discontinued operation | |
|         (net of $21,000 tax benefit) | (39,000) |
|         Net income | $546,000 |

**Panel (b): When Assets Are "Held for Sale" at Year-End**

| | |
|---|---:|
| Income from continuing operations | $800,000 |
| Income tax expense | (280,000) |
| Income from continuing operations after tax | 520,000 |
| Discontinued operations | |
|     Operating income (net of taxes of $42,000) from | |
|         January 1, 2008 through December 31, 2008 | 78,000 |
|     Impairment loss (net of $17,500 tax benefit) | |
|         on assets held for sale | (32,500) |
|         Net income | $565,500 |

but has not sold it by the end of the reporting period, the income effects of the discontinued operations are reported in two elements as follows:

1. Operating income or loss (that is, revenues minus expenses) from operating the component from the beginning of the reporting period to the end of the reporting period, net of tax effects.

2. An impairment loss[16] (net of tax effects) if the book value of the net assets in the disposal group is more than the fair value minus cost to sell.

Panel (b) of Exhibit 2.2 illustrates a typical income statement disclosure for this situation with an after-tax impairment loss on assets "held for sale" of $32,500.

It is important to notice that both the income (loss) from operating the discontinued component and any gain (loss) from sale (or impairment loss) are reported net of tax effects. This "net of tax" treatment is called **intraperiod income tax allocation.** The reason for this net of tax treatment is the belief that the income tax burden or benefit should be matched with the item giving rise to it. The allocation of the tax burden or benefit across components of income is believed to make the income figures more informative to users.

Here's why: If income tax were not matched with the item giving rise to it, total reported income tax expense would combine taxes arising both from items that were transitory as well as from other items that were more sustainable. Mixing together the tax effect of continuing activities with the tax effect of single occurrence events would make it difficult for statement readers to forecast future tax outflows arising from ongoing events. Under intraperiod income tax

*APB Opinion No. 30* allowed companies to estimate profits (losses) from operating a discontinued segment in future periods and to include these estimated amounts as part of Gain (loss) on disposal of discontinued operations. This flexibility invited income shifting and/or income smoothing behavior by management. *SFAS No. 144* effectively eliminates this potential for opportunistic behavior.

---

[16] See Chapter 10 for further details on determining whether an asset has become impaired and, if so, the amount of the loss.

allocation, the income tax associated with the (presumably) transitory items ③ and ④ are not included in Mythical's $406 million income tax expense figure for 2008 (Exhibit 2.1) related to income from continuing operations, thus facilitating forecasts of expected future flows after tax.

## Extraordinary Items (Item ④)

Another category of transitory items reported separately on the income statement is extraordinary items (item ④ in Exhibit 2.1). To be treated as an extraordinary item, the event or transaction must meet *both* of the following criteria:[17]

1. *Unusual nature:* The underlying event or transaction possesses a high degree of abnormality, and considering the environment in which the company operates, that event or transaction is unrelated to the business's ordinary activities.

2. *Infrequent occurrence:* The underlying event or transaction is a type that would not reasonably be expected to recur in the foreseeable future, again considering the environment in which the business operates.[18]

The justification for defining extraordinary items so precisely and for requiring separate disclosure of special or unusual items is to prevent statement manipulation. Without such requirements, management might, in a "down" earnings year, be tempted to treat nonrecurring gains as part of income from continuing operations and nonrecurring losses as extraordinary. Precise guidelines preclude this.

Like discontinued operations, extraordinary items are reported net of tax. Given the stringency of the criteria, few events qualify as extraordinary items. Examples of qualifying items include losses resulting from natural disasters (for example, hurricane Katrina) or losses arising from new laws or edicts (for example, an expropriation by a foreign government), and, in some cases, gains and losses on early debt retirement.

Income statement reporting of gains and losses resulting from the retirement of debt prior to its scheduled maturity is covered in *SFAS No. 145*.[19] It calls for gains and losses from early debt retirement to be classified as extraordinary only if they meet the criteria in *APB Opinion No. 30*. Accordingly, firms that use early debt retirement on a recurring basis as part of their ongoing risk management practices report the associated gains and losses as part of income from continuing operations with separate line-item disclosure. Other firms, for which early debt retirement is an unusual and infrequent occurrence, are required to report associated gains and losses as an extraordinary item.

---

**RE**CAP

**To be categorized as extraordinary and to appear below the Income from continuing operations line, an item must be unusual in nature *and* occur infrequently. Special or unusual items that do not meet both criteria, but are considered material, must be disclosed separately as part of pre-tax income from continuing operations.**

---

[17] *APB Opinion No. 30,* para. 20.

[18] The business environment in which an enterprise operates is a primary consideration in determining whether an underlying event or transaction is unusual in nature and infrequent in occurrence. The environment of an enterprise includes such factors as the characteristics of the industry or industries in which it operates, the geographical location of its operations, and the nature and extent of government regulation. For example, a plant explosion that results in uninsured losses would be considered an extraordinary loss by most businesses. But for a company that manufactures explosive materials (for example, dynamite), losses from such an event may not be considered unusual in nature or infrequent in occurrence given the environment in which the entity conducts its operations.

[19] *SFAS No. 145,* op. cit., paras. 1, 6a, A4–A6.

## Frequency and Magnitude of Various Categories of Transitory Income Statement Items

As Exhibit 2.1 illustrates, financial reporting rules for presenting operating results are designed to isolate transitory and nonsustainable components of earnings to assist users in predicting future earnings and cash flows. Research evidence confirms that the GAAP income statement classification framework we have discussed is useful to statement users. Specifically, subdividing earnings into three transitory components—special or unusual items, discontinued operations, and extraordinary items—and disclosing these amounts separately so that they are distinguished from the income that comes from continuing operations improves forecasts of future earnings.[20]

Figure 2.5(a) reveals that the proportion of firms reporting one or more of the types of transitory earnings components highlighted in the previous discussion has generally increased over time. In 1996, roughly 37% of firms listed on either the New York Stock Exchange

### Figure 2.5

PROPORTION OF NYSE/ AMEX FIRMS REPORTING NONRECURRING ITEMS (1996–2005)

*Source: Standard and Poor's Compustat® Annual Industrial File* as data source; methodology not verified or controlled by *Standard & Poor's*.

**Panel (a)**

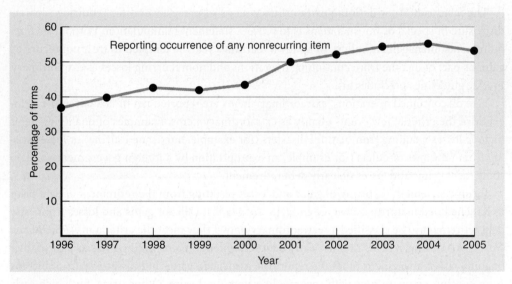

**Panel (b)**

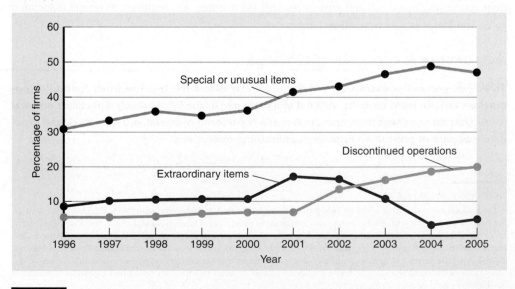

---

[20] Evidence that special items are likely to recur in the aggregate is provided by Fairfield et al., op. cit.

| EXHIBIT 2.3 | Percentage of Nonrecurring Items That are Losses (1996–2005) | | | | | | | | | |
| --- | --- | --- | --- | --- | --- | --- | --- | --- | --- | --- |
| | 1996 | 1997 | 1998 | 1999 | 2000 | 2001 | 2002 | 2003 | 2004 | 2005 |
| Special or unusual items | 68.4% | 70.4% | 73.7% | 69.2% | 68.7% | 80.5% | 75.6% | 74.0% | 74.2% | 72.9% |
| Discontinued operations | 48.1 | 35.2 | 46.8 | 45.8 | 46.6 | 53.0 | 50.5 | 44.7 | 42.2 | 39.0 |
| Extraordinary items | 83.1 | 86.7 | 85.0 | 79.0 | 71.7 | 71.7 | 87.6 | 66.5 | 61.7 | 76.1 |
| Any nonrecurring item (net) | 68.1 | 70.7 | 73.2 | 68.0 | 66.4 | 77.1 | 73.9 | 66.7 | 67.1 | 65.0 |

*Source: 2005 Compustat Annual Industrial File, Standard and Poor's Compustat® Services, Inc., Englewood, CO.*

(NYSE) or American Stock Exchange (AMEX) reported at least one of the transitory earnings components on their income statement. Ten years later, in 2005, that proportion had risen to nearly 53%. Clearly, material, separately disclosed gains and losses have become increasingly common elements of firms' earnings statements in recent years.

Figure 2.5(b) displays the proportion of NYSE and AMEX firms reporting (1) Special or unusual items, (2) Discontinued operations, or (3) Extraordinary items on their income statement from 1996–2005. The most common category of separately disclosed earnings components is for special or unusual items reported as part of income from continuing operations. Slightly less than 47% of the sample firms reported such items in 2005, compared to 31% in 1996. Discontinued operations is the next most common separately disclosed item, appearing on approximately 20% of the earnings statements of firms in 2005 compared to 5% in 1996. The proportion of firms disclosing extraordinary items decreased slightly from roughly 9% in 1996 to 5% in 2005.

Exhibit 2.3 shows that over the 1996–2005 period, the majority of special or unusual items and extraordinary items were losses (for example, 72.9% of special items in 2005; see highlight). The preponderance of losses for special or unusual items reflects two things:

1. The conservative bias of accrual accounting rules encourages early recognition of declines in asset values below cost or book value but tends to delay recognition of increases in value until the asset is sold.

2. Firms have a stronger incentive to separately disclose and clearly label losses than they do gains. To include (undisclosed) nonrecurring losses as part of the income from continuing operations line would cause statement users to underestimate future income. To avoid this understatement firms opt for separate line-item disclosure of losses.

## Reporting Accounting Changes

In Chapter 1 (Figure 1.2), we discussed the qualitative characteristics of accounting that enhance its decision usefulness. We learned that *consistency*, which is using the same accounting methods to describe similar economic events from period to period, enhances accounting's decision usefulness by allowing users to identify trends or turning points in a company's performance over time. However, because we live in a dynamic and ever-changing business environment, consistency in application of accounting standards over time is not always possible. Firms sometimes voluntarily switch methods of accounting or revise estimates used in computing net income because they believe that the alternative method or estimate better reflects the firm's underlying economics. Also, accounting standard-setting bodies, such as the FASB, frequently issue new standards in response to changes in the business environment that require companies to change accounting methods. When firms use different accounting principles to account for similar business transactions or events in adjacent periods, the period-to-period consistency of the reported numbers can be compromised. Below we describe how accounting method changes are

| EXHIBIT 2.4 | Types of Accounting Changes | |
|---|---|---|
| **Type of Change** | **Description** | **Examples** |
| Change in accounting principle | Change from one generally accepted accounting principle to another. This change can be voluntary (initiated by the firm) or mandatory (required by a standard-setting body such as the FASB). | Voluntary<br>• Change in methods of inventory costing<br>• Change from completed contract to percentage-of-completion method for recognizing revenues and profits on long-term construction contracts<br>Mandatory<br>• Adoption of a new FASB standard |
| Change in accounting estimate | Revision of an estimate because of new information or new experience. | • Change in estimated percentage of uncollectible accounts (bad debts)<br>• Change in depreciation method (e.g., straight line to accelerated method)*<br>• Change in service life or salvage values of depreciable assets |
| Change in accounting entity | Change in the economic units that compose the reporting entity. | • Reporting consolidated financial statements in place of financial statements for individual entities<br>• Adding a subsidiary not previously included in prior years' consolidated financial statements |

\* Under *SFAS No. 154*, a change in depreciation methods is treated as a change in estimate that is achieved by a change in accounting principle.

recorded and disclosed under *SFAS No. 154*, "Accounting Changes and Error Corrections."[21] These disclosures are designed to enhance the comparability and consistency of the numbers over time and to alert statement users about the effects of the change on the current period results.

Accounting changes fall into one of three categories as shown in Exhibit 2.4: change in accounting principle, change in accounting estimate, and change in reporting entity. A fourth type of change, correction of an accounting error, is not considered an accounting change but is treated as a change in accounting principle under *SFAS No. 154*. We discuss and illustrate the accounting and disclosure requirements for accounting error corrections in Chapter 3 in the section Accounting Errors, Earnings Restatements, and Prior Period Adjustments.

*SFAS No. 154* specifies two approaches for reporting accounting changes depending on the type of change. Under the **retrospective approach,** which is used for a change in accounting principle and change in reporting entity, numbers presented in financial statements issued in previous years are revised to reflect the impact of the change whenever those statements are presented for comparative purposes. The advantage of this approach is that the financial statements in the year of the change and for prior years presented for comparative purposes are prepared on the same basis of accounting. This enhances the comparability and consistency of the accounting numbers over time. The downside of this approach is that firms may use an aggressive accounting method in earlier years that overstates income and asset values in an effort to lower new debt or equity financing costs and subsequently change to a more appropriate (conservative) method. In such instances, public confidence in the integrity of accounting data may suffer when numbers previously reported and relied on for decision making are later revised.

---

[21] "Accounting Changes and Error Corrections: A Replacement of APB Opinion No. 20 and FASB Statement No. 3," *SFAS No. 154* (Norwalk, CT: FASB, 2005).

A second approach to account for accounting changes is the **prospective approach,** which is used for changes in accounting estimates. This approach requires no adjusting entry to modify prior years' financial statements, and prior years' numbers presented for comparative purposes are not restated. Instead, the new estimate is used in determining the income for the year of the change (i.e., the current year) and is applied to all future years. The effect of using the new estimate versus the old estimate on the current period income is disclosed in the footnote explaining the change in estimate.

We now provide a more detailed discussion of these two approaches that are selectively applied to the three types of accounting changes that are summarized in Exhibit 2.4.

## Change in Accounting Principle

A change in an accounting principle occurs when (1) a firm *voluntarily* changes from one generally accepted accounting principle to another generally accepted accounting principle or (2) when the accounting principle that was formerly used is no longer generally accepted because the accounting standard-setting body (FASB) issues a standard that requires firms to follow a new approach or method of accounting for certain transactions or events (*mandatory* change). An example of a voluntary change is a firm switching from using the completed contract to percentage-of-completion method of accounting for long-term construction contracts or switching from the first-in, first-out (FIFO) to last-in, first out (LIFO) method for valuing inventories. An example of a mandatory accounting change is the FASB's recently adopted standard requiring firms to expense employee stock option grants on the income statement rather than disclosing the value of such grants only in footnotes to the financial statements as was previously required.[22]

As indicated, *SFAS No. 154* requires firms to use the *retrospective approach* to account for changes in accounting principles unless it is impracticable to do so.[23] Under this approach, prior years' financial statements (balance sheet, income statement, cash flow statement, and statement of stockholders' equity) that are presented for comparative purposes are revised in the year of the change to reflect the impact of the accounting principle change. This means that for each year in the comparative statements reported, the balance of each account affected is revised to reflect what that balance would have been under the new principle. The income statement, cash flow statement, and balance sheet amounts for the year of the change are based on the application of the new accounting principle.

Besides reporting revised amounts in the comparative financial statements, a journal entry is made to adjust all account balances to reflect what those amounts would have been under the new method as of the beginning of the current year (i.e., the change year). In addition to adjusting existing asset or liability accounts, the entry to record the accounting principle change typically requires an adjustment to the firm's Retained earnings balance (as of the beginning of the year in which the change takes place) to reflect the **cumulative effect** of the accounting principle change on all prior periods reported income. The cumulative effect is the difference between what the reported earnings would have been in prior years if the new method had always been used versus what the reported earnings were under the old method.[24]

Exhibit 2.5 illustrates how the retrospective approach was used by Eastman Kodak Company in 2006 for its change from the LIFO inventory method to the average cost method. Panel (a)

---

[22] "Share-Based Payment," *SFAS No. 123 (Revised)* (Norwalk, CT: FASB, 2004).

[23] Changes in principles that are deemed to be impracticable to apply retrospectively occur when information needed to estimate the effects on affected accounts is not available or would require assumptions about management's intent in a prior period that cannot be independently verified (*SFAS No. 154,* para. 11).

[24] The cumulative effect on beginning retained earnings reflects only the direct effects on earnings, which includes related tax effects. Indirect effects (e.g., profit sharing or royalty payments based on reported income) are not included under the retrospective application (*SFAS No. 154,* para. 10).

| EXHIBIT 2.5 | Eastman Kodak Company |

**Disclosures for Change in Accounting Principle**

**Note 3: Inventories, Net**

**Panel (a)**

| ($ in millions) | December 31, 2006 | December 31, 2005 |
|---|---|---|
| Finished goods | $ 745 | $ 893 |
| Work in process | 213 | 243 |
| Raw materials | 244 | 319 |
| Total | $1,202 | $1,455 |

On January 1, 2006, the Company elected to change its method of costing its U.S. inventories to the average cost method, which approximates FIFO, whereas in all prior years most of the Company's inventory in the U.S. was costed using the LIFO method. As a result of this change, the cost of all of the Company's inventories is determined by either the FIFO or average cost method. The new method of accounting for inventory in the U.S. is deemed preferable as the average cost method provides better matching of revenue and expenses given the rapid technological change in the Company's products. The average cost method also better reflects more current costs of inventory on the Company's Statement of Financial Position. As prescribed in *SFAS No. 154*, "Accounting Changes and Error Corrections," retrospective application of the change in accounting method is disclosed below.

**Panel (b)**

Components of the Company's Consolidated Statement of Operations [Income Statement] affected by the change in costing methodology as originally reported under the LIFO method and as adjusted for the change in inventory costing methodology from the LIFO method to the average cost method are as follows:

| ($ in millions, except per share data) | Year Ended December 31, 2005 | | |
|---|---|---|---|
| | As Previously Reported | LIFO to Average Cost Change in Costing Methodology Adjustment (1) | As Adjusted |
| Cost of goods sold | $10,617 | $ 33 | $10,650 |
| Gross profit | 3,651 | (33) | 3,618 |
| Loss from continuing operations before interest, other income (charges), net and income taxes | (599) | (33) | (632) |
| Loss from continuing operations before income taxes | (766) | (33) | (799) |
| Provision (benefit) for income taxes | 689 | (134) | 555 |
| (Loss) earnings from continuing operations | (1,455) | 101 | (1,354) |
| Net (loss) earnings | $(1,362) | $101 | $(1,261) |
| Basic and diluted net (loss) earnings per share: | $ (4.73) | $ .35 | $ (4.38) |
| Continuing operations | $ (5.05) | $ .35 | $ (4.70) |

| EXHIBIT 2.5 | Eastman Kodak Company *(continued)* |
| --- | --- |

**Panel (b)** *continued*

| | Year Ended December 31, 2004 | | |
| --- | --- | --- | --- |
| | As Previously Reported | LIFO to Average Cost Change in Costing Methodology Adjustment | As Adjusted |
| Cost of goods sold | $9,582 | $ 19 | $9,601 |
| Gross profit | 3,935 | (19) | 3,916 |
| Loss from continuing operations before interest, other income (charges), net and income taxes | (87) | (19) | (106) |
| Loss from continuing operations before income taxes | (94) | (19) | (113) |
| Benefit for income taxes | (175) | (7) | (182) |
| Earnings (loss) from continuing operations | 81 | (12) | 69 |
| Net earnings (loss) | $ 556 | $(12) | $ 544 |
| Basic and diluted net earnings (loss) per share: | $ 1.94 | $(.04) | $ 1.90 |
| Continuing operations | $ .28 | $(.04) | $ .24 |

**Panel (c)**

Components of the Company's Consolidated Statement of Financial Position affected by the change in costing methodology as of December 31, 2005, as originally reported under the LIFO method and as adjusted for the change in inventory costing methodology from the LIFO method to the average cost method are as follows (in millions):

| | As Previously Reported | LIFO to Average Cost Change in Costing Methodology Adjustment | As Adjusted |
| --- | --- | --- | --- |
| Assets | | | |
| Current Assets | | | |
| Inventories, net | $ 1,140 | $315 | $ 1,455 |
| Total Current Assets | 5,781 | 315 | 6,096 |
| Total Assets | 14,921 | 315 | 15,236 |
| Shareholders' Equity | | | |
| Retained earnings | 6,402 | 315 | 6,717 |
| Total Shareholders' Equity | 1,967 | 315 | 2,282 |
| Total Liabilities & Shareholders' Equity | $14,921 | $315 | $15,236 |

shows the Finished goods, Work in process, and Raw materials inventory values at the end of the 2006 and 2005 fiscal years based on the newly adopted average cost method along with an explanation for why the change was made. Panel (b) shows the effect of the change on various income statement line items for 2005 and 2004, the two years for which Eastman Kodak provided comparative income statement data. Because the 2006 income statement is based on the newly adopted average cost method, having the restated income statement line items for 2005 and 2004 allows statement users to compare operating results over these three years using a consistent basis of inventory accounting. Panel (c) shows the effect of the change on the ending balance sheet values for 2005, the only year for which comparative balance sheet information was provided in Kodak's 2006 annual report. Note that the $315 million increase in the December 31, 2005, inventory values is offset by a $315 million increase in Retained earnings because prior years' income would have been higher if Kodak had been using the average cost method rather than the LIFO method in those years (Chapter 9 explains why).[25]

**Retroactive Effect Indeterminable**    In some cases, it is impracticable to determine the cumulative effect of applying a change in accounting principle to prior periods. For example, the LIFO inventory accounting method requires that firms maintain records of when inventory is increased as well as the cost of these new inventory layers. Therefore, LIFO entails more detailed inventory recordkeeping than either the FIFO or average cost methods. A firm that switches to LIFO would have no reason to have kept detailed inventory data on new layers of inventory costs prior to LIFO adoption. Accordingly, computing what income would have been for previous years under LIFO could be difficult or even impossible. *SFAS No. 154* states that if it is impracticable to determine the cumulative effect of applying a change in accounting principle to prior periods, the new accounting principle is to be applied as if the change was made prospectively as of the earliest date practicable. In most cases, this amounts to disclosing only the effect of the change on the current period income. Exhibit 2.6 illustrates the disclosure of a change to the LIFO method of inventory accounting for Mittal Steel USA Inc. for which the retroactive effect is indeterminable.

**Change in Accounting Estimate**    Estimates are used extensively in accounting. Examples of items for which estimates are necessary include uncollectible receivables, inventory

---

| **EXHIBIT 2.6** | Mittal Steel USA Inc. |
| --- | --- |

**Accounting Change—Retroactive Effect Indeterminable**

**Excerpt from Note (g) Inventories**

Inventories are stated at the lower of cost or market, which approximates replacement cost. Costs include the purchase costs of raw materials, conversion costs, and an allocation of fixed and variable production overhead. The components of inventories follow ($ in millions):

| | December 31 | |
| --- | --- | --- |
| | **2005** | **2004** |
| FIFO or average cost | | |
| Raw materials | $1,005 | $180 |
| Finished and semi-finished goods | 1,510 | 413 |
| | 2,515 | 593 |
| LIFO reserve | (7) | — |
| Total | $2,508 | $593 |

Effective January 1, 2005, [the Company] has changed its accounting policies for valuing inventory from FIFO to LIFO. We believe the LIFO method is preferable to the FIFO method because it provides better matching of current revenues and costs in the income statement, primarily as a result of the volatility in the key steel related energy and commodity markets and because it provides better comparability to the LIFO method used by many of the Company's competitors.

Only the 2005 financial statements present amounts determined under LIFO. The effect of changing from FIFO to LIFO resulted in a reduction of net income of $4 million in 2005. The cumulative effect of implementing LIFO on prior periods and the pro forma effects of retroactive application is not determinable primarily because the necessary accounting records since the inception of the Company in 1998, which would be required to compute the cumulative effect, are no longer available.

---

[25] Kodak also disclosed the effect of the change on its 2005 and 2004 cash flow statement, but we have omitted these disclosures to save space. They can be found in Kodak's 2006 10-K report at www.sec.gov/edgar/searchedgar/webusers.htm.

obsolescence, service lives, and salvage values of depreciable assets and warranty obligations. Changes in accounting estimates come about because new information that indicates the previous estimate is no longer valid becomes available. In some cases, a change in accounting estimate results from a change in accounting principle. For example, a change from using straight-line depreciation to an accelerated depreciation method may occur because management concludes that the pattern of consumption of an asset's expected benefits has changed and that a new depreciation method better reflects that pattern. Changes in accounting estimates that result from a change in accounting principle are accounted for as a change in estimate under *SFAS No. 154.*

*When accounting estimates are changed, past income is never adjusted;* instead, the income effects of the changed estimate are accounted for in the period of the change and in future periods if the change affects both. This is called the *prospective approach* to reporting an accounting change. If the change in estimate has a material effect on current and future income, the dollar amount of the effect must be disclosed. Exhibit 2.7 shows how National Semiconductor Corporation (NSC) disclosed the effect of a change in accounting estimate, one that increased the useful lives of some of its factory machinery and equipment.

We use another example to illustrate how current and future period numbers are adjusted when a change in an accounting estimate is made. Miles Corporation purchases a production machine on January 1, 2006 for $6 million. The machine has no salvage value, an expected useful life of 10 years, and is being depreciated on a straight-line basis. On January 1, 2008, the machine's book value is $4.8 million (that is, $6 million of original cost minus two years of accumulated depreciation at $0.6 million per year). At that date, it becomes evident that due to changes in demand for the machine's output, its *remaining* useful life is six years, not eight years. If Miles Corporation had perfect foresight, the annual depreciation charge should have been $0.75 million ($6 million divided by eight years), amounting to $1.5 million over the first two years. Consequently, there is $0.3 million too Little accumulated depreciation ($1.5 million minus $1.2 million) on January 1, 2008, and pre-tax income for the previous two years is overstated by $0.3 million. Rather than forcing Miles to retroactively adjust reported

---

**EXHIBIT 2.7**     **National Semiconductor Corp**

**Change of Accounting Estimate**

**Excerpt from 2007 annual report**

*Property, Plant and Equipment*

Effective May 30, 2005, we prospectively changed the estimated useful life of our factory machinery and equipment from 5 years to 9 years for machinery and equipment placed in service on or after that date. We will continue to use a straight-line method to depreciate machinery and equipment. The change in useful life was adopted because we had completed the sale of our PC Super I/O and cordless businesses and announced the closure of our assembly and test plant in Singapore, all key actions associated with the implementation of our strategy to focus on analog product capabilities. The life cycles of analog products and the process technology associated with analog are longer than the non-analog products that were historically a part of our product portfolio. As a result, the average product life of our current portfolio is longer than it was previously. Therefore, the equipment used to manufacture our now-predominantly analog product portfolio will have a longer productive life. The effect of the change in fiscal 2007 was an increase to net income of $7.3 million and to diluted earnings per share of $0.02 and in fiscal 2006 it was an increase to net income of $1.9 million and to diluted earnings per share of $0.01. Factory machinery and equipment placed in service prior to fiscal 2006 continue to be depreciated over 5 years using a straight-line method.

> Because NSC is required to use the prospective approach for its change in accounting estimates, none of the prior years' comparative financial statement amounts are revised.

past income, the GAAP disclosure rules require the change in estimate to be reflected in higher depreciation charges over the new remaining life of the asset, in this case, from 2008 to 2013.[26] Depreciation in those years will be $0.8 million per year (that is, the remaining book value of $4.8 million divided by the remaining useful life of six years). Over the eight-year life of the asset, depreciation will appear as follows:

| | | | |
|---|---|---|---|
| 2006–2007 | 2 years × $0.6 million per year | = | $1.2 million |
| 2008–2013 | 6 years × $0.8 million per year | = | 4.8 million |
| Total cost of the asset | | | $6.0 million |

From the perspective of perfect foresight in which depreciation would have been $0.75 million per year, depreciation in the first two years is understated by $0.15 million annually, and in each of the last six years, it is overstated by $0.05 million annually. Obviously, over the asset's eight-year life, depreciation totals $6.0 million.

Why are changes in estimates "corrected" in this peculiar fashion? The reason is that accrual accounting requires many estimates; because the future is highly uncertain, a high proportion of these estimates turns out to be wrong. If past income were corrected for each misestimate, income statements would be cluttered with numerous retroactive adjustments. The approach illustrated by this example provides an expedient way to deal with the uncertainty in financial statements without generating burdensome corrections.

### Change in Reporting Entity

Another type of accounting change can arise when a company acquires another company. In such circumstances, the newly combined entity presents consolidated financial statements in place of the previously separate statements of each party to the merger. Such combinations result in what is called a **change in reporting entity.**

When a change in a reporting entity occurs, comparative financial statements for prior years must be restated for comparative purposes to reflect the new reporting entity as if it had been in existence during all the years presented.[27] In addition, the effect of the change on income before extraordinary items, net income, other comprehensive income, and any related per share amounts are disclosed for all periods presented.

Comparative financial statements represent an important resource for analysts, because they provide potentially valuable data for assessing trends and turning points. However, under current GAAP, not all business combinations or spin-offs result in a change in the reporting entity. Consequently, analysts must understand the circumstances under which retroactive restatement takes place (and when it does not) to ensure that the data being used are indeed comparable. These matters are discussed in more detail in Chapter 16.

## RECAP

**Accounting changes can dramatically affect reported earnings and distort year-to-year comparisons. For these reasons, GAAP requires special disclosures to improve interperiod comparability and to help the statement user understand what effect the accounting change has had on the current period's reported profits. The three basic types of accounting changes are:**

1. **Change in accounting principles.**

2. **Change in accounting estimates.**

3. **Change in reporting entity.**

---

[26] *SFAS No. 154,* para. 19.
[27] *SFAS No. 154,* para. 23.

## Earnings per Share

One of the most commonly reported measures of a company's operating performance is **earnings per share** (EPS). All publicly traded companies must report EPS numbers on the face of their income statement. Exhibit 2.8 illustrates the EPS disclosures for Hewlett-Packard Company. Note that two sets of numbers are reported: one set for **basic EPS** and another set for **diluted EPS.** Basic EPS is computed by dividing income available to common shareholders (that is, net income minus dividends to preferred shareholders) by the weighted average common shares outstanding for the period. Diluted EPS reflects the EPS that would result if all potentially dilutive securities were converted into common shares. It is reported for firms with complex capital structures, that is, firms with convertible debt, convertible preferred stock, options, or warrants outstanding. The calculations involved for diluted EPS

| **EXHIBIT 2.8** | **Hewlett-Packard Company** |
| --- | --- |

**Condensed Income Statements**

| | Years Ended October 31 | | |
| --- | --- | --- | --- |
| ($ in millions, *except per share amounts*) | Year 2 | Year 1 | Year 0 |
| Net revenue | $56,588 | $45,226 | $48,870 |
| Total costs and expenses | 57,600 | 43,787 | 44,845 |
| (Loss) earnings from operations | (1,012) | 1,439 | 4,025 |
| Total interest and other income, net | (40) | (737) | 600 |
| (Loss) earnings from continuing operations before extraordinary item, cumulative effect of change in accounting principle and taxes | (1,052) | 702 | 4,625 |
| (Benefit from) provision for taxes | (129) | 78 | 1,064 |
| Net (loss) earnings from continuing operations before extraordinary item, cumulative effect of change in accounting principle | (923) | 624 | 3,561 |
| Net earnings from discontinued operations | — | — | 136 |
| Extraordinary item gain on early extinguishment of debt, net of taxes | 20 | 56 | — |
| Cumulative effect of change in accounting principle, net of taxes* | — | (272) | — |
| Net (loss) earnings | $ (903) | $ 408 | $ 3,697 |
| | | | |
| Earnings (loss) per share: | | | |
| Basic: | | | |
| Continuing operations | $ (0.37) | $ 0.32 | $ 1.80 |
| Discontinued operations | — | — | 0.07 |
| Extraordinary item gain on early extinguishment of debt, net of taxes | 0.01 | 0.03 | — |
| Cumulative effect of change in accounting principle, net of taxes | — | (0.14) | — |
| Net (loss) earnings | $ (0.36) | $ 0.21 | $ 1.87 |
| Diluted: | | | |
| Continuing operations | $ (0.37) | $ 0.32 | $ 1.73 |
| Discontinued operations | — | — | 0.07 |
| Extraordinary item gain on early extinguishment of debt, net of taxes | 0.01 | 0.03 | — |
| Cumulative effect of change in accounting principle, net of taxes | — | (0.14) | — |
| Net (loss) earnings | $ (0.36) | $ 0.21 | $ 1.80 |
| Weighted average shares used to compute net (loss) earnings per share: | | | |
| Basic | 2,499 | 1,936 | 1,979 |
| Diluted | 2,499 | 1,974 | 2,077 |

* Note that this illustration also discloses EPS amounts for the cumulative effect of a change in accounting principle. Prior to issuance of *SFAS No. 154* in 2005, the cumulative effect of accounting principle changes was reported on the income statement.

are complex and are covered in detail in Chapter 15. Here we simply illustrate the financial statement presentation of EPS.

Note that each set of EPS numbers includes separately reported numbers for income from continuing operations, discontinued operations, extraordinary items, and bottom-line net income. Therefore, it is important for the statement user to be aware of how the number being reported in companies' earnings announcements is defined. This caution applies both to announcements in the financial press and to analysts' forecasts of firms' performance.

## COMPREHENSIVE INCOME

Generally, items included in net income result from **completed** or **closed transactions.** A closed transaction is one whose ultimate "payoff" results from events (1) that have already occurred and (2) whose dollar flows can be predicted fairly accurately. Recollect that income recognition automatically triggers a corresponding change in the carrying amount (book value) of net assets.

Sometimes balance sheet carrying amounts change even though the transaction is not yet completed or closed. Let's consider a specific example, such as a bank or other financial institution that has investments in stocks or other financial instruments with readily determinable market values. Assume that these securities are held in the firm's available-for-sale portfolio and that their current market values exceed original purchase prices. In 1993, the FASB decided that the fair value of the securities—rather than invested historical cost (the amount originally invested in them)—should appear on the balance sheet. To recognize a market value increase, the following accounting entry must be made:

> **DR**  Marketable securities . . . . . . . . . . . . . . . . . . . . . . . . . . . . . . . . . . . . . . . . . . . . .    XXX
>     **CR**  Owners' equity—unrealized holding gain
>             on investment securities . . . . . . . . . . . . . . . . . . . . . . . . . . . . . . . . . .    XXX

Obviously, the credit to offset the increase in the marketable securities account must be made to some account that increases stockholders' equity. Notice, however, that this is not a closed transaction because the securities have not been sold. Because such transactions are still *open* or incomplete, the FASB does not require the credit to run through the income statement. Instead, the owners' equity increase is reported directly as a separate component of stockholders' equity in the balance sheet.[28] Thus, selected unrealized gains (or losses) arising from incomplete (or open) transactions sometimes bypass the income statement and are reported as direct adjustments to stockholders' equity. Such items are called **other comprehensive income** components and fall into one of the four following categories:

1. Unrealized gains (losses) on marketable securities held in firms' available-for-sale portfolios (discussed more fully in Chapter 16).

2. Unrealized gains (losses) resulting from translating foreign currency financial statements of majority-owned subsidiaries into U.S. dollar amounts for the purpose of preparing consolidated financial statements (discussed in Chapter 16).

---

Thompson Financial (First Call) is a leading provider of analyst EPS forecasts in the United States. The EPS forecasts reported by Thompson are typically basic EPS for income from continuing operations excluding the effects of special, nonrecurring gains or losses and certain other noncash charges (for example, depreciation and goodwill amortization). Such earnings are frequently referred to as pro forma or "Street" earnings because they do not strictly correspond to a GAAP earnings number.

A market value decrease would be debited to Owners' equity—unrealized holding loss on investment securities account with an offsetting credit to the Marketable securities account.

[28] "Accounting for Certain Investments in Debt and Equity Securities," *SFAS No. 115* (Norwalk, CT: FASB, 1993), para. 13.

**EXHIBIT 2.9**   Arden Group, Inc. and Consolidated Subsidiaries

**Consolidated Statements of Operations and Comprehensive Income**

| ($ in thousands) | 2006 | 2005 | 2004 |
|---|---|---|---|
| Sales | $482,737 | $470,354 | $502,898 |
| Cost of sales | 296,401 | 289,931 | 310,582 |
| Gross profit | 186,336 | 180,423 | 192,316 |
| Selling, general and administrative expense | 149,656 | 148,607 | 157,737 |
| Operating income | 36,680 | 31,816 | 34,579 |
| Interest and dividend income | 2,560 | 1,722 | 1,986 |
| Other income (expense), net | 2 | 36 | 1,787 |
| Interest expense | (123) | (152) | (182) |
| Income before income taxes | 39,119 | 33,422 | 38,170 |
| Income tax provision | 15,895 | 13,571 | 15,498 |
| Net income | $ 23,224 | $ 19,851 | $ 22,672 |
| Other comprehensive loss, net of tax: | | | |
| Unrealized loss from available-for-sale securities: | | | |
| Net unrealized holding loss arising during the period | (38) | (381) | (161) |
| Reclassification adjustment for realized gain included in net income | (1) | (11) | (86) |
| Net unrealized loss, net of income tax benefit of $28 for 2006, $269 for 2005 and $169 for 2004 | (39) | (392) | (247) |
| Comprehensive income | $ 23,185 | $ 19,459 | $ 22,425 |

3. Unrealized actuarial gains and losses on pension assets and liabilities and increases (decreases) in pension obligations due to prior service cost adjustments under *SFAS No. 158* (discussed in Chapter 14).

4. Unrealized gains (losses) on derivatives used to hedge certain risks (discussed in Chapter 11).[29]

*SFAS No. 130* requires firms to report comprehensive income in a statement that is displayed with the same prominence as other financial statements. Firms are permitted to display the components of other comprehensive income in one of several alternative formats:

1. In a single-statement format, one in which net income and other comprehensive income are added to disclose (total) comprehensive income.

2. In a two-statement approach, one in which net income composes one statement and a second, which presents a separate statement of comprehensive income.

3. As part of the statement of changes in stockholders' equity.

Exhibit 2.9 from Arden Group's 2006 annual report (shown above) illustrates the first approach, Exhibit 2.10 shows the two-statement approach for Merck & Company, and Exhibit 2.11 demonstrates the disclosure of other comprehensive income components as part of Deere & Company's 2006 Statement of Changes in Stockholders' Equity.

> In "Elements of Financial Statements," *Statement of Financial Accounting Concepts Statement No. 6* (Stamford, CT: FASB, 1985), para. 70, comprehensive income is defined as
>
> the change in equity (net assets) of a business enterprise during a period from transactions and other events and circumstances from nonowner sources. It includes all changes in equity during a period except those resulting from investments by owners and distributions to owners.

[29] "Reporting Comprehensive Income," *SFAS No. 130* (Norwalk, CT: FASB, 1997).

## EXHIBIT 2.10    Merck & Co., Inc. and Subsidiaries

### Consolidated Statement of Income

|  | Years Ended December 31 | | |
| --- | --- | --- | --- |
| ($ in millions) | 2006 | 2005 | 2004 |
| Sales | $22,636.0 | $22,011.9 | $22,972.8 |
| Costs, Expenses and Other |  |  |  |
|   Materials and production | 6,001.1 | 5,149.6 | 4,965.7 |
|   Marketing and administrative | 8,165.4 | 7,155.5 | 7,238.7 |
|   Research and development | 4,782.9 | 3,848.0 | 4,010.2 |
|   Restructuring costs | 142.3 | 322.2 | 107.6 |
|   Equity income from affiliates | (2,294.4) | (1,717.1) | (1,008.2) |
|   Other (income) expense, net | (382.7) | (110.2) | (344.0) |
|  | 16,414.6 | 14,648.0 | 14,970.0 |
| Income Before Taxes | 6,221.4 | 7,363.9 | 8,002.8 |
| Taxes on Income | 1,787.6 | 2,732.6 | 2,172.7 |
| Net Income | $ 4,433.8 | $ 4,631.3 | $ 5,830.1 |

### Consolidated Statement of Comprehensive Income

|  | Years Ended December 31 | | |
| --- | --- | --- | --- |
| ($ in millions) | 2006 | 2005 | 2004 |
| Net Income | $ 4,433.8 | $ 4,631.3 | $ 5,830.1 |
| Other Comprehensive Income (Loss) |  |  |  |
|   Net unrealized (loss) gain on derivatives, net of tax and net income realization | (50.9) | 81.3 | (31.7) |
|   Net unrealized gain (loss) on investments, net of tax and net income realization | 26.1 | 50.3 | (100.9) |
|   Minimum pension liability, net of tax | 22.5 | (7.0) | (4.9) |
|   Cumulative translation adjustment relating to equity investees, net of tax | 18.9 | (26.4) | 26.1 |
|  | 16.6 | 98.2 | (111.4) |
| Comprehensive Income | $ 4,450.4 | $ 4,729.5 | $ 5,718.7 |

## EXHIBIT 2.11    Deere & Company

### Statement of Changes in Consolidated Stockholders' Equity

| | For the Year Ended October 31, 2006 | | | | | |
| --- | --- | --- | --- | --- | --- | --- |
| (In millions of dollars) | Total Equity | Common Stock | Treasury Stock | Unamortized Restricted Stock | Retained Earnings | Other Comprehensive Income (Loss) |
| **Balance October 31, 2005** | $6,851.5 | $2,081.7 | $(1,743.5) | $(16.4) | $6,556.1 | $(26.4) |
| Comprehensive income |  |  |  |  |  |  |
|   Net income | 1,693.8 |  |  |  | 1,693.8 |  |
|   Other comprehensive income (loss) |  |  |  |  |  |  |
|     Minimum pension liability adjustment | 21.3 |  |  |  |  | 21.3 |
|     Cumulative translation adjustment | 79.7 |  |  |  |  | 79.7 |
|     Unrealized gain on derivatives | .6 |  |  |  |  | .6 |
|     Unrealized loss on investments | (.9) |  |  |  |  | (.9) |
|   Total comprehensive income | 1,794.5 |  |  |  |  |  |
| Repurchases of common stock | (1,299.3) |  | (1,299.3) |  |  |  |
| Treasury shares reissued | 369.4 |  | 369.4 |  |  |  |
| Dividends declared | (363.4) |  |  |  | (363.4) |  |
| Other stockholder transactions | 138.5 | 130.3 |  | 7.9 | .3 |  |
| **Balance October 31, 2006** | $7,491.2 | $2,212.0 | $(2,673.4) | $ (8.5) | $7,886.8 | $ 74.3 |

Comprehensive income measures a company's change in equity (net assets) that results from all nonowner transactions and events. It is composed of both bottom-line accrual income that is reported on the income statement and other comprehensive income components. Other comprehensive income comprises selected unrealized gains and losses on incomplete (or open) transactions that bypass the income statement and that are reported as direct credits or debits to stockholders' equity. Firms are required to report comprehensive income in a statement that is displayed with the same prominence as other financial statements. But firms are free to choose the format of presentation, either as a separate statement or as part of a statement that is combined with the income statement or a statement of changes in stockholders' equity.

## SUMMARY

- This chapter highlights the key differences between cash and accrual income measurement.

- In most instances, accrual-basis revenues do not equal cash receipts and accrual expenses do not equal cash disbursements.

- The principles that govern revenue and expense recognition under accrual accounting are designed to alleviate the mismatching of effort and accomplishment that occurs under cash-basis accounting.

- Revenue is recognized when *both* the critical event and measurability conditions are satisfied.

- The critical event establishes when the entity has done something to earn the asset being received, and measurability is established when the revenue can be measured with a reasonable degree of assurance.

- The critical event and measurability conditions may be satisfied before or after the point of sale.

- The matching principle determines how and when the assets that are used up in generating the revenue or that expire with the passage of time are expensed.

- Relative to current operating cash flows, accrual earnings generally provide a more useful measure of firm performance and serve as a more useful benchmark for predicting future cash flows.

- Predicting future cash flows and earnings is critical to assessing the value of a firm's shares and its creditworthiness.

- Multiple-step income statements are designed to facilitate this forecasting process by isolating the more recurring or sustainable components of earnings from the nonrecurring or transitory earnings components.

- GAAP disclosure requirements for various types of accounting changes also facilitate the analysis of company performance over time.

- All publicly traded companies must report EPS numbers on the face of their income statement. All firms are required to report basic EPS based on the weighted average number of shares actually outstanding during the period.

- In addition to basic EPS, firms with complex capital structures that include convertible debt, convertible preferred stock, options, or warrants are required to disclose diluted EPS, which reflects the EPS that would result if all potentially dilutive securities were converted into common shares.

- Occasionally, changes in assets and liabilities resulting from incomplete or open transactions bypass the income statement and are reported as direct adjustments to stockholders' equity. These direct adjustments are called *other comprehensive income components*.

- Comprehensive income provides a measure of all changes in equity of an enterprise that result from transactions with nonowners.

- When used with related disclosures in the financial statements, comprehensive income and its components can provide valuable information to investors and creditors for assessing the magnitude and timing of an entity's future cash flows.

## APPENDIX

# REVIEW OF ACCOUNTING PROCEDURES AND T-ACCOUNT ANALYSIS

The basic accounting equation is the foundation of financial reporting:

$$A = L + OE$$

The basic accounting equation says that at all times, the dollar sum of a firm's assets (A) must be equal to the dollar sum of the firm's liabilities (L) plus its owners' equity (OE). To understand why this equality must always hold, keep two things in mind:

1. Assets don't materialize out of thin air; they have to be financed from somewhere.
2. Only two parties can provide financing for a firm's assets:
   a. Creditors of the company—for example, when a supplier ships inventory to a firm on credit (an asset—inventory—is received).
   b. Owners of the company—for example, when owners buy newly issued shares directly from the firm (an asset—cash—is received).

> For simplicity, we ignore nuances of the par value of the stock, etc., and simply treat the entire amount as "common stock." The details of stock transactions are explored further in Chapter 15.

Putting these two things together explains why the two sides of the basic accounting equation must be equal. The equation says the total resources a firm owns or controls (its assets) must, by definition, be equal to the total of the financial claims against those assets held by either creditors or owners.

We'll now use the basic accounting equation to show how various transactions affect its components. Notice that each transaction maintains the basic equality; for example, any increase in an asset must be offset by (1) a corresponding increase in a liability or owners' equity account or (2) a decrease in some other asset.

Assume that Chicago Corporation sells office furniture and provides office design consulting services. It is incorporated on January 1, 2008, and issues $1 million of stock to investors for cash. Here's how this and subsequent transactions will affect the basic accounting equation:

## Transaction 1

| Assets | = | Liabilities | + | Owners' equity |
|---|---|---|---|---|
| +$1,000,000 Cash | | | | +$1,000,000 Common stock |

On the next day, Chicago Corporation buys a combination office building and warehouse for $330,000, paying $30,000 in cash and taking out a $300,000 loan at 8% interest per year.

## Transaction 2

| Assets | = | Liabilities | + | Owners' equity |
|---|---|---|---|---|
| −$30,000 Cash | | +$300,000 Loan | | |
| +$330,000 Building | | payable | | |

Suppliers ship a wide assortment of inventory costing $97,000 to the firm on credit on January 11.

## Transaction 3

| Assets | = | Liabilities | + | Owners' equity |
|---|---|---|---|---|
| +$97,000 Inventory | | +$97,000 Accounts payable | | |

On January 15, Chicago Corporation sells a portion of its inventory costing $50,000 to several customers for $76,000.

## Transaction 4

| Assets | = | Liabilities | + | Owners' equity |
|---|---|---|---|---|
| +$76,000 Accounts receivable | | | | +$76,000 Sales revenue |
| −$50,000 Inventory | | | | −$50,000 Cost of goods sold |

A sale causes assets to flow into the company. Who benefits from this inflow of assets? The owners do. That's why owners' equity is increased by $76,000 in Transaction 4. The source of this increase is labeled; in this case, the source of the increase is Sales revenue. But in making a sale, the firm must relinquish an asset, inventory. Whose claims are reduced as a result of this outflow of assets? The owners'. That's why owners' equity is decreased by $50,000 in the second part of Transaction 4. Again, the reason for the decrease in owners' equity is labeled; in this case, the need to deliver inventory to the customer reduces owners' equity claims on the firm's assets by $50,000, the Cost of goods sold.

In addition to the balance sheet (which follows the balancing format of the basic accounting equation), there is another financial statement called the *income statement*. Recollect that Sales revenue is the top line of the income statement and that Cost of goods sold is deducted from revenues. So Transaction 4, which was illustrated in a basic accounting equation (that is, balance sheet) format, really includes income statement accounts. ***Another way to say the same thing is that the revenue and expense accounts that appear on the income statement are really owners' equity accounts. Revenues are owners' equity increases; expenses are owners' equity decreases.*** (Later in this appendix, we'll show how these accounts are closed into Retained earnings, a component of owners' equity, as part of the adjusting and closing process.)

## Understanding Debits and Credits

Keeping track of transactions using the basic accounting equation as we did in Transaction 1–4 is cumbersome. For this reason, a streamlined approach is used to record how transactions either increase or decrease financial statement accounts. Increases and decreases in accounts are based on the convention of *debits* and *credits*. Debit (abbreviated DR) means left side of accounts, and credit (abbreviated CR) means right side of accounts.

We now depict the basic accounting equation in T-account form and show the rules for how debits and credits operate to reflect increases or decreases to various accounts.

| Asset Accounts | | = | Liability Accounts | | + | Owners' Equity Accounts | |
|---|---|---|---|---|---|---|---|
| Debits | Credits | | Debits | Credits | | Debits | Credits |
| **(DR)** increase the account balance | **(CR)** decrease the account balance | | **(DR)** decrease the account balance | **(CR)** increase the account balance | | **(DR)** decrease the account balance | **(CR)** increase the account balance |

Because Transaction 4 showed us that revenue accounts increase owners' equity and expense accounts decrease it, the DR and CR rules treat revenue and expense accounts just like any other owners' equity accounts. The rules can be summarized as follows:

| Revenues (that is, OE increases) | | Expenses (that is, OE decreases) | |
|---|---|---|---|
| Debits | Credits | Debits | Credits |
| **(DR)** decrease the account balance | **(CR)** increase the account balance | **(DR)** increase the account balance | **(CR)** decrease the account balance |

Let's elaborate on the debit and credit rules for expense accounts. Expense accounts are increased by debits. An increase in an expense *decreases* owners' equity. Owners' equity is decreased by debits. That's why increases in an expense account (which decrease owners' equity) are debits.

The basic accounting equation must always be "in balance"—that is, the total of the assets must always equal the total of the liabilities plus owners' equity. *Similarly, for each transaction, the dollar total of the debits must equal the dollar total of the credits.* Adherence to the debit and credit rules for each transaction automatically keeps the basic accounting equation in balance. To help you visualize how this happens, we redo Transactions 1–4 in debit and credit format and show (in brackets to the right of the account name) what happens to the basic accounting equation:

### Transaction 1:  Stock issued for cash

| | | | |
|---|---|---|---|
| **DR** | Cash [+A] .......................................... | $1,000,000 | |
| | **CR**  Common stock [+OE] .......................... | | $1,000,000 |

### Transaction 2:  Purchase of building

| | | | |
|---|---|---|---|
| **DR** | Building [+A] ...................................... | $330,000 | |
| | **CR**  Cash [−A] ..................................... | | $ 30,000 |
| | **CR**  Loan payable [+L] ............................ | | 300,000 |

### Transaction 3:  Purchase of inventory on credit

| | | | |
|---|---|---|---|
| **DR** | Inventory [+A] ..................................... | $97,000 | |
| | **CR**  Accounts payable [+L] ......................... | | $97,000 |

### Transaction 4:  Sale of inventory on account

| | | | |
|---|---|---|---|
| **DR** | Accounts receivable [+A]............................ | $76,000 | |
| **DR** | Cost of goods sold [−OE]............................ | 50,000 | |
| | **CR**  Sales revenue [+OE]............................ | | $76,000 |
| | **CR**  Inventory [−A] ................................ | | 50,000 |

As the pluses and minuses to the right of the account names show, adherence to the DR/CR rules automatically maintains the balance of the basic accounting equation.

We next introduce four additional transactions for Chicago Corporation. Assume that the company purchases a one-year fire and theft insurance policy on the building and its contents on January 15, 2008, for $6,000. It makes the following journal entry upon purchasing the policy:

**Transaction 5:**    **Purchase of prepaid insurance**

| | | |
|---|---|---|
| **DR** | Prepaid insurance [+A] ..................................... | $6,000 |
| **CR** | Cash [−A] .......................................... | $6,000 |

Prepaid insurance is an asset account because the policy provides a valuable benefit to the company: insurance coverage for the ensuing 12 months.

Next, assume that the company receives a $10,000 fee in advance from a law firm to help the firm design its new office space. The fee is received on January 17, and the consulting/design services are to be provided over the next month. Chicago Corporation makes the following journal entry:

**Transaction 6:**    **Receipt of consulting fees in advance**

| | | |
|---|---|---|
| **DR** | Cash [+A] ............................................... | $10,000 |
| **CR** | Fee received in advance [+L] ........................... | $10,000 |

The credit is to the liability account Fee received in advance because the firm has an obligation to provide the consulting services (or return the fee). Until those services are provided, no revenue can be recognized.

Further assume that Chicago pays certain suppliers $37,000 for inventory recorded in Transaction 3. Other suppliers will be paid in ensuing periods.

**Transaction 7:**    **Payment on account**

| | | |
|---|---|---|
| **DR** | Accounts payable [−L] ..................................... | $37,000 |
| **CR** | Cash [−A] .......................................... | $37,000 |

Finally, $30,000 is received from one of the customers to whom inventory was sold in Transaction 4.

**Transaction 8:**    **Collections on account**

| | | |
|---|---|---|
| **DR** | Cash [+A] ............................................... | $30,000 |
| **CR** | Accounts Receivable [−A] ........................... | $30,000 |

# Adjusting Entries

Before financial statements are prepared (either monthly, quarterly, or annually), a firm's financial accounts must be reviewed to determine whether all economic events that have occurred are reflected in the accounts. It is usually the case that certain readily identifiable types of events will *not* be reflected in the accounts. To include these events in the accounts, **adjusting entries** must be made. These adjusting entries fall into four categories:

1. Adjustments for prepayments.
2. Adjustments for unearned revenues.
3. Adjustments for accrued expenses.
4. Adjustments for accrued revenues.

We now assume that Chicago is preparing financial statements for the month ended January 31, 2008. Adjusting entries in each of the four categories are necessary and discussed next.

**Adjustments for Prepayments**    The insurance policy acquired for $6,000 on January 15 in Transaction 5 has partially expired. One-half of one month's coverage has now elapsed; consequently, 1/24 of the original *annual* premium payment is no longer an asset. The passage of time means that *past* insurance coverage has no future value. So, the following adjusting entry is made:

> **Adjusting Entry A1:**
>
> **DR**    Insurance expense [−OE] ...............................    $250
>       **CR**    Prepaid insurance [−A] ...........................    $250
>           ($6,000/12 months = $500; $500 × 1/2 month = $250)

After this entry is made, the balance in the Prepaid insurance account is $5,750; this is the original $6,000 balance minus the $250 credit in Adjusting Entry A1. The $5,750 represents the remaining asset, insurance coverage for the ensuing 11½ months. The adjusting entry has *simultaneously* accomplished two things:

1. The DR recognizes that portion of the premium that has expired, that is, the portion that is a January expense. This is the matching principle in action because the expense is matched against January revenues.

2. The CR reduces the carrying amount in the asset account by $250. As a result of this reduction, the Prepaid insurance account is shown at $5,750; this is the portion of the original $6,000 insurance premium that has not yet expired.

The building acquired in Transaction 2 also represents a prepayment. Chicago paid for the building in early January 2008, and this building is expected to be used in operations over a series of *future* years. As the building is used, a portion of its future service potential declines. This decline in service potential value is an expense of the period called **depreciation.** Assume that Chicago estimates building depreciation for January totaled $1,250. The following adjusting entry is then made:

> We will discuss the various methods for estimating depreciation in Chapter 10.

> **Adjusting Entry A2:**
>
> **DR**    Depreciation expense [−OE] ..........................    $1,250
>       **CR**    Accumulated depreciation [−A] ...................    $1,250

(The Accumulated depreciation account represents a contra-asset account that is deducted from the cost of the building, as we shall see later.)

> A **contra** account is an account that is *subtracted* from another account to which it relates. Contra-asset accounts carry credit balances because they are subtracted from asset accounts that carry debit balances.

**Adjustments for Unearned Revenues**    By the end of January, let's assume that 60% of the design work for the law firm has been completed. Consequently, the following adjusting entry is made:

> **Adjusting Entry A3:**
>
> **DR**    Fee received in advance [−L] ..........................    $6,000
>       **CR**    Consulting fees revenue [+OE] ....................    $6,000

Notice that this entry also accomplishes two things. First, the debit lowers the balance in the liability account Fee received in advance to $4,000 (that is, the original $10,000 minus the $6,000 liability reduction arising from the debit). Second, the credit properly recognizes that 60% of the $10,000 advance has been earned in January and thereby increases owners' equity.

**Adjustments for Accrued Expenses**   Salaries and wages for the month of January totaled $16,000. The paychecks will not be issued to employees until Monday, February 3. Because the expense arose in January, a liability exists for money owed to the employees and the following entry must be made:

**Adjusting Entry A4:**

| | | |
|---|---|---|
| **DR** | Salary and wages expense [−OE] ........................ | $16,000 |
| **CR** | Salary and wages payable [+L] ..................... | $16,000 |

Adjusting entries such as this one must be made for a wide range of expenses that *accrue* over the reporting period. ***Accrual accounting recognizes expenses as the underlying real economic event occurs, not necessarily when the cash flows out.*** Consequently, adjusting entries for accrued expenses must be made not only for accrued wages payable but also for items such as heat, light, and power used during the month and for interest that has accumulated during the period but has not yet been paid. Assume that the utility bill arrives on January 31 but will not be paid until February 9, its due date. If the utility bill for January totaled $9,000, the following additional adjusting entry is necessary:

**Adjusting Entry A5:**

| | | |
|---|---|---|
| **DR** | Heat, light, and power expense [−OE] .................... | $9,000 |
| **CR** | Accounts payable [+L] .......................... | $9,000 |

Furthermore, interest of $2,000 has accrued on the loan principal that was used to buy the building. (The accrued interest is determined as follows: $300,000 × 8% per year = $24,000 × 1/12 of year = $2,000.) The following entry is made:

**Adjusting Entry A6:**

| | | |
|---|---|---|
| **DR** | Interest expense [−OE] ............................... | $2,000 |
| **CR** | Accrued interest payable [+L] ..................... | $2,000 |

## Adjustments for Accrued Revenues   During the last week in January, Chicago

Corporation provides design consulting services to a physician who is remodeling her office. The physician is billed for the $2,100 due. The adjusting entry is:

**Adjusting Entry A7:**

| | | |
|---|---|---|
| **DR** | Accounts receivable [+A] ............................. | $2,100 |
| **CR** | Consulting fees revenue [+OE] .................... | $2,100 |

Again, the adjusting entry simultaneously accomplishes two things:

1. The DR reflects the asset that the firm expects to collect as a result of consulting services rendered in January.
2. The CR shows the corresponding increase in owners' equity that arises when the asset write-up is recognized.

## Posting Journal Entries to Accounts and Preparing Financial
## Statements   Throughout this book, we use journal entries as a streamlined mechanism

for showing you how economic events affect financial statement accounts. In this section of the appendix, we provide a terse overview of how professional accountants use journal entries

| EXHIBIT 2.12 | Posting to T-Accounts |
| --- | --- |

| Assets | = | Liabilities | + | Owners' Equity |

**Cash**

| (1) $1,000,000 | (2) | $30,000 |
| (6) | 10,000 | (5) | 6,000 |
| (8) | 30,000 | (7) | 37,000 |
| Bal. $967,000 | | |

**Accounts Payable**

| (7) | $37,000 | (3) | $97,000 |
| | | (A5) | 9,000 |
| | | Bal. | $69,000 |

**Common Stock**

| | (1) $1,000,000 |
| | Bal. $1,000,000 |

**Retained Earnings**

(Revenue and expense account balances will be closed out to this account at end of the accounting period.)

**Accounts Receivable**

| (4) | $76,000 | (8) | $30,000 |
| (A7) | 2,100 | | |
| Bal. | $48,100 | | |

**Salary and Wages Payable**

| | (A4) | $16,000 |
| | Bal. | $16,000 |

**Consulting Fees Revenue**

| | (A3) | $6,000 |
| | (A7) | 2,100 |
| | Bal. | $8,100 |

**Sales Revenue**

| | (4) | $76,000 |
| | Bal. | $76,000 |

**Inventory**

| (3) | $97,000 | (4) | $50,000 |
| Bal. | $47,000 | | |

**Accrued Interest Payable**

| | (A6) | $2,000 |
| | Bal. | $2,000 |

**Cost of Goods Sold**

| (4) | $50,000 | |
| Bal. | $50,000 | |

**Insurance Expense**

| (A1) | $250 | |
| Bal. | $250 | |

**Prepaid Insurance**

| (5) | $6,000 | (A1) | $250 |
| Bal. | $5,750 | | |

**Loan Payable**

| | (2) | $300,000 |
| | Bal. | $300,000 |

**Depreciation Expense**

| (A2) | $1,250 | |
| Bal. | $1,250 | |

**Salary and Wages Expense**

| (A4) | $16,000 | |
| Bal. | $16,000 | |

**Building**

| (2) | $330,000 | |
| Bal. | $330,000 | |

**Fee Received in Advance**

| (A3) | $6,000 | (6) | $10,000 |
| | | Bal. | $4,000 |

**Heat, Light, and Power Expense**

| (A5) | $9,000 | |
| Bal. | $9,000 | |

**Interest Expense**

| (A6) | $2,000 | |
| Bal. | $2,000 | |

**Accumulated Depreciation**

| | (A2) | $1,250 |
| | Bal. | $1,250 |

as the building blocks for preparing financial statements. We use T-accounts to demonstrate this. We also show how analysis of T-accounts can be used to infer what transactions (and dollar amounts) a firm entered into between two balance sheet dates.

The DRs and CRs in each journal entry that is made are posted to T-accounts. **Posting** means the DR or CR is entered in the appropriate left (or right) side of the affected T-account. A separate T-account is maintained for each asset, liability, and owners' equity account. (Remember: Revenue and expense accounts are effectively owners' equity accounts, too. The balances accumulated in these accounts for a particular reporting period will be closed out, or transferred to owners' equity at the end of the period.)

Exhibit 2.12 shows all T-accounts that arise from Chicago's transactions during January 2008. The journal entry DR or CR that gave rise to the amount posted in the T-account is indicated by a number to the left of each item. For example, in the Cash T-account, the (1) to the left of the DR of $1,000,000 indicates that this item arose from the $1,000,000 DR in transaction 1. The (1) to the left of the $1,000,000 credit to common stock indicates that this item resulted from the balancing CR in Transaction 1. Posting *both* the DR and CR to the T-accounts reflected in the original entry maintains the equality of the basic accounting equation.

The adjusting entries are also posted to the T-accounts shown in those entries. For example, in Exhibit 2.12, the (A1) to the left of the $250 DR to the Insurance expense T-account tells us that this item arose from adjusting entry A1. (Notice the CR from that

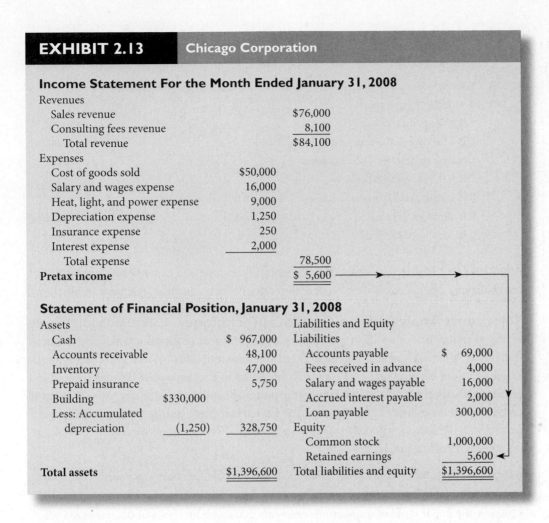

**EXHIBIT 2.13**     Chicago Corporation

**Income Statement For the Month Ended January 31, 2008**

| Revenues | | |
|---|---|---|
| Sales revenue | | $76,000 |
| Consulting fees revenue | | 8,100 |
| Total revenue | | $84,100 |
| Expenses | | |
| Cost of goods sold | $50,000 | |
| Salary and wages expense | 16,000 | |
| Heat, light, and power expense | 9,000 | |
| Depreciation expense | 1,250 | |
| Insurance expense | 250 | |
| Interest expense | 2,000 | |
| Total expense | | 78,500 |
| **Pretax income** | | $ 5,600 |

**Statement of Financial Position, January 31, 2008**

| Assets | | | Liabilities and Equity | |
|---|---|---|---|---|
| Cash | | $ 967,000 | Liabilities | |
| Accounts receivable | | 48,100 | Accounts payable | $ 69,000 |
| Inventory | | 47,000 | Fees received in advance | 4,000 |
| Prepaid insurance | | 5,750 | Salary and wages payable | 16,000 |
| Building | $330,000 | | Accrued interest payable | 2,000 |
| Less: Accumulated | | | Loan payable | 300,000 |
| depreciation | (1,250) | 328,750 | Equity | |
| | | | Common stock | 1,000,000 |
| | | | Retained earnings | 5,600 |
| **Total assets** | | $1,396,600 | Total liabilities and equity | $1,396,600 |

entry was posted as a credit to the Prepaid insurance account, with the A1 designation to the left of the posting.)

The accountant preparing the financial statements would use the balances in the revenue and expense accounts (highlighted in Exhibit 2.12) to prepare the January 2008 income statement. As in Exhibit 2.13, income for January (ignoring taxes) is $5,600. This amount represents the **net** increase in owners' equity for the month arising from operations. Consequently, the $5,600 appears again *in the balance sheet* as an owners' equity increase labeled Retained earnings (shown by the arrows). The asset, liability, and common stock T-accounts (entered in black) compose the other balance sheet accounts. (Notice that the credit balance in Accumulated depreciation is deducted from the Building account. That's why this is a contra-asset account.)

## Closing Entries

After the income statement for the month of January 2008 has been prepared, the revenue and expense accounts have served their purpose. So, balances in these accounts are "zeroed out" (or closed) to get them ready to reflect February transactions. To get the revenue and expense account balances to zero, a **closing journal entry** is made. All revenue account balances (which are credits) are *debited* (to get them to zero); all expense account balances (which are debits) are *credited* (to get them to zero). The difference between the closing

This is true because revenues increase owners' equity and expenses decrease owners' equity (review Transaction 4). So, the excess of revenues over expenses represents the **net** increase in owners' equity.

entry debits and credits—in this case, a credit of $5,600—is made to Retained earnings. Here's the entry:

| | | | |
|---|---|---|---|
| **DR** | Sales revenue | $76,000 | |
| **DR** | Consulting fees revenue | 8,100 | |
| | **CR** Cost of goods sold | | $50,000 |
| | **CR** Salary and wages expense | | 16,000 |
| | **CR** Heat, light, and power expense | | 9,000 |
| | **CR** Depreciation expense | | 1,250 |
| | **CR** Insurance expense | | 250 |
| | **CR** Interest expense | | 2,000 |
| | **CR** Retained earnings | | 5,600 |

After this entry has been posted to the accounts, all revenue and expense accounts will have zero balances. The accounts are now clear to receive February income statement transactions.

### T-accounts Analysis as an Analytical Technique

Understanding the various events or transactions that affect individual account balances is critical to analyzing financial statements. Users of financial statements can't "see" the individual transactions that underlie various account balances and changes in account balances in comparative balance sheets. Nevertheless, it's often possible to "get behind the numbers" and deduce the aggregate amount of certain common events or transactions that have taken place during the reporting period. Armed with the following knowledge, one can reconstruct transactions that have occurred during a given reporting period.

- Start with beginning and ending balances in various balance sheet T-accounts (which are always available from comparative balance sheets).
- Know the major types of transactions or events that cause increases or decreases in individual T-accounts.
- Know how various accounts and financial statement items articulate with one another.

T-account analysis also can be used to gain insights into why accrual-basis earnings and cash-basis earnings (that is, cash flows from operations) differ.

Let's use a new example, Trevian Corporation, to illustrate how T-account analysis can be used to infer or deduce unknown or unobservable transactions. Consider the following analysis of Accounts receivable (net of the Allowance for doubtful accounts):

**Accounts Receivable—Net**

| | | | |
|---|---|---|---|
| Beginning Balance | $1,000,000 | | |
| | | Collections on account | (B) |
| Sales on account | (A) | | |
| Ending Balance | $1,200,000 | | |

Note that the major transaction that increases Accounts receivable (debits to this account) is sales on account, and the major transaction causing a decrease in Accounts receivable (credits to this account) is the collections on account. Assuming that these are the only events that affected Accounts receivable during the period, we can infer from the $200,000 increase in Trevian's Accounts receivable that sales on account exceeded collections on account during the period by $200,000. Can we go a step further and deduce the aggregate amounts of the debits

---

A comparative balance sheet reflects the asset, liability, and owners' equity account balances as of the end of the current reporting period (typically a quarter or year) and for one previous reporting period. Firms are required by the SEC to show two years of comparative balance sheet data and three years of comparative income statement data in annual 10-K reports.

---

Other transactions that can affect the Accounts receivable account include write-offs of specific accounts determined to be uncollectible, sales returns and allowances, and customers that take advantage of sales discounts by paying off their account balance within the discount period. Typically, these events have a minimal effect on the Accounts receivable balance for the period.

(A) and credits (B) to this account? Yes, we can. However, to do so, we need to understand how parts of the income statement and balance sheet articulate with one another.

Recall that the first line of the income statements of most companies is Sales revenue. Typically, when one business sells a product or service to another company, the sale is a credit sale, meaning that the sale is "on account" and will be collected within 30, 60, or 90 days, depending on industry credit terms. Suppose Trevian's sales revenue was $3,500,000 and all sales were credit sales. We can re-create the following entry that summarizes the credit sales for the period and shows directly how income statement and balance sheet accounts reflect opposite sides of the same transaction and, thus, articulate with one another.

| | | | |
|---|---|---|---|
| **DR** | Accounts receivable | $3,500,000 | |
| | **CR** Sales revenue | | $3,500,000 |

Knowing that all sales on account are reflected in an offsetting debit to Accounts receivable allows us to deduce the amount (A) = $3,500,000 in the Accounts receivable T-account just presented. Next, we can combine this information with the fact that the net increase in Accounts receivable was $200,000 to deduce that the collections on account during the period—unknown amount (B)—must have been $3,300,000. In other words,

| | |
|---|---|
| Beginning accounts receivable balance | $1,000,000 |
| + Sales on account | 3,500,000 |
| − Collections on account | (3,300,000) ← (Plug to balance = B) |
| = Ending accounts receivable balance | $1,200,000 |

Analysis of the Accounts receivable T-account also provides information for understanding differences between accrual-basis income and cash from operations. The important insight from the analysis of the Accounts receivable T-account is that sales on account (reflected as revenue in accrual-basis income) are recorded on the debit side of this account while collections on account (reflected as revenue in cash-basis income measurement—that is, cash flow from operations) are recorded on the credit side of this account. Knowing that Trevian's Accounts receivable has increased by $200,000 tells us that accrual-basis revenue exceeded cash-basis revenue for the period by $200,000. Therefore, we would need to *subtract* this increase in Accounts receivable from the accrual-basis income number to convert accrual earnings to cash flow from operations. Conversely, if collections on account had exceeded sales on account by $200,000, this *decrease* in Accounts receivable would have to be *added* to accrual-basis net income to arrive at cash flow from operations.

Analogous reasoning can be used to gain insights into transactions that affect Accounts payable and the differences between accrual-basis expenses and cash-basis expenses. The following T-account summarizes the key events that cause changes in Trevian's Accounts payable for a period:

**Accounts Payable**

| | | | |
|---|---|---|---|
| | | Beginning balance | $2,000,000 |
| Payments on account | (B) | | |
| | | Purchases of inventory on account | (A) |
| | | Ending balance | $1,500,000 |

Here we can see that payments on account exceeded purchases of inventory on account by $500,000, resulting in a decrease in the Accounts payable T-account for the period. We can deduce the amount of purchases on account by again referring to the income statement and recalling the components that comprise the cost of goods sold computation for a merchandising firm. For purposes of this illustration, assume that Trevian's cost of goods sold is $2,100,000, and the beginning and ending inventory from its comparative balance sheets are $1,500,000 and $1,800,000, respectively. Purchases of inventory for the period can be deduced as follows:

| | |
|---|---|
| Beginning inventory | $1,500,000 |
| + Purchases of inventory | 2,400,000 ← (Plug to balance = A) |
| − Ending inventory | (1,800,000) |
| = Cost of goods sold | $2,100,000 |

Assuming that all purchases of merchandise inventory were purchased on credit (generally the case for most businesses), we can determine through T-account analysis that payments on account must have been $2,900,000 determined as follows:

| | |
|---|---|
| Beginning accounts payable balance | $2,000,000 |
| + Purchases on account (see above) | 2,400,000 |
| − Payments on account | (2,900,000) ← (Plug to balance = B) |
| = Ending accounts payable balance | $1,500,000 |

Changes in the Accounts payable and Inventory T-accounts help us understand the differences between accrual accounting's cost of goods sold expense and the cash-basis expense for inventory purchases. We'll use the preceding schedules for Trevian's cost of goods sold and accounts payable to demonstrate this point:

| | |
|---|---|
| Accrual accounting cost of goods sold deduction included in determining income | $2,100,000 |
| + Inventory increase | 300,000 |
| = Total inventory purchases in 2008 | 2,400,000 |
| + Accounts payable decrease | 500,000 |
| = Cash basis expense for inventory purchases | $2,900,000 |

As shown, two adjustments are required to convert accrual-basis cost of goods sold ($2,100,000) to cash-basis expense for inventory purchases ($2,900,000). The first adjustment for the inventory increase is because beginning inventory is a *non-cash addition* to cost of goods sold, while ending inventory is a *non-cash deduction* in arriving at cost of goods sold (see cost of goods sold schedule above). Therefore, to remove the net non-cash effects of beginning and ending inventory from cost of goods sold, we must add the increase in inventory. (If inventory had declined, we would subtract the decrease.) Making this adjustment to cost of goods sold gives us the total inventory purchased in 2008. (We've assumed that all inventory purchases are on account. Consequently, all inventory purchases during the year would be credited to Accounts payable.)

The second adjustment, for the decrease in Accounts payable, is made because Trevian's cash *payments* for inventory purchased on account exceeded new inventory *purchases* on account in the current period (see Accounts payable schedule on page 95). Thus, Trevian's cash payments for inventory actually exceeded the credit purchases of inventory that are included in the accrual-basis cost of goods sold number. Accordingly, to convert the accrual-basis cost of goods sold expense to a cash-basis expense, the decrease in Accounts payable must be added. (If Accounts payable had increased, this change would have been subtracted.)

Note that in the previous discussion, the adjustments made are to convert accrual-basis *expense* to cash-basis *expense*. To adjust accrual-basis *income* to obtain cash-basis *income* (cash flow from operations), the adjustment for the changes in Inventory and Accounts payable would be in the opposite direction. That is, the increase in Inventory and the decrease in

Accounts payable would be *subtracted* from accrual income to obtain cash flow from operations. This is so because adjustments to expense have the opposite effect on income.

In general, analyses similar to that used for Accounts receivable and Accounts payable can be carried out for Accrued revenue, Accrued expense, Deferred (unearned) revenue, and Deferred (prepaid) expense accounts to deduce other differences between accrual-basis income and cash-basis income. Understanding that differences between accrual-basis and cash-basis income can be gleaned from most working capital accounts (that is, current asset and current liability accounts reported on the balance sheet) is one of the key lessons in financial statement analysis that we will return to repeatedly throughout later chapters in this book.

## EXERCISES

In November and December 2008, Gee Company, a newly organized magazine publisher, received $36,000 for 1,000 three-year subscriptions at $12 per year, starting with the January 2009 issue of the magazine.

**Required:**

How much should Gee report in its 2008 income statement for subscriptions revenue on an accrual basis? How much revenue would be reported in 2008 on a cash basis?

**E2-1**

Determining accrual- and cash-basis revenue

**AICPA**
ADAPTED

Aneen's Video Mart sells one- and two-year mail-order subscriptions for its video-of-the-month business. Subscriptions are collected in advance and credited to sales. An analysis of the recorded sales activity revealed the following:

|  | 2007 | 2008 |
|---|---|---|
| Sales | $420,000 | $500,000 |
| Less cancellations | (20,000) | (30,000) |
| Net sales | $400,000 | $470,000 |
| Subscription expirations |  |  |
| 2007 | $120,000 |  |
| 2008 | 155,000 | $130,000 |
| 2009 | 125,000 | 200,000 |
| 2010 |  | 140,000 |
|  | $400,000 | $470,000 |

**Required:**

What amount of unearned subscription revenue should Aneen report on its December 31, 2008, balance sheet?

**E2-2**

Determining unearned subscription revenue

**AICPA**
ADAPTED

Regal Department Store sells gift certificates redeemable for store merchandise that expire one year after their issuance. Regal has the following information pertaining to its gift certificates sales and redemptions:

| Unredeemed at 12/31/07 | $ 75,000 |
|---|---|
| 2008 sales | 250,000 |
| 2008 redemptions of prior year sales | 25,000 |
| 2008 redemptions of current year sales | 175,000 |

Regal's experience indicates that 10% of gift certificates sold will not be redeemed.

**Required:**

In its December 31, 2008, balance sheet, what amount should Regal report as unearned revenue?

**E2-3**

Determining unearned revenue

**AICPA**
ADAPTED

<table>
<tr><td>

**E 2-4**

Determining when to recognize revenue

AICPA
ADAPTED

</td><td>

On October 1, 2008, Hawkeye Company sold 100,000 gallons of heating oil to Johnson Co. at $3 per gallon. On December 15, 2008, 50,000 gallons were delivered, and the remaining 50,000 gallons were delivered on January 15, 2009. Payment terms were: 50% due on October 1, 2008; 25% due on first delivery; and the remaining 25% due on final delivery.

**Required:**

What amount of revenue should Hawkeye recognize from this sale during 2008 on an accrual basis?

</td></tr>
</table>

<table>
<tr><td>

**E 2-5**

Converting from accrual- to cash-basis revenue

AICPA
ADAPTED

</td><td>

In its accrual-basis income statement for the year ended December 31, 2008, Dart Company reported revenue of $1,750,000. Additional information follows:

| | |
|---|---|
| Accounts receivable 12/31/07 | $375,000 |
| Uncollectible accounts written off during 2008 | 20,000 |
| Accounts receivable 12/31/08 | 505,000 |

**Required:**

Under the cash basis of income determination, how much should Dart report as revenue for 2008?

</td></tr>
</table>

<table>
<tr><td>

**E 2-6**

Converting from accrual- to cash-basis revenue

AICPA
ADAPTED

</td><td>

Tara Company reported accrual-basis revenue of $1,980,000 in its income statement for the year ended December 31, 2008. Additional information follows:

| | **2007** | **2008** |
|---|---|---|
| Accounts receivable | $415,000 | $550,000 |
| Allowance for doubtful accounts | 25,000 | 40,000 |

No uncollectible accounts were written off during 2008.

**Required:**

Had the cash basis of accounting been used instead, how much revenue would Tara Company have recognized for 2008?

</td></tr>
</table>

<table>
<tr><td>

**E 2-7**

Converting from cash- to accrual-basis revenue

AICPA
ADAPTED

</td><td>

John Tracey, M.D., keeps his accounting records on the cash basis. During 2008, he collected $150,000 in fees from his patients. At December 31, 2007, Dr. Tracey had accounts receivable of $20,000. At December 31, 2008, he had accounts receivable of $35,000 and unearned fees of $5,000.

**Required:**

On the accrual basis, what was Dr. Tracey's patient service revenue for 2008?

</td></tr>
</table>

<table>
<tr><td>

**E 2-8**

Converting from cash- to accrual-basis revenue

AICPA
ADAPTED

</td><td>

Marr Corporation reported rental revenue of $2,210,000 in its cash-basis income statement for the year ended November 30, 2008. Additional information follows:

| | |
|---|---|
| Rents receivable—November 30, 2008 | $1,060,000 |
| Rents receivable—November 30, 2007 | 800,000 |
| Uncollectible rents written off during the fiscal year | 30,000 |

**Required:**

On the accrual basis, how much gross rental revenue should Marr report in 2008?

</td></tr>
</table>

<table>
<tr><td>

**E 2-9**

Converting from accrual- to cash-basis expense

AICPA
ADAPTED

</td><td>

Under Hart Company's accounting system, all insurance premiums paid are debited to Prepaid insurance. For interim financial reports, Hart makes monthly estimated charges to Insurance expense with credits to Prepaid insurance. Additional information for the year ended December 31, 2008 follows:

| | |
|---|---|
| Prepaid Insurance at December 31, 2007 | $210,000 |
| Charges to Insurance expense during 2008, including a year-end adjustment of $35,000 | 875,000 |
| Unexpired insurance premiums at December 31, 2008 | 245,000 |

</td></tr>
</table>

**Required:**

What was the total amount of insurance premiums Hart paid during 2008?

---

Dix Company operates a retail store and must determine the proper December 31, 2008, year-end accrual for the following expenses:

- The store lease calls for fixed rent payments of $1,200 per month, payable at the beginning of the month, and additional rent equal to 6% of net sales over $250,000 per calendar year, payable on January 31 of the following year. Net sales for 2008 are $450,000.

- An electric bill of $850 covering the period December 16, 2008 through January 15, 2009 was received January 22, 2009.

- A $400 telephone bill was received January 7, 2009 covering:

| | |
|---|---|
| Service in advance for January 2009 | $150 |
| Local and toll calls for December 2008 | 250 |

**Required:**

What amount should Dix Company report as accrued liabilities on its December 31, 2008 balance sheet?

**E2-10**

Determining accrued liabilities

**AICPA**
ADAPTED

---

Munn Corporation's income statements for the years ended December 31, 2008 and 2007 included the following information before adjustments:

| | 2008 | 2007 |
|---|---|---|
| Operating income | $ 800,000 | $600,000 |
| Gain on sale of division | 450,000 | — |
| | 1,250,000 | 600,000 |
| Provision for income taxes | (375,000) | (180,000) |
| Net income | $ 875,000 | $420,000 |

On January 1, 2008, Munn Corporation agreed to sell the assets and product line of one of its operating divisions for $1,600,000. The sale was consummated on December 31, 2008, and it resulted in a gain on disposition of $450,000. This division's pre-tax net losses were $320,000 in 2008 and $250,000 in 2007. The income tax rate for both years was 30%.

**Required:**

Starting with operating income (before tax), prepare revised comparative income statements for 2008 and 2007 showing appropriate details for gain (loss) from discontinued operations.

**E2-11**

Determining gain (loss) from discontinued operations

**AICPA**
ADAPTED

---

On September 1, 2008, Revsine Co. approved a plan to dispose of a segment of its business. Revsine expected that the sale would occur on March 31, 2009, at an estimated gain of $350,000. The segment had actual and estimated operating profits (losses) as follows:

| | |
|---|---|
| Realized loss from 1/1/08 to 8/31/08 | $(300,000) |
| Realized loss from 9/1/08 to 12/31/08 | (200,000) |
| Expected profit from 1/1/09 to 3/30/09 | 400,000 |

Assume that the marginal tax rate is 30%.

**Required:**

In its 2008 income statement, what should Revsine report as profit or loss from discontinued operations (net of tax effects)?

**E2-12**

Determining loss on discontinued operations

---

**E2-13**

Determining period versus product costs

**Required:**

Classify the following costs as period or product costs. If a product cost, indicate which will be matched with sales as part of cost of goods sold and which will be shown as a direct deduction from sales.

| | |
|---|---|
| Depreciation on office building | Depreciation on factory |
| Insurance expense for factory building | Bonus to factory workers |
| Product liability insurance premium | Salary to marketing staff |
| Transportation charges for raw materials | Administrative expenses |
| Factory repairs and maintenance | Bad debt expense |
| Rent for inventory warehouse | Advertising expenses |
| Cost of raw materials | Research and development |
| Factory wages | Warranty expense |
| Salary to chief executive officer | Electricity for plant |

---

**E2-14**

Converting from cash to accrual basis

The following information is provided for Kelly Plumbing Supply.

| | |
|---|---|
| Cash received from customers during December 2008 | $387,000 |
| Cash paid to suppliers for inventory during December 2008 | 131,000 |

Cash received from customers includes November accounts receivables of $139,000. Sales totaling $141,000 were made on account during December and are expected to be collected in January 2009. Cash paid to suppliers in December included payments of $19,000 for inventory purchased and used in November. All inventory purchased in December and $39,000 of inventory purchased in November was used in December.

**Required:**

What is gross profit for the month of December under accrual accounting?

---

**E2-15**

Accrual-basis revenue recognition

Runway Care, Inc. provides contract mowing services for private airfields with grass runways. Some clients prepay for their mowing services early in the spring and their payment is credited to Unearned revenue. The following information was taken from Runway's 2008 financial statements.

| | **Balance at** | |
|---|---|---|
| | **June 30** | **July 31** |
| Accounts receivable | $30,000 | $29,000 |
| Unearned revenue | 5,000 | 3,000 |

Runway received $73,000 of payments on accounts receivable during July.

**Required:**

How much revenue should Runway report for the month of July?

---

**E2-16**

Determining effect of omitting year-end adjusting entries

Hentzel Landscaping commenced its business on January 1, 2008.

1. During the first year of its operations, Hentzel purchased supplies in the amount of $12,000 (debited to Supplies inventory), and of this amount, $3,000 were unused as of December 31, 2008.

2. On March 1, 2008, Hentzel received $18,000 for landscaping services to be rendered for 18 months (beginning July 1, 2008). This amount was credited to Unearned landscaping revenue.

3. The company's gasoline bill for $2,500 for the month of December 2008 was not received until January 15, 2009.

4. The company had borrowed $50,000 from HomeTown Financing on April 1, 2008, at a 12% interest rate per annum. The principal, along with all the interest, is due on April 1, 2009.

5. On January 1, 2008, the company purchased 10 lawnmowers at $3,000 per unit. They are expected to last for three years with no salvage value.

On December 31, 2008, Hentzel did not record any adjusting entries with respect to these transactions.

**Required:**

Using the following table format, show the effect of the *omission* of each year-end adjusting entry on the following. (Indicate both the amount and the direction of the effect.) Use OS for overstated, US for understated, and NE for no effect.

| Item Number | Assets | Liabilities | Net Income |
|---|---|---|---|
| Direction of effect | | | |
| Dollar amount of effect | | | |

---

Presented below is a combined single-step income and retained earnings statement for Amalgamated Steel Co. for 2008.

**E2-17**

Preparing a multiple-step income statement

**Income Statement**
**Year Ended December 31, 2008**

| ($ in 000) | |
|---|---|
| Net sales | $4,801,776 |
| Costs and expenses | |
| Cost of products sold | 4,332,277 |
| Marketing, administrative and other expenses | 175,588 |
| Interest expense | 14,286 |
| Other, net | 49,572 |
| Total expenses before taxes | 4,571,723 |
| Earnings before income taxes | 230,053 |
| Provision for income taxes | (69,016) |
| Net income | 161,037 |
| Retained earnings at 1/1/08 | 2,538,883 |
| Dividends on common stock | (59,383) |
| Retained earnings at 12/31/08 | $2,640,537 |

Additional facts gleaned from Amalgamated's financial statement footnotes follow:

a. "Other, Net" for 2008 included a corporate restructuring charge of $9,753,000 and a gain of $11,000,000 resulting from compensation paid by the U.S. government for company property taken under the right of eminent domain. The remainder of the caption is comprised of investment losses.

b. "Marketing, administrative, and other expenses" for 2008 included a loss on currency translation of $50,000.

c. All of these transactions were subject to Amalgamated's income tax rate of 30%.

d. Amalgamated disclosed earnings per share data only in the notes to the financial statements. The company had 10,000,000 shares of common stock outstanding throughout 2008.

**Required:**

Recast this single-step combined income statement and retained earnings statement as a multi-step income statement in appropriate form. Include appropriate per share amounts.

| E2-18 |
|-------|

**Preparing an income statement with irregular items**

KEW Corp. has 500,000 shares of common stock outstanding. In 2008, KEW reports income from continuing operations before taxes of $4,350,000. Additional transactions from 2008—and not considered in the $4,350,000—are as follows:

1. The company reviewed its notes receivable and discovered that a note carried at $16,000 was 18 months past due. The note was not likely to be collected.

2. KEW sold machinery for $85,000 that originally cost $300,000. Accumulated depreciation at the time of the sale amounted to $225,000. KEW sells unneeded machinery occasionally when retooling one of its production processes.

3. KEW sold a division during 2008 resulting in a pre-tax loss of $890,000. The operating loss incurred by the discontinued division prior to its sale was $650,000; the loss from its disposal was $240,000. This transaction meets the *SFAS No. 144* criteria for discontinued operations.

4. KEW lost $395,000 (pre-tax) when a plant it operated in a third-world country was expropriated following a revolution. The company had no other foreign operations.

**Required:**

Based on this information, prepare an income statement for the year ended December 31, 2008, starting with income from continuing operations before income taxes; include proper earnings per share disclosures. KEW's total effective tax rate on all items was 35%.

| E2-19 |
|-------|

**Analyzing income statement presentation**

During 2008, the following various events (consider each to be independent and material) occurred at several of your CPA firm's clients.

1. Martin Manufacturing's production facility is located near Miami, Florida. Two hurricanes (one considered major) struck southern Florida in 2008. One of the storms caused extensive damage to Martin's plant.

2. ACF, Inc. manufactures railroad tank cars and has been doing so since the 1960s. Because some of ACF's production equipment had become obsolete, the equipment was sold at a loss and new equipment acquired.

3. Furman Foods produces canned and frozen foods that are private labeled for various supermarket chains. Because profit margins on the frozen food operation were disappointing, Furman sold it to a competitor, taking a loss on the sale.

4. *SFAS No. 142,* issued in June 2001, altered accounting for goodwill. Annual amortization of goodwill is no longer required; instead, goodwill must be periodically evaluated for impairment. If no impairment has occurred, goodwill should not be amortized. Unfortunately, the controller at Jensen Company overlooked this mandated change in accounting principles and continued to amortize goodwill in keeping with past practices. This fact was discovered only this year. (Assume that Jensen's goodwill is not impaired.)

5. Smithfield Corporation restructured its operations. The company consolidated its five regional offices into three operating districts, thus enabling two regional headquarters facilities to be closed and staff to be reassigned or terminated. Although Smithfield believes this restructuring will save money in the long term, it incurred a loss when these facilities were closed.

6. Magnum Motors changed its method of inventory valuation. As the only "FIFO company" in the industry, Magnum's management believed that readers of the company's financial statements would find them more useful if Magnum used LIFO as do its competitors.

7. Andy's Colors, a paint manufacturer, decided to discontinue the manufacture of latex paints. The company's line of oil-based paints will be continued. These two paint lines are separable both operationally and financially. Andy's management found a buyer for the latex paint manufacturing facilities. Unfortunately, some environmental problems were discovered during the buyer's examination of these facilities and the sale is on hold pending a resolution of this matter. Andy's management believes this problem can be satisfactorily dealt with, but that it may take a few years to do so.

**Required:**

Briefly discuss the 2008 financial statement presentation of each of the preceding events. Ignore earnings per share disclosures.

---

Krewatch, Inc. is a vertically integrated manufacturer and retailer of golf clubs and accessories (gloves, shoes, bags, etc.). Krewatch maintains separate financial reporting systems for each of its facilities. The company experienced the following events in 2008:

| E2-20 |
| --- |

**Income statement presentation**

1. After several years of production problems at the accessories manufacturing plant, Krewatch sold the plant to an investor group headed by a former manager at the plant. Krewatch plans to continue to carry the accessory line in its retail stores and is committed to purchase the plant's entire annual output.
2. Krewatch incurred restructuring costs of $12,562,990 when it eliminated a layer of middle management.
3. Krewatch extinguished $200 million in 30-year bonds issued 18 years ago. These bonds were the only ones issued in the company's history. Krewatch recognized a gain on this transaction.
4. Krewatch changed its method of accounting for inventory from FIFO to the average cost method.
5. Due to technological advances in golf club manufacturing, management determined that production equipment would need to be upgraded more frequently than in the past. Consequently, the useful lives of equipment for depreciation purposes were reduced.
6. The company wrote off inventory that was not salable at the insistence of its auditors.
7. Equipment was sold at a loss.

**Required:**

For each event, (1) identify the appropriate reporting treatment from the following list (consider each event to be material), and (2) indicate whether it would be included in income from continuing operations, would appear on the income statement below that subtotal, or would require retrospective application.

a. Change in accounting estimate.
b. Change in accounting principle.
c. Discontinued operation.
d. Special or unusual item.
e. Extraordinary item.

---

Joanna Danielle Corporation reported the following for 2008: net sales $3,255,000; cost of goods sold $1,985,550; selling and administrative expenses $651,000; and an unrealized holding loss on available-for-sale securities $18,000. Joanna Danielle's tax rate was 35%.

| E2-21 |
| --- |

**Preparing comprehensive income statement**

**Required:**

Prepare a multiple-step income statement and a statement of comprehensive income using the two-income statement format. Ignore earnings per share.

| | |
|---|---|
| **E 2-22**<br><br>Determining comprehensive income | Andrew's Extreme Sports reported the following information for 2008: net sales, $1,680,000; cost of goods sold, $1,041,600; selling and administrative expenses, $369,600; and an unrealized holding gain from foreign currency translations of $4,900. Andrew's issued common stock for $500,000 and paid a dividend of $0.10 per share on the weighted average number of shares outstanding for the year (250,000 shares). The company has January 1, 2008 balances in Common stock, $1,500,000; Retained earnings, $985,100; and Other comprehensive income −$14,800.<br><br>**Required:**<br><br>Prepare a multiple-step income statement and a statement of stockholders' equity that includes comparative income effects for Andrew's Extreme Sports. Assume a 35% income tax rate. |
| **E 2-23**<br><br>Calculating EPS | An analyst gathered the following information about a company whose fiscal year end is December 31:<br><br>• Net income for the year was $10.5 million.<br><br>• Preferred stock dividends for $2 million were paid for the year.<br><br>• Common stock dividends of $3.5 million were paid for the year.<br><br>• There were 20 million shares of common stock outstanding on January 1, 2008.<br><br>• The company issued 6 million new shares of common stock on April 1, 2008.<br><br>• The capital structure does not include any potentially dilutive convertible securities, options, warrants, or other contingent securities.<br><br>**Required:**<br><br>What would the company's basic earnings per share be for 2008? |

## PROBLEMS / DISCUSSION QUESTIONS

| | |
|---|---|
| **P 2-1**<br><br>Determining royalty revenue<br><br>**AICPA**<br>ADAPTED | Seldin Company owns a royalty interest in an oil well. The contract stipulates that Seldin will receive royalty payments semiannually on January 31 and July 31. The January 31 payment will be for 20% of the oil sold to jobbers between the previous June 1 and November 30, and the July 31 payment will be for oil sold between the previous December 1 and May 31. Royalty receipts for 2008 amounted to $80,000 and $100,000 on January 31 and July 31, respectively. On December 31, 2007, accrued royalty revenue receivable amounted to $15,000. Production reports show the following oil sales:<br><br><table><tr><td>June 1, 2007–November 30, 2007</td><td>$400,000</td></tr><tr><td>December 1, 2007–May 31, 2008</td><td>500,000</td></tr><tr><td>June 1, 2008–November 30, 2008</td><td>425,000</td></tr><tr><td>December 1, 2008–December 31, 2008</td><td>70,000</td></tr></table><br>**Required:**<br><br>What amount should Seldin report as royalty revenue for 2008? |
| **P 2-2**<br><br>Preparing journal entries and statement | a. On January 1, 2008, Frances Corporation started doing business and the owners contributed $200,000 capital in cash.<br><br>b. The company paid $24,000 to cover the rent for the office space for the 24-month period from January 1, 2008, to December 31, 2009.<br><br>c. On March 1, 2008, MSK Inc. entered into a consulting contract under which Frances Corporation promised to provide consulting to MSK Inc. for the 10-month period from March 1, 2008, to December 31, 2008. In return, MSK promised to pay a monthly consulting fee of $15,000, which was to be paid in January 2009. Frances fulfilled its contractual obligation during 2008.<br><br>d. On July 1, 2008, Frances purchased office equipment for $100,000 cash. The equipment has an estimated useful life of five years and no salvage value. The equipment was immediately |

placed into use. Frances uses the straight-line method of depreciation. It records depreciation expense in proportion to the number of months' usage.

e. Through November 30, 2008, the company had paid $66,000 to its employees for 11 months of salaries. Accrued salaries on December 31, 2008 were $6,000.

f. On December 31, 2008, Norbert Corporation advanced $20,000 to Frances Corporation for consulting services to be provided during 2009.

**Required:**

1. Provide journal entries for each of these transactions.

2. Provide adjusting entries at the end of the year.

3. Prepare an income statement for the year ended December 31, 2008.

4. Prepare a balance sheet as of December 31, 2008.

---

The following information pertains to Baron Flowers, a calendar-year sole proprietorship, which maintained its books on the cash basis during the year.

### Trial Balance December 31, 2008

| | DR | CR |
|---|---|---|
| Cash | $ 25,600 | |
| Accounts receivable 12/31/07 | 16,200 | |
| Inventory 12/31/07 | 62,000 | |
| Furniture and fixtures | 118,200 | |
| Land improvements | 45,000 | |
| Accumulated depreciation 12/31/07 | | $ 32,400 |
| Accounts payable 12/31/07 | | 17,000 |
| Baron, drawings | | –0– |
| Baron, capital 12/31/07 | | 124,600 |
| Sales | | 653,000 |
| Purchases | 305,100 | |
| Salaries | 174,000 | |
| Payroll taxes | 12,400 | |
| Insurance | 8,700 | |
| Rent | 34,200 | |
| Utilities | 12,600 | |
| Living expenses | 13,000 | |
| | $827,000 | $827,000 |

**P 2-3**

Converting accounting records from cash basis to accrual basis

**AICPA**
ADAPTED

mhhe.com/revsine4e

The "Baron, drawings" account is used to record any distributions to Mark Baron. The "Baron, capital" account is used to record any capital contributions that Baron makes to the business and any profits or losses retained in the business.

Baron has developed plans to expand into the wholesale flower market and is in the process of negotiating a bank loan to finance the expansion. The bank is requesting 2008 financial statements prepared on the accrual basis of accounting from Baron. During the course of a review engagement, Sue Muir, Baron's accountant, obtained the following additional information:

1. Amounts due from customers totaled $32,000 at December 31, 2008.

2. An analysis of the receivables revealed that an allowance for uncollectible accounts of $3,800 should be provided.

3. Unpaid invoices for flower purchases totaled $30,500 and $17,000 at December 31, 2008, and December 31, 2007, respectively.

4. A physical count of the goods at December 31, 2008 determined that the inventory totaled $72,800. The inventory was priced at cost, which approximates market value.

5. On May 1, 2008, Baron paid $8,700 to renew its comprehensive insurance coverage for one year. The premium on the previous policy, which expired on April 30, 2008, was $7,800.

6. On January 2, 2008, Baron entered into a 25-year operating lease for the vacant lot adjacent to his retail store, which was to be used as a parking lot. As agreed to in the lease, Baron paved and fenced in the lot at a cost of $45,000. The improvements were completed on April 1, 2008, and have an estimated useful life of 15 years. No provision for depreciation or amortization has been recorded. Depreciation on furniture and fixtures was $12,000 for 2008.

7. Accrued expenses at December 31, 2007 and 2008 follows:

|  | 2007 | 2008 |
|---|---|---|
| Utilities | $ 900 | $1,500 |
| Payroll taxes | 1,100 | 1,600 |
|  | $2,000 | $3,100 |

8. Baron was notified late in the year of a lawsuit filed against his business for an injury to a customer. His attorney believes that the unfavorable outcome is probable and that a reasonable estimate of the settlement exclusive of amounts covered by insurance is $50,000.

9. The Salaries account includes $4,000 per month paid to the proprietor. He also receives $250 per week for living expenses. These amounts should have been charged to Baron's drawing account.

**Required:**

1. Determine the adjustments required to convert Baron Flowers' trial balance to the accrual basis of accounting for the year ended December 31, 2008. Prepare formal journal entries to support your adjustments.

2. Write a brief memo to Baron explaining why the bank would require financial statements prepared on the accrual basis instead of the cash basis.

---

**P 2-4**

Making adjusting entries and statement preparation

mhhe.com/revsine4e

The following is the preclosing trial balance of Antonia Retailers, Inc.:

## Preclosing Trial Balance as of December 31, 2008

|  | DR | CR |
|---|---|---|
| Cash | $ 42,000 |  |
| Accounts receivable | 67,500 |  |
| Prepaid rent | 15,000 |  |
| Inventory | 100,000 |  |
| Equipment | 60,000 |  |
| Building | 90,000 |  |
| Allowance for doubtful accounts |  | $ 5,000 |
| Accumulated depreciation—equipment |  | 30,000 |
| Accumulated depreciation—building |  | 9,000 |
| Advance from customers |  | 25,000 |
| Accounts payable |  | 18,000 |
| Salaries payable |  | 4,000 |
| Capital stock |  | 70,000 |
| Retained earnings 1/1/08 |  | 187,500 |
| Sales revenue |  | 350,000 |
| Cost of goods sold | 185,000 |  |
| Salaries expense | 50,000 |  |
| Bad debt expense | 10,500 |  |
| Rent expense | 30,000 |  |
| Insurance expense | 18,000 |  |
| Depreciation expense—building | 5,000 |  |
| Depreciation expense—equipment | 2,000 |  |
| Dividends | 23,500 |  |
| Totals | $698,500 | $698,500 |

The following additional information is provided:

a. The company paid a salary advance of $10,000 to one of its employees, a total that was debited to the Salaries expense account. This was an advance against the employee's salary for the year 2009.

b. On January 1, 2008, the company paid an insurance premium of $18,000, which was debited to the Insurance expense account. The premium provided insurance coverage for 18 months beginning on January 1, 2008.

c. The company decided to revise its estimate of bad debts expense by calculating it at 10% of its sales revenue.

d. On January 1, 2009, the company's board of directors declared an additional dividend of $10,000 for the year 2008.

**Required:**

1. Prepare the necessary adjusting entries for the year ended December 31, 2008.

2. Prepare an income statement for the year ended December 31, 2008.

3. Prepare a balance sheet as of December 31, 2008.

**Required:**

Following is selected information from the balance sheet for Flaps Inc. Solve for the missing amounts for each of the five years.

**P2-5**

Understanding the accounting equation

| | **Year** | | | | |
|---|---|---|---|---|---|
| | **2007** | **2008** | **2009** | **2010** | **2011** |
| Total liabilities and stockholders' equity | $13,765 | F | K | P | U |
| Current liabilities | A | 3,420 | 3,467 | 3,517 | V |
| Common stock | 138 | 139 | L | 142 | 144 |
| Contributed capital | 2,340 | G | 2,387 | 2,422 | W |
| Noncurrent assets | 8,667 | 8,721 | M | 8,968 | X |
| Retained earnings | 2,795 | 2,813 | 2,851 | Q | Y |
| Total assets | B | H | 14,040 | R | 14,351 |
| Noncurrent liabilities | 5,231 | I | 5,335 | S | 5,454 |
| Additional paid-in capital | C | 2,216 | 2,247 | T | 2,296 |
| Current assets | D | J | 5,200 | 5,275 | 5,315 |
| Total liabilities | 8,630 | 8,683 | N | 8,929 | Z |
| Total stockholders' equity | E | 5,168 | O | 5,314 | 5,354 |

The following is selected information from Flightscape Adventures' financial statements. Solve for the missing amounts for each of the five years. You may have to use some numbers from the year before or the year after to solve for certain current year numbers. (NA = not available.)

**P2-6**

Understanding the accounting equation

| | **Year** | | | | |
|---|---|---|---|---|---|
| | **2007** | **2008** | **2009** | **2010** | **2011** |
| Current assets (CA) | A | $2,285 | L | $2,150 | X |
| Noncurrent assets | 3,665 | F | 3,604 | R | 3,732 |
| Total assets | 5,821 | G | M | 5,805 | Y |
| Current liabilities (CL) | 1,437 | H | N | S | 1,463 |
| Noncurrent liabilities | B | 2,345 | O | 2,206 | 2,252 |
| Contributed capital | 990 | I | P | 1,049 | Z |
| Retained earnings (ending) | 1,182 | J | 1,087 | T | 1,204 |
| Total stockholder's equity | C | 2,302 | 2,136 | U | AA |
| Total liabilities and stockholders' equity | D | K | 5,724 | 5,805 | BB |
| Working capital (CA − CL) | E | 762 | 707 | V | 732 |
| Net income (loss) | NA | 85 | Q | 40 | 99 |
| Dividends | 11 | 14 | 9 | W | 12 |

| | |
|---|---|
| **P 2-7**<br><br>Converting from cash to accrual basis | During August 2008, Packer Manufacturing had the following cash receipts and disbursements: |

|  |  |
|---|---|
| Cash received from customers | $319,000 |
| Cash received from selling equipment | 11,200 |
| Cash paid for salaries | 47,000 |
| Cash paid to suppliers for inventory purchases | 130,000 |

In addition, the following balance sheet account balances were shown on Packer's books:

|  | July 31 | August 31 |
|---|---|---|
| Accounts receivable | $128,000 | $135,000 |
| Inventory | 33,000 | 25,000 |
| Accounts payable | 21,000 | 25,000 |
| Salaries payable | 8,000 | 5,000 |

Assume all sales and purchases are on account.

**Required:**

1. Determine sales for August 2008.

2. Determine salary expense for August 2008.

3. Determine cost of goods sold for August 2008.

| | |
|---|---|
| **P 2-8**<br><br>Converting from cash to accrual basis | During the month of October 2008, HAWK-I Rentals had the following cash receipts and payments: |

|  |  |
|---|---|
| Rental receipts (cash) received | $43,000 |
| Cash paid for insurance | 5,000 |
| Cash paid for taxes | 6,000 |
| Cash received from sale of used equipment | 11,000 |

Of the rental receipts collected, $2,000 was reported as Rent receivable at September 30, and $3,500 was a prepayment of November's rent. An insurance premium of $1,000 was owed at the end of October. Taxes of $1,000 and $700 were owed at October 1 and October 31, respectively. Equipment sold in October had a book value (cost − accumulated depreciation) of $12,200 at the time of sale.

**Required:**

1. Determine rental income for October 2008.

2. Determine insurance expense for October 2008.

3. Determine tax expense for October 2008.

4. Assuming that the accumulated depreciation on the equipment sold was $1,300, what is the appropriate journal entry to record the sale of the used equipment?

| | |
|---|---|
| **P 2-9**<br><br>Journal entries and statement preparation | Bob's Chocolate Chips and More, a bakery specializing in gourmet pizza and chocolate chip cookies, started business October 1, 2008. The following transactions occurred during the month. |

a. Common stock of $90,000 was sold to start the business.

b. Equipment consisting of mixers and ovens was acquired October 1 for $30,000 cash. The equipment is expected to last five years and can be sold at that time for $5,000. Management uses the straight-line method to calculate depreciation expense.

c. Ingredients costing $15,000 were purchased on account during the month and all but $5,000 was paid for by the end of the month.

d. Rent is $500 a month. October, November, and December's rent was paid October 5.

e. A payment of $800 for utilities was made during the month.

f.  Sixty percent of the ingredients purchased in part c were prepared and sold for $35,000 on account; $26,000 was collected on accounts receivable during the month.

g.  Wages of $5,200 were paid during the month. Moreover, wages for the last three days of the month amounted to $400 and will be paid during the first week of November.

h.  Borrowed $12,000 from the bank for additional working capital requirements, and $3,000 was repaid by month-end. Interest on the unpaid loan balance amounted to $450 at the end of October and was paid on November 5.

**Required:**

Prepare the required journal entries and adjusting entries as well as an income statement and a balance sheet for Bob's Chocolate Chips and More as of October 31, 2008. (*Hint:* You may want to consider using T-accounts to classify and accumulate the preceding transactions before preparing the statements.)

---

The following is the pre-adjusted trial balance of JetCo Fuel Services as of December 31, 2008.

**P2-10**

Journal entries and statement preparation

## Pre-Adjusted Trial Balance December 31, 2008

| | Debits | Credits |
|---|---|---|
| Cash | $ 39,800 | |
| Accounts receivable, net | 70,700 | |
| Fuel inventory | 42,600 | |
| Equipment | 30,000 | |
| Fuel tanker | 75,000 | |
| Accumulated depreciation | | $ 3,000 |
| Accounts payable | | 35,100 |
| Accrued expenses | | 12,500 |
| Customer deposits | | 2,400 |
| Notes payable | | 75,000 |
| JetCo capital stock | | 75,000 |
| Retained earnings | | 15,300 |
| Fuel sales | | 840,000 |
| Fuel expense | 641,200 | |
| Salary expense | 75,000 | |
| Insurance expense | 72,000 | |
| Rent expense | 12,000 | |
| | $1,058,300 | $1,058,300 |

**Additional Information:**

a.  A fuel tanker was purchased July 1, 2008 by issuing a three-year 10% interest-bearing note payable for $75,000. The tanker is expected to last 10 years and then be scrapped. JetCo uses the straight-line depreciation method.

b.  After taking a physical inventory, it was discovered that fuel inventories were overstated by $6,100.

c.  Equipment on the balance sheet was acquired January 1, 2007 and has a 10-year life.

d.  A search of unrecorded liabilities reveals unrecorded fuel expenses of $4,800.

e.  A 36-month insurance policy was acquired for $72,000 on August 31, 2008, and charged to Insurance expense.

f.  On June 1, 2008, one-year's rent ($12,000) was paid and charged to rent expense.

g.  The balance in the Customer deposits account was earned in 2008.

h.  During 2008, JetCo paid a dividend of $75,000, which was subtracted from Retained earnings.

**Required:**

1. Prepare any required adjustments as of December 31, 2008.

2. Prepare JetCo's income statement for the year ending 2008 and its balance sheet.

---

**P2-11**

IVAX Corporation:
Determining missing amounts
on income statement

The following information was taken from a recent income statement of IVAX Corporation. IVAX is a holding company with subsidiaries providing research, development, manufacturing, and marketing of brand name pharmaceutical products.

| | ($ in 000) |
|---|---:|
| Amortization of intangible assets | $    ? |
| Cost of goods sold | ? |
| Extraordinary gain on extinguishment of debt, net of taxes | 1,121 |
| General and administrative expenses | 88,434 |
| Gross profit | 241,171 |
| Net income | 74,642 |
| Income before extraordinary item | ? |
| Income from continuing operations | ? |
| Income from continuing operations before income taxes | 34,664 |
| Income from discontinued operations, net of taxes | 48,904 |
| Interest expense | ? |
| Interest income | 11,972 |
| Net income | ? |
| Net revenues | ? |
| Operating income | ? |
| Other income, net | 20,830 |
| Provision for income taxes | (10,047) |
| Research and development | 48,615 |
| Restructuring costs and asset write-downs | 12,222 |
| Selling expenses | 79,508 |
| Gross profit as percent of sales | 37.81% |
| Total operating expenses | $232,452 |

**Required:**

1. Recast IVAX's income statement and present it in good form. Fill in the missing data.

2. Consider the item Restructuring costs and asset write-downs. What impact did this charge have on IVAX's cash flows?

3. IVAX's income statements over the last three years report research and development expenses averaging $51.3 million per year. IVAX incurred these expenses to enhance current products and to develop new products in the hope of generating higher future sales. GAAP requires that all such costs be expensed in the year incurred. Consider the following statement:

   *Research and development expenditures are really assets because they will benefit the future operations of the firm (that is, lead to higher sales).*

   If you agree, suggest an alternative way to account for research and development expenditures rather than expensing them in the year incurred. If you disagree, what are your reasons?

4. Assume that you are a financial analyst for IVAX. Your boss has asked you to project next year's net earnings. What earnings number from the information provided here would you use as the basis for your projection? Why?

The following condensed statement of income of Helen Corporation, a diversified company, is presented for the two years ended December 31, 2008 and 2007:

|  | 2008 | 2007 |
|---|---|---|
| Net sales | $10,000,000 | $9,600,000 |
| Cost of sales | (6,200,000) | (6,000,000) |
| Gross profit | 3,800,000 | 3,600,000 |
| Operating expenses | (2,200,000) | (2,400,000) |
| Operating income | 1,600,000 | 1,200,000 |
| Gain on sale of division | 900,000 | — |
| Net income before taxes | 2,500,000 | 1,200,000 |
| Provision for income taxes | (1,250,000) | (600,000) |
| Net income | $ 1,250,000 | $ 600,000 |

**P2-12**

Determining income from continuing operations and gain (loss) from discontinued operations

**AICPA**
ADAPTED

On January 1, 2008, Helen entered into an agreement to sell for $3,200,000 the assets and product line of one of its separate operating divisions. The sale was consummated on December 31, 2008 and resulted in a gain on disposition of $900,000. This division's contribution to Helen's reported income before taxes for each year was as follows:

| 2008 | $640,000 loss |
|---|---|
| 2007 | $500,000 loss |

Assume an income tax rate of 50%.

**Required:**

1. In preparing a revised comparative statement of income, Helen should report income from continuing operations after income taxes for 2008 and 2007, respectively, amounting to how much?

2. Starting with the revised income from continuing operations numbers you obtained in requirement 1, prepare the revised comparative income statements for 2008 and 2007 showing appropriate details for gain (loss) from discontinued operations.

Jordan Wing, Inc., a sporting goods retailer, began operations on January 2, 2006. It reported net income of $3,091,660 during 2008. Additional information about transactions occurring in 2008 follows:

**P2-13**

Preparing an income statement with irregular items

1. Jordan Wing realized $175,000 from settling a trademark infringement lawsuit.

2. The corporation disposed of its catalog sales component at a pre-tax loss of $345,000. This transaction meets the criteria for discontinued operations specified in *SFAS No. 144.*

3. Sale of 10,000 shares of Xerox stock held as a short-term investment resulted in a gain of $23,450.

4. The firm changed its method of depreciating fixed assets from the straight-line method to the declining balance method, which was used to determine income in 2008.

5. Jordan Wing suffered a $23,000 impairment loss in 2007, which it failed to record.

6. The firm experienced an (extraordinary) uninsured tornado pre-tax loss in the amount of $83,500.

**Required:**

Prepare an income statement for the year ended December 31, 2008, starting with income from continuing operations before taxes; include proper earnings per share disclosures. Jordan Wing had 150,000 common shares outstanding for the year. Assume a 35% tax rate on all items.

---

<table>
<tr><td>

**P2-14**

Discontinued operations
components held for sale

</td><td>

For 2008, Silvertip Construction, Inc. reported income from continuing operations (after tax) of $1,650,000 before considering the following information. On November 15, 2008, the company adopted a plan to dispose of a component of the business. This component qualifies for discontinued operations treatment under *SFAS No. 144*. During 2008, the component had pre-tax operating losses of $95,000. The component's assets have a book value of $760,000 on December 31, 2008. A recent market value analysis of these assets placed their estimated selling price at $735,000, less a 6% brokerage commission. Management appropriately determines that these assets are impaired and expects to find a buyer for the component and complete the sale early in 2009.

**Required:**

Prepare a partial income statement for Silvertip including EPS disclosures for the year ended December 31, 2008. Begin at income from continuing operations. Assume a 35% income tax rate and 1,000,000 shares of outstanding common stock.

</td></tr>
</table>

---

<table>
<tr><td>

**P2-15**

Preparing a multiple-step
income statement

</td><td>

The preliminary 2008 income statement of Athletic Footwear, Inc. follows.

## Income Statement For the Year Ended December 31, 2008

*($ in 000, except earnings per share)*

|  |  |
|---|---:|
| Revenues and gains: |  |
| Net sales | $257,348 |
| Other income | 26,533 |
| Interest | 790 |
|   Total revenue and gains | $284,671 |
| Expenses and losses: |  |
| Cost of goods sold | $159,556 |
| Selling and administrative | 48,896 |
| Discontinued operations | 30,882 |
| Income taxes | 17,228 |
|   Total expenses | $256,562 |
|   Net income | $ 28,109 |
| Earnings per share | $    0.56 |

</td></tr>
</table>

Additional facts pertaining to the company's 2008 operations follow:

1. Selling and administrative expenses included $6,231,000 in restructuring costs.
2. Other income represents a gain on the early extinguishment of debt.
3. Early debt extinguishment is part of Athletic Footwear's risk management strategy.
4. A tax rate of 38% applies to all items.
5. Athletic Footwear had 50,000,000 shares of common stock outstanding throughout 2008.
6. Discontinued operations, as reported, resulted from the sale of Athletic Footwear's manufacturing facility (in addition to selling brand name shoes, the company sold shoes of its own manufacture under the AFRules brand). In the future, Athletic Footwear will carry only brand name footwear in its stores. Included in the reported loss was a loss of $19,402,000 attributable to the sale of the manufacturing division's assets; the remainder of the loss stems from the division's pre-sale operations.

**Required:**

Prepare a revised multiple-step income statement reflecting the additional facts in the preceding information (include required EPS data).

The following information was taken from the records of Liz's Theatrical Supplies for 2008. In addition to selling theatrical supplies, Liz owned and operated a theater until October 15, 2008, when Liz sold this component of the business. All listed amounts are pre-tax, but are subject to a 38% income tax rate.

**P 2 - 1 6**

Preparing comprehensive income under single-step format

| | |
|---|---|
| Cost of goods sold | $490,823 |
| Extraordinary loss | 50,000 |
| Income from discontinued operations | 70,000 |
| Interest income | 4,650 |
| Loss from disposal of discontinued component | 95,000 |
| Loss on write-off of obsolete inventory | 23,500 |
| Net sales | 791,650 |
| Rent revenue | 16,000 |
| Selling and administrative expenses | 158,330 |
| Unrealized holding loss on available-for-sale securities | 15,000 |

**Required:**

Prepare a single-step income statement and statement of comprehensive income for 2008 using a single-statement format.

---

The income statement of Smithfield Beverage, Inc. that follows does not include any required reporting related to a $62,000 pre-tax gain that was realized in 2008 when Smithfield repurchased and retired $1 million of its 8% term bonds (scheduled to mature in 2015). Smithfield's income tax rate is 35%; 250,000 shares of common stock were outstanding during 2008.

**P 2 - 1 7**

Extinguishing debt early

### Income Statement for the Year Ended December 31, 2008

| | |
|---|---|
| Sales | $3,512,000 |
| Cost of goods sold | (2,177,440) |
| Gross profit | 1,334,560 |
| Selling and administrative expenses | (772,640) |
| Income from operations, before income taxes | 561,920 |
| Income taxes | (196,672) |
| Net income | $ 365,248 |
| Earnings per share | $ 1.46 |

**Required:**

Discuss any modifications to Smithfield's income statement necessitated by this gain under each of the following independent assumptions (do not produce "corrected" income statements):

1. Such early debt retirements are part of Smithfield's risk management strategy.

2. Smithfield has been in business for 65 years. The company occasionally issues term bonds, but has not previously retired bonds prior to normal maturity.

---

Roger's Plumbing, Inc. operates two segments: (1) a division that installs residential and commercial plumbing in buildings being constructed and (2) a service division that has both residential and commercial components. A recent construction boom has kept Roger's so busy that it has been unable to handle all of the service work on a timely basis. Growing tired of phone messages from irritated customers who wanted their leak fixed yesterday (and unable to hire additional qualified employees), management decides in October to sell the service business, begins to advertise its availability, and has the division's assets appraised. Ted Roger, CEO, believes the service business will be easier to sell if it is split into residential and

**P 2 - 1 8**

Reporting discontinued operations

commercial components. The appraisal results in the following information. Goodwill is the appraiser's estimate of the value of the company's customer base as Roger's Plumbing plans to forward all service calls for a period of three years to whoever buys each component of the service business. Roger's Plumbing has income before taxes of $2,756,000 for 2008 (the year management decides to sell the service division). This amount includes $185,400 residential service income and $215,000 commercial service income. Roger's Plumbing is subject to an income tax rate of 35%.

| Assets | Book Value | Fair Market Value |
|---|---|---|
| **Residential service component:** | | |
| Service vehicles | $ 40,000 | $ 45,000 |
| Repair parts inventory | 25,000 | 22,000 |
| Tool and equipment | 9,500 | 8,000 |
| Goodwill | — | 20,000 |
| Total—Residential service | $ 74,500 | $ 95,000 |
| **Commercial service component:** | | |
| Service vehicles | 55,000 | 53,500 |
| Repair parts inventory | 21,000 | 21,000 |
| Tool and equipment | 14,500 | 12,000 |
| Goodwill | — | 25,000 |
| Total—Commercial service | $ 90,500 | $111,500 |
| Total for service division | $165,000 | $206,500 |

**Required:**

Assume that Roger's Plumbing sells the residential service component on December 5, 2008 for $99,500 (less disposal costs of $2,000). By year-end, the company has received three firm offers for the commercial service component that ranged from $82,500 to $87,000. Management is still actively seeking a better offer, but if none is obtained plans to sell the component to the highest bidder before the end of January 2009. The company's auditors tell management that the consistency of the bids to date indicates an error in the appraisal and that an impairment loss should be recognized to comply with *SFAS No. 144*. Assume estimated costs of $2,500 to sell the commercial service component. Prepare an income statement for Roger's Plumbing, Inc. (for 2008) beginning with income from continuing operations. For purposes of working this problem, report the various components of the gains/losses for discontinued operations separately for actual sales versus assets held for sale. Ignore per share disclosures.

---

**P2-19**

Restatements for error correction

Bettner, Inc. operates a hardwood lumber export business. It began operations as a family business in 1997 and incorporated in 1999. On January 3, 2000, Bettner acquired Needham Bros. lumber and appropriately recorded $1 million of goodwill related to this transaction. Bettner's accounting policy at the time was to amortize goodwill over a 10-year period. Unfortunately, Bettner's CFO neglected to change this policy when the FASB issued *SFAS No. 142*, "Goodwill and Other Intangible Assets," in 2001. Had Bettner implemented *SFAS No. 142*, goodwill would not have been amortized in 2002 and subsequent years; instead, Bettner would have conducted annual impairment tests to determine whether goodwill required a write-off. (These tests would have indicated that no impairment write-off was necessary.) Bettner's failure to comply with *SFAS No. 142* was not discovered until the company, considering a public stock offering, was audited for the first time in 2008. Bettner's comparative financial statements (unaudited) follow:

## Income Statements

|  | For Years Ending December 31, | | |
| --- | --- | --- | --- |
|  | 2006 | 2007 | 2008 |
| Sales | $1,953,251 | $2,126,251 | $2,207,251 |
| Cost of goods sold | 1,230,548 | 1,339,538 | 1,390,568 |
| Gross profit | 722,703 | 786,713 | 816,683 |
| Selling, general & administrative expenses | 390,650 | 425,250 | 441,450 |
| Goodwill amortization | 100,000 | 100,000 | 100,000 |
| Income before income taxes | 232,053 | 261,463 | 275,233 |
| Income tax expense | 81,219 | 91,512 | 96,332 |
| Net income | $ 150,834 | $ 169,951 | $ 178,901 |

## Balance Sheets

|  | December 31, | |
| --- | --- | --- |
|  | 2007 | 2008 |
| Current assets | $1,352,628 | $1,402,109 |
| Property, plant, & equipment | 875,240 | 982,630 |
| Goodwill | 200,000 | 100,000 |
| Total assets | $2,427,868 | $2,484,739 |
| Current liabilities | $ 795,663 | $ 824,770 |
| Long-term debt | 525,000 | 500,000 |
| Common stock | 150,000 | 150,000 |
| Retained earnings | 957,205 | 1,009,969 |
| Total liabilities & stockholders' equity | $2,427,867 | $2,484,739 |

Assume that goodwill is deductible for income tax purposes and that Bettner's income tax rate is 35%.

**Required:**

1. Restate Bettner's financial statements to bring them into compliance with *SFAS No. 142*.

2. Draft the disclosures required by *SFAS No. 154* related to this restatement.

---

**P2-20**

**Reporting a change in accounting principle**

Barden, Inc. operates a retail chain that specializes in baby clothes and accessories that are made to its specifications by a number of overseas manufacturers. Barden began operations in 1998 and has always employed the FIFO method to value its inventory. Since 1998, prices have generally declined as a result of intense competition among Barden's suppliers. In 2007, however, prices began to rise significantly as these suppliers succumbed to international pressure and addressed sweatshop conditions in their factories. The improved working conditions and benefits led to increased costs that are being passed on to Barden. In turn, Barden's management believes that FIFO no longer is the best method to value its inventories and thus switched to LIFO on January 1, 2008. This accounting change was justified because of LIFO's better matching of current costs with current revenues. Barden judges it impractical to apply the LIFO method on a retrospective basis because the company never maintained records on a LIFO basis. As a result of this change, ending inventory was reported at $275,000 instead of its $345,000 FIFO value. Barden reported 2008 net income of $825,000; the company's income tax rate is 35%. Barden has 10,000 shares of stock outstanding.

**Required:**

1. How should Barden's 2008 comparative financial statements reflect this change in accounting principle?

2. Prepare whatever disclosure *SFAS No. 154* requires as a result of this change.

## CASES

| C2-1 |
| --- |

Conducting financial reporting research: Discontinued operations

The Mohegan Tribe is a federally recognized Native American tribe with an approximately 405-acre reservation located in southeastern Connecticut. Under the Indian Gaming Regulatory Act of 1988, or IGRA, federally recognized Native American tribes are permitted to conduct full-scale casino gaming operations on tribal land.

In October 1996, the tribe opened a gaming and entertainment complex known as Mohegan Sun. The tribe substantially completed a major expansion of Mohegan Sun known as Project Sunburst. The first phase of Project Sunburst, the Casino of the Sky, which included increased gaming, restaurant and retail space, and an entertainment arena, opened on September 25, 2001. The remaining components, including the majority of a 1,200-room luxury hotel and approximately 100,000 square feet of convention space, opened in April 2002 with substantial completion of construction occurring in June 2002. Gambling operations include slot machines, table games, off-track wagering, and (until recently) bingo.

Loss from discontinued operations for a recent fiscal year was $591,000. The loss was the result of the Tribe's decision to cease bingo operations to convert the floor space into the 637-unit Hall of the Lost Tribes smoke-free slot machine venue. The loss related to severance pay and disposal of bingo inventory.

**Required:**

1. Review *SFAS No. 144*, "Accounting for the Impairment or Disposal of Long-Lived Assets," using the FASB's Financial Accounting Research System (FARS), PricewaterhouseCooper's Comperio® authoritative financial reporting database, or other reference sources in your local library. Does the loss referenced here qualify as a loss from discontinued operations? Explain your answer citing relevant paragraphs from *SFAS No. 144*.

2. Would the loss qualify as a loss from discontinued operations if the Tribe had turned the bingo operation over to the Mohawks? The Mohawks do not currently have a casino on their tribal lands but are considering getting into the business. To gain experience with casino operations, the Mohawks have arranged with the Mohegan Tribe to take over the bingo operation at Mohegan Sun for an indefinite period. While the bingo profits will go to the Mohawks, the Mohegan Tribe will pay facilities rent and a training fee of 10% of gaming revenues. Again, explain your answer citing relevant paragraphs from *SFAS No. 144*.

| C2-2 |
| --- |

Conducting financial reporting research: Discontinued operations

Corrpro Companies, Inc., founded in 1984, provides corrosion control–related services, systems, equipment, and materials to the infrastructure, environmental, and energy markets. Corrpro's products and services include (a) corrosion control engineering services, systems, and equipment, (b) coatings services, and (c) pipeline integrity and risk assessment services. The following information was abridged from the company's March 31, 2003, Form 10-K.

**Assets and Liabilities Held for Sale**

In July 2002, the Company's Board of Directors approved a formal business restructuring plan. The multi-year plan includes a series of initiatives to improve operating income and reduce debt. The Company intends to sell non-core business units and use the proceeds to reduce debt. The Company has engaged outside professionals to assist in the disposition of the domestic and international non-core business units. Prior to the quarter ended September 30, 2002, the Company's non-core domestic and international units were reported as the Other Operations and International Operations reporting segments. Effective for the quarter ended September 30,

2002, the Other Operations and the International Operations reporting segments have been eliminated and the non-core domestic and international units are reported as Discontinued operations. Prior year financial statements have been reclassified to reflect these non-core units as Discontinued operations, which are also referred to as "assets and liabilities held for sale."

## Corrpro, Inc.

### Consolidated Statements of Operations For the years ended March 31,

| ($ in 000s) | 2003 | 2002 | 2001 |
|---|---|---|---|
| Revenues | $104,220 | $123,058 | $120,489 |
| Operating costs and expenses | | | |
| Cost of sales | 71,607 | 87,326 | 85,325 |
| Selling, general, and administrative | 29,788 | 32,327 | 35,535 |
| Operating income (loss) | 2,825 | 3,405 | (371) |
| Interest expense | 5,907 | 5,055 | 4,401 |
| Loss from continuing operations | | | |
| before income taxes | (3,082) | (1,650) | (4,772) |
| Provision (benefit) for income taxes | (331) | 10,669 | (934) |
| Loss from continuing operations | (2,751) | (12,319) | (3,838) |
| Discontinued operations | | | |
| Loss from operations, net of taxes | (9,931) | (5,898) | (4,443) |
| Gain on disposals, net of taxes | 2,095 | — | — |
| Loss before cumulative effect of change in | | | |
| accounting principle | (10,587) | (18,217) | (8,281) |
| Cumulative effect of change in | | | |
| accounting principle | (18,238) | — | — |
| Net loss | $(28,825) | $(18,217) | $ (8,281) |

**Required:**

Refer to *SFAS No. 144,* "Accounting for the Impairment or Disposal of Long-Lived Assets," when answering the following questions about Corrpro's discontinued operations.

1. What criteria must be met to warrant reclassifying the noncore business units as discontinued operations effective with the quarter ending September 30, 2002?

2. Suppose that in March 2003 a buyer signed a purchase commitment for Corrpro's Rohrback Cosasco Systems division. This sale requires regulatory approval that is expected to take at least 18 months to obtain. Should Corrpro's 2003 financial statements include this division in assets and liabilities held for sale? Explain.

3. Assume that in February 2003 a potential buyer of another of the domestic noncore business units insisted on a site assessment prior to signing a purchase commitment. The assessment's purpose was to determine whether the site was environmentally impaired. Unfortunately for Corrpro, trace amounts of a suspected carcinogen were discovered, causing the buyer to terminate the purchase. The buyer is willing to reconsider its decision if the site is remediated. While the site can be remediated using existing technology, doing so will be costly enough to negate the purpose of the sale, which is to raise funds to reduce debt. Management believes that employing new remediation methods currently being tested will make this sale economically feasible and thus places the sale of this business unit on hold. Should Corrpro's 2003 financial statements include this division in Assets and liabilities held for sale?

4. Is there any reason for management to prefer discontinued operations treatment for these noncore business units?

**C2-3**

Baldwin Piano and Organ I:
Identifying critical events for
revenue recognition

The following information is based on the annual report and 10-K statement of Baldwin Piano and Organ Company.

The company is the largest domestic manufacturer of keyboard musical instruments, and it manufactures or distributes all major product classes of pianos and electronic organs. The company believes that the breadth and quality of its line of keyboard musical instruments, its large and well-established dealer distribution networks, and its efficient and low-cost manufacturing capabilities have enabled it to maintain its strong market share in the keyboard musical instrument market.

Over the company's 131-year history, its principal products have been pianos and organs. The company significantly expanded its principal business lines through its 1988 acquisition of the keyboard operations of The Wurlitzer Company, which now operates as a wholly owned subsidiary of the company. Over the years, the company has also expanded and diversified its product line to utilize excess capacity and its woodworking, electronics, and technical expertise. The company manufactures printed circuit boards, electronic assemblies, grandfather and other quality clocks, and wooden cabinets.

The company ships keyboard instruments and clocks to its dealer network on a consignment basis. Accordingly, revenue is recognized when the dealer sells the instrument to a third party. The company charges a monthly display fee on all consigned inventory held by dealers longer than 90 days. On an annual basis, this display fee ranges from 12% to 16% of the selling price of such inventory to the dealer. Display fee income is included under the component Other operating income, net.

The company distributes its Baldwin keyboard musical instruments in the United States through approximately 500 independent dealers (600 outlets) and 11 company-owned stores operating in six major metropolitan areas. Most of the independent dealers carry Baldwin products as their principal line and often their exclusive one.

The company has been engaged in financing the retail purchase of its products for more than 80 years. In the current year, approximately 35% of the company's domestic sales were financed by the company in retail installment programs offered through its dealers. Installment contract receivables are recorded at the principal amount of the contracts. Interest on the contracts is recorded as income over the life of the contracts. The company has entered into agreements with an independent financial institution to sell substantially all of its installment receivable contracts. The company continues to service (collect cash and perform other administrative services) all installment receivables sold. Over the lives of the contracts, the difference between the original interest earned on the contracts and the interest paid to the independent financial institution is recognized as the component labeled "Income on the sale of installment receivables." The installment contracts are written generally at fixed rates ranging from 12% to 16% with terms extending over three to five years. The interest paid to the independent financial institution is around 5%. Under the agreement with the independent financial institution, the company is required to repurchase either installment receivables that become more than 120 days past due or accounts that are deemed uncollectible.

Wurlitzer and the electronic contract business transfer title and recognize revenue at the time of shipment to their dealers and customers, respectively.

The company distributes its Wurlitzer products through approximately 400 independent dealers. Its networks of Baldwin dealers and Wurlitzer dealers are separate and distinct with no significant overlap. Certain Wurlitzer dealers finance their inventory from an independent bank. Dealers can borrow money from the bank based on the value of the inventory purchased from Wurlitzer with the musical instruments pledged as collateral. The dealers are required to pay the bank monthly interest payments and pay the principal balance after inventory is sold or if it is held longer than 12 months. The bank may request Wurlitzer to repurchase notes due from delinquent dealers. The company believes that its financial statements contain adequate provisions for any loss that may be incurred as a result of this commitment.

The electronic contract business consists of manufacturing printed circuit boards and electro-mechanical assemblies for manufacturers outside the music industry. These products were a natural extension of the company's production and those research and development capabilities developed in connection with its electronic keyboard musical instrument business. The company currently produces printed circuit boards and other electronic assemblies for a diverse group of original equipment manufacturers, which sell to the medical electronics, telecommunications, computer peripheral, specialty consumer, data communications, and industrial control markets.

**Required:**

1. Baldwin uses different critical events to recognize revenue from the sale of inventory for its different business segments. Identify the critical events and rank them from the most to the least conservative policy based on your judgment of the circumstances. For each source of revenue, does the chosen revenue recognition method satisfy both the critical event and the measurability criteria? If you don't have enough information, discuss what additional information is needed to form a judgment on this issue.

2. In addition to income from the sale of inventory, Baldwin also earns income from financing the sale of some of its inventories. Identify the critical event Baldwin used to record the financing income. Discuss whether the revenue recognition method for the financing income satisfies the critical event and measurability criteria. Total financing income includes gain or loss on sale of installment receivables and interest income.

---

Neville Company decides at the beginning of 2008 to adopt the FIFO method of inventory valuation. It had used the LIFO method for financial and tax reporting since its inception on January 1, 2006, and had maintained records that are sufficient to retrospectively apply the FIFO method. Neville concluded that the FIFO method is the preferable inventory valuation method for its inventory (it was the lone member of its industry that used LIFO; its competitors all valued inventory using FIFO).

The effects of the change in accounting principle on inventory and cost of sales are presented in the following table:

**C 2-4**

Retrospectively applying a change in accounting principle

| Date | Inventory Determined By | | Cost of Sales Determined By | |
|------|-----------------|-----------------|-----------------|-----------------|
|      | LIFO Method | FIFO Method | LIFO Method | FIFO Method |
| 1/1/2006 | $ — | $ — | $  — | $  — |
| 12/31/2006 | 200 | 160 | 1,600 | 1,640 |
| 12/31/2007 | 400 | 480 | 2,000 | 1,880 |
| 12/31/2008 | 640 | 780 | 2,260 | 2,200 |

For each year presented, assume that sales are $6,000 and selling, general, and administrative expenses are $1,800. Neville Company's effective income tax rate for all years is 35% (there are no permanent or temporary differences under *SFAS No. 109*, "Accounting for Income Taxes," prior to the change). Neville's annual report provides two years of financial results. The company's income statements as originally reported under the LIFO method follow.

| Income Statements | 2007 | 2006 |
|---|---|---|
| Sales | $6,000 | $6,000 |
| Cost of goods sold | 2,000 | 1,600 |
| Selling, general, & administrative expenses | 1,800 | 1,800 |
| Income before income taxes | 2,200 | 2,600 |
| Income taxes | 770 | 910 |
| Net income | $1,430 | $1,690 |

**Required:**

1. Prepare Neville Company's 2008 and 2007 income statements reflecting the retrospective application of the accounting change from the LIFO method to the FIFO method.

2. Prepare Neville Company's disclosure related to the accounting change; limit disclosure of financial statement line items affected by the change in accounting principle to those appearing on the company's income statements for the years presented.

# COLLABORATIVE LEARNING CASE

**C2-5**

Baldwin Piano and Organ II: Analyzing and interpreting the income statement

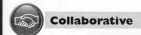 Collaborative

In addition to the information provided in Baldwin Piano I, consider the following information provided with information from the annual report and 10-K statement of Baldwin Piano and Organ company.

## Income Statements for the Years Ended December 31

| | Year 3 | Year 2 | Year 1 |
|---|---|---|---|
| Net sales | $120,657,455 | $110,076,904 | $103,230,431 |
| Cost of goods sold | (89,970,702) | (79,637,060) | (74,038,724) |
| **Gross profit** | 30,686,753 | 30,439,844 | 29,191,707 |
| Income on the sale of installment receivables | 5,746,125 | 5,256,583 | 4,023,525 |
| Interest income on installment receivables | 443,431 | 308,220 | 350,058 |
| Other operating income, net | 3,530,761 | 3,803,228 | 3,768,760 |
| | 40,407,070 | 39,807,875 | 37,334,050 |
| **Operating expenses** | | | |
| Selling, general, and administrative expense | (26,187,629) | (25,118,465) | (23,970,568) |
| Provision for doubtful accounts | (1,702,234) | (2,053,189) | (2,131,644) |
| **Operating profit** | 12,517,207 | 12,636,221 | 11,231,838 |
| Interest expense | (2,232,258) | (2,610,521) | (3,932,830) |
| Income before income taxes | 10,284,949 | 10,025,700 | 7,299,008 |
| Income taxes | (4,120,000) | (4,090,000) | (2,884,000) |
| Income before cumulative effects of change in accounting principles | 6,164,949 | 5,935,700 | 4,415,008 |
| Cumulative effect of changes in postretirement and postemployment benefits | (1,604,000) | — | — |
| **Net income** | $ 4,560,949 | $ 5,935,700 | $ 4,415,008 |

Interest income on installment receivables represents interest on receivables not sold to the independent financial institution.

The following summary table was prepared on the basis of the business segment data reported by Baldwin:

| Business | Segment Revenue as a Percentage of Total Revenue | | Segment Profit as a Percentage of Segment Revenue | |
|---|---|---|---|---|
| | Year 3 | Year 2 | Year 3 | Year 2 |
| Musical products | 72.70% | 81.50% | 5.00% | 7.60% |
| Electronic | 22.20 | 13.30 | 14.80 | 13.90 |
| Financing services | 5.20 | 5.10 | 52.80 | 49.20 |

The cash flow statement indicates that the company has repaid long-term debt of about $8.6 million, $5.6 million, and $8.3 million during Year 1, Year 2, and Year 3, respectively. The balance sheet indicates that the book value of the company's finished goods inventory decreased by about 8% from Year 2 to Year 3.

In March Year 3, the contents of one of the company's finished goods warehouses were damaged by exposure to smoke from a fire adjacent to the warehouse. The company has received insurance proceeds equal to the wholesale value of the destroyed inventory. Accordingly, a gain of approximately $1,412,000 on the insurance settlement is included in the Year 3 consolidated statements of earnings in the component labeled Other operating income, net.

On January 27, Year 3, the company entered into an agreement in principle whereby Peridot Associates, Inc. (Peridot) would acquire all outstanding shares of the company's common stock at a per share price of $18.25, subject to certain contingencies. The agreement expired on May 16, Year 3. Under the agreement, the company was obligated to reimburse Peridot $800,000 for certain expenses incurred by Peridot. Additionally, the company incurred other expenses of approximately $305,000 related to the proposed acquisition. These combined expenses are included in the Year 3 consolidated statements of earnings as the component labeled Other operating income, net.

**Required:**

Identify and explain the sources of the change in Baldwin's profitability from Year 2 to Year 3 with a view to evaluating its current earnings quality and future prospects. To what extent can this change be attributed to changes in the management's estimates?

(*Hint:* Preparing a common-size income statement and/or year-to-year percentage change analysis of income statement items will help you formulate your response.) Additional information regarding Baldwin Piano can be found in case C2–3.

**.mhhe.com/revsine4e**

**Remember to check the book's companion Web site
for additional study material.**

# Additional Topics in Income Determination | 3

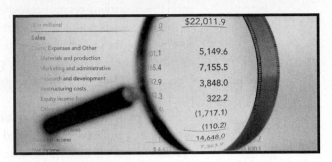

| ($ in millions) | | $22,011.9 |
|---|---|---|
| **Sales** | | |
| Costs, Expenses and Other | | |
| Materials and production | 01.1 | 5,149.6 |
| Marketing and administrative | 65.4 | 7,155.5 |
| Research and development | 32.9 | 3,848.0 |
| Restructuring costs | 2.3 | 322.2 |
| Equity income fr | 4) | (1,717.1) |
| Oth | | (110.2) |
| | | 14,648.0 |
| Net Income | 5.4 | 7,363 830.1 |

This chapter covers special topics in income determination. The first part of the chapter outlines the conditions and describes the accounting procedures for recognizing revenue and profit either before a sale occurs or after a sale occurs. We also discuss selected transactions or circumstances when the timing and amount of revenue recognition presents significant challenges. The second part of the chapter looks at earnings management and how firms can sometimes exploit the flexibility in GAAP to manage annual earnings up or down. We conclude with a discussion of accounting errors and irregularities and how these errors are corrected and reported once they are discovered.

Because revenue is usually recognized at the time of sale in most industries, some people erroneously conclude that the sale is itself the *sole* criterion in recognizing revenue. This is not correct! The correct rule for recognizing revenue is more complicated and subtle. As noted in Chapter 2, revenue is recognized at the earliest moment in time that Condition 1 (the "critical event") *and* Condition 2 ("measurability") are *both* satisfied. That is, at what point in the earnings process is the revenue "earned" and when do the benefits received become realized or realizable? ***The earliest moment at which Conditions 1 and 2 are both satisfied is usually the time of sale.*** That is why revenue is usually recognized when the sale is made.

In some cases Conditions 1 and 2 are satisfied *before* the sale, for example, as production takes place on a long-term construction contract. When this happens and when expenses are *also* measurable with a reasonable degree of assurance, GAAP allows income to be recognized before the sale.

In other circumstances, Conditions 1 and 2 may not both be satisfied until *after* the time of sale, for instance, not until the cash is received on installment sales when considerable uncertainty exists regarding ultimate collection. In these cases, GAAP disallows revenue recognition when the sale occurs; instead, revenue recognition is deferred until cash is received.

## REVENUE RECOGNITION PRIOR TO SALE
### Percentage-of-Completion Method

Long-term construction projects—such as roads and bridges, military hardware, and costly items such as oil tankers—frequently satisfy both revenue recognition conditions prior to the time of sale.

### LEARNING OBJECTIVES

**After studying this chapter, you will understand:**

1. The conditions under which it is appropriate to recognize revenues and profits either before or after the point of sale.

2. The procedures for recognizing revenue and adjusting associated asset values in three specific settings: long-term construction contracts, agricultural commodities, and installment sales.

3. Specialized application of revenue recognition principles for franchise sales, sales with right of return, and "bundled" software sales with multiple deliverables.

4. How the flexibility in GAAP for income determination invites managers to manipulate or manage earnings.

5. The various techniques used to manage earnings.

6. SEC guidance on revenue recognition designed to curb earnings management.

7. How error corrections and restatements of prior period financial statements are reported.

*Chapter*

**123**

These types of projects are usually begun only after a formal contract with a purchaser has been signed. Because a buyer for the completed project is assured, the critical event in the earning of revenue is the actual construction; that is, revenue recognition Condition 1 is satisfied as construction progresses. Furthermore, because the contract price is specified, the amount of the revenue that has been earned is measurable with a reasonable degree of assurance, thus satisfying revenue recognition Condition 2.

In many construction projects, it is also possible to estimate with reasonable accuracy the cost of the project and to measure its stage of completion. Furthermore, construction contracts usually require purchasers to make progress payments to the contractor as construction progresses. These interim payment requirements help ensure that the contractor will receive payment for the work performed.

When long-term construction contracts possess all of these attributes, revenue recognition Conditions 1 and 2 are both satisfied as construction progresses, and expenses can be matched against revenues to determine income. This is called the **percentage-of-completion method.** Here's how it works.

Solid Construction Corporation signs a contract with the City of Springfield on January 1, 2008 to build a highway bridge over Stony Creek. The contract price is $1,000,000; construction costs are estimated to be $800,000, and the project is scheduled to be completed by December 31, 2010. Periodic cash payments are to be made by the City of Springfield as construction progresses. Here is a summary of the Stony Creek project's progress each year:

| | **Actual Experience on the Project as of December 31** | | |
| --- | --- | --- | --- |
| | **2008** | **2009** | **2010** |
| Costs incurred to date | $240,000 | $544,000 | $ 850,000 |
| Estimated future costs | 560,000 | 306,000 | — |
| Billings to date | 280,000 | 650,000 | 1,000,000 |
| Cash collections to date | 210,000 | 600,000 | 1,000,000 |

Under the percentage-of-completion method, the profit to be recognized in any year is based on the ratio of incurred contract costs divided by estimated total contract costs. Using the data in the example, we compute the profit for 2008 using the following steps:

> In this example, we use costs incurred to date divided by the total estimated cost of the project to estimate the percentage of completion. Output measures are sometimes used as we discuss below.

### Step 1: **Compute the percentage-of-completion ratio by dividing costs incurred to date by estimated total costs.**

This is done to estimate the percentage of completion at any given point during the project. At the end of 2008, estimated total costs on the project are $800,000, comprising $240,000 of costs incurred in 2008 plus $560,000 of estimated future costs. The cost ratio is:

$$\frac{\$240,000}{\$800,000} = 0.30 \text{ or } 30\%$$

### Step 2: **Determine the estimated total profit on the contract by comparing the contract price with the estimated total costs.**

At the end of 2008, the estimated profit on the contract is still $200,000, that is, the difference between the contract price of $1,000,000 and estimated total costs of $800,000.

### Step 3: **Compute the estimated profit earned to date.**

The estimated profit earned to date is the cost ratio (or percentage of completion) computed in Step 1 multiplied by the estimated profit computed in Step 2, that is, 0.30 × $200,000 = $60,000.

Notice that 30% of the total estimated costs of $800,000 has been incurred by the end of 2008, so 30% of the total estimated profit of $200,000 can be recognized in that same year. That is, profit is recognized in proportion to costs incurred. Because no profit has been recognized prior to 2008, all of the $60,000 is recognizable in 2008.

Because cost estimates and completion stages change, these computations must be repeated in each subsequent year. Furthermore, the profit computation for each subsequent contract year must incorporate an additional step. The computation for 2009 illustrates this.

**Step 1: Compute the percentage-of-completion ratio, determined by dividing incurred costs to date by estimated total costs.**

At the end of 2009, estimated total costs on this contract have risen to $850,000: $544,000 of costs incurred through 2009 plus $306,000 of estimated future costs. The cost ratio (or percentage of completion) is:

$$\frac{\$544,000}{\$850,000} = 0.64 \text{ or } 64\%$$

**Step 2: Determine the estimated profit on the contract.**

The estimated profit on the contract has now dropped to $150,000—the difference between the contract price of $1,000,000 and the newly estimated total costs of $850,000 as of the end of 2009:

**Step 3: Compute the estimated profit earned to date.**

Because 64% of the total estimated costs has already been incurred (Step 1), 64% of the revised estimated profit of $150,000 (Step 2), or $96,000, has been earned through December 31, 2009.

Be sure to notice that a portion of the profit on this contract—$60,000—has already been recognized in 2008. Therefore, only the *incremental profit* earned in 2009 should be recognized. This requires an additional computation.

**Step 4: Compute the incremental profit earned in the current year.**

The estimated total profit earned through December 31, 2009 is $96,000 (Step 3). Because $60,000 of the estimated profit was recognized on this contract in 2008, only $36,000 ($96,000 − $60,000) of additional profit can be recognized in 2009.

These four steps can be expressed succinctly using the following profit computation formula:

$$\underbrace{\left[ \underbrace{\frac{\text{Costs incurred to date}}{\text{Estimated total costs}} \times \frac{\text{Estimated}}{\text{total profit}}}_{\text{Profit earned to date}} \right] - \underbrace{\frac{\text{Profit recognized}}{\text{in previous years}}}_{\substack{\text{Previously recognized} \\ \text{profit}}}}_{} = \frac{\text{Profit recognized}}{\text{in current year}}$$

(3.1)

The previously recognized profit is the sum of all profits (or losses) recognized on the contract in prior years, that is, the sum of all profits (or losses) that were determined by multiplying the cost-completion ratio by the total profit estimated at those earlier dates. Again, the reason for subtracting this amount from the profit-earned-to-date figure is to avoid double counting profits recognized in prior years.

Repeating the computations for 2008 and 2009 using the formula in equation (3.1) gives the following results:

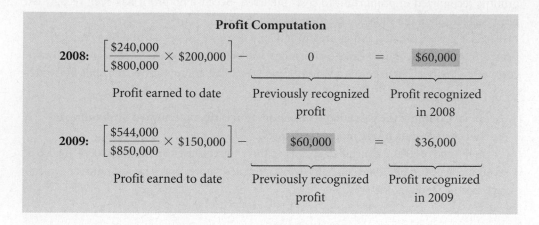

**Profit Computation**

**2008:** $\left[\dfrac{\$240,000}{\$800,000} \times \$200,000\right]$ − 0 = $60,000

Profit earned to date    Previously recognized profit    Profit recognized in 2008

**2009:** $\left[\dfrac{\$544,000}{\$850,000} \times \$150,000\right]$ − $60,000 = $36,000

Profit earned to date    Previously recognized profit    Profit recognized in 2009

Of course, these results are identical to those derived using the multiple-step approach illustrated previously. The computation for 2010 would be:

**2010:** $\left[\dfrac{\$850,000}{\$850,000} \times \$150,000\right]$ − $96,000 = $54,000

Profit earned to date    Previously recognized profit    Profit recognized in 2010

Using the percentage-of-completion method, the cumulative profit recognized over the three years totals $150,000 ($60,000 + $36,000 + $54,000). This total equals the difference between the contract price of $1,000,000 and the actual costs of $850,000.

The journal entries shown in Exhibit 3.1 would be used to record these events on the books of Solid Construction Corporation.

Entries (2) and (3) of Exhibit 3.1 require elaboration. Income is recognized in entry (2) using the income recognition formula of equation (3.1). An alternative to entry (2), which provides more detailed information, is to separately record the construction expense as shown in Exhibit 3.1. The amount debited to the account Construction expense each period is for the actual construction costs incurred in that period. The credit to Construction revenue is determined by multiplying the total contract price by the completion percentage and then subtracting any revenue recognized in prior periods. For example, the revenue recognized in 2009 is determined by multiplying the contract price of $1,000,000 times the completion percentage as of the end of 2009 (64%), giving total revenue earned to date of $640,000. Subtracting the $300,000 of revenue recognized in 2008 yields Construction revenue of $340,000 recognized in 2009.

Consistent with linking asset valuation and income determination together, as discussed in Chapter 2, the carrying value of net assets is also increased as income is recognized. This is why the entry (2) debit increases the Construction in progress account, which is a part of inventory. Thus, entry (2) reflects the dual financial statement impact of income recognition: *both net assets and income increase.*

In entry (3), the account Billings on construction in progress is a contra account (reduction) to the inventory subcomponent Construction in progress. The net of these two accounts is shown as a current asset (if there is a debit balance) or as a current liability (if there is a

| EXHIBIT 3.1 | Solid Construction Corporation |
|---|---|

**Journal Entries**
**Percentage-of-Completion Method**

| | 2008 | 2009 | 2010 |
|---|---|---|---|
| (1) To record costs incurred | | | |
|    **DR**  Inventory: Construction in progress.......................... | $240,000 | $304,000 | $ 306,000 |
|      **CR**  Accounts payable, cash, etc. ...................... | | $240,000 | $304,000 | $ 306,000 |
| (2) To record income recognized | | | |
|    **DR**  Inventory: Construction in progress.......................... | $ 60,000 | $ 36,000 | $ 54,000 |
|      **CR**  Income on long-term construction contract .......... | | $ 60,000 | $ 36,000 | $ 54,000 |
|   Alternative entry | | | |
|    **DR**  Inventory: Construction in progress.......................... | $ 60,000[a] | $ 36,000[a] | $ 54,000[a] |
|    **DR**  Construction expense ............... | 240,000[b] | 304,000[b] | 306,000[b] |
|      **CR**  Construction revenue .......... | $300,000[c] | $340,000[c] | $ 360,000[c] |
| (3) To record customer billings | | | |
|    **DR**  Accounts receivable ................. | $280,000 | $370,000 | $ 350,000 |
|      **CR**  Billings on construction in progress ................... | $280,000 | $370,000 | $ 350,000 |
| (4) To record cash received | | | |
|    **DR**  Cash .............................. | $210,000 | $390,000 | $ 400,000 |
|      **CR**  Accounts receivable ........... | $210,000 | $390,000 | $ 400,000 |
| (5) To record completion and acceptance of the project | | | |
|    **DR**  Billings on construction in progress ........................ | | | $1,000,000 |
|      **CR**  Inventory: Construction in progress ................... | | | $1,000,000 |

| | | 2008 | 2009 | 2010 |
|---|---|---|---|---|
| [a] | Gross profit earned in current period | 30% × ($1,000,000 − $800,000) | 64% × ($1,000,000 − $850,000) − $60,000 | ($1,000,000 − $850,000) − $96,000 |
| [b] | Actual construction costs incurred in current period | $240,000 | $544,000 − $240,000 | $850,000 − $544,000 |
| [c] | Revenues earned in current period | 30% × $1,000,000 | (64% × $1,000,000) − $300,000 | $1,000,000 − $300,000 − $340,000 |

credit balance). In our example, the balance sheet presentation for Solid Construction Corporation would be as follows for 2008 and 2009:

| **2008** | | |
|---|---|---|
| **Current Assets** | | |
| Accounts receivable | | $70,000 |
| Inventory: Construction in progress | $300,000 | |
| Less: Billings on construction in progress | (280,000) | |
| Inventory in excess of contract billings | | 20,000 |

| 2009 | | |
|---|---|---|
| **Current Assets** | | |
| Accounts receivable | | $50,000 |
| **Current Liabilities** | | |
| Inventory: Construction in progress | $(640,000) | |
| Less: Billings on construction in progress | 650,000 | |
| Contract billings in excess of inventory | | $10,000 |

The component Billings on construction in progress must be treated as a contra-inventory account (that is, shown as a deduction from inventory) to avoid balance sheet double counting. Here's why. Typically, a sale results in an asset (Accounts receivable) being increased for the selling price of the goods with a simultaneous decrease in another asset, Inventory, for the cost of goods sold. However, inventory is not reduced at the time the receivable is recorded under long-term construction accounting. Rather, the Inventory: Construction in progress account remains on the company's books until the project is complete and the sale is finalized. Treating the Billings on construction in progress account as an offset (contra) to Inventory: Construction in progress account avoids including certain costs and profits twice on the balance sheet—once in Inventory: Construction in progress and a second time in the Accounts Receivable account.

Finally, although profits are recognized proportionately to percentage of completion as construction progresses, *estimated losses on a contract are recognized in their entirety as soon as it becomes known that a contract loss will ensue.*

In our example, cumulative income to date is determined by using the ratio of incurred costs to date divided by estimated total costs. This cost ratio is widely used because it provides a simple index of progress toward completion, that is, work done to date. However, there are situations in which this cost ratio may not accurately reflect construction progress. For example, consider a case in which raw materials to be used in construction are stockpiled in advance of use. In such situations, costs are being incurred as the raw materials are received and recorded on the books, yet these costs do not increase the stage of completion until the raw materials are actually *used*. In projects in which this stockpiling is significant, some other means for measuring progress toward completion would be preferable. Possibilities include labor hours worked or various output measures (such as miles of roadway completed).

## Completed-Contract Method

In some cases, it is not possible to determine expected costs with a high degree of reliability under long-term construction contracts (for example, building underground street tunnels in Boston), making the use of the percentage-of-completion method inappropriate. In these situations, the **completed-contract method** is used instead.

The completed-contract method postpones recognition of income until the project is completed. Journal entries under the completed-contract method are identical to the journal entries illustrated previously for the percentage-of-completion method except that entry (2) in Exhibit 3.1, which records income as construction progresses, is omitted. Instead, all of the income on the contract is recognized when the contract is completed. The entry for recognizing income under the completed-contract method in 2010 follows:

| | | |
|---|---|---|
| **DR** Billings on construction in progress | $1,000,000 | |
| **CR** Inventory: Construction in progress | | $850,000 |
| **CR** Income on long-term construction contract | | 150,000 |

| EXHIBIT 3.2 | Yearly Income Comparison of Two Long-Term Contract Accounting Methods | |
|---|---|---|

| Year | Completed-Contract Method | Percentage-of-Completion Method |
|---|---|---|
| 2008 | –0– | $ 60,000 |
| 2009 | –0– | 36,000 |
| 2010 | $150,000 | 54,000 |
| Total income | $150,000 | $150,000 |

Although income is recognized only on completion, losses are recognized in their entirety as soon as their probable existence is known.

Exhibit 3.2 illustrates that total income for the three years is the same under both the completed-contract method and the percentage-of-completion method ($150,000). However, the timing of income recognition differs considerably.

The net asset balance at intermediate construction stages will also differ with the two methods. As shown in column (g) of Exhibit 3.3, *the amount of this net asset balance difference in any year is precisely equal to the difference in cumulative profit recognized on each basis.* This difference in net asset balances exists because the recognition of income has a corresponding effect on net asset balances.

## Revenue Recognition on Commodities

The timing of revenue recognition for producers of agricultural and mining commodities raises some interesting issues. There is general agreement that in both mining and farming, the critical event in adding value usually comes *before* the actual sale. The critical event in mining is extracting the resource from the ground. In agriculture, the critical event is harvest.

| EXHIBIT 3.3 | Comparative Account Balances | |
|---|---|---|

**Percentage-of-Completion versus Completed-Contract Method**

**December 31, Year-End Account Balances**

| | Completed-Contract Method | | | Percentage-of-Completion Method | | | |
|---|---|---|---|---|---|---|---|
| | (a) Construction in Progress | (b) Billings | (c) Net Asset (Liability) Balance Col. (a) − Col. (b) | (d) Construction in Progress | (e) Billings | (f) Net Asset (Liability) Balance Col. (d) − Col. (e) | (g) Difference in Net Asset Balances Between Methods Col. (f) − Col. (c) |
| 2008 | $240,000 | $280,000 | $ (40,000) | $300,000 | $280,000 | $ 20,000 | $60,000* |
| 2009 | 544,000 | 650,000 | (106,000) | 640,000 | 650,000 | (10,000) | 96,000† |
| 2010 | –0– | –0– | –0– | –0– | –0– | –0– | –0– |

* Also equals difference between cumulative profit on percentage-of-completion method ($60,000) and the completed-contract method ($0) from Exhibit 3.2.
† Also equals difference between cumulative profit on percentage-of-completion method ($60,000 + $36,000 = $96,000) and the completed-contract method ($0 + $0) from Exhibit 3.2.

(The critical event is harvest because prior to harvest, the crop may still be lost because of drought, hail, insects, or disease. Only after the crop is safely out of the field have these income-threatening possibilities been avoided.) Thus, revenue recognition Condition 1 is satisfied prior to the sale itself.

However, the precise time at which revenue recognition Condition 2 ("measurability") is satisfied for commodities producers is open to some dispute. The following example explores the issues.

> A farmer harvests 110,000 bushels of corn on September 30, 2008. On this date, the posted market price per bushel was $3.50. The total cost of growing the crop was $220,000, or $2.00 per bushel. The farmer decides to sell 100,000 bushels for cash on September 30 at the posted price of $3.50 and stores the remaining 10,000 bushels. On January 2, 2009, the market price drops to $3.00. Fearing further price declines, the farmer immediately sells the bushels in storage at a price of $3.00 per bushel.

**Completed-Transaction (Sales) Method**   The timing of revenue recognition on the 100,000 bushels of corn that were sold on September 30 is straightforward. Revenue recognition Conditions 1 and 2 are both satisfied at September 30, and income would be recognized at the time of sale. The income statement would show:

### 2008 Income Statement
*Completed-transaction (sales) method*

| | |
|---|---:|
| Revenues (sale of 100,000 bushels at a market price of $3.50 per bushel) | $350,000 |
| Expenses (costs of $2.00 per bushel for 100,000 bushels sold) | (200,000) |
| Income from sale | $150,000 |

> As costs are incurred during the year, the direct costs of crop production—things such as seed, fertilizer, fuel, and depreciation on machinery—are charged to a Production in process or Crop inventory account with offsetting credits to Cash, Accounts payable, or Accumulated depreciation.

Under the traditional view, which we call the **completed-transaction (sales) method,** no income would be recognized at September 30 on the 10,000 bushels that were harvested but not sold. For these 10,000 bushels, revenue recognition Condition 2 is considered not to have been met because the eventual selling price is unknown: That is, the sale transaction is not yet completed. The bushels in storage would be reflected on the farmer's balance sheet at their *cost* of $20,000 ($2.00 per bushel × 10,000 bushels).

When the bushels in storage are sold in 2009, the income statement would show the profit on the sale of the 10,000 bushels:

### 2009 Income Statement
*Completed-transaction (sales) method*

| | |
|---|---:|
| Revenues (sale of 10,000 bushels at a market price of $3.00 per bushel) | $30,000 |
| Expenses (costs of $2.00 per bushel for 10,000 bushels sold) | (20,000) |
| Income from sale | $10,000 |

Note that the traditional approach avoids recognizing any income on the 10,000 unsold bushels until the sales transaction is completed in 2009.

## Market Price (Production) Method

There is another way for measuring income in the previous example. This alternative recognizes that well-organized markets exist for most agricultural and many mining commodities. In addition, the quantities offered for sale by any individual producer are usually very small in relation to the total size of the market. Producers face an established price for as many units as they choose to sell. These factors mean that a readily determinable market price at which output *could be sold* is continuously available. In this view, revenue recognition Condition 2 ("measurability") is satisfied prior to the actual sale of actively traded commodities.

Because revenue recognition Condition 1 ("critical event") occurs at harvest, both conditions necessary to recognize revenue are satisfied as soon as the crop is safely out of the field (that is, at the point of production or harvest). Thus, farming income on all 110,000 bushels is recognized under this approach on September 30 (when grain is harvested):

> The International Accounting Standards Board (IASB) requires agricultural produce harvested by an enterprise to be measured at its fair value at time of harvest less estimated cost to transport the grain to the local elevator. The difference is referred to as **net realizable value.** Any gain or loss arising from initial recognition of harvested assets and from the change in fair value less estimated transportation costs of harvested assets are to be included in net profit or loss for the period in which it arises. See "Agriculture," *IAS 41* (London: International Accounting Standards Board [IASB], 2002).

### 2008 Income Statement
*Market price (production) method*

**International**

| | |
|---|---:|
| Revenues (100,000 bushels sold at a market price of $3.50) | $350,000 |
| Expenses (costs of $2.00 per bushel for 100,000 bushels sold) | (200,000) |
| Market gain on unsold inventory (10,000 bushels times the difference between the $3.50 market price at the date of harvest and the $2.00 cost per bushel) | 15,000 |
| Total income from farming activities | $165,000 |

This **market price (production) method** recognizes farming income on the 10,000 unsold bushels as well as on the 100,000 bushels sold. This view emphasizes the fact that the farmer *could have sold* these 10,000 bushels at the time of harvest for a readily determinable price of $3.50 per bushel. Because the critical event in farming is harvest and the potential sales price at the time of harvest is known, both revenue recognition conditions relating to farming are deemed to be satisfied on September 30. Therefore, farming income of $165,000 is immediately determinable.

> The market price used in this calculation is the **net realizable value**—that is, the market price at point of delivery less any delivery costs. Thus, if it costs the farmer $0.10 per bushel to transport the grain from the farm to the local elevator, the net realizable value would be $3.40 ($3.50 − $0.10). This would be the price used to compute the gain on the unsold inventory.

Under the market price method, the farmer's balance sheet reflects the bushels in storage at $35,000 ($3.50 market price at harvest times 10,000 bushels). If the corn was initially carried at its *cost* of $20,000 ($2.00 per bushel times 10,000 bushels), the entry necessary to reflect the value added by farming is:

| **DR** Crop inventory | $15,000 | |
|---|---|---|
| **CR** Market gain on unsold inventory | | $15,000 |

The credit would appear as shown on the income statement for 2008.

After the corn is harvested, the activity called *farming* has ended. However, the farmer is actually engaged in another business in addition to farming. By withholding 10,000 bushels from the market, the farmer is also pursuing a separate (nonfarming) activity called **speculation.** This speculation is undertaken in the hope that prices will rise above their September 30 level of $3.50 per bushel. Subsequent changes in the market price of corn will thus give rise to speculative gains or losses—also called **inventory holding gains and losses.**

To illustrate, recollect that at the start of 2009, the market price of corn drops from $3.50 to $3.00 per bushel. This decline in price gives rise to a speculative (holding) loss in 2009 of

$5,000 (a decline of $0.50 per bushel times 10,000 bushels). The inventory is **marked-to-market,** and the journal entry to reflect the loss is:

| DR | Inventory (holding) loss on speculation | $5,000 | |
|----|----------------------------------------|--------|--------|
| | CR Crop inventory | | $5,000 |

After this entry is posted, the inventory's carrying value is now reduced to $30,000 (10,000 bushels times $3.00 per bushel).

Fearing further price declines, the farmer immediately sells the remaining 10,000 bushels at $3 on January 2. The entry is:

| DR | Cost of goods sold | $30,000 | |
|----|-------------------|---------|---------|
| | CR Crop inventory | | $30,000 |
| DR | Cash | $30,000 | |
| | CR Crop revenue | | $30,000 |

## Comparison: Completed-Transaction (Sales) and Market Price (Production) Methods

Although total income over the two periods is the same under each approach, the income recognized in each period is *not* the same, and the activities to which the income is attributed also differ:

| Completed-Transaction (Sales) Method | | | Market Price (Production) Method | |
|--------------------------------------|-----------|------|----------------------------------|----------|
| Income from sales | $150,000 | 2008 | Income from farming activities | $165,000 |
| Income from sales | 10,000 | 2009 | Holding loss on speculation | (5,000) |
| Total income | $160,000 | | Total income | $160,000 |

The completed-transaction (sales) method avoids recognizing any income on the 10,000 unsold bushels until the transaction is completed (when the grain is sold). However, in emphasizing completed transactions, this traditional approach—the completed-transaction method—merges the results of the farmer's speculative and farming activities and does not reflect the separate results of either.

This example illustrates why income recognition can be controversial: Should the farmer recognize market-price changes on agricultural commodities prior to sale? In practice, the completed-transaction method is far more prevalent. However, the market price method is deemed to be in conformity with generally accepted accounting principles when readily determinable market values are continuously available. The market price method has the dual advantages of:

1. Explicitly recognizing the separate results arising from the farming and speculative activities that the farmer is engaged in.
2. Conforming more closely to the income recognition conditions introduced in Chapter 2.

## RECAP

For long-term construction contracts and commodities (natural resources and agricultural products), the two conditions for revenue recognition—"critical event" and "measurability"—are frequently satisfied prior to sale. The percentage-of-completion method recognizes revenue and profits (losses) on long-term construction contracts as work progresses. The market price (production) method recognizes the difference between the cost of the natural resource or agricultural commodity and its prevailing market price as income at the time of production or harvest. In both cases, an inventory account—Construction in progress (for long-term construction contracts) and Crop inventory (for commodities)—is debited to reflect the increase in value recognized on the income statement, thereby maintaining the linkage between income determination and asset valuation.

# REVENUE RECOGNITION SUBSEQUENT TO SALE
## Installment Sales Method

Sometimes revenue is not recognized at the point of sale even though a valid sale has taken place. This accounting treatment is acceptable only under highly unusual circumstances. One instance in which revenue recognition might be delayed beyond the point of sale is when sales are made under very extended cash collection terms. Examples include installment sales of consumer durables and retail land sales of vacation or retirement property. A lengthy collection period considerably increases the risk of nonpayment. ***When the risk of noncollection is unusually high and when there is no reasonable basis for estimating the proportion of installment accounts likely to prove uncollectible, then revenue recognition may be deferred.***

When these extreme risk situations exist, neither of the two revenue recognition conditions is satisfied. Specifically, when it's highly uncertain whether customers will make the cash payments called for in the contract, then the sale itself is not the critical event in creating value. In such circumstances, the actual cash collection is the critical event, and revenue recognition Condition 1 is satisfied only as the amounts due from customers are received. Similarly, revenue recognition Condition 2 is not satisfied because the amount ultimately collectible from customers is not measurable with a reasonable degree of assurance at the time of sale.

Because Conditions 1 and 2 are both satisfied only over time as cash collections take place, a revenue recognition method tied to cash collections has been devised to deal with such situations. This revenue recognition approach is called the **installment sales method.**

**Installment Sales Method Illustrated**    The installment sales method recognizes revenue and income proportionately as cash is collected. The amount recognized in any period is based on two factors:

1.  The installment sales gross-profit percentage (gross profit/sales).
2.  The amount of cash collected on installment accounts receivable.

Here's an example of revenue and income recognition under the installment sales method:

|  | 2008 | 2009 |
|---|---|---|
| Installment sales | $1,200,000 | $1,300,000 |
| Cost of installment goods sold | 840,000 | 884,000 |
| Gross profit | $ 360,000 | $ 416,000 |
| Gross-profit percentage | 30% | 32% |
| Cash collections | | |
| On 2008 installment sales | $ 300,000 | $ 600,000 |
| On 2009 installment sales | | 340,000 |

During 2008, installment sales of $1,200,000 were made. The potential gross profit on these sales was $360,000. The installment contracts call for cash payments over each of the next four years. Because of the extreme uncertainties regarding ultimate collectibility, this gross profit will be recognized only as customers pay on their accounts. Because $300,000 of cash was collected in 2008, the gross profit recognized in 2008 will be $90,000—that is, $300,000 multiplied by 30%, the gross-profit percentage (gross profit/sales) on 2008 installment sales. This $90,000 is shown on the 2008 income statement as 2008 income from installment sales. The difference between the total potential gross profit of $360,000 and the $90,000 of recognized income, or $270,000, is deferred gross profit (see entries [4] and [5] in Exhibit 3.4).

---

| EXHIBIT 3.4 | Installment Sales Method |
|---|---|

**Journal Entries**

| | 2008 | | 2009 | |
|---|---|---|---|---|
| (1) To record installment sales | | | | |
| **DR** Accounts receivable—2008 installment sales .......... | $1,200,000 | | | |
| **DR** Accounts receivable—2009 installment sales .......... | | | $1,300,000 | |
| **CR** Installment sales revenue ..................... | | $1,200,000 | | $1,300,000 |
| (2) To record cost of goods sold | | | | |
| **DR** Cost of installment goods sold ..................... | $ 840,000 | | $ 884,000 | |
| **CR** Inventory................................... | | $ 840,000 | | $ 884,000 |
| (3) To record cash collections | | | | |
| **DR** Cash .......................................... | $ 300,000 | | $ 940,000 | |
| **CR** Accounts receivable—2008 installment sales..... | | $ 300,000 | | $ 600,000 |
| **CR** Accounts receivable—2009 installment sales..... | | | | 340,000 |
| (4) To defer gross profit on portion of current-period sales that are not yet collected | | | | |
| **DR** Deferred gross profit (income statement)............. | $ 270,000 | | $ 307,200 | |
| **CR** Deferred gross profit—Adjustment to accounts receivable ......................... | | $ 270,000 | | $ 307,200 |
| (5) To recognize realized gross profit on installment sales of prior periods | | | | |
| **DR** Deferred gross profit—Adjustment to accounts receivable....................................... | | | $ 180,000 | |
| **CR** Recognized gross profit on installment sales—prior year............................ | | | | $ 180,000 |

Income recognized in 2009 from installment sales comprises two components:

1. A component relating to 2009 cash collections on 2008 installment sales.
2. A component relating to 2009 cash collections on 2009 installment sales.

The computation for installment sales income recognized in 2009 is:

**Total 2009 Installment Sales Income**

| | Gross Profit Recognized |
|---|---|
| Component relating to 2008 sales: | |
| Cash collections in 2009 from 2008 sales | $600,000 |
| Multiplied by 2008 gross-profit percentage | 30% |
| | $180,000 |
| Component relating to 2009 sales: | |
| Cash collections in 2009 from 2009 sales | $340,000 |
| Multiplied by 2009 gross-profit percentage | 32% |
| | $108,800 |
| Total installment sales income recognized in 2009 | $288,800 |

See Exhibit 3.4 for journal entries to record these facts for years 2008 and 2009.

The income statement would appear as follows:

|  | 2008 | 2009 |
| --- | --- | --- |
| Installment sales | $1,200,000 | $1,300,000 |
| Cost of installment goods sold | (840,000) | (884,000) |
| Gross profit | 360,000 | 416,000 |
| *Less:* Deferred gross profit on installment sales of current year | (270,000) | (307,200) |
| Gross profit recognized on current year's sales | 90,000 | 108,800 |
| *Plus:* Gross profit recognized on installment sales of prior years | — | 180,000 |
| Total gross profit recognized this year | $ 90,000 | $ 288,800 |

Some additional internal recordkeeping is necessary when applying the installment sales method. Installment sales and the related cost of goods sold must be tracked by individual year in order to compute the gross-profit percentage that applies to each year. In addition, the accounting system must match cash collections with the specific sales year to which the cash collections relate. This matching is needed to apply the correct gross-profit percentage to cash receipts.

On the balance sheet, the Accounts receivable—installment sales components are classified as current assets if they are due within 12 months of the balance sheet date. Amounts not expected to be collected within the next year may also be classified as current assets if installment sales are a normal part of the company's operations because the company's operating cycle would include the installment collection period. Existing practice typically classifies the deferred gross-profit account as a contra-asset, which is shown as a reduction to accounts receivable.

Selling, general, and administrative expenses relating to installment sales are treated as period costs—that is, as costs that are expensed in the period in which they are incurred—because they provide no future benefits. This treatment is consistent with the manner in which period costs are handled for normal (noninstallment) sales.

**Interest on Installment Contracts**   The essence of an installment sales contract is that the cash payments arising from the sale are spread over multiple periods. Because of this delay in receiving the sales proceeds, sellers charge interest on installment sales contracts. Consequently, the required monthly or quarterly installment payments include both interest and principal. This complication was omitted from the example we just illustrated. GAAP requires that the interest component of the periodic cash proceeds must be recorded separately as interest revenue. This means that interest payments are not considered when computing the recognized gross profit on installment sales. Chapter 8 outlines the procedures for differentiating between principal and interest payments on customer receivables.

## Cost Recovery Method

When collections on installment sales occur over an extended period and there is no reasonable basis for estimating collectibility, GAAP allows companies to use the **cost recovery method** for recognizing profits on such sales.[1] This method is commonly used when a high degree of uncertainty exists regarding the collection of receivables (for example, for retail land development sales). Under this method, no profit is recognized until cash payments received from the buyer exceed the seller's cost of goods sold. After the cost of the merchandise has

---

[1] "Omnibus Opinion—1966," *Accounting Principles Board Opinion No. 10* (New York: AICPA, 1969).

been recovered, any cash collected in excess of this amount is recorded as recognized gross profit on the seller's income statement.

The following example illustrates the accounting treatment under the cost recovery method.

---

In 2008, Florida Swamp Land Development Company sells 100 1-acre lots for $12,000 each. One-third of the sales price, $4,000 per lot, or $400,000 total, is collected when the contract is signed and the remainder is to be collected in two equal installments in the following two years. The cost of acquiring and developing the land was $600,000. Because most of the sales are made to individuals who reside outside the State of Florida, there tends to be a high rate of default on collections, which is difficult to estimate.

---

If the cost recovery method is applied to these sales and the cash is collected on schedule, the accounting entries would be as follows:

2008

| | | | | |
|---|---|---|---|---|
| **DR** | Installment receivables | | $1,200,000 | |
| | **CR** | Land inventory | | $600,000 |
| | **CR** | Deferred gross profit | | 600,000 |

To record sale of 100 lots at $12,000 each.

| | | | | |
|---|---|---|---|---|
| **DR** | Cash | | $ 400,000 | |
| | **CR** | Installment receivables | | $400,000 |

To record collections on account.

2009

| | | | | |
|---|---|---|---|---|
| **DR** | Cash | | $ 400,000 | |
| | **CR** | Installment receivables | | $400,000 |

To record collections on account.

| | | | | |
|---|---|---|---|---|
| **DR** | Deferred gross profit | | $ 200,000 | |
| | **CR** | Realized gross profit | | $200,000 |

To record realized gross profit equal to cumulative cash collections in excess of cost of land sold = $800,000 − $600,000 = $200,000.

2010

| | | | | |
|---|---|---|---|---|
| **DR** | Cash | | $ 400,000 | |
| | **CR** | Installment receivables | | $400,000 |

To record collections on account.

| | | | | |
|---|---|---|---|---|
| **DR** | Deferred gross profit | | $ 400,000 | |
| | **CR** | Realized gross profit | | $400,000[a] |

[a] To record realized gross profit determined as follows:

| | |
|---|---|
| Cumulative cash collections | $1,200,000 |
| Cost of land sold | (600,000) |
| Gross profit recognized in prior periods | (200,000) |
| Amount recognized in 2010 | $ 400,000 |

Note that the cost recovery method is more conservative than the regular installment sales method because the regular installment method recognizes gross profit on each dollar collected while the cost recovery method recognizes profit only when the cumulative cash collections exceed the total cost of land sold.

**The installment sales method of revenue recognition is used when the risk of noncollection is high or when it is impractical to estimate the amount of uncollectibles. Under the installment sales method, the gross profit on sales is deferred and recognized as income in subsequent periods, that is, when the installment receivables are collected in cash. The linkage between income determination and asset valuation is maintained by showing deferred gross profit as a contra account (reduction) to Installment accounts receivable.**

## Revenue Recognition for Specialized Sales Transactions

In this section, we briefly review accounting requirements for industries or transactions that have specialized applications of revenue recognition principles. Specifically, we consider the unique revenue recognition issues for the following areas:

- Franchise sales.
- Sales with right of return.
- Bundled sales (software sales).

## Franchise Sales

**Franchising** is a popular way to expand sales of products and services in a variety of industries. In 2006, franchise operations accounted for more than $1 trillion of sales in the United States. Exhibit 3.5 identifies the 10 fastest growing franchise operations for 2008 and the industries in which they operate.

In franchise arrangements, the franchisor (seller) gives the franchisee (buyer) the exclusive right to sell a product or service in a given locale or area and use the franchisor's name for a specified period of time. Typically, franchise agreements call for both of the following two types of payments:

1. An initial franchise fee, all or part of which is paid to the franchisor when the franchise agreement is signed, with the remainder due in installments (with interest) over a specified period; and

2. Continuing or periodic fees generally based on a percentage of sales generated by the franchisee.

| EXHIBIT 3.5 | Ten Fastest Growing Franchise Operations for 2008 |
|---|---|
| **Franchise** | **Industry** |
| Jan Pro Franchising International Inc. | Commercial cleaning (service) |
| 7-Eleven Inc. | Convenience store |
| Subway | Restaurants/Fast food |
| Jani-King | Commercial cleaning (service) |
| Dunkin Donuts | Restaurants/Doughnut shop |
| Jackson Hewitt Tax Service | Tax preparation (service) |
| Bonus Building Care | Commercial cleaning (service) |
| Instant Tax Service | Tax preparation & electronic filing (service) |
| Liberty Tax Service | Tax preparation & electronic filing (service) |
| ReMax International Inc. | Real estate agents |

*Source:* www.entrepreneur.com/franchise500

Accounting for continuing periodic fees received by the franchisor poses little difficulty. These fees are recorded as revenue in the period they are earned and received. Accounting for the initial franchise fee, however, raises some challenging revenue recognition issues as you will see.

The initial franchise fee typically comprises two elements:

1. Payment for the right to operate a franchise in a given area.
2. Payment for services to be performed by the franchisor.

Examples of initial services include:

- Finding and securing a site for the franchise.
- Overseeing construction of the facilities.
- Training employees.
- Setting up and maintaining a recordkeeping system.
- Sales promotion and advertising.

Occasionally, initial franchise fees may also include payment for tangible property such as signs, equipment, inventory, land, and buildings. Fees received for tangible assets are recognized when title to the property passes to the franchisee.

The key issue in franchise fee accounting centers on when and how much of the initial franchise fee should be recognized up front as revenue by the franchisor. *Statement of Financial Standards (SFAS) No. 45* specifies that revenue from initial franchise fees should be recognized when all material services or conditions relating to the sale have been substantially performed or satisfied by the franchisor.[2] Essentially, the question is—when are the initial franchise fees earned by the franchisor? The answer is not always easily discernable, opening the way for possible abuses from recognizing revenue before it is earned.

The following example illustrates the key measurement and recognition issues related to franchise fee revenue.

---

On January 1, 2008 Diet Right sells a dieting/weight loss franchise for an initial fee of $25,000 with $10,000 due at the signing of the franchise agreement and the remainder due in three annual installments (due December 31) of $5,000 each plus interest at 8% on the unpaid balance. The $10,000 up-front payment gives the franchisee the right to use Diet Right's name and sell prepackaged healthy meals prepared at Diet Right's corporate headquarters. In return for the initial franchise fee, Diet Right agrees to train employees, set up a recordkeeping system, maintain a Web site with online dietary counseling by a registered dietician, and provide advertising and various promotional materials. In addition to the initial franchise fee, Diet Right will receive 2% of the franchise's annual sales for allowing the franchisee to purchase prepackaged meals at below market prices.

---

**Recording Initial Franchise Fees**    Assuming that the deferred payments under the franchise agreement are for services not yet performed (for example, training employees, maintaining Web site, and advertising), Diet Right would record the following entry for the initial franchise fee when the franchise agreement is signed.

---

[2] "Accounting for Franchise Fee Revenue," *Statement of Financial Accounting Standards (SFAS) No. 45* (Stamford, CT: FASB, 1981).

**January 1, 2008:**

| | | | |
|---|---|---|---|
| **DR** | Cash.............................................. | $10,000 | |
| **DR** | Note receivable...................................... | 15,000[a] | |
| | **CR** Earned franchise fee revenue....................... | | $10,000[b] |
| | **CR** Unearned franchise fees............................ | | 15,000 |

[a] Initial fee of $25,000 minus $10,000 received at signing of franchise agreement
[b] Amount received for right to use Diet Right name and to sell Diet Right's prepackaged meals

The unearned franchise fees will be recognized as earned when the initial services are performed. These services could be performed evenly over time or at one point in time.

Assuming that one-half of the deferred payment ($7,500) is for employee training and recordkeeping system installation completed by Diet Right before the franchise opens, the following entry would be made on Diet Right's books when the franchise commences operations on March 1, 2008.

**March 1, 2008:**

| | | | |
|---|---|---|---|
| **DR** | Unearned franchise fees................................. | $7,500 | |
| | **CR** Earned franchise fees............................... | | $7,500 |

Note that this portion of the initial franchise fee is recognized even though the amount has not been received in cash. This treatment is appropriate assuming that the collectibility of the note receivable from the franchisee is reasonably assured.

If the remaining $7,500 of the initial franchise fee is for services provided by Diet Right on an ongoing basis over the term of the note (for example, maintenance of Web site and advertising), the following adjusting entry would be made at the end of each year to record franchise fee revenue earned during the period.

**December 31, 2008 (2009 and 2010):**

| | | | |
|---|---|---|---|
| **DR** | Unearned franchise fees................................. | $2,500 | |
| | **CR** Earned franchise fee revenue........................ | | $2,500 |

In addition, the entry to record the receipt of payment on the note receivable and interest earned at 8% on the outstanding note balance would be as follows at December 31:

| | | 2008 | | 2009 | | 2010 | |
|---|---|---|---|---|---|---|---|
| **DR** | Cash ................ | $5,000 | | $5,000 | | $5,000 | |
| | **CR** Notes receivable | | $5,000 | | $5,000 | | $5,000 |
| **DR** | Cash ................ | $1,200[a] | | $ 800[b] | | $ 400[c] | |
| | **CR** Interest revenue | | $1,200 | | $ 800 | | $ 400 |

[a] 0.08 × $15,000 = $1,200   [b] 0.08 × $10,000 = $800   [c] 0.08 × $5,000 = $400

**Recording Continuing Franchise Fees**   If the franchisee sales were $100,000 in 2008, the entry for the continuing or periodic fee (0.02 × $100,000 = $2,000) would be:

| | | | |
|---|---|---|---|
| **DR** | Cash ...................................................... | $2,000 | |
| | **CR** Earned franchise fee revenue........................... | | $2,000 |

These returns may be made by the ultimate customer or by a party who resells the product to the final customer (that is, a distributor).

Costs incurred by the franchisor to provide initial and continuing services (for example, counseling by a registered dietician or advertising) are expensed in the same periods as the franchise revenue following the matching principle.

## Sales with Right of Return

Due to the nature of their products, certain companies such as book publishers, packaged software companies, and semiconductor manufacturers experience high rates of return of their products. For example, book publishers commonly have rates of return in excess of 25% for hardcover books. Because of rapid obsolescence of their product, semiconductor manufacturers such as Motorola and Intel grant distributors the right to return semiconductors they are unable to sell.

When the frequency and magnitude of returns are high, a question arises as to whether an entity should recognize revenue at the time of sale or defer recognition until the uncertainty regarding product returns is resolved. *SFAS No. 45* specifies that for a seller to record revenue at time of sale when **right of return** exists, all the following criteria must be met:[3]

- The seller's price to the buyer is substantially fixed or determinable at the date of sale.
- The buyer has paid the seller or the buyer is obligated to pay the seller and the obligation is not contingent on the resale of the product.
- The buyer's obligation to the seller does not change in the event of theft or physical destruction or damage of the product.
- The buyer acquiring the product for resale has economic substance and exists separate and distinct from the seller. That is, the buyer cannot be a **special purpose entity** established by the seller for the sole purpose of buying and reselling the seller's product and thus allowing the seller to recognize revenue.
- The seller does not have significant obligations for future performance to directly bring about resale of the product to the buyer.
- The amount of future returns can be reasonably estimated.

This is perhaps the most important of these criteria and the one subject to greatest uncertainty. Because estimation of future product returns entails considerable judgment, it can lead to manipulation and revenue overstatement. Statement users need to be particularly wary of unusual patterns in return provisions for those entities that operate in industries with high levels and variability of product returns.

When all six of these conditions are met, an entity will debit Sales returns and credit Allowance for sales returns for the estimated returns from sales made during the period. The sales returns account is netted against (shown contra to) the gross sales figure for the period to avoid overstatement of sales revenue, and the allowance account is shown contra to Accounts receivable to avoid overstating this asset account.

When any of these conditions is not met, then sales revenue and the related cost of sales are deferred and recognized either when the return privilege has substantially expired or when the conditions listed above are met, whichever comes first.

## Bundled Sales

Software vendors such as Microsoft and Oracle often package their products in "bundles" of more than one product or service ("multiple deliverables") that are sold for a lump-sum

---

[3] "Revenue Recognition When Right of Return Exists," *SFAS No. 48* (Stamford, CT: FASB 1981).

contract price. In addition to the software itself (or the license to use the software), other deliverables include such things as training in the use of the software, upgrades and enhancements, and postcontract customer support. The key accounting issue related to bundled sales transactions is the timing of revenue recognition. That is, how much of the lump-sum contract price should be recognized up front when the product is delivered to the customer, and how much should be deferred and recognized as the seller satisfies its commitment for other deliverables specified in the contract?

Authoritative guidance on this issue is provided in *Statement of Position (SOP) 97-2* issued in 1997.[4] It states that if a software sales arrangement includes multiple, distinct elements, the revenue from the arrangement should be allocated to the various elements based on vendor-specific objective evidence of the elements' relative fair value. As a practical matter, vendor-specific objective evidence is obtained from observed prices charged when the elements are sold separately.

To illustrate how revenue is allocated with multiple deliverables, assume that Oracle sells its database management software system to a corporate client for $1 million. The contract stipulates that in addition to the software, Oracle will provide staff training on the use of the software, a free upgrade on a when-and-if-available basis, and customer support over the five years of the licensing agreement. Objective evidence of relative fair market values, based on what Oracle would charge for these individual elements if sold separately, is as follows:

> Statements of Position (SOPs) on accounting issues present the conclusions of at least two-thirds of the Accounting Standards Executive Committee (AcSEC) of the American Institute of CPAs (AICPA). AcSEC is the senior technical body of the AICPA authorized to speak for it on financial accounting and reporting matters. AICPA SOPs that have been cleared by the FASB are deemed to be part of GAAP.

| | Fair Value | Percentage of Total Fair Value |
|---|---|---|
| Database management software | $ 600,000 | 40% |
| Training | 450,000 | 30 |
| Upgrades | 300,000 | 20 |
| Customer support | 150,000 | 10 |
| Total estimated fair values if sold separately | $1,500,000 | 100% |

In this example, Oracle would recognize $400,000 (0.40 × $1 million) of revenue when the software is delivered and installed for the client, $300,000 (0.30 × $1 million) when the training is complete, $200,000 (0.20 × $1 million) when upgrades are installed and $100,000 (0.10 × $1 million) recognized evenly over the five years of the contract as the customer service is provided.

Exhibit 3.6 is an excerpt from Oracle's footnote on significant accounting policies that explains its revenue recognition policies for software licensing revenues and service revenues. The amount of sales revenue that Oracle deferred and reported as unearned revenue amounted to $3.492 billion as of May 31, 2007.

Because the determination of relative fair values of multiple deliverables requires considerable judgment on the part of companies' management, there is potential for premature revenue recognition and/or arbitrary income shifting from period to period. Accordingly, statement users need to be particularly vigilant when assessing companies' revenue and profits with significant amounts of bundled sales.

---

[4] "Software Revenue Recognition," *Statement of Position 97-2* (New York: AICPA, 1997).

**EXHIBIT 3.6**   Oracle Corporation Excerpts from Significant Accounting Policies on Revenue Recognition

### Revenue Recognition

We derive revenues from the following sources: (1) software, which includes new software license and software license updates and product support revenues, and (2) services, which include consulting, On Demand and education revenues.

New software license revenues represent fees earned from granting customers licenses to use our database, middleware and applications software, and exclude revenues derived from software license updates, which are included in software license updates and product support. While the basis for software license revenue recognition is substantially governed by the provisions of Statement of Position No. 97-2, *Software Revenue Recognition,* issued by the American Institute of Certified Public Accountants, we exercise judgment and use estimates in connection with the determination of the amount of software and services revenues to be recognized in each accounting period.

For software license arrangements that do not require significant modification or customization of the underlying software, we recognize new software license revenue when: (1) we enter into a legally binding arrangement with a customer for the license of software; (2) we deliver the products; (3) customer payment is deemed fixed or determinable and free of contingencies or significant uncertainties; and (4) collection is probable. Substantially all of our new software license revenues are recognized in this manner.

The vast majority of our software license arrangements include software license updates and product support, which are recognized ratably over the term of the arrangement, typically one year. Software license updates provide customers with rights to unspecified software product upgrades, maintenance releases and patches released during the term of the support period. Product support includes internet access to technical content, as well as internet and telephone access to technical support personnel located in our global support centers. Software license updates and product support are generally priced as a percentage of the net new software license fees. Substantially all of our customers purchase both software license updates and product support when they acquire new software licenses. In addition, substantially all of our customers renew their software license updates and product support contracts annually.

For arrangements with multiple elements, we allocate revenue to each element of a transaction based upon its fair value as determined by "vendor specific objective evidence." Vendor specific objective evidence of fair value for all elements of an arrangement is based upon the normal pricing and discounting practices for those products and services when sold separately and for software license updates and product support services is additionally measured by the renewal rate offered to the customer. We may modify our pricing practices in the future, which could result in changes in our vendor specific objective evidence of fair value for these undelivered elements. As a result, our future revenue recognition for multiple element arrangements could differ significantly from our historical results.

We defer revenue for any undelivered elements, and recognize revenue when the product is delivered or over the period in which the service is performed, in accordance with our revenue recognition policy for such element. If we cannot objectively determine the fair value of any undelivered element included in bundled software and service arrangements, we defer revenue until all elements are delivered and services have been performed, or until fair value can objectively be determined for any remaining undelivered elements. When the fair value of a delivered element has not been established, we use the residual method to record revenue if the fair value of all undelivered elements is determinable. Under the residual method, the fair value of the undelivered elements is deferred and the remaining portion of the arrangement fee is allocated to the delivered elements and is recognized as revenue.

*Source:* 2006 Oracle Annual Report.

# EARNINGS MANAGEMENT

*"Executives rarely have to violate the law to put a gloss on dreary earnings. Accepted accounting principles leave ample room for those who want to fudge the numbers."*[5]

The criteria for revenue and expense recognition outlined in Chapter 2 provide general guidelines for accrual accounting income determination. Applying these rules in specific settings still leaves room, however, for considerable latitude and judgment. For example, determining when revenue has been earned (critical event) and is realizable (measurability)—the two conditions for revenue recognition—are often judgment calls. Managers can sometimes exploit the flexibility in GAAP to manipulate reported earnings in ways that mask the company's underlying performance. Some managers have even resorted to outright financial fraud to inflate reported earnings, but this is relatively rare.

The increasing propensity of managers to bolster earnings by exploiting the flexibility in GAAP or by resorting to financial fraud led former SEC Chairman Arthur Levitt to warn:

> Increasingly, I have become concerned that the motivation to meet Wall Street earnings expectations may be overriding common sense business practices. Too many corporate managers, auditors, and analysts are participating in a game of nods and winks. In the zeal to satisfy consensus earnings estimates and project a smooth earnings path, wishful thinking may be winning the day over faithful representation. As a result, I fear that we are witnessing an erosion in the quality of earnings, and therefore, the quality of financial reporting. Managing may be giving way to manipulation; integrity may be losing to illusion.[6]

Earnings management is not new. But the perception is that it has become increasingly common in today's marketplace because of pressure to meet analysts' earnings forecasts. Companies that miss analysts' earnings per share estimates by even a few pennies frequently experience significant stock price declines. Several highly publicized examples of alleged accounting "irregularities"[7] and several research studies[8] lend support to Chairman Levitt's concerns about earnings management.

One way to avoid a decline in stock price for reporting a loss is to make sure to report an accounting profit. Ideally, this should be accomplished through real economic events that are accounted for correctly. When all else fails, however, managers sometimes resort to various sorts of accounting "tricks" (described more fully later) to artificially inflate earnings. Results from a recent research study suggest that artificially inflating earnings is a common occurrence, especially for firms that would otherwise report small losses.[9] Figure 3.1 is a frequency distribution of annual reported earnings for a large number of firms over a 20-year period. The horizontal axis represents groupings of individual firms' reported earnings stated as a percentage of their beginning-of-year market value of equity.

[5] F. S. Worthy, "Manipulating Profits: How It's Done," *Fortune,* June 25, 1984, pp. 50–54.

[6] Statements made by Arthur Levitt, chairman of the Securities and Exchange Commission, in a speech entitled, "The Numbers Game," delivered at the New York University Center for Law and Business, September 28, 1998.

[7] D. Bank, "Informix Says Accounting Problems Were More Serious Than First Disclosed," *The Wall Street Journal,* September 23, 1997; T. O'Brien, "KnowledgeWare Accounting Practices Are Questioned," *The Wall Street Journal,* September 7, 1994; M. Maremont, "Anatomy of a Fraud: How Kurzweil's Straight-Arrow CEO Went Awry," *BusinessWeek,* September 16, 1996, pp. 90–93; S. Lipin, "How Telxon Corp. Came to Restate Earnings," *The Wall Street Journal,* December 23, 1998; J. Laing, "Dangerous Games: Did 'Chainsaw Al' Dunlap Manufacture Sunbeam's Earnings Last Year?" *Barron's Online,* June 8, 1998, pp. 1–8; and E. Nelson and J. Lublin, "Whistle-Blowers Set Off Cendant Probe," *The Wall Street Journal,* August 13, 1998.

[8] D. Burgstahler and I. Dichev, "Earnings Management to Avoid Earnings Decreases and Losses," *Journal of Accounting and Economics,* December 1997, pp. 99–126; F. Degeorge, J. Patel, and R. Zeckhauser, "Earnings Management to Exceed Thresholds," *Journal of Business,* January 1999, pp. 1–33; and P. Dechow, S. Richardson, and A. Tuna, "Are Benchmark Beaters Doing Anything Wrong?" Working Paper, University of Michigan Business School, July 2000.

[9] Dechow et al., Ibid.

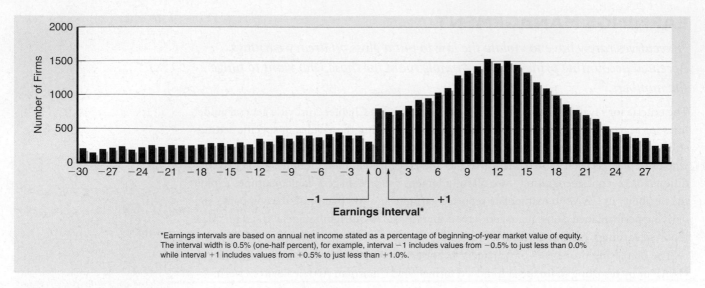

**Figure 3.1** DISTRIBUTION OF ANNUAL NET INCOME

SOURCE: P. Dechow, S. Richardson, and A. Tuna, "Why Are Earnings Kinky? A Reexamination of the Earnings Management Explanation," *Review of Accounting Studies*, Vol. 8, 2003, pp. 335–84.

> Let's use a numerical example for clarity. Assume Hong Company reports 2008 earnings of $500,000 and the market value of its equity on January 1, 2008 was $62,500,000. Thus, $500,000/$62,500,000 = .008 or 0.8%. Since 0.8% is within the interval of 0.5% to 1.0%, Hong Company would appear in interval +1.

The interval width of each grouping (that is, the interval width for each bar on the graph) is 0.5%, or half of 1 percent. Thus, the grouping labeled −1 includes firms whose earnings stated as a percentage of beginning-of-year market value of equity falls in the range from −0.5% to just less than the negative side of 0.00%. Grouping 0 contains values from 0.00% to just less than +0.5% while grouping +1 contains values from +0.5% to just less than 1.0%. The vertical axis measures the number of firms whose reported earnings fall into the various categories.

The striking feature of this graph is the discontinuity in the number of firms reporting slightly negative earnings versus slightly positive earnings. Substantially fewer firms fall just below zero (grouping −1) while a substantially higher number of firms report earnings at or just above zero (groupings 0 and +1). What appears to be happening is that managers of firms that would otherwise report small losses (group −1) are finding ways to prop up earnings to move the firm's reported profits into the group 0 or group 1 range (that is, slightly positive range). One way of doing so, even in troubled times, is to exploit the flexibility in GAAP or to resort to a variety accounting gimmicks to push earnings into the positive range.

> The analysts' consensus EPS estimates come from Institutional Brokers Estimate System (I/B/E/S) which provides analyst earnings per share forecasts (both annual and quarterly) for more than 18,000 companies in more than 50 countries.

As has been noted, investors often penalize companies that fail to meet analysts' earnings expectations. Figure 3.2 provides indirect evidence on the strong incentive managers have to meet or beat analysts' earnings estimates. This graph shows the distribution of analysts' annual earnings per share (EPS) forecast errors, that is, actual EPS minus analysts' consensus EPS estimate. The interval width of each bar is 1 cent. Thus, the forecast error bar labeled −1 cent (+1 cent) reflects the number of firm-years when actual earnings per share falls below (above) the analysts' consensus forecasts by 1 cent. Note the large number of observations clustered in the zero forecast error interval where actual EPS equals the consensus estimate. Also note the much smaller number of forecast errors that fall in the bar just below zero (−1 cent) compared to the number that fall just above zero (+1 cent). One explanation of

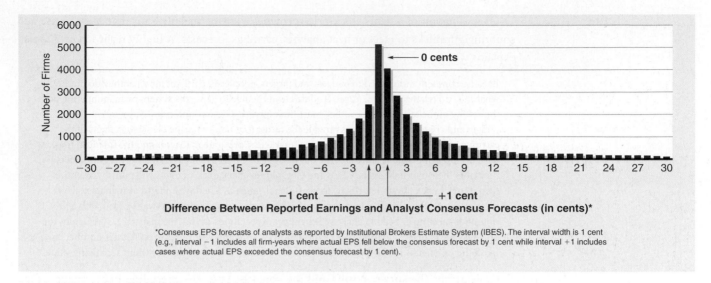

**Figure 3.2** DISTRIBUTION OF ANNUAL FORECAST ERRORS (IN CENTS) AS REPORTED BY I/B/E/S

*SOURCE:* P. Dechow, S. Richardson, and I. Tuna, "Are Benchmark Beaters Doing Anything Wrong?" Working Paper. Copyright © 2000 Irem Tuna. Reprinted by permission of the author. July 2000.

this result is that some companies are managing earnings upward to "meet or beat" analysts' earnings projections.

A recent survey of more than 400 chief financial officers (CFOs) and treasurers of major U.S. companies provides evidence that corroborates the data displayed in Figures 3.1 and 3.2.[10] More than 65% of the financial executives surveyed indicated that reporting a profit was an important earnings benchmark while approximately 74% indicated that meeting or beating analysts' consensus EPS forecasts for the current quarter was an important benchmark.

When asked why their company tries to meet earnings benchmarks, more than 86% of the financial executives surveyed indicated that they did so to help build credibility with the capital market. In addition, 82% indicated that benchmark beating was important to maintain or increase stock price while 74% indicated that beating benchmarks helped to convey future growth prospects to investors. Managers say they willingly sacrifice firm value to appease Wall Street analysts: more than 80% of the CFOs surveyed indicted that they would delay research and development, advertising, and maintenance spending; 55% acknowledged that they would delay the start of positive net present value projects to achieve earnings targets. Earnings can also be managed with a variety of accrual estimates and year-end adjustments. Clearly, real transaction management or accrual management seems more consistent with managing earnings to disguise the firm's true underlying economic performance than with managing earnings to convey value-relevant private information to investors about the firm's future growth prospects.

> For years, Wall Street has known that companies manage earnings. Academic studies have found that actual earnings do not fall randomly around the consensus estimate. Instead, they tend to come in at or above the forecast. Some companies, like General Electric, almost always seem to beat estimates by a penny or two a share, no matter what the economic conditions. . . . Managements try to give investors what they want, and companies whose earnings are predictable are prized on Wall Street, which does not like unhappy surprises.
>
> *Source:* A. Berenson, "Tweaking Numbers to Meet Goals Comes Back to Haunt Executives," *The New York Times,* June 29, 2002.

---

[10] J. Graham, C. Harvey, and S. Rajgopal, "The Economic Implications of Corporate Financial Reporting," *Journal of Accounting & Economics,* December 2005, pp. 3–73.

Overvaluation of a firm's stock price provides a strong incentive for managers to use accounting gimmicks to meet or beat analysts' earnings forecasts. A highly regarded economist explains why:

> Because compensation is tied to budgets and targets, people are paid not for what they do but for what they do relative to some target. And this leads people to game the system by manipulating both the setting of the targets and how they meet their targets. These counterproductive target-based budget and compensation systems provide the fertile foundation for the damaging effects of the earnings management game with the capital markets. Corporate managers and the financial markets have been playing a game similar to the budgeting game. Just as managers' compensation suffers if they miss their internal targets, CEOs and CFOs know that capital markets will punish the entire firm if they miss analysts' [earnings] forecasts by as much as a penny. And just as managers who meet or exceed their internal targets receive a bonus, the capital markets reward a firm with a premium for meeting or beating analysts' [earnings] expectations during the quarter.... Generally, the only way for managers to meet those expectations year in and year out is to cook their numbers to mask the inherent uncertainty in their business. And that cannot be done without sacrificing value.[11]

Collectively, the survey results and the conjectures in the preceding quote suggest that when capital market-based incentives to manage earnings to meet or beat analysts' forecasts are present, the representational faithfulness and predictive usefulness of the resultant accounting numbers may be compromised.[12] As a user of financial statements, you should be aware of managements' incentives to distort reported earnings and the ways in which this is done, a subject to which we turn in the next section and throughout the remainder of the book.

## Popular Earnings Management Devices

What are some of the more popular techniques firms use to manage earnings? Former Chairman Levitt singles out five areas that the SEC finds particularly troublesome and pervasive.[13]

- *"Big Bath" restructuring charges:* The 1990s was the decade of **restructuring** in corporate America. To remain competitive and become more efficient, hundreds of companies closed plants, consolidated operations, reduced their labor force, and sold off noncore business units. Once a decision to restructure is made, GAAP requires companies to estimate the future costs they expect to incur to carry out the restructuring for such things as employee severance payments and plant closings. These estimated restructuring costs are then charged to an expense account with an offsetting credit to a liability account (Restructuring reserve) in the current period. In an effort to "clean up" company balance sheets, managers have often taken excessive restructuring write-offs and overstated estimated charges for future expenditures. Examples of questionable items that the SEC has found in restructuring charges include services to be provided in some future period by lawyers, accountants, and investment bankers; special bonuses for officers; and expenses for retraining and relocating people. Amazingly, some companies even took charges for training people not yet hired!

---

[11] M. Jensen, "Agency Costs of Overvalued Equity," *Financial Management,* Spring 2005, p. 5–19. Copyright © 2005 Wiley-Blackwell. Used with permission.

[12] For empirical evidence consistent with this concern, see B. Badertscher, "Overvaluation and Its Effect on Managements' Choice of Alternative Earnings Management Mechanisms," Working Paper, University of Iowa, June 2007; B. Badertscher, C. Collins, and T. Lys, "Earnings Management and the Predictive Ability of Accruals with Respect to Future Cash Flows," Working Paper, University of Iowa, October 2007; and J. Efendi, A. Srivastava, and E. Swanson, "Why Do Corporate Managers Misstate Financial Statements? The Role of In-the-Money Options and Other Incentives, *Journal of Financial Economics,* September 2007, pp. 667–708.

[13] Levitt, "The Numbers Game," op. cit.

Why are companies tempted to overstate restructuring charges? The conventional wisdom is that investors look beyond one-time special charges and write-offs and, instead, value a company's stock based on sustainable operating earnings (see Chapter 6). So, many believe that taking "big bath" charges does not adversely affect stock price.[14] Moreover, these restructuring charges and associated liability reserves are sometimes reversed in future years when earnings fall short of targets, thereby providing a boost to the bottom line at opportune times.

- *Creative acquisition accounting and purchased R&D:* When one company buys another company and uses the **purchase method** of accounting for the combination (see Chapter 16), the buyer must allocate a portion of the purchase price to the acquired firm's identifiable net assets, including intangibles such as in-process (incomplete) research and development (R&D) activities (that is, **in-process R&D**). *SFAS No. 2* states that "while future benefits from a particular research and development project may be foreseen, they generally cannot be measured with a reasonable degree of certainty."[15] Accordingly, values assigned to R&D projects that have no alternative future use are immediately expensed (that is, in the period in which the acquisition occurs). This treatment results in an economic asset (potential benefits from in-process R&D) that never appears on the balance sheet. If and when revenues from these R&D investments materialize, there are no offsetting expenses because the cost of the purchased R&D was written off in the period acquired. This is a classic example of mismatching revenues and expenses that gives the appearance of excessive profitability in later years.

  The fair value of in-process R&D is difficult to measure and, therefore, difficult to verify. This creates considerable opportunity to manage postacquisition earnings by allocating a disproportionate share of the initial purchase price to in-process R&D. This problem has been particularly acute for acquisitions of technology and software development companies where a major portion of the purchase price has been allocated to in-process R&D activities that are then immediately written off.

- *Miscellaneous "cookie jar reserves":* Accrual accounting allows companies to estimate and accrue for obligations that will be paid in *future periods* as a result of transactions or events in the *current period*. Similar reserves are allowed for estimated declines in asset values. Examples include provisions for bad debts and loan losses, warranty costs, sales returns, and reserves for various future expenditures related to corporate restructuring. Some companies use unrealistic assumptions to arrive at these estimated charges. They overreserve in good times and cut back on estimated charges, or even reverse previous charges, in bad times. As a result, these "cookie jar reserves" become a convenient income smoothing device.

> Beginning in 2009, firms will no longer be allowed to immediately write off purchased in-process R&D acquired in a business combination. Rather, *SFAS No. 141R* requires the acquiring firm to capitalize in-process R&D as an intangible asset that is subject to periodic impairment reviews under *SFAS No. 144* (see Chapter 16).

> A report prepared by outside investigators for the Board of Freddie Mac, a big mortgage financier, highlights how management used a variety of cookie jar reserves to artificially smooth earnings.
>
> Freddie Mac, which for most of the last few years has faced the uncommon problem of having profits that substantially exceeded Wall Street forecasts, did not want to deviate too much from those expectations, the report said. So it used techniques to make its underlying business of insuring and buying mortgages seem less profitable and to create a reserve of earnings for later years. . . . Freddie Mac said it had understated its pre-tax profits by as much as $6.9 billion in 2002 and previous years as a result of serious accounting problems, and the company ousted its three top executives. The report offers more evidence of what regulators and many investors say is a culture of earnings management in corporate America. Like many other big publicly traded companies, Freddie Mac put a premium on meeting analysts' forecasts of its profits and providing consistent growth in reported earnings.
>
> *Source:* A. Berenson, "Report Says Freddie Mac Misled Investors," *New York Times,* July 24, 2003. Copyright © 2003. Used by permission of The New York Times Co., Inc.

---

[14] J. Elliott and D. Hanna, "Repeated Accounting Write-Offs and the Information Content of Earnings," *Journal of Accounting Research, Supplement,* 1996, pp. 135–55.

[15] "Accounting for Research and Development Costs," *SFAS No. 2* (Stamford, CT: FASB, 1974), para. 45.

- *Intentional errors deemed to be "immaterial" and intentional bias in estimates:* Material-ity thresholds are another way of using financial reporting flexibility to inflate earnings. Sometimes, companies intentionally misapply GAAP, for example, capitalizing an ex-penditure that should be expensed. If the auditor subsequently catches this incorrect treatment, management might justify the error by arguing that the earnings effect is "immaterial" and, therefore, not worth correcting. The problem, of course, is that a se-ries of these "immaterial" errors spread across several accounts can, in the aggregate, have a material effect on bottom-line earnings.

  Intentional misstatement of estimates is another area of abuse. Estimates abound in accrual accounting. Examples include estimated useful lives and salvage values for fixed assets, estimates of bad debts, and the amount of write-down for obsolete inventory. Man-agement can often shade these estimates in one direction or the other to achieve a desired earnings target. As long as these estimates fall within "acceptable" ranges, the biased esti-mate is unlikely to draw attention from the external auditor.

- *Premature or aggressive revenue recognition:* Another common abuse is to recognize revenues before they have been "earned" (the critical event criterion) or become "real-ized" (the measurability criterion). The next section discusses this important earnings management device.

### Revenue Recognition Abuses

The SEC says that revenue is earned (critical event) and is realized or realizable (measurability)—and, therefore, can be recognized—when all of the following criteria are met:

1. Persuasive evidence of an exchange arrangement exists.
2. Delivery has occurred or services have been rendered.
3. The seller's price to the buyer is fixed or determinable.
4. Collectibility is reasonably assured.

> "Arrangement" means there is a final understanding be-tween the parties as to the specific nature and terms of the agreed-upon transaction.

The following scenarios taken from *SEC Staff Accounting Bulletin (SAB) No. 104* illustrate some troublesome areas of revenue recognition as well as the SEC's recommendation regard-ing the appropriate treatment.[16]

- *Scenario 1—Goods shipped on consignment:* A software manufacturer (seller) ships 100,000 copies of a new video game to distributors, charging $50 per copy. Under terms of the signed agreement, distributors have the right (a) to return unsold copies of the video game and (b) not to pay the seller until they resell the product to final cus-tomers through their retail outlets. The software manufacturer wants to recognize $5,000,000 of revenue upon delivery of the video games to the distributors. Can the company do this?

  **SEC interpretive response:** No revenue can be recognized on delivery. The reason is that the seller retains the risks and rewards of ownership of the product. Title does not pass to the distributor when the goods are shipped. Also, under criterion 4 in the preced-ing list, there is considerable uncertainty as to ultimate collectibility of the sales price on the goods shipped.

- *Scenario 2—Sales with delayed delivery:* Prior to the close of its September 30 fiscal quarter, a manufacturer (seller) completes production of 50,000 specialized gas valves. The valves sell for $60 each and were ordered by customers that assemble and sell gas

---

[16] "Revenue Recognition," *Staff Accounting Bulletin No. 104* (Washington, DC: SEC, December 17, 2003).

fireplaces. The customers are unable to take delivery by September 30 for reasons that include (1) lack of available storage space, (2) having ample inventory on hand to cover production for the next month, and (3) delayed production schedules. The seller segregates the valves awaiting shipment from other unsold products in its own warehouse and wishes to recognize $3,000,000 of revenue in the current quarter from these goods produced but not shipped.

*SEC interpretive response:* Without evidence of an exchange being spelled out in the sales agreement (criterion 1), the seller cannot recognize revenue until delivery has taken place (criterion 2). Generally, delivery is *not* considered to have occurred unless the customer (1) takes title and (2) assumes the risks and rewards of ownership of the products. Typically, these conditions are met when a product is received at the customer's place of business or when the product is shipped to the customer and the customer assumes responsibility for the product once it leaves the seller's premises. If the buyer requests in the sales agreement that the transaction be on a "bill and hold" basis and has a substantial business purpose for doing so, the seller may recognize revenue when the production of the goods is complete.

- *Scenario 3—Goods sold on layaway:* Company R, a retailer, offers layaway sales to its customers. It collects an initial cash deposit from the customer but retains the merchandise and sets it aside in its inventory. Although a date may be specified within which the customer must finalize the purchase, Company R does not require the customer to sign a fixed payment agreement. The merchandise is not released to the customer until full payment is received. Company R wants to recognize revenue equal to a pro rata portion of the merchandise sales price as cash is collected.

  *SEC interpretive response:* Company R should postpone recognizing revenue until merchandise is delivered to the customer (criterion 2 delivery has not occurred). Until then, the cash received to date should be recognized as a liability such as Deposits from layaway customers. Because Company R retains the risks of ownership, receives only deposits, and does not have an enforceable right to the remainder of the purchase price, it is not entitled to recognize revenue until the sales price is received in full.

- *Scenario 4—Nonrefundable up-front fees:* Increasingly, service providers negotiate agreements with customers that require the customer to pay a nonrefundable up-front "initiation" or service "activation" fee. For example, companies that provide telecommunications services typically charge each new customer a nonrefundable activation fee. Once enrolled for service, customers then pay monthly usage fees that just cover the company's operating costs. The costs to activate the telecommunications service are minimal. Thus, the up-front fee customers pay more than covers these costs. The key question here involves when revenue from nonrefundable up-front activation fees should be recognized.

  *SEC interpretive response:* Unless the up-front fee is in exchange for products delivered or services performed that represent the culmination of a separate earnings process, deferral of revenue is appropriate because service has not been rendered (criterion 2, delivery). In such circumstances, the up-front fees, even if nonrefundable, are deemed to be earned as the services are delivered over the service agreement's full term. This means that the up-front fees should be deferred and recognized pro rata over the periods when services are provided because that's when the fees are earned.

- *Scenario 5—Gross versus net basis for Internet resellers:* Another troublesome area is the method used to record sales by certain Internet companies that simply act as an agent or broker in a transaction. For example, assume that Dot-com Company operates an Internet site from which it sells airline tickets. Customers place orders by selecting a specific flight from Dot-com's Web site and providing a credit card number for payment. Dot-com receives the order and credit card authorization and passes this information along to the airline. The airline sends the tickets directly to the customer. Dot-com does not take title to the tickets and, therefore, has no ownership risk or other responsibility for the tickets. The airline is fully responsible for all returned tickets and disputed credit card charges. (So, Dot-com is just an agent or broker that facilitates the transaction between the customer and the airline.) The average ticket price is $500, of which Dot-com receives a $25 commission. In the event a credit card sale is rejected, Dot-com loses its $25 commission on sale. Because its management believes that revenue growth is what drives its share price, it seeks to report the revenue from this transaction on a "gross" basis at $500, along with cost of sales of $475.

*SEC interpretive response:* Dot-com should report the revenue from this transaction on a "net" basis: $25 as commission revenue and $0 for cost of sales. In determining whether revenue should be reported gross (with separate display of cost of sales) or on a net basis, the SEC stipulates that the following factors be considered:

1. Is Dot-com acting as a principal or as an agent/broker in the transaction?
2. Does Dot-com take title to the ticket?
3. Does Dot-com assume the risks of ownership such as possible losses from bad debts or returns?

If Dot-com acts as a principal in the transaction, takes title to the tickets or assumes the ownership risks, then the gross method is deemed appropriate. Otherwise, the net method must be used.

- *Scenario 6—Capacity swaps:* Over the past decade, revenue growth has been a major factor that affects the value of telecommunications companies. In an effort to bolster quarter-over-quarter revenue growth and build capacity for future expected customer demand, several telecommunication companies entered into a series of **"capacity swap"** transactions exchanging access to each other's networks. As an example, assume that on January 1, 2008, San Francisco Telecom agrees to exchange $150 million worth of capacity over its fiber optic network between San Francisco and Asia for $175 million of capacity on Boston Telecom's communications network between New York and Europe. Company engineers estimate that current customer demand would have to increase five-fold (not a likely outcome for the foreseeable future) before the capacity being acquired would be needed. On signing the agreement, each company seeks to book revenue equal to the capacity rights being sold while booking the capacity bought as a capital expense that will be written off on a straight-line basis over the 10-year term of the swap agreement. As a consequence, San Francisco Telecom plans to book $150 million of revenue and $17.5 million per year ($175 million/10 years) of expenses resulting in increased pre-tax profits of $132.5 million in the year the swap agreement is signed. Boston Telecom would book $175 million of revenue, $15 million of expenses, and $160 million in pre-tax profits. Thus, both companies stand to report substantially higher revenues and profits in the current period despite the fact that none, or very little, of the capacity exchanged is likely to be used by paying customers in the current period.

  *SEC interpretive response:*[17] The SEC position is that rather than recognize the entire amount of the swapped capacity as revenue up front when the contract is signed, revenues should be deferred and recognized over the term of the swap agreement as the capacity is brought on line and used by the acquiring firm's customers. Capacity acquired is to be charged against earnings over the life of the swap agreement as indicated earlier.

---

[17] This interpretative response was issued subsequent to *SAB 104* as part of enforcement actions brought against companies deemed to have violated GAAP. The SEC publishes details of major enforcement actions against firms with accounting irregularities in a series called Accounting and Auditing Enforcement Releases.

It is important to note that *SAB 104* was not meant to change GAAP. Instead, it is intended to close some loopholes and eliminate gray areas in how GAAP is being applied in practice. A recent survey of annual reports indicates that the SEC guidelines have diminished abuses.[18] However, aggressive revenue recognition still occurs, so analysts must be vigilant for firms that overstate true earnings performance by bending revenue recognition rules.

---

**The criteria for revenue and expense recognition are intended to provide general guidance for accrual accounting income determination. However, these general criteria leave ample room for judgment and interpretation that create flexibility in GAAP. Analysts and investors must be alert for management's attempts to exploit this flexibility in ways that push the boundaries of acceptable revenue and expense recognition.**

**RECAP**

## Accounting Errors, Earnings Restatements, and Prior Period Adjustments

Accounting errors or irregularities[19] can occur for a variety of reasons. Sometimes they occur because of simple oversight. For example, a buyer may fail to include in its ending inventory the cost of merchandise in transit for which title transfers at the time goods are shipped by the seller (see Chapter 9). Errors can also occur because different parties disagree on how to account for a given transaction, resulting in misapplication of GAAP. For example, practicing accountants looking at a given set of facts can sometimes disagree on when the "critical event" and "measurability" conditions have been satisfied for revenue recognition. Finally, errors sometimes occur because management attempts to exploit the flexibility in GAAP or commits outright financial fraud to inflate earnings and overstate net assets. The Enron and WorldCom restatements in 2001 and 2002 that led to the largest corporate failures in U.S. history provide examples.

Several different parties are charged with the responsibility for discovering accounting errors and irregularities:

- The company's internal audit staff and audit committee of the board of directors are charged with the responsibility for evaluating internal controls, overseeing the preparation of the financial statements, and ensuring that their content fully and accurately depicts the company's financial condition and results of operations. As part of their ongoing review of control systems and financial reporting process, the audit committee and the company's internal audit staff provide the first-line defense against accounting errors/irregularities.

- External auditors provide an additional safeguard in identifying and correcting accounting errors and irregularities. Although the company's management is responsible for the preparation and content of the published financial statements, the independent external auditor is charged with the responsibility for auditing the financial statements to ensure that they are fairly presented in all material respects in accordance with GAAP. As part of the interim review and year-end audit, the external auditor will occasionally uncover accounting errors and irregularities that require correction of current period results or restatement of prior period financial statements.

- As noted in Chapter 1, the Securities Act of 1933 and the Securities Exchange Act of 1934 require companies that sell securities in the United States to register with the SEC and

---

[18] P. McConnell, J. Pegg, and D. Zion, "Revenue Recognition 101," *Accounting Issues* (New York: Bear, Stearns & Co. Inc., March 10, 2000).

[19] Some characterize an *accounting error* as an unintentional mistake in applying GAAP while an *accounting irregularity* is an accounting choice that management knowingly makes that is subsequently determined to have gone beyond the boundaries of acceptable GAAP. In this section, we use the terms *accounting error* and *irregularity* without making a distinction because they both have the same reporting consequence in terms of required restatements.

## Figure 3.3

TOTAL NUMBER OF RESTATEMENT ANNOUNCEMENTS IDENTIFIED, 1997–SEPTEMBER 2005

*SOURCE:* U.S. Government Accountability Office: "Financial Restatements: Update of Public Company Trends, Market Impacts and Regulatory Enforcement Activities" (July 2006).

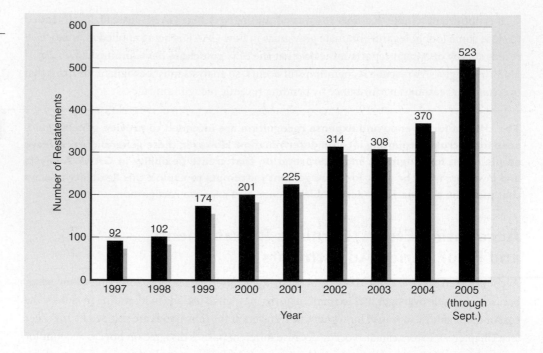

make periodic financial filings with the Commission. As part of its oversight of the registration and filing process, the SEC staff reviews selected issuers' filings to ensure compliance with SEC accounting and disclosure requirements. Through this process, the SEC staff sometimes identifies accounting irregularities that require correction.

A recent report issued by the U.S. Government Accountability Office (GAO) demonstrates a dramatic increase in the incidence of accounting irregularities leading to earnings restatements from 1997 through 2005.[20] Figure 3.3 shows that the number of restatements due to accounting errors and irregularities among firms listed on the AMEX, NYSE, and Nasdaq exchanges rose from 92 in 1997 to 523 restatements through September 2005—an increase of roughly 470%. From 2002 through September 2005, approximately 16% of all listed companies announced at least one restatement.

WorldCom provides an example of this type of accounting irregularity. During 2001 and the first quarter of 2002, it improperly capitalized more than $3.8 billion of operating line costs. After announcing this improper accounting treatment, WorldCom's market value plummeted nearly $29 billion, and the company was forced into bankruptcy.

Figure 3.4 summarizes the major reasons for the restatements. Revenue recognition irregularities constitute the most frequently cited reason for restatements during the period January 1997 to June 2002, accounting for 38% of the 919 announced restatements during the sample period. Restatements due to revenue recognition irregularities include recognizing revenue sooner or later than is allowed under GAAP, or recognizing questionable or fictitious revenue. Cost- or expense-related errors and irregularities were the most common reason for restatement during the period July 2002 to September 2005, constituting 35% of the restatements during this period. This category includes improper recognition of costs or expenses, improperly capitalizing as assets expenditures that should be expensed on the income statement, and improper treatment of tax liabilities, income tax reserves, and other tax-related items. Other reasons for restatements include improper restructuring charges and asset write-offs, improper accounting for acquisitions and mergers including under- or overstatement of gains/losses related to acquisitions, and improper valuations of in-process R&D at acquisition.

---

[20] "Financial Restatements: Update of Public Company Trends, Market Impacts, and Regulatory Enforcement Activities," *Report to the Ranking Minority Member, Committee on Banking, Housing, and Urban Affairs, U.S. Senate* (Washington, DC: U.S. General Accountability Office, 2006).

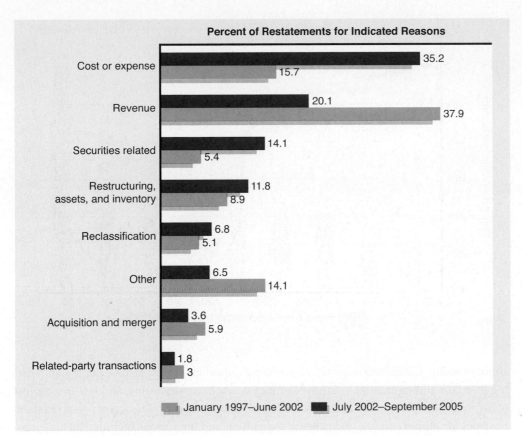

**Percent of Restatements for Indicated Reasons**

Cost or expense — 35.2 / 15.7
Revenue — 20.1 / 37.9
Securities related — 14.1 / 5.4
Restructuring, assets, and inventory — 11.8 / 8.9
Reclassification — 6.8 / 5.1
Other — 6.5 / 14.1
Acquisition and merger — 3.6 / 5.9
Related-party transactions — 1.8 / 3

January 1997–June 2002   July 2002–September 2005

**Figure 3.4**

REASONS FOR EARNINGS RESTATEMENTS: JANUARY 1997–SEPTEMBER 2005

*Source:* U.S. Government Accountability Office: "Financial Restatements: Update of Public Company Trends, Market Impacts and Regulatory Enforcement Activities" (July 2006).

Once discovered, accounting errors and irregularities must be corrected and disclosed. Material errors discovered after the year in which the error is made are corrected through a **prior period adjustment**.[21] This adjustment results in an addition to, or subtraction from, the company's beginning Retained earnings balance (for the year the error is detected) and correction of related asset or liability balances. In addition to making the prior period adjustment to Retained earnings, previous years' financial statements that are presented for comparative purposes are retroactively restated to reflect the specific accounts that are corrected, and the impact of the error on current and prior period reported net income is disclosed in the footnotes to the financial statements.

Recent studies find that firms forced to restate earnings suffer a dramatic decline in stock prices.[22] Figure 3.5 on page 154 plots the average cumulative abnormal daily stock returns of firms that announced earnings restatements from 1971 to 2000. Day 0 in the plot is the day that the restatement is announced in the financial press. The figure shows the returns from 120 days before to 120 days after the announcement. The striking feature of this graph is that restatement firms lose, on average, 25% of their market value over the time period examined with most of the decline occurring in the narrow three-day window surrounding the restatement

---

[21] "Accounting Changes and Error Corrections: A Replacement of APB Opinion No. 20 and FASB Statement No. 3," *SFAS No. 154* (Norwalk, CT: FASB, 2005).

[22] S. Richardson, I. Tuna and M. Wu, "Predicting Earnings Management: The Case of Earnings Restatements," Working Paper, University of Pennsylvania, 2002; Z. Palmrose, V. Richardson and S. Scholz, "Determinants of Market Reactions to Restatement Announcements," *Journal of Accounting and Economics*, February 2004, pp. 59–90.

Restatements can also affect the share prices of nonrestating firms as well. See C. Gleason, N. Jenkins, and B. Johnson, "The Contagion Effects of Accounting Restatements," *The Accounting Review,* January 2008, pp. 83–110.

**Figure 3.5**

CUMULATIVE ABNORMAL
RETURNS FOR FIRMS
RESTATING EARNINGS
1971–2000

*SOURCE:* Richardson, et al., op. cit.

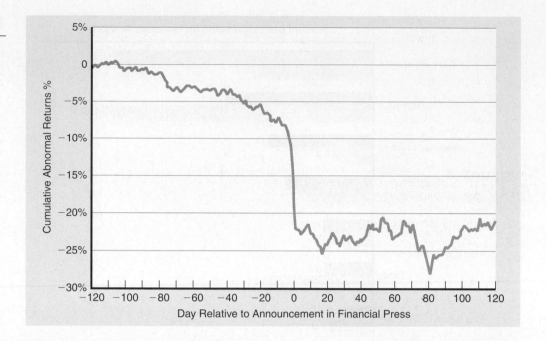

announcement. Clearly, earnings restatements are important events. Firms caught manipulating their accounting numbers suffer a significant loss in market value, and lawsuits against firms' management and their auditors often ensue. That's why it's so important you understand the rules for proper revenue and expense recognition and the various methods that management sometimes uses to circumvent these rules to manipulate earnings.

Exhibit 3.7 provides an example of a restatement disclosure for Apple Computer Inc. from its 2006 10-K report. Apple's restatement was prompted by discovery of a series of irregularities related to stock option grants made to employees from 1997 to 2001 that resulted in misstated earnings in those years and subsequent years. Some option grants were "backdated" to an earlier point in time when the firm's stock price was lower than when the actual grant occurred. Because stock options typically have an exercise price that is set to the stock's market price on the grant date, such backdating allows executives to receive in-the-money options, thereby enhancing the value of their option grants. The relevant accounting standard at the time required Apple to report compensation expense equal to the number of options granted times the difference between the market price of Apple's stock on the actual grant date (when the stock price was higher) minus the stock price on the reported (incorrect) backdated grant date (when the stock price was lower).[23] Accordingly, by failing to properly record compensation expense related to these backdated option grants, Apple overstated after-tax income by a total of $80 million for fiscal years 1997 through 2005 with an additional $4 million after-tax adjustment in 2006.

Panel (a) of Exhibit 3.7 provides excerpts from Note 2 of Apple's 2006 10-K statement that describes the nature of the accounting irregularity and its effect on after-tax income for 2006, 2005, and 2004. Panel (b) shows the restatements to various expense categories on Apple's 2005 and 2004 income statements, and Panel (c) shows the adjustments to various 2005 balance sheet accounts, including the $80 million (prior period) adjustment to the Retained earnings balance for overstatement of income in 2005 and prior years. As explained on the

---

[23] "Accounting for Stock-Based Compensation," *SFAS No. 123* (Norwalk, CT: FASB, 1995). See Chapter 15 for further discussion of accounting for stock option grants and more on backdating.

next page, the entry that Apple made in 2006 to correct the 2005 ending balance sheet accounts was as follows (in millions of dollars):

| | | | |
|---|---|---|---|
| **DR** | Retained earnings | $80 | |
| **DR** | Deferred stock compensation | 1 | |
| | **CR** Common stock | | $43 |
| | **CR** Accrued expenses | | 3 |
| | **CR** Other assets | | 35 |

---

## EXHIBIT 3.7    Apple Computer, Inc.

### Accounting Restatement

**Panel (a)**

*Note 2—Restatement of Consolidated Financial Statements*

The Company is restating its consolidated balance sheet as of September 24, 2005, and the related consolidated statements of operations, shareholders' equity, and cash flows for each of the fiscal years ended September 24, 2005 and September 25, 2004, and each of the quarters in fiscal year 2005.

Previously filed annual reports on Form 10-K and quarterly reports on Form 10-Q affected by the restatements have not been amended and should not be relied on.

On June 29, 2006, the Company announced that an internal review had discovered irregularities related to the issuance of certain stock option grants made between 1997 and 2001, including a grant to its Chief Executive Officer ("CEO") Steve Jobs. The Company also announced that a Special Committee of outside directors ("Special Committee") had been formed and had hired independent counsel to conduct a full investigation of the Company's past stock option granting practices.

As a result of the internal review and the independent investigation, management has concluded, and the Audit and Finance Committee of the Board of Directors agrees, that incorrect measurement dates were used for financial accounting purposes for certain stock option grants made in prior periods. Therefore, the Company has recorded additional non-cash stock-based compensation expense and related tax effects with regard to past stock option grants, and the Company is restating previously filed financial statements in this Form 10-K. These adjustments, after tax, amounted to $4 million, $7 million, and $10 million in fiscal years 2006, 2005 and 2004, respectively. The adjustment to 2006 was recorded in the fourth quarter of fiscal year 2006 due to its insignificance.

### Apple Computer Income Statement Restatements For Fiscal Years Ending September 24, 2005 and 2004

**Panel (b)**

The following table presents the effects of the stock-based compensation and related tax adjustments made to the Company's previously reported consolidated statements of operations ($ in millions):

| | Fiscal Year Ended September 24, 2005 | | | Fiscal Year Ended September 25, 2004 | | |
|---|---|---|---|---|---|---|
| | **As Reported** | **Adjustments** | **As Restated** | **As Reported** | **Adjustments** | **As Restated** |
| Net sales | $13,931 | $— | $13,931 | $8,279 | $ — | $8,279 |
| Cost of sales (1) | 9,888 | 1 | 9,889 | 6,020 | 2 | 6,022 |
| Gross margin | 4,043 | (1) | 4,042 | 2,259 | (2) | 2,257 |
| Operating expenses: | | | | | | |
| Research and development (1) | 534 | 1 | 535 | 489 | 2 | 491 |
| Selling, general, and administrative (1) | 1,859 | 5 | 1,864 | 1,421 | 9 | 1,430 |
| Restructuring costs | — | — | — | 23 | — | 23 |
| Total operating expenses | 2,393 | 6 | 2,399 | 1,933 | 11 | 1,944 |
| Operating income | 1,650 | (7) | 1,643 | 326 | (13) | 313 |
| Other income and expense | 165 | — | 165 | 57 | — | 57 |
| Income before provision for income taxes | 1,815 | (7) | 1,808 | 383 | (13) | 370 |
| Provision for income taxes | 480 | — | 480 | 107 | (3) | 104 |
| Net income | $ 1,335 | $(7) | $ 1,328 | $ 276 | $(10) | $ 266 |

*(continued)*

| EXHIBIT 3.7 | Apple Computer, Inc. *(continued)* |
|---|---|

## Apple Computer Balance Sheet Restatements as of September 24, 2005

**Panel (c)**

The following table presents the effects of the stock-based compensation and related tax adjustments made to the Company's previously reported consolidated balance sheet as of September 24, 2005 ($ in millions):

| | September 24, 2005 | | |
|---|---|---|---|
| | As Reported | Adjustments | As Restated |
| **Assets** | | | |
| Current assets: | | | |
| Cash and cash equivalents | $ 3,491 | $ — | $ 3,491 |
| Short-term investments | 4,770 | — | 4,770 |
| Accounts receivable, less allowance of $46 | 895 | — | 895 |
| Inventories | 165 | — | 165 |
| Deferred tax assets | 331 | — | 331 |
| Other current assets | 648 | — | 648 |
| Total current assets | 10,300 | — | 10,300 |
| Property, plant, and equipment, net | 817 | — | 817 |
| Goodwill | 69 | — | 69 |
| Acquired intangible assets, net | 27 | — | 27 |
| Other assets | 338 | (35) | 303 |
| Total assets | $11,551 | (35) | $11,516 |
| **Liabilities and Shareholders' Equity** | | | |
| Current liabilities: | | | |
| Accounts payable | $ 1,779 | $ — | $ 1,779 |
| Accrued expenses | 1,705 | 3 | 1,708 |
| Total current liabilities | 3,484 | 3 | 3,487 |
| Non-current liabilities | 601 | — | 601 |
| Total liabilities | 4,085 | 3 | 4,088 |
| Commitments and contingencies | | | |
| Shareholders' equity: | | | |
| Common stock, no par value; 1,800,000,000 shares authorized; 835,019,364 shares issued and outstanding | 3,521 | 43 | 3,564 |
| Deferred stock compensation | (60) | (1) | (61) |
| Retained earnings | 4,005 | (80) | 3,925 |
| Accumulated other comprehensive income | — | — | — |
| Total shareholders' equity | 7,466 | (38) | 7,428 |
| Total liabilities and shareholders' equity | $11,551 | (35) | $11,516 |

The $80 million debit to Retained earnings reflects the fact that Apple's net income in 2005 and prior years was overstated because employee compensation expense was understated. This adjustment to Retained earnings is net of tax effects. The $1 million debit to Deferred stock compensation reflects compensation related to the option issuances that had not yet been earned as of the balance sheet date (September 24, 2005). The credit of $43 million to Common stock reflects additional paid-in capital that should have been recognized when the in-the-money options were granted to employees. The credit to Accrued expenses is difficult to trace. One possibility is that this represents an accrual of a tax penalty that Apple expects to pay to the IRS because it failed to withhold taxes on compensation paid to employees when they received the backdated in-the-money options. Finally, the credit to Other assets is needed because Apple overstated the expected tax benefit associated with the backdated option grants.

- This chapter outlines the special accounting procedures used when revenue recognition doesn't occur at the point of sale.

- The "critical event" and "measurability" conditions for revenue recognition are typically satisfied at point of sale.

- In some circumstances—long-term construction contracts, production of natural resources and agricultural commodities—it is appropriate to recognize revenue prior to sale.

- Revenue recognition may also be delayed until after the sale, specifically, when cash is collected. The installment sales method or cost recovery method is used when considerable uncertainty exists about the collectibility of the sales price or when significant costs that are difficult to predict will be incurred after the sale.

- Franchise sales, sales with right of return, and bundled sales (software sales) pose particularly challenging revenue recognition issues and statement users need to be aware of potential accounting abuses.

- The broad criteria for revenue and expense recognition leave room for considerable latitude and judgment. This flexibility in GAAP can sometimes be exploited by management to hide or misrepresent the underlying economic performance of a company.

- This chapter outlines some of the more common ways to manage earnings that have come under SEC scrutiny. Later chapters provide further examples of how earnings can be manipulated.

- Auditors and financial statement users must be aware of management's incentives to manage earnings and the ways in which this is accomplished. Armed with this knowledge, you will be in a much better position to spot potential "accounting irregularities" and to avoid their unpleasant consequences.

- Once discovered, accounting errors or irregularities must be corrected and disclosed. Errors discovered after the year in which they occur are corrected through a prior period adjustment to Retained earnings.

**EXERCISES**

The following data pertain to Pell Company's construction jobs, which commenced during 2008:

**E3-1**

Long-term construction contract accounting

**AICPA**
ADAPTED

| | Project 1 | Project 2 |
|---|---|---|
| Contract price | $420,000 | $300,000 |
| Costs incurred during 2008 | 240,000 | 280,000 |
| Estimated cost to complete | 120,000 | 40,000 |
| Billed to customers during 2008 | 150,000 | 270,000 |
| Received from customers during 2008 | 90,000 | 250,000 |

**Required:**

1. If Pell used the completed-contract method, what amount of gross profit (loss) would it report in its 2008 income statement?

2. If Pell used the percentage-of-completion method, what amount of gross profit (loss) would it report in its 2008 income statement?

| | |
|---|---|
| **E3-2**<br><br>Determining gross profit under percentage of completion<br><br>AICPA<br>ADAPTED | Haft Construction Company has consistently applied the percentage-of-completion method. On January 10, 2008, Haft began work on a $3,000,000 construction contract. At the inception date, the estimated cost of construction was $2,250,000. The following data relate to the progress of the contract: |

|  |  |
|---|---|
| Income recognized at 12/31/08 | $ 300,000 |
| Costs incurred 1/10/08 through 12/31/09 | 1,800,000 |
| Estimated cost to complete at 12/31/09 | 600,000 |

**Required:**

In its income statement for the year ended December 31, 2009, what amount of gross profit should Haft report?

---

| | |
|---|---|
| **E3-3**<br><br>Determining gross profit using installment sales<br><br>AICPA<br>ADAPTED | Lang Company uses the installment method of revenue recognition. The following data pertain to its installment sales for the years ended December 31, 2008 and 2009: |

| | **2008** | **2009** |
|---|---|---|
| Installment receivables at year-end on 2008 sales | $60,000 | $30,000 |
| Installment receivables at year-end on 2009 sales | — | 69,000 |
| Installment sales | 80,000 | 90,000 |
| Cost of sales | 40,000 | 60,000 |

**Required:**

What amount should Lang report as deferred gross profit in its December 31, 2008 and 2009 balance sheets?

---

| | |
|---|---|
| **E3-4**<br><br>Determining gross profit using the installment sales method<br><br>AICPA<br>ADAPTED | Because there is no reasonable basis for estimating the degree of collectibility, Astor Company uses the installment method of revenue recognition for the following sales: |

| | **2008** | **2007** |
|---|---|---|
| Sales | $900,000 | $600,000 |
| Collections from: | | |
| 2007 sales | 100,000 | 200,000 |
| 2008 sales | 300,000 | — |
| Accounts written off: | | |
| 2007 sales | 150,000 | 50,000 |
| 2008 sales | 50,000 | — |
| Gross profit percentage | 40% | 30% |

**Required:**

What amount should Astor report as deferred gross profit in its December 31, 2008 balance sheet for the 2007 and 2008 sales?

---

| | |
|---|---|
| **E3-5**<br><br>Determining realized gross profit using the installment method<br><br>AICPA<br>ADAPTED | On January 2, 2008, Yardley Company sold a plant to Ivory Inc. for $1,500,000. On that date, the plant's carrying cost was $1,000,000. Ivory gave Yardley $300,000 cash and a $1,200,000 note, payable in four annual installments of $300,000 cash plus 12% interest. Ivory made the first principal and interest payment of $444,000 on December 31, 2008. Yardley uses the installment method of revenue recognition. |

**Required:**

In its 2008 income statement, what amount of realized gross profit should Yardley report?

Taft Corporation, which began business on January 1, 2008, appropriately uses the installment sales method of accounting. The following data are available for December 31, 2008 and 2009:

| | 2008 | 2009 |
|---|---|---|
| Balance of deferred gross profit on sales on account for: | | |
| 2008 | $300,000 | $120,000 |
| 2009 | | 440,000 |
| Gross profit on sales | 30% | 40% |

**Required:**

The Installment accounts receivable balances at December 31, 2008 and 2009 would be how much?

**E3-6**

Determining installment accounts receivable

AICPA
ADAPTED

Kul Company, which began operations on January 1, 2008, appropriately uses the installment sales method of accounting. The following information is available for 2008:

| | |
|---|---|
| Installment accounts receivable, December 31, 2008 | $400,000 |
| Deferred gross profit, December 31, 2008 | |
| (before recognition of realized gross profit for 2008) | 280,000 |
| Gross profit on sales | 40% |

**Required:**

For the year ended December 31, 2008, cash collections and realized gross profit on installment sales should be how much?

**E3-7**

Determining realized gross profit on installment sales

AICPA
ADAPTED

On December 31, 2008, Rice, Inc. authorized Graf to operate as a franchise for an initial franchise fee of $150,000. Of this amount, $60,000 was received upon signing the agreement and the balance, represented by a note, is due in three annual payments of $30,000 each, beginning December 31, 2009. The present value on December 31, 2008 of the three annual payments appropriately discounted is $72,000. According to the agreement, the nonrefundable down payment represents a fair measure of the services already performed by Rice; however, substantial future services are required of Rice. Collectibility of the note is reasonably certain.

**Required:**

In Rice's December 31, 2008 balance sheet, unearned franchise fees from Graf's franchise should be reported as how much?

**E3-8**

Determining deferred franchise fee revenue

AICPA
ADAPTED

For $50 a month, Rawl Company visits its customers' premises and performs insect control services. If customers experience problems between regularly scheduled visits, Rawl makes service calls at no additional charge. Instead of paying monthly, customers may pay an annual fee of $540 in advance.

**Required:**

For a customer who pays the annual fee in advance, Rawl should recognize the related revenue in what amounts and when?

**E3-9**

Determining revenue recognized with advanced fees

AICPA
ADAPTED

Dunne Company sells equipment service contracts that cover a two-year period. Each contract's sales price is $600. Dunne's past experience is that, of the total dollars spent for repairs on service contracts, 40% is incurred evenly during the first contract year and 60% evenly during the second contract year. Dunne sold 1,000 contracts evenly throughout 2008.

**Required:**

In its December 31, 2008 balance sheet, what amount should Dunne report as deferred service contract revenue?

**E3-10**

Determining deferred service contract revenue

AICPA
ADAPTED

| | | |
|---|---|---|
| **E3-11** | | |

Determining account
balances under installment
sales method

**AICPA**
ADAPTED

Bear Company, which began operations on January 2, 2008, appropriately uses the installment sales method of accounting. The following information is available for 2008:

| | |
|---|---|
| Installment sales | $1,400,000 |
| Realized gross profit on installment sales | 240,000 |
| Gross profit percentage on sales | 40% |

**Required:**
For the year ended December 31, 2008, what amounts should Bear report as accounts receivable and deferred gross profit?

**E3-12**

Determining gross profit and
deferred gross profit under
the installment method

**AICPA**
ADAPTED

Baker Company is a real estate developer that began operations on January 2, 2008. It appropriately uses the installment method of revenue recognition. Baker's sales are made on the basis of a 10% down payment with the balance payable over 30 years. Baker's gross profit percentage is 40%. Relevant information for Baker's first two years of operations follows:

| | 2009 | 2008 |
|---|---|---|
| Sales | $16,000,000 | $14,000,000 |
| Cash collections | 2,020,000 | 1,400,000 |

**Required:**
1. At December 31, 2008, Baker's deferred gross profit was how much?
2. Baker's realized gross profit for 2009 was how much?

**E3-13**

Determining unearned
franchise fees

**AICPA**
ADAPTED

Each of Potter Pie Co.'s 21 new franchisees contracted to pay an initial franchise fee of $30,000. By December 31, 2008, each franchisee had paid a nonrefundable $10,000 fee and signed a note to pay $10,000 principal plus the market rate of interest on December 31, 2009, and December 31, 2010. Experience indicates that one franchisee will default on the additional payments. Services for the initial fee will be performed in 2009.

**Required:**
What amount of net unearned franchise fees would Potter report at December 31, 2008?

**E3-14**

Cost recovery method

**AICPA**
ADAPTED

Several of Fox, Inc.'s customers are having cash flow problems. Information pertaining to these customers for the year ended March 31, 2007 and 2008 follows:

| | 3/31/07 | 3/31/08 |
|---|---|---|
| Sales | $10,000 | $15,000 |
| Cost of sales | 8,000 | 9,000 |
| Cash collections | | |
| on 2007 sales | 7,000 | 3,000 |
| on 2008 sales | — | 12,000 |

**Required:**
If the cost recovery method is used, what amount would Fox report as gross profit from sales for the year ended March 31, 2008?

**E3-15**

Journal entries: Point-of-sale,
cost recovery, and installment
sales methods

On August 19, 2008, Lewisburg Steel Company sold building materials to Coyne Construction for $600,000, collecting $200,000 on delivery of the materials. The $400,000 balance due plus interest at a market rate on the unpaid balance will be repaid as follows:

| Payment Date | Payment Amount |
|---|---|
| August 19, 2009 | $150,000 |
| August 19, 2010 | 150,000 |
| August 19, 2011 | 100,000 |

The building materials cost Lewisburg Steel $390,000. The company uses a perpetual inventory system (that is, cost of the goods is subtracted from inventory when the sale occurs).

**Required:**

1. Prepare the required journal entries for 2008, 2009, and 2010 using point-of-sale revenue recognition (ignore interest revenue).

2. Repeat requirement 1 using the cost recovery method.

3. Repeat requirement 1 using the installment sales method.

---

On August 1, 2008, Flintstone Company sold inventory to Rubble Company for $400,000. This inventory's original cost was $100,000. The sales contract stipulates that Rubble make a 10% down payment followed by four annual installments on each August 1, beginning August 1, 2009. Flintstone employs a perpetual inventory system under which inventory is decreased by the cost of merchandise sold at time of sale.

| **E 3-16** |

Journal entries: Point-of-sale, installment sales, and cost recovery methods

**Required:**

1. Prepare the necessary journal entries for 2008 and 2009 using point-of-sale revenue recognition.

2. Repeat requirement 1 using the installment sales method.

3. Repeat requirement 1 using the cost recovery method.

4. Typically, interest charges are also included in financing arrangements like this one between Flintstone and Rubble. How would the consideration of interest impact your answer to requirement 1?

---

On April 1, 2008, Oversized Burrito Company entered into a 10-year franchise agreement with a group of individuals. The company receives a $300,000 initial franchise fee and agrees to assist in the design of the building, help secure financing, and provide management advice over the first half of the franchise agreement. A down payment of 20% of the franchise fee is due on April 1, 2008. The remaining 80% is to be payable in eight equal installments beginning on April 1, 2009.

| **E 3-17** |

Franchise sales: Revenue recognition

Assume that services to be performed by Oversized Burrito between April 1, 2008 and August 15, 2008, the date that the franchise opened, are substantial and that the installment receivable is reasonably collectible. Also assume that substantial performance of the initial services has occurred as of August 15, 2008.

**Required:**

1. Prepare the necessary journal entries for Oversized Burrito for April 1, 2008 (ignore interest).

2. Prepare the necessary journal entries for August 15, 2008 (ignore interest).

---

Healthy & Tasty Food Company entered into an agreement with a franchisee on July 1, 2008. The agreement specified that Healthy & Tasty receive an initial franchise fee of $150,000 (20% due at signing; the balance to be paid in equal annual installments plus interest at 9% of the unpaid balance beginning July 1, 2009). The franchise fee comprises (1) consideration for the right to operate the franchise and (2) payment for services to be performed by Healthy & Tasty that include site selection and building design, employee training, and management training. Substantial performance of these services is deemed to have occurred when the franchise opens for business in March 2009. Healthy & Tasty allocates the fee equally between the two elements.

| **E 3-18** |

Franchise sales

**Required:**

1. Prepare the entry to record the signing of the franchise agreement and receipt of the payment due at that time.

2. Prepare any adjusting journal entries necessitated by this agreement at December 31, 2008.

3. Prepare the entry Healthy & Tasty should make when the franchise opens in March 2009.

| | |
|---|---|
| **E3-19**<br><br>Revenue recognition:<br>Bundled sales | Megabyte Software Developers shipped its tax return preparation product to a customer on September 15, 2008. In addition to the software, Megabyte's contract requires the company to provide (1) training to the customer's accounting staff during October of 2008, (2) technical product support for one year starting October 1, 2008, and (3) an upgrade early in 2009 to the software that reflects last-minute changes in tax laws affecting tax returns for 2008. The customer paid the total contract price of $85,000 prior to product shipment. Megabyte would charge the following if these individual contract elements were sold separately: |

|  | **Fair Value** |
|---|---|
| Tax return preparation software | $ 70,000 |
| Training customer's staff | 10,000 |
| Customer support | 15,000 |
| Software upgrade | 5,000 |
| Total fair value | $100,000 |

**Required:**

1. Prepare a journal entry to record receipt of the cash payment.

2. Determine the amount of revenue to be recognized in 2008 and prepare the necessary journal entry.

| | |
|---|---|
| **E3-20**<br><br>Installment sales and cost<br>recovery methods | York's Rustic Furniture began operations on January 1, 2008. To build its customer base, the company permitted customers, regardless of their credit history, to pay in installments when they made a major purchase. Installment sales amounted to $750,000 in 2008; these items cost York's Rustic Furniture $400,000. Given the questionable credit histories of many of its customers and its inability to use past history to estimate collection rates, the company adopted the cost recovery method and accordingly recognized $75,000 in gross profit. |

**Required:**

1. How much cash did the company collect on installment sales in 2008?

2. Assume that York's Rustic Furniture had instead used the installment sales method. What amount of gross profit would it have deferred in 2008?

| | |
|---|---|
| **E3-21**<br><br>Error correction/Prior<br>period adjustment | Terry, Inc. is a calendar year corporation whose financial statements for 2006 and 2007 included errors as follows: |

| Year | Ending<br>Inventory | Depreciation<br>Expense |
|---|---|---|
| 2006 | $15,000 overstated | $12,500 overstated |
| 2007 | 5,000 understated | 4,000 understated |

Assume that purchases were recorded correctly and that no correcting entries were made at December 31, 2006, or December 31, 2007.

**Required:**

1. Ignoring income taxes, what amount should Terry report as a prior period adjustment to the beginning Retained earnings in its statement of retained earnings at January 1, 2008?

2. Give the journal entries that Terry would make in 2008 to correct the errors.

| | |
|---|---|
| **E3-22**<br><br>Error correction/Prior<br>period adjustment | Tack, Inc. reported a Retained earnings balance of $150,000 at December 31, 2007. In June 2008, Tack's internal audit staff discovered two errors that were made in preparing the 2007 financial statements that are considered material: |

a. Merchandise costing $40,000 was mistakenly omitted from the 2007 ending inventory.

b. Equipment purchased on July 1, 2007 for $70,000 was mistakenly charged to a repairs expense account. The equipment should have been capitalized and depreciated using straight-line depreciation, a 10-year useful life, and $10,000 salvage value.

**Required:**

1. What amount should Tack report as a prior period adjustment to beginning Retained earnings at January 1, 2008? (Ignore taxes.)

2. Give the journal entries that Tack would make in June 2008 to correct the errors made in 2007. Assume that depreciation for 2008 is made as a year-end adjusting entry. (Ignore taxes.)

---

Krafty Kris, Inc. discovered the following errors after the 2008 financial statements were issued:

**E3-23**

**Correction of errors/Prior period adjustment**

a. A major supplier shipped inventory valued at $8,550 to Krafty Kris on consignment. This merchandise was mistakenly included in the inventory taken by Krafty Kris on December 31, 2007. (Goods shipped on consignment are the property of the consignor and should be included in its inventory.)

b. Krafty Kris renewed its liability insurance policy on October 1, 2007, paying a $36,000 premium and debiting Insurance expense. No further entries have been made. The premium purchased insurance coverage for a period of 36 months.

c. Repair expense was debited at the time equipment was purchased for $100,000 on January 8, 2008. The equipment has a life of five years; its salvage value is considered immaterial. Krafty uses straight-line depreciation method.

**Required:**

1. Prepare journal entries to correct these errors. Ignore income taxes.

2. Assuming that these errors remain uncorrected, explain their effects on the 2009 financial statements issued by Krafty Kris, Inc.

## PROBLEMS / DISCUSSION QUESTIONS

Mai Fuji started a business on January 1, 2008. Key operating statistics for 2008 were as follows:

**P3-1**

**Income measurement under alternative revenue recognition rules**

| | |
|---|---|
| Beginning inventory | 0 |
| Number of units produced | 20,000 |
| Number of units sold (delivery basis) | 16,000 |
| Number of units sold for which cash has been received by December 31, 2008 | 14,000 |

Direct production costs were $12 per unit. There were no fixed costs or selling/delivery expenses. The selling price per unit was $16.

On January 1, 2009, Fuji decided to liquidate the business. She sold the remaining inventory at $13 per unit for cash. By January 15, 2009, she collected the amount due from customers for sales made during 2008.

**Required:**

Based on the preceding information, compute Fuji's net income for the years 2008 and 2009 under

1. Production basis.

2. Sales (or delivery) basis.

3. Cash collection basis.

---

Agri Pro, a farm corporation, produced 15,000 bushels of wheat in its first year of operations. During the year, it sold 10,000 bushels of the grain produced for $2.40 per bushel and collected three-fourths of the selling price on the grain sold; the balance is to be collected in equal amounts during each of the two following years. The local grain elevator is quoting

**P3-2**

**Income determination under alternative bases of revenue recognition**

a year-end market price of $3.00 per bushel. Additional data for the first year are as follows:

| | |
|---|---:|
| Depreciation on equipment | $ 3,000 |
| Other production costs (cash)—per bushel | 0.50 |
| Miscellaneous administrative costs (cash) | 4,000 |
| Selling and delivery costs (incurred and paid at | |
| time of sale), per bushel | 0.10 |
| Dividends paid to stockholders during year | 10,000 |
| Interest on borrowed money (1/2 paid in cash) | 5,000 |

Agri Pro is enthusiastic about the accountant's concept of matching product costs with revenues.

**Required:**

Compute net income under each of the following methods and determine the carrying (book) value of inventory and accounts receivable at the end of the first year of operation for each of these methods.

1. Recognize revenue when production is complete.

2. Recognize revenue at point of sale.

3. Recognize revenue on an installment (cash collection) basis.

---

| | |
|---|---|
| **P 3 - 3**<br><br>Determining pre-tax income and accounts receivable using the installment method | Lowery, Inc., an Arizona land speculator, started business on May 1, 2008. It sold 700 acres of desert sand to a local developer for $960 an acre. Lowery is paid 60% of the selling price when the contract is signed, with the balance due in 24 months; however, collection is not assured. Lowery's property acquisition costs were $350 per acre and property taxes of $75,000 were paid during the year. |

**Required:**

Compute Lowery's 2008 pre-tax income and determine its Accounts receivable balance at December 31, 2008, using the installment sales method.

---

| | |
|---|---|
| **P 3 - 4**<br><br>Determining pre-tax income, inventory carrying value, and accounts receivable under sales and production basis | Howe, Inc., a Texas crude oil producer, started business on May 1, 2008. It sells all of its production, F.O.B. shipping point, to a single customer at the current spot price for West Texas crude. The customer pays Howe 60% of the selling price on delivery with the remaining to be paid in 10 months. Throughout 2008, the oil spot market price was $28 per barrel; however, on December 31, 2008, the market price jumped to $31 per barrel, where it is expected to remain. Howe's direct production costs are $12 per barrel, drilling equipment depreciation expense totaled $180,000 for the eight-month period ending December 31, and property taxes of $75,000 were paid during the year. Howe produced 30,000 barrels of oil of which 6,000 barrels were included in January 1, 2009 opening inventory. |

**Required:**

Compute Howe's 2008 pre-tax income and determine its inventory carrying value and Accounts receivable balance at December 31, 2008 under the following:

1. Production basis.

2. Sales (completed transaction) basis.

3. Installment (cash collection) basis.

---

| | |
|---|---|
| **P 3 - 5**<br><br>Percentage-of-completion accounting | In 2008, Long Construction began work under a three-year contract whose price is $800,000. Long uses the percentage-of-completion method for financial accounting purposes. The income to be recognized each year is based on the proportion of cost incurred to total estimated |

costs for completing the contract. The financial statement presentations relating to this contract at December 31, 2008, follow:

AICPA
ADAPTED

**Balance Sheet**

| | |
|---|---|
| Accounts receivable—construction contract billings | $15,000 |
| Construction in progress | 50,000 |
| Less: Contract billings | (47,000) |
| Construction in progress less billings | $ 3,000 |

**Income Statement**

| | |
|---|---|
| Income (before tax) on the contract recognized in 2008 | $10,000 |

**Required:**

1. How much cash was collected in 2008 on this contract?
2. What was the initial estimated total cost on this project?
3. What is the estimated total income (before tax) on this contract?

---

MSK Construction Company contracted to construct a factory building for $525,000. Construction started during 2008 and was completed in 2009. Information relating to the contract follows:

**P3-6**

Long-term construction contract accounting

| | 2008 | 2009 |
|---|---|---|
| Costs incurred during the year | $290,000 | $150,000 |
| Estimated additional cost to complete | 145,000 | — |
| Billings during the year | 260,000 | 265,000 |
| Cash collections during the year | 240,000 | 285,000 |

**Required:**

Record the preceding transactions in MSK's books under the completed-contract and the percentage-of-completion methods. Determine amounts that will be reported on the balance sheet at the end of 2008.

---

Maple Corporation sells farm machinery on the installment plan. On July 1, 2008, it entered into an installment sale contract with Agriculture, Inc., for an eight-year period. Equal annual payments under the installment sale are $100,000 and are due on July 1. The first payment was made on July 1, 2008. Additional information follows:

**P3-7**

Determining income under installment sales method

AICPA
ADAPTED

- The amount that would be realized on an outright sale of similar farm machinery is $556,000.
- The cost of the farm machinery sold to Agriculture is $417,000.
- The finance charges relating to the installment period are $244,000 based on a stated interest rate of 12%, which is appropriate.
- Circumstances are such that the collection of the installments due under the contract is reasonably assured.

**Required:**

What income or loss before income taxes should Maple record for the year ended December 31, 2008 as a result of this transaction? Show supporting computations in good form.

---

Englewood Marine builds 30-foot fiberglass fishing boats, which it markets through a network of third-party dealers on a consignment basis. The consignment agreement stipulates that Englewood retains title to the boats until final sale to the customer. Dealers can return unsold boats to Englewood by paying shipping expenses and a financing fee for the time held. Each boat's cost to dealers is fixed at $28,000. Englewood's gross profit margin per boat is 30%.

**P3-8**

Revenue recognition for goods on consignment

Englewood shipped 41 boats to dealers during the six months ending October 31. Shipments were:

| Monthly Boat Shipments to Dealers | |
| --- | --- |
| May—3 | August—9 |
| June—6 | September—8 |
| July—8 | October—7 |

Dealers had three Englewood boats on hand for the quarter ended July 31 and two boats on hand at October 31.

**Required:**

1. Prepare a schedule showing Englewood's revenues, cost of goods sold, and gross profit for the quarters ending July 31 and October 31.

2. Indicate how Englewood would report the unsold boats and for how much at July 31 and October 31.

---

**P3-9**

Revenue recognition based on delivery performance

Composite, Inc. manufactures modular homes. Due to lack of storage space for raw material inventories, Composite implemented a just-in-time inventory process in early 2006. Composite contracts with qualified vendors to be sole suppliers for a given raw material. In return, the vendors guarantee performance in accordance with Composite's purchase order.

On Friday, November 2, 2008, Composite placed a purchase order with Mogul Chemical Company for plastic resins. Composite's purchase order specifically states that all material is shipped so that Composite takes title to the goods when they are received. Delivery is to be made at 6:00 a.m. on the designated delivery date. Designated delivery date, number of pounds, and selling price per pound are:

| Delivery Date | Pounds | Selling Price per Pound |
| --- | --- | --- |
| Friday, November 30, 2008 | 75,000 | $1.00 |
| Friday, December 7, 2008 | 80,000 | 1.00 |
| Friday, December 14, 2008 | 60,000 | 1.10 |
| Friday, December 21, 2008 | 50,000 | 1.20 |
| Friday, January 4, 2009 | 50,000 | 1.20 |

In December, Mogul Chemical experienced a slowdown in sales and decided to produce Composite's January 2009 order over the Christmas holidays. After completing the production on December 29, the material was promptly loaded on a staged trailer, which was immediately locked and sealed. An invoice and a bill of lading were prepared. The invoice was then sent to Composite on a "bill and hold" basis.

Upon receiving the invoice, Composite contacted Mogul and was told that the material was invoiced because Mogul wanted to include the sale in the quarter ended December 31, 2008. However, actual delivery would take place according to the purchase order terms. Composite accepted the explanation.

**Required:**

1. Determine the sales revenue that Mogul should recognize on transactions with Composite for the quarter ended December 31, 2008.

2. What would Mogul's justification be for including the production on December 29 in its December sales?

3. Should Mogul include the December 29 production in its December sales? Why or why not?

DW Hooks is a customer-oriented retailer of high-definition televisions and other similar electronic and computer equipment. Hooks accepts layaway sales provided the customer makes a minimum down payment of 20% of the retail price and pays the balance off within 90 days. After the customer makes the initial deposit, Hooks transfers the merchandise from the Retail inventory account to the Layaway—Merchandise inventory account. Inventory is valued at approximately 80% of the retail selling price. When the layaway sale is paid in full, Hooks delivers the merchandise to the customer.

At January 31, 2008, Hooks had $72,000 of merchandise on layaway for which customers had made cash deposits totaling $55,000. For the quarter ending April 30, 2008, Hooks had the following layaway transactions:

| Month | Amounts Added to Layaway Inventory | Deposits Made During Month | Deliveries Cost | Deliveries Retail |
|---|---|---|---|---|
| February | $49,000 | $45,000 | $24,000 | $30,000 |
| March | 50,000 | 67,000 | 56,000 | 70,000 |
| April | 40,000 | 51,000 | 48,000 | 60,000 |

**Required:**

1. Prepare the journal entries required to record these transactions.

2. Prepare a schedule showing sales revenue earned for the period, and reconcile the balances in layaway and customer deposits at January 31, 2008 to April 30, 2008.

3. How should Hook report the customer deposits in its financial statements?

**P3-10**

Revenue recognition on layaways

On July 1, 2008, Quincy Company sold a piece of industrial equipment to Tana Company for $200,000. The equipment cost Quincy $80,000 to manufacture. Per the sales agreement, Tana made a 20% down payment and paid the remaining balance in four equal quarterly installments plus 10% on the unpaid balance, starting October 1, 2008.

**Required:**

1. Identify and explain three alternative methods for revenue and cost recognition available to Quincy in this scenario.

2. Calculate the amount of gross profit recognized in 2008 under each of the alternatives identified in requirement 1.

3. Elaborate on what circumstances would have to exist for each alternative to be employed.

**P3-11**

Alternative bases of revenue recognition

Founded in 1989, Brio Software, Inc. helps Global 3000 companies improve business performance by creating new value from existing information systems and, ultimately, aligning everyone in the enterprise with key corporate goals. Brio's business intelligence software lets companies access, analyze and share information, offering users relevant, accurate and timely insight into the variables that impact their business. With this insight, companies can make superior business decisions.

The following information appears in Brio Software's 10-K report regarding its revenue recognition policies:

**P3-12**

Bundled services

## Revenue Recognition

Brio derives revenues from two sources, perpetual license fees and services. Services include software maintenance and support, training and consulting, and system implementation services. Maintenance and support consist of technical support and software upgrades and enhancements. Significant management judgments and estimates are made and used to determine the revenue recognized in any accounting period. Material differences may result in the amount and timing of Brio's revenue for any period if different conditions were to prevail.

Brio applies the provisions of *Statement of Position (SOP) 97-2*, "Software Revenue Recognition," as amended by *SOP 98-9*, "Modification of SOP 97-2, Software Revenue Recognition, With Respect to Certain Transactions" and related technical practice aids to all transactions involving the sale of software products.

Brio recognizes product revenue when persuasive evidence of an arrangement exists, the product has been delivered, the fee is fixed or determinable, and collection of the resulting receivable is probable. In software arrangements that include rights to multiple elements, such as software products and services, Brio uses the residual method under which revenue is allocated to the undelivered elements based on vendor-specific objective evidence (VSOE) of the fair value of such undelivered elements. VSOE of the undelivered elements is determined based on the price charged when such elements are sold separately. The residual amount of revenue is allocated to delivered elements and recognized as revenue. Such undelivered elements in these arrangements typically consist of services.

Brio uses a purchase order or a signed contract as persuasive evidence of an arrangement for sales of software, maintenance renewals, and training. Sales through Brio's value added resellers, private label partners, resellers, system integrators, and distributors (collectively "resellers") are evidenced by a master agreement governing the relationship with binding purchase orders on a transaction-by-transaction basis. Brio uses a signed statement of work to evidence an arrangement for consulting and system implementation services.

Software is delivered to customers electronically or on a CD-ROM. Brio assesses whether the fee is fixed or determinable based on the payment terms associated with the transaction. Brio's standard payment terms are generally less than 90 days. When payments are subject to extended payment terms, revenue is deferred until payments become due, which is generally when the payment is received. Brio assesses collectibility based on a number of factors, including the customer's past payment history and its current creditworthiness. If Brio determines that collection of a fee is not probable, it defers the revenue and recognizes it when collection becomes probable, which is generally on receipt of cash payment. If an acceptance period is other than in accordance with standard user documentation, revenue is recognized on the earlier of customer acceptance or the expiration of the acceptance period.

When licenses are sold with consulting and system implementation services, license fees are recognized upon shipment provided that (1) the preceding criteria have been met, (2) payment of the license fees does not depend on the performance of the consulting and system implementation services, (3) the services are not essential to the functionality of the software, and (4) VSOE exists for the undelivered elements. For arrangements that do not meet these criteria, both the product license revenues and services revenues are recognized in accordance with the provisions of *SOP 81-1*, "Accounting for Performance of Construction Type and Certain Production Type Contracts." Brio accounts for the arrangements under the completed-contract method pursuant to *SOP 81-1* because reliable estimates are typically not available for the costs and efforts necessary to complete the consulting and system implementation services.

The majority of Brio's consulting and system implementation services qualify for separate accounting. Brio uses VSOE of fair value for the services and maintenance to account for the arrangement using the residual method, regardless of any separate prices stated within the contract for each element. Brio's consulting and system implementation service contracts are bid either on a fixed-fee basis or on a time-and-materials basis. For a fixed-fee contract, Brio recognizes revenue using the completed-contract method. For time-and-materials contracts, Brio recognizes revenue as services are performed.

Maintenance and support revenue is recognized ratably over the term of the maintenance contract, which is typically one year. Training revenue is recognized when the training is provided.

---

Assume that Brio enters into a contract with a customer for deliverable software and services as follows. The prices listed are those quoted in the contract.

| | |
|---|---:|
| Perpetual license fee | $ 650,000 |
| Elements undelivered at contract signing: | |
|    Technical support | 120,000 |
|    Training | 80,000 |
|    System implementation services | 100,000 |
|    Software upgrades and enhancements | 50,000 |
| Total contract price | $1,000,000 |

These contract elements, if purchased separately, would be priced as follows:

| | |
|---|---:|
| Perpetual license fee | $ 840,000 |
| Elements undelivered at contract signing: | |
| Technical support | 120,000 |
| Training | 72,000 |
| System implementation services | 108,000 |
| Software upgrades and enhancements | 60,000 |
| Total contract price | $1,200,000 |

**Required:**

1. Following Brio's stated revenue recognition policies, how much revenue would it recognize on this contract?

2. Prepare the journal entry to record receipt of the signed contract and electronic delivery of the software. Assume that the sale conforms to Brio's normal billing terms and that collectibility is not an issue.

3. How much revenue would Brio recognize on this contract if the various elements included in the contract were not sold separately?

---

Roxio, Inc. is a leading provider of digital media software and services for the consumer market. The company provides software that enables individuals to record digital content onto CDs and DVDs and offers photo and video editing products. Roxio's Form 10-K for the year ended March 31, 2003 reported the following information:

**P3-13**

Sales with right of return

### Roxio, Inc.

| | Selected Financial Data for the Years Ended March 31 | | |
|---|---|---|---|
| ($ in 000s) | 2001 | 2002 | 2003 |
| Net revenues | $121,908 | $142,521 | $120,408 |
| Net income | 3,570 | 2,349 | (9,944) |
| Allowance for sales returns and certain sales incentives: | | | |
| Balance at beginning of period | 2,186 | 4,602 | 5,492 |
| Additions | 8,351 | 16,286 | 18,333 |
| Deductions | 5,935 | 15,396 | 16,749 |
| Balance at the end of period | 4,602 | 5,492 | 7,076 |

### Business Risks

We rely on distributors and retailers to sell our products. If our distributors attempt to reduce their levels of inventory or if they do not maintain sufficient levels to meet customer demand, our sales could be negatively impacted. If we reduce the prices of our products to our distributors, we may have to compensate them for the difference between the higher price they paid to buy their inventory and the new lower prices. In addition, we are exposed to the risk of product returns from distributors through their exercise of contractual return rights.

### Revenue Recognition

For software product sales to distributors, revenues are recognized on product shipment to the distributors or receipt of the products by the distributor, depending on the shipping terms, provided that all fees are fixed or determinable, evidence of an arrangement exists, and collectibility is probable. Our distributor arrangements provide distributors certain product rotation rights. Additionally, we permit our distributors to return products in certain circumstances, generally during periods of product transition. End users additionally have the right to return their product within 30 days of the purchase. We establish allowances for expected product returns in accordance with *SFAS No. 48,* "Revenue Recognition When

Right of Return Exists," and *SAB 101*. These allowances are recorded as a direct reduction of revenues and accounts receivable. Management applies significant judgment and relies on historical experience in establishing these allowances. If future return patterns differ from past return patterns due to reduced demand for our product or other factors beyond our control, we may be required to increase these allowances in the future and may be required to reduce future revenues. If at any point in the future we become unable to estimate returns reliably, we could be required to defer recognizing revenues until the distributor notifies us that the product has been sold to an end user. We provide for estimated product returns and pricing adjustments in the period in which the revenues are recognized.

**Required:**

1. Re-create (in summary form) the journal entries Roxio made in the Allowance for sales returns and certain sales incentives account for fiscal years 2001–2003. Explain the rising balance in this account.

2. Are opportunities for "earnings management" present in Roxio's stated accounting policies for expected product returns? Is there any evidence in the data presented that Roxio's management has availed themselves of any of the opportunities you identify?

3. Determine Roxio's gross revenues for fiscal years 2001–2003.

---

## P3-14
### Manipulation of receivables

Holman Electronics manufactures audio equipment, selling it through various distributors. Holman's days sales outstanding (Accounts receivable / Average daily credit sales) figures increased steadily in 2008 and then spiked dramatically in 2009, peaking at 120 days in the second quarter. In the third quarter of 2009, Holman's days sales outstanding figure dropped to 90 days. Its chief financial officer engineered this drop by artificially reducing the amount of outstanding accounts receivable. Channel partners with large outstanding receivables were pressured into signing notes for those amounts. Once sales personnel secured the notes, the CFO directed a reclassification entry to the general ledger converting more than $30 million in trade receivables into notes receivable, which are not included in the days sales outstanding calculation. This reclassification was not disclosed in the Form 10-Q that Holman filed for that quarter.

**Required:**

What might be the motive for the CFO's actions? Explain your answer.

---

## P3-15
### Correction of errors and worksheet preparation

GWH Enterprises began operations in January 2006 to manufacture a cleaning solution that promised to be more effective and less toxic than existing products. Family members, one of whom was delegated to be the office manager and bookkeeper, staffed the company. Although conscientious, the office manager lacked formal accounting training, which became apparent when the growing company was forced in March 2009 to hire a CPA as controller. Although ostensibly brought in to relieve some of the office manager's stress, management made it clear to the new controller that they had some concerns about the quality of information they were receiving. Accordingly, the controller made it a priority to review the records of prior years, looking for ways to improve the accounting system. From this review, the following errors were uncovered.

1. The office manager expensed rent on equipment and facilities when paid. Amounts paid in 2006, 2007, and 2008 that represent prepaid rent are $3,000, $3,500, and $4,600, respectively.

2. No adjusting entries were ever made to reflect accrued salaries. The amounts $7,000, $9,500, and $6,200 should have been accrued in each of the three prior years, respectively.

3. Errors occurred in the depreciation calculations that resulted in depreciation expense being understated by $2,500 in 2006, understated by $5,000 in 2007, and overstated by $4,000 in 2008.

4. In February 2009, some surplus production equipment was sold for $2,000 that originally had cost $7,000, and $6,000 in depreciation had correctly been taken on this equipment. The office manager made this entry to record the sale:

To record sale of surplus equipment

| | | |
|---|---|---|
| **DR** Cash ............................................... | $2,000 | |
| **DR** Accumulated Depreciation ........................... | 5,000 | |
| **CR** Equipment ....................................... | | $7,000 |

5. Utility expenses in the amount of $1,800 were incorrectly classified as selling expenses in 2008.

**Required:**

Complete the following worksheet to assist in preparing the correcting entry. (By way of example, the first required entry on the worksheet has been made.)

## Error Corrections Worksheet

| | Effect on Income | | | | Accounts to be Adjusted | |
|---|---|---|---|---|---|---|
| Description | 2006 | 2007 | 2008 | 2009 | Dr. | Cr. |
| Reported Income | $(18,000) | $27,000 | $25,000 | N/A | | |
| Item 1: | | | | | | |
| Prepaid rent—2006 | 3,000 | (3,000) | | | Counterbalancing error | |
| Prepaid rent—2007 | | | | | | |
| Prepaid rent—2008 | | | | | | |
| Item 2: | | | | | | |
| Accrued wages—2006 | | | | | | |
| Accrued wages—2007 | | | | | | |
| Accrued wages—2008 | | | | | | |
| Item 3: | | | | | | |
| Depreciation | | | | | | |
| Item 4: | | | | | | |
| Gain on machinery | | | | | | |
| Item 5: | | | | | | |
| Expense classification | | | | | | |
| Adjusted income | — | — | — | | | |

**P3-16**

Correcting errors/Prior period adjustment

In 2008, the new CEO of Watsontown Electric Supply became concerned about the company's apparently deteriorating financial position. Wishing to make certain that the grim monthly reports he was receiving from the company's bookkeeper were accurate, the CEO engaged a CPA firm to examine the company's financial records. The CPA firm discovered the following facts during the course of the engagement, which was completed prior to any adjusting or closing entries being prepared for 2008.

1. A new digital imaging system was acquired on January 5, 2007 at a cost of $5,000. Although this asset was expected to be in use for the next four years, the purchase was inadvertently charged to office expense. Per the company's accounting manual, office equipment of this type should be depreciated using the straight-line method with no salvage value assumed.

2. A used truck, purchased on November 18, 2008, was recorded with this entry:

To record truck expenditure:

| | | |
|---|---|---|
| **DR** Vehicle Expense ......................................... | $18,000 | |
| **CR** Cash ............................................ | | $18,000 |

Management plans to use this truck for three years and then trade it in on a new one. Salvage is estimated at $3,000. Watsontown has always used straight-line depreciation for fixed assets, recording a half-year of depreciation in the year the asset is acquired.

3. On July 1, 2008, the company rented a warehouse for three years. The lease agreement specified that each year's rent be paid in advance, so a check for the first year's rent of $18,000 was issued and recorded as an addition to the Buildings account.

4. Late in 2007, Watsontown collected $23,500 from a customer in full payment of his account. The cash receipt was credited to revenue. Two months before the audit, Watsontown's bookkeeper was reviewing outstanding receivables and noticed the outstanding balance. Knowing the customer in question had recently died, she wrote off the account. Because Watsontown seldom has bad debts, the company uses the direct write-off method whereby it charges Bad debts expense and credits Accounts receivable when an account is deemed uncollectible.

5. A three-year property and casualty insurance policy was purchased in January 2007 for $30,000. The entire amount was recorded as an insurance expense at the time.

6. On October 1, 2007, Watsontown borrowed $100,000 from a local bank. The loan terms specified annual interest payments of $8,000 on the anniversary date of the loan. The first interest payment was made on October 1, 2008 and expensed in its entirety.

**Required:**

Prepare any journal entry necessary to correct each error as well as any year-end adjusting entry for 2008 related to the described situation. Ignore income tax effects.

---

**P 3 - 1 7**

**General Motors restatement**

General Motors (GM) disclosed in a Form 8-K dated November 9, 2005, that it would restate its financial statements to correct the accounting for credits and other lump-sum payments from suppliers. Typically, suppliers offer an up-front payment in exchange for the customer's promise to purchase certain quantities of merchandise over time. Per GAAP, such "rebates" cannot be recognized until after the promised purchases occur.

As GM noted,

> GM erroneously recorded as a reduction to cost of sales certain payments and credits received from suppliers prior to completion of the earnings process. GM concluded that the payments and credits received were associated with agreements for the award of future services or products or other rights and privileges and should be recognized when subsequently earned.

Assume that GM signed a procurement contract on January 2, 2004, that obligated it to purchase 1 million tires each year for the next three years from one of its suppliers. As part of this agreement, GM received a cash payment of $75 million on January 5, 2004.

**Required:**

1. Given GM's past accounting practices for such rebates, what journal entry did the company make when it received the payment?

2. Had GM followed GAAP, what would the appropriate journal entry have been? Where would the account credited be shown on GM's financial statements?

3. Assume that GM made the entry you suggested in requirement 2. What adjusting entry, if any, would have been required at December 31, 2004? (Assume that GM reports on a calendar year basis and makes annual adjusting entries.)

4. Assume that GM "discovered" the error in its approach to recording supplier rebates on November 1, 2005. What entry would be necessary to restate GM's 2004 balance sheet? (Ignore income tax effects.)

5. What impact did GM's past accounting practices related to supplier credits and rebates have on reported net income in the year in which the rebate was received and in subsequent years?

Thomas Smith owns and operates a farm in Kansas. During 2008, he produced and harvested 40,000 bushels of wheat. He had no inventory of wheat at the start of the year. Immediately after harvesting the wheat in the late summer of 2008, Smith sold 30,000 bushels to a local grain elevator operator. As of December 31, 2008, he had received payment for 20,000 bushels. Additional information relating to the farm follows:

**C3-1**

Smith's Farm: Alternative bases of income determination

| | |
|---|---|
| **Price:** | |
| Market price per bushel at the time of harvest and sale to the grain elevator operator | $ 3.60 |
| Market price per bushel at December 31, 2008 | 3.60 |
| **Costs:** | |
| Variable production costs per bushel | 0.50 |
| Delivery costs per bushel | 0.20 |
| Annual fixed cost of operating the farm that are unrelated to the volume of production | $25,000 |

**Required:**

1. Prepare a 2008 income statement for Smith's farm under each of the following assumptions regarding what constitutes the "critical event" in the process of recognizing income:

   a. Assuming that production is the critical event.

   b. Assuming that the sale is the critical event.

   c. Assuming that cash collection is the critical event.

   (For simplicity, treat the fixed operating costs as period rather than product costs.)

2. Determine the December 31, 2008 balances for Wheat inventory and Accounts receivable under each of the three income recognition methods in requirement 1.

3. Assume that the farm is left idle during 2009. With no harvest, Smith's only transaction consists of an October 2009 sale of the 10,000 bushels in inventory at $2.80 per bushel. Further assume that no fixed costs are incurred while the farm is idle.

   Compute 2009 income on both the sale and production basis. Discuss the causes for any profit or loss reported under each income determination alternative.

London, Inc. began operation of its construction division on October 1, 2008 and entered into contracts for two separate projects. The Beta project contract price was $600,000 and provided for penalties of $10,000 per week for late completion. Although during 2009 the Beta project had been on schedule for timely completion, it was completed four weeks late in August 2010. The Gamma project's original contract price was $800,000. Change orders during 2010 added $40,000 to the original contract price. The following data pertain to the separate long-term construction projects in progress:

**C3-2**

London, Inc.: Determining gross profit under the percentage-of-completion method

**AICPA**
ADAPTED

| | Beta | Gamma |
|---|---|---|
| **As of September 30, 2009:** | | |
| Costs incurred to date | $360,000 | $410,000 |
| Estimated costs to complete | 40,000 | 410,000 |
| Billings | 315,000 | 440,000 |
| Cash collections | 275,000 | 365,000 |
| **As of September 30, 2010:** | | |
| Cost incurred to date | 450,000 | 720,000 |
| Estimated costs to complete | — | 180,000 |
| Billings | 560,000 | 710,000 |
| Cash collections | 560,000 | 625,000 |

### Additional Information

London accounts for its long-term construction contracts using the percentage-of-completion method for financial reporting purposes and the completed-contract method for income tax purposes.

### Required:

1. Prepare a schedule showing London's gross profit (loss) recognized for the years ended September 30, 2009 and 2010 under the percentage-of-completion method.

2. Prepare a schedule showing London's balances in the following accounts at September 30, 2009 under the percentage-of-completion method:

   • Accounts receivable

   • Costs and estimated earnings in excess of billings

   • Billings in excess of costs and estimated earnings

3. Determine how much income would be recognized if London used the completed-contract method for the 2009 and 2010 fiscal years.

---

**C3-3**

Stewart & Stevenson Services, Inc.: Understanding accounts used for long-term construction contract accounting

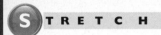

Stewart & Stevenson Services, Inc. manufactures motors and generators. The following is extracted from the Year 2 financial statements of Stewart & Stevenson Services, Inc.

|  | Year 2 | Year 1 |
|---|---|---|
| **Balance Sheet Items** | | |
| Accounts receivable | $143,166 | $121,030 |
| Costs incurred on uncompleted contracts | 190,670 | 70,766 |
| Accrued profits | 13,117 | 9,857 |
| Cost incurred + accrued profits | 203,787 | 80,623 |
| Less: Customer progress payments | (164,078) | (55,258) |
| Cost in excess of billings (net) | $ 39,709 | $ 25,365 |
| **Income Statement Items** | | |
| Sales revenue | $812,526 | $686,363 |
| Cost of sales | 685,879 | 569,695 |
| Gross margin | $126,647 | $116,668 |
| Gross margin rate | 15.6% | 17.0% |

Assumption: All sales revenue is from long-term construction contracts.

## Stewart & Stevenson Services, Inc.

### Construction in Process Inventory

| Beginning balance | $ 80,623 | |
|---|---|---|
| Ending balance | 203,787 | |

### Billings on Contract (Progress Payments)

| | $ 55,258 | Beginning balance |
|---|---|---|
| | 164,078 | Ending balance |

### Accounts Receivable

| Beginning balance | $121,030 | |
|---|---|---|
| Ending balance | 143,166 | |

### Required:

1. Using the preceding information, reconstruct the following T-accounts, showing how the accounts changed from their beginning to ending balances in Year 2.

2. Compute sales revenue, cost of goods sold, and gross margin assuming the company was using the completed-contract method during Year 2.

3. Assuming a tax effect rate of 40% and that the company switched from the percentage-of-completion method to the completed-contract method at the end of Year 2, provide the effect of this change of accounting principle on the accounting equation at the end of Year 2.

4. Assuming that the information on accrued profits is not available, estimate the gross margin assuming the company was using the completed-contract method during Year 2.

5. Explain the difference in the gross margins obtained from requirements 2 and 4.

6. Assuming that the information on accrued profits is not available, estimate the gross margin if revenue were recognized on a cash-collection basis.

---

**C3-4**

Revenue recognition:
Membership fees

Uncle Mike's is a discount club retailer that generates revenues from membership fees and selling products at discounted prices to its club members. To shop at its stores, the customer must purchase a $40 annual membership, which expires on December 31. The cost of the membership is prorated over the remaining months of the year; for example, the cost of a membership purchased in July would be $20 ($40 × 6 months/12 months). However, the customer has the right to cancel the membership at any time during the year and receive a full refund of the membership fee originally paid at the end of the respective calendar quarter.

Based on historical data and industry averages, Uncle Mike's estimates that 30% of its members will request a refund before the end of their membership period. Uncle Mike's data for the past 10 years indicates that significant variations between actual and estimated cancellations have not occurred. Furthermore, Uncle Mike's does not expect significant variations to occur in the foreseeable future.

During the calendar year ended December 31, 2008, Uncle Mike's quarterly membership refunds were as follows: March $54,900; June $18,715; September $8,803; and December $4,667. Memberships issued during the year were:

| Month | Number | Month | Number |
| --- | --- | --- | --- |
| January | 2,000 | July | 500 |
| February | 2,000 | August | 500 |
| March | 1,500 | September | 1,000 |
| April | 1,000 | October | 800 |
| May | 900 | November | 900 |
| June | 500 | December | 800 |

**Required:**

1. Prepare a schedule showing quarterly and annual membership fees earned by Uncle Mike's during 2008.

2. How would you initially classify the membership fees in Uncle Mike's financial statements?

3. How would your answer in requirement 1 change if Uncle Mike's could not accurately predict membership refunds?

---

**C3-5**

Revenue recognition: Goods
shipped to distributors with
right of return

GiveThree Inc., a maker of a popular series of video games for various systems, shipped several thousand units to three distributors of its games on December 20, 2008, to ensure that the anticipated heightened demand for its games would be met during the last two weeks of the calendar and fiscal year. The distributors were told to hold the shipments and to return any part of them that they couldn't sell after the first of the new year. The company planned to book the revenue associated with these shipments at the point of delivery to the distributors and to make an entry debiting Sales returns and allowances, which is a contra-revenue account (shown as a deduction from Sales revenue), in 2009 for any parts of the shipments that are ultimately returned.

**Required:**

1. Critically evaluate Give Three's proposed accounting treatment.

2. How should revenue related to these shipments be recognized in light of GAAP regarding revenue recognition?

3. Locate *The Wall Street Journal* article from February 14, 2002 entitled, "TakeTwo Announces SEC Investigation," and identify the primary accounting issue discussed in the article. You may be able to access it through Dow Jones News Retrieval or www.factiva.com if your library subscribes to these services.

---

**C3-6**

Channel stuffing

ClearOne Communications, Inc. is a provider of end-to-end video and audio conferencing services, including the manufacture and sale of video and audio conferencing products. From its inception as a manufacturer of this equipment through 2001, ClearOne sold its products through a nationwide network of manufacturer's representatives. Sometime in early 2001, ClearOne decided to alter its business model and instead of utilizing manufacturer's representatives, began selling its products through a nationwide network of distributors complemented by a direct sales force. Through early 2001, ClearOne experienced robust growth and increased product sales every quarter. From the selected financial data extracted from ClearOne's Form 10-Ks that follow, this growth appeared to continue through fiscal 2002. However, a complaint filed by the SEC against ClearOne alleges that things may not be as rosy as they seem.

### ClearOne Communications

| | Selected Financial Data Years Ended June 30 | | |
| --- | --- | --- | --- |
| | **2002** | **2001** | **2000** |
| Product sales | $37,215,161 | $28,189,612 | $22,226,504 |
| Service sales | 17,327,525 | 11,688,793 | 5,891,909 |
| Cost of goods sold—products | 15,057,167 | 10,633,956 | 8,033,867 |
| Cost of goods sold—services | 7,942,952 | 5,869,106 | 2,974,456 |
| Operating expenses | 20,809,281 | 14,904,460 | 10,568,861 |
| Pre-tax operating income | 10,733,286 | 8,470,883 | 6,541,229 |
| Income from continuing operations | 7,410,752 | 5,525,185 | 4,301,742 |
| Net accounts receivable at June 30 | $20,316,730 | $ 7,212,970 | $ 4,153,677 |
| Cost of goods sold %—products | 40.5% | 37.7% | 36.1% |

**Required:**

1. Retrieve the SEC's complaint against ClearOne Communications, Inc. (www.sec.gov/litigation/complaints/comp17934.htm). Describe management's scheme for inflating revenue.

2. The SEC alleges that by the end of fiscal 2002, ClearOne had stuffed approximately $11.5 million of inventory into the distribution channel. On the basis of this assertion, what was the approximate amount of its alleged revenue overstatement by the end of 2002?

3. Does the financial statement data presented support your estimate? Why or why not?

---

**C3-7**

Financial reporting case:
Revenue recognition—
Software sales

Indus International, Inc. (the Company) develops, markets, implements, and supports a proprietary line of Enterprise Asset Management (EAM) software and service solutions for capital-intensive industries (for example, the utilities and energy industry) worldwide. The following was extracted from Forms 10-Q and 10-K filed by the company for Year 1.

## Revenue Recognition

The Company provides its software to customers under contracts, which provide for both software license fees and system implementation services. Revenues from system implementation services, which generally are time and material-based, are recognized as direct contract costs are incurred. The revenues from software license fees have been recognized as earned revenue in accordance with AICPA Statements of Position 97-2, and 98-4 relating to software revenue recognition, when persuasive evidence of arrangement exists, delivery has occurred, the license fee is fixed and determinable, and collection is probable. Prior to Year 0, the Company began to report applicable new license fees on standard software products not requiring substantial modification or customization as earned revenue upon shipment to customers. Previously, because substantial modification and customization of software products was expected by customers, The Indus Group, Inc. had deferred the applicable license fees initially and recognized those fees as earned over the period of modification, customization and other installation services. Maintenance and support services are subject to separate contracts for which revenue is recognized ratably over the contract period. Unbilled accounts receivable represent amounts related to revenue which has been recorded either as deferred revenue or earned revenue but which has not been billed. Generally, unbilled amounts are billed within 60 to 90 days of the sale of product or performance of services. Deferred revenue represents primarily unearned maintenance and support fees and unearned license fees, for which future performance obligations remain.

## Indus International, Inc.

### Condensed Consolidated Statements of Operations

| ($ in 000s, except per share amounts) | Three Months Ended September 30 | |
| --- | --- | --- |
| | **Year 1** | **Year 0** |
| **Revenues:** | | |
| Software license fees | $ 9,935 | $13,042 |
| Service and maintenance | 40,945 | 37,291 |
| Total revenues | 50,880 | 50,333 |
| Cost of revenues | 25,292 | 25,994 |
| Gross profit | 25,588 | 24,339 |
| **Operating expenses:** | | |
| Research and development | 8,874 | 8,171 |
| Sales and marketing | 7,232 | 8,778 |
| General administrative | 4,930 | 4,379 |
| Total operating expenses | 21,036 | 21,328 |
| Income from operations | 4,552 | 3,011 |
| Interest and other income (expense), net | 1,126 | (206) |
| Income before income taxes | 5,678 | 2,805 |
| Income taxes | 2,158 | — |
| Net income | $ 3,520 | $ 2,805 |
| EPS (basic) | $ 0.11 | $ 0.09 |
| EPS (diluted) | $ 0.10 | $ 0.08 |
| Shares used in computing EPS (basic) | 32,196 | 30,990 |
| Shares used in computing EPS (diluted) | 34,750 | 34,739 |

### Required:

1. Reported third quarter income includes more than $2 million in revenue from two contracts for which the CEO had "side letters" written to the customers giving each a right to cancel its contracts. Should this revenue have been recognized at that time? Cite appropriate authoritative literature in support of your answer.

2. On October 28, Year 1, Indus issued a press release announcing its third quarter Year 1 financial results. The company reported that it had met quarterly targets with revenues of $50.88 million and earnings of $3.52 million, or 10 cents per share on a diluted basis. What would be the approximate effect on reported EPS of not including revenue from the two contracts referred to in requirement 1?

---

**C3-8**

Ethical issues: Earnings management

Symbol Technologies, Inc. is a leading manufacturer of bar code scanners and related information technology whose stock is traded on the New York Stock Exchange. In 2003, the SEC filed allegations that during the period 1998 to 2002, the company manipulated millions of dollars in revenue, net income, and other measures of financial performance. These manipulations were designed to meet financial projections driven by Wall Street expectations and were allegedly engineered and/or facilitated by the company's chief accounting officer (a CPA).

An example of the various ploys used by Symbol occurred in 2001 when a Symbol officer and other employees created an excessive reserve of $10 million for obsolete inventory. This $10 million cushion was a "cookie jar" reserve designed for use when the company failed to meet its quarterly forecast, and it exceeded any reasonable estimate of the company's exposure for obsolete inventory. This reserve was released into earnings in the fourth quarter of 2001. By making this and other adjustments that quarter, Symbol reported net income of $13.4 million rather than a $2.4 million loss and hit the quarterly forecast right on the nose. The reversal of this "cookie jar" inventory reserve and the favorable impact on reported earnings were not disclosed to the public.

**Required:**

Identify the ethical issues involved with the "cookie jar" reserves and the economic consequences for parties affected by the chief accounting officer's actions. (*Hint:* Reference the AICPA's Code of Professional Conduct for CPAs.)

---

**C3-9**

Franchise sales

Austins Steaks & Saloon, Inc. (Austins) operates and/or franchises restaurants. It currently has approximately 118 franchisees operating 186 Western Sizzlin, Western Sizzlin Wood Grill, Market Street Buffet and Bakery, and Great American Steak & Buffet restaurants in 22 states.

Austins' standard franchise agreement has a 20-year term, with one 10-year renewal option. It provides for a one-time payment of an initial franchise fee and a continuing royalty fee based on gross sales. Sales reports and financial statements are regularly collected from franchisees.

Each franchisee is responsible for selecting the location for its restaurant, subject to Austins' approval (based on demographics, competition, traffic volume, etc.). Each franchised restaurant must have a designated manager and assistant manager who have completed Austins' six-week manager training program or who have been otherwise approved by the company. For the opening of a restaurant, Austins provides consultation and makes company personnel generally available to a franchisee. In addition, the company sends a team of personnel to the restaurant for up to two weeks to assist the franchisee and its managers in the opening and the initial marketing and training effort as well as the over-all operation of the restaurant.

Initial franchise fees are recognized when the company has substantially performed all material services and the restaurant has opened for business. Franchise royalties, which are based on a percentage of monthly sales, are recognized as income on the accrual basis. Costs associated with franchise operations are recognized on the accrual basis.

Assume that:

a. Austins entered into a standard franchise agreement on July 1, 2008 with Stacey Spitko to open a Market Street Buffet and Bakery in Lewisburg, PA.

b. The agreement called for an initial franchise fee of $500,000 and a 2.5% royalty. Of the fee, $100,000 is payable immediately; the remainder is to be paid in equal annual installments each July 1 over the life of the franchise agreement.

c. Interest of 6% on the unpaid franchise fee balance is also payable each July 1.

d. Royalty payments are to be submitted with accompanying financial statements 15 days after the end of each quarter.

e. The restaurant opened on September 30, 2008. Austins management sent a team to assist with the opening. Because Spitko felt that this assistance would be more valuable if rendered primarily after the restaurant opened, the team scheduled its arrival in Lewisburg for September 26, 2008 and was on site until October 10. Management estimated that $34,000 in costs was incurred to provide the entire package of "restaurant opening" services.

f. In keeping with the agreement, the restaurant reported the following gross sales in 2008 and 2009 and made the required payments:

|  | Quarter | | | |
| --- | --- | --- | --- | --- |
|  | **First** | **Second** | **Third** | **Fourth** |
| 2008 |  |  |  | $185,000 |
| 2009 | $208,500 | $242,000 | $243,500 | $271,000 |

**Required:**

1. Should Austins recognize revenue from the initial franchise fee in its quarter ending September 30, 2008? Explain.

2. For Austins, prepare summary journal entries for 2008 and 2009 necessitated by this franchise agreement.

---

The following was excerpted from *The Wall Street Journal Online*:

The Dallas technology outsourcer [Affiliated Computer Services] acknowledged May 10, after a preliminary internal probe, that it had issued executive stock options that carried "effective dates" preceding the written approval of the grants. ACS said it plans a charge of as much as $32 million to rectify its accounting related to the grants. It is being examined by the Securities and Exchange Commission. On Aug. 7, the company announced that investors should no longer rely on its prior disclosures about the findings of its continuing internal probe. It had previously said a preliminary review suggested no intentional backdating occurred and any charges were likely to be minor. Noncash compensation costs related to backdating will be about $51 million, plus additional tax-related expenses.

Certain executives have repeatedly received stock options on favorable dates—just ahead of sharp gains in the price of the company stock. Below [are shown] the number of option grants [Jeffrey Rich, ACS former chief executive] received between roughly 1995 and 2002 and the odds—by a *Wall Street Journal* analysis—that such a favorable pattern of grants would occur by chance. Charts show three especially propitious grants to [Mr. Rich], and what the stock did two months before the grant and two months after.

Total grants: 6

Odds: About 1 in 300 billion

**C3-10**

Affiliated Computer Services (ACS): Restatements due to options backdating

**Examples of Options Granted** *(stock prices adjusted for splits)*

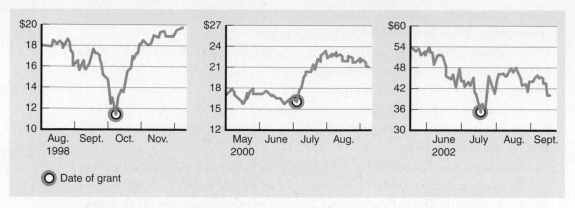

O Date of grant

**Company's Response at Date of Publication (March 18, 2006)**

> Mr. Rich said no grants were backdated, called his favorable dates "blind luck." Company spokes-woman said, "We did grant options when there was a natural dip in the stock price." Mr. Rich stepped down as chief executive last fall.

**Required:**

Visit the SEC's Web site (www.sec.gov) and retrieve ACS's form 10-K/A for the fiscal year that ended June 30, 2006. Read footnote 2 to the financial statements entitled "Review of Stock Option Grant Practices," and then address the following:

1. ACS conducted an internal investigation into its stock options–granting practices. What did this investigation reveal?

2. Locate the tables (toward the end of footnote 2) that reflect options-related adjustments to ACS's consolidated financial statements.

   a. What financial statements were affected, and in what manner, by ACS's options granting practices?

   b. Re-create the journal entry that ACS made to restate the company's balance sheet at June 30, 2005.

**Remember to check the book's companion Web site for additional study material.**

# Structure of the Balance Sheet | 4
## and Statement of Cash Flows

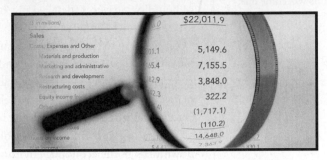

| ($ in millions) | | $22,011.9 |
|---|---|---|
| **Sales** | | |
| Costs, Expenses and Other | | |
| Materials and production | 01.1 | 5,149.6 |
| Marketing and administrative | 65.4 | 7,155.5 |
| Research and development | 82.9 | 3,848.0 |
| Restructuring costs | 2.3 | 322.2 |
| Equity income f | 4) | (1,717.1) |
| Other | | (110.2) |
| | | 14,648.0 |
| on income | | |

T he **balance sheet**—sometimes called the *statement of financial position*—contains a summation of the assets owned by the firm, the liabilities incurred to finance these assets, and the shareholders' equity representing the amount of financing provided by owners at a specific date.

The Financial Accounting Standards Board (FASB) defines the three basic elements of the balance sheet:[1]

1. *Assets:* Probable future economic benefits obtained or controlled by an entity as a result of past transactions or events.

2. *Liabilities:* Probable future sacrifices of economic benefits arising from an entity's *present* obligations to transfer assets or provide services to other entities in the *future* as a result of *past* transactions or events.

3. *Equity:* The residual interest in an entity's assets that remains after deducting its liabilities. For a corporate form of organization, this interest is referred to as *shareholders'* or *stockholders' equity.*

The balance sheet tells us how management has invested the firm's money and where the money came from. It provides information for assessing rates of return, capital structure, liquidity, solvency, and financial flexibility of an enterprise.

Two **rate of return** measures for evaluating operating efficiency and profitability of an enterprise are return on assets (ROA) and return on common equity (ROCE). (The precise calculation of these two performance measures is detailed in Chapter 5.) By comparing ROA to ROCE, statement users can see whether debt financing is being used to enhance the return earned by shareholders.

The balance sheet provides critical information for understanding an entity's **capital structure,** which refers to how much of an entity's assets are financed from debt versus equity sources. An important decision in corporate finance is determining the proper mix of debt and equity financing. Management must weigh the benefits of using debt financing (with tax-deductible interest) against the dangers of becoming overleveraged (that is, having too much debt) and the possibility of defaulting on required interest and principal payments.

## LEARNING OBJECTIVES

**After studying this chapter, you will understand:**

1. How the various asset, liability, and stockholders' equity accounts on a typical corporate balance sheet are measured and classified.

2. How to use balance sheet information to understand key differences in the nature of firms' operations and how those operations are financed.

3. Differences in balance sheet terminology and presentation format in countries outside the United States.

4. The information provided in footnotes on significant accounting policies, subsequent events, and related party transactions.

5. How successive balance sheets and the income statement can be used to determine cash inflows and outflows for a period.

6. How information provided in the cash flow statement can be used to explain changes in noncash accounts on the balance sheet.

7. The distinction between operating, investing, and financing sources and uses of cash.

8. How changes in current asset and current liability accounts can be used to adjust accrual earnings to obtain cash flows from operations.

*Chapter*

---

[1] "Elements of Financial Statements of Business Enterprises," *Statement of Financial Accounting Concepts No. 6* (Stamford, CT: Financial Accounting Standards Board [FASB] 1985), para. 25, 35, 49.

In addition to assessing the mix of debt versus equity financing, the balance sheet and related footnotes provide information for evaluating the **maturity structure** of the various obligations within the liability section. This information is critical to assessing the **liquidity** of an entity. Liquidity measures how readily assets can be converted to cash relative to how soon liabilities will have to be paid in cash. The balance sheet is the source of information for a variety of liquidity measures (detailed in Chapter 5) used by analysts and commercial loan officers to assess an entity's creditworthiness.

> *Maturity structure* refers to how far into the future the obligations will come due.

In addition to the liquidity measures that focus on short-term cash inflows and cash needs, balance sheets provide information for assessing long-term **solvency**—a company's ability to generate sufficient cash flows to maintain its productive capacity and still meet interest and principal payments on long-term debt. A company that cannot make debt payments when due is technically insolvent and may be forced to reorganize or liquidate.

**Operating and financial flexibility** refers to an entity's ability to adjust to unexpected downturns in the economic environment in which it operates or to take advantage of profitable investment opportunities as they arise. Balance sheets provide information for making these assessments. A firm that has most of its assets invested in specialized manufacturing facilities (for example, a foundry) has limited ability to adjust to economic downturns and, thus, has limited operating flexibility. Similarly, a firm with minimal cash reserves and large amounts of high interest debt will have limited ability to take advantage of profitable investment opportunities that may arise.

Now that we have outlined the information contained in balance sheets and how it is used, we turn our attention to how various balance sheet accounts are measured and classified.

> As part of a joint effort with the IASB, the FASB is currently working on a project on financial statement presentation that would require firms to use the term "statement of financial position" in place of "balance sheet" and to report selected line items and subtotals that are typically not currently provided. Further details on proposed changes to the format of the statement of financial position (balance sheet) can be found on the FASB Web site at www. fasb.org under Project Updates—Financial Statement Presentation.

## CLASSIFICATION CRITERIA AND MEASUREMENT CONVENTIONS FOR BALANCE SHEET ACCOUNTS

We will use Motorola's financial statements to illustrate the classification criteria and measurement methods used in a typical balance sheet. While many people characterize generally accepted accounting principles (GAAP) balance sheet carrying amounts as **historical costs,** what they really represent is more complicated. In fact, carrying amounts in a GAAP balance sheet are a mixture of historical costs, **current costs** (also called **fair value**), **net realizable value,** and **discounted present values.**

Exhibit 4.1 shows Motorola's balance sheet, which uses a typical U.S. disclosure format. In the Assets section, cash and any other assets expected to be converted into cash within the next 12 months (or within the **operating cycle,** if the operating cycle is longer than 12 months) are classified as current assets. Assets not expected to be converted into cash within this period are categorized separately. Within the current assets category, items are disclosed in descending order of liquidity—how quickly the items will be converted into cash through the normal course of business. In the Liabilities section of the balance sheet, items expected to be settled from current assets within the next 12 months (or within the operating cycle, if longer) are categorized as Current liabilities. All other liabilities appear in a separate section as noncurrent or long-term obligations. Equity claims also appear in their own separate section of the balance sheet, which is often referred to as the Stockholders' Equity section.

> A firm's **operating cycle** is the elapsed time beginning with the initiation of production and ending with the cash collection of the receivables from the sale of the product.

To convey a feeling for the diversity of the measurement bases used in a typical balance sheet, we will discuss selected accounts from Motorola's 2006 comparative balance sheet (see Exhibit 4.1). Many of the measurement issues discussed below are explored in greater depth in subsequent chapters.

| EXHIBIT 4.1 | Motorola, Inc. and Subsidiaries Consolidated Balance Sheets |

|  | December 31 | |
| --- | --- | --- |
| ($ in millions) | **2006** | **2005** |
| **Assets** | | |
| **Current assets** | | |
| Cash and cash equivalents | $ 3,212 | $ 3,774 |
| Sigma Funds[1] | 12,204 | 10,867 |
| Short-term investments | 224 | 144 |
| Accounts receivable, net | 7,509 | 5,652 |
| Inventories, net | 3,162 | 2,422 |
| Deferred income taxes | 1,731 | 2,355 |
| Other current assets | 2,933 | 2,496 |
| Current assets "held for sale"[2] | — | 312 |
| **Total current assets** | 30,975 | 28,022 |
| Property, plant and equipment, net | 2,267 | 2,020 |
| Investments | 895 | 1,644 |
| Deferred income taxes | 1,325 | 1,196 |
| Other assets | 3,131 | 2,597 |
| Non-current assets "held for sale" | — | 323 |
| **Total assets** | $38,593 | $35,802 |
| **Liabilities and Stockholders' Equity** | | |
| **Current liabilities** | | |
| Notes payable and current portion of long-term debt | $ 1,693 | $ 448 |
| Accounts payable | 5,056 | 4,295 |
| Accrued liabilities | 8,676 | 7,529 |
| Current liabilities "held for sale" | — | 320 |
| **Total current liabilities** | 15,425 | 12,592 |
| Long-term debt | 2,704 | 3,806 |
| Other liabilities | 3,322 | 2,727 |
| Non-current liabilities "held for sale" | — | 4 |
| **Stockholders' equity** | | |
| Preferred stock, $100 par value | | — |
| Common stock, $3 par value | 7,197 | 7,508 |
| Issued shares: 2006—2,399.1 and 2005—2,502.7 | | |
| Outstanding shares: 2006—2,397.4 and 2005—2,501.1 | | |
| Additional paid-in capital | 2,509 | 4,691 |
| Retained earnings | 9,086 | 5,897 |
| Non-owner changes to equity | (1,650) | (1,423) |
| **Total stockholders' equity** | 17,142 | 16,673 |
| **Total liabilities and stockholders' equity** | $38,593 | $35,802 |

[1] Sigma Funds is a money market–like fund managed by four investment management firms that invests in high quality investment grade debt obligations.

[2] "Held for sale" assets and liabilities relate to operating units that Motorola expects to discontinue within one year (see Chapter 2).

## Cash and Cash Equivalents

The balance sheet carrying amount for this account reflects the amount of money or currency the firm has on hand in bank accounts or in certificates of deposit. If cash consists exclusively of U.S. dollar amounts, the balance sheet Cash account reflects the *historical* amount of net dollar units arising from past transactions. Due to the unique liquidity of cash, however, this historical amount of net dollar units is identical to the current market value of the cash.

**Monetary assets** are fixed in dollar amounts regardless of price changes. A $300,000 cash deposit remains fixed at $300,000 even if the general level of prices goes up and the purchasing power of that $300,000 declines. **Nonmonetary assets** such as inventory and buildings are *not* fixed in dollar amounts; that is, inventory purchased for $300,000 can conceivably increase in value if prices go up. While not assured, this potential for changing value is the distinguishing characteristic of nonmonetary items—their value is *not* measured in a fixed number of monetary units.

If some of the cash amounts are denominated in foreign currency units (likely for Motorola, a multinational firm), those amounts in foreign currency units must be *translated* into U.S. dollar equivalents. For **monetary assets** such as cash, accounts receivable, and notes receivable, the current rate of exchange in effect at the balance sheet date is used to translate foreign currency units into dollars. As a consequence of using the current rate of exchange (rather than the historical rate of exchange that was in effect at the time of the foreign currency cash inflows), this portion of the Cash account is carried at its **current market price,** *not* at its historical transaction amount. For these foreign currency deposits, current market exchange values are used regardless of whether they are higher or lower than the historical rate. Consequently, the GAAP measurement convention for cash is, in reality, current market price rather than historical cost.

A U.S. company with 1 million pesos in the bank account of its Mexican manufacturing subsidiary would value the cash at $92,593 U.S. dollars on December 31, 2006, when the exchange rate was 10.80 pesos to the dollar. This same bank account (with 1 million pesos) would have been valued at $94,073 U.S. dollars on December 31, 2005 when the exchange rate was 10.63 pesos to the dollar.

**Short-Term Investments**   This category of assets comprises items such as U.S. Treasury bills, notes, equity securities, or other financial assets that companies use to earn a return on funds not currently needed in operations. The FASB measurement rules for certain investments in debt and equity securities distinguishes between debt securities, which the reporting company intends to hold to maturity, and all other securities (both debt and equity), which an entity intends to hold only for short periods of time.[2]

The rules are:

1. Debt securities the company intends to hold to maturity are carried at amortized cost. (When debt securities are sold at a premium or discount, the premium or discount is amortized over time, hence, the term **amortized cost.**)

2. Debt and equity securities held for short-range investment purposes are carried at market value at each balance sheet date (that is, the price at which these securities can be bought and sold), regardless of whether the market price is above or below cost.

When the balance sheet carrying amount of the securities investment is written up or down to current market value, the offsetting gain or loss appears on the income statement if the securities are **trading securities** for which the intent is to generate profits on short-term differences in price. When less actively traded securities (termed **available-for-sale securities**) are marked-to-market, the offsetting gain or loss goes directly to stockholders' equity rather than through the income statement. (These accounting rules are discussed further in Chapter 16.)

*How long the company intends to hold the debt securities determines how they are measured on the balance sheet. Some will be carried at amortized cost and others at current market prices. Equity securities held for the short term are always measured at current market prices (fair value).*

**Net Accounts Receivable**   This account reflects credit sales that have not yet been collected. The balance sheet carrying amount for gross accounts receivable equals the face amount due that arises from past credit sales transactions. Thus, if a company sold goods with a $100,000 sales price on November 15, 2008, the following entry would be made:

| | | |
|---|---|---|
| **DR** | Accounts receivable ................................... | $100,000 |
| | **CR** Sales revenue ......................................... | $100,000 |

---

[2] "Accounting for Certain Investments in Debt and Equity Securities," *Statement of Financial Accounting Standards (SFAS) No. 115* (Norwalk, CT: FASB 1993). Under the old rules that *SFAS No. 115* replaced, short-term investments were carried at lower of cost or market.

If the receivable is still outstanding at December 31, 2008, it would be shown on the balance sheet at $100,000. However, accrual accounting requires that any future costs be matched against the revenues recognized in the period of sale. When sales are made for credit (on account), some sales may unknowingly be made to customers who will be incapable of making the required payment. The expense associated with these uncollectible accounts must be recognized—on an estimated basis—in the period in which the sales arise. This compels companies to prepare an estimate of the proportion of existing accounts receivable balances that they reasonably believe will ultimately not be collected. In Motorola's case, the 2006 accounts receivable footnote disclosure shows the details behind the Accounts receivable, net balance shown on its balance sheet as follows:

---

The accounting entry to recognize estimated uncollectible accounts is:

**DR**  Bad debt expense . . . . . . . . . . . . . . . . . . . . . . . .     $XXX

    **CR**  Allowance for doubtful accounts . . . . . . .          $XXX

The debited account reduces income in the current period, but the account credited appears as a deduction from gross accounts receivable. Such deductions from asset accounts are called **contra-asset** accounts. (Estimating and recognizing bad debt expense is discussed in Chapter 8.)

---

*($ in millions)*

| | |
|---|---|
| Gross accounts receivable | $7,587 |
| Less: Allowance for doubtful accounts | (78) |
| Net accounts receivable reported on balance sheet | $7,509 |

Notice that as a consequence of this "netting" of accounts, the total for net accounts receivable $7,509 million) is carried at expected **net realizable value** as of the balance sheet date, not at original historical cost ($7,587 million).

## Inventories

The inventory account for a manufacturing firm such as Motorola comprises three components: (1) raw materials, (2) work-in-process, and (3) finished goods. In the notes to its financial statements, Motorola discloses that inventories are carried at **lower of cost or market,** where cost is computed using the weighted average method (discussed in Chapter 9). Therefore, the measurement basis for inventories depends on the relationship between historical cost and current market price.

> For a wholesale or retail company, this account reflects only finished goods, that is, merchandise held for resale.

- When costs are lower than market price, the carrying amounts for inventory conform to the historical cost convention.
- When cost exceeds market, inventories on the balance sheet are carried at current market price, where that market price is the cost to replace the item (subject to special GAAP rules described in Chapter 9).

## Deferred Income Taxes

This asset account represents taxes paid by Motorola to the government on income that (1) was recognized for tax purposes in the current or prior periods but (2) will not be recognized for financial reporting purposes until some future period. Because this future expense has already been paid, it is reported as a **deferred tax asset.** In the United States, the rules used to determine income for financial reporting purposes (called **book income**) frequently do not conform to the rules used to determine income for taxation purposes (called **taxable income**). Book income also diverges from taxable income in many other industrialized countries. Income determination rules for financial reporting differ from rules for determining income for taxation purposes because of the very different objectives of the two computations. The objective in measuring book income is to reflect a firm's underlying economic success: Was the firm profitable during the period? The objective in measuring taxable income is to conform to laws designed to provide a basis for funding government operations. Because the rules that govern income determination for tax purposes result from a national political process, these rules do not necessarily measure changes in firms' underlying economic condition. Most companies maintain two sets of accounting records (or books) to facilitate both accurate financial reporting and compliance with tax laws.

The amount reported as book income is the basis for the deduction reported on the income statement for tax expense. However, the amount actually owed and paid to the government—that is, the sum of the credits to cash and to income taxes payable on the balance sheet—is determined by firms' taxable income. As a consequence, the debit to the income statement account (Tax expense) and the credit to the balance sheet accounts (Cash or Taxes payable) **will usually be for different amounts.** To balance the entry, deferred income taxes—reflecting the difference in the *timing* of revenue and expense in computing book income versus taxable income—must be debited or credited. (The measurement and reporting rules for deferred taxes are covered in Chapter 13.)

> In 2000 Motorola also reported Deferred income taxes totaling $1,504 million in the liability section of its balance sheet. This amount arises because certain timing differences caused book income to be *higher* than taxable income in prior years.

In Motorola's case, the Deferred income tax asset account has a debit balance of $1,731 million due to the **timing differences** that caused taxable income to exceed book income in past years.[3] Taxable income can exceed book income for at least two possible reasons:

1. Internal Revenue Service (IRS) rules do not allow Motorola to claim deductions for tax purposes until after these items are reflected as GAAP expenses on the books.
2. IRS rules require Motorola to recognize revenues on its tax return before they are recognized on its GAAP income statement.

> There are other reasons why book income may differ from taxable income—called *permanent differences*—but they do not give rise to deferred taxes. For example, U.S. income tax law does not tax municipal bond interest. Consequently, if a firm owns municipal bonds and receives interest on these bonds, the interest is tax free. Book income will include the interest income, but taxable income will not.

Because these timing differences are expected to reverse in subsequent years, *future* book income will exceed taxable income. Even though these reversals may be expected to take place in, say, three years in the future, GAAP reflects these amounts at their *undiscounted amount.* In other words, existing GAAP ignores the time value of money and treats expected reversals in the years 2010 and 2015 identically.

**Property, Plant and Equipment—Net** This account reflects the tangible long-lived assets that Motorola uses in its operations. This item appears on the balance sheet at its net amount: historical cost minus accumulated depreciation. Motorola, like most companies, provides information about the components of this figure in the financial statement notes.

| | December 31 | |
| --- | --- | --- |
| ($ in millions) | **2006** | **2005** |
| Land | $ 129 | $ 147 |
| Buildings | 1,705 | 1,697 |
| Machinery and equipment | 5,885 | 5,416 |
| | 7,719 | 7,260 |
| Less: Accumulated depreciation | (5,452) | (5,240) |
| Property, plant and equipment—net | $ 2,267 | $ 2,020 |

---

[3] *Debits* to deferred income tax arise because the credit to Taxes payable exceeds the debit to Taxes expense. Because tax expense is based on book income and taxes payable is based on taxable income, this means that in past years, book income for Motorola was less than taxable income.

When a long-lived asset becomes impaired—that is, when its carrying amount may no longer be recoverable—the fixed asset account is reduced to its lower **fair value**.[4] If available, quoted current market prices represent the best measure of fair value. However, market prices for long-lived assets are not always readily available. So, fair value may need to be estimated by discounting expected future net operating cash flows. (This topic is covered in Chapter 10.)

> *SFAS No. 121* (para. 7) defines *fair value* of an asset as "the amount at which the asset could be bought or sold in a current transaction between willing parties, that is, other than a forced or liquidation sale." *SFAS No. 157* extends this definition in ways described in Chapter 6.

**Notes Payable and Current Portion of Long-Term Debt**   Notes payable are formal written promises to pay cash at some future date issued in connection with loans from a bank or for the purchase of goods or services. The current portion of long-term debt represents the portion of long-term borrowings that fall due within one year of the balance sheet date. Because these amounts will be paid within a relatively short period of time (within one year), they are reported at their (undiscounted) face amount, that is, the amount due at the payment date.

**Accounts Payable and Accrued Liabilities**   Accounts payable represent amounts owed to suppliers of merchandise or services purchased on open account (that is, for credit). Payment is typically due within 30 to 90 days. Accrued liabilities represent expenses that have been incurred, but not yet paid. Examples include accrued wages and accrued interest expense. These items are reflected on the balance sheet at the amount of the original liability, that is, at the amount arising at the transaction's inception. Consequently, the numbers are shown at historical cost.

**Long-Term Debt**   This account represents obligations that fall due beyond one year from the balance sheet date. Examples include notes, bonds, lease obligations, and pension obligations. When long-term debt (typically, notes or bonds) is issued, the initial balance sheet carrying amount is determined by computing the **discounted present value** of the sum of (1) the future principal repayment *plus* (2) the periodic interest payments. The rate used for discounting these amounts is the effective yield on the notes or bonds at the date they were issued. Here, we'll simply provide a brief overview of the general measurement rules for long-term debt. More on bonds and other long-term debt instruments is presented in Chapter 11.

When bonds are sold at par, the amount received equals the recorded face amount of the debt. For example, if Motorola sells $100,000,000 of 15-year, 10% coupon bonds for $100,000,000, the accounting entry is:

| | | | |
|---|---|---|---|
| **DR** | Cash | $100,000,000 | |
| | **CR**  Bonds Payable | | $100,000,000 |

The $100,000,000 carrying amount equals the present value of the principal *and* interest payments over the life of the bond discounted at 10%, the effective yield at the time of issue. The effective yield is 10% because the effective yield on bonds sold at par equals the coupon rate. (We'll show why in Chapter 11.) When bonds are sold at a premium (say, $105 million) or at a discount (say, $95 million), the initial carrying amount is again equal to the present value of the future payments when the discount rate is the effective yield on the bonds. In general, at balance sheet dates after the bonds' issuance date, the subsequent carrying amount of *all* bonds outstanding equals the present value of the future principal and interest flows discounted at the

---

[4] "Accounting for the Impairment of Long-Lived Assets and for Long-Lived Assets to Be Disposed of," *SFAS No. 121* (Norwalk, CT: FASB, 1995).

*original effective yield rate*. This carrying amount will differ from the bonds' current market price whenever interest rates have changed subsequent to issuance. Consequently, long-term debt is also carried at historical cost when the carrying amount is determined by calculating the discounted present value of the future principal and interest cash flows using the original effective yield on the bonds as the discount rate.

### Common Stock

This account represents the **par value** of shares issued and outstanding. The par value is determined by the company's articles of incorporation. Par values were originally established to ensure that a corporation would maintain a minimum level of investment by shareholders to protect the interests of creditors. For example, some states preclude companies from paying dividends to shareholders that would result in a reduction of stockholders' equity below the par value of shares issued and outstanding. As a practical matter, debt covenant provisions in the borrower's lending agreements generally place restrictions on firms' distributions to shareholders that are more stringent than the statutory par-value restrictions. Therefore, the par value of shares has limited economic significance, as discussed in Chapter 15. The common stock account is carried at the historical par value of the shares.

### Additional Paid-in Capital

This account reflects the amounts in excess of par or stated value that the corporation received when the shares were originally issued. For example, if Motorola issued 100,000 shares of $3 par-value stock for $15 per share, the Additional paid-in capital component would be credited for

$$(\$15 - \$3) \times 100,000 = \$1,200,000$$

Thus, additional paid-in capital is also shown at historical cost (that is, the amount above par value paid to the firm when the shares were originally issued).

### Retained Earnings

This account measures the net of cumulative earnings less cumulative dividend distributions of the company since inception. Therefore, it represents the cumulative earnings that have been reinvested in the business. The Retained earnings account is increased (decreased) by the net income (net loss) for the period and is decreased for dividends that are declared in the period. For many firms, like Motorola, retained earnings represents the major portion of stockholders' equity. Thus, the book value of equity is largely determined by the past earnings that have been retained and reinvested in the business. As we will see in Chapters 5 and 6, book value of equity is a key element of many performance measures—such as return on common equity (ROCE)—and it plays an important role in equity valuation.

Different measurement bases pervade the balance sheet. Because these items ultimately appear on the income statement, income is a mixture of historical costs, current values, and present values. This means that retained earnings is also a mixture of many different measurement bases.

### Non-owner Changes to Equity

This account measures the cumulative unrealized gains and losses from *other comprehensive income components* (see Chapter 2) recognized in current and prior years. This component of stockholders' equity is also called Accumulated other comprehensive income. As noted in Chapter 2, the most common components of other comprehensive income are:

1. Fair value adjustments made to securities classified as "available-for-sale" (see Chapter 16).
2. Fair value changes on derivatives that meet certain conditions for hedge accounting (see Chapter 11).

3. Foreign currency translation adjustments (see Chapter 16).

4. Unrealized actuarial gains and losses on pension assets and liabilities and increases (decreases) in pension obligations due to prior service cost adjustments under *SFAS No. 158* (see Chapter 14).

The non-owner changes to this equity account are credited for unrealized gains and debited for unrealized losses. All amounts are shown net of tax effects. For Motorola, this account balance increased from a $1,423 million debit balance at the end of 2005 to a $1,650 million debit balance at the end of 2006, an increase of $227 million. Motorola's consolidated statement of stockholders' equity (not shown) explains the components of this change:

| ($ in millions) | Unrealized Gain (Loss) | |
| --- | ---: | --- |
| 1. Unrealized loss on available-for-sale securities | $ (60) | **DR** |
| 2. Foreign currency translation adjustments | 127 | **CR** |
| 3. Minimum pension liability adjustment | (308) | **DR** |
| 4. Gain on derivative instruments, net | 14 | **CR** |
| Total 2006 increase | $(227) | **DR** |

## Analytical Insights: Understanding the Nature of a Firm's Business

One tool for gaining insights into the nature of a company's operations and for analyzing its asset and financial structure is to prepare a **common-size balance sheet.** In it, each balance sheet account is expressed as a percentage of total assets or, equivalently, as a percentage of total liabilities plus shareholders' equity. Exhibit 4.2 presents common-size balance sheets for four companies operating in four distinctly different industries: E-Trade Group, an Internet company specializing in online investing services; Deere & Company, a manufacturer of agricultural and heavy construction equipment with a large finance subsidiary; Wal-Mart, a well-known discount retailer; and Potomac Electric Power Company, an electrical utility providing service to Washington, D.C., and the surrounding area. Can you match up the common-size statements with each of these companies? Think about the industry in which each firm operates and about the economic activities the firms might engage in. Then try to figure out how these activities might impact a typical balance sheet.

 **Analysis**

Note that Company C has a very large proportion of its assets in cash, marketable securities, and accounts receivable with no inventory, and a relatively small amount of property, plant, and equipment (PP&E). Most of Company C's debt financing comes from short-term liabilities, because the company carries no long-term debt. Finally, note that Retained earnings is negative (a deficit), indicating that the company has suffered cumulative losses since it was formed. The lack of inventory rules out Deere and Wal-Mart as the source of Company C's data because both would hold significant inventories. Also, the relatively low amount of PP&E further rules out these two firms as well as Potomac Power because all three need significant amounts of fixed assets to conduct business. This leaves E-Trade Group as the obvious match. A corroborating piece of evidence is the deficit in Retained earnings. Because of heavy start-up costs, many of the relatively young Internet companies such as E-Trade have yet to turn a profit.

Both Company A and Company B have relatively high amounts of current assets, but the mix of current assets is quite different. For Company A, current receivables represent nearly

# EXHIBIT 4.2 Common-Size Balance Sheet Comparison

| | Company A $ in Millions | % | Company B $ in Millions | % | Company C $ in Millions | % | Company D $ in Millions | % |
|---|---|---|---|---|---|---|---|---|
| **Assets** | | | | | | | | |
| Current assets | | | | | | | | |
| Cash and marketable securities | $ 1,206.2 | 5.3 | $ 2,161.0 | 2.6 | $ 5,157.5 | 28.4 | $ 676.7 | 12.8 |
| Current receivables | 12,826.9 | 56.6 | 2,000.0 | 2.4 | 10,149.7 | 55.8 | 401.2 | 7.6 |
| Inventories | 1,505.7 | 6.6 | 22,614.0 | 27.1 | — | — | 37.8 | 0.7 |
| Other current assets | 1,939.3 | 8.6 | 1,471.0 | 1.8 | — | — | 24.2 | 0.5 |
| Total current assets | 17,478.1 | 77.1 | 28,246.0 | 33.9 | 15,307.2 | 84.2 | 1,139.9 | 21.6 |
| Noncurrent assets | | | | | | | | |
| Property, plant, and equipment, net | 2,052.3 | 9.0 | 45,750.0 | 54.8 | 331.7 | 1.8 | 2,753.4 | 52.1 |
| Goodwill and intangibles, net | 874.0 | 3.9 | 8,595.0 | 10.3 | 684.4 | 3.8 | — | — |
| Other assets, net | 2,258.7 | 10.0 | 860.0 | 1.0 | 1,849.1 | 10.2 | 1,392.6 | 26.3 |
| **Total assets** | $22,663.1 | 100.0% | $83,451.0 | 100.0% | $18,172.4 | 100.0% | $5,285.9 | 100.0% |
| **Liabilities and Stockholders' Equity** | | | | | | | | |
| Current liabilities | | | | | | | | |
| Total current liabilities | $ 9,456.6 | 41.7 | $27,282.0 | 32.7 | $16,532.0 | 91.0 | $ 965.4 | 18.2 |
| Long-term liabilities | 9,214.3 | 40.7 | 21,067.0 | 25.2 | — | — | 2,287.5 | 43.3 |
| **Total liabilities** | 18,670.9 | 82.4 | 48,349.0 | 57.9 | 16,532.0 | 91.0 | 3,252.9 | 61.5 |
| Redeemable preferred stock | — | — | — | — | 69.5 | 0.4 | 209.8 | 4.0 |
| Stockholders' equity | | | | | | | | |
| Contributed capital and other equity items | 157.4 | 0.7 | 661.0 | 0.8 | 1,818.0 | 10.0 | 849.1 | 16.1 |
| Retained earnings (deficit) | 3,834.8 | 16.9 | 34,441.0 | 41.3 | (247.1) | (1.4) | 974.1 | 18.4 |
| **Total liabilities and stockholders' equity** | $22,663.1 | 100.0% | $83,451.0 | 100.0% | $18,172.4 | 100.0% | $5,285.9 | 100.0% |

57% of total assets while Company B has no current receivables, but 27% of its assets are in inventory. Because many of Deere's agricultural and heavy construction equipment products sell for well in excess of $100,000, dealers and customers often need to finance their purchases. Deere offers this financing through its wholly owned finance subsidiary whose operations are included in the consolidated numbers. Thus, the large receivables balance for Company A coupled with significant amounts invested in inventories and PP&E provide strong clues that Deere is Company A.

Like most national discount retailers, Wal-Mart would be expected to have large amounts of inventory. Because most sales are for cash or paid through bank credit cards (for example, Visa or Master Card), Wal-Mart would likely have little or no current receivables on its balance sheet. Moreover, with a large number of stores either purchased or leased under capital lease arrangements, we would expect to see relatively large investments in PP&E. This profile seems to match up well with Company B's data.

This leaves Potomac Power as Company D. Note the relatively low amount of current assets and the large investment in PP&E to generate electricity. The large amount of long-term debt financing is also quite common for utilities. Regulated utilities are allowed to build a "reasonable and fair return" to stockholders into the energy rates charged customers. Therefore, they have a relatively steady and predictable earnings and cash flow stream. This allows utilities such as Potomac Power to use proportionately more long-term debt to finance their operations relative to companies with more volatile earnings patterns.

The preceding exercise demonstrates how statement readers can extract useful information from common-size balance sheets to learn about the underlying economics of an industry and the nature of the firm's operations. Chapter 5 will introduce additional analytical tools for conducting in-depth analyses of companies.

## International Differences in Balance Sheet Presentation

The account titles and format of balance sheets prepared in other countries can sometimes differ rather dramatically from those prepared under U.S. GAAP.[5] In contrast to the United States where assets are presented in decreasing order of liquidity, in the United Kingdom, Germany, Netherlands, and some other European countries, non-current (fixed) assets are presented first followed by the current assets displayed in increasing order of liquidity. This format is illustrated in Exhibit 4.3, which presents the 2006 balance sheet of Burberry PLC, a British company that designs, manufactures, and distributes luxury apparel for men, women, and children throughout the world.

Note that within the fixed assets category, Intangible assets are presented first followed by tangible assets (that is, Property, plant, and equipment), Deferred tax assets and finally Trade and other receivables. The British balance sheet format is presented in a way that emphasizes the firm's liquidity by placing current assets and current liabilities in close proximity to one another.

The Burberry balance sheet also introduces some account titles unique to British (U.K.) accounting that can be confusing to the unwary. For example, the Stocks account shown in the Current asset section is the common terminology for inventory. Although Burberry uses familiar terminology for Trade and other receivables, some British companies use the term Debtors for this account. The Equity section contains several account titles unique to British

---

[5] In addition, the measurement bases used for various accounts can sometimes be quite different from country to country. Throughout the book, we will alert you to these important differences as we discuss the recognition, measurement, and disclosure rules that govern financial reporting.

## EXHIBIT 4.3    Burberry PLC

### Group Balance Sheet

| (Amounts reported in millions of British pounds) | As at 31 March 2007 £m | As at 31 March 2006 £m |
|---|---|---|
| **Assets** | | |
| **Non-current assets** | | |
| Intangible assets | 133.6 | 135.4 |
| Property, plant and equipment | 162.7 | 167.0 |
| Deferred taxation assets | 24.6 | 16.6 |
| Trade and other receivables | 5.1 | 4.2 |
| | 326.0 | 323.2 |
| | | |
| **Current assets** | | |
| Stock | 149.8 | 124.2 |
| Trade and other receivables | 137.2 | 108.0 |
| Derivative financial assets | 5.3 | 2.8 |
| Income tax recoverable | — | 0.2 |
| Cash and cash equivalents | 131.4 | 113.7 |
| | 423.7 | 348.9 |
| **Total assets** | 749.7 | 672.1 |
| **Liabilities** | | |
| **Non-current liabilities** | | |
| Long-term liabilities | (10.4) | (14.6) |
| Deferred taxation liabilities | (10.2) | (10.5) |
| Retirement benefit obligations | (1.8) | (1.8) |
| Provisions for liabilities and charges | — | (2.8) |
| | (22.4) | (29.7) |
| | | |
| **Current liabilities** | | |
| Bank overdrafts and borrowings | (134.2) | (101.2) |
| Derivative financial liabilities | (0.5) | (2.1) |
| Trade and other payables | (170.7) | (126.9) |
| Income tax liabilities | (25.0) | (25.6) |
| | (330.4) | (255.8) |
| **Total liabilities** | (352.8) | (285.5) |
| **Net assets** | 396.9 | 386.6 |
| **Equity** | | |
| **Capital and reserves attributable to the Company's equity holders** | | |
| Ordinary share capital | 0.2 | 0.2 |
| Share premium account | 167.3 | 151.8 |
| Capital reserve | 26.0 | 25.8 |
| Hedging reserve | 1.8 | (0.2) |
| Foreign currency translation reserve | (6.2) | 21.2 |
| Retained earnings | 207.8 | 187.8 |
| **Total equity** | 396.9 | 386.6 |

*Source:* Burberry Group PLC Annual Report 2006/2007.

accounting. Exhibit 4.4 shows the accounts under U.S. GAAP that correspond to these British accounts. One of the British equity accounts that requires brief elaboration since it has no U.S. counterpart is the Capital reserve. In the United Kingdom, when a company repurchases its own shares, these shares are canceled. When the repurchase is paid for from profits, an amount equivalent to the par or stated value of the shares repurchased is

| EXHIBIT 4.4 | Comparison of U.K. and U.S. Account Titles |
| --- | --- |
| **U.K. Equity Accounts** | **Equivalent U.S. Accounts** |
| Ordinary share capital | Common stock—par |
| Share premium | Capital in excess of par |
| Capital reserve | No equivalent in U.S. GAAP |
| Revaluation reserve | No equivalent in U.S. GAAP |

transferred from the Ordinary share capital account to a Capital reserve account, which is not available for dividend distribution. Although not shown on Burberry's balance sheet, some British companies report a Revaluation reserve as part of shareholders' equity. U.K. GAAP allows companies to periodically revalue both tangible and intangible fixed assets upward. Any surplus arising from a revaluation is credited to the Revaluation reserve (see Chapter 10 for further details).[6]

Finally, note that Burberry reports the numbers on its balance sheet for the "Group." The Group numbers reflect the financial position of Burberry and all of its subsidiaries. This is equivalent to the "consolidated" financial statement numbers of a parent and its subsidiaries under U.S. GAAP.

This example provides a brief glimpse of how balance sheet format and terminology used in other countries differ from those used under U.S. GAAP. Examples of differences in accounting standards across countries appear throughout the book and are discussed further in Chapter 18.

**The balance sheet provides a snapshot of a company's financial position at a given point in time. It shows the various types of assets held at the balance sheet date and the claims against those assets (that is, how those assets have been financed).**

**Balance sheet accounts reflect a variety of measurement bases, including historical cost, current costs (also called fair value), net realizable value, and discounted present value. Therefore, users of balance sheet information must be careful to recognize the effects that these different measurement bases can have both when aggregating numbers across accounts as well as when computing ratios that are used in making intercompany comparisons.**

**With the tremendous growth in international business and the increased frequency of cross-border financing, it is likely that you will encounter financial statements prepared under non–U.S. GAAP sometime during your career. When you do, you must be aware of differences in recognition and measurement criteria, statement format, and terminology to properly interpret and analyze those statements.**

## Financial Statement Footnotes

Footnotes are an integral part of companies' financial reports. Financial statement footnotes provide a wealth of information that allows statement users to better understand and interpret the numbers presented in the body of the financial statements. In some instances, footnotes contain important information not found in the financial statements themselves. For example, the lease footnote shows a firm's future commitments under noncapitalized operating leases, which is useful in assessing a firm's future cash flow needs and creditworthiness. Throughout the remainder of the book, we illustrate the type of information typically found in footnotes, and we discuss how this information can be used to evaluate a company's future prospects and creditworthiness.

---

[6] "Property, Plant and Equipment," *IAS 16* (London: International Accounting Standards Board [IASB], revised 2003). "Intangible Assets," *IAS 38* (London: IASB, 2004).

Here we briefly discuss and illustrate three important notes typically found in companies' financial reports:

1. Summary of significant accounting policies.
2. Disclosure of important subsequent events.
3. Related-party transactions.

## Summary of Significant Accounting Policies

As you will see in later chapters, in many areas of accounting, management is free to choose from equally acceptable alternative accounting methods. Examples include different cost flow assumptions for valuing inventory (FIFO versus LIFO), different methods for determining depreciation expense (straight-line versus accelerated), and different methods of accounting for long-term construction contracts (percentage-of-completion versus completed contract). To make valid intercompany comparisons, it is important for statement users to recognize and understand the alternative accounting methods that a reporting entity has selected to account for its economic activities.

The **Summary of Significant Accounting Policies** explains the important accounting choices that the reporting entity uses to account for selected transactions and accounts.[7] Exhibit 4.5 shows excerpts from the accounting policy footnote in Motorola's 2006 annual report.

## Subsequent Events Footnote

Events or transactions that have a significant effect on a company's financial position or results of operations sometimes occur after the close of its fiscal year-end but before the financial statements are issued. Disclosure of these **subsequent events** is required if they are material and are likely to influence investors' appraisal of the risk and return prospects of the reporting entity.[8] Examples of such events include loss of a major customer, a business combination, issuance of debt or equity securities, or a catastrophic loss. Exhibit 4.6 illustrates a subsequent event disclosure provided by Xerox Corporation in its 2006 annual report related to the board of directors' authorizing repurchase of the company's common stock in the subsequent year.

## Related-Party Transactions

A **related-party transaction** occurs when a company enters into a transaction with individuals or other businesses that are in some way connected with it or its management or board of directors. Examples include transactions between:

1. The reporting entity and its principal owners, management or members of their immediate families, and members of the board of directors.
2. Subsidiaries of a common parent.
3. The reporting entity and nonconsolidated affiliates in which it holds a significant ownership stake.

Because related-party transactions are not entered into at arm's length, these events pose greater risks. Therefore, companies are required to disclose in a footnote any related-party transactions, including the nature of the relationship, a description of the transaction, and any

> Enron's dealings with several special purpose entities set up as limited partnerships that were headed up by Andrew Fastow, Enron's chief financial officer, provide an example of this type of related-party transaction.

---

[7] "Disclosure of Accounting Policies," *Accounting Principles Board Opinion No. 22* (New York: American Institute of Certified Public Accountants [AICPA] 1972).

[8] "Codification of Auditing Standards and Procedures," *Statement on Auditing Standards No. 1* (New York: AICPA, 1972).

**EXHIBIT 4.5**    Motorola Inc.

**Excerpts from 2006 Accounting Policies Footnote**

1. Summary of Significant Accounting Policies

**Revenue Recognition:**  The Company recognizes revenue when persuasive evidence of an arrangement exists, delivery has occurred, the sales price is fixed or determinable, and collectibility of the sales price is reasonably assured. In addition to these general revenue recognition criteria, the following specific revenue recognition policies are followed:

*Products and Equipment*—For product and equipment sales, delivery generally does not occur until the products or equipment have been shipped, risk of loss has transferred to the customer, and objective evidence exists that customer acceptance provisions have been met. The Company records revenue when allowances for discounts, price protection, returns and customer incentives can be reliably estimated. Recorded revenues are reduced by these allowances. The Company bases its estimates on historical experience taking into consideration the type of products sold, the type of customer, and the type of transaction specific in each arrangement.

*Long-Term Contracts*—For long-term contracts that involve customization or modification of the Company's equipment or software, the Company generally recognizes revenue using the percentage of completion method based on the percentage of costs incurred to date compared to the total estimated costs to complete the contract. In certain instances, when revenues or costs associated with long-term contracts cannot be reliably estimated or the contract involves unproven technologies or other inherent hazards, revenues and costs are deferred until the project is complete and customer acceptance is obtained.

*Services*—Revenue for services is generally recognized ratably over the contract term as services are performed.

*Software and Licenses*—Revenue from pre-paid perpetual licenses is recognized at the inception of the arrangement, presuming all other relevant revenue recognition criteria are met. Revenue from non-perpetual licenses or term licenses is recognized ratably over the period that the licensee uses the license. Revenue from software maintenance, technical support and unspecified upgrades is generally recognized over the period that these services are delivered.

**Inventories:** Inventories are valued at the lower of average cost (which approximates computation on a first-in, first-out basis) or market (net realizable value or replacement cost).

**Property, Plant and Equipment:** Property, plant and equipment are stated at cost less accumulated depreciation. Depreciation is recorded using straight-line and declining-balance methods, based on the estimated useful lives of the assets (buildings and building equipment, 5–40 years; machinery and equipment, 2–12 years) and commences once the assets are ready for their intended use.

**EXHIBIT 4.6**    Xerox Corp.

**Footnote on Subsequent Event
2006 Annual Report**

Note 22—Subsequent Event

In February 2007, the Board of Directors authorized an additional repurchase of up to $500 million of the Company's common stock over the next 12 months. The repurchases may be made on the open market, or through derivative or negotiated transactions. The Company expects the stock to be repurchased primarily through open-market purchases. Open-market repurchases will be made in compliance with the Securities and Exchange Commission's Rule 10b-18, and are subject to market conditions as well as applicable legal and other considerations.

**EXHIBIT 4.7**    USA Technologies

**Excerpts from 2006 Footnote on Related-Party Transactions**

**7. Related-Party Transactions**

During the years ended June 30, 2006, 2005, and 2004, the Company incurred approximately $258,000, $284,000, and $391,000, respectively, in connection with legal services provided by a member of the Company's Board of Directors. At June 30, 2006 and 2005, approximately $28,000 and $25,000, respectively, of the Company's accounts payable and accrued expenses were due to this Board member. During the year ended June 30, 2005, the Company incurred approximately $72,600 in connection with consulting services provided by another member of the Company's Board of Directors. At June 30, 2006 and 2005, approximately $0 and $73,000, respectively, of the Company's accrued expenses were due to this Board member. During the years ended June 30, 2006, 2005, and 2004, certain Board members and executives participated in various debt or equity offerings of the Company for total investments of approximately $53,000, $245,000, and $266,000, respectively. As of June 30, 2006 and 2005, Mr. Illes, an accredited investor, held $1,000,000 of Senior Notes.

dollar amounts involved.[9] Exhibit 4.7 illustrates a related-party footnote disclosure from USA Technologies' 2006 annual report detailing transactions that the company entered into with board members and executive officers.

## STATEMENT OF CASH FLOWS

The balance sheet shows a firm's investment (assets) and financial structure (liabilities and stockholders' equity) at a given *point in time*. By contrast, the **statement of cash flows** shows the user why a firm's investments and financial structure have *changed* between two balance sheet dates. The connection between successive balance sheet positions and the statement of cash flows can be demonstrated through simple manipulation of the basic accounting equation:

$$\text{Assets} = \text{Liabilities} + \text{Stockholders' equity} \qquad (4.1)$$

Partitioning the assets into cash and all other assets yields:

$$\text{Cash} + \text{Noncash assets} = \text{Liabilities} + \text{Stockholders' equity} \qquad (4.2)$$

Rearranging yields:

$$\text{Cash} = \text{Liabilities} - \text{Noncash assets} + \text{Stockholders' equity} \qquad (4.3)$$

From basic algebra, we know that an equality like this must also hold for the algebraic sum of the changes on both sides of the equation. Representing equation (4.3) in the form of the change ($\Delta$) in each term results in

$$\Delta\text{Cash} = \Delta\text{Liabilities} - \Delta\text{Noncash assets} + \Delta\text{Stockholders' equity} \qquad (4.4)$$

Thus, the cash flow statement, which provides an explanation of why a firm's cash position has changed between successive balance sheet dates, simultaneously explains the changes that

---

[9] "Related Party Disclosures," *SFAS No. 57* (Stamford, CT: FASB, 1982).

have taken place in the firm's noncash asset, liability, and stockholders' equity accounts over the same time period.

The change in a firm's cash position between successive balance sheet dates will *not* equal the reported earnings for that period for three reasons:

1. Reported net income usually will not equal cash flow from **operating activities** because (a) noncash revenues and expenses are often recognized as part of accrual earnings, and (b) certain operating cash inflows and outflows are not recorded as revenues or expenses under accrual accounting in the same period the cash flows occur.

2. Changes in cash are also caused by nonoperating **investing activities** such as the purchase or sale of fixed assets.

3. Additional changes in cash are caused by **financing activities** such as the issuance of stock or bonds, the repayment of a bank loan, or dividends paid to stockholders.

Cash flows are critical to assessing a company's liquidity and creditworthiness. Firms with cash flows that are smaller than currently maturing obligations can be forced into bankruptcy or liquidation. Because cash flows and accrual earnings can differ dramatically, current reporting standards mandate that firms prepare a statement of cash flows as well as an income statement and balance sheet. The cash flow statement is designed to explain the causes for year-to-year changes in the balance of cash and cash equivalents.[10] We provide a brief introduction to the statement of cash flows here, focusing on the format of the statement and on the nature of some of the basic adjustments that are needed to convert accrual earnings to cash flow from operations. Later, after you have reviewed the accrual and cash flow effects of the transactions that affect various balance sheet and income statement accounts in the intervening chapters, you will find a more detailed explanation of the cash flow statement in Chapter 17.

> **Cash equivalents** include short-term, highly liquid investments that are readily convertible to cash such as demand deposits, savings accounts, certificates of deposit, money market funds, and U.S. treasury bills.

The cash flow statement summarizes the cash inflows and outflows of a company broken down into its three principal activities:

- *Operating activities:* Cash flows from operating activities result from the cash effects of transactions and events that affect operating income: both production and delivery of goods and services.

- *Investing activities:* Cash flows from investing activities include making and collecting loans; investing in and disposing of debt or equity securities of other companies; and purchasing and disposing of assets, such as equipment, that are used by a company in the production of goods or services.

- *Financing activities:* Cash flows from financing activities include obtaining cash from new issues of stock or bonds, paying dividends or buying back a company's own shares (treasury stock), borrowing money, and repaying amounts borrowed.

***Companies that are able to satisfy most of their cash needs from operating cash flows are generally considered to be in stronger financial health and better credit risks.***

Exhibit 4.8 presents Wal-Mart's 2006 cash flow statement broken into operating, investing, and financing activities. Note that operating activities generated $20.164 billion in cash flows, investing activities used $14.463 billion, and financing activities used $4.839 billion of cash, resulting in a net cash increase of $959 million after adjusting for a $97 million foreign currency exchange rate change on cash. Wal-Mart uses the so-called **indirect approach**

---

[10] The format for preparing the cash flow statement is specified in "Statement of Cash Flows," *SFAS No. 95* (Stamford, CT: FASB, 1987).

| EXHIBIT 4.8 | Wal-Mart Stores, Inc. |
| --- | --- |
|  | Consolidated Statements of Cash Flows |

|  | Fiscal Year Ended January 31, | | |
| --- | --- | --- | --- |
| (Amounts in millions) | 2007 | 2006 | 2005 |
| **Cash flows from operating activities** | | | |
| Net income | $11,284 | $11,231 | $10,267 |
| Loss from discontinued operations, net of tax | 894 | 177 | 215 |
| Income from continuing operations | 12,178 | 11,408 | 10,482 |
| Adjustments to reconcile income from continuing operations to net cash provided by operating activities: | | | |
| Depreciation and amortization | 5,459 | 4,645 | 4,185 |
| Deferred income taxes | 89 | (129) | 263 |
| Other operating activities | 1,039 | 613 | 388 |
| Changes in certain assets and liabilities, net of effects of acquisitions | | | |
| Increase in accounts receivable | (214) | (466) | (302) |
| Increase in inventories | (1,274) | (1,761) | (2,515) |
| Increase in accounts payable | 2,344 | 2,425 | 1,681 |
| Increase in accrued liabilities | 588 | 1,002 | 997 |
| Net cash provided by operating activities of continuing operations | 20,209 | 17,737 | 15,179 |
| Net cash used in operating activities of discontinued operations | (45) | (102) | (135) |
| Net cash provided by operating activities | 20,164 | 17,635 | 15,044 |
| **Cash flows from investing activities** | | | |
| Payments for property and equipment | (15,666) | (14,530) | (12,803) |
| Proceeds from disposal of property and equipment | 394 | 1,042 | 925 |
| Proceeds from disposal of certain international operations, net | 610 | — | — |
| Investment in international operations, net of cash acquired | (68) | (601) | (315) |
| Other investing activities | 223 | (67) | (99) |
| Net cash used in investing activities of continuing operations | (14,507) | (14,156) | (12,292) |
| Net cash provided by (used in) investing activities of discontinued operations | 44 | (30) | (59) |
| Net cash used in investing activities | (14,463) | (14,186) | (12,351) |
| **Cash flows from financing activities** | | | |
| (Decrease) increase in commercial paper | (1,193) | (704) | 544 |
| Proceeds from issuance of long-term debt | 7,199 | 7,691 | 5,832 |
| Dividends paid | (2,802) | (2,511) | (2,214) |
| Payment of long-term debt | (5,758) | (2,724) | (2,131) |
| Purchase of Company stock | (1,718) | (3,580) | (4,549) |
| Payment of capital lease obligations | (340) | (245) | (204) |
| Other financing activities | (227) | (349) | 113 |
| Net cash used in financing activities | (4,839) | (2,422) | (2,609) |
| Effect of exchange rate changes on cash | 97 | (101) | 205 |
| Net increase in cash and cash equivalents | 959 | 926 | 289 |
| Cash and cash equivalents at beginning of year | 6,414 | 5,488 | 5,199 |
| Cash and cash equivalents at end of year | $ 7,373 | $ 6,414 | $ 5,488 |

to calculate cash flows from operations by adjusting accrual-basis earnings for differences between accrual revenues and expenses and cash inflows and outflows related to operating activities during the period. The rationale for the depreciation and amortization adjustment and why changes in various working capital accounts capture the differences between accrual earnings and operating cash flows is explained with a simplified example in the following section.

Wal-Mart's major investing cash outflow ($15.666 billion) was for purchase of property, plant, and equipment. In the financing section, the issuance of long-term debt provided $7.199

billion of cash. Major financing cash outflows were used for repayment of loans obtained through commercial paper ($1.193 billion), dividend payments ($2.802 billion), repayment of long-term debt ($5.758 billion), and purchase of company stock ($1.718 billion).

## Cash Flows versus Accrual Earnings

The following example illustrates the major differences between cash flows and accrual earnings, why a cash flow statement is needed to fully understand the distinction between the two, and why certain adjustments are made to accrual earnings to obtain cash flows from operations.

HRB Advertising Company opened for business on April 1, 2008. The corporation's activities and transactions for the remainder of 2008 are summarized as follows:

1. Herb Wilson, Robin Hansen, and Barbara Reynolds each contributed $3,500 cash on April 1 for shares of the company's common stock.

2. HRB rented office space beginning April 1, and paid the full year's rental of $2,000 per month, or $24,000, in advance.

3. The company borrowed $10,000 from a bank on April 1. The principal plus accrued interest is payable January 1, 2009 with interest at the rate of 12% per year.

4. HRB purchased office equipment with a five-year life for $15,000 cash on April 1. Salvage value is zero and the equipment is being depreciated using the straight-line method.

5. HRB sold and billed customers for $65,000 of advertising services rendered between April 1 and December 31. Of this amount, $20,000 was still uncollected by year-end.

6. By year-end, the company incurred and paid the following operating costs: (a) utilities, $650; (b) salaries, $36,250; and (c) supplies, $800.

7. The company had accrued (unpaid) expenses at year-end as follows: (a) utilities, $75; (b) salaries, $2,400; and (c) interest, $900.

8. Supplies purchased on account and unpaid at year-end amounted to $50. When supplies are purchased, they are charged to an asset account.

9. Supplies inventory on hand at year-end amounted to $100.

10. Annual depreciation on office equipment is $15,000/5 = $3,000. Because the equipment was acquired on April 1, the depreciation expense for 2008 is $3,000 × 9/12 = $2,250.

Herb, Robin, and Barbara were delighted to discover that the company earned a profit (before taxes) of $3,725 in 2008. However, they were shocked to learn that the company's checking account was overdrawn by $11,200 at year-end. This overdraft was particularly disconcerting because the bank loan had become due.

Is HRB Advertising Company profitable, or is it about to go bankrupt? What are its prospects for the future? Exhibit 4.9 helps us examine these issues.

While HRB Advertising generated *positive* accrual accounting earnings of $3,725 during 2008, its operating cash flow was a *negative* $16,700. Columns (b) and (c) show the causes for the divergence between the components of accrual income (column [a]) and operating cash flows (column [d]). Because of a net infusion of cash from financing activities (column [d]), the net change in cash (a negative $11,200) was much smaller than the negative cash flow of $16,700 from operating activities.

We now discuss the rationale behind the adjustments in columns (b) and (c). We examine each adjustment in terms of how it affects bottom-line *accrual-basis net income*, not how the adjustment affects revenues or expenses that compose net income. Because expenses are treated as negative amounts in computing net income, an adjustment that reduces (increases) an expense is treated as a plus (negative) amount in columns (b) and (c). This way of designating

| EXHIBIT 4.9 | HRB Advertising Company |
|---|---|

**Analysis of Accrual Income versus Change in Cash for Year Ended December 31, 2008**

| Item | (a)<br>Accrual<br>Income | (b)<br>Noncash Accruals:<br>Revenue Earned (or<br>Expenses Incurred) | (c)<br>Prepayments<br>and Supplies<br>Buildup | (d)<br>a + b + c<br>Cash Received<br>(or Paid) During<br>2008 |
|---|---|---|---|---|
| **Operating activities** | | | | |
| Advertising revenues | $65,000 | −$20,000[5] | | $45,000 |
| Salaries | −38,650 | +2,400[7b] | | −36,250 |
| Rent | −18,000 | | −$6,000[2] | −24,000 |
| Utilities | −725 | +75[7a] | | −650 |
| Supplies | −750 | +50[8] | −100[9] | −800 |
| Interest | −900 | +900[7c] | | –0– |
| Depreciation | −2,250 | +2,250[10] | | –0– |
| Operating cash flow | | | | −$16,700 |
| **Net income** | $ 3,725 | | | |
| | | | | |
| **Investing activities** | | | | |
| Equipment purchase | | | | −$15,000[4] |
| | | | | |
| **Financing activities** | | | | |
| Stock issuance | | | | $10,500[1] |
| Bank borrowing | | | | 10,000[3] |
| | | | | $20,500 |
| **Change in cash** | | | | −$11,200 |

Note: Numbers in parentheses refer to numbered transactions on page 199.

positive and negative amounts will facilitate our discussion of the adjustments to accrual basis income needed to arrive at operating cash flows.

- Advertising revenues recognized under accrual accounting totaled $65,000. However, $20,000 of this remains as uncollected accounts receivable at year-end. Thus, the ending balance in the Accounts receivable account must be *subtracted* from the accrual basis revenues to derive the cash received during the year for advertising services.

- The salaries expense of $38,650 for the year includes the $36,250 of salaries incurred and paid in cash plus the $2,400 of salary expense accrued at year-end. Therefore, the accrued (unpaid) salaries, which is the ending balance in the Accrued salaries payable (liability) account, must be *added back* to total salaries expense to derive the salaries paid in cash.

- HRB recognized rent expense of $2,000 × 9 months = $18,000 in 2008. The difference between the amount paid out in cash and the amount recognized as expense under accrual accounting ($24,000 − $18,000, or $6,000) would be the ending balance in the Prepaid rent (asset) account. This amount is shown as a negative adjustment (*subtraction*) in column (c) because the cash outflow for rent was higher than the amount of rent expense recognized.

- The utilities expense of $725 for the year includes the $650 of utilities paid in cash plus $75 of utilities expense accrued at year-end. The utilities expense incurred but not yet paid, which is the ending balance in the Accrued utilities payable (liability) account, must be *added back* to the total utilities expense to obtain the cash payments for utilities in 2008.

- Total supplies purchased during the year included $800 paid in cash and $50 purchased on account (Accounts payable). Of the amount purchased, $100 of supplies remains on hand in the Supplies inventory account at year-end. So, supplies expense under accrual accounting is $800 + $50 − $100 = $750. To adjust the accrual-basis expense to derive the cash outflow for supplies requires that we *add back* the ending balance in Accounts payable (which was a noncash increase to the supplies expense) and *subtract* the $100 ending balance in Supplies inventory (which was a noncash decrease to the supplies expense).

- Accrued interest expense for the year is $10,000 × 12% × 9/12 = $900. Because none of this has been paid in cash, the ending balance in the Accrued interest payable (liability) account must be *added back* to the Interest expense account to obtain the cash paid out for interest in 2008.

- Depreciation is a noncash expense under accrual accounting. So, this amount, which is reflected in the increase in the Accumulated depreciation (contra-asset) account, must be *added back* to depreciation expense.

> Remember, for a start-up company, beginning account balances are zero.

Except for depreciation, each of the adjustments we just outlined uses the ending balance (which is also the *change* in the account balance in the first year of a company's life) of a current asset account (for example, Accounts receivable, Supplies inventory, or Prepaid rent) or a current liability account (for example, Accounts payable, Salaries payable, Utilities payable, or Interest payable) to adjust accrual-basis revenues or expenses to derive cash flows from operations. The adjustments to accrual-basis income (revenues − expenses) for changes in current asset and current liability accounts that represent accrued revenues, deferred (unearned) revenues, accrued expenses, or deferred (prepaid) expenses are summarized in Figure 4.1.

> Only adjustments for changes in working capital accounts are summarized in Figure 4.1 Other adjustments (such as depreciation and gains/losses on asset sales) will be discussed in Chapter 17.

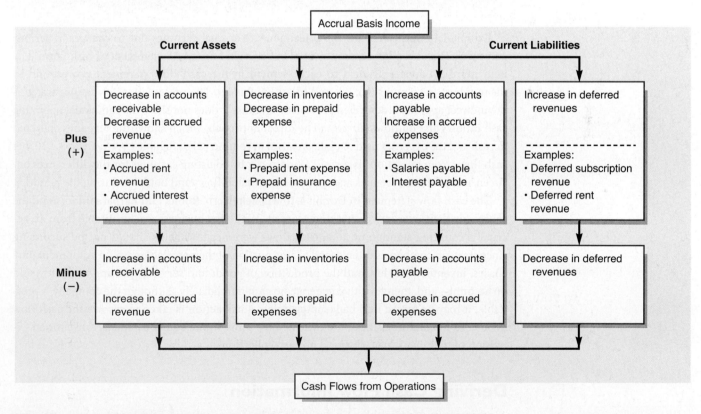

**Figure 4.1** ADJUSTMENTS TO ACCRUAL EARNINGS FOR CHANGES IN WORKING CAPITAL ACCOUNTS TO OBTAIN CASH FLOWS FROM OPERATIONS

### EXHIBIT 4.10    HRB Advertising Company

**Statement of Cash Flows for Year Ended December 31, 2008**

**Operating cash flows**

| | | |
|---|---|---|
| Net income | | $ 3,725 |
| Plus | | |
| Depreciation[10] | $ 2,250 | |
| Increase in salaries payable[7b] | 2,400 | |
| Increase in accounts payable[8] | 50 | |
| Increase in utilities payable[7a] | 75 | |
| Increase in interest payable[7c] | 900 | 5,675 |
| Minus | | |
| Increase in receivables[5] | (20,000) | |
| Increase in prepaid rent[2] | (6,000) | |
| Increase in supplies inventory[9] | (100) | (26,100) |
| Cash flows from operations | | $(16,700) |
| | | |
| **Investing cash flows** | | |
| Equipment purchase[4] | | $(15,000) |
| | | |
| **Financing cash flows** | | |
| Stock issuance[1] | | $ 10,500 |
| Bank borrowing[3] | | 10,000 |
| | | $ 20,500 |
| **Change in cash** | | $(11,200) |

Note: Numbers in parentheses refer to numbered transactions on page 199.

Exhibit 4.10 illustrates how the adjustments to accrual earnings due to *changes* in various current asset and liability accounts would be reflected in a GAAP statement of cash flows. The item numbers appearing next to each element in the cash flow statement correspond to the numbers in columns (b), (c), and (d) of Exhibit 4.9. The presentation format illustrated is the indirect approach (described previously) because it does not show the individual operating cash inflows and outflows *directly*. (The **direct approach,** which shows the revenues collected in cash and the expenses paid in cash, is shown in column [d] of Exhibit 4.9.) In Exhibit 4.10, net cash flows from operations is arrived at indirectly by adjusting earnings for the differences between accrual-basis revenues and expenses and cash inflows and outflows during the period.

The cash flow statement in Exhibit 4.10 will help Herb, Robin, and Barbara understand the causes for their overdrawn checking account. While the business was profitable from an accrual accounting standpoint, total cash flows were negative. This should not be surprising since start-up companies often spend a large portion of their available cash on equipment purchases, inventory buildup, and the production of goods and services that are frequently sold on account—and, therefore, that generate no cash immediately. Although the company is profitable, it may be forced into bankruptcy unless quick action is taken to resolve the cash flow deficit. To remain in business, the owners must infuse more equity capital, arrange for an extension of their bank loan, or speed up cash collections.

## Deriving Cash Flow Information

The three owners were able to convince their banker to refinance the loan but only after they each agreed to contribute another $2,000 to the company, a total of $6,000. The loan was replaced by a three-year note, but the interest rate was increased to 13.50% to reflect the

## EXHIBIT 4.11 HRB Advertising Company

### Comparative Balance Sheets December 31, 2008 and 2009

| | 2008 | 2009 |
|---|---|---|
| **Assets** | | |
| Cash | $(11,200) | $ 500 |
| Accounts receivable | 20,000 | 15,775 |
| Supplies inventory | 100 | 225 |
| Prepaid rent | 6,000 | 6,000 |
| Office equipment | 15,000 | 16,500 |
| Less: Accumulated depreciation | (2,250) | (5,500) |
| Total assets | $ 27,650 | $33,500 |
| **Liabilities and Equities** | | |
| Utilities payable | $ 75 | $ 50 |
| Interest payable | 900 | 675 |
| Accounts payable (supplies) | 50 | 75 |
| Salaries payable | 2,400 | 4,200 |
| Bank loan | 10,000 | — |
| Note payable | — | 10,000 |
| **Total liabilities** | $ 13,425 | $15,000 |
| Common stock | 10,500 | 16,500 |
| Retained earnings | 3,725 | 2,000 |
| **Total liabilities and stockholders' equity** | $ 27,650 | $33,500 |

additional risk associated with the refinanced borrowing. Herb, Robin, and Barbara felt confident that with careful attention to both earnings and cash flow, they could successfully grow the business and repay the note before its maturity.

During 2009, the second year of business, revenues increased and operating cash flows were positive, but the company recorded a loss for the year. Exhibit 4.11 contains HRB Advertising's comparative balance sheets for 2008 and 2009, and Exhibit 4.12 presents the company's earnings and cash flow statements for the two years.

We can see from the balance sheet that the $10,000 bank loan was refinanced as a Note payable (Exhibit 4.11) and that additional common stock of $6,000 was issued during 2009. Also notice that the company's Cash account ended the year with a positive balance of $500.

Highlights from the income statement (Exhibit 4.12 [a]) include substantial growth in advertising revenues from $65,000 to $92,000, a 41.5% increase. At the same time, the company was able to speed up its collection of credit sales and reduce its Accounts receivable balance, as shown in Exhibit 4.11. Unfortunately, salary expense increased nearly 63%, from $38,650 to $62,875, which seems to be the major factor contributing to the company's $1,725 loss for the year. From the cash flow statement (see Exhibit 4.12 [b]), we see that 2009 cash flows from operations totaled a positive $7,200 even though the business sustained a loss for the year. The company's overall cash balance increased by $11,700 during the year with $6,000 of that amount representing cash contributed by the owners in exchange for additional common stock.

Although U.S. companies must now include a cash flow statement similar to Exhibit 4.12 (b) in their annual report to shareholders, this was not always the case. Moreover, quarterly cash flow statements are not required, although most companies voluntarily make them available to shareholders. Companies that don't provide quarterly cash flow statements challenge the analyst. How can cash flow information be derived from a company's balance sheet and income statement when the cash flow statement itself is not available?

| EXHIBIT 4.12 | HRB Advertising Company | | |
| --- | --- | --- | --- |

**Comparative Income and Cash Flow Statements for Years Ended December 31, 2008 and 2009**

| | 2008 | 2009 |
| --- | --- | --- |
| **Panel (a)** | | |
| **Income Statement** | | |
| Revenue from advertising services | $ 65,000 | $ 92,000 |
| Less | | |
| Salaries expense | (38,650) | (62,875) |
| Supplies expense | (750) | (1,200) |
| Rent expense | (18,000) | (24,000) |
| Utilities expense | (725) | (1,050) |
| Interest expense | (900) | (1,350) |
| Depreciation | (2,250) | (3,250) |
| **Net income** | $  3,725 | $ (1,725) |
| **Panel (b)** | | |
| **Cash Flow Statement** | | |
| Net income | $  3,725 | $ (1,725) |
| Depreciation | 2,250 | 3,250 |
| | 5,975 | 1,525 |
| Working capital adjustments | | |
| Accounts receivable decrease (increase) | (20,000) | 4,225 |
| Supplies inventory (increase) | (100) | (125) |
| Prepaid rent decrease (increase) | (6,000) | — |
| Utilities payable increase (decrease) | 75 | (25) |
| Accounts payable (supplies) increase | 50 | 25 |
| Interest payable increase (decrease) | 900 | (225) |
| Salaries payable increase | 2,400 | 1,800 |
| **Cash flow from operations** | $(16,700) | $  7,200 |
| Equipment purchases | $(15,000) | $ (1,500) |
| **Cash flow from investing activities** | $(15,000) | $ (1,500) |
| Bank loan (repayment) | $ 10,000 | $(10,000) |
| Note payable issued | — | 10,000 |
| Common stock issued | 10,500 | 6,000 |
| **Cash flow from financing activities** | $ 20,500 | $  6,000 |
| **Change in cash balance** | $(11,200) | $ 11,700 |

The answer is not very complicated, as we will see. Deriving information about a company's cash receipts and disbursements from balance sheet and income statement information involves little more than a careful and systematic analysis of the changes in individual balance sheet accounts and their corresponding income statement effects. From this analysis, you can deduce individual cash flows and construct a summary schedule of cash receipts (inflows) and disbursements (outflows) that closely resembles the cash flow statement presented in Exhibit 4.12(b).

The starting point for this analysis is the Cash account itself. Notice from the balance sheet (Exhibit 4.11) that the company's cash position increased by $11,700 during 2009, from the $11,200 deficit at the beginning of the year to a $500 positive balance at year-end. Consequently, we know that total cash receipts for the year must have been $11,700 higher than total cash payments. Now let's uncover some individual cash flow items.

Exhibit 4.13 illustrates the general T-account analysis that can be used to derive cash flow information from selected balance sheet accounts of HRB Advertising for 2009. From the comparative balance sheet in Exhibit 4.11, the beginning and ending balances can be obtained for each *balance sheet* account that is affected when a revenue or expense item is recorded. The accrual-basis revenue or expense that results in a debit or credit to the related balance sheet account can then be entered (see circled items in Exhibit 4.13). The cash received or cash paid, which results in an offsetting entry to each of these accounts, is the "plug" figure (in blue) that is needed to arrive at the ending balance that is given. We now illustrate this analysis for selected accounts in Exhibit 4.13.

The company's only source of operating cash inflows is customer receipts, so we begin with an analysis of the Accounts receivable account. As shown in Exhibit 4.13, the balance in Accounts receivable declined by $4,225 during 2009, from a beginning balance of $20,000 to a year-end balance of $15,775. Because billings for advertising services performed during 2009 totaled $92,000 (that is, Advertising revenues in the income statement of Exhibit 4.12[a]), HRB must have collected $96,225 from its customers. To see this, note that collections must have been $4,225 higher than new billings because the Accounts receivable balance decreased by this amount during the year. Another way to think about this calculation is to assume that all customers pay on a timely basis. In this case, HRB would have collected $20,000 cash from customers billed in 2008 and another $76,225 from customers billed in 2009 (or $92,000 billings minus the $15,775 that was uncollected at year-end).

Salary payments represent the company's largest operating cash outflow. Exhibit 4.13 shows that Salaries payable increased by $1,800 during the year, from a beginning balance of $2,400 to $4,200 at year-end. Consequently, salary payments must have been $61,075 for the year, or $1,800 less than the total salaries expense of $62,875 that shows up in the income statement in Exhibit 4.12 (a).

Some cash inflows and outflows involve more than one balance sheet account. Exhibit 4.13 shows this for supplies. As shown there, Accounts payable (supplies) increased $25 during the year, from a beginning balance of $50 to $75 at year-end. This means that payments for supplies must have been $25 less than purchases. But where can we find information about purchases? Certainly not from the income statement (Exhibit 4.12 [a]) because it reports the cost of supplies *used* during the year regardless of when they were purchased. Because purchases increase the total supplies on hand, we turn our attention to the Supplies inventory account. As we see in Exhibit 4.13, Supplies inventory increased by $125 during the year, from $100 at the start to $225 at year-end. Purchases must therefore have been $125 more than the amount of supplies used during the year (that is, the supplies expense from Exhibit 4.12[a]). In other words, purchases must have totaled $1,325 (or the $1,200 supplies expense plus the $125 Supplies inventory increase), and consequently, supplier payments must have totaled $1,300 (or $1,325 purchases minus the $25 Accounts payable increase).

The same type of analysis just outlined is illustrated for the Prepaid rent, Accounts payable (utilities), and Accrued interest payable accounts in Exhibit 4.13. The process continues until all balance sheet accounts are fully reconciled and the company's cash receipts and disbursements are identified. In addition, analysis of changes in the Notes payable, Common stock, and Equipment accounts (not shown) can identify cash inflows and outflows from investing and financing activities.

The derived cash inflows and outflows for HRB Advertising are listed in Exhibit 4.14, by major sources: operating, investing, and financing activities. This schedule explains why the company's cash balance increased by $11,700 during the year. Operating activities contributed $7,200 of cash, $1,500 was spent on new equipment, and financing activities added another $6,000. These are precisely the cash inflows and outflows listed in the company's cash flow statement in Exhibit 4.12 (b).

These investing and financing activities will be discussed in Chapters 10 and 11.

The analysis in Exhibit 4.14 has focused on the adjustments to accrual earnings that are required as a result of changes in various working capital (current assets minus current liabilities)

EXHIBIT 4.13　HRB Advertising Company

**Analysis of Income Statement and Balance Sheet Accounts for Year Ended December 31, 2009**

| INCOME STATEMENT | BALANCE SHEET |
|---|---|

**Advertising revenues** — **Accounts receivable**

| | | | |
|---|---|---|---|
| | *Beginning balance* | $20,000 | |
| $92,000 | *Advertising revenues (accrual basis)* | $92,000 | $96,225 *Collections (cash basis)* |
| | *Ending balance* | $15,775 | |

**Salaries expense** — **Salaries payable**

| | | | |
|---|---|---|---|
| | | | $ 2,400 *Beginning balance* |
| $62,875 | *Salaries paid (cash basis) (accrual basis)* | $61,075 | $62,875 *Salaries expense* |
| | | | $ 4,200 *Ending balance* |

**Rent expense** — **Prepaid rent**

*Rent expense from 1/1/09 to 3/31/09* — $ 6,000

| | | | |
|---|---|---|---|
| | *Beginning balance* | $ 6,000 | Amortized from beginning balance |
| | *Rent paid in advance on 4/1/09* | $24,000 | $ 6,000 Rent expense from 1/1/09 to 3/31/09 |

*Rent expense from 4/1/09 to 12/31/09* — $18,000   *(accrual basis)*   $18,000 Amortized from 4/1/09 payment Rent expense from 4/1/09 to 12/31/09

*Total expense* $24,000   *Ending balance*   $ 6,000

**Utilities expense** — **Accounts payable (utilities)**

| | | | |
|---|---|---|---|
| | | | $ 75 *Beginning balance* |
| $ 1,050 | *Payments (cash basis) (accrual basis)* | $ 1,075 | $ 1,050 *Utilities expense* |
| | | | $ 50 *Ending balance* |

**Accounts payable (supplies)**

| | | | |
|---|---|---|---|
| | *Payments (cash basis)* | $ 1,300 | $ 50 *Beginning balance* |
| | | | $ 1,325 *Purchases on accounts* |
| | | | $ 75 *Ending balance* |

**Supplies expense** — **Supplies inventory**

| | | | |
|---|---|---|---|
| | *Beginning balance* | $ 100 | |
| $ 1,200 | *Purchases on account (accrual basis)* | $ 1,325 | $ 1,200 *Supplies used up* |
| | *Ending balance* | $ 225 | |

**Interest expense** — **Accrued interest payable**

| | | | |
|---|---|---|---|
| | | | $ 900 *Beginning balance* |
| $ 1,350 | *Payments (cash basis)* | $ 1,575 | $ 1,350 *Accrued expense* |
| | *(accrual basis)* | | $ 675 *Ending balance* |

**Depreciation expense** — **Accumulated depreciation**

| | | | |
|---|---|---|---|
| | | | $ 2,250 *Beginning balance* |
| $ 3,250 | *(accrual basis)* | | $ 3,250 *Depreciation expense* |
| | | | $ 5,500 *Ending balance* |

---

**EXHIBIT 4.14** | **HRB Advertising Company**

**Schedule of Cash Receipts and Disbursements for the Years Ended December 31, 2008 and 2009**

|  | 2008 | 2009 | |
|---|---|---|---|
| **Operating activities** | | | |
| Advertising services | $ 45,000 | $ 96,225 | ← *from Accounts receivable* |
| Salaries | (36,250) | (61,075) | ← *from Salaries payable* |
| Rent | (24,000) | (24,000) | ← *from Prepaid rent* |
| Utilities | (650) | (1,075) | ← *from Utilities payable* |
| Supplies | (800) | (1,300) | ← *from Supplies payable* |
| Interest | — | (1,575) | ← *from Interest payable* |
| Operating cash flow | $(16,700) | $ 7,200 | |
| **Investing activities** | | | |
| Equipment purchase | $(15,000) | $ (1,500) | ← *from Office equipment* |
| **Financing activities** | | | |
| Bank borrowing | $ 10,000 | $(10,000) | ← *from Notes payable* |
| Note issuance | — | 10,000 | ← *from Notes payable* |
| Stock issuance | 10,500 | 6,000 | ← *from Common stock* |
| | 20,500 | 6,000 | |
| Change in cash | $(11,200) | $ 11,700 | ← *from Cash* |

accounts to derive operating cash flows under the indirect method. Obviously, many other adjustments are required to fully reconcile accrual earnings and cash flows from operations. These will be discussed in Chapter 17 after you have had a chance to review in some detail the accrual accounting entries related to noncurrent asset and liability accounts.

---

**Accrual earnings and cash flows capture different aspects of a firm's performance and often differ by a wide margin from year to year. Cash flows are critical to assessing a company's liquidity and creditworthiness. The cash flow statement provides a detailed summary of the cash inflows and outflows that are derived from a company's three primary activities: operations, investing, and financing. This section has outlined the basic techniques for deriving operating cash flows from an analysis of comparative balance sheets and income statement information. To do this, you must analyze changes in current asset and current liability accounts (as well as other noncash revenues and expenses such as depreciation) that capture differences between the cash flow effects and accrual earnings effects of revenue and expense transactions.**

 RE CAP

---

### SUMMARY

- The balance sheet and statement of cash flows are two of the primary financial statements required under GAAP.

- The balance sheet shows the assets owned by a company at a given point in time and how those assets are financed (debt versus equity). A variety of measurement bases are used to report the various asset, liability, and stockholders' equity accounts.

- When making intercompany comparisons, financial statement users must be careful to recognize how the different measurement bases affect key financial ratios and how account titles and statement formats vary across countries.

- Financial statement footnotes are an integral part of companies' financial reports and provide a wealth of information that allows statement users to better understand and interpret the numbers presented in the body of the financial statements.

- The statement of cash flows shows the change in cash for a given period broken down into operating, investing, and financing activities.

- Successive balance sheets and the statement of cash flows articulate with one another meaning changes in noncash balance sheet accounts can be used to explain changes in cash for a period.

- Analysis of changes in selected balance sheet accounts also can be used to explain why operating cash flows differ from accrual income.

- Conversely, the statement of cash flows provides information that enables users to understand changes in balance sheet accounts that have occurred over the reporting period.

- Understanding the interrelationships between successive balance sheets and the statement of cash flows and being able to exploit these interrelationships to derive unknown account balances are important skills for analysts and lending officers.

# EXERCISES

**E4-1**

Analyzing balance sheet classification

Typical balance sheet classifications appear follow:

| | |
|---|---|
| a. Current assets | f. Current liabilities |
| b. Long-term investments and funds | g. Long-term debt |
| c. Property, plant and equipment | h. Paid-in capital |
| d. Intangible assets | i. Retained earnings |
| e. Other assets | |

**Required:**

Use the preceding letters to indicate the proper classification for each of the following December 31, 2008, balance sheet items. Place brackets around the chosen letter for items that are contra accounts.

| | | |
|---|---|---|
| 1. | _____ | Accounts payable |
| 2. | _____ | Accrued salaries payable |
| 3. | _____ | Accumulated depreciation |
| 4. | _____ | Cash |
| 5. | _____ | Class B Preferred stock |
| 6. | _____ | Common stock |
| 7. | _____ | Installment note, payable in annual installments until 2009 |
| 8. | _____ | Investment in joint venture |
| 9. | _____ | Land, site of current manufacturing facility |
| 10. | _____ | Leaseholds |
| 11. | _____ | Long-lived assets classified as "held for sale" |
| 12. | _____ | Note payable, March 25, 2009 maturity date |
| 13. | _____ | Note receivable, October 12, 2010, maturity date |
| 14. | _____ | Office supplies |

15. _____ Prepaid rent, for 2009

16. _____ Short-term investments

17. _____ Term bonds payable, 2015 maturity date

18. _____ Trademarks

19. _____ Unearned revenue on 3-year subscriptions

20. _____ Vehicles

---

The following balance sheet for Northumberland Farm Machinery and Supply, Inc. was prepared by an inexperienced accountant and contains several errors.

**E 4-2**

Preparing a Balance sheet

## Balance Sheet December 31, 2008

| Assets | |
| --- | ---: |
| Cash | $ 15,000 |
| Short-term investments | 8,000 |
| Inventory | 175,000 |
| Accounts receivable | 70,000 |
| Fixed assets | 575,000 |
| Trademark | 5,000 |
| Goodwill | 65,000 |
| **Total assets** | **$913,000** |

| Liabilities and Shareholders' Equity | |
| --- | ---: |
| Accounts payable | $ 40,000 |
| Wages payable | 6,500 |
| Allowance for bad debts | 2,500 |
| Mortgage payable | 180,000 |
| Bonds payable | 300,000 |
| Common stock | 127,000 |
| Retained earnings | 257,000 |
| **Total liabilities and shareholders' equity** | **$913,000** |

### Additional Information:

1. Inventory is valued at cost (FIFO). At December 31, 2008, the inventory could have been replaced at a total cost of $165,000.

2. Fixed assets is comprised of land, buildings, and machinery that cost $85,000, $840,000, and $250,000, respectively. Accumulated depreciation on the buildings and machinery was $480,000 and $120,000, respectively.

3. Accounts receivable include a $5,000 note receivable from the company president due in June 2010.

4. The mortgage is payable in monthly installments; $15,000 in principal will be repaid in 2009.

5. The company's common stock has a $1 par value; 50,000 shares have been issued and are outstanding at year-end.

6. Short-term investments consists of other companies' shares that are appropriately valued at current market prices. These shares are appropriately classified as available-for-sale because management plans to sell them if the company needs additional operating cash in the next few months.

7. The bonds payable mature in 2013 and pay interest semiannually. The accountant forgot to record $6,000 in interest that had accrued since the last semiannual payment was made.

### Required:

Prepare a classified balance sheet in proper form. Make any necessary corrections.

| | |
|---|---|
| **E4-3**<br><br>Making financial disclosures | Examples of typical disclosures that would appear in the notes accompanying financial statements follow: |

Example      _____AP_____    Cash equivalents

   1.   _____   Components of inventory

   2.   _____   Computer software capitalization

   3.   _____   Depreciation methods

   4.   _____   Foreign currency translation

   5.   _____   Maturities of long-term debt issues

   6.   _____   Postretirement benefits

   7.   _____   Restructuring and asset impairment charges

   8.   _____   Revenue recognition

   9.   _____   Schedule of other expense (income)

 10.   _____   Use of estimates

**Required:**

Indicate where the disclosure pertaining to each item would likely appear: either in the accounting policies note (AP) or a separate note (SN).

| | |
|---|---|
| **E4-4**<br><br>Balance sheet classifications | A number of balance sheet accounts for Harvey's Heavy Metals, Inc. follow. |

1. Raw materials inventory
2. Available-for-sale securities
3. 5,000 shares of XYZ common stock
4. Property taxes payable
5. Prepaid customer orders
6. Accrued salaries
7. Machinery held for sale
8. Treasury stock
9. Cash dividends payable
10. Certificates of deposit
11. Supplies
12. Accumulated depreciation
13. Franchise
14. Cash surrender value of life insurance
15. Long-term debt maturing within one year

**Required:**

Indicate the proper balance sheet classification for each of these accounts. If more than one classification is potentially possible, indicate what additional information would be needed to make a determination.

| | |
|---|---|
| **E4-5**<br><br>Classifying balance sheet accounts | Bunny's Fashions, Inc. used the following headings on the company's December 31, 2008 balance sheet. |

a. Current assets

b. Long-term investments

c. Property, plant, and equipment

d. Intangible assets

e. Other assets

f. Current liabilities

g. Long-term obligations

h. Capital stock

i. Additional paid-in-capital

j. Retained earnings

**Required:**

For each of the following, indicate its normal classification category. Use (NA) for items that would not appear on the face of the balance sheet but would be discussed in the notes to the financial statements. Indicate by (NR) any items that would not be reported.

| | | |
|---|---|---|
| 1. | _____ | Accounts receivable |
| 2. | _____ | Accrued interest on notes payable (2009 maturity) |
| 3. | _____ | Accumulated depreciation |
| 4. | _____ | Bonds issued in 1996 the company plans to retire in 2016. No sinking fund exists. |
| 5. | _____ | Class B common stock |
| 6. | _____ | Deposits on designer fashions ordered by customers |
| 7. | _____ | Depreciation methods |
| 8. | _____ | Investment in affiliated company |
| 9. | _____ | Maturities of long-term debt issues |
| 10. | _____ | New 40-year bonds were issued on January 5, 2009 |
| 11. | _____ | Obsolete production machinery held for sale |
| 12. | _____ | Office building owned by the company |
| 13. | _____ | Preferred stock |
| 14. | _____ | Premium on Class B common stock |
| 15. | _____ | Prepaid insurance |
| 16. | _____ | Salaries payable |
| 17. | _____ | Taxes payable |
| 18. | _____ | The company president announced plans to retire in 2010 |
| 19. | _____ | Trademarks |
| 20. | _____ | Unrestricted savings account |

During 2008, Kew Company, a service organization, had $200,000 in cash sales and $3,000,000 in credit sales. The accounts receivable balances were $400,000 and $485,000 at December 31, 2007 and 2008, respectively.

**Required:**

What was Kew Company's cash receipts from sales in 2008?

**E4-6**

Determining collections on account

**AICPA**
ADAPTED

| **E4-7**

**Determining cash from operations**

**AICPA**
ADAPTED

The following information is available from Sand Corporation's accounting records for the year ended December 31, 2008:

| | |
|---|---|
| Cash received from customers | $870,000 |
| Rent received | 10,000 |
| Cash paid to suppliers and employees | 510,000 |
| Taxes paid | 110,000 |
| Cash dividends paid | 30,000 |

**Required:**

Compute cash flow provided by operations for 2008.

---

| **E4-8**

**Determining cash collections on account**

**AICPA**
ADAPTED

Fresh Company is preparing its cash budget for the month of May. The following information is available concerning its accounts receivable:

| | |
|---|---|
| Estimated credit sales for May | $200,000 |
| Actual credit sales for April | $150,000 |
| Estimated collection in May for credit sales in May | 20% |
| Estimated collection in May for credit sales in April | 70% |
| Estimated collection in May for credit sales prior to April | $ 12,000 |
| Estimated write-offs in May for uncollectible credit sales | $ 8,000 |
| Estimated bad debts expense in May for credit sales in May | $ 7,000 |

**Required:**

What are the estimated cash receipts from accounts receivable collections in May?

---

| **E4-9**

**Determining ending accounts receivable**

**AICPA**
ADAPTED

The following information is available for Alex Corporation's first year of operation:

| | |
|---|---|
| Payment for merchandise purchases | $200,000 |
| Ending merchandise inventory | 60,000 |
| Accounts payable (balance at end of year) | 40,000 |
| Collections from customers | 170,000 |

All merchandise items were marked to sell at 30% above cost.

**Required:**

What should be the ending balance in Accounts receivable, assuming all accounts are deemed collectible?

---

| **E4-10**

**Determining cash disbursements**

**AICPA**
ADAPTED

Serven Corporation has estimated its accrual-basis revenue and expenses for June 2008 and would like your help in estimating cash disbursements. Selected data from these estimated amounts are as follows:

| | |
|---|---|
| Sales | $700,000 |
| Gross profit (based on sales) | 30% |
| Increase in trade accounts receivable for the month | $ 20,000 |
| Change in accounts payable during month | 0 |
| Increase in inventory during month | $ 10,000 |

Variable selling, general, and administrative expenses include a charge for uncollectible accounts of 1% of sales.

Total selling, general, and administrative expenses are $71,000 per month plus 15% of sales.

Depreciation expense of $40,000 per month is included in fixed selling, general, and administrative expense.

**Required:**

On the basis of the preceding data, what are the estimated cash disbursements from operations for June?

The following information was taken from the 2008 financial statement of Planet Corporation:

E4-11

Determining cash collections on account

AICPA
ADAPTED

| | |
|---|---:|
| Accounts receivable, January 1, 2008 | $ 21,600 |
| Accounts receivable, December 31, 2008 | 30,400 |
| Sales on accounts and cash sales | 438,000 |
| Uncollectible accounts (bad debts) | 1,000 |

No accounts receivable were written off or recovered during the year.

**Required:**

Determine the cash collected from customers by Planet Corporation in 2008.

Lance Corporation's statement of cash flows for the year ended September 30, 2008, was prepared using the indirect method, and it included the following items:

E4-12

Determining cash received from customers

AICPA
ADAPTED

| | |
|---|---:|
| Net income | $60,000 |
| Noncash adjustments | |
| Depreciation expense | 9,000 |
| Increase in accounts receivable | (5,000) |
| Decrease in inventory | 40,000 |
| Decrease in accounts payable | (12,000) |
| Net cash flows from operating activities | $92,000 |

Lance reported revenues from customers of $75,000 in its 2008 income statement.

**Required:**

What amount of cash did Lance receive from customers during the year ended September 30, 2008?

The following information was taken from the 2008 financial statements of Eiger Corporation, a maker of equipment for mountain and rock climbers:

E4-13

Determining cash from operations and reconciling with accrual net income

| | |
|---|---:|
| Net income | $100,000 |
| Depreciation | 30,000 |
| Increase (decrease) in | |
| Accounts receivable | 110,000 |
| Inventories | (50,000) |
| Prepaid expenses | 15,000 |
| Accounts payable | (150,000) |
| Salaries payable | 15,000 |
| Other current liabilities | (70,000) |

**Required:**

1. Calculate Eiger's cash flow from operating activities for 2008.

2. Explain the reasons for the difference between the firm's net income and its cash flow from operating activities in 2008.

The following information was taken from the 2008 financial statements of Zurich Corporation, a maker of fine Swiss watches:

E4-14

Determining cash from operations and reconciling with accrual net income

| | |
|---|---:|
| Net income | $(200,000) |
| Depreciation | 50,000 |
| Increase (decrease) in | |
| Accounts receivable | (140,000) |
| Inventories | 25,000 |
| Other current assets | 10,000 |
| Accounts payable | 120,000 |
| Accrued payables | (25,000) |
| Interest payable | 50,000 |

**Required:**

1. Calculate Zurich's cash flow from operating activities for 2008.

2. Explain the reasons for the difference between the firm's net income and its cash flow from operating activities in 2008.

| | |
|---|---|
| **E4-15** | |
| Determining amounts shown on statements of cash flows | |

The following information was taken from Abbott Laboratory's financial statements. Abbott makes a variety of health care products and uses the indirect method to determine cash flows from operations:

| | |
|---|---:|
| Cost of goods sold | $ 6,563,978 |
| Acquisitions of property, plant, and equipment | 1,007,247 |
| Decrease in inventories | 109,087 |
| Repayments of obligations under long-term leases | 112,876 |
| Decrease in salaries payable | 534,281 |
| Gain on sale of land | 271,986 |
| Increase in receivables | 181,085 |
| Purchases of long-term investment securities | 178,727 |
| Repayments of long-term borrowings | 234,848 |
| Increase in accrued payables | 154,873 |
| Proceeds from short-term borrowings | 196,487 |
| Decrease in accounts payable | 121,741 |
| Proceeds from sales of property, plant, and equipment | 23,878 |
| Proceeds from the sale of long-term borrowings | 381,848 |
| Proceeds from sales of long-term investment securities | 496,120 |
| Decrease in other current assets | 114,009 |
| Purchases of common stock for treasury | 607,598 |
| Increase in prepaid expenses | 34,875 |
| Dividends paid | 488,413 |
| Sales | 10,978,387 |
| Depreciation and amortization | 427,782 |
| Repayments of short-term borrowings | 213,833 |
| Increase in current assets | 3,978,911 |
| Proceeds from the exercise of executive stock options | 74,027 |

**Required:**

Determine which of the preceding items would appear as a separate line-item on Abbott Laboratory's statement of cash flows. In each case, indicate whether the item is related to cash flows from operations, from investing activities, or from financing activities.

# PROBLEMS / DISCUSSION QUESTIONS

| | |
|---|---|
| **P4-1** | |
| Preparing a balance sheet | |

Bambi's House Wares, Inc. produced the unadjusted trial balance shown below at December 31, 2008.

| | Debits | Credits |
|---|---:|---:|
| Accounts payable | | $ 796,050 |
| Accounts receivable | $2,175,000 | |
| Accrued interest payable | | 3,190 |
| Accrued salaries payable | | 13,450 |
| Accumulated depreciation—building | | 3,590,150 |
| Accumulated depreciation—production equipment | | 4,750,000 |
| Additional paid-in capital | | 520,000 |
| Administrative expenses | 1,377,500 | |
| Allowance for uncollectible accounts | | 97,875 |
| Available-for-sale securities (at cost, $91,000) | 96,000 | |
| Bond sinking fund | 155,000 | |
| Bonds payable (maturing 2013) | | 2,500,000 |
| Buildings | 9,845,000 | |

*(continued)*

| | Debits | Credits |
|---|---|---|
| Cash | 67,500 | |
| Cash dividends payable | | 34,000 |
| Common stock ($10 par) | | 4,000,000 |
| Cost of goods sold | 8,845,000 | |
| Dividends | 68,000 | |
| Goodwill | 390,000 | |
| Interest expense | 168,750 | |
| Inventories | 1,105,625 | |
| Investment in affiliated company | 250,000 | |
| Investment revenue | | 31,500 |
| Land | 417,800 | |
| Leasehold | 2,350 | |
| Loss on discontinued operations before tax | 68,500 | |
| Notes payable (maturing 6/15/2009) | | 16,500 |
| Notes payable (maturing 8/15/2012) | | 200,000 |
| Production equipment | 5,500,000 | |
| Retained earnings, January 1, 2008 | | 689,510 |
| Sales | | 14,500,000 |
| Selling expenses | 1,160,000 | |
| Trademark | 8,100 | |
| Treasury stock at cost | 47,100 | |
| Unrealized holding gain on available-for-sale securities | — | 5,000 |
| Totals | $31,747,225 | $31,747,225 |

**Required:**

Prepare a balance sheet at December 31, 2008 for Bambi's House Wares, Inc. The company's tax rate is 35%.

---

Shawn Mikeska, Inc. prepared the following balance sheet at December 31, 2007.

**P 4-2**

Preparation of a statement of cash flows and a balance sheet

## Balance Sheet December 31, 2007

| | |
|---|---|
| Cash | $ 50,000 |
| Accounts receivable | 27,000 |
| Inventory | 80,000 |
| Long-term investments | 10,000 |
| Land | 32,000 |
| Plant and equipment (net) | 91,000 |
| **Total assets** | $290,000 |
| Accounts payable | $ 17,000 |
| Taxes payable | 3,000 |
| Bonds payable | 100,000 |
| Capital stock | 75,000 |
| Retained earnings | 95,000 |
| **Total liabilities and stockholders' equity** | $290,000 |

The following occurred during 2008.

1. Exchanged $25,000 in cash and a $35,000 note payable for land valued at $60,000.

2. Bonds payable (maturing in 2012) in the amount of $20,000 were retired by paying $18,000 cash.

3. Capital stock in the amount of $50,000 was issued at par value.

4. The company sold surplus equipment for $18,000. The equipment had a book value of $14,000 at the time of the sale.

5. Net income was $31,000.

6. Cash dividends of $2,500 were paid to the stockholders.

7. Purchased 100 shares of stock (considered short-term investments) for $8,300.

8. A new building was acquired through the issuance of $50,000 in bonds.

9. Recorded $8,000 of depreciation on the plant and equipment.

10. At December 31, 2008, Cash was $87,200, Accounts receivable had a balance of $30,000, Inventory had increased to $82,000, and Accounts payable had fallen to $12,000. Long-term investments and Taxes payable were unchanged from 2007.

**Required:**

1. Prepare a statement of cash flows for 2008 using the indirect method.

2. Prepare the December 31, 2008 balance sheet for Shawn Mikeska, Inc.

---

**P4-3**

Preparing a balance sheet

A December 31, 2008, post-closing trial balance for Short Erin Company follows.

| Account Title | Debits | Credits |
|---|---|---|
| Cash | $ 61,500 | |
| Short-term investments | 47,000 | |
| Accounts receivable | 95,600 | |
| Inventory | 175,000 | |
| Prepaid expenses | 13,500 | |
| Land | 241,800 | |
| Buildings | 584,900 | |
| Accumulated depreciation—buildings | | $ 132,500 |
| Production equipment | 477,700 | |
| Accumulated depreciation—production equipment | | 239,600 |
| Patents | 50,000 | |
| Leasehold | 7,000 | |
| Accounts payable | | 38,400 |
| Accrued salaries | | 3,400 |
| Taxes payable | | 65,800 |
| Notes payable | | 200,000 |
| Installment note payable | | 84,200 |
| Bonds payable | | 250,000 |
| Common stock | | 300,000 |
| Retained earnings | | 440,100 |
| Totals | $1,754,000 | $1,754,000 |

Additional information about Short Erin's account balances:

1. Cash includes $12,000 in U.S. treasury bills purchased on December 21, 2008 that mature in January 2009. The account also includes $8,500 in stock purchased just before year-end that the company plans to sell in a few days.

2. The Account receivable balance consists of:

| | |
|---|---|
| Trade receivables | $84,700 |
| Allowance for doubtful trade accounts | (4,600) |
| Note receivable from Short Erin's president due in 2010 | 15,500 |
| | $95,600 |

Trade receivables includes $1,400 of customer accounts with credit balances.

3. Notes payable consists of two notes. One, in the amount of $50,000, is due on March 19, 2009. The other note matures on October 27, 2011.

4. The Taxes payable account contains deferred income taxes amounting to $61,250.

5. The installment note payable bears an annual interest rate of 10%. Semiannual payments of $6,756.43 are due each June 30 and December 31 and include principal and accrued interest. These payments will reduce the Installment note balance by $5,220 in 2009.

6. Of the 1,000,000 authorized shares of no par common stock, 300,000 shares are issued and outstanding.

7. The company recently announced plans to sell its operating facility in Katy, Texas, consisting of land (cost $82,000) and a building (cost $175,000; book value $110,000). Production equipment has already been removed from the Katy plant and is being used in other company facilities.

**Required:**

Prepare a classified balance sheet for the Short Erin Company at December 31, 2008.

---

Consider the following transactions pertaining to Retail Traders Company. Amounts in parentheses indicate a decrease in the account.

**P 4 - 4**

Preparing the income statement and statement of cash flows

| | **Assets** | = | **Liabilities** | + | **Owners' Equity** | |
| | | | | | | |
| **Explanation** | **Cash** | **Inventory** | **Accounts Payable** | **Common Stock** | **Retained Earnings** |
|---|---|---|---|---|---|
| Beginning balance | | $ 10,000 | $ 5,000 | $3,000 | $ 2,000 |
| Credit purchases | | 100,000 | 100,000 | | |
| Cash sales | $115,000 | | | | 115,000 |
| Cost of goods sold | | (90,000) | | | (90,000) |
| Cash paid to suppliers | (85,000) | | (85,000) | | |
| Ending balance | $ 30,000 | $ 20,000 | $ 20,000 | $3,000 | $ 27,000 |

**Required:**

1. Based on this information, prepare an income statement and statement of cash flows.

2. Provide an intuitive explanation of how the adjustments made to net income in the cash flow statement convert the accrual numbers to cash flow numbers.

---

In reviewing Graceland Rock Company's financial statements, you note that net income increased but cash flow from operations decreased from 2008 to 2009.

**P 4 - 5**

Explaining the differences between cash flow from operations and accrual net income

**CMA**
ADAPTED

**Required:**

1. Explain how net income could increase for Graceland while cash flow from operations decreased. Your answer must include three illustrative examples.

2. Explain why cash flow from operations may be a good indicator of a firm's "quality of earnings" when analyzed in conjunction with accrual-basis earnings.

---

The common-size balance sheets from four companies follow: Amazon.com, an Internet book retailer; Alcoa, a major producer of aluminum products; Wendy's, a fast-food services organization; and Delta Air Lines, a major supplier of air transportation.

**P 4 - 6**

Analyzing common-size financial statements

**Required:**

Based on your general business knowledge, the economic activities of these four firms, and information derived from the following balance sheet analysis, match the company with its respective balance sheet. Explain your reasoning for the choices that you make.

## Common-Size Balance Sheet Comparisons

| | Company A | Company B | Company C | Company D |
|---|---|---|---|---|
| **Assets** | | | | |
| Current assets | | | | |
| Cash and marketable securities | 1.84% | 6.91% | 28.57% | 11.19% |
| Current receivables | 13.85 | 3.64 | — | 4.22 |
| Inventories | 9.48 | — | 8.93 | 2.14 |
| Other current assets | 2.95 | 5.60 | 3.45 | 1.02 |
| **Total current assets** | 28.12% | 16.15% | 40.95% | 18.57% |
| Noncurrent assets | | | | |
| Property, plant and equipment, net | 53.52% | 69.32% | 12.85% | 73.76% |
| Goodwill and intangibles, net | 7.78 | 9.56 | 29.55 | 2.56 |
| Other assets, net | 10.58 | 4.97 | 16.65 | 5.11 |
| **Total assets** | 100.00% | 100.00% | 100.00% | 100.00% |
| **Liabilities and Stockholders' Equity** | | | | |
| Current liabilities | | | | |
| Total current liabilities | 17.60% | 32.20% | 29.90% | 15.09% |
| Long-term liabilities | 36.84 | 39.73 | 59.33 | 17.73 |
| **Total liabilities** | 54.44 | 71.93 | 89.23 | 32.82 |
| Minority interest | 8.53 | — | — | — |
| Redeemable preferred stock | — | — | — | 10.62 |
| Stockholders' Equity | | | | |
| Contributed capital and other equity items | 1.51 | 11.41 | 46.46 | (0.18) |
| Retained earnings (deficit) | 35.52 | 16.66 | (35.69) | 56.74 |
| **Total liabilities and stockholders' equity** | 100.00% | 100.00% | 100.00% | 100.00% |

---

**P4-7**

Analyzing common-size financial statements

Following are the common-size balance sheets from four companies: Merck & Co., a global research-driven pharmaceutical manufacturing company; Target, a national discount retailer; Gannett, a newspaper publisher and broadcasting company; and Wisconsin Electric Power Company, a regional electric utility.

**Required:**

Based on your general business knowledge, the environment in which the above firms operate, and information derived from the balance sheet analysis, match the company with its respective balance sheet. Explain your reasoning for the choices that you make.

## Common-Size Balance Sheet Comparisons

| | Company A | Company B | Company C | Company D |
|---|---|---|---|---|
| **Assets** | | | | |
| Current assets | | | | |
| Cash and marketable securities | 1.28% | 8.99% | 0.40% | 0.51% |
| Current receivables | 10.72 | 11.47 | 5.91 | 9.80 |
| Inventories | 22.16 | 7.99 | 3.16 | 1.05 |
| Other current assets | 3.66 | 3.15 | 1.61 | 0.58 |
| **Total current assets** | 37.82 | 31.60 | 11.08 | 11.94 |
| Noncurrent assets | | | | |
| Property, plant and equipment, net | 57.74 | 27.15 | 62.75 | 24.69 |
| Goodwill and intangibles, net | — | 21.28 | — | 59.94 |
| Other assets, net | 4.44 | 19.97 | 26.17 | 3.43 |
| **Total assets** | 100.00% | 100.00% | 100.00% | 100.00% |

*(continued)*

|  | Company A | Company B | Company C | Company D |
|---|---|---|---|---|
| **Liabilities and stockholders' equity** | | | | |
| Current liabilities | | | | |
|    Total current liabilities | 34.13% | 24.58% | 13.41% | 9.81% |
| Long-term liabilities | 31.68 | 28.55 | 50.04 | 38.79 |
|    **Total liabilities** | 65.81 | 53.13 | 63.45 | 48.60 |
| Redeemable preferred stock | — | — | 3.23 | — |
| Stockholders' equity | | | | |
| Contributed capital and other equity items* | 4.70 | (18.93) | 14.37 | (9.72) |
| Retained earnings (deficit) | 29.49 | 65.80 | 18.95 | 61.12 |
|    **Total liabilities and stockholders' equity** | 100.00% | 100.00% | 100.00% | 100.00% |

\* Net of cost of shares repurchased for treasury.

---

Karr, Inc. reported net income of $300,000 for 2008. Changes occurred in several balance sheet accounts as follows:

| | | | |
|---|---|---|---|
| Equipment | $25,000 increase | Inventories | $20,000 decrease |
| Accumulated depreciation | 40,000 increase | Accounts receivable | 15,000 increase |
| Note payable | 30,000 increase | Accounts payable | 5,000 decrease |

**Additional Information:**

a. During 2008 Karr sold equipment costing $25,000, with accumulated depreciation of $12,000, for a gain of $5,000.

b. In December 2008 Karr purchased equipment costing $50,000, with $20,000 cash and a 12% note payable of $30,000.

c. Depreciation expense for the year was $52,000.

**Required:**

1. In Karr's 2008 statement of cash flows, calculate net cash provided by operating activities.

2. In Karr's 2008 statement of cash flows, calculate net cash used in investing activities.

**P 4-8**

Determining cash flows from operating and investing activities

AICPA
ADAPTED

---

The following data have been extracted from the financial statements of Prentiss, Inc., a calendar-year merchandising corporation:

| | December 31 | |
|---|---|---|
| **Balance Sheet Data** | **2008** | **2009** |
| Trade accounts receivable—net | $ 84,000 | $ 78,000 |
| Inventory | 150,000 | 140,000 |
| Accounts payable—merchandise (credit) | (95,000) | (98,000) |

- Total sales for 2009 were $1,200,000 and for 2008 were $1,100,000. Cash sales were 20% of total sales each year.

- Cost of goods sold was $840,000 for 2009.

- Variable general and administrative (G&A) expenses for 2009 were $120,000. These expenses have varied in proportion to sales and have been paid at the rate of 50% in the year incurred and 50% the following year. Unpaid G&A expenses are *not* included in accounts payable.

- Fixed G&A expenses, including $35,000 depreciation and $5,000 bad debt expense, totaled $100,000 each year. The amount of such expenses involving cash payments was paid at the rate of 80% in the year incurred and 20% the following year. In each year, there was a $5,000 bad debt estimate and a $5,000 write-off. Unpaid G&A expenses are *not* included in accounts payable.

**P 4-9**

Determining operating cash flow components

AICPA
ADAPTED

**Required:**

Compute the following:

1. The amount of cash collected during 2009 that resulted from total sales in 2008 and 2009.

2. The amount of cash disbursed during 2009 for purchases of merchandise.

3. The amount of cash disbursed during 2009 for variable and fixed G&A expenses.

---

**P4-10**

Understanding the relation between the income statement, cash flow statement, and changes in balance sheet accounts

The following cash flow information pertains to the 2008 operations of Matterhorn, Inc., a maker of ski equipment:

| | |
|---|---|
| Cash collections from customers | $ 16,670 |
| Cash payments to suppliers | 19,428 |
| Cash payments for various operating expenses | 7,148 |
| Cash payments for current income taxes | 200 |
| Cash provided (used) by operating activities | (10,106) |

The following additional information comes from Matterhorn's 2008 income statement:

| | |
|---|---|
| Net income | $ 609 |
| Depreciation of equipment | 2,256 |
| Amortization of patents | 399 |
| Loss on sale of equipment | 169 |

The following additional information comes from Matterhorn's 2007 and 2008 comparative balance sheets (decreases are in parentheses):

| | |
|---|---|
| Change in accounts receivable | $ 3,630 |
| Change in inventory | 3,250 |
| Change in accounts payable | (3,998) |
| Change in accrued operating expenses | (2,788) |
| Change in deferred taxes payable | 127 |

**Required:**

1. Use the preceding information to derive Matterhorn's 2008 income statement.

2. Use the same information to compute Matterhorn's 2008 cash flow from operating activities under the indirect method (that is, derive cash flow from operating activities by making the necessary adjustments to net income).

3. Provide a brief explanation for the difference observed between net income and cash provided by operating activities.

---

**P4-11**

Understanding the relation between the income statement, cash flow statement, and changes in balance sheet accounts

The following cash flow information pertains to the 2008 operations of Divemaster, Inc., a maker of scuba diving equipment:

| | |
|---|---|
| Cash collections from customers | $72,481 |
| Cash payments to suppliers | 51,768 |
| Cash payments for selling and administrative expenses | 9,409 |
| Cash payments for interest | 1,344 |
| Cash payments for current income taxes | 671 |
| Cash provided by operating activities | 9,289 |

The following additional information comes from Divemaster's 2008 income statement:

| | |
|---|---|
| Net income | $1,085 |
| Depreciation of equipment | 7,380 |
| Gain on sale of equipment | 327 |

The following additional information comes from Divemaster's 2007 and 2008 comparative balance sheets (decreases are in parentheses):

| | |
|---|---|
| Change in accounts receivable | $(4,603) |
| Change in inventory | 7,400 |
| Change in accounts payable | 3,146 |
| Change in accrued selling and administrative expenses | 772 |
| Change in deferred taxes payable | (87) |
| Change in accrued interest payable | 117 |

**Required:**

1. Use the preceding information to derive Divemaster's 2008 income statement.

2. Use the same information to compute Divemaster's 2008 cash flow from operating activities under the indirect method (that is, derive cash flow from operating activities by making the necessary adjustments to net income).

3. Provide a brief explanation for the difference observed between net income and cash provided by operating activities.

---

The following information is taken from the operating section of the statement of cash flows (direct method) of Battery Builders, Inc.:

**P4-12**

Understanding the relation between operating cash flows and accrual earnings

| | |
|---|---|
| Collections from customers | $ 28,000 |
| Payments to suppliers for purchases | (13,000) |
| Payments for operating expenses | (9,000) |
| Payments for current period income taxes | (4,000) |
| Cash provided by operating activities | 2,000 |

The following information is obtained from the income statement of Battery Builders:

| | |
|---|---|
| Net income | $4,000 |
| Depreciation expense | 4,000 |
| Gain on sale of equipment | 2,000 |
| Write-off of intangibles | 1,000 |

In addition, the following information is obtained from the comparative balance sheets of Battery Builders (decreases in parentheses):

| | |
|---|---|
| Change in accounts receivable | $ 3,000 |
| Change in inventory | 3,000 |
| Change in accounts payable | 2,000 |
| Change in accrued payable (related to operating expense) | (2,000) |
| Change in deferred income taxes payable | 1,000 |

**Required:**

1. Prepare a complete accrual-basis income statement for the current year.

2. Compute the cash flows from operations using the indirect approach (that is, start with accrual-basis net income and adjust for various items to obtain cash flows from operations).

**P4-13**

Microsoft: Finding missing values on a classified balance sheet and analyzing balance sheet changes

The following information was taken from Microsoft Corporation's Year 2 balance sheet; Microsoft is one of the largest independent computer software makers in the United States.

| ($ in millions) | June 30, Year 2 |
|---|---|
| Total current liabilities | $ 5,730 |
| Other current assets | ? |
| Equity investments | ? |
| Property, plant, and equipment, net | 1,505 |
| Common stock and paid-in capital | ? |
| Other assets | 260 |
| Cash and short-term investments | 13,927 |
| Total stockholders' equity | ? |
| Accounts payable | 759 |
| Retained earnings | 7,622 |
| Unearned revenue | ? |
| Accrued compensation | 359 |
| Accounts receivable, net | 1,460 |
| Total assets | ? |
| Other current liabilities | 809 |
| Preferred stock | 980 |
| Total current assets | 15,889 |
| Income taxes payable | 915 |
| Total liabilities and stockholders' equity | 22,357 |

The following is Microsoft's Year 1 balance sheet.

## Consolidated Balance Sheets

| ($ in millions) | June 30, Year 1 |
|---|---|
| **Assets** | |
| Current assets | |
|   Cash and short-term investments | $ 8,966 |
|   Accounts receivable, net | 980 |
|   Other | 427 |
|     **Total current assets** | 10,373 |
| Property, plant and equipment | 1,465 |
| Equity investments | 2,346 |
| Other assets | 203 |
|     **Total assets** | $14,387 |
| **Liabilities and Stockholders' Equity** | |
| Current liabilities | |
|   Accounts payable | $ 721 |
|   Accrued compensation | 336 |
|   Income taxes payable | 466 |
|   Unearned revenue | 1,418 |
|   Other | 669 |
|     **Total current liabilities** | 3,610 |
| Stockholders' equity | |
|   Convertible preferred stock: shares | |
|     authorized 100; issued and outstanding 13 | 980 |
|   Common stock and paid-in capital: shares | |
|     authorized 8,000; issued and outstanding 2,408 | 4,509 |
|   Retained earnings | 5,288 |
|     **Total stockholders' equity** | 10,777 |
|     **Total liabilities and stockholders' equity** | $14,387 |

**Required:**

1. Solve for the missing values and present Microsoft's Year 2 balance sheet in good form.

2. Microsoft has recently become a customer of your firm. In fact, its accounts receivable is one of your firm's largest current assets. The amount is so large that the chief executive

officer (CEO) of your firm is concerned because if Microsoft doesn't pay in a timely fashion, your firm would experience severe cash flow problems. Use Microsoft's balance sheet to assess Microsoft's ability to make timely payment of its current liabilities.

3. Using your Year 2 and the Year 1 balance sheets provided, compare and contrast the firm's financial position at the end of these two years. For example, were there any major changes in Microsoft's financial position from the end of Year 1 to the end of Year 2? In what ways did the firm's financial position improve or deteriorate over this time period?

4. Assume that you are a financial analyst. Based on the financial position of Microsoft as portrayed in the Year 1 and Year 2 balance sheets, would you advise your clients to invest in the firm's common stock? Why or why not?

5. Before advising your clients about whether or not to purchase the common stock of Microsoft, what information beyond the Year 1 and Year 2 balance sheets would you seek?

---

The following information was taken from one of Hewlett-Packard Company's recent balance sheets. Hewlett-Packard is a major designer and manufacturer of electronic measurement and computing equipment, including workstations, PCs, and laser printers.

**P4-14**

Finding missing values on a classified balance sheet and analyzing balance sheet accounts

mhhe.com/revsine4e

| *($ in millions)* | |
|---|---:|
| Total liabilities and shareholders' equity | ? |
| Inventories: Finished goods | $ 1,100 |
| Other current assets | 347 |
| Employee compensation and benefits payable | 837 |
| Total current assets | 6,716 |
| Land | ? |
| Total shareholders' equity | 7,269 |
| Long-term debt | ? |
| Machinery and equipment | 2,792 |
| Taxes payable | 381 |
| Long-term receivables and other assets | 1,912 |
| Other long-term liabilities | 210 |
| Cash and cash equivalents | 625 |
| Total assets | 11,973 |
| Notes payable and short-term borrowings | ? |
| Deferred revenues (current) | 375 |
| Short-term investments | 495 |
| Buildings and leasehold improvements | 2,779 |
| Total current liabilities | 4,063 |
| Inventories: Purchased parts and fabricated assemblies | 1,173 |
| Deferred taxes payable | 243 |
| Common stock and capital in excess of $1 par value | 1,010 |
| Accumulated depreciation | 2,616 |
| Other accrued liabilities | 583 |
| Retained earnings | ? |
| Accounts and notes receivable | ? |
| Accounts payable | 686 |

**Required:**

1. Use the information in the problem to determine the missing amounts, and present Hewlett-Packard's balance sheet in good form.

2. Does Hewlett-Packard obtain financing primarily from stockholders or from creditors? Explain.

3. What is Hewlett-Packard's largest current asset?

4. What is Hewlett-Packard's largest current liability?

5. Calculate the ratio of Hewlett-Packard's current assets to current liabilities, and comment on Hewlett-Packard's short-term liquidity position.

6. Hewlett-Packard's balance sheet lists an item called Other current assets. What assets might be included under this heading?

---

**P4-15**

Analyzing the difference between operating cash flows and accrual earnings

mhhe.com/revsine4e

The following are Food Tiger's 2007 and 2008 balance sheets and 2008 income statement.

## Comparative Balance Sheets

| | December 31 | |
| --- | --- | --- |
| | **2008** | **2007** |
| **Assets** | | |
| Current assets | | |
| Cash and cash equivalents | $      6,804 | $        428 |
| Receivables | 97,106 | 76,961 |
| Inventories | 844,539 | 673,606 |
| Prepaid expenses | 9,401 | 16,684 |
| Total current assets | 957,850 | 767,679 |
| Property, at cost | 1,446,896 | 1,094,804 |
| Less: Accumulated depreciation | (407,641) | (303,027) |
| **Total assets** | $1,997,105 | $1,559,456 |
| **Liabilities and Shareholders' Equity** | | |
| Current liabilities | | |
| Accounts payable—trade | $  343,163 | $  290,064 |
| Accrued expenses | 184,017 | 138,921 |
| Accrued interest payable | 1,067 | 3,394 |
| Income taxes payable | 37,390 | 42,958 |
| Total current liabilities | 565,637 | 475,337 |
| Long-term debt | 504,913 | 415,561 |
| Total liabilities | $1,070,550 | $  890,898 |
| Shareholders' equity | | |
| Common stock | $  263,155 | $  162,298 |
| Retained earnings | 663,400 | 506,260 |
| **Total shareholders' equity** | $  926,555 | $  668,558 |
| **Total liabilities and shareholders' equity** | $1,997,105 | $1,559,456 |

## Income Statement for Year Ended December 31, 2008

| | |
| --- | --- |
| Net sales | $6,438,507 |
| Cost of goods sold | (5,102,977) |
| Gross profit | 1,335,530 |
| Selling and administrative expenses | (855,809) |
| Interest expense | (34,436) |
| Depreciation | (104,614) |
| Income before income taxes | 340,671 |
| Provision for income taxes | (135,500) |
| **Net income** | $ 205,171 |

**Additional Information:**

1. The Accounts payable—trade account is used only for purchases of merchandise inventory.

2. The balance in the Prepaid Expenses account represents prepaid selling and administrative expenses for the following year.

3. Except for the prepaid selling and administrative expenses noted in (2), the company records all selling and administrative expenses in the Accrued expenses account prior to making payment.

4. The company records all interest expense in the Accrued interest payable account prior to making payment.

5. The company records all income tax expense in the Income taxes payable account prior to making payment.

6. Cash dividends declared and paid during 2008 were $48,031.

7. No long-term assets were disposed of in 2008.

**Required:**

1. Prepare an analysis of Food Tiger's 2008 operating cash flows and accrual-based net income by completing the following table. The table follows the format of Exhibit 4.9 in this chapter.

2. Prepare Food Tiger's Statement of Cash Flows for 2008. Follow the format of Exhibit 4.10 in this chapter.

## Table 1 Food Tiger, Inc.

**Analysis of Change in Cash versus Income for 2008**

| Item | (a) Accrual Income | (b) Noncash Accruals: Revenue Earned or Expenses Incurred | (c) Prepayments/ Buildups/Other Adjustments | (d) (a + b + c) Cash Received (+) or Paid (−) |
|------|--------|--------|--------|--------|
| Operating activities | | | | |
| . | | | | |
| . | | | | |
| . | | | | |
| Operating cash flow | | | | |
| Net income | | | | |
| Investing activities | | | | |
| . | | | | |
| . | | | | |
| . | | | | |
| Financing activities | | | | |
| . | | | | |
| . | | | | |
| Change in cash | | | | |

---

Vanguard Corporation is a distributor of food products. The corporation has approximately 1,000 stockholders, and its stock, which is traded "over-the-counter," is sold throughout 2008 at about $7 a share with little fluctuation. The corporation's balance sheet at December 31, 2007 follows.

**P4-16**

Preparing the balance sheet and income statement

**AICPA**
ADAPTED

## Balance Sheet December 31, 2007

**Assets**

Current assets

| | | |
|---|---|---|
| Cash | | $ 4,386,040 |
| Accounts receivable | $3,150,000 | |
| Less allowance for doubtful accounts | (94,500) | 3,055,500 |
| Inventories—at the lower of cost (FIFO) or market | | 2,800,000 |
| Total current assets | | 10,241,540 |
| Fixed assets—at cost | $3,300,000 | |
| Less accumulated depreciation | (1,300,000) | 2,000,000 |
| **Total assets** | | $12,241,540 |

**Liabilities and Stockholders' Equity**

Current liabilities

| | | |
|---|---|---|
| Notes payable due within one year | | $ 1,000,000 |
| Accounts payable and accrued liabilities | | 2,091,500 |
| Federal income taxes payable | | 300,000 |
| Total current liabilities | | 3,391,500 |
| Notes payable due after one year | | 4,000,000 |

Stockholders' equity

| | | |
|---|---|---|
| Capital stock—authorized 2,000,000 shares of $1 par value; issued and outstanding 1,000,000 shares | $1,000,000 | |
| Additional paid-in capital | 1,500,000 | |
| Retained earnings | 2,350,040 | |
| **Total stockholders' equity** | | 4,850,040 |
| **Total liabilities and stockholders' equity** | | $12,241,540 |

Information concerning the corporation and its activities during 2008 follows:

1. Sales for the year were $15,650,000. The gross profit percentage for the year was 30% of sales. Merchandise purchases and freight-in totaled $10,905,000. Depreciation and other expenses do not enter into cost of goods sold.

2. Administrative, selling, and general expenses (including provision for state taxes) other than interest, depreciation, and provision for doubtful accounts amounted to $2,403,250.

3. The December 31, 2008, accounts receivable amounted to $3,350,000, and the corporation maintains an allowance for doubtful accounts equal to 3% of the accounts receivable outstanding. During the year $50,000 of 2007 receivables were deemed uncollectible and charged off to the allowance account.

4. The rate of depreciation of fixed assets is 13% per annum, and the corporation consistently follows the policy of taking one-half year's depreciation in the year of acquisition. The depreciation expense for 2008 was $474,500.

5. The notes are payable in 20 equal quarterly installments commencing March 31, 2008, with interest at 5% per annum also payable quarterly.

6. Accounts payable and accrued liabilities at December 31, 2008, were $2,221,000.

7. The balance of the 2007 federal income tax paid in 2008 was in exact agreement with the amount accrued on the December 31, 2007, balance sheet.

8. The 2008 estimated tax payments made in 2008 totaled $400,000. Income tax expense for 2008 on an accrual accounting basis was $530,000.

9. During the second month of each quarter of 2008, dividends of $0.10 a share were declared and paid. In addition, in July 2008, a 5% stock dividend was declared and paid.

**Required:**

Prepare the following statements in good form and support them by well-organized and developed computations for the year ending December 31, 2008:

a. Balance sheet

b. Income statement

---

The purpose of this problem is to familiarize you with the statement of cash flows of a publicly held company. Its primary objective is to test your understanding of the relationships underlying the cash flow statement. It also serves as a natural way to expand your understanding of accounting terminology. This is an important feature because the financial statements of publicly held companies often use terms that are different from those appearing in financial accounting textbooks.

The information that follows was taken from Snap-On-Tools Corporation's Year 2 statement of cash flows. Snap-On-Tools makes and sells hand tools for mechanics, tool storage units, and related items. Most of the company's sales come from dealers who visit customer locations with their walk-in vans.

**P 4 - 1 7**

Snap-On-Tools Corporation: Determining missing amounts on the cash flow statement

mhhe.com/revsine4e

| ($ in thousands) | |
| --- | --- |
| Cash and cash equivalents at beginning of year | $ 10,930 |
| Increase in notes payable | 52,503 |
| Decrease in deferred income taxes | 6,005 |
| Decrease in accounts payable | 8,202 |
| Net cash provided by operating activities | ? |
| Capital expenditures | 21,081 |
| Depreciation | 25,484 |
| Acquisition of Sun Electric, net of cash acquired | 110,719 |
| Increase in receivables | 5,458 |
| Net cash used in investing activities | ? |
| Payment of long-term debt | 8,332 |
| Increase in other noncurrent assets | 3,609 |
| Decrease in inventories | 5,928 |
| Proceeds from stock option plans | 4,940 |
| Net earnings | 65,975 |
| Increase in accruals, deposits, and other liabilities | 23,330 |
| Cash dividends paid | 45,718 |
| Increase in long-term debt | 78,650 |
| Net cash provided by (used in) financing activities | ? |
| Effect of exchange rate changes | 1,916 |
| Increase in cash and cash equivalents | ? |
| Disposal of property and equipment | 3,379 |
| Cash and cash equivalents at end of year | ? |
| Amortization | 3,973 |
| Increase in prepaid expenses | 4,829 |
| Gain on sale of assets | 250 |

**Required:**

Use the information provided here to solve for the missing values, and recast Snap-On-Tools's Year 2 statement of cash flows in proper form. (*Note:* The item "Effect of exchange rate changes" captures gains or losses that arise when a firm converts its foreign subsidiaries' financial statements from the respective currencies [for example, French francs] into U.S. dollars.) In Snap-On's case, these translations were not favorable in Year 2. While the amount of this item reflects events and transactions affecting various items in the statement of cash flows, it is not separately identified with any individual section of the statement. Rather, it is treated as an adjustment to aggregate net cash flows to arrive at the change in cash. This adjustment usually appears near the bottom of the statement of cash flows.

## CASES

### C4-1
Conducting financial reporting research: Subsequent events

Alpha Manufacturing, Inc. issued audited financial statements on March 10, 2009, for its year ended December 31, 2008. The following events occurred after December 31, 2008, but before the financial statements were issued.

1. Alpha Manufacturing received legal notification on January 18, 2009 that Conner Co. (one of the company's customers) had filed for bankruptcy. Alpha Manufacturing's December 31, 2008 Accounts receivable balance included receivables from Conner Co. in the amount of $92,500.

2. On February 23, 2009, Alpha's board of directors voted to secure $50,000,000 in additional debt financing through an issue of 25-year debentures. Management has been working with an investment bank on this matter and plans to market the securities in the next month or two.

3. Alpha signed a contract with a major retailer on January 12, 2009 that is expected to increase sales by 20% over the next few years.

4. February 15, 2009 was not a good day for Alpha Manufacturing. On that date, a competitor introduced a new product that will render $27 million of Alpha's inventory obsolete. Alpha will also be forced to idle one of its production facilities and retool another as a result of this development.

**Required**

Review *Statement on Auditing Standards No. 1* on "Subsequent Events" from your library. Determine the appropriate treatment of each of these events in Alpha Manufacturing's 2008 financial statements. Assume that each of these events is considered material.

### C4-2
Conducting financial reporting research: Related-party matters

John Rigas founded Adelphia Communications Corporation with a $300 license in 1952, took the company public in 1986, and built it into the sixth largest cable television operator by acquiring other systems in the 1990s. As the company grew, it also expanded into other fields. It operated a telephone business, a sports radio station, a sports cable channel, and many other smaller subsidiaries. Despite being a publicly held firm, the company remained a family-run business; five of the firm's nine board members were Rigas family members who also held various executive posts. John was the CEO and chairman of the board. His sons, Tim (CFO), Michael (VP of operations), and James (VP of strategic planning), made up much of the firm's leadership team. In addition, John Rigas's son-in-law sat on Adelphia's board of directors. The company filed for bankruptcy in June 2002 after it disclosed $2.3 billion in off-balance-sheet debt. The Rigases are among a number of former corporate executives who have faced criminal charges since Enron's fall in 2001 touched off a series of white-collar scandals.

At John's trial, prosecutors said the Rigases used complicated cash management systems (CMS) to spread money around to various family-owned entities to cover stealing about $100 million for themselves. Rigas Entities consisted of approximately 63 different entities organized as partnerships, corporations, or limited liability companies exclusively owned or controlled by members of the Rigas family. Adelphia managed and maintained virtually every aspect of the approximately 14 companies comprising the Rigas Cable Entities, including maintaining their books and records on a general ledger system shared with Adelphia and its subsidiaries. Adelphia and the Rigas Entities participated jointly in a CMS operated by Adelphia, which resulted in commingling funds among the participants and greatly facilitating the fraud at Adelphia.

A complaint filed by the SEC stated:

> The commission charges that Adelphia, at the direction of the individual defendants: (1) fraudulently excluded billions of dollars in liabilities from its consolidated financial statements by hiding them in off-balance sheet affiliates; (2) falsified operations statistics and inflated Adelphia's earnings to meet Wall Street's expectations; and (3) concealed rampant self-dealing by the Rigas

Family, including the undisclosed use of corporate funds for Rigas Family stock purchases and the acquisition of luxury condominiums in New York and elsewhere. The Commission seeks a final judgment ordering the defendants to account for and disgorge all ill-gotten gains including . . . all property unlawfully taken from Adelphia through undisclosed related-party transactions.[11]

The SEC also alleges that since at least 1986, Adelphia improperly netted, or offset, related-party payables and related-party receivables as of year-end. As a result of this offset, gross related-party receivables of $1.351 billion and gross related-party payables of $1.348 billion were reported as a mere $3 million net receivable.[12]

**Required:**

1. Review *SFAS No. 57*, "Related Party Disclosures" (available on the FASB's Web site: www.FASB.org).

2. Use EDGAR (www.SEC.gov) to access the 2000 Form 10-K for Adelphia Communications Corporation. Examine Adelphia's balance sheet and locate a line item called Related-party receivables—net. Next, look up and read the "related-party" footnote (note 13). Do you believe that this footnote adequately explains the nature of these related-party receivables or meets *SFAS No. 57's* disclosure requirements? Justify your answer.

3. What is the significance of Adelphia's treatment of related-party receivables and payables and the company's failure to adequately disclose its related-party transactions?

4. Why is it important that companies disclose related-party transactions?

---

A recent balance sheet for Pittards, PLC, a British company, follows. The company's principal activities are the design, production, and procurement of technically advanced leather. The Group financial statements consolidate the accounts of Pittards, PLC, and all its subsidiary undertakings. (Footnote references appearing on the original balance sheet have been omitted.)

**C 4-3**

Analyzing international reporting

**Required:**

1. Examine the Pittards balance sheet and identify at least three differences between balance sheets as presented in the United Kingdom and the United States.

2. Compare the Pittards balance sheet with the Burberry Group balance sheet in Exhibit 4.3 and identify at least three differences between them.

3. Review Pittards' balance sheet and discuss how its format provides useful information to investors and creditors.

## Pittards, PLC

### Balance Sheet as at 31 December 2006

| (£ in 000) | Group | Company |
|---|---|---|
| **Fixed assets** | | |
| Tangible fixed assets | £ 6,235 | £ 631 |
| Investments | — | 3,368 |
| | 6,235 | 3,999 |
| **Current assets** | | |
| Stocks | 6,086 | — |
| Debtors | 3,509 | 11,943 |
| Cash at bank and in hand | 21 | — |
| | 9,616 | 11,943 |
| | | *(continued)* |

---

[11] Securities and Exchange Commission, *Accounting and Auditing Enforcement Release No. 1599*, July 24, 2002.

[12] Securities and Exchange Commission, *Accounting and Auditing Enforcement Release No. 2326*, September 30, 2005.

| (£ in 000) | Group | Company |
|---|---|---|
| **Creditors—amounts falling due within one year** | | |
| Bank loans and overdrafts | (971) | (971) |
| Trade creditors | (3,137) | — |
| Other creditors | (3,733) | (13,889) |
| | (7,841) | (14,860) |
| **Net current assets (liabilities)** | 1,775 | (2,917) |
| Total assets less current liabilities | 8,010 | 1,082 |
| **Creditors—amounts falling due after more than one year** | (3,004) | (428) |
| **Provisions for liabilities and charges** | (520) | (13) |
| **Net assets before pension scheme liability** | 4,486 | 641 |
| **Pension scheme liability** | — | — |
| Net assets (liabilities) after pension scheme liability | 4,486 | 641 |
| **Capital and reserves** | | |
| Called up share capital | 2,233 | 2,233 |
| Share premium account | 4,214 | 4,214 |
| Capital redemption reserve | 8,158 | 8,158 |
| Revaluation reserve | 2,335 | — |
| Capital reserve | 6,475 | — |
| Profit and loss account | (18,434) | (13,469) |
| Own shares | (495) | (495) |
| **Shareholders' funds** | 4,486 | 641 |

---

**C4-4**

Debbie Dress Shops, Inc.:
Determining cash flow
amounts from comparative
balance sheets and income
statement

AICPA
ADAPTED

 **STRETCH**

The balance sheet and income statement for Debbie Dress Shops are presented along with some additional information about the accounts. You are to answer the questions that follow concerning cash flows for the period.

## Balance Sheet

| | December 31 | |
|---|---|---|
| | **2008** | **2007** |
| **Assets** | | |
| Current assets | | |
| Cash | $ 300,000 | $ 200,000 |
| Accounts receivable—net | 840,000 | 580,000 |
| Merchandise inventory | 660,000 | 420,000 |
| Prepaid expenses | 100,000 | 50,000 |
| Total current assets | 1,900,000 | 1,250,000 |
| Long-term investments | 80,000 | — |
| Land, building, and fixtures | 1,130,000 | 600,000 |
| Less: Accumulated depreciation | (110,000) | (50,000) |
| | 1,020,000 | 550,000 |
| **Total assets** | $3,000,000 | $1,800,000 |
| **Liabilities and Stockholders' Equity** | | |
| Current liabilities | | |
| Accounts payable | $ 530,000 | $ 440,000 |
| Accrued expenses | 140,000 | 130,000 |
| Dividends payable | 70,000 | — |
| Total current liabilities | 740,000 | 570,000 |
| Note payable—due year 2011 | 500,000 | — |
| **Stockholders' equity** | | |
| Common stock | 1,200,000 | 900,000 |
| Retained earnings | 560,000 | 330,000 |
| Total stockholders' equity | 1,760,000 | 1,230,000 |
| **Total liabilities and stockholders' equity** | $3,000,000 | $1,800,000 |

*(continued)*

## Income Statements

| | Years Ended December 31 | |
|---|---|---|
| | **2008** | **2007** |
| Net credit sales | $6,400,000 | $4,000,000 |
| Cost of goods sold | 5,000,000 | 3,200,000 |
| Gross profit | 1,400,000 | 800,000 |
| Expenses (including income taxes) | 1,000,000 | 520,000 |
| **Net income** | $ 400,000 | $ 280,000 |

a. All accounts receivable and accounts payable are related to trade merchandise. Accounts payable are recorded net and always are paid to take all the discounts allowed. The allowance for doubtful accounts at the end of 2008 was the same as at the end of 2007; no receivables were charged against the allowance during 2008.

b. The proceeds from the note payable were used to finance a new store building. Capital stock was sold to provide additional working capital.

**Required:**

1. Calculate cash collected during 2008 from accounts receivable.
2. Calculate cash payments during 2008 on accounts payable to suppliers.
3. Calculate cash provided from operations for 2008.
4. Calculate cash inflows during 2008 from financing activities.
5. Calculate cash outflows from investing activities during 2008.

---

Following is Drop Zone Corporation's balance sheet at the end of 2007 and its cash flow statement for 2008. Drop Zone manufactures equipment for sky divers.

### Balance Sheet December 31, 2007

| Assets | |
|---|---|
| Current assets | |
| Cash | $ 7,410 |
| Accounts receivable—net | 6,270 |
| Inventory | 13,395 |
| Prepaid assets | 1,995 |
| **Total current assets** | 29,070 |
| Land | 27,930 |
| Buildings and equipment | 194,655 |
| Less: Accumulated depreciation, buildings and equipment | (40,185) |
| **Total assets** | $211,470 |
| **Liabilities and Stockholders' Equity** | |
| Current liabilities | |
| Accounts payable | $ 11,400 |
| Accrued payables | 3,135 |
| **Total current liabilities** | 14,535 |
| Long-term debt | 19,950 |
| Stockholders' equity | |
| Common stock, $10.00 par value | 18,525 |
| Paid-in capital | 31,920 |
| Retained earnings | 144,780 |
| Less: Treasury stock | (18,240) |
| **Total liabilities and stockholders' equity** | $211,470 |

**C4-5**

Drop Zone Corporation: Understanding the relation between successive balance sheets and the cash flow statement

mhhe.com/revsine4e

**S** T R E T C H

## Statement of Cash Flows for Year Ended December 31, 2008

**Operating activities**

| | |
|---|---:|
| Net income | $ 11,400 |
| Plus (minus) noncash items | |
| +Depreciation expense | 5,415 |
| Plus (minus) changes in current asset and liability accounts | |
| +Decrease in inventory | 1,425 |
| +Decrease in prepaid assets | 855 |
| +Increase in accrued payables | 1,140 |
| −Increase in accounts receivable | (3,990) |
| −Decrease in accounts payable | (2,850) |
| Cash provided by operating activities | $ 13,395 |
| **Investing activities** | |
| Purchase of equipment | $ (39,615) |
| Proceeds from the sale of land | 8,550 |
| Cash used by investing activities | $ (31,065) |
| **Financing activities** | |
| Issuance of long-term debt | $ 16,245 |
| Issuance of common stock | 12,825 |
| Cash dividends paid | (6,270) |
| Purchase of treasury stock | (2,565) |
| Cash provided by financing activities | $ 20,235 |
| **Net cash flow** | $ 2,565 |

**Additional Information:**

a. During 2008, 500 shares of common stock were sold to the public.

b. Land was sold during 2008 at an amount that equaled its original cost.

**Required:**

Use the preceding information to derive Drop Zone Corporation's balance sheet at the end of 2008.

# COLLABORATIVE LEARNING CASE

**C4-6**

Kellogg Company: Determining missing amounts on the cash flow statement and explaining the causes for change in cash

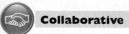
**Collaborative**

The following information was taken from Kellogg Company's Year 2 statement of cash flows. Kellogg is the world's largest maker of ready-to-eat cereals. Its cereal products account for about 38% of the U.S. market and 52% of the non-U.S. market. Some of its more famous brand-name products include Frosted Flakes, Rice Krispies, Fruit Loops, and Apple Jacks.

*($ in millions)*

| | |
|---|---:|
| Increase (decrease) in cash and temporary investments | $77.5 |
| Issuance of common stock | 17.7 |
| Other noncash expenses | 16.8 |
| Decrease in accounts receivable | 10.2 |
| Additions to properties | ? |
| Purchase of treasury stock | 83.6 |
| Depreciation | 222.8 |
| Increase in prepaid expenses | 22.9 |
| Cash and temporary investments at end of year | ? |
| Decrease in deferred income taxes | 5.4 |

*(continued)*

*($ in millions)*

| | |
|---|---|
| Borrowings on notes payable | 182.1 |
| Cash used by investing activities | 319.9 |
| Issuance of long-term debt | 4.3 |
| Cash dividends | ? |
| Property disposals | 25.2 |
| Cash provided by operations | 934.4 |
| Increase in accounts payable | 42.7 |
| Other financing activities | 1.1 |
| Reduction of long-term debt | 126.0 |
| Increase in inventories | 41.4 |
| Cash used by financing activities | ? |
| Effect of exchange rate changes on cash | 0.7 |
| Net earnings | ? |
| Cash and temporary investments at beginning of year | 100.5 |
| Increase in accrued liabilities | 105.6 |
| Other acquisitions | 11.6 |
| Reduction of notes payable | 274.0 |

**Required:**

1. Determine the missing values and recast Kellogg's Year 2 statement of cash flows, showing in good form cash flows from operations, investing, and financing activities. (*Note:* The item "Effect of exchange rate changes on cash" captures the gains or losses that arise when a firm converts its foreign subsidiaries' financial statements from the respective currencies (for example, French francs) into U.S. dollars. In Kellogg's case, these translations were favorable in Year 2. This item should be treated as an adjustment to aggregate net cash flows to arrive at the change in cash. This adjustment usually appears near the bottom of the statement of cash flows.)

2. How did Kellogg fund its investing activities during Year 2?

3. How much cash did depreciation provide during Year 2?

4. Cash provided by operations was $934.4 million in Year 2, yet Kellogg's Cash account balance increased by only $77.5 million during the year. How can this be?

 **.mhhe.com/revsine4e**

**Remember to check the book's companion Web site
for additional study material.**

# Essentials of Financial Statement Analysis | 5

> "*Investors would be well advised to shut out all the yammering about earnings expectations, consensus forecasts, and whisper numbers and focus instead on the financial information reported by companies themselves.*"[1]

A firm's financial statements are like an optical lens. If you know how to look through them, you can more clearly see what is going on at the firm. Has profitability improved? Are customers paying their bills more promptly? How was the new manufacturing plant financed? Financial statements hold the answers to these and other questions. They can tell us how the company got to where it is today, and they can help us forecast where the company might be tomorrow.

This chapter provides an overview of three financial analysis tools—**common-size statements, trend statements,** and **financial ratios.** We show how each tool is used to analyze profitability and credit risk, and we explain how to interpret the results from each. But the important message in this chapter is that all financial analysis tools are built around reported accounting data, and these tools can be no better than the data from which they are constructed. *What financial data a company chooses to report and how the data are reported affect not only the financial statements themselves but also the ratios and other numbers used to analyze those statements.*

Introducing financial analysis tools at this early point prepares you for later chapters in which we describe various financial reporting alternatives and their impact on ratios, trends, and other comparisons.

## BASIC APPROACHES

Analysts use financial statements and financial data in many ways and for many different purposes. Two purposes you should know are time-series analysis and cross-sectional analysis.

**Time-series analysis** helps identify financial trends over time for a *single* company or business unit. The analyst might be interested in determining the rate of growth in sales for Intel Corporation or the degree to which Intel's earnings have fluctuated historically

*Chapter*

---

[1] G. Morgenson, "Flying Blind in a Fog of Data," *The New York Times,* June 18, 2000.

in relation to inflation, business cycles, foreign currency exchange rates, or changes in economic growth in domestic or foreign markets.

**Cross-sectional analysis** helps identify similarities and differences *across* companies or business units at a single moment in time. The analyst might compare the 2008 profitability of one company in an industry to a competitor's profitability. A related analytic tool—**benchmark comparison**—measures a company's performance or health against some predetermined standard. For example, commercial lending agreements often require the borrowing company to maintain minimum dollar levels of working capital or tangible net worth. Once the loan has been granted, the lender—a bank or insurance company—monitors compliance by comparing the borrower's reported financial amounts and ratios to those specified in the loan agreement.

> **Tangible net worth** is usually defined as total *tangible* assets minus total liabilities; tangible assets exclude things such as goodwill, patents, trademarks, and other *intangible* items.

## Financial Statement Analysis and Accounting Quality

Financial ratios, common-size statements, and trend statements are extremely powerful tools for understanding how a company got where it is today and where the company might be tomorrow. But because these tools are built around reported accounting data, they can be no better than the data from which they are constructed. Analysts need a thorough understanding of accounting rules and a keen eye for information in the financial statement footnotes before they can use the tools to their full advantage.

Analysts use financial statement information to "get behind the numbers"—that is, to see more accurately the economic activities and condition of the company and its prospects (see Figure 5.1). However, financial statements do not always provide a complete and faithful picture of a company's activities and condition. The raw data needed for a complete and faithful picture do not always reach the financial reports because the information is filtered by generally accepted accounting principles (GAAP) and by management's accounting discretion. Both factors can distort the quality of the reported information and the analyst's view of the company.

Let's see how the financial reporting "filter" phenomenon works with equipment leases. GAAP requires each lease to be classified as either a **capital lease** or an **operating lease,** and it

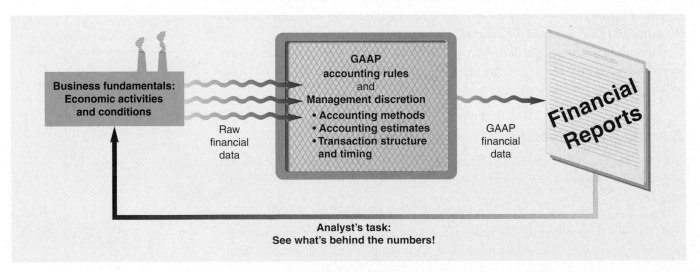

**Figure 5.1**   THE FINANCIAL REPORTING FILTER AND THE ANALYST'S TASK

requires only capital leases to be reported as balance sheet assets and liabilities. Operating leases are "off-balance-sheet" items—meaning they are not included in the reported asset and liability numbers but are instead disclosed in supplemental footnotes that accompany the financial statements. (We'll see how and why this is so in Chapter 12.) So GAAP lets capital leases pass to the balance sheet, but it filters out operating leases, sending them to the statement footnotes. Analysts can—and do—use these footnotes to recast the balance sheet so that all equipment leases are treated the same way. The GAAP filter is then overcome.

**Management discretion** can cloud financial analysis in several ways. For example, managers who understand GAAP can use it to structure business transactions so that financial reporting goals are achieved. Do you, as a manager, want to keep equipment leases off the balance sheet? Then just make certain your company's lease contracts meet the GAAP rules for an operating lease. Doing so keeps the leases off your balance sheet and lowers reported debt.

Management discretion can also complicate the analyst's task in such areas as inventory accounting for which GAAP allows managers to freely choose among several alternative reporting methods. Some companies account for inventory using the first-in first-out (FIFO) method; others use last-in first-out (LIFO). These alternative methods can produce very different balance sheet and income statement figures and, as a result, numerous financial ratios and comparisons can be affected (Chapter 9). Here, too, the analyst can sometimes use footnote information to recast the reported financial results and thereby eliminate management discretion as an information filter.

Management also has discretion over accounting estimates and the timing of business transactions. Consider estimated bad debt expense, management's forecast of the amount of current credit sales that will never be collected from customers. A reduction in estimated bad debt expense could mean that customer credit quality has improved—that is, more credit customers are now expected to pay their bills. Or it could mean that bad debt expense was temporarily reduced to meet a quarterly earnings goal. Similar questions arise over the timing of discretionary expenditures for advertising, research and development (R&D), or information technology. Did advertising expense decline because the current ad program was a resounding success or because management curtailed spending this quarter just to meet an earnings goal? In other words, have business fundamentals improved, or is the appearance of improvement due simply to "earnings management"?

> GAAP and management discretion can sometimes make the analyst's task easier by illuminating aspects of the company's activities and condition. For example, GAAP requires companies to disclose sales and operating income by business segment—information that some companies would not otherwise make available. Similarly, management sometimes goes far beyond GAAP's minimum reporting requirements by disclosing financial and nonfinancial operating details that are invaluable to analysts.

**Conflicts of interest** pose another potential threat to the quality of financial reports. Conflicts of interest arise when what is good for one party (for example, management) isn't necessarily good for another party (say, lenders or outside investors). Take the case of Adelphia Communications, a provider of cable entertainment and communication services. In March 2002, Adelphia revealed for the first time the existence of $2.6 billion in previously unreported off-balance-sheet liabilities. Over the next several months, lenders and investors learned that Adelphia's top executives—including the company's founder and his family members—had deliberately shifted bank loans totaling $2.6 billion from Adelphia's books to the books of unconsolidated affiliates controlled by the family. What happened to the $2.6 billion that was originally borrowed? Family members used it to buy Adelphia stock, construct a golf course, pay off personal loans, and purchase luxury condominiums in Colorado, Mexico, and New York City—uses unrelated to the original business purpose of the bank loans. By June 2002, Adelphia and more than 200 of its subsidiaries and affiliates had filed bankruptcy.

When related-party transactions occur, *Statement of Financial Accounting Standards (SFAS) No. 57*\* requires companies to disclose the nature of the relationship, provide a description of the transactions, and report the dollar amount of the transactions and any amounts due to or from related parties. *SFAS No. 57* requires a high level of disclosure because related-party transactions cannot be presumed to have been the result of an "arm's-length" negotiation between an independent buyer and seller in a competitive marketplace.

\* "Related-Party Disclosures," *SFAS No. 57* (Stamford, CT: FASB, 1982).

Companies have an obligation to disclose business transactions that involve potential conflicts of interest. By concealing from lenders and investors that billions of dollars had been given to affiliates controlled by the founder's family and how the money was being spent, Adelphia violated guidelines of the Financial Accounting Standards Board (FASB) and the Securities and Exchange Commission (SEC). Adelphia violated GAAP by systematically hiding the debt on the books of the affiliates. Lenders and investors were caught unaware.

## RECAP

**The message here is simply that analysts must always be vigilant about the possibility that accounting distortions are present and complicate the interpretation of financial ratios, percentage relations, and trend indices. That's why each chapter of this book alerts you to potential accounting distortions and then shows you how to eliminate those distortions. Only then can you accurately assess a company's true profitability and credit risk. So, remember that the first step to informed financial statement analysis is a careful evaluation of the quality of the company's reported accounting numbers. No tool of financial statement analysis is completely immune to distortions caused by GAAP or by management's reporting choices.**

## A CASE IN POINT: GETTING BEHIND THE NUMBERS AT WHOLE FOODS MARKET

In 1978, twenty-five year old college dropout John Mackey and Rene Lawson, his twenty-one year old girlfriend, borrowed $45,000 from family and friends to open the doors of a small natural foods store called SaferWay in Austin, Texas (the name being a spoof of Safeway, which operated grocery stores in Austin at that time). When the couple got booted out of their apartment for storing food products there, they decided to simply live at the store. Since it was zoned commercial, there was no shower stall. Instead, they bathed in the Hobart dishwasher, which had an attached water hose. Two years later, John Mackey partnered with Craig Weller and Mark Skiles to merge SaferWay with their Clarksville Natural Grocery, resulting in the opening of the original Whole Foods Market on September 20, 1980.[2]

Natural and organic food is one of the fastest growing segments of food retailing today, and Whole Foods Market is the dominant player with nearly 200 retail stores. The company's business model is built around offering an extensive selection of high-quality food products that promote a healthy lifestyle, and high levels of customer service. Flagship Whole Foods stores combine an old-fashioned neighborhood grocery with an organic farmers' market, a European bakery, a New York deli, and a modern supermarket.[3] Patrons select from among more than 30,000 natural and organic items that include an extensive selection of fruits, vegetables, cheese, fish, and seafood as well as meat and poultry. Perishable foods account for about 67% of sales.

Competition in the grocery business is local. So, each Whole Foods store offers patrons a customized product mix. The Austin store has all types of products from small local producers and vendors—from salsas to tofu to tabbouleh to humus, to hundreds of other items unique to that

---

[2] Whole Foods Market, Inc. corporate Web site.

[3] In addition to its signature banner, the company also operates stores under the trade names of Bread & Circus, Fresh Fields, Wellspring Grocery, and Merchant of Vino.

store. Some stores also offer special services such as massage, valet parking, and home delivery. The retail stores are supported by regional offices and distribution centers, bake house facilities, commissary kitchens, seafood processing facilities, produce procurement centers, a national meat purchasing office, a confectionary, and a specialty coffee and tea procurement and brewing operation.

New store openings, acquisitions of competitors, and organic growth—more customers spending more dollars at existing stores—have contributed to the company's rapid growth. Sales increased at a 27% compound annual growth rate between 1991 and 2006. Sales in 2006 totaled just over $5.6 billion, up 19% from 2005. Net income that year was nearly $204 million, up almost 50% from 2005, and operating cash flows were strong at $453 million.

Food retailing was once an intensely personalized business. People bought food directly from local farmers or neighborhood shops. Owners of the early mom-and-pop stores often lived in the same neighborhood where their businesses were located. They were "close to the customer" and knew their customers' names and ages, where they lived and worked, and their grocery likes and dislikes. In the 1950s, people in large numbers began migrating from cities to suburbs. Merchants followed them, leading to explosive growth in shopping centers and, eventually, to the formation of giant grocery chains. Large supermarkets came to dominate the retail landscape.

Today, retail grocery chains act as intermediaries that bring producers and consumers together. They buy products from a large number of suppliers in wide enough assortments to satisfy their customers, they move those products to retail stores where customers can choose among them, they maintain the products' freshness, and they complete the sales by checking out and bagging merchandise at the cash register. Store hours are often long to suit the varying schedules of a complex society.

The grocery industry remains one of the most fragmented U.S. retail sectors. With total sales of $906.7 billion in 2006, the industry includes a range of businesses from small grocery shops and convenience stores to supermarket chains. The top five food retailers—Wal-Mart, Kroger, SUPERVALUE, Safeway, and Ahold USA—accounted for 30.7% of total food industry sales in 2006. Supermarket chains comprised only 17.6% of grocery store units in 2006 but 55.1% of food item sales by grocery stores.

Grocery retailing has always been a low-margin business. Rival stores compete for each consumer food dollar based on product assortment, quality, convenience, service, and price. Cost control is a key management imperative because price competition is intense. Labor accounts for more than 50% of total operating expenses.

The organic food category generated $16.9 billion in sales in 2006, up from $13.8 billion in 2005. With nearly 40% of consumers purchasing items labeled "organic," most who buy natural and organic products do so in their primary supermarkets. As a result of growing consumer interest in natural and organic foods, major food retailers not only are increasing the square footage devoted to this product category but also are testing plans to open natural and organic food stores.

Now that you have an understanding of the business and the industry, let's take a look at Whole Foods' financial statements.

## Examining Whole Foods Market's Financial Statements

See Exhibit 5.1 for comparative income statements for Whole Foods Market. Sales increased from $3.149 billion in 2003 to more than $5.607 billion in 2006. These figures reflect revenue from natural and organic grocery products and other items sold at the company's retail stores. But sales growth is only part of the story at Whole Foods. Exhibit 5.1 data also show that net income increased from about $99 million in 2003 to nearly $204 million in 2006.

A closer look at Whole Foods' income statements reveals that 2006 net income was helped by two nonoperating items: $20.7 million of investment and other income, more than double

| EXHIBIT 5.1 | Whole Foods Market | | | |
|---|---|---|---|---|

**Comparative Income Statements**

| ($ in thousands) | 2006 | 2005 | 2004 | 2003 |
|---|---|---|---|---|
| Sales | $5,607,376 | $4,701,289 | $3,864,950 | $3,148,593 |
| Cost of goods sold and occupancy costs | 3,647,734 | 3,052,184 | 2,523,816 | 2,070,334 |
| Gross profit | $1,959,642 | $1,649,105 | $1,341,134 | $1,078,259 |
| Direct store expenses | 1,421,968 | 1,223,473 | 986,040 | 794,422 |
| General and administrative expenses | 181,244 | 158,864 | 119,800 | 100,693 |
| Pre-opening and relocation costs | 37,421 | 37,035 | 18,648 | 15,765 |
| Operating income | $ 319,009 | $ 229,733 | $ 216,646 | $ 167,379 |
| Interest expense | (32) | (2,223) | (7,249) | (8,114) |
| Investment and other income | 20,736 | 9,623 | 6,456 | 5,593 |
| Income before income taxes | $ 339,713 | $ 237,133 | $ 215,853 | $ 164,858 |
| Provision for income taxes | 135,885 | 100,782 | 86,341 | 65,943 |
| Net income | $ 203,828 | $ 136,351 | $ 129,512 | $ 98,915 |

the amount reported in 2005, and a $2.2 million reduction in interest expense. Based on the company's effective tax rate of 40%, these two items contributed $5.322 million to net income that year—the $11.113 million *increase* in investment and other income plus the $2.191 million decrease in interest expense multiplied by the 40% effective tax rate. In other words, Whole Foods would have reported net income of $198.507 million ($203.829 − $5.322) for 2006 without these nonoperating item improvements. Financial statement readers are always on the alert for changes in the contribution made by nonoperating items to overall net income. A failure to spot such changes can sometimes lead readers to draw mistaken inferences about firm profitability.

**Common-Size and Trend Analysis Income Statements**   Financial analysts use common-size and trend statements of net income to help spot changes in a company's cost structure and profit performance. **Common-size income statements** (top of Exhibit 5.2) recast each statement item as a percentage of sales. Common-size income statements show you how much of each sales dollar the company spent on operating expenses and other business costs and how much of each sales dollar hit the bottom line as profit. For example, Whole Foods Market's direct store expenses for 2006 are shown as 25.4% of 2006 sales (25.4% = $1,421,968 direct store expenses$_{2006}$/$5,607,376 sales$_{2006}$) instead of $1,421,968 million. This means that 25.4 cents of each 2006 sales dollar was spent on direct store costs. That leaves 74.6 cents of each 2006 sales dollar to cover the wholesale cost of grocery products sold and other business costs and to provide a profit for the year.

The trend statements (bottom of Exhibit 5.2) also recast each statement item in percentage terms, but they do so using a base year number rather than sales. Trend statements help you spot increases (and decreases) over time in each income statement item. For instance, the trend statement of income shows Whole Foods Market's 2006 net income as 206.1% of base year 2003 net income (206.1% = $203.828 net income$_{2006}$/$98.915 net income$_{2003}$ expressed as a percentage). This means that profits in 2006 are more than twice as much as they were in 2003.

The common-size and trend statements of net income reveal several interesting aspects of the company's profit performance:

- The trend statements indicate that sales increased steadily over the four-year period and in 2006 were 178.1% higher than in 2003.

| EXHIBIT 5.2 | Whole Foods Market |
|---|---|

### Common-Size and Trend Analysis of Income

**Common-Size Statements**

| (% of sales) | 2006 | 2005 | 2004 | 2003 |
|---|---|---|---|---|
| Sales | 100.0% | 100.0% | 100.0% | 100.0% |
| Cost of goods sold and occupancy costs | 65.1 | 64.9 | 65.3 | 65.8 |
| Gross profit | 34.9 | 35.1 | 34.7 | 34.2 |
| Direct store expenses | 25.4 | 26.0 | 25.5 | 25.2 |
| General and administrative expenses | 3.2 | 3.4 | 3.1 | 3.2 |
| Pre-opening and relocation costs | 0.7 | 0.8 | 0.5 | 0.5 |
| Operating income | 5.7 | 4.9 | 5.6 | 5.3 |
| Interest expense | 0.0 | 0.0 | (0.2) | (0.3) |
| Investment and other income | 0.4 | 0.2 | 0.2 | 0.2 |
| Income before income taxes | 6.1 | 5.0 | 5.6 | 5.2 |
| Provision for income taxes | 2.4 | 2.1 | 2.2 | 2.1 |
| Net income | 3.6% | 2.9% | 3.4% | 3.1% |

**Trend Statements (2003 = 100%)**

| | 2006 | 2005 | 2004 | 2003 |
|---|---|---|---|---|
| Sales | 178.1% | 149.3% | 122.8% | 100.0% |
| Cost of goods sold and occupancy costs | 176.2 | 147.4 | 121.9 | 100.0 |
| Gross profit | 181.7 | 152.9 | 124.4 | 100.0 |
| Direct store expenses | 179.0 | 154.0 | 124.1 | 100.0 |
| General and administrative expenses | 180.0 | 157.8 | 119.0 | 100.0 |
| Pre-opening and relocation costs | 237.4 | 234.9 | 118.3 | 100.0 |
| Operating income | 190.6 | 137.3 | 129.4 | 100.0 |
| Interest expense | 0.4 | 27.4 | 89.3 | 100.0 |
| Investment and other income | 370.7 | 172.1 | 115.4 | 100.0 |
| Income before income taxes | 206.1 | 143.8 | 130.9 | 100.0 |
| Provision for income taxes | 206.1 | 152.8 | 130.9 | 100.0 |
| Net income | 206.1% | 137.8% | 130.9% | 100.0% |

*Note:* Percentages are rounded.

- The trend statements also indicate that net income growth exceeded sales growth because 2006 net income was 206.1% more than in 2003. Two previously mentioned nonoperating items were partially responsible for this bottom-line net income growth, but operating income in 2006 was also 190.6% more than in 2003.

- According to the common-size statements, over time only small fluctuations occurred in the amount spent on individual operating expense items such as direct store expenses, cost of goods sold, and occupancy costs.

The years shown in the statements were particularly successful ones for Whole Foods and its employees. The trend statements show that sales increased 178.1% over four years and that operating income was up 190.6%. What factors contributed to the company's tremendous sales growth? It was a combination of increased sales at existing retail stores—11% in 2006 alone—plus sales from newly opened stores. Why did operating income grow faster than sales? Apparently, the company benefited from operating and administrative efficiencies that resulted in lower expenses per dollar of sales. For example, cost of goods sold and occupancy costs fell from

## EXHIBIT 5.3     Krispy Kreme Doughnuts, Inc.

### Panel (a): Information about Operations by Business Segment

| ($ in millions) | Year 3 | Year 2 | Year 1 |
|---|---|---|---|
| Revenues: | | | |
|   Company store operations | $319.6 | $266.2 | $213.7 |
|   Franchise operations | 19.3 | 14.0 | 9.4 |
|   KKM&D* | 152.6 | 114.2 | 77.6 |
|     Total revenues | $491.5 | $394.4 | $300.7 |
| Operating income: | | | |
|   Company store operations | $ 58.2 | $ 42.9 | $ 27.4 |
|   Franchise operations | 14.3 | 9.0 | 5.7 |
|   KKM&D* | 26.8 | 19.0 | 11.7 |
|   Unallocated general and administrative expenses | (39.5) | (29.0) | (21.3) |
|     Total operating income | $ 59.8 | $ 41.9 | $ 23.5 |

### Panel (b): Revenue Contribution and Operating Margin by Business Segment

| | Year 3 | Year 2 | Year 1 |
|---|---|---|---|
| Revenue contribution | | | |
|   Company store operations | 65% | 67% | 71% |
|   Franchise operations | 4 | 4 | 3 |
|   KKM&D* | 31 | 29 | 26 |
| Operating margin | | | |
|   Company store operations | 18% | 16% | 13% |
|   Franchise operations | 74 | 64 | 61 |
|   KKM&D* | 18 | 17 | 15 |

* KKM&D sells flour mix, doughnut-making equipment, and supplies to franchised stores.

65.8 cents per dollar of sales in 2003 to 65.1 cents in 2006 as the common-size statements show. This means 0.7 cents more gross profit for each dollar of sales.

Common-size and trend statements can also be helpful in identifying where a company makes money. The top portion of Exhibit 5.3 reproduces information found in the annual report footnote of Krispy Kreme Doughnuts, Inc. on its three business segments—company-owned stores that sell doughnuts to the public, franchise operations that generate license and royalty income, and the manufacturing segment (called "KKM&D") that sells flour mix, doughnut-making equipment, and supplies to franchised stores. The top portion of Panel (a) shows how much revenue each business segment produced each year. The bottom portion of Panel (a) shows the operating income—sales minus operating expenses including selling, general, and administration costs—earned by each segment along with corporate general and administrative expenses not allocated to segments. For example, revenue from company-owned stores totaled $319.6 million in Year 3, and operating income was $58.2 million.

> Whole Foods Market operates in a single business segment. It does not provide details about product line profitability because competitors might then use the information to their advantage.

Panel (b) of Exhibit 5.3 uses a common-size approach to isolate each segment's contribution to total company revenue and then computes an operating profit margin (that is, operating income divided by revenue) for each segment. As you can now easily see, 65% ($319.6/$491.5) of Krispy Kreme's revenue for Year 3 came from company-owned stores while only 4% came from franchise licenses and fees. But the franchise segment had a higher operating margin (74% = $14.3/$19.3) when compared to company-owned stores and KKM&D (18% each). Although the franchise segment makes a smaller contribution to overall company revenue, it makes a larger percentage contribution to overall operating income.

Now let's see what we can learn from a balance sheet.

| EXHIBIT 5.4 | Whole Foods Market |
|---|---|

## Comparative Balance Sheets

| ($ in thousands) | 2006 | 2005 | 2004 | 2003 |
|---|---|---|---|---|
| **Assets** | | | | |
| Current assets: | | | | |
| Cash and cash equivalents | $ 2,252 | $ 308,524 | $ 198,377 | $ 165,779 |
| Short-term investments | 193,847 | | | |
| Restricted cash | 60,065 | 36,922 | 23,160 | |
| Accounts receivable | 82,137 | 66,682 | 64,972 | 45,947 |
| Merchandise inventories | 203,727 | 174,848 | 152,912 | 123,904 |
| Prepaid expenses and other current assets | 33,804 | 45,965 | 16,702 | 12,447 |
| Deferred income taxes | 48,149 | 39,588 | 28,894 | 15,607 |
| Total current assets | $ 623,981 | $ 672,529 | $ 485,017 | $ 363,684 |
| Property and equipment, net | 1,236,133 | 1,054,605 | 877,457 | 718,240 |
| Goodwill | 113,494 | 112,476 | 112,186 | 80,548 |
| Intangible assets, net | 34,767 | 21,990 | 24,831 | 26,569 |
| Other assets | 34,621 | 27,696 | 20,302 | 7,779 |
| Total assets | $2,042,996 | $1,889,296 | $1,519,793 | $1,196,820 |
| **Liabilities and Shareholders' Equity** | | | | |
| Current liabilities: | | | | |
| Current installments of long-term debt | $ 49 | $ 5,932 | $ 5,973 | $ 5,806 |
| Accounts payable | 121,857 | 103,348 | 90,751 | 72,715 |
| Accrued wages, bonuses, and benefits | 153,014 | 126,981 | 100,536 | 70,875 |
| Dividends payable | | 17,208 | 9,361 | |
| Other current liabilities | 234,850 | 164,914 | 124,641 | 90,188 |
| Total current liabilities | $ 509,770 | $ 418,383 | $ 331,262 | $ 239,584 |
| Long-term debt, less current installments | 8,606 | 12,932 | 164,770 | 162,909 |
| Deferred lease liabilities | 120,421 | 91,775 | 13,566 | 13,349 |
| Other long-term liabilities | 56 | 530 | 21,756 | 4,802 |
| Total liabilities | $ 638,853 | $ 523,620 | $ 531,354 | $ 420,644 |
| Shareholders' equity: | | | | |
| Common stock, no par value | 1,147,872 | 874,972 | 535,107 | 423,297 |
| Common stock in treasury | (99,964) | | | |
| Accumulated other comprehensive income | 6,975 | 4,405 | 2,053 | 1,624 |
| Retained earnings | 349,260 | 486,299 | 451,279 | 351,255 |
| Total shareholders' equity | $1,404,143 | $1,365,676 | $ 988,439 | $ 776,176 |
| Total liabilities and shareholders' equity | $2,042,996 | $1,889,296 | $1,519,793 | $1,196,820 |

## Common-Size and Trend Analysis Balance Sheets

Exhibit 5.4 shows Whole Foods Market's comparative balance sheets using reported dollar amounts. The company's assets are concentrated in the stores themselves (represented by the Property and equipment and Merchandise inventories accounts) and, to a lesser degree, in Short-term investments. Consumers pay cash for their grocery items, so Accounts receivable must represent amounts retail customers such as local restaurants owe the company. Restricted cash is money the company has set aside as collateral to support a portion of its projected workers' compensation claims. To finance its various operating assets, the company has relied on a combination of vendor payables (in the Accounts payable account), long-term debt, and common stock along with internally generated resources represented by Retained earnings.

| EXHIBIT 5.5 | Whole Foods Market |
| --- | --- |

## Common-Size and Trend Analysis of Assets

### Common-Size Statements

| (% of total assets) | 2006 | 2005 | 2004 | 2003 |
| --- | --- | --- | --- | --- |
| **Assets** | | | | |
| Current assets: | | | | |
| Cash and cash equivalents | 0.1% | 16.3% | 13.1% | 13.9% |
| Short-term investments | 9.5 | — | — | |
| Restricted cash | 2.9 | 2.0 | 1.5 | |
| Accounts receivable | 4.0 | 3.5 | 4.3 | 3.8 |
| Merchandise inventories | 10.0 | 9.3 | 10.1 | 10.4 |
| Prepaid expenses and other current assets | 1.7 | 2.4 | 1.1 | 1.0 |
| Deferred income taxes | 2.4 | 2.1 | 1.9 | 1.3 |
| Total current assets | 30.5% | 35.6% | 31.9% | 30.4% |
| Property and equipment, net | 60.5 | 55.8 | 57.7 | 60.0 |
| Goodwill | 5.6 | 6.0 | 7.4 | 6.7 |
| Intangible assets, net | 1.7 | 1.2 | 1.6 | 2.2 |
| Other assets | 1.7 | 1.5 | 1.3 | 0.6 |
| Total assets | 100.0% | 100.0% | 100.0% | 100.0% |

### Trend Statements (2003 = 100%)

| | 2006 | 2005 | 2004 | 2003 |
| --- | --- | --- | --- | --- |
| **Assets** | | | | |
| Current assets: | | | | |
| Cash and cash equivalents | 1.4% | 186.1% | 119.7% | 100.0% |
| Short-term investments | | | | |
| Restricted cash | — | — | — | |
| Accounts receivable | 178.8 | 145.1 | 141.4 | 100.0 |
| Merchandise inventories | 164.4 | 141.1 | 123.4 | 100.0 |
| Prepaid expenses and other current assets | 271.6 | 369.3 | 134.2 | 100.0 |
| Deferred income taxes | 308.5 | 253.7 | 185.1 | 100.0 |
| Total current assets | 171.6% | 184.9% | 133.4% | 100.0% |
| Property and equipment, net | 172.1 | 146.8 | 122.2 | 100.0 |
| Goodwill | 140.9 | 139.6 | 139.3 | 100.0 |
| Intangible assets, net | 130.9 | 82.8 | 93.5 | 100.0 |
| Other assets | 445.1 | 356.0 | 261.0 | 100.0 |
| Total assets | 170.7% | 157.9% | 127.0% | 100.0% |

*Note:* Percentages are rounded. The — denotes a trend percentage that cannot be computed because the 2003 base year value is zero.

Several important changes in the company's asset mix and financial structure have occurred since 2003. These changes are apparent from the common-size and trend statements in Exhibits 5.5 (Assets) and 5.6 (Liabilities and Shareholders' Equity).

Consider the composition of Whole Foods' assets in 2006. According to the common-size statements in Exhibit 5.5, property and equipment made up 60.5% of that year's total assets. Inventories represented 10.0% of total 2006 assets while accounts receivable contributed another 4.0%. The trend statements in Exhibit 5.5 reveal that accounts receivable growth (178.8% in 2006) kept pace with sales growth (178.1% from Exhibit 5.4). Growth in property and equipment (172.1%) and inventories (164.4%) was somewhat slower than sales growth.

| EXHIBIT 5.6 | Whole Foods Market |
| --- | --- |

## Common-Size and Trend Analysis of Liabilities and Shareholders' Equity

### Common-Size Statements

| (% of total assets) | 2006 | 2005 | 2004 | 2003 |
| --- | --- | --- | --- | --- |
| **Liabilities and Shareholders' Equity** | | | | |
| Current liabilities: | | | | |
| Current installments of long-term debt | 0.0% | 0.3% | 0.4% | 0.5% |
| Accounts payable | 6.0 | 5.5 | 6.0 | 6.1 |
| Accrued wages, bonuses, and benefits | 7.5 | 6.7 | 6.6 | 5.9 |
| Dividends payable | | 0.9 | 0.6 | |
| Other current liabilities | 11.5 | 8.7 | 8.2 | 7.5 |
| Total current liabilities | 25.0% | 22.1% | 21.8% | 20.0% |
| Long-term debt, less current installments | 0.4 | 0.7 | 10.8 | 13.6 |
| Deferred lease liabilities | 5.9 | 4.9 | 0.9 | 1.1 |
| Other long-term liabilities | 0.0 | 0.0 | 1.4 | 0.4 |
| Total liabilities | 31.3% | 27.7% | 35.0% | 35.1% |
| Shareholders' equity: | | | | |
| Common stock, no par value | 56.2% | 46.3% | 35.2% | 35.4% |
| Common stock in treasury | (4.9) | 0.0 | 0.0 | 0.0 |
| Accumulated other comprehensive income | 0.3 | 0.2 | 0.1 | 0.1 |
| Retained earnings | 17.1 | 25.7 | 29.7 | 29.3 |
| Total shareholders' equity | 68.7% | 72.3% | 65.0% | 64.9% |
| Total liabilities and shareholders' equity | 100.0% | 100.0% | 100.0% | 100.0% |

### Trend Statements (2003 = 100%)

| | 2006 | 2005 | 2004 | 2003 |
| --- | --- | --- | --- | --- |
| **Liabilities and Shareholders' Equity** | | | | |
| Current liabilities: | | | | |
| Current installments of long-term debt | 0.8% | 102.2% | 102.9% | 100.0% |
| Accounts payable | 167.6 | 142.1 | 124.8 | 100.0 |
| Accrued wages, bonuses, and benefits | 215.9 | 179.2 | 141.8 | 100.0 |
| Dividends payable | | — | — | |
| Other current liabilities | 260.4 | 182.9 | 138.2 | 100.0 |
| Total current liabilities | 212.8% | 174.6% | 138.3% | 100.0% |
| Long-term debt, less current installments | 5.3% | 7.9 | 101.1 | 100.0 |
| Deferred lease liabilities | 902.1 | 687.5 | 101.6 | 100.0 |
| Other long-term liabilities | 1.2 | 11.0 | 453.1 | 100.0 |
| Total liabilities | 151.9% | 124.5% | 126.3% | 100.0% |
| Shareholders' equity: | | | | |
| Common stock, no par value | 271.2% | 206.7% | 126.4% | 100.0% |
| Common stock in treasury | — | | | |
| Accumulated other comprehensive income | 429.5 | 271.2 | 126.4 | 100.0 |
| Retained earnings | 99.4 | 138.4 | 128.5 | 100.0 |
| Total shareholders' equity | 180.9% | 175.9% | 127.3% | 100.0% |
| Total liabilities and shareholders' equity | 170.7% | 157.9% | 127.0% | 100.0% |

*Note:* Percentages are rounded. The — denotes a trend percentage that cannot be computed because the 2003 base year value is zero.

The company's cash balance fell from $308.524 million in 2005 (16.3% of total assets) to just $2.252 million in 2006 (0.1% of total assets). At the same time, Whole Foods made a substantial short-term investment: $193.847 million in 2006, or 9.5% of total assets. A financial statement note tells us that this amount likely represents investments in money-market savings accounts, certificates of deposits, and publicly traded securities. These highly liquid investments generate income and could be sold to raise cash if the company were to need money for future growth.

The company's investment in accounting **goodwill**—$113.494 million in 2006—is the acquisition price premium paid for a target company over and above the value of its identifiable assets. (Chapter 16 has more on goodwill.) Whole Foods has acquired a number of other natural and organic grocery stores over the years including Bluebonnet Natural Foods Grocery, Wellspring Grocery, Sourdough: A European Bakery, and Mrs. Gooch's Natural Foods Markets.

What changes in the company's financial structure occurred between 2003 and 2006? Did the mix of debt and equity remain constant over the four years? What happened to the proportion of short-term versus long-term borrowing? The common-size and trend statements in Exhibit 5.6 provide the answers. We can see the following from the common-size statements:

- Total current liabilities were 25.0% in 2006, up from only 20.0% in 2003, and this increase was concentrated in the category Other current liabilities.

- Long-term debt stood at 13.6% in 2003 but declined steadily to 0.4% in 2006.

- Common stock exhibits the opposite pattern. It stood at 35.4% in 2003 and then increased to 56.2% in 2006.

The central message from the common-size statements in Exhibit 5.6 is that Whole Foods reduced its reliance on long-term debt and increased its reliance on investor capital (Common stock) over the four-year period.

The trend statements in Exhibit 5.6 support this view of the company's changing financial structure. Long-term debt in 2006 was only 5.3% of the amount the company owed in 2003 whereas common stock increased 271.2% since 2003. On the other hand, the growth in accounts payable (167.6%) roughly parallels sales growth. *Trend statements often indicate a company's growth (and decline) more clearly than do common-size statements.*

### Common-Size and Trend Analysis Cash Flow Statements

See Exhibit 5.7 for comparative cash flow statements. Some statement items are shown as combined figures to simplify the presentation. Common-size and trends for selected cash flow items are in Exhibit 5.8. The common-size statements are constructed by dividing each cash flow item by sales for the year. For example, Whole Foods Market's operating activities generated $452.664 million cash (Exhibit 5.7) in 2006, or 8.1% of the $5.607 billion in sales that year (Exhibit 5.8). In other words, cash from operations equaled 8.1 cents per sales dollar, down from 9.0 cents in 2003 (Exhibit 5.8).

How does Whole Foods use these operating cash flows? Like most growing retail companies, it devotes some financial resources to expanding the store base. Therefore, a major use of its cash goes for new store location development costs and capital expenditures for property, plant and equipment. These two activities consumed $340.202 million ($208.588 + $131.614 from Exhibit 5.7) in 2006, or 6.0 cents per sales dollar (3.7% + 2.3% from Exhibit 5.8). Notice that the cash generated that year by operating activities (8.1 cents per sales dollar) was more than enough to fund retail store expansion. But wait a moment! Where did Whole Foods get the additional cash needed that year to fund its other investment activities ($229.053 million) and dividend payments ($358.075 million)? Some money came from leftover operating cash flow,

| EXHIBIT 5.7 | Whole Foods Market |
|---|---|

### Comparative Cash Flow Statements

| ($ in thousands) | 2006 | 2005 | 2004 | 2003 |
|---|---|---|---|---|
| Net income | $ 203,828 | $ 136,351 | $ 129,512 | $ 98,915 |
| Adjustments | 248,836 | 274,468 | 199,314 | 183,586 |
| Net cash provided by operating activities | $ 452,664 | $ 410,819 | $ 328,826 | $ 282,501 |
| Development costs of new store locations | (208,588) | (207,792) | (155,214) | (89,007) |
| Other property, plant and equipment expenditures | (131,614) | (116,318) | (109,739) | (84,103) |
| Other | (229,053) | (1,762) | (54,201) | (2,693) |
| Net cash used in investing activities | $(569,255) | $(325,872) | $(319,154) | $(175,803) |
| Dividends paid | (358,075) | (54,683) | (27,728) | |
| Issuance of common stock | 222,030 | 85,816 | 59,518 | 52,270 |
| Purchase of treasury stock | (99,964) | | | |
| Excess tax benefit from exercised stock options | 52,008 | | | |
| Payments on long-term debt and capital | (5,680) | (5,933) | (8,864) | (5,835) |
| Net cash provided by (used in) financing | $(189,681) | $ 25,200 | $ 22,926 | $ 46,435 |
| Net change in cash and cash equivalents | $(306,272) | $ 110,147 | $ 32,598 | $ 153,133 |

| EXHIBIT 5.8 | Whole Foods Market |
|---|---|

### Common-Size and Trend Analysis of Selected Cash Flow Items

**Common-Size Statements**

| (% of sales) | 2006 | 2005 | 2004 | 2003 |
|---|---|---|---|---|
| Selected items | | | | |
| Net cash provided by operating activities | 8.1% | 8.7% | 8.5% | 9.0% |
| Development costs of new store locations | (3.7) | (4.4) | (4.0) | (2.8) |
| Other property, plant and equipment expenditures | (2.3) | (2.5) | (2.8) | (2.7) |

**Trend Statements (2003 = 100%)**

| | 2006 | 2005 | 2004 | 2003 |
|---|---|---|---|---|
| Selected items | | | | |
| Net cash provided by operating activities | 160.2% | 145.4% | 116.4% | 100.0% |
| Development costs of new store locations | 234.4 | 233.5 | 174.4 | 100.0 |
| Other property, plant and equipment expenditures | 156.5 | 138.3 | 130.5 | 100.0 |

some from issuing stock ($222.030 million), and some from drawing down the company's cash balance ($306.272 million).

The trend statements in Exhibit 5.8 reveal that operating cash flow increased 160.2% over four years compared to net income growth of 206.1% (Exhibit 5.2) during the same period. Development costs rose at an even faster pace (234.4%). In addition, the company spent large amounts of cash on other investment activities and dividends in 2006. Despite some imbalance in 2006 cash inflows and outflows, the company is on a solid financial footing. Operating cash flows each year were more than sufficient to cover retail store expansion, and the company used its accumulated excess cash to pay down debt, make short-term investments, and pay dividends.

RECAP

From our analysis of Whole Foods Market and its financial statements, we can come to three conclusions:

- Informed financial statement analysis begins with knowledge of the company and its industry.
- Common-size and trend statements provide a convenient way to organize financial statement information so that major financial components and changes can be easily recognized.
- Financial statements help the analyst gain a sharper understanding of the company's economic condition and its prospects for the future.

# PROFITABILITY, COMPETITION, AND BUSINESS STRATEGY

> *"The mechanics of running a business are not really very complicated when you get down to essentials. You have to make some stuff and sell it to somebody for more than it cost you. That's about all there is, except for a few million details."*
>
> —John L. McCaffey

> Analysts sometimes make income statement and balance sheet adjustments intended to isolate core operating activities—think of selling grocery products at Whole Foods Market—from nonoperating activities. The resulting profit performance measure is return on operating net assets, or RONA. Whole Foods Market's short-term investments and the income produced by those investments would not be included in RONA.

## Financial Ratios and Profitability Analysis

Financial ratios provide other powerful tools analysts use in evaluating profit performance and assessing credit risk. Most evaluations of profit performance begin with the **return on assets (ROA)** ratio,

$$\text{ROA} = \frac{\text{Earnings before interest (EBI)}}{\text{Average assets}}$$

where *EBI* refers to the company's *earnings before interest* for a particular period (such as a year), and *average assets* represents the average book value of total assets over that same time period. Before computing ROA, analysts may adjust the company's reported earnings and asset figures. These adjustments fall into three broad categories:

1. Adjustments aimed at *isolating a company's sustainable profits* by removing nonrecurring items from reported income.
2. An adjustment that *eliminates after-tax interest expense* from the profit calculation so that profitability comparisons over time or across companies are not clouded by differences in financial structure.[4]

---

[4] To illustrate how financial structure can affect profitability comparisons, consider two companies that have (a) identical after-tax operating profits of $500 before interest expense is considered and (b) the same total asset base of $5,000. One company has no interest-bearing debt; the other has $2,000 of 12% debt outstanding. Annual interest expense on this debt is $240 = $2,000 × 0.12, but the deductibility of interest expense for tax purposes saves the company $96 = $240 × 0.40 each year when the corporate income tax rate is 40%. Consequently, the company with debt would report net income of $356 or $500 − $240 × (1 − 0.40). If financing costs are ignored, the all-equity company would have an ROA of 10% ($500/$5,000) while the company with debt would have an ROA of only 7.12% ($356/$5,000). The analyst might mistakenly conclude that one company's profit performance is superior to the other when, in fact, the only difference between these two companies is their choice of financing. The "adjusted" ROA for the company with debt would confirm that identical levels of *operating* profit performance had been achieved:

$$\text{ROA} = \frac{\text{After-tax operating profits} + \text{Interest expense} \times (1 - \text{Tax rate})}{\text{Average assets}}$$

$$= \frac{\$356 + \$240 \times (1 - 0.40)}{\$5,000} = .10 \text{ or } 10\%$$

| EXHIBIT 5.9 | Whole Foods Market | | | |
|---|---|---|---|---|

**Return on Assets**

| | 2006 | 2005 | 2004 | 2003 |
|---|---|---|---|---|
| Net income as reported | $ 203,828 | $ 136,351 | $ 129,512 | $ 98,915 |
| Nonrecurring items | 0 | 0 | 0 | 0 |
| Interest expense (after-tax) | 19 | 1,334 | 4,349 | 4,868 |
| Earnings before interest (EBI) | $ 203,847 | $ 137,685 | $ 133,861 | $ 103,783 |
| | | | | |
| Assets at end of year | $2,042,996 | $1,889,296 | $1,519,793 | $1,196,820 |
| Assets at beginning of year | 1,889,296 | 1,519,793 | 1,196,820 | 943,201 |
| Average assets | $1,966,146 | $1,704,545 | $1,358,307 | $1,070,011 |
| | | | | |
| Return on assets (EBI/Average assets) | 10.4% | 8.1% | 9.9% | 9.7% |

*Note:* Following common practice, the company's effective tax rate (40% in this case) is used to compute the after-tax impact of interest expense.

3. Adjustments for **distortions related to accounting quality concerns,** which involve potential adjustments to both earnings and assets for items such as the off-balance-sheet operating leases mentioned earlier.

Exhibit 5.9 summarizes the ROA calculations for Whole Foods using the company's earnings and balance sheet information from Exhibits 5.1 and 5.4. The adjustments made to reported earnings each year eliminate interest expense ($0.032 million in 2006) on an after-tax basis. ROA for 2006 thus becomes:

$$\text{ROA}_{2006} = \frac{\text{Net income} + \text{Interest expense} \times (1 - \text{Tax rate})}{\text{Average assets}}$$

$$= \frac{\$203.828 + \$0.032 \times (1 - 0.40)}{(\$2,042.996 + \$1,889.296)/2} = .104 \text{ or } 10.4\%$$

Notice that the company's effective tax rate (40%) was used in the ROA calculation. After all adjustments, Whole Foods' ROA increased from 9.7% in 2003 to 10.4% in 2006. Here's why.

A company can increase its operating profits per asset dollar in just two ways. One is to increase the profit yield on each sales dollar. The other is to expand the amount of sales generated from each asset dollar. In other words, a company that wants to **increase its rate of return on assets** can strive to do so in two different ways:

1. *By increasing the profit margin.* For instance, a large manufacturing company might use its bargaining power to negotiate favorable price reductions from raw material suppliers. Lower raw material costs would reduce operating expenses for the same level of sales and thus yield an increase in the manufacturing company's profit margin.

2. *By increasing the intensity of asset utilization.* For instance, a restaurant that was previously open for only lunch and dinner might decide to stay open 24 hours each day. Doing so would allow the restaurant to generate more sales per dollar invested in restaurant assets and thus yield an increase in asset utilization.

Both approaches are embedded in the ROA calculation:

$$\text{ROA} = \frac{\text{EBI}}{\text{Average assets}} = \left(\frac{\text{EBI}}{\text{Sales}}\right) \times \left(\frac{\text{Sales}}{\text{Average assets}}\right)$$

$$= \text{Profit margin} \times \text{Asset turnover}$$

Changes in the profit yield per sales dollar show up as changes in the **profit margin,** and changes in the amount of sales generated from each asset dollar are reflected as **asset turnover** changes.

Consider a company that earns $9 million of EBI on sales of $100 million and has an average asset base of $50 million. The ROA for this company is:

$$\text{ROA} = \left(\frac{\text{EBI}}{\text{Sales}}\right) \times \left(\frac{\text{Sales}}{\text{Average assets}}\right)$$

$$= \left(\frac{\$9}{\$100}\right) \times \left(\frac{\$100}{\$50}\right) = 0.09 \times 2 = 0.18, \text{ or } 18\%$$

Now suppose that some efficiencies in inventory and accounts receivable management are achieved so that average assets can be reduced to $45 million without sacrificing sales. Assets turnover will increase to 2.22, and ROA will rise to 20%:

$$\text{ROA} = \left(\frac{\text{EBI}}{\text{Sales}}\right) \times \left(\frac{\text{Sales}}{\text{Average assets}}\right)$$

$$= \left(\frac{\$9}{\$100}\right) \times \left(\frac{\$100}{\$45}\right) = 0.09 \times 2.22 = 0.20, \text{ or } 20\%$$

However, there is another way to boost ROA from 18% to 20%—that is, increase the profit margin to 10% through aggressive expense reductions. Sales are unchanged and asset turnover stays at 2, but ROA is now:

$$\text{ROA} = \left(\frac{\text{EBI}}{\text{Sales}}\right) \times \left(\frac{\text{Sales}}{\text{Average assets}}\right)$$

$$= \left(\frac{\$10}{\$100}\right) \times \left(\frac{\$100}{\$50}\right) = 0.10 \times 2 = 0.20, \text{ or } 20\%$$

Exhibit 5.10 extends the ROA analysis of Whole Foods by presenting profit margin and asset turnover figures for each of the four years. Here we learn that the company's improved profitability stems from better profit margins because asset turnover actually declined.

| **EXHIBIT 5.10** | **Whole Foods Market** |
| --- | --- |

**ROA Decomposition**

|  | 2006 | 2005 | 2004 | 2003 |
| --- | --- | --- | --- | --- |
| Sales | $5,607,376 | $4,701,289 | $3,864,950 | $3,148,593 |
| Earnings before interest (EBI) | 203,847 | 137,685 | 133,861 | 103,783 |
| Average assets | 1,966,146 | 1,704,545 | 1,358,307 | 1,070,011 |
| Profit margin (EBI/Sales) | 3.6% | 2.9% | 3.5% | 3.3% |
| Asset turnover (Sales/Average assets) | 2.85 | 2.76 | 2.85 | 2.94 |
| ROA = Margin × Asset turnover | 10.4% | 8.1% | 9.9% | 9.7% |

Whole Foods' profit margin increased from 3.3% in 2003 to 3.6% in 2006. However, asset turnover fell from 2.95 to 2.85 over this same period. In other words, in 2003, Whole Foods Market generated $2.94 of sales from each asset dollar, and each sales dollar produced 3.3 cents of EBI, for an ROA of 9.7%. By contrast, the company generated only $2.85 of sales for each asset dollar in 2006, but each sales dollar produced 3.6 cents of EBI, so the ROA that year was 10.4%.

> If Whole Foods had been able to keep its asset turnover at the 2003 level and still improve the operating margin to 3.6%, the company's ROA for 2006 would then have been 10.6%, or 3.6% times 2.94.

The explanation for Whole Foods Market's profitability improvement lies in the numbers—and in the business decisions that lurk behind the numbers. Whole Foods grew from 145 stores to 186 stores by the end of 2006. This expanded store base, along with increased sales from existing stores, allowed the fixed costs of grocery procurement, marketing, and store operations to be spread over a larger number of individual stores. The result was in an improved profit margin. But there is another part to the story. More stores meant more resources tied up operating cash, receivables, inventories, and facilities (property, plant and equipment). Whole Foods' asset base was less productive in 2006 ($2.85 of sales per dollar of assets) than it was in 2003 ($2.94 of sales per asset dollar).

Can Whole Foods sustain its 2006 level of profitability? It's hard to say. Increased wholesale costs of grocery items, brand erosion, and competitive price pressures may reduce the company's ROA. For example, an increase in the cost of perishable foods, which account for 67% of sales, could easily cause the profit margin to slip to 3.0% from its 2006 level of 3.6%. This small change when amplified by the asset turnover ratio would cause ROA to decline from 10.4% to 8.6% ($3.0\% \times 2.85$). To sustain ROA at 10.4%, Whole Foods would then need to generate $3.45 of sales per asset dollar (10.4%/3.0%), or an additional $0.65 over its $2.85 of sales per asset dollar in 2006. However, achieving continued sales growth from existing stores is a challenge for any retail company operating in a mature industry.

Many analysts find it helpful to further decompose ROA by isolating individual factors that contribute to a company's profit margin and asset turnover. For example, the profit margin for Whole Foods Market can be expressed as:

> Using the information in Whole Foods' 2006 income statement to illustrate the tax expense adjustment, we find that adjusted taxes would equal $135,898 instead of the reported income tax expense of $135,885 shown in the statement. The various adjustments made in arriving at EBI also cause the tax component of ROA to differ from the reported figure. The correct figure for *Taxes* is computed by solving:
>
> $$EBI = Sales - COGS - OpEx + Other - Taxes$$
>
> Substitution for EBI and the other statement items yields:
>
> $$\$203{,}847 = \$5{,}607{,}376 - \$3{,}647{,}734 - \$1{,}640{,}633 + \$20{,}736 - Taxes$$
>
> meaning that *Taxes* = $135,898 that year.

$$\text{Profit margin} = \frac{EBI}{Sales} = \frac{(Sales - COGS - OpEx + Other - Taxes)}{Sales}$$

$$= \left(\frac{Sales}{Sales}\right) - \left(\frac{COGS}{Sales}\right) - \left(\frac{OpEx}{Sales}\right) + \left(\frac{Other}{Sales}\right) - \left(\frac{Taxes}{Sales}\right)$$

$$= 100\% \quad - \left(\frac{COGS}{Sales}\right) - \left(\frac{OpEx}{Sales}\right) + \left(\frac{Other}{Sales}\right) - \left(\frac{Taxes}{Sales}\right)$$

where, from Exhibit 5.1, *COGS* is the company's cost of goods sold and occupancy costs; *OpEx* is Whole Foods' other operating expenses (direct store expenses, general and administrative expenses, and preopening and relocating costs); *Other* is non-operating investment and other income, and *Taxes* is adjusted income tax expense. (Some income statement items are combined for brevity.) These margin components (which happen to correspond to the common-size income statement items we've already described) can help the analyst identify areas where cost reductions have been achieved or where cost improvements are needed.

The asset turnover component of ROA can be decomposed as:

$$\frac{1}{\text{Asset turnover}} = \frac{\text{Average assets}}{\text{Sales}}$$

$$= \left( \frac{\text{Average current assets} + \text{Average long-term assets}}{\text{Sales}} \right)$$

$$= \left( \frac{\text{Average current assets}}{\text{Sales}} \right) + \left( \frac{\text{Average long-term assets}}{\text{Sales}} \right)$$

$$= \left( \frac{1}{\text{Current asset turnover}} \right) + \left( \frac{1}{\text{Long-term asset turnover}} \right)$$

The **current asset turnover** ratio helps the analyst spot efficiency gains from improved accounts receivable and inventory management; the **long-term asset turnover** ratio captures information about property, plant and equipment utilization. We have much more to say about these and other asset utilization ratios later.

## ROA and Competitive Advantage

Our analysis of Whole Foods' profit performance has thus far revealed that the company's ROA for 2006 was 10.4%, up from 9.7% in 2003. This profitability increase was traced to a higher profit margin because asset utilization fell. Now we want to know how Whole Foods' profit performance compares with that of other firms in the industry.

One of Whole Foods' most important direct competitors in 2006 was Wild Oats Market.[5] The company was formed in 1987 with the purchase of the Crystal Market vegetarian natural foods store in Boulder, Colorado. In 1993 and 1994, *Inc.* magazine named Wild Oats one of the 500 Fastest-Growing Private Companies in America. The company went public in 1996, and its stock began trading on the NASDAQ market. By 2006, Wild Oats operated 109 stores in 23 states and British Columbia, Canada.

Exhibit 5.11 presents a decomposition of 2006 ROA for Whole Foods and Wild Oats Market. Also shown are the average ROA and component values for the industry—retail grocery—to which these two companies belong. Industry data such as these are available from a variety of sources, including Standard & Poor's *Industry Survey,* Robert Morris and Associate's *Annual Statement Studies,* and many online financial information services.

Whole Foods was more profitable than both Wild Oats and the average grocery chain in 2006, earning an ROA of 10.4% compared to (2.8)% for Wild Oats and 5.7% for the industry.

| EXHIBIT 5.11 | Whole Foods Market | | |
|---|---|---|---|

**2006 ROA Decomposition**

| | Whole Foods Market | Wild Oats Market | Grocery Industry |
|---|---|---|---|
| Profit margin (EBI/Sales) | 3.6% | (1.0)% | 2.1% |
| Asset turnover (Sales/Average assets) | 2.85 | 2.73 | 2.72 |
| ROA = Margin × Asset turnover | 10.4% | (2.8)% | 5.7% |

[5] Whole Foods Market acquired Wild Oats in 2007.

The ROA decomposition reveals that the company's profit margin was 3.6 cents per sales dollar—better than the industry average profit margin of 2.1% and far superior to the (1.0)% margin loss at Wild Oats. Superior asset utilization also helped Whole Foods beat the competition. It generated $2.85 in sales per asset dollar compared to $2.73 at Wild Oats and $2.72 for the industry. So, the keys to the company's success in 2006 lay in both its profit margin and its asset turnover. Whole Foods outperformed the competition by earning a higher profit margin on each sales dollar and by generating more sales per asset dollar.

Can Whole Foods maintain this level of ROA performance? The answer can be found only by identifying the company's competitive advantage—that is, the source of its superior profit margin and turnover rate—and by determining whether that competitive advantage is sustainable over time. Several factors can explain why companies operating in the same industry—and that therefore confront similar economic conditions—can earn markedly different rates of return on their assets. Some companies gain a competitive advantage over rivals by developing unique products or services. Others do so by providing consistent quality or exceptional customer service and convenience. Still others get ahead because of their innovative production technologies, distribution channels, or sales and marketing efforts. The sustainability of these advantages, however, varies.

Competition in an industry continually works to drive down the rate of return on assets toward the competitive floor—that is, the rate of return that would be earned in the economist's "perfectly competitive" industry.[6] Companies that consistently earn rates of return above the floor are said to have a **competitive advantage.** However, rates of return that are higher than the industry floor stimulate more competition as existing companies innovate and expand their market reach or as new companies enter the industry. These developments lead to an erosion of profitability and advantage.

To see how these forces work, consider the simplified representation of the restaurant industry comprising four firms in Figure 5.2.

Firm A and Firm B earn exactly the same competitive floor rate of return, which we assume to be 6%, but they do so in different ways. Firm A, a casual dining restaurant chain, earns a 6% ROA by combining a high margin (say 6%) with low turnover (say 1). Firm B, a fast-food burger chain, has a low margin (say 2%) and a high turnover (3 times). Despite their differences, both companies achieve the same level of economic success: ROA = 6% = 6% × 1 = 2% × 3.

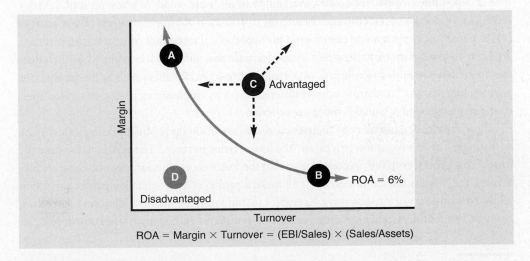

**Figure 5.2**

ILLUSTRATION OF HOW MARGIN AND TURNOVER AFFECT RETURN ON ASSETS (ROA)

ROA = Margin × Turnover = (EBI/Sales) × (Sales/Assets)

[6] This competitive floor represents the industry-average **cost of capital** and is approximated by the yield on long-term government securities (that is, the **risk-free rate of return**) adjusted upward for the risk of business failure and capital loss in the industry.

Firm C enjoys a competitive advantage that allows it to earn a return of more than 6%; D is disadvantaged and earns a return of less than 6%.

Suppose C's superior profitability stems from the widespread acceptance of its new Healthy Breakfast menu among health-conscious consumers. C's current edge is that the breakfast menu items are unique in the marketplace.

The particular competitive advantage C now enjoys may not persist. Other restaurant companies can and will develop menu items that rival the Healthy Breakfast menu in taste and nutritional benefits. As rival menu items become available, they will compete directly with Healthy Breakfast for each consumer dollar, and C's sales volume will thus decline. This will prompt a reduction in C's asset turnover, and it will shift C leftward (dashed arrow) in Figure 5.2 toward the competitive ROA of 6%. Of course, C's management is unlikely to ignore the introduction of rival breakfast items. Faced with the threatened loss of its competitive advantage, C could respond by reducing prices or by increasing advertising expenditures. Both responses could stimulate additional consumer sales and increase turnover, causing a shift back to the right. However, price reductions and increased advertising costs also lower the company's EBI margin, and thus they produce a downward shift (dashed arrow) toward the competitive ROA floor.

While the challenge to C is sustaining its Healthy Breakfast advantage in the face of escalating competition or creating a new competitive advantage source, D is facing different challenges. D's current level of profitability is below the industry floor of 6%. Investors and creditors will be reluctant to commit additional financial resources to D unless its profit picture improves. Why? Because D is not currently earning a rate of return large enough to compensate investors for business and financial risk. If D is unable to rectify the situation quickly, its cost of capital will increase, its profit margin will become even lower, and its long-term financial viability may be threatened. What turnaround strategies can D pursue?

According to most observers, there are only two strategies for achieving superior performance in any business. One strategy is product and service **differentiation;** the other is **low-cost leadership.**[7] A differentiation strategy focuses customer attention on "unique" product or service attributes to gain brand loyalty and attractive profit margins. The idea is quite simple: People are willing to pay premium prices for things they value and can't get elsewhere.

Differentiation can take several forms. Examples include advanced technology and performance capabilities, consistent quality, availability in multiple colors or sizes, prompt delivery, technical support services, customer financing, distribution channels, or some other factor of real or perceived importance to customers. Our hypothetical restaurant companies, for instance, are likely to focus customer attention on superior taste and nutritional benefits when introducing menu items intended to compete with Healthy Breakfast. Retailers such as Bloomingdales, Neiman Marcus, and Nordstrom achieve differentiation by emphasizing customer service, merchandise quality, and a "unique" shopping experience.

A low-cost leadership strategy focuses customer attention on product pricing, often using such slogans as "everyday low prices" or "the lowest price in town." The goal is to become the lowest cost producer in the marketplace so that the business can underprice the competition, achieve the highest sales volumes, and still make a profit on each sale. Companies can attain a low-cost position in various ways. Examples include making quantity discount purchases, having a lean administrative structure, and using production efficiencies from outsourcing or

---

[7] See W. K. Hall, "Survival Strategies in a Hostile Environment," *Harvard Business Review,* September–October 1980, pp. 78–85; and M. E. Porter, *Competitive Strategy* (New York: Free Press, 1980). Porter also describes a "niche" or "focused" strategy by which companies achieve uniqueness within a narrowly defined market segment.

vigorous cost containment. Large retailing companies such as Home Depot are able to negotiate steep quantity discounts with manufacturers because their size gives them more bargaining power; such discounts then allow the retailer to offer merchandise to customers at comparatively low prices.

Few companies actually pursue one strategy to the exclusion of the other. Most companies try to do both—developing customer loyalty while controlling costs. Understanding the relative emphasis a company places on differentiation versus low-cost leadership can be important for competitive analysis. ***Differences in the business strategies companies adopt give rise to economic differences, which are reflected as differences in profit margins, asset utilization, and profitability.*** For example, consider in Figure 5.2 the two restaurant companies A and B, which earn exactly the same 6% competitive ROA. Company A achieved this profitability level through a combination of high margin (6%) and low asset turnover (1), a combination often associated with companies that adopt a differentiation strategy. Company B achieved the same ROA level through a combination of low margin (2%) and high turnover (3), a pattern consistent with low-cost leadership.

The choice confronting D's management should now be clear. D can return to a competitive profit level in three ways: (1) improve the profit margin, (2) increase asset turnover (more sales volume or fewer assets), or (3) both. Margin improvements will shift D upward in Figure 5.2, whereas better turnover will shift it horizontally to the right. In both cases, D moves closer to the industry ROA of 6%. So, D's managers must choose one path or the other—or a combination of the two. That's all they need to do—and attend to a few million details to do it.

---

**RECAP**

**Not every company in an industry earns the same rate of return on its assets. Some earn more than the industry average ROA while others earn less. Companies that fall below the industry average ROA strive to grow sales, improve operating efficiency, and better manage assets so that they can become competitive again. Those who are fortunate enough to earn more than the industry average ROA struggle to maintain their competitive advantage—through differentiation or low-cost leadership—and to stay on top. This ebb and flow of competition shows up as differences in ROA and in its profit margin and asset turnover components.**

## RETURN ON COMMON EQUITY AND FINANCIAL LEVERAGE

If you want to gauge a company's profit performance from its shareholders' viewpoint, use ROCE. ***ROCE measures a company's performance in using capital provided by common shareholders to generate earnings.***[8] It explicitly considers how the company finances its assets. Interest charged on loans and dividends on preferred stock are both subtracted in arriving at net income available to common shareholders. So too are minority interest earnings, the net income earned by affiliated business and assigned to minority investors in those businesses. Of course, interest expense and minority interest earnings are always deducted in arriving at GAAP net income. The capital provided by common shareholders during the period can be computed by averaging the aggregate par value of common stock, capital contributed in excess of par, and retained

---

[8] If the analysts' goal is to isolate *sustainable* ROCE, Net income available to common shareholders must be purged of nonoperating and nonrecurring items and corrected for accounting quality distortions. These adjustments are discussed in later chapters.

earnings (minus common treasury shares) at the beginning and end of the period. For example, using the data in Exhibit 5.1 and Exhibit 5.4, the ROCE for Whole Foods Market in 2006 was:

$$ROCE = \frac{\text{Net income} - \text{Preferred dividends}}{\text{Average common shareholders' equity}}$$

$$ROCE_{2006} = \frac{\$203,828 - \$0}{\dfrac{\$1,404,143 + \$1,365,676}{2}} = \frac{\$203,828}{\$1,384,909.5} = 0.147, \text{ or } 14.7\%$$

Whole Foods' ROCE was a respectable 14.7% in 2006.

Profitability and financial leverage both influence the return that common shareholders earn on their investment in the company. To see how, let's look at what happens when a successful company borrows money to fund its growth.

ParsTech develops and distributes home financial planning software nationwide. Assume the company has $1 million in assets and no debt; it is an "all-equity" firm. Earnings in 2008 are $150,000 and the entire amount is paid to shareholders as a dividend. These events are summarized in the first row of Exhibit 5.12.

ParsTech's ROA for 2008 is 15% ($150,000 in earnings/$1 million in assets). Because the company has no debt, all earnings belong to shareholders, so ROCE is also 15%.

Early in 2009, the company borrows $1 million to expand its manufacturing, distribution, and customer support facilities. Lenders charge only 10% interest on the loan because the company has steady cash flows and a track record of successful new product introductions.

Strong consumer demand plus expanded plant capacity produce a banner year for the company. Earnings before interest total $300,000 in 2009, and ParsTech's ROA is again 15% (shown in the second row of Exhibit 5.12). Who gets the $300,000? Lenders must receive their share—$100,000 in interest on the loan—but the rest belongs to common shareholders. Shareholders receive $200,000, and ROCE is 20%.

Why did ROCE increase while ROA was unchanged? The answer is **financial leverage.** ParsTech borrowed $1 million at 10% (or $100,000 annual interest) but earned 15% (or $150,000) on the money. After the company paid interest charges, common shareholders gained $50,000 without investing more of their own money in the company. Financial leverage benefits shareholders whenever the cost of debt (10% in our example) is less than what the company earns on the borrowed funds (15% in our example).

> More precisely, it's the *after-tax* cost of debt that must be less than what the company earns on borrowed funds. If the corporate income tax rate is 40%, ParsTech has an after-tax cost of debt of 6.0% [10% × (1 − 0.40)] even though lenders are charging 10% interest. Financial leverage benefits ParsTech shareholders as long as the company earns more than 6.0% after tax on its debt-financed investment.

| EXHIBIT 5.12 | ParsTech |
| --- | --- |

**Financial Leverage**

| | Earnings before Interest* | Assets | Common Shareholders' Equity | Return on Assets (ROA) | Interest Charges | Net Income Available to Common Stockholders | Return on Common Equity (ROCE) |
| --- | --- | --- | --- | --- | --- | --- | --- |
| 2008 | $150,000 | $1 million | $1 million | 15% | — | $150,000 | 15% |
| 2009 | 300,000 | 2 million | 1 million | 15 | $100,000 | 200,000 | 20 |
| 2010 | 450,000 | 3 million | 1 million | 15 | 300,000 | 150,000 | 15 |

* Earnings are before interest but after taxes, and they are distributed to lenders (as interest) and shareholders (as dividends) each year.

There's a downside here, however, because financial leverage can sometimes be costly to shareholders. For instance, suppose that ParsTech borrowed another $1 million in 2010 to further expand its facilities. But this time, lenders assign a higher credit risk to the company and charge 20% interest. Earnings before interest but after taxes are $450,000 in 2010 and ParsTech's ROA is again 15%. What is ROCE?

Now lenders receive $300,000 in interest—$100,000 for the first loan plus $200,000 for the second—leaving only $150,000 of earnings for common shareholders. ROCE in 2010 is 15% ($150,000/$1 million in common equity), down from the previous year. Stockholders are no better off now than they were two years earlier when the company was smaller and earnings were lower. What happened?

The second loan cost more (20%, or $200,000 in annual interest) than ParsTech was able to earn ($150,000) on the borrowed funds, and shareholders had to make up the difference. *Financial leverage is beneficial—but only when the company earns more than the incremental after-tax cost of debt.* If the cost of debt becomes too high, increased leverage can actually harm shareholders.

## Components of ROCE

We can break down ROCE into several components to aid in our interpretation, much as we did earlier with ROA. The components of ROCE are ROA, common earnings leverage, and financial leverage:

$$\text{ROCE} = \text{ROA} \times \text{Common earnings leverage} \times \text{Financial structure leverage}$$

$$= \left(\frac{\text{EBI}}{\text{Average assets}}\right) \times \left(\frac{\text{Net income available to common shareholders}}{\text{EBI}}\right)$$

$$\times \left(\frac{\text{Average assets}}{\text{Average common shareholders' equity}}\right)$$

$$= \frac{\text{Net income available to common shareholders}}{\text{Average common shareholders' equity}}$$

ROA measures profitability before considering how the company's assets are financed. The **common earnings leverage ratio** shows the proportion of EBI (earnings before interest but after taxes) that belongs to common shareholders. The **financial structure leverage ratio** measures the degree to which the company uses common shareholders' capital to finance assets.

To see how the components of ROCE work together, consider two companies—NoDebt and HiDebt—each with $2 million in assets. NoDebt raised all its capital from common shareholders; HiDebt borrowed $1 million at 10% interest. Both companies pay income taxes at a combined federal and state rate of 40%.

Exhibit 5.13 shows how the two companies compare in different earnings years. Let's start with a good earnings year, one in which both companies earn $240,000 before interest but after taxes. This represents an ROA of 12% for each company, and 12% is also NoDebt's ROCE. HiDebt's ROCE is 18% because $180,000 of earnings ($240,000 − $60,000 after-tax interest) is available to common shareholders. Leverage increased the return to HiDebt's shareholders because the capital contributed by lenders earned 12% but required an after-tax interest payment of only 6%—that is, a 10% rate of interest × (1 − 40% tax rate). The extra 6% earned on each borrowed asset dollar increased the return to common shareholders.

What happens when earnings are low? That situation is illustrated by the bad earnings year in Exhibit 5.13. Both companies earn $60,000 before interest but after taxes for a 3% ROA. All

## EXHIBIT 5.13   NoDebt and HiDebt

**Profitability and Financial Leverage**

| | Total Assets | Shareholders' Equity | Earnings before Interest* | After-Tax Interest | Available to Common Shareholders | ROA | ROCE |
|---|---|---|---|---|---|---|---|
| Good earnings year | | | | | | | |
| HiDebt | $2 million | $1 million | $240,000 | $60,000 | $180,000 | 12.0% | 18.0% |
| NoDebt | 2 million | 2 million | 240,000 | — | 240,000 | 12.0 | 12.0 |
| Neutral earnings year | | | | | | | |
| HiDebt | 2 million | 1 million | 120,000 | 60,000 | 60,000 | 6.0 | 6.0 |
| NoDebt | 2 million | 2 million | 120,000 | — | 120,000 | 6.0 | 6.0 |
| Bad earnings year | | | | | | | |
| HiDebt | 2 million | 1 million | 60,000 | 60,000 | — | 3.0 | 0.0 |
| NoDebt | 2 million | 2 million | 60,000 | — | 60,000 | 3.0 | 3.0 |

\* Earnings are before interest but after taxes. HiDebt has after-tax interest charges of $60,000—that is, $1 million × 10% × (1 − 40%)—each year.

of these earnings are available to NoDebt shareholders, so ROCE for that company is also 3%. At HiDebt, after-tax interest charges wipe out earnings, and ROCE becomes 0% because there's nothing left for shareholders. HiDebt earns 3% on each asset dollar but must pay 6% to lenders for each dollar borrowed. In this case, leverage decreases the return to common equity and harms shareholders.

In the neutral year, leverage neither helps nor harms shareholders. That's because the 6% return earned on each asset dollar just equals the 6% after-tax cost of borrowing. Figure 5.3 illustrates the key results from this example.

## RECAP

**Financial leverage works two ways. It can make good years better by increasing the shareholders' return, but it can also make bad years worse by decreasing the shareholders' return. The result depends on whether the company earns more on each borrowed dollar than it pays out in interest.**

## Figure 5.3

FINANCIAL LEVERAGE AND ROCE

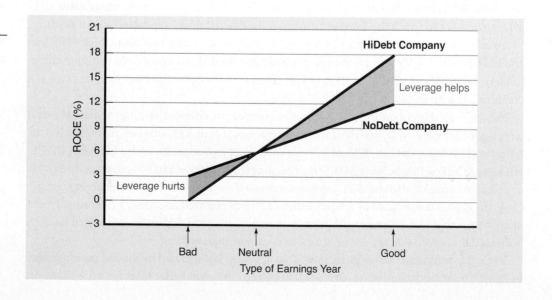

# LIQUIDITY, SOLVENCY, AND CREDIT ANALYSIS

**Credit risk** refers to the risk of payment default by the borrower, and the resulting loss to the lender of interest and loan principal. Put differently, credit risk refers to the ability and willingness of a borrower (an individual or organization) to pay its debt. Ability and willingness influence the likelihood that the lender (typically a bank or insurance company) will receive promised principal and interest payments when due. In the corporate arena, two factors must be kept in mind:

- A company's *ability to repay debt* is determined by its capacity to generate cash from operations, asset sales, or external financial markets in excess of its cash needs.

- A company's *willingness to pay* depends on which of the competing cash needs management believes are most pressing at the moment. Those needs include working capital and plant capacity requirements to sustain existing operating activities; capital expenditures for new products, service development or market expansion; and shareholder dividends or debt service requirements.

Figure 5.4 summarizes these ideas.

Numerous and interrelated risks influence a company's ability to generate cash. Multinational companies, for example, must cope with possible changes in host government regulations, potential political unrest, and fluctuating currency exchange rates. Domestic companies are exposed to the risks of political or demographic changes, recession, inflation, and interest rate fluctuations. Companies within a particular industry confront risks related to technological change, shifting competition, regulation, and availability of raw materials and labor. Management competency, litigation, and the company's strategic direction are additional sources of risk. Each of these risks ultimately affects a company's operating performance, net income, and cash flows. In fact, the statement of cash flows—which reports the net amount of cash generated or used by operating, investing, and financing activities—is an important source of information for analyzing a company's credit risk.

For instance, the comparative cash flow statements for Whole Foods Market in Exhibit 5.7 reveal strong and growing operating cash flows. In fact, the amount of cash generated by operating activities is more than sufficient to fund the company's store expansion needs at current levels. What about the company's debt burden and its credit risk? The comparative balance sheets (Exhibit 5.4) reveal that Whole Foods had about $8.6 million of long-term debt outstanding at the end of 2006 compared to $452.664 million of operating cash flow (Exhibit 5.7)

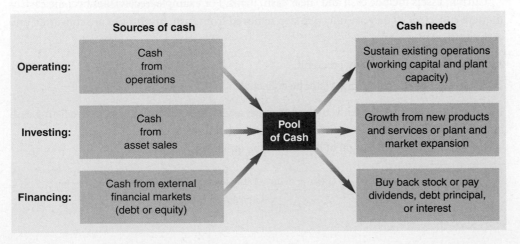

## Figure 5.4

BALANCING CASH
SOURCES AND NEEDS

that year. Moreover, $193.847 million in short-term investments could have been tapped if the company needed cash. So, Whole Foods is characterized by minimal credit risk: the balance owed lenders represents just a small fraction of annual operating cash flows, and other highly liquid assets are available to service the debt.

Although cash flow statements contain information enabling a user to assess a company's credit risk, financial ratios are also useful for this purpose. *Credit risk analysis using financial ratios typically involves an assessment of liquidity and solvency.* **Liquidity** refers to the company's *short-term* ability to generate cash for working capital needs and immediate debt repayment needs. **Solvency** refers to the *long-term* ability to generate cash internally or from external sources to satisfy plant capacity needs, fuel growth, and repay debt when due. Our discussion of financial ratios as an analytical tool for assessing credit risk is based on the distinction between concerns for short-term liquidity and for long-term solvency.

## Short-Term Liquidity

Short-term liquidity problems arise because operating cash inflows don't match outflows. To illustrate the mismatching problem, consider the **operating cycle** of a retailer such as Wal-Mart. It acquires merchandise from suppliers on credit, promising to pay within 30 or 60 days. The merchandise is first shipped to Wal-Mart warehouses. Later it is sent on to Wal-Mart stores where it is displayed for purchase and promoted through in-store and media advertising. Wal-Mart pays for some transportation, labor, and advertising costs immediately and delays payment of other costs. Eventually, Wal-Mart sells the merchandise to customers, who pay by cash or charge card; receivables (if any) are collected some time later; and the company then pays the remaining amounts owed to suppliers and others. Liquidity problems arise when cash inflows from customers lag behind the cash outflows to employees, suppliers, and others.

The operating cycle must not only generate sufficient cash to supply working capital needs, but also provide cash to service debt as payments become due. Interest expense is the largest single debt cost for some companies. Other companies may discover that operating cash flows are sufficient to cover periodic interest payments but that the need to repay loan principal causes a liquidity problem. Companies that are not liquid—and are therefore not able to pay obligations as they come due—may be forced into bankruptcy.

One index of a company's short-term liquidity is its **current ratio:**

$$\text{Current ratio} = \frac{\text{Current assets}}{\text{Current liabilities}}$$

Current assets include cash and "near cash" items. For example, receivables become cash as they are collected, so they are only one step removed from cash. Inventories are converted into cash in two steps:

1. They must be sold, usually on credit.
2. The resulting receivable must later be collected.

By including receivables and inventory in current assets, the current ratio reflects existing cash as well as amounts soon to be converted to cash in the normal operating cycle.

A more short-run reflection of liquidity is the **quick ratio:**

$$\text{Quick ratio} = \frac{\text{Cash} + \text{Marketable securities} + \text{Receivables}}{\text{Current liabilities}}$$

Few businesses can instantaneously convert their inventories into cash. So, the quick ratio does not include inventory in the numerator. It therefore provides a measure of *very* immediate liquidity.

**Activity ratios** tell us how efficiently the company is using its assets. Activity ratios can highlight efficiencies in asset management—accounts receivable collections, inventory levels, and vendor payment—and help the company spot areas needing improvement. They can also highlight causes for operating cash flow mismatches. For example, the **accounts receivable turnover** ratio is an activity ratio that can help analysts determine whether receivables are excessive when compared to existing levels of credit sales:

$$\text{Accounts receivable turnover} = \frac{\text{Net credit sales}}{\text{Average accounts receivable}}$$

To illustrate how to interpret this ratio, suppose that annual credit sales totaled $10 million and customer accounts receivable were $2 million at the beginning of the year and $3 million at year-end. The accounts receivable turnover ratio value is then:

$$\frac{\$10}{(\$2 + \$3)/2} = 4 \text{ times per year}$$

The average annual balance of receivables ($2.5 million) represents one-fourth of yearly credit sales ($2.5/$10 = 1/4), so receivables must turn over four times per year.

The analyst can also use the accounts receivable turnover ratio to spot changing customer payment patterns. For example, if we divide the accounts receivable turnover ratio into 365 days, the result tells us the number of days that the average customer receivable is "on the books" before it is collected:

$$\text{Days accounts receivable outstanding} = \frac{365 \text{ days}}{\text{Accounts receivable turnover}}$$
$$= \frac{365 \text{ days}}{4} = 91.25 \text{ days}$$

In our example, the average accounts receivable is collected about 91 days after the credit sale occurs. This is the same as saying accounts receivable "turn over" four times per year.

Another activity ratio is the **inventory turnover ratio,** which tells us how effectively inventories are managed:

$$\text{Inventory turnover} = \frac{\text{Cost of goods sold}}{\text{Average inventory}}$$

Assume that beginning inventory was $8 million, that year-end inventory was $9 million, and that cost of goods sold was $43.35 million. Therefore inventory turnover is:

$$\frac{\$43.35}{(\$8 + \$9)/2} = 5.1 \text{ times per year}$$

Take for example, the inventory turnover ratio for Amazon.com and other e-commerce companies. The business models used by e-commerce companies avoid the need to stock inventory in brick-and-mortar stores. As a result, inventory turnover ratios for e-tailers tend to be quite large. Amazon's inventory turnover ratio (14.6) has a

Most companies just report a single "sales" number that is the sum of cash plus credit sales. Using total sales instead of "credit sales" in the accounts receivable turnover calculation can sometimes produce misleading results. Companies for which cash sales comprise a large proportion of total sales will have relatively low accounts receivable balances and correspondingly large receivable turnover ratios. Fortunately, cash sales are rare in a surprisingly large number of businesses today. In certain industries such as discount retailing (Wal-Mart) and groceries (Whole Foods Market), however, cash sales are the rule rather than the exception.

Calculating inventory turnover and days inventory held for a manufacturing firm is more complicated than for the merchandising firm illustrated here. That's because inventory in a manufacturing firm must pass through three stages of the operating cycle:

1. As *raw material*, from purchase to the start of production.
2. As *work in process*, over the length of the production cycle.
3. As *finished goods*, from completion of production until it is sold.

Inventory in a merchandising firm passes only through Stage 3.

To calculate how long inventory is held at each stage, analysts use the following activity ratios:

Raw materials: $365 \text{ days} \times \dfrac{\text{Average raw materials inventory}}{\text{Raw materials used}}$

Work in process: $365 \text{ days} \times \dfrac{\text{Average work-in-process inventory}}{\text{Cost of goods manufactured}}$

Finished goods: $365 \text{ days} \times \dfrac{\text{Average finished goods inventory}}{\text{Cost of goods sold}}$

Cost of goods sold and the breakdown of inventory into raw materials, work in process, and finished goods is reported in the financial statements. Cost of goods manufactured can be calculated as cost of goods sold *plus* ending finished goods inventory *minus* beginning finished goods inventory. However, the amount of raw materials used in production is rarely disclosed in financial statements. It may be available in the company's fact book or obtained by contacting the company's investor relations group.

large numerator ($2,324 million, reflecting high sales volume) and a small denominator ($159 million, reflecting low inventory levels).

The inventory turnover ratio can also be used to determine the average **days inventory held** as follows:

$$\text{Days inventory held} = \frac{365 \text{ days}}{\text{Inventory turnover}}$$

$$= \frac{365 \text{ days}}{5.1} = 71.57 \text{ days}$$

In our example, it takes about 72 days for inventory to move from the company to its customers. In other words, average inventory is sufficient to cover almost 72 days of customer sales. This is just another way to say that inventory turns over 5.1 times (that is, 365 days/71.57 days) each year. By contrast, Amazon's inventory is held for about 25 days (or 365 days divided by 14.6 inventory turns).

The **accounts payable turnover** ratio—and its **days payable outstanding** counterpart—helps analysts understand the company's pattern of payments to suppliers:

$$\text{Accounts payable turnover} = \frac{\text{Inventory purchases}}{\text{Average accounts payable}}$$

$$\text{Days accounts payable outstanding} = \frac{365 \text{ days}}{\text{Accounts payable turnover}}$$

Suppose that trade accounts payable averaged $7.3 million and inventory purchases totaled $44.350 million during the year. The accounts payable turnover ratio would then equal almost 6 (that is, it would turn over six times per year), and the days accounts payable outstanding would be about 60 days. (You should verify both calculations!) *More timely payment of accounts payable would lead to a lower average payable balance, a higher turnover ratio, and fewer days outstanding.*

Let's piece these activity ratios together to get a picture that will help us analyze the financial condition of our company.

> For retail companies such as Amazon.com and Wal-Mart, inventory purchases equal cost of goods sold expense plus the year's inventory increase—that is, $44.350 = $43.350 + ($9 − $8) in our example.

- Inventory remains on hand for about 72 days.
- Inventory is sold, and another 91 days elapse before cash is collected from the customer.
- Suppliers are paid about 60 days after inventory is purchased.

Cash outflows and inflows seem dangerously mismatched. Suppliers are paid 60 days after inventory is purchased by the company, but it takes 72 days to sell the inventory and another 91 days to collect cash from customers. That's a mismatch of 103 days (72 + 91 − 60). Here's how that number was obtained: The company's **operating cycle** spans 163 days—that is how long it takes to sell inventory (72 days) and collect cash from the customers (91 days). But the company pays for inventory purchases in just 60 days, so its **cash conversion cycle** is 103 days—suppliers are paid 103 days before the company has received cash from product sales. This

## EXHIBIT 5.14 · Amazon.com, Wal-Mart, and Nordstrom

### Comparison of Operating and Cash Conversion Cycles

|  | Amazon.com | Wal-Mart | Nordstrom |
|---|---|---|---|
| Working capital activity ratios: |  |  |  |
| 1. Days inventory held | 25.0 | 50.0 | 88.8 |
| 2. Days accounts receivable outstanding | 0.0 | 3.0 | 46.0 |
| 3. Days accounts payable outstanding | 74.0 | 33.9 | 47.1 |
| Operating cycle (1 + 2) | 25.0 | 53.0 | 134.8 |
| Cash conversion cycle (1 + 2 − 3) | (49.0) | 19.1 | 87.7 |

hypothetical company may face a short-term liquidity problem because cash outflows and inflows are mismatched by 103 days. It must rely on other cash sources—for example, bank loans—to sustain its operating working capital requirements over the 103-day gap.

Exhibit 5.14 reports the operating cycle and cash conversion cycle for three retailers: Amazon.com, Wal-Mart, and Nordstrom. Each company has adopted a different business model, and differences in these business models appear as differences in working capital activity ratios, operating cycles, and cash conversion cycles. Amazon.com is an e-commerce retailer that doesn't stock inventory on store shelves, although its distribution centers do stock inventory. Consequently, inventory levels at Amazon.com are quite low—just 25 days. Amazon's customers pay by bank credit card so Amazon gets cash (from the customer's credit card company) almost instantaneously when it makes a sale. The operating cycle at Amazon.com is 25 days, but the cash conversion cycle is *minus* 49 days. That's because Amazon waits 74 days after buying inventory to pay its suppliers.

Wal-Mart and Nordstrom are traditional brick-and-mortar retailers that target different market segments. Wal-Mart carries a broad line of merchandise, emphasizes low prices, and most customers pay cash or use a credit card. Nordstrom is known for its fashion apparel and shoes. The company emphasizes product quality and customer service and promotes its in-store credit card. Wal-Mart has a 53-day operating cycle compared to 134.8 days at Nordstrom. It takes Nordstrom longer to sell inventory (88.8 days compared to 50 days at Wal-Mart) and longer to collect cash from customers once the sale has been made (46 days, compared to 3 days at Wal-Mart). However, Wal-Mart pays suppliers in about 34 days while Nordstom's suppliers wait 47 days for payment. So, the difference in cash conversion cycle at the two companies—19.1 days at Wal-Mart compared to 87.7 days at Nordstrom—can be traced back to Nordstrom's emphasis on fashion apparel (slower to sell) and its in-store credit card (slower to collect cash). Both companies must carefully manage their short-term liquidity because cash outflows and inflows are mismatched.

> The company's restricted cash is excluded from the current ratio computation because these dollars cannot be used to pay short-term creditors. Of course, that's why the cash is restricted. Similarly, the company's short-term investments are included in the quick ratio computation because these dollars can be used to pay creditors. Analytical adjustments of this type are common in credit risk analysis.

Let's return to our analysis of Whole Foods Market. See Exhibit 5.15 for data on the company's short-term liquidity ratios. Whole Foods' current ratio was 1.11 in 2006, down from 1.52 four years earlier. The quick ratio was 0.55, which also is less than the 0.88 level in 2003. The quick ratio means that Whole Foods' cash, short-term investments, and accounts receivable were sufficient to cover only 55% of the company's 2006 current liabilities. Adding inventories and other current assets further improves the picture—a current ratio of 1.11 means that total current assets (adjusted for restricted cash) cover 111% of Whole Foods Market's current liabilities.

---

**EXHIBIT 5.15** Whole Foods Market

**Credit Risk Analysis: Short-Term Liquidity**

|  | 2006 | 2005 | 2004 | 2003 |
|---|---|---|---|---|
| Current ratio | 1.11 | 1.52 | 1.39 | 1.52 |
| Quick ratio | 0.55 | 0.90 | 0.79 | 0.88 |
| Working capital activity ratios |  |  |  |  |
|   1. Days inventory held | 75.8 | 78.4 | 80.1 | 81.8 |
|   2. Days accounts receivable outstanding | 4.8 | 5.1 | 5.2 | 4.5 |
|   3. Days accounts payable outstanding | 11.2 | 11.5 | 11.7 | 11.6 |
|   Operating cycle (1 + 2) | 80.6 | 83.5 | 85.3 | 86.3 |
|   Cash conversion cycle (1 + 2 − 3) | 69.4 | 72.0 | 73.6 | 74.7 |

*Note:* The current ratio excludes the company's restricted cash whereas short-term investments are included in the quick ratio.

---

Inventory turnover improved in that inventory levels were down from 81.8 days in 2003 to 75.8 days in 2006. Several factors may have contributed to this inventory turnover improvement: a more appealing merchandise mix, warehouse distribution efficiency gains, or reduced inventory levels on store shelves. There was little change in the apparent payment pattern of Whole Foods' credit customers. Days receivable outstanding in 2006 was 4.8, compared to 4.5 in 2003. Of course, this unusually prompt payment pattern—credit customers paying their bills within 5 days—is distorted by our inability to break out true credit sales from cash sales at the company. Days payable outstanding held steady at just over 11 throughout the four years described in Exhibit 5.15.[9]

Some misalignment of operating cash flows exists because payments to suppliers occurred about 11 days after inventory was purchased but it took about 81 days (75.8 + 4.8) to generate a sale and collect cash from credit customers. In view of the company's overall level of positive operating cash flow, this misalignment is unlikely to cause concerns.

## Long-Term Solvency

Solvency refers to a company's ability to generate a stream of cash inflows sufficient to maintain its productive capacity and still meet the interest and principal payments on its long-term debt. A company that cannot make timely payments in the amount required becomes insolvent and may be compelled to reorganize or liquidate.

*Debt ratios provide information about the amount of long-term debt in a company's financial structure.* The more a company relies on long-term borrowing to finance its business activities, the higher is its debt ratio and the greater is the long-term solvency risk. There are several variations in debt ratios. Two commonly used ratios are **long-term debt to assets** and **long-term debt to tangible assets**:

$$\text{Long-term debt to assets} = \frac{\text{Long-term debt}}{\text{Total assets}}$$

$$\text{Long-term debt to tangible assets} = \frac{\text{Long-term debt}}{\text{Total tangible assets}}$$

---

[9] As you may recall from Whole Foods Market's comparative income statement (Exhibit 5.1), the company lumps cost of goods sold and occupancy costs into a single expense item. This creates distortions in both inventory turnover and accounts payable turnover in that the resulting figures reflect too few days of actual activity.

Suppose that a company has $20 million of outstanding long-term debt and $100 million of total assets, of which $35 million are intangibles such as goodwill or purchased patents, trademarks, or copyrights. The two debt ratios would be:

$$\text{Long-term debt to assets} = \frac{\$20}{\$100} = 0.200$$

$$\text{Long-term debt to tangible assets} = \frac{\$20}{\$100 - \$35} = 0.308$$

These results tell us that only 20 cents of each asset dollar was financed using long-term debt. The remaining 80 cents came from other sources—internally generated resources, short-term borrowing, or equity capital in the form of common and preferred stock. This level of debt—only 20 cents of each asset dollar—would be surprisingly high for a discount retailer such as Wal-Mart but surprisingly low for an electric utility company. Retailers use short-term debt and trade credit to finance their inventory purchases, and they usually lease (but don't own) their retail stores. Electric utilities, on the other hand, rely on long-term debt to support their sizable investment in power-generating facilities and transmission lines. Electric utilities also have relatively predictable operating cash flows because energy demand is reasonably stable and competition is limited by regulators. Companies whose sales fluctuate widely due to changing economic conditions generally prefer to avoid debt because the fixed interest charges can be difficult to meet during bad times. These cyclical companies tend to have smaller debt-to-asset ratios.

Most analysts add the current portion of long-term debt to the numerator in long-term debt solvency ratios, although this debt is classified as a current liability on the balance sheet. Some analysts go so far as to include *all* short-term interest bearing debt (such as notes payable) in their solvency ratio calculations. Several arguments favor this approach: (1) Long-term debt repayable over several years will always have some portion shown as a current liability, and this current portion should not be ignored; (2) long-term debt is shown as a current liability when loan covenants have been violated, but this does not mean that the firm's solvency risk has improved; (3) a firm with significant short-term debt but no long-term debt is not necessarily less risky than one with only long-term debt outstanding. Adding short-term debt to the ratio numerator overcomes distortions that can affect the interpretation of solvency risk.

Analysts devote considerable attention to refining both the numerator and denominator of debt ratios. For example, analysts include in the numerator "hybrid" securities, or obligations that have the cash flow characteristics of regular balance sheet debt although they may not be classified as such on the balance sheet. Operating leases and other off-balance-sheet obligations are routinely included as debt "equivalents" in the numerator. The exclusion of intangible assets from the solvency ratio denominator is also common. This adjustment is intended to remove "soft" assets—those difficult to value reliably—from the analysis.

Comparative debt ratios for Whole Foods Market are shown in Exhibit 5.16. The company's debt-to-assets ratio was 0.004 in 2006, meaning that each total asset dollar supported less than 1 cent of long-term debt. This represented a sharp improvement from the 0.141 debt-to-assets level in 2003. A similar picture emerges when the solvency is measured using tangible (rather

**EXHIBIT 5.16**  Whole Foods Market

**Credit Risk Analysis: Long-Term Solvency**

| | 2006 | 2005 | 2004 | 2003 |
|---|---|---|---|---|
| Long-term debt to assets ratio | 0.004 | 0.010 | 0.112 | 0.141 |
| Long-term debt to tangible-assets ratio | 0.005 | 0.011 | 0.123 | 0.155 |
| Interest coverage ratio | 9,969.031 | 103.344 | 29.886 | 20.628 |
| Operating cash flow to total liabilities | 0.958 | 1.059 | 0.730 | 0.762 |

*Note:* Current installments are included in long-term debt for purposes of these ratios.

than total) assets. The company's debt-to-tangible-assets ratio was 0.005 in 2006, down from 0.155 in 2003. These two debt ratios moved in the same direction and were consistent with a financially sound company that relies on internally generated cash for growth and is trimming its debt load.

Although debt ratios are useful for understanding a company's financial structure, they provide no information about its ability to generate a stream of inflows sufficient to make principal and interest payments. One financial ratio commonly used for this purpose is the **interest coverage ratio:**

$$\text{Interest coverage} = \frac{\text{Operating income before taxes and interest}}{\text{Interest expense}}$$

This ratio indicates how many times interest expense is covered by operating profits before taxes and interest are factored in. It reflects the cushion between operating profit inflows and required interest payments. If the company must also make periodic principal payments, the analyst could include those amounts in the calculation.

> Many analysts use an *adjusted* operating income figure that removes nonrecurring items from reported income and that corrects for accounting quality distortions.

Suppose that a company has $200 million of operating income before taxes and interest and $50 million of interest expense. The company's interest coverage ratio is $200/$50 = 4. This shows that operating profit is four times larger than interest expense—a substantial cushion for the lender. But now suppose that our company is also required to make a $100 million debt principal payment. The revised interest coverage ratio is $200/($50 + $100) = 1.33. When required debt payments are factored in, the lender's cushion now looks thin.

A criticism of the traditional interest coverage ratio is that it uses earnings rather than operating cash flows in the numerator. Some analysts prefer to compute a **cash flow coverage ratio** in which the numerator represents operating cash flows before interest and tax payments are factored in. When operating profits and cash flows move in tandem, both versions of the ratio will yield similar results. However, when the two measures do diverge—for example, during a period in which the company experiences rapid growth—income may be a poor substitute for cash flow. In that case, the cash flow coverage ratio is preferable as a solvency measure. After all, real cash (not just operating profits) is what the company needs to make its required interest payments.

Another useful measure of long-term solvency compares a company's **operating cash flow** to its **total liabilities** (excluding deferred taxes):

$$\frac{\text{Operating cash flow}}{\text{to total liabilities}} = \frac{\text{Cash flow from continuing operations}}{\text{Average current liabilities plus long-term debt}}$$

This ratio shows a company's ability to generate cash from operations to service both short-term and long-term borrowings.

Referring to Exhibit 5.16, we see that Whole Foods Market's interest coverage ratio was 20.628 in 2003. This means that pre-tax operating income was about 21 times more than interest expense that year, indicating that the company had ample coverage. The coverage ratio ballooned to nearly 10,000 by 2006 because operating income was then much higher and interest expense much lower as a result of the company's reduced debt burden.

Whole Foods' operating cash flow to total liabilities ratio clearly demonstrates why most analysts regard the company as financially solvent and a low credit risk. Operating cash flows in 2006 were alone sufficient to repay 95.8% of the company's total liabilities, meaning that Whole Foods could afford to repay all of its debt in about one year if it so chose. Of course, the company is unlikely to do so because it needs cash—from operations and other sources—to fuel growth and sustain its dividend payments.

# Cash Flow Analysis

Although a company's earnings are important, an analysis of its cash flows is central to all credit evaluations and lending decisions. This is because a company's earnings include many noncash accruals such as accounts receivable. Obviously, a company cannot make interest and principal payments with its accounts receivable. Rather, the company must pay its lenders with hard, cold cash!

Consider the situation confronting your client, G. T. Wilson Company. Wilson Company has been a client of your bank for more than 40 years. The company owns and operates nearly 850 retail furniture stores throughout the United States and has more than 38,000 employees. Sales and earnings growth have exceeded the industry average until recently, and the company has paid dividends consistently for almost 100 years. Prior to 2001, Wilson built its reputation on sales of moderately priced upholstered furniture, case goods (wooden tables, chairs, and bookcases), and decorative accessories. The company's stores were located in large urban centers where occupancy costs were quite low. Increased competition and changing consumer tastes caused Wilson to alter its strategy beginning in 2001. One aspect of this strategic shift involved expanding the company's product line to include higher quality furniture, consumer electronics, and home entertainment systems. To complement its expanded product line, Wilson also introduced a credit card system so that customers could more easily pay for their purchases. Wilson used commercial paper, bank loans, and trade credit to finance the growth of receivables and inventories. The company's strategy also focused on closing unprofitable downtown stores; at the same time, it expanded by opening new stores in suburban shopping centers.

Your bank has extended two loans to Wilson, a $50 million secured construction loan that matures in 2012 and a $200 million revolving credit line that is currently up for renewal. Wilson has always complied with the terms of the revolving line of credit, but the company's borrowing has been at or near the maximum amount allowed for the past two years. See Exhibit 5.17 for the company's comparative cash flow statements and Exhibit 5.18 for selected financial statistics. What do these cash flow statements and summary statistics tell us about the company's credit risk?

## Cash Flow from Operations

A company's cash flow from operations refers to the amount of cash it is able to generate from ongoing core business activities. Generating cash from operations is essential to any company's long-term economic viability. However, not every company can be expected to produce positive operating cash flows every year. Even financially healthy companies must sometimes spend more cash on their operating activities than they receive from customers.

According to the comparative cash flow statements in Exhibit 5.17, Wilson produced positive operating cash flows in 2001 and 2002. Since then, its operating cash flows have been consistently negative and declining, with the average level for the last three years equal to about *minus* $100 million. This sharply contrasts with the company's sales and earnings performance as shown in Exhibit 5.18. Sales have increased steadily from $980 million in 2001 to $1.85 billion in 2007 with a small decline in 2008. Net income (Exhibit 5.17) increased from $33.0 million in 2001 to a peak of $41.9 million in 2003 followed by three years of relative stability where earnings averaged about $33 million each year. Net income declined in 2007 to $10.9 million, and the company reported a $145.4 million loss in 2008.

What aspects of Wilson's operations consumed cash during the company's profitable years? Data in Exhibit 5.17 show that the primary factors contributing to the company's negative operating cash flows were increases in accounts receivable and increases in inventories.

| EXHIBIT 5.17 | G. T. Wilson Company |
|---|---|

## Comparative Statements of Cash Flow

| | | | | Years Ended January 31 | | | | |
|---|---|---|---|---|---|---|---|---|
| ($ in thousands) | 2001 | 2002 | 2003 | 2004 | 2005 | 2006 | 2007 | 2008 |
| **Operating:** | | | | | | | | |
| Net income | $ 33,000 | $ 38,200 | $ 41,900 | $ 36,400 | $ 31,600 | $ 34,950 | $ 10,900 | $(145,400) |
| Depreciation | 8,200 | 8,400 | 9,000 | 9,600 | 10,600 | 12,000 | 13,600 | 14,600 |
| Other adjustments to income | (850) | (1,100) | (1,600) | (2,500) | (1,800) | (1,700) | (1,350) | (17,000) |
| (Increase) Decrease in receivables | (42,000) | (40,300) | (55,500) | (12,000) | (49,900) | (60,300) | (72,200) | 9,600 |
| (Increase) in inventories | (9,100) | (24,900) | (13,500) | (38,400) | (38,200) | (100,850) | (51,100) | (4,350) |
| (Increase) Decrease in prepayments | 100 | (400) | (650) | (200) | (150) | (1,250) | (650) | 700 |
| Increase (Decrease) in accounts payable | 3,800 | 22,400 | 2,050 | 13,900 | 6,900 | (12,100) | (8,000) | 42,400 |
| Increase (Decrease) in other current liabilities | 11,900 | 8,500 | 15,400 | (21,900) | 13,900 | 14,950 | 15,650 | (1,500) |
| Cash flow from operations | $ 5,050 | $ 10,800 | $ (2,900) | $ (15,100) | $ (27,050) | $(114,300) | $ (93,150) | $(100,950) |
| **Investing:** | | | | | | | | |
| Acquisition of property, plant and equipment | $ (7,800) | $ (10,600) | $ (14,400) | $ (16,100) | $ (25,900) | $ (26,250) | $ (23,150) | $ (15,500) |
| Acquisition of investments | (400) | — | — | (450) | (6,000) | (2,200) | (5,700) | (5,300) |
| Cash flow from investing | $ (8,200) | $ (10,600) | $ (14,400) | $ (16,550) | $ (31,900) | $ (28,450) | $ (28,850) | $ (20,800) |
| **Financing:** | | | | | | | | |
| Increase (Decrease) in short-term borrowing | 1,600 | 18,900 | 64,000 | 64,300 | (8,650) | 152,300 | 63,050 | 147,600 |
| Increase (Decrease) in long-term borrowing | (1,500) | (1,500) | (1,650) | (1,500) | 98,450 | (1,600) | 93,900 | (4,000) |
| Increase (Decrease) in capital stock | 4,000 | 850 | (17,900) | (8,900) | 7,400 | (8,200) | 1,800 | 850 |
| Dividends | (14,400) | (17,700) | (19,700) | (20,800) | (21,100) | (21,150) | (21,100) | (4,500) |
| Cash flow from financing | $ (10,300) | $ 550 | $ 24,750 | $ 33,100 | $ 76,100 | $ 121,350 | $137,650 | $ 139,950 |
| Other | (400) | (100) | — | (400) | (1,350) | 2,450 | (650) | (700) |
| Change in cash | $ (13,850) | $ 650 | $ 7,450 | $ 1,050 | $ 15,800 | $ (18,950) | $ 15,000 | $ 17,500 |

It is interesting to note that Wilson's allowance for uncollectibles actually declined in percentage terms after 2003 (Exhibit 5.18) even though the average collection period increased. So, bad debt expense accruals apparently fell.

Some increase in receivables and inventories is to be expected because of the company's decision to expand its product line and introduce a customer credit card. However, increases in receivables or inventories can sometimes signal unfavorable business conditions. For example, the average collection period for customer accounts (days receivables in Exhibit 5.18) increased from 95.3 days in 2001 to 142.5 days in 2008. This trend could reflect expanded credit card use, more lenient credit policies toward customers, or a deterioration in customers' ability to pay. Similarly, the increase in days inventory (Exhibit 5.18) from

| EXHIBIT 5.18 | G. T. Wilson Company |
|---|---|

**Selected Financial Statistics**

| | Years Ended January 31 | | | | | | | |
|---|---|---|---|---|---|---|---|---|
| | **2001** | **2002** | **2003** | **2004** | **2005** | **2006** | **2007** | **2008** |
| Operations | | | | | | | | |
| Sales ($ millions) | $980 | $1,095 | $1,210 | $1,250 | $1,375 | $1,665 | $1,850 | $1,762 |
| Number of new stores | | | | | | | | |
| (net of closures) | 6 | 13 | 21 | 52 | 40 | 37 | 41 | 21 |
| Gross profit/sales | 32.1% | 32.8% | 33.0% | 36.5% | 35.8% | 35.3% | 35.1% | 30.1% |
| Selling, general, and | | | | | | | | |
| administrative/Sales | 25.1% | 25.2% | 25.2% | 29.9% | 30.7% | 30.6% | 30.4% | 41.3% |
| Net income/Sales | 3.4% | 3.5% | 3.5% | 2.9% | 2.3% | 2.1% | 0.6% | (8.3)% |
| Dividends/net income | 43.6% | 46.3% | 47.0% | 57.1% | 66.8% | 60.5% | 193.6% | (3.1)% |
| Short-Term Liquidity | | | | | | | | |
| Current assets/Current liabilities | 3.6 | 3.3 | 3.4 | 3.7 | 4.6 | 4.5 | 5.0 | 6.2 |
| Operating cash flows | | | | | | | | |
| as a % of sales | 0.5% | 1.0% | (0.2)% | (1.2)% | (2.0)% | (6.9)% | (5.0)% | (5.7)% |
| Days receivable | 95.3 | 104.1 | 115.1 | 126.2 | 131.1 | 130.5 | 140.0 | 142.5 |
| Allowance for uncollectibles (%) | 4.1% | 3.8% | 4.0% | 3.6% | 3.2% | 2.8% | 3.0% | 3.3% |
| Days inventory | 100.2 | 102.7 | 104.3 | 112.8 | 117.1 | 129.6 | 131.2 | 130.5 |
| Days payable | 42.5 | 48.6 | 45.7 | 48.9 | 47.1 | 33.6 | 30.7 | 42.6 |
| Long-Term Solvency | | | | | | | | |
| Total debt as a % of assets | 29.3% | 25.9% | 30.8% | 37.3% | 41.8% | 49.8% | 56.4% | 75.7% |
| Interest coverage | 8.1 | 8.7 | 6.4 | 4.7 | 4.5 | 3.9 | 1.2 | (2.4) |
| Short-term debt as a % | | | | | | | | |
| of total debt | 46.5% | 59.4% | 70.8% | 81.6% | 64.0% | 75.8% | 70.0% | 78.3% |

100.2 in 2001 to 130.5 in 2008 could be due to product line extensions, escalating merchandise costs, or slack consumer demand. The credit analyst must evaluate each possible explanation to discover what economic forces are responsible for the company's negative operating cash flows and whether positive cash flows from operating activities are likely to be generated in the future.

A business such as G. T. Wilson that spends more cash on its operating activities than it generates must find ways to finance the operating cash shortfall. Typically, this means using up cash reserves, borrowing additional cash, issuing additional equity, or liquidating investments such as real estate and other fixed assets. None of these options can be sustained for prolonged periods of time. For example, Wilson could finance the company's continued operating cash flow deficit by selling some retail stores. Doing this might jeopardize the company's ability to generate positive operating cash flows in the future. Similarly, creditors are unlikely to keep lending to a business that continuously fails to generate an acceptable level of cash flow from its operations. In this regard, Wilson's inability to generate positive operating cash flows in recent years is troublesome.

**Investing Activities** In this section of the cash flow statement, companies disclose capital expenditures, acquisitions of other firms, and investments in marketable securities. Of course, disinvestment generates cash (examples include the sale of buildings, equipment, or investment securities).

Wilson Company's cash flow statements (Exhibit 5.17) show sustained investment in property, plant and equipment that is consistent with the company's expansion into new stores (Exhibit 5.18). Analysts should carefully investigate the company's capital expenditures and any fixed asset retirements during the year. Capital expenditures and asset sales should be consistent with the company's business strategy and growth opportunities. For example, consider the following scenarios.

- *Emerging companies* require substantial investments in property, plant and equipment at a stage when operating cash flows are typically negative.
- *Established growth companies* also require substantial fixed asset investments to further expand their market presence. Operating cash flows for established growth companies can be positive or negative depending on the pace of expansion, the degree to which expansion also requires working capital investment, and the ability of the company to generate a positive operating cash flow from markets in which it is established.
- *Mature companies'* capital expenditures, on the other hand, are limited to the amount needed to sustain current levels of operation. Mature companies usually rely on internal sources (operating cash flows and fixed asset sales) to finance their capital expenditure needs.

Consequently, changes in a company's capital expenditures or fixed asset sales over time must be carefully analyzed. For example, a sharp reduction in capital expenditures for an emerging growth company may indicate that the company is suffering from a temporary cash shortage. Decreased capital expenditures may also signal a more fundamental change in management's expectations about the company's growth opportunities and its competitive environment. Similarly, an unexplained increase in fixed asset sales could mean that management needs to raise cash quickly or that it is eliminating excess production capacity. The analyst needs to evaluate each of these possibilities because they have very different implications for the company's future operating cash flows.

**Financing Activities**　The most significant source of external financing for most companies is debt. A large amount of research has been conducted that explores the "optimal" amount of debt financing that companies should include in their capital structure. Determining this optimal debt level involves a trade-off between two competing economic forces—taxes and bankruptcy costs.[10] The advantage of debt financing is that interest on debt is tax deductible. The disadvantage is that highly leveraged firms have a higher risk of bankruptcy. The precise point at which these two forces counterbalance one another varies from company to company and over time. One way analysts can assess the optimal debt level is to evaluate the company's historical and estimated future ability to meet scheduled debt payments. In this regard, Wilson Company's situation appears bleak.

The financing section of Wilson's cash flow statements (Exhibit 5.17) reveals a heavy reliance on short-term debt to finance the company's capital expenditures and operating cash flow deficits. The company issued $98.45 million of long-term debt in 2005 and $93.9 million in 2007. But the vast majority of Wilson's external financing has been in the form of short-term debt. Total debt as a percentage of assets (Exhibit 5.18) increased from 29.3% in 2001 to 75.7% in 2008; short-term debt as a percentage of total debt increased from 46.5% in 2001 to 78.3% in 2008, and the company's interest coverage ratio deteriorated from 8.1 times to *minus* 2.4 times.

---

[10] See Ross, Westerfield, and Jaffe, op. cit. These and other authors identify a third economic force that influences firms' capital structure decisions—that is, agency costs. These costs are considered in more detail in Chapter 7.

Wilson's cash flow needs and growing debt burden raise questions about the wisdom of its dividend policy. Recall that Wilson has paid cash dividends to shareholders for almost 100 years and continued to do so during 2008 when the company reported a $145.4 million loss. Cash dividend payments totaled $14.4 million in 2001, increased to $20.8 million in 2004, and then held steady at that level until falling to $4.5 million in 2008. These cash flows could instead have been used to finance the company's operating deficits and capital expenditures—or to pay down debt.

Why was management so reluctant to curtail dividends? The payment of a cash dividend is viewed as an important signal by many financial analysts and investors. Management presumably "signals" its expectations about the future through its dividend policy. A cash dividend increase is viewed as an indication that management expects future operating cash flows to be favorable—to the extent it can sustain the higher dividend. A reduction in cash dividends is interpreted as an indication that management expects future operating cash flows to decrease and remain at this decreased level. Research tends to corroborate dividend signaling. Increases and decreases in cash dividend payments are (on average) associated with subsequent earnings and operating cash flow changes in the same direction. Of course, the degree of association between dividend changes and future earnings or operating cash flow performance is less than perfect. So, financial analysts and investors must carefully evaluate the specific circumstances confronting each company.

> This illustration is based loosely on the financial statements of a real company, W. T. Grant, for the years 1968 through 1975. At the time that it filed for bankruptcy in late 1975, Grant was the seventeenth largest retailer in the United States. The company's collapse has been traced to a failed business strategy that involved rapid store expansion, product line extensions, and customer credit terms that contributed to delayed payment and increased customer default risk.
>
> *Source:* J. Largay and C. Stickney, "Cash Flows, Ratio Analysis and the W. T. Grant Company Bankruptcy," *Financial Analysts Journal,* July–August 1980, pp. 51–84.

**Recommendation**  Wilson's use of short-term debt financing coupled with its inability to generate positive cash flows from operations places the company in a precarious position. Unless other external financing sources are identified or unless operating activities start to generate positive cash flows, the company will be forced to declare bankruptcy if (and when) short-term creditors demand payment on existing loans. Wilson Company is a serious credit risk to the bank, and renewal of the $200 million revolving credit line is probably not justified. In fact, the bank may consider taking immediate steps to improve the likelihood of loan repayment and to protect its creditor position in the event of bankruptcy.

---

**Timing differences between cash inflows and cash outflows create the need to borrow money. Cash flow analysis helps lenders identify why cash flow imbalances occur and whether the imbalance is temporary. Commercial banks, insurance companies, pension funds, and other lenders will lend the needed cash only if there is a high probability that the borrower's future cash inflows will be sufficient to repay the loan. Credit analysts rely on their understanding of the company, its business strategy and the competitive environment, and the adequacy of its past cash flows as a basis for forecasting future cash flows and assessing the company's financial flexibility under stress.**

RECAP

## Financial Ratios and Default Risk

A company is in **default** when it fails to make a required loan principal or interest payments on time. Lenders can respond to a default in one of several ways. At one end of the spectrum, lenders may simply adjust the loan payment schedule to better suit the company's anticipated operating cash flows. This response would seem appropriate when the default stems from a temporary cash flow shortfall. If the borrower's cash flow problem is more serious, lenders modify the payment schedule, increase the loan interest rate, or require loan collateral (such as

## Figure 5.5

DEFAULT RATES AMONG PUBLIC COMPANIES BY MOODY'S CREDIT RATING: 1983–1999

*SOURCE:* RiskCalc for Private Companies: Moody's Default Model Rating Methodology, Moody's Investors Service (May 2000).

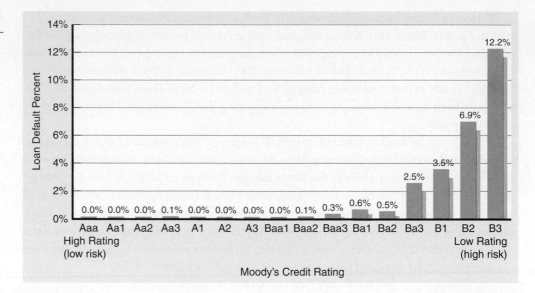

receivables, inventory, or equipment) as additional protection. If the borrower's cash flow problem is extreme, lenders may petition a court to judge the borrower insolvent. The court-appointed trustee then can either liquidate or reorganize the business—and restructure its loans—in an effort to settle all obligations in an orderly and equitable manner. Insolvency (or *bankruptcy,* as it is more commonly known) thus becomes the ultimate form of default.

**Credit analysis** is intended to help lenders assess a borrower's default risk or the likelihood of loan default. Financial ratios play two crucial roles in credit analysis. First, they help lenders quantify a potential borrower's default risk before a loan decision is finalized. Second, after a loan is granted, financial ratios serve as an early warning device that alerts lenders to changes in the borrower's credit risk. But which specific financial ratios are most useful for these purposes? In other words, which particular financial ratios best predict default risk and how well do they do so?

Predicting loan default and bankruptcy is not an easy task because both events are relatively rare, especially among public companies. For example, Figure 5.5 shows the one-year default rates for 1983 to 1999 among public companies covered by Moody's Investors Services, a credit-rating agency. Moody's assigns a credit rating to each of several thousand companies. For example, a Moody's Aaa rating represents the lowest credit risk.

The power of Moody's ratings is immediately clear in the ability to group companies by low and high default rates. Companies assigned the top rating (Aaa) seem never to default on their loans while those assigned the bottom rating (B3) default 12.2% of the time. In fact, the default rates associated with most of the rating categories shown in Figure 5.5 are quite small. Remember, too, that most public companies are financially sound and thus earn a relatively high credit rating; 80% of the companies covered by Moody's receive a rating of B1 or higher. This means that only a few companies fall into the high credit risk (B3) pool, and of those, only about 12% default within one year.

Figure 5.6 shows default frequency graphs for four common financial ratios: return on assets (ROA), debt to tangible assets, interest coverage, and the quick ratio. Notice that ROA is a profitability measure, and the other financial ratios measure solvency (debt-to-tangible-assets ratio and interest coverage ratio) or liquidity (quick ratio). Each graph was estimated using financial data from public companies in Moody's loan default database over the 1980–1999 period. To generate the ROA graph, the data were first divided into 50 groups that ranged from very low ROA to very high ROA. The companies in each group were then examined to determine

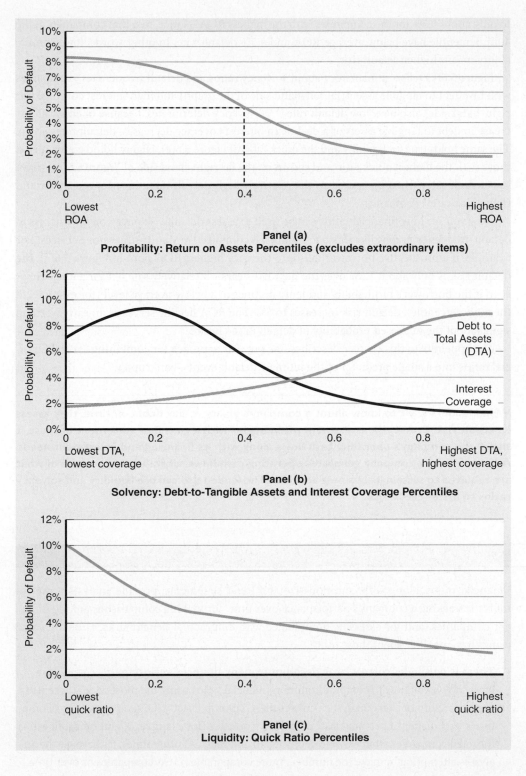

## Figure 5.6

PROBABILITY OF DEFAULT WITHIN FIVE YEARS AMONG PUBLIC COMPANIES: 1980–1999

*Source:* RiskCalc for Private Companies: Moody's Default Model Rating Methodology, Moody's Investors Service (May 2000).

whether or not a default occurred in 90 days to five years from the financial statement date. Default frequencies were then compiled for each group and statistically smoothed to aid interpretation. Graphs for the other three ratios were constructed in a similar manner.

The pattern of default frequencies in Figure 5.6(a) confirms our intuition: Default risk goes up as profitability declines. Highly *unprofitable* companies—those with the lowest ROA shown on the far left-hand side of Figure 5.6(a)—have a five-year default rate of about 8% compared to only about 1.5% for the companies with the highest ROA. Notice, too, that companies in the 40th percentile have below average ROA and a 5% default rate. In other words, lower profitability means higher default risk.

Figure 5.6(b) tells a similar story about solvency ratios and default frequencies. Companies with low debt to tangible assets (far left-hand side of the graph) and high interest coverage (far right-hand side) also have low default rates. As solvency deteriorates, because of either an increase in debt to tangible assets or a decline in interest coverage decreases, default rates go up. The same holds true for liquidity and the quick ratio in Figure 5.6(c). Highly liquid companies—those with the highest quick ratio and shown on the far right-hand side of Figure 5.6(c)—have low default rates when compared to the relatively high default rates experienced by illiquid (low quick ratio) companies.

Now you see how financial ratios can be used to assess default risk once you have access to default-frequency graphs like those in Figure 5.6 compiled by Moody's Investor Services. For example, if a prospective borrower falls into the very highest ROA pool in Figure 5.6(a), the default risk is only about 1.5% over the next five years—a relatively safe bet for a loan. However, if the borrower's profitability suddenly declines to a below-average level (for example, to the 40th percentile), default risk increases to 5%. The ROA decline serves as an early warning signal about the increased probability of default in the future.

The appendix to this chapter describes one popular approach for combining several financial ratios into a single predictor of the ultimate default event—bankruptcy.

 RECAP

**When lenders want to know about a company's ability to pay debts on time, they assess its credit risk. Credit risk assessment often begins with a cash flow statement because it shows the company's operating cash flows along with its financing and investment needs. A low credit risk company generates operating cash flows substantially in excess of what are required to sustain its business activities. The lender also can use liquidity and solvency ratios to assess credit risk.**

## SUMMARY

Financial ratios, along with common-size and trend statements, provide analysts powerful tools for tracking a company's performance over time, for making comparisons among different companies, and for assessing compliance with contractual benchmarks. Here are some things to remember about those tools:

- **There is no single "correct" way to compute many financial ratios.** In this chapter, we have shown you how to compute common financial ratios using the most widely accepted methods. But not every analyst calculates these ratios in exactly the same way. Why? Sometimes it's a matter of personal taste or industry practice (for example, operating profit ratios for retail companies often exclude depreciation and rent). At other times, it's because the analyst is attempting to make the numbers more comparable across companies or over time.

- **Financial ratios don't provide the answers, but they can help you ask the right questions.** It's useful to know that a company's profitability or credit risk has improved (or declined), but it's even more important to know *why* the change occurred. Did consumer demand increase, or was the company stealing market share from competitors? Were operating costs reduced and, if so, which ones? Use the financial ratios and the other tools in this chapter to guide your analysis. They can help you to ask the right questions and tell you where to look for answers.

- **Is it the economics of the business or is it the accounting?** Watch out for accounting distortions that can complicate your interpretation of financial ratios and other comparisons. Remember that the analyst's task is to "get behind the numbers"—that is, to develop a solid understanding of the company's economic activities and how industry fundamentals have shaped where the company is today and where it will be tomorrow.

**APPENDIX**

# ALTMAN'S Z-SCORE AND THE PREDICTION OF BANKRUPTCY

The best-known bankruptcy prediction model is Altman's Z-score model—a set of five financial ratios that are combined in a precise way to estimate a company's default risk.[11] Altman faced several challenges when developing the Z-score model: which financial ratios to use, how to combine them into a composite index of bankruptcy risk, and where to draw the line between companies predicted to be financially solvent in the future and those likely to go bankrupt.

Altman first searched for individual ratios that showed promise as predictors of bankruptcy. He assembled a large sample of bankrupt and nonbankrupt firms, calculated the ratio value for each sample firm using financial statement data prior to the bankruptcy, and then compared default frequencies across the range of ratio values much as we did in Figure 5.6. If bankrupt firms tended to cluster at one extreme of the ratio (for example, at very high ratio values) while nonbankrupt firms tended to cluster at the other extreme, the ratio was retained for further consideration. Altman next used statistical techniques to further reduce the list of candidate ratios to only those that added new information to the bankruptcy risk estimate. These same techniques identified the best way to combine the surviving ratios into a composite index of bankruptcy risk.

The final Z-score model is:

$$\text{Z-score} = 1.2 \times \text{Working capital/Total assets}$$
$$+ 1.4 \times \text{Retained earnings/Total assets}$$
$$+ 3.3 \times \text{EBIT/Total assets}$$
$$+ 0.6 \times \text{Market value of equity/Book value of debt}$$
$$+ 1.0 \times \text{Sales/Total assets}$$

where EBIT is earnings before interest and taxes. Notice how the model combines information about a company's current profitability (EBIT/Total assets), long-term profitability (Retained earnings/Total assets), liquidity (Working capital/Total assets), solvency (Market value of equity/Book value of debt), and asset turnover (Sales/Total assets) into a single measure of bankruptcy risk. Notice also that the five surviving ratios are not simply added together to form the overall Z-score value. Instead, each ratio has its own unique weight in the final calculation.

Now suppose that you applied the Z-score formula to a real company and got 2.4 as your answer. As you can probably guess by looking carefully at the formula, high Z-scores are good and low Z-scores are bad. (High Z-scores arise when profitability, liquidity, solvency, and turnover are also high.) But what does a Z-score value of 2.4 mean? Is a value of 2.4 above or below the cutoff for predicted bankruptcy? Before we see how Altman answered this question, let's look at some hypothetical data so that we can better understand the problem Altman faced.

---

[11] E. Altman, "Financial Ratios, Discriminant Analysis and the Prediction of Corporate Bankruptcy," *Journal of Finance*, September 1968, pp. 589–609.

## Figure 5.7

FREQUENCY DISTRIBUTION OF Z-SCORES FOR TWO TYPES OF CREDIT CUSTOMER

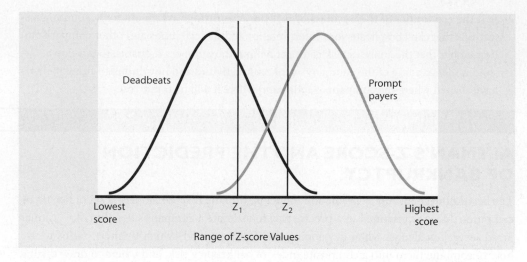

Suppose your company sells merchandise on credit and that it has only two types of credit customers: "deadbeats" who fail to pay their bills and "prompt payers" who always pay the full amount on time. Of course, you can't know for certain which customer types you are dealing with until it comes time for them to pay their bills. You can, however, use historical information about your customers and their payment patterns to identify characteristics that seem to predict whether a customer will be a deadbeat or prompt payer. If your customers are companies, financial ratios might do the trick, especially if those ratios are combined according to the Z-score formula. Refer to Figure 5.7 for the historical frequency distribution of Z-score values for the deadbeats and prompt-paying customers. As you might suspect, deadbeats tend to have low Z-scores (high default risk) while prompt paying customers tend to have high Z-scores (low default risk).

Now suppose that you were to set the cutoff point at $Z_1$, meaning that customers with Z-score values below that point would be denied credit and could buy your merchandise for cash only. Almost all of your prompt-paying customers would still qualify for credit at your store because the vast majority of these customers have Z-scores above $Z_1$. Unfortunately, so do many deadbeats. If you want to deny credit to more deadbeats, you need to set the cutoff higher. The value $Z_2$ in Figure 5.7 is one possibility. Using this cutoff, fewer deadbeats will qualify for credit, but you will also be denying credit to a larger number of prompt-paying customers.

The research evidence led Altman to conclude that firms having a Z-score higher than 2.99 (think $Z_2$) clearly fell into the "prompt payer" category—our label, not his—and were predicted to remain solvent. Firms having a Z-score of less than 1.81 (think $Z_1$), on the other hand, clearly fell into the deadbeat category and were predicted to go bankrupt. Firms with Z-scores that fell between these two cutoff points landed in a gray area, where classification mistakes can be large (because the two distributions overlap) and costly. Altman recommends that these firms be given additional, in-depth scrutiny using conventional financial analysis tools and information beyond just that contained in the published financial statements.

The original Z-score model was designed for publicly traded manufacturing firms. Altman has since developed models for private companies and public service–sector firms.[12] Credit-rating agencies like Dun and Bradstreet have used a similar approach to develop their credit-rating scores, although these agencies are often silent about the specific factors they consider and how much weight each factor is given in the composite score.

---

[12] See E. Altman, *Corporate Financial Distress and Bankruptcy* (New York: Wiley, 1993).

Motley Company's merchandise inventory and other related accounts for 2008 follow:

| Sales | $3,000,000 |
|---|---|
| Cost of goods sold | 2,200,000 |
| Merchandise inventory | |
| Beginning of year | 500,000 |
| End of year | 600,000 |

**Required:**

Assuming that the merchandise inventory buildup was relatively constant during the year, how many times did the merchandise inventory turn over during 2008?

Selected data of Islander Company follow:

| | As of December 31 | |
|---|---|---|
| **Balance Sheet Data** | **2008** | **2007** |
| Accounts receivable | $500,000 | $470,000 |
| Allowance for doubtful accounts | (25,000) | (20,000) |
| Net accounts receivable | $475,000 | $450,000 |
| | | |
| Inventories—lower of cost or market | $600,000 | $550,000 |
| | **Year Ended December 31** | |
| **Income Statement Data** | **2008** | **2007** |
| Net credit sales | $2,500,000 | $2,200,000 |
| Net cash sales | 500,000 | 400,000 |
| Net sales | $3,000,000 | $2,600,000 |
| | | |
| Cost of goods sold | $2,000,000 | $1,800,000 |
| Selling, general, and administrative expenses | 300,000 | 270,000 |
| Other | 50,000 | 30,000 |
| Total operating expenses | $2,350,000 | $2,100,000 |

**Required:**

1. What is the accounts receivable turnover for 2008?

2. What is the inventory turnover for 2008?

On January 1, 2008, River Company's beginning inventory was $400,000. During 2008, the company purchased $1,900,000 of additional inventory, and on December 31, 2008 its ending inventory was $500,000.

**Required:**

What is the inventory turnover for 2008?

Utica Company's net accounts receivable was $250,000 at December 31, 2007 and $300,000 at December 31, 2008. Net cash sales for 2008 were $100,000. The accounts receivable turnover for 2008 was 5.0, which was computed from net credit sales for the year.

**Required:**

What was Utica's total net sales for 2008?

| | |
|---|---|
| **E5-5**<br><br>Analyzing current and quick ratios<br><br>AICPA<br>ADAPTED | Todd Corporation wrote off $100,000 of obsolete inventory at December 31, 2008.<br><br>**Required:**<br>What effect did this write-off have on the company's 2008 current and quick ratios? |
| **E5-6**<br><br>Analyzing effects on current ratio<br><br>AICPA<br>ADAPTED | Gil Corporation has current assets of $90,000 and current liabilities of $180,000.<br><br>**Required:**<br>Compute the effect of each of the following transactions on Gil's current ratio:<br><br>1. Refinancing a $30,000 long-term mortgage with a short-term note.<br>2. Purchasing $50,000 of merchandise inventory with short-term accounts payable.<br>3. Paying $20,000 of short-term accounts payable.<br>4. Collecting $10,000 of short-term accounts receivable. |

| | |
|---|---|
| **E5-7**<br><br>Calculating interest coverage<br><br>AICPA<br>ADAPTED | The following data were taken from the financial records of Glum Corporation for 2008: |

| | |
|---|---|
| Sales | $3,600,000 |
| Bond interest expense | 120,000 |
| Income taxes | 600,000 |
| Net income | 800,000 |

**Required:**
How many times was bond interest earned in 2008?

| | |
|---|---|
| **E5-8**<br><br>Analyzing why inventory turnover increased<br><br>AICPA<br>ADAPTED | In a comparison of 2008 to 2007 performance, Neir Company's inventory turnover increased substantially although sales and inventory amounts were essentially unchanged.<br><br>**Required:**<br>Which of the following statements best explains the increased inventory turnover ratio?<br><br>1. Cost of goods sold decreased.<br>2. Accounts receivable turnover increased.<br>3. Total asset turnover increased.<br>4. Gross profit percentage decreased. |

| | |
|---|---|
| **E5-9**<br><br>Calculating days sales outstanding<br><br>AICPA<br>ADAPTED | Selected information taken from the accounting records of Vigor Company follows: |

| | |
|---|---|
| Net accounts receivable at December 31, 2007 | $ 900,000 |
| Net accounts receivable at December 31, 2008 | $1,000,000 |
| Accounts receivable turnover | 5 to 1 |
| Inventories at December 31, 2007 | $1,100,000 |
| Inventories at December 31, 2008 | $1,200,000 |
| Inventory turnover | 4 to 1 |

**Required:**
1. What was Vigor's gross margin for 2008?
2. Suppose that there are 360 business days in the year. What were the number of days sales outstanding in average receivables and the number of days sales outstanding in average inventories, respectively, for 2008?

## PROBLEMS / DISCUSSION QUESTIONS

The following table presents ROA calculations for three companies in the retail grocery industry using earnings (EBI) and balance sheet data for each company. These companies compete on price, quality of goods and service, convenience, and product mix. 7-Eleven operates convenience stores and generates approximately 25% of its revenue from gasoline sales. Publix Super Markets operates retail food supermarkets in Florida, Georgia, South Carolina, Alabama, and Tennessee. Albertson's is the second largest U.S. supermarket chain.

**P5-1**

Comparing profitability

### 7-Eleven Corp.

|  | Year 1 | Year 2 | Year 3 | Year 4 |
|---|---|---|---|---|
| Sales | $ 8,251,700 | $ 9,178,711 | $ 9,622,301 | $10,109,744 |
| Profit margin (EBI/Sales) | 1.7% | 1.8% | 1.4% | 0.9% |
| Asset turnover (Sales/Average assets) | 3.20 | 3.38 | 3.41 | 3.39 |
| ROA = Margin × Asset turnover | 5.5% | 6.0% | 4.9% | 3.1% |

### Publix Super Markets

|  | | | | |
|---|---|---|---|---|
| Sales | $13,068,900 | $14,575,031 | $15,284,229 | $15,930,602 |
| Profit margin (EBI/Sales) | 3.5% | 3.6% | 3.5% | 4.0% |
| Asset turnover (Sales/Average assets) | 3.38 | 3.49 | 3.53 | 3.46 |
| ROA = Margin × Asset turnover | 11.9% | 12.7% | 12.3% | 13.8% |

### Albertson's

|  | | | | |
|---|---|---|---|---|
| Sales | $37,478,000 | $35,501,000 | $36,605,000 | $35,626,000 |
| Profit margin (EBI/Sales) | 1.6% | 2.7% | 2.7% | 3.1% |
| Asset turnover (Sales/Average assets) | 2.43 | 2.23 | 2.28 | 2.28 |
| ROA = Margin × Asset turnover | 3.9% | 6.1% | 6.3% | 7.0% |

**Required:**

1. Which company has shown the strongest sales growth over the past three years?

2. Which company has shown the greatest improvement in profitability over the past three years?

3. Which company was the most profitable in Year 4? What was the source of that superior profitability—a profit margin advantage or better turnover?

Electronic Arts develops, markets, publishes, and distributes interactive software games. An abridged "lease commitments" footnote from the company's 2002 annual report reads:

**P5-2**

Determining accounting quality

In 2001, we renewed the lease on our headquarters facility in Redwood City, California and account for this arrangement as an operating lease. We have an option to purchase the property (land and facilities) for $145.0 million, or, at the end of the lease in 2006, to arrange for (1) an additional extension of the lease or (2) sale of the property to a third party. In December 2000, we entered into a second lease for a five-year term to expand our Redwood Shores, California headquarters facilities and develop adjacent property. We also accounted for this arrangement as an operating lease and have an option to purchase this property for $127.0 million.

Operating leases are "off-balance-sheet" obligations, meaning that GAAP does not include the debt among the liabilities shown on a company's balance sheet. Operating lease obligations are only disclosed in the financial statement footnotes. Capital leases, on the other hand, are included among balance sheet liabilities. This liability increase is offset by a corresponding increase to a balance sheet asset representing the leased property or equipment. (Chapter 12 provides the details.)

### Electronic Arts

| ($ in thousands) | Selected financial data | 2002 |
|---|---|---|
| | EBI | $ 110,374 |
| | Average assets | 1,539,146 |
| | Long-term debt | 0 |
| | ROA (EBI/Average assets) | 7.17% |

**Required:**

1. Suppose that Electronic Arts had entered into a capital lease rather than an operating lease. Describe in qualitative terms how this change would alter the company's balance sheet.

2. Describe in qualitative terms what impact a capital lease would have on the company's ROA and long-term debt to assets ratios.

3. Would the changes in these ratios, if any, be favorable from management's perspective? Why or why not?

---

**P5-3**

Assessing short-term liquidity

The following table reports the operating cycle, cash conversion cycle, and current ratio for three retailers in the apparel business. The GAP built its brand name on basic, casual clothing styles (T-shirts, jeans, and khakis). Over the years, the company expanded by opening Banana Republic and Old Navy stores. Spiegel is a top U.S. direct retailer, selling through its namesake catalog and its Eddie Bauer unit. The majority of J. Crew's sales come from classic-styled jeans, khakis, and other basic items sold to young professionals through catalogs, a Web site, and the company's retail and factory outlets.

| | GAP | Spiegel | J. Crew |
|---|---|---|---|
| Working capital activity ratios: | | | |
| 1. Days inventory held | 73.0 | 108.2 | 93.9 |
| 2. Days accounts receivable outstanding | 0.0 | 90.2 | 0.0 |
| 3. Days accounts payable outstanding | 43.8 | 116.5 | 49.6 |
| Operating cycle (1 + 2) | 73.0 | 198.4 | 93.9 |
| Cash conversion cycle (1 + 2 − 3) | 29.2 | 81.9 | 44.3 |
| Current ratio | 2.11 | 0.74 | 1.32 |

**Required:**

1. Do any of these companies appear to have a short-term liquidity problem?

2. Which company has the most mismatched cash flow?

3. All three companies are in the same industry. Why is Spiegel the only one with accounts receivable?

---

**P5-4**

Analyzing credit risk and long-term solvency

AK Steel is a fully integrated producer of steel. It operates seven manufacturing and finishing plants in Indiana, Kentucky, Ohio, and Pennsylvania. These plants produce cold-rolled and hot-rolled steel products as well as specialty stainless and electrical steels that are sold to the domestic automotive, appliance, industrial machinery and equipment, and construction markets. Comparative debt ratios for AK Steel are shown in the following table.

### AK Steel Corporation

| | 2005 | 2006 | 2007 | 2008 |
|---|---|---|---|---|
| Long-term debt to assets ratio | 0.28 | 0.28 | 0.27 | 0.24 |
| Long-term debt to tangible assets ratio | 0.29 | 0.28 | 0.28 | 0.25 |
| Interest coverage ratio | 1.98 | 2.50 | (0.13) | (5.44) |
| Cash flow coverage ratio | 3.07 | 3.44 | 2.11 | 3.02 |
| Operating cash flow to total liabilities | 0.11 | 0.15 | 0.07 | 0.14 |

**Required:**

1. Does AK Steel appear to be able to easily make its interest payments? How can you tell?

2. Does AK Steel rely heavily on debt to finance asset purchases? Has the company's reliance on debt changed significantly over the past several years?

3. Does AK Steel have significant amounts of intangible assets? How can you tell?

---

The following table breaks down ROCE for Best Buy, a retailer of consumer electronics.

**P 5 - 5**

Decomposing return on common shareholders' equity (ROCE)

| Best Buy | | | |
|---|---|---|---|
| | **2001** | **2002** | **2003** |
| ROA | 0.10 | 0.10 | 0.08 |
| Common earnings leverage | 0.99 | 0.97 | 0.98 |
| Financial structure leverage | 2.69 | 2.81 | 2.86 |
| ROCE | 0.27 | 0.27 | 0.22 |

**Required:**

How did Best Buy's profitability change over the three years?

---

Georgia-Pacific and Weyerhaeuser are forest products companies. Georgia-Pacific manufactures and distributes building products, consumer products (Brawny, Coronet, Dixie, and Quilted Northern brand-name products), and paper and packaging. Weyerhaeuser produces wood products (lumber, plywood, oriented stand board, and engineered wood), containerboard and packaging, pulp, and papers. Weyerhaeuser also recycles paper and develops real estate. Financial statement data for these two companies follow.

**P 5 - 6**

Interpreting accounts receivable turnover

| Georgia-Pacific | | | | |
|---|---|---|---|---|
| ($ in millions) | **Year 1** | **Year 2** | **Year 3** | **Year 4** |
| Sales | | $22,050 | $25,016 | $23,271 |
| Accounts receivable | $2,158 | 2,705 | 2,352 | 1,777 |
| Accounts receivable turnover | | 9.07 | 9.89 | 11.27 |

| Weyerhaeuser | | | | |
|---|---|---|---|---|
| Sales | | $14,603 | $13,084 | $16,771 |
| Accounts receivable | $1,296 | 1,247 | 1,024 | 1,413 |
| Accounts receivable turnover | | 11.48 | 11.52 | 13.76 |

**Required:**

1. Which company collects its accounts receivable more quickly?

2. Which company showed better improvement in accounts receivable turnover from Year 2 to Year 4?

3. What factors might explain why these two companies—which appear to operate in similar markets—have different accounts receivable turnover ratios?

---

Danaher Corporation has two business segments. The process/environmental controls group produces monitoring, sensing, controlling, and testing products. The company's tools and components segment manufactures mechanics' hand tools, automotive specialty tools, and accessories under various brand names. Selected financial statement data and related performance indicators follow.

**P 5 - 7**

Analyzing inventories

## Danaher Corporation

| ($ in thousands) | Year 1 | Year 2 | Year 3 |
|---|---|---|---|
| Sales | $3,777,777 | $3,782,444 | $4,577,232 |
| Cost of goods sold | 2,315,731 | 2,338,027 | 2,791,175 |
| Average inventory | 392,642 | 434,423 | 446,912 |
| Selected performance measures: | | | |
| Sales growth rate | 0.18 | 0.00 | 0.21 |
| Average inventory growth rate | 0.19 | 0.11 | 0.03 |
| Gross profit (%) | 0.39 | 0.38 | 0.39 |
| Inventory turnover ratio | 5.90 | 5.38 | 6.25 |

**Required:**

How well did Danaher manage its inventories over the three-year period?

---

**P5-8**

**Analyzing fixed asset turnover**

Lennox International makes air conditioning, heating, and fireplace systems for residential and commercial uses, as well as commercial refrigeration equipment. American Standard Companies is a leading maker of air conditioning systems, plumbing products, and automotive braking systems. Selected financial statement data and asset utilization ratios for each company follow.

## American Standard Companies

| | Year 1 | Year 2 | Year 3 |
|---|---|---|---|
| Sales | $7,598,370 | $7,465,300 | $7,795,400 |
| ROA | 0.09 | 0.08 | 0.09 |
| Current assets turnover | 4.22 | 3.96 | 3.99 |
| Fixed (long-term) assets turnover | 2.61 | 2.57 | 2.57 |
| Total assets turnover | 1.61 | 1.56 | 1.56 |

## Lennox International

| | Year 1 | Year 2 | Year 3 |
|---|---|---|---|
| Sales | $3,242,204 | $3,113,649 | $3,025,767 |
| ROA | 0.05 | (0.01) | 0.05 |
| Current assets turnover | 3.62 | 3.86 | 4.36 |
| Fixed (long-term) assets turnover | 3.33 | 2.79 | 3.14 |
| Total assets turnover | 1.73 | 1.62 | 1.83 |

**Required:**

1. Compare the asset utilization effectiveness of these two companies. Which company seems to be doing the better job? Are any important industry trends apparent from these data?
2. Why does Lennox International have a lower ROA than does American Standard?

---

**P5-9**

**Comparing profitability for three companies**

The following table shows six profitability measures derived from the financial statements of three real companies, labeled A, B, and C in the table. (They are not listed in the table in any particular order.) The real companies are:

- Brunswick Corporation, a leader in the leisure products industry that manufactures boats and marine engines, bowling and billiard products, as well as fitness equipment.
- Consolidated Edison, an electricity and natural gas company whose nonutility operations include energy marketing and fiber-optic telecommunications.
- Foot Locker, a shoe retailer with about 3,600 specialty stores in North America, Australia, and Europe. It also operates Champs Sports, an athletic wear retail chain, and Eastbay, a catalog retailer of athletic equipment and apparel.

|                              | A    | B    | C    |
|------------------------------|------|------|------|
| Operating profit margin      | 0.12 | 0.04 | 0.04 |
| Asset turnover ratio         | 0.47 | 1.13 | 1.88 |
| ROA                          | 0.06 | 0.04 | 0.07 |
| Common earnings leverage     | 0.68 | 0.79 | 0.90 |
| Financial structure leverage | 3.09 | 2.97 | 2.28 |
| ROCE                         | 0.12 | 0.09 | 0.15 |

**Required:**

Which company is which? Explain how you identified each company from the data in the table.

---

Nucor Corporation produces steel and steel products at its eight mills and is a major recycler of scrap metal. The following data relate to Nucor for four years.

**P5-10**

Determining profitability

## Nucor Corporation

| ($ in thousands)            | Year 1      | Year 2      | Year 3      | Year 4      |
|-----------------------------|-------------|-------------|-------------|-------------|
| Total assets                | $3,729,848  | $3,721,788  | $3,759,348  | $4,381,001  |
| Common stockholders' equity | 2,262,248   | 2,130,952   | 2,201,460   | 2,322,989   |
| Sales                       |             | 4,756,521   | 4,333,707   | 4,801,776   |
| Net income                  |             | 310,908     | 112,961     | 162,080     |
| Interest expense            |             | 22,449      | 22,002      | 22,918      |
| Income tax rate             |             | 0.37        | 0.37        | 0.296       |

**Required:**

1. Calculate Nucor's ROA for Year 2, Year 3, and Year 4. Decompose ROA into operating profit margin and asset turnover components.

2. Has Nucor's profitability changed over the three years? If so, how?

3. Calculate the rate of return on common stockholders' equity for Year 2, Year 3, and Year 4. Decompose ROCE into ROA, common earnings leverage, and financial structure leverage.

4. What seem to be the reasons for the change in ROCE over the three years?

---

Daley, Inc. is consistently profitable. Its normal financial statement relationships are as follows:

**P5-11**

Analyzing why financial ratios change

AICPA
ADAPTED

| Current ratio               | 3 to 1   |
|-----------------------------|----------|
| Inventory turnover          | 4 times  |
| Total debt/total assets ratio | 0.5 to 1 |

**Required:**

Determine whether each transaction or event that follows increased, decreased, or had no effect on each ratio.

1. Daley declared but did not pay a cash dividend.

2. Customers returned invoiced goods for which they had not paid.

3. Accounts payable were paid at year-end.

4. Daley recorded both a receivable from an insurance company and a loss from fire damage to a factory building.

5. Early in the year, Daley increased the selling price of one of its products because customer demand far exceeded production capacity. The number of units sold this year was the same as last year.

**P 5 - 1 2**

Explaining changes in financial ratios

**AICPA**
ADAPTED

Audit engagement partners were comparing notes about changes in clients' financial statement ratios or amounts from the prior year's figures. Here is what the partners had discovered.

Client 1. Inventory turnover increased substantially from the prior year. (Select three explanations.)

Client 2. Accounts receivable turnover decreased substantially from the prior year. (Select three explanations.)

Client 3. Allowance for doubtful accounts increased in dollars from the prior year but decreased from the prior year as a percentage of accounts receivable. (Select three explanations.)

Client 4. Long-term debt increased from the prior year, but interest expense increased more than the percentage increase in long-term debt. (Select one explanation.)

Client 5. Operating income increased from the prior year although the company was less profitable than in the prior year. (Select two explanations.)

Client 6. Gross margin percentage was unchanged from the prior year although gross margin increased from the prior year. (Select one explanation.)

**Required:**
Select from the following list the most likely explanation for each audit client.

a. Items shipped on consignment during the last month of the year were recorded as sales.

b. A significant number of credit memos for returned merchandise issued during the last month of the year were not recorded.

c. Year-end inventory purchases were overstated because items received in the first month of the subsequent year were incorrectly included.

d. Year-end inventory purchases were understated because items received before year-end were incorrectly excluded.

e. A larger percentage of sales occurred during the last month of the year compared to the prior year.

f. A smaller percentage of sales occurred during the last month of the year compared to the prior year.

g. The same percentage of sales occurred during the last month of the year compared to the prior year.

h. Sales increased at the same percentage as cost of goods sold compared to the prior year.

i. Sales increased at a lower percentage than cost of goods sold increased compared to the prior year.

j. Sales increased at a higher percentage than cost of goods sold increased compared to the prior year.

k. Interest expense decreased compared to the prior year.

l. The effective income tax rate increased compared to the prior year.

m. The effective income tax rate decreased compared to the prior year.

n. Short-term borrowing was refinanced on a long-term basis at the same interest rate.

o. Short-term borrowing was refinanced on a long-term basis at lower interest rates.

p. Short-term borrowing was refinanced on a long-term basis at higher interest rates.

The December 31, 2008 balance sheet of Ratio, Inc. follows. These are the *only* accounts in Ratio's balance sheet. Amounts indicated by a question mark (?) can be calculated from the additional information given.

**P5-13**

Working backward to the statements

**AICPA**
ADAPTED

| **Assets** | |
|---|---|
| Cash | $ 25,000 |
| Accounts receivable (net) | ? |
| Inventory | ? |
| Property, plant, and equipment (net) | 294,000 |
| | $432,000 |
| | |
| **Liabilities and Stockholders' Equity** | |
| Accounts payable (trade) | ? |
| Income taxes payable (current) | 25,000 |
| Long-term debt | ? |
| Common stock | 300,000 |
| Retained earnings | ? |
| | $432,000 |

**Additional Information:**

| | |
|---|---|
| Current ratio at year-end | 1.5 to 1 |
| Total liabilities divided by total stockholders' equity | 0.8 |
| Inventory turnover based on sales and ending inventory | 15 times |
| Inventory turnover based on cost of goods sold and ending inventory | 10.5 times |
| Gross margin for 2008 | $315,000 |

**Required:**

Compute the December 31, 2008 balance for each missing item.

$$\text{Hint:}\ \frac{\text{Gross margin}}{\text{Inventory}} = \frac{\text{Sales} - \text{CGS}}{\text{Inventory}} = \left(\frac{\text{Sales}}{\text{Inventory}}\right) - \left(\frac{\text{CGS}}{\text{Inventory}}\right)$$

Griffin and Lasky, Inc. (G&L) supplies industrial automation equipment and machine tools to the automotive industry. G&L uses the percentage of completion method for recognizing revenue on its long-term contracts. Customer orders have long lead times because they involve multiyear capital investment programs. Sometimes orders are canceled. Selected items from the company's financial statements follow.

**P5-14**

EBITDA and revenue recognition

| ($ in millions) | 2006 | 2007 | 2008 |
|---|---|---|---|
| Sales | $571.5 | $619.5 | $730.6 |
| Accounts receivable—billed | 141.6 | 94.5 | 147.9 |
| Accounts receivable—unbilled | 104.5 | 249.4 | 202.7 |
| Total accounts receivable | 246.1 | 343.9 | 350.6 |
| Inventory | 57.4 | 74.8 | 102.3 |
| Earnings before interest and taxes (EBIT) | 74.8 | 75.8 | 38.1 |
| Depreciation and amortization | 14.8 | 15.4 | 19.3 |
| Plant write-down | –0– | –0– | 30.3 |

**Required:**

1. Compute earnings before interest, taxes, depreciation, and amortization (EBITDA) and adjusted EBITDA—after excluding the plant write-down—for each year in the schedule.

2. Are profits at G&L keeping pace with sales?

3. Compute the days receivables outstanding using year-end receivables for each year in the schedule.

4. Why might analysts be concerned about earnings quality at G&L?

**P5-15**

Toys "Я" Us: Analyzing common-size statements of cash flow

mhhe.com/revsine4e

Following are the comparative statements of cash flows for Toys "Я" Us for 2002, 2001, and 2000. The company reported sales (in millions) of $11,305, $11,019, and $11,332, respectively, in those years.

### Toys "Я" Us

## Consolidated Statement of Cash Flows

| ($ in millions) | 2002 | 2001 | 2000 |
|---|---|---|---|
| Net income | $ 229 | $ 67 | $ 404 |
| Adjustments: | | | |
| Depreciation and amortization | 317 | 308 | 290 |
| Deferred income taxes | 99 | (58) | 67 |
| Noncash operating gains and losses | (45) | 56 | (379) |
| Other gains and losses | 0 | 0 | 81 |
| Changes in operating assets and liabilities: | | | |
| Accounts receivable | 8 | 15 | (69) |
| Inventories | (100) | 217 | (486) |
| Accounts payable | 112 | (241) | (178) |
| Other | (46) | 140 | 119 |
| Cash flows from operating activities | $ 574 | $ 504 | $(151) |
| Capital expenditures | $(398) | $ (705) | $(402) |
| Investments | 0 | 0 | 252 |
| Cash flows from investing activities | $(398) | $ (705) | $(150) |
| Debt issues | $ 548 | $1,214 | $ 566 |
| Stock issued | 266 | 19 | 12 |
| Debt repayments | (141) | (998) | (45) |
| Stock repurchased | 0 | (44) | (632) |
| Dividends | 0 | 0 | 0 |
| Other | (60) | 0 | 97 |
| Cash flows from financing activities | $ 613 | $ 191 | $ (2) |
| Effect of exchange rate changes | (49) | 18 | (6) |
| Change in cash | $ 740 | $ 8 | $(309) |

**Required:**

1. What is the purpose of preparing common-size statements of cash flows? For example, what can a financial analyst learn about a firm by preparing them?

2. Prepare common-size statements of cash flows (expressed as a percentage of sales) for the fiscal years ending 2002, 2001, and 2000 for Toys "Я" Us.

3. Interpret your common-size statements of cash flows. For example, what interesting features of the company's operating, financing, and investing activities do they reveal?

**P5-16**

Maytag Corporation: Analyzing profitability

Maytag Corporation manufactures and distributes a broad line of home appliances including gas and electric ranges, dishwashers, refrigerators, freezers, laundry equipment, and vacuum cleaning products. The home appliance segment contributes about 87% of Maytag's total sales. The company's other two segments are commercial appliances and international appliances, both of which have been scaled back over the last three years. Roughly 89% of Maytag's sales come from North American markets.

Refer to Maytag's 2002 financial statements. Consolidated sales increased 1.8% from 2000 to 2001 and 7.9% from 2001 to 2002. Earnings varied considerably over these years with net income falling from $201 million in 2000 to $48 million in 2001 and then rebounding to $188 million in 2002. Whirlpool, a competitor, acquired Maytag in 2006.

**Required:**

Prepare an analysis of Maytag's profitability for 2002, 2001, and 2000 using the four steps below. For all ratios requiring balance sheet values, use the average of beginning and ending balances. Base ratios using earnings numbers on net income before extraordinary items. Use "adjusted" rather than "as reported" earnings and balance sheet numbers where appropriate. Assume a 35% tax rate.

**Step 1:** Calculate average total assets, liabilities, and stockholders' equity for 2002.

|  | 2002 | 2001 | 2000 |
|---|---|---|---|
| Average total assets | ? | $2,912.5 | $2,653.0 |
| Average total liabilities and minority interest | ? | 2,890.0 | 2,329.0 |
| Average total shareholders' equity | ? | 22.5 | 224.5 |

**Step 2:** Calculate Maytag's ROA for each year. Use margin and turnover analysis with common-size income statements to explain the year-to-year change in ROA.

**Step 3:** What after-tax interest rate has Maytag been paying for its debt? Analyze the portion of average total assets that Maytag has been financing with debt over the three-year period and comment on any apparent strategy.

**Step 4:** Calculate Maytag's ROCE for each year. Has leverage benefited Maytag shareholders? How can you tell?

## Maytag Corporation

### Consolidated Statements of Income

| ($ in millions) | 2002 | 2001 | 2000 |
|---|---|---|---|
| Sales | $4,666 | $4,324 | $4,248 |
| Cost of goods sold | 3,661 | 3,320 | 3,102 |
| Gross profit | 1,005 | 1,004 | 1,146 |
| Selling, general, and administrative expenses | 578 | 705 | 678 |
| Special items* | 67 | 21 | 67 |
| Operating income | 360 | 278 | 401 |
| Interest expense | 62 | 65 | 64 |
| Other expenses (income), net | 2 | — | 4 |
| Tax expense | 101 | 30 | 115 |
| Minority interest | 4 | 15 | 16 |
| Net income before extraordinary items and discontinued operations | 191 | 168 | 202 |
| Loss from discontinued operations | (3) | (111) |  |
| Extraordinary Item—loss on early debt retirement | — | (5) | — |
| Cumulative effect of accounting change | — | (4) | — |
| Net income | $ 188 | $ 48 | $ 202 |

* Special items include expenses associated with plant closings and other nonrecurring charges.

*(continued)*

## Consolidated Balance Sheets

| ($ in millions) | 2002 | 2001 | 2000 |
|---|---|---|---|
| Cash | $ 8 | $ 109 | $ 27 |
| Accounts receivable | 587 | 619 | 538 |
| Inventories | 468 | 448 | 409 |
| Other current assets | 261 | 194 | 103 |
| Current Assets | 1,324 | 1,370 | 1,077 |
| Property, plant and equipment (net) | 1,066 | 1,036 | 970 |
| Intangibles (net) | 396 | 399 | 465 |
| Other assets | 318 | 351 | 157 |
| Total assets | $3,104 | $3,156 | $2,669 |
| Accounts payable | $ 364 | $ 316 | $ 285 |
| Current interest-bearing debt | 374 | 282 | 423 |
| Other current liabilities | 426 | 477 | 264 |
| Current liabilities | 1,164 | 1,075 | 972 |
| Long-term debt | 739 | 932 | 451 |
| Deferred taxes | — | 25 | 22 |
| Minority interest | — | 100 | 365 |
| Other liabilities | 1,159 | 1,001 | 837 |
| Total liabilities | 3,062 | 3,133 | 2,647 |
| Common stockholders' equity | 42 | 23 | 22 |
| Total liabilities and equity | $3,104 | $3,156 | $2,669 |

---

**P5-17**

Analyzing ratios

CFA
ADAPTED

mhhe.com/revsine4e

Margaret O'Flaherty, a portfolio manager for MCF Investments, is considering investing in Alpine Chemical 7% bonds, which mature in 10 years. She asks you to analyze the company to determine the riskiness of the bonds.

## Alpine Chemical Company Financial Statements

| ($ in millions) | Years Ended December 31 | | | | | |
|---|---|---|---|---|---|---|
| | 2003 | 2004 | 2005 | 2006 | 2007 | 2008 |
| Assets | | | | | | |
| Cash | $ 190 | $ 55 | $ 0 | $ 157 | $ 249 | $ 0 |
| Accounts receivable | 1,637 | 2,087 | 1,394 | 2,143 | 3,493 | 3,451 |
| Inventories | 2,021 | 945 | 1,258 | 1,293 | 1,322 | 1,643 |
| Other current assets | 17 | 27 | 55 | 393 | 33 | 171 |
| Current assets | 3,865 | 3,114 | 2,707 | 3,986 | 5,097 | 5,265 |
| Gross fixed assets | 4,650 | 5,038 | 5,619 | 5,757 | 6,181 | 7,187 |
| Less: Accumulated depreciation | 2,177 | 2,543 | 2,841 | 3,138 | 3,465 | 3,893 |
| Net fixed assets | 2,473 | 2,495 | 2,778 | 2,619 | 2,716 | 3,294 |
| Total assets | $ 6,338 | $ 5,609 | $ 5,485 | $ 6,605 | $ 7,813 | $ 8,559 |
| Liabilities and net worth | | | | | | |
| Notes payable | $ 525 | $ 750 | $ 0 | $ 1,300 | $ 1,750 | $ 1,900 |
| Accounts payable | 673 | 638 | 681 | 338 | 743 | 978 |
| Accrued liabilities | 303 | 172 | 359 | 359 | 483 | 761 |
| Current liabilities | 1,501 | 1,560 | 1,040 | 1,997 | 2,976 | 3,639 |

*(continued)*

| ($ in millions) | 2003 | 2004 | 2005 | 2006 | 2007 | 2008 |
|---|---|---|---|---|---|---|
| | | | **Years Ended December 31** | | | |
| Long-term debt | 1,985 | 1,044 | 1,401 | 1,457 | 1,542 | 1,491 |
| Deferred tax credits | 352 | 347 | 363 | 336 | 345 | 354 |
| Total liabilities | 3,838 | 2,951 | 2,804 | 3,790 | 4,863 | 5,484 |
| Common stock | 50 | 50 | 100 | 100 | 100 | 100 |
| Capital surplus | 100 | 100 | 0 | 0 | 0 | 0 |
| Retained earnings | 2,350 | 2,508 | 2,581 | 2,715 | 2,850 | 2,975 |
| Net worth | 2,500 | 2,658 | 2,681 | 2,815 | 2,950 | 3,075 |
| Total liabilities and net worth | $ 6,338 | $ 5,609 | $ 5,485 | $ 6,605 | $ 7,813 | $ 8,559 |

| Income statement | 2003 | 2004 | 2005 | 2006 | 2007 | 2008 |
|---|---|---|---|---|---|---|
| Net sales | $14,100 | $15,508 | $13,875 | $14,750 | $19,133 | $19,460 |
| Cost of goods sold | 10,200 | 11,220 | 9,366 | 10,059 | 13,400 | 13,117 |
| Gross profit | 3,900 | 4,288 | 4,509 | 4,691 | 5,733 | 6,343 |
| Operating expense | 2,065 | 2,203 | 2,665 | 2,685 | 3,472 | 3,885 |
| Operating profit | 1,835 | 2,085 | 1,844 | 2,006 | 2,261 | 2,458 |
| Interest expense | 275 | 465 | 275 | 319 | 376 | 318 |
| Depreciation expense | 475 | 477 | 479 | 478 | 495 | 511 |
| Profit before tax | 1,085 | 1,143 | 1,090 | 1,209 | 1,390 | 1,629 |
| Income taxes | 193 | 115 | 265 | 145 | 192 | 150 |
| Net income | $ 892 | $ 1,028 | $ 825 | $ 1,064 | $ 1,198 | $ 1,479 |

**Required:**

1. Using the data provided in the accompanying financial statement, calculate the following ratios for Alpine Chemical for 2008:

   a. EBIT/Interest expense

   b. Long-term debt/Total capitalization

   c. Funds from operations/Total debt

   d. Operating income/Sales

   Use the following conventions: EBIT is earnings before interest and taxes; Total capitalization is interest-bearing long-term debt plus net worth; Funds from operations means net income plus depreciation expense; and Total debt includes interest-bearing short-term and long-term debt.

2. Briefly explain the significance of each ratio calculated in requirement 1 to the assessment of Alpine Chemical's creditworthiness.

3. Insert your answers to requirement 1 into Table 1 that follows. Then from Table 2 on the next page, select an appropriate credit rating for Alpine Chemical.

| TABLE I | Alpine Chemical Company | | | | | |
|---|---|---|---|---|---|---|
| | 2003 | 2004 | 2005 | 2006 | 2007 | 2008 |
| EBIT/Interest expense | 4.95 | 3.46 | 4.96 | 4.79 | 4.70 | ? |
| Long-term debt/Total capitalization | 44% | 28% | 34% | 34% | 34% | ? |
| Funds from operations/Total debt | 54% | 84% | 93% | 56% | 51% | ? |
| Operating income/Sales | 13% | 13% | 13% | 14% | 12% | ? |

## TABLE 2 Industry Data

### Three-Year Medians (2005–2008) by Credit-Rating Category

|  | Aaa | Aa | A | Bbb | Bb | B |
|---|---|---|---|---|---|---|
| EBIT/Interest expense | 11.0 | 9.5 | 4.5 | 3.0 | 2.0 | 1.0 |
| Long-term debt/Total capitalization | 13.0 | 16.5 | 29.5 | 39.0 | 45.5 | 63.5 |
| Funds from operations/Total debt | 83.0 | 74.0 | 45.5 | 31.5 | 18.5 | 8.0 |
| Operating income/Sales | 21.5 | 16.0 | 15.0 | 12.0 | 11.0 | 9.0 |

**P5-18**

Analyzing financial statements

AICPA
ADAPTED

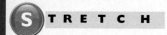 **S TRETCH**

A cash flow statement and partial balance sheet for Woods Company and supplemental information follow. The omitted items are numbered from (1) through (16) and can be calculated from the other information given.

### 2008 Statement of Cash Flows

| | |
|---|---:|
| Operations | |
| Net loss for 2008 | $ (2,885) |
| Adjustments: | |
| Bond premium amortization | (500) |
| Deferred income taxes | (200) |
| Depreciation expense | 3,000 |
| Amortization of intangibles | 2,000 |
| Increase in (noncash) working capital | (700) |
| Total from operations | 715 |
| Proceeds from equipment sold | 10,000 |
| Proceeds from reissue of treasury stock | 11,400 |
| Par value of common stock issued to reacquire preferred stock | 7,500 |
| Purchase of land | (14,715) |
| Payment on long-term bond debt | (7,200) |
| Par value of preferred stock reacquired by issuing common stock | (7,500) |
| Increase in cash | $ 200 |

### Supplemental Information—Selected 2008 Income Statement Items

| | |
|---|---:|
| Bond interest expense (net of amortization) | $ 3,500 |
| Loss before tax adjustment | (3,900) |
| Less: Income tax adjustment for refund due | 815 |
| Deferred income taxes | 200 |
| Net loss after tax adjustment | $ (2,885) |

### Selected Ratios

| | January 1, 2008* | December 31, 2008 |
|---|---|---|
| Current ratio | ? | 3:1 |
| Total stockholders' equity divided by total liabilities | 4:3 | ? |

* The preceding ratios were computed prior to the error correction (described next).

Woods Company neglected to amortize $2,000 of intangibles in 2007. The correction of this material error was appropriately made in 2008. The book value and selling price of the equipment sold was two-thirds of the cost of the equipment.

## Woods Company

### Balance Sheets

|  | January 1, 2008* | December 31, 2008 |
|---|---|---|
| Current assets | $ 22,000 | $    (5) |
| Building and equipment | 92,000 | (6) |
| Accumulated depreciation | (25,000) | (7) |
| Land | (1) | (8) |
| Intangibles and goodwill | 12,000 | (9) |
| Total assets | $      (?) | $    (?) |
| Current liabilities | $      (2) | (10) |
| Bonds payable (8%) | (3) | (11) |
| Bond premium | (?) | (12) |
| Deferred income taxes | (4) | 1,700 |
| Common stock | 66,000 | (13) |
| Paid-in capital | 13,000 | (14) |
| Preferred stock | 16,000 | (15) |
| Retained earnings (deficit) | (6,000) | (16) |
| Treasury stock (at cost) | (9,000) | 0 |
| Total liabilities and stockholders' equity | $      (?) | $    (?) |

\* The January 1, 2008 items are shown prior to the error correction.

**Required:**

Number your answer sheet from (1) through (16). Place the correct balance for each balance sheet item next to the corresponding number on your answer sheet. Question mark (?) amounts may be needed to calculate the numbered balances. Do not restate the January 1 balance sheet for the error. Working capital was $16,500 at January 1, 2008.

**Required:**

Use the following information and your knowledge of financial ratios and balance sheet relationships to fill in the missing items on the balance sheet of Clapton Corporation. Round all amounts to the nearest dollar.

**P5-19**

Determining financial ratios and analyzing the balance sheet

**Additional Information:**

1. Days accounts payable outstanding was 45.6 in 2008 compared to 66.3 in 2007.

2. The current ratio at the end of 2008 was 2.5 compared to 2.0 at the end of 2007.

3. The firm's gross profit rate was 25% in 2008 and 28% in 2007.

4. Net income for 2008 was $1,250,000 compared to $1,000,000 in 2007.

5. No common or preferred stock was issued during 2008.

6. Return on average assets was 5% for 2008 compared to 8% in 2007.

7. Cash dividends declared and paid in 2008 were $250,000; in 2007 they were $200,000.

8. Days accounts receivable outstanding was 36.5 in 2008 and 50.5 in 2007.

9. The long-term debt to total asset ratio at the end of 2008 was 0.40 compared to 0.30 at the end of 2007.

10. The quick ratio at the end of 2008 was 1.6875 compared to 1.5 at the end of 2007.

11. Days inventory held was 60.8 in 2008 and 75.7 in 2007.

12. Net sales in 2008 were $20,000,000 compared to $18,000,000 in 2007.

13. Earnings before interest (EBI) for 2008 was $1,750,000, compared to $1,400,000 in 2007.

## Clapton Corporation

### Consolidated Balance Sheets

| | As of December 31 | |
|---|---|---|
| | **2008** | **2007** |
| **Assets** | | |
| Current assets | | |
| Cash | $       (a) | $   950,000 |
| Marketable securities | 3,200,000 | (b) |
| Accounts receivable | (c) | 1,800,000 |
| Inventories | (d) | (e) |
| Total current assets | 10,000,000 | (f) |
| Property, plant and equipment (net) | (g) | 18,000,000 |
| Noncurrent assets | | |
| Long-term receivables | 2,500,000 | 2,000,000 |
| Investments | 1,500,000 | 1,000,000 |
| Other | 1,000,000 | (h) |
| Total assets | $       (i) | $       (j) |
| **Liabilities and Stockholders' Equity** | | |
| Current liabilities | | |
| Accounts payable | $       (k) | $       (l) |
| Wages and employee benefits payable | 775,000 | (m) |
| Income taxes | 300,000 | 750,000 |
| Advances and deposits | 100,000 | 200,000 |
| Other current liabilities | 200,000 | 400,000 |
| Total current liabilities | (n) | (o) |
| Long-term liabilities | | |
| Long-term debt | (p) | 9,000,000 |
| Deferred income taxes | 3,000,000 | 2,000,000 |
| Other | (q) | 500,000 |
| Total liabilities | (r) | 15,000,000 |
| Stockholders' equity | | |
| Preferred stock | 1,000,000 | (s) |
| Common stock | (t) | 2,000,000 |
| Paid-in capital | (u) | 9,000,000 |
| Retained earnings | (v) | (w) |
| Total stockholders' equity | (x) | (y) |
| Total liabilities and stockholders' equity | $       (z) | $       (zz) |

**Helpful Hints:**

- Start by calculating the missing values for common and preferred stock. Then compute total assets for 2007.

- Total assets for 2008 can be found using 2007 total assets and the additional information in items (6) and (13).

- Accounts receivable for 2008 can be found using 2007 accounts receivable along with the information in items (8) and (12).

Kroger operates retail food and drug stores, multidepartment stores, jewelry stores, and convenience stores throughout the United States. These stores are operated under banners such as Kroger, Ralphs, Fred Meyer, Food 4 Less, King Soopers, Dillons, and City Market. The company operated 2,468 supermarkets and multidepartment stores, 779 convenience stores, and 412 jewelry stores at the end of 2006. Safeway and its subsidiaries operate as food and drug retailers in the United States and Canada. At the end of 2006, the company operated 1,761 stores.

Financial ratios for each company follow. EBI denotes after-tax earnings before interest expense and excluding nonoperating gains or losses.

**C5-1**

Kroger and Safeway: Comparing two grocery retailers

## Selected Financial Ratios

| | Kroger | | | | Safeway | | | |
|---|---|---|---|---|---|---|---|---|
| | **2003** | **2004** | **2005** | **2006** | **2003** | **2004** | **2005** | **2006** |
| **Annual growth rate** | | | | | | | | |
| Sales | 3.9% | 4.9% | 7.3% | 9.2% | 9.7% | 0.8% | 7.2% | 4.6% |
| Operating earnings (before taxes) | (12.1) | (20.2) | 7.3 | 9.9 | (32.8) | 3.8 | (21.7) | 25.6 |
| Assets | 3.3 | (1.3) | 0.0 | 3.6 | (5.9) | 1.9 | 2.5 | 3.3 |
| **Return on common equity (ROCE)** | | | | | | | | |
| EBI/Sales margin | 0.027 | 0.020 | 0.020 | 0.020 | 0.026 | 0.027 | 0.020 | 0.024 |
| Asset turnover | 2.633 | 2.736 | 2.956 | 3.171 | 2.283 | 2.351 | 2.468 | 2.509 |
| Return on assets (ROA) | 0.070 | 0.055 | 0.060 | 0.064 | 0.060 | 0.064 | 0.049 | 0.060 |
| Common earnings leverage | 0.219 | (0.088) | 0.785 | 0.831 | (0.181) | 0.574 | 0.734 | 0.907 |
| Financial structure leverage | 5.216 | 5.482 | 5.167 | 4.477 | 4.283 | 3.833 | 3.374 | 3.026 |
| ROE | 0.080 | (0.027) | 0.242 | 0.239 | (0.047) | 0.141 | 0.122 | 0.164 |
| **Selected expense items (% sales)** | | | | | | | | |
| Cost of goods sold | 73.4% | 74.4% | 75.2% | 75.8% | 67.7% | 67.9% | 68.6% | 68.7% |
| Selling, general, and administrative | 20.0 | 20.0 | 19.3 | 18.9 | 25.4 | 25.0 | 25.6 | 24.8 |
| Interest expense | 1.1 | 1.0 | 0.8 | 0.7 | 1.3 | 1.2 | 1.1 | 1.0 |
| **Selected asset utilization ratios** | | | | | | | | |
| Days receivables are outstanding | 4.808 | 5.071 | 4.563 | 4.041 | 4.088 | 3.679 | 3.276 | 3.687 |
| Days inventory held | 38.590 | 37.036 | 35.415 | 33.121 | 38.912 | 40.372 | 38.110 | 35.746 |
| Days payables outstanding | 31.977 | 32.358 | 29.435 | 26.846 | 24.590 | 24.617 | 27.092 | 30.372 |

**Required:**

1. Which company was the more profitable in 2006? (*Hint:* Compare ROE and ROA performance for the two grocery retailers.)

2. What was the likely source of that company's superior profit performance in 2006? (*Hint:* Decompose ROE and ROA into their individual component parts.)

3. Which company was the more profitable in 2004?

4. Both companies have EBI/Sales margins that hover around 2%. What aspect of the retail grocery industry contributes to such low margins?

5. Which company better manages its receivables, inventories, and payables?

Crocs designs, develops, and manufactures consumer products from specialty resins. The company's primary product line is Crocs-branded footwear for men, women, and children. It sells its products through traditional retail channels, including specialty footwear stores. Deckers Outdoor designs and produces sport sandals as well as sheepskin and sustainable footwear. The company's products are marketed under three proprietary brands: Teva,

**C5-2**

Crocs and Deckers Outdoor: Comparing footwear manufacturers

Simple, and UGG. It sells its products through domestic retailers and global distributors and directly to consumers via the Internet.

Financial ratios for each company follow. EBI denotes after-tax earnings before interest expense and excluding nonoperating gains or losses.

## Selected Financial Ratios

| | Crocs | | | Deckers Outdoor | | |
|---|---|---|---|---|---|---|
| | **2004** | **2005** | **2006** | **2004** | **2005** | **2006** |
| Annual growth rate | | | | | | |
| Sales | 1055.6% | 703.1% | 226.7% | 77.4% | 23.3% | 15.0% |
| Operating earnings (before taxes) | 30.8 | (1812.7) | 254.6 | 124.2 | 23.1 | 28.6 |
| Assets | 1128.8 | 381.1 | 283.7 | 45.9 | 18.7 | 19.3 |
| Profitability | | | | | | |
| EBI/Sales margin | (0.070) | 0.149 | 0.161 | 0.119 | 0.118 | 0.132 |
| Asset turnover | 1.542 | 2.304 | 1.879 | 1.444 | 1.371 | 1.325 |
| Return on Assets (ROA) | (0.107) | 0.342 | 0.303 | 0.171 | 0.162 | 0.175 |
| Selected expense items (% sales) | | | | | | |
| Cost of goods sold | 47.8% | 40.9% | 41.7% | 57.1% | 56.9% | 52.6% |
| Selling, general, and administrative | 58.1 | 30.8 | 29.2 | 21.7 | 21.7 | 23.5 |
| Interest expense | 0.4 | 0.6 | 0.2 | 0.7 | 0.0 | 0.0 |
| Selected asset utilization ratios | | | | | | |
| Days receivables are outstanding | 46.300 | 35.767 | 43.020 | 51.583 | 57.129 | 54.249 |
| Days inventory held | 80.797 | 126.896 | 141.476 | 71.856 | 77.036 | 74.931 |
| Days payables outstanding | 141.133 | 237.369 | 130.687 | 45.894 | 38.359 | 40.276 |

**Required:**

1. Which company was the more profitable in 2006?

2. What was the likely source of that company's superior profit performance in 2006?

3. Which company was the more profitable in 2004? What seems to have been the problem at the underperforming company that year?

4. Which company better manages its receivables, inventories, and payables?

5. Is it likely that Crocs will continue to grow in the next several years at the same rate it grew between 2004 and 2006?

---

**C5-3**

Argenti Corporation:
Evaluating credit risk

mhhe.com/revsine4e

It's late Tuesday evening, and you've just received a phone call from Dennis Whiting, your boss at GE Capital. Dennis wants to know your reaction to the Argenti loan request before tomorrow's loan committee meeting. Here's what he tells you:

> We've provided seasonal loans to Argenti for the past 20 years, and they've always been a first-rate customer, but I'm troubled by several recent events. For instance, the company just reported a $141 million loss for the first quarter of 2008. This comes on top of a $237 million loss in 2007 and a $9 million loss in 2006. What's worse, Argenti changed inventory accounting methods last year, and this change reduced the 2007 loss by $22 million. I can't tell if the company's using other accounting tricks to prop up earnings, but I doubt it.
>
> I believe Argenti's problem lies in its core business—customers just aren't buying its merchandise these days. Management's aggressive price discount program in the fourth quarter of 2007 helped move inventory, but Argenti doesn't have the cost structure needed to be competitive as a discounter. Take a look at the financials I'm sending over, and let me know what you think.

Argenti Corporation operates a national chain of retail stores (Argenti's) selling appliances and electronics, home furnishings, automotive parts, apparel, and jewelry. The company's first store opened in New York City in 1904. Today, the company owns or leases more than

900 stores located in downtown areas of large cities and in suburban shopping malls. Customer purchases are financed in house using ArgentiCredit cards. The company employs more than 58,000 people.

The Seasonal Credit Agreement with GE Capital—dated October 4, 2007—provides a revolving loan facility in the principal amount of $165 million. The purpose of this facility is to provide backup liquidity as Argenti reduces its inventory levels. Under the credit agreement, Argenti may select among several interest rate options, which are based on market rates. Unless GE Capital agrees, loans may be made under the seasonal credit facility only after the commitments under the company's other debt agreements are fully used.

## Argenti Corporation

### Balance Sheets and Selected Other Data

| ($ in millions) | 2007 | 2006 | 2005 | 2004 | 2003 |
|---|---|---|---|---|---|
| **Assets** | | | | | |
| Cash and securities | $ 35 | $ 38 | $ 36 | $ 117 | $ 92 |
| Receivables | 213 | 166 | 112 | 62 | 47 |
| Inventories | 1,545 | 1,770 | 1,625 | 1,242 | 1,038 |
| Other current assets | 13 | 22 | 6 | 4 | 312 |
| | 1,806 | 1,996 | 1,779 | 1,425 | 1,489 |
| Property, plant and equipment—net | 1,308 | 1,366 | 1,396 | 1,263 | 1,222 |
| Investments | 317 | 345 | 314 | 296 | 277 |
| Other assets | 1,448 | 1,177 | 1,048 | 851 | 445 |
| | $4,879 | $4,884 | $4,537 | $3,835 | $3,433 |
| **Liabilities and shareholders' equity** | | | | | |
| Notes payable | $1,028 | $ 160 | $ 144 | $ 0 | $ 0 |
| Accounts payable | 1,812 | 2,040 | 1,955 | 1,595 | 1,399 |
| Accrued expenses | 1,232 | 1,201 | 1,248 | 1,204 | 1,148 |
| | 4,072 | 3,401 | 3,347 | 2,799 | 2,547 |
| Long-term debt | 87 | 423 | 228 | 213 | 125 |
| Other liabilities | 112 | 185 | 203 | 216 | 208 |
| Preferred stock | 175 | 175 | 75 | 0 | 0 |
| Common stock | 54 | 46 | 23 | 19 | 16 |
| Retained earnings | 518 | 768 | 750 | 661 | 583 |
| Less: Treasury stock | (139) | (114) | (89) | (73) | (46) |
| | $4,879 | $4,884 | $4,537 | $3,835 | $3,433 |
| **Selected earnings and cash flow data** | | | | | |
| Sales | $6,620 | $7,085 | $7,029 | $6,023 | $5,806 |
| Cost of goods sold | 4,869 | 5,211 | 5,107 | 4,258 | 4,047 |
| Gross margin | 1,751 | 1,874 | 1,922 | 1,765 | 1,759 |
| Net income | (237) | (9) | 137 | 101 | 60 |
| Operating cash flow | (356) | (182) | 153 | 132 | 157 |
| Dividends | 9 | 4 | 24 | 23 | 19 |

Argenti management has asked GE Capital for a $1.5 billion refinancing package that would be used to pay off all or a substantial portion of its outstanding debt. Excerpts from the company's financial statements footnotes follow.

### Management Discussion and Analysis (2007 Annual Report)

The company has obtained waivers under the Long-Term Credit Agreement and the Short-Term Credit Agreement with respect to compliance for the fiscal quarter ending March 29, 2008—with covenants requiring maintenance of minimum consolidated shareholders' equity, a minimum ratio of debt to capitalization, and minimum earnings before interest, taxes, depreciation, amortization, and rent (EBITDAR). These waivers and amendments reduce the maximum amount of debt permitted to be incurred, and the maturity of the Long-Term Agreement was changed from February 28, 2009 to August 29, 2008.

The company is currently in discussions with financing sources with a view toward both a longer term solution to its liquidity problems and obtaining refinancing for all or a substantial portion of its outstanding indebtedness, including a total of $1,008 million, which will mature on or about August 29, 2008. This would include repayment of the current bank borrowings and amounts outstanding under the Note Purchase Agreements. The company's management is highly confident that the indebtedness can be refinanced. Its largest shareholder, GE Capital, also expects the company to be able to refinance such indebtedness. However, there can be no assurance that such refinancing can be obtained or that amendments or waivers required to maintain compliance with the previous agreements can be obtained.

### Footnote to Financial Statements (2007 Annual Report)

The company intends to improve its financial condition and reduce its dependence on borrowing by slowing expansion, controlling expenses, closing certain unprofitable stores, and continuing to implement its inventory reduction program. Management is in the process of reevaluating the company's merchandising, marketing, store operations, and real estate strategies. The company is also considering the sale of certain operating units as a means of generating cash. Future cash is also expected to continue to be provided by ongoing operations, sale of receivables under the Accounts Receivable Purchase Agreement with GE capital, borrowings under revolving loan facilities, and vendor financing programs.

### Quarterly Income

|  | Mar. 08 | Dec. 07 | Sep. 07 | Jun. 07 | Mar. 07 |
|---|---|---|---|---|---|
| Sales | $ 1,329 | $ 2,084 | $ 1,567 | $ 1,534 | $ 1,435 |
| Cost of goods sold | 997 | 1,525 | 1,096 | 1,210 | 1,038 |
| Gross profit | $ 332 | $ 559 | $ 471 | $ 324 | $ 397 |
| Net income | $ (141) | $ (165) | $ (35) | $ 11 | $ (48) |
| Gross profit (% sales) | 25.0% | 26.8% | 30.1% | 21.1% | 27.7% |
| Net income (% sales) | (10.6)% | (7.9)% | (2.2)% | 0.7% | (3.3)% |

**Required:**

1. Why did Argenti need to increase its notes payable borrowing to more than $1 billion in 2007?

2. What recommendation would you make regarding the company's request for a $1.5 billion refinancing package?

**Remember to check the book's companion Web site for additional study material.**

# The Role of Financial Information in Valuation and Credit Risk Assessment | 6

We introduced the key financial ratios used to assess a company's operating performance, liquidity, and solvency in the previous chapter. In this chapter, we examine the role that financial accounting information plays in valuation and credit risk assessment. We also examine the expanding use of fair value accounting in company financial statements, and explain why accountants and auditors must be skilled at valuation. Along the way, we will also build a framework for understanding what academic and professional research has to say about how useful accounting numbers are to investors and creditors.

**Corporate valuation** involves estimating the worth—or intrinsic value—of a company, one of its operating units, or its ownership shares. Although there are several approaches to valuation, equity investors and analysts often use **fundamental analysis** to estimate a company's value. This valuation approach uses basic accounting measures, or "fundamentals," to assess the amount, timing, and uncertainty of a firm's *future* operating cash flows or earnings. Data from a firm's financial statements, along with industry and economywide data, are used to develop projections of future earnings or cash flows. These projections are then discounted at a risk-adjusted cost of capital to arrive at an initial valuation estimate. This initial estimate is further refined by adding the current value of nonoperating assets (such as a corporate art collection) and subtracting off-balance-sheet obligations. This refined valuation becomes the basis for investment (buy, hold, or sell) decisions.

**Cash flow assessment** plays a central role in analyzing a company's **credit risk.** Lenders and credit analysts use the firm's financial statements and other information to estimate its *future* cash flows. They then compare these cash flow projections to the firm's future debt-service requirements. Companies with projected operating cash flows that comfortably exceed required future debt principal and interest payments are deemed good credit risks. Less favorable operating cash flow prospects may suggest that the firm is a high credit risk. In this case, the firm may be charged higher rates of interest, have more stringent conditions placed on its loans, or be refused credit.

## LEARNING OBJECTIVES

**After studying this chapter, you will understand:**

1. The basic steps in corporate valuation using free cash flows and abnormal earnings.

2. Why *current* earnings are considered more useful than *current* cash flows for assessing *future* cash flows.

3. What factors contribute to variation in price-earnings multiples.

4. How the permanent, transitory, and valuation-irrelevant components of earnings each affects price-earnings multiples.

5. The notion of earnings quality and what factors influence the quality of earnings.

6. The expanding use of *fair value* measurements in IFRS and GAAP financial statements.

7. How stock returns relate to "good news" and "bad news" earnings surprises.

8. The importance of credit risk assessment in lending decisions and how credit ratings are determined.

9. How to forecast a company's financial statements.

*Chapter*

297

# ENTERPRISE VALUATION

Valuing an entire company, an operating division of that company, or its ownership shares involves three basic steps:

1. **Forecasting** future amounts of some financial attribute—what we call a **value-relevant attribute**—that ultimately determine how much a company is worth. Common value-relevant attributes include:

   - Distributable or free cash flows (defined and discussed in the next section).
   - Accounting earnings.
   - Balance sheet book values.

2. Determining the **risk** or **uncertainty** associated with the forecasted future amounts.

3. Determining the **discounted present value** of the expected future amounts using a discount rate that reflects the risk or uncertainty from Step 2.

> Dividends are another value-relevant attribute discussed in finance texts. However, the dividend discount valuation approach described in many finance texts is of limited practical use despite its intuitive appeal. This is so because dividends represent the *distribution* of wealth. The accounting measures considered here focus on wealth *creation*, the prosperity and growth of the business.

## The Discounted Free Cash Flow Approach to Equity Valuation

The **distributable—or free—cash flow valuation approach** combines the elements in these three steps to express current stock price as the discounted present value of expected future distributable cash flows. **Free cash flow**—a term popular among analysts—is often defined as the company's operating cash flows (before interest) minus cash outlays for operating capacity such as buildings, equipment, and furnishings. It's the amount available to finance further expansion of operating capacity, to reduce debt, to pay dividends, or to repurchase stock. This is the best way to measure free cash flows if you are interested in valuing the company as a whole without regard to its capital structure.

But what if you want to value just the company's common stock? Then you would need to refine the free cash flow measure by also subtracting cash interest payments, debt repayments, and preferred dividends. What's left is the free cash flow (denoted *CF*) that's available to common stockholders.[1] Of course, *CF* can be used to pay common dividends, buy back common stock, or expand operating capacity. The free cash flow equity valuation model can be written as:[2]

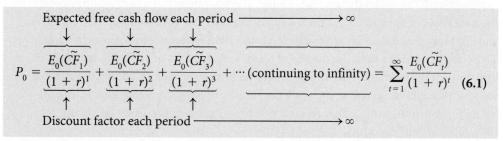

$$P_0 = \frac{E_0(\widetilde{CF}_1)}{(1+r)^1} + \frac{E_0(\widetilde{CF}_2)}{(1+r)^2} + \frac{E_0(\widetilde{CF}_3)}{(1+r)^3} + \cdots \text{(continuing to infinity)} = \sum_{t=1}^{\infty} \frac{E_0(\widetilde{CF}_t)}{(1+r)^t} \quad (6.1)$$

The math may look complex, but the intuition is straightforward. The free cash flow valuation model says that the price ($P_0$) that the market assigns today (at time $t = 0$) to a company's stock equals the sum ($\Sigma$) of the stream of *expected future free cash flows* (the $E_0[\widetilde{CF}]$ terms) per

---

[1] One of the earliest accounting treatments of this concept appeared in L. Revsine, *Replacement Cost Accounting* (Upper Saddle River, NJ: Prentice Hall, 1973), pp. 33–35 and 95–100. There, free cash flow was defined as "the portion of net operating flows that can be distributed as a dividend without reducing the level of future physical operations" (p. 34).

[2] See E. F. Fama and M. H. Miller, *The Theory of Finance* (New York: Holt, Rinehart & Winston, 1972); R. Brealey and S. Myers, *Principles of Corporate Finance* (New York: McGraw-Hill, 2006); S. A. Ross, R. W. Westerfield, and J. F. Jaffee, *Corporate Finance* (New York: McGraw-Hill, 2005); L. Soffer and R. Soffer, *Financial Statement Analysis: A Valuation Approach* (Upper Saddle River, NJ: Prentice Hall, 2003).

share of stock *discounted back to the present* (the $[1 + r]^t$ terms).[3] Each periodic expected future free cash flow has its own unique discount factor $(1/[1 + r]^t)$, which reflects the risk $(r)$ and timing $(t)$ of the free cash flow. The $E_0$ signifies that the expected future cash flows are based on investors' *current assessment* (at time $t = 0$) of the company's future business activities.

The cash flow stream begins one period from now at $t = 1$, and it continues over an infinite horizon to $t = \infty$, but each future free cash flow is currently unknown and therefore uncertain.[4]

The discount rate $(r)$, commonly referred to as the **equity cost of capital,** is adjusted to reflect the uncertainty or riskiness of the expected cash flow stream.[5] Streams that are more uncertain or risky will be discounted at a higher rate.

Simply put, the free cash flow valuation model in equation (6.1) says that today's market price of each common share depends on investors' current *expectations* about the firm's future economic prospects as measured by free cash flows available to common shareholders. These future cash flows are discounted by a factor that reflects the risk (or uncertainty) and timing of the anticipated flows.[6]

Here's an illustration of the discounted free cash flow approach to valuation.

---

Willard Brown is thinking about starting a truck rental business. He plans to buy four trucks now and to then add a fifth truck in two years. Each truck will cost $20,000. Willard has carefully evaluated the local market for rental trucks and believes that each truck will generate $5,000 of net operating cash flows each year. At the end of five years, Willard believes that he can sell the trucks for $30,000 in total. How much is the business worth?

---

Exhibit 6.1 shows you each step in the valuation process. First, Willard must forecast the expected future free cash flows associated with the truck rental business. These include the expected net operating cash flows of $5,000 per truck or $20,000 in the first two years (from four trucks) and then $25,000 in the final three years (when the fifth truck is added). Then there's the additional $30,000 cash flow Willard expects to receive when he sells the trucks at the end of Year 5, and the $20,000 he must spend at the end of Year 2 to buy the final truck. The expected future free cash flows range from a low of $0 in Year 2, to a high of $55,000 in Year 5.

Next, Brown must assess the cash flow risk associated with the truck rental business and determine the appropriate discount rate. For now, let's just say it's 10%.

---

[3] We denote uncertain future amounts with a tilde (~). Thus, $E_0 (\widetilde{CF}_3)$ indicates the currently expected but uncertain free cash flow for Period 3 in the future. By contrast, the already known past cash flow in Period 0 would be shown without the tilde (that is, as $CF_0$).

[4] An alternative representation of the discounted cash flow valuation model presumes that the future cash flow stream continues only through some finite terminal period, $T$, at which point the company is liquidated and a liquidating or terminal distribution $\widetilde{CF}_T$) is paid to stockholders:

$$P_0 = \sum_{t=1}^{T-1} \frac{E_0(\widetilde{CF}_t)}{(1 + r)^t} + \frac{F_0(\widetilde{CF}_T)}{(1 + r)^T}$$

[5] There is no clear consensus in the finance literature on how best to estimate the cost of equity capital. However, one popular approach is to use the **capital asset pricing model** (CAPM), which expresses the equity cost of capital as the sum of the return on a riskless asset $(r_f)$ plus an equity risk premium $(E[r_M] - r_f)$ multiplied by the company's systematic (beta) risk:

$$r_e = r_f + \beta(E[r_M] - r_f)$$

See J. Pettit, "Corporate Capital Costs: A Practitioners' Guide," *Journal of Applied Corporate Finance*, Spring 1999, pp. 115–20.

[6] Some finance textbooks adopt a slightly different cash flow approach to enterprise valuation. This alternative approach uses a *weighted average cost of capital* (WACC) to discount the expected future free cash flows available to all capital providers—both lenders and equity investors. The WACC discount rate is a blended rate that combines the equity cost of capital and the debt cost of capital. When enterprise value has been determined, it is apportioned into the value of debt and the value of equity. When done currectly, this alternative approach always yields the same share price estimate as the equity cash flow approach in equation (6.1).

| EXHIBIT 6.1 | Illustration of the Discounted Free Cash Flow Approach to Valuation |
|---|---|

**Step 1:** Forecast expected future free cash flows

|  | Year 1 | Year 2 | Year 3 | Year 4 | Year 5 |
|---|---|---|---|---|---|
| Net cash flows from operations | $20,000 | $20,000 | $25,000 | $25,000 | $25,000 |
| Cash from selling all trucks in Year 5 |  |  |  |  | 30,000 |
| Capital expenditure in Year 2 for the fifth truck |  | (20,000) |  |  |  |
| Future free cash flows | $20,000 | $    0 | $25,000 | $25,000 | $55,000 |

**Step 2:** Determine the cash flow risk (discount rate)                                          10%

**Step 3:** Determine the discounted present value of future free cash flows

|  | Year 1 | Year 2 | Year 3 | Year 4 | Year 5 |
|---|---|---|---|---|---|
| Expected future free cash flows | $20,000 | $    0 | $25,000 | $25,000 | $55,000 |
| Present value factor $1/(1 + 0.10)^t$ | 0.90909 | 0.82645 | 0.75131 | 0.68301 | 0.62092 |
| Present value of each future free cash flow | $18,182 | $    0 | $18,783 | $17,075 | $34,151 |

| Value of business opportunity (sum of all present values) | $88,191 |
|---|---|
| Value per share (1,000 shares) | $88.19 |

> This is the value that Brown would attach to the stream. Because it cost him $80,000 to create the stream, the *net* present value of the business opportunity for him is $88,191 minus $80,000, or $8,191.

The final step involves determining the discounted present value of each future free cash flow. The discount factors shown in Exhibit 6.1 are computed as $1/(1 + 0.10)^t$ and thus capture information about the risk of the business opportunity (10%, or 0.10) and about the timing of each cash flow (the exponent $t$). The present value of the $20,000 Year 1 free cash flow is therefore $18,182. The present value of the entire free cash flow stream (the sum of the free cash flow present values for Year 1 through 5) is $88,191. So, if 1,000 shares of common stock are outstanding, the truck rental business is worth $88.19 per share using Brown's free cash flow forecasts.

To apply discounted free cash flow valuation approach as represented in equation (6.1), we would need to estimate free cash flows for each and every future period, starting one year hence and going forward forever. Obviously, this would be a daunting task. In practice, some simplifying assumptions are made to facilitate the valuation process.[7]

One simplification for a mature firm with a stable cash flow pattern is to assume that the *current level* of cash flows ($CF_0$) will continue unchanged forever—a zero-growth perpetuity. This means the *expected* free cash flows in each future period will equal the *known* current period cash flow so that equation (6.1) becomes:

> For example, we assumed that Brown sold all of his trucks at the end of Year 5 and ceased doing business.

$$
\begin{array}{c}
\text{Expected free cash flow in each year set} \\
\text{equal to the free cash flow realized in Year 0} \longrightarrow \infty \\
\downarrow \qquad \downarrow \qquad \downarrow \qquad\qquad \downarrow \\
P_0 = \dfrac{CF_0}{(1 + r)^1} + \dfrac{CF_0}{(1 + r)^2} + \dfrac{CF_0}{(1 + r)^3} + \cdots \text{(continuing to infinity)} \qquad \textbf{(6.2)} \\
\uparrow \qquad \uparrow \qquad \uparrow \qquad\qquad \uparrow \\
\text{Discount factor each year} \longrightarrow \infty
\end{array}
$$

---

[7] These simplifying assumptions and other detailed aspects of the valuation process are described in B. Cornell, *Corporate Valuation* (Homewood, IL: R. D. Irwin, 1993); T. Koller, M. Goedhart, and D. Wessels, *Valuation: Measuring and Managing the Value of Companies* (New York: Wiley, 2005); A. Damadoran, *Investment Valuation* (New York: Wiley, 2002); S. Penman, *Financial Statement Analysis and Security Valuation* (New York: McGraw-Hill/Irwin, 2007); and L. Soffer and R. Soffer, *Financial Statement Analysis: A Valuation Approach* (Upper Saddle River, NJ: Prentice Hall, 2003).

The present value of the same dollar cash flow each period over an infinite horizon—called a **constant perpetuity**—simplifies to:[8]

$$P_0 = \frac{CF_0}{r} \qquad (6.3)$$

Thus, if a company is currently generating a free cash flow of $5 per share which is expected to continue indefinitely, and if the discount rate is 10%, the estimated share price would be $5/0.10 = $50.

## Goodwill Impairment and Free Cash Flow Valuation

You may think that the details of free cash flow valuation are important only for stock analysts and investors. If so, you would be mistaken. Because of recent changes in U.S. financial reporting practices for goodwill, accountants and auditors must also know how to use the discounted free cash flow valuation approach.

For example, here's a footnote from the Corning, Inc., 2002 annual report to shareholders. It is a leading manufacturer of fiber-optic cable and other equipment for the telecommunications industry.

### Impairment of Goodwill

*SFAS No. 142,* "Goodwill and Other Intangible Assets," requires management to make judgments about the fair value of its reporting unit. Corning measures fair value on the basis of **discounted expected future cash flows.** The determination of expected future cash flows involves judgment. Corning's judgment was based upon our historical experience in the telecommunications business, our current knowledge from our commercial relationships, and available external information about future trends. With this input, it is management's expectation that there will be minimal volume growth in the short term, volume growth is assumed to accelerate beginning in 2005 commensurate with overall market recovery. Terminal value of the business assumes a growth in perpetuity of 3%. These cash flows are also used to value intangible and tangible assets which determine the implied value of reporting unit goodwill. . . . Corning used a discount rate of 12% in its calculation of fair value of the expected future cash flows and recorded an impairment charge of $400 million. . . . [Emphasis added.]

*Source: Corning, Inc., 2002 Annual Report to Shareholders.*

---

[8] A constant perpetuity is a stream of constant cash flows without end. To see why the present value of a cash flow perpetuity

$$PV = \frac{CF}{(1 + r)^1} + \frac{CF}{(1 + r)^2} + \frac{CF}{(1 + r)^3} + \cdots + \frac{CF}{(1 + r)^\infty}$$

reduces to

$$PV = \frac{CF}{r}$$

consider this example. Suppose an investment's market price (that is, the present value) is $1,000 and that this investment will yield a return of 9%, or $90, forever. Because the amount of this perpetual cash flow is $PV \times r$, we can express the amount of the perpetuity as:

$$PV \times r = CF$$

Dividing both sides of the equation by $r$ immediately yields the formula for the present value of a perpetuity:

$$PV = \frac{CF}{r}$$

In our example,

$$\$1,000 = \frac{\$90}{0.09}$$

Accounting **goodwill** arises when one company buys another company and pays more than the fair market value of the acquired company's individual net assets. (You will learn more about goodwill in Chapter 16.) For example, suppose Corning pays $800 million for another telecommunications equipment manufacturer. If the acquired company's identifiable net assets (cash, receivables, inventories, equipment, buildings, patents, and so on *minus* debt) have a **fair value** of only $50 million, then Corning must record the $750 million balance of the purchase price as goodwill.

*Statement of Financial Accounting Standards (SFAS) No. 142* requires companies to "test" for impairment of this goodwill at least once a year.[9] That's what Corning's accountants and auditors did using the free cash flow valuation approach. Continuing our example, assume that Corning estimated the expected future free cash flows associated with its telecommunications reporting unit (the acquired company) and discovered the unit is now worth only $400 million. Why? Because few companies today are spending money on new telecommunications equipment. This downturn in demand has lowered Corning's forecasts of the acquired company's future sales, earnings, and future free cash flows from what they were when Corning bought the unit.

If the reporting unit's fair value of identifiable net assets is still $50 million, then Corning can show only $350 million of goodwill. Corning's original goodwill ($750 million) has become impaired and must be written down by $400 million—a direct charge to net income for the year. (We've skipped certain details of *SFAS No. 142* but they are described in Chapter 10.)

Corning goes on to say that the impairment charge would have been $225 million higher if the company had used a discount rate of 12.5% rather than 12% to compute the present value of the reporting unit's expected future free cash flows. On the other hand, no impairment charge would have been recorded in 2002 if an 11% discount rate had been used.

Next year, Corning's accountants and auditors will again test for goodwill impairment using the discounted free cash flow valuation approach.

## The Role of Earnings in Valuation

We have just described a free cash flow valuation approach linking investors' expectations about a company's future cash flow prospects to today's stock price. *But what role does earnings play in valuation?* If investors are truly interested in knowing the company's future cash flows, why would they care about current earnings? The answer hinges on the belief that *current* accrual accounting earnings are more useful than *current* cash flows in predicting *future* cash flows. The Financial Accounting Standards Board (FASB), for example, makes this assertion. It states:

> Information about enterprise earnings and its components measured by accrual accounting generally provides a better indication of enterprise performance than information about current cash receipts and payments.[10]

The Board stresses that the primary objective of financial reporting is to provide information useful to investors and creditors in assessing the *amount, timing,* and *uncertainty* of future net cash flows.[11] The FASB contends that users pay attention to firms' accounting earnings because this accrual measure of periodic firm performance improves their ability to forecast companies' future cash flows.

---

*Fair value* is the price that would be received on selling each asset in an orderly market transaction. We will have more to say about fair value later in this chapter.

---

The following quote from the "Intrinsic Value" column of *The Wall Street Journal* underscores the importance of accrual earnings as an indicator of future free cash flows:

> As per usual, this column values stocks by their expected future free cash flow, discounted back to the present. Earnings are a proxy—imperfect but the best we have— for free cash flow, which is the spare change that the underlying business throws off to their owners after paying for salaries, interest, capital maintenance, taxes and Danish for their chief executives, in addition to their eight-figure bonuses.

*Source:* R. Lowenstein, "S&P 500: Cheap, Fair, Going, Gone....," *The Wall Street Journal,* June 19, 1997. Copyright © 1997 Dow Jones & Company, Inc. All rights reserved worldwide. Reprinted with permission.

---

[9] "Goodwill and Other Intangible Assets," *Statement of Financial Accounting Standards No. 142* (Norwalk, CT: FASB, 2001).

[10] "Objectives of Financial Reporting by Business Enterprises," *Statement of Financial Accounting Concepts (SFAC) No. 1* (Stamford, CT: FASB, 1978), para. 43.

[11] Ibid., para. 37. The term **net cash flows** refers to the difference between cash receipts (inflows) and cash payments (outflows).

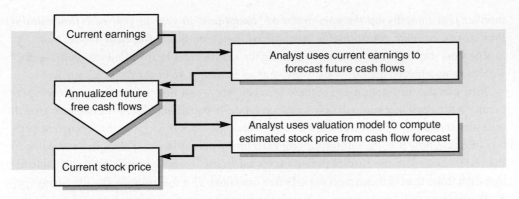

**Figure 6.1**

LINKAGE BETWEEN STOCK
PRICE AND ACCRUAL
EARNINGS

The FASB's belief that *current* earnings outperform *current* cash flows in predicting *future* cash flows stems from the *forward-looking* nature of accrual accounting. To illustrate, consider this example. Under generally accepted accounting principles (GAAP), a $100,000 cash expenditure for production equipment is not expensed in its entirety when purchased. Instead, this expenditure is charged to an asset account, and the asset is depreciated over future years as it is used to produce the products that are sold to customers. Both the depreciable life and depreciation method are chosen to reflect the *expected future benefit pattern* that arises from the use of the asset. Accrual accounting automatically incorporates this long-horizon, multiple-period view for capital expenditure transactions.

Consider another example. Under accrual accounting, an up-front cash advance from a customer is recognized as income not when the cash is received but rather over a series of future periods as the advance is earned (recall the Canterbury Publishing example from Chapter 2).

Cash flows are "lumpy." But as these examples illustrate, accrual accounting earnings measurement takes a long-horizon perspective that smooths out the "lumpiness" in year-to-year cash flows. This explains why the FASB contends that current earnings provide a much better measure of long-run expected operating performance than do current cash flows.

The FASB's contention is supported by empirical research that shows two results:

- Current earnings are a better forecast of future cash flows than are current cash flows.[12]
- Stock returns correlate better with accrual earnings than with realized operating cash flows.[13]

These results imply that investors are better able to predict a company's future free cash flows using the company's accrual earnings than by using realized cash flows.

Figure 6.1 illustrates the linkage between a company's current earnings, future free cash flows, and current stock price, as suggested by the FASB and by the empirical evidence.[14]

As Figure 6.1 shows, the analyst combines information about the company's current earnings, its business strategy, and the industry's competitive dynamics to forecast future free cash flows. ***Through the use of accruals and deferrals, accrual accounting produces an earnings***

---

[12] See M. Barth, C. Cram, and K. Nelson, "Accruals and the Prediction of Future Cash Flows," *The Accounting Review,* January 2001, pp. 27–58; and P. Dechow, S. P. Kothari, and R. Watts, "The Relation Between Earnings and Cash Flows," *Journal of Accounting and Economics,* May 1998, pp. 133–68. Additional evidence on the usefulness of *current earnings* in predicting *future cash flows* is provided by R. Greenberg, G. Johnson, and K. Ramesh, "Earnings versus Cash Flow as a Predictor of Future Cash Flow," *Journal of Accounting, Auditing and Finance,* Fall 1986, pp. 266–77; and C. Finger, "The Ability of Earnings to Predict Future Earnings and Cash Flow," *Journal of Accounting Research,* Autumn 1994, pp. 210–23.

[13] B. Lev and P. Zorowin, "The Boundaries of Financial Reporting and How to Extend Them," *Journal of Accounting Research,* Autumn 1999, pp. 353–85; J. Callen and D. Segal, "Do Accruals Drive Stock Returns? A Variance Decomposition Analysis," *Journal of Accounting Research,* June 2004, pp. 527–60; J. Watson and P. Wells, "The Association between Various Earnings and Cash Flow Measures of Firm Performance and Stock Returns: Some Australian Evidence," Working Paper, University of Technology, Sydney, AU, 2005; P. Dechow, "Accounting Earnings and Cash Flows as Measures of Firm Performance: The Role of Accounting Accruals," *Journal of Accounting and Economics,* July 1994, pp. 3–42.

[14] For a slightly different discussion of these linkages, see W. Beaver, *Financial Reporting: An Accounting Revolution* (Upper Saddle River, NJ: Prentice Hall, 1981), Ch. 4.

*number that smooths out the unevenness or "lumpiness" in year-to-year cash flows, and it provides an estimate of sustainable "annualized" long-run future free cash flows.*

The final step in this process involves using the annualized free cash flow estimate together with the risk-adjusted discount rate to arrive at an estimated value for the firm's stock.

To appreciate the implications of these linkages, let's revisit the simplified zero-growth perpetuity setting and our free cash flow valuation model in equation (6.2). Assuming zero growth means that one way to estimate a firm's equity value (or stock price) is to use its current period's free cash flow ($CF_0$) as our forecast for each future period free cash flow. But according to the FASB's assertion, the current period's accrual income is a better proxy for sustainable future cash flows than is the current period's free cash flow. This means replacing the current period's cash flow ($CF_0$) in equation (6.2) with the current period's earnings (denoted $X_0$). In this case, the free cash flow valuation equation simplifies to:

Expected future free cash flow set equal to current cash flow

Expected future free cash flow set equal to current accrual earnings in Year 0 $\longrightarrow \infty$

Zero-growth free cash flow discount model from equation (6.1)

$$P_0 = \sum_{t=1}^{\infty} \frac{CF_0}{(1+r)^t} = \frac{X_0}{(1+r)^1} + \frac{X_0}{(1+r)^2} + \frac{X_0}{(1+r)^3} + \cdots + \frac{X_0}{(1+r)^\infty} \qquad \textbf{(6.4)}$$

Discount factor each year $\longrightarrow \infty$

As in equation (6.2), the right-hand side of equation (6.4) is a perpetuity with a discounted present value of $X_0/r$. Given our simplifying assumptions, the current stock price estimate can thus be expressed as a capitalization rate ($1/r$) times a perpetuity equal to current earnings:

$$P_0 = \frac{1}{r}(X_0) = \frac{X_0}{r} \qquad \textbf{(6.5)}$$

or alternatively:

$$\frac{P_0}{X_0} = \frac{1}{r} \qquad \textbf{(6.6)}$$

The left-hand side of equation (6.6) is the **price/earnings (P/E) ratio**—also called the **earnings multiple**—which is a measure of the relation between a firm's current earnings and its share price. Under the assumption of zero growth, the P/E ratio in equation (6.6) is the reciprocal of the equity cost of capital (risk-adjusted interest rate) used to discount future earnings. If the current equity cost of capital is 8%, the earnings multiple is $1/0.08 = 12.5$, which is the rate at which \$1 of current earnings is capitalized into share price. If the company reports current earnings of \$5 per share and if investors believe this earnings level will persist forever as a perpetuity of \$5 per share, then the present value of the future earnings stream implies a share price of \$5 × 12.5 = \$62.50.

 RECAP

In theory, equity valuation involves discounting the expected value of some measure of wealth creation—such as free cash flow or earnings—over an infinite horizon using a risk-adjusted discount rate that reflects the equity cost of capital. In practice, simplifying assumptions are made to facilitate the valuation process. One simplification is to assume that future periods' free cash flows will be a perpetuity equal to the current period's accrual earnings. Accrual accounting produces an earnings number that smooths out the unevenness in year-to-year cash flows, thereby providing a measure of firm performance that is generally a better indicator of a company's long-run sustainable free cash flows. By using this valuation approach, stock price is stated as a multiple of the current period's earnings, where the multiple (in the no-growth case) is the reciprocal of the firm's equity cost of capital.

# RESEARCH ON EARNINGS AND EQUITY VALUATION

Over the past 35 years, researchers have investigated the **value-relevance** of financial accounting information.[15] This research seeks to further our understanding of the relation between stock prices and earnings.

To illustrate, let's consider equation (6.5). That equation says that current earnings ($X_0$) can "explain" current stock price ($P_0$) in the sense that a perpetual earnings stream of $5 per share gives rise to a $62.50 share price. It immediately follows that *differences* in current earnings across firms should help explain *differences* in stock prices across firms at a particular point in time. ***That is, if investors view accounting earnings as an important piece of information for assessing firm value, then earnings differences across firms should help explain differences in firms' stock prices.*** This is just another way of saying that earnings are value-relevant.

One way to test whether reported earnings are value-relevant is to examine the statistical association between stock prices and earnings across many firms at a given point in time. Researchers have explored this statistical association using the following simple earnings valuation equation:

$$P_i = \alpha + \beta X_i + e_i \qquad (6.7)$$

where $P_i$ is the end-of-period closing stock price for firm $i$, and $X_i$ is the firm's reported accounting earnings per share for that same period; the intercept ($\alpha$) and slope ($\beta$) terms in the equation represent coefficients to be estimated using standard regression analysis or similar techniques; $e_i$ denotes a random error that reflects the variation in stock prices that cannot be explained by earnings.

If accounting earnings are relevant for determining stock prices, then the estimated slope coefficient $\beta$, which measures the relationship between earnings and prices, should be positive. A statistically positive $\beta$ means that differences in earnings across firms explain a significant portion of the variation in firms' share prices. Moreover, if current earnings were a perfect forecast of expected future free cash flows and if all companies had the same cost of equity capital and conformed to the zero-growth assumption, current earnings would explain 100% of the variation in share prices.

> For now, earnings per share (EPS) can be taken to mean a company's net income divided by its number of outstanding common shares. As you will discover in Chapter 15, EPS calculations in practice are a little more complicated than this.

Figure 6.2 plots 2006 year-end stock prices (shown on the vertical axis) against annual EPS (shown on the horizontal axis) for 48 restaurant companies. The upward-sloping line represents the estimated price-earnings relation for the regression equation (6.7) for this group of companies at the end of 2006. The regression line has a vertical axis intercept ($\alpha$) estimate of $9.57 per share and a slope ($\beta$) coefficient estimate of 14.28—that is:

$$
P_i \;=\; \underset{\substack{\uparrow \\ \text{Implied stock} \\ \text{price at} \\ \$0\ \text{EPS}}}{\overset{\overset{\text{Intercept}}{\downarrow}}{\$9.57}} \;+\; \underset{\substack{\uparrow \\ \text{Earnings} \\ \text{multiple}}}{\overset{\overset{\text{Slope}}{\downarrow}}{14.28}} \;\times\; \underset{\substack{\uparrow \\ \text{EPS}}}{(\$X_i)} \qquad (6.8)
$$

---

[15] For an overview of this research, see B. Lev and J. Ohlson, "Market-Based Empirical Research in Accounting: A Review, Interpretation, and Extension," *Journal of Accounting Research,* Supplement 1982, pp. 249–322; B. Lev, "On the Usefulness of Earnings and Earnings Research: Lessons and Directions from Two Decades of Empirical Research," *Journal of Accounting Research,* Supplement 1989, pp., 153–92; S. Kothari, "Capital Markets Research in Accounting," *Journal of Accounting and Economics,* September 2001, pp. 105–232; and R. Holthausen and R. Watts, "The Relevance of the Value-Relevance Literature for Financial Accounting Standard Setting," *Journal of Accounting and Economics,* September 2001, pp. 3–76.

## Figure 6.2

2006 STOCK PRICE AND
ACTUAL 2006 EPS FOR 48
RESTAURANT COMPANIES

Regression Result:

$$P_i = \$9.57 + 14.28X_i$$
$$R^2 = 61.7\%$$

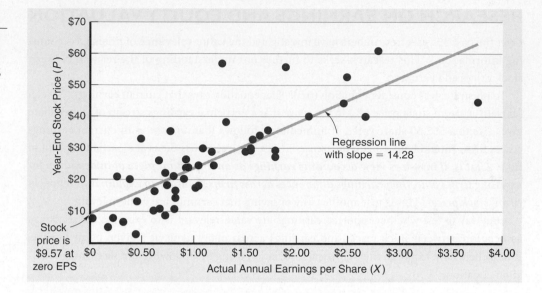

A restaurant firm that reported EPS of $X_i = \$1$ in 2006 would be predicted to have a stock price of $\$23.85 = \$9.57 + 14.28 \times \$1$. The estimated slope coefficient ($\beta = 14.28$) is positive and statistically significant, indicating that reported earnings explains some of the variation in stock prices of restaurant companies. In fact, the proportion of variation in share prices explained by earnings (the $R^2$ for the regression) is 61.7%. However, some points lie well above the average price-earnings relation in Figure 6.2 while others fall far below the regression line.[16] The next section discusses reasons why current earnings do not explain 100% of the variation in current prices and why some firms' P/E ratios are well above (or below) average.

## Sources of Variation in P/E Multiples

### Current Earnings, a Poor Forecast of Future Expected Earnings    Two firms with identical current earnings can have very different stock prices if investors believe that the firms' future earnings will not be the same. Investors care most about where a firm is headed (future earnings and free cash flows), not where it has been (past earnings and cash flows). To illustrate, suppose that Firms A and B both earn $1.50 per share in the current year. However, investors expect Firm A to earn $2.50 per share next year (and every year thereafter) whereas they expect Firm B to earn only $1.50 in perpetuity. If the equity cost of capital for both firms is 10% and we apply equation (6.5), Firm A will command a stock price of $25 (= $2.50/0.10), but Firm B will sell for only $15 (= $1.50/0.10) per share. Even though both firms earn $1.50 per share this year, Firm A has a higher stock price because its expected future earnings are higher.

What happens when expected future earnings replace current earnings in Figure 6.2? The answer can be found in Figure 6.3, which plots the relation between 2006 year-end stock prices (shown on the vertical axis) and professional stock analysts' consensus forecasts of 2007 EPS (shown on the horizontal axis) for 43 restaurant firms where analysts' forecasts are available. Stock prices and EPS forecasts are both from December 2006. The upward-sloping regression line in Figure 6.3 now has an intercept ($\alpha$) estimate of $6.65 and a slope ($\beta$) coefficient

---

[16] The error term ($e_i$) in equation (6.7) does not show up in equation (6.8). That's because equation (6.8) is the expression for the *fitted regression line*. The vertical distance between the fitted regression line and the data points for individual firms in Figure 6.2 are the $e_i$ error terms in equation (6.7).

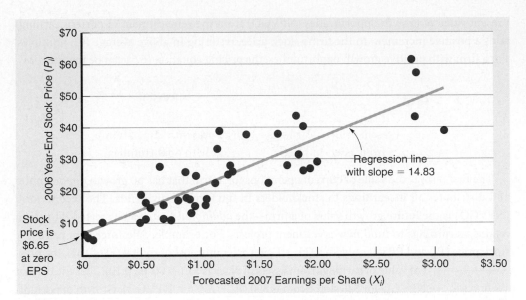

**Figure 6.3**

2006 STOCK PRICE AND
FORECASTED 2007 EPS
FOR 43 RESTAURANT
COMPANIES

Regression Result:

$P_i = \$6.65 + 14.83\,X_i$
$R^2 = 74.4\%$

estimate of 14.83. This means that a restaurant firm that analysts forecast to earn \$1 per share in 2007 would also be predicted to have a stock price of \$21.48 = \$6.65 + 14.83 × \$1. Notice that the percentage of share price variation explained by *expected* future earnings (the regression $R^2$) is 74.4%, more than that for *actual* current earnings (61.7%) but still less than 100%.

**Risk Differences**    Two firms with the same level of current *and* future expected earnings can sell for different prices because of differences in the risk or uncertainty associated with those earnings. Riskier firms have a higher risk-adjusted cost of capital, which means that the discount rate for capitalizing their earnings will be *higher,* resulting in *lower* share prices for those companies.

To illustrate, suppose that Firm A and Firm B both report current earnings of \$10 per share, and investors expect that these earnings will, on average, persist into the future forever. However, Firm A's earnings exhibit greater volatility over time—and therefore, greater risk—which results in a 15% cost of equity capital for Firm A. Firm B's earnings are more stable—that is, they represent a lower risk—so Firm B's cost of equity capital is only 10%.

The estimated share price for each firm would be:

| Firm A | Firm B |
|---|---|
| $\dfrac{\$10}{0.15} = \$66.67$ | $\dfrac{\$10}{0.10} = \$100$ |

Thus, despite having equal earnings, Firm A's share price will be one-third less than Firm B's (\$66.67 versus \$100) because Firm A is riskier and its cost of capital (15%) is higher than Firm B's (10%).

**Growth Opportunities**    Most firms' P/E ratios run between 10 and 30. However, it is not uncommon to find young companies such as Salesforce.com and high-tech companies such as PMC-Sierra trading at share prices 400 or 500 times more than their current EPS. What explains these exceptionally high P/E ratios?

In addition to valuing earnings generated from existing assets, the market values **growth opportunities**—that is, the firm's *potential earnings* from reinvesting current earnings in new projects that will eventually earn a rate of return in excess of the cost of equity capital. The net present value of growth opportunities (NPVGO) from the reinvestment of current earnings adds a positive increment to the firm's stock price, resulting in above average P/E multiples. For a firm with positive growth opportunities, the pricing equation (6.5) can be rewritten as:

$$P_0 = \underbrace{\frac{X_0}{r}}_{\substack{\text{Present value of earnings} \\ \text{from assets in place}}} + \underbrace{\text{NPVGO}}_{\substack{\text{Net present value of future} \\ \text{growth opportunities}}} \tag{6.9}$$

The first term is the value of current operations for a firm that has no growth opportunities and distributes all its earnings to stockholders in the form of dividends. The second term (NPVGO) is the future growth value of a firm—the *additional* share value created if the firm retains its earnings to fund new investment projects. For example, Salesforce.com has a $51 stock price ($P_0$) and EPS of only $0.10 ($X_0$). Using an equity cost of capital ($r$) of 10%, the present value of earnings from assets in place is $1 (= $0.10/0.10). This means that NPVGO for Salesforce.com is $50 ($P_0 - X_0/r = $ NPVGO). Growth opportunities thus comprise 98% of the company's stock price.

> If on the one hand, investors believe the firm will put money into worthwhile projects (that is, those with a *positive* net present value), NPVGO will be positive. On the other hand, if investors believe the firm will invest in unprofitable projects (that is, those with a *negative* net present value), NPVGO will be negative.

To illustrate the incremental value derived from growth opportunities, suppose that Firm A has 100,000 shares outstanding and can generate earnings of $1 million per year in perpetuity if it undertakes no new investment projects. Thus, its EPS now and in the future is $10 ($1 million/100,000 shares). If Firm A's cost of equity capital is 10%, the price per share is:

$$P_0 = \frac{X_0}{r} = \frac{\$10}{0.10} = \$100$$

Now assume that Firm A can reinvest all earnings from Period 0 in a project that is expected to increase earnings in Period 1 and *in every subsequent period* by $150,000, or $1.50 per share. This represents a 15% return on the reinvested earnings ($150,000/$1 million). If Firm A's cost of capital remains at 10%, the net present value of this investment project as of the start of period 1 is:

$$\underbrace{-\$1,000,000}_{\substack{\text{Earnings invested} \\ \text{at beginning of} \\ \text{Period 1}}} + \underbrace{\frac{\$150,000}{0.10}}_{\substack{\text{Present value at beginning of} \\ \text{Period 1 of incremental return} \\ \text{from reinvested earnings}}} = \$500,000$$

Because $500,000 is the project's net present value as of the beginning of Period 1, the value of the project today (time 0) can be determined by discounting back one period:

$$\frac{\$500,000}{(1 + 0.10)^1} = \$454,545$$

Thus, NPVGO per share is $454,545/$100,000 = $4.55. Firm A's price per share with this particular growth opportunity is:

$$P_0 = \frac{X_0}{r} + \text{NPVGO}$$

$$= \frac{\$10}{0.10} + \$4.55 = \$104.55$$

Note that the stock is now more valuable than it was with no growth ($100). That's because the firm is able to reinvest earnings in a project expected to earn a 15% rate of return (forever) when the firm's cost of capital or discount rate is only 10%. In this simplified example, the retention rate on earnings was 100%—meaning that none of the earnings were paid as dividends to shareholders. But this need not be the case for a firm to have growing earnings.

In general, the growth rate in earnings will depend on:

- The portion of earnings reinvested each period, called the **earnings retention rate.**[17]
- The rate of return earned on new investment ($r^*$).

As long as the retention rate is positive and as long as the return earned on new investment is more than the firm's cost of equity capital ($r^* > r$), NPVGO will be positive and will contribute to the P/E multiple. Return on common equity (ROCE), one of the key accounting performance measures introduced in Chapter 5, can be used to assess whether a firm is likely to earn a return on reinvested earnings that exceeds its cost of equity capital.

> Equation (6.7) is our simple earnings valuation equation: $P_i = \alpha + \beta X_i + e_i$ where $P$ is stock price, $X$ is earnings per share, $\alpha$ and $\beta$ are regression coefficients, and $e$ is the error term.

## Permanent, Transitory, and Valuation-Irrelevant Components of Earnings

If investors view firms' current earnings levels as likely to persist in perpetuity, then the slope coefficient ($\beta$) in equation (6.7) should equal the average earnings multiple for the particular companies and time period being examined. This prediction follows directly from the equity valuation model in equation (6.5), in which current earnings are translated into share price using an earnings multiple based on the risk-adjusted cost of equity capital. For example, if the average risk-adjusted cost of capital is 8%, then $\beta$ should be $1/0.08$, or 12.5. However, for many firms, the earnings multiple falls well below this theoretical value.[18] Why?

One explanation is that reported earnings numbers often contain three distinctly different components, each subject to a different earnings capitalization rate:

1. A **permanent earnings** component ($X_t^P$), which is expected to persist into the future and is therefore valuation-relevant. In theory, the multiple for this component should approach $1/r$.

2. A **transitory earnings** component ($X_t^T$), which is valuation relevant but is not expected to persist into the future. Because transitory earnings result from one-time events or transactions, the multiple for this component should approach 1.0.

3. A **value-irrelevant earnings** (or **noise**) component ($X_t^{VI}$), which is unrelated to future free cash flows or future earnings and, therefore, is *not* pertinent to assessing current share price. Such earnings components should carry a multiple of zero.[19]

> Investors may correctly view some items that comprise income from continuing operations as highly transitory and/or value-irrelevant and would be capitalized accordingly. Analysts call these "special" items. Examples include inventory holding gains and losses embedded in First-In, First-Out (FIFO) earnings and Last-In, First-Out (LIFO) liquidation profits that result when old LIFO inventory layers are sold. Later chapters discuss the value-relevance of these and other earnings and balance sheet items in considerable detail.

These three earnings components correspond roughly to the three broad classifications in the multiple-step income statements as described in Chapter 2. For example:

- *Income from continuing operations* (with the possible exception of certain so-called special items) is generally regarded as a recurring, sustainable component of a company's profit performance, and thus it would fall into the permanent earnings category.

---

[17] The earnings retention rate ($k$) is [(Earnings − Dividends)/Earnings]. One minus the retention rate ($1 − k$) is the **dividend payout ratio.**

[18] Notice that the slope coefficient of 14.28 for restaurants in Figure 6.2 suggests an earnings capitalization rate of 7.00% because $1/0.0700 = 14.28$.

[19] For a more formal discussion of these three earnings components and their valuation implication, see R. Ramakrishnan and J. Thomas, "Valuation of Permanent, Transitory, and Price-Irrelevant Components of Reported Earnings," *Journal of Accounting, Auditing and Finance*, Summer 1998, pp. 301–36.

- ***Income (loss) from discontinued operations and extraordinary gains and losses,*** on the other hand, are nonrecurring. These items are more likely to be viewed as transitory components of earnings and, therefore, to be valued at a much lower multiple than those items associated with permanent earnings components.

- A ***change in accounting principles,*** which has no future cash flow consequences to shareholders, may be viewed as "noise" that is valuation-irrelevant.

The idea that reported earnings may sometimes contain permanent, transitory, and value-irrelevant components suggests that $X_i$ (total earnings) in the simple P/E regression model of equation (6.7) should be rewritten as the sum of permanent, transitory, and valuation-irrelevant components—that is:

$$X_i = X_i^P + X_i^T + X_i^{VI}$$

This modification allows for a different multiple or capitalization rate for each earnings component in the valuation equation.[20]

$$P_i = \alpha + \underset{\uparrow}{\beta_P X_i^P} + \underset{\uparrow}{\beta_T X_i^T} + \underset{\uparrow}{\beta_{VI} X_i^{VI}} + e_i \quad \textbf{(6.10)}$$

Permanent component of earnings ↓ ; Transitory component of earnings ↓ ; Value-irrelevant component of earnings ↓

Earnings multiples for permanent ($\beta_P$), transitory ($\beta_T$), and value-irrelevant ($\beta_{VI}$) components of earnings

Equation (6.10) expresses share price as a function of the permanent, transitory, and valuation-irrelevant components of earnings. Each earnings component has a different earnings multiple—$\beta_P$, $\beta_T$, and $\beta_{VI}$, respectively.

In theory, permanent (sustainable) earnings should have a higher earnings multiple than transitory earnings because we expect the former to persist longer into the future—that is, $\beta_P$ should be higher than $\beta_T$.[21] Likewise, the multiple for transitory earnings should exceed the multiple for value-irrelevant earnings because the latter have no bearing on future cash flows and, therefore, have no bearing on price—that is, $\beta_{VI}$ should be 0 while $\beta_T$ should be approximately 1.0. Figure 6.4 illustrates these predictions about earnings multiples for different earnings components. The slope of each line corresponds to the earnings multiple for that particular earnings component, where $r$ equals 20%.

To illustrate the importance of distinguishing between permanent, transitory, and value-irrelevant earnings components, let's suppose that two companies report identical bottom-line earnings of $10 per share as in Exhibit 6.2. Does this mean they would necessarily sell for the same price? Perhaps not, as we will see.

A careful analysis of Firm A's financial statements and related footnotes reveals that its total earnings fall into three categories: (1) 60% that is judged to be value-relevant and permanent,

---

[20] You may wonder about the distinction between the value-irrelevant component ($X_i^{VI}$) and the error term ($e_i$) in equation (6.10). $X_i^{VI}$ is an earnings component that is not relevant to assessing share price. However, $e_i$ represents "other information" that is *not* a component of current earnings but *is* relevant to assessing price. For example, $e_i$ may represent news about a new scientific breakthrough or discovery the firm has just made. Such news would have a positive effect on share price, but it would not yet be reflected in current earnings.

[21] Lipe presents evidence consistent with this conjecture. He finds a greater stock price reaction to earnings components that exhibit greater permanence than to those components that are more transitory in nature. See R. Lipe "The Information Contained in the Components of Earnings," *Journal of Accounting Research,* Supplement 1986, pp. 33–64.

**Figure 6.4**

P/E MULTIPLES FOR
PERMANENT, TRANSITORY,
AND VALUE-IRRELEVANT
EARNINGS COMPONENTS
WITH $r = 20\%$

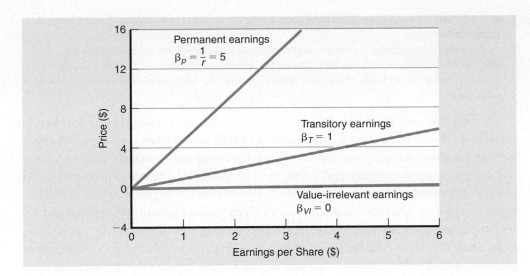

(2) 30% that is value-relevant but transitory, and (3) 10% that is considered value-irrelevant. Analysis of Firm B's financial report indicates its earnings composition is 50% permanent, 20% transitory, and 30% value-irrelevant. This decomposition of each firm's reported EPS is shown in Exhibit 6.2.

Using a 20% cost of capital to capitalize the permanent component of earnings, we find that the valuation model in equation (6.10) implies a stock price of $33 for Firm A and $27 for Firm B. Firm A's stock price is 22% higher than Firm B's price, even though both companies report the same EPS. In the vernacular of the analyst community, Firm A's stock sells for a higher earnings multiple because investors perceive its **earnings quality** to be superior to that of Firm B.

**The Concept of Earnings Quality**     A *Wall Street Journal* article described earnings quality and its implications for stock prices:

> Quality of earnings measures how much the profits companies publicly report diverge from their true operating earnings. Low quality means the bottom line is padded with paper gains—such as the profit-fattening effect of inflation on a company's reported inventory values, or gains produced

| EXHIBIT 6.2 | Applying P/E Multiples to Earnings Components | |
|---|---|---|
| | **Firm A** | **Firm B** |
| EPS as reported | $10 | $10 |
| Analyst's EPS decomposition | | |
| Permanent component | 60% of $10 = $6 | 50% of $10 = $5 |
| Transitory component | 30% of $10 = $3 | 20% of $10 = $2 |
| Value-irrelevant component | 10% of $10 = $1 | 30% of $10 = $3 |
| Earnings multiple applied to each earnings component at cost of capital of $r = 20\%$ | | |
| Permanent component ($\beta_p = 5 = 1/0.20$) | 5 × $6 = 30 | 5 × $5 = 25 |
| Transitory component ($\beta_T = 1$) | 1 × $3 = 3 | 1 × $2 = 2 |
| Value-irrelevant component ($\beta_{VI} = 0$) | 0 × $1 = 0 | 0 × $3 = 0 |
| Implied share price | $33 | $27 |
| Implied total earnings multiple (share price/EPS as reported) | 3.3 | 2.7 |

by "underdepreciation," when a company doesn't write off plant and equipment as fast as their real value is falling.

Because a decline in quality means companies' reported earnings are weaker and less sustainable than they appear, it indicates likely trouble for future earnings—whether or not a recession arrives. If history is any guide, those lower quality earnings also will come home to roost in lower stock prices. . . .[22]

The notion of earnings quality is multifaceted, and there is no consensus on how best to measure it.[23] Basically, earnings are considered to be high quality when they are *sustainable*— for example, those that are generated from repeat customers and from high-quality products that enjoy steady consumer demand. Examples of *un*sustainable earnings items include gains or losses from debt retirement; asset write-offs from corporate restructuring and plant closings; or temporary reductions in discretionary expenditures for advertising, research and development, or employee training. Accrual accounting treats these discretionary expenditures as expenses. One way a firm can boost earnings temporarily is by cutting back on the amount spent for these activities. However, earnings increases of this type are not sustainable because the expenditures are critical to creating future demand for the firm's products and to creating new products or developing competent management—all important determinants of long-run sustainable earnings.

Earnings quality is also affected by the accounting methods management chooses to describe routine, ongoing business activities (such as using LIFO rather than FIFO for inventory accounting). Earnings quality is also affected by the subjectivity—it's unavoidable!—of accounting estimates (for example, the estimated allowance for future uncollectibles).

Does earnings quality matter? One study finds that when reported earnings are adjusted for quality differences—for example, subtracting (or adding back) transitory gains (or losses) or adjusting for differences in inventory methods (FIFO versus LIFO)—the "quality-adjusted" earnings numbers better explain why firms' stocks sell for different prices.[24] These results suggest that differences in earnings quality are associated with differences in the overall earnings capitalization rate (earnings multiple) that investors assign to reported earnings when determining share prices. Notice carefully that as transitory ($X_t^T$) or value-irrelevant ($X_t^{VI}$) components become a larger part of a firm's reported earnings:

- The quality of those reported earnings is eroded.
- Reported earnings become a less reliable indicator of the company's long-run sustainable cash flows.
- Hence, earnings are a less reliable indicator of fundamental value.

This is illustrated in Exhibit 6.2, where we see that Firm B (with a higher proportion of transitory or value-irrelevant components of earnings) has an overall earnings multiple of 2.7 compared to 3.3 for Firm A. Suppose that all of the reported earnings were considered

---

[22] B. Donnelly, "Profits' 'Quality' Erodes, Making Them Less Reliable," *The Wall Street Journal,* October 18, 1990.

[23] See L. Bernstein and J. Siegel, "The Concept of Earnings Quality," *Financial Analysts Journal,* July–August 1979, pp. 72–75; and J. Siegel, "The 'Quality of Earnings' Concept—A Survey," *Financial Analysts Journal,* March–April 1982, pp. 60–68.

[24] See B. Lev and R. Thiagarajan, "Fundamental Information Analysis," *Journal of Accounting Research,* Autumn 1993, pp. 190–215. To arrive at "quality-adjusted" earnings the researchers start with reported earnings and then eliminate revenue or expense items thought to be transitory or value-irrelevant. Additional research insights about earnings quality can be found in D. Cohen, "Quality of Financial Reporting Choice: Determinants and Economic Consequences," Working Paper, New York University, December 2003; K. Schipper and L. Vincent, "Earnings Quality," *Accounting Horizons,* Supplement 2003, pp. 97–110; and S. Whisenant and P. Fairfield, "Using Fundamental Analysis to Assess Earnings Quality: Evidence from the Center for Financial Research and Analysis," *Journal of Accounting, Auditing and Finance,* Fall 2001, pp. 273–95.

permanent. Then the stock would sell for $10/0.20 = $50$, and the earnings multiple would be 5. Low-quality earnings will be assigned a lower overall earnings multiple and capitalized at a lower rate.

The research to date suggests that the capital market is rather sophisticated—it does not react naively to reported earnings, but instead it appears to distinguish among permanent, transitory, and value-irrelevant earnings components. Investors recognize differences in the quality of reported earnings numbers and consider these differences when assessing the implications of earnings reports for share prices. From time to time throughout this book, we will come back to this idea as we discuss alternative accounting treatments both for on-going events and for specialized transactions and as we review the academic and professional research literature on the valuation-relevance of alternative accounting methods and footnote disclosures.

---

RE CAP

**Firms' shares often sell at prices that differ from multiplying current reported earnings by the average earnings multiple for their industry. A variety of factors contribute to variation in P/E multiples. These include differences in risk; in growth opportunities; and in what proportions of current earnings are considered to be permanent, transitory, and value-irrelevant. The persistence of earnings is related to earnings quality—higher quality earnings are more persistent and sustainable. Assessing earnings quality involves using information from a multiple-step income statement, a balance sheet, a cash flow statement, financial footnotes, and Management's Discussion and Analysis (MD&A) to identify components of current earnings that are likely to be sustainable in contrast to those that are transitory or price irrelevant.**

## The Abnormal Earnings Approach to Equity Valuation

In the previous section, we found that the role of accounting earnings information in equity valuation is *indirect*—earnings are useful only because they help generate forecasts of future free cash flows. These future free cash flow estimates were then discounted to arrive at an estimated value for the company and its shares. Recently, another valuation approach has emerged in practice that uses earnings and equity book value numbers themselves as *direct* inputs in the valuation process. Under many circumstances, this new earnings-based approach leads to valuation estimates that are equivalent to the free cash flow approach. So, why is it important to learn about this new approach? Because it helps us better understand the economic forces that influence share prices over time and across firms.

This new approach is based on the notion that a company's value (and its share price) is driven not by the level of earnings themselves but by the level of earnings *relative to a fundamental economic benchmark*. That benchmark is the cost of capital expressed in dollars, and it reflects the level of earnings investors demand from the company as compensation for the risks of investment. Investors willingly pay a premium only for those firms that earn more than the cost of capital—meaning firms that produce **positive abnormal earnings.** For firms whose earnings are "ordinary" or "normal"—that is, have an earnings rate equal to the cost of capital—investors are willing to pay only an amount equal to the underlying book value of net assets. Firms that earn less than the cost of capital—that is, that produce **negative abnormal earnings**—have a share price *below* book

> In theory, the abnormal earnings approach and the free cash flow approach *always* produce the same valuation estimate. In practice, however, the two approaches sometimes produce different valuation estimates. When this occurs, it's because the analyst has introduced shortcuts and simplifications that produce errors in one or both valuation estimates.

value and thus sell at a discount. This relationship between share prices, book value, and abnormal earnings performance is expressed mathematically as:[25]

$$P_0 \;=\; \underset{\substack{\uparrow \\ \text{Book value of}\\ \text{equity at Time 0}}}{BV_0} \;+\; \sum_{t=1}^{\infty} \frac{\overset{\substack{\text{Expected future abnormal}\\ \text{earnings}}}{E_0(\text{abnormal earnings}_t)}}{(1+r)^t} \qquad (6.11)$$

Share price at Time 0 ↑ ($P_0$)

Discount factors for each future period ↑ ($(1+r)^t$)

where $BV$ denotes the equity book value (assets minus liabilities, or net assets) per share that shareholders have invested in the firm, $E_0$ denotes the expectation about future abnormal EPS formed at Time 0, and $r$ is the equity cost of capital.

The cost of equity capital, $r$, also corresponds to the risk-adjusted return that stockholders *require* from their investment. So, the earnings level the company must generate in period $t$ to satisfy stockholders is $r \times BV_{t-1}$, or stockholders' required rate of return multiplied by the beginning of period $(t-1)$ invested capital. Any difference between actual earnings for the period $(X_t)$ and stockholders' required dollar return on invested capital for the period $(r \times BV_{t-1})$ represents **abnormal earnings.**

$$\text{Abnormal earnings}_t \;=\; \underset{\substack{\uparrow \\ \text{Actual}\\ \text{earnings}}}{X_t} \;-\; \underset{\substack{\uparrow \\ \text{Required}\\ \text{earnings}}}{(r \times BV_{t-1})} \qquad (6.12)$$

To illustrate, suppose a company's equity book value ($BV$) at the beginning of the year is $100 per share, and the cost of equity ($r$) is 15%. Stockholders therefore require earnings of at least $100 × 15%, or $15 per share. If investors expect the company to report earnings equal to the benchmark earnings of $15 per share, but the company does even better and earns $20 per share—thus exceeding the benchmark—its stock price will increase to reflect its superior performance. If actual earnings are only $10—thus falling short of the benchmark expected earnings—the stock price will fall. The amount of the stock price increase (or decline) depends on the degree to which stockholders believe that abnormal earnings (earnings above *or* below the benchmark) are permanent rather than transitory.

Exhibit 6.3 shows how the abnormal earnings approach can be used to assign a value to Willard Brown's truck rental business. You remember Brown? Here's a description of the business opportunity along with some additional information pertinent to the abnormal earnings valuation approach.

---

[25] Several variations of the abnormal earnings valuation model have appeared in the literature. Recent examples include J. Ohlson, "Earnings, Book Values, and Dividends in Equity Valuation," *Contemporary Accounting Research,* Spring 1995, pp. 661–87; T. Koller, M. Goedhart, and D. Wessels, *Valuation: Measuring and Managing the Value of Companies* (New York: Wiley, 2005); R. Lundholm and R. Sloan, *Equity Valuation and Analysis* (New York: McGraw-Hill, 2007); B. Madden, *CFROI Valuation* (Boston, MA: Butterworth-Heinemann, 1999); S. Penman, *Financial Statement Analysis and Security Valuation* (New York: McGraw-Hill, 2007); L. Soffer and R. Soffer, *Financial Statement Analysis: A Valuation Approach* (Upper Saddle River, NJ: Prentice Hall, 2003); and G. B. Stewart III, *The Quest for Value* (New York: Harper Business, 1991).

| EXHIBIT 6.3 | Illustration of the Abnormal Earnings Approach to Valuation |
| --- | --- |

| | Year 1 | Year 2 | Year 3 | Year 4 | Year 5 |
| --- | --- | --- | --- | --- | --- |
| Summary earnings and equity book value | | | | | |
| Beginning book value of equity | $80,000 | $67,830 | $75,660 | $60,440 | $45,220 |
| Net income for the year | 7,830 | 7,830 | 9,780 | 9,780 | 9,780 |
| Dividends paid to shareholders | (20,000) | — | (25,000) | (25,000) | (25,000) |
| Ending book value of equity | $67,830 | $75,660 | $60,440 | $45,220 | $30,000 |

**Step 1:** Forecast expected future abnormal earnings

| | Year 1 | Year 2 | Year 3 | Year 4 | Year 5 |
| --- | --- | --- | --- | --- | --- |
| Expected future earnings (net income) | $ 7,830 | $ 7,830 | $ 9,780 | $ 9,780 | $ 9,780 |
| | | | | | |
| Beginning equity book value | $80,000 | $67,830 | $75,660 | $60,440 | $45,220 |
| Investors required rate of return | 10% | 10% | 10% | 10% | 10% |
| Required ("normal") earnings | $ 8,000 | $ 6,783 | $ 7,566 | $ 6,044 | $ 4,522 |
| Expected future abnormal earnings | $ (170) | $ 1,047 | $ 2,214 | $ 3,736 | $ 5,258 |

**Step 2:** Determine the present value of expected future abnormal earnings

| | Year 1 | Year 2 | Year 3 | Year 4 | Year 5 |
| --- | --- | --- | --- | --- | --- |
| Expected future abnormal earnings | $ (170) | $1,047 | $ 2,214 | $ 3,736 | $ 5,258 |
| Present value factor | 0.90909 | 0.82645 | 0.75131 | 0.68301 | 0.62092 |
| Present value of each future abnormal earnings | $ (155) | $ 865 | $ 1,663 | $ 2,552 | $ 3,265 |

| | |
| --- | --- |
| Sum of all present values | $ 8,191 |
| Beginning equity book value | $80,000 |
| Value of business opportunity | $88,191 |
| Value per share | $ 88.19 ◄ |

> This is the same value estimate we obtained using the discounted free cash flow approach in Exhibit 6.1.

---

Willard Brown is thinking about starting a truck rental business. If you recall, he plans to buy four trucks now and then to add a fifth truck in two years. Each truck will cost $20,000, and he believes each will generate $5,000 of net operating cash flows every year. At the end of five years, he thinks he can sell the trucks for $30,000 in total.

Additional information:

- Brown will put $80,000 cash into the business. This amount represents his beginning equity.
- The company will pay out all excess cash as dividends each year. The cash needed to buy the last truck in Year 2 will come from operating cash flows that year. No new investment will be required.
- Net income includes truck depreciation and is estimated to be $7,830 in Years 1 and 2 and $9,780 each year in the final three years.
- The $30,000 received for the trucks at the end of five years equals their book value at that point in time. No gain or loss is to be recorded on the sale of the trucks.

---

If we use the abnormal earnings approach instead of the free cash flow approach to determine the value of Brown's business, how much will it be worth?

The top portion of Exhibit 6.3 describes how the book value of equity is forecasted to change over time. Equity book value is increased by net income for the year and decreased when dividends are paid to shareholders. Notice that Brown's company does not pay a dividend in Year 2. Why? Because the entire $20,000 of operating cash flows generated that year (4 trucks × $5,000 operating cash flow per truck) is needed to buy the fifth and final truck.

Step 1 of Exhibit 6.3 illustrates the computation of expected future abnormal earnings from the truck business. Each year the beginning book value of equity is multiplied by the rate of return required by investors (10% in this example) to arrive at required or "normal" earnings. For example, the required earnings threshold in Year 1 is $8,000, or $80,000 of initial equity capital multiplied by the 10% required rate of return. The $8,000 required earnings is then subtracted from the $7,830 of forecasted earnings for the year to arrive at expected abnormal earnings of −$170.

Step 2 of Exhibit 6.3 then determines the present value of expected future abnormal earnings over the life of the truck rental business (5 years). The discount factors shown are the same ones used in the discounted free cash flow approach described earlier (see Exhibit 6.1). The individual present values are then summed, and this amount ($8,191) is added to the beginning book value of equity ($80,000) to arrive at the estimated value of the truck rental business ($88,191, or $88.19 per share). This is the same value estimate we developed using the free cash flow approach!

Financial statements and related footnotes provide a wealth of information for assessing the relationships expressed by abnormal earnings valuation equations (6.11) and (6.12). The balance sheet provides detailed information on the book value of equity (assets minus liabilities). The income statement provides detailed information for assessing a firm's earnings. As you have seen, we can use these numbers from a firm's financial statements to determine its worth via the abnormal earnings approach.

### Abnormal Earnings and ROCE

ROCE combines information about earnings and equity book value—two financial statement items essential to the abnormal earnings valuation approach. A firm's ROCE can be compared to its required rate of return on common equity (cost of equity capital) or to the ROCEs of other companies in the industry to evaluate its prospects for generating "abnormal earnings." Companies with ROCEs that consistently exceed the industry average generally have shares that sell for a premium relative to book value (that is, a higher market-to-book ratio).

Figure 6.5 plots the relationship between the 2006 ROCE (measured on the horizontal axis) and the 2006 year-end market-to-book ratio (measured on the vertical axis) for 48 restaurant

## Figure 6.5

RELATIONSHIP BETWEEN ROCE PERFORMANCE AND MARKET-TO-BOOK (M/B) RATIOS FOR 48 RESTAURANT COMPANIES

Regression Result:

$$M/B = 1.31 + 0.13\,ROCE$$
$$R^2 = 59.1\%$$

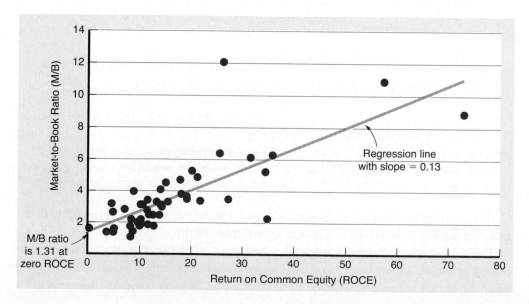

companies. The upward-sloping line represents the estimated regression line of ROCE versus market-to-book ratio for these companies. The regression line has an intercept estimate of 1.31 and a slope coefficient estimate of 0.13. According to the regression line, a restaurant company that earned an ROCE of 20% should have a market-to-book ratio of 3.91 (or 1.31 + [0.13 × 20]). A market-to-book ratio of 3.91 means that the company's shares sell for a substantial premium of almost three times their equity book value.

In making comparisons across firms, the analyst must be careful to gauge the quality and comparability of the accounting policies or methods used. For example, does the company being analyzed tend to select liberal accounting methods (those that may increase earnings and net asset values) or more conservative methods (those that may decrease earnings and net asset values). The degree of conservatism associated with a firm's accounting choices has a direct bearing on the relationship among share price, earnings, and equity book value components of equation (6.11). To see this, let us consider a company that has a $10 share price and an $8 per share equity book value. Analysts who understand the accounting complexities described later in this book know there are two reasons why this company's stock may be valued at a $2 premium to equity book value. One reason is that shareholders believe the company will produce abnormal earnings in the future, and those future earnings are worth—according to equation (6.11)—$2 today. A second possibility, however, is that stockholders expect the company to produce only "normal" earnings in the future (that is, zero abnormal earnings), but they recognize that the company's conservative accounting methods understate equity book value by $2 per share.[26]

Much of the information needed for assessing the quality and value relevance of a company's reported accounting numbers appears in footnotes to its financial statements. These footnotes describe accounting policies for matters such as revenue recognition (completed contract versus percentage of completion), depreciation (straight line versus accelerated), and inventory valuation (LIFO versus FIFO). Later chapters will clarify the important differences in these and other accounting methods and their impact on earnings and balance sheet book values. In certain instances, we show how you can adjust reported numbers to put firms that use different methods on a more equal footing before using those numbers for valuation purposes.

RECAP

**The abnormal earnings approach to valuation says a company's future earnings are determined by (1) the resources (net assets) available to management and (2) the rate of return or profitability earned on those net assets. If a firm can earn a return on net assets (common equity book value) that *exceeds* its cost of equity capital, it will generate positive abnormal earnings. Its stock will then sell at a premium relative to book value. However, if the firm earns a return on net assets that falls *below* its cost of equity capital, it will generate negative abnormal earnings. Its stock will then sell at a discount relative to book value. A key feature of this valuation model is that it explicitly takes into account a cost for the capital (net assets) provided by the owners of the business. Value is added only if the earnings generated from those net assets exceed the equity cost of capital benchmark. Appendix A to this chapter illustrates how to use this valuation model for a real company.**

---

[26] For a further discussion of these points and the implications of the abnormal earnings valuation model, see G. Feltham and J. Ohlson, "Valuation and Clean Surplus Accounting for Operating and Financial Assets," *Contemporary Accounting Research*, Spring 1995, pp. 689–731; V. Bernard. "The Feltham-Ohlson Framework: Implications for Empiricists," *Contemporary Accounting Research*, Spring 1995, pp. 733–47; Lundholm and Sloan, ibid.; Penman, ibid.; Soffer and Soffer, ibid.; and Stewart, ibid.

## Application: Valuing a Business Opportunity

Allen Ford's passion for literature motivated him to consider opening a neighborhood bookstore. Ford convinced a colleague who was an expert in market research to look at the economic viability of a general title bookstore. The results of his analysis fueled Ford's enthusiasm: The market demographics were favorable, and there was little competition. Annual sales were projected to ultimately reach $350,000.

Ford rejected the notion of opening his own independent bookstore, however, and instead focused on several franchise opportunities. By affiliating with a national or regional company, he would enjoy brand-name recognition, economies of scale in purchasing and advertising, and employee training and support programs. After investigating several possibilities, Allen settled on The BookWorm, an expanding regional chain of franchised bookstores that emphasized convenience, price, selection, and neighborhood friendliness. Each store had a coffee bar surrounded by soft seating. Abundant natural light encouraged patrons to browse in a leisurely fashion. The franchise had a proven record of success in similar communities, and it appealed to Ford's tastes.

Ford learned that a BookWorm store could be established for about $100,000, including the initial franchise fee of $21,000, store fixtures of $20,000 to $25,000, and an inventory cost of $55,000 to $60,000. The inventory and fixtures would be purchased from the corporate parent, BookWorm, Inc. Corporate staff would conduct a site location study, assist in negotiating lease terms for retail space, help with store layout and renovation, train employees on operating policies and procedures, and provide all grand opening advertising and promotional materials. Once a new BookWorm franchise opened, the corporate parent received royalties (typically as a percentage of sales) determined in accordance with a 15-year renewable franchise contract.

The prospectus that Ford obtained from the parent company contained the selected financial highlights for a typical BookWorm franchise store shown in Exhibit 6.4. The notes accompanying the exhibit indicated that store fixtures are depreciated over 10 years; the initial franchise fee is amortized over 15 years; operating expenses include a competitive salary for a store manager; and income taxes have been ignored because they are owner specific, thus making them highly variable across locations.

| EXHIBIT 6.4 | BookWorm Franchise |
|---|---|

**Projected Sales, Earnings, Free Cash Flows, and Owner's Investment**

|  | Year 1 | Year 2 | Year 3 | Year 4 | Year 5 |
|---|---|---|---|---|---|
| Sales | $200,000 | $250,000 | $300,000 | $325,000 | $350,000 |
| Franchise royalty (5%) | 10,000 | 12,500 | 15,000 | 16,250 | 17,500 |
| Pre-tax earnings | (6,832) | 3,600 | 13,750 | 22,000 | 26,000 |
| Free cash flows* | (3,000) | 5,500 | 15,000 | 16,000 | 24,500 |
| Assets at year-end | 100,000 | 100,000 | 100,000 | 100,000 | 100,000 |
| Owner's investment: |  |  |  |  |  |
| Beginning of year | 100,000 | 100,000 | 100,000 | 100,000 | 100,000 |
| + Pre-tax earnings | (6,832) | 3,600 | 13,750 | 22,000 | 26,000 |
| − Distribution to owner | 6,832 | (3,600) | (13,750) | (22,000) | (26,000) |
| = End of year | $100,000 | $100,000 | $100,000 | $100,000 | $100,000 |

* Free cash flows are cash from operations minus required capital expenditures.

With these financial projections and his understanding of the marketplace, Allen Ford had to decide whether to invest $100,000 in a BookWorm franchise. Influencing the decision were several nonfinancial considerations such as his confidence in BookWorm's corporate staff and the proposed interior design and ambiance of the shop. However, viewed through the stark lens of economics, Ford's decision problem simplifies to the standard **net present value rule**— invest if the estimated value of the franchise (adjusted for the risk of investment) exceeds its $100,000 cost. From trade sources, Ford learned that 16% was a reasonable estimate of the cost of equity capital for franchised neighborhood bookstores. Allen used two different approaches to estimate the value of the bookstore, relying on predictions contained in the **pro forma,** or forecasted, financial statements whenever possible.

The first approach, based on expected future *free cash flows,* is summarized in Exhibit 6.5. Sales and free cash flow projections for Years 1 through 5 are taken directly from the pro forma financial statement data in Exhibit 6.4. Ford believes that sales will remain flat after Year 5 and that free cash flows will average about $24,500 per year thereafter. These assumptions produce a Year 5 **terminal value** estimate of $153,125—that is, the present value (at the end of Year 5) of the perpetual $24,500 free cash flow per year, discounted at a 16% cost of equity capital.

When the terminal value at the end of Year 5 is discounted back to the present (beginning of Year 1) and added to the sum of the present value of expected free cash flows for Year 1 through Year 5, the result is a free cash flow value estimate for the bookstore of $104,517, as shown in Exhibit 6.5. This amount is *higher* than Ford's required capital investment of $100,000—this means Ford will be earning a return in excess of 16% per year on his investment *if* he opens the bookstore and the financial projections underlying the valuation estimate prove correct.

A second approach for estimating the value of Ford's business opportunity relies on expected future *abnormal earnings*—the amount by which operating earnings each year exceed the dollar cost of capital for the bookstore. This valuation, also based on projections contained in the pro forma financial statements, is summarized in Exhibit 6.6. In addition to flat sales

---

| EXHIBIT 6.5 | BookWorm Franchise |
|---|---|

**Valuation of Expected Future Cash Flows**

| | Year 1 | Year 2 | Year 3 | Year 4 | Year 5 | Beyond Year 5 |
|---|---|---|---|---|---|---|
| **(a) Financial Projections** | | | | | | |
| Sales | $200,000 | $250,000 | $300,000 | $325,000 | $350,000 | $350,000 |
| Free cash flows | $ (3,000) | $ 5,500 | $ 15,000 | $ 16,000 | $ 24,500 | $ 24,500 |
| *As a percentage of sales* | *−1.5%* | *2.2%* | *5.0%* | *4.9%* | *7.0%* | *7.0%* |
| | | | | | *Estimated terminal value* = $24,500/0.16 | |
| **(b) Valuation Estimate at 16%** | | | | | | |
| Expected future cash flow | $ (3,000) | $ 5,500 | $ 15,000 | $ 16,000 | $ 24,500 | $153,125* |
| × Discount factor at 16% | 0.86207 | 0.74316 | 0.64066 | 0.55229 | 0.47611 | 0.47611 |
| = Present value of each flow | $ (2,586) | $ 4,087 | $ 9,610 | $ 8,837 | $ 11,665 | $ 72,904 |
| **(c) Estimated Value** (sum of all present values above) | $104,517 | | | | | |

* Rounded

| EXHIBIT 6.6 | BookWorm Franchise |
|---|---|

### Valuation of Expected Abnormal Earnings

|  | Year 1 | Year 2 | Year 3 | Year 4 | Year 5 | Beyond Year 5 |
|---|---|---|---|---|---|---|
| **(a) Computation of Abnormal Earnings** |  |  |  |  |  |  |
| Equity book value (beginning of year) | $100,000 | $100,000 | $100,000 | $100,000 | $100,000 | $100,000 |
| × Cost of equity capital = 16% | 0.16 | 0.16 | 0.16 | 0.16 | 0.16 | 0.16 |
| = Normal earnings | $ 16,000 | $ 16,000 | $ 16,000 | $ 16,000 | $ 16,000 | $ 16,000 |
| Projected pre-tax earnings (loss) | $ (6,832) | $ 3,600 | $ 13,750 | $ 22,000 | $ 26,000 | $ 25,000 |
| − Normal earnings | (16,000) | (16,000) | (16,000) | (16,000) | (16,000) | (16,000) |
| = Abnormal earnings (loss) | $ (22,832) | $ (12,400) | $ (2,250) | $ 6,000 | $ 10,000 | $ 9,000 |
| **(b) Valuation Estimate at 16%** |  |  |  |  | *Estimated terminal value* = $9,000/0.16 |  |
| Expected abnormal earnings (loss) | $ (22,832) | $ (12,400) | $ (2,250) | $ 6,000 | $ 10,000 | $ 56,250 |
| × Discount factor at 16% | 0.86207 | 0.74316 | 0.64066 | 0.55229 | 0.47611 | 0.47611 |
| = Present value of each abnormal earnings flow | $ (19,683) | $ (9,215) | $ (1,441) | $ 3,314 | $ 4,761 | $ 26,781 |
| **(c) Estimated Value** |  |  |  |  |  |  |
| Sum of all present values | $ 4,517 |  |  |  |  |  |
| Capital to start the business | 100,000 |  |  |  |  |  |
| Estimated value | $104,517 |  |  |  |  |  |

Before investing, Ford should perform a **sensitivity analysis** of the free cash flow and abnormal earnings valuation estimates. Sensitivity analysis involves constructing "best-case" and "worst-case" scenarios for the business that incorporate alternative assumptions about sales, costs, and competitor behavior. Each scenario produces financial forecasts that become the basis for revised free cash flow and abnormal earnings valuation estimates. In this way, Ford could learn how alternative economic conditions might affect the bookstore's value and his return on investment.

and free cash flow in Year 5, Ford is projecting flat pre-tax earnings of $25,000 for each year beyond Year 5.

Part (a) of Exhibit 6.6 describes the calculation of yearly abnormal earnings. First, the 16% Cost of equity capital is multiplied by the beginning book value of equity to produce a figure called **Normal earnings** in each year. The component Normal earnings is the profit level that investors (including Ford) demand from the business to earn their 16% per year required rate of return. Then Normal earnings is subtracted from Projected pre-tax earnings to produce an estimate of expected Abnormal earnings for each year.

In part (b), the Beyond Year 5 Terminal value estimate of $56,250 represents the present value (at the end of Year 5) of the perpetual $9,000 per year abnormal earnings flow from Year 6 to infinity, discounted at a 16% cost of equity capital. The present value (as of the beginning of Year 1) of all abnormal earnings sums to $4,517. This amount, when added to the $100,000 of capital required to start the business, yields a valuation estimate for the bookstore of $104,517. Once again, the analysis supports opening the bookstore.

## EARNINGS SURPRISES

Both the earnings capitalization model (equation [6.4]) and the abnormal earnings model (equation [6.11]) share a common characteristic: Each requires estimates of future earnings. But estimates can (and usually do) prove to be incorrect. When this happens, an "earnings surprise" results.

Two recent examples follow:

- *October 22, 2007*: Apple Inc.—the maker of iPods, iPhones, and Macintosh computers—reports fourth quarter EPS of $1.42, or 3 cents more than Wall Street analysts are forecasting. Apple shares rise 7% on the Nasdaq stock market.
- *October 23, 2007*: Arrow Electronics, a distributor of electronic components, reports third quarter EPS of $0.79, or 3 cents less than Wall Street analysts' consensus forecast. Arrow shares fall 9% on the New York Stock Exchange.

If securities markets are rational and efficient in the sense that they fully and correctly impound all available information into a company's stock price, the price will reflect investors' *unbiased* expectations about the company's future earnings and cash flows. These expectations take into account a vast array of information available to the public, including information about the company's earnings and cash flow history, product market conditions, competitor actions, and other factors. For example, the stock prices of General Motors and Ford incorporate information about unit sales figures published weekly in the financial press as well as expectations about changes in interest rates because interest rates influence consumers' car-buying behavior. Stock prices move up or down as investors receive new information and then revise their expectations about the future earnings and cash flow prospects of the company. Financial reports are an important source of information that investors use to update their expectations.

> *Unbiased* means that, on average, the market's earnings expectations will be correct—not too high or too low.

Consider a typical General Motors quarterly earnings announcement that is released through major financial wire services. If reported quarterly earnings correspond exactly to the earnings investors expected before the announcement, the investors have no reason to alter their expectations about GM's future earnings or cash flows. The reported quarterly earnings simply *confirm* the market's expectations. In other words, although the earnings release may resolve market uncertainty about current earnings, it does not provide new information to investors. On the other hand, if reported quarterly earnings deviate from investors' expectations, this **earnings surprise** represents new information that investors will use to revise their expectations about the company's future earnings and cash flow prospects. Of course, this change in investor expectations will cause the company's stock price to change following the earnings announcement. That's what happened at Apple and Arrow Electronics.

> Stock price changes can also occur because of unanticipated changes in interest (discount) rates over time.

The way stock prices change in response to new information about earnings can be expressed mathematically as follows:

> The change in stock price from one point in time to another can also be influenced by dividends. Consequently, some versions of equation (6.13) include a dividend term so that the resulting price change (defined as $P_t + D_t - P_{t-1}$) better isolates the impact of new earnings information. A similar (but more complicated) expression for earnings announcement stock price changes can be derived from the abnormal earnings valuation equation (6.10). Until recently, however, most "earnings surprise" research has used variations of equation (6.13).

$$
\underset{\substack{\text{Price change from}\\ \text{period } t-1 \text{ to } t \\ \downarrow}}{P_t - P_{t-1}} = \underset{\substack{\text{Current earnings}\\ \text{surprise}\\ \downarrow}}{\overbrace{X_t - E_{t-1}(\widetilde{X}_t)}} + \underset{\substack{\text{Change } (\Delta) \text{ in expectations}\\ \text{about future earnings}\\ \downarrow}}{\sum_{k=1}^{\infty} \frac{\Delta E_t(\widetilde{X}_{t+k})}{(1+r)^k}}
\tag{6.13}
$$

where:

- $P_t - P_{t-1}$ is the stock price change from just before to just after the earnings announcement.
- $X_t - E_{t-1}(\widetilde{X}_t)$ is the earnings "surprise" or deviation of reported earnings from the market's expectation just *before* the earnings announcement.
- $\sum_{k=1}^{\infty} \dfrac{\Delta E_t(\widetilde{X}_{t+k})}{(1+r)^k}$, the summation term, represents the valuation impact of revised expectations about all future earnings.

## Figure 6.6

STOCK RETURNS AND
QUARTERLY EARNINGS
"SURPRISES"

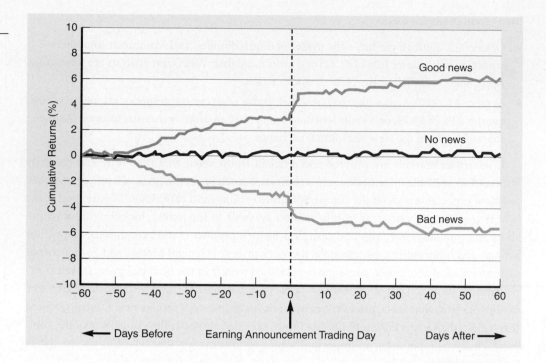

Figure 6.6 illustrates the typical behavior of stock returns (the price change divided by $P_{t-1}$) leading up to and following quarterly earnings announcements for three different scenarios:

1.  Reported earnings are viewed as a *good news* earnings surprise because they exceed market expectations (think Apple Inc.).

2.  Reported earnings contain *no news* because they correspond exactly to market expectations.

3.  Reported earnings are viewed as a *bad news* earnings surprise because they fall below market expectations (think Arrow Electronics).[27]

Companies that report good news earnings (a positive earnings surprise) tend to have an upward drift in stock returns before the actual earnings announcement date (Day 0 in Figure 6.6), followed by another stock return increase on announcement. The stock returns of companies reporting bad news earnings surprises exhibit a negative drift before the announcement followed by another decrease in stock returns at the announcement date. Modest postannouncement drifts in stock returns are also not uncommon, especially when the earnings surprise is quite large.[28] Quarterly earnings announcements that contain "no news" lead to stock returns that hover around zero before and after announcement.

It's easy to explain why stock prices sometimes exhibit a positive or negative drift *before* the actual earnings announcement date. Consider General Motors. Investors learn about the

---

[27] For early research on the association between earnings surprises and stock returns, see R. Ball and P. Brown, "An Empirical Evaluation of Accounting Income Numbers," *Journal of Accounting Research,* Autumn 1968, pp. 159–78; and G. Foster, C. Olsen, and T. Shevlin, "Earnings Releases, Anomalies, and the Behavior of Security Returns," *The Accounting Review,* October 1984, pp. 574–603. Recent research is summarized in S. Kothari, "Capital Market Research in Accounting," *Journal of Accounting and Economics,* September 2001, pp. 105–232.

[28] A number of studies investigate whether postearnings announcement drift is a profit opportunity for investors. For a review of this literature, see V. Bernard, "Stock Price Reactions to Earnings Announcements: A Summary of Recent Anomalous Evidence and Possible Explanations," in R. Thaler (ed.), *Advances in Behavioral Finance* (New York: Russell Sage Foundation, 1992); and V. Bernard, J. Thomas, and J. Abarbanell, "How Sophisticated Is the Market in Interpreting Earnings News?" *Journal of Applied Corporate Finance,* Summer 1993, pp. 54–63.

company's automobile sales on a weekly basis and therefore can anticipate fairly well the actual quarterly earnings number prior to its formal announcement by GM. The fact that GM's stock price changes at the announcement date indicates that not all of the information contained in the earnings release is fully anticipated by investors. Small companies—and those followed by just a few securities analysts—tend to exhibit less preannouncement stock return drift because investors usually have very limited information about the company and its earnings prospects for the quarter. Large companies, whose performance is tracked by many analysts, are more likely to exhibit the preannouncement stock return behavior illustrated in Figure 6.6.

You should understand one more feature of quarterly earnings surprises. Sometimes the earnings surprise and its associated stock return are in opposite directions. Here is a recent example.

- *October 23, 2007:* Coach Inc., the leather goods and accessories company, reports first quarter EPS of $0.41, up 21% from the same quarter a year earlier. Sales increased 28%. Coach shares fall 12% on the New York Stock Exchange.

Why did the stock price fall despite the apparent good news about sales and earnings performance for the quarter? The answer can be found in the company's earnings press release. In addition to reporting strong performance for the quarter, Coach said it was becoming "more conservative" in its outlook and thus lowering its sales and earnings forecasts for the rest of the fiscal year. Investors responded to the bad news about future earnings by selling Coach shares.

How common is this phenomenon? Quarterly earnings surprises and their associated stock returns are in the opposite direction roughly 40% of the time, although the reasons why are not well understood.[29]

---

**RECAP**

**A company's stock price at any given point in time reflects investors' aggregate expectations about the company's future earnings. Information that changes investors' expectations about future earnings will cause the stock price to rise or fall depending on whether the information represents good news or bad news. Research evidence demonstrates that quarterly and annual earnings announcements are important information events. Stock prices tend to increase (or decrease) when the reported earnings turn out to be higher (or lower) than expected. The degree of the surprise conveyed by an earnings announcement depends on the amount of pre-earnings announcement information provided by the financial press.**

## FAIR VALUE ACCOUNTING

For decades, GAAP balance sheet carrying amounts were based primarily on **historical cost,** or what had been paid for a particular asset. As you may recall from Chapter 4, today's GAAP balance sheet is more complicated and contains a mixture of historical cost and other measurements. In fact, more than 40 accounting standards allow or require **fair value** measurement. One example, already mentioned in this chapter, is *SFAS No. 142,* which requires that fair value be used to assess goodwill impairment. Others are described throughout the book. In some ways, this growing use of fair value accounting parallels a shift in the United States from a manufacturing to a service economy in which intangible assets are more important than the plant and equipment that previously defined a company's financial strength.

> Carrying amounts in a GAAP balance sheet are measured using historical cost, net realizable value, discounted present value, and fair value.

---

[29] W. Kinney, D. Burgstahler, and R. Martin, "Earnings Surprise Materiality as Measured by Stock Returns," *Journal of Accounting Research,* December 2002, pp. 1297–1329; and W. B. Johnson and R. Zhou, "Contrarian Share Price Reactions to Earnings Surprises," Working Paper, University of Iowa, 2007.

Until recently, accountants and auditors had little agreement about how to determine fair value. Consider, for example, a truck rental firm and the various ways in which the fair value for a single used truck could be measured. One approach is to find the **exit price,** or the amount the firm would *receive* if it sold the truck. A second approach is to find the **entry price,** the amount the firm would *pay* if it bought a truck of the same type and condition. Accountants and auditors rely on **market price** to determine entry or exit fair values when the asset (rental truck) is traded in an active market. But what if there is no active market for the asset? Then fair value can be determined only by using a valuation model such as those described in the chapter (e.g., by discounting the expected future net cash flows from renting the truck for the duration of its useful life). So, at least three different approaches could be used to measure the rental truck's fair value.

In September 2006, the FASB issued *SFAS No. 157*, "Fair Value Measurements," to increase consistency and comparability in the way fair values are determined for financial reporting purposes. *SFAS No. 157* defines fair value, establishes a framework for measuring fair value, and requires expanded disclosure of fair value measurements. However, it does not establish any new instances that require fair value measurement.

*SFAS No. 157* defines fair value as "the price that would be received to sell an asset or paid to transfer a liability in an orderly transaction between market participants at the measurement date."[30] This means that, for accounting purposes, fair value is an exit price, not an entry price. *SFAS No. 157* also says that the hypothetical transaction of selling the asset or transferring the liability is presumed to occur in the ordinary course of business (i.e., not a forced sale or transfer) and in the item's principal market. Transaction costs do not reduce fair value. *SFAS No. 157* further states that an asset's fair value must reflect its "highest and best use" by others, not how the company uses it. This distinction can be important when, for example, valuable California ocean-front real estate is used as a company parking lot. A liability's fair value must incorporate the company's credit risk.

*SFAS No. 157* provides a hierarchy that prioritizes the information used to arrive at fair value. The hierarchy addresses the difference between assets or liabilities that trade on an active market (e.g., a share of stock in Ford) and those not actively traded (e.g., a grain silo). The hierarchy has three levels:

- *Level 1* uses *quoted prices* from active markets for *identical* assets or liabilities to determine fair value. This is the preferred level.
- *Level 2* includes *observable* inputs other than Level 1 quoted prices. These are quoted prices from an active market for similar assets or liabilities, quoted prices from less-than-active markets, and observable inputs other than quoted prices (such as interest rate yield curves or stock price volatility measures).
- *Level 3* covers *unobservable* inputs such as management's estimates of expected future cash flows or abnormal earnings, which are then used in valuation model approaches to fair value measurement. These are often referred to as **mark-to-model** valuation inputs.

Under *SFAS No. 157,* firms must disclose the fair values at each reporting date, the hierarchy level at which the fair values were determined, a reconciliation of beginning Level 3 inputs to ending inputs, and the amount of unrealized gains or losses that are included in earnings. The Level 3 reconciliation alerts financial statement readers to any changes in management forecasts and valuation model assumptions. Research evidence tends to support the FASB's emphasis on observable market inputs (Levels 1 and 2) and the importance

---

[30] "Fair Value Measurements," *SFAS No. 157* (Norwalk, CT: FASB, 2006), para. 5.

of disclosing the extent to which fair values rely on management judgment and discretion (Level 3).[31]

*SFAS No. 157* gives companies, auditors, and investors much needed guidance on how to measure fair values. It also reopens the door to potential accounting abuses. The accounting irregularities uncovered at Enron in late 2001 led the FASB to ban the use of mark-to-model (Level 3) fair value accounting for most energy contracts. Why? Because the use of subjective, internal valuation models when quoted market prices were not available invited Enron and other energy companies to artificially inflate their earnings through unreasonably optimistic assumptions about future events. Critics then and now claim that mark-to-model fair value accounting is "a license for management to invent the financial statements to be whatever they want them to be."[32] Level 3 fair values add an additional layer of uncertainty and subjectivity as well as risk of material misstatement to financial reports.

Fair value accounting poses a significant challenge for auditors who must evaluate how companies came up with their numbers. Expanded use of fair value accounting means that auditors must have technical knowledge of the valuation tools described in this chapter and how the tools are used in practice. That is one reason why valuation is an important component of this book.

**A number of people mistakenly believe that GAAP balance sheet carrying amounts are based on historical cost, but many of these carrying amounts are instead now shown at fair value. *SFAS No. 157* provides fair value guidance for companies, their auditors, and investors. It also serves as a wake-up call to accountants and auditors about the need to become more skilled in valuing balance sheet assets and liabilities.**

## CREDIT RISK ASSESSMENT

Equity investors analyze financial statements to determine the value of a firm's shares. Creditors, on the other hand, are primarily concerned with assessing a firm's ability to meet its debt obligations through timely payment of principal and interest. Commercial banks, insurance companies, pension funds, and other lenders form opinions about a company's **credit risk** by comparing current and future debt-service requirements to estimates of the company's current and expected future cash flows.

### Financing the BookWorm Franchise

After careful review, Allen Ford decided to purchase a BookWorm franchise. The evaluation process was lengthy. It included interviews with 10 current franchise owners. These interviews helped Ford gain a deeper understanding of the business and its key risks and success factors. He was able to identify several proven marketing and promotion strategies for launching the franchise. With this information and an assessment of local market conditions, Ford refined the financial projections supplied by the parent company, BookWorm, Inc.; performed a valuation analysis; and concluded that the franchise was likely to earn an acceptable risk-adjusted rate of return over time. There was still one hurdle—financing a portion of the $100,000 franchise purchase price.

[31] See AAA Financial Accounting Standards Committee, "Response to the FASB's Exposure Draft on Fair Value Measurements," *Accounting Horizons*, September 2005, pp. 187–96.

[32] Damon Silvers, associate general counsel for the AFL-CIO, as quoted in D. Reilly, "FASB to Issue Retooled Rule for Valuing Corporate Assets," *The Wall Street Journal*, September 15, 2006.

Ford needed a bank loan for two reasons. First, his personal investment portfolio was worth only $50,000. Second, his interviews with other franchise owners revealed that a $100,000 initial investment might not provide an adequate cash cushion during the first year of operation.

Ford described the business opportunity to a local banker and said his cash needs would be in the $50,000 to $100,000 range. The banker said a loan of this size would not be a problem because ample funds were currently available at attractive interest rates. Ford had to complete a detailed loan application, including a personal credit history and business plan, and to prepare monthly earnings and cash flow projections for the first two years of franchise operations. Filled with optimism, Ford began assembling the financial and other information required and thinking about the kind of loan he would request from the bank.

## Traditional Lending Products

Commercial bank loans are a common source of cash for most companies today. These loans can be structured either as short-term or long-term, fixed or floating rate, payable on demand or with fixed maturity, and secured or unsecured.

### Short-Term Loans

Loans with maturities of one year or less, called *short-term loans*, comprise more than half of all commercial bank loans. **Seasonal lines of credit** and special purpose loans are the most common short-term borrowing. Short-term loans are used primarily to finance working capital needs when inventory or receivables increase temporarily. They may be **secured** by the inventories or receivables themselves, or they may be **unsecured**. Loan repayment usually comes from the routine conversion of these current assets into cash.

> Companies with sales cycles that are seasonal (e.g., lawn and garden equipment retailers) commonly use seasonal lines of credit. These loans provide the cash to support increases in current assets during the peak selling period. The borrower draws on the seasonal credit line as funds are required and later repays as seasonal sales produce net cash inflows. **Special purpose business loans** are often used to finance, on a temporary basis, increases in current assets resulting from unusual or unexpected circumstances.

### Long-Term Loans

Called **term lending agreements,** long-term loans have a maturity of more than one year with maturities ranging from two to five years being the most common. The principal and interest repayment schedule, along with other conditions of the loan, are detailed in a signed contractual agreement between the borrower and the bank. Term loans are often used to finance the purchase of fixed assets, the acquisition of another company, the refinancing of existing long-term debt, or permanent working capital needs. They are frequently secured by pledging the assets acquired with the loan proceeds, although lenders rarely look to asset liquidation as the primary source of funds for loan repayment. Scheduled principal and interest payments are generally presumed to come from the borrower's future operating cash flows.

### Revolving Loans

Revolving loans are a variation on the seasonal credit line. They allow borrowing up to a maximum level at any time over the life (usually more than one year) of the loan commitment. Revolving loans are often used to finance cash imbalances that arise in day-to-day operations, seasonal needs, or permanent working capital needs when normal trade credit is inadequate to support a company's sales volume. Borrowers can *prepay* the revolving loan and later reborrow those funds, but they must comply with the terms and conditions specified in the loan agreement. The interest rate on the revolving line of credit is usually the bank's prime lending rate plus an additional percentage, and the rate will usually change (or "float") as the prime rate rises or falls over the life of the credit line. In addition to interest, the borrower pays a "commitment fee" that is based on the total amount of the credit extended.

**Commercial Paper**    Commercial banks are not the only source of debt financing for businesses. Another source of financing is **commercial paper**—short-term notes sold directly to investors by large and financially sound companies. These notes usually mature in 270 days or less and carry a fixed interest rate. Because commercial paper is issued directly to institutional investors (such as insurance companies) and is usually secured by a bank credit line, the interest rate the borrowing company pays is often significantly below the rate a bank would charge for a comparable direct loan.

**Public Debt**    Long-term forms of public debt financing include bonds, debentures, or notes. Long-term debt securities are promises the issuing company makes to pay principal when due and to make timely interest payments on the unpaid balance. Bonds can have numerous special features. For example, **secured bonds** specify collateral that protects the bondholder if and when the borrower defaults. Other bonds contain **seniority** features that specify which bondholders will be paid first in the event of bankruptcy. Some may contain **sinking fund provisions** that require the borrowing company to make annual payments to a trustee (usually a bank), who then uses the funds to retire a portion of the debt prior to its maturity. Still others may contain **call provisions** that allow the borrowing company to "call" (meaning repurchase) part of all of the debt at stated prices over a specific period.

> The word **bond** is commonly used to refer to all types of secured and unsecured debt although, strictly speaking, a bond is a secured debt. A **debenture** is an *unsecured* bond for which no specific pledge of property is made, although the debenture holder does have a claim on property not otherwise pledged as collateral or security. The term **note** is generally used for unsecured debt instruments issued with a maturity of 10 years or less.

Regardless of the special features attached, virtually all bonds or notes contain numerous **protective covenants** designed to protect the lender's interests. These covenants place restrictions on the borrower's activity and are described in the **indenture,** a written agreement between the borrowing company and its lenders. The role that accounting numbers play in these debt covenants is described in Chapter 7.

## Credit Analysis

To lend funds to a company, a commercial loan officer of a bank must first evaluate the prospective borrower's ability to repay the proposed loan at maturity. This evaluation typically involves financial analysis and includes the preparation of forecasted financial statements, "due diligence" (a qualitative assessment of the business, its customers and suppliers, and management's character and capability), and analysis of credit risk.

Financial analysis of a potential borrower begins with an understanding of the firm, its business, its key risks and success factors, and the competitive dynamics of its industry. Next, an evaluation of the quality of its accounting earnings and financial reporting choices is made to determine whether traditional ratios and statistics derived from the financial statements can be relied on to measure accurately the company's economic performance and financial condition. However, lenders and credit analysts frequently adjust a company's reported financial statement numbers. For example, nonrecurring gains and losses and other transitory components of earnings are removed from the reported bottom-line earnings number to arrive at a measure of operating performance that is more representative of a firm's long-run sustainable profitability. Off-balance-sheet obligations (such as operating lease commitments) are frequently added to a firm's reported debt. Finally, other adjustments are made to improve the comparability of the financial data across potential loan candidates.

The next step is evaluating the company's profit performance and balance sheet strength. Financial, operating, and leverage ratios (discussed in Chapter 5) as well as trends in revenues and expenses are examined and compared to industry averages. This phase of the analysis identifies positive and negative changes in the prospective borrower's profitability, financial health, and industry position. However, the historical performance and condition of the borrower is only a partial indication of creditworthiness. Loan approval is largely determined by the borrower's ability to repay the proposed loan from *future* operating cash flows. ***Consequently, an estimate of the company's future financial condition is indispensable to most lending decisions.*** Analysts accomplish this assessment by constructing pro forma financial statement projections (forecasts) of borrower cash flows.

> Appendix B shows how you can construct pro forma financial statement projections.

The credit analyst prepares pro forma or "as if" financial statement projections to assess the borrower's ability to generate sufficient cash flows to make interest and principal payments when due. These projections incorporate the analyst's understanding of the company's plans and business strategy, the likely responses of rival companies, and other factors that shape the prospective borrower's economic environment. The pro forma financial statements and their underlying assumptions are then tested to establish the borrower's vulnerability to changing economic circumstances. This testing involves examining plausible "worst-case" scenarios that indicate just how poorly the company can perform before it defaults. This enables the analyst to gauge the company's **financial flexibility**—that is, the degree to which the company can satisfy its cash needs during periods of fiscal stress by drawing on existing credit lines, accessing financial markets, curtailing discretionary cash expenditures, or selling assets.

A **due diligence** evaluation is like "kicking the tires" of the prospective borrower. The analyst does a due diligence evaluation by conducting plant tours, trade checks, and interviews with competitors, suppliers, customers, and employees. Comprehensive due diligence may also include asset appraisals; reviews of the company's other debt obligations, internal controls, planned capital expenditures, and potential environmental liabilities; and other matters that bear on the company's future success and ability to repay debt at maturity.

The final step of credit analysis is a **comprehensive risk assessment** that involves evaluating and summarizing the various individual risks associated with the loan. Some risks are unique to the specific borrower (for example, a pharmaceutical company may run the risk that a new drug it has developed may ultimately prove ineffective during clinical test trials); other risks are associated with potential changes in the economy or industry, new regulations, or unanticipated events. The credit analyst evaluates the severity of each risk in terms of (1) its probability of occurrence, (2) how it could affect the borrower's ability or willingness to repay, and (3) the bank's estimated costs if the borrower defaults.[33]

If the prospective borrower is judged to be creditworthy, it negotiates the final terms and conditions of the loan with the borrower. Obviously, a lender is compensated for *anticipated* credit risks by the interest rate it charges on the loan. The interest rate must be sufficient to cover the lender's (1) cost of borrowing funds, (2) costs of administering, monitoring, and servicing the loan, (3) normal (competitive) return on the capital needed to support the bank's lending operations, and (4) premium for exposure to default risk. Collateralized loans or loans with personal guarantees lower credit risk and enable lenders to lower the borrower's cost of debt.

Comprehensive credit analysis of the type we have just described is an expensive and time-consuming activity. Sometimes lenders find it more cost effective to use less rigorous and detailed approaches to assessing borrower creditworthiness. For example, manufacturers such as Xerox routinely provide equipment lease financing to business customers. Because the dollar amount involved is often small (say less than $25,000 per copier) and Xerox retains ownership of the equipment during the lease period, the lender (Xerox) has minimal risk exposure.

---

[33] For additional insights about the tools and techniques of credit analysis, see B. Ganguin and J. Bilardello, *Fundamentals of Corporate Credit Analysis* (New York: McGraw-Hill, 2005).

Lenders such as Xerox adopt more streamlined approaches to credit analysis to avoid costly scrutiny of financial statement details, ratios, and cash flow projections for each potential business customer. One streamlined approach is to rely on credit reports issued by companies such as Dun & Bradstreet. These third-party reports include financial statements for the business along with information about existing loans, payment histories, pending litigation, other pertinent data, and a **credit score** that predicts future payment habits and financial stability. Lenders such as Xerox can then use the Dun & Bradstreet credit score to set the price, terms, and condition of the equipment lease contract.

## Credit-Rating Agencies

Large companies often borrow money by selling commercial paper, notes, bonds, or debentures to individual and institutional investors. Investors' beliefs about borrower credit risk, influence the price paid—and thus the amount borrowed. The riskier the borrower is perceived to be, the less investors are willing to pay for the security. How do these investors assess credit risk? One way is to rely on the opinion of a credit-rating agency.

> Standard & Poor's, for example, now rates more than $13 trillion in bonds and other financial obligations of borrowers in more than 50 countries.

In the United States, three agencies (Moody's Investors Service, Standard & Poor's Corp., and Fitch Inc.) assess and grade the creditworthiness of companies and public entities—individual states, counties, municipalities—that sell debt to investors. Credit ratings are letter-based grades (e.g., AAA) that express the rating agency's opinion about default risk or the borrower's capacity and willingness to meet its financial commitments on time and in accordance with the terms of the debt security. The higher the credit rating, the lower is the default risk as judged by the rating agency.

John Moody invented credit ratings in 1909 when he first published the *Manual of Railroad Securities,* which rated 200 U.S. railroad companies and their debt securities. The Standard Company began grading bonds in 1916. Poor's and Fitch followed in the 1920s. Poor's and Standard merged in 1941. All rating agencies initially made money by charging investors for their ratings. They began charging borrowers instead in the 1970s because photocopiers made it easy for nonpaying investors to obtain the ratings. Credit-rating agencies are independent of any investment banking company, commercial bank, and similar organization.

### Credit Ratings and Default Risk
See Exhibit 6.7 for the credit-rating levels used by Standard & Poor's, along with a credit quality description and historical default rate for each level. The default rates in Exhibit 6.7 refer to the percentage of borrowers that failed to make all promised debt payments based on the credit rating initially assigned. If credit ratings predict default risk, borrowers whose debt is highly rated should default less often than those with low-rated debt. This is indeed the case.

Standard & Poor's highest rating (AAA), for example, means that the borrower's capacity to meet its financial commitment on the debt is judged to be "extremely strong." Less than 1% of AAA borrowers default. A BBB rating, on the other hand, means that the debt has "adequate protection" against nonpayment but that adverse economic conditions or changing circumstances could weaken the borrower's capacity to meet its debt repayment obligation. In other words, Standard & Poor's credit analysis judge BBB-rated debt to be riskier than AAA debt. And they are correct! The historical default rate on BBB debt is slightly more than 6%. Even riskier is debt rated CCC—meaning "currently vulnerable" to nonpayment—for which the historical default rate is about 54%. Slightly more than one of every two borrowers issuing CCC speculative grade debt later default.

| EXHIBIT 6.7 | Standard & Poor's Credit Ratings | |
| --- | --- | --- |

| Rating | Credit Quality | Historical Default Rate (%)* |
| --- | --- | --- |
| Investment grade | | |
| AAA | Extremely strong | 0.52% |
| AA | Very strong | 1.13 |
| A | Strong | 2.32 |
| BBB | Adequate protection | 6.64 |
| Speculative (or "junk") grade | | |
| BB | Less vulnerable | 19.52 |
| B | More vulnerable | 35.76 |
| CCC | Currently vulnerable | 54.38 |
| CC | Highly vulnerable | |
| C | Currently highly vulnerable | |
| D | In default | |

*Note:* Defaults on investment grade bonds—those rated BBB or better—seldom happen.

* Historical default rates are the percentages of defaults by issuers rated by Standard & Poor's during 1987–2002 based on the rating they were initially assigned.

*Source:* See A. Borrus, "The Credit Rates: How They Work and How They Might Work Better," *BusinessWeek,* April 8, 2002; and D. Henry, "Anatomy of a Ratings Downgrade," *BusinessWeek,* October 1, 2007.

**The Credit-Rating Process**    The ratings process involves much more than just a detailed examination of financial statements, notes, and ratios:[34]

> Credit ratings often are identified with financial analysis, and especially ratios. But it is critical to realize that ratings analysis starts with the assessment of the business and competitive profile of the company. Two companies with identical financial metrics are rated very differently, to the extent that their business challenges and prospects differ.[35]

Each rating agency has teams of analytical experts who grill corporate executives about operating and financial plans, management policies, risk tolerance, and the firm's competitiveness within the industry. The team also conducts a thorough review of business fundamentals, including an assessment of industry prospects for growth, pattern of business cycles, and vulnerability to technological change, labor unrest, and regulatory action.

Organizational considerations can also adversely impact assessed credit risk. Standard & Poor's credit analysts, for example, regard the following situations as involving increased default risk:

- The company has a highly aggressive business model and is growing through large acquisitions or expanding into unproven markets.

- The company has made frequent and significant changes to its strategy or has excessive management turnover.

- The organization relies significantly on an individual, especially one who may be nearing retirement.

---

[34] For a more detailed description of the credit-rating process at Standard & Poor's, see *Corporate Ratings Criteria 2005* (New York: Standard & Poor's Corp.).

[35] Ibid., p. 19.

- Management compensation is excessive or poorly aligned with stakeholders' interests.
- The company has an excessively complex legal structure, perhaps employing intricate off-balance-sheet structures.

Credit risk also increases when firms are deemed to be aggressive in their application of accounting standards or when their financial statements lack transparency to business fundamentals.

At Standard & Poor's, the financial statement analysis phase of the credit-rating process begins by assessing accounting quality. The purpose is to determine whether ratios and statistics derived from the statements reliably indicate economic performance and financial condition. High-quality financial statements help credit analysts see what's really going on at the company; low-quality statements mask true performance and condition. Among the accounting quality issues that credit analysts at Standard & Poor's routinely review are revenue and expense recognition (Chapters 2 and 3 of this book); receivables and the provision for doubtful accounts (Chapter 8); LIFO inventory (Chapter 9); fixed asset depreciation methods and asset lives (Chapter 10); operating leases (Chapter 12); environmental liabilities and contingent obligations not yet recognized on the balance sheet (Chapter 11); research and development or interest costs that are capitalized rather than expensed (Chapter 10); derivatives and hedges (Chapter 11); and nonrecurring items that affect operating cash flow (Chapter 17).

To the extent possible, analytical financial statement adjustments are made to better portray economic reality and to level the differences among companies. At Standard & Poor's, nonrecurring gains and losses are eliminated from earnings. Unusual cash flow items similar in origins to nonrecurring gains and losses are also reversed. Operating leases are added to the balance sheet so that companies that buy all of their plant and equipment are put on a more comparable basis with those that lease part or all of their operating assets. Although it is rarely possible to completely recast a company's financial statements, it is important for credit analysts to have at least some notion of the extent to which different financial metrics are overstated or understated.

The financial statement analysis phase of the credit-rating process then proceeds using the tools and techniques described in Chapter 5. When this phase has been completed, analytical team members meet with the rating committee to discuss their recommendation and pertinent facts supporting the rating. The committee then votes on the rating recommendation. The borrower is then notified of the rating and can appeal. When a final rating is assigned, it is disseminated to the public through the news media.

All ratings are monitored after they have been assigned. Surveillance is intended to spot changes in borrower credit risk. The surveillance process includes continually reviewing new financial or economic information and possibly meeting with management. When it becomes necessary to reassess the rating, the analytical team undertakes an initial review. The borrower may then be placed on Standard & Poor's *CreditWatch* listing if the likelihood of rating change is sufficiently high. This is followed by a comprehensive credit rating analysis—including, if warranted, a meeting with management—and a presentation to the rating committee. The committee then decides whether to confirm the existing rating, issue a downgrade (say from AA to A), or upgrade (say from BBB to A). Rating downgrades and upgrades thus signal changes in borrower credit risk.

> In most markets outside the United States, ratings are assigned only on the borrower's request, so the borrower can choose to make the rating public or keep it confidential. In the United States, Standard & Poor's assigns and publishes ratings regardless of borrower request if the debt security is to be sold publicly. In the case of private placements, the borrower retains publication rights.

**Financial Ratios and Debt Ratings** The key financial statement ratios tracked by credit analysts at Standard & Poor's are described in Exhibit 6.8 along with the median ratio value for U.S. corporate borrowers in each rating level. These key financial ratios measure profitability (return on capital); the

| EXHIBIT 6.8 | Standard & Poor's Key Financial Ratios and Ratings of Corporate Debt |
| --- | --- |

| | Three-Year (2001 to 2003) Medians | | | | | | |
| --- | --- | --- | --- | --- | --- | --- | --- |
| | **AAA** | **AA** | **A** | **BBB** | **BB** | **B** | **CCC** |
| EBIT interest coverage | 23.8 | 13.6 | 6.9 | 4.2 | 2.3 | 0.9 | 0.4 |
| EBITDA interest coverage | 25.3 | 17.1 | 9.4 | 5.9 | 3.1 | 1.6 | 0.9 |
| FFO/Total debt (%) | 167.8 | 77.5 | 43.2 | 34.6 | 20.0 | 10.1 | 2.9 |
| Free operating cash flow/Total debt (%) | 104.1 | 41.1 | 25.4 | 16.9 | 7.9 | 2.6 | (0.9) |
| Total debt/EBITDA | 0.2 | 1.1 | 1.7 | 2.4 | 3.8 | 5.6 | 7.4 |
| Return on capital (%) | 35.1 | 26.9 | 16.8 | 13.4 | 10.3 | 6.7 | 2.3 |
| Total debt/Capital (%) | 6.2 | 34.8 | 39.8 | 45.6 | 57.2 | 74.2 | 101.2 |

**Formulas**

| | |
| --- | --- |
| EBIT interest coverage | Earnings from continuing operations* before interest and taxes/Gross interest incurred before subtracting capitalized interest and interest income |
| EBITDA interest coverage | Adjusted earnings from continuing operations† before interest, taxes, depreciation, and amortization/Gross interest incurred before subtracting capitalized interest and interest income |
| Funds from operations (FFO)/Total debt | Net income from continuing operations, depreciation, and amortization, deferred income taxes, and other noncash items/Long-term debts + Current maturities + Commercial paper and other short-term borrowings |
| Free operating cash flow/Total debt | FFO − Capital expenditures +(−) increase (decrease) in working capital (excluding changes in cash, marketable securities, and short-term debt)/Long-term debts + Current maturities, commercial paper, and other short-term borrowings |
| Total debt/EBITDA | Long-term debts + Current maturities, commercial paper, and other short-term borrowings/Adjusted earnings from continuing operations before interest, taxes, and depreciation and amortization |
| Return on capital | EBIT/Average of beginning-of-year and end-of-year capital, including short-term debt, current maturities, long-term debt, noncurrent deferred taxes, minority interest, and equity (common and preferred stock) |
| Total debt/Capital | Long-term debt + Current maturities, commercial paper, and other short-term borrowings/Long-term debts + Current maturities, commercial paper, and other short-term borrowings + Shareholder's equity (including preferred stock) + Minority interest |

*Note:* Standard & Poor's uses different ratios to rate debt issued by utilities and financial services companies. The universe of rated companies includes about 1,000 industrial firms. See *Corporate Ratings Criteria 2005* (New York: Standard & Poor's Corp.), pp. 43–44.

* Including interest income and equity earnings; excluding nonrecurring items.

† Excludes interest income, equity earnings, and nonrecurring items; also excludes rental expense that exceeds the interest component of capitalized operating leases. Includes amounts for operating lease debt equivalent, and debt associated with accounts receivable sales/securitization programs.

extent to which operating earnings exceed interest costs (EBIT interest coverage and EBITDA interest coverage); financial structure (Total debt/Capital); and cash flow capacity (Funds from operations/Total debt, Free operating cash flow/Total debt, and Total debt/EBITDA). Each ratio has a precise Standard & Poor's definition so that every credit analyst at the rating agency is computationally consistent.

Notice how the ratio median values in Exhibit 6.8 rise or fall across credit-rating levels. For example, the median borrower assigned a AAA rating is quite profitable (return on capital of 35.1%) with little debt (Total debt/Capital of 6.2%) and sizable operating cash flow (Free operating cash flow/Total debt of 104.1%). By comparison, the median BB speculative grade borrower is substantially less profitable (return on capital of 10.3%) with much more debt (Total debt/Capital of 57.2%) and significantly less operating cash flow (Free operating cash flow/Total debt of only 7.9%). These patterns are consistent with the notion, discussed in Chapter 5, that certain financial statement ratios are quite useful in predicting loan default.

Commercial banks, insurance companies, pension funds, and other lenders lend needed cash only if the probability of repayment is high. Consequently, the central question to be answered is whether the borrower's future cash inflows will be sufficient to repay the loan. Credit analysts rely on their understanding of the company, its business strategy, and the competitive environment when they apply the tools and techniques of financial statement analysis and cash flow forecasting to assess credit risk and the company's financial flexibility under stress. Credit-rating agencies use a similar approach to assess default risk.

RE**CAP**

## SUMMARY

In *Concepts Statement No. 1,* the FASB sets forth the primary objectives of financial reporting. One of those objectives states:

> Financial reporting should provide information to help present and potential investors and creditors and others in assessing the amounts, timing and uncertainty of prospective cash receipts from dividends or interest and the proceeds from the sale, redemption, or maturity of securities or loans. Since investors' and creditors' cash flows are related to enterprise cash flows, financial reporting should provide information to help investors, creditors, and others assess the amounts, timing, and uncertainty of prospective net cash inflows to the related enterprise.[36]

- This chapter provides a framework for understanding how financial reporting meets this important objective.
- Specifically, we show how accounting numbers are used in valuation, cash flow analysis, and credit risk assessment, and then illustrate what it means to "assess the amounts, timing, and uncertainty of prospective net cash inflows" of a business.
- A critical part of understanding the **decision-usefulness** of accounting information—a major focus of this book—is understanding *which* accounting numbers are used, *why* they are used, and *how* they are used in making investment and credit decisions.
- Knowing how earnings, book values, and cash flows are used in investment and credit decisions will help you to evaluate the alternative accounting measures discussed in subsequent chapters of this book—not only those recognized in the financial statements but also those disclosed outside the financial statements in footnotes.

## APPENDIX A

## ABNORMAL EARNINGS VALUATION

This appendix illustrates how the abnormal earnings valuation model can be combined with security analysts' published earnings forecasts to produce an **intrinsic stock price estimate** for a company. To make this illustration real, we focus on Whole Foods Market, Inc. and those analysts' earnings forecasts that were available in October 2007 when the company's common stock was trading at $48.00 per share.

**Share Price Valuation**　The five steps to deriving a share price estimate using analysts' earnings forecasts and the abnormal earnings valuation model are:

1. Obtain analysts' EPS forecasts for some finite horizon, say the next five years.
2. Combine the EPS forecasts with projected dividends to forecast common equity book value over the horizon.

---

[36] Objectives of Financial Reporting by Business Enterprises," *SFAC No. 1* (Stamford, CT: FASB, 1978), p. viii.

3. Compute yearly *abnormal* earnings by subtracting *normal* earnings (that is, beginning equity book value multiplied by the equity cost of capital) from analysts' EPS forecasts.

4. Forecast the perpetual (terminal year) *abnormal* earnings flow that will occur beyond the explicit forecast horizon.

5. Add the current book value and the present value of the two abnormal earnings components—the first five years and for years beyond the terminal period—to obtain an intrinsic value estimate of the company's share price.

Each of these steps is illustrated in the Whole Foods Market valuation in Exhibit 6.9.

Our forecast horizon—and the one used by analysts covering the company—is the five-year period from 2007 through 2011. Analysts focus on the short- to intermediate-term forecast horizon in valuing a company for at least three reasons. First, competitive pressures make it difficult for the company to sustain growth in sales, profits, and cash flows in the long run. Thus, it is unrealistic to forecast that a growing company can maintain high short-term growth rates for an indefinite period. Second, long-range projections are more uncertain and, therefore, subject to greater error. Simply put, projected earnings or dividend payouts to shareholders become less and less reliable the further removed they are from the current forecast date. And third, because of the time value of money, the discounted present values of future abnormal earnings (or free cash) flows become smaller as the forecast horizon increases. In other words, longer range forecasts often do not matter very much in terms of determining current share price. For example, the present value of a dollar received 25 years from now discounted at 15%—a very realistic estimate for the cost of equity capital—is equal to $1/(1 + 0.15)^{25} = \$0.03$.

In late October 2007, securities analysts who covered Whole Foods Market were forecasting EPS of $1.35 for 2007 and $1.51 for 2008. These same analysts were forecasting annual EPS growth of 15.6% for 2009 through 2011. Based on the company's projected EPS of $1.51 for 2008, this means that analysts were forecasting 2009 EPS of $1.75 (or $1.51 × 1.156). These same analysts were forecasting 2010 EPS of $2.02 (or $1.75 × 1.156), and so on. These EPS forecasts are presented in part (a) of Exhibit 6.9.

Next, we need to compute the book value of common equity for each year of the five-year forecast horizon. From the historical information contained in part (b) of the exhibit and a detailed look at the company's 2006 financial statements (Chapter 5), we learn that Whole Foods Market has paid annual dividends of $0.60 per share beginning in the second quarter of 2005. The company also paid a "special" dividend of $1.85 per share in 2006, which explains why the total dividend payment that year was $2.45. We assume that the special dividend payment is a one-time event and thus forecast dividends at $0.60 per share for 2007 through 2011. To simplify matters, we also assume that stock issuances and comprehensive income adjustments are zero over the forecast horizon. These assumptions are combined with the EPS forecasts from part (a) to produce the equity book value forecasts of $10.81 per share at the end of 2007 and $16.02 per share at the end of 2011.

The abnormal earnings calculations for each of the five years in our forecast horizon are shown in part (c) of Exhibit 6.9. Here, normal earnings are subtracted from the annual EPS forecasts. Normal earnings are just Whole Foods Market's common equity book value at the *beginning* of each year—as computed in part (b)—multiplied by the company's cost of equity capital, which is 10.25%.[37] For example, Whole Foods Market's normal earnings for 2007

---

[37] This figure was derived from the CAPM using the then-current risk-free rate of 4.60% for 30-year treasury bonds, Whole Foods Market's equity beta of 0.94 as reported by *Zacks Investment Research* and a long-term market risk premium of 6%. The CAPM formula applied to Whole Foods Market is:

$$4.60\% + (0.94 \times 6\%) = 10.24\%, \text{ or about } 10.25\%$$

| EXHIBIT 6.9 | Whole Foods Market, Inc. |
|---|---|

## Abnormal Earnings Valuation

| | Actual Results | | Forecasted Results | | | | | Beyond 2011 |
|---|---|---|---|---|---|---|---|---|
| | 2005 | 2006 | 2007 | 2008 | 2009 | 2010 | 2011 | |
| **(a) Earnings Forecasts** | | | | | | | | |
| Reported earnings per share | $0.99 | $1.41 | | | | | | |
| Last year's earnings per share | | | $1.41 | $1.35 | $1.51 | $1.75 | $2.02 | |
| × (1 + Forecasted earnings growth) | | | 0.9574 | 1.1185 | 1.1560 | 1.1560 | 1.1560 | |
| = Forecasted earnings per share | | | $1.35 | $1.51 | $1.75 | $2.02 | $2.33 | |
| **(b) Equity Book Value Forecasts** (per share amounts) | | | | | | | | |
| Equity book value at beginning of year | $7.61 | $10.05 | $10.06 | $10.81 | $11.72 | $12.87 | $14.28 | |
| + Earnings per share | 0.99 | 1.41 | 1.35 | 1.51 | 1.75 | 2.02 | 2.33 | |
| + Stock issued (repurchased) | 0.81 | 0.71 | 0.00 | 0.00 | 0.00 | 0.00 | 0.00 | |
| + Other comprehensive income[1] | 1.11 | 0.34 | 0.00 | 0.00 | 0.00 | 0.00 | 0.00 | |
| − Dividends | (0.47) | (2.45) | (0.60) | (0.60) | (0.60) | (0.60) | (0.60) | |
| = Equity book value at year-end | $10.05 | $10.06 | $10.81 | $11.72 | $12.87 | $14.28 | $16.02 | |
| ROCE = EPS/Equity book value at beginning of year | 13.0% | 14.0% | 13.4% | 14.0% | 14.9% | 15.7% | $16.3% | |
| **(c) Abnormal Earnings** | | | | | | | | |
| Equity book value at beginning of year | $7.61 | $10.05 | $10.06 | $10.81 | $11.72 | $12.87 | $14.28 | |
| × Equity cost of capital | 10.25% | 10.25% | 10.25% | 10.25% | 10.25% | 10.25% | 10.25% | |
| = Normal earnings | $0.78 | $1.03 | $1.03 | $1.11 | $1.20 | $1.32 | $1.46 | |
| Actual or forecasted earnings | $0.99 | $1.41 | $1.35 | $1.51 | $1.75 | $2.02 | $2.33 | |
| − Normal earnings | 0.78 | 1.03 | 1.03 | 1.11 | 1.20 | 1.32 | 1.46 | |
| = Abnormal earnings | $0.21 | $0.38 | $0.32 | $0.40 | $0.54 | $0.70 | $0.87 | |
| **(d) Valuation** | | | | | | | | |
| Future abnormal earnings in forecast horizon | | | $0.32 | $0.40 | $0.54 | $0.70 | $0.87 | |
| × Discount factor at 10.25% | | | 0.90703 | 0.82270 | 0.74622 | 0.67684 | 0.61391 | |
| = Abnormal earnings discounted to present | | | $0.29 | $0.33 | $0.41 | $0.47 | $0.53 | |
| Abnormal earnings in year 2012[2] | | | | | | | | $0.90 |
| Assumed long-term growth rate | | | | | | | | 4.0% |
| Perpetuity factor for year 2011 | | | | | | | | 16.00 |
| Discount factor | | | | | | | | 0.61391 |
| Present value of terminal year abnormal earnings[3] | | | | | | | | $8.87 |
| **(e) Estimated share price** | | | | | | | | |
| Sum of discounted abnormal earnings over horizon | | | $2.03 | | | | | |
| + Present value of terminal year abnormal earnings | | | $8.87 | | | | | |
| = Present value of all abnormal earnings | | | $10.91 | | | | | |
| + Current equity book value | | | $10.06 | | | | | |
| = Estimated current share price at October, 2007 | | | $20.97 | | | | | |
| Actual share price at October, 2007 | | | $48.00 | | | | | |

[1] Also includes adjustments for share-based compensation and the tax benefit of exercised employee stock options.

[2] This is forecasted abnormal earnings in 2011 multiplied by 1 plus the long-term growth rate: $0.87 × (1 + 0.04) = $0.9033$, or $0.90 rounded.

[3] This is just $0.90 × 16.00 × 0.61391 = $8.87$ (rounded).

would be calculated by multiplying its equity book value at the beginning of the year, which is $10.06, by the equity cost of capital, which is 0.1025. The result is $1.03. These normal earnings ($1.03) are then subtracted from forecasted earnings of $1.35. The difference between the two, or $0.32, is Whole Foods Market's abnormal earnings for 2007.

These abnormal earnings forecasts from part (c) become the basic inputs to the valuation calculation in part (d), where abnormal earnings are discounted at the company's 10.25% equity cost of capital. A *terminal value* calculation intended to represent the value of the company's abnormal earnings flow beyond our five-year forecast horizon is also shown in part (d). To arrive at this terminal value estimate, we assume that Whole Foods Market's abnormal earnings of $0.87 in 2011 will continue to grow by 4% each year for the foreseeable future. The present value of this growing perpetual flow at the beginning of 2012 is $14.48 (not shown in Exhibit 6.9), which is the 2011 abnormal earnings multiplied by 1 plus the long-term growth rate (1 + 0.04), and then multiplied again by the perpetuity factor 16.00.[38] This quantity is then discounted using the present value factor for five periods discounted at 10.25% (0.61391), which translates the present value of abnormal earnings at the beginning of 2011 into a present value at the beginning of 2007 of $8.87. Part (e) shows that the sum of all discounted abnormal earnings flows ($10.91) plus the company's 2006 year-end equity book value ($10.06) produces an estimated share price of $20.97; this contrasts with Whole Foods Market's actual $48.00 share price in October 2007.

What does this tell us? For one thing, Whole Foods Market's $48.00 per share stock price in October 2007 was considerably higher than that implied by securities analysts' five-year EPS and dividend payout forecasts coupled with our own predictions about earnings growth beyond the forecasts horizon (Year 2011). In this regard, Whole Foods Market's stock may appear to be somewhat overpriced in the marketplace. However, the market may have been anticipating abnormal earnings to increase even faster and for a longer time period than our projections would indicate. The rub, of course, is that we cannot know at the time which of the forecasts will prove correct in the future.

The abnormal earnings valuation model in Exhibit 6.9 can be used to value almost any publicly traded company. It's easy to implement because it requires just a handful of data items—earnings forecasts from analysts, a beginning book value of equity, forecasts of dividends and stock repurchases, an equity cost of capital (discount rate), and a long-term growth rate for abnormal earnings beyond the terminal year. But how well does it work?

This question has several answers. One approach compares the accuracy of stock price estimates from several different valuation models—for example, the abnormal earnings model versus the free cash flow valuation model. A study did just that using a sample of nearly 3,000 firm-year observations from 1989 through 1993.[39] Earnings, dividends, and cash flow forecasts were gathered from *Value Line* for each sample firm and year. These forecasts were then used as inputs to an abnormal earnings valuation model (like the one in Exhibit 6.9) and as inputs to a separate free cash flow valuation model. The two value estimates—one based on abnormal earnings and the other based on free cash flows—were then compared to actual stock prices. Which valuation model was best? Abnormal earnings value estimates were more accurate and explained more of the variation in actual stock prices than did free cash flow value estimates.

> In theory, both valuation models should produce the same stock price estimate. But in practice, the two valuation models often do not produce the same stock price estimate.

---

[38] This perpetuity discount factor is equal to 1 divided by the difference between the equity cost of capital (10.25%) and the abnormal earnings growth rate (4%), or $1/(.1025 - .04)$.

[39] J. Francis, P. Olsson, and D.R. Oswald, "Comparing the Accuracy and Explainability of Dividends, Free Cash Flow, and Abnormal Earnings Equity Value Estimates," *Journal of Accounting Research,* Spring 2000, pp. 45–70.

A related study asked if money can be made from the abnormal earnings valuation model in Exhibit 6.9.[40] Using a sample of nearly 18,000 firm-year observations covering 1979 to 1991, the researchers computed valuation estimates for each firm and year. These estimates were then used to construct a *value index*—the estimated value divided by the actual share price—for each company and year. (The value index for Whole Foods Market would be 0.437, or $20.97/$48.00). The simulated trading strategy involved "buying" the most undervalued companies (high value index) and "selling short" the most overvalued companies (low value index). This strategy produced a three-year portfolio return of 35%, which implies investors can profit from using the abnormal earnings valuation model.

**APPENDIX B**

# FINANCIAL STATEMENT FORECASTS

Financial statement forecasts (or projections) are essential ingredients of equity valuation and credit risk analysis. This appendix illustrates the construction of *comprehensive* financial statement forecasts.[41] Our approach has two advantages. First, it uses information about the company's complete operating, investing, and financing activities to yield a forecast of each individual financial statement item. Second, the approach ensures that the forecasted financial statements—sometimes called *pro forma projections*—are internally consistent. Nothing is overlooked, and the projected financial statements fit together as they should.

The starting point for developing comprehensive financial statement forecasts is a detailed understanding of the company, its recent financial performance, and health. (Chapter 5 shows you how!) This involves learning about the company and its industry conditions, competitors, customers, and suppliers. Armed with this knowledge, the analyst can then develop plausible predictions about future economic conditions in the industry and about how the company and its competitors will respond to those conditions. The analyst then incorporates these predictions into the forecasted financial statements.

> Sometimes the analyst is interested in forecasting only a single financial statement item, such as EPS. Shortcuts that circumvent the need to construct comprehensive financial statement forecasts are often used in such cases, but the resulting single-item forecasts may prove highly unreliable.

Preparing comprehensive financial statement forecasts involves six steps:

1. Project sales revenue for each period in the forecast horizon (say, two years).

2. Forecast operating expenses such as cost of goods sold (but not depreciation, interest, or tax expense, which are handled separately), and derive projected pre-tax operating income before depreciation and amortization. Expense margins—for example, cost of goods sold expressed as a percentage of sales—are useful for this purpose.

3. Forecast the level of balance sheet operating assets and liabilities—cash, inventories, accounts receivable, accounts payable, and the like—needed to support the projected operations in Steps 1 and 2. Turnover ratios (also called *utilization*) ratios can help guide these projections.

4. Forecast depreciation expense and tax expense each period. These are two of the last three items needed to construct projected income statements.

---

[40] R. Frankel and C. Lee, "Accounting Valuation, Market Expectation, and Cross-Sectional Stock Returns," *Journal of Accounting and Economics,* June 1998, pp. 283–320.

[41] Techniques for constructing financial statement forecasts are described in T. Koller et al., op. cit.; R. Lundholm and R. Sloan, op. cit.; K. Palepu, V. Bernard, and P. Healy, *Business Analysis and Valuation* (Cincinnati, OH: South-Western Publishing, 2008); L. Soffer and R. Soffer, op. cit.; and C. Stickney and P. Brown, *Financial Statement Analysis: A Strategic Perspective* (Fort Worth, TX: Dryden Press, 1999).

5. Forecast the company's financial structure (mix of debt and equity financing) and dividend policy each period. Then use this information, along with an estimate of the interest rate charged on debt financing, to project interest expense and complete the income statement.

6. Derive projected cash flow statements from the forecasted income statements and balance sheets.

## Illustration of Comprehensive Financial Statement Forecasts

Veto Equipment Supply Company manufactures original equipment parts for the U.S. automobile industry. The company has been in business for more than 50 years. Although sales rise and fall with the ebb and flow of consumer demand for U.S. automobiles, the company has remained profitable throughout most of its history. In 2008, Veto reported sales of $25.2 million, an increase of 5% from the previous year. Net income that year was $1.056 million, an increase of 20% from 2007.

The company has a $2.5 million revolving credit loan with Commerce First Bank. At the end of 2008, Veto had drawn only $2.077 million of the available credit, but management is still concerned about the amount of money it will need to borrow over the next two years. The reason for this concern is that Veto has developed a successful new product that is expected to increase its sales significantly. However, the new product will require that Veto expand its operations. Management wants to know whether Veto will need to negotiate a higher credit limit to support the planned expansion. How much more money will the company need?

Exhibit 6.10 shows the company's income statements and balance sheets for the past two years. An abbreviated statement of retained earnings is included to provide an explicit link between income statement and balance sheet amounts. Our task is to "fill in the blanks" by preparing forecasted financial statements for 2009 and 2010 using the six-step process described above. Let's get started!

**Step 1:**   **Project sales revenue.** Management is forecasting sales growth of 10% in 2009 and another 15% in 2010. This compares to 4% sales growth in 2007 and 5% in 2008. We will use management's sales growth estimates to compute projected sales revenue for the next two years. This means that sales in 2009 are expected to be $27.720 million, or $25.200 million $\times$ 1.10. Similarly, sales in 2010 are projected to be $31.878 million, or $27.720 $\times$ 1.15.

|  | Historical | | Projected | |
|---|---|---|---|---|
|  | **2007** | **2008** | **2009** | **2010** |
| **Sales growth** | 4.0% | 5.0% | 10.0% | 15.0% |

**Step 2:**   **Forecast operating expenses (except depreciation and interest expense, and taxes).** A good jumping-off point for this step in the forecasting process is to assemble information about the company's historical expense margins. These data then provide a basis for projecting future expense amounts.

The historical expense margins and our projected margins follow.

|  | Historical (%) | | Projected (%) | |
|---|---|---|---|---|
|  | **2007** | **2008** | **2009** | **2010** |
| Expense margins |  |  |  |  |
| Cost of goods sold | 65.7% | 65.0% | 65.0% | 65.0% |
| Research and development expense | 0.0 | 0.0 | 0.0 | 0.0 |
| Selling, general, and administrative expense | 23.3 | 23.0 | 23.0 | 23.0 |
| Nonoperating income (loss) | 0.0 | 0.0 | 0.0 | 0.0 |

| EXHIBIT 6.10 | Veto Equipment Supply Company |
|---|---|

## Historical Financial Statements

| ($ in thousands) | Historical 2007 | Historical 2008 | Projected 2009 | Projected 2010 |
|---|---|---|---|---|
| **Income Statement** | | | | |
| Sales | $24,000 | $25,200 | | |
| Cost of goods sold | 15,760 | 16,380 | | |
| Research and development expense | — | — | | |
| Selling, general, and administrative expense | 5,600 | 5,796 | | |
| Depreciation expense | 1,080 | 1,147 | | |
| Pre-tax operating income | 1,560 | 1,877 | | |
| Interest expense | 240 | 277 | | |
| Nonoperating income (loss) | — | — | | |
| Pre-tax earnings | 1,320 | 1,600 | | |
| Tax expense | 440 | 544 | | |
| Net income | $   880 | $ 1,056 | | |
| | | | | |
| **Balance Sheet** | | | | |
| Operating cash and equivalents | $ 1,160 | $ 1,134 | | |
| Accounts receivable | 2,120 | 2,016 | | |
| Inventories | 3,240 | 3,528 | | |
| Other current assets | — | — | | |
| Current assets | 6,520 | 6,678 | | |
| Property, plant and equipment (gross) | 16,600 | 17,640 | | |
| Accumulated depreciation | (10,080) | (11,227) | | |
| Other assets | 600 | 756 | | |
| Total assets | $13,640 | $13,847 | | |
| | | | | |
| Current portion of long-term debt | $   180 | $   208 | | |
| Accounts payable | 2,820 | 2,520 | | |
| Other payables | 160 | 252 | | |
| Current liabilities | 3,160 | 2,980 | | |
| Long-term debt | 1,800 | 1,869 | | |
| Other liabilities | 800 | 504 | | |
| Shareholders' equity | | | | |
| Contributed capital | 5,000 | 5,358 | | |
| Retained earnings | 2,880 | 3,136 | | |
| Total shareholders' equity | 7,880 | 8,494 | | |
| Total liabilities and equity | $13,640 | $13,847 | | |
| | | | | |
| **Retained Earnings** | | | | |
| Beginning retained earnings | $ 2,800 | $ 2,880 | | |
| + Net income | 880 | 1,056 | | |
| − Dividends | (800) | (800) | | |
| = Ending retained earnings | $ 2,880 | $ 3,136 | | |

Notice that cost of goods sold was 65.7% of sales in 2007 but then declined to only 65.0% of sales in 2008. You can see from the table that we are projecting a continuation of this lower margin for the next two years. Consequently, cost of goods sold is expected to be $18.018 million in 2009, or 65.0% of the $27.720 million in projected sales for that year. The 2010 cost of goods sold forecast ($20.721 million) is constructed in a similar manner.

Research and development expenses are projected to remain at zero for the next two years, as are nonoperating items. Selling, general, and administrative expenses are projected to be

23.0% of sales. In other words, our expense forecasts presume that management will continue to operate the business over the next two years in the same manner it did in 2008.

**Step 3:**    **Forecast the level of balance sheet operating assets and liabilities.** Here, too, information about the company's historical asset and liability utilization ratios—for example, operating cash or accounts receivable as a percent of sales—is helpful as a starting point in this step. Here are the historical (and projected) utilization ratios for each operating asset and liability.

> To simplify the forecasting task, utilization ratios are computed using year-end balance sheet amounts.

|  | Historical (%) | | Projected (%) | |
|---|---|---|---|---|
|  | **2007** | **2008** | **2009** | **2010** |
| Operating asset and liability utilization (% of sales) | | | | |
| Operating cash and equivalents/Sales | 4.8% | 4.5% | 4.5% | 4.5% |
| Accounts receivable/Sales | 8.8 | 8.0 | 8.0 | 8.0 |
| Inventory/Sales | 13.5 | 14.0 | 17.0 | 17.0 |
| Other current assets/Sales | 0.0 | 0.0 | 0.0 | 0.0 |
| Property, plant, and equipment (gross)/Sales | 69.2 | 70.0 | 65.0 | 70.0 |
| Other assets/Sales | 2.5 | 3.0 | 3.0 | 3.0 |
| Accounts payable/Sales | 11.8 | 10.0 | 10.0 | 10.0 |
| Other current liabilities/Sales | 0.7 | 1.0 | 1.0 | 1.0 |
| Other liabilities/Sales | 3.3 | 2.0 | 2.0 | 2.0 |

Notice, for example, that accounts receivable at the end of 2007 amounted to 8.8% of sales that year. However, accounts receivable were only 8.0% of sales at the end of 2008. We are projecting that receivables will maintain their current 8.0% level over the next two years. This means that accounts receivable are forecasted to be $2.218 million at the end of 2009 (or 8.0% of the $27.720 in expected 2009 sales). A similar computation determines the forecasted balance of accounts receivable at the end of 2010.

Most of the operating assets and liabilities are forecasted to remain at their 2008 utilization ratios for the next two years. However, there are two exceptions. Inventory levels are expected to increase from 14.0% of sales in 2008 to 17.0% of sales in 2009 and 2010. At the same time, Veto's investment in gross property, plant, and equipment is expected to decline from 70.0% of sales in 2008 to 65.0% of sales in 2009 and then rise back again to 70.0% in 2010.

**Step 4:**    **Forecast Depreciation expense and Tax expense.** Historical and projected information about Depreciation expense (as a percent of the year-end cost of property, plant, and equipment) and Tax expense (as a percent of pre-tax earnings) is shown in the following table.

|  | Historical (%) | | Projected (%) | |
|---|---|---|---|---|
|  | **2007** | **2008** | **2009** | **2010** |
| Depreciation expense/PP&E gross cost | 6.5% | 6.5% | 6.5% | 6.5% |
| Tax expense/Pre-tax earnings | 33.3 | 34.0 | 34.0 | 34.0 |

Depreciation expense has been running at 6.5% of the company's year-end investment in property, plant, and equipment. Depreciation is expected to remain at this level for the next two years. So, Depreciation expense is forecasted to be $1.171 million in 2009 (or 6.5% of the

$18.018 million invested in property, plant, and equipment at the end of that year). This amount of Depreciation expense is shown on the company's 2009 income statement, and as an increase to the Accumulated depreciation balance sheet account in 2009. Tax expense is projected to be 34.0% of pre-tax earnings for the next two years, a level equal to that in 2008. This means that tax expense is forecasted to be $0.634 million in 2009 (or 34% of the $1.864 million in pre-tax earnings that year including interest expense from Step 5).

**Step 5:**   **Forecast the company's financial structure.** This forecasting step develops projections for dividends, debt, and interest expense. Here's an historical snapshot of each financial statement component and our projections for 2009 and 2010.

|  | Historical (%) | | Projected (%) | |
|---|---|---|---|---|
|  | **2007** | **2008** | **2009** | **2010** |
| Financial structure |  |  |  |  |
| Debt/Assets | 14.5% | 15.0% | 15.0% | 15.0% |
| Current portion of long-term debt/Debt | 9.1 | 10.0 | 10.0 | 10.0 |
| Interest rate on beginning debt | 12.1 | 14.0 | 14.0 | 14.0 |
| Dividends ($ in thousands) | $800 | $800 | $800 | $800 |

The debt (current portion plus long-term portion) to asset ratio at Veto Equipment Supply was 14.5% in 2007, and 9.1% of the company's debt that year was listed as a current liability on the balance sheet. The debt to asset ratio increased to 15% in 2008 and is projected to remain at that percentage level over the next two year. The current portion of long-term debt is projected to stay at 10%. This means that Veto is projected to have debt of $2.194 million in 2009 (or 15.0% of the $14.629 in forecasted total assets). Of that amount, $0.219 (or 10%) is classified as a current liability.

Interest expense as a percent of beginning debt was 12.1% in 2007 but then increased to 14.0% in 2008. We are projecting interest expense to remain at this percentage level over the next two years. So, interest expense in 2009 is projected to be $0.291 million (or 14.0% of the $2.077 million in *beginning* debt that year). Dividends have been $0.800 million each year and are expected to remain so for the next two years.

We have now completed the forecasting steps necessary to construct projected income statements and balance sheets for Veto Equipment Supply Company. See Exhibit 6.11 for our detailed forecasts.

In 2010, the company is projected to have sales of $31.878 million and net income of $1.365 million. However, the revolving credit line needs are expected to reach $2.823 million (or $0.282 in current debt plus another $2.541 million in long-term debt). This amount exceeds the company's existing credit limit for the Commerce First Bank loan. Let's take a look at Veto's projected cash flow statements to learn the reason for this projected increase in borrowing.

> We did not forecast one financial statement item—Contributed capital—directly. Instead, we used the balance sheet equation that requires total assets to equal total liabilities plus shareholders' equity. The projected contributed capital figure was set equal to an amount that ensured that the balance sheet equation held for each forecast year.

**Step 6:**   **Derive projected cash flow statements.** Projected cash flow statements can now be derived directly from the company's projected income statements and balance sheets. See Exhibit 6.12 for the company's historical and projected cash flows.

The historical cash flow statements reveal that Veto enjoyed positive free cash flows—Cash from operations *minus* Cash used in investing activities—in both 2007 and 2008. The statements also indicate that the company paid dividends and increased its long-term debt in both years. From a credit risk perspective, this is not good news because it suggests that the company is borrowing money to maintain a stable dividend payout.

**EXHIBIT 6.11**  Veto Equipment Supply Company

## Historical and Projected Income Statements and Balance Sheets

| | Historical | | Projected | |
|---|---|---|---|---|
| ($ in thousands) | 2007 | 2008 | 2009 | 2010 |
| **Income Statement** | | | | |
| Sales | $24,000 | $25,200 | $27,720 | $31,878 |
| Cost of goods sold | 15,760 | 16,380 | 18,018 | 20,721 |
| Research and development expense | — | — | — | — |
| Selling, general, and administrative expense | 5,600 | 5,796 | 6,375 | 7,332 |
| Depreciation expense | 1,080 | 1,147 | 1,171 | 1,450 |
| Pre-tax operating income | 1,560 | 1,877 | 2,156 | 2,375 |
| Interest expense | 240 | 277 | 291 | 307 |
| Nonoperating income (loss) | — | — | — | — |
| Pre-tax earnings | 1,320 | 1,600 | 1,865 | 2,068 |
| Tax expense | 440 | 544 | 634 | 703 |
| Net income | $    880 | $ 1,056 | $ 1,231 | $ 1,365 |
| **Balance Sheet** | | | | |
| Operating cash and equivalents | $ 1,160 | $ 1,134 | $ 1,247 | $ 1,435 |
| Accounts receivable | 2,120 | 2,016 | 2,218 | 2,550 |
| Inventories | 3,240 | 3,528 | 4,712 | 5,419 |
| Other current assets | — | — | — | — |
| Current assets | 6,520 | 6,678 | 8,177 | 9,404 |
| Property, plant and equipment (gross) | 16,600 | 17,640 | 18,018 | 22,315 |
| Accumulated depreciation | (10,080) | (11,227) | (12,398) | (13,848) |
| Other assets | 600 | 756 | 832 | 956 |
| Total assets | $13,640 | $13,847 | $14,629 | $18,827 |
| Current portion of long-term debt | $    180 | $    208 | $    219 | $    282 |
| Accounts payable | 2,820 | 2,520 | 2,772 | 3,188 |
| Other payables | 160 | 252 | 277 | 319 |
| Current liabilities | 3,160 | 2,980 | 3,268 | 3,789 |
| Long-term debt | 1,800 | 1,869 | 1,975 | 2,541 |
| Other liabilities | 800 | 504 | 554 | 638 |
| Shareholders' equity | | | | |
| Contributed capital | 5,000 | 5,358 | 5,265 | 7,727 |
| Retained earnings | 2,880 | 3,136 | 3,567 | 4,132 |
| Total shareholders' equity | 7,880 | 8,494 | 8,832 | 11,859 |
| Total liabilities and equity | $13,640 | $13,847 | $14,629 | $18,827 |
| **Retained Earnings** | | | | |
| Beginning retained earnings | $ 2,800 | $ 2,880 | $ 3,136 | $ 3,567 |
| + Net income | 880 | 1,056 | 1,231 | 1,365 |
| − Dividends | (800) | (800) | (800) | (800) |
| = Ending retained earnings | $ 2,880 | $ 3,136 | $ 3,567 | $ 4,132 |

The projected cash flow statements indicate that Veto is facing a significant cash flow problem in 2010. Even though operating cash flows that year are projected to be $2.233 million, free cash flows are expected to be in a deficit position of $2.188 million (or $2.233 million in operating cash flows minus $4.421 million in required investment).

| EXHIBIT 6.12 | Veto Equipment Supply Company |
|---|---|

**Historical and Projected Cash Flow Statements**

| | Historical | | Projected | |
|---|---|---|---|---|
| ($ in thousands) | 2007 | 2008 | 2009 | 2010 |
| Cash Flow Statement | | | | |
| Net income | $ 880 | $ 1,056 | $ 1,231 | $ 1,365 |
| Noncash expenses | | | | |
| Depreciation | 1,080 | 1,147 | 1,171 | 1,450 |
| Changes in noncash working capital accounts | | | | |
| Accounts receivable decrease | 65 | 104 | (202) | (332) |
| Inventory decrease (increase) | (158) | (288) | (1,184) | (707) |
| Other current asset decrease | — | — | — | — |
| Accounts payable increase (decrease) | 100 | (300) | 252 | 416 |
| Other current liabilities increase | (20) | 92 | 25 | 42 |
| Cash from operations | $ 1,947 | $ 1,811 | $ 1,293 | $ 2,234 |
| Increase in property, plant, and equipment | $ (985) | $(1,040) | $ (378) | $(4,297) |
| Increase in other assets | (67) | (156) | (76) | (124) |
| Cash used in investing activities | $(1,052) | $(1,196) | $ (454) | $(4,421) |
| Increase in long-term debt | $ 200 | $ 97 | $ 117 | $ 629 |
| Increase in other liabilities | (50) | (296) | 50 | 83 |
| Increase in contributed capital | — | 358 | (93) | 2,463 |
| Dividends paid | (800) | (800) | (800) | (800) |
| Cash from financing activities | $ (650) | $ (641) | $ (726) | $ 2,375 |
| Net increase (decrease) in cash | $ 245 | $ (26) | $ 113 | $ 188 |

Add the continued dividend payment of $800,000, and the cash flow deficit approaches $3 million.

According to our forecasts, Veto will make up this deficit by borrowing $0.630 million, as shown by the increase in long-term debt and by raising another $2.463 million from stockholders as the increase in contributed capital shows. But what if stockholders are unwilling to buy more shares from the company? Then management must either scale back the company's operating plans to free up more cash or negotiate a substantially larger credit line with Commerce First Bank.

## PROBLEMS / DISCUSSION QUESTIONS

**Required:**
1. Define the term *quality of earnings*.
2. List the techniques that management can use to improve a company's *reported* earnings performance in the short run.
3. Give examples of low-quality earnings components.

P 6 - 1

Earnings quality

**Required:**
1. Describe the role of accounting numbers in corporate valuation.
2. What does *sustainable earnings* mean? What types of earnings are not sustainable?
3. Briefly describe what the process of valuation involves.

P 6 - 2

Identifying the role of accounting numbers in valuation

*(continued)*

4. What are free cash flows? Describe the key features of the free cash flow approach to valuation.

5. Explain the difference between a company's operating cash flow and its free cash flow.

6. What are abnormal earnings? Describe the key features of the abnormal earnings approach to valuation.

7. What is an earnings surprise? How does an earnings surprise impact the value of a firm's equity?

| | |
|---|---|
| **P6-3**<br><br>Identifying components of earnings | This chapter discusses these three components of earnings: permanent, transitory, and valuation-irrelevant.<br><br>**Required:**<br><br>1. Provide a one-sentence explanation for each component.<br><br>2. Provide some examples of each component. (You might examine the income statements of two or three publicly traded companies to aid your answer.) |

---

**P6-4**

Explaining differences in P/E ratios

The price/earnings (P/E) ratios in October 2007 for two groups of companies were

| Company | P/E Ratio |
|---|---|
| **Group A** | |
| Amazon.com | 90 |
| Microsoft | 22 |
| Toyota Motors | 11 |
| Whole Foods Market | 34 |
| | |
| **Group B** | |
| Kroger | 17 |
| Pantry | 12 |
| Safeway | 11 |
| Whole Foods Market | 34 |

**Required:**

1. What factors might explain the difference in the P/E ratios of the firms in Group A?

2. What factors might explain the difference in the P/E ratios of the grocery firms in Group B?

---

**P6-5**

Credit risk and cash flow volatility

The quarterly cash flows from operations for two software companies are

| | 2006 | | | | 2007 |
|---|---|---|---|---|---|
| | **Q1** | **Q2** | **Q3** | **Q4** | **Q1** |
| Firm A | $406.1 | $204.2 | $729.1 | $440.2 | $ 587.8 |
| Firm B | $136.7 | $243.1 | $708.2 | $(87.9) | $(161.4) |

**Required:**

1. Explain why Firm B has more credit risk than Firm A.

2. Suppose that Firm B's cash flow was $200 higher each quarter (e.g., $336.7 in Q1 of 2006). Explain why Firm B might still be judged to have higher credit risk than Firm A.

---

**P6-6**

Assessing credit risk using cash flow forecasts

Randall Manufacturing has requested a $2 million, four-year term loan from Farmers State Bank. It will use the money to expand its warehouse and to upgrade its assembly line. Randall supplied the following cash flow forecasts as part of the loan application.

| ($ in thousands) | Year 1 | Year 2 | Year 3 | Year 4 |
|---|---|---|---|---|
| Cash provided by operations | $ 685 | $715 | $720 | $735 |
| Cash used for investing activities | (2,590) | (50) | (50) | (50) |
| Cash used for financing activities | 2,000 | (100) | (100) | (100) |
| Net change in cash | $ 95 | $565 | $570 | $585 |

The forecasts assume that the loan is granted in Year 1 and that $2.590 million will be spent that year on the expansion and upgrade. Randall plans to spend $50,000 each year to replace worn-out manufacturing equipment and $100,000 each year for dividends.

**Required:**

1. As the bank's chief loan officer, what is your opinion about the degree of credit risk associated with this $2 million loan?

2. How can Randall Manufacturing lower its credit risk?

---

As discussed in the chapter, abnormal earnings (AE) are

$$AE_t = \text{Actual earnings}_t - \text{Required or "normal" earnings}_t$$

which may be expressed as

$$AE_t = \text{NOPAT}_t - (r \times BV_{t-1})$$

where NOPAT is the firm's net operating profit after taxes, $r$ is the cost of equity capital, and $BV_{t-1}$ is the book value of equity at time $t - 1$.

**Required:**

Solve the following problems:

1. If NOPAT is $5,000, $r = 15\%$, and $BV_{t-1}$ is $50,000, what is AE?

2. If NOPAT is $25,000, $r = 18\%$, and $BV_{t-1}$ is $125,000, what is AE?

3. Assume that the firm in requirement 2 can increase NOPAT to $30,000 by instituting some cost-cutting measures. What is the new AE?

4. Assume that the firm in requirement 2 can divest $25,000 of unproductive capital with NOPAT falling by only $2,000. What is the new AE?

5. Assume that the firm in requirement 2 can add a new division at a cost of $40,000, which will increase NOPAT by $7,600 per year. Would adding the new division increase AE?

6. Assume that the firm in requirement 1 can add a new division at a cost of $25,000, which will increase NOPAT by $3,500 per year. Would adding the new division increase AE?

**P 6 - 7**

Determining abnormal earnings—Some examples

---

As discussed in the chapter, abnormal earnings (AE) are

$$AE_t = \text{Actual earnings}_t - \text{Required earnings}_t$$

which may be expressed as

$$AE_t = \text{NOPAT}_t - (r \times BV_{t-1})$$

where NOPAT is the firm's net operating profit after taxes, $r$ is the cost of equity capital, and $BV_{t-1}$ is the book value of equity at $t - 1$.

Appearing next is the NOPAT, $BV_{t-1}$, and cost of equity capital for two firms.

**P 6 - 8**

Calculating value creation by two companies

mhhe.com/revsine4e

| Company A | 2004 | 2005 | 2006 | 2007 | 2008 |
|---|---|---|---|---|---|
| NOPAT | $ 66,920 | $ 79,632 | $ 83,314 | $ 89,920 | $ 92,690 |
| $BV_{t-1}$ | 478,000 | 504,000 | 541,000 | 562,000 | 598,000 |
| Cost of equity capital | 0.152 | 0.167 | 0.159 | 0.172 | 0.166 |

| Company B | 2004 | 2005 | 2006 | 2007 | 2008 |
|---|---|---|---|---|---|
| NOPAT | $192,940 | $176,341 | $227,700 | $ 198,900 | $ 282,964 |
| $BV_{t-1}$ | 877,000 | 943,000 | 989,999 | 1,020,000 | 1,199,000 |
| Cost of equity capital | 0.188 | 0.179 | 0.183 | 0.175 | 0.186 |

**Required:**

1. Calculate each firm's AE each year from 2004 to 2008.
2. Which firm was better managed over the 2004–2008 period? Why?
3. Which firm is likely to be the better stock investment in 2009 and beyond? Why?

---

**P6-9**

Identifying P/E ratio determinants

A firm's P/E ratio can be written using equation (6.9) as:

$$P/E = \frac{\text{Market price per share}}{\text{Earning per share}} = \frac{1}{r} + \frac{\text{Present value of growth opportunities per share}}{\text{Earning per share}}$$

where $r$ is the cost of equity capital (discount rate).

**Required:**

Briefly discuss how a firm's P/E ratio is related to (1) the present value of growth opportunities, (2) risk, and (3) the firm's choice of accounting methods.

---

**P6-10**

Valuing growth opportunities

As shown in equation (6.9), the price equation for a firm with positive growth opportunities is

$$P_0 = \frac{X_0}{r} + \text{NPVGO}$$

where $P_0$ is the current stock price, $X_0$ is current reported earnings per share, $r$ is the cost of equity capital, and NPVGO is the net present value of future growth opportunities. The recent values of $P_0$, $X_0$, and $r$ for several companies are:

|  | $P_0$ | $X_0$ | $r$ |
|---|---|---|---|
| Dell Computer | $26.74 | $0.82 | 0.138 |
| eBay | 67.82 | 0.82 | 0.198 |
| Ford Motor | 9.30 | 0.99 | 0.114 |
| Home Depot | 24.02 | 1.55 | 0.121 |
| Wal-Mart | 50.51 | 1.83 | 0.090 |

**Required:**

1. Why does eBay have a higher cost of equity capital ($r$) than Wal-Mart?
2. Compute NPVGO for each company.
3. Why is eBay's NPVGO larger than that for Home Depot?
4. Why do Ford Motor and Wal-Mart have such different NPVGO amounts?

---

**P6-11**

Earnings-based equity

**Required:**

In each of the following situations, assume a zero-growth rate for earnings and dividends (NPVGO is zero), that all earnings are paid out as dividends, and that the earnings-based valuation model in equation (6.9) is being used.

1. Dennison Corporation's earnings are expected to be $7 per share and its stock price is $28. What is the required rate of return on the firm's equity?
2. Sampson Corporation's earnings are expected to be $5 per share and its required rate of return on equity is 22%. What is the current price of the stock?
3. Johnson Corporation's current stock price is $40 and its required rate of return on equity is 15%. What is the firm's expected earnings?

---

**P6-12**

Interpreting stock price changes

Assume that General Motors (GM) announces on September 30, 2008 that it expects its EPS to be $4.50 for the year ending December 31, 2008. At the time of the announcement, financial analysts are forecasting GM's annual EPS to be $5.00.

**Required:**

1. Would GM's earnings guidance announcement cause a change in its stock price on September 30? Explain why or why not.

2. Consider the following two scenarios:

   a. The $0.50 difference between GM's management forecast and analysts' forecast is completely attributable to a previously reported month-long labor strike at one of GM's parts plants, a strike that disrupted production at most of the firm's car manufacturing facilities.

   b. The $0.50 difference between GM's management forecast and analysts' forecast is attributable to GM's (previously undisclosed) decision to discontinue production of its line of sports utility vehicles and small trucks.

   Do you expect the magnitude of the stock price change to be more in case (a) or case (b)? Why?

---

**P6-13**

**Stock price and earnings information**

Figure 6.6 in this chapter illustrates the behavior of stock returns over the period before a quarterly earnings announcement (from trading days $-60$ to $-1$); at the time of an earnings announcement (on day 0); and over the period following an earnings announcement (from trading days $+1$ to $+60$) for three groups of firms. (*Note:* A 60-trading-day period is almost equal to the 90 calendar days that make up a fiscal quarter.) The three groups are "good news" firms (firms whose earnings are higher than the market expected), "no news" firms (firms whose earnings are what the market expected), and "bad news" firms (firms whose earnings are lower than what the market expected).

**Required:**

1. Why do the stock returns of good news firms drift upward before the earnings announcement date?

2. Why do the stock returns of bad news firms drift downward before the earnings announcement date?

3. Why don't the stock returns of no news firms drift upward or downward during the $-60$ to $-1$ trading day period?

4. For each group, explain the behavior of the stock returns at the time of the earnings announcement (on trading day 0).

5. While not immediately obvious from Figure 6.6, the stock returns of good news firms tend to continue to drift upward after the earnings announcement, and the stock returns of bad news firms tend to continue to drift downward after the earnings announcement. Explain why these postannouncement drifts occur.

6. Suppose a separate Figure 6.6 were produced for a sample of large publicly traded firms and for a sample of small publicly traded firms. Would you expect the two figures to look the same? Explain why or why not.

---

**P6-14**

**Assigning credit ratings using financial ratios**

Exhibit 6.8 describes the key financial ratios that Standard & Poor's analysts use to assess credit risk and assign credit ratings to industrial companies. The same financial ratios for three firms follow.

|  | Firm 1 | Firm 2 | Firm 3 |
|---|---|---|---|
| EBIT interest coverage | 2.7 | 12.8 | 16.7 |
| EBITDA interest coverage | 3.7 | 18.7 | 24.6 |
| FFO/Total debt | 19.8 | 80.2 | 135.1 |
| Free operating cash flow/Total debt | 8.2 | 40.6 | 87.9 |
| Total debt/EBITDA | 4.0 | 1.0 | 0.3 |
| Return on capital | 9.9 | 29.2 | 32.7 |
| Total debt/Capital | 54.8 | 30.2 | 8.1 |

**Required:**

1. What credit rating would be assigned to Firm 1?

2. What credit rating would be assigned to Firm 2?

3. Does Firm 3 have more or less credit risk than Firm 2? How can you tell?

---

**P6-15**

Making credit-rating changes

Exhibit 6.8 describes the key financial ratios that Standard & Poor's analysts use to assess credit risk and assign credit ratings to industrial companies. Those same financial ratios for a single company over time follow. The company was assigned a AAA credit rating at the beginning of 2008.

| | 2008 | | | | 2009 | |
|---|---|---|---|---|---|---|
| | **QI** | **Q2** | **Q3** | **Q4** | **QI** | **Q2** |
| EBIT interest coverage | 23.8 | 22.1 | 21.6 | 20.8 | 20.6 | 12.4 |
| EBITDA interest coverage | 25.3 | 26.4 | 25.6 | 23.2 | 22.9 | 16.5 |
| FFO/Total debt | 167.8 | 150.8 | 130.7 | 128.4 | 80.2 | 76.2 |
| Free operating cash flow/Total debt | 104.1 | 107.3 | 103.7 | 98.6 | 61.5 | 45.3 |
| Total debt/EBITDA | 0.2 | 0.2 | 0.2 | 0.6 | 0.8 | 1.0 |
| Return on capital | 35.1 | 34.3 | 30.6 | 28.1 | 25.9 | 24.7 |
| Total debt/Capital | 6.2 | 6.8 | 7.5 | 15.4 | 27.2 | 35.6 |

**Required:**

1. Did the company's credit risk increase or decrease over these six quarters?

2. What credit rating should be assigned to the company as of Q2 in 2009?

3. In what quarter should the company's credit rating be downgraded from AAA?

---

**P6-16**

Applying P/E multiples to earnings components

Consider the following information:

| | **ABC Corporation** | **XYZ Corporation** |
|---|---|---|
| Reported EPS | $5.00 | $5.00 |
| EPS decomposition | | |
| Permanent | 75% | 55% |
| Transitory | 20% | 25% |
| Value-irrelevant | 5% | 20% |

**Required:**

1. Use a risk-adjusted cost of capital of 15% to calculate each firm's implied share price and earnings multiples. Why are the implict share prices and earnings multiples for the two firms different?

2. Repeat requirement 1 using a risk-adjusted cost of capital of 8%.

---

**P6-17**

Calculating sustainable earnings

mhhe.com/revsine4e

Colonel Electric Company is one of the largest and most diversified industrial corporations in the world. From the time of its incorporation in 1892, the company has engaged in developing, manufacturing, and marketing a wide variety of products for the generation, transmission, distribution, control, and utilization of electricity.

Appearing in the following table are the 2006–2008 income statements of Colonel Electric Company.

## Comparative Income Statement for Years Ended December 31

| ($ in millions) | 2008 | 2007 | 2006 |
|---|---|---|---|
| **Revenues** | | | |
| Sales of goods | $54,196 | $53,177 | $52,767 |
| Sales of services | 11,923 | 10,836 | 8,863 |
| Royalties and fees | 1,629 | 753 | 783 |
| **Total revenues** | 67,748 | 64,766 | 62,413 |
| **Costs and expenses** | | | |
| Cost of goods sold | (24,594) | (24,308) | (22,775) |
| Cost of services sold | (8,425) | (6,785) | (6,274) |
| Restructuring (charges) reversals | 1,000 | — | (2,500) |
| Interest charges | (595) | (649) | (410) |
| Other costs and expenses | (6,274) | (5,743) | (5,211) |
| Litigation charges (income) | 550 | — | (250) |
| (Losses) gains on sales of investments | (75) | — | 25 |
| (Losses) gains on asset sales | 25 | 55 | (35) |
| Inventory write-offs | — | (18) | — |
| Asset impairment write-offs | — | — | (24) |
| Special item charges | (34) | — | (8) |
| Loss from labor strike | — | (20) | — |
| **Total costs and expenses** | (38,422) | (37,468) | (37,462) |
| Earnings from continuing operations before income taxes | 29,326 | 27,298 | 24,951 |
| Provision for income taxes (34%) | (9,971) | (9,281) | (8,483) |
| Earnings from continuing operations | $19,355 | $18,017 | $16,468 |
| Income (loss) from discontinued operations (net of tax) | — | (250) | 1,100 |
| Gain (loss) on sale of discontinued operations (net of tax) | 750 | — | — |
| Extraordinary gain (loss) on early debt retirement (net of tax) | (50) | — | 10 |
| **Net earnings** | $20,055 | $17,767 | $17,578 |

In 2008 the company earned Royalties and fees revenue of $1 billion from a one-time, six-month contract with the U.S. government. The company does not expect to do any further business with the U.S. government in the future.

**Required:**

1. Calculate Colonel Electric's sustainable earnings for each year. (Although there is no consensus on how best to measure sustainable earnings, one common approach is to start with GAAP reported earnings and then eliminate unsustainable earnings items.)

2. How do Colonel Electric's sustainable earnings compare to its reported net earnings in each year?

---

Companies that want to "manage" their reported earnings can do so through real transactions that alter operating cash flows or through accounting gimmicks that change only net income accruals (the noncash revenue and expense components of GAAP earnings).

The 2007–2008 balance sheets and 2008 income statement of Runner's World follow. The company's operating cash flow for 2008 was ($38,460) a net outflow.

**P6-18**

Assessing earnings quality: net accruals and discretionary accruals

## Income Statement for the Year Ended December 31, 2008

| | |
|---|---:|
| Sales | $120,000 |
| Cost of goods sold | (60,000) |
| Selling, general, and administrative expenses | (22,000) |
| Depreciation expense | (14,000) |
| Operating income | 24,000 |
| Interest expense | (6,000) |
| Interest income | 1,000 |
| Income before taxes | 19,000 |
| Income taxes (34%) | (6,460) |
| **Net income** | **$ 12,540** |

## Balance Sheet

| | December 31 | |
|---|---|---|
| | **2008** | **2007** |
| **Assets** | | |
| Cash | $ 100,000 | $ 80,000 |
| Accounts receivable | 95,000 | 75,000 |
| Inventories | 120,000 | 90,000 |
| Prepaid expenses | 15,000 | 20,000 |
| Plant, property, and equipment (net) | 924,000 | 850,000 |
| Long-term investments | 175,000 | 232,000 |
| Total assets | $1,429,000 | $1,347,000 |
| | | |
| **Liabilities and stockholders' equity** | | |
| Liabilities | | |
| Accounts payable | $ 220,000 | $ 155,000 |
| Accrued payables | 195,000 | 275,000 |
| Interest payable | 22,000 | 10,000 |
| Income tax payable | 45,000 | 62,000 |
| Long-term debt | 350,000 | 270,000 |
| Total liabilities | 832,000 | 772,000 |
| Stockholders' equity | | |
| Common stock | 175,000 | 145,000 |
| Retained earnings | 422,000 | 430,000 |
| Total stockholders' equity | 597,000 | 575,000 |
| Total liabilities and stockholders' equity | $1,429,000 | $1,347,000 |

**Required:**

1. Calculate the net accruals (the difference between accrual earnings and operating cash flows) recorded by Runner's World in 2008.

2. Identify the individual components of net accruals in requirement 1.

3. Which accruals identified in requirement 2 are subject to the greatest degree of management discretion?

4. Why might managers manipulate the firm's discretionary accruals?

**P6-19**

Growth, expansion, and equity valuation

Allison Manufacturing and BSJ Manufacturing both produce after-market accessories for sports utility vehicles. Both companies are about to launch strategic initiatives that will increase sales and net income for the foreseeable future. Allison has decided to launch an expensive advertising campaign that will increase sales from $20 million to $30 million a year and net income from $2 million to $2.5 million a year. BSJ has decided to issue an additional $10 million of common stock and then use the proceeds to buy a smaller accessories manufacturer. The acquisition is expected to increase BSJ's sales by $10 million a year and net income by $1 million. Key financial statement figures for both companies follow. The "before" amounts describe each company's current operations, and the "after" amounts incorporate the expected results from the strategic initiatives.

|  | Before | After |
|---|---|---|
| **Allison Manufacturing** | | |
| Annual sales | $20 million | $ 30 million |
| Annual net income | $ 2 million | $2.5 million |
| Equity book value | $10 million | $ 10 million |
| Number of shares outstanding | 100,000 | 100,000 |
| **BSJ Manufacturing** | | |
| Annual sales | $20 million | $ 30 million |
| Annual net income | $ 2 million | $ 3 million |
| Equity book value | $10 million | $ 20 million |
| Number of shares outstanding | 100,000 | 200,000 |

Both companies pay all net income out as dividends each year and have a 10% cost of equity capital. Use the abnormal earnings valuation model from equation (6.11) to answer the required questions.

**Required:**

1. Calculate the per share value of each company *before* it undertakes its strategic initiatives assuming that its current levels of annual net income can be sustained forever.

2. Calculate the percentage growth rate in sales and net income that each company will experience as a result of its strategic initiatives. What is the ROCE for each company before and after its strategic initiative?

3. Calculate the per share value of each company after it implements its strategic initiative assuming that the new expected level of annual net income can be sustained forever.

4. Explain why the per share value of one company increases while the per share value of the other company declines.

---

In August 2007, analysts were expecting Whole Foods Market's sales to be $6,450 million in 2007 and $7,500 million in 2008. Net income was expected to be $147 million and $151 million in 2007 and 2008, respectively. The company's financial statements through 2006 are described and analyzed in Chapter 5.

**P6-20**

Whole Foods Market: Making financial statement forecasts

mhhe.com/revsine4e

**Required:**

1. Using the steps outlined in Appendix B to this chapter and the spreadsheet template available on the textbook Web site, prepare 2007 and 2008 forecasted financial statements (balance sheets, income statements, and cash flow statements) for Whole Foods Market. Your forecasts should incorporate the following assumptions:

   a. Sales for 2007 and 2008 will equal $6,450 million and $7,500 million, respectively. Investment and other income will be $20 million each year.

   b. All other income statement items (except pre-opening and relocation costs and interest expense) are expected to equal their 2006 levels as a percentage of sales. Interest expense is expected to be close to zero (see item [e] below). Pre-opening and relocation costs are expected to be $40 million each year.

   c. The company's income tax rate will be 40%.

   d. Cash and cash equivalents are expected to be 2.0% of sales.

   e. Long-term debt and capital lease obligations are expected to remain at around $10 million each year. Current installments of long-term debt will be $50,000 each year. Interest expense will be essentially zero each year because amounts are rounded to the nearest $100,000.

   f. All other balance sheet items except Common stockholders equity are expected to equal their 2006 levels as a percentage of sales. Depreciation expense (included in item [b]) is estimated to be $178.0 million and $207.0 million in 2007 and 2008, respectively. Accumulated depreciation was $706.1 million and $589.2 million in 2006 and 2005, respectively.

g. Development costs of new store locations (included in Direct store expenses in item [b]) are expected to be $200 million each year, and are classified as an investing (not operating) cash flow item by the company.

h. The company will continue to pay dividends of about $60 million each year. The company will issue or buy back stock during 2007 and 2008 to meet its cash flow needs or to distribute excess cash. Additional forecast assumptions may be needed.

i. Round all percentage calculations to the nearest one-half of a percent for forecasting purposes (e.g. 2.35% becomes 2.5%).

2. How do your net income forecasts from requirement 1 compare with those of the analysts ($147 million and $151 million in 2007 and 2008)? What does this tell you about your forecasting assumptions compared to those used by the analysts?

3. How do your sales, net income, accounts receivable, total assets, and operating cash flow forecasts for 2007 and 2008 compare to the amounts actually reported by the company in those two years? What factors are likely to explain sizable differences between the actual figures and your forecasts?

---

| **P6-21** |
|---|

Krispy Kreme Doughnuts:
Preparing financial statement
forecasts

mhhe.com/revsine4e

**S** TRETCH

In October 2003, analysts were expecting sales at Krispy Kreme Doughnuts, Inc. to be $657 million in 2003 and $819 million in 2004. Net income was expected to be $50.7 million in 2003 and $65.9 million in 2004. The company's financial statements through 2002 are contained in the spreadsheet template available on the textbook Web site.

**Required:**

1. Using the steps outlined in Appendix B to this chapter and the spreadsheet template, prepare 2003 and 2004 forecasted financial statements (income statements, balance sheets, and cash flow statements) for Krispy Kreme. Your forecasts should incorporate the following assumptions:

   • Sales for 2003 and 2004 will equal $657 million and $819 million, respectively.

   • Nonoperating expenses and income will be zero.

   • The company's income tax rate will be 35%.

   • All other income statement items are expected to equal their 2002 levels as a percentage of sales. Depreciation expense was $12.3 million in 2002 ($10.3 in cost of goods sold and $2.0 in selling, general, and administration [SG&A]) and $8.0 million in 2001 ($6.0 in cost of goods sold and $2.0 in SG&A).

   • All balance sheet items except Common stockholders' equity are expected to equal their 2002 levels as a percentage of sales. Accumulated depreciation was $43.9 million and $50.2 million in 2001 and 2002, respectively. Combine Long-term investments, Intangibles, and Other assets into a single balance sheet item (Other assets).

   • Debt is expected to be 15% of assets, and the current portion of long-term debt will be 10% of total debt each year. Interest expense will be 6% of debt at the beginning of each year.

   • The company will issue or buy back stock during 2003 and 2004 to meet its cash flow needs or to distribute excess cash. Dividends and Other comprehensive income will be zero.

2. How do your net income forecasts from requirement 1 compare with those of the analysts ($50.7 million and $65.9 million)? What does this tell you about your forecasting assumptions compared to those used by the analysts?

3. Why is it important to assume the company will issue or buy back stock when constructing financial statement forecasts?

4. How do your sales, net income, accounts receiveable, total assets, and operating cash flow forecasts for 2003 and 2004 compare to the amounts actually reported by the company in those two years? What factors are likely to explain sizable differences between the actual figures and your forecasts?

---

In August 2003, Krispy Kreme's common stock was trading at $44 per share. Several analysts and investors believed at the time that its shares were worth considerably less. They were right because by November 2007, the stock was trading below $3 per share.

This problem illustrates how the abnormal earnings valuation model described in Appendix A of this chapter can be combined with security analysts' published earnings forecasts and used to spot potentially overvalued stocks.

**Required:**

1. Use the abnormal earnings valuation model from Appendix A of this chapter to derive an estimate of Krispy Kreme's stock price as of August 2003. A spreadsheet template is available on the textbook Web site. You will need this additional information:

   • Actual EPS for 2001 and 2002 were $0.49 and $0.70, respectively.

   • The per share amount of stock issued in 2001 and 2002 was $0.65 and $0.39, respectively. No stock is expected to be issued or bought back during the next five years.

   • Other comprehensive income per share was $0.32 in 2002 and zero in 2001. Analysts are forecasting other comprehensive income to be zero each year during the next five years.

   • Krispy Kreme does not pay dividends.

   • Return on equity, calculated using the beginning-of-year equity book value, was 21.1% and 20.2% in 2001 and 2002, respectively.

   • Analysts are forecasting EPS to be $0.70 and $0.89 in 2003 and 2004, respectively. The estimated long-term EPS growth rate is 13.25% for 2005 through 2007.

   • Krispy Kreme's equity cost of capital is 11%, and the long-term growth rate (beyond 2007) is assumed to be 3%.

2. Why might your value estimate from requirement 1 differ from the company's stock price in August 2003?

**P 6-22**

Krispy Kreme Doughnuts: Valuing abnormal earnings

mhhe.com/revsine4e

---

Dell Computer Corporation designs, manufactures, and markets a wide range of computer systems, including desktops, notebooks, and network servers; it also markets software, peripherals, and service and support programs. The company is the world's leading direct-computer systems company and one of the top five computer vendors in the world.

Dell was founded on the principle that delivering computers custom built to specific customer orders is the best business model for providing solutions that truly meet end-user needs. This build-to-order, flexible manufacturing process enables the company to achieve faster inventory turnover and reduced inventory levels. It also allows the company to rapidly incorporate new technologies and components into its product offerings. Dell also offers a broad range of service and support programs through its own technical personnel and its direct management of specialized service suppliers. These services range from telephone support to onsite customer-dedicated systems engineers.

1. Appearing in the following table are Dell's EPS and equity book value per share for fiscal years 2000–2002. (Dell's fiscal year ends on January 31.)

2. Dell has not been paying any dividends on its common stock. Assume that it won't in the future.

3. Dell has issued common stock and also repurchased some common stock in the open market. Assume that no stock will be issued or repurchased in the future.

**P 6-23**

Dell Computer: Valuing abnormal earnings

mhhe.com/revsine4e

4. In August 2003, financial analysts following Dell were forecasting annual EPS of $1.00 in 2003, $1.21 in 2004, and an annual EPS growth rate of 15% for 2005–2007.

5. After an initial five-year horizon, assume that Dell's abnormal earnings will grow by 8% per year.

6. Dell's beta is 1.20 and the risk-free rate of return is 4%. Use this information, along with a market risk premium of 5.5%, to estimate Dell's cost of equity capital. (See footnote 37 in this chapter for a description of how to calculate the equity cost of capital.)

7. Dell's actual stock price was $32 at the end of August 2003.

| **Dell Computer** | | | |
|---|---|---|---|
| | **2000** | **2001** | **2002** |
| As reported earnings per share | $0.79 | $0.46 | $0.80 |
| Equity book value beginning of year | 2.08 | 2.17 | 1.80 |
| + Earnings per share | 0.79 | 0.46 | 0.80 |
| + Stock issued (repurchased) | (0.70) | (0.83) | (0.71) |
| − Dividends per share | 0 | 0 | 0 |
| = Equity book value, end of year | $2.17 | $1.80 | $1.89 |

**Required:**

1. Use the abnormal earnings valuation model from Appendix A of this chapter to derive an estimate of Dell's stock price as of August 2003. How does the price you derive compare to the company's actual stock price of $32.00?

2. Some analysts were forecasting the company's EPS to be $1.20 in 2003 and $1.50 in 2004 and to grow at 20% each year from 2005 to 2007. Repeat requirement 1 using these analysts' forecasts in your calculation.

3. Why might Dell's actual stock price differ from the share price estimates you derived in requirements 1 and 2?

---

**P6-24**

Determining the usefulness of management earnings forecasts to financial analysts and investors

The following excerpt is from an article appearing in *The Wall Street Journal*.

## LOW-BALLING: HOW SOME COMPANIES SEND STOCKS ALOFT

What makes a stock a high flyer? Consistently beating the analysts' estimates helps a lot. And many companies seem to have figured out a way to try to help ensure that happens.

Each quarter, after securities analysts estimate what the companies they follow will earn, the game begins. Chief financial officers or investor relations representatives traditionally "give guidance" to analysts, hinting whether the analysts should raise or lower their earnings projections so the analysts won't be embarrassed later.

And these days, many companies are encouraging analysts to deflate earnings projections to artificially low levels, analysts and money managers say. If the game is played right, a company's stock will rise sharply on the day it announces its earnings—and beats the analysts' too-conservative estimates.

Take U.S. Healthcare Inc. Late last year, some analysts say, executives of the health-care services company led them to figure it would post fourth-quarter earnings of about 45 cents a share. On Jan. 28, U.S. Healthcare announced a "preliminary" earnings estimate of 55 cents a share. Then, only two weeks later, U.S. Healthcare shocked Wall Street by posting a

*(continued)*

whopping 68 cents a share for the quarter. The company's stock surged 10% that day, closing at $40.625.

Several analysts think that they were misled. "U.S. Health-care may have beat its own internal estimates, but it also wanted to guide analysts to numbers they knew they could beat," says Kenneth Abramowitz, a health-care analyst who follows the company for Sanford Bernstein and Co.

Costas Nicolaides, the company's chief financial officer, says U.S. Healthcare simply did better than it expected. "I don't guide analysts," he says. "But if someone were to come up with a ridiculous figure, I might raise my eyebrow, or my body language would be such that they'd know."

Money managers and analysts say an increasing number of companies are leading analysts to underestimate their earnings. "More companies," especially those in such growth areas as health-care and technology, "are starting to coerce us to a high degree about what our estimates should be," says Michael Stark, a research analyst with Robertson Stephens & Co. in San Francisco. "They're always low-balling."

Analysts and portfolio managers say that some companies consistently report earnings that are just a little bit better than what they lead analysts to believe. They mention T2 Medical Inc. and Cirrus Logic Inc.; both "understate by pennies," says

Robert Czepial, who runs the Robertson Stephens & Co. Growth Fund. "Of course they're managing the information," he says.

A spokesman for T2 declines to comment. Cirrus's chief financial officer, Sam Srinivasan, says that "Cirrus doesn't play the game of being conservative with the numbers for the analysts."

One corporate chief financial officer, speaking on the condition of anonymity, says that analysts, not the company he works for, are to blame for the company's low-balling its projected earnings. "If the Street's looking for 10 cents and you do nine, you're a moron," he says. "If they're looking for 10 and you do 11, you're a hero."

But low-balling may not work forever. That's the conclusion that some analysts draw from the case of AST Research Inc. For more than five quarters, several analysts and money managers say, the Irvine, Calif., computer maker consistently led them to believe it would earn at least five cents a share less than the actual results.

But for this year's first quarter, analysts lifted their projections, running far ahead of the company's "guidance."

Last month, when AST announced its earnings for the quarter, its stock fell $1.875 to $28.125—even though AST's results were in line with numbers it had given analysts.

*Source:* "Lowballing: How Some Companies Send Stock Aloft," *The Wall Street Journal,* May 6, 1991. Copyright © 1991 Dow Jones & Company, Inc. All rights reserved worldwide. Reprinted with permission.

**Required:**

1. Briefly discuss why managers' forecasts of earnings may be useful to financial analysts and investors.

2. Why might managers steer analysts toward conservative earnings estimates by issuing earnings forecasts that they know are below the earnings they expect to report?

3. As an analyst, what action(s) would you take with firms that consistently issue conservative earnings forecasts?

4. Are there any disadvantages to firms (or their managers) issuing conservative earnings forecasts?

5. The article claims that firms can consistently "low-ball" analysts by issuing conservative earnings forecasts and then expect to see their stock prices increase when reported earnings are "higher than expected." Do you agree or disagree with this claim? Why?

---

**CASES**

As described in the chapter, the abnormal earnings approach for estimating common share value is

$$P_0 = BV_0 + \sum_{t=1}^{\infty} \frac{E_0(X_t - r \times BV_{t-1})}{(1 + r)^t}$$

where $P$ is the total value of all outstanding shares, $BV$ is the (beginning) book value of stockholders' equity, $r$ is the cost of equity capital, $E$ is the expectations operator, and $X$ is

**C 6-1**

Illinois Tool Works: Valuing abnormal earnings

mhhe.com/revsine4e

net income. In words, the model says that share value equals the book value of stockholders' equity plus the present value of future expected abnormal earnings (where abnormal earnings is net income minus the cost of equity capital multiplied by the beginning-of-period book value of stockholders' equity).

The approach is amazingly simple. Two "rubs" are that the model is silent on just how one comes up with expected net income for future years (and therefore future expected abnormal earnings) and just how many future years should be used. Because of the way present value is calculated, abnormal earnings amounts expected for years in the distant future have a small present value and are essentially irrelevant to valuation. In addition, competitive market forces tend eventually to drive abnormal earnings to zero. Thus, it isn't important to make the forecasting horizon terribly long. Professional analysts rarely use more than 15 years, often fewer than 10.

Comparative income statements and retained earnings statements for Illinois Tool Works (ITW) for 2000–2002 follow.

**Required:**

1. Assume a 10-year forecasting horizon. Also assume that ITW's 2002 return on beginning stockholders' equity (net income without extraordinary items divided by beginning 2002 stockholders' equity) of 9.5% is expected to persist throughout the forecasting horizon (that is, that expected net income is always equal to 0.095 multiplied by beginning-of-the-year stockholders' equity). Also assume that no additional stock issuances or repurchases are made and that dividends equal 25% of net income in each year. (This is ITW's approximate historical dividend payout ratio.) Given these assumptions, the book value of stockholders' equity at the *end* of 2003 equals book value at the *beginning* of 2003 plus $(1 - 0.25)$ times 2003 net income. Finally assume that the cost of equity capital is 9%. (This is ITW's approximate cost of equity capital.) With these relatively simple assumptions, use the abnormal earnings model to estimate the total value of Illinois Tool Works' common shares as of the end of 2002. Ignore terminal values at the end of the 10-year forecast horizon in your calculations.

2. As of the end of 2002, 307 million common shares were outstanding. Convert your estimate in requirement 1 to a per share estimate. For purposes of comparison, the actual market value of ITW's common shares ranged from $56 to $64 during the first quarter of 2003.

3. Now assume that ITW will maintain a 20% return on beginning stockholders' equity over the 10-year forecast horizon. What would the company's shares then be worth?

## Illinois Tool Works

## Consolidated Statement of Income

| ($ in millions) | 2002 | 2001 | 2000 |
|---|---|---|---|
| Sales | $9,468 | $9,293 | $9,984 |
| Cost of goods sold | 5,936 | 5,910 | 6,192 |
| Gross profit | 3,532 | 3,383 | 3,792 |
| Selling and administrative expenses | 1,720 | 1,691 | 1,814 |
| Depreciation and amortization | 306 | 385 | 414 |
| Operating profit | 1,506 | 1,307 | 1,564 |
| Interest expense | 68 | 68 | 72 |
| Nonoperating income (expense) | (4) | (7) | (13) |
| Special items | 0 | 3 | 0 |
| Pre-tax income | 1,434 | 1,235 | 1,479 |
| Total income taxes | 502 | 429 | 521 |
| Extraordinary items | (219) | 0 | 0 |
| Net income | $ 713 | $ 806 | $ 958 |

## Illinois Tool Works

### Consolidated Statement of Shareholders' Equity

| ($ in millions) | 2002 | 2001 | 2000 |
|---|---|---|---|
| Balance at beginning of year | $ 9,823 | $9,604 | $9,061 |
| Net income (loss) | 713 | 806 | 958 |
| Stock issued (repurchased) | 361 | (337) | (192) |
| Common stock dividends | (273) | (250) | (223) |
| Balance at end of year | $10,624 | $9,823 | $9,604 |

The following excerpt is from an article that appeared in *The Wall Street Journal*.

**C6-2**

Nike: Firm-specific information releases and large stock price changes

### NIKE'S STOCK DROPS 13% AS FIRM SEES QUARTERLY NET FALLING SHORT OF FORECASTS

Nike Inc. warned that shifts in order patterns and other factors would drag fiscal fourth-quarter earnings below Wall Street forecasts. The news hammered the Beaverton, Ore., athletic-footwear maker's highflying shares. In New York Stock Exchange composite trading yesterday, Nike dropped $8.625, or 13%, to $55.375.

The issues crimping profits for the period ending tomorrow are relatively minor and short term, analysts said. But Wall Street and investor expectations about Nike have been high because of the company's turbocharged growth over the past several quarters. Moreover, the stock has surged in recent days on unconfirmed rumors that investor Warren Buffett has been buying Nike shares. The developments do represent the first stumble in a long time for Nike, which has had profit increases as high as 80% in recent quarters.

Nike said that it expects earnings of between 51 and 56 cents a share for the fourth quarter, including a one-time pretax charge of $18 million for the planned shutdown of a manufacturing facility. Wall Street had been expecting earnings of 69 cents a share. In the year-earlier fourth quarter, Nike earned $156.4 million, or 53 cents a share, on revenue of $1.92 billion.

Nike said several factors damped fourth-quarter profits. One was a shift in order patterns, particularly in Europe. Nike said more retailers bought more items in advance. Typically, Nike retailers buy shoes in advance, and if they sell out, make emergency "at once" orders that are delivered quickly. But Nike said retailers are making fewer "at once" orders in the current quarter. That implies that retailers' sales are lower than they

expected. Some analysts said that, because of Nike's torrid growth in recent quarters, Nike retailers ordered aggressively, betting that sales would continue to surge. "Some got stuck because sales may not have gone up as rapidly as they have," said Jennifer Black Groves, an analyst with Black & Co.

Nike also said it had a "slight" increase in order cancellations in the U.S. Nike's international business has been booming, but U.S. sales still make up more than 60% of total revenue. In an analysts call, the company said it had about $30 million of canceled orders in the quarter, slightly more than it has typically had in recent quarters. Analysts said the domestic market for Nike is mature, and suggested Nike may have priced shoes at a point where competitors can cut into Nike sales. Reebok, Converse, and Adidas all have recently introduced shoes that sell in the $80 to $110 a pair range; many Nike models cost more. "They've been walking up the price ladder and they may have gone up as far as they can go," said Alice Ruth, an analyst at Montgomery Securities.

Even with pinched fourth-quarter profit, Nike said it expects a record year, with revenue and profit increasing 40% from year-earlier levels. It also said it expects revenue growth in 1998 to surpass the company's stated goal of 15%. Last fiscal year, Nike earned $553.2 million, or $3.77 a share, on sales of $6.5 billion.

Nonetheless, the fourth-quarter projection prompted many analysts to adjust their fiscal 1997 and 1998 projections. Shelly Hale Young, analyst at Hambrecht & Quist, lowered her 1997 projection to $2.68 a share from $2.83, and dropped her 1998 forecast to $3.24 from $3.40.

**Required:**

1. What aspects of *The Wall Street Journal* article are likely to have caused Nike's stock price to change?

2. Assume that you are a financial analyst. Would the information in the article cause you to alter your forecast of Nike's earnings for next year (1998)? Why? Would the article alter your earnings forecasts for each of the next five years? Why?

3. Do you think that the stock prices of Nike's competitors (Reebok, Converse, L.A. Gear, and Adidas) would change on the day that Nike made the announcement? If so, how and why? If not, why not?

4. Firms often release important news after the market has closed for the day. Why might they do this? What are the costs and benefits of such a strategy?

## COLLABORATIVE LEARNING CASE

**C6-3**

Microsoft Corporation: Unearned revenues and earnings management

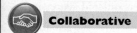 **Collaborative**

Microsoft develops, manufactures, licenses, sells, and supports a wide range of software products, including operating systems for personal computers (PCs) and servers; server applications for client/server environments; business and consumer productivity applications; software development tools; and Internet and intranet software and technologies. The company has expanded its interactive content efforts, including MSN (the Microsoft Network online service), various Internet-based services, and entertainment and information software programs. Microsoft also sells PC books and input devices, and it researches and develops advanced technologies for future software products.

The following excerpt is from an article that appeared in *The Wall Street Journal*.

### MICROSOFT'S EARNINGS GROWTH SLOWED IN THE LATEST QUARTER

Microsoft Corp.'s growth juggernaut slowed in its fiscal fourth quarter, but the numbers masked a surprisingly potent performance by the software giant.

The Redmond, Wash., company's earnings barely topped Wall Street's consensus, breaking a pattern of dramatic upside surprises for the company. But the company's profit would have been considerably higher had it not salted away revenue in a special reserve account for use in future quarters. That account, dubbed "unearned revenues," continued to swell and underscore the returns Microsoft is reaping as a near-monopoly supplier of personal computer operating-software and key application programs.

The account represents revenues Microsoft has collected but hadn't yet reported. It was established because the company faces future costs to deliver up-grades and customer support for products that already have been paid for. The policy helps smooth out sharp swings in the company's quarterly results.

Microsoft reported net income of $1.06 billion, or 80 cents a share, for the quarter ended June 30, an increase of 89% from $559 million, or 43 cents a share, a year earlier. Analysts had expected per-share earnings of about 79 cents, according to First Call Corp. Quarterly revenue was $3.18 billion, up 41% from $2.26 billion a year earlier.

*Source:* Microsoft's Earnings Growth Slowed in the Latest Quarter," *The Wall Street Journal*, July 18, 1997. Copyright © 1997 Dow Jones & Company, Inc. All rights reserved worldwide. Reprinted with permission.

**Other Information:**

1. Appearing in the accompanying tables are the comparative income statements for the fourth quarters of fiscal 1996 and 1997 and for the fiscal years 1996 and 1997. Also shown are comparative balance sheets for fiscal 1996 and 1997.

2. The balance in the unearned revenues account on March 31, 1997 (the end of the third fiscal quarter of 1997) was $1,285 million.

3. The following description of Microsoft's unearned revenues account is taken from the company's SEC filings:

The portion of the Company's revenues that are earned later than billed is reflected in the unearned revenues account. Of the March 31, 1997 balance of $1,285 million, approximately $765 million represented the unearned portion of Windows desktop operating systems revenues and $150 million represented the unearned portion of Office 97 revenues. Unearned revenues associated with upgrade rights for Microsoft Office 97 were $190 million, and the balance of unearned revenues was primarily attributable to maintenance and other subscription contracts.

## Microsoft Corporation

### Income Statements

| ($ in millions, except earnings per share) | Three Months Ended June 30 | | Years Ended June 30 | |
|---|---|---|---|---|
| | **1996** | **1997** | **1996** | **1997** |
| Net revenues | $2,255 | $3,175 | $8,671 | $11,358 |
| Cost of revenues | 241 | 242 | 1,188 | 1,085 |
| Research and development | 453 | 516 | 1,432 | 1,925 |
| Sales and marketing | 661 | 744 | 2,657 | 2,856 |
| General and administrative | 90 | 94 | 316 | 362 |
| Total operating expenses | 1,445 | 1,596 | 5,593 | 6,228 |
| Operating income | 810 | 1,579 | 3,078 | 5,130 |
| Interest income | 92 | 127 | 320 | 443 |
| Other expenses | (42) | (80) | (19) | (259) |
| Income before income taxes | 860 | 1,626 | 3,379 | 5,314 |
| Provision for income taxes | 301 | 569 | 1,184 | 1,860 |
| Net income | $ 559 | $1,057 | $2,195 | $ 3,454 |
| Preferred stock dividends | –0– | 7 | –0– | 15 |
| Net income available for common shareholders | $ 559 | $1,050 | $2,195 | $ 3,439 |
| Earnings per share | $ 0.43 | $ 0.80 | $ 1.71 | $ 2.63 |
| Average shares outstanding | 1,290 | 1,327 | 1,281 | 1,312 |

### Balance Sheets

| ($ in millions) | June 30, 1996 | June 30, 1997 |
|---|---|---|
| **Assets** | | |
| Current assets | | |
| Cash and short-term investments | $ 6,940 | $ 8,966 |
| Accounts receivable | 639 | 980 |
| Other | 260 | 427 |
| Total current assets | 7,839 | 10,373 |
| Property, plant, and equipment | 1,326 | 1,465 |
| Investments | 675 | 2,346 |
| Other assets | 253 | 203 |
| Total assets | $10,093 | $14,387 |
| **Liabilities and Stockholders' Equity** | | |
| Current liabilities | | |
| Accounts payable | $ 808 | $ 721 |
| Accrued compensation | 202 | 336 |
| Income taxes payable | 484 | 466 |
| Unearned revenues | 560 | 1,418 |
| Other | 371 | 669 |
| Total current liabilities | 2,425 | 3,610 |

*(continued)*

## Balance Sheets

| ($ in millions) | June 30, 1996 | June 30, 1997 |
|---|---|---|
| **Liabilities and Stockholders' Equity** | | |
| Minority interest | $ 125 | $ — |
| Put warrants | 635 | — |
| Stockholders' equity | | |
| Convertible preferred stock | — | 980 |
| Common stock and paid-in capital | 2,924 | 4,509 |
| Retained earnings | 3,984 | 5,288 |
| Total stockholders' equity | 6,908 | 10,777 |
| Total liabilities and stockholders' equity | $10,093 | $14,387 |

### Required:

1. Calculate Microsoft's net profit margin for the fourth quarter of 1996 and 1997 and for the fiscal years 1996 and 1997. Comment on the results.

2. Calculate Microsoft's working capital and current ratio. Comment on the results.

3. Did Microsoft fall short of, meet, or exceed analysts' expectations for fourth-quarter 1997 EPS?

4. If no reductions were made from the Unearned revenues account during the fourth quarter of fiscal 1997, how much did Microsoft add to the account during that quarter?

5. Continuing requirement 4, how much higher or lower would Microsoft's fourth-quarter income before tax have been (on a per share basis) if this accrual adjustment had not been made?

6. Assume that Microsoft reduced its Unearned revenues account by $188.0 million during the first three quarters of fiscal 1997. How much did Microsoft add to the account during the fiscal year?

7. Continuing requirement 6, how much higher or lower would Microsoft's annual income before tax have been (on a per share basis) if this accrual adjustment had not been made?

8. How much income before tax (on a per share basis) does Microsoft have "stored" in the Unearned revenues account at the end of 1997?

9. How can the Unearned revenues account be used to manage EPS?

10. How can analysts monitor the extent to which the Unearned revenues account is being used to manage EPS?

11. Does the existence of the Unearned revenues account necessarily mean that Microsoft intends to manage its reported earnings? Explain.

**Remember to check the book's companion Web site for additional study material.**

# The Role of Financial Information in Contracting | 7

| ($ in millions) | | $22,011.9 |
|---|---|---|
| **Sales** | | |
| Costs, Expenses and Other | 01.1 | 5,149.6 |
| Materials and production | 65.4 | 7,155.5 |
| Marketing and administrative | 82.9 | 3,848.0 |
| Research and development | 2.3 | 322.2 |
| Restructuring costs | | (1,717.1) |
| Equity income fr... | | (110.2) |
| Oth... | | 14,648.0 |
| ...s income | | |

*"A verbal contract isn't worth the paper it's written on."*

—Sam Goldwyn, film producer

**A** *contract* is a legally binding exchange of promises between parties. The vast majority of contracts can and are made orally, as when you buy coffee from the corner barista. Sometimes written contracts are required, for example, when buying an automobile or house. Business contracts include formal written agreements, such as Allen Ford's franchise contract with BookWorm, Inc.[1] Financial accounting numbers are often used to define contract terms in these business agreements and to monitor compliance with those terms.

Commercial lending agreements, for example, may require the borrower to maintain an interest coverage ratio above a certain level (say, 5) for the duration of a loan. This requirement protects the lender from a deterioration of the borrower's creditworthiness. The lender then uses earnings, cash flow, and balance sheet data to monitor the borrower's compliance with the loan covenants. If the covenants are violated—for example, because the borrower's interest coverage ratio falls below 5—the lender can then act swiftly to recover the loan.

Financial data are also used in executive compensation contracts and in formal agreements with government agencies, joint-venture partners, suppliers, distributors, and customers. Figure 7.1 identifies the parties in each of these contractual relationships.

The usefulness of financial statement data for contracting purposes depends on the accounting methods the company uses and its freedom to change them. For example, an interest coverage provision is *unlikely* to protect the lender if the borrowing company can achieve the required coverage level by changing its accounting methods or through other artificial means. Contracting parties understand that financial reporting flexibility affects how contracts are written and enforced. This chapter describes these influences and addresses the following questions:

- What role do accounting numbers play in contracts?
- What incentives do accounting-based contracts create for the parties involved?

## LEARNING OBJECTIVES

**After studying this chapter, you will understand:**

1. What conflicts of interest arise between managers and shareholders, lenders, or regulators.

2. How and why accounting numbers are used in debt agreements, in compensation contracts, and for regulatory purposes.

3. How accounting-based contracts and regulations influence managerial incentives.

4. What role contracts and regulations play in shaping managers' accounting choices.

5. How and why managers cater to Wall Street using their accounting discretion.

*Chapter*

---

[1] Chapter 6 explains why Allen Ford decided to purchase a BookWorm franchise. In this chapter, Ford must obtain a bank loan to finance the purchase.

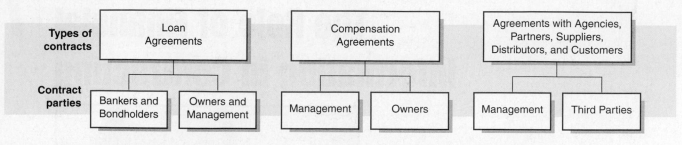

**Figure 7.1** SIGNIFICANT CONTRACTING RELATIONSHIPS IN CORPORATE ORGANIZATIONS

- How do these incentives help us understand why managers choose certain accounting methods and avoid others?
- How do these incentives influence when transactions are recorded?

## Finalizing the BookWorm Loan

Allen Ford assembled the monthly cash flow projections and other materials requested by the loan officer. This was not easy, but it produced an unintended benefit: Ford was forced again to evaluate the economic viability of the bookstore and the financial challenges ahead. His detailed financial projections revealed the need for a $75,000 loan, slightly larger than he anticipated originally. Otherwise, the prospects for the business seemed bright.

Several days after Ford completed the loan application, the bank phoned him to indicate preliminary approval of both the term loan and the revolving credit line. Ford was elated with the approval but surprised by the interest rate. It seemed higher than other local banks were charging for similar business loans. Ford and the loan officer agreed to meet to discuss the final terms and conditions of both loans. The loan officer advised Ford to consider accepting more stringent loan covenant restrictions in exchange for a more flexible repayment schedule or a lower rate of interest.

Ford was not quite sure what the loan officer had in mind, but it seemed worth exploring. He knew that some loan covenants were tied directly to the borrower's financial statements, and he wanted to be certain that the accounting-based covenants proposed by the bank agreed with his financial projections for the bookstore. In preparation for this negotiation, Ford decided to spend some time understanding how loan covenants work and what types of covenants are commonly used in commercial bank loans.

## CONFLICTS OF INTEREST IN BUSINESS RELATIONSHIPS

Delegating decision-making authority is an essential feature of the modern corporation and most business relationships. Capital providers (stockholders and lenders) delegate to professional managers the authority to make decisions about how the firm's assets are deployed and financed. In turn, managers delegate authority over aspects of a company's business affairs to others—inside and even outside the company—who have expertise or timely access to information that is critical for decision making. (Wal-Mart and Costco, for example, allow some suppliers to monitor product sales electronically at the checkout stand and to replenish shelf inventory without first seeking company approval.) But delegation of authority can cause **conflicts of interest,** which arise when one party to the business relationship can take actions for his or her own benefit that harm other parties in the relationship.

Suppose that rather than operating the store himself, Allen Ford hired a bookstore manager. Would the bookstore manager always make decisions that are in Ford's (the owner's) best interest? Probably not, because some business decisions that benefit the owner may not always benefit the manager. Conversely, other business decisions directly benefit the manager at Ford's expense. Consider this example: A longtime friend of the manager arrives in town unexpectedly and suggests a leisurely lunch at the country club. The manager is tempted to agree even though it would mean closing the bookstore for several hours. Ford would prefer to keep the bookstore open because he absorbs the profit lost from closing the store and receives no benefit from the manager's luncheon reunion. Ford, the owner, and the manager have conflicting interests when it comes to keeping the bookstore open during lunch.

Potential conflicts of interest permeate many business relationships. Ford's franchise loans provide an illustration. The interest rate on each loan compensates the bank for the credit risk and other costs associated with providing financial capital to the BookWorm business. Once the loans are granted, however, Ford might be tempted to divert the cash toward other, more risky investment opportunities such as buying tickets in the state lottery. The lender's risk of nonpayment jumps if the loan proceeds are diverted because the chance of winning $40 million is quite remote.

***Contract terms can be designed to eliminate or reduce conflicting incentives that arise in business relationships.*** Ford's loan agreements will describe the business purpose for each loan and require that the borrowed funds be used only for those purposes. By agreeing to such conditions, Ford is providing the bank a written assurance that borrowed funds will not be diverted to other unspecified uses—such as buying lottery tickets. Business contracts specify the mutual expectations—the rights and responsibilities—of each participant in the relationship. Thus, they provide a low-cost mechanism for addressing any conflicts of interest that can occur.

## NEWS CLIP

### EDIFICE COMPLEX

"When you go to the track, you study the horse," says David Yermack, a New York University finance professor. "Investing is not that different. You want to know as much as you can about the jockey."

A study he co-wrote looked at executives' home purchases. It found that, on average, the stocks of companies run by leaders who buy or build megamansions sharply underperform the market. The researchers don't claim to know why. They theorize that some of these executives might be focused more on enjoying their wealth and less on working hard.

One CEO looked at was Trevor Fetter of Tenet Healthcare Corp., who bought a 10,057-square-foot manse in the Dallas area around the start of 2005. Since then, Tenet's stock is off more than 60% while the broader market has risen. . . .

The new research is part of a more nuanced approach to studying management. Instead of assuming all CEOs are devoted to maximizing wealth for themselves or shareholders, researchers posit that executives can have other aims, like building a legacy or showing off wealth through a mammoth house. They may be perfectly rational behaviors but hardly ones that are in shareholders' interests. . . .

A key finding [in the Yermack study] was that stock performance tended to deteriorate after a CEO bought or built an extremely large or costly estate, which they defined as over 10,000 square feet or sited on more than 10 acres. On average, these companies' stocks underperformed the S&P 500 index by about 25 percentage points over the three years after the purchase. . . .

*Source:* M. Maremont, "Scholars Link Success of Firms to Lives of CEOs," *The Wall Street Journal*, September 5, 2007. Copyright © 2007 Dow Jones & Company, Inc. All rights reserved worldwide. Reprinted with permission.

# DEBT COVENANTS IN LENDING AGREEMENTS

Most companies have debt in the form of either commercial bank loans or bonds. In addition, managers frequently own shares of the companies they manage. Unfortunately, the interests of creditors and stockholders often diverge, particularly after the lender has handed over the cash. This divergence creates incentives for managers to take actions that transfer part of the company's value from creditors to the managers themselves as well as to other stockholders.

Here is an example that illustrates the conflicting incentives of creditors and owner–manager borrowers. Recall that Allen Ford needs about $125,000 to launch his BookWorm store. He plans to invest $50,000 of his own money and borrow the remaining $75,000 from the bank. Once the loan is granted, however, a natural conflict of interests arises between Ford, the borrower, and the bank, the creditor. This conflict of interests occurs because Ford, not the bank, decides just how the money will be spent.

> These conflicts of interest between creditors and owner-managers are spelled out in detail in the appendix to this chapter.

Suppose Ford immediately pays himself a $75,000 dividend instead of using the bank's money to buy inventory and equipment for the store. After all, he is the owner–manager of the business and as such can declare a dividend at any time. A $75,000 dividend payment would increase Ford's personal wealth but surely spell disaster for the BookWorm store because the cash needed to launch the business would no longer be available. The bank would have a $75,000 loan outstanding to a business consisting of only $50,000 in cash. The dividend payment benefits Ford but harms the bank.

Creditors know that their interests will sometimes conflict with those of borrowers, and they protect themselves in several ways. One way is to charge a higher rate of interest on the loan as compensation for the risky actions that owner–managers like Ford might take. ***Another way to reduce conflicts of interest between lenders and borrowers is by writing contracts that restrict—explicitly or implicitly—the borrowers' ability to harm lenders.*** For instance, the bank might require Ford to personally guarantee the business loan. A personal guarantee would require him to repay the bank loan from his own funds if the bookstore failed. This would certainly make paying himself a $75,000 dividend less attractive. Alternatively, the loan agreement might prohibit any dividend payments without prior approval by the bank, or it might limit dividends to some fraction (say, 50%) of net income.

Lending agreements contain restrictions called **debt covenants** that help guard against conflicts of interest between creditors and borrowers.

Debt covenants serve three broad functions:

1. *Preservation of repayment capacity:* Some covenants place strict limits on new borrowing, prohibit stock repurchases and dividends without prior lender approval, or ensure that cash generated both from ongoing operations and from asset sales will not be diverted from servicing debt.

2. *Protection against credit-damaging events:* All lenders are concerned with the risk of a sudden deterioration in repayment ability that can result from a merger, acquisition, takeover, or recapitalization. Some covenants prevent these adverse events from happening unless the debt is first repaid, the interest rate is adjusted upward, or prior lender approval is obtained.

3. *Signals and triggers:* Many covenants are in place to ensure the steady flow of information from borrower to lender. This information flow can reveal declining sales and profits, diminished operating cash flows, or other facets of the business that signal increased repayment risk. When deterioration occurs, triggers bring borrower and lender to the negotiation table and place the lender in a position of influence. Triggers enable the lender to decide whether it might be appropriate to modify or waive restrictions or to demand immediate repayment.

Debt covenants benefit both creditors and borrowers. Creditors benefit because the covenants reduce default risk. Borrowers benefit because a lower default risk means a lower cost of debt. *This cost savings occurs because creditors face less default risk and can afford to offer loans at lower rates of interest.*

## Affirmative Covenants, Negative Covenants, and Default Provisions

Debt covenants are intensively negotiated. They require the borrower to maintain a certain financial status for the loan's duration, and they set minimum standards for the borrower's future conduct and performance. Covenants vary with the borrower's business characteristics, financial condition, and the length of the loan. If credit risk is high, covenants may be tied directly to detailed financial projections provided by the borrower; if credit risk is low, a few general financial benchmarks may be sufficient. In either case, covenants are designed to protect the creditor and to sound an early warning if the borrower's financial condition deteriorates.

**Affirmative covenants** stipulate actions the borrower *must* take. Generally, these include:

1. Using the loan for the agreed-upon purpose.
2. Complying with financial covenants and reporting requirements.
3. Complying with laws.
4. Allowing the lender to inspect business assets and business contracts.
5. Maintaining business records and business properties and carrying insurance on them.

For example, loan agreements place restrictions on how the money borrowed can be used, often saying that it can be used only for a specific agreed-upon purpose spelled out in the loan contract. This type of covenant can be found in a recent loan agreement involving TCBY Enterprises, "The Country's Best Yogurt," as the borrower.

> Borrower will use the proceeds of the term loans for the loan purposes set forth . . . in Section 1.1 of this agreement. (para. 5.5 of TCBY term loan agreement).

To keep the lender informed about the company's financial and operating performance, another covenant in TCBY's loan agreement states that it is required to provide financial reports to the lender in a timely manner:

> [The company] will furnish . . . not later than one hundred twenty days (120) after the close of each fiscal year . . . consolidated balance sheets, income statements and statements of cash flow . . . and such other comments and financial details as are usually included in similar reports. (para. 5.1 of TCBY term loan agreement).

Financial covenants establish minimum financial tests with which a borrower must comply. These tests can specify dollar amounts (such as required minimum levels of net worth and working capital) or ratios (such as minimum debt-to-equity and interest coverage ratios). Financial covenants are intended to signal financial difficulty and to trigger intervention by the creditor—we explain how later—long before bankruptcy or liquidation become necessary. However, financial covenants often do not stipulate the accounting methods to be used when preparing the statements, except that they must comply with generally accepted accounting principles (GAAP):

> Such reports shall be prepared in accordance with GAAP and shall be audited by independent certified public accountants of recognized standing . . . and shall contain unqualified opinions . . . (para. 5.1 of TCBY term loan agreement).

The financial covenants also define the financial terms and ratios mentioned in the contract:

> Borrower will at all times maintain a ratio of Current Assets to Current Liabilities . . . that is greater than 2.0 to 1.0 . . . a Profitability Ratio greater than 1.5 to 1.0 . . . [defined as] the ratio of Net Income for the immediately preceding period of twelve calendar months to Current Maturities of Long Term Debt . . . a Fixed Charge Coverage Ratio greater than 1.0 to 1.0 . . . [defined as] the ratio of Net Income of the Borrower and Subsidiaries for the immediately preceding period of twelve calendar months plus Noncash Charges of the Borrower and Subsidiaries for the same period to Current Maturities of Long Term Debt of the Borrower and Subsidiaries plus cash dividends paid by TCBY to the shareholders of TCBY for the preceding period of twelve calendar months plus Replacement CapEx of the Borrower and Subsidiaries for the preceding twelve calendar months . . . (para. 5.7, 5.8, and 5.9 of TCBY term loan agreement).

Notice that TCBY is required to maintain a **fixed-charge coverage** ratio greater than 1.0, measured over the most recent 12 months:

$$\text{Fixed-charge coverage} = \frac{\text{Net income} + \text{Noncash charges}}{\text{Current maturities} + \text{Dividends} + \text{Replacement CapEx}}$$

Noncash charges—such as depreciation and goodwill amortization—are added back to net income because they don't reduce the cash available for debt repayment. TCBY's lender views Replacement CapEx—capital expenditures required to maintain (but not expand) the business—as a necessary cash outflow like debt repayment.

Also notice how the fixed-charge coverage requirement indirectly limits the company's ability to pay dividends. Suppose TCBY had net income of $50, noncash charges of $35, current loan maturities of $40, and replacement capital expenditures of $30. How large a dividend could TCBY pay to shareholders? A simple calculation shows the answer to be $15.

$$\text{Fixed-charge coverage} = \frac{\$50 + \$35}{\$40 + \text{Dividend} + \$30} = 1.0$$

$$= \frac{\$50 + \$35}{\$40 + \$15 + \$30} = 1.0$$

Dividends in excess of $15 would put TCBY in violation of its fixed-charge coverage requirement.

**Negative covenants** tend to be more significant and even more intensively negotiated than affirmative covenants because they place direct *restrictions* on the actions borrowers can take. These restrictions prevent actions that might impair the lender's claims against the company's cash flows, earnings, and assets. Negative covenants include limits on total indebtedness, investment of funds, capital expenditures, leases, and corporate loans as well as restrictions on the payment of cash dividends, share repurchases, mergers, asset sales, voluntary prepayment of other indebtedness, and new business ventures. This example is from the TCBY loan agreement:

> [Borrower agrees that it will not] sell, lease, transfer, or otherwise dispose of any assets . . . except the sale of inventory in the ordinary course of business and disposition of obsolete or worn-out equipment upon the replacement thereof . . . [or to] repurchase the stock of TCBY using, directly or indirectly, the proceeds of any loan. (paras. 6.6 and 6.12 of TCBY term loan agreement).

Covenants restricting the use of funds for dividend payments, share repurchases, capital expenditures, and other business purposes are included so the creditor has greater assurance that cash will be available to make interest and principal payments when due. In limiting the borrower's ability to sell, merge, or transfer operating assets, the creditor is ensuring the survival of the borrower's repayment potential.

Restrictions on total indebtedness limit the amount of additional debt the company may incur over the loan term. These restrictions are stated as a dollar amount or as a ratio (examples include total debt to assets, working capital, or tangible net worth):

> [Borrower agrees that it will not take on any new loans if] the aggregate amount of all such loans, advances and extensions of credit . . . would exceed twenty-five percent (25%) of the consolidated Tangible Net Worth of the Borrower . . . (para. 6.3 of TCBY term loan agreement).

It is also common for a borrower to agree not to use any of its existing property as collateral on future loans without first obtaining consent from the current lender:

> [Borrower agrees that it will not] create, incur, assume or suffer to exist any Lien, encumbrance, or charge of any kind (including any lease required to be capitalized under GAAP) upon any of its properties and/or assets other than Permitted Liens. (para. 6.1 of TCBY term loan agreement).

An unusual feature of this **negative pledge**—a promise to not take a particular action—is that TCBY agrees to limit its property leasing activities, but it does so only for leases required to be capitalized under GAAP. The agreement does not restrict TCBY from utilizing other operating leases, which are not capitalized under GAAP (Chapter 12 explains why).

The **events of default** section of a loan agreement describes circumstances in which the creditor has the right to terminate the lending relationship. Situations leading to default include the failure to pay interest or principal when due, inaccuracy in representations, failure to abide by a covenant, failure to pay other debts when due (known as *cross default*), impairment of collateral, change in management or ownership, and bankruptcy.

Most lending agreements require the borrower to periodically provide a **certificate of compliance,** which affirms that the borrower's managers have reviewed the financial statements and found no violation of any covenant provision. If a covenant has been violated, the nature and status of the violation must be specified.[2] Remedies for breach of covenant restrictions include renegotiating the debt contract terms such as an increase in the interest rate, seizing collateral, accelerating the maturity of the debt, or initiating legal bankruptcy proceedings.

The common remedy creditors exercise in the event of default is renegotiation of the loan agreement. All aspects of the loan—payment schedule, interest rate, collateral, affirmative and negative covenants—may be renegotiated. When the circumstances of default are considered relatively insignificant, the creditor may waive the violation or give the borrower a period of time—a *grace period*—to correct its covenant breach. When the default is severe, the creditor may accelerate loan repayment (with interest) and terminate its relationship with the borrower. Although creditors rarely exercise the right to accelerate repayment, having this right substantially strengthens a lender's negotiating position with the borrower if problems arise.

> For example, TCBY would be in default on the bank loan if the company reported net income of $120 and had $100 in current maturities of long-term debt. These figures would equate to a profitability ratio (as defined in the loan agreement) of 1.2, which is less than the 1.5 required minimum.

---

**When it comes to a company's business decisions, what's best for managers and shareholders isn't always best for creditors. Debt covenants—including those based on accounting numbers—help reduce this conflict of interest. Creditors benefit because debt covenants reduce default risk, and shareholders benefit from the lowered cost of debt financing.**

---

[2] Any covenant breach that existed at the date of the most recent balance sheet and that subsequently has not been cured (that is, remedied or corrected) should be disclosed in the notes to the financial statements (Rule 4–08[c] of Securities and Exchange Commission [SEC] Regulation S-X). When covenants are violated, the related debt must be reclassified as current if it is probable that the borrower will not be able to cure the default within the next 12 months. See "Classification of Obligations that are Callable by the Creditor," *Statement of Financial Accounting Standards (SFAS) No. 78* (Stamford, CT: Financial Accounting Standards Board [FASB] 1983) and "Classification of Obligations When a Violation Is Waived by the Creditor," *Emerging Issues Task Force 86–30* (Stamford, CT: FASB, 1986).

# NEWS CLIP

### PENSION SHIFT THREATENS COVENANTS

A proposed new rule for how companies account for employee pension plans could cause some firms problems with their loans and other debt outstanding.

The rule, proposed by the Financial Accounting Standards Board in March and slated to take effect at year's end, will require companies to report pension and retiree-benefit-plan surpluses or deficits as assets or liabilities on their balance sheets. That's worrisome enough for companies whose balance sheets will end up looking worse.

But the new bookkeeping could put some companies in jeopardy of breaching covenants, the terms a company must meet or surpass to prove to lenders they are good risks. Covenants often require minimum levels of shareholder equity, a measure of a company's net worth that subtracts liabilities from assets. Another common covenant demands that the borrow-

ing company keep debt below a specified ratio to capital, defining capital as shareholder equity plus debt.

So a company that piles a big pension liability onto the balance sheet and thus cuts its shareholder equity—the effect the new pension rule will have at many companies—could be in danger of violating its covenants.

Some companies have written language into their loan agreements that prevents covenants from being tripped solely by accounting changes, and banking and accounting executives expect lenders will be willing to waive or renegotiate covenants for others.

Still, the new accounting rule is going to give lenders more leverage over some companies, allowing banks to charge higher interest rates or add fees in exchange for renegotiating covenants. . . .

*Source:* M. Rapoport, "Tracking the Numbers: Pension Shift Threatens Covenants," *The Wall Street Journal*, May 3, 2006. Copyright © 2006 Dow Jones & Company, Inc. All rights reserved worldwide. Reprinted with permission.

## Mandated Accounting Changes as a Trigger of Debt Covenant Violation

When accounting regulators such as the FASB or International Accounting Standards Board (IASB) issue new reporting standards, their goal is to improve the relevance and reliability of firms' financial statements. But new reporting standards can sometimes have unintended consequences: Adoption may trigger a debt covenant violation.

The news article above mentions that Electronic Data Systems Corporation (EDS) is one company that could be adversely affected by the new pension accounting rule. EDS has a loan covenant that requires a minimum amount of shareholders' equity (called *net worth* in the loan agreement), adjusted for net income and any money raised by selling new shares. A note in the 2005 annual report provides details about this covenant and two others with which EDS must comply:

> The new rules are described in *SFAS No. 158* and discussed in Chapter 14.

Following is a summary of the financial covenant requirements under our unsecured credit facilities and the calculated amount or ratios at December 31, 2005 (dollars in millions):

|  | As of and for the Year Ended December 31, 2005 | |
|---|---|---|
|  | Covenant | Actual |
| Minimum net worth | $6,420 | $7,512 |
| Leverage ratio | 2.25 | 1.67 |
| Fixed charge coverage ratio | 1.15 | 2.37 |

The loan agreements (called *unsecured credit facilities* in the note) stipulate that EDS must maintain a minimum net worth of at least $6.420 billion, a maximum leverage ratio of 2.25, and a minimum fixed charge coverage ratio of 1.15 as of the end of 2005. EDS is in compliance with each covenant. Actual net worth, for example, was $7,512 million at the end of 2005, or

17% above the required minimum. This means that EDS had a net worth safety margin of $1,092 million (= $7,512 − $6,420), the dollar amount by which this particular financial statement item can decline before triggering covenant violation.

What will happen to this safety margin when EDS adopts the newly mandated pension accounting rule? According to one analyst who looked at the company's pension disclosures, net worth may fall by as much as $1,060 million. The safety margin all but evaporates, placing EDS in a rather precarious position.

Borrowers and lenders recognize that covenant compliance can be jeopardized by mandated changes in accounting practices even though real credit risk is unchanged. That is why many loan agreements have financial covenants that rely on *fixed GAAP*, that is, the accounting rules in place when the loan is first granted. This approach would allow EDS to continue using old GAAP for covenant compliance tests even though new GAAP is used in the company's audited financial statements. Loan covenants with fixed GAAP insulate the company from any adverse effects of mandatory accounting changes.

How often is fixed GAAP used in loan agreements? One study found that roughly 25% of the loans examined did not include any covenants tied to financial statement amounts. Of the remaining 75% of loans with accounting-based covenants, roughly half used fixed GAAP and thus were insulated from mandatory accounting changes.[3]

When the loan agreement does not permit fixed GAAP, lenders still have the option to waive or renegotiate covenants harmed by a new accounting standard. That is what may have happened at EDS in 2006. The annual report that year indicated that EDS had renegotiated its unsecured credit facilities midyear, and the new loan does not contain a minimum net worth covenant. Renegotiation thus alleviates the covenant violation problem caused when EDS began using the new pension accounting rule.

There may be more to the story, however. Elsewhere in the 2006 annual report, EDS revealed that the new pension accounting rule reduced net worth by only $0.566 billion, a princely sum but far less than the analyst had estimated. The covenant safety margin was reduced but a substantial margin remained intact. EDS may well have negotiated a new credit facility for other reasons such as to obtain a lower interest rate.

## Managers' Responses to Potential Debt Covenant Violations

*Violating a covenant is costly, so managers have strong incentives to make accounting choices and/or manipulate discretionary accruals in ways to reduce the likelihood of technical default.* Accounting choices include not only the selection of alternative accounting techniques (for example, LIFO versus FIFO inventory methods) but also accrual adjustments, such as changing the amount of bad debt provisions, and decisions about when to initiate transactions that result in accounting gains or losses (for example, when assets are sold or the corporation is restructured). *Readers of financial statements must be able to recognize and understand these incentives and their effect on managers' accounting choices.*

> A **technical default** occurs when the borrower violates one or more loan covenants but has made all interest and principal payments. A **payment default** occurs when the borrower is unable to make the scheduled interest or principal payment.

A number of studies have examined how debt-covenant-related incentives affect managers' accounting choices. One study looked at voluntary accounting changes made by 130 companies reporting covenant violations from 1980 to 1989.[4] The study found that net

---

[3] M. B. Mohrman, "The Use of Fixed GAAP Provisions in Debt Contracts," *Accounting Horizons*, September 1996, pp. 78–91.
[4] A. P. Sweeney, "Debt-Covenant Violations and Managers' Accounting Responses," *Journal of Accounting and Economics*, May 1994, pp. 281–308.

worth and working capital restrictions are the most frequently violated accounting-based covenants and that companies approaching default often make accounting choices that increase reported earnings. The most common techniques used at these companies to increase earnings are changes in pension cost assumptions (discussed in Chapter 14), the liquidation of LIFO layers, and the adoption of the FIFO inventory method (both discussed in Chapter 9).

Another study examined **discretionary accounting accruals,** noncash financial statement adjustments that "accrue" revenue (like debits to Accounts receivable and credits to Sales) or accrue expenses (such as debits to Warranty expense and credits to Accrued warranties payable).[5] This study, which looked at discretionary accruals by 94 companies reporting covenant violations from 1985 to 1988, found that "abnormal" accruals in the year prior to violation significantly increased reported earnings by accelerating revenue and postponing expenses. (Normal accruals were determined by examining each company's past accruals and by benchmarking against average accruals reported by other firms in the same industry that year.) Moreover, these accrual adjustments were also more likely to increase working capital in the year of the covenant violation.[6]

One recent study provides novel and compelling evidence that borrowers take actions to avoid debt covenant violations.[7] The evidence comes from a detailed look at the accounting-based covenants in roughly 1,600 commercial loans made to U.S. companies from 1989 through 1999. It singled out two covenants for analysis: a minimum net worth covenant and a minimum current ratio covenant. For each loan and covenant, the researchers calculate the amount of "slack" available each quarter over the life of the loan. For example, a firm with $11 million in net worth and a loan that stipulates a $10 million net worth minimum has $1 million of slack, or 10 percent of the covenant requirement. The data are then sorted into 19 bins based on the amount of slack available each quarter. If managers try to avoid covenant violations, we should see relatively few data points just below zero slack and relatively many data points just above zero.

Figure 7.2 depicts the results for minimum net worth covenants. As predicted, there are an unusually small number of loan/quarters where net worth falls just below the covenant minimum (i.e., slack is zero or negative) and an unusually large number of loan/quarters with net worth just above the minimum. A similar pattern is evident for minimum current ratio covenants. Managers apparently take actions to avoid violating the accounting-based covenants in commercial loans, but exactly how they sidestep a violation is less clear. As the researchers are quick to point out, borrowers can achieve the required covenant benchmark through their accounting choices, "real" actions such as issuing more stock to increase net worth, or other means.

Borrowers appear to willingly pay substantially higher interest rates to retain accounting flexibility that may help them avoid covenant violations. One study of 206 bank loans found that interest rates were 75 basis points higher when the loan agreement allowed "floating GAAP," meaning that accounting method changes could be used to increase covenant slack, rather than fixed GAAP.[8]

---

[5] M. L. DeFond and J. Jiambalvo, "Debt Covenant Violation and Manipulation of Accruals," *Journal of Accounting and Economics,* January 1994, pp. 145–76.

[6] Two early studies do not find support for the hypothesized influence of debt covenants on managers' accounting choices. See P. M. Healy and K. Palepu, "Effectiveness of Accounting-Based Dividend Covenants," *Journal of Accounting and Economics,* January 1990, pp. 97–133; and H. DeAngelo, L. DeAngelo, and D. J. Skinner, "Accounting Choice in Troubled Companies," *Journal of Accounting and Economics,* January 1994, pp. 113–43.

[7] L. D. Dichev and D. J. Skinner, "Large-Sample Evidence on the Debt Covenant Hypothesis," *Journal of Accounting Research,* September 2002, pp. 1091–1124.

[8] A. Beatty, K. Ramesh, and J. Weber, "The Importance of Accounting Changes in Debt Contracts: The Cost of Flexibility in Covenant Calculations," *Journal of Accounting and Economics,* June 2002, pp. 173–204.

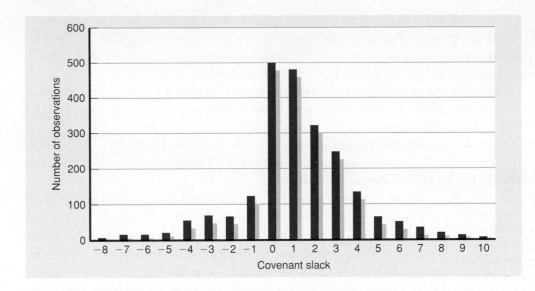

**Figure 7.2**

HISTOGRAM OF NET WORTH COVENANT SLACK

Each column (bin) shows the frequency of loan/quarters ($N = 2{,}339$) when the borrowers' actual net worth falls below (negative slack) or above (positive slack) the minimum net worth level stipulated in each of 1,600 commercial loans.

*SOURCE:* L. D. Dichev and D. J. Skinner, "Large-Sample Evidence on the Debt Covenant Hypothesis," *Journal of Accounting Research,* September 2002, pp. 1091–1124. Copyright © 2002. Used by permission of Wiley-Blackwell Publishing, Ltd.

These and other studies suggest that *management tends to make accounting changes and/ or to manipulate discretionary accruals that increase income to avoid violating debt covenants.* However, earnings increases due to maneuvers to avoid covenant violations are unlikely to reflect the true economic condition of the company and, therefore, are not likely to be sustainable. Unsustainable earnings increases are unlikely to translate into permanent cash flow increases. Consequently, these "tenuous" earnings should be interpreted with caution.

Throughout the remainder of the book, we highlight how alternative accounting methods and accrual adjustments affect earnings and key financial ratios. We'll alert you to accounting choices that can have substantial implications for debt covenants that you should keep in mind as you go about interpreting and using accounting numbers for making economic decisions.

## MANAGEMENT COMPENSATION

Most modern corporations are not run by the descendants of those who founded the organization but instead by professional managers, that is, "hired hands" who may lack the passion for corporate excellence that comes with substantial share ownership. This separation of ownership and control creates potential conflicts of interest between shareholders and managers.[9]

Consider a top executive whose job requires extensive travel and who, for reasons of "comfort and convenience," prefers the corporate jet to a commercial airline. Who receives the benefits of the comfort and convenience? And who pays the cost? If the comfort and convenience that comes from using the corporate jet leads to increased managerial productivity, both parties stand to gain. Shareholders lose, however, when the benefits of comfort and convenience accrue only to the executive and no productivity improvements result from it. That's because shareholders alone bear the added cost of travel by corporate jet.

Obviously, managers have incentives to use corporate assets for their personal benefit at owners' expense. Potential conflicts of interest can be overcome if managers are given incentives that cause them to behave as

> The corporate jet example illustrates one type of conflict between owners and managers: managers' tendency to "overconsume" corporate resources. But there are others. For example, managers who are near retirement age may have little incentive to adopt a long-term focus by investing in R&D.

[9] For more information about conflicts of interest between owners and managers see J. Boyd, R. Parrino, and G. Pritsch, "Stockholder-Manager Conflicts and Firm Value," *Financial Analysts Journal,* May/June 1998, pp. 14–30.

owners. One way is to give them a compensation package that links their pay to improvements in firm value.[10] If a manager's compensation goes up as the organization's value increases, he or she has an incentive to take actions that lead to such an increase. As a result, both the manager and the owners will benefit simultaneously.

Two ways to align managers' incentives with owners' interests are to link compensation to stock returns and/or financial performance measures such as accounting earnings. Both are widely used. Neither is perfect.

Consider stock returns. Managerial strategies and decisions clearly affect share prices in the long run. But in the short run, share prices could rise or fall due to such factors as interest rate changes that are beyond management's control.

> Changes in interest rates affect stock prices for two reasons. To see why, consider the effect of a *decrease* in marketwide interest rates. First, notice that a decrease in them will reduce the company's cost of equity capital. As you know from Chapter 6, this will increase share price. Second, as interest rates decrease, the yields on fixed-rate bond investments fall, making them less attractive to investors. Both factors contribute to an increase in the demand for stocks and an increase in stock prices.

Similar problems cloud the linkage between compensation and financial performance measures such as earnings. On the positive side, earnings are probably less susceptible to the influence of temporary and external economic forces and, unlike stock returns, accounting-based financial performance measures can be tied to a manager's specific responsibilities, such as the profitability of a single product line or geographical region. On the other hand, using accounting earnings as a measure is frequently criticized for its reliance on accruals, deferrals, allocations, and valuations that involve varying degrees of subjectivity and judgment.

A good compensation plan must overcome the incentive alignment problems we have discussed and motivate managers to act like owners.[11]

## How Executives Are Paid

Most compensation packages involve a base salary, an annual incentive, and a long-term incentive:

- **Base salary** is typically dictated by industry norms and the executive's specialized skills.
- **Annual incentives** set yearly financial performance goals that must be achieved if the executive is to earn various bonus awards. For example, a plan may stipulate that a bonus of 50% of salary is earned only if the after tax return on assets for the company exceeds 12%. But a 100% bonus can be earned if the return on assets is 15% or more. Such plans link pay to performance; because compensation is "at risk," managers have an incentive to achieve plan goals.
- **Long-term incentives** motivate and reward executives for the company's long-term growth and prosperity (typically three to seven years). Long-term incentives are designed to counterbalance the inherently short-term orientation of other incentives.

Figure 7.3 shows the mix of compensation for chief executive officers in 1985, 1995, 2000, and 2005 based on annual surveys of pay practices at large U.S. companies. In 1985, base salary

---

[10] A more complete discussion of compensation incentives and owner-manager conflicts of interest is contained in M. Jensen and W. Meckling, "Theory of the Firm: Managerial Behavior, Agency Costs and Ownership Structure," *Journal of Financial Economics,* October 1976, pp. 305–60; P. Milgrom and J. Roberts, *Economics, Organization, and Management* (Upper Saddle River, NJ: Prentice Hall, 1992); and R. Watts and J. Zimmerman, *Positive Accounting Theory* (Upper Saddle River, NJ: Prentice Hall, 1986).

[11] Certain features of executive compensation packages are also designed to reduce the combined tax liability of the company and its managers. Tax considerations undoubtedly contribute to the popularity of certain pay practices and help explain their use by some companies but not others. See C. W. Smith and R. L. Watts, "Incentive and Tax Effects of Executive Compensation Plans," in R. Ball and C. W. Smith (eds), *The Economics of Accounting Policy Choice* (New York: McGraw-Hill, 1992).

## Figure 7.3

### CEO COMPENSATION MIX

Annual incentive is a yearly performance-based bonus payment. Long-term incentive is a yearly award in cash, stock, or stock options for multi-year performance.

*Source:* The Conference Board, "Executive Annual Incentive Plans—1996" (New York: 1997); The Conference Board, "Top Executive Compensation in 2000" (New York: 2001); and Mercer Human Resource Consulting, *2006 CEO Compensation Survey and Trends* (New York: May 2007).

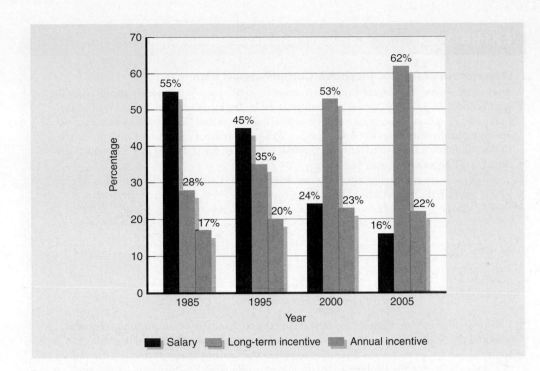

was 55% of the median total pay. Annual bonus payments and long-term incentive awards that year comprised 28% and 17%, respectively, of total pay. In other words, each dollar of compensation paid to CEOs in 1985 was made up of $0.55 in base salary and $0.45 in performance-related incentive pay.

Several trends are evident in Figure 7.3. One trend is that base salary has become a smaller component of total CEO compensation (55% in 1985 versus 16% in 2005), while long-term incentive awards have become a larger part of CEO pay (28% in 1985 versus 62% in 2005). This shift in compensation mix can be traced to the increased use of stock options in executive pay packages. Figure 7.3 also shows that $0.84 of each dollar of pay in 2005 comes from annual incentives ($0.22) and long-term incentives ($0.62). This means that the amount of "at-risk" pay—the combined percentage of short-term and long-term incentive compensation—is substantially greater in 2005 (84%) than it was in 1985 (45%).

Within a given organization, the proportion of pay "at risk" falls off steeply for executives on lower rungs of the corporate ladder. One compensation survey found that corporate executives in large industrial companies had 71% of their 1997 pay at risk, mid-level managers had 20%, and nonmanagerial professionals had only 8%.[12]

One of the earliest annual incentive plans was the General Motors Bonus Plan adopted in 1918. According to a former CEO of the company, "the interests of the corporation and its stockholders are best served by making key employees parties in the corporation's prosperity . . . each individual should be rewarded in proportion to his [sic] contribution to the profit of his [sic] own division and of the corporation as a whole."

*Source:* Alfred P. Sloan, Jr., *My Years with General Motors* (New York: Doubleday & Company, 1964), p. 407.

### Annual (Short-term) Incentives

The most common financial performance measure used in these bonus plans is GAAP net income or some variation of it. For example, Exhibit 7.1 shows you what Computer Associates International says about its annual incentive plan.

Notice that Computer Associates' shareholders approved the annual incentive plan (see ①). This means that the basic features of the plan—who participates, how performance will be measured, the maximum payout as a percent of salary, and so on—were submitted to shareholders

---

[12] Hay Group, Inc., *1998 Hay Compensation Report* (1998).

---

**EXHIBIT 7.1**     **Computer Associates International**

### Description of Annual Incentive Compensation Plan

*Annual Incentives.* [U]nder the Company's annual incentive plan ① **previously approved by the stockholders,** targeted payouts are determined at the beginning of each fiscal year based on the Company's ② achievement of (a) a minimum level of **revenue** and (b) threshold amounts of **net operating profit after taxes** (**NOPAT**), relative to the performance of the Company's peers. The NOPAT thresholds are derived from the financial forecasts of the Company that are publicly disclosed at the beginning of each fiscal year.

No payouts are made unless the minimum revenue level is achieved. If the minimum revenue level is reached, the **payout amount can range from 0% to 200%,** based on the percentage of NOPAT that is ③ achieved as compared to the threshold, as follows:

|  | % Target Payout |
|---|---|
| Below threshold | 0% |
| At threshold | Up to 50% |
| Between threshold and target | Up to 100% |
| Between target and maximum | Up to 200% |

The [Compensation] **Committee must certify the achievement of the minimum revenue level and the NOPAT thresholds** prior to each annual payout under the annual incentive plan. In addition, the ④ Committee has **discretion to reduce the amount of any payout** if it determines that, notwithstanding the achievement of the minimum amounts, a reduction is appropriate.

In fiscal 2003, the Company exceeded the minimum revenue level and the NOPAT target amounts. The amounts paid under the annual incentive plan reflected those results, as well as **individual contributions and customer satisfaction.**

*Source:* Computer Associates International, 2003 Proxy Statement. (Emphasis and circled numbers added.)

---

and approved by a formal vote at an annual meeting. Most companies do not request shareholder approval of their annual incentive plans, but a growing number are doing so.

Computer Associates uses two accounting-based performance measures, revenue and NOPAT, to determine managers' annual incentive pay (see ② and ③). The bonus formula has two components.

1. The company must achieve a minimum revenue goal each year before any bonus will be paid.
2. Once this revenue goal has been achieved, the amount of the bonus is determined by corporate profits (NOPAT) compared to a minimum and maximum profit threshold and a target profit amount.

Figure 7.4 illustrates how the second (or NOPAT) component of the bonus formula works. Suppose the minimum NOPAT threshold for the year is set at $10 million, the target NOPAT is $20 million, and the maximum threshold is $30 million. To complete the illustration, let's assume that the CEO's target bonus is $2 million, or a 10% share of the $20 million NOPAT. One more thing: Revenue for the year is assumed to exceed the minimum requirement for bonus payments.

As Figure 7.4 shows, no bonus is paid if actual NOPAT for the year falls below the $10 million threshold. If NOPAT falls at the minimum threshold, the CEO will receive a bonus of $0.5 million (50% payout × 10% NOPAT bonus share × $10 million NOPAT). If NOPAT falls between the minimum threshold and the target, the payout rate increases from 50% up to 100%. So, if the company reports NOPAT of $20 million, the CEO earns a bonus of $2 million (100% payout × 10% NOPAT bonus share × $20 million NOPAT).

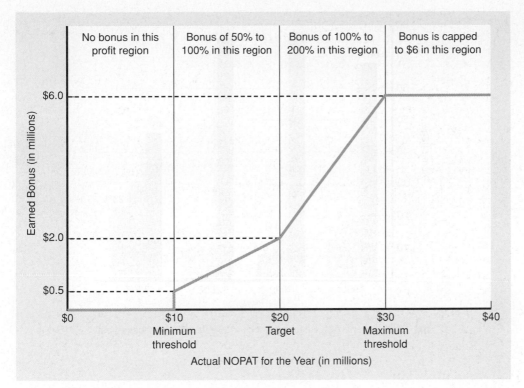

**Figure 7.4**

COMPUTER ASSOCIATES
INTERNATIONAL

How the annual bonus
formula works.

Once NOPAT exceeds the $20 million target level, the payout rate grows further from 100% up to 200%. For example, the CEO earns a bonus of $6 million when NOPAT at the company reaches $30 million ($6 million = 200% payout × 10% NOPAT bonus share × $30 million NOPAT). But there's a catch! The bonus formula puts a cap on the *maximum* amount of annual incentive pay the CEO can earn. Even though actual NOPAT may be above $30 million (the maximum threshold), the CEO's bonus will still be just $6 million that year.

At Computer Associates and most other companies today, it's the compensation committee that is responsible for implementing the executive pay plan (see ④). This committee is comprised of the company's outside (nonmanagement) directors. It selects the performance metrics to be used and sets the annual or multiyear performance goals for each executive. (At some companies, the pay plan is then submitted to shareholders for their approval.) This avoids the conflict of interest that would naturally arise if the executives themselves were to set annual threshold and target profit levels. The committee can sometimes override the bonus formula when circumstances warrant. Computer Associates' compensation committee is allowed to reduce or eliminate the calculated award, but it may not increase the award. As we will see in a moment, compensation committees play an important role in reducing managers' incentives to meet the performance target using accounting "gimmickry."

> Notice how important one more profit dollar can be if it enables the company to report NOPAT of $10 million rather than $9,999,999. In our example, that one extra profit dollar causes the CEO's bonus to jump from $0 to $500,000.

## Long-Term Incentives

Long-term incentives comprise a large portion of total compensation for most CEOs, although many long-term plans are not tied directly to accounting numbers. Figure 7.5 shows the mix of long-term incentives by type.

**Stock options** are the most common long-term incentive device. Stock options come in various forms, the choice of which depends largely on the tax treatment for the executive and

## Figure 7.5

LONG-TERM
INCENTIVE MIX

*SOURCE:* Annual survey of 350 large U.S. companies conducted by Mercer Human Resource Consulting.

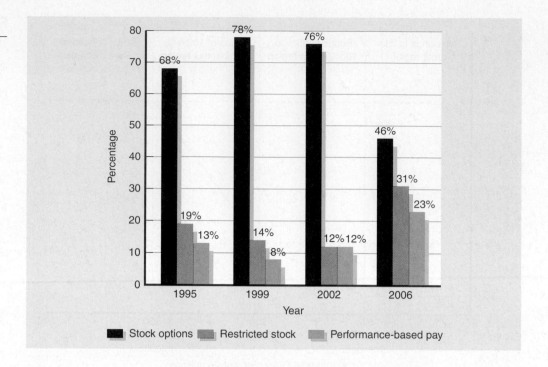

the company. Stock options give the executive the right (but not the obligation) to buy shares at a stated (exercise) price, typically the market price on the option grant date, for a period of years. If the stock price rises, the executive may trade in (or "exercise") each option plus pay the stated exercise price in exchange for a share of company stock. Because the option has value only if the market price of the underlying stock rises, the executive has an incentive to increase shareholder value as measured by stock price.

So-called **incentive stock options** qualify for favorable tax treatment; that is, the executive is taxed at the capital gains rate when the option is exercised, which is usually lower than the ordinary income tax rate. So-called **nonqualified stock options** do not have this personal tax advantage. Instead, the executive pays ordinary income tax on the difference between the exercise price and the stock's market value at the exercise date. In turn, the company receives a tax deduction equal to this same amount.

Stock grants give the executive outright ownership of company shares. **Restricted stock** is typically an award of stock that is nontransferable or subject to forfeiture for a period of years. The most prevalent restriction is one of continued employment, although performance-related conditions are sometimes applied. Dividends can be paid to the executive even when the stock is restricted, and some restricted stock awards carry immediate voting rights. Restricted stock grants provide a set of "golden handcuffs" for retaining executives with desirable skills, at least during the restriction period.

**Performance-based pay plans** require the manager to achieve certain multiyear financial performance goals such as a three-year average return on common equity (ROCE) of at least 20%. The payout could be either cash or company shares. From a financial reporting perspective, these plans are important because performance goals are often tied to financial targets such as earnings per share growth or return-on-equity hurdles. Occasionally, the performance goals are strategic: increasing market share, reducing costs, or raising product quality. Performance goals are established at the beginning of the award period, which usually ranges from four to seven years, and may be stated in absolute terms or relative to the performance levels achieved by peer companies over the award period.

Performance plans have been a key element of long-term incentive compensation in many companies for a number of years. However, passage of the Tax Reform Act of 1993 provided further impetus to link pay plans to specific performance goals. The act limits to $1 million the federal income tax deduction that public companies may claim for compensation paid to any of the top five executives except in certain circumstances. One such exception is for compensation that is based solely on the attainment of one or more performance criteria that an independent compensation committee established. By linking top executive pay to specific performance goals, firms gain valuable tax deduction benefits when compensation payments exceed the $1 million threshold.

Figure 7.5 has two important messages. First, stock options are the dominant form of long-term incentive pay for top executives in the United States. In 1996, for example, stock options contributed 68 cents of each long-term incentive dollar paid out that year. Restricted stock grants added 13 cents, and performance plan payouts added another 19 cents. The popularity of stock options increased during the late 1990s to the point in 2002 when options contributed 76 cents of each long-term incentive dollar. This brings us to the second message in Figure 7.5. Since 2002, there has been a fundamental shift in the mix of long-term incentive pay for top executives of U.S. firms. Stock options are now a smaller component of long-term incentive pay, contributing only 46 cents of each long-term pay dollar in 2006 while restricted stock grants and performance plan payouts have increased. One reason for the decreased popularity of stock options as a long-term incentive device is that they no longer receive favorable accounting treatment. Chapter 15 explains why.

> In 2006, a scandal involving potentially abusive stock options grants erupted in the United States. By July of that year, the SEC was investigating more than 80 companies for backdating, or illegally timing the option grant to increase the eventual payout. Options offer the right to buy stock at a specified exercise price, usually equal to the market price on the date the options were granted, so backdating them to a date when the price was low makes them potentially more valuable. The details are in Chapter 15.

## Proxy Statements and Executive Compensation

Information about a company's executive compensation practices can be found in the annual **proxy statement,** a notification of the annual shareholders meeting, filed each year with the SEC. Among other disclosures, this document describes both the compensation payments and awards made to the five highest paid executives of the company and any new executive compensation plans.

Although top executive compensation disclosures were mandated in 1933, a year before the SEC was created, the information provided was quite sparse. In the late 1980s, as top executive pay routinely began to exceed $1 million, major stockholders and the news media expressed outrage over the amounts paid, their questionable link to firm performance, and the inadequacy of required disclosures. This outrage is one reason why the Tax Reform Act of 1993 included a $1 million cap on the corporate tax deduction for top executive pay. The SEC also stepped into the fray in 1992 by dramatically expanding the required pay disclosures when Section 402 of Regulation S-K was first introduced. The stock option backdating scandal of 2006 led the SEC to further increase the required disclosures for executive compensation.[13]

Firms now must provide a **compensation discussion and analysis (CD&A)** in the proxy statement. This disclosure requirement is similar in nature to the long-standing **management's discussion and analysis (MD&A)** for 10-K and 10-Q filings, which requires a report on the operations of the business "as seen through the eyes of management." Among other things, the CD&A must describe the specific items of corporate performance that are considered in making compensation decisions, how specific forms of compensation are structured and

---

[13] SEC Release 33-8765, *Executive Compensation Disclosure,* December 22, 2006; and Release 33-8732a, *Executive Compensation and Related Party Disclosure,* August 29, 2006. Release 33-8732a is 436 pages in length.

implemented to reflect performance, and the impact of accounting and tax treatments of the particular form of compensation.

In addition to the CD&A, firms must now provide detailed disclosure of three broad executive pay categories:

1. Compensation for the last fiscal year and the two preceding years.
2. Holdings of equity-related interests that relate to compensation.
3. Retirement and other postemployment compensation.

The first pay category involves compensation paid currently or deferred and includes stock options, restricted stock, and any other forms of compensation that are parts of the executive's pay plan. Equity-related holdings are stock options and restricted stock shares awarded in prior years. Retirement compensation includes pension and health care benefits as well as benefits payable in the event of a change in corporate control (so-called golden parachute payments). Compensation information must be disclosed for the chief executive officer and the chief financial officer regardless of the total amount of their compensation and for the next three most highly paid executives serving as corporate officers if their total compensation is more than $100,000.

Some groups had hoped the SEC would go further and lobbied for an annual advisory shareholder vote on executive pay. Although the SEC is unlikely to require an advisory vote, shareholders are now much better informed about executive compensation and how it is determined.

> Whole Foods Market is one company that links incentive pay to economic value added, or EVA, performance (see Case 7-3). EVA is a performance metric popularized by the consulting firm Stern Stewart & Company. In its simplest form, EVA is just net operating profit after taxes (or NOPAT) minus a charge for the financial capital lenders and investors have put into the business ($c^* \times$ Capital, where $c^*$ is the company's weighted average cost of capital). So, a company that earns $150 of NOPAT using $1,000 of capital with a $c^*$ of 10% will have generated $50 of EVA ($150 $-$ 0.10 $\times$ $1,000). Stern Stewart and most other economic value practitioners advocate making a variety of adjustments to GAAP income statements and balance sheets before performing the EVA calculation. These adjustments are intended to eliminate certain accounting "distortions," many of which we describe in later chapters of this book.

## Incentives Tied to Accounting Numbers

Many companies today use performance plans that are usually tied to accounting numbers as *long-term* compensation incentives. For *annual* bonus plans, accounting numbers become overwhelmingly important. Let's take a closer look at how these at-risk compensation components—annual bonus plans and long-term compensation—are tied to accounting numbers.

The common performance measures used in annual and multiyear (long-term) incentive plans for senior corporate executives are shown in Figure 7.6. Most plans link incentive pay to one or more accounting-based performance measures, such as revenue, earnings per share, or return on equity. Economic value added (EVA) is used in 12% of the plans, while operating cash flow is used in 10% of the plans.

In addition to accounting-based performance measures, data in Figure 7.6 indicate that many annual and multiyear plans also use nonfinancial performance measures to determine incentive pay. Financial metrics including last year's return on assets or earnings per share tell us about the past. However, nonfinancial metrics such as sales orders booked are lead indicators of future economic performance.[14] Many companies today combine nonfinancial performance metrics with accounting-based financial metrics (i.e., gross margin, operating income, and revenue) and market-based metrics (such as total shareholder return and stock price) to produce a "balanced scorecard" for evaluating managerial performance.[15]

---

[14] To learn more about the use of nonfinancial performance measures in bonus plans, see C. D. Ittner, D. F. Larcker, and M. U. Rajan, "The Choice of Performance Measures in Annual Bonus Contracts," *The Accounting Review,* April 1997, pp. 231–55.

[15] See R. S. Kaplan and D. P. Norton, *The Balanced Scorecard* (Boston, MA: Harvard Business School Press, 1996).

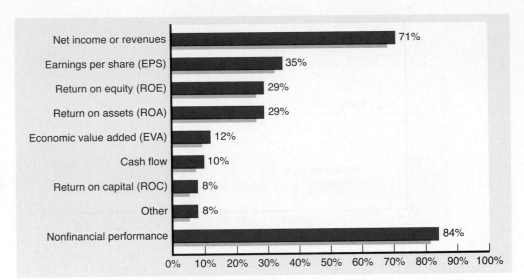

**Figure 7.6**

PERFORMANCE MEASURES USED IN ANNUAL AND MULTIYEAR CASH INCENTIVE PLANS

The individual percentages sum to more than 100% because many companies use multiple measures of performance. The results are based on a comprehensive survey of 2,700 U.S. companies.

*Source:* "Executive Annual Incentive Plans—1996." Copyright © 1996. Used with permission of The Conference Board. www.conference-board.org

This wide use of accounting-based incentives is controversial for at least four reasons:

First, earnings growth does not automatically translate into increased shareholder value. Management can grow earnings by expanding the size of the business through acquisitions or new investment. This strategy can produce substantial dollar increases in sales volume, operating earnings, and EPS. But these added profits don't always increase shareholder value. For shareholder value to increase, the company must earn more on new investments than its incremental cost of capital. Alas, not all acquisitions and investments clear the cost of capital "hurdle" even though they may show an accounting profit. So, earnings-based incentive compensation plans can reward managers for launching new investments that increase earnings but not shareholder value. Notice that EVA overcomes this problem by incorporating an explicit charge for the cost of capital.

Second, the accrual accounting process itself can sometimes distort traditional measures of company performance. Take return on assets (ROA), for example. Companies that show improving ROA often do so because of real profitability gains: higher revenues or lower expenses. However, some ROA improvements are due to nothing more than depreciation accounting. To see this, consider a business that generates $100 of net income each year and pays that same amount out as a dividend. The business opens on January 1, 2008, with total assets of $1,000 and no debt. Half of those assets ($500) are invested in new equipment. The annual depreciation charge for the equipment is $50. The company's ROA for 2008 is 10% ($100 of net income divided by $1,000 of beginning assets). But next year ROA will increase to about 10.5%. And the year after that, ROA will be 11.1%. Why? Not because profits at the company have increased but because depreciation accounting has reduced the book value of total assets. (Inflation exacerbates this problem, as discussed in Chapter 10.)

As a stockholder in the company, you probably don't want to pay an ROA bonus for nothing more than depreciation accounting. It's better instead to reward management for real profitability improvement and to ignore the profit growth illusion created by depreciation accounting. That's why some companies prefer return on gross investment (ROGI, or net income divided by total *gross* assets) as a performance metric in their bonus plans.

> ROA for 2009 equals the $100 of net income, divided by net assets of $950 (after subtracting $50 of accumulated depreciation) or 10.5%. The 11.1% ROA calculation for 2010 is $100 of net income, divided by net assets of $900 (after subtracting $100 of accumulated depreciation).

Third, accounting-based incentive plans can encourage managers to adopt a short-term business focus. Consider the typical bonus plan in Figure 7.7. The executive receives a bonus equal to 100% of base salary if annual EPS reaches the $3.50 target. The bonus award declines

**Figure 7.7**

TYPICAL STRUCTURE OF
ANNUAL PERFORMANCE
BONUSES

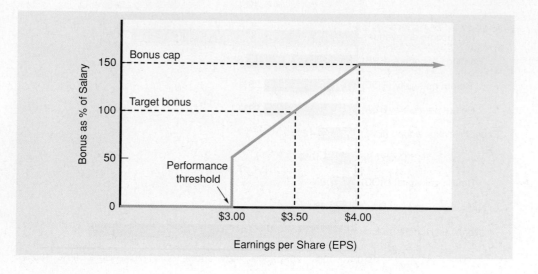

to 50% of base salary for EPS performance at the $3.00 level, and it escalates to 150% for EPS at the $4.00 level. If EPS falls below $3.00, no bonus is awarded; at EPS above $4.00, the bonus remains 150% of base salary.

To see how accounting-based incentives might contribute to a short-term focus, consider an executive who believes current business conditions will allow the company to earn only $2.80 EPS for the year. Despite these unfavorable (no bonus) conditions, the executive can still achieve the $3.00 EPS minimum required for a bonus by curtailing needed expenditures, say, simply by cutting back on critical research and development. Research expenses go down, reported earnings go up, and bonuses are paid! This short-term strategy can prove costly in the long term if a competitor introduces a new product based on the technology the company had been researching. Of course, the same unsustainable short-term earnings increase can be achieved by delaying essential maintenance and repairs or by postponing other key operating expenditures.

Executives also have an incentive to "manage down" reported earnings when the accounting benchmark (EPS in this example) is *above* the upper bonus limit. Suppose our executive believes that current business conditions will enable the company to earn $4.20 EPS this year. Here the executive has an incentive to reduce reported earnings to $4.00, deferring the excess to the future. After all, the same bonus is awarded no matter whether EPS is at the $4.00 or $4.20 level!

How can excess earnings be deferred? It's easy! Delay some fourth-quarter customer shipments until the beginning of next year. Current year's sales decline and earnings fall without affecting this year's bonus; the delayed sales and earnings count toward next year's bonus. You don't lose anything this year, and you increase the probability of earning the bonus next year.

Fourth, executives have some discretion over the company's accounting policies, and they can use that discretion to achieve bonus goals. For example, an executive falling short of the $3.00 EPS minimum might deliberately reduce fourth-quarter inventories, report a "LIFO liquidation" gain, and boost earnings to a level above the bonus threshold. (LIFO liquidations are discussed in Chapter 9.) On the other hand, if earnings performance is so low that reaching the bonus threshold is impossible, the manager has an incentive to further reduce earnings. The objective of these deliberate earnings reductions, called *big baths,* is simple. Today's write-offs lower future expenses, thereby increasing future earnings—and future bonuses! Examples of big-bath write-offs include asset impairments and large restructuring charges. Accounting discretion also allows managers who believe earnings will exceed the $4.00 ceiling to play bonus "games": reduce reported earnings down to the bonus maximum and defer the excess.

**Research Evidence**   Do managers use accounting flexibility to achieve bonus goals? One study, which looked at annual bonus plans like the one in Figure 7.7, revealed two things:

1. When annual earnings already exceeded the $4.00 bonus ceiling, managers used discretionary accounting options to *reduce* earnings.

2. When it was clearly evident that earnings would be below the bonus threshold ($3.00 in Figure 7.7), managers used their financial reporting flexibility to reduce earnings still further.[16]

These reductions in earnings had no impact on that year's bonus but improved managers' chances of receiving bonuses the following year. That's because taking a larger discretionary expense this year often meant a smaller expense next year, and that helped to ensure that next year's earnings would meet or beat the bonus target.[17]

Another study examined motivations for a controversial, debt extinguishment transaction called **insubstance defeasances**.[18] These transactions were widely believed to generate artificial profits, and the FASB subsequently forbade them in 1996.[19] The evidence is that some firms used these transactions to window-dress earnings and to avoid restrictions in bond covenants. Again, the research findings show that managers sometimes use accounting flexibility to evade contract constraints to gain bonus benefits.

Several studies show that incoming CEOs have an incentive to decrease earnings in the year of the executive change and increase earnings in the next year.[20] Doing so presumably allows the new CEO to take credit for the company's apparent (but not necessarily real) performance improvement.

Another research study found evidence that R&D expenditures tend to decline during the years immediately prior to a CEO's retirement.[21] Existing GAAP requires R&D expenditures to be expensed as incurred, thereby reducing income and bonuses.[22] By reducing R&D expenditures before they retired, CEOs were able to increase their final bonus payouts.

---

**Compensation plans should align managers' incentives with shareholders' objectives. Many compensation plans link incentive pay to accounting numbers. This linkage is an effective management incentive because improved financial performance generally translates into greater shareholder wealth. Unfortunately, accounting numbers can be manipulated. Consequently, compensation plans tied to financial goals sometimes backfire because of the short-term, self-interest focus of executives.**

---

[16] P. Healy, "The Effect of Bonus Schemes on Accounting Decisions," *Journal of Accounting and Economics,* April 1985, pp. 85–108. Later studies find mixed evidence on managers' use of accounting discretion around bonus thresholds. See T. Fields, T. Lys, and L. Vincent, "Empirical Research on Accounting Choice," *Journal of Accounting and Economics,* September 2001, pp. 255–308.

[17] When current earnings are poor but future earnings are expected to be strong, managers borrow earnings from the future for use in the current period. See M. L. DeFond and C. W. Park, "Smoothing Income in Anticipation of Future Earnings," *Journal of Accounting and Economics,* July 1997, pp. 115–39.

[18] J. R. M. Hand. P. J. Hughes, and S. E. Sefcik, "Insubstance Defeasances: Security Price Reactions and Motivations," *Journal of Accounting and Economics,* May 1990, pp. 47–89. The transaction allowed a company to account for a liability "as if extinguished" when cash or other assets were placed irrevocably in a trust that then made all remaining principal and interest payments on the debt.

[19] "Accounting for Transfers and Servicing of Financial Assets and Extinguishments of Liabilities," *SFAS No. 125* (Norwalk, CT: FASB, 1996), para. 16.

[20] J. Elliott and W. Shaw, "Write-offs as Accounting Procedures to Manage Perceptions," *Journal of Accounting Research,* Supplement 1988, pp. 91–119; J. Francis, D. Hanna, and L. Vincent, "Causes and Effects of Discretionary Accounting Write-offs," *Journal of Accounting Research,* Supplement 1996, pp. 117–34; S. Pourciau, "Earnings Management and Non-routine Executive Changes," *Journal of Accounting and Economics,* January–July 1993, pp. 317–36.

[21] P. M. Dechow and R. G. Sloan, "Executive Incentives and The Horizon Problem: An Empirical Investigation," *Journal of Accounting and Economics,* March 1991, pp. 51–89.

[22] "Accounting for Research and Development Costs," *SFAS No. 2* (Stamford, CT: FASB, 1974).

### Protection Against Short-Term Focus

> It is essential for financial statement users to identify companies that achieve incremental increases in earnings resulting from strength in business fundamentals rather than earnings management techniques or accounting "gimmickry." [23]

These abuses explain why compensation plans must also be designed to include long-term incentive components (primarily stock options) that are specifically intended to mitigate the short-term focus of executives. Stock options (and stock ownership) give managers a strong incentive to avoid shortsighted business decisions and instead operate the company in ways that create shareholder value. That's why today stock and stock option portfolios rather than cash compensation and other benefits are the major determinants of top executives' wealth.

Another factor that can reduce short-term focus is the fact that incentive compensation plans are administered by a compensation committee comprised of the company's outside (nonmanagement) directors. The committee can intervene when circumstances warrant modification of the scheduled incentive award. For example, intervention might arise when a mandatory change in an accounting principle occurs. In general, the compensation committee can adjust the incentive award whenever it believes that current earnings have been unduly influenced by special items or other possible accounting distortions.

For example, language of the following sort is typical in many compensation agreements:

> At any time prior to the payment of performance awards, the compensation committee may adjust previously established performance targets and other terms and conditions . . . to reflect major unforeseen events such as changes in laws, regulations, or accounting practices, mergers, acquisitions, divestitures, or extraordinary, unusual, or nonrecurring items or events. [24]

Compensation committees *can* adjust incentive awards for unusual or nonrecurring items and events, but do they? One study looked at the pay practices of 376 large public companies and found that nonrecurring gains tend to flow through to compensation, but losses do not. [25] Compensation committees apparently do shield top managers from bonus reductions when net income is decreased by nonrecurring losses. But when net income is increased by nonrecurring gains, top managers reap the benefits in the form of higher bonus awards.

## Catering to Wall Street

> Many companies, at one time or another, massage their numbers using creative accounting techniques, and probably do it now more than ever. . . . The issue isn't so much whether many companies are committing fraud—that's likely confined to a small group of dishonest executives. For most companies, it isn't even a matter of stretching the rules to wildly inflate their results. It's more a question of how many companies, following standard accounting guidelines, use loopholes to tweak their earnings numbers here and there just to make the crucial number, earnings per share, look better. [26]

The prevalence of stock options in executive pay packages may actually contribute to, rather than moderate, managers' short-term focus. Penny differences in EPS matter a lot to investors;

---

[23] G. Napolitano, *Earnings Management Revisited: Minimizing the Torpedoes in Financial Reports* (New York: Goldman Sachs, November 1998), p. 3.

[24] J. D. England, "Executive Pay, Incentives and Performance," in D. E. Logue (ed.), *Handbook of Modern Finance* (Boston: Warren, Gorham & Lamont, 1996), p. E9–18.

[25] J. J. Gaver and K. M. Gaver, "The Relation Between Nonrecurring Accounting Transactions and CEO Cash Compensation," *The Accounting Review,* April 1998, pp. 235–54.

[26] K. Brown, "Tweaking Results Is Hardly a Sometime Thing," *The Wall Street Journal,* February 6, 2002.

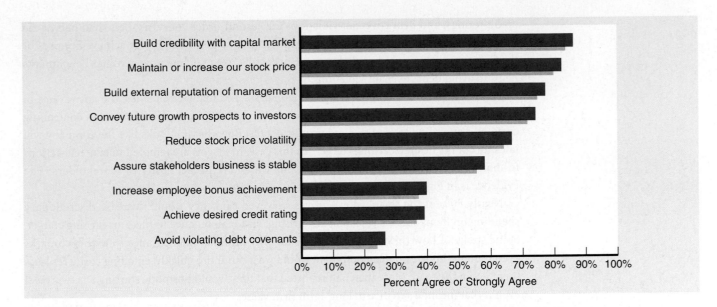

**Figure 7.8** WHY MEET EARNINGS BENCHMARKS?

How 401 financial executives at U.S. companies responded to the question: "Meeting earnings benchmarks helps ..."

*SOURCE:* J. R. Graham, C. R. Harvey, and S. Rajgopal, "The Economic Implications of Corporate Financial Reporting," *Journal of Accounting and Economics*, December 2005, p. 27. Copyright © 2005 with permission from Elsevier Ltd.

just watch what happens to a company's share price when quarterly EPS comes in one cent below analysts' expectations.[27] And when investors penalize firms that fail to meet analysts' EPS targets, the penalty—a lower stock price—makes executive stock options less valuable. On the other hand, firms that report continuous growth in annual EPS are priced at a premium relative to other firms.[28] This price premium translates into more valuable executive stock options.

Critics argue that stock options thus encourage managers to cater to Wall Street's short-term earnings expectations. And managers appear to willingly do so. As you may recall from Chapter 3, actual EPS numbers do not fall randomly around analysts' consensus EPS estimates. Instead, too many firms report EPS numbers that just meet or beat the estimate while too few report EPS that falls just short of the estimate (see Figure 3.1b). As one commentator notes, "Managements try to give investors what they want, and companies whose earnings are predictable are prized on Wall Street, which does not like unhappy surprises."[29]

A recent survey of more than 400 financial executives at U.S. companies paints a telling picture about why managers cater to Wall Street.[30] The findings are summarized in Figure 7.8. When asked why it is important to meet earnings benchmarks, an overwhelming 86% said that it helps build credibility with the capital market. More than 80% agreed that meeting benchmarks helps maintain or increase the firm's stock price. They also believe that meeting earnings benchmarks helps enhance their external reputation, conveys favorable information about the firm's future growth prospects, and reduces stock price volatility. Compensation,

[27] In February 2001, Cisco Systems lost 13% of its market value over the two days after it announced earnings that fell one cent short of expectations. For large-sample evidence, see D. Skinner and R. Sloan, "Earnings Surprises, Growth Expectations, and Stock Returns or Don't Let an Earnings Torpedo Sink Your Portfolio," *Review of Accounting Studies*, June 2002, pp. 289–312.

[28] M. E. Barth, J. A. Elliott, and M. W. Finn, "Market Rewards Associated with Patterns of Increasing Earnings," *Journal of Accounting Research*, Autumn 1999, pp. 387–413.

[29] A. Berenson, "Tweaking Numbers to Meet Goals Comes Back to Haunt Executives," *The New York Times*, June 29, 2002.

[30] J. R. Graham, C. R. Harvey, and S. Rajgopal, "The Economic Implications of Corporate Financial Reporting," *Journal of Accounting and Economics*, December 2005, pp. 3–73.

credit ratings, and debt covenant violations are second-order concerns. Less than half of the financial executives said meeting earnings benchmarks helps employees achieve bonuses or the firm to achieve desired credit ratings. Fewer still (26%) said meeting earnings benchmarks helps to avoid debt covenant violations.

How do firms meet their earnings benchmarks? For many companies, the answer lies in operational excellence: providing customers highly valued products and services, controlling costs, and attending to a myriad of business details. But what if it looks like the company will fall short of the desired earnings target? In this case, managers are tempted to take real actions to maintain accounting appearances, actions which are in fact costly to shareholders. The evidence is in Figure 7.9.

Nearly 80% of the financial executives surveyed said they would decrease discretionary spending on items such as research, advertising, and maintenance to meet an earnings target. Some spoke of how they would put off or do only minimal maintenance to hit benchmarks even though this meant that equipment would wear out more quickly, entailing costly replacement down the road. More than half reported that they would postpone starting a new project even if that meant a sacrifice in long-term firm value.

The surveyed executives voiced little support for taking accounting actions to hit earnings targets. Less than half said they would borrow revenue from next quarter and use it to bolster current period revenue. Fewer still said they would draw down accounting reserves (28%), postpone taking an accounting charge (21%), or alter accounting assumptions such as those relating to the allowance for doubtful accounts (8%). As one executive explained, auditors can second-guess the firm's accounting policies, but they can't readily challenge real economic actions to meet earnings targets that are taken in the ordinary course of business.

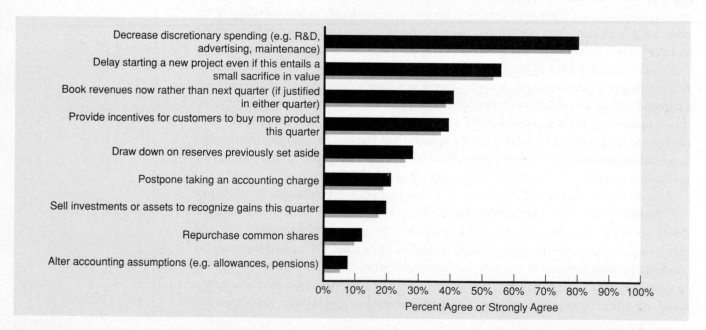

**Figure 7.9** HOW EARNINGS BENCHMARKS ARE SOMETIMES MET

How 401 financial executives at U.S. companies responded to the question: "Near the end of the quarter, it looks like your company might come in below the desired earnings target. Within what is permitted by GAAP, which of the following choices might your company make?"

SOURCE: J. R. Graham, C. R. Harvey, and S. Rajgopal, "The Economic Implications of Corporate Financial Reporting," *Journal of Accounting and Economics*, December 2005, p. 35.

Managers have strong incentives to achieve short-term earnings benchmarks. Some do so through operational excellence. For others, the path to benchmark beating involves taking real actions that may harm shareholders in the long term or using accounting gimmicks that mask underlying firm performance.

## REGULATORY AGENCIES

Financial statements used by creditors and shareholders are prepared using GAAP. But banks, insurance companies, public utilities, and many others must also provide financial statements to the government agencies that regulate them. Those statements are prepared on another basis—RAP—to satisfy specific regulatory objectives.

**RAP** stands for **regulatory accounting principles,** the methods and procedures that must be followed when assembling financial statements for regulatory agencies. RAP tells a company how to account for its business transactions from when to record revenue and in what amount to how depreciation expense must be calculated and what account title to use.

Regulators use RAP financial reports to set the prices customers are charged, as a basis for supervisory action, as a source of statistical information, and as an early warning signal for monitoring a company's financial health. To achieve these goals, regulators sometimes require the use of accounting principles that deviate from GAAP. Here's an example of a disclosure related to such a deviation:

> Under regulatory accounting, the company capitalizes both interest and equity costs during periods of construction. (SBC Communications, annual report)

GAAP allows the cost of debt (called *interest*) to be treated as just another construction project cost, but "equity costs" are not capitalized under GAAP (see Chapter 10). So, SBC Communications is telling annual report readers that its treatment of equity cost complies with RAP but deviates from GAAP. As a result, the company's completed construction projects—its telephone lines and related facilities—are shown at higher book values than would be the case if GAAP were used.

Why do shareholders, creditors, and other statement readers care about RAP if companies use it only when preparing financial reports for regulatory agencies? The answer is that *RAP sometimes shows up in the company's GAAP financial statements too.* Why? Because *SFAS No. 71* allows rate-regulated companies such as SBC Communications to account for and report assets and liabilities consistent with the way in which regulators establish rates as long as:

- the rates are designed to recover the costs of providing the regulated service, and
- the competitive environment makes it reasonable to assume that such rates can be charged and collected.[31]

So, SBC Communications not only capitalized equity costs in its financial reports to industry regulators but also did so in its published financial statements for shareholders and creditors.

*Knowing how a company accounts for its business transactions—whether it uses GAAP or RAP—is essential to gaining a clear understanding of its financial performance and condition.*

There's another reason why shareholders and creditors need to understand RAP as well as GAAP. Regulated companies can suffer because financial reports affect the regulatory process; for example, a rate increase may be denied based on the reported numbers. This possibility can influence both (1) management's GAAP accounting choices and (2) when transactions are recorded.

To see how, let's take a look at banks, savings institutions, and credit unions.

> The published balance sheets of rate-regulated companies will also contain **regulatory assets and liabilities** that reflect anticipated future rate adjustments, deferred costs, and delayed obligations specific to the regulatory process.

---

[31] "Accounting for the Effects of Certain Types of Regulation," *SFAS No. 71* (Stamford, CT: FASB, 1982).

# Capital Requirements in the Banking Industry

Federal and state regulatory agencies require banks and other financial institutions to meet **minimum capital requirements.** The purpose of these requirements is to ensure that the bank (or institution) remains financially sound and can meet its obligations to depositors.

The test for capital adequacy is a simple one: Does the amount of investor capital (think of "adjusted" stockholders' equity) or the ratio of investor capital to gross assets—both defined by RAP—exceed the minimum level allowed by the regulator? If it does, the bank is in compliance and considered to have adequate capital. If bank capital falls below the minimum allowed, regulatory intervention can be triggered.

Suppose that Hometown Bank & Trust has gross assets of $900 million and investor capital of $135 million, and suppose the bank's regulators set a 10% minimum capital ratio. Hometown is in compliance with the capital requirement because it has a capital adequacy ratio of 15%, calculated as:

$$\text{Capital adequacy ratio} = \frac{\text{Invested capital (as defined by RAP)}}{\text{Gross assets (as defined by RAP)}}$$

$$= \frac{\$135 \text{ million}}{\$900 \text{ million}} = 15\%$$

which is above the 10% minimum allowed.

*Regulators have a powerful weapon to encourage compliance with minimum capital guidelines.* They can impose costs on banks and financial institutions found to be in noncompliance. For example, a noncomplying bank:

- Is required to submit a comprehensive plan describing how and when its capital will be increased.
- Can be examined more frequently by the regulator.
- Can be denied a request to merge, open new branches, or expand services; and
- Can be subject to dividend payment restrictions if it has inadequate or "potentially inadequate" capital (for example, Hometown Bank & Trust might be prohibited from paying any dividends if its capital adequacy ratio falls to the minimum 10% level allowed).

Because regulators can restrict bank operations, a bank with inadequate capital incurs greater regulatory costs than does a bank with adequate capital.

> A bank's **loan loss provision** is just the estimated bad debt expense associated with its loan receivables. Loan loss provisions are expenses that reduce bank net income but (under RAP) have no impact on invested capital. **Loan charge-offs** are loans the bank no longer expects to collect. Loan charge-offs decrease bank capital but have no impact on bank net income.

Bank managers can avoid the regulatory costs of failing to meet minimum capital requirements in several ways. The best approach is to operate profitably and invest wisely so that the bank remains financially sound. Another way is to choose accounting policies that increase RAP–invested capital or decrease RAP gross assets so that the bank can pass its capital adequacy test. Let's examine this "artificial" approach to regulatory compliance.

The cash that banks receive from depositors is used to make loans. These loans show up as balance sheet receivables; they typically represent the bank's single largest asset. Uncollected loans are a significant cost in the banking industry. But bank managers have some discretion over the timing and amount of recorded uncollectibles. This discretion can be used to improve the bank's capital adequacy ratio. How?

It's easy: Understate the true loan loss provision and loan charge-offs for the year. This improves the bank's capital adequacy ratio and simultaneously increases the net income figure reported to shareholders. But these improvements are just an illusion. In reality, the bank expects more uncollectibles than are shown on the financial reports. Understanding loan loss provisions and charge-offs may help avoid noncompliance with bank capital requirements, but this strategy hides the bank's true performance and condition from both regulators and shareholders. So, evading RAP guidelines can impede accurate financial analysis.

## Rate Regulation in the Electric Utilities Industry

State and federal agencies known as public utility commissions set the prices charged by electric utility companies. The rate formulas of most commissions use accounting-determined costs and asset values. A typical rate formula for an electric utility looks like this:

Allowed revenue = Operating costs + Depreciation + Taxes + (ROA × Asset base)

where ROA is the return on assets allowed by the regulator. The rate formula sets total allowed revenues equal to an amount that covers the company's operating costs (fuel, labor, and administrative expenses plus depreciation and taxes) and provides a "fair" return on the capital invested in operating assets (things such as generating stations, transmission lines, fuel inventory, and so on). This "fair return" component of the rate formula is (ROA × Asset base).

Suppose that Midwest Power & Light has annual operating costs, depreciation, and taxes of $300 million. Suppose also that $500 million of capital is invested in operating assets. Finally, suppose that the state public service commission sets ROA at 10%. The annual allowed revenue would be:

$$\text{Allowed revenue} = \$300 \text{ million} + (10\% \times \$500 \text{ million})$$
$$= \$300 \text{ million} + \$50 \text{ million} = \$350 \text{ million}$$

To arrive at a rate per kilowatt-hour of electricity, the $350 million of revenue allowed is divided by the company's *estimate* of total kilowatt-hours to be sold during the year.

Industry RAP governs which items can be included in a regulated utility's operating costs and asset base and which cannot be included. The difference is important because included items are charged to customers, but disallowed items are charged to shareholders. Consider this example: Suppose that Midwest Power & Light spends $10 million on customer safety advertising and $50 million on corporate "image" advertising. Customer safety advertising is an allowed operating cost, so it is included in the rate formula. Customers ultimately pay for the $10 million spent on safety advertising through higher electricity rates.

Corporate image advertising is not an allowed cost in most states, so the $50 million that Midwest Power & Light spent promoting itself cannot be passed on to customers in the form of higher electricity rates. Who pays the bill? Shareholders do because the company has $50 million less cash. Regulators apparently see image advertising as unnecessary. Consequently, they do not require customers to pay for it through higher electricity rates.

The example illustrates how RAP can influence rate regulation and the revenues ultimately received by utility companies. But there's another important point to the example. Industry RAP treats customer safety advertising and corporate image advertising differently. GAAP does not; both types of advertising would be included in operating costs on the company's income statement. Other differences between public utility RAP and GAAP are:

- **Deferring costs** that would otherwise be charged to expense by nonregulated companies: Utilities can postpone expensing storm damage costs, for example, as long as it is *probable* that those specific deferred costs are subject to recovery in future revenues,
- **Capitalization of equity costs** on construction projects whereas interest alone can be capitalized by nonregulated companies.

Because of *SFAS No. 71*, RAP gets included in the financial statements that utility companies prepare for shareholders and creditors.

Rate regulation also creates incentives for public utility managers to artificially increase the asset base. Suppose Midwest Power & Light signs a $700,000, one-year rental agreement for service vehicles. If the rental payment is an allowed operating cost for rate-making purposes, customers would pay $700,000 in higher electricity rates. On the other hand, if the rental could be included in the company's regulatory asset base, customers would pay $770,000, or 10% more: $700,000 for depreciation (the full cost of the one-year asset) plus another $70,000 so that shareholders receive the allowed 10% return on the $700,000 asset.

> In 2002, Duke Energy agreed to pay $25 million to its customers to settle allegations that the company had *underreported* its net income to avoid having to reduce its electricity rates. Profits were underreported by $123 million (pre-tax) because the company overstated RAP expenses. See Case 7-4.

Given the choice, utility company shareholders would prefer to have the rental payment treated as an asset for rate-making purposes. The company could then charge customers an extra $70,000 and use the cash to cover "disallowed" costs—such as image advertising—or to pay stockholder dividends. One way to make this happen is to design the rental contract so that it qualifies for RAP treatment as an asset. (We show you how in Chapter 12.) Another approach is to lobby regulators to relax the rules governing when a rental contract qualifies for asset treatment. ***Change the contract or change the accounting rules:*** The result is the same. Adding more dollars to the asset base increases the allowed revenue stream for a rate-regulated company.

## Taxation

All companies are regulated by state and federal tax agencies. When it comes to income taxes and the U.S. government, the regulators are Congress and the Internal Revenue Service (IRS). Congress writes the rules, but the IRS interprets and administers them, and it collects the income tax.

IRS regulations govern the computation of net income for tax purposes. These IRS accounting rules are just another type of RAP. Many IRS accounting rules are the same as GAAP rules. Consider this example: Revenue is generally recognized for tax and GAAP purposes at the time of sale, not later when cash is collected from customers. However, there are situations in which IRS accounting rules differ from GAAP.

> Chapter 10 explains GAAP depreciation expense and the straight-line method, and Chapter 13 sheds further light on IRS depreciation expense.

A case in point is depreciation expense. GAAP requires companies to spread the cost of assets like equipment and buildings over the entire period of intended use (or economic life). The amount charged to depreciation each year can be computed using one of several different methods. IRS rules, on the other hand, require companies to use a strict schedule called the Modified Accelerated Cost Recovery System to determine their annual depreciation tax deduction. The result is that GAAP depreciation expense will rarely (if ever) equal the IRS depreciation tax deduction, which means that taxable net income will most often differ from GAAP net income.

> LIFO means **"last-in, first-out,"** and here's how it works. Suppose a start-up bicycle retailer begins the year with no inventory. Ten bicycles are purchased for $150 each during the first week of operations and another five bicycles are purchased mid-month for $180 each: same brand and model, just a higher price from the manufacturer. Eight bicycles are sold during the month, leaving seven still in inventory. Using LIFO, the retailer would calculate the cost of goods sold to be $1,350 (or five bicycles at $180 each plus three more at $150 each). Notice that this calculation presumes the *last* bicycles to come into the shop (those bought for $180 each) are the *first sold.* Notice also that with rising inventory costs, LIFO produces a larger cost of goods sold expense ($1,350 in our example) than does FIFO, or **"first-in, first-out"** (eight bicycles at $150 each, or $1,200). A higher cost of goods sold expense means a lower taxable income, Chapter 9 tells you more.

Sometimes the IRS requires firms to use identical tax and GAAP accounting methods. When inventory costs are rising, companies like to use LIFO for tax purposes because it lowers their taxable income. But the IRS rules on LIFO inventory accounting contain an unusual requirement: Companies that elect to use LIFO for tax purposes must also use LIFO in their shareholder reports. So, the tax benefits of LIFO can be obtained only when LIFO is also used in GAAP financial statements, but doing so lowers GAAP net income when prices are rising. Because the LIFO method is widely used, many corporate managers must believe that the tax benefits of LIFO outweigh its negative impact on GAAP net income.

Taxation and GAAP accounting are related in another way. Companies reporting large GAAP earnings sometimes attract the attention of politicians who threaten to impose "windfall profits" taxes. This has been true for big U.S. oil companies during periods of rapidly increasing oil prices and/or during oil shortages caused by governmental policies.

For example, during the 1970s, the federal government controlled the price of gasoline in an effort to reduce consumption and to dampen the inflationary impact of escalating oil prices. In 1979, the price of gasoline at the pump was decontrolled one week before big oil companies announced record third-quarter profits that were labeled by politicians as "obscene." After the earnings announcements, a windfall profits tax on oil company earnings was proposed, and politicians voted to reinstate gasoline price controls. These actions occurred even though part of the reported profit increase was due to an accounting change required by the FASB; most of the rest of the increase was due to overseas operations and inventory holding gains.

Sometimes it just doesn't pay to be seen as a highly profitable company. When that's the case, managers have incentives to use accounting methods that make the company look less profitable than it really is. That way they can avoid attracting the attention of politicians and regulators who might impose a windfall profits tax or other cost on the company.

---

**Government regulatory agencies and taxing authorities can write their own accounting rules, and many do. The result is that some financial statements for shareholders and creditors contain special regulatory items or use regulatory accounting methods that deviate from normal GAAP. Accounting-based regulations including IRS rules also influence the choice of GAAP accounting methods for shareholder reports and when transactions are recorded.**

## ANALYTICAL INSIGHTS: IDENTIFYING "MANAGED" EARNINGS

The message from this chapter is that managers sometimes have powerful incentives to "manage" their companies' reported profitability and financial condition. These incentives are motivated by loan covenants, compensation contracts, regulatory agency oversight, tax avoidance efforts, a desire to meet or beat analysts' quarterly earnings forecasts, and to increase the company's stock price. Financial statement gimmicks are likely to be most prevalent when these accounting incentives are especially strong, for example, when the company is in danger of violating its debt covenants, when a large portion of top management pay comes from bonuses tied to earnings per share or sales growth, or when management has a lengthy record of beating "the street's" earnings forecast by a penny. What's the penalty for failing to make the numbers? Loan default, lost bonuses, and an abrupt stock price decline.

So, now you know *when* to look for potential accounting distortions, but what exactly do you look *for* and *where* do you look? How do companies "manage" earnings? What accounting gimmicks are used?

The remaining chapters of this book answer these questions in detail. For now, we'll simply give you a broad overview to sensitize you to the danger areas.

Look to areas where subjective judgments or estimates have a significant impact on the financial statements. For some companies, the areas to scrutinize might be revenue recognition, deferred marketing and customer acquisition costs, or reserves for bad debts and inventory obsolescence. For other companies, the critical areas may involve intangible asset valuation, asset impairment, warranty and product liability reserves, restructuring charges, or litigation and environmental contingencies. Also take a close look at areas where it is difficult to evaluate the company's accounting practices because no authoritative standards exist or because established practices are controversial. And watch out for large business transactions, especially those that are unusually complex in structure or in their financial statement effects. Also take a magnifying glass to the financial statement footnotes and other financial disclosures. They should be complete and transparent, allowing you to look behind the numbers to see what's really going on in the company. If not, there may be an accounting torpedo headed in your direction.[32]

> A recent professional pronouncement requires independent auditors to adopt this incentives-driven financial analytic perspective when conducting audits.
>
> *Source:* "Consideration of Fraud in a Financial Statement Audit," *Statement on Auditing Standards No. 99* (New York: American Institute of Certified Public Accountants, 2002), paras. 16–17.

## SUMMARY

- Conflicts of interest among managers, shareholders, lenders, or regulators are natural features of business.

- Contracts and regulations help address these conflicts of interest in ways that are mutually beneficial to the parties involved.

- Accounting numbers often play an important role in contracts and regulations because they provide useful information about the company's performance and financial condition as well as about the management team's accomplishments.

- Accounting-based lending agreements, compensation contracts, and regulations shape managers' incentives; after all, that's why accounting numbers are included in contracts and regulations. They also help explain the accounting choices managers make.

- Understanding why and how managers exercise their discretion in implementing GAAP can be extremely helpful to those who are analyzing and interpreting a company's financial statements.

- What happened to Allen Ford? The bank provided the loans he needed to open his first BookWorm, and the concept proved so successful he now owns three stores.

## EXERCISES

**E7-1**

Identifying conflicts of interest and agency costs

Suppose you and two friends each invested $100,000 in an oil and gas partnership. The general partner, Huge Gamble, Inc., invests no cash but makes all operating decisions for the partnership, including where and how deep to drill for oil. Drilling costs plus a management fee are charged against the $300,000 of cash you and your friends invested. If oil is found, you each get 15% of partnership net income with the remaining 55% going to Huge Gamble. But if the wells are dry, you get nothing except any cash that remains.

**Required:**

What is an agency relationship, and what are agency costs? How do these concepts apply to your investment in the oil and gas partnership?

---

[32] Examples of accounting torpedoes can be found in U.S. General Accounting Office (GAO) report "Financial Statement Restatements: Trends, Market Impacts, Regulatory Responses, and Remaining Challenges," GAO-03-138 (October 2002). This report chronicles the accounting abuses uncovered at Enron, Sunbeam, Xerox, and other companies.

**Required:**

What is a debt covenant? Why do lenders include them in loan agreements? Why do borrowers agree to include covenants in loan agreements?

**E 7-2**

Understanding debt covenants

---

**Required:**

What are affirmative debt covenants? What are negative covenants? Provide two examples of each.

**E 7-3**

Affirmative and negative debt covenants

---

The debt covenants in TCBY's loan agreement do not explicitly mention the accounting methods that must be used when it prepares financial statements for submission to the lender.

**Required:**

Why don't lenders require the use of specific accounting methods rather than letting management pick from among GAAP alternatives?

**E 7-4**

Debt covenants and accounting methods

---

**Required:**

What are the advantages of loan agreements that contain covenants tied to accounting numbers? Are there any disadvantages? Explain.

**E 7-5**

Tying contracts to accounting numbers

---

**Required:**

What are regulatory costs, and why are they important for understanding a company's financial reporting choices?

**E 7-6**

Regulatory costs

---

Some public service commissions let utilities include construction in progress—construction dollars spent for projects not yet completed—in their rate-making asset bases. Other states allow only completed projects to be included.

**Required:**

Which approach favors shareholders? Why?

**E 7-7**

Regulatory accounting principles

---

Illinois Power & Heat just spent $5 million repairing one of its electrical generating stations that was damaged by a tornado. The loss was uninsured. Management has asked the public service commission for approval to treat the $5 million as an asset for rate-making purposes rather than as an allowed expense.

**Required:**

What difference will this make to customers and shareholders?

**E 7-8**

Equipment repairs and rate regulation

---

**Required:**

Why do regulators require banks and insurance companies to maintain minimum levels of investor capital? What impact does this type of regulatory requirement have on the financial statements that banks and insurance companies prepare for shareholders?

**E 7-9**

Maintaining capital adequacy.

---

The top five executives at Marvel Manufacturing are paid annual bonuses based on predetermined earnings goals. These bonuses can be as much as 500% of salary. As a member of the company's compensation committee, you've been asked to comment on the following proposed changes to the annual bonus plan:

**E 7-10**

Incentive design

- Use after-tax income from continuing operations as the earnings performance measure instead of bottom-line net income.
- Set performance goals based on return on assets (ROA) rather than on earnings.

- Set performance goals, net income or ROA, based on beating the industry average rather than using an absolute performance target.

**Required:**

What are the advantages and disadvantages of each suggested change?

---

**E7-11**

**Medical malprofits**

**Required:**

Explain the potential conflict of interest that arises when doctors own the hospitals in which they work. The following news article may help.

The executive who became the most visible symbol of profit-driven medical care stepped down yesterday as the top officer of the Columbia/HCA Healthcare Corporation amid a criminal investigation of whether the company's pursuit of profits has stretched beyond the legal limits. . . . [He] will be replaced by Thomas F. Frist, Jr., a surgeon by training, who has made his career in the hospital business. . . . Dr. Frist said he was ending Columbia's practice of selling ownership stakes in its hospitals to its doctors. That has been a critical piece of the strategy that helped propel Columbia's growth but led to great legal and ethical criticism that the company was compromising the medical independence of its doctors.

*Source: The New York Times, July 26, 1997.*

---

**E7-12**

**Stock options**

**Required:**

1. During the late 1990s, stock options were a substantial component of executive pay packages. How might the use of stock options contribute to accounting gimmickry and financial statement abuses?

2. GE's new "performance share" plan described here ties CEO compensation to (a) cash flow performance and (b) stock return performance over the next five years. Does the use of these performance measures rather than net income or earnings per share increase or reduce the likelihood of accounting gimmickry? Explain why.

### SIGN OF TIMES: GE CHIEF IMMELT TO GET STOCK—NOT OPTIONS

For General Electric Co. chief Jeffrey Immelt, stock-option grants—those wealth generators of the 1990s—will be a thing of the past.

In another move to reshape its executive-compensation and corporate governance policies, General Electric said yesterday it no longer would grant its chairman and chief executive either stock options or restricted stock. Instead, it will tie the majority of his pay to a new type of stock award that requires him to meet specific performance targets.

Under the plan, which could set a precedent for other corporations, Mr. Immelt has been granted 250,000 "performance share units." These financial instruments eventually will turn into stock shares if Mr. Immelt and the company meet two performance measures. If they miss, he will still get his base salary, currently $3 million, an undetermined bonus . . . and dividends . . . on his stock units.

Each stock unit equals one share, and under GE's current price, the value of the new grants is about $7.5 million. If Mr. Immelt meets his targets, the performance-share units would contribute a significant portion of his pay.

Half of the units will vest in five years if GE's cash flow increases at an average of at least 10% each year. The other 125,000 shares will vest at the same time if GE's shareholder return meets or outperforms the five-year cumulative total return of companies in the Standard & Poor's 500 stock index. . . .

*Source: "Sign of the Times: GE Chief Immelt to Get Stock—Not Options," The Wall Street Journal, September 18, 2003. Copyright © 2003 Dow Jones & Company, Inc. All rights reserved worldwide. Used with permission.*

**Required:**

1. The company's bonus plan for top executives follows. One way Krispy Kreme executives can achieve their earnings growth target is to open new stores as fast as possible. Explain why this might alarm shareholders.

2. Describe how Krispy Kreme's executive bonus plan might lead to accounting abuses at the company.

For fiscal 2003, bonuses for all executive officers were contingent upon meeting or exceeding targets for two performance measures: (1) a percentage increase in earnings per share of common stock; and (2) a percentage return on revenues as measured by dividing earnings before interest and taxes (EBIT) by total Krispy Kreme revenues. Both targets were met or exceeded for fiscal 2003 though not to the extent they were met or exceeded in fiscal 2002 or fiscal 2001.

*Source:* Krispy Kreme Doughnuts, Inc. 2003 proxy.

**E7-13**

Krispy Kreme's bonus plan

# PROBLEMS / DISCUSSION QUESTIONS

**Required:**

1. Suppose David Johnson received a base salary (before personal income taxes) of $800,000 in 1993. His personal tax rate was 35% that year, and the year-end value of his Campbell stock was $1.6 million. How much of his after-tax salary for 1993 would go toward buying more stock in the company?

2. What are the advantages and disadvantages of Campbell's stock ownership plan?

3. Do you think that institutional investors such as pension portfolio managers and mutual fund managers would favor or oppose Campbell's plan? Why?

**P7-1**

Managerial incentives and stock ownership

## CAMPBELL'S SOUP EXECUTIVES MUST OWN FIRM'S STOCK

Campbell Soup Co. said Tuesday it is introducing a stock ownership plan for its chief executive and about 70 other senior executives. Under the plan, David Johnson, president and chief executive officer, is required to hold three times his 1992 base salary of $757,500 in shares by the end of 1994. He must maintain the three-times-earnings stake every year until he leaves the company. Executive or senior vice presidents are expected to buy and hold at least two times their annual base salary by 1994. Corporate vice presidents who have been with the company for three or more years will buy and hold the equivalent of one year's base salary. Senior executives will buy shares equal to at least one-half their annual salary. All corporate officers must hold at least 1,000 shares of Campbell stock by the end of this year.

*Source:* Reprinted with permission of Bloomberg L.P.; © 2001. *Bloomberg Business News,* May 1993. All rights reserved.

**Required:**

1. The following article describes a shareholder proposal made by one ConAgra investor. The investor, Donald Hudgens, has five minutes to speak on his proposal at the ConAgra shareholders' meeting. What key points do you think Hudgens will make?

2. ConAgra's vice president for human resources will also have five minutes to defend the current incentive plan and to oppose the Hudgens proposal. What arguments will the vice president make?

**P7-2**

Managerial pay and performance

3. Will ConAgra's institutional investors (for example, pension portfolio managers and mutual fund managers) favor or oppose the Hudgens plan? Why?

4. How do you think the shareholder vote turned out?

## CONAGRA HOLDER IS SEEKING CHANGES IN INCENTIVE PLAN

Donald Hudgens thinks ConAgra, Inc.'s chairman and chief executive officer, Philip B. Fletcher, has it too easy. "Maybe I'm naive," says Mr. Hudgens, a retired railroad chemist. "I've never had a high-powered job." Still, he contends that ConAgra's CEO should be working harder for his millions.

As a consequence, ConAgra shareholders will vote later this month on Mr. Hudgens's proposal that the company revise a special long-term incentive plan directors approved for Mr. Fletcher last year. Under that plan, the chairman would receive 50,000 ConAgra common shares for every percentage point over 10% that the company's per-share earnings rise during the next four fiscal years.

For example, if earnings grow at a compound annual rate of 14%, as they did last year, Mr. Fletcher would get 200,000 shares of stock—that is, four percentage points times 50,000 shares. The payout would occur in July 1998. At ConAgra's current price, every 50,000 shares would be valued at $1.6 million.

"They'll do it [exceed 10%] in spite of any incentive award," Mr. Hudgens says. He has some statistical support. Prudential Securities food analyst John McMillin calculates that over the past five years ConAgra's per-share earnings have grown at a 15.4% compounded annual rate; ConAgra's longtime internal goal is for per-share earnings growth to exceed 14% a year, on average.

Thus, Mr. Hudgens wants ConAgra to compare its performance with that of other food companies, and he has drawn up a list of 13—Archer-Daniels-Midland Co., Borden, Inc., CPC International, Inc., Campbell Soup Co., General Mills, Inc., H.J. Heinz Co., Kellogg Co., PepsiCo, Inc., Philip Morris Co., Quaker Oats Co., Ralston Purina Co., Sara Lee Corp., and Tyson Foods, Inc. Moreover, per-share growth must come from continuing operations, the 54-year-old shareholder says.

"I have no problem with management making a lot of money," Mr. Hudgens says. "More power to 'em. But I want them to work their tails off for us."

---

**P 7-3**

**Foot Locker, Inc.:** anticipating covenant violation

Foot Locker, Inc. reported an $18 million loss on sales of $1,283 million for the quarter ended August 4, 2007. The quarterly financial filing (10-Q) also contained this warning for investors and creditors.

Management believes operating cash flows will be adequate to fund its working capital requirements, future pension contributions for the Company's retirement plans, anticipated quarterly dividend payments, scheduled debt repayments, potential share repurchases, and to support the development of its short-term and long-term operating strategies. . . . Under the Company's revolving credit and term loan agreement, the Company is required to satisfy certain financial and operating covenants, including a minimum fixed charge coverage ratio. In addition, this agreement restricts the amount the Company may expend in any year for dividends to 50 percent of its prior year's net income. Based upon the Company's second quarter financial results and business uncertainties for the second half of the year, the Company may not continue to be in compliance with the fixed charge coverage ratio. In addition, the restricted payment provision may prohibit the Company from the payment of the dividend at the current rate in 2008.

**Required:**

1. What is a minimum fixed charge coverage ratio, and what purpose does it serve in the company's loan agreements?

2. Why would Foot Locker agree to restrict dividends to just 50% of its prior year's net income?

3. In general terms, explain how a company such as Foot Locker might use accounting tricks to avoid violating debt covenants tied to financial statement numbers.

4. What is likely to happen if Foot Locker does not satisfy one or more of the loan covenants at year-end?

---

**P7-4**

Frisby Technologies:
Violating a covenant

## FRISBY IN DEFAULT ON LOAN COVENANTS

Frisby Technologies has received a notice of default from two of its secured creditors. DAMAD Holdings AG and Bluwat AG have notified the company that it is in default of the tangible net worth covenant contained in its respective loan agreements with the lenders. The covenant requires the company to maintain a tangible net worth of not less than $1,250,000 as of the end of each fiscal quarter. A similar covenant is contained in the company loan agreements with its other secured lenders, MUSI Investments S.A. and Fin.part International S.A. As of September 30, 2002, the company's tangible net worth, calculated as provided in the respective loan agreements, was a negative $663,402.

Under the terms of the DAMAD and Bluwat loan agreements, the company has until December 18 to cure the default or such longer period as it is diligently prosecuting a cure to the reasonable satisfaction of the lenders. The company does not currently expect that it will be able to cure the default within the prescribed cure period.

If the default is not cured prior to the end of the cure period, then (i) the entire unpaid balance owed to the lenders, $1.25 million plus accrued interest, would become due and payable; (ii) the interest rate, to the extent permitted by law, could be increased by either or both lenders up to the maximum rate allowed by law;

(iii) any accrued and unpaid interest, fees or charges could be deemed by either or both lenders to be a part of the principal balance, with interest to accrue on a daily compounded basis until the entire outstanding principal and accrued interest is paid in full; (iv) either or both lenders could foreclose on its security interest in substantially all of the company's assets; and (v) each lender would have all rights available to it at law or in equity.

In addition, repayment of the loans is secured by a limited guaranty by COB/CEO Gregory Frisby of up to one-third of the total amount outstanding under the loans.

The company has requested waiver of compliance of the tangible net worth covenant from each of the lenders, but no such waiver has been granted. The company will continue to pursue a waiver or otherwise to seek to negotiate a forbearance agreement or other satisfactory resolution with the lenders. If the company is unsuccessful, it may voluntarily seek protection from its creditors under federal bankruptcy laws, which would have a material adverse effect on the company's business, financial condition and prospects.

*Source*: R. Craver, "Default of Credit Agreement Adds to Frisby's Woes," *Winston-Salem Journal*, November 22, 2002. Copyright © 2002 Winston-Salem Journal. Used with permission.

**Required:**

1. What is a minimum tangible net worth covenant, and what purpose does it serve in the Frisby loan agreements?

2. Why might lenders be reluctant just to waive Frisby's covenant violation?

3. Among the options available to Frisby's lenders is foreclosure: shuttering the company and selling off all assets. Why might lenders prefer to avoid this action?

Delhaize America operates retail food supermarkets in the southeastern and mid-Atlantic regions of the United States. The Company's stores, Food Lion, Kash 'n' Karry, and Save 'n' Pack, sell a wide variety of groceries, including produce, meats, dairy products, seafood, frozen food, delicatessen and bakery foods, and nonfood items such as health and beauty care products, prescriptions, and other household and personal products.

In 1999 the company entered into a credit agreement with a group of banks. Excerpts taken from the loan agreement follow:

### Section 6.07. Fixed Charges Coverage

At the end of each Fiscal Quarter set forth below, the ratio of (i) Consolidated EBITDAR for the period of four Fiscal Quarters then ended to (ii) Consolidated Fixed Charges for such period, shall not have been less than the ratio set forth below opposite such Fiscal Quarter:

| Fiscal Quarter | Ratio |
| --- | --- |
| First Fiscal Quarter ended on or immediately after the Effective Date—Third Fiscal Quarter 2001 | 2.25:1 |
| Fourth Fiscal Quarter 2001—Third Fiscal Quarter 2002 | 2.50:1 |
| Fourth Fiscal Quarter 2002—Third Fiscal Quarter 2003 | 2.75:1 |
| Fourth Fiscal Quarter 2003 and thereafter | 3.00:1 |

### Section 6.08. Ratio of Consolidated Adjusted Debt to Consolidated EBITDAR

At no date will the ratio of (i) Consolidated Adjusted Debt at such date to (ii) Consolidated EBITDAR for the period of four consecutive Fiscal Quarters ended on or most recently prior to such date exceed the ratio set forth below opposite the period in which such date falls:

| Period | Ratio |
| --- | --- |
| Effective Date—day immediately preceding last day of Fourth Fiscal Quarter 2001 | 4.50:1 |
| Last day of Fourth Fiscal Quarter 2001—day immediately preceding last day of Fourth Fiscal Quarter 2002 | 4.00:1 |
| Last day of Fourth Fiscal Quarter 2002—day immediately preceding last day of Fourth Fiscal Quarter 2003 | 3.75:1 |
| Last day of Fourth Fiscal Quarter 2003 and thereafter | 3.50:1 |

*Source:* Delhaize America loan agreement.

EBITDAR is earning before interest, taxes, depreciation, amortization, and rent, and consolidated fixed charges means debt payments and interest expenses plus rent payments.

**Required:**

1. Why does the loan agreement include rent as a fixed charge in the EBITDAR coverage ratio described in Section 6.07?

2. The minimum acceptable EBITDAR coverage ratio (Section 6.07) increases from 2.25 at inception of the loan to 3.00 in the fourth quarter of 2003. How does the company benefit from this requirement? How does the lender benefit?

3. The debt-to-EBITDAR ratio described in Section 6.08 serves what purpose?

4. The maximum acceptable debt-to-EBITDAR ratio (Section 6.08) decreases from 4.50 at inception of the loan to 3.50 in the fourth quarter of 2003. How does the company benefit from this requirement? How does the lender benefit?

John Brincat is the president and chief executive of Mercury Finance, an auto lender that specializes in high credit-risk customers. The company's proxy statement contains the following description of Brincat's pay package.

**P 7-6**

Tying bonus to EPS performance

Mr. Brincat is eligible for an annual incentive bonus equal to 1% of Net After-tax Earnings of the Company and is eligible for an additional bonus based upon annual increases in Net After-tax Earnings per share only after earnings exceed 20% over the prior year. The additional bonus is determined as follows:

- Earnings per share increases of 0% to 19.99%, no additional bonus is paid.

- Earnings per share increases of 20% to 29.99%, additional bonus will be equal to 2.5% of the amount of increase from the prior year.

- Earnings per share increases of 30% to 39.99%, additional bonus will be equal to 3.0% of the amount of increase from the prior year.

- Earnings per share increases of 40% or more, additional bonus will be equal to 3.5% of the amount of increase from the prior year.

In addition, at the time the employment contract was entered into, Mr. Brincat was issued a stock option grant . . . of 2,500,000 shares at a price of $17.375 per share, the fair market value on the date of the grant. The options vest equally during the next five years of the contract and are exercisable in increments of 500,000 shares annually only if earnings per share each year exceeds the prior year's earnings per share by 20%. If earnings per share do not increase by 20%, Mr. Brincat forfeits that year's options and has no further right or claim to that year's options.

*Source:* Mercury Finance 1995 proxy.

**Required:**

1. Suppose that Mercury Finance had $50 million of net after-tax earnings for the year. How much of a bonus would Brincat receive if the EPS increase that year was only 10%?

2. How much of a bonus would Brincat receive if the EPS increase was 30%?

3. As a shareholder, how comfortable would you be if your company's managers had contracts with these types of bonus and stock option incentives? Why?

Following your retirement as senior vice president of finance for a large company, you joined the board of Cayman Grand Cruises, Inc. You serve on the compensation committee and help set the bonuses paid to the company's top five executives. According to the annual bonus plan, each executive can earn a bonus of 1% of annual net income.

**P 7-7**

Earnings quality and pay

No bonuses were paid in 2006 because the company reported a net loss of $6,588,000.

Shortly after the end of the year, the compensation committee received a letter signed by all five executives, indicating that they felt the company had performed well in 2006. The letter identified the following items from the 2006 income statement that the executives felt painted a less favorable view of performance than was actually the case:

## Proposed Adjustments to 2006 Earnings

| *($ in thousands)* | |
|---|---|
| Restructuring and other nonrecurring charges | $63,000 |
| Loss from discontinued operations | 22,851 |
| Extraordinary charge, early retirement of debt | 6,824 |
| Cumulative effect of required changes in accounting principles for postretirement benefits other than pensions | 88,847 |

*(continued)*

*($ in thousands)*

| | |
|---|---:|
| Cumulative effect of management-initiated changes in accounting principles for: | |
| Depreciation | 14,180 |
| Warehouse and catalog costs | 2,110 |

The letter asked the compensation committee to add these items back to the reported net loss and to then recalculate the bonus awards for 2006. The fiscal year 2006 income statement follows. Assume the tax rate is 34%.

**Required:**

1. As a member of the compensation committee, how would you respond to each suggested adjustment? Why?

2. What 2006 net income figure do you suggest be used to determine bonuses for the year?

## Cayman Grand Cruises, Inc.

### Consolidated Statement of Income

| *($ in thousands)* | **June 30, 2006** |
|---|---:|
| Net revenues | $1,024,467 |
| Cost of sales | 535,178 |
| Gross margin | 489,289 |
| Selling, general, and administrative | 299,101 |
| Research, development, and engineering | 94,172 |
| Gain on sale of joint venture | (33,000) |
| Restructuring and other nonrecurring charges | 63,000 |
| Operating income | 66,016 |
| Gain on sale of investment | 40,800 |
| Interest expense | (7,145) |
| Interest income | 2,382 |
| Other income (expense)—net | (2,121) |
| Income before income taxes | 99,932 |
| Provision for income taxes | (29,980) |
| Income from continuing operations | 69,952 |
| Income (loss) from discontinued operations (net of tax effect) | (22,851) |
| Gain on disposal of discontinued operations (net of tax effect) | 38,343 |
| Extraordinary charge, early retirement of debt (net of tax effect) | (6,824) |
| Income before cumulative effect of changes in accounting principles | 78,620 |
| Cumulative effect on prior years of changes in accounting principles for:* | |
| Postretirement benefits other than pensions (net of tax effect) | (88,847) |
| Income taxes (net of tax effect) | 19,929 |
| Depreciation (net of tax effect) | (14,180) |
| Warehouse and catalog costs (net of tax effect) | (2,110) |
| Net income (loss) | $ (6,588) |

---

* This approach to reporting the prior period ("cumulative") impact of a change in accounting principles was discontinued by the FASB in 2005.

---

**P 7 - 8**

Avoiding debt covenant violations

Food Lion, Inc. operates a chain of retail supermarkets principally in the southeastern United States. The supermarket business is highly competitive, and it is characterized by low profit margins. Food Lion competes with national, regional, and local supermarket chains; discount food stores; single-unit stores; convenience stores; and warehouse clubs.

Food Lion recently entered into a credit agreement with a group of banks. Excerpts taken from the loan agreement follow.

### Section 5.19. Limitation on Incurrence of Funded Debt

The Borrower will not create, assume or incur or in any manner be or become liable in respect of any [additional] Funded Debt . . . [unless] the ratio of Income Available for Fixed Charges for the immediately preceding four Fiscal Quarters to Pro Forma Fixed Charges for such four Fiscal Quarters shall have been at least 2.00 to 1.00.

### Section 5.20. Fixed Charges Coverage

At the end of each Fiscal Quarter . . . the ratio of Income Available for Fixed Charges for the immediately preceding four Fiscal Quarters then ended to Consolidated Fixed Charges for the immediately preceding four Fiscal Quarters then ended, shall not be less than . . . 1.75 to 1.0.

### Section 5.21. Minimum Consolidated Tangible Net Worth

Consolidated Tangible Net Worth will at no time be less than (i) $706,575,475 plus (ii) 30.0% of the cumulative Consolidated Net Income of the Borrower during any period after [the new loan agreement is signed], calculated quarterly but excluding from such calculations of Consolidated Net Income for purposes of this clause (ii), any quarter in which the Consolidated Net Income of the Borrower and its Consolidated Subsidiaries is negative.

*Source:* Food Lion, Inc. loan agreement.

**Required:**

1. In two more weeks, the company's books will be closed for the quarter, and the *fixed charges coverage* might fall below the level required by the loan agreement. How can management avoid violating this covenant?

2. The company's *tangible net worth* may also fall below the amount specified in the loan agreement. How can management avoid violating this covenant?

3. Elsewhere in the loan agreement it says that the company's *ratio of consolidated debt to total capitalization* must be no more than 0.75 to 1.0. How can management avoid violating this covenant?

4. Suppose you were one of Food Lion's bankers, and you were thinking about making changes to the loan covenants. What management activities would you most want to limit? Why?

---

A 1999 *Wall Street Journal* article described how Microsoft records revenue from software sales.

**P7-9**

Microsoft's "unearned revenue" account

### SOME SAVVY FANS COOL TO MICROSOFT

Some savvy investors, detecting fissures in Microsoft's armor, are pulling back from the world's most highly valued company.

The concern: the first-ever drop in an arcane but closely watched indicator of Microsoft's future results.

The balance in Microsoft's "unearned revenue" account, which declined to $4.13 billion on Sept. 30 from $4.24 billion in June, has become a lighting rod for more general concerns about the price of the company's shares. . . . Managers of several large funds . . . are shedding part of their Microsoft holdings. The immediate trigger was the first quarter-to-quarter decline in Microsoft's unearned revenue account. . . .

In the software industry, Microsoft pioneered the practice of recording a portion of the revenue from some products as "unearned," starting with the release of Windows 95. The

*(continued)*

practice is common in some other fields: Many magazine publishers, for instance, record subscription revenues only when issues are shipped.

Similarly, Microsoft now holds back a portion of revenues from Windows 98, Windows NT and Office until it "earns" the revenue by delivering interim upgrades, bug fixes and other customer support. The account also includes the value of coupons that customers receive, which entitle them to free upgrades when they buy a Microsoft product before the next version is ready.

A delay in the shipment of Office 2000 earlier this year caused the company to add $400 million to the unearned revenue account in the March quarter to cover the coupons issued to buyers of Office 97. As copies of Office 2000 were shipped, half of that amount flowed into the June quarterly results; another $150 million was transferred in the fiscal quarter ended in September.

The effect was to bolster earned revenues in those quarters and lower unearned revenues. . . .

## FUTURE OR FALLOUT?

Microsoft's unearned revenue account consists of revenues set aside from the sales of Windows 98, Windows NT and Office to pay for future improvements. It also includes the value of coupons that entitle users to upgrade to newer versions of Microsoft software.

SOURCE: "Some Savvy Fans Cool to Microsoft," *The Wall Street Journal,* October 28, 1999. Copyright © 1999 Dow Jones & Company, Inc. All rights reserved worldwide. Reprinted with permission.

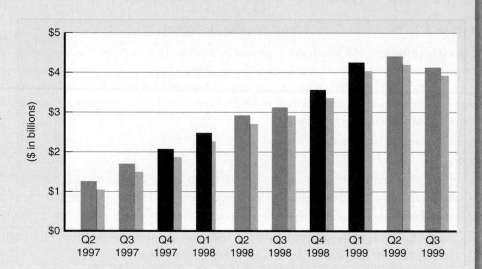

**Required:**

1. Based on the revenue recognition principles discussed in Chapters 2 and 3, explain why a company such as Microsoft would set aside some software sales revenues as "unearned"?

2. How would you determine how much sales revenue to set aside each quarter? Is this number easy to calculate?

3. Suppose the Unearned revenue account is reduced by $100 million. Where do these dollars go? (The Unearned revenue account is reduced by a debit. What account receives the offsetting credit?)

4. Describe how contracting and regulatory incentives might influence how much revenue is set aside as unearned. How might these incentives influence when the Unearned revenue account is reduced and by how much?

5. Why do analysts and investors pay such close attention to changes in Microsoft's Unearned revenue account?

---

**P7-10**

Understanding rate regulation and accounting choices

Alliant Energy just received regulatory approval for its 2008 electricity rate. The company has been authorized to charge customers $0.10 per kilowatt-hour (kwh), a rate lower than other utilities in the state charge. Details of the rate calculation follow:

## Alliant Energy

|  |  | **2008 Rate Authorization** |
|---|---|---|
| Allowed operating costs |  | $ 1,120 million |
| Assets in service | $3,200 million |  |
| × Allowed rate of return | 8.75%   = | 280 million |
| Revenue requirement |  | $ 1,400 million |
| ÷ Estimated energy demand |  | 14,000 million kwh |
| Rate allowed per kwh |  | $   0.10 |

Shortly after the 2008 rate was set, the company's financial reporting staff circulated an internal memo recommending the following accounting changes:

1. Extend plant depreciation life by five years to reflect current utilization forecasts. This would add $175 million to the asset base and reduce annual depreciation (an operating cost) by $5 million.

2. Increase estimated bad debt expense from 1% to 1.5% of sales to reflect current forecasts of customer defaults. This would add $7 million to operating costs and reduce total assets by the same amount.

3. Amortize 2007 hostile takeover defense costs of $4.5 million over three years rather than take the entire expense in 2007. This would increase 2008 operating costs by $1.5 million and add $3 million to the asset base.

4. Write up fuel and materials inventories to their current replacement value. This would add $60 million to the asset base, but it would have no impact on 2008 operating costs.

**Required:**

1. Assess the impact of each proposed change on the company's 2008 revenue requirement and rate per kilowatt-hour, assuming that regulators will approve the accounting changes and adjust the allowed rate accordingly.

2. As a member of the state utility commission, comment on the merits of each proposed accounting change.

---

Here's how Level 3 Communication's "moving target" stock option plan works. Suppose options are granted on January 1, 2000, when the company's stock is selling for $50 a share. The options cannot be exercised until January 1, 2003, and the exercise price on that date is $50 plus a factor reflecting the change in the S&P Index between the grant date and the exercise date. If the Index increases 50%, so does the exercise price (to $75). If the Index falls by 10% between the grant date and the exercise date, the exercise price also falls (to $45).

**P7-11**

Relative performance and stock options

**Required:**

1. On January 1, 2003, the company's stock is trading at $90 a share. The S&P Index has increased 60 percent from its level at the grant date. What is the exercise price of Level 3's options? Have employees benefited from the company's stock option plan?

2. What if the January 1, 2003, stock price was only $70? Calculate the option exercise price and determine whether employees have benefited from the stock option plan. How well have Level 3 stockholders done since the grant date?

3. Stock prices and the S&P Index tend to increase when the Chairman of the Federal Reserve Bank lowers interest rates. What is the rationale for raising the exercise price when interest rates decline? What other macroeconomic risks can influence the value of employee stock options at Level 3?

4. Why haven't other companies adopted the Level 3 plan?

## THE MOVING TARGET OPTION

Nineteen ninety-eight was a good year for Harvey Golub, the chief executive of American Express. His stock options zoomed from $45 million to $60 million in value. But it was a bad year for Golub's shareholders. They underperformed the S&P 500 by 13 percentage points.

The disappointed Amex holders have a lot of company. It's common these days for executives to get rich off options even as they deliver subpar results to their investors. It's the simple arithmetic of a bull market: Options can be worth a lot of money on a stock that rises, even if it badly lags the averages. . . .

How do we stop this madness? One bold telecom executive, James Crowe, shows how. When he founded fiber-optics network Level 3 Communications three years ago, he vowed to align his interests with investors'. His option plan, which covers all employees, ties exercise prices to the S&P 500 Index. If Level 3 just keeps up with the average, the options are worthless. If it outperforms, the options are worth a decent amount to rank and file employees and big money to top managers.

Level 3 investors aren't hurting and neither is Chief Executive Crowe. Since the stock was first offered to the public just under two years ago, it has tripled in price. Crowe has a $300 million paper profit so far on his options.

Crowe thinks every company should adopt an option plan like this one. "All kinds of companies have hurt their investors, yet managements are getting enormous payoffs," he scolds.

Crowe is a lonely crusader. We don't know of a single other public company that ties option prices to the S&P.

Former Securities & Exchange Commissioner Joseph Grundfest, now a Stanford Law School professor, presented Level 3's plan at his annual directors' conference last year. Directors of companies like American International Group, Bank America, Lucent and Time Warner attended. Grundfest reports their reaction: "Many thought it was a great idea—for other companies." He adds: "A Level 3-style plan would eliminate the Lake Wobegon effect, where all CEOs are above average. Which is why it's frightening to many."

*Source:* T. Mack, "The Moving Target Option," *Forbes,* March 20, 2000. Copyright © 2000 Forbes, Inc. Reprinted with permission.

---

Determining whether citizens should have a say in CEO pay: Practices in Europe

## CEO LEADS SWISS BACKLASH OVER EXECUTIVE PAY

In Switzerland, long a haven for big money, a backlash is developing against outsized executive compensation.

The push is being spurred by an unlikely source: a CEO. Thomas Minder, a 47-year-old chief executive of small cosmetics manufacturer Trybol AG, is going to shareholder meetings at Swiss giants like Novartis SA to challenge their CEO pay packages.

Mr. Minder has been collecting signatures to call a national vote—as permitted under the Swiss constitution—to amend Swiss law to force more transparency and accountability on executive compensation. He says his goal is to create ways for shareholders to veto pay packages and create more "sensible" pay practices in Switzerland, a country where wealth has traditionally been welcomed, rather than frowned upon.

Across Europe, growing disenchantment with high executive pay is increasingly a political issue. In France, the losing candidate for the presidency, Ségolène Royal, called on Airbus to withdraw its proposed 10,000 job cuts after it disclosed that Noël Forgeard, former chief executive of Airbus and its parent, European Aeronautic Defence & Space Co., received €6.1 million ($8.2 million) in an exit pay package. The company said the package was provided for in his contract, but Ms. Royal called the payment a "scandal."

In Germany, Finance Minister Peer Steinbrück has said Europe's social model couldn't be sustained if the wages of low earners fall as company profits rise.

Switzerland is set to introduce greater disclosure of executive compensation for companies listed on the Swiss exchange. Starting next year, companies must disclose the salaries of the highest paid member of the management board. Previously, Swiss companies released only the total salaries of the combined board and the individual salary of the highest paid member of the supervisory board, which is akin to a U.S. board of directors. . . .

*(continued)*

Current law allows Swiss companies to disclose less detail on executive pay than U.S. companies. They aren't required to disclose individual pay packages for chief executives and often don't have to mention benefits such as personal loans or housing allowances. . . .

Mr. Minder says he pays himself "far less" than 100,000 Swiss francs, or about $81,000, a year and took on his campaign because pay levels are so high that "executives don't suffer personal hardships even if their performance at the helm of the company is miserable." . . .

Among his 25 proposals: giving shareholders the right to block or approve pay packages; a complete ban on "golden parachutes" or pay packages given to executives upon leaving a company; and measures that would force institutional shareholders to disclose how they voted on issues such as approving bonuses. . . .

If Mr. Minder collects 100,000 signatures, his proposals will be put to the Swiss Parliament and federal councilors. They can come up with a counter-proposal or allow a popular vote on Mr. Minder's proposals, thanks to the Swiss tradition of direct democracy. Mr. Minder has until May 2008 to hand in the signatures, and he says he is "very well on track," without being specific. A national vote may not follow for at least a year.

While the chances of success for a popular vote, known as a plebiscite, are very slim, the move to force a vote makes the issue part of the mainstream political agenda. . . .

**Required:**

1. Do shareholders vote on the compensation packages paid to top executives of U.S. companies?

2. One of Minder's proposals would ban the use of golden parachutes. How might this ban harm shareholders?

3. In the United States, the average big company CEO made $11.6 million in 2005, or 411 times the typical U.S. worker, according to the Institute for Policy Studies. That same year, average CEO compensation for companies with approximately $500 million in worldwide annual sales was $2.2 million in the United States, $1.4 million in Switzerland, and $1.2 million in France, the United Kingdom, and Germany. With these statistics as a backdrop, provide (a) three reasons in support of giving European shareholders the right to approve CEO pay packages and (b) three reasons why you are against doing so.

4. Should citizens have the right to approve CEO pay packages? Why or why not?

## CASES

### C7-1

Sunny Day Stores, Inc.: Analyzing debt covenants and financial distress

Sunny Day Stores operates convenience stores throughout much of the United States. The industry is highly competitive, with low profit margins. The company's competition includes national, regional, and local supermarkets; oil companies; and convenience store operators.

A footnote to the 2005 financial statements described the company's long-term debt:

Note payable to the Prudential Insurance Company of America ("Prudential") with annual principal payments of $900,000, interest at 8.93%. Amount outstanding: $5,700,000 in 2005 and $6,600,000 in 2004.

Term note payable to First Florida Bank ("First Florida") maturing in September 2010, with quarterly principal payments of $125,000 through June 30, 2006 and $250,000 thereafter, with interest at 1% in excess of prime (5.5% at December 26, 2005). Amount outstanding $3,563,956 in 2005 and $3,000,000 in 2004.

Revolving note payable to First Florida Bank with interest at 1% in excess of prime (5.5% at December 26, 2005). Amount outstanding: $7,400,000 in 2005 and 2004.

Certain of the Company's loan agreements pertaining to the borrowings from the Prudential Insurance Company of America ("Prudential") and First Florida Bank ("First Florida") require the

Company to maintain minimum interest coverage ratio, working capital, and net worth levels, impose restrictions on additional borrowings, and prohibit the payment of dividends. Specifically, at the end of fiscal 2005 Sunny Day must have a net worth of $22,850,000, working capital (on a FIFO inventory basis) must be at least $1,300,000, and the interest coverage ratio must be at least 1.6.

The company's 2005 financial statements that follow show that Sunny Day Stores was not in compliance with these loan covenants at year end.

## Sunny Day Stores, Inc.

### Comparative Balance Sheets

| | 2005 | 2004 | | 2005 | 2004 |
|---|---|---|---|---|---|
| Cash and cash equivalents | $ 1,451,688 | $ 2,971,457 | Accounts payable | | |
| Accounts receivable less | | | Trade | $ 9,237,416 | $ 6,208,733 |
| allowances for doubtful | | | Money orders | 1,637,255 | 1,442,811 |
| accounts of $82,000 | | | Fuel taxes | 1,106,713 | 635,556 |
| and $63,000 in 2005 | | | Accrued liabilities | | |
| and 2004, respectively | 985,987 | 705,923 | Salaries and wages | 774,519 | 846,131 |
| Refundable income taxes | 400,000 | 135,831 | Self-insurance reserves | 1,186,613 | 966,770 |
| Inventories—FIFO basis | 10,640,125 | 8,690,734 | State and local taxes | 1,136,241 | 569,160 |
| Less: LIFO reserve | (3,057,715) | (2,845,703) | Current portion of long- | | |
| Total inventories | 7,582,410 | 5,845,031 | term debt | 1,956,369 | 1,082,429 |
| Prepaid expenses and | | | Total current liabilities | $17,035,126 | $11,751,590 |
| other assets | 764,627 | 547,705 | | | |
| Refundable deposits | 700,000 | 380,522 | | | |
| Total current assets | $11,884,712 | $10,586,469 | | | |
| Property and equipment | | | Deferred income taxes | 400,000 | 1,477,323 |
| Land | 11,016,168 | 13,603,304 | Unearned revenue | 111,426 | 179,224 |
| Buildings | 19,673,636 | 19,801,221 | | | |
| Fixtures and equipment | 32,232,643 | 32,749,133 | Long-term debt, less | | |
| Leaseholds and | | | current portion | 13,969,745 | 16,693,772 |
| improvements | 5,084,679 | 4,929,748 | | | |
| | $68,007,126 | $71,083,406 | | | |
| Less: Allowances for | | | | | |
| depreciation and | | | | | |
| amortization | (31,008,778) | (28,988,173) | Stockholders' equity | | |
| | $36,998,348 | $42,095,233 | Common stock | 170,165 | 170,165 |
| Other assets | | | Additional paid-in capital | 5,124,245 | 5,124,245 |
| Land held for sale | 2,641,735 | | Retained earnings | 15,171,001 | 17,735,240 |
| Other | 456,913 | 449,857 | | $20,465,411 | $23,029,650 |
| | | | Total liabilities and | | |
| Total assets | $51,981,708 | $53,131,559 | stockholders' equity | $51,981,708 | $53,131,559 |

## Sunny Day Stores, Inc.

### Statement of Cash Flows

| | 2005 | 2004 | 2003 |
|---|---|---|---|
| **Cash Flows from Operating Activities** | | | |
| Net income (loss) | $(2,564,239) | $(1,042,297) | $ 613,423 |
| Adjustments | | | |
| Depreciation and amortization | 3,980,186 | 4,460,529 | 3,793,119 |
| Deferred income taxes | (1,077,323) | (512,995) | 577,235 |
| Gain on sale of property | (532,570) | (174,657) | (100,322) |
| Decrease in unearned revenue | (67,798) | (83,804) | (84,235) |
| | | | *(continued)* |

## Statement of Cash Flows

| | 2005 | 2004 | 2003 |
|---|---|---|---|
| Changes in assets and liabilities | | | |
| (Increase) in accounts receivable | (280,064) | 53,121 | (358,982) |
| (Increase) in refundable income taxes | (264,169) | 244,085 | (113,675) |
| (Increase) in inventories | (1,737,379) | 2,908,024 | 412,647 |
| (Increase) in other assets | (263,981) | (141,910) | (241,347) |
| Increase in refundable deposits | (319,478) | (15,107) | (145,866) |
| Increase in accounts payable and other liabilities | 4,409,596 | (4,304,076) | 3,807,200 |
| Total adjustments | 3,847,020 | 2,433,210 | 7,545,774 |
| Net cash flow from operations | $ 1,282,781 | $ 1,390,913 | $ 8,159,197 |
| **Cash Flows from Investing Activities** | | | |
| Purchase of property and equipment, net | (2,390,832) | (2,871,399) | (9,593,270) |
| Sale of property and equipment | 1,428,051 | 668,656 | 821,641 |
| Collections of notes and loans receivables | 10,318 | (103,610) | 7,775 |
| Net cash used in investing activities | $ (952,463) | $(2,306,353) | $(8,763,854) |
| **Cash Flows from Financing Activities** | | | |
| Issuance of long-term debt | 82,515 | 2,633,454 | 4,528,915 |
| Dividends | –0– | –0– | (204,198) |
| Payment of long-term debt | (1,932,602) | (3,108,251) | (1,588,391) |
| Net cash provided by financing activities | $(1,850,087) | $ (474,797) | $ 2,736,326 |
| Net increase (Decrease) in Cash | $(1,519,769) | $(1,390,237) | $ 2,131,669 |

### Sunny Day Stores, Inc.

## Statement of Operations

| | 2005 | 2004 | 2003 |
|---|---|---|---|
| Net revenue | $217,710,782 | $202,393,136 | $191,243,016 |
| Cost and expenses | | | |
| Costs of goods sold | 176,102,027 | 158,643,287 | 146,652,853 |
| Selling, general, and administrative | 44,631,749 | 43,687,704 | 41,805,330 |
| Interest expense—net | 1,551,138 | 1,728,650 | 1,658,732 |
| Net gain from sale of property | (532,570) | (174,657) | (100,322) |
| | 221,752,344 | 203,884,984 | 190,016,593 |
| Income (loss) before taxes | (4,041,562) | (1,491,848) | 1,226,423 |
| Provision (benefit) for income taxes | | | |
| Current | (400,000) | 63,444 | 50,000 |
| Deferred | (1,077,323) | (512,995) | 563,000 |
| | (1,477,323) | (449,551) | 613,000 |
| Net income (loss) | $ (2,564,239) | $ (1,042,297) | $ 613,423 |
| Earnings per common share | $(1.51) | $(0.61) | $0.36 |

### Required:

It's late January 2006, and Prudential and First Florida have hired you to act on their behalf in negotiations with Sunny Day Stores. Both lenders want to restructure their loans to address the company's current financial problems, and the restructured loans may require covenant changes.

Prudential and First Florida seek your advice on the type and amount of collateral to be required, revised interest rates, and possible changes to the payment schedules. In addition, the lenders have asked you to suggest new minimum net worth, working capital, and interest coverage ratios for 2006 and 2007. Specifically:

1. What type and amount of collateral do you suggest be required?
2. Should a higher interest rate be charged? Why or why not?

3. What changes would you suggest be made to the payment schedule?

4. What new minimum net worth, working capital, and interest coverage limits would you suggest the lenders set?

5. Suppose the company asked permission to resume payment of its $0.12 per share dividend, which was suspended in 2004. What advice would you give Prudential and First Florida?

---

**C7-2**

Maxcor Manufacturing: Compensation and earnings quality

Margaret Magee has served both as an outside director to Maxcor Manufacturing since 2000 and as a member of the company's compensation committee since 2004. Margaret has been reviewing Maxcor's 2007 preliminary earnings statement in preparation for the February 2008 board and compensation committee meetings. She is uneasy about the company's definition and computation of operating profits for 2007, particularly because management bonuses at Maxcor are based on achieving specific operating profit goals.

## Maxcor Manufacturing

### Consolidated Results of Operations

|  | Years Ended December 31 | |
| --- | --- | --- |
| ($ in millions) | **2007** | **2006** |
| Sales | $98.4 | $111.2 |
| Operating costs | | |
|    Cost of goods sold | (81.5) | (92.2) |
|    Selling, general, and administrative expenses | (12.5) | (12.9) |
| Operating profit | 4.4 | 6.1 |
| Research and development expenses (see note) | (5.7) | (2.4) |
| Provision for plant closings (see note) | (2.6) | –0– |
| Interest expense | (2.9) | (2.6) |
| Other income | 0.7 | 1.2 |
| Profit (loss) before taxes | (6.1) | 2.3 |
| Provision (credit) for income taxes | 2.1 | (0.8) |
| Profit (loss) of consolidated companies | (4.0) | 1.5 |
| Equity in profit of affiliated companies | 0.2 | 0.3 |
|    Profit (loss) | $(3.8) | $ 1.8 |

The preliminary financial statements also contained the following notes:

**Research and Engineering Expenses.** Research and engineering expenses include both Research and development expenses for new product development and charges originally made to Cost of goods sold for ongoing product improvements. The amounts (in millions) for 2007 and 2006 were:

|  | **2007** | **2006** |
| --- | --- | --- |
| Research and development expenses | $5.7 | $2.4 |
| Cost of goods sold | 2.9 | 6.3 |
| Research and engineering expense | $8.6 | $8.7 |

**Plant Closing Costs.** In 2007, the Company recorded provisions for plant closing and staff consolidation costs totaling $2.62 million. Included in this total are charges related to the probable closing of the Company's York, Pennsylvania, facility ($1.75 million), the consolidation of the North American operations of the Building Construction Products Division ($0.63 million), and charges to reflect lower estimates of the market value of previously closed U.S. facilities ($0.24 million). These costs include the estimated costs of employee severance benefits, net losses on disposal of land, buildings, machinery and equipment, and other costs incidental to the closing and planned consolidation.

Maxcor Manufacturing is an established, privately held manufacturer that operates in two principal business segments: *Building construction products,* which involves the design, manufacturing, and marketing of construction and materials-handling machinery, and *Engines* for various off-highway applications. Before 2007, the company had experienced 15 years of steadily increasing sales and operating profits.

The company was founded in 1938 by Hugh Maxwell, a former Ford Motor Company engineer. Neither Maxwell nor any members of his family are currently company officers. Maxcor's common stock is held by the Maxwell Family Trust (35%), the Maxwell Employee Stock Ownership Plan (ESOP) Trust (50%), a venture capital firm (13%), and current management (2%). Magee also serves as an outside trustee for the Maxwell ESOP Trust.

Maxcor's senior management participates in an incentive bonus plan that was first adopted in 2001. The bonus formula for 2007 was approved by the compensation committee at its February 2007 meeting. According to the plan, each senior manager's 2007 bonus is to be determined as follows:

| Bonus as Percentage of 2007 Salary | 2007 Operating Profits (*$ in millions*) |
|---|---|
| 0% | Below $4.0 |
| 100 | At least $4.0 |
| 200 | At least $6.0 |
| 300 | At least $8.0 |

The compensation committee can award a lower amount than that indicated by the plan formula if circumstances warrant such action. No bonus reductions have occurred since the plan was adopted in 2001.

**Required:**

Why might Magee feel uneasy about Maxcor's computation of 2007 operating profits? Should she approve the 100% bonus payment for 2007 as specified by the plan formula? What changes (if any) would you recommend be made to the bonus formula for next year?

---

Whole Foods Market is one of many companies today that use economic value added (EVA) as the performance metric for determining managerial compensation. Here's what Whole Foods Market has to say about its EVA-based compensation plan.

**C7-3**

Whole Foods Market:
EVA-based compensation

## What Our Compensation Program Is Designed to Reward

Our compensation program is designed to reward teamwork and each Team Member's contribution to the Company. In measuring the executive officers' contribution to the Company, the Compensation Committee considers numerous factors including the Company's growth and financial performance through reference to the following metrics. All of our executive officers participate in an incentive compensation plan based primarily on improvement in Economic Value Added ("EVA"). EVA is the primary basis for the Company's financial decision-making tools and incentive compensation systems. In its simplest definition, EVA is equivalent to net operating profits after taxes minus a charge for the cost of capital necessary to generate those profits. High EVA correlates with high returns on invested capital. The incentive compensation paid to the executive officers for fiscal year 2006 was based upon the incremental improvement in the Company's overall EVA, the number of new stores opened or acquired during the fiscal year, and the number of new stores opened with total development costs within the development budget minus a charge for the new stores opened with costs in excess of the development budget during the fiscal year. Fiscal year 2006 incentive compensation averaged approximately 49% of the total cash compensation earned by the executive officers.

Stock price performance has not been a factor in determining annual compensation because the price of the Company's common stock is subject to a variety of factors outside our control. The Company does not have an exact formula for allocating between cash and non-cash compensation. Other than EVA pool and Benefit Hours pool balances (see below), compensation is generally paid as earned.

We also have a policy that limits the total cash compensation paid to any Team Member in each calendar year. The compensation cap is calculated each year as an established multiple of the average cash compensation of all full-time Team Members employed during such year. For fiscal year 2006, the Company increased the cap from 14 to 19 times the above described average. Employee benefits, stock options and any other form of non-cash compensation, such as the 401(k) match, are not counted in determining and applying the salary cap. Payouts under any EVA Incentive Compensation Plan ("EVA Plan") fall within the scope of the Company's salary cap policy. Per the EVA Plan, amounts are contributed annually to a "pool" for each Team Member based on EVA results. A portion of the annual EVA pool contribution may remain in the pool and a portion is paid out annually. Annual payouts are calculated as 100% of the pool up to certain job-specific dollar amounts plus a portion of the excess. If the EVA bonus to be paid out will cause the Team Member's cash compensation to exceed the annual salary cap, the amount above the cap is forfeited; the full amount which would otherwise be paid out (including amounts not actually paid to the Team Member) is still subtracted from the pool balance. The accumulated balance in any Team Member's pool account is limited to the amount of the salary cap. Team Members may take time off without pay in order to reduce their salary earned and increase the amount of bonus that can be paid within the cap. The salary cap does not apply in the Team Member's year of termination or retirement.

*Source:* Whole Foods Market, Proxy Statement, January 22, 2007.

### Required:

1. Compared to GAAP earnings, what advantage does EVA provide as a performance metric for incentive compensation purposes? Why might this advantage be particularly important for companies such as Whole Foods Market?

2. Explain why Whole Foods Market does not use stock price performance to determine annual compensation for its executives. What mechanisms other than annual compensation might the company use to encourage managers to create shareholder value?

3. What impact (if any) does EVA use have on earnings management? In other words, will managers be more likely or less likely to use accounting tricks to achieve EVA bonus targets than is the case for traditional GAAP earnings targets?

4. Explain how the EVA pool works and why it might help overcome management's tendency to focus on the short term.

---

| **C7-4** |
|---|

**Duke Energy Corp.: Rate regulation and earnings management**

Regulated utilities such as Duke Energy are authorized to earn a specific rate of return on their capital investments. Energy regulators set a rate that the utility can charge its customers for the electricity. If the cost of fuel and other operations decreases and a utility earns more than its authorized rate of return, regulators could cut the rate a utility charges its customers.

### DUKE ENERGY SETTLES WITH STATES ON CHARGES IT UNDERSTATED NET

Duke Energy Corp.'s regulated electric utility, Duke Power, agreed to pay $25 million to its customers to settle allegations the company had underreported profit in order to avoid having to reduce its electricity rates.

Energy regulators in North Carolina and South Carolina had ordered an audit of Duke Power's books. The inquiry, conducted by accounting firm Grant Thornton LLP, found the utility had failed to report about $123 million in pre-tax income from 1998 to 2000. . . .

"They manipulated their earnings in an effort to ensure that they didn't report numbers above the authorized rate of return,"

*(continued)*

said Gary Walsh, executive director of the South Carolina [Public Service] commission.

Grant Thornton concluded that the $123 million in accounting entries were "inconsistent with applicable accounting principles, inconsistent with Duke Power's past practice and without proper justification." The report says there was a coordinated effort by the utility unit's top management to underreport net income by overreporting expenses, specifically insurance for its nuclear operations.

Duke Energy, in a written statement, said it had reached "different professional opinions" than Grant Thornton on the accounting issues but had agreed to change the way it accounts for certain items, specifically nuclear insurance, as part of the proposed settlement. Duke Energy, which hasn't admitted to any wrongdoing, said it would take a $19 million charge in the fourth quarter in connection with the settlement if it is approved. . . .

The utility's underreporting to regulators didn't affect Duke Energy's report of net income, the Grant Thornton report said. . . .

Duke Power's accounting problems started in late 1998 when a neighboring utility was ordered to cut rates to its customers after it had earned more than the amount allowed by state regulators. According to the audit of Duke Power's books, as well as Duke internal documents cited in the report, Duke executives at that point realized their utility risked a similar order and decided they had to change the handling of certain accounting items to avoid showing too high a rate of return.

*Source:* E. K. Kranhold, "Duke Energy Settles with States on Charges It Understated Net," *The Wall Street Journal,* October 23, 2002. Copyright © 2002 Dow Jones & Company, Inc. All rights reserved worldwide. Reprinted with permission.

**Required:**

1. Many earnings management devices are intended to accelerate revenue or delay expenses and thus increase current earnings. Explain how electricity rate regulation sometimes creates incentives for utility executives to *overstate* expenses and *understate* earnings.

2. Documents produced by Duke Energy in connection with this matter indicate that some personnel at the company characterized "above-the-line" expenses as those that Duke's electric customers paid—meaning they were accounted for and included in the electric rates paid by customers—while "below-the-line" expenses were characterized as "paid" by Duke's shareholders. Suppose Duke Energy spent $10 million hiring a consulting company to develop a new logo for the company. Explain why customers and shareholders care whether the cost of logo development is classified by the company as above or below the line.

3. According to the news article, "The utility's underreporting to regulators didn't affect Duke Energy's report of [GAAP] net income." Explain why.

---

**C7-5**

Computer Associates International: Compensation and accounting irregularities

### CA'S EX-CEO PLEADS GUILTY TO SECURITIES FRAUD

Sanjay Kumar, the former chief executive of CA Inc., pleaded guilty to securities fraud and obstruction of justice charges stemming from a scheme that used backdated contracts to falsify the U.S. company's quarterly earnings reports.

The plea ends the career of a Sri Lankan immigrant who climbed to the top of the corporate ladder and made a fortune in the U.S. high-technology boom. Mr. Kumar now faces a maximum 90 years in prison if the eight counts to which he pleaded result in consecutive sentences. However, lighter sentencing of 10 to 30 years might be dictated under federal guidelines.

*(continued)*

At the software company formerly known as Computer Associates, Mr. Kumar first gained note as the protégé of company founder Charles Wang. Together, the two built a fast-growing enterprise adept at taking over smaller companies specializing in software for corporate back offices.

But in 2000, when the company abruptly announced a change in auditors and accounting methodology, revenue started to plummet. The Securities and Exchange Commission began investigating in 2002 and eventually referred the case to the U.S. Justice Department, which has secured a number of guilty pleas of top CA Executives.

In September 2004, Mr. Kumar, 44 years old, was indicted with former sales chief Stephen Richards, 41, who also pleaded guilty yesterday. Mr. Kumar had left the company earlier in the year.

The defense decision to plead guilty followed the Friday arrest of Tommy Bennett, a former CA executive who recently has been working for Mr. Kumar. Mr. Bennett was charged with conspiracy to obstruct justice.

According to Mr. Bennett's arrest warrant, Mr. Bennett, who was senior vice president in change of business development and who worked at CA from 1988 to 2004, became involved after prosecutors told the court they planned to introduce evidence that Mr. Kumar had erased the hard drive on his personal computer in 2003—after CA had advised employees to preserve all evidence. Mr. Bennett was arrested for approaching a former CA technician, who allegedly had helped Mr. Kumar erase the drive. . . .

Mr. Wang, 60, first spotted the younger Mr. Kumar when Mr. Kumar was a poor teenage immigrant. The two immigrants eventually became wealthy together, once sharing with another executive a $1 billion award of shares in the company. . . .

CA admitted in 2004 that it had improperly inflated quarterly revenue over several years. Four top officers and three financial officers of CA have pled guilty in connection with the case. CA itself was also charged, but it avoided an indictment by reaching a deferred prosecution agreement with the Justice Department. Under that agreement, CA has continued to cooperate with prosecutors, paid $225 million in restitution to shareholders and agreed to have a court-appointed independent examiner while restating some $2.2 billion in revenue, which was booked in the wrong periods. . . .

According to evidence presented by the government and described by CA in its restatements, much of the predictability of revenue was due to fraudulent accounting. According to the government, Mr. Kumar orchestrated "35-day months" at the end of each quarter, during which sales executives and Mr. Kumar himself frantically cut deals to persuade customers to sign needed contracts, which were then backdated to make it appear they had been signed in the previous quarter.

*Source:* W. M. Bulkeley and P. Davies, "CA's Ex-CEO Pleads Guilty to Securities Fraud," *The Wall Street Journal,* April 25, 2006. Copyright © 2006 Dow Jones & Company, Inc. All rights reserved worldwide. Reprinted with permission.

**Required:**

1. Refer to Exhibit 7.1, which describes the 2003 annual incentive compensation plan for top executives at Computer Associates International. What features of this plan might have contributed to the illegal backdating of sales contracts?

2. Stock options and company shares comprised a substantial portion of Kumar's personal wealth. How might these equity-based incentives have contributed to the illegal backdating of sales contracts?

3. Why would Computer Associate's outside auditor have difficulty spotting the contract backdating?

**Remember to check the book's companion Web site for additional study material.**

# Receivables | 8

| ($ in millions) | | $22,011.9 |
|---|---|---|
| Sales | | |
| Costs, Expenses and Other | 01.1 | 5,149.6 |
| Materials and production | 65.4 | 7,155.5 |
| Marketing and administrative | | |
| Research and development | 82.9 | 3,848.0 |
| Restructuring costs | | |
| Equity income fr... | 2.3 | 322.2 |
| Oth... | 4) | (1,717.1) |
| ...xes | | (110.2) |
| ...gn income | | 14,648.0 |
| | $4... | 7,363.9 ...830.1 |

R eceivables are amounts that outsiders owe to a business firm. In U.K. financial reports, receivables are called "debtors"—a term clearly connoting the legal obligation of outsiders to make payments to a firm. Most receivables arise from credit sales and are called **trade receivables** or **accounts receivable**. Receivables that result from other types of transactions and events (for example, insurance claims from casualty losses) are separately disclosed, if significant, on the balance sheet. This separate disclosure facilitates informed financial analysis.

## ASSESSING THE NET REALIZABLE VALUE OF ACCOUNTS RECEIVABLE

Generally accepted accounting principles (GAAP) require that accounts receivable be reflected in the balance sheet at their **net realizable value.**[1] Two things must be estimated to determine the net realizable value of receivables:

1. The amount that will not be collected because customers are unable to pay—called **uncollectibles.**

2. The amount that will not be collected because customers return the merchandise for credit or are allowed a reduction in the amount owed—called **returns** and **allowances.**

The next sections discuss financial reporting issues relating to uncollectibles, returns, and allowances.

## Estimating Uncollectibles

Receivables arising from some credit sales are never collected. These losses are an unavoidable cost of doing business. Companies could adopt such stringent credit standards that "bad debt" losses would be virtually zero. But if they sold only to customers with impeccable credit records, they would forgo many otherwise profitable sales opportunities.

Most companies establish credit policies by weighing the expected cost of credit sales—customer billing and collection costs plus potential bad debt losses—against the benefit of increased sales. Companies choose what they believe is a profit-maximizing

---

[1] *Net realizable value* refers to the selling price of an item minus reasonable further costs both to make the item ready to sell and to sell it. When applied to trade receivables, *net realizable value* refers to the amount of money the business can reasonably expect to collect from its credit customers.

*Chapter*

balance. This trade-off between increased costs and additional profits from credit sales illustrates that bad debts are often unavoidable. Consequently, the accrual accounting matching principle requires that some *estimate* of uncollectible accounts be offset against current period sales—that is, **estimated losses from customers who are ultimately unable to pay are treated as an expense of the period in which the sale is made.** Obviously, companies can't know at the time of sale which customers will ultimately be unable to pay. So, the proper matching of revenues and expenses is achieved by estimating the proportion of the current period's credit sales that will not be collected in the future and then by charging this estimated amount as an expense.

Suppose that Bristol Corporation estimates that, based on current industry trends and the company's experience, bad debt losses arising from first quarter 2008 sales are expected to be $30,000. The entry Bristol makes under GAAP is:

| | | |
|---|---|---|
| **DR** Bad debt expense ........................................... | $30,000 | |
| **CR** Allowance for uncollectibles ........................... | | $30,000 |

The Allowance for uncollectibles is a contra-asset account that is subtracted from gross accounts receivable. If Bristol's Accounts receivable (gross) and Allowance for uncollectibles balance *before* recording this bad debt entry were $1,500,000 and $15,000, respectively, after recording bad debts, its balance sheet shows:

| | | |
|---|---|---|
| Accounts receivable (gross) | $1,500,000 | |
| Less: Allowance for uncollectibles | (45,000) | { (15,000) Initial balance |
| Accounts receivable (net) | $1,455,000 | { (30,000) Addition |

Companies can use two alternative approaches to estimate uncollectible accounts. One multiplies a specific loss percentage by sales revenues; the other multiplies a (usually different) loss percentage by gross accounts receivable. Each approach is illustrated as follows.

> A third approach, which is used only for tax reporting purposes, is the **direct write-off method.** Under this approach, Bad debt expense is recorded at the time a specific account is written off, with an offsetting credit to Accounts receivable. No allowance account is used under this approach. Because tax reporting rules require the direct write-off method for recognizing uncollectible accounts while GAAP requires one of the two allowance methods described here, a temporary or timing difference between book income and taxable income is created (see Chapter 13 for further discussion).

1. *The sales revenue approach.* Assume that Bristol Corporation prepares quarterly financial statements and must estimate bad debt expense at the end of each quarter. Analyzing past customer payment patterns, Bristol determined that bad debt losses average about 1% of sales. If first quarter sales in 2008 total $3,000,000, bad debt losses from those sales are expected to total $30,000. Bristol then makes the entry previously illustrated to record its estimate of bad debt expenses arising from current quarter sales.

**Sales Revenue Approach**

**Estimate the current period bad debt expense as a percentage of current period sales. For Bristol Corporation, the estimate is:**

$$0.01 \times \$3,000,000 \text{ Sales for the quarter} = \$30,000 \text{ Bad debt expense}$$

So, the entry is:

| | | |
|---|---|---|
| **DR** Bad debt expense ............................. | $30,000 ← | |
| **CR** Allowance for uncollectibles ............... | | $30,000 |

2. *The gross accounts receivable approach.* Suppose that instead of estimating bad debts as a percentage of sales, Bristol determined that at any given time, approximately 3% of gross accounts receivable eventually prove uncollectible. Gross receivables at March 31, 2008 total $1,500,000, which means that on that date the required allowance for uncollectibles is 3% of this amount, or $45,000. Because the allowance account balance is only $15,000,

$30,000 must be added to the uncollectibles account at the end of the quarter. Doing this brings the allowance for uncollectibles balance up to $45,000.

### Gross Receivables Approach

Estimate the required allowance account balance as a percentage of gross receivables and then adjust the allowance upward or downward to this figure. For Bristol Corporation, the required allowance account balance is:

0.03 × $1,500,000 Outstanding receivables = $45,000 Allowance for uncollectibles

The allowance account currently has a $15,000 balance, so $30,000 is added:

| | | |
|---|---|---|
| **DR** | Bad debt expense ............................ | $30,000 |
| **CR** | Allowance for uncollectibles .............. | $30,000 |

## Writing Off Bad Debts

When a specific account receivable is known to be definitely uncollectible, the entire account must be removed from the books. For example, if Bristol determines that a $750 receivable from Ralph Company cannot be collected, it makes the following entry:

| | | |
|---|---|---|
| **DR** | Allowance for uncollectibles ................................ | $750 |
| **CR** | Account receivable—Ralph Company ................... | $750 |

Notice that this entry has no effect on income. A specific account receivable (Ralph Company) is eliminated from the books and the allowance contra-account is reduced, *but no bad debt expense is recorded.* This is consistent with the accrual accounting philosophy of recording estimated bad debt expense when the sale was made rather than at some later date when the nonpaying customer is identified. Of course, Bristol Corporation does not know at the time of each sale which particular customers will be unable to pay. That's why the offsetting credit for bad debt expense was originally made to the contra-asset account, Allowance for uncollectibles. *Only when the seller knows which specific receivable is uncollectible can the individual account (Ralph Company) be written off.* This is what the preceding entry accomplishes.

"Backing into" the $30,000 with the use of a T-account is shown as follows:

**Allowance for uncollectibles**

| | |
|---|---|
| $15,000 | Current balance |
| 30,000 | Required adjustment |
| $45,000 | Computed new balance |

## Assessing the Adequacy of the Allowance for Uncollectibles Account Balance

No matter which method—percentage of sales or percentage of gross receivables—is used to estimate bad debts, management must periodically assess the reasonableness of the allowance for uncollectibles balance. Given existing economic conditions and customer circumstances, is the balance in the Allowance for uncollectibles account adequate, excessive, or insufficient?

To make this judgment, management performs an **aging of accounts receivable.** As the name implies, an aging of receivables is simply a determination of how long each receivable has been on the books. Receivables that are long past due often exist because customers are experiencing financial difficulties and may ultimately be unable to pay. An aging is performed by subdividing total accounts receivable into several age categories (see Exhibit 8.1).

Obviously, considerable judgment goes into evaluating the adequacy of the Allowance for uncollectibles balance. Most companies carefully appraise this area because audit guidelines are well developed and auditors' scrutiny is intense.

---

**EXHIBIT 8.1** **Bristol Corporation**

**Allowance for Uncollectibles Based on Aging of Receivables**

On December 31, 2008, Bristol Corporation's gross accounts receivable are $1,600,000, and the balance of the Allowance for uncollectibles is $39,000. Bristol's normal sales terms require payment within 30 days after the sale is made and the goods are received by the buyer. Bristol determines that the receivables have the following age distribution:

| | Current | 31–90 days old | 91–180 days old | Over 180 days old | Total |
|---|---|---|---|---|---|
| Amount | $1,450,000 | $125,000 | $15,000 | $10,000 | $1,600,000 |

Once the receivables have been grouped by age category, a separate estimate of uncollectibles by category is developed. Based on past experience, Bristol determines the following estimate of expected bad debt losses by category:

| | | | | |
|---|---|---|---|---|
| Estimated % of bad debt losses | 2.5% | 6% | 20% | 40% |

The required balance in the Allowance for uncollectibles account would then be as follows:

| | Current | 31–90 days old | 91–180 days old | Over 180 days old | Total |
|---|---|---|---|---|---|
| Amount | $1,450,000 | $125,000 | $15,000 | $10,000 | $1,600,000 |
| × Estimated % of bad debt losses | 2.5% | 6% | 20% | 40% | |
| = Allowance for uncollectibles | $ 36,250 | $ 7,500 | $ 3,000 | $ 4,000 | $ 50,750 |

Because the balance of the Allowance for uncollectibles is only $39,000 on December 31, 2008, the account must be increased by $11,750. This is the difference between the $50,750 required balance (as computed) and the existing $39,000 balance. To bring the balance up to the $50,750 figure indicated by the aging, Bristol makes the following adjusting entry:

**DR** Bad debt expense . . . . . . . . . . . . . . . . . . . . . . . . . . . . . . . . . . . . . . . . . . . . $11,750

    **CR** Allowance for uncollectibles . . . . . . . . . . . . . . . . . . . . . . . . . . . . . $11,750

---

Exhibit 8.2 contains selected financial statement figures taken from the 2001 annual report of The Scotts Company, a leading manufacturer and marketer of consumer branded products for lawn and garden care.

Scotts had a lackluster year in 2001. Sales increased 2.2% (from $1,709.0 million to $1,747.7 million), but pre-tax income fell 75.3% (from $116.3 million to $28.7 million). Earnings declined because of a small decrease in gross profit and costs associated with plant closures and relocations. Despite the income decline, both the bad debt expense (as a percentage of sales) and the allowance for uncollectibles (as a percentage of gross customer receivables) increased

---

**EXHIBIT 8.2** **The Scotts Company**

**Analysis of Uncollectible Accounts Receivable**

| ($ in millions) | 2001 | 2000 |
|---|---|---|
| **A. Reported Amounts** | | |
|   Net sales | $1,747.7 | $1,709.0 |
|   Pre-tax income | 28.7 | 116.3 |
|   Customer receivables (gross) | 244.7 | 227.7 |
|   Allowance for uncollectibles | 23.9 | 11.7 |
|   Bad debt expense | 20.9 | 4.8 |
| **B. Analysis** | | |
|   Bad debt expense as % of sales | 1.2% | 0.3% |
|   Allowance as % of customer receivables | 9.8 | 5.1 |

*Source:* The Scotts Company 2001 annual report to shareholders.

in 2001. This suggests that Scotts was taking a more conservative view of receivable collections than it had in the past perhaps because the customer credit quality had recently deteriorated.

What impact did this conservative view have on the company's 2001 pre-tax earnings? The data in Exhibit 8.2 provide the answer.

Suppose that Scotts had maintained 2001 bad debt expense at 0.3% of sales (the same rate used in 2000). Bad debt expense would then have been $5.2 million (0.3% of $1,747.7 million sales)—or $15.7 million lower. This would have meant a corresponding $15.7 million (or 54.7%) increase in pre-tax income for the year.

Now suppose that Scotts had kept the allowance for uncollectibles at 5.1% of gross receivables (the rate used in 2000). In this case, the allowance account balance for 2001 would have been $12.5 million (5.1% of $244.7 million gross customer receivables)—or $11.4 million lower than what the company actually reported. Of course, this would have meant an $11.4 million reduction in bad debt expense for the year and an $11.4 million (or 39.7%) increase in pre-tax income.

This analysis shows that the decision to be more conservative about receivable collections penalized reported earnings in what was already a down profit year.

For companies such as Scotts, a modest change in the percentage rate used to estimate bad debt expense or the allowance for uncollectibles can have a big impact on reported earnings.

Determining whether the allowance for uncollectibles is adequate requires judgment. Consequently, the temptation to "manage" earnings by using bad debt accruals can be strong. As the Scotts example illustrates, not all companies succumb to this temptation. However, research evidence does show that companies tend to reduce bad debt expense (and thereby increase earnings) when earnings are otherwise low—and then to increase the expense when earnings are high.[2]

## Estimating Sales Returns and Allowances

Sometimes a company ships the wrong goods to customers or the correct goods arrive damaged. In either case, the customer returns the item or requests a price reduction. When goods are returned or a price allowance granted, the customer's account receivable must be reduced and an income statement charge made. Assume that Bristol Corporation agrees to reduce by $8,000 the price of goods that arrived damaged at Bath Company. Bristol records this price adjustment as:

**DR**  Sales returns and allowances . . . . . . . . . . . . . . . . . . . . . . . . . . . . . . . . .  $8,000
      **CR**  Accounts receivable—Bath Company . . . . . . . . . . . . . . . . . . . .  $8,000

Bath now owes $8,000 less than the amount it previously had been billed, as reflected by the reduction to Accounts receivable. The account that is debited here is an offset to sales revenues—termed a **contra-revenue account.** Sales revenues are not reduced directly; the contra-revenue account allows Bristol Corporation to keep a running record of the frequency

---

[2] See M. McNichols and G. P. Wilson, "Evidence of Earnings Management From the Provision for Bad Debts," *Journal of Accounting Research,* Supplement 1988, pp. 1–31; S. Moyer, "Capital Adequacy Ratio Regulations and Accounting Choices in Commercial Banks," *Journal of Accounting and Economics,* July 1990, pp. 123–54; M. Scholes, P. Wilson, and M. Wolfson, "Tax Planning, Regulatory Capital Planning and Financial Reporting Strategy for Commercial Banks," *Review of Financial Studies* 3, no. 4 (1990), pp. 625–50; J. Collins, D. Shackelford, and J. Wahlen, "Bank Differences in the Coordination of Regulatory Capital, Earnings, and Taxes," *Journal of Accounting Research,* Autumn 1995, pp. 263–91; A. Beatty, S. Chamberlain, and J. Magliolo, "Managing Financial Reports of Commercial Banks: The Influence of Taxes, Regulatory Capital, and Earnings," *Journal of Accounting Research,* Autumn 1995, pp. 231–61. As the titles of these studies suggest, regulatory capital requirements in commercial banks and financial services companies also influence bad debt accruals.

and amount of returns and price reductions because these events represent potential breakdowns in customer relations.

At the end of the reporting period, companies estimate the expected amount of future returns and allowances arising from receivables currently on the books. If the estimated number is large in relation to the accounts receivable balance or to earnings, the adjusting entry is:

| | | |
|---|---|---|
| **DR** Sales returns and allowances..................................... | XXX | |
| **CR** Allowance for sales returns and allowances................. | | XXX |

The debit is to a contra-revenue account that reduces net sales by the estimated amount of returns and allowances. Because it is not yet known which *specific* customer accounts will require future returns and allowances, the credit entry must be made to a contra-asset account that offsets gross accounts receivable. In practice, estimated sales returns and allowances are seldom material in relation to receivables. Consequently, no end-of-period accrual is typically made for these items.

Ordinary returns and allowances are seldom a major issue in financial reporting. On the other hand, companies occasionally adopt "aggressive" revenue recognition practices—meaning that they recognize revenue either prematurely or inappropriately. Examples include recognizing revenue on goods shipped on consignment or recognizing revenue when delivery is delayed, as discussed in Chapter 3. This revenue recognition aggressiveness generates significant returns in later periods. Aggressive revenue recognition overstates both accounts receivable and income. Consequently, analysts must understand that a sudden spurt in accounts receivable may be a danger signal, as we see next.

> Ignoring *estimated* future returns and allowances has a trivial effect on income when the amount of *actual* returns and allowances does not vary greatly from year to year.

**Analysis**

## Analytical Insight: Do Existing Receivables Represent Real Sales?

When a company's sales terms, customer creditworthiness, and accounting methods do not change from period to period, the growth rates in sales and in accounts receivable are roughly equal. If sales increase by 10%, accounts receivable should also increase by about 10%. Statement readers who understand this carefully monitor the relationship between sales growth and receivables growth. When receivables increase faster than sales, those statement readers see a potential "red flag." Receivables could increase at a higher rate than sales for several reasons. One reason is that the disparity in growth rates might reflect something positive such as a deliberate change in sales terms designed to attract new customers. Suppose that instead of requiring payment within 30 days of shipment, Hmong Company allows customers to pay in four months. Such changes broaden the potential market for the company's products and services by allowing slightly less creditworthy customers to buy the firm's products. In this case, receivables growth will far outpace sales growth. To illustrate, consider the following example:

> Assume that before introducing more lenient credit terms, Hmong Company had annual sales of $12 million and customers, on average, paid within 30 days. Outstanding accounts receivable, therefore, represent one month's sales, or $1 million. Under the new credit program, customer receivables would represent four months' sales, or $4 million; this represents a 300% increase in receivables even if total sales remain unchanged.

Another reason for receivables growth exceeding sales growth could be due to deteriorating creditworthiness among existing customers, which could represent an emerging problem. If customers are unable to pay, receivables will not be collected when due and accounts receivable will increase at a faster rate than sales. However, the company's independent auditor should uncover this problem in careful audits. Accordingly, when the cause for the unusual growth in receivables is due to an inability of customers to pay on time, GAAP financial statements would ordinarily show a large increase in estimated uncollectibles.

So, growth in accounts receivables can outstrip growth in sales revenues either because firms allow customers more time to pay or because customers are unable to pay due to their own cash flow problems.

Another reason why receivables growth could exceed sales growth is that the firm has changed its financial reporting procedures, which determine *when* sales are recognized. To illustrate this possibility, let's consider an automobile manufacturer that builds cars and ships them to a dealer who ultimately sells them to you and other individuals. Assume that the manufacturer in past years has recognized revenue from sales only when an automobile was sold to the final customer. But if the auto manufacturer in the current year suddenly decides to recognize automobile sales revenue when the cars are shipped to the dealer, *this represents a significant change in financial reporting principles.* To see how such a financial reporting change affects the relationship between receivables growth and sales growth, consider Exhibit 8.3, which presents selected financial statement data for Bausch & Lomb Inc. for the years 1990–1993.

In Exhibit 8.3 net trade accounts receivable increased dramatically in both 1992 and 1993. This increase shows up in absolute dollar amounts (an increase of $72,076 in 1992 and $107,635 in 1993) as well as in relation to total balance sheet assets (11.8% in 1991 versus 14.8% in 1992 and 15.3% in 1993). What makes this growth seem "unusual," however, is the disparity in growth rates between sales and receivables. While sales grew 12.43% in 1992 and 9.54% in 1993, receivables jumped by 35.11% and 38.81% in those same years, respectively (highlighted areas in Exhibit 8.3). Clearly, something unusual was happening in

> Collectibility of receivables requires forecasts of future conditions. Forecasts are often inaccurate. However, existing auditing procedures for accounts receivable are very detailed and stringent, requiring auditors to send confirmations to randomly chosen customers verifying the legitimacy of the recorded receivables. Aging schedules to uncover payment problems are also required. Furthermore, auditors undertake credit checks on the company's largest customers to ascertain the probability of eventual collection. As a consequence of these procedures, while collectibility requires forecasts that could be wrong, extreme overstatement of net (collectible) receivables is rare. An exception to the general rule occurred in 2007 when the default rate on subprime loans was much higher than expected. See our discussion of subprime loans on page 433.

| EXHIBIT 8.3 | Bausch & Lomb, Inc | | | |
|---|---|---|---|---|

**Selected Financial Statement Data, 1990–1993**

| ($000 omitted) | 1990 | 1991 | 1992 | 1993 |
|---|---|---|---|---|
| Net sales | $1,368,580 | $1,520,104 | $1,709,086 | $1,872,184 |
| Net trade accounts receivable | $202,967 | $205,262 | $277,338 | $384,973 |
| Days sales outstanding* | 54 days* | 49 days | 59 days | 75 days |
| Receivables as a % of total assets | 12.1% | 11.8% | 14.8% | 15.3% |
| Year-to-year growth in | | | | |
|   Net sales | | $151,524 | $188,982 | $163,098 |
|   Net trade accounts receivable | | $2,295 | $72,076 | $107,635 |
|   Net sales | | 11.07% | 12.43% | 9.54% |
|   Net trade accounts receivable | | 1.13% | 35.11% | 38.81% |

* *Days sales outstanding* is Net trade accounts receivables divided by Net sales per day. For example, the calculation for 1990 Days sales outstanding is $202,967 net trade receivables/($1,368,580 net sales/365 days) = 54 days

*Source:* Bausch & Lomb Inc. Annual Reports.

both years. A partial explanation was provided one year later in the company's 1994 annual report, which stated:

> In the fourth quarter of 1993, the Company adopted a business strategy to shift responsibility for the sale and distribution of a portion of the U.S. traditional contact lens business to optical distributors. A 1993 fourth quarter marketing program to implement this strategy was developed, contributing one-time net income of approximately $10 million. Subsequently, this strategy proved unsuccessful.

Prior to this change in Bausch & Lomb's business strategy, revenues and associated receivables were recognized when sales were made to retailers or ultimate consumers. In the fourth quarter of 1993, however, shipments to distributors appear to have been treated as sales. This change in revenue recognition was in keeping with the shift in sales strategy, but the worry is that if distributors are unable to sell their inventory, they will return it to Bausch & Lomb for credit. This is exactly what happened, as described in the company's 1994 annual report:

> *In October 1994, the Company announced it had implemented a new pricing policy for traditional contact lenses and agreed on a one-time basis to accept returns from these distributors.* As a result, the Company recorded sales reserves and pricing adjustments which reduced operating earnings by approximately $20 million in the third quarter. The new pricing policy sought to enhance the Company's competitive position in a market segment where industry prices had declined since the business strategy was implemented. *The returns program allowed U.S. distributors to send back the excess portion of unsold traditional lenses and balance their overall contact lens inventories.* [Emphasis added.]

---

*Statement of Financial Accounting Standards No. 48* lists six criteria that must be satisfied before revenue is recognized when a sales agreement contains conditions that may allow the buyer to return the product.* The most important of these criteria for Bausch & Lomb are:

1. The return privilege has substantially expired because of performance by the seller, or other conditions, and

2. The amount of future returns can be reasonably estimated.

These guidelines are imprecise and abuses of the rules have occurred, as discussed in Chapter 3.

* "Revenue Recognition When Right of Return Exists," *SFAS No. 48* (Stamford CT: FASB, 1981).

---

So, we see that like our hypothetical automobile manufacturer, Bausch & Lomb began recognizing revenue when output was shipped to distributors rather than waiting until units were sold to final consumers.

Although the first 1994 annual report excerpt above suggests that the changes in sales strategy and revenue recognition began only in 1993, the data in Exhibit 8.3 reveal that a large disparity in sales and receivables growth rates occurred earlier. What explains this pre-1993 disparity?

A *Business Week* article published six months after Bausch & Lomb released its 1994 annual report suggests several possible explanations.[3] The article asserts that top-down pressure to achieve sales and profit goals caused Bausch & Lomb managers to loosen revenue recognition standards in the early 1990s, an assertion that top Bausch & Lomb executives vehemently denied. Specifically, Bausch & Lomb sales representatives allegedly "gave customers extraordinarily long payment terms, knowingly fed gray markets, and threatened to cut off distributors unless they took on huge quantities of unwanted products. Some also shipped goods before customers ordered them and booked the shipments as sales. . . ."[4] The article further contends that this type of deal making "became frantic" from the last quarter of 1992 through early 1994 and that the U.S. contact lens division "had a habit of constantly rolling over unpaid bills so that customers wouldn't return unwanted goods for credit."[5] If *Business Week's* interpretations are correct, these practices would explain the unusual pre-1993 receivables growth.

See Figure 8.1 for the company's days sales outstanding (DSO) for receivables by quarter for March 1989 through the end of 1995. DSO receivables represent just the dollar amount of

---

[3] M. Maremont "Blind Ambition," *Business Week,* October 23, 1995, pp. 78–92.

[4] Ibid., pp. 79–80.

[5] Ibid., p. 86.

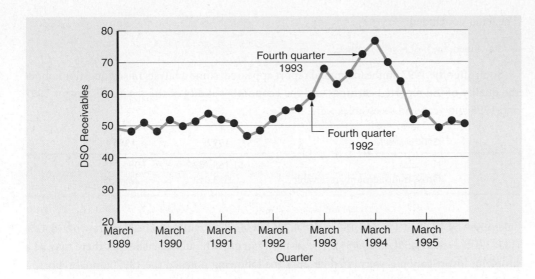

**Figure 8.1**

BAUSCH & LOMB INC.

DSO Receivables* by Quarter

* DSO Receivables is Days sales outstanding for receivables and is defined as Net trade accounts receivables divided by Net sales per day.

outstanding receivables divided by average daily sales. From March 1989 to March 1992, Bausch & Lomb's DSO receivables averaged about 50 days and fluctuated little from quarter to quarter. By the end of 1992, however, DSO receivables had increased to 59 days, and by the fourth quarter of 1993, it stood at 72 days. This unusual pattern of increase in Bausch & Lomb's DSO receivables undoubtedly caused some financial statement readers to become skeptical about the company's revenue recognition practices.

One last point regarding Bausch & Lomb. The *BusinessWeek* article contends that the reported December 31, 1993 accounts receivable number of $385 million (see Exhibit 8.3) *understates* the real growth of outstanding customer credit. The understatement occurs, according to the article, because Bausch & Lomb sold some receivables to a third-party financing company for cash. Receivable sales of this sort are called **factoring:** Factoring transactions are discussed later in this chapter. Factored receivables are removed from the balance sheet. If the receivables had not been factored, the accounts receivable balance would have been higher and the disparity in sales and receivables growth rates for 1992 and 1993 would have been even larger!

Scrutiny of changes in accounts receivable balances is essential. Large increases in accounts receivable relative to sales frequently represent a danger signal. The two most likely causes are collection difficulties and sales contingencies or disputes that may lead to potential returns. Another possible explanation, however, as you just saw, is a change in revenue recognition methods.

Many revenue recognition "irregularities" can be discovered by tracking the relationship between changes in sales and changes in receivables. Sunbeam Corporation's 1997 annual report provides another example.

Albert J. Dunlap joined Sunbeam Corporation as chairman and chief executive officer in July 1996. He had earned a reputation as a "turnaround" specialist because of his aggressiveness in restructuring and downsizing companies he had previously run, such as Scott Paper. By cutting costs and eliminating waste, Dunlap restored the companies to profitability. Sunbeam had mediocre performance in the years prior to Dunlap's arrival. But reported 1997 quarterly and annual financial results seemed to indicate considerable improvement.

At the start of his letter to shareholders in the 1997 annual report, Dunlap stated:

> We had an amazing year in 1997! During the past 12 months we set new records in almost every facet of the Company's operations. We experienced significant sales growth and concurrently increased margins and earnings.

The letter concluded:

> Stay tuned, the best is yet to come!

Soon after the 1997 Sunbeam annual report appeared, some analysts raised questions about the quality of the reported earnings and the economic validity of the results.[6] Sales for 1997 and 1996 and year-end receivables were:

| ($000 omitted) | 1997 | 1996 |
|---|---|---|
| Net sales | $1,168,182 | $984,236 |
| Gross trade accounts receivable | 313,013 | 229,455 |

Sales grew by 18.69% ([$1,168,182 − $984,236]/$984,236) while receivables grew by 36.42% ([$313,013 − $229,455]/$229,455). The disparity in growth rates is a clue that there may be a problem. Investigation is warranted because the following notes to the 1997 annual report in Exhibit 8.4 disclose "bill and hold sales" and disposal of receivables—events that affect both sales and receivables.

Let's look at bill and hold sales. In a **bill and hold** sale, the company recognizes revenue and the associated account receivable but does not ship the product to the customer until later. One issue is whether these are real sales. The annual report note states that these bill and hold terms were at the customer's request and legal title to the inventory had passed. So, it's reasonable to conclude that the sales were legitimate even though the inventory hadn't been shipped. But the other issue is whether these are really sales of 1997 or instead 1998 sales that have been pulled into 1997 by the bill and hold terms. The amount in question isn't trivial—3% of Sunbeam's 1997 sales ($1,168,182,000) is $35,045,460. This represents 19.05% of the reported $183,946,000 sales increase between 1996 and 1997.

Furthermore, the true growth in receivables is understated by the amount of receivables sold at the end of 1997. The $59 million cash received is the book value of the receivables minus a financing charge. So, $59 million roughly approximates the amount of receivables removed from the books.

---

## EXHIBIT 8.4    Sunbeam Corporation Footnotes

### Revenue Recognition

The Company recognizes revenues from product sales principally at the time of shipment to customers. In limited circumstances, at the customer's request the Company may sell seasonal product on a bill and hold basis provided that the goods are completed, packaged and ready for shipment, such goods are segregated, and the risks of ownership and legal title have passed to the customer. *The amount of such bill and hold sales at December 29, 1997 was approximately 3% of consolidated revenues.*

### Credit Facilities

In December 1997, the Company entered into a revolving trade accounts receivable securitization program to sell without recourse, through a wholly-owned subsidiary, certain trade accounts receivable. The maximum amount of receivables that can be sold through this program is $70 million. *At December 28, 1997, the Company had received approximately $59 million from the sale of trade accounts receivable.*

*Source:* Sunbeam Corporation 1997 annual report. [Emphasis and highlighting added.]

---

[6] See Jonathan R. Laing, "Dangerous Games," *Barron's,* June 8, 1998.

Let's summarize the clues that were available to the careful auditor and/or analyst:

1. Receivables growth greatly exceeded sales growth.
2. Bill and hold sales raise the possibility that some of this disparity is because sales were booked too early, thus generating receivables that won't be collected quickly. Worse yet, collection may never occur if delivery of "sold" items is ultimately refused.
3. Had Sunbeam not sold approximately $59 million of receivables, the "real" growth rate of receivables would have exceeded the reported rate of 36.42%, further increasing the disparity between sales and receivables growth rates. This even larger disparity increases the likelihood that some "channel stuffing"—that is, overly aggressive revenue recognition on items "sold" to dealers—was occurring.

These, as well as other issues unrelated to receivables, prompted a reaudit of Sunbeam's financial statements from the fourth quarter of 1996 through the first quarter of 1998. The reaudit disclosed that 1997 sales had been overstated by $95,092,000 (or 8.1%) with profits of $38,301,000 rather than $109,415,000, as reported.[7]

And it was careful scrutiny by informed analysts that led to inquiries that resulted in these corrections!

> Sunbeam's board of directors fired Albert J. Dunlap on June 15, 1998. He personally paid $15 million as part of a $141 million settlement of a shareholder class action fraud lawsuit against Sunbeam. In addition, he later paid a $500,000 penalty to the SEC to settle civil allegations of accounting fraud. As part of the settlement, Dunlap agreed to a permanent ban on serving as an official of a public company.
>
> *Source:* Michael Schroeder, "Dunlap Settles Fraud Charges with the SEC," *The Wall Street Journal,* September 5, 2002.

**RECAP**

**Evaluating the net realizable value of accounts receivable requires analyzing the adequacy of estimated uncollectibles and provisions for returns and price adjustments. An increase in receivables growth exceeding sales growth could indicate aggressive revenue recognition policies. Statement readers who carefully examine receivables trends and levels can discern potential problems as they evolve.**

## IMPUTING INTEREST ON TRADE NOTES RECEIVABLE

In certain industries, the seller sometimes extends long-term credit to the buyer, who then signs a note. If the note bears an interest rate that approximates prevailing borrowing and lending rates, the accounting is straightforward. Assume that Michele Corporation manufactures and sells a machine to Texas Products Company. The machine's cash selling price is $50,000. Michele accepts a three-year, $50,000 note signed by Texas Products with 10% interest per annum to be paid in quarterly installments each year. Assume that 10% approximates prevailing borrowing rates for companies as creditworthy as Texas Products. Upon making the sale, Michele records:

| **DR** Note receivable—Texas Products Company | $50,000 | |
|---|---|---|
| **CR** Sales revenues | | $50,000 |

Interest income accrues each quarter, and upon receipt of the cash payment, the accrued interest receivable is reduced. These are the entries:

| **DR** Accrued interest receivable | $1,250 | |
|---|---|---|
| **CR** Interest income | | $1,250 |

To accrue three months' interest = [$50,000 × 0.10]/4.

[7] See Dana Canedy, "Sunbeam Restates Results, and 'Fix' Shows Significant Warts," *The New York Times,* October 21, 1998.

| DR | Cash | $1,250 | |
|---|---|---|---|
| | **CR** Accrued interest receivable | | $1,250 |

To record receipt of the interest payment.

A complication arises for a note that does not state an interest rate or when the stated rate is lower than prevailing rates for loans of similar risk. Suppose that Monson Corporation sells equipment it manufactured to Davenport Products in exchange for a $50,000 note due in three years. The note bears no explicit interest. It says only that the entire $50,000 is to be paid at the end of three years. Monson's published cash selling price for the equipment is $37,566, and the current borrowing rate for companies like Davenport is 10%.

The present value factor for a payment three years away at a 10% rate is 0.75132 (see Appendix 1, Table 1). Therefore, the note's present value is $50,000 times 0.75132, or $37,566—which exactly equals the equipment's cash selling price. Although the $50,000 note itself does not contain any mention of interest, Monson will earn a return of 10% per year for financing Davenport's long-term credit purchase. This is easily demonstrated in Exhibit 8.5.

At the end of Year 3, Monson receives a $50,000 payment, which consists of the cash sales price ($37,566) plus interest ($12,434 = $3,756.60 + $4,132.26 + $4,545.14).

Monson Corporation records the sale to Davenport Products as:

| DR | Note receivable—Davenport | $37,566.00 | |
|---|---|---|---|
| | **CR** Sales revenue | | $37,566.00 |

Over the next three years, the note receivable is increased and interest income recognized. For example, at the end of Year 1, the entry is:[8]

| DR | Note receivable—Davenport | $3,756.60 | |
|---|---|---|---|
| | **CR** Interest income | | $3,756.60 |

| **EXHIBIT 8.5** | **Demonstration that Monson Earns 10% Interest for Three Years on Cash Sales Price of $37,566.00** |
|---|---|

| | |
|---|---:|
| Present value of $50,000 payment in 3 years (cash sales price) | $37,566.00 |
| Plus: Year 1 interest: 10% × $37,566.00 | 3,756.60 |
| Equals: Present value of $50,000 payment due in 2 years | 41,322.60 |
| Plus: Year 2 interest: 10% × $41,322.60 | 4,132.26 |
| Equals: Present value of $50,000 payment due in 1 year | 45,454.86 |
| Plus: Year 3 interest: 10% × $45,454.86 | 4,545.14* |
| Equals: Davenport payment at the end of Year 3 | $50,000.00 |

* Rounded.

[8] For simplicity, we ignore the periodic recording of interest on a monthly or quarterly basis during the year. In reality, if quarterly financial statements were prepared, the first year interest income of $3,756.60 would be apportioned to each quarter.

Notice that after Monson records interest income of $4,132.26 in Year 2 and $4,545.14 in Year 3, the carrying amount of the note receivable is exactly $50,000, as shown in Exhibit 8.5. When Davenport makes the required payment at the note's maturity, Monson Corporation records:

| | | |
|---|---|---|
| **DR** Cash .................................................... | $50,000.00 | |
| **CR** Note receivable—Davenport ......................... | | $50,000.00 |

This process of allocating the $50,000 proceeds of the note between sales revenue and interest income is called **imputed interest.**

A complication also arises when the note receivable contains a stated interest rate *but the stated rate is lower than prevailing borrowing rates at the time of the transaction.* When this happens, interest must again be imputed. Assume that Quinones Corporation sells a machine to Linda Manufacturing in exchange for a $40,000, three-year, 2.5% note from Linda. At the time of the sale, the interest rate normally charged to companies with Linda's credit rating is 10%. Because the note's stated interest rate is far below Linda's normal borrowing rate, Quinones must determine the machine's implied sales price by computing the note's present value at the 10% rate. The computation of this implied sales price is shown in Exhibit 8.6.

This computation shows that the implied selling price of the machine is $32,539.66 because this amount equals the discounted present value of the note Quinones received in exchange for the machine. Quinones makes the following entry:

| | | |
|---|---|---|
| **DR** Note receivable—Linda Mfg. ............................. | $32,539.66 | |
| **CR** Sales revenue ....................................... | | $32,539.66 |

Because payment is deferred, Quinones will earn 10% over the duration of the note on the amount of the credit sale ($32,539.66). The interest earned consists of three $1,000 payments over each of the ensuing years and another imputed interest payment of $7,460.34 ($40,000 minus the $32,539.66 implied cash selling price) at maturity.

---

**EXHIBIT 8.6**     **Computation of Implied Sales Price in Conjunction with a Nominal Interest-Bearing Note**

**Calculation of Present Value at 10% Effective Interest Rate**

Present value of $40,000 principal repayment in three years at 10%:

| | | | | |
|---|---|---|---|---|
| $40,000 | × | 0.75132 | = | $30,052.80 |

Present value of three interest payments of $1,000 (that is, $40,000 × 0.025), each at 10%:

| | | | | |
|---|---|---|---|---|
| Year 1 | $1,000 | × | 0.90909 | = | 909.09 |
| Year 2 | $1,000 | × | 0.82645 | = | 826.45 |
| Year 3 | $1,000 | × | 0.75132 | = | 751.32 |
| Implied sales price of machine | | | | $32,539.66 |

---

(*Note:* All present value factors are from Appendix 1, Table 1, 10% column.)

See Exhibit 8.7 for the composition of yearly interest income, and Figure 8.2 for the note receivable from the time of sale to maturity.

As shown in Exhibit 8.7 and Figure 8.2, the present value of the note, and thus its carrying value, increases each year (see column [d] of Exhibit 8.7). The increase in the carrying value of the note equals the difference between the annual 10% interest income earned—Column (a)—and the cash received—Column (b). For example, in Year 1, Quinones records:

| | | | |
|---|---|---|---|
| **DR** | Note receivable—Linda Mfg. ............................ | $2,253.97 | |
| **DR** | Cash ................................................. | 1,000.00 | |
| | **CR**   Interest income ....................................... | | $3,253.97 |

Similar entries are made in Years 2 and 3 using the amounts shown in Exhibit 8.7. At the end of Year 3, the note's carrying amount will be $40,000. When Linda pays the note on maturity, Quinones records the payment as:

| | | | |
|---|---|---|---|
| **DR** | Cash ................................................. | $40,000.00 | |
| | **CR**   Note receivable—Linda Mfg. ......................... | | $40,000.00 |

## EXHIBIT 8.7   Quinones Corporation

### Computation of Interest on Note Receivable

| | (a) Interest Income—10% of Column (d) Balance for Prior Year | (b) Cash Interest Received | (c) Increase in Present Value of Note (a) Minus (b) | (d) End-of-Year Present Value of Note |
|---|---|---|---|---|
| Inception | — | — | — | $32,539.66 |
| Year 1 | $ 3,253.97 | $1,000.00 | $2,253.97 | 34,793.63 |
| Year 2 | 3,479.36 | 1,000.00 | 2,479.36 | 37,272.99 |
| Year 3 | 3,727.01* | 1,000.00 | 2,727.01 | 40,000.00 |
| Total | $10,460.34 | | | |

* Rounded.

## Figure 8.2

QUINONES CORPORATION

Carrying Value of Note Receivable

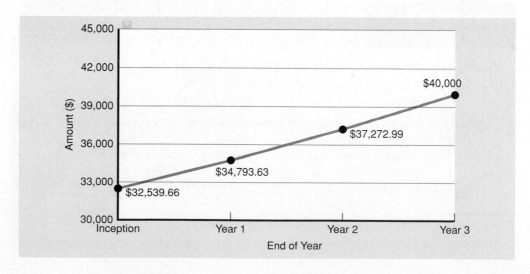

**For long-term credit sales transactions utilizing notes receivable:**

- **Sales revenue is recorded at the known cash price (Monson Corporation) or at the implied cash price (Quinones Corporation) of the item sold. The implied cash price is determined by computing the note receivable's present value using the prevailing borrowing rate (that is, the effective market rate of interest).**

- **Interest income is recorded each period over the note's term to maturity using the prevailing borrowing rate.**

This approach achieves a clear separation between the two income sources—credit sales and interest earned. Income from the credit sale is recorded when the sale is made. Interest income from financing the customer's purchase, on the other hand, is recorded over time as it is earned. This separation of income sources makes it possible to assess the degree to which a company's overall earnings are due to profitable credit sales versus profitable customer financing—a potentially important distinction.

## ACCELERATING CASH COLLECTION: SALE OF RECEIVABLES AND COLLATERALIZED BORROWINGS

Companies collect cash from their credit customers according to the payment schedule called for in the note or trade receivable. Sometimes companies prefer not to wait until customer payments arrive in the normal course of business. Instead, they accelerate cash collection with the help of a bank or financing company.

There are two ways to accelerate cash collections as depicted in Figure 8.3, **factoring** and **collateralized borrowings.** In factoring, the company sells its receivables outright to a bank in exchange for cash. Customer payments flow directly to the bank in most cases. Factoring can be **without recourse** (also called **nonrecourse**), meaning that the bank cannot turn to the company for payment in the event that some customer receivables prove uncollectible. Factoring can also be **with recourse,** meaning that the company must buy back any bad receivables from the bank.

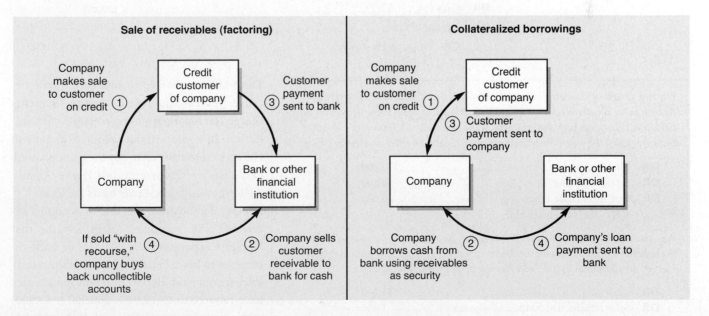

**Figure 8.3**  SALE OF RECEIVABLES AND COLLATERALIZED BORROWINGS

The other way to accelerate cash collection is through a collateralized borrowing, where the receivables are the collateral. The company obtains cash from the bank and is responsible for repaying the loan.

Reasons why companies might accelerate cash collections include:

1. *Competitive conditions require credit sales but the company is unwilling to bear the cost of processing and collecting receivables.* Restaurants are an example of this. Customers of upscale restaurants expect to be able to charge meals rather than pay cash, yet most restaurants are reluctant to incur the costs of servicing receivables. Consequently, restaurants rely on third parties such as VISA, American Express, and Diners' Club, companies that, in effect, "buy" the customer receivable from the restaurant.

2. *There may be an imbalance between the credit terms of the company's suppliers and the time required to collect customer receivables.* Suppliers might extend credit on three-month terms to a company while inventory turnover (cost of goods sold/average inventory) plus receivables turnover (net credit sales/average accounts receivable) total six months. To pay suppliers within the due date, cash collection must be accelerated.

3. *The company may have an immediate need for cash but be short of it.* Selling receivables to a financial institution allows the company to raise cash quickly. Using receivables as collateral for a bank loan also represents a way to obtain quick cash (and perhaps low-cost financing).

Let's look at the accounting issues that arise when receivables are either sold or used in a collateralized borrowing.

> Credit card companies "buy" the receivables at a discount—they pay the restaurant, say, 97 cents for every dollar of receivables. The three-cent "discount" is the fee the credit card company charges for accelerating cash receipts.

## Sale of Receivables (Factoring)

To illustrate a factoring transaction *without* recourse, suppose that Hervey Corporation sells $80,000 of its customer receivables to Leslie Financing. The purchaser (Leslie Financing) is called the **factor**. Leslie charges a 5% fee (0.05% × $80,000 = $4,000) for this service and pays Hervey $76,000. The entry to record the nonrecourse sale of the receivables on Hervey Corporation's books is:

| | | |
|---|---|---|
| **DR** | Cash ................................................. | $76,000 |
| **DR** | Interest expense ........................................... | 4,000 |
| | **CR** Accounts receivable .................................... | $80,000 |

> Usually, a bank or financing company refuses to bear the costs of sales returns, discounts, or allowances. Consequently, a holdback to cover these items may be included in the transaction. For example, if the holdback is $3,000 and if all other facts regarding the nonrecourse sale are unchanged, the entry on Hervey's books is:
>
> | | | |
> |---|---|---|
> | **DR** | Cash .................................. | $73,000 |
> | **DR** | Interest expense ...................... | 4,000 |
> | **DR** | Due from Leslie Financing ............... | 3,000 |
> | | **CR** Accounts receivable................ | $80,000 |
>
> Any returns, discounts, or allowances reduce the amount Leslie pays to Hervey. If these items totaled $1,800 on the sold receivables, Leslie would ultimately pay Hervey an additional $1,200, and Hervey makes the following entry:
>
> | | | |
> |---|---|---|
> | **DR** | Cash .................................. | $1,200 |
> | **DR** | Sales returns, discounts, and allowances..... | 1,800 |
> | | **CR** Due from Leslie Financing........... | $3,000 |

The $4,000 is charged to Interest expense because this amount represents the financing charge Hervey incurred to accelerate cash collection. In a sale without recourse, if some of Hervey's customers fail to pay the amount owed, Leslie has no recourse against Hervey (hence the term)—and thus, Leslie bears the loss.

Next we illustrate the sale of accounts receivable *with* recourse. Again, assume that Hervey Corporation sells $80,000 of trade receivables to Leslie Financing. If any of the receivables are not paid, Hervey bears the loss. Leslie's fee is reduced to 4% (0.04 × $80,000 = $3,200) with a recourse transaction rather than 5% because the risk to Leslie is lower. Assume that

Leslie withholds $5,000 to cover possible noncollections. The entry on Hervey Corporation's books is:

| | | | |
|---|---|---|---|
| **DR** | Cash | $71,800 | |
| **DR** | Interest expense | 3,200 | |
| **DR** | Due from Leslie Financing | 5,000 | |
| | **CR** Accounts receivable | | $80,000 |

The $5,000 holdback account, Due from Leslie Financing, represents a cushion to absorb credit losses that Hervey must ultimately bear in a sale with recourse.

Assume that all but $3,750 of receivables are collected. Once collections are known, the financing company remits the final settlement amount. The entry on Hervey's books is:

| | | | |
|---|---|---|---|
| **DR** | Cash | $1,250 | |
| **DR** | Allowance for uncollectibles | 3,750 | |
| | **CR** Due from Leslie Financing | | $5,000 |

## Borrowing Using Receivables as Collateral

If the transaction between Hervey Corporation and Leslie Financing had been a **collateralized loan** rather than a sale of receivables, the accounts receivable would not be removed from Hervey's books. Instead, it would create a liability account to reflect the loan. Suppose that $80,000 of receivables was pledged as collateral for a loan; interest is 4% of $80,000. Then the entry is:

| | | | |
|---|---|---|---|
| **DR** | Cash | $76,800 | |
| **DR** | Prepaid interest | 3,200 | |
| | **CR** Loan payable—Leslie Financing | | $80,000 |

> The $3,750 debit to Allowance for uncollectibles is appropriate if normal allowances had been accrued on the receivables that were sold. Allowance accounts are usually maintained when the sale is with recourse. If no allowance was maintained, the debit of $3,750 would be made to an account entitled Loss on sale of receivables or some other similarly titled income statement loss account.

The fact that the receivables have been pledged as collateral for this loan must be disclosed in the notes to the financial statements if material.[9] Once the loan is due, Hervey makes these entries:

| | | | |
|---|---|---|---|
| **DR** | Loan payable—Leslie Financing | $80,000 | |
| | **CR** Cash | | $80,000 |
| **DR** | Interest expense | $ 3,200 | |
| | **CR** Prepaid interest | | $ 3,200 |

Notes receivable can also be assigned or sold. Accelerating cash collection on notes in this way is called **discounting** because the financial institution advances cash to the company based on the *discounted* present value of the notes. For example, suppose Abbott Manufacturing received a $9,000, six-month, 8% per year interest-bearing note from Weaver Company, a customer. That same day, Abbott discounted the note at Second State Bank. If the bank

---

[9] "Accounting for Contingencies," *SFAS No. 5* (Stamford, CT: Financial Accounting Standard Board [FASB], 1975), para. 12.

discounts the note at 12%, Abbott receives only $8,798.40. The cash proceeds to Abbott are computed as follows:

| | |
|---|---:|
| Face amount of the note | $9,000.00 |
| Interest to maturity ($9,000 × 0.08 × 6/12) | 360.00 |
| Maturity amount of the note | 9,360.00 |
| Interest charge by bank | |
| ($9,360 × 0.12 × 6/12) | 561.60 |
| Cash proceeds | $8,798.40 |

Abbott makes the following entry when the note is discounted:

| | | | |
|---|---|---:|---:|
| **DR** | Cash . . . . . . . . . . . . . . . . . . . . . . . . . . . . . . . . . . . . . . . . . . . . . . . . . . . . . . . | $8,798.40 | |
| **DR** | Interest expense . . . . . . . . . . . . . . . . . . . . . . . . . . . . . . . . . . . . . . . . . | 201.60 | |
| | **CR**  Note receivable . . . . . . . . . . . . . . . . . . . . . . . . . . . . . . . . . . . . . . . . | | $9,000.00 |

Accelerating cash collection generates interest expense of $201.60, the difference between the note's book value and the cash proceeds.

At maturity, the bank will present the note to Weaver Company for payment. Notes can be discounted either with or without recourse. If discounted *with* recourse, Second State Bank would collect $9,360 ($9,000 principal + $360 interest) from Abbott if Weaver failed to pay the note at maturity. When notes are discounted with recourse and the note is removed from the seller's books, a contingent liability must be disclosed in the footnotes.[10]

## Ambiguities Abound: Is It a Sale or a Borrowing?

Usually, the nature of a transaction involving receivables is clear. But in some situations, it is not obvious whether the receivables have been sold or are instead being used as collateral for a loan. The ambiguity arises when certain obligations, duties, or rights regarding the transferred receivables are retained by the firm undertaking the transfer (which is called the **transferor**).

The FASB has provided guidelines in *SFAS No. 140* for distinguishing between sales and collateralized borrowings involving receivables.[11] The guidelines hinge on the issue of whether the transferor **surrenders control over the receivables.** If control is surrendered, the transaction is treated as a sale, and any gain or loss is recognized in earnings. However, if the criteria for a sale are not met because control has not been surrendered, the transaction is accounted for as a collateralized borrowing.

The issues addressed in *SFAS No. 140* have assumed great importance with the growth of **financial asset securitization.** *Securitization occurs when receivables (such as mortgages and automobile loans) are bundled together and sold or transferred to another organization, which issues securities that are collateralized by the transferred receivables.* For example, the financing subsidiary of General Motors (General Motors Acceptance Corporation) bundles large numbers of automobile loans together. It then uses these loans as collateral for interest-bearing notes that it sells to outside investors. The outside investors often earn a higher return than would otherwise be available to them because auto loans usually carry a relatively high rate of interest. By

> *SFAS No. 140* states that the transferor surrenders control over the receivables when *all* of the following conditions are met:*
>
> 1. The transferred assets are beyond the reach of the transferor and its creditors.
> 2. The transferee has the right to dispose of the assets.
> 3. There is no agreement obligating the transferor to repurchase or redeem the transferred assets in the future, nor can the transferor unilaterally force the holder to return the assets.
>
> * See para. 9 and paras. 27–28.

---

[10] Ibid., para. 12.

[11] "Accounting for Transfers and Servicing of Financial Assets and Extinguishments of Liabilities," *SFAS No. 140* (Norwalk, CT: FASB, 2000).

bundling large numbers of receivables, GM creates value because the portfolio effect of the bundling itself reduces the risk of loss.

Home mortgages, car loans, and credit card debt are just a few of the receivables that have been securitized and sold to investors. An estimated $3.2 trillion of securitized instruments were outstanding in the United States at the end of 2005.[12] As more of these transactions were undertaken, the FASB felt compelled to provide guidelines for when to treat securitizations as sales and for when to treat them as borrowings.

Ambiguities arise, for example, when a bank transfers a group of mortgages (which, to the bank, are receivables) to some other organization but retains the responsibility for servicing the mortgages. The bank often continues to collect the mortgage payments or to handle customer inquiries, or it even promises to buy back the mortgages at some future date if certain conditions occur.

The accounting treatment of these receivable transactions has important financial reporting implications. For example:

1. If the transaction is really a borrowing but is erroneously treated as a sale, both assets and liabilities are understated (that is, the loan liability does not appear on the company's balance sheet and neither do the receivables that were transferred). The understatements consequently distort ratios such as debt to equity and rate of return on assets.

2. If the transaction is really a sale, a gain or loss on the transaction should be recognized. To erroneously treat such transactions as borrowings misrepresents the company's net assets.

## A Closer Look at Securitizations

Securitizations are popular for two reasons:

1. Investors have a strong appetite for acquiring securitized assets.
2. Firms with large amounts of receivables have powerful incentives to engage in securitizations.

It's a "win–win" situation for investors and firms; both parties benefit.

Investors benefit because they are able to obtain highly liquid financial instruments that diversify their risk. A simple example shows this. Suppose that the prevailing rate of return on debt instruments with "moderate" risk is 6% per year. The 6% yield is determined by the credit standing of large corporate and government issuers of bonds and other instruments. By contrast, people who take out home mortgages with banks do not have the same high credit standing as these bond issuers. Understandably, the rates people pay on their mortgages are higher—let's say 7% per year.

Assume that a bank forms a bundled portfolio of these home mortgages and is prepared to sell them at a price that yields the investor a return of 6%. The risk associated with the individual mortgages ranges from "low" to "moderately high" *but the risk of the bundled portfolio in the aggregate is moderate.* So, the investors have a new investment option that also provides a 6% per year yield at the same moderate risk level but responds differently than other debt instruments to changes in interest rates and other economic events. This diversifies risk, and that's attractive. Furthermore, the investors could not form a moderate-risk, 6% return mortgage portfolio themselves because the costs of identifying potential mortgagees and assessing credit are high and would lower their return below 6%. Even if they could construct their own portfolio, they'd have difficulty finding buyers for individual mortgages if investors later wanted to liquidate the

[12] Fitch, Inc., "U.S. Structured Finance Rating Comparability Survey," *Credit Market Research* (New York, March 24, 2006).

When the expected interest and principal payments are discounted at a rate lower than the stated rate, the present value exceeds the face amount of the loans. The computational approach is similar to the one given in Exhibit 8.6 except that the discount rate is lower than the stated rate. Consequently, the present value is higher not lower than the note's face amount. Computational issues will be discussed in more detail in Chapter 11 in conjunction with bond payable premiums.

investment. So, investors benefit from securitizations by gaining liquid portfolio diversification opportunities that they could not achieve on their own.

A bank may reduce risk further by paying an independent third party, a **guarantor,** to bear some of the default risk. For example, a guarantor may agree to pay security holders interest and principal payments for loans that default. Government-sponsored entities, such as Fannie Mae and Freddie Mac, are the primary guarantors for mortgage-backed securities. In its 2006 annual report, Fannie Mae states that it receives upfront fees and ongoing fees based on the amount and risk of the loans. In 2006, its effective fee rate was 0.22% of the amounts guaranteed.

Both the investors and the bank benefit from the reduction in risk. If the bank sells the 7% mortgages at a price that yields the purchasers a return of 6%, the selling price is higher than the carrying value of the mortgages on the bank's books. So, the bank records a gain on the sale of the receivables. *This gain exists because the bank has created value.* As you just saw, the individual investors would never consider lending directly to, say, two or three home purchasers. (It's too risky. Who knows how many will default?) But the large portfolio is much less risky. Thus, investors who are unable to duplicate the bank's return on their own without assuming high risks (and costs) are very willing to accept the 6% return.

Banks and other firms that engage in securitization transactions do not transact directly with the investors. The process of securitization is somewhat convoluted for reasons we'll soon explain. See Figure 8.4 for how a typical securitization is structured.

## Figure 8.4

STRUCTURE OF A
SECURITIZATION

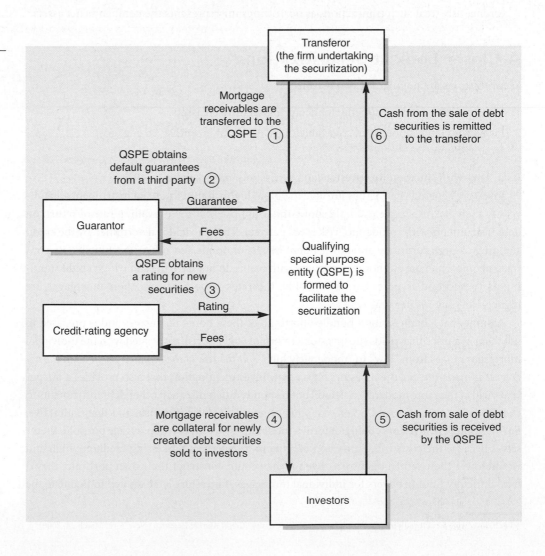

The transferor forms what is called a **special purpose entity,** or **SPE.** Securitizations are carefully designed to meet conditions under *SFAS No. 140* that enable the transferor to keep the SPE off its balance sheet. SPEs that meet these conditions are called **qualifying special purpose entities (QSPEs).** The QSPE is usually a trust or corporation that is legally distinct from the transferor and is created solely for the purpose of undertaking the securitization transaction. The transferor then sells (transfers) the receivables (mortgages in our example) to the QSPE (① in Figure 8.4). At the time of the transfer, the QSPE may also obtain guarantees from an outside entity (②). Before the QSPE markets the new debt securities, it usually obtains a credit rating for the new securities (③). Because the QSPE is legally separate from the transferor, the QSPE's credit rating depends on the quality of the transferred receivables and can differ from the rating of the transferor's general debt. The QSPE pays fees to the rating agency for its rating opinion.[13] The QSPE then creates and issues debt securities that it sells to outside investors (④ and ⑤). The cash that the QSPE receives from the investors is then remitted to the transferor (⑥). In many situations, the transferor continues to service the assets (that is, handle cash collections, recordkeeping, etc.), usually for a fee that the QSPE pays.

The cash flows from the mortgages themselves (that is, principal repayment and interest) are later used to make the periodic interest and principal repayments to the investors who bought the debt securities.

The QSPE is created for two reasons. One is to protect the investors who bought the debt securities. Because the receivables were sold to the QSPE, they are beyond the reach of the transferor and its creditors. ***So, even if the transferor were to declare bankruptcy, the collateral underlying the notes is safe from seizure.*** The other reason for creating the QSPE is because its existence allows the transferor to demonstrate that it has given up control and keep the QSPE off its balance sheet. If there were no QSPE, the transferor would issue the notes directly to investors, constituting a collateralized borrowing; the receivables would appear on the transferor's books and so would the notes (as a liability). Creating the qualifying legally distinct entity, however, removes the receivables from the transferor's books. Furthermore, the notes are the QSPE's debt, not the transferor's. Because the QSPE is not consolidated, the debt securities never appear on the transferor's balance sheet. ***So, both the receivables and the debt are "off balance sheet."***

Why does the FASB allow favorable off-balance-sheet treatment for these contorted transactions? One reason is that they are economically

---

To meet the criteria to be a QSPE, the trust must satisfy four conditions stated in *SFAS No. 140,* para. 35:

1. *It is demonstrably distinct from the transferor.* This condition is met if the transferor cannot unilaterally dissolve the SPE and either of two other highly technical circumstances apply.

2. *Its activities are narrowly limited.* These are restricted to holding title to the transferred assets, issuing the collateralized debt securities, collecting cash flows from the transferred assets, and making interest and principal payments to holders of the debt securities.

3. *It holds only rigidly defined types of assets.* The assets must not require decision making by the SPE.

4. *Its ability to dispose of assets is limited to narrowly defined circumstances.* This means that the SPE must be an unthinking robot that cannot exercise discretion.

The FASB has tightened the rules for what constitutes a QSPE. These additional rules would deny QSPE treatment when the transferor retains certain risks and rewards in the transferred assets.

---

International Financial Reporting Standards (IFRS) and *SFAS No. 140* define "control" differently. Under IFRS, control exists when the SPE's activities are expressly designed to satisfy the business needs of the enterprise that created it. Consequently, QSPEs would be consolidated under IFRS, and both the mortgage receivables and the new debt securities would remain on the balance sheet.

*Source:* "Consolidation—Special Purpose Entities," *SIC-12* (London: International Accounting Standards Board [IASB], Standing Interpretations Committee, 2004).

---

[13] The largest credit-rating agencies are Fitch Ratings, Moody's Investor Service, and Standard & Poor's. For more information on institutional features related to ratings, see Chapter 6 and U.S. Securities and Exchange Commission, *Report on the Role and Function of Credit Rating Agencies in the Operation of the Securities Markets, As Required by Section 702(b) of the Sarbanes-Oxley Act of 2002* (Washington, DC, January 2003).

**International**

beneficial. That is, the transferor creates value through the portfolio effect of bundling the assets, and investors diversify their risk and earn slightly higher returns.

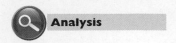
**Analysis**

To illustrate these financial statement effects of the off-balance-sheet treatment of securitizations, consider the following example.

---

Doyle National Bank has the following account balances at December 31, 2008:

| | |
|---|---|
| Assets | |
|   Mortgages receivable | $1,200,000 |
|   All other assets | 1,800,000 |
| Total assets | $3,000,000 |
| Liabilities and equity | |
|   Liabilities | $2,700,000 |
|   Equity | 300,000 |
| Total liabilities and equity | $3,000,000 |
| After-tax income for the year | |
|   ended December 31, 2008 | $ 40,000 |

On December 30, 2008, Doyle securitized $1,000,000 of mortgages using a QSPE it had established. The cash received from the QSPE was exactly $1,000,000, so it recognized no gain or loss on the transaction. The receivables were removed from the books because this transaction conformed to the *SFAS No. 140* rules for securitizations.

The journal entry Doyle made to remove the receivables on December 30, 2008 was:

**DR** Cash ............................................. $1,000,000
    **CR** Mortgages receivable .......................... $1,000,000

Now let's see what the financial statement effect would have been had the $1,000,000 transaction instead been treated as a borrowing with the mortgages used as collateral. With this changed assumption, the entry *would have been:*

**DR** Cash ............................................. $1,000,000
    **CR** Loan payable ................................. $1,000,000

Under this alternative scenario, the account balances at December 31, 2008 (assuming no *other* transactions) would have been:

| | Amounts under Securitization Scenario | Change in Balance If $1,000,000 Transaction Is Accounted for as a Borrowing | Amounts under Collateralized Borrowing Scenario |
|---|---|---|---|
| Assets | | | |
|   Mortgages receivable | $1,200,000 | +$1,000,000 | $2,200,000 |
|   All other assets | 1,800,000 | — | 1,800,000 |
| Total assets | $3,000,000 | | $4,000,000 |
| Liabilities and equity | | | |
|   Liabilities | $2,700,000 | +$1,000,000 | $3,700,000 |
|   Equity | 300,000 | — | 300,000 |
| Total liabilities and equity | $3,000,000 | | $4,000,000 |
| After-tax income for the year ended December 31, 2008 | $ 40,000 | — | $ 40,000 |

---

Doyle National Bank's return-on-assets ratio and debt-to-equity ratio after completing this $1,000,000 transaction are computed in the following table. The left column shows the ratio values reflected after the securitized receivables have been removed from the balance sheet.

The right column shows the ratio balances *that would have been reflected* if the transaction had been treated as a borrowing with the mortgages serving as collateral. (Remember that under a borrowing, the receivables remain on Doyle's books and a liability for the borrowing is recorded.)

|  | Ratios under Securitization Scenario | Ratios under Collateralized Borrowing Scenario |
|---|---|---|
| Return-on-assets ratio | $\dfrac{\$40,000}{\$3,000,000} = 0.013$ | $\dfrac{\$40,000}{\$4,000,000} = 0.01$ |
| Debt-to-equity ratio | $\dfrac{\$2,700,000}{\$300,000} = 9.000$ | $\dfrac{\$3,700,000}{\$300,000} = 12.33$ |

So, you see that treating the transaction as a securitization (which removes the mortgage assets from the balance sheet and does not put a loan payable on the balance sheet) improves the return-on-assets ratio from 1% to 1.3%—a 30% increase. Similarly, the securitization treatment improves (reduces) the debt-to-equity ratio from 12.33 to 9—a 27% reduction. If a gain had been recognized on the securitization, both ratios would have been improved even further.

A gain would arise if investors accept a rate which is lower than the face rate on the mortgages (e.g., the mortgages bear a 7% rate but investors accept a 6% rate—as was discussed on page 430).

The off-balance-sheet treatment of QSPEs illustrated in this section applies only when *financial assets*—that is, receivables, mortgages, and so on—are transferred. More stringent rules apply when firms try to use SPEs to remove nonfinancial assets such as equipment from their financial statements. The FASB issued these rules in response to the notorious SPE transactions that Enron utilized to misrepresent its indebtedness and income. In Chapter 16, we discuss the rules for determining when these nonfinancial asset SPEs (called **variable interest entities**) can legitimately be removed from the transferor's books.

## Securitization and the 2007 Subprime Mess

In its 2007 third quarter filing (p. 55), the mortgage lender Fannie Mae defines a **subprime loan** as:

> a mortgage loan made to a borrower with a weaker credit profile than that of a prime borrower. As a result of the weaker credit profile, subprime borrowers have a higher likelihood of default than prime borrowers. (p. 55)

Subprime loans can be securitized as part of a general portfolio of loans or can be put into a pool of subprime loans. Sometimes when loans are securitized, classes of securities with different levels of credit risk may be created. The senior securities receive payments first if there are defaults, and the junior securities receive payments last. Each class of security is then rated and sold. As the article on the next page notes, these senior securities could be rated AAA. The junior securities also could be bundled and resecuritized so that a senior class of junior loans could be created. This senior class of junior securities could also receive high credit ratings.[14]

To increase returns, banks and money market funds invested heavily in these highly rated subprime securities. When housing prices fell and interest rates on adjustable rate mortgages increased in 2007, the default rate in the subprime market was much higher than expected. Consequently, subprime defaults affected securities with high credit ratings. In some instances, money market funds were holding these securities, and investors, who thought that they had highly rated (low-risk) investments suddenly lost money.[15] In prior home price declines, the banks incurred most of the losses, but because of securitization, many small investors also suffered losses in 2007.

---

[14] See J. Tiemann, "A Pyramid of Little Golden Crumbs," Tiemann Investment Advisors, LLC (August 31, 2007), p. 7.

[15] See D. Evans, "Subprime Infects $300 Billion of Money Market Funds, Hikes Risk," August 20, 2007, Bloomberg.com.

# NEWS CLIP

## MARKET SHOCK: AAA RATING MAY BE JUNK

The great stock market rally of 2002 through 2007 has been built on liquidity—and much of the liquidity has been based on financial engineering that allowed highly risky investments to be financed by investors who thought they were taking no risks.

They were wrong.

Now the question is whether the market can continue rising as investors learn that the financial innovations that helped to build the boom were constructed on sand.

When *Bear Stearns* admitted this week that two hedge funds were expected to lose, in round numbers, 100 percent of their value, it blamed "unprecedented declines in the valuations of a number of highly rated (AA and AAA) securities."

Those securities were nothing like the bonds issued by companies with triple-A or double-A ratings. Such bonds almost never plunge in value because the companies borrowing the money are financially solid.

But the money invested by the hedge funds went to finance mortgage loans to subprime customers, borrowers as close to being a triple-A credit as Moscow is to Maui as a beach resort.

By the magic of securitization, sow's ears could become silk purses, or at least look like them. Most subprime mortgages would never default, went the theory, and rising home prices would minimize losses when there were defaults. So if a security was protected from the first 10 or 20 percent of losses in a mortgage portfolio, then it was as safe as a loan to *General Electric*. Such securities got AAA ratings.

Securities with a greater exposure to loss could still get investment-grade ratings. All told, the vast majority of the money that financed risky loans appeared to be invested in investment-grade paper.

Those who made the mortgage loans—or who made junk-rated loans to leveraged buyout companies—found that they could securitize the loans and sell the highly rated securities for enough money to assure themselves a profit before any homeowners could default. Any profit that came later from the riskier securities, which the lenders often kept, was icing on the cake.

*Source:* Floyd Norris, "Market Shock: AAA Rating May Be Junk," *New York Times*, July 20, 2007. Copyright © 2007 New York Times Company Inc. Used with permission.

## Some Cautions for Statement Readers

Factoring, assignment, and securitization of receivables raise some issues for those who analyze financial statements. The main issue is the level of disclosure in statement footnotes when receivables have been transferred during the reporting period. When the transfer is with recourse (the "selling" company is still responsible for uncollected receivables), *SFAS No. 5* requires footnote disclosure of the contingent liability.[16] ***But there is no similar unequivocal disclosure requirement when receivables are sold without recourse.*** Some observers contend that receivables sold without recourse are a financing transaction that must be separately disclosed in the cash flow statement.[17] But even if this interpretation is correct, GAAP requires that disclosures be made only when they are **material.** The FASB has defined materiality as:

 **Analysis**

> A decision not to disclose certain information may be made, say, . . . because the amounts involved are too small to make a difference (they are not material). . . . The Board's present position is that no general standards of materiality can be formulated to take into account all the considerations that enter into an experienced human judgment.[18]

---

[16] "Accounting for Contingencies," *SFAS No. 5* (Stamford, CT: FASB, 1975), para. 12.

[17] This position is based on an interpretation of "Statement of Cash Flows," *SFAS No. 95* (Stamford, CT: FASB, 1987), para. 16.

[18] "Qualitative Characteristics of Accounting Information," *Statement of Financial Accounting Concepts No. 2* (Stamford, CT: FASB, 1980), paras. 125 and 131.

*Materiality* is defined loosely as information that, if disclosed, would change the decision maker's conclusion. But because the guidelines are unclear, some companies could purposely not disclose sales of receivables and, if asked about the omission, declare the information "immaterial."

Here's what this means for statement readers. Earlier in this chapter, you learned that one way to assess whether reported receivables arose from legitimate sales was to compare the growth rate of sales and the growth rate of receivables. This comparison in Exhibit 8.3 for Bausch & Lomb showed that receivables growth far outstripped sales growth between 1991 and 1993. Our conclusion—based on disclosures from the 1994 Bausch & Lomb annual report—was that the leap in receivables growth arose from "forcing" inventory on distributors and treating these shipments as sales. The way to recognize these potential trouble areas is to monitor receivables growth. ***But when firms sell receivables, the receivables number reported in the ending balance sheet includes only the remaining receivables and thus understates the true growth in receivables over the period.***

This is precisely what *BusinessWeek* says happened at Bausch & Lomb, whose "internal financial documents" it claims show year-end 1993 receivables to be $506 million rather than the $385 million reported on the company's balance sheet (see again Exhibit 8.3). According to *BusinessWeek*, Bausch & Lomb felt the factored receivables didn't need to be disclosed under GAAP.[19]

If the *BusinessWeek* assertion is correct and Bausch & Lomb didn't disclose the removal of $121 million of receivables from the balance sheet (that is, $506 − $385) through factoring, assignment, or securitization, the reported 1993 receivables growth rate is understated. Specifically:

> The Securities and Exchange Commission (SEC) has issued a Staff Accounting Bulletin (SAB) on materiality to establish clearer guidelines.* (SABs inform registrants about the criteria the SEC staff will use in resolving reporting issues.) *SAB No. 99* rejects arbitrary, across-the-board percentages such as 5% as the materiality threshold. Instead, through a series of examples, the SEC reaffirms that materiality is contextual. Consider then a firm for which the consensus analysts' quarterly earnings per share (EPS) forecasts are $1.00 per share. The firm knows that actual earnings will fall short at 99¢ per share. If the firm evades GAAP rules to raise earnings by 1¢ per share, *in that specific context*, the inappropriate earnings boost is material because it is designed to change investors' perceptions of whether the firm is performing up to expectations.
>
> \* *SEC Staff Accounting Bulletin: No. 99—Materiality,* August 12, 1999.

|  | 1992 | 1993 |
|---|---|---|
| Receivables growth computed in Exhibit 8.3 using Bausch & Lomb balance sheet data | $277,338 | $384,973 |
|  | +38.81% | |
| Receivables growth computed by adding $121 million to reported 1993 receivables based on the *BusinessWeek* assertion | $277,338 | $506,000 |
|  | +82.45% | |

So, the receivables growth rate computed from the financial statements was "only" 38.81% rather than 82.45%—the figure *BusinessWeek* claims would have resulted had Bausch & Lomb disclosed the receivables transaction.

Regardless of whose interpretation of disclosure requirements is correct here, the opportunity to transfer receivables provides a way for companies to disguise the *real* extent of receivables growth. Suppose that a company is "aggressively" booking sales to artificially raise current earnings. To avoid discovery, the company could factor or securitize some of its "good" receivables—those that don't arise from the questionable sales—and thus understate the true disparity in the growth rates of receivables and sales. So, the receivables remaining on the books are the "bad" ones and the factoring has disguised the deterioration in the *quality* of reported receivables. Consequently, statement readers must scrutinize footnotes and the

---

[19] M. Maremont, op. cit., p. 90.

financing activities section of the cash flow statement for evidence of dispositions of receivables that may be masking overly aggressive revenue recognition policies or bad receivables management.

The transferred receivables "disappear" from the balance sheet. Because receivables are lower, certain ratios such as return on assets and receivables turnover improve when compared to previous periods. But is the ratio improvement sustainable? Should the analyst "undo" the transfer and recompute the ratios with the receivables included? At a minimum, the analyst must be aware of the extent of the disruption in the year-to-year ratio pattern and its impact on financial forecasts. Other adjustments depend on the circumstances. Also, did the transferor "cherry-pick" the best receivables to make the transaction attractive to the purchasers? If it did, the analyst must scrutinize the quality of the remaining receivables as well as the adequacy of the allowance for uncollectibles.

One additional point on securitizations and receivables sales in general is needed. As you remember from Chapter 4, a decline in receivables is a source of operating cash flow. But when that decline in receivables does not arise from ordinary collections—instead, say, from a securitization—should this receivables decrease still be considered an operating cash inflow? Because receivables (assets) were sold, should this be classified as an investing cash inflow instead?

GAAP on this point has been unclear. However, most firms undertaking receivables securitizations classify the inflows as *cash from operating activities*. This is how Sunbeam classified the $59 million of cash inflow from its securitization in 1997. Many view the opportunity to do this as a deficiency in "Statement of Cash Flows," *SFAS No. 95*.[20] These analysts believe that categorizing the asset sales proceeds as operating cash flows gives a potentially misleading picture of long-term sustainable inflows arising from current operations. Consequently, they believe that when evaluating operating cash flows, analysts should remove the effect of receivable sales.

Because of the increased usage of receivable sales and securitizations, the SEC provided additional guidance about statement of cash flow classifications in a recent speech.[21] SEC staff believe that sales of customer receivables or sales of loans acquired specifically for resale should be classified as operating activities. The staff also stated that *manufacturing* firms should classify sales of receivables as investing activities only if the receivables are being held as an investment and do not relate to sales of inventory. *Finance* firms should classify proceeds as investing cash flows if the loans were originally acquired for investments as opposed to resale.[22] Even with the additional guidance from the SEC, sale of receivables is clearly an area that auditors and analysts must carefully evaluate when analyzing the statement of cash flows.

## TROUBLED DEBT RESTRUCTURING

What happens to a lender when a customer is financially unable to make the interest and principal payments required by an installment loan or other receivable? Rather than force the customer into bankruptcy, lenders frequently agree to **restructure** the loan receivable, thus

> The Sunbeam sale of trade accounts receivable on page 420 was a securitization. Sunbeam fully disclosed the transaction. But if the securitization had not taken place, the year-to-year increase in Sunbeam's receivables would have approximated 60%, not the 36.42% reported on the comparative financial statements themselves.

---

[20] See C. W. Mulford and K. Shkonda, "The Impact of Securitizations of Customer-Related Receivables on Cash Flows and Leverage: Implications for Financial Analysis," College of Management, Georgia Institute of Technology, www.mgt.gatech.edu/finlab (June 2006).

[21] See J. Levine, "Remarks before the 2005 Thirty-Third AICPA National Conference on Current SEC and PCAOB Developments" (n.d.), www.sec.gov/news/speech/spch120605j1.htm and related PowerPoint slides at www.sec.gov/news/speech/slides120605j1.pdf.

[22] These beliefs are based on *SFAS No. 95*, para. 22 and *SFAS No. 102*, para. 9. See "Statement of Cash Flows—Exemption of Certain Enterprises and Classification of Cash Flows from Certain Securities Acquired for Resale, an Amendment of FASB Statement No. 95," *SFAS No. 102* (Norwalk, CT: FASB, 1989). The speeches also provided guidance regarding reclassifying securities and retained interests in securitized loans.

allowing the customer to remain in business. The restructured loan can differ from the original loan in several ways:

- Scheduled interest and principal payments may be reduced or eliminated.
- The repayment schedule may be extended over a longer time period.
- The customer and lender can settle the loan for cash, other assets, or equity interests.

Lenders are willing to restructure a customer's loan to help the customer resolve present financial difficulties and stay in business. And lenders often receive more through restructuring than they would from foreclosure or bankruptcy.

Consider the debt restructuring described in Exhibit 8.8. On December 31, 2008, Harbor Hotels Corporation owned and/or managed 47 hotel properties located primarily in the northeastern and southeastern United States. It financed these investments using long-term debt—a convertible subordinated debenture. During 2008, the company suffered operating losses and cash flow difficulties. The convertible subordinated debenture originally carried an interest rate of 7.5% per year and a maturity date of January 1, 2010. The conversion price on December 31, 2008 was $4.50 per common share. Because Hudson could not make the required loan payments, the lender (a mutual fund) canceled $4.5 million of the debt in exchange for the following:

- An acceleration of the maturity date by 8 1/2 months.
- An increase in the annual interest rate from 7.5% to 18.75%.
- A decrease in the conversion price of $2.70 per share (that is, $4.50 − $1.80).

Obviously, the lender would have preferred that Harbor Hotels pay the original debt principal and interest on time. Faced with the company's inability to do so, it chose to restructure the debt rather than force the company into bankruptcy. The enormous leap in the interest rate from 7.5% to 18.75% reflects Harbor Hotels' precarious financial condition and the resulting risk of the restructured loan.

This example illustrates a key feature of **troubled debt restructurings** not present in ordinary debt refinancings. *SFAS No. 15* gives this definition:

> A restructuring of debt constitutes a troubled debt restructuring . . . if the creditor for economic or legal reasons related to the debtor's financial difficulties grants a **concession** to the debtor that it would not otherwise consider [Emphasis added.].[23]

In other words, for the restructuring to be "troubled," the borrower (Harbor Hotels) must be unable to pay off the original debt and the lender (the mutual fund) must grant a concession

---

### EXHIBIT 8.8    Harbor Hotels Corporation

#### Debt Restructuring

In July 2008, the Company replaced its outstanding $7.5 million Convertible Subordinated Debenture to Oppenheimer Convertible Securities Fund with a new Convertible Subordinated Debenture bearing the following terms: principal balance of $3.0 million; interest rate of 18.75%; maturity date of April 15, 2009; and a conversion price of $1.80 per share. As a result, the Company reported an extraordinary gain from the debt restructuring, net of expenses, of approximately $4 million or $0.64 per common share—basic.

---

To help you understand this financial instrument, we'll define each of the three words, in reverse order. **Debentures** are bonds that have no underlying collateral that could be seized if Harbor Hotels defaulted on the debt. It is an unsecured borrowing. **Subordinated** means that Harbor has other debt issues that "ranked ahead" of this debt in the event of liquidation—that is, investors in the other debt would be paid before investors in the convertible subordinated debenture. **Convertible** bonds allow the investor—at the investor's option—to convert the bond into equity shares of Harbor. A conversion price of $4.50 on December 31, 2008 means that each $1,000 bond could be converted into 222.222 shares ($1,000/$4.50 = 222.222). This is an attractive feature for bond investors because it provides a potentially valuable "upside" option if the issuer prospers.

---

[23] "Accounting by Debtors and Creditors for Troubled Debt Restructurings," *SFAS No. 15* (Stamford, CT: FASB, 1977), para. 2.

to the borrower. What the FASB means by "concession" is quite specific: In exchange for canceling the original debt, the lender must accept *new debt or assets with an economic value less than the book value of the original debt plus any accrued interest.*

Our Harbor Hotels example meets these guidelines. The company was unable to make its interest and principal payments. The lender then agreed to restructure the debt, and in so doing, granted the company a substantial economic concession—the $4.5 million of debt cancellation.

Troubled debt restructurings can be accomplished in two different ways:

- **Settlement,** which cancels the original loan by a transfer of cash, other assets, or equity interests (borrower's stock) to the lender.
- **Continuation with modification** of debt term by canceling the original loan and signing a new loan agreement.

Some troubled debt restructurings contain elements of both settlement and modification.

The accounting issues related to troubled debt restructuring encompass both the measurement of the new (modified) loan and the recognition of any gain or loss. The following example illustrates these issues.[24]

Assume that Harper Companies purchased $75,000 of corn milling equipment from Farmers State Cooperative on January 1, 2005. Harper paid $25,000 cash and signed a five-year, 10% installment note for the remaining $50,000 of the purchase price. The note calls for annual payments of $10,000 plus interest on December 31 of each year. Harper made the first two installment payments on time but was unable to make the third annual payment on December 31, 2007. After much negotiation, Farmers State agreed to restructure the note receivable. At that time, Harper owed $30,000 in unpaid principal plus $3,000 in accrued interest. We assume that the restructuring was agreed to on January 1, 2008 and that both companies have already recorded interest up to that date.

## Settlement

Suppose Farmers State agrees to cancel the loan if Harper pays $5,000 cash and turns over a company car. The car was purchased 18 months ago for $21,000 cash, has a current fair value of $18,000, and is carried on Harper's books at $16,000 ($21,000 original cost minus $5,000 accumulated depreciation). Notice that the combined economic value of the cash ($5,000) and automobile ($18,000) is $23,000—or $10,000 less than the $33,000 Harper owes Farmers State.

The January 1, 2008 entries made to record settlement of the troubled debt are:

| Harper Companies (Borrower) | | |
|---|---|---|
| **DR** Automobile | $ 2,000 | |
| **CR** Gain on disposal of asset | | $ 2,000 |
| To increase the net carrying amount of the automobile ($16,000) to its fair value ($18,000). | | |

---

[24] Troubled debt restructurings often involve complexities that are beyond the scope of our discussion here. See *SFAS No. 15*, ibid.; "Accounting by Creditors for Impairment of a Loan," *SFAS No. 114* (Norwalk, CT: FASB, 1993); and "Accounting by Creditors for Impairment of a Loan—Income Recognition and Disclosures," *SFAS No. 118* (Norwalk, CT: FASB, 1994).

| **DR** | Note payable | $30,000 | |
|---|---|---|---|
| **DR** | Interest payable | 3,000 | |
| **DR** | Accumulated depreciation | 5,000 | |
| | **CR** Cash | | $ 5,000 |
| | **CR** Automobile | | 23,000 |
| | **CR** Gain on debt restructuring | | 10,000 |

To record the settlement.

**Farmers State Cooperative (Lender)**

| **DR** | Cash | $ 5,000 | |
|---|---|---|---|
| **DR** | Automobile | 18,000 | |
| **DR** | Loss on receivable restructuring | 10,000 | |
| | **CR** Note receivable | | $30,000 |
| | **CR** Interest receivable | | 3,000 |

To record the settlement.

What do these entries accomplish? The settlement creates two earnings gains for Harper:

- A gain on asset disposal of $2,000—the difference between the car's fair value ($18,000) and its book value ($16,000).

- A debt restructuring gain of $10,000—the difference between the note's book value plus accrued interest ($30,000 + $3,000) and the fair value of assets transferred ($5,000 cash plus $18,000 automobile).

> Farmers State's settlement loss would not be extraordinary but would instead be included in computating income from continuing operations. Because it's a lender, restructurings are a normal part of its business and are likely to recur. So, these transactions meet *neither* of the two criteria for extraordinary items—unusual nature and infrequency of occurrence—discussed in Chapter 2, Harper Companies' gain would be treated as extraordinary only if it met both of these criteria for extraordinary items.

Farmers State's has a debt restructuring loss for the same $10,000 figure. Both companies record all interest up to the restructuring date and then cancel the note and related interest receivable and payable.

## Continuation with Modification of Debt Terms

Instead of reaching a negotiated settlement of the note receivable, Harper and Farmers State could have resolved the troubled debt by modifying the terms of the original loan. The possibilities are endless. For accounting purposes, what matters is whether the **undiscounted sum of future cash flows under the restructured note is more or less than the note's carrying value (including accrued interest) at the restructuring date.**

### Sum of Restructured Flows Exceeds Carrying Value of Payable

Suppose that Farmers State agrees to postpone all principal and interest payments on the note receivable to maturity. Harper's final (and only) payment on December 31, 2009 would total $39,000 (the $30,000 principal plus $9,000 representing three years interest at 10%). Harper and Farmers State have already recorded $3,000 in accrued interest as of January 1, 2008. So, the book value of the note plus accrued interest is $33,000 at the restructuring date.

Because the sum of future cash flows on the restructured note ($39,000) is *greater* than the carrying value of the original payable ($33,000), Harper will not show a restructuring gain.

To see this, notice that the restructured note calls for Harper to make a single payment of $39,000 on December 31, 2009—*two* years from the January 1, 2008 restructuring date. We need to find a discount rate that equates the present value of this $39,000 payment with the $33,000 carrying value of the note receivable. This means finding the rate $r$ that solves the following equation:

$$\underbrace{\text{Carrying value}} = \underbrace{\text{Present value of future cash flows (in 2 years)}}$$

$$\$33,000 = \frac{\$39,000}{(1 + r)^2}$$

The value of $r$ that satisfies this equation is 0.087. To verify this, go to our Web site—www.mhhe.com/resvine4e—and use the present value calculator to see that the present value factor for a single payment due in two periods at 8.7% is 0.84615, and $39,000 multiplied by this factor equals $33,000 (rounded).

Instead, Harper will compute a new (and lower) effective interest rate for the restructured note and accrue interest at that new rate until the loan is fully paid. The new effective interest rate is the rate that equates the present value of the restructured cash flows to the carrying value of the debt at the date of restructure.[25] The new effective interest rate for Harper Companies is 8.7% per year.

Farmers State will continue using the 10% interest rate on the original note.[26] To do so, it must value the restructured note payments using a 10% effective interest rate. Farmers State will then show a loss for the difference between the present value of the restructured note, which is $32,232, and the carrying value of the original note ($33,000). The entries made by both companies are:

> The present value factor for a single payment due in two years at 10% is 0.82645. The value of the note is $39,000 × 0.82645, or $32,232 (rounded).

**Harper Companies (Borrower)**

| | | | |
|---|---|---|---|
| **DR** | Note payable | $30,000 | |
| **DR** | Interest payable | 3,000 | |
| | **CR** Restructured note payable | | $33,000 |

To record the modified note (when sum of restructured cash flows is greater than note carrying value).

**Farmers State Cooperative (Lender)**

| | | | |
|---|---|---|---|
| **DR** | Restructured note receivable | $32,232 | |
| **DR** | Loss on receivable restructuring | 768 | |
| | **CR** Note receivable | | $30,000 |
| | **CR** Interest receivable | | 3,000 |

To record the modified note (when sum of restructured cash flows is greater than note carrying value).

Both companies accrue interest beginning on the debt restructuring date (January 1, 2008) and ending on the restructured note's maturity date (December 31, 2009). But they will *not* use the same interest rate, as you just saw. The borrower, Harper, will record annual interest at 8.7% of the note's carrying value at the beginning of each year, whereas Farmers State will use a 10% annual rate.

The FASB's choice of two different interest rates, one for the borrower and another for the lender, illustrates the role of conservatism in financial reporting. If the lender, Farmers State, used the 8.7% rate, it would continue to carry the note at $33,000 (see the present value calculation in the sidebar above) and recognize no loss although the cash inflows have been reduced. If the borrower, Harper, used the original 10% rate, this would cause it to reduce the note carrying value to $32,232 and recognized an up-front gain. So, to obtain conservative outcomes, the FASB required the parties to use different interest rates.

---

[25] *SFAS No. 15,* para. 16.

[26] *SFAS No. 114,* para. 14.

The entries for the next two years are:

---

**Harper Companies (Borrower)**

| | | | |
|---|---|---|---|
| **DR** | Interest expense | $2,871 | |
| | **CR** Restructured note payable | | $2,871 |

($2,871 = $33,000 × 0.087)

To record interest on December 31, 2008.

| | | | |
|---|---|---|---|
| **DR** | Interest expense | $3,121 | |
| | **CR** Restructured note payable | | $3,121 |

($3,121 = [$33,000 + $2,871] × 0.087)

To record interest on December 31, 2009.

**Farmers State Cooperative (Lender)**

| | | | |
|---|---|---|---|
| **DR** | Restructured note receivable | $3,223 | |
| | **CR** Interest income | | $3,223 |

($3,223 = $32,232 × 0.10)

To record interest on December 31, 2008.

| | | | |
|---|---|---|---|
| **DR** | Restructured note receivable | $3,546 | |
| | **CR** Interest income | | $3,546 |

($3,546 = [$32,232 + $3,223] × 0.10)

To record interest on December 31, 2009.

---

Over time, Harper Companies' note payable and Farmers State Cooperative's note receivable increase to the final balance of $39,000, the required payment at maturity (see Exhibit 8.9). The entry to record the payment is:

---

**Harper Companies (Borrower)**

| | | | |
|---|---|---|---|
| **DR** | Restructured note payable | $39,000 | |
| | **CR** Cash | | $39,000 |

To record payment of balance on December 31, 2009.

**Farmers State Cooperative (Lender)**

| | | | |
|---|---|---|---|
| **DR** | Cash | $39,000 | |
| | **CR** Restructured note receivable | | $39,000 |

To record receipt of balance on December 31, 2009.

---

This example illustrates a restructured loan in which the total restructured cash flows are *greater* than the carrying value of the troubled debt. Next let's examine a situation in which the sum of the future cash flows is *less* than the carrying value of the troubled debt.

## Sum of Restructured Flows Is Less Than Payable's Carrying Value

Suppose that Farmers State waives all interest payments (that is, the $3,000 unpaid accrued interest for 2007 as well as the 2008 and 2009 interest) and defers all principal payments until December 31, 2009. The restructured cash payments (now only $30,000) are *lower* than the receivable's carrying value ($33,000). Harper will show a gain on the debt restructuring and will

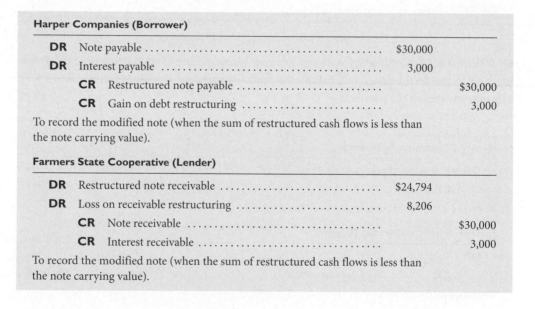

**EXHIBIT 8.9**    Growth of Note Carrying Amount

|  | Harper Companies | Farmers State Cooperative |
|---|---|---|
| Restructured note, initial carrying amount | $33,000 | $32,232 |
| Accrued interest expense, Harper |  |  |
| 2008 | 2,871 |  |
| 2009 | 3,121 |  |
| Accrued interest revenue, Farmers State |  |  |
| 2008 |  | 3,223 |
| 2009 |  | 3,546 |
| Note carrying amount, December 31, 2009 | $39,000* | $39,000* |

* Rounded.

The $24,794 is just the present value of $30,000 received in two years at 10%, or $24,794 = $30,000 × 0.82645.

treat the subsequent payment as a reduction of the restructured principal. Harper records no interest expense. But Farmers State follows the procedures outlined in the previous example. It values the restructured note at $24,794 (using the 10% effective interest rate from the original note), records a debt restructuring loss, and accrues interest income to maturity. The entries made at the restructuring date are:

**Harper Companies (Borrower)**

| | | | |
|---|---|---|---|
| **DR** | Note payable | $30,000 | |
| **DR** | Interest payable | 3,000 | |
| | **CR** Restructured note payable | | $30,000 |
| | **CR** Gain on debt restructuring | | 3,000 |

To record the modified note (when the sum of restructured cash flows is less than the note carrying value).

**Farmers State Cooperative (Lender)**

| | | | |
|---|---|---|---|
| **DR** | Restructured note receivable | $24,794 | |
| **DR** | Loss on receivable restructuring | 8,206 | |
| | **CR** Note receivable | | $30,000 |
| | **CR** Interest receivable | | 3,000 |

To record the modified note (when the sum of restructured cash flows is less than the note carrying value).

**International**

IFRS for debt restructurings from the lender's perspective are similar to U.S. GAAP. (See "Financial Instruments: Recognition and Measurement," *IAS 39* [London, 2005], para. 63.) No explicit international standards govern troubled debt restructuring from the borrower's perspective.

Harper would not record any interest over the life of the restructured note. The $30,000 cash payment on December 31, 2009 would reduce the outstanding balance of Harper's restructured note payable. Farmers State still records interest income over the life of the note. These entries would be:

**Harper Companies (Borrower)**

| | | | |
|---|---|---|---|
| **DR** | Restructured note receivable | $30,000 | |
| | **CR** Cash | | $30,000 |

(No entries are made until the cash payment at maturity.)

**Farmers State Cooperative (Lender)**

| | | |
|---|---|---|
| **DR** Restructured note receivable ............................. | $ 2,479 | |
| **CR** Interest income....................................... | | $ 2,479 |

($2,479 = $24,794 × 0.10)

To record interest on December 31, 2008.

| | | |
|---|---|---|
| **DR** Restructured note receivable ............................. | $ 2,727 | |
| **CR** Interest income ...................................... | | $ 2,727 |

($2,727 = [$24,794 + $2,479] × 0.10)

To record interest on December 31, 2009.

The note receivable balance at Farmers State has now increased to $30,000 (that is, $24,794 + $2,479 + $2,727).

| | | |
|---|---|---|
| **DR** Cash ................................................. | $30,000 | |
| **CR** Restructured note receivable ......................... | | $30,000 |

To record payment of receivable balance on December 31, 2009.

## Evaluating Troubled Debt Restructuring Rules

The GAAP rules for troubled debt restructurings are subject to several criticisms.

First, an obvious (and uncomfortable) lack of symmetry exists in the financial reporting of the borrower and lender. Different measurement rules are used to value the borrower's restructured note payable and the lender's restructured receivable when there is continuation with modification of debt terms. Consequently, the initial book value that GAAP assigns to the payable is not the same as the initial book value assigned to the receivable. This also results in a difference between the borrower's restructuring gain and the lender's restructuring loss. We explained this as an instance of the FASB's opting for a conservative measurement method.

Second, the GAAP restructuring gains and losses do not always correspond to real economic gains and losses for the companies involved. For one thing, GAAP often assigns the gain or loss to the wrong time period. Although the accounting loss the case of Farmers State Cooperative was shown in 2008, most of the economic loss occurred earlier when Harper became unable to make the loan payments.

Third, it's possible to question GAAP's use of the original loan's effective interest rate to value the restructured receivable and the lender's restructuring loss. Turning again to Farmers State, its original 10% loan to Harper used an interest rate that reflected the borrower's credit risk when the loan was first made. Over the ensuing three years, Harper's credit risk undoubtedly increased to the point where lenders would charge a higher rate of interest (say 15%) on new loans to the company. After all, Harper failed to meet its financial obligations in 2007. A higher effective interest rate on the restructured receivable will produce a lower initial book value and a larger restructuring loss for the lender. The GAAP approach is a practical solution because it avoids the sometimes difficult task of estimating the borrower's real effective interest rate at the restructuring date. However, this approach also fails to fully reflect the economic realities of troubled debt restructurings and results in the conservatism discussed earlier.

**Exhibit 8.10 summarizes, in general terms, the accounting illustrated in each of the Harper–Farmers State troubled debt restructurings.**

RECAP

**EXHIBIT 8.10**    Summary of Accounting Procedures for Troubled Debt Restructurings

| | Settlement Gain or Loss | Restructured Loan Cash Flows Are | |
| --- | --- | --- | --- |
| | | Lower Than Current Carrying Value of Loan* | Higher Than Current Carrying Value of Loan* |
| **Borrower** | | | |
| New loan payable | — | Total of restructured cash flows | Current book value |
| Gain on debt restructuring | Ordinary† | Ordinary† | None |
| Gain (loss) on transfer of assets | Ordinary | — | — |
| Future interest expense | — | None, all payments applied to principal | Based on rate that equates current carrying value and restructured cash flows |
| **Lender** | | | |
| New loan receivable | — | Present value of new cash flows at original effective interest rate | Present value of new cash flows at original effective interest rate |
| Loss on debt restructuring | Ordinary | Ordinary | Ordinary |
| Future interest income | — | Based on original loan rate | Based on original loan rate |

\* Includes unpaid accrued interest.

† Unless it meets both criteria for extraordinary items.

# THE FAIR VALUE OPTION

IFRS allow firms to voluntarily opt to measure financial assets (such as mortgage receivables) and financial liabilities at fair value (rather than cost).[27] Changes in fair value are included in periodic income. This fair value option is permitted only under narrowly specified circumstances. Here's one example. Firms sometimes have financial assets and liabilities that are economically "matched." For instance, mortgages are deliberately financed by debt whose fair value decreases (increases) offset increases (decreases) in the value of the mortgages due to interest rate changes. (More about this in Chapter 11.) Despite this economic matching, accounting rules and/or differences in the timing of transactions can produce an income timing inconsistency. The IASB illustrates this possibility:[28]

**International**

> [For example,] the entity has financed a specified group of loans by issuing traded bonds whose changes in fair value tend to offset each other. If, in addition, the entity regularly buys and sells the bonds but rarely, if ever, buys and sells the loans, reporting both the loans and the bonds at fair value through profit or loss eliminates the inconsistency in the timing of recognition of gains and losses that would otherwise result from measuring them both at amortised cost and recognizing a gain or loss each time a bond is repurchased.

So, using the IFRS fair value option in this case would reflect the economic changes in the matched loans and bonds better.

To achieve a similar consistency in the treatment of matched items, the FASB issued *SFAS No.159* that also allows firms to choose a fair value option.[29] Chapter 11 discusses *SFAS No. 159* in more detail.

---

[27] "Financial Instruments: Recognition and Measurement," *IAS 39* (London: International Accounting Standards Board, 2005), para. 9.

[28] Ibid., para. AG4E (d)(ii).

[29] "The Fair Value Option for Financial Assets and Financial Liabilities, Including an Amendment of FASB Statement No. 115," *SFAS No.159* (Norwalk, CT: FASB, February 2007).

- GAAP requires that accounts receivable be shown at their net realizable value.

- Companies use one of two methods to estimate uncollectible accounts: (1) the sales revenue approach or (2) the gross accounts receivable approach. Under either approach, firms must periodically assess the reasonableness of the uncollectibles balance by performing an aging of accounts receivable.

- Analysts should scrutinize the allowance for uncollectibles balance over time. Significant increases in the allowance could indicate collection problems while significant decreases in the allowance could be a sign of earnings management.

- Receivables growth can exceed sales growth for several reasons, including a change in customer mix or credit terms. But a disparity in the growth rate of receivables and sales could also indicate that aggressive revenue recognition practices are being used.

- In certain long-term credit sales transactions, interest must be imputed by determining the note receivable's present value.

- Firms sometimes transfer or dispose of receivables before their due date to accelerate cash collection. Sales of receivables—also called *factoring*—can be with or without recourse.

- Receivables are also used as collateral for a loan.

- In analyzing receivables transactions, it is sometimes not obvious whether the transaction to accelerate cash collection represents a sale or a borrowing; however, the FASB provided guidelines in *SFAS No. 140* for distinguishing between sales (when the transferor surrenders control over the receivables) and borrowings (when control is not surrendered).

- Analysts should examine receivables transfer transactions to determine whether they represent a sale or a borrowing. Any divergence between the accounting treatment and the economics of the transaction misstates assets and liabilities. Furthermore, sales of receivables change ratios such as receivables turnover as well as potentially masking the underlying real growth in receivables.

- Banks and other holders of receivables frequently restructure the terms of the receivable when a customer is unable to make required payments. These troubled debt restructurings can take one of two forms: (1) settlement or (2) continuation with modification of debt terms.

- When terms are modified, the precise accounting treatment depends on whether the sum of future cash flows under the restructured note is more or less than the note's carrying value at the restructuring date.

- The interest rate used in troubled debt restructurings may not reflect the real economic loss suffered by the lender.

# ROOMKIN & JURIS DEPARTMENT STORES SECURITIZATION

Roomkin & Juris is a department store chain in the western United States. In September 2008, it created a legally separate trust (R & J Trust) to serve as the special purpose entity for securitizing $1,000,000 of customer receivables. It charges customers an interest rate of 12% per year on unpaid receivable balances. The receivables were sold to the trust, which in turn issued $1,000,000 of two-year 9% per annum notes collateralized by the receivables. Interest on the notes is paid quarterly. Roomkin & Juris services the accounts and remits a portion of the cash collected to the trust. The R & J Trust uses this cash to make all required payments to the investors. Because the receivables are constantly turning over, this is called a **revolving securitization.** The amount of collateral must be maintained at the original amount (here $1,000,000) less any credit losses (which, we assume, the investors bear). Three transactions in 2008 were related to the securitization:

- *September 30:* Roomkin & Juris sold receivables with a book value of $980,000 (that is, gross receivables of $1,000,000 and an allowance for uncollectibles of $20,000) to the trust for $995,000.

- *October 1–December 29:* Roomkin & Juris collected $692,500 from customers on the receivables sold to the trust. This amount represents payment of both the principal portion of the receivables and interest.

- *December 30:* Roomkin & Juris transferred $692,500 of new receivables and cash to the trust to replenish the collateral base and to allow the trust to make required interest payments.

1. **Record the sale of the receivables on Roomkin & Juris' books.**

   The journal entry is:

   | | | |
   |---|---|---|
   | **DR** Cash | $995,000 | |
   | **DR** Allowance for uncollectibles | 20,000 | |
   | **CR** Accounts receivable | | $1,000,000 |
   | **CR** Gain on sale of receivables | | 15,000 |

   Because the investors bear all credit losses, the allowance that relates to the sold receivables is removed from the books. The journal entry presumes that Roomkin & Juris do not charge a fee for servicing the accounts. The $15,000 gain is the value created by securitization—it's what investors are willing to pay over and above the receivables' book value.

2. **Record Roomkin & Juris' cash collections on the sold receivables.**

   The journal entry is:

   | | | |
   |---|---|---|
   | **DR** Cash | $692,500 | |
   | **CR** Due to R & J Trust | | $692,500 |

   The collateral must be maintained at $1,000,000 less any credit losses. (Remember that investors bear all credit losses in this securitization.) So, Roomkin & Juris must replace the receivables principal that has been repaid by the customers plus $22,500 cash to cover the fourth quarter 2008 interest payment on the notes ($1,000,000 × 0.09 × 0.25 = $22,500). This total is $692,500.

3. **Record the asset transfer to the R & J Trust.**

   The journal entry is:

   | | | |
   |---|---|---|
   | **DR** Due to R & J Trust | $692,500 | |
   | **CR** Accounts receivable | | $670,000 |
   | **CR** Cash | | 22,500 |

Because some original accounts receivable have been collected, the collateral is now replenished by a transfer of $670,000 of *new* receivables to the R & J Trust. The $22,500 cash enables the trust to make the quarterly interest payment on the notes.

4. **What happens in September 2010 when the R & J Trust repays the principal amount of the notes?**

Over the two years, the collateral has been maintained at $1,000,000 minus any credit losses. Let's assume that the receivables collateral balance is $984,000 on September 30, 2010 when the notes are due; that is, credit losses were $16,000 ($1,000,000 − $984,000). The amount of principal repayment that the investors will receive is $984,000. Roomkin & Juris will remit that amount in cash to the R & J Trust. Because the securitization has terminated, collateral is no longer needed and the receivables are transferred back from the R & J Trust to the department store. The entry on Roomkin & Juris' books is:

| | | | |
|---|---|---|---|
| **DR** | Accounts receivable | $984,000 | |
| **CR** | Cash | | $984,000 |

---

# TIME VALUE OF MONEY

Cash is an economic resource. When firms borrow cash—for example, take a two-year bank loan—they are renting the use of that economic resource for the two-year term of that loan. The lender's charge for renting its cash to the borrower is **interest.**

Interest is an important concept because many business transactions involve borrowing, lending, or investing. Because of interest, a dollar amount invested today increases (or accumulates) to a higher amount in the future. The amount that that dollar grows to in the future is the **future value.** Similarly, because of interest, a dollar amount that will be received in the future—say, two years from now—is less valuable than that same dollar amount in hand today. Calculating today's value of a future dollar amount is called **discounting.** The result of that discounting calculation is the **present value** of that future dollar amount.

The time at which cash inflows and cash outflows occur determines the ultimate future value or the present value of those flows. Correctly valuing these flows is necessary to represent properly the value of the assets, liabilities, revenues, and expenses arising from various business transactions.

> The concepts of present value and future value are totally driven by the role of interest. These concepts are unrelated to the buying power of money—inflation or deflation—which is a distinct and separate topic that we do not discuss in this appendix.

## Future Value

Assume that Alice Han's parents give her a $1,000 check for her twenty-first birthday. She wants to invest the money for graduate school, which she will attend in two years. Three local banks advertise that their savings accounts pay 6% interest per year, although how that interest is computed differs among them. Bank A pays 6% **simple interest** on the cash in a depositor's savings account. *Simple interest* means that each year's interest is computed on the original amount invested, which is called the **principal.** So, interest each year would be $1,000 × 0.06, or $60. At the end of two years, the account at Bank A will have a future value of $1,120, calculated as:

Future value with simple interest = $1,000 + $60 + $60 = $1,120

Bank B pays 6% compound interest on savings accounts. **Compound interest** means that interest is paid not just on the initial principal but also on the interest that has been earned each period to date. So, the accumulated amount would be computed as follows:

| Date | Interest Calculation | Accumulated Amount |
|---|---|---|
| Initial principal | | $1,000.00 |
| Year 1 | $1,000 × 0.06 = $60.00 | $1,060.00 |
| Year 2 | $1,060 × 0.06 = $63.60 | $1,123.60 |

Future value with interest compounded annually = $1,123.60

Bank B has compounded the interest annually; that is, interest is computed only once a year.

Bank C pays 6% interest compounded semiannually. This means that interest is computed every six months at a rate of 3%. The accumulated amount is:

| Date | Interest Calculation | Accumulated Amount |
|---|---|---|
| Initial principal | | $1,000.00 |
| Year 1—First 6 months | $1,000 × 0.03 = $30.00 | $1,030.00 |
| —Last 6 months | $1,030 × 0.03 = $30.90 | $1,060.90 |
| Year 2—First 6 months | $1,060.90 × 0.03 = $31.83 | $1,092.73 |
| —Last 6 months | $1,092.73 × 0.03 = $32.78 | $1,125.51 |

Future value with interest compounded semiannually = $1,125.51

Because most business transactions use compound interest, so will our examples. The formula for computing compound interest is

$$FV = P(1 + r)^n$$

Where:

$FV$ = future value

$P$ = present value

$r$ = interest rate per compounding period

$n$ = number of compounding periods

For simplicity, let's assume that interest is compounded annually. So, the compounding period is a year. Using the formula to compute the future amount of a $1,000, two-year deposit in Bank B:

$$FV = \$1,000 (1 + 0.06)^2$$

$$FV = \$1,123.60$$

Of course, $1,123.60 equals the same future amount computed previously by the earlier more tedious calculation.

## Present Value

As you just saw, if interest is compounded annually at 6%, the future value of $1,000.00 after two years is $1,123.60. This means that $1,123.60 to be received two years in the future is equivalent to $1,000 today—its present value—when the interest rate is 6% per year. To be sure you understand this concept of present value, we'll look at it from another perspective.

Assume that Alice Han's parents, knowing that she wanted to enroll in graduate school in two years, gave her a choice of birthday gifts:

- $1,000 cash immediately.
- $1,123.60 to be received in exactly two years.

Which option should she choose? If she is determined to spend the money for graduate school (that is, she doesn't need the cash immediately) and if she knows that 6% per year is the prevailing interest rate, **she should be indifferent between the two options.** Here's why. If she chooses the $1,000 today, she could put it in a savings account at Bank B at 6% per year compounded annually where it would accumulate to $1,123.60 in two years.[30] So, the two alternative gift amounts are identical at 6% per year compounded annually. *Being indifferent between $1,000 today and $1,123.60 in two years means that the present value of $1,123.60 due in two years is $1,000 at a 6% interest rate compounded annually.*

By rearranging the formula for computing compound interest, we can represent this notion of present value:

$$FV = P(1 + r)^n$$

Solving this formula for $P$, we find the present value:

$$P = \frac{FV}{(1 + r)^n}$$

Table 1 in Appendix 1 at the end of the book shows the present value factors for various compounding periods and various interest rates per period. These present value factors result from solving the present value equation for $P$. This table provides the factor for computing

| TABLE 1 | Present Value of $1 |
|---------|---------------------|

**(Selected Excerpts)**

$$P = \frac{1}{(1 + r)^n} = (1 + r)^n$$

| (n) Periods | 2% | 3% | 4% | 5% | 6% | 7% | 8% | 9% | 10% | 11% | 12% | 15% |
|---|---|---|---|---|---|---|---|---|---|---|---|---|
| 1 | 0.98039 | 0.97087 | 0.96154 | 0.95238 | 0.94340 | 0.93458 | 0.92593 | 0.91743 | 0.90909 | 0.90090 | 0.89286 | 0.86957 |
| 2 | 0.96117 | 0.94260 | 0.92456 | 0.90703 | 0.89000 | 0.87344 | 0.85734 | 0.84168 | 0.82645 | 0.81162 | 0.79719 | 0.75614 |
| 3 | 0.94232 | 0.91514 | 0.88900 | 0.86384 | 0.83962 | 0.81630 | 0.79383 | 0.77218 | 0.75132 | 0.73119 | 0.71178 | 0.65752 |
| 4 | 0.92385 | 0.88849 | 0.85480 | 0.82270 | 0.79209 | 0.76290 | 0.73503 | 0.70843 | 0.68301 | 0.65873 | 0.63552 | 0.57175 |
| 5 | 0.90573 | 0.86261 | 0.82193 | 0.78353 | 0.74726 | 0.71299 | 0.68058 | 0.64993 | 0.62092 | 0.59345 | 0.56743 | 0.49718 |

[30] For simplicity, we focus on annual compounding and ignore the possibility of depositing money in Bank C.

the present value of a dollar to be received *n* periods in the future at interest rate *r*. (A portion of that table is reproduced here for convenience.)

Using Han's two gift options as a concrete example, we can show you how to use Table 1. Look at the intersection of the Period 2 row and the 6% column and you will see the number 0.89000 (highlighted). This number is the factor that represents the present value of a dollar to be received at the end of two years at a 6% per period **discount rate**. To verify this, notice that if 89¢ were invested at 6% compounded annually for two years, it would accumulate to:

> Discount rate is what the interest rate is called when computing present values.

| Date | Interest Calculation | Accumulated Amount |
|---|---|---|
| Initial principal | | $0.89 |
| Year 1 | $0.89 × 0.06 = 0.0534. Then, $0.89 + 0.0534 | =$0.9434 |
| Year 2 | $0.9434 × 0.06 = 0.0566. Then, $0.9434 + 0.0566 | =$1.00 |

Because 0.89000 is the present value factor for one dollar, the present value for 1,123.60 dollars (Alice's parents' second birthday choice amount) is $1,123.60 × 0.89000 = $1,000. So, you see how Table 1 helps us verify that the two gift amounts have identical present values.

Careful examination of Table 1 reveals two general characteristics of present value computations. First, looking *down any column,* you can see that the numbers become smaller. For example, in the 6% column, the number in the Period 3 row is 0.83962, which is smaller than 0.89000—the number in the Period 2 row. This illustrates that the further in the future is the dollar flow, the smaller is its present value. Second, looking to the right *across any row,* the numbers again become smaller. For example, in the Period 2 row, in the 7% column, the number 0.87344 is smaller than 0.89000—the number in the 6% column. This illustrates that the higher the discount rate is (7% versus 6%), the smaller the present value of $1 is. Why? Because the higher the discount rate is, the smaller is the amount that must be invested at *r*% to equal $1 in *n* periods. At 7%, only 87.344¢ must be invested to equal $1 in two periods, whereas at 6%, 89¢ must be invested to equal $1 in two periods.

## Present Value of an Ordinary Annuity

Jacquie Henderson has just won the state lottery's $100,000 Bonanza. The winnings are paid out in four equal installments. Each $25,000 installment is mailed to the winner on the one-year anniversary of the lottery drawing beginning 365 days from now. Jacquie understands that the discounted present value of the prize is less than $100,000 and wishes to compute its exact value using a discount rate of 5%. One way she can do this is to list each of the four payments separately and use the present value factors from Table 1. Doing it this way, the computation is:

| Payment Number | Payment Amount | Present Value Factor | Present Value |
|---|---|---|---|
| 1 | $25,000 | 0.95238 | $23,809.50 |
| 2 | 25,000 | 0.90703 | 22,675.75 |
| 3 | 25,000 | 0.86384 | 21,596.00 |
| 4 | 25,000 | 0.82270 | 20,567.50 |
| Total | | | $88,648.75 |

As the computation shows, the present value of the advertised $100,000 prize is only $88,648.75. Notice that the $25,000 undiscounted dollar amount received each period is the same. When each payment in a series is the same dollar amount, the series is called an **annuity**. When each payment is made at the *end* of each period, as in our example, that payment series is an **ordinary annuity** (also called an **annuity in arrears**).

| TABLE 2 | Present Value of an Ordinary Annuity of $1 |
|---------|--------------------------------------------|

**(Selected Excerpts)**

$$P_{OA} = \left(1 - \frac{1}{(1 + r)^n}\right)/r$$

| (n) Periods | 2% | 3% | 4% | 5% | 6% | 7% | 8% | 9% | 10% | 11% | 12% | 15% |
|-------------|------|------|------|------|------|------|------|------|------|------|------|------|
| 1 | 0.98039 | 0.97087 | 0.96154 | 0.95238 | 0.94340 | 0.93458 | 0.92593 | 0.91743 | 0.90909 | 0.90090 | 0.89286 | 0.86957 |
| 2 | 1.94156 | 1.91347 | 1.88609 | 1.85941 | 1.83339 | 1.80802 | 1.78326 | 1.75911 | 1.73554 | 1.71252 | 1.69005 | 1.62571 |
| 3 | 2.88388 | 2.82861 | 2.77509 | 2.72325 | 2.67301 | 2.62432 | 2.57710 | 2.53129 | 2.48685 | 2.44371 | 2.40183 | 2.28323 |
| 4 | 3.80773 | 3.71710 | 3.62990 | 3.54595 | 3.46511 | 3.38721 | 3.31213 | 3.23972 | 3.16987 | 3.10245 | 3.03735 | 2.85498 |
| 5 | 4.71346 | 4.57971 | 4.45182 | 4.32948 | 4.21236 | 4.10020 | 3.99271 | 3.88965 | 3.79079 | 3.69590 | 3.60478 | 3.35216 |

To compute the present value of an ordinary annuity, it isn't necessary to compute the present value of each payment separately as we just did. Instead, Table 2 of Appendix 1 at the back of the book provides present value factors for ordinary annuities of various lengths at selected discount rates. A portion of Table 2 is reproduced here for convenience.

Notice in Table 2 that the intersection of the Period 4 row and the 5% column contains the factor 3.54595 (highlighted). This number is simply the sum of the four present value factors we just used in the lottery computation. Specifically:

| Payment Number | Present Value Factor |
|:--------------:|:--------------------:|
| 1 | 0.95238 |
| 2 | 0.90703 |
| 3 | 0.86384 |
| 4 | 0.82270 |
| Total | 3.54595 |

So, you see that 3.54595 is the present value of an ordinary annuity of $1.00 each period for four periods. To determine the present value of an ordinary annuity of $25,000 each period for four periods, we multiply 3.54595 times $25,000. The product, $88,648.75, is identical to the number we just computed more tediously for the present value of Jacquie Henderson's lottery winnings.

## Present Value of an Annuity Due

Let's return to the lottery example and assume now that Henderson receives the first lottery check immediately. The next three checks follow at one-year intervals, that is, at the start of each of the next three periods. When each payment is made at the *beginning* of the period, as we now assume in this example, that payment series is an **annuity due** (also called an **annuity in advance**).

To determine the present value of the lottery winnings when the payout is an annuity due, we can again compute from Table 1 the present value at 5% of each of the $25,000 checks, remembering that the present value factor for the first payment received *today* is 1.0000:

| Payment Number | Payment Amount | Present Value Factor | Present Value |
|:--------------:|:--------------:|:--------------------:|:-------------:|
| 1 | $25,000 | 1.00000 | $25,000.00 |
| 2 | 25,000 | 0.95238 | 23,809.50 |
| 3 | 25,000 | 0.90703 | 22,675.75 |
| 4 | 25,000 | 0.86384 | 21,596.00 |
| Total | | | $93,081.25 |

## TABLE 3                    Present Value of an Annuity Due of $1

### (Selected Excerpts)

$$P_{AD} = 1 + \left(1 - \frac{1}{(1 + r)^{n-1}}\right)/r$$

| (n) Periods | 2% | 3% | 4% | 5% | 6% | 7% | 8% | 9% | 10% | 11% | 12% | 15% |
|---|---|---|---|---|---|---|---|---|---|---|---|---|
| 1 | 1.00000 | 1.00000 | 1.00000 | 1.00000 | 1.00000 | 1.00000 | 1.00000 | 1.00000 | 1.00000 | 1.00000 | 1.00000 | 1.00000 |
| 2 | 1.98039 | 1.97087 | 1.96154 | 1.95238 | 1.94340 | 1.93458 | 1.92593 | 1.91743 | 1.90909 | 1.90090 | 1.89286 | 1.86957 |
| 3 | 2.94156 | 2.91347 | 2.88609 | 2.85941 | 2.83339 | 2.80802 | 2.78326 | 2.75911 | 2.73554 | 2.71252 | 2.69005 | 2.62571 |
| 4 | 3.88388 | 3.82861 | 3.77509 | 3.72325 | 3.67301 | 3.62432 | 3.57710 | 3.53129 | 3.48685 | 3.44371 | 3.40183 | 3.28323 |
| 5 | 4.80773 | 4.71710 | 4.62990 | 4.54595 | 4.46511 | 4.38721 | 4.31213 | 4.23972 | 4.16987 | 4.10245 | 4.03735 | 3.85498 |

When the lottery payments are made at the start of the year rather than at the end of the year (that is, an annuity due rather than an ordinary annuity), the present value of those payments is higher—$93,081.25 versus only $88,648.75 for the ordinary annuity.

Tables for computing the present value of an annuity due are also available; see Table 3 of Appendix 1 at the back of this book. A portion of Table 3 is reproduced here for convenience.

The highlighted present value factor at the intersection of the Period 4 row and the 5% column is 3.72325. Multiplying 3.72325 times $25,000 yields $93,081.25, the answer we just computed. And, if you have suspected that the 3.72325 factor is simply the sum of 1.00000 + 0.95238 + 0.90703 + 0.86384, your suspicion is not only correct but also you understand annuities, discount rates, and present value.

## EXERCISES

### E8-1

Analyzing accounts receivable

AICPA
ADAPTED

For the month of December 2008, Ranger Corporation's records show the following information:

| | |
|---|---:|
| Cash received on accounts receivable | $35,000 |
| Cash sales | 30,000 |
| Accounts receivable, December 1, 2008 | 80,000 |
| Accounts receivable, December 31, 2008 | 74,000 |
| Accounts receivable written off as uncollectible | 1,000 |

**Required:**
Determine the gross sales for the month of December 2008.

### E8-2

Analyzing accounts receivable

AICPA
ADAPTED

At the close of its first year of operations on December 31, 2008, Walker Company had accounts receivable of $250,000, which were *net* of the related allowance for doubtful accounts. During 2008, the company had charges to bad debt expense of $40,000 and wrote off, as uncollectible, accounts receivable of $10,000.

**Required:**
What should the company report on its balance sheet at December 31, 2008 as accounts receivable *before* the allowance for doubtful accounts?

### E8-3

Determining ratio effects of write-offs

AICPA
ADAPTED

Delta Corporation wrote off a $100 uncollectible account receivable against the $1,200 balance in its allowance account.

**Required:**
For the following amounts or ratios, determine the relationship between the amount or ratio before the write-off (x) with the amount or ratio after the write-off (y):

| Amount or Ratio | Possibilities |
|---|---|
| 1. Current ratio | a. *x* more than *y* |
| 2. Net accounts receivable balance | b. *x* equals *y* |
| 3. Gross accounts receivable balance | c. *x* less than *y* |
| | d. Cannot be determined |

---

The following information is available for Parker Company:

| | |
|---|---|
| Credit sales during 2008 | $100,000 |
| Allowance for doubtful accounts at December 31, 2007 | 1,200 |
| Accounts receivable deemed worthless and written off during 2008 | 1,600 |

During 2008, Parker estimated that its bad debt expense should be 1% of all credit sales.

As a result of a review and aging of accounts receivable in early January 2009, it has been determined that an allowance for doubtful accounts of $1,100 is needed at December 31, 2008.

**Required:**

What is the total amount that Parker should record as Bad debt expense for the year ended December 31, 2008?

**E 8-4**

Determining bad debt expense

**AICPA**
ADAPTED

---

Lake Company sold some machinery to View Company on January 1, 2008 for which the cash selling price was $758,200. View entered into an installment sales contract with Lake at a 10% interest rate. The contract required payments of $200,000 a year over five years with the first payment due on December 31, 2008.

**Required:**

Prepare an amortization schedule that shows what portion of each $200,000 payment will be shown as interest income over the period 2008–2012.

**E 8-5**

Preparing an amortization schedule

**AICPA**
ADAPTED

---

Weaver, Inc. received a $60,000, six-month, 12% interest-bearing note from a customer. The note was discounted the same day at Third National Bank at 15%.

**Required:**

Compute the amount of cash Weaver received from the bank.

**E 8-6**

Discounting a note

**AICPA**
ADAPTED

---

On January 1, 2008, Carpet Company loaned $100,000 to its supplier, Loom Corporation, which was evidenced by a note, payable in five years. Interest at 5% is payable annually with the first payment due on December 31, 2008. The going rate of interest for this type of loan is 10%. The parties agreed that Loom will meet Carpet's inventory needs for the loan period at favorable prices. Assume that the present value (at the going rate of interest) of the $100,000 note is $81,000 at January 1, 2008.

**Required:**

1. Show the journal entry that Carpet would make to record interest and the receipt of cash at December 31, 2008.

2. What is the nature of the account that arises as a consequence of the difference between the 5% cash interest and the effective yield of 10%?

**E 8-7**

Recording note receivable carrying amount

**AICPA**
ADAPTED

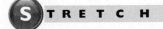

---

On December 31, 2008, Vale Company had an unadjusted credit balance of $1,000 in its Allowance for uncollectible accounts. An analysis of Vale's trade accounts receivable at that date revealed the following:

| Age | Amount | Estimated Uncollectible |
|---|---|---|
| 0–30 days | $60,000 | 5% |
| 31–60 days | 4,000 | 10 |
| Over 60 days | 2,000 | 70 |

**E 8-8**

Aging accounts receivables

**AICPA**
ADAPTED

**Required:**

What amount should Vale report as allowance for uncollectible accounts in its December 31, 2008 balance sheet?

---

**E 8-9**

Analyzing accounts receivable

**AICPA**
ADAPTED

The following information relates to Jay Company's accounts receivable for 2008:

| | |
|---|---|
| Accounts receivable, 1/1/08 | $ 650,000 |
| Credit sales for 2008 | 2,700,000 |
| Sales returns for 2008 | 75,000 |
| Accounts written off during 2008 | 40,000 |
| Collections from customers during 2008 | 2,150,000 |
| Estimated future sales returns at 12/31/08 | 50,000 |
| Estimated uncollectible accounts at 12/31/08 | 110,000 |

**Required:**

What amount should Jay report for accounts receivable before allowances for sales returns and uncollectible accounts at December 31, 2008?

---

**E 8-10**

Valuing outstanding consignments

**AICPA**
ADAPTED

Mare Company's December 31, 2008 balance sheet reported the following current assets:

| | |
|---|---|
| Cash | $ 70,000 |
| Accounts receivable | 120,000 |
| Inventories | 60,000 |
| Total | $250,000 |

An analysis of the accounts disclosed that accounts receivable consisted of the following:

| | |
|---|---|
| Trade accounts | $ 96,000 |
| Allowance for uncollectible accounts | (2,000) |
| Selling price of Mare's unsold goods | |
| out on consignment, at 130% of cost, | |
| not included in Mare's ending inventory | 26,000 |
| Total | $120,000 |

**Required:**

What are the correct totals for cash, accounts receivable, and inventories at December 31, 2008?

---

**E 8-11**

Determining whether it's a real sale

Blue, Inc. sells playground equipment to schools and municipalities. It mails invoices at the end of each month for all goods shipped during that month; credit terms are net 30 days. Sales and accounts receivable data for 2008, 2009, and 2010 follow:

| | Years Ending December 31 | | |
|---|---|---|---|
| | **2008** | **2009** | **2010** |
| Sales | $1,785,980 | $1,839,559 | $1,986,724 |
| Accounts receivable at year-end | 220,189 | 227,896 | 267,094 |

**Required:**

1. Calculate the rates of increase in sales and in receivables during 2009 and 2010.

2. Do your calculations indicate any potential problems with Blue's receivables?

3. If so, suggest a possible explanation for your findings and indicate what action, if any, would then be needed to bring Blue's financial statements into conformity with GAAP.

---

**E 8-12**

Calculating imputed interest on noninterest-bearing note

On December 31, 2008, Fenton Company sold equipment to Denver, Inc., accepting a $275,000 noninterest-bearing note receivable in full payment on December 31, 2011. Denver, Inc., normally pays 12% for its borrowed funds. The equipment is carried in Fenton's perpetual inventory records at 65% of its cash selling price.

**Required:**

1. Prepare Fenton's journal entries to record the sale on December 31, 2008.
2. Prepare Fenton's journal entry on December 31, 2008 necessitated by this transaction. (*Hint:* Prepare an amortization schedule for the loan.)
3. Show Fenton's balance sheet presentation of Denver's note at December 31, 2009.

---

Slifer, Inc. sells $125,000 of its accounts receivable to M&T Finance with recourse. M&T charges a 3% fee and withholds 10% of the face amount of the receivables to cover possible uncollectible accounts and sales returns.

**E8-13**

**Factoring receivables**

**Required:**

1. Prepare the journal entry Slifer would make to record the factoring.
2. Prepare Slifer's journal entry to record any subsequent cash received from M&T if M&T collects all of the factored receivables except for two accounts: $2,500 (due to a sales return) and $2,000 (resulting from a bad debt).

---

Smithfield Farms purchased a combine from John Deere for $175,000 on January 2, 2008. Smithfield paid $25,000 in cash and signed an installment note calling for five annual payments of $39,569.58 beginning on December 31, 2008. Deere based the payments on a 10% rate of interest. Smithfield made the first payment, but a failed harvest in 2009 left it unable to make the upcoming payment. Deere agreed to repossess the combine—which had a market value of $132,000—on December 31, 2009—and cancel the note. Deere accrued interest on the loan for 2009 prior to canceling the note.

**E8-14**

**Recording troubled debt settlement**

**Required:**

Prepare the journal entry John Deere would make on December 31, 2009 to record the settlement.

---

Central Valley Construction (CVC) purchased $80,000 of sheet metal fabricating equipment from Buffalo Supply on January 1, 2008. CVC paid $15,000 cash and signed a five-year, 10% note for the remaining $65,000 of the purchase price. The note specifies that payments of $13,000 plus interest be made each year on the loan's anniversary date. CVC made the required January 1, 2009 payment but was unable to make the second payment on January 1, 2010 because of a downturn in the construction industry. At this time, CVC owed Buffalo Supply $52,000 plus $5,200 interest that had been accrued by both companies. Rather than write off the note and repossess the equipment, Buffalo Supply agreed to restructure the loan as one payment of $50,000 on January 1, 2012 to satisfy the restructured note.

**E8-15**

**Recording troubled debt restructuring**

**Required:**

Prepare the entries CVC and Buffalo Supply would make on January 1, 2010 to record the restructuring.

## PROBLEMS / DISCUSSION QUESTIONS

Aardvark, Inc. began 2008 with the following receivables-related account balances:

| | |
|---|---|
| Accounts receivable | $575,000 |
| Allowance for uncollectibles | 43,250 |

**P8-1**

**Determining balance sheet presentation and preparing journal entries for various receivables transactions**

Aardvark's transactions during 2008 include the following:

1. On April 1, 2008, Aardvark accepted an 8%, 12-month note from Smith Bros. in settlement of a $17,775 past due account.
2. Aardvark finally ceased all efforts to collect $23,200 from various customers and wrote off their accounts.

3. Total sales for the year (80% on credit) were $1,765,000. Cash receipts from customers as reported on Aardvark's cash flow statement were $1,925,000.

4. Sales for 2008 as reported included $100,000 of merchandise that Jensen, Inc. ordered from Aardvark. Unfortunately, a shipping department error resulted in items valued at $150,000 being shipped and invoiced to Jensen. Because Jensen believed that it could eventually use the unordered items, it agreed to keep them in exchange for a 10% reduction in their price to cover storage costs.

5. On February 1, 2008, Aardvark borrowed $65,000 from Sun Bank and pledged receivables in that amount as collateral for the loan. Interest of 5% was deducted from the cash proceeds. In June, Aardvark repaid the loan.

6. Aardvark estimates uncollectible accounts using the sales revenue approach. In past years, bad debt expense was estimated at 1% of gross sales revenue, but a weaker economy in 2008 led management to increase the estimate to 1.5% of gross sales revenue.

7. On July 1, 2008, Aardvark sold equipment to Zebra Company and received a $100,000 noninterest-bearing note receivable due in three years. The equipment normally sells for $79,383. Assume that the appropriate rate of interest for this transaction is 8%.

**Required:**

1. Prepare journal entries for each of the preceding events. Also prepare any needed entries to accrue interest on the notes at December 31, 2008.

2. Show Aardvark's balance sheet presentation for accounts and notes receivable at December 31, 2008.

---

**P8-2**

Determining balance sheet presentation and preparing journal entries for various receivables transactions

Baer Enterprises's balance sheet at October 31, 2008 (fiscal year-end) includes the following:

| | |
|---|---|
| Accounts receivable | $379,000 |
| Less: Allowance for uncollectible accounts | (33,000) |
| Accounts receivable (net) | $346,000 |

Transactions for fiscal year 2009 include the following:

1. Due to a product defect, previously sold merchandise totaling $10,500 was returned.

2. Customer accounts totaling $29,750 were written off during the year.

3. On November 1, 2008, Baer sold teleconferencing equipment and received a $75,000 noninterest-bearing note receivable due in three years. The normal cash selling price for the equipment is $56,349. Assume that the appropriate interest rate for this transaction is 10%.

4. Credit sales during the year were $395,000; collections totaled $355,000.

5. Baer sold Hartman, Inc. $45,000 of accounts receivable without recourse. Hartman's fee for factoring receivables is 9%.

6. Utilizing the gross receivables approach, Baer determined that the 2009 fiscal year-end allowance for uncollectible accounts should be $35,000.

**Required:**

1. Prepare journal entries for each of these events. Also prepare the entry to accrue interest income on the note.

2. Show Baer's balance sheet presentation for accounts and notes receivable at October 31, 2009.

---

**P8-3**

Determining allowance for uncollectibles

Avillion Corporation had a $45,000 debit balance in accounts receivable and a $3,500 credit balance in allowance for uncollectibles on December 31, 2008. The company prepared the following aging schedule to record the adjusting entry for bad debts on December 31, 2008.

| Age of Receivables | Amount | Expected Bad Debts |
|---|---|---|
| 0–30 days old | $30,000 | 5% |
| 31–90 days old | 10,000 | 11 |
| Over 90 days old | 5,000 | 30 |

1. On January 1, 2009, the company learned that one of its customers (Smith Corporation), which owed $2,000, had filed for bankruptcy and could be unable to pay the amount due.

2. On March 1, 2009, Smith Corporation's bankruptcy was finalized and the bankruptcy court notified all of its creditors (including Avillion Corporation) that Smith Corporation will pay 60 cents on the dollar for the amount owed to its creditors.

3. On May 7, 2009, Avillion Corporation received a check from Smith Corporation for the amount indicated by the court.

**Required:**

1. Provide journal entries to record the preceding transactions in Avillion's books. In addition, using the following table format, show the effects of each transaction on the following financial statement items. Clearly indicate the amount and the direction of the effects (use "+" for increase, "−" for decrease, and "NE" for no effect).

| | Assets | Liabilities | Net Income | Cash Flow from Operations |
|---|---|---|---|---|
| Direction of effect | | | | |
| Dollar amount of effect | | | | |

2. Assume that Avillion had instead prepared the following aging schedule on December 31, 2008:

| Age of Receivables | Amount | Expected Bad Debts |
|---|---|---|
| 0–30 days old | $30,000 | 3% |
| 31–90 days old | 10,000 | 8 |
| Over 90 days old | 5,000 | 22 |

Redo requirement (1) using the revised aging schedule.

---

At December 31, 2007, Oettinger Corporation, a premium kitchen cabinetmaker for the home remodeling industry, reported the following accounts receivable information on its year-end balance sheet:

**P 8-4**

Preparing journal entries, aging analysis, and balance sheet presentation

| | |
|---|---|
| Gross accounts receivable | $850,000 |
| Less: Allowance for uncollectibles | (25,000) |
| Accounts receivable (net) | $825,000 |

During 2008, the company had credit sales of $8,200,000 of which it collected $7,975,000. Oettinger employs the sales revenue approach to estimate bad debt expense and, continuing to use the same 1% used in previous years, made the normal adjustment at the end of 2008.

Although 2008 started off well, the industry experienced a slowdown in the last four months of the year, and cash collections consequently dropped off substantially. Moreover, a major customer, which owed Oettinger $85,000, unexpectedly filed for bankruptcy and went out of business during November at which time its account was written off. Oettinger's controller is concerned that some customers are experiencing cash flow problems and that the company's allowance for uncollectible accounts is too low. As a result, she prepared the following schedule:

| % of Accounts Receivable Balance | Number of Days Past Due | Estimated % Collectible |
|---|---|---|
| 20% | 0–30 | 98% |
| 40 | 31–60 | 95 |
| 35 | 61–90 | 85 |
| 3 | 91–120 | 75 |
| 2 | Over 120 | 50 |

**Required:**

1. Determine Oettinger's accounts receivable balance at December 31, 2008. Prepare a journal entry for each transaction affecting the accounts receivable balance for 2008.

2. Prepare an aging analysis to compute the required balance in the Allowance for uncollectible accounts at December 31, 2008.

3. Prepare any other required journal entries affecting the Allowance for uncollectible accounts for the year ended December 31, 2008. (Do not duplicate any entries from requirement 1.)

4. Show Oettinger's balance sheet presentation of accounts receivable at December 31, 2008.

---

**P 8-5**

Analyzing accounts receivable

AICPA
ADAPTED

The following information is available for Hokum Company:

| ($ in thousands) | 2008 | 2009 | 2010 |
|---|---|---|---|
| Charge sales | $900 | $1,100 | $1,000 |
| Cash sales | 600 | 800 | 700 |
| Total | $1,500 | $1,900 | $1,700 |
| Accounts receivable (end of year) | $170 | $230 | $220 |
| Allowance for doubtful accounts (end of year) | 47 | 30 | 56 |
| Accounts written off as uncollectible (during the year) | 2 | 50 | 4 |

**Required:**

Assuming *no* change in the method used for estimating doubtful accounts during 2008–2010, determine the balance in the Allowance for doubtful accounts at the beginning of 2008. (*Hint:* Use T-accounts.)

---

**P 8-6**

Analyzing accounts receivable

The following information pertains to the financial statements of Buffalo Supply Company, a provider of plumbing fixtures to contractors in central Pennsylvania.

| | Fiscal Years Ended October 31 | | |
|---|---|---|---|
| | 2008 | 2007 | 2006 |
| **From Income Statements** | | | |
| Revenues | $3,519,444 | $3,877,135 | $2,969,981 |
| Bad debt expense | 45,753 | 50,403 | 38,610 |
| **From Balance Sheets** | | | |
| Gross accounts receivable | $ 345,044 | $ 362,349 | $ 282,855 |
| Less: Allowance for doubtful accounts | (54,654) | (74,365) | (47,612) |
| Net accounts receivable | $ 290,390 | $ 287,984 | $ 235,243 |

**Required:**

Reconstruct all journal entries pertaining to Gross accounts receivable and Allowance for doubtful accounts for the fiscal year ended October 31, 2008. Assume that all revenues are from credit sales. (*Hint:* Begin by doing a T-account analysis of both accounts, starting with the allowance account.)

On December 31, 2002, Sea Containers Ltd., a company located in Hamilton, Bermuda, reported notes receivable of $63,930,000. This amount represents the present value of future cash flows (both principal and interest) discounted at a rate of 11.12% per annum. The schedule of collections of the receivables is provided next:

**P 8-7**

Scheduling interest received

mhhe.com/revsine4e

| ($ in thousands) | Year Ending December | Collections |
|---|---|---|
| | 2003 | $20,724 |
| | 2004 | 15,896 |
| | 2005 | 11,559 |
| | 2006 | 7,179 |
| | 2007 | 8,559 |
| | 2008 | 13 |
| | | $63,930 |

Assume that the interest due is paid along with the face value of the receivables at the end of each year.

**Required:**

Provide journal entries to record the interest received and the notes receivable collected in each year.

On January 2, 2008, Healthy Farms purchased from Deerfield Ag Center a new piece of machinery that had a cash selling price of $127,255. As payment, Healthy gave Deerfield a $150,000, five-year note that provided for annual interest payments at 6%. At the time of the sale, the interest rate normally charged to farms with Healthy's credit rating is 10%.

**P 8-8**

Imputing interest on a nominal interest-bearing note

mhhe.com/revsine4e

**Required:**

1. Prepare Deerfield's journal entry to record the sale.

2. Prepare the journal entry to record the first interest payment Deerfield received on December 31, 2008.

3. Determine the note receivable balance that Deerfield will report on December 31, 2009.

The following information is adapted from the financial statements of Buck Hill Falls Company. The company provides recreational facilities, water and sewage services, and miscellaneous maintenance services to residents of Buck Hill Falls, Monroe County, Pennsylvania.

**P 8-9**

Analyzing accounts receivable

### Buck Hill Falls Company

| | Fiscal Years Ended October 31 | | |
|---|---|---|---|
| | **Year 3** | **Year 2** | **Year 1** |
| **From Income Statements** | | | |
| Revenues | $2,175,475 | $2,218,139 | $2,203,529 |
| Provision for doubtful accounts | 20,585 | 150,631 | 95,241 |
| **From Balance Sheets** | | | |
| Gross accounts receivable | $ 353,723 | $ 325,229 | $ 210,758 |
| (−) Allowance for doubtful accounts | (100,445) | (79,860) | (35,000) |
| Net accounts receivable | $ 253,278 | $ 245,369 | $ 175,758 |

*Note:* Bad debt expense is frequently referred to as Provision for doubtful accounts.

**Required:**

1. Reconstruct all journal entries pertaining to Gross accounts receivable and Allowance for doubtful accounts (that is, Allowance for uncollectibles) for the fiscal years ended October 31, Year 2 and October 31, Year 3. You may assume that all revenues are from credit sales. (*Hint:* Use T-accounts.)

2. Try to identify scenarios consistent with the allowance and write-off activity reported over the Year 1–Year 3 period.

---

**P8-10**

Recording cash discounts and sales returns

On February 7, 2008, Jilian Company sold 20,000 sweatshirts to customers for $130,000 using credit terms of 2/10, n/30. These credit terms mean that customers will receive a 2% cash discount of the invoice price for payments made within 10 days of the sale (this is what the 2/10 signifies). If payment is not made within 10 days, the entire invoice price is due no later than the 30th day (this is what the n/30 signifies). On February 16, 2008, various customers made payment on one-half of the total receivables (discounts are recorded in a Cash discounts account that is reported as a contra-revenue item on the income statement). A customer returned goods with a $5,000 selling price on February 25, 2008. It paid the balance due (from the remaining receivables) on March 5, 2008.

**Required:**

1. Provide journal entries to record the preceding transactions in Jilian's books; assume that Jilian records sales returns when customers actually return the goods.

2. Assume that the borrowing rate for Jilian's customers is 18%. Demonstrate that the customers not paying within 10 days would be better off borrowing the money if necessary to make payment within the discount period.

---

**P8-11**

Recording cash discounts and sales returns

On January 1, 2008, Hillock Brewing Company sold 50,000 bottles of beer to various customers for $45,000 using credit terms of 3/10, n/30. These credit terms mean that customers receive a cash discount of 3% of invoice price for payments made within 10 days of the sale (this is what the 3/10 signifies). If payment is not made within 10 days, the entire invoice price is due no later than the 30th day (this is what the n/30 signifies). At the time of sale, Hillock expects sales returns of 5%. On January 9, 2008, customers made payment on one-half of the total receivables. They returned goods with a selling price of $2,000 on January 15, 2008. They paid the balance due on January 28, 2008.

**Required:**

1. Provide journal entries to record the preceding transactions in Hillock's books; assume that Hillock records *expected sales* returns at the time of sales.

2. Redo requirement (1) assuming that customers returned goods with a selling price of $3,000 on January 15, 2008.

3. Provide journal entries to record the preceding transactions in Hillock's books; assume that Hillock records sales returns when customers *actually* return the goods.

4. Because the net sales revenue is the same under both methods—requirements (1) and (3)—what is the advantage of recording anticipated sales returns rather than waiting to record them when the customers actually return the goods?

5. Assuming that the incremental annualized borrowing rate for a customer is 18%, are customers better off paying within 10 days to receive the discount or should they wait to pay until the 30th day?

Mik-Gen Corporation has a $100,000 bond sinking fund payment due in early August. To meet its obligation, it decided on August 1 to accelerate collection of accounts receivable by assigning $130,000 of specified accounts to a commercial lender as collateral for a loan. Under the agreement, Mik-Gen guarantees the accounts and will notify its customers to make their payments directly to the lender; in return, the lender advances Mik-Gen 85% of the accounts assigned. The remaining 15% will be paid to Mik-Gen once the commercial lender has recovered its fees and related cash advances. The lender receives a fee of 5% of the total accounts assigned, which is immediately deducted from the initial cash advance. The lender also assesses a monthly finance charge of one-half of 1% on any uncollected balances. Finance charges are to be deducted from the first payment due Mik-Gen after the lender has recovered its cash advances.

On August 31, Mik-Gen received a statement from the lender saying it had collected $80,000. On September 30, Mik-Gen received a check from the lender with a second statement saying it has collected an additional $40,000.

**Required:**

1. Prepare all necessary journal entries.

2. Show the balance sheet presentation of the assigned accounts receivable and any related liabilities at August 31.

| | |
|---|---|
| **P8-12** | |
| **Balance sheet effects of collateralized borrowing** | |

---

Atherton Manufacturing Company sold $200,000 of accounts receivable to a factor. Pertinent facts about this transaction include the following:

1. The factored receivables had a corresponding $4,000 balance in Allowance for uncollectibles.

2. The receivables were factored on a without recourse basis with notification (that is, the customers were instructed to mail their checks directly to the factor).

3. Atherton remained responsible for sales returns, and the factor retained a 5% holdback for this purpose.

4. The factor charged 1% interest on the gross receivables factored plus a 6% factoring fee, both of which the factor deducted from the value of receivables.

5. Customers returned inventory with a $3,000 selling price. All remaining accounts were settled, and the factor paid the balance due. Assume that Atherton records sales returns only when goods are returned (that is, it does not record an allowance for sales returns).

6. The factor incurred actual bad debts of $7,500.

**Required:**

Provide journal entries to record:

1. The receipt of proceeds from the factor.

2. Treatment of sales returns.

3. Any other items related to the pertinent facts, including the final cash settlement from the factor.

| | |
|---|---|
| **P8-13** | |
| **Factoring receivables** | |

---

The following information is taken from the financial statements of Ramsay Health Care Inc.:

| | Year 3 | Year 2 |
|---|---|---|
| | **Excerpts from Balance Sheets as of End of** | |
| Gross accounts receivable | $26,944,000 | $31,651,000 |
| Allowance for doubtful accounts | (3,925,000) | (4,955,000) |
| Net accounts receivable | $23,019,000 | $26,696,000 |

*(continued)*

| | |
|---|---|
| **P8-14** | |
| **Reconstructing T-accounts** | |
| **S TRETCH** | |

| | Excerpts from Income Statements for the Years Ended | | |
|---|---|---|---|
| | Year 3 | Year 2 | Year 1 |
| Revenue | $137,002,000 | $136,354,000 | $136,946,000 |
| Provision for doubtful accounts | 5,846,000 | 8,148,000 | 8,628,000 |
| Operating income before taxes | 6,900,000 | (1,048,000) | 9,321,000 |

*Note:* Bad debt expense is frequently referred to as Provision for doubtful accounts.

**Required:**

1. Reconstruct all journal entries relating to Gross accounts receivable and Allowance for doubtful accounts (that is, Allowance for uncollectibles) for the year ended December 31, Year 3. You may assume that all revenues are from credit sales.

2. Assume that the company computes its bad debt expense by multiplying sales revenues by some percentage (called the *sales revenue approach*). Recalculate the bad debt expense (that is, Provision for doubtful accounts) for Year 3; assume that Ramsay estimated the Year 3 bad debts at the same percentage of revenue as it did in Year 2. Based on the revised figure, show how to present Gross accounts receivable and Allowance for doubtful accounts as of the end of Year 3. Also calculate a revised operating income before taxes using the revised figure for bad debt expense.

3. In answering this part, assume that the company is using the gross accounts receivable approach to estimate its bad debt expense (that is, assume that Allowance for doubtful accounts is fixed as a percentage of gross receivables). Recalculate the bad debts expense for Year 3 *and* the ending balance in Allowance for doubtful accounts at the end of Year 3; assume that Ramsay estimated the expected bad debts at the same percentage of receivables as it did in Year 2. Also, calculate the revised operating income before taxes using the revised figure for bad debt expense.

4. Based on your answers to requirements (2) and (3), what inferences can be drawn about Ramsay's accounts receivables management and the adequacy of the Allowance for doubtful accounts?

---

**P8-15**

Restructuring a note receivable

mhhe.com/revsine4e

Fish Spotters, Inc. purchased a single-engine aircraft from National Aviation on January 1, 2008. Fish Spotters paid $55,000 cash and signed a three-year, 8% note for the remaining $45,000. Terms of the note require Fish Spotters to pay accrued interest annually on December 31 with the remaining $45,000 balance due with the last interest payment on December 31, 2010. Fish Spotters made the first two interest payments but was unable to make the principal and interest payment due December 31, 2010. On January 1, 2011 National Aviation agreed to restructure the note receivable.

**Required:**

Provide the journal entries that National Aviation would record under each of the following independent scenarios.

1. It agrees to take the aircraft back in return for the outstanding note. Assume that the aircraft has a market value of $40,000.

2. It agrees to accept a $5,000 cash payment and a new $35,000 note receivable due in five years. The note stipulates payment of $4,200 annual interest each December 31. Prepare the note receivable amortization table through December 31, 2015 and all entries through December 31, 2013.

Warren Companies purchased equipment for $72,000 from General Equipment Manufacturers on January 1, 2006. Warren paid $12,000 in cash and signed a five-year, 5% installment note for the remaining $60,000 of the purchase price. The note calls for annual payments of $12,000 plus interest on December 31 of each year. Warren made the first installment on time, but it was not able to make the next installment (due on December 31, 2007). On January 1, 2008 General Equipment agreed to restructure the note receivable.

**P8-16**

Restructuring a note receivable

**Required:**

Provide journal entries in the books of both Warren Companies and General Equipment Manufacturers for the period 2008–2010 under the following *independent* scenarios:

1. General Equipment accepted $20,000 in cash and old equipment fully depreciated in Warren's books (with a market value of $14,000) in exchange for the outstanding note.

2. General Equipment agreed to receive a total of $57,600 ($48,000 plus $9,600, representing four years' interest at 5%) on December 31, 2010 in exchange for the outstanding note. (Interpolate for Warren's new effective interest rate.)

3. General Equipment decides to waive all interest and defers all principal payments until December 31, 2010.

---

The following footnotes are excerpted from the financial statements of three companies:

**P8-17**

Accounting for transfer of receivables

## Ricoh Company Ltd., March 31, Year 2

### Note No. 7—Short-term Borrowings and Trade Notes Receivable Discounted with Banks

The Company and certain of its domestic subsidiaries regularly discount trade notes receivable on a full recourse basis with banks. These trade notes receivable discounted are contingent liabilities. The weighted average interest rates on these trade notes receivable discounted were 4.2% and 3.2% as of March 31, Year 1 and Year 2, respectively.

## Crown Crafts Inc., March 31, Year 2

### Note No. 4—Financing Arrangements

**Factoring Agreement** The Company assigns substantially all of its trade accounts receivable to a commercial factor. Under the terms of the factoring agreement, the factor remits invoiced amounts to the Company on the approximate due dates of the factored invoices. The Company does not borrow funds from its factor or take advances against its factored receivables balances. Accounts are factored without recourse as to credit losses but with recourse as to returns, allowances, disputes, and discounts. Factoring fees included in marketing and administrative expenses in the consolidated statements of earnings were $1,501,000 (Year 2), $1,223,000 (Year 1), and $1,077,000 (Year 0).

## Foxmeyer Corporation, March 31, Year 2

### Note C—Accounts Receivable Financing

On October 29, Year 1, the Corporation entered into a one-year agreement to sell a percentage ownership interest in a defined pool of the Corporation's trade accounts receivable with limited recourse. Proceeds of $125.0 million from the sale were used to reduce amounts outstanding under the Corporation's revolving credit facilities. Generally, an undivided interest in new accounts receivable will be sold daily as existing accounts receivable are collected to maintain the participation interest at $125.0 million. Such accounts receivable sold are not included in the accompanying consolidated balance sheet at March 31, Year 2. An allowance for doubtful accounts has been retained on the participation interest sold based on estimates of the Corporation's risk of credit loss from its obligation under the recourse provisions. The cost of the accounts receivable financing program is based on a 30-day commercial paper rate plus certain fees. The total cost of the program in Year 2 was $2.2 million and was charged against Other income in the accompanying consolidated statements of income. Under the agreement, the Corporation also acts as agent for the purchaser by performing recordkeeping and collection functions on the participation interest sold. The agreement contains certain covenants regarding the quality of the accounts receivable portfolio, as well as other covenants which are substantially identical to those contained in the Corporation's credit facilities.

**Required:**

How do the three companies record the transfer of their receivables—that is, as a sale or borrowing? Is their accounting treatment consistent with the economics of the transactions? Explain.

---

**P8-18**

Determining whether existing receivables represent real sales

Moto-Lite Company is an original equipment manufacturer of high-quality aircraft engines that it traditionally has sold directly to aero clubs building their own aircraft. The engine's selling price depends on its size and horsepower; Moto-Lite's average gross profit per engine is 35%.

To expand its sales, Moto-Lite entered into an agreement with Macco Corporation, a British manufacturer of light aircraft, to be the sole supplier of its 80 horsepower, 2 stroke engines. Under the terms of the agreement, Moto-Lite will stock a minimum of 10 engines at Macco's production facility to service aircraft production requirements. Each engine has a firm selling price of $6,000. Title to the engines does not pass until Macco uses the engine in its production process.

During its quarter ending October 31, Moto-Lite shipped and billed 19 engines (DR Accounts receivable, CR Sales) to Macco Corporation. As of that date, Macco had used 9 engines in its production process. All but three of the engines used had been paid for prior to October 31. The remaining 10 engines will be used in November.

**Required:**

1. What type of agreement does this appear to be? Was Moto-Lite correct to record all 19 motors shipped as sales in the quarter ending October 31?

2. How should the transaction be accounted for and by how much, if at all, were Moto-Lite's sales, receivables, and gross profit overstated at October 31?

---

**P8-19**

Determining whether existing receivables represent real sales

Aurora Aluminum, a vendor to Bostian Enterprises, receives Bostian's purchase order for computer drill sheets. Bostian, a maker of electronic circuit boards, implemented a production process designed to take advantage of just-in-time inventory management techniques. Accordingly, its purchase order specifically states that delivery is to be made to Bostian's assembly plant at 1 P.M. on January 16, 2009 and that payment will be 30 days after delivery.

Aurora had a lull in production activity and decided to produce Bostian's order over the Christmas holidays. After producing the material on December 27, it promptly loaded the order on a staged trailer, which was immediately locked and sealed. An invoice and a bill of lading were prepared. The invoice was immediately sent to Bostian on a "bill and hold" basis.

Upon receiving the invoice, Bostian contacted Aurora, which said that the material was invoiced because Aurora wanted to include the sale in its just closed calendar year-end; however, actual delivery would take place in accordance with the purchase order terms and that payment would be expected 30 days after delivery. Moreover, risk of ownership would remain with Aurora until delivery. Bostian accepted the explanation and reminded Aurora that it could not accept the material prior to its scheduled delivery date due to space constraints.

**Required:**

Was Aurora correct to include the Bostian transaction as a sale and account receivable in calendar year 2008? Explain.

---

The following facts pertain to the year ended December 31, 2008 of Grosse Pointe Corporation, a manufacturer of power tools.

**P8-20**

Channel stuffing

1. Based on year-to-date sales through early December, management projected 2008 sales to be 5% below their forecast target for the year.

2. The 2008 sales forecast included projected sales of a new string trimmer that it introduced late in the third quarter of 2008; unfortunately for Grosse Pointe, actual customer orders for the new product through early December had been disappointing.

3. Effective December 15, 2008, Grosse Pointe began providing the following incentives to boost sales of the new string trimmer: (a) normal 2/10, n/30 payment terms were extended to n/90 and (b) full right of return for 90 days was granted on all trimmers purchased during the last two weeks of December.

4. Grosse Pointe has never before been forced to offer such incentives and thus has no basis for estimating return rates or default rates on these sales.

5. Sales of the new trimmer for October 1 to December 15, 2008 were $1,265,000.

6. The marketing department began aggressively promoting the new trimmer by stressing the incentives' "no-risk" nature ("if you can't sell them, just return them") and generated sales for December 15 to 31, 2008 of $2,391,000. Management included all of this revenue to make the company's sales target for 2008. Grosse Pointe uses a perpetual inventory system and charged $1,650,000 to Cost of goods sold when these sales were made.

**Required:**

1. Is Grosse Pointe correct to recognize the Incentive sales and related Accounts receivable in 2008? Explain.

2. If Grosse Pointe's auditors do not concur with management's desired accounting treatment, what correcting entries are needed?

---

## CASES

Appearing next is information pertaining to Garrels Company's Allowance for doubtful accounts. Examine this information and answer the following questions.

**C8-1**

Garrels Company: Analyzing allowances—Comprehensive

| | **Years Ended December 31** | | |
|---|---|---|---|
| ($ in thousands) | **2006** | **2005** | **2004** |
| Allowance for doubtful accounts | | | |
| Balance, beginning of year | ? | ? | $1,324 |
| Provision charged to expense | ? | 502 | 1,349 |
| Write-offs, less recoveries | 1 | 622 | ? |
| Balance, end of year | 1,453 | ? | 1,302 |

**Required:**

1. Solve for the unknowns in the preceding schedule. (*Hint:* Use T-accounts.)

2. Make all entries related to the Allowance for doubtful accounts account for 2004–2006.

3. Make all entries for bad debts for 2004–2006 assuming that Garrels did not accrue for estimated bad debt losses but instead recorded bad debt expense once receivables were determined to be uncollectible. (This is called the *direct write-off method.*)

4. Why does GAAP require the allowance method over the direct write-off method?

5. Calculate the cumulative difference in reported pre-tax income under the allowance and direct write-off methods over the 2004–2006 period.

6. Assume that it is the end of 2007 and Garrels management is trying to decide on the amount of the bad debt expense for 2007. Based on an aging of accounts receivable, the accounting department feels that a $400,000 provision is appropriate. However, the company just learned that a customer with an outstanding accounts receivable of $300,000 may have to file for bankruptcy. The decision facing Garrels management is whether to increase the initial provision of $400,000 by $300,000, by some lesser amount, or by nothing at all. What is your recommendation?

7. Continuing the scenario from requirement (6) now consider the following additional information. Assume that you are a member of the company's compensation committee. Assume further that the company's chief financial officer (CFO) is solely responsible for deciding the amount of bad debt expense to record and that the CFO has a cash bonus plan that is a function of reported earnings before income taxes. Specifically, assume that the CFO receives an annual cash bonus of zero if earnings before income taxes is below $17 million and 10.0% of the amount by which earnings before income taxes exceeds $17 million and up to a maximum bonus of $1 million (that is, when net income reaches $27 million, no further bonus is earned). What adjustment to the initial $400,000 bad debt provision might the CFO make in each of the following scenarios? Assume that the following earnings before income taxes include the initial $400,000 provision for bad debts.

   a. $11 million

   b. $18.2 million

   c. $38.25 million

   d. $27.15 million

8. What other scenarios can you identify in which managers might use the provision for bad debts to accomplish some contract-related strategy?

9. Identify other items in the financial statements (besides the bad debt provision) that managers have the ability to "manage."

---

**C8-2**

Comerica, Inc.: Analyzing allowance for loan losses

Access Comerica's 2005 annual report (10-K) on the SEC Web site (www.sec.gov).

**Required:**

1. Examine Note 4—Allowance for Loan Losses.

   a. How does the dollar amount of Loans charged-off in 2005 compare with that in 2004?

   b. How much was added to the Provision for loan losses in 2005?

   c. What is the trend in the ratio of Provision for loan losses to Total loans over the 2003–2005 period?

2. As a consequence of your findings in requirement (1), how (if at all) does this new information affect your expectation regarding the future performance of Comerica's existing loans? To answer this question, it will be helpful to read the portion of Management's Discussion and Analysis entitled "Provision and Allowance for Credit Losses" (pp. 28–30).

Thompson Traders started its business on January 1, 2004. The following information pertains to the company's accounts receivable during the first five years of its operations:

| | | | Bold Debts Pertaining to Sales Made During | | | | |
| Year | Revenue | Bad Debts Written Off | 2004 | 2005 | 2006 | 2007 | 2008 |
|---|---|---|---|---|---|---|---|
| 2004 | $30,000 | $ 600 | $600 | | | | |
| 2005 | 40,000 | 1,000 | 300 | $700 | | | |
| 2006 | 60,000 | 1,500 | –0– | 500 | $1,000 | | |
| 2007 | 80,000 | 2,400 | –0– | –0– | 800 | $1,600 | |
| 2008 | 90,000 | 3,000 | –0– | –0– | –0– | 800 | $2,200 |

The company typically sells on credit to its customers. All sales made in a given calendar year are fully settled by the following year, by which time all uncollected receivables are written off. Since inception, Thompson has recorded bad debts expense at 2.75% of its revenue. After five years of operation, the company is now considering a reevaluation of its bad debts formula before finalizing its financial statements for the year 2008. The following are excerpts taken from a recent meeting of Thompson's managers discussing this issue:

> Tony Barclay, Corporate Accounting: Our experience suggests that the bad debts written off have ballooned from 2% of revenues to almost 3.5%. So, while we were being very conservative in the earlier years, currently our provisions are much below our actuals. Conservatively, I recommend a formula of 3.5% of revenues.

> Ian Spencer, manager, Accounts Receivable: While I agree with Tony's computations, my experience suggests that the quality of our receivables has pretty much remained the same and I don't expect them to change in the near future. Therefore, I recommend that we retain our current formula.

> Brian Joshi, outside consultant: If you believe that you have under- or overprovided for bad debts over the last four years, you have to revise the formula to reflect your past experience and current expectations. While revising the formula will lead to correct expensing in the future, you also have to adjust the allowance account for past estimation errors. More important, because this will be considered as a change in accounting methods, you have to restate the past financial statements.

**Required:**

You have been hired as a summer intern in the corporate controller's office to examine Thompson's bad debt accounting. Based on the information provided, write a report to top management assessing the company's bad debt formula and provide specific recommendations to improve its accounting, if needed. In completing the report, please address all issues raised during the recent company meeting.

**www .mhhe.com/revsine4e**

**Remember to check the book's companion Web site
for additional study material.**

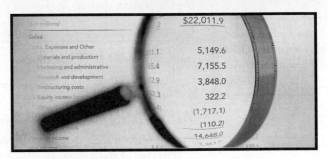

| (in millions) | | $22,011.9 |
|---|---|---|
| **Sales** | | |
| Costs, Expenses and Other | | |
| Materials and production | 01.1 | 5,149.6 |
| Marketing and administrative | 65.4 | 7,155.5 |
| Research and development | 82.9 | 3,848.0 |
| Restructuring costs | 2.3 | 322.2 |
| Equity income | 4) | (1,717.1) |
| | | (110.2) |
| | | 14,648.0 |
| income | | |

## LEARNING OBJECTIVES

**After studying this chapter, you will understand:**

1. The two methods used to determine inventory quantities: the perpetual inventory system and the periodic inventory system.

2. What specific items and types of costs are included in inventory.

3. What absorption costing is and how it complicates financial analysis.

4. The difference between various inventory cost flow assumptions: weighted average, FIFO, and LIFO.

5. How to use the LIFO reserve disclosure to transform LIFO firms to a FIFO basis and improve analytical comparability.

6. How LIFO liquidations distort gross profit and how to adjust for these distortions to improve forecasts.

7. How LIFO affects firms' income taxes.

8. What research tells us about the economic incentives guiding the choice of inventory accounting methods.

9. How to eliminate realized holding gains from FIFO income.

10. How to apply the lower of cost or market method and on what assumptions the method rests.

11. How and why the dollar-value LIFO method is applied.

A wholesaler or retailer buys assets such as business suits or shoes that are immediately salable in their current form. Assets held for sale are called **inventories.** A typical wholesaler or retailer will have only one inventory account, called **Merchandise inventory,** on its balance sheet.

A manufacturing firm making a final product such as dishwashers uses inputs from many different suppliers. Consequently, manufacturers' balance sheets typically include three categories of inventory accounts:

1. **Raw materials inventory,** which consists of components such as steel that will eventually be used in the completed product.

2. **Work-in-process inventory,** which contains the aggregate cost of units that have been started but not completed as of the balance sheet date. Work-in-process inventory includes the cost of the raw materials, direct labor, and overhead that has been incurred in the manufacture of the partially completed units.[1]

3. **Finished goods inventory,** which represents the total costs incorporated in completed but unsold units.

For most firms, inventories are a significant asset, both in absolute size and in proportion to all of a company's other assets. Furthermore, selling inventories for a price more than their cost represents the main source of a firm's sustainable income. For these reasons, inventory accounting is exceedingly important.

## AN OVERVIEW OF INVENTORY ACCOUNTING ISSUES

We will use an example of a retailer who sells refrigerators to illustrate the basic issues in inventory accounting. Assume that the retailer starts the year with a beginning inventory of one refrigerator it purchased for $300. During the year, the retailer's cost of identical refrigerators increases to $340, and the retailer purchases another refrigerator at this $340 cost. At the end of the year, the retailer sells one of the refrigerators to a consumer for $500. Assume also that it is not possible to ascertain which of the two refrigerators was actually sold.

---

[1] Manufacturing overhead includes items such as depreciation of production equipment and buildings, power, indirect labor, and so on.

*Chapter*

It is easy to determine the total cost of the goods that were available for sale. This total cost is determined by adding the cost of the beginning inventory and the cost of any purchases during the period, that is:

The total cost of the goods available for sale during the period was $640, a total that represents the aggregate *historical cost* of the two refrigerators.

The cost of the refrigerator that has been sold must be removed from the Inventory account and charged to Cost of goods sold, while the cost of the other refrigerator remains in inventory. In other words, the total cost of the goods available for sale ($640) must be allocated between ending inventory and cost of goods sold. This allocation process can be represented as follows:

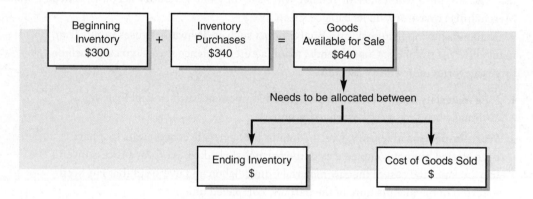

***The choice of the method for making this allocation between ending inventory and cost of goods sold represents the major issue in inventory accounting.***

Even in this simple case, the total for the goods available for sale ($640) can be allocated between ending inventory and cost of goods sold in at least three ways:

1.  One way is to assume that the refrigerator that was sold should reflect the average of the cost of the two refrigerators ($640/2 = $320), which makes the allocation:

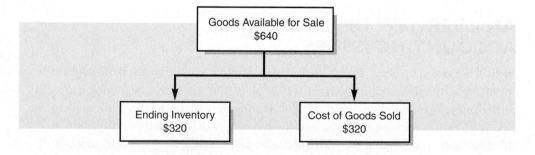

This is called the **weighted average** inventory costing method.

2.  Another possibility is to assume that the refrigerator that was sold was the oldest refrigerator in stock, the $300 unit from the beginning inventory. This means the cost assigned to the refrigerator still on hand at the end of the year is the $340 cost of the most recently purchase unit. Here, the allocation is:

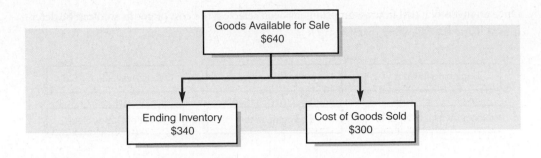

This method assumes that the first unit purchased is the first unit sold. Accountants call this **first-in, first-out (FIFO)**.

3. Another alternative is to assume that the refrigerator that was sold was the most recently purchased refrigerator, the one costing $340. This means the cost assigned to the refrigerator still on hand at the end of the year is the $300 cost of the oldest available unit that was in inventory at the start of the year, making the allocation:

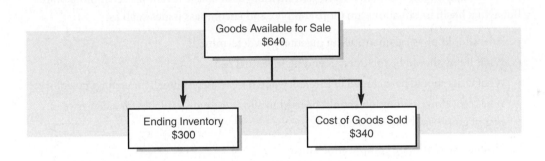

This method assumes the last unit purchased is the first unit sold. This is called **last-in, first-out (LIFO)**.

Each of these cost allocations assumes a different flow of inventory costs—average cost, FIFO, or LIFO—from goods available for sale to the ending Inventory account and to the Cost of goods sold expense account; this is why these methods are called *cost flow assumptions*. Generally accepted accounting principles (GAAP) do not require the *cost flow* assumption to correspond to the actual *physical flow* of inventory. ***If the cost of inventory never changed, all three cost flow assumptions would yield the same financial statement result.*** Also, under historical cost accounting, no matter what cost flow assumption is used, the total dollar amount allocated between cost of goods sold and ending inventory always equals the historical dollar cost of the goods available for sale ($640 in this case). This important point is shown in the following schedule:

> Although many firms use the LIFO cost flow accounting assumption, very few examples exist in which the real physical flow of units sold is also last-in, first-out. To see why, consider a grocery store. If the store actually sold the most recently acquired items first—a LIFO flow—the unsold items that were received earlier would soon become stale!

| Cost Flow Assumption | Total Historical Cost of Goods Available for Sale | = | Amount Allocated to Ending Inventory | + | Amount Allocated to Cost of Goods Sold |
|---|---|---|---|---|---|
| Weighted average | $640 | = | $320 | + | $320 |
| FIFO | $640 | = | $340 | + | $300 |
| LIFO | $640 | = | $300 | + | $340 |

Once an inventory cost flow assumption has been selected, the cost of goods sold can be determined using the following formula:

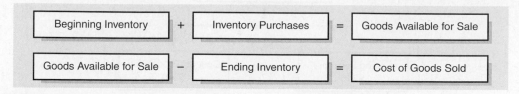

| Beginning Inventory | + | Inventory Purchases | = | Goods Available for Sale |
| Goods Available for Sale | − | Ending Inventory | = | Cost of Goods Sold |

For example, assume that the FIFO cost flow assumption is selected, so ending inventory is $340. Then, cost of goods sold is calculated as:

| | |
|---|---:|
| Beginning inventory | $300 |
| Inventory purchases | +340 |
| Goods available for sale | 640 |
| Ending FIFO inventory | −340 |
| Cost of goods sold | $300 |

This simple example should refresh your memory about basic inventory accounting points.[2] But actual business situations are more complex and encompass issues such as:

- How should physical quantities in inventory be determined?
- What items should be included in ending inventory?
- What costs should be included in inventory purchases (and eventually in ending inventory)?
- What cost flow assumption should be used to allocate goods available for sale between cost of goods sold and ending inventory?

We discuss each of these complications next.

## DETERMINATION OF INVENTORY QUANTITIES

There are two different methods for determining inventory quantities, perpetual and periodic. A **perpetual inventory system** keeps a running (or "perpetual") record of the amount of inventory on hand. Purchases are debited to the Inventory account itself, and the cost of units sold is removed from the Inventory account as sales are made. Usually, these inventory records are maintained in both physical units and dollars. The physical amount of inventory on hand at any point in time should correspond to the unit balance in the Inventory account.

The Inventory T-account for a merchandising firm under a perpetual inventory system contains the following information at any point in time:

**Inventory**

| | |
|---|---|
| Beginning inventory (units and $s) <br> Plus: <br>     Cost of units purchased <br>       (units and $s) | Minus: <br>     Cost of units transferred to <br>       Cost of goods sold (units and $s) |
| Equals: <br>     Ending inventory <br>       on hand (units and $s) | |

---

[2] We don't discuss the weighted average method in the cost flow assumptions section later in the chapter because it generates numbers that are between the LIFO and FIFO approaches, and it introduces no additional issues. However, we do illustrate weighted average in more detail in the self-study problem at the end of the chapter.

A **periodic inventory system** does not keep a running record of the amount of inventory on hand. Purchases are accumulated in a separate Inventory purchases account (often called Purchases), and no entry is made at the time of sale to reflect cost of goods sold. The T-accounts for a periodic inventory system look like this:

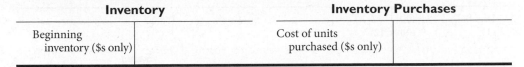

| Inventory | | Inventory Purchases | |
|---|---|---|---|
| Beginning inventory ($s only) | | Cost of units purchased ($s only) | |

In a periodic inventory system, ending inventory and cost of goods must be determined by physically counting the goods on hand at the end of the period. The computation is:

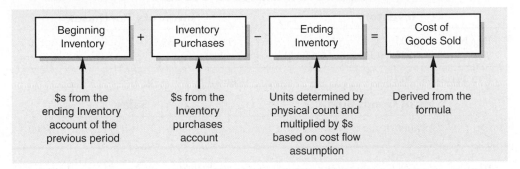

| Beginning Inventory | + | Inventory Purchases | − | Ending Inventory | = | Cost of Goods Sold |
|---|---|---|---|---|---|---|
| $s from the ending Inventory account of the previous period | | $s from the Inventory purchases account | | Units determined by physical count and multiplied by $s based on cost flow assumption | | Derived from the formula |

To illustrate the accounting entries under each system, assume the following data:

| | |
|---|---|
| Sales | $10,000 |
| Beginning inventory | 1,400 |
| Inventory purchases | 9,100 |
| Ending inventory | 3,500 |

The following compares entries under the perpetual and periodic inventory systems.

## Comparison of Entries—Perpetual versus Periodic Inventory System

| Perpetual Inventory System | | Periodic Inventory System | |
|---|---|---|---|
| **Entry (1) To Record Purchases:** | | | |
| **DR** Inventory ..................... $ 9,100 | | **DR** Inventory purchases ........... $ 9,100 | |
| **CR** Accounts payable ......... | | **CR** Accounts payable | |
| (or Cash) ................ | $9,100 | (or Cash). ............... | $ 9,100 |
| **Entry (2) To Record Sales:** | | | |
| **DR** Cash or Accounts receivable...... $10,000 | | **DR** Cash or Accounts receivable .... $10,000 | |
| **CR** Sales revenues ............ | $10,000 | **CR** Sales revenues .......... | $10,000 |
| **DR** Cost of goods sold ............. $ 7,000 | | | |
| **CR** Inventory................. | $ 7,000 | (NO ENTRY) | |
| **Entry (3) To Close the Accounts:** | | | |
| (NO ENTRY) | | **DR** Inventory (ending) ............ $ 3,500 | |
| | | **DR** Cost of goods sold ............ 7,000* | |
| | | **CR** Inventory (beginning).... | $ 1,400 |
| | | **CR** Inventory purchases...... | 9,100 |

---

* Computed as Beginning inventory ($1,400) + Purchases ($9,100) − Ending inventory ($3,500) = Cost of goods sold ($7,000). Under a perpetual inventory system, cost of goods sold is just the per unit cost of each sold item and is recorded when the item is sold. Over the period in our example, the unit costs of sold items total $7,000.

The inventory-related accounts appear as follows under each method (entry numbers are indicated in parentheses):

## PERPETUAL INVENTORY SYSTEM

| Inventory | | | | Cost of Goods Sold | | | |
|---|---|---|---|---|---|---|---|
| Beg. bal. | $1,400 | | | (2) | $7,000 | | |
| (1) | 9,100 | (2) | $7,000 | | | | |
| | | | | **Sales** | | | |
| End. bal. | $3,500 | | | | | (2) | $10,000 |

## PERIODIC INVENTORY SYSTEM

| Inventory | | | | Inventory Purchases | | | |
|---|---|---|---|---|---|---|---|
| Beg. bal. | $1,400 | | | (1) | $9,100 | (3) | $9,100 |
| (3) | 3,500 | (3) | $1,400 | | | | |
| End. bal. | $3,500 | | | End. Bal. | –0– | | |

| Cost of Goods Sold | | | | Sales | | | |
|---|---|---|---|---|---|---|---|
| (3) | $7,000 | | | | | (2) | $10,000 |

Periodic inventory systems reduce recordkeeping, making these systems less costly to maintain. However, this cost advantage is achieved at the expense of far less management control over inventory. For those firms that use a periodic inventory system, there is no running inventory record, and quantities on hand must be determined by physical count. Furthermore, the cost of goods sold number under the periodic system is a "plug" figure; that is, the computation assumes that goods not on hand when the physical count is taken were sold. But some of the goods not on hand may have been stolen or wasted. Under the periodic system, there is no way to determine the extent of these potential losses.

When the physical count reveals inventory shortages, the accounting records must be adjusted to conform to the actual amount on hand. If a shortage of $310 was indicated, the adjustment is:

**DR**    Loss from inventory shortage
      (or Cost of goods sold).................... $310
    **CR**    Inventory ...........................            $310

A perpetual inventory system is more complicated and usually more expensive. It does not eliminate the need to take a physical inventory because the book inventory figures must be verified for accuracy at least annually. But a perpetual system gives management greater control over inventories. For example, the running balance in inventory allows careful monitoring of stock levels. This is useful in avoiding stockouts, particularly in manufacturing where just-in-time inventory purchasing is practiced. Furthermore, the comparisons that must be made between book inventories and physical count figures reveal discrepancies that may be attributable to theft, employee carelessness, or natural shrinkage.

Choosing between the two systems depends on weighing their costs and benefits. Perpetual inventory systems are typically used where:

- *A small number of inventory units, each with a high unit value, exists.* An example is vehicles at an automobile dealership.

- *Continuous monitoring of inventory levels is essential.* An example is a production line where raw materials shortages would shut the operation down.

Periodic systems are used when inventory volumes are high and per unit costs are low. However, the widespread use of computerized optical scanning equipment has led to the

## NEWS CLIP

### KIMBERLY-CLARK KEEPS COSTCO IN DIAPERS

One morning, a Costco store in Los Angeles began running a little low on size one and size two Huggies. Crisis loomed.

So what did Costco managers do? Nothing. They didn't have to, thanks to a special arrangement with Kimberly-Clark Corp., the company that makes the diapers.

Under this deal, responsibility for replenishing stock falls on the manufacturer, not Costco. In return, the big retailer shares detailed information about individual stores' sales. So, long before babies in Los Angeles would ever notice it, diaper dearth was averted by a Kimberly-Clark data analyst working at a computer hundreds of miles away in Neenah, Wisconsin. . . . A Kimberly-Clark spokeswoman says the benefits of the program "more than offset" additional labor costs. Last year, Kimberly-Clark posted a 51% rise in net income to $1.67 billion on $13 billion in sales, capping three years of improving results.

For Costco, the benefits of such close cooperation with a major supplier are equally clear: Costco saves money not only on staffing in its inventory department but also on storage.

*Source:* E. Nelson and A. Zimmerman, "Kimberly-Clark Keeps Costco in Diapers," *The Wall Street Journal,* September 7, 2000. Copyright © 2000 Dow Jones & Company, Inc. All rights reserved worldwide. Reprinted with permission.

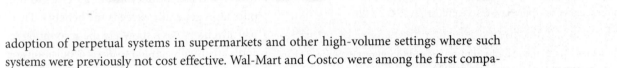

adoption of perpetual systems in supermarkets and other high-volume settings where such systems were previously not cost effective. Wal-Mart and Costco were among the first companies to utilize optical scanning and perpetual inventory systems. These firms share the information captured by their electronic inventory management systems with suppliers who are authorized to automatically ship new merchandise directly to these retailers' stores when their inventory levels fall below prescribed minimum levels. This approach shortens inventory restocking cycles at Wal-Mart and Costco and reduces their need to warehouse inventories.

## ITEMS INCLUDED IN INVENTORY

All inventory items to which the firm has legal title should be included in the Inventory account. However, in day-to-day operations, most firms do not attempt to use the passage of legal title as the criterion for including items in their inventory records because this would be a time-consuming process. Instead, most firms record inventory only when they physically receive it.

This physical-receipt system creates no difficulties except when it comes time to prepare financial statements. At that time, the firm must determine whether all goods that were in fact legally owned have been included in the Inventory account. Goods in transit are the primary concern because legal title to such goods may transfer to the purchaser before the purchaser physically receives them. The purchaser determines the legal status of goods in transit by examining invoices pertaining to goods received during the first few days of the next accounting period and then uses this information to determine precisely when title passed.

Sometimes a firm may physically possess goods but does not legally own them. One example is goods shipped on **consignment.** Here the firm that holds the goods (the consignee) acts as an agent for the owner (the consignor) in selling the goods. The consignee receives a sales commission and forwards the net sales price (after deducting the commission and any selling expenses) to the consignor. Consignment goods should not be included in the consignee's inventory; but they must appear as part of the inventory of the consignor, the legal owner.

Consignment goods also raise potential revenue recognition issues for the consignor that analysts must consider. For example, manufacturers may ship products to their dealers on consignment and nevertheless try to treat such shipments as sales, thereby recognizing income prematurely. Consequently, if "sales" terms provide the "purchaser" the right to return unsold goods or if the cash payment terms are unusually long, it is possible that the manufacturer has inappropriately treated consignment shipments as sales, thereby overstating both sales revenues and income and understating inventory (see Chapter 3).

# COSTS INCLUDED IN INVENTORY

The carrying cost of inventory should include all costs required to obtain physical possession of the merchandise and to make it salable. This includes the purchase cost, sales taxes and transportation costs paid by the purchaser, insurance costs, and storage costs. For a manufacturing firm, inventory costs also include those production costs, such as labor and overhead, that are incurred in making a finished salable product.[3]

---

To illustrate, assume that on February 9, 2008, Hernandez Company purchased inventory with a list price of $1,000 subject to a 2% cash discount if the invoice was paid within 10 days. Hernandez, like most companies, records the purchase at its net (after discount) cost of $980:

**DR** Inventory . . . . . . . . . . . . . . . . . . . . . . . . . . . . . . . $980
    **CR** Accounts payable . . . . . . . . . . . . . . . . . . . . .     $980

Due to an administrative oversight, the invoice is not paid until March 15, 2008. The entry Hernandez then makes is:

**DR** Accounts payable . . . . . . . . . . . . . . . . . . . . . . . . $980
**DR** Interest expense—purchase discount lost . . . . . .   20
    **CR** Cash . . . . . . . . . . . . . . . . . . . . . . . . . . . . . . .     $1,000

So the cost associated with the lost discount is charged to Interest expense. The inventory carrying amount of these goods is $980.

---

In principle, inventory costs should also include the costs of the purchasing department and other general administrative costs associated with the acquisition and distribution of inventory. As a practical matter, however, such costs are extremely difficult to associate with individual purchases and would have to be allocated on some arbitrary basis. From a cost-benefit perspective, the effort expended in trying to assign these indirect inventory costs to unit purchases generally exceeds the benefits. That's why inventory costs shown in the accounting records are usually limited to *direct* acquisition and processing costs that can be objectively associated with specific goods. Costs that do not meet this criterion, such as purchasing department costs, are generally expensed in the period in which they arise. Furthermore, a cash purchase discount that is lost because of a late payment is recorded as interest expense rather than as a cost of acquiring inventory.

## Manufacturing Costs

The inventory costs of a manufacturer include raw material, labor, and certain overhead items. Costs of this type are called **product costs;** they are assigned to inventory and treated as assets until the inventory is sold. When sold, the inventory carrying value is charged to cost of goods sold, and at that point all inventoried costs become an expense.

A manufacturer also incurs costs not considered to be closely associated with production. Examples include general administrative costs (such as the president's salary) and selling costs (say, the commissions earned by the firm's salespeople). These costs are not inventoried. Instead, they are treated as expenses of the period in which they are incurred and are called **period costs.**

The flow of product costs through the inventory accounts and, eventually, to the Cost of goods sold account is illustrated in Exhibit 9.1.

## ABSORPTION COSTING VERSUS VARIABLE COSTING

As indicated in Exhibit 9.1, manufacturing overhead costs comprise one element of product costs and are accordingly included in inventory. However, there are two views regarding the appropriate treatment of *fixed* manufacturing overhead costs. One view is called **variable costing** (or direct costing), while the other view is called **absorption costing** (or full costing).

Variable costing includes only the variable costs of production in inventory. **Variable costs** are those that change in proportion to the level of production. Examples include raw materials

---

[3] In certain cases, interest incurred during the time that inventory is being developed for sale can be capitalized, as described in Chapter 10. Examples include discrete projects such as shipbuilding or real estate development; that is, cases in which money is borrowed to finance construction over several reporting periods. See *Statement of Financial Accounting Standards (SFAS) No. 34*, "Capitalization of Interest Cost" (Stamford, CT: Financial Accounting Standards Board [FASB], October 1979).

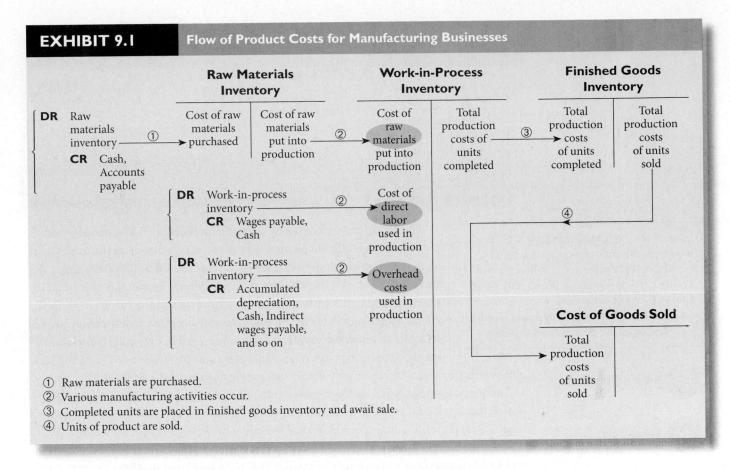

**EXHIBIT 9.1**   Flow of Product Costs for Manufacturing Businesses

① Raw materials are purchased.
② Various manufacturing activities occur.
③ Completed units are placed in finished goods inventory and await sale.
④ Units of product are sold.

cost, direct labor, and certain overhead items such as electricity used in running production equipment. **Fixed costs** of production are costs that do not change as production levels change. Examples include rental of production facilities, depreciation of production equipment, and property taxes. ***When variable costing is used, these fixed production overhead costs are not included as part of inventory cost.*** Instead, fixed production overhead costs are treated as period costs and are expensed in the period in which they are incurred.

The logic underlying variable costing is that incurred costs are includable in inventory only if they provide future benefits to the firm. Proponents of variable costing argue that fixed production overhead costs are *not* assets because they expire in the period in which they are incurred and thus do not provide a future benefit to the firm. For example, factory insurance carried in June provides no benefit after June 30; for insurance protection in July, another month's premium must be paid. But future benefits *do* derive from variable costs such as materials used in production; once materials have been purchased and used in making an inventory unit, that cost can be "stored" and will provide a future benefit when the inventory is eventually sold. These types of costs are includable in inventory under variable costing.

***Under absorption costing, all production costs are inventoried.*** Fixed production overhead costs are not written off to expense as incurred. Instead they are treated as product costs and carried as assets in the appropriate inventory accounts. The rationale is that *both* variable and fixed production costs are assets because *both* are needed to produce a salable product.

Both absorption costing and variable costing treat all selling, general, and administrative (SG&A) costs as period costs. These SG&A costs are *never* inventoried under *any* circumstances under either method. Exhibit 9.2 shows the treatment of costs by category under each inventory costing approach. The only cost category treated differently is fixed production overhead, which is highlighted in the table.

**EXHIBIT 9.2** Summary of Cost Treatment by Category under Variable and Absorption Costing

| Cost Category | Inventoried under Variable Costing? | Inventoried under Absorption Costing? |
|---|---|---|
| Production materials | Yes | Yes |
| Production labor | Yes | Yes |
| Variable production overhead | Yes | Yes |
| Fixed production overhead | No | Yes |
| Selling, general and administrative | No | No |

International Accounting Standards (IAS) also require the use of absorption costing. See *IAS 2* (revised 2003), "Inventories" (London: International Accounting Standards Board, 2003, paras. 12–13). GAAP in most non-U.S. settings also requires absorption costing but there are exceptions; e.g., Mexican GAAP permits variable costing.

**International**

**Valuation**

The variable and absorption costing alternatives provide statement readers potentially very different pictures of year-to-year changes in performance; that is, the trend of earnings over a series of years can differ markedly under the two approaches, as we will illustrate. These different earnings trends could influence analysts' forecasts. Analysts must understand the financial statement effects of *both* methods even though ***generally accepted accounting principles (GAAP) do not allow variable costing to be used in external financial statements.*** Accounting rules require inventory cost to include both fixed and variable production costs; therefore, ***only absorption costing is permitted under GAAP.***

Unfortunately, absorption costing makes it difficult to interpret year-to-year changes in reported income. These problems arise when inventory levels change between one year and the next. This is illustrated in the example whose basic assumptions are shown in Exhibit 9.3.

Over the two years in the example, selling price, variable production costs per unit, and total fixed production costs were constant. Units produced increased in 2009 (125,000 versus 100,000 in 2008), but units sold in 2009 dropped (90,000 versus 110,000 units in 2008).

Exhibit 9.4 shows that the reported GAAP gross margin under FIFO absorption costing increases from $110,000 in 2008 to $130,000 in 2009, an 18.2% increase. Income *increases* despite the fact that variable production cost and selling price per unit were constant, fixed costs did not change in total, and unit sales decreased.

Why do we get this strange result? The answer reveals a major deficiency of absorption cost financial statements. Production increased in 2009 to 125,000 units and exceeded sales, which totaled 90,000 units. Inventory therefore increased by 35,000 units (125,000 minus 90,000) to

**EXHIBIT 9.3** Absorption versus Variable Costing Illustration

**Selling price and cost data**
Selling price = $8 per unit in both 2008 and 2009
Variable production costs = $3 per unit in both 2008 and 2009
Fixed production costs = $400,000 per year in both 2008 and 2009
Beginning inventory (FIFO basis), January 1, 2008 = 50,000 units @ $7

| Production and Sales Volume Data | 2008 | 2009 |
|---|---|---|
| Units produced | 100,000 | 125,000 |
| Units sold | 110,000 | 90,000 |
| Ending inventory (in units)* | 40,000 | 75,000 |

\* Computations: 2008: 50,000 + 100,000 − 110,000 = 40,000 units
2009: 40,000 + 125,000 − 90,000 = 75,000 units

| EXHIBIT 9.4 | Absorption versus Variable Costing Statements: Contrasting the Outcomes |
|---|---|

## Absorption Cost Income Statements (GAAP)

| | 2008 | | | | 2009 |
|---|---|---|---|---|---|
| Sales revenues (110,000 @ $8) | | $880,000 | Sales revenues (90,000 @ $8) | | $720,000 |
| Cost of goods sold | | | Cost of goods sold | | |
| From beginning inventory | | | From beginning inventory | | |
| (50,000 @ $7) | $350,000 | | (40,000 @ $7) | $280,000 | |
| From 2008 production (60,000 @ $7*) | 420,000 | | From 2009 production (50,000 @ $6.20†) | 310,000 | |
| | | (770,000) | | | (590,000) |
| GAAP gross margin | | $110,000 | GAAP gross margin | | $130,000 |
| Gross margin % | | 12.50% | Gross margin % | | 18.06% |
| Ending inventory: 40,000 units @ $7* | | | Ending inventory: 75,000 units @ $6.20† | | |

| * This cost is determined as follows: | | † This cost is determined as follows: | |
|---|---|---|---|
| Variable productions costs (given) | $3.00/unit | Variable production costs (given) | $3,00/unit |
| Fixed production costs, unitized $400,000/100,000 = | 4.00/unit | Fixed production costs, unitized $400,000/125,000 = | 3,20/unit |
| Total production cost for 2008 | $7.00/unit | Total production cost for 2009 | $6.20/unit |

## Variable Cost Income Statements (Not GAAP)

| | 2008 | | | | 2009 |
|---|---|---|---|---|---|
| Sales revenues (110,000 @ $8) | | $880,000 | Sales revenues (90,000 @ $8) | | $720,000 |
| Variable cost of goods sold | | | Variable cost of goods sold | | |
| From beginning inventory | | | From beginning inventory | | |
| (50,000 @ $3) | $150,000 | | (40,000 @ $3) | $120,000 | |
| From 2008 production (60,000 @ $3) | 180,000 | | From 2009 production (50,000 @ $3) | 150,000 | |
| | | (330,000) | | | (270,000) |
| Variable contribution margin | | 550,000 | Variable contribution margin | | $450,000 |
| Less: Fixed production | | | Less: Fixed production | | |
| costs treated as a period expense | | (400,000) | costs treated as a period expense | | (400,000) |
| Variable cost gross margin | | $150,000 | Variable cost gross margin | | $ 50,000 |
| Gross margin % | | 17.05% | Gross margin % | | 6.94% |
| Ending inventory: 40,000 units @ $3 | | | Ending inventory: 75,000 units @ $3 | | |

a year-end total of 75,000 units. When inventory increases under absorption costing, as in this illustration, the amount of fixed cost assigned to inventory increases. In Exhibit 9.4, the fixed costs in inventory at January 1, 2009 totaled $160,000 (that is, 40,000 units times $4 of fixed cost per *unit*). At December 31, 2009, fixed cost included in inventory had increased to $240,000 (that is, 75,000 units times $3.20 of fixed cost per unit). *As inventory absorbs more fixed cost, less fixed cost gets charged to the income statement and income goes up.* Very large inventory increases produce a favorable absorption costing income effect that can offset an unfavorable income effect caused, say, by a sales decrease. This is what happened in Exhibit 9.4, and it is this effect that explains the jump in 2009 income.

By contrast, variable cost income in Exhibit 9.4 falls from $150,000 in 2008 to $50,000 in 2009. Critics of absorption costing contend that in situations similar to this example, variable costing better reflects underlying economics. Nonetheless, external financial statements must conform to absorption costing, as required by GAAP.

> A research study found that firms in danger of producing zero earnings resort to (among other things) overproducing inventory to reduce cost of goods sold and thereby boost profits. So, the evidence suggests that absorption costing provides opportunities for firms to manipulate profits opportunistically.
>
> Source: S. Roychowdhury, "Earnings Management through Real Activities Manipulation," *Journal of Accounting and Economics,* December 2006, pp. 335–70.

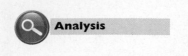

Generalizing from this example, the mechanics of absorption costing can lead to year-to-year income changes that may delude the unwary. This can happen whenever production and sales are not in balance, that is, whenever physical inventory levels (in units) are either increasing or decreasing. When the number of units in inventory is increasing, absorption cost gross margins tend to rise. This effect may be so large that it could obscure offsetting unfavorable effects (for example, sales decreases or deteriorating efficiency) that are taking place simultaneously. When physical inventory levels decrease absorption cost income tends to fall because fixed overhead that was previously in inventory is charged against income as part of the cost of goods sold.

Here's an example of how an understanding of absorption costing can help careful analysts. In 2001 Intel Corporation's gross margin was 49.2%. According to a *New York Times* story, Intel management initially predicted that gross margins in the second quarter of 2002 would be 53%.[4] But one analyst warned his clients "that Intel's impressive margins were mostly a result of a buildup in inventory, not sales to end users, and that the margins were therefore unsustainable unless demand picked up."[5] Late in the second quarter, Intel reduced its profit margin forecast to 49% because of weak demand. "They continued to produce at high levels, which improved their gross margins, and then talked about efficiencies and productivity when it was only an inventory buildup," the analyst concluded.[6]

> Companies rarely disclose absorption costing effects on income. But Vacu-Dry Company did in its 1996 Annual Report:
>
> In fiscal 1995, the increase in the cost of sales percentage was predominantly due to the lower production volume as a result of the decreased sales volume and the resultant *decrease in overhead absorption.* [Emphasis added.]

## Mitigation of the Absorption Costing Effect

To reduce year-to-year fluctuations in fixed manufacturing overhead charged to inventory, as in Exhibit 9.4, the FASB specified how production volume should be defined:

> The allocation of fixed production overhead to the costs of conversion is based on the **normal capacity** of the production facilities. Normal capacity refers to a range of production levels. Normal capacity is the production expected to be achieved over a number of periods or seasons under normal circumstances. Some variation in production levels from period to period is expected and establishes the range of normal capacity. The range of normal capacity will vary based on business- and industry-specific factors. Judgment is required to determine when a production level is abnormally low (that is, outside the range of expected variation in production).[7]

So, the basis for allocating fixed overhead should be normal capacity, but the FASB's definition of normal capacity is very broad and subjective. In practice, *SFAS No. 151* is unlikely to affect the computation of fixed production overhead in inventory even when production volume does fluctuate from period to period. Thus, the potential time-series distortions generated by absorption costing will likely persist despite the issuance of *SFAS No. 151*.

## Vendor Allowances

It is common practice in certain industries such as retail sales for manufacturers of products (vendors) to provide cash payments and/or credits to their customers. These arrangements are called **vendor allowances**. An example of a vendor allowance appears below:

> Competition for shelf space in the supermarket soft drink section is intense. To gain access to space, Super Cola signs a contract with Plaid and Stripes, a national supermarket chain, to pay $50,000 per month for 20 lineal feet of prominent shelf space in each of Plaid and Stripes stores throughout the country.

---

[4] G. Morgenson, "Far From Wall Street, Intel's Bad News Was No Surprise," *The New York Times,* June 9, 2002.

[5] Ibid.

[6] Ibid.

[7] "Inventory Costs: An Amendment of ARB No. 43, Chapter 4," *SFAS No. 151* (Norwalk, CT: FASB, 2004), para. 2.

In this example, the $50,000 per month is clearly a reduction in the cost of the Super Cola purchased by Plaid and Stripes.[8] So, the financial statement effect of the vendor allowance should be to lower cost of goods sold. Equivalently, the $50,000 should be used to reduce Super Cola's inventory carrying value.

Managers at recipient firms have used some vendor allowance arrangements to manage earnings. One example occurred at Kmart several years ago. In 2001, a supplier issued Kmart a $2 million vendor allowance in exchange for Kmart's agreement to purchase an additional $15 million worth of goods in 2001 and beyond.

In an administrative proceeding, the Securities and Exchange Commission (SEC) stated:

> A significant number of allowances were recognized prematurely—or "pulled forward"—on the basis of incorrect information provided to Kmart's accounting department, while the correct terms of the payments were undisclosed. As a result of these accounting irregularities . . . Kmart's cost of goods sold was understated by $2 million in fiscal year 2000.[9]

So, although the $2 million vendor allowance was given to induce purchases in 2001 and beyond, they were recognized in income in 2000, according to the SEC. Other earnings management activities using vendor allowance occurred at Ahold, the Dutch supermarket operator; Saks Inc.; and CSK Auto Corporation, among others.

**To analyze comparative income statements, you must understand the mechanics of absorption costing and bear in mind that any imbalance between units produced and units sold may have a pronounced effect on reported income. Furthermore, the absorption cost income effect can obscure underlying economic changes of interest to statement readers. For example, a sudden, unexpected sales jump, clearly a good news event, may cause an inventory depletion. With GAAP absorption costing, the inventory reduction forces an additional dose of fixed overhead through the income statement, thereby masking part of the income benefit arising from the sales jump.**

## COST FLOW ASSUMPTIONS: THE CONCEPTS

For most publicly held firms, inventory is continuously purchased in large quantities. It is difficult to determine which purchase lots correspond to the units that have been sold, especially in firms whose manufacturing alters the form of the raw materials acquired. Consider an automobile manufacturer. It's not easy to know what specific steel purchase batch was used in the hood of a specific car.

In a few industries, however, it is possible to identify which particular units have been sold. In retail businesses such as jewelry stores and automobile dealerships, which sell a small number of high-value items, cost of goods sold can be measured by reference to the known cost of the actual units sold. This inventory accounting method is called **specific identification.** But this method suffers from a serious deficiency because it makes it relatively easy to manipulate income. Consider a large jewelry dealer with three identical watches in inventory that were acquired at three different purchase costs. Under the specific identification method, the reported profit on a sale can be raised (or lowered) by simply delivering the lowest (or highest) cost watch. An inventory method allowing such latitude is open to criticism.

---

[8] "Accounting by a Customer (including a Reseller) for Certain Consideration Received from a Vendor," *Emerging Issues Task Force (EITF) Issue No. 02-16* (Norwalk, CT: FASB, 2003), para. 4.

[9] SEC, *Account and Auditing Enforcement Release No. 2300,* August 30, 2005, paras. 1 and 3.

Specific identification is usually not feasible for most businesses. Even when it is feasible, it has some serious drawbacks, as just illustrated. For these reasons, a **cost flow assumption** is usually required to allocate goods available for sale between ending inventory and cost of goods sold, that is,

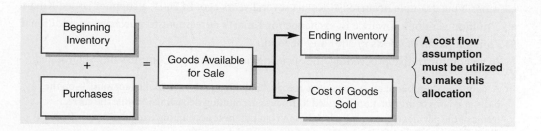

*It is important to understand that GAAP does not require the cost flow assumption to conform to the actual physical flow of the goods.*

The American Institute of Certified Public Accounting (AICPA) surveyed 600 companies and the inventory cost flow assumptions that they use indicate two things (see Exhibit 9.5). First, the most popular inventory costing method is FIFO, followed closely by LIFO; weighted average cost is the next most popular method. Second, the total frequencies of all methods exceed the total number of firms surveyed (600), which means most firms use a combination of inventory costing methods. For example, of the 229 firms using LIFO in 2005, only 16 firms (7%) exclusively used LIFO for all inventories, largely because it is prohibited in most countries outside the United States. Thus, U.S.-domiciled multinational companies that use LIFO for domestic inventories would usually be required to use some other cost flow assumption for their foreign subsidiary inventories.

> IAS permit the use of either the FIFO or weighted average cost flow assumption (see *IAS 2,* para. 25). In special circumstances, the specific identification method can also be used (para. 23), but LIFO is prohibited (see para. BC 19).

**International**

| EXHIBIT 9.5 | Frequency of Inventory Cost Flow Assumptions (2002–2005) | | | |
|---|---|---|---|---|

| | Number of Companies | | | |
|---|---|---|---|---|
| | **2005** | **2004** | **2003** | **2002** |
| **Methods** | | | | |
| First-in, first-out (FIFO) | 385 | 386 | 384 | 380 |
| Last-in, first-out (LIFO) | 229 | 239 | 251 | 255 |
| Average cost | 155 | 169 | 167 | 165 |
| Other | 30 | 27 | 31 | 28 |
| **Use of LIFO** | | | | |
| All inventories | 16 | 20 | 26 | 17 |
| 50% or more of inventories | 113 | 108 | 120 | 121 |
| Less than 50% of inventories | 76 | 85 | 77 | 88 |
| Not determinable | 24 | 26 | 28 | 29 |
| **Companies Using LIFO** | **229** | **239** | **251** | **255** |

*Source:* Y. Iofe and M. C. Calderisi (eds.), *Accounting Trends and Techniques,* 2006. Copyright © 2006 by the American Institute of Certified Public Accountants, Inc. Reprinted with permission.

Let's revisit the refrigerator dealer to explore the underlying cost flow concepts. This simple example highlights key issues without cluttering the analysis with details that hinder comprehension. Recall the facts of the example.

> The retailer started the year with a beginning inventory of one refrigerator, which had an invoice cost of $300. During the year, the dealer cost of identical refrigerators increased to $340. Assume that the retailer purchases another refrigerator at this $340 cost. At the end of the year, one of the two refrigerators is sold for $500.

## First-In, First-Out (FIFO) Cost Flow

The FIFO method assumes the oldest units available in inventory are the first units that are sold. This means that ending inventory on the FIFO basis always consists of the cost of the most recently acquired units. In the refrigerator example, the computations are:

| **Income statement** | | |
|---|---|---|
| Sales revenues | $500 | |
| Cost of goods sold (FIFO) | 300 | (Cost of oldest unit) |
| Net income | $200 | |
| | | |
| **Balance sheet** | | |
| Ending inventory (FIFO) | $340 | (Cost of newest unit) |

See Figure 9.1 for a more realistic FIFO cost flow case in which numerous purchases and sales are made throughout the year. The FIFO cost flow in this diagram illustrates that sales are presumed to have been made from the oldest available goods (in this case, from beginning inventory and the goods purchased in January through September) and that ending inventory consists of the most recently acquired goods (October through December).

FIFO charges the oldest costs against revenues on the income statement. This characteristic is often viewed as a deficiency of the FIFO method because the current cost of replacing the units sold is not being matched with current revenues. However, on the balance sheet, FIFO inventory represents the most recent purchases, and if inventory turnover is reasonably rapid, usually approximates current replacement cost.

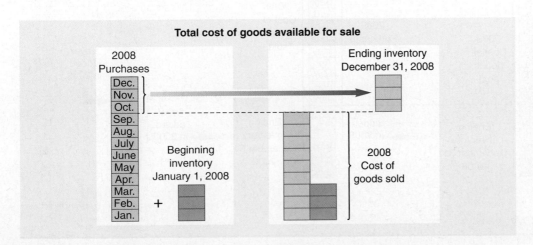

**Figure 9.1**

FIFO COST FLOW

# Last-In, First-Out (LIFO) Cost Flow

The LIFO method presumes that sales were made from the most recently acquired units. In the refrigerator example, the computations are:

| **Income statement** | | |
|---|---|---|
| Sales revenues | $500 | |
| Cost of goods sold (LIFO) | 340 | (Cost of newest unit) |
| Net income | $160 | |
| | | |
| **Balance sheet** | | |
| Ending inventory (LIFO) | $300 | (Cost of oldest unit) |

This method seldom corresponds to the actual physical flow of goods, but remember that GAAP does not require conformity between the assumed cost flow and the physical flow of units.

LIFO matches the most recently incurred costs against revenues. When purchases and sales occur continuously, the most recently incurred costs are virtually identical to current replacement cost. So, LIFO provides a good match between current costs and current revenues. On the balance sheet, however, LIFO inventory consists of the oldest costs ($300 in the refrigerator example), which usually does not approximate the current replacement cost of inventory.

For firms that have used the LIFO method for many years, the LIFO inventory amount may reflect only a small fraction of what it would cost to replace this inventory at today's prices. A diagram of LIFO cost flow in Figure 9.2 shows how old **layers** can accumulate in ending inventory.

As in Figure 9.2, when purchases exceed sales in any year, a new LIFO layer is formed. New inventory layers are valued using the *oldest* costs incurred during that year. For example, the LIFO layer added in 2008 is comprised of the inventory purchase costs expended from January through March 2008. Because sales under LIFO are always presumed to have been made from the most recent purchases, the 2008 LIFO layer remains on the books at the end of 2009 as long as units sold in 2009 do not exceed units purchased in 2009. As in Figure 9.2, not only did the 2008 LIFO layer remain but also a small additional LIFO layer was added in 2009 because unit purchases again exceeded unit sales. A firm that has been on LIFO since, say, 1954 could still be carrying a portion of its inventory at 1954 costs, a portion at 1955 costs, and so on.

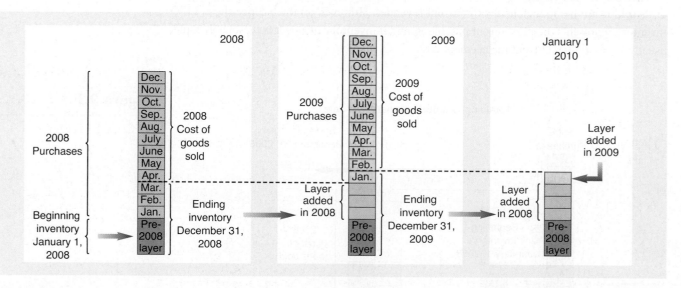

**Figure 9.2** LIFO COST FLOW

# FIFO, LIFO, and Inventory Holding Gains

FIFO and LIFO give different financial statement results because each method treats inventory holding gains and losses in a different way. To understand the differences, we first need to understand inventory holding gains and losses.

**Inventory holding gains and losses** are the input cost changes that occur following the purchase of inventory. Let's go back to the refrigerator example. Assume that the replacement cost of each refrigerator at the end of the year was $340. However, both FIFO and LIFO are historical cost methods, and, therefore, goods available for sale reflect only the *historical cost* that was paid to acquire the two units on hand:

| | |
|---|---|
| Beginning inventory (1 unit @ $300) | $300 |
| Purchases (1 unit @ $340) | +340 |
| Historical cost of goods available for sale | $640 |

Notice that historical cost accounting ignores the $40 holding gain that arose on the unit of beginning inventory as its replacement cost increased from $300 to $340. Thus, goods available for sale are shown at their historical cost of $640 rather than at their current replacement cost of $680 (that is, to replace the two units would cost $340 each).

An accounting method called **current cost accounting** (also called **replacement cost accounting**) records holding gains on financial statements as they arise. ***Because it is a departure from historical cost, current cost accounting is not permitted in the basic financial statements.*** However, the FASB does allow voluntary supplementary disclosure of current cost data in the annual report.[10]

In a current cost (non-GAAP) accounting system, the following entry is made at the time that inventory replacement cost increases:

| | | | |
|---|---|---|---|
| **DR** | Inventory . . . . . . . . . . . . . . . . . . . . . . . . . . . . . . . . . . . . . . . . . . . . . . . . . . . . . | $40 | |
| | **CR** Unrealized holding gain . . . . . . . . . . . . . . . . . . . . . . . . . . . . . . . . . . | | $40 |

The Unrealized holding gain account represents an owners' equity increase. Whether these holding gains should be treated as a component of net income or included in other comprehensive income is a controversial issue that we revisit in Chapter 18. In this chapter, we ignore the controversy and treat holding gains as an element of other comprehensive income.

> The holding gain takes place as the replacement cost of the inventory increases. But because the gain has not yet been included in income, it is an **unrealized holding gain.** Once the gain is included in income (as described in this section), it is a **realized holding gain.**

After the holding gains entry has been made, the current cost of goods available for sale is:

| | |
|---|---|
| Beginning inventory (1 unit @ $300) | $300 |
| Increase in the replacement cost of beginning inventory | +40 |
| Purchases (1 unit @ $340) | +340 |
| Current cost of goods available for sale (2 units @ $340) | $680 |

> You may want to read Chapter 2, pages 82–85, to review other comprehensive income.

When the unit is sold for $500, the partial financial statements under current cost accounting are:

**Income statement**

| | |
|---|---|
| Sales revenues | $500 |
| Replacement cost of goods sold (1 unit @ $340) | 340 |
| Current cost operating profit | $160 |

**Balance sheet**

| | |
|---|---|
| Ending inventory | $340 |

---

[10] "Financial Reporting and Changing Prices," *SFAS No. 89* (Stamford, CT: FASB, 1986).

## Figure 9.3

ALLOCATION OF GOODS
AVAILABLE FOR SALE:
HISTORICAL COSTING
VERSUS CURRENT
COSTING

(a) Historical Cost of Goods
Available for Sale = $640 and
(b) Current Cost of Goods
Available for Sale = $680.

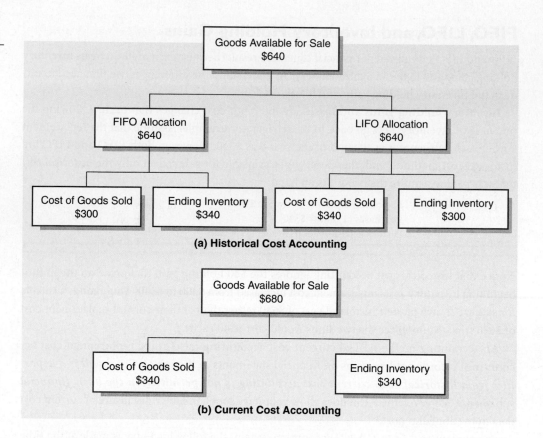

(a) Historical Cost Accounting

(b) Current Cost Accounting

The current (or replacement) cost operating profit figure is the margin that results from matching current replacement cost against current revenues. It reflects the expected ongoing profitability of current operations at current levels of costs and selling prices.

Figure 9.3 contrasts the treatment of goods available for sale under (a) historical cost accounting and (b) current cost accounting. Notice that the total amount to be allocated between inventory and cost of goods sold is $40 higher under current costing ($680 versus $640). This difference is attributable to the $40 holding gain that was added to goods available for sale under current costing (highlighted in the earlier table). With current costing, the total to be allocated is carried at current cost (two units at $340 each, for a total of $680). *This means that the balance sheet inventory number and the cost of goods sold number are both shown at current cost.*

By contrast, the historical cost figures for goods available for sale under both FIFO and LIFO ($640) are $40 less than the total current cost of the two units available ($680). This means that under either LIFO or FIFO it is impossible to simultaneously reflect both the balance sheet inventory *and* cost of goods sold at current cost: One can be shown at current cost, but the other must then be shown at historical cost. *The primary difference between FIFO and LIFO is that each method makes a different choice regarding which financial statement element is shown at the out-of-date cost.* FIFO shows inventory at approximately current cost but is then forced to reflect cost of goods sold at historical cost.[11] LIFO shows cost of goods sold at approximately current cost but is then forced to reflect inventory on the balance sheet at historical cost.

---

[11] In our example, FIFO inventory is shown at *exactly* current cost because the purchase cost ($340) equals the end-of-year replacement cost. In more complicated situations that occur in real organizations, FIFO inventory amounts *approximate* current costs. The faster the inventory turnover (cost of goods sold divided by average inventory), the closer is the correspondence between inventory at FIFO cost and inventory at current (replacement) cost.

When input costs are rising, LIFO income is lower than FIFO income as long as inventory quantities remain constant or increase. In the refrigerator example, LIFO income is $160, whereas FIFO income is $200 (see pages 483–484). Income is *lower under LIFO because LIFO charges the new, higher cost units to cost of goods sold.*

> Inventory quantity decreases—reductions in physical units in inventory—can produce a distortion known as a *LIFO liquidation,* discussed later in the chapter.

The income number under LIFO *usually* (but not always) closely approximates the income number under current costing:

| LIFO Income | | Current Cost Income | |
|---|---|---|---|
| Sales revenues | $500 | Sales revenues | $500 |
| Cost of goods sold | 340 | Replacement cost of goods sold | 340 |
| LIFO operating profit | $160 | Current cost operating profit | $160 |

When purchases occur continuously, this near equivalence exists because LIFO charges the most recently acquired goods to cost of goods sold.

Now let's reexamine the FIFO income number. **By charging the oldest costs to the income statement, FIFO automatically includes in income the holding gain on the unit that was sold.** This result is seen by comparing the total income figures under FIFO and current costing:

| FIFO Income | | Current Cost Income | |
|---|---|---|---|
| Sales revenues | $500 | Sales revenues | $500 |
| Cost of goods sold | 300 | Replacement cost of goods sold | 340 |
| FIFO operating profit | $200 | Current cost operating profit | $160 |

$40 difference

A comparison of the two income numbers shows that FIFO income is $40 higher. This $40 difference is, of course, the holding gain on the oldest refrigerator, which is the one that the FIFO assumption considers to have been sold. Another way to visualize this income difference is to decompose FIFO income into its component parts.

| Components of FIFO Income | |
|---|---|
| Current (replacement) cost operating profit | $160 |
| Holding gain on unit considered sold | 40 |
| FIFO operating profit | $200 |

This reformulation tells us that FIFO income consists of two components:

- Current (replacement) cost operating profit of $160
- A realized holding gain of $40 on the unit that was sold.

> Remember, "current cost operating profit" represents a matching against sales revenue of the then-current replacement cost of the inventory at the time of sale.

While these components are easy to extract in the simple refrigerator example, in actual financial statements, the components of FIFO profit are not disclosed and only the total figure is reported.

Some analysts argue that by merging current cost profit and realized holding gains, FIFO gives misleading signals about the company's sustainable operating profits. For example, operating profit is generally considered to be potentially sustainable if existing conditions continue. By contrast, holding gains depend on external prices increases, which may or may not be sustainable. But FIFO gives the impression that operating profit is $200, thus suggesting that $200, not $160, is sustainable. Because the higher FIFO income number includes potentially unsustainable gains, that $40 portion of FIFO income is considered to represent low-quality earnings.[12]

In Chapter 1, page 13, we discussed political costs arising from reported profits in certain politically sensitive industries such as oil. All of us who fill our vehicle gas tanks are painfully aware of the steady rise in gasoline prices beginning in 2004. This made consumers unhappy, and human nature being what it is, many looked for a scapegoat. When multinational oil companies soon after began reporting record profits, they were an obvious target. Critics made charges (largely unsubstantiated) of price gouging. Some in the U.S. Congress proposed imposition of a "Windfall Profits" tax on oil companies.[13]

All U.S. oil firms use LIFO in an effort to better match revenues and expenses and thereby keep inventory holding gains out of income.[14] However, IAS do not permit LIFO. This poses a serious political dilemma for a non-U.S. oil company such as BP (formerly known as British Petroleum), a U.K.–based multinational that reports using IAS. BP uses FIFO, so realized holding gains on inventory increase its bottom-line income. In an effort to reflect sustainable profits more clearly, BP provides in its annual report a supplemental disclosure of the amount of inventory holding gains included in FIFO historical cost income. Here is an excerpt:

### BP Reconciliation of Pre-Tax Historical Cost (FIFO) Profit

**Pre-Tax to Replacement Cost Profit**

|  | $ in Millions | | |
| --- | --- | --- | --- |
|  | **2005** | **2004** | **2003** |
| Pre-tax FIFO profit | $22,341 | $17,075 | $12,448 |
| Inventory holding (gains) losses | (3,027) | (1,643) | (16) |
| Replacement cost profit | 19,314 | 15,432 | 12,432 |
| Inventory holding gains as a percent of FIFO profit* | 13.5% | 9.6% | 0.1% |

* Added by the authors.

This reconciliation shows that the increase in worldwide crude oil prices over the period, in conjunction with FIFO accounting, diminished the quality (sustainability) of BP's earnings. In 2003, virtually no inventory holding gains were included in reported income, but by 2005, inventory holding gains constituted 13.5% of reported pre-tax FIFO profit.

## The LIFO Reserve Disclosure

The previous section discussed income statement matching problems under FIFO. Remember, however, LIFO is also an historical cost accounting method with its own deficiencies. There is only $640 (rather than $680) to allocate between cost of goods sold and inventory in our refrigerator example. Because LIFO allocates the most recent cost of $340 to the income

[12] See, for example, J. G. Siegel, "The 'Quality of Earnings' Concept—A Survey," *Financial Analysts Journal,* March–April 1982, pp. 60–68.

[13] K. Phillips and J. Bosman, "Industry Thinks It Has a Message, but It Isn't Reaching Consumers," *The New York Times,* May 3, 2006.

[14] D. Reilly, "Big Oil's Accounting Methods Fuel Criticism—LIFO Leaves the Likes of Exxon with Big Balance-Sheet Reserves as Gas-Pump Prices Slam Drivers," *The Wall Street Journal,* August 8, 2006.

statement, that leaves only $300—the old historical cost—for allocation to the balance sheet. Therefore, the LIFO balance sheet inventory number does not reflect current replacement cost. This leads to another set of issues that further cloud financial reporting. Let's examine them.

Because LIFO inventory costs on the balance sheet frequently include old inventory layers, the LIFO balance sheet amounts are much lower than FIFO inventory amounts. This can make it very difficult to compare LIFO versus FIFO firms meaningfully. To remedy this difficulty, the SEC adopted a disclosure policy in 1974 that requires LIFO firms to disclose the dollar magnitude of the difference between LIFO and FIFO (or current replacement cost) inventory costs. This disclosure, called the **LIFO reserve,** must be reported at each balance sheet date. Exhibit 9.6 illustrates a typical disclosure of this divergence between LIFO and FIFO inventory amounts for Aral Company. (This example is loosely based on the actual financial statements of a food-processing firm that is no longer a free-standing entity.)

> Technically, the SEC rule requires firms to disclose "the excess of replacement cost or current cost over stated LIFO value . . ." (see Regulation S-X, Rule 5-02). In practice, most firms do measure the LIFO reserve as the difference between the LIFO inventory carrying amount and the replacement cost of the inventory. However, some firms compute the LIFO reserve by taking the difference between inventory book value at LIFO and inventory book value at FIFO. Presumably, this is justified if inventory turnover is reasonably rapid because FIFO inventory will then approximate replacement cost. Consequently, both of these alternative computations of the LIFO reserve will usually result in similar amounts and thus comply with the SEC directive.

The disclosure in Exhibit 9.6 provides statement readers an important tool. By adding the reported LIFO reserve amount at December 31, 2008 to the December 31, 2008 balance sheet LIFO inventory number, we can estimate the December 31, 2008 FIFO inventory. Specifically, the sum of the ending LIFO inventory ($4,980,000) and the year-end LIFO reserve ($1,720,000) totals $6,700,000. This sum represents an estimate of Aral Company's December 31, 2008 FIFO ending inventory. Notice that this result immediately follows from the definition of the LIFO reserve, which is the difference between FIFO inventory amounts and LIFO inventory amounts, that is,

$$\text{Inventory}_{\text{FIFO}} - \text{Inventory}_{\text{LIFO}} = \text{LIFO Reserve}$$
$$\$6,700,000 - \$4,980,000 = \$1,720,000$$

Therefore, rearranging the equation yields the following:

$$\text{Inventory}_{\text{FIFO}} = \text{Inventory}_{\text{LIFO}} + \text{LIFO Reserve}$$
$$\$6,700,000 = \$4,980,000 + \$1,720,000$$

Thus, we can think of the FIFO inventory cost as being comprised of LIFO inventory cost plus a LIFO reserve adjustment that measures the difference between the current cost of inventory

| EXHIBIT 9.6 | Aral Company |
|---|---|

**Inventories Footnote Disclosure**

| | December 31 | |
|---|---|---|
| | **2008** | **2007** |
| Raw materials | $ 792,000 | $ 510,000 |
| Work-in-process | 1,808,000 | 1,315,000 |
| Finished goods | 4,100,000 | 4,425,000 |
| Inventory at FIFO cost | 6,700,000 | 6,250,000 |
| Less: LIFO reserve | 1,720,000 | 2,375,000 |
| Inventory at LIFO cost | $4,980,000 | $3,875,000 |

| **EXHIBIT 9.7** | Adjusting Cost of Goods Sold from LIFO to FIFO |
|---|---|

| (1) | (2) | (3) |
|---|---|---|
| Beginning Inventory$_{LIFO}$<br>Plus<br>  Purchases<br>Equals<br>  Goods available$_{LIFO}$<br>Minus<br>  Ending inventory$_{LIFO}$<br>Equals | + Beginning LIFO reserve | = Beginning inventory$_{FIFO}$<br>Plus<br>  Purchases<br>Equals<br>  Goods available$_{FIFO}$<br>Minus |
| | + Ending LIFO reserve | = Ending inventory$_{FIFO}$<br>Equals |
| Cost of goods sold$_{LIFO}$ $\Bigg\{$ | − Increase in LIFO reserve<br>or<br>+ Decrease in LIFO reserve | = Costs of goods sold$_{FIFO}$ |

Remember that this conversion to FIFO is an approximation. As long as inventory turns fairly rapidly, the approximation is close.

units and the historical cost of all LIFO layers. The LIFO reserve disclosure allows the analyst to convert reported LIFO inventory amounts to approximate FIFO amounts. This adjustment can be performed for all dates for which LIFO reserve amounts are disclosed. For example, using the beginning LIFO reserve disclosure in Exhibit 9.6, Aral's December 31, 2007 FIFO inventory can be estimated as:

$$\begin{array}{ccccc} \text{Inventory}_{FIFO} & = & \text{Inventory}_{LIFO} & + & \text{LIFO Reserve} \\ \$6{,}250{,}000 & = & \$3{,}875{,}000 & + & \$2{,}375{,}000 \end{array}$$

FIFO inventory at December 31, 2007 equals $6,250,000. This number is also, of course, the FIFO beginning inventory for January 1, 2008.

Using the LIFO reserve disclosure in this way also makes it possible for analysts to convert LIFO cost of goods sold to a FIFO basis. This is most easily understood by looking at the basic cost of goods sold formula in column (1) of Exhibit 9.7. Notice that both the beginning and ending inventory *and* the cost of goods sold amounts in column (1) are measured at LIFO. (Inventory purchases represent the actual transactions and events of the period and do not require a cost flow assumption.) Column (2) shows the addition of the respective LIFO reserves to beginning and ending LIFO inventory. As we just saw, the sum that results from this addition yields FIFO inventory amounts shown in column (3). Using the basic cost of goods sold formula on the column (3) FIFO numbers plus actual purchases yields FIFO cost of goods sold. Thus, the LIFO reserve disclosures make it possible to convert LIFO cost of goods sold to a FIFO basis.

We apply this adjustment process to convert Aral Company's reported LIFO cost of goods sold number to a FIFO basis in Exhibit 9.8. Inventory purchases during 2008 are $22,165,000. FIFO cost of goods sold is $21,715,000. To make valid comparisons across firms that use different inventory accounting methods, you must make the adjustments like those in Exhibit 9.8.

A shortcut procedure can be used to convert cost of goods sold from LIFO to FIFO. The shortcut focuses on the *change* in the LIFO reserve between the beginning and end of the year, as reflected in the bracketed area at the bottom of column (2) in Exhibit 9.7. (This shortcut avoids the need to successively add the respective LIFO reserve amounts to beginning and ending inventory.) Applying this shortcut adjustment to the Aral Company data in Exhibit 9.8, we see that the change in the LIFO reserve was a *decrease* of $655,000 (that is, $2,375,000 at the start of the year versus $1,720,000 at the end of the year) and that FIFO cost of goods sold

| EXHIBIT 9.8 | Aral Company |
| --- | --- |

**Adjusting from LIFO to FIFO Cost of Goods Sold**

| ($ in thousands) | As Reported in Financial Statements (LIFO) | | LIFO Reserve | | Adjusted to FIFO Basis |
| --- | --- | --- | --- | --- | --- |
| Beginning inventory, | | | | | |
| January 1, 2008 | $ 3,875 | + | $2,375 | = | $ 6,250 |
| Purchases | 22,165 | | | | 22,165 |
| Goods available | 26,040 | | | | 28,415 |
| Ending inventory, | | | | | |
| December 31, 2008 | 4,980 | + | 1,720 | = | 6,700 |
| Cost of goods sold | $21,060 | + | $ 655 decrease | = | $21,715 |

exceeds LIFO cost of goods sold by $655,000. So, when the LIFO reserve amount *decreases,* the shortcut conversion procedure is:

$$\text{Cost of goods sold}_{\text{LIFO}} \quad + \quad \text{Decrease in LIFO reserve} \quad = \quad \text{Cost of goods sold}_{\text{FIFO}}$$

When the LIFO reserve amount *increases,* the conversion is:

$$\text{Cost of goods sold}_{\text{LIFO}} \quad - \quad \text{Increase in LIFO reserve} \quad = \quad \text{Cost of goods sold}_{\text{FIFO}}$$

Aral uses LIFO for all of its inventory. But as in Exhibit 9.5, most companies use a combination of inventory cost flow assumptions. The following disclosure from the 2005 Huttig Building Products, Inc. annual report illustrates this:

Inventories are valued at the lower of cost or market. The Company's entire inventory is comprised of finished goods. Approximately 83% of inventories were determined by using the LIFO (last-in, first-out) method of inventory valuation as of December 31, 2005 and 90% as of December 31, 2004. The LIFO percentage in 2005 decreased due to the acquisition of the Dallas branch in 2005, which utilizes the average cost method. The balance of all other inventories is determined by the average cost method, which approximates costs on a FIFO (first-in, first-out) method. The replacement cost would be higher than the LIFO valuation by $8.9 million in 2005 and $9.2 million in 2004.

*Source:* Huttig Building Products 2005 Form 10-K.

The LIFO-to-FIFO adjustment for a company such as Huttig Building Products, which uses LIFO for only a portion of its inventory, is identical to the method used in Exhibit 9.8 for Aral Company. The beginning and ending LIFO reserves are added, respectively, to beginning and ending reported inventory amounts. It doesn't matter that LIFO was used for only 90% of the beginning inventory and 83% of the ending inventory. By adding the LIFO reserve to the reported inventory, *the LIFO portion is adjusted,* and what results is inventory on a 100% FIFO basis.

There is no standardized GAAP format for disclosing the LIFO reserve. The format shown in Exhibit 9.6 for Aral Company is often seen. Other firms disclose the LIFO reserve amount in narrative form, as Huttig did. Indeed, Huttig never used the term "LIFO reserve"; instead it revealed the reserve obliquely by stating the amount by which inventory replacement cost exceeds the LIFO valuation. Exhibit 9.9 shows another disclosure format, this one from Finlay Enterprises, Inc., a jewelry retailer that uses LIFO for inventory reporting.

## EXHIBIT 9.9 — Illustrative LIFO Reserve Disclosure Format

**Finlay Enterprises, Inc.**
Note 3—Merchandise Inventories consisted of the following:

| ($ in thousands) | Merchandise Inventories | |
| --- | --- | --- |
| | **January 28, 2006** | **January 29, 2005** |
| Jewelry goods—rings, watches, and other fine jewelry (first-in, first-out [FIFO] basis) | $353,009 | $297,266 |
| Less: Excess of FIFO cost over LIFO inventory value | 21,252 | 18,677 |
| LIFO cost | $331,757 | $278,589 |

*Source:* Finlay Enterprises, Inc. 2005 annual report.

Notice that Finlay, like Huttig, did not use the phrase "LIFO reserve."

A self-study problem intended to solidify your understanding of the different inventory accounting methods appears at the end of the chapter. You may wish to refer to it now.

**Under both FIFO and LIFO, the allocation of costs between ending inventory and cost of goods sold is limited to the *historical costs* incurred. As costs change, LIFO puts the "oldest" costs on the balance sheet while FIFO runs the "oldest" costs through the income statement. The LIFO reserve disclosure permits analysts to transform LIFO financial statements to a FIFO basis, thus making comparisons between firms more meaningful when one firm is using LIFO and the other FIFO.**

## INFLATION AND LIFO RESERVES

Figure 9.4 provides descriptive statistics on the magnitude of LIFO reserves and inflation for a broad cross-section of firms that used LIFO for all or part of their inventories from 1976 to 2001.[15] Figure 9.4(a) shows the median LIFO reserve amount stated as a percentage of owners' equity along with the 25th and 75th percentile values.[16] Figure 9.4(b) relates the annual inflation rates (as measured by the percentage change in the Consumer Price Index) to the LIFO reserve amounts reported in Figure 9.4(a) over the 1976 to 2001 time period.

The median LIFO reserve in Figure 9.4(a) ranged from a high of 13.3% of owners' equity in 1980 to a low of 2.6% in 2001. Because owners' equity equals the book value of net assets (that is, assets minus liabilities), the results in Figure 9.4(a) also reveal how much *higher* the reported net assets of firms would have been had they valued their LIFO inventories under the FIFO method. Clearly, the decision to use the LIFO inventory method reduces the net asset values below what they would have reported under the FIFO inventory method.

Compare Panels (a) and (b) in Figure 9.4 and notice how the LIFO reserve amounts increase in response to upticks in annual inflation rates during the late 1970s. As the rate of inflation

---

[15] The 1995 to 1996 data for these graphs are adapted from R. Jennings, P. J. Simko, and R. B. Thompson, II, "Does LIFO Inventory Accounting Improve the Income Statement at the Expense of the Balance Sheet?" *Journal of Accounting Research,* Spring 1996, pp. 85–109. The data from 1992–2001 came from Standard & Poor's Compustat®.

[16] The 75th percentile value is the value that is equal to or greater than the observation for 75% of the firms in the sample. In other words, 25% of the firms will have an observed value that is higher than the 75th percentile.

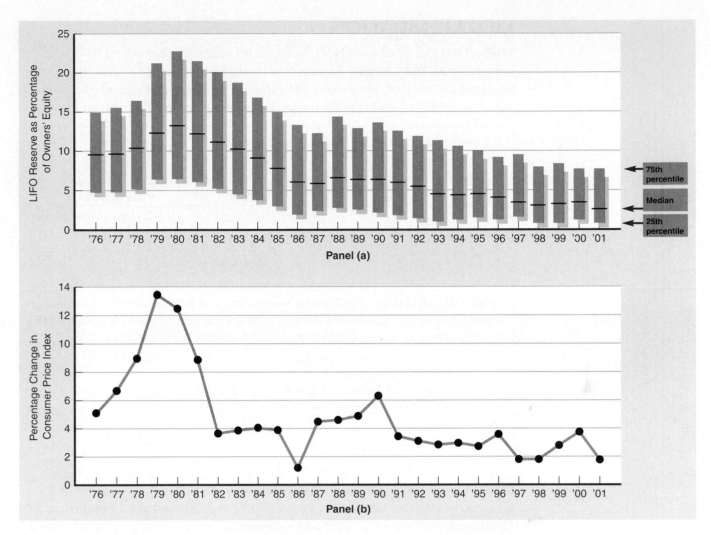

**Figure 9.4** MAGNITUDE OF LIFO RESERVES AND LIFO EARNINGS EFFECT

(a) Distribution of LIFO Reserve Amounts as a Percentage of Owners' Equity and (b) Percentage Change in CPI for Benchmark.

*Source:* (a) R. Jennings, P. J. Simko, and R. B. Thompson, II, op. cit., 1976 to 1991; Standard & Poor's Compustat®, 1992–2001.

increases from about 5% in 1976 to more than 12% in 1980, the median LIFO reserve increases from 9.5% to 13.3% of owners' equity. This pattern should not surprise you. When inflation heats up, the disparity between old LIFO inventory costs and current FIFO costs increases. This disparity creates the LIFO reserve and, as long as inventory *levels* in units do not fall, when the disparity increases, so too must the LIFO reserve amount.

You may ask why the LIFO reserve amounts as a percentage of owners' equity show a general downward trend through the 1980s and early 1990s despite annual inflation rates from 4% to 6% in most years. With constant inventory *levels* (in units) and positive price increases from year to year, you would expect to see LIFO reserves that continue to increase through time. The general downward trend in the LIFO reserve as a percentage of owners' equity from 1981–2001 can be explained by a combination of (1) the growth in owners' equity through time from profitable operations and (2) the increasing tendency of firms to reduce inventory levels as they downsize, restructure, or adopt just-in-time inventory management.

# LIFO LIQUIDATION

When a LIFO firm liquidates old LIFO layers, the net income number under LIFO can be seriously distorted. This is because the older (and usually lower) costs in the LIFO layers that are liquidated are "matched" against sales dollars that are stated at higher current prices. This results in an inflated or illusory profit margin. The following example illustrates the point.

---

The Bernazard Company had the following layers in its LIFO inventory at January 1, 2008 at which time the replacement cost of the inventory was $600 per unit.

| Year LIFO Layer Added | Units | Unit Cost | Total | LIFO Reserve as of 1/1/08 |
|---|---|---|---|---|
| 2005 | 10 | $300 | $ 3,000 | ($600 − $300) × 10 = $ 3,000 |
| 2006 | 20 | 400 | 8,000 | ($600 − $400) × 20 = 4,000 |
| 2007 | 30 | 500 | 15,000 | ($600 − $500) × 30 = 3,000 |
| | 60 | | $26,000 | $10,000 |

Bernazard sets its selling price by adding a $400 per unit markup to replacement cost at the time of sale. As of January 1, 2008, the replacement cost was $600 per unit; this cost remained constant throughout 2008. During 2008 the company purchased 45 units at a cost of $600 per unit, and it sold 80 units at a price of $1,000 per unit. Pre-tax LIFO income for 2008 is:

| | | |
|---|---|---|
| Sales revenues, 80 @ $1,000 | | $80,000 |
| Cost of goods sold | | |
| 2008 purchases, 45 @ $600 | $27,000 | |
| 2007 purchases, 30 @ $500 | 15,000 | |
| 2006 purchases, 5 @ $400 | 2,000 | |
| | | 44,000 |
| LIFO gross margin | | $36,000 |

---

Because the number of units sold (80) exceeded the number of units purchased in 2008 (45), Bernazard was forced to liquidate its entire 2007 LIFO layer (30 units) and 5 units from its 2006 LIFO layer. In such situations, LIFO's income statement matching advantages disappear. Indeed, a "mismatching" occurs because the reported LIFO margin per unit is only $36,000/80, or $450; this overstates the "real" current cost operating margin of $400 per unit. This $50 per unit overstatement of the margin occurs because some 2006 and 2007 purchase costs are being matched against 2008 revenues. If analysts use past margin numbers as a starting point in generating future profit or cash flow estimates, the LIFO income number is misleading when dipping occurs. That is, the $450 *reported* LIFO unit margin overstates the current cost *real* margin of $400 used for pricing purposes and thus does not represent a sustainable future per unit margin number. LIFO earnings that include LIFO dipping profits are considered to be lower quality earnings.[17] The illusory profit elements would generally be assigned a lower earnings multiple for valuation purposes. Research shows that security price reactions to earnings numbers that contain LIFO liquidation profits are smaller than the price reactions to earnings numbers that are devoid of these illusory profits.[18]

 **Valuation**

To understand better what happens when LIFO dipping occurs, let's examine the reported current cost operating margin for 2008:

| | |
|---|---|
| Sales revenues (80 × $1,000) | $80,000 |
| Replacement cost of goods sold (80 × $600) | 48,000 |
| Current cost operating margin (80 × $400) | $32,000 |

---

[17] For example, see Siegel, op. cit., pp. 60–68.

[18] T. Carroll, D. W. Collins, and W. B. Johnson, "The LIFO-FIFO Choice and the Quality of Earnings Signals," Working paper, University of Iowa, August 1997.

## EXHIBIT 9.10 — Calculation of LIFO Liquidation Profits

LIFO Layer Liquidated

| Year Added | Units Liquidated | | Current Cost | | Historical Cost | | Effect on Earnings |
|---|---|---|---|---|---|---|---|
| 2007 | 30 | × | ($600 | − | $500) | = | $3,000 |
| 2006 | 5 | × | ($600 | − | $400) | = | 1,000 |
| Total increase in pre-tax earnings due to LIFO liquidation | | | | | | | $4,000 |

The 2008 LIFO gross margin of $36,000 in the example on page 494 exceeds the 2008 current cost margin of $32,000. ***This "extra" LIFO income of $4,000 is the result of mismatching.*** In more technical terms, as LIFO layers are liquidated, some of the inventory holding gains of 2007 and 2006 that were ignored under historical cost LIFO in the years they occurred suddenly are recognized as income as the old, lower cost inventory layers are matched against current selling prices. This can be seen by examining the December 31, 2008, LIFO inventory computation:

| Year LIFO Layer Added | Remaining Units | Unit Cost | Ending Inventory 12/31/08 Total | LIFO Reserve as of 12/31/08 |
|---|---|---|---|---|
| 2005 | 10 | $300 | $3,000 | ($600 − $300) × 10 = $3,000 |
| 2006 | 15 | 400 | 6,000 | ($600 − $400) × 15 = 3,000 |
| | 25 | | $9,000 | $6,000 |

The LIFO reserve was $10,000 at January 1, 2008 (see page 494). Notice that the LIFO dipping has reduced the LIFO reserve to $6,000 at December 31, 2008. This $4,000 reduction in the LIFO reserve represents another way to visualize how LIFO dipping creates a mismatching on the income statement. Previously ignored unrealized holding gains are included in income as Bernazard liquidates the old LIFO layers. The $4,000 earnings "boost" equals the difference between the current cost to replace the liquidated layer of LIFO inventory (at date of sale) and the original cost of those units. This is demonstrated in Exhibit 9.10. When old LIFO layers are invaded, LIFO income jumps, but the increase is not sustainable.

When the income effect of a LIFO liquidation is material, the SEC requires that firms disclose the dollar impact of LIFO dipping on income. Most companies that provide the 10-Q or 10-K disclosure also disclose the dollar impact of dipping in the report. The statement user should be alert to the fact that the earnings effect of LIFO dipping can be reported on either a *before-tax* or *after-tax* basis. Exhibit 9.11 shows this disclosure (on both a before- and after-tax basis) from Aral Company's 2008 annual report.

The LIFO dipping disclosure in Exhibit 9.11 indicates that 2008 earnings before income taxes increased by $2,600,000 as a consequence of matching old LIFO layer costs against 2008 revenues. This number represents the *pre-tax* effect of LIFO liquidation, indicating that the reported

## EXHIBIT 9.11 — Aral Company

### 2008 Annual Report Disclosure of LIFO Dipping

During 2008, the Company liquidated certain LIFO inventories that were carried at lower costs prevailing in prior years. The effect of this liquidation was to increase earnings before income taxes by $2,600,000 ($1,690,000 increase in net earnings, or an increase of $.08 per share).

> **EXHIBIT 9.12**    Aral Company
>
> **Change in the LIFO Reserve**
>
> | | |
> |---|---:|
> | Beginning LIFO reserve, January 1, 2008 | $2,375,000 |
> | Decrease in LIFO reserve due to LIFO dipping (Exhibit 9.11) | (2,600,000) |
> | Increase in LIFO reserve due to increases in input costs during the year (plug) | 1,945,000 |
> | Ending LIFO reserve, December 31, 2008 | $1,720,000 |

LIFO gross margin in 2008 overstated sustainable earnings by $2,600,000. Equivalently, the LIFO cost of goods sold number was lower than current cost of goods sold by $2,600,000.

## Reconciliation of Changes in LIFO Reserve

We are now able to explain more precisely what factors drive the LIFO–FIFO cost of goods sold difference computed for Aral in Exhibit 9.8. As we see in that exhibit, FIFO cost of goods sold exceeds LIFO cost of goods sold by $655,000, the dollar decrease in the LIFO reserve. LIFO dipping reduces the LIFO reserve because old, lower cost LIFO layers are eliminated. But the LIFO reserve increases when input costs increase. So, to explain what causes the LIFO versus FIFO cost of goods sold difference, we need to explain what causes both upward and downward changes in the LIFO reserve. This is done in Exhibit 9.12.

We know the beginning and ending balance of the reserve as well as the decrease caused by LIFO dipping. To reconcile to the December 31, 2008 LIFO reserve amount, the reserve had to increase by $1,945,000, (the highlighted the "plug" figure in Exhibit 9.12). This increase is attributable to rising input costs. So, the $655,000 difference between the LIFO and FIFO cost of goods sold numbers can be explained as:

| | |
|---|---:|
| 1. Rising input costs *increased* LIFO cost of goods sold by | $1,945,000 |
| 2. LIFO dipping undercharged expense and thus *reduced* cost of goods sold by | (2,600,000) |
| 3. Result: FIFO cost of goods sold exceeds LIFO cost of goods sold by | $ 655,000 |

Reconciling the LIFO reserve as in Exhibit 9.12 provides auditors and other analysts information about the direction of input costs. When linked to other data, this cost information can be valuable. For example, if the auditor/analyst knows that input costs are rising but competition limits output price increases, it is likely that the firm's future margins will suffer. This will reduce future operating cash flows, adversely affecting the firm's value and perhaps even viability as a going concern.

## Improved Trend Analysis

**Analysis**

The LIFO to FIFO adjustment is also used in trend analysis as illustrated in Exhibit 9.13, where comparative gross profit data for Aral are shown for 2006 to 2008.

The Exhibit 9.13(a) data show that the gross profit percentage rose slightly in 2007 and more dramatically in 2008. But we have also seen (Exhibit 9.11) that in 2008 there was LIFO dipping, which increased the reported gross profit in 2008 over what it would have been without the liquidation. You might ask what the profit trend looks like after adjusting for LIFO dipping. We can extend the previous analysis to address this question; see Exhibit 9.13(b).

| EXHIBIT 9.13 | Aral Company |
| --- | --- |

## a. Comparative Gross Profit Data as Reported

| | Years Ended December 31 | | |
| --- | --- | --- | --- |
| ($ in thousands) | **2008** | **2007** | **2006** |
| Net sales | $26,000 | $25,000 | $24,000 |
| Cost of goods sold | 21,060 | 21,000 | 20,400 |
| Gross profit | $ 4,940 | $ 4,000 | $ 3,600 |
| Gross profit as a percentage of sales | 19.0% | 16.0% | 15.0% |

## b. Gross Profit Data Adjusted for LIFO Dipping

| | Years Ended December 31 | | |
| --- | --- | --- | --- |
| ($ in thousands) | **2008** | **2007** | **2006** |
| Gross profit as reported | $ 4,940 | $ 4,000 | $ 3,600 |
| Pre-tax effect of LIFO dipping on gross profit | 2,600 | — | — |
| Gross profit after eliminating LIFO dipping effect | $ 2,340 | $ 4,000 | $ 3,600 |
| Net sales (as reported) | $26,000 | $25,000 | $24,000 |
| Adjusted gross profit percentage | 9.0% | 16.0% | 15.0% |
| Exhibit 9.13 gross profit percentage | 19.0% | 16.0% | 15.0% |
| Difference | −10% | N/A | N/A |

**Valuation**

The computations reveal that after removing the illusory income effect arising from LIFO dipping, the gross profit percentage for Aral shows a sharp decline in 2008. The adjusted gross profit percentage (highlighted in Exhibit 9.13[b]) fell from 15.0% in 2006 to 9.0% in 2008. This deterioration is not immediately evident in the *reported* gross margin figures. Analysis of trend data provides potentially important information regarding management's performance in adapting to new market conditions. Neglecting to adjust the year-to-year data for nonsustainable factors (such as the artificial margin improvement that results from LIFO dipping) could easily lead to erroneous conclusions.

Consider one final point regarding Exhibit 9.13(b). Many analysts believe that the most recent margin percentage provides the least biased estimate of the next year's margin percentage. (This belief is correct when margins follow a random-walk pattern. When they do, the best estimate of the next period's value is generated by simply extrapolating the most recently observed past value.) *After eliminating the effects of LIFO dipping, the adjusted gross margin percentage provides a clearer picture of the underlying real sustainable gross margin in each year.* Analysts trying to estimate Aral Company's future performance must understand that it is the 9.0% adjusted margin percentage, not the 19.0% unadjusted figure, that represents the starting point for estimating the sustainable margin in subsequent periods.

---

The Aral disclosure revealed both the pre-tax *and* after-tax income effect of LIFO dipping. Some companies disclose only the increase in net (after-tax) earnings. In these instances, analysts can still easily convert the LIFO dipping effect to a pre-tax basis and evaluate year-to-year changes in gross margin.

Here's how. Assume that a company discloses that LIFO dipping increased its (after-tax) net income by $1,690,000. Also assume that the income tax rate is 35%. Then:

$$\text{After-tax effect} = \text{Pre-tax effect} \times (1 - \text{Marginal tax rate})$$

or

$$\$1,690,000 = \text{Pre-tax effect} \times (1 - 0.35)$$

or

$$\frac{\$1,690,000}{0.65} = \text{Pre-tax effect of } \$2,600,000$$

The $2,600,000 pre-tax impact of LIFO dipping would then be used to undertake an analysis similar to Exhibit 9.13(b).

Of course, LIFO liquidations don't occur only at the end of the year. When liquidations occur midyear, both the accounting treatment and accompanying 10-Q disclosure can differ slightly from the Aral Company example. The reason is that management must determine whether the midyear inventory reduction will persist to year-end or just be temporary.

Here's what one oil refining company said about its midyear LIFO liquidations (dollar amounts are in millions):

During the second quarter of 2006, we incurred a **temporary** LIFO liquidation gain in our Refinery inventory in the amount of $178. This gain decreased by $19 during the third quarter and we expect it to be fully restored by the end of the year. The temporary LIFO liquidation gain has been deferred as a component of accrued expenses and other current liabilities in the accompanying September 30, 2006 condensed consolidated balance sheet.

During the second quarter of 2006, we also incurred a **permanent** reduction in a LIFO layer resulting in a liquidation gain in our Refinery inventory in the amount of $1,026. In the third quarter, this gain decreased by $11. This liquidation gain, which represents a reduction of approximately 77,000 barrels, was recognized as a component of cost of goods sold in the nine month period ended September 30, 2006. [Emphasis added.]

*Source:* Delek US Holdings, Inc. Form 10-Q filing for the period ended June 30, 2007.

As this example illustrates, midyear LIFO liquidation gains that are deemed to be permanent flow directly to cost of goods sold and thereby increase earnings in the quarter when they occur. However, temporary midyear LIFO liquidation gains don't flow to cost of goods sold in the quarter when they occur. These temporary gains are instead parked on the balance sheet. If inventory quantities increase to their former level by year-end, the temporary gain is reversed and eliminated. This accounting approach thus eliminates from quarterly earnings any volatility that would otherwise arise because of seasonal fluctuations in LIFO inventory levels. But what if inventory quantities remain low at year-end? In this case, the temporary LIFO liquidation gain is now deemed permanent and flows from the balance sheet to year-end cost of goods sold. Delayed recognition distorts fourth quarter net income, but that's the trade-off that results from an accounting approach that eliminates quarterly earnings volatility when inventory reductions are truly temporary.

## The Frequency of LIFO Liquidations

Figure 9.5 provides information regarding the frequency of LIFO liquidations from 1985 through 2001 for manufacturing and merchandising firms using LIFO. The vertical axis

### Figure 9.5

PERCENTAGE OF MANUFACTURING AND MERCHANDISING FIRMS USING LIFO AND EXPERIENCING A LIFO LIQUIDATION

*SOURCE:* 1985–1993 data, *National Automated Accounting Research System (NAARS).* The NAARS service is offered jointly by Lexis-Nexis, a division of Reed Elsevier, Inc., and the American Institute of Certified Public Accountants; 1995–2001 data, 10-K Wizard® and Compustat®.

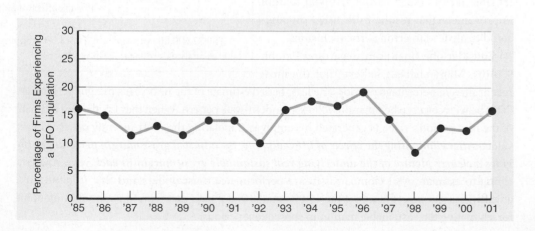

represents the percentage of firms that reported a LIFO liquidation in any given year. In most years, between 10% and 20% of firms using LIFO experience a LIFO liquidation; clearly, liquidations are not uncommon. Inventory costs tended to increase over this period.

When LIFO dipping occurred, the older costs that were matched against current revenues were below current replacement costs roughly 60% to 80% of the time. This causes a transitory boost to earnings. How large is this earnings boost? The median effect of LIFO dipping on pre-tax earnings ranged from a high of 10.4% in 1991 to a low of 2.0% in 2000. But 25% of the firms with 1991 LIFO liquidations boosted pre-tax earnings by 36.8% or more. Clearly, LIFO liquidations occur frequently, and their impact on earnings is large enough to warrant close attention.

> What about the remaining LIFO liquidations? They either had an "immaterial" effect on pre-tax earnings or (in rare cases) they reduced pre-tax earnings. LIFO liquidations reduce pre-tax earnings when current replacement cost of inventory falls below the older LIFO cost.

To avoid being misled by transitory LIFO liquidation profits, statement users should carefully scrutinize the LIFO inventory footnote. The objective is to determine whether a LIFO liquidation occurred during the period and, if so, what impact it had on reported profits for the period.

---

**LIFO liquidations occur frequently and often have a large impact on reported earnings. The earnings effect arises from a mismatching since LIFO layers carried at "old" costs are matched against current period revenues. Reported margins are distorted and so is the income trend.**

RE**CAP**

---

## ELIMINATING LIFO RATIO DISTORTIONS

LIFO inventory costing can lead to ratio distortions that can be corrected easily. For example, on its December 31, 2008 balance sheet, Aral Company reported total current assets of $14,460,000 and total current liabilities of $5,784,000, Utilizing these numbers, the current ratio at December 31, 2008 is:

$$\frac{\text{Current assets}}{\text{Current liabilities}} = \frac{\$14,460,000}{\$5,784,000} = 2.5$$

However, Exhibit 9.6 disclosed that the LIFO inventory carrying amount understated FIFO (and replacement cost) inventory by $1,720,000. This amount is the LIFO reserve that we must add to the numerator to reflect the current ratio in truly *current* terms. The adjusted current ratio is ($000 omitted):

**Analysis**

$$\frac{\$14,460 + \$1,720}{\$5,784} = 2.80$$

The current ratio improves after making the LIFO adjustment. Most other ratios deteriorate once the adjustments for LIFO effects have been included. To illustrate the general deterioration, consider the inventory turnover ratio:

$$\frac{\text{Cost of goods sold}}{\text{Average inventory}} = \text{Inventory turnover}$$

The inventory turnover ratio is designed to reflect the physical turnover of product, that is, how long the typical unit remains in inventory. Most firms have many inventory categories. This diversity renders unit measures of inventory turnover meaningless because unit turnover is difficult to interpret in a diversified firm. That's why dollar, rather than unit, inventory measures are used to compute the turnover ratio. For Aral, using the inventory amounts from

Exhibit 9.6 and cost of goods sold from Exhibit 9.8, inventory turnover for 2008 is ($000 omitted):

$$\frac{\$21,060}{(\$3,875 + \$4,980)/2} = 4.76 \text{ times per year}$$

The typical unit turns over 4.76 times per year. Another way to understand what this means is to divide 4.76 into 365, the number of days in a year. The result $365/4.76 = 76.7$ shows that the typical unit remains in inventory for 76.7 days.

The inventory turnover ratio is structured to approximate *physical* unit flow. The numerator is the cumulative dollar cost of units that have been sold; the denominator is the average cost of units on hand during the year. Under "normal" circumstances, the quotient should reflect the physical unit turnover. Unfortunately, LIFO frequently distorts the representation of physical unit flow. To see why, consider the denominator of the Aral ratio; it does *not* reflect the then-current cost of the inventory at either the beginning or end of 2008 because there was a LIFO reserve at both times: $2,375,000 and $1,720,000, respectively. For a firm using LIFO.

- The numerator of the ratio—cost of goods sold—is predominantly current period costs, here, 2008, and
- The denominator—average inventory—consists of old LIFO costs.

The quotient will not capture physical unit turnover unless an adjustment is made to the denominator. Furthermore, an adjustment to the numerator is also required here because the pre-tax impact of the LIFO dipping ($2,600,000) causes the cost of goods sold numerator to understate *current* cost of goods sold by this amount. To correctly gauge physical turnover, the analyst must *always* adjust the denominator of LIFO firms' turnover by adding the LIFO reserve amounts to beginning and ending inventory. In addition, the numerator must also be adjusted for LIFO liquidation profits whenever LIFO dipping occurs. The Aral 2008 inventory turnover ratio adjusting both the numerator and the denominator is ($000 omitted):

$$\frac{\overset{\text{(Reported cost of goods sold)}}{\$21,060} + \overset{\text{(Pre-tax effect of LIFO dipping)}}{\$2,600}}{[(\underset{\substack{\text{Beginning} \\ \text{inventory}}}{\$3,875} + \underset{\substack{\text{Beginning LIFO} \\ \text{reserve}}}{\$2,375}) + (\underset{\substack{\text{Ending} \\ \text{inventory}}}{\$4,980} + \underset{\substack{\text{Ending} \\ \text{LIFO reserve}}}{\$1,720})]/2} = 3.65$$

Dividing this LIFO–adjusted turnover (3.65) into 365 days reveals that the typical unit, in fact, remains in inventory for 100 days—considerably longer than the 76.7 days suggested by the unadjusted analysis.

## TAX IMPLICATIONS OF LIFO

In the United States, the accounting principles that a firm uses in preparing its external financial statements need not be the same as the principles used in computing income taxes. The only exception to this statement occurs under LIFO. U.S. tax rules specify that if LIFO is used for tax purposes, the external financial statements must also use LIFO. This is called the **LIFO conformity rule.**

The LIFO conformity rule partially explains the widespread use of LIFO for financial reporting purposes. To gain the tax advantage of LIFO, firms must also use this method in their external financial statements.

LIFO's tax advantage is that it provides a lower income number than FIFO during periods of rising prices and nondecreasing inventory quantities, thus lowering the immediate tax liability. However, this effect can be reversed if LIFO layers are liquidated or if future purchase costs fall.

> Footnote disclosure of the LIFO reserve, as required by GAAP, is allowed by the IRS.

The dollar amount of the tax saving provided by LIFO can easily be computed by reference to the LIFO reserve number. For example, in Exhibit 9.6 we saw that Aral's LIFO reserve at December 31, 2008 was $1,720,000. This number equals the cumulative excess of LIFO cost of goods sold over what the cost of goods sold would have been had FIFO been used. The $1,720,000 also represents the cumulative unrealized holding gain on the old LIFO layers. Under FIFO, the old, lower cost inventory would have been charged to cost of goods sold, thereby raising cumulative pretax income by this amount. Assuming an average tax rate over the past years of 40%. Aral has *postponed* approximately $688,000 in taxes (that is, $1,720,000 × 40%) since it began using LIFO.

> The marginal federal corporate tax rate immediately prior to 1986 was 46% and from 1986 to 1992 the rate was 34%. Since 1992 the rate has been 35%. With state and local taxes, the overall marginal tax rates obviously would be even higher. We use a flat 40% rate to simplify the calculations.

The amount of taxes that companies can postpone by using LIFO can be substantial; see Exhibit 9.14. This table lists the 12 firms with the largest LIFO reserves as of year-end 2005 with their estimated tax savings (based on using a 40% marginal tax rate). As shown, the LIFO tax benefit ranges from $6.160 billion for ExxonMobil to $403.6 million for Ford Motor Company. The average amount of taxes postponed by these 12 firms was $1,289.9 million. Clearly, these companies have received substantial cumulative cash flow benefit from using LIFO rather than FIFO.

Although clear cash flow benefits result from using LIFO, critics argue that LIFO could induce undesirable managerial behavior. This could happen if a firm has depleted its inventory quantities toward the end of a year. If inventories are allowed to remain at the depleted level, the tax liability could increase considerably because the liquidation of old, low-cost LIFO layers increases income. However, a manager can avoid this increase in taxes by simply

| **EXHIBIT 9.14** | **Estimated Tax Savings for Firms with the Largest LIFO Reserves** | |
|---|---|---|
| ($ in millions) | 2005 LIFO Reserve | Estimated Cumulative Tax Benefit* |
| ExxonMobil | $15400.0 | $6160.0 |
| Chevron | 4846.0 | 1938.4 |
| ConocoPhillips | 4721.0 | 1888.4 |
| Caterpillar | 2345.0 | 938.0 |
| Sunoco | 2304.0 | 921.6 |
| Phelps Dodge | 1540.0 | 616.0 |
| Marathon Oil | 1535.0 | 614.0 |
| General Motors | 1491.0 | 596.4 |
| Imperial Oil Ltd. | 1226.0 | 490.4 |
| Dow Chemical | 1149.0 | 459.6 |
| Deere & Co. | 1132.0 | 452.8 |
| Ford Motor Co. | 1009.0 | 403.6 |

* Based on an average marginal tax rate of 40%.

*Source:* Compustat® as data source; methodology not verified or controlled by Standard & Poor's.

purchasing a large amount of inventory at the end of the year to bring the inventory back up to beginning-of-year levels. Doing this to avoid tax increases may cause unwise purchasing behavior: Excessive stocks could be carried, or year-end purchases could be made despite the fact that future purchase costs are expected to fall.[19]

# ELIMINATING REALIZED HOLDING GAINS FOR FIFO FIRMS

**Analysis**

LIFO puts realized holding gains into income when old LIFO layers are eliminated. In contrast, reported income for FIFO firms *always* includes some realized holding gains during periods of rising inventory costs because FIFO charges the *oldest* inventory to Cost of goods sold. Another way to say the same thing is that FIFO cost of goods sold is understated because of the inventory holding gains that have occurred during the period. Because holding gains are potentially unsustainable, astute analysts try to remove them from reported FIFO income (or, equivalently, add them to FIFO costs of goods sold).

The size of divergence between FIFO cost of goods sold and replacement cost of goods sold depends on two factors:

1. *The severity of input cost changes:* All other factors being equal, the greater the amount of cost change, the larger the divergence between FIFO and replacement cost of goods sold.

2. *The rapidity of physical inventory turnover:* The slower inventory turnover, the larger the divergence.

We illustrate a simple procedure to convert cost of goods sold from FIFO to replacement cost and thereby eliminate realized holding gains from FIFO income.[20] The procedure requires estimating the inventory cost change and assumes rapid inventory turnover. Consider the following example.

Ray Department Store experienced the following inventory transactions during 2008.

| | |
|---|---:|
| Beginning inventory (FIFO basis) | $1,000,000 |
| Merchandise purchases | +8,000,000 |
| Goods available for sale | 9,000,000 |
| Ending inventory (FIFO basis) | −1,100,000 |
| Cost of goods sold (FIFO basis) | $7,900,000 |

Assume that, on average, Ray's input costs for inventory increased by 10% during 2008. The adjustment procedure comprises three steps:

1. Determine FIFO cost of goods sold. In the example, this is $7,900,000. This amount is *not* adjusted.

2. Adjust the *beginning* inventory for one full year of specific price change. In the example, this is $1,000,000 times 10%, or $100,000.

3. Determine the replacement cost of goods sold, which is the sum of the amount in Step 1 ($7,900,000) and the amount in Step 2 ($100,000), that is, $8,000,000.

The difference between the computed replacement cost of goods sold ($8,000,000) and FIFO cost of goods sold ($7,900,000) equals the amount of realized holding gains included in the

---

[19] Results consistent with the potential for tax-driven inventory management inefficiencies are reported in M. Frankel and R. Trezevant, "The Year-End LIFO Inventory Purchasing Decision: An Empirical Test," *The Accounting Review,* April 1994, pp. 382–98.

[20] See A. Falkenstein and R. L. Weil, "Replacement Cost Accounting: What Will Income Statements Based on the SEC Disclosures Show?—Part II," *Financial Analysts Journal,* March–April 1977, pp. 48–57. We have altered the Falkenstein and Weil procedural description slightly to simplify the exposition.

FIFO income figure ($100,000). This simple procedure gives results that accurately approximate tedious calculation approaches.

In Appendix A to this chapter, we provide an intuitive explanation for why this procedure for isolating realized holding gains for FIFO firms "works." We also discuss how analysts can use either price indices or competitors' data to estimate the rate of inventory cost change—10% in the Ray Department Store example.

## INVENTORY ERRORS

Errors in computing inventory are rare and almost always accidental. For example, a computer programming mistake might assign the wrong costs to inventory items. But in occasional instances, companies deliberately (and fraudulently) misstate inventories to manipulate reported earnings. You must first understand how inventory errors affect reported results to understand why some managers use this misrepresentation technique.

To visualize the effect of inventory errors, let's assume that due to a miscount in the 2008 year-end physical inventory, Jones Corporation's ending inventory is *overstated* by $1 million. Also assume there are no other inventory errors. Using the cost of goods sold formula, we see that this error *understates* 2008 cost of goods sold by $1 million:

|  | Effect of 2008 Error on |
|---|---|
| Beginning inventory | No error |
| + Purchases | No error |
| = Goods available | No error |
| − Ending inventory | Overstated by $1 million |
| = Cost of goods sold | Understated by $1 million |

Because ending inventory is subtracted in the cost of goods sold computation, an overstatement of ending inventory leads to an understatement of cost of goods sold. Understating cost of goods sold by $1 million overstates pre-tax income by $1 million. Furthermore, if the error is not detected and corrected in 2008, it will also cause 2009 pre-tax income to be misstated. The reason that the error carries over into 2009 is that the December 31, 2008 ending inventory becomes the January 1, 2009 beginning inventory. So, the carryforward effect (assuming no other 2009 inventory errors) is:

|  | Effect of 2008 Error on the 2009 COGS Computation |
|---|---|
| Beginning inventory | Overstated by $1 million |
| + Purchases | No error |
| = Goods available | Overstated by $1 million |
| − Ending inventory | No error |
| = Cost of goods sold | Overstated by $1 million |

The 2009 cost of goods sold overstatement results in a $1 million understatement of 2009 pre-tax income. The carryforward effect in 2009 is equal in amount but in the opposite direction from the 2008 effect. Because the first year's income is overstated by $1 million and the second year's income is understated by the same amount, by December 31, 2009, the end of the two-year cycle, the Retained earnings account (which is cumulative, of course) will be correct.

If an inventory error is discovered during the reporting year, it is corrected immediately. However, if an error is not discovered until a subsequent year (say, 2009 in our example), then the Retained earnings balance as of the beginning of the discovery year (2009) is corrected. If the error has a material effect on the company's financial statements, it must be separately disclosed.

> If we assume that Jones Corporation's inventory error was discovered in January 2009 after the 2008 books were closed and that the income tax rate is 35%, the entry to correct the error is:
>
> | | | | |
> |---|---|---|---|
> | **DR** | Retained earnings..................... | $650,000 | |
> | **DR** | Income tax payable.................... | 350,000 | |
> | **CR** | Inventory......................... | | $1,000,000 |

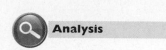

In recent years, the media have coined the phrase "accounting irregularities." Some of these irregularities simply relate to exuberant use of the flexibility within GAAP; others involve fraud. Accounting fraud is relatively rare, but it does happen. And some of the more spectacular frauds involve inventory misstatement. Leslie Fay Companies, Inc., is an example. The company, which manufactures women's apparel, expected 1992 to be a difficult year because of pricing and style issues. To offset the emerging profit shortfall, it overstated quarter-end inventory. As we just saw, overstating ending inventory decreases cost of goods sold, increases income, and masks the adverse real conditions facing the company. Subsequent shareholder litigation alleged that this behavior was partly motivated by a bonus plan tied to reported profits.[21] But as our numerical example illustrates, the phony earnings boost in the overstatement year reverses in the following year. So, if the economic adversity that motivated the deliberate initial inventory overstatement continues, the inventory overstatements have to continue as well.

This is exactly what happened at Comptronix Corporation, an electronics manufacturer that lost an important customer in 1989.[22] After succumbing to the temptation to overstate profits by overstating inventory, the practice could not be abandoned without causing a reversal. So, the overstatement continued until late 1992.[23] The fraud was eventually discovered at both companies. Can auditors and other analysts be successful detectives and uncover these situations? For outsiders, fraud is difficult to detect, but sometimes there are clues.[24] For example, the reduction in cost of goods sold arising from inventory overstatement increases gross margins. ***So, an unexplained increase in gross margins during troubled economic times is suspicious and warrants investigation.***

## ANALYTICAL INSIGHTS: LIFO DANGERS

LIFO makes it possible to manage earnings. To see how, consider a firm that has an executive bonus plan linked to earnings per share (see Figure 7.7, page 380). Assume that it is December 15, 2008, the firm reports on a calendar year basis, and the managers expect EPS for 2008 to be $4.40. (Because the year-end is only two weeks away, this estimate is likely to be very accurate.) As described in Chapter 7, let's assume the bonus "tops out" at $4.00 per share. From the managers' perspective, 40¢ of expected earnings is wasted in the sense that it doesn't increase bonus payouts. So, the executives have an incentive to manage down reported earnings back toward $4.00. LIFO makes this easy to do when input costs are rising. Here's why.

LIFO is applied using the periodic inventory method. Firms wait until the end of the year to compute cost of goods sold. So inventory purchased on December 31, 2008 is the "last in" and is considered to be the "first out" when LIFO cost of goods sold is computed. Similarly, inventory purchased on

> Using the perpetual method defeats the purpose of LIFO. Here's why. Suppose a calendar year firm makes a sale on January 4 and uses the perpetual method; under LIFO, the units sold are presumed to come from the most recent purchase, say January 3. But if the firm instead uses the periodic method and computes cost of goods sold on December 31, those early-in-the-year January purchases will be the *oldest* purchases and less likely to be considered sold. So, perpetual LIFO is seldom used.

[21] L. Vickery, "Leslie Fay's Ex-Financial Chief, Polishan, Is Found Guilty of Fraud," *The Wall Street Journal*, July 7, 2000.

[22] See C. Mulford and E. Comiskey, *Financial Warnings* (New York: John Wiley & Sons, Inc., 1996), pp. 228–33.

[23] For a comprehensive discussion of the accounting issues at Comptronix, see J. L. Boockholdt, "Comptronix, Inc.: An Audit Case Involving Fraud," *Issues in Accounting Education*, February 2000, pp. 105–28.

[24] For a discussion of these clues, see Mulford and Comiskey, op. cit.

December 30 is considered to have been sold next, and so on. Because input costs are rising, if the managers buy unneeded, higher cost inventory during the last two weeks of 2008, this will raise cost of goods sold, lower income, and drive EPS down toward $4.00. Lowering earnings in this way doesn't decrease their bonus so long as they don't let EPS fall below $4.00. But this unneeded inventory *does* increase inventory carrying costs as well as the risk of loss from obsolescence and spoilage. So, managers don't suffer from the inventory buildup, but shareholders do.

But the story isn't over. In 2009, the firm has too much inventory; remember that the purchases at the end of 2008 were unneeded. So, in 2009, managers reduce inventory down to proper levels—a LIFO liquidation occurs. If input costs and output prices move together (that's the norm), then 2009 selling prices are higher than those in 2008. The LIFO dipping in 2009 results in old, lower-cost, early 2008 purchases being matched against higher 2009 selling prices. This artificially raises 2009 income. So, it's a win-win situation for the managers! Playing this 2008 year-end LIFO game costs the managers no 2008 bonus and promises to increase 2009 income. At the end of 2008, they can't accurately forecast 2009 income. It might be below $3.00 per share, out of the bonus range. But the LIFO dipping income could be enough to raise 2009 income above $3.00 per share, back into the bonus range. The effect of the income shift from 2008 into 2009 improves the likelihood that the managers will earn a bonus in 2009 as well.

To see the full range of earnings management "dangers" using LIFO, let's go to a totally new scenario. It's November 15, 2008. Again there's a bonus plan like the one in Figure 7.7 and input costs and output prices have been rising. But here, assume that forecasted EPS is only $2.60. At this earnings level, the managers won't qualify for a bonus. But if they deliberately stop normal purchases for the last six weeks of the year, LIFO layers will be depleted. Again a mismatching occurs as December sales revenues are matched against pre-November 15 costs. When this is done aggressively, EPS can be driven into the bonus area above $3.00 per share. Do managers engage in this type of deliberate LIFO dipping? Unfortunately, research evidence here is sparse. However, if bonus contracts do not subtract out LIFO dipping "profits," there is an incentive to dip deliberately.

> Remember that under LIFO, 2008 cost of goods sold assumed that December purchases were sold first, then November, and so on, working backward through the year. The new LIFO inventory layers added during the last two weeks of 2008 are costed out at cost levels in effect early in 2008, say, costs incurred in January and February.

## EMPIRICAL EVIDENCE ON INVENTORY POLICY CHOICE

LIFO provides significant tax benefits when costs are rising. To obtain these tax benefits, Congress specified that companies must use LIFO not just for tax purposes but also for financial reporting. Despite this constraint, only about 40% of companies in an AICPA survey use LIFO (refer to Exhibit 9.5). Because costs have tended to rise consistently over most of the past 60 years, you can ask why the other 60% of companies do *not* use LIFO. Are they squandering available tax benefits? Why many companies do not use LIFO has intrigued accounting researchers for years. Conjectures about the reason for this include the following:[25]

1. The estimated tax savings from using LIFO are too small to justify the added complexity of the LIFO approach. There are two possible reasons for small tax savings:
   a. Inventory holding gains are trivial for non-LIFO firms.
   b. These non-LIFO firms have large tax loss carryforwards and are not currently paying taxes.

---

[25] See B. E. Cushing and M. J. LeClere, "Evidence on the Determinants of Inventory Accounting Policy Choice," *The Accounting Review,* April 1992, pp. 355–66.

2. Firms in cyclical industries that are subject to extreme fluctuations in physical inventory levels would find LIFO unattractive because of the high probability of LIFO liquidations and consequent adverse tax effects.

See the discussion of LIFO and the lower of cost or market rule in Appendix B.

3. Inventory obsolescence poses difficult issues under LIFO; consequently, firms subject to a high rate of inventory obsolescence may be reluctant to adopt LIFO.

4. During periods of generally rising prices, LIFO leads to lower profits. Managers may be reluctant to adopt LIFO under these conditions for either one or both of the following reasons:

   a. They believe that lower LIFO earnings will lead to lower stock price.

   b. They believe that the lower LIFO earnings will lead to lower compensation because management bonuses are often linked to reported earnings.

5. In a period of rising prices, LIFO causes certain ratios—such as the leverage ratio—used in loan agreements to deteriorate. Firms might be reluctant to adopt LIFO because adoption could result in loan covenant violations.

6. Smaller firms might not adopt LIFO because of the higher costs associated with maintaining the more complicated LIFO accounting records.

Research evidence is consistent with many (but not all) of these conjectures about why some firms don't use LIFO. Several studies have found that the potential inventory holding gains are much higher for LIFO firms than for non-LIFO firms.[26] Accordingly, the tax saving for LIFO adopters is much higher than the potential savings for firms not using LIFO. Furthermore, non-LIFO firms generally have significantly larger tax loss carryforwards than LIFO firms, thereby obviating the need to adopt LIFO.[27] Research evidence is also generally consistent with the fact that LIFO adopters have lower levels of inventory fluctuations[28] and lower leverage in comparison with non-LIFO adopters.[29] In the aggregate, these studies suggest rational economic explanations for the decision by some firms to not adopt LIFO.

Another aspect of inventory accounting that has intrigued researchers is whether the stock market differentiates between LIFO earnings and FIFO earnings. In inflationary periods, LIFO firms would on average report lower profits than FIFO firms but would have higher after-tax cash flows. From an economic perspective, the LIFO firms are better off despite the lower reported earnings. Furthermore, the quality of reported LIFO earnings is presumably higher than FIFO earnings because LIFO earnings usually exclude inventory holding gains from net income; accordingly, LIFO earnings are presumably more sustainable than FIFO earnings during inflationary periods. Thus, the research question is whether investors differentiate between the quality of LIFO versus FIFO earnings or, instead, simply penalize LIFO firms for their lower reported earnings.

Many of the early studies of market reaction to LIFO versus FIFO examined instances in which firms switched from FIFO to LIFO as inflation accelerated. The research question frequently posed was:

 **Valuation**

> If the market simply reacts to bottom-line earnings, then stock prices of firms shifting to LIFO should, on average, fall. On the other hand, if the market considers earnings *quality*, then the relatively higher reported (and expected future) after-tax cash flows of new LIFO adopters should lead on average to stock price increases as the switch is announced.

---

[26] Two examples of such studies are Cushing and LeClere, ibid., and N. Dopuch and M. Pincus, "Evidence on the Choice of Inventory Accounting Methods: LIFO vs. FIFO," *Journal of Accounting Research,* Spring 1988, pp. 28–59.

[27] Cushing and LeClere, op. cit., and F. W. Lindahl, "Dynamic Analysis of Inventory Accounting Choice," *Journal of Accounting Research,* Autumn 1989, pp. 201–26.

[28] Examples include Dopuch and Pincus, op. cit., and C. J. Lee and D. A. Hsieh, "Choice of Inventory Accounting Methods: Comparative Analysis of Alternative Hypotheses," *Journal of Accounting Research,* Autumn 1985, pp. 468–85.

[29] Examples include Lindahl, op. cit., and Cushing and LeClere, op. cit.

Early research studied the stock price reaction to announcements by firms that switched to LIFO as well as to the announcements of the new LIFO earnings numbers. These studies generated conflicting results, probably because of the failure to control for other factors influencing stock price behavior during the year of the inventory switch.

A more recent study that included such controls found consistent evidence that the market perceives LIFO earnings to be of higher quality than FIFO earnings.[30] This study produced the following findings:

1. When reported earnings included highly transitory inventory holding gains (either under FIFO or when LIFO liquidation occurs), the market perceives these earnings to be of lower quality. Thus, the share price increase is small relative to when high-quality (sustainable) earnings are reported.

2. The market response to earnings news is greater after LIFO adoption. This suggests that the market believes that LIFO produces a higher quality earnings signal.

3. Across all firms, there is a higher market response to a given dollar amount of earnings surprise under LIFO in comparison to FIFO. Again, this result is consistent with LIFO being perceived as the higher quality earnings number.

## SUMMARY

This chapter helps readers understand existing GAAP inventory methods and disclosures. It can also help readers compare and analyze profitability and net asset positions across firms that use different inventory methods. Here are the important messages from this chapter.

- Absorption costing can lead to potentially misleading period-to-period income changes when inventories increase or decrease sharply.

- Financial reporting rules allow firms latitude in selecting a cost flow assumption for determining the cost of goods sold reported on the income statement and the inventory values reported on the balance sheet. Some firms use FIFO, some use LIFO, and some use weighted average costing; others use a combination of these methods.

- This diversity in practice can severely hinder interfirm comparisons when inventory purchase costs are changing over time, which is usually the case. Before undertaking interfirm comparisons, numbers for the LIFO firms should be transformed to the FIFO basis.

- Reported FIFO income merges sustainable operating profits and potentially unsustainable realized holding gains. Analysts must disentangle these elements when preparing earnings and cash flow forecasts.

- Similarly, LIFO dipping distorts reported margins because it matches "old" costs with current selling prices.

- Old, out-of-date LIFO inventory carrying amounts can distort various ratios such as inventory turnover. Analysts should use the LIFO reserve to adjust inventories before computing ratio values.

- Users of financial statements must understand these differences and know how to adjust for them using various footnote disclosures. Only by doing so can they make valid comparisons across firms that utilize different inventory cost flow assumptions.

---

[30] Carroll, Collins, and Johnson, op. cit. Additional evidence on how the market values LIFO versus FIFO earnings can be found in Jennings, Simko, and Thompson, op. cit.

## SELF-STUDY PROBLEM

### MITSURU CORPORATION

Mitsuru Corporation began business operations on January 1, 2008, as a wholesaler of macadamia nuts. Its purchase and sales transactions for 2008 are listed in Exhibit 9.15. Mitsuru uses a periodic inventory system.

1. **Compute 2008 ending inventory and cost of goods sold for Mitsuru Corporation using the weighted average cost flow assumption.**

   Ending inventory totals 4,000 pounds, that is, purchases of 23,000 pounds minus sales of 19,000 pounds. The average cost per pound (rounded) is:

   $$\frac{\text{Total cost of goods available for sale} \rightarrow \$238,900}{\text{Total pounds available for sale} \quad \rightarrow 23,000} = \$10.39/\text{pound}$$

   Ending inventory is 4,000 pounds times $10.39, or $41,560. Cost of goods sold is then determined as follows:

   | | |
   |---|---|
   | Total cost of goods available for sale | $238,900 |
   | Less: Ending inventory just computed | (41,560) |
   | Cost of goods sold (weighted average method) | $197,340 |

2. **Compute 2008 ending inventory and cost of goods sold for Mitsuru using the FIFO cost flow assumption.**

   Under the first-in, first-out (FIFO) cost flow assumption, the ending inventory consists of the 4,000 most recently purchased pounds of macadamia nuts. This ending inventory amount consists entirely of the December 18 purchase of 4,000 pounds for $42,400. Accordingly, FIFO cost of goods sold is:

   | | |
   |---|---|
   | Total cost of goods available for sale | $238,900 |
   | Less: Ending FIFO inventory | (42,400) |
   | FIFO cost of goods sold | $196,500 |

---

### EXHIBIT 9.15 — Mitsuru Corporation

**Inventory Purchases and Sales**

| Date | Purchases Pounds | Purchases Dollars/Pound | Purchases Total Dollars | Sales Pounds |
|---|---|---|---|---|
| January 1 | 1,000 | $10.00 | $ 10,000 | |
| February 3 | 4,000 | 10.20 | 40,800 | |
| February 9 | | | | 3,600 |
| April 1 | 4,000 | 10.30 | 41,200 | |
| May 29 | | | | 3,500 |
| June 28 | 5,000 | 10.40 | 52,000 | |
| July 20 | | | | 4,100 |
| September 14 | 5,000 | 10.50 | 52,500 | |
| September 17 | | | | 4,200 |
| December 18 | 4,000 | 10.60 | 42,400 | |
| December 22 | | | | 3,600 |
| | 23,000 | | $238,900 | 19,000 |

3. **Compute 2008 ending inventory and cost of goods sold for Mitsuru using the LIFO cost flow assumption.**

   Under last-in, first-out (LIFO), the ending inventory comprises the 4,000 pounds of oldest macadamia nut purchases. This 4,000 pounds would consist of two layers:

   | | | | | | | |
   |---|---|---|---|---|---|---|
   | January 1 | 1,000 pounds | @ | $10.00 | = | $10,000 |
   | February 3 | 3,000 pounds | @ | $10.20 | = | 30,600 |
   | | 4,000 pounds | | | | $40,600 |

   Thus, LIFO cost of goods sold is:

   | | |
   |---|---|
   | Total cost of goods available for sale | $238,900 |
   | Less: Ending LIFO inventory | (40,600) |
   | LIFO cost of goods sold | $198,300 |

4. **Assume that the December 31, 2008 macadamia nut replacement cost is $10.60 per pound. Compute Mitsuru's LIFO reserve and use the beginning and ending LIFO reserve amounts to reconcile between LIFO and FIFO cost of goods sold.**

   The LIFO reserve at a given point in time is the difference between the LIFO inventory book value and its then-current replacement cost. At January 1, 2008, Mitsuru's LIFO reserve was $0 because the LIFO book value and replacement cost both equaled $10,000. At December 31, 2008, the LIFO reserve was $1,800, computed as follows:

   | | |
   |---|---|
   | December 31, 2008 inventory replacement cost; 4,000 pounds @ $10.60 | $42,400 |
   | December 31, 2008 LIFO inventory | (40,600) |
   | December 31, 2008 LIFO reserve | $ 1,800 |

   Using the formula for converting cost of goods sold (COGS) from a LIFO to FIFO basis in conjunction with the answers to Parts 2 and 3 of this self-study problem yields:

   | $COGS_{LIFO}$ | + | Beginning LIFO reserve | − | Ending LIFO reserve | = | $COGS_{FIFO}$ |
   |---|---|---|---|---|---|---|
   | $198,300 | + | 0 | − | $1,800 | = | $196,500 |

   Notice that $196,500 equals the FIFO cost of goods sold number computed in Part 2.

   As the text discussed, the reconciliation procedure is an approximation. Adding the LIFO reserve to the LIFO inventory equals replacement cost. If the inventory turns quickly, then inventory replacement cost *approximates* FIFO inventory. In this self-study problem, ending FIFO inventory at $10.60 per pound exactly equals replacement cost. Hence, the adjustment is precise.

**APPENDIX A**

# ELIMINATING REALIZED HOLDING GAINS FROM FIFO INCOME

In the chapter, we show a simple way to estimate the amount of realized holding gains included in the FIFO income figure. In this appendix, we provide a simple example to illustrate why this method works.

Consider a firm buying and selling inventory *in equal amounts* daily as you contemplate Figure 9.6. The *quantity* of inventory purchased during the year is the area denoted P. Beginning inventory *quantity* is the area denoted B, and ending inventory *quantity* is the area

**Figure 9.6**

FIFO TO LIFO COST
OF GOODS SOLD
APPROXIMATION
TECHNIQUE

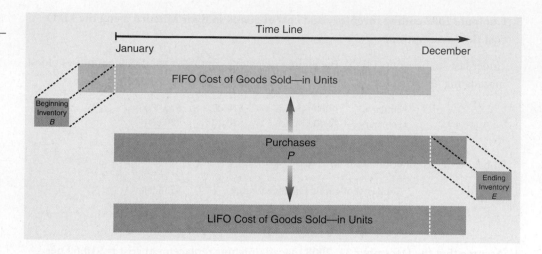

denoted $E$. Let's assume that $B$ equals $E$; that is, the firm had exactly as many units in inventory at the year-end as it did at the start of the year. Under these conditions the *units* comprising FIFO cost of goods sold consists of the area $B + (P - E)$. In other words, under the FIFO cost flow assumption, cost of goods sold consists of the first, or oldest, units available, which is beginning inventory plus the earliest purchases. Under LIFO, cost of goods sold would comprise the area $P$, that is, the most *recently* purchased units. The difference between the units comprising the two cost of goods sold (COGS) measures is the area $E$ minus $B$. Expressed in units:

$$\text{COGS}_{\text{LIFO}} = \text{COGS}_{\text{FIFO}} + E - B \tag{9.1}$$

Expressed in dollars:

$$\$\text{COGS}_{\text{LIFO}} = \$\text{COGS}_{\text{FIFO}} + \$E - \$B \tag{9.2}$$

Notice that if inventory costs do not change over the year, $\$E = \$B$ and $\$\text{COGS}_{\text{LIFO}} = \$\text{COGS}_{\text{FIFO}}$. In general, it's reasonable to expect inventory costs to change from the beginning to the end of the year. If we assume that inventory purchase costs changed over the year at the rate $r$, then $\$E$ will not equal $\$B$ although $E$ units equal $B$ units. Specifically, the dollar amount of ending inventory will equal $(1 + r)$ times the dollar amount of beginning inventory, that is,

$$\$E = \$B \times (1 + r) \tag{9.3}$$

Substituting the equation (9.3) value of $\$E$ into equation (9.2) yields:

$$\$\text{COGS}_{\text{LIFO}} = \$\text{COGS}_{\text{FIFO}} + \$B \times (1 + r) - \$B \tag{9.4}$$

or

$$\$\text{COGS}_{\text{LIFO}} = \$\text{COGS}_{\text{FIFO}} + \$B \times r \tag{9.5}$$

In this example, daily unit purchases and sales are equal. Under these conditions, LIFO cost of goods sold equals current cost of goods sold, so equation (9.5) can be rewritten:

$$\$\text{COGS}_{\text{CC}} = \$\text{COGS}_{\text{FIFO}} + \$B \times r \tag{9.6}$$

where $\$\text{COGS}_{\text{CC}}$ is current cost of goods sold. The difference between FIFO pretax income and current cost income (or, equivalently, FIFO cost of goods sold and current cost of goods sold) is the inventory holding gain or loss. Thus, the product $\$B \times r$ provides an estimate of the inventory holding gain (or loss) that is embedded in the FIFO earnings number.[31]

Notice that equation (9.6) is equivalent to the simple holding gain estimation procedure used in the chapter. This approximation works as long as the total number of inventory units on hand does not fluctuate much during the year and as long as inventory purchases and sales take place frequently. If these conditions aren't met for a specific firm, the conversion from FIFO cost of goods sold to current cost of goods sold will not be accurate.

To eliminate realized holding gains from FIFO income, we must estimate $r$, the percentage change in inventory purchase costs. One means for estimating this rate is to use some input cost price index, such as one of the various producer price indices (PPI) prepared by the U.S. Department of Labor, Bureau of Labor Statistics. Another approach is to select a competitor that is in the same industry as the FIFO firm being adjusted but that utilizes the LIFO inventory procedure. The rate $r$ can then be estimated using the following ratio computed from the LIFO competitor's disclosures:

$$\text{Rate of Inventory Input Cost Change } (r) = \frac{\text{Change in LIFO Reserve}}{\text{Beginning inventory}_{\text{LIFO}} + \text{Beginning LIFO Reserve}}$$

The denominator of the ratio is the initial current cost of the inventory, and the numerator is the change in current cost over the period. The quotient is an estimate of the desired rate, $r$. However, if the competitor dipped into LIFO layers over the period, the disclosed decrease in cost of goods sold because of the dipping must be added back to the numerator. The reason is that LIFO dipping reduces the LIFO reserve. Adding back the dipping effect generates a more accurate measure of $r$. But, if the competitor's year-to-year inventory levels changed substantially, the derived rate will differ from the true rate of inventory cost increase.

# LOWER OF COST OR MARKET METHOD

This appendix covers a widely used method in inventory accounting, the lower of cost or market method.

An asset represents a cost that has been incurred to create future service value for a firm. If subsequent events cause the future service value of an asset to drop below its cost, its carrying value must be reduced. In inventory accounting, this is called the **lower of cost or market method.**

It is more complicated than its name implies, although the reasoning underlying lower of cost or market is simple. Whenever the **replacement cost** of inventory declines below its original cost, the presumption is that the inventory's service value has been impaired and a write-down is warranted. If a unit of inventory originally cost $10 but its replacement cost falls to $8, a decrease in carrying value of $2 is required. *What's implied here is that inventory replacement cost and eventual selling price move together.* The decline in replacement cost is

---

[31] Analysts generally perceive such inventory holding gains as low-quality earnings items because they cannot be sustained in the future unless inventory costs continue to increase; see Siegel, op. cit. Consistent with this view, Carroll, Collins, and Johnson, op. cit., find that the market price adjustments associated with earnings surprises of firms whose earnings contain relatively large inventory holding gains are substantially smaller than those of firms with relatively smaller FIFO inventory holding gains.

presumed to signal that the price at which the inventory can be sold—its future service value—has fallen. Thus, a loss has occurred that must be recognized in the accounts.

In practice, the relationship between cost decreases and selling price decreases is unlikely to be perfect. For this reason, the market value used in applying lower of cost or market is subject to two constraints:

1. **Ceiling:** *Market* should not exceed the inventory's **net realizable value,** that is, the estimated selling price of the inventory in the ordinary course of business less the reasonably predictable costs of completing and selling it.

2. **Floor:** *Market* should not be less than the inventory's net realizable value reduced by an allowance for an approximately normal profit margin.[32]

The ceiling constraint (that market should not exceed net realizable value) is designed to avoid overstating obsolete goods. For example, assume that a motor originally costing $80 is now obsolete and has a net realizable value of only $50. Even if its replacement cost is $65, the inventory should be valued at its net realizable value of $50. To value the motor at its $65 replacement cost fails to recognize the full extent of the expected loss that has occurred.

The floor constraint covers situations in which declines in input replacement cost do not move perfectly with declines in selling price. To illustrate, assume the following:

|  | Original Cost | Replacement Cost | Net Realizable Value | Net Realizable Value Less Normal Profit of $11 |
|---|---|---|---|---|
| Inventory item | $60 | $46 | $70 | $59 |

This scenario assumes that the normal per unit profit margin is $11. An inventory write-down to $46 would lead to an abnormally high unit profit margin of $24 (net realizable value of $70 less the $46 replacement cost) when the inventory is sold in a later period. This $24 profit exceeds the $11 normal profit margin. A write-down to $59 would still afford the company a normal profit margin; any larger write-down would result in excess profits in future periods. The floor provides a lower bound for write-downs in situations when input replacement cost and selling price do not move together.

Together, these two constraints mean that *market* (the market value used in applying the lower of cost or market rule) is the *middle value* of (1) replacement cost, (2) net realizable value, and (3) net realizable value less a normal profit margin. This is depicted in Figure 9.7.

Applying the lower of cost or market rule is illustrated in Exhibit 9.16 using four scenarios. The inventory value used in each scenario is highlighted.

**Scenario 1.**    The inventory is valued at cost ($20). The reason is that $23 is the middle value of the three market values—$23 is between $21 and $27—and cost ($20) is lower than market ($23). This illustrates the straightforward lower of cost or market rule for inventory carrying values in historical cost accounting: Inventories are carried at original cost unless the item's future service value has been impaired. Of course, nothing here suggests impairment because the replacement cost of inventory ($23) exceeds the original cost ($20).

**International**

IAS also incorporate a lower of cost or market rule. *Market* is defined as net realizable value; see *IAS 2,* paras. 8–29.

---

[32] "Restatement and Revision of Accounting Research Bulletins," *Accounting Research Bulletin No. 43* (New York: American Institute of Accountants, 1953), Chapter 4, para. 8.

**Figure 9.7**

LOWER OF COST OR
MARKET RULE FOR
INVENTORIES

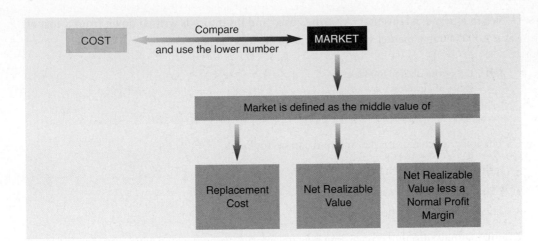

**Scenario 2.** The inventory is carried at replacement cost ($19). Market is again defined as the middle value of the three market value measures in Figure 9.7. The values are 18, 19, and 24; because 19 is between 18 and 24, it is market. Market is less than the original cost of $20 so it is presumed that a portion of the inventory's original service value has been impaired. Therefore, the inventory is written down from $20 to $19.

**Scenario 3.** The inventory is valued at net realizable value ($18) because net realizable value is the middle *market* value (that is, 18 is between 12 and 19) and is below cost. Here we see the operation of the ceiling. This rule is intended to avoid carrying obsolete goods at a cost in excess of the net value that will be realized on sale. If the rule were not invoked, inventory would be carried at $19 (its replacement cost), which is more than the $18 that it is expected to yield.

**Scenario 4.** The inventory is valued at net realizable value less a normal profit margin ($19) because this number is lower than original cost and is the middle value of the market price constraints. Scenario 4 illustrates the floor. If the rule were not invoked, inventory would be carried at $15 (its replacement cost). This would be an excessive write-down, because a $15 carrying cost would result in an above normal margin when the goods were later sold.

| EXHIBIT 9.16 | | | Application of Lower of Cost or Market Rule | | | |
|---|---|---|---|---|---|---|
| | | | Market | | | |
| Scenario | Original Cost | Replacement Cost | Net Realizable Value | Net Realizable Value less a Normal Profit Margin | Middle of the Three Market Values | Inventory Value Used |
| 1 | $20 | $23 | $27 | $21 | $23 | $20 |
| 2 | 20 | 19 | 24 | 18 | 19 | 19 |
| 3 | 20 | 19 | 18 | 12 | 18 | 18 |
| 4 | 20 | 15 | 25 | 19 | 19 | 19 |

When a perpetual inventory system is used and inventory is written down from a cost of, say, $1,000,000 to a market value of $970,000, the entry is:

| | | | |
|---|---|---|---|
| **DR** | Loss from decline in market value of inventory.......................................... | $30,000 | |
| | **CR** Inventory............................................. | | $30,000 |

The lower of cost or market method can be applied to:

- Individual inventory items.
- Classes of inventory, say, fertilizers versus weed killers.
- The inventory as a whole.

Companies have discretion regarding how inventories are aggregated when applying the lower of cost or market rule (see Exhibit 9.17). Depending on whether the aggregation is by item of inventory, inventory class, or total inventory, the lower of cost or market value could be $27,000, $31,000, or $32,000.

Income tax regulations do not permit the use of the lower of cost or market rule in conjunction with LIFO. The reason for this prohibition is that LIFO provides tax advantages when prices are rising; if LIFO firms were permitted to use lower of cost or market, they would also gain tax advantages when prices are falling. Congress is unwilling to provide LIFO firms with tax savings that would occur regardless of the direction of input cost movements.

### The Contracting Origins of the Lower of Cost or Market Method

The lower of cost or market method for inventories was widely practiced in the United States before the 1920s. Presumably, it evolved in the formative years of modern financial reporting to satisfy the information needs of what was then the most important external user group: commercial lenders. Banking in that era consisted mainly of securitized lending. Loans required collateral from the borrower, primarily in the form of inventory, accounts receivable, or fixed assets. Clearly, lenders wanted to avoid basing their decision on overstated asset values because they resulted in inadequate amounts of collateral. The conservatism inherent in lower of cost or market represented a mechanism for protecting the then-dominant user group

> If a periodic inventory system is used, this entry would not be made. Instead, the inventory's ending *market* value ($970,000) would be used as ending inventory in the cost of goods sold computation. This treatment essentially "buries" the $30,000 loss as an undisclosed element of cost of goods sold.

 **Contracting**

| **EXHIBIT 9.17** | **Aggregation Alternatives in Applying the Lower of Cost or Market Rule** |
|---|---|

| Inventory item | Cost | Market | Lower of Cost or Market Aggregated by | | |
|---|---|---|---|---|---|
| | | | Item | Class | Total |
| Class 1 | | | | | |
|    Item 1 | $10,000 | $ 6,000 | $ 6,000 | | |
|    Item 2 | 3,000 | 8,000 | 3,000 | | |
| | $13,000 | $14,000 | | $13,000 | |
| Class 2 | | | | | |
|    Item 3 | 20,000 | 18,000 | 18,000 | 18,000 | |
| | $33,000 | $32,000 | $27,000 | $31,000 | $32,000 |

from unpleasant surprise—lower than expected collateral values.[33] Thus, the lower of cost or market rule evolved because of the dominant form of lending contracts used years ago.

### Evaluation of the Lower of Cost or Market Rule
Individual and institutional equity investors are now important users of financial statements. The conservative bias built into the lower of cost or market rule protects lenders, but it may sometimes harm these other statement users. Suppose you own stock in a company whose inventory is written down to market. If the write-down was unwarranted (for example, because the decline in replacement cost did not portend a decline in the inventory's eventual selling price), your financial position is worsened by lower of cost or market accounting. Why? Because the share price you could get if you sold your stock may be lower than the price you could sell the shares for if the accounting were less conservative. Clearly, conservative rules designed to systematically understate asset amounts favor lenders and equity purchasers over borrowers and equity sellers. This absence of neutrality that pervades lower of cost or market has troubled numerous financial reporting experts and has led to repeated criticisms of the approach.

In addition to its bias against those seeking loans and those selling equity securities, the lower of cost or market rule has another deficiency. It assumes that input costs and output prices generally move together. Therefore, a decline in input cost triggers a loss recognition because it is presumed that the cost decrease portends a selling price decrease. But there is little empirical evidence to corroborate this assumption. It is indeed possible that input costs and selling prices move together, but it is also possible that they do not. When input costs and selling prices do not move together, a loss may be recognized when, in fact, no loss has occurred. Consider, for example, the following illustration:

| | Original Cost | Replacement Cost | Net Realizable Value | Net Realizable Value Less Normal Profit Margin |
|---|---|---|---|---|
| Cost relationships on January 1, 2008 | $100 | $100 | $115 | $90 |
| Cost relationships on December 31, 2008 | 100 | 95 | 115 | 90 |

---

[33] Evidence about the role that lenders played in the evolution of modern financial reporting and the lower of cost or market rule is contained in a proposal from the Federal Reserve Board that was designed to standardize financial reporting (*Federal Reserve Bulletin*, April 1, 1917, p. 270):

> *Because this matter was clearly of importance to banks and bankers, and especially to the Federal Reserve Banks* which might be asked to rediscount commercial paper based on borrowers' statements, the Federal Reserve Board has taken an active interest in the consideration of the suggestions which have developed as a result of the Trade Commission's investigation, and now submits in the form of a tentative statement certain proposals in regard to suggested standard forms of statements for merchants and manufacturers. [Emphasis added.]
>
> The problem naturally subdivides itself into two parts. (1) The improvement in standardization of the forms of statements; (2) the adoption of methods which will insure greater care in compiling the statements and the proper verification thereof.

The proposal (which was subsequently adopted) contained a specific reference to the importance of the lower of cost or market rule for inventories (p. 275):

> . . . The auditor should satisfy himself that inventories are stated at cost or market prices, whichever are the lower at the date of the balance sheet. No inventory must be passed which has been marked up to market prices and a profit assumed that is not and may never be realized. . . . It may be found that inventories are valued at the average prices of raw materials and supplies on hand at the end of the period. *In such cases the averages should be compared with the latest invoices in order to verify the fact that they are not in excess of the latest prices.* . . . [Emphasis added.]

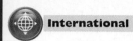

Strict application of the lower of cost or market rule at year-end would require a write-down of the inventory to $95 from its original cost of $100. However, the selling price of the inventory has not changed, since its net realizable value is still $115. Therefore, no loss exists but GAAP would require a $5 write-down!

In summary, the lower of cost or market rule reflects conservatism. But as financial statement users have become more diverse, the rule has been subjected to mounting criticism. First, conservatism is itself an elusive concept. While inventory write-downs may initially be conservative, the resulting higher margin in the period following the write-down provides opportunities for earnings management. Second, as the use of published financial statements has broadened over the years, conservatism strikes many observers as a violation of the neutrality posture that financial reporting rules are designed to achieve. For example, if downward changes in replacement cost are considered to be reliable evidence of a loss, logic suggests that upward changes in replacement cost should similarly be considered reliable evidence of a gain. Finally, the lower of cost or market rule relies on an implicit relationship between input costs and output prices that may not prevail. When the input/output relationship does not exist, inventory losses may be recognized even though no real loss has occurred. As a consequence of these limitations, the lower of cost or market approach constitutes GAAP but it does not hold a secure place in accounting theory.

> Worse yet, after a write-down, IAS permit inventory to be *written back up* to a number not exceeding original cost if selling prices recover (see *IAS 2*, para. 33). So companies might conceivably recognize losses in "good" earnings years that can comfortably absorb the "hit" and then write the inventory back up in "bad" earnings years (recognizing gains) to mask the real extent of earnings deterioration.

---

## APPENDIX C

# DOLLAR-VALUE LIFO

The LIFO inventory method requires data on each separate product or inventory item, and it therefore has two drawbacks. First, item-by-item inventory records are *costly* to maintain; and second, when LIFO records are kept by individual item, the likelihood of *liquidating* a LIFO layer is greatly increased.

- *Cost:* Traditional LIFO systems kept by individual item require considerable clerical work. Detailed records for each separate product or item in beginning inventory must be kept both in terms of physical units and unit cost. Similar detail must be accumulated for all purchases during the period. Finally, ending inventory must also be costed individually by item. These data requirements quickly become unwieldy for firms with numerous inventory categories.

- *Liquidation:* One of the motivations for adopting LIFO is that it tends to keep inventory holding gains out of income and thereby lowers taxes. However, when old LIFO layers are liquidated, this objective is subverted and both income and income taxes rise. The possibility of liquidating a LIFO layer is very high when item-by-item LIFO is used. Consider the case of computer stores that sell printers. As laser printers were introduced, these stores reduced their inventories of older technology dot-matrix printers. If LIFO always had to be kept on a per item basis, this decrease in the obsolete models would cause a liquidation of old LIFO layers and negate the benefits of LIFO.

To overcome both the clerical cost and liquidation problems associated with LIFO, the **dollar-value LIFO** method has been developed in which LIFO cost can be estimated for broad categories of inventory from simple inventory records that are kept in terms of end-of-period costs.

# Overview of Dollar-Value LIFO

Dollar-value LIFO avoids much of the detailed recordkeeping required under standard LIFO. Ending inventory is determined in terms of year-end prices, just as it is under FIFO. The ending inventory at year-end prices is then adjusted by a price index to estimate LIFO inventory.[34] To illustrate the procedure in simplified form, let's assume that a firm first adopts LIFO on January 1, 2008 and elects to use dollar-value LIFO. The time of initial LIFO adoption is termed the **base period.** The facts of the example are:

| | |
|---|---|
| Beginning inventory, LIFO, at base-period (1/1/08) costs | $100,000 |
| Ending inventory at 12/31/08 costs | $140,000 |
| Inventory price index at base period (1/1/08) | 1.00 |
| Inventory price index at 12/31/08 | 1.12 |

Under LIFO, a new LIFO layer is added only when the unit (or physical) quantity of inventory increases. In this example, we cannot compare the ending inventory dollars ($140,000) with the beginning inventory dollars ($100,000) to determine whether physical quantities increased. Why? Because the December 31 inventory is stated at year-end costs while the beginning inventory is stated at base-period costs.

However, we can use the inventory price index to restate ending inventory (expressed in year-end costs) to base-period costs by dividing $140,000 by 1.12. The result, $125,000, is the December 31, 2008, inventory expressed in base-period (January 1, 2008) costs.

Once ending inventory is restated, it is possible to determine whether the physical quantity of inventory has increased during 2008:

| | |
|---|---|
| Ending inventory expressed in base-period costs ($140,000/1.12) | $125,000 |
| Beginning inventory expressed in base-period costs | 100,000 |
| Inventory increase expressed in base-period costs | $ 25,000 |

---

[34] A *price index* is simply a ratio that compares prices during the current period with prices during some base period. Separate indices are computed for each period. If a price index for a given year is 1.12, this means that prices in that year are 12% higher than they were in the base period.

In applying dollar-value LIFO, the index used must reflect price changes for the specific inventory. General price indices are not permitted except in unusual situations. One method for computing the index is to determine the following ratio by reference to detailed purchase records:

$$\frac{\text{Cost of ending inventory at end-of-period prices}}{\text{Cost of ending inventory at base-period prices}} = \text{Index for Year}$$

However, this computation can be burdensome when the inventory consists of many different types of items. In such situations, an index can be computed based on a sample of representative purchases. One such approach is:

| | Ending Inventory Units (1) | Base-Period Cost per Unit (2) | Current Period's Cost per Unit (3) | Total Base-Period Cost (1) × (2) | End-of-Period Cost (1) × (3) |
|---|---|---|---|---|---|
| Item A | 20,000 | $3 | $ 4 | $ 60,000 | $ 80,000 |
| Item B | 5,000 | 7 | 8 | 35,000 | 40,000 |
| Item C | 11,000 | 9 | 10 | 99,000 | 110,000 |
| | | | | $194,000 | $230,000 |

The resulting index is

$$\frac{\$230,000}{\$194,000} = 1.186$$

and measures the current cost of the purchase basket relative to the base-period cost of that same basket.

Clearly, a new LIFO layer was added in 2008. However, the new LIFO layer must be recorded at the cost level that was in effect when the layer was added. Because the inventory increase expressed in terms of base-period costs was $25,000—and because costs increased 12% during 2008—the new LIFO layer would be costed at $25,000 × 1.12, or $28,000. Therefore, the December 31, 2008, ending inventory computed under the dollar-value LIFO method would be comprised of two layers:

| | Base-Period Costs | Adjustment Factor | Dollar-Value LIFO Carrying Amount |
|---|---|---|---|
| Beginning inventory (1/1/08) | $100,000 | 1.00 | $100,000 |
| 2008 layer | 25,000 | 1.12 | 28,000 |
| Ending inventory, dollar-value LIFO | | | $128,000 |

To continue the example, let's assume that the December 31, 2009 inventory price index is 1.20 and that ending inventory at December 31, 2009 is $146,400 (expressed in year-end 2009 costs).

As before, it is necessary to determine whether a new LIFO layer was added in 2009. To do this, we must restate the December 31, 2009 inventory in terms of base-period costs and compare it to the January 1, 2009 inventory (expressed in base-period costs):

| | | |
|---|---|---|
| Ending inventory expressed in base-period costs ($146,400/1.20) | | $122,000 |
| Beginning inventory expressed in base-period costs | | |
| Base-period layer | $100,000 | |
| 2009 layer ($28,000/1.12) | 25,000 | |
| | | 125,000 |
| Inventory decrease expressed in base-period costs | | $ (3,000) |

Expressed in base-period costs, inventory decreased in 2009. Because the cost flow is LIFO, this decrease is assumed to have come from the 2008 layer. At base-period costs, the 2008 layer would be reduced to $22,000, that is, $25,000 minus the $3,000 inventory decrease. The December 31, 2009 dollar-value LIFO inventory would again be comprised of two layers:

| | Base-Period Costs | Adjustment Factor | Dollar-Value LIFO Carrying Amount |
|---|---|---|---|
| Beginning inventory | $100,000 | 1.00 | $100,000 |
| 2008 layer | 22,000 | 1.12 | 24,640 |
| Ending inventory, dollar-value LIFO | | | $124,640 |

Finally, assume that inventory at December 31, 2010 totals $170,100 at year-end costs and that the inventory price index at that date is 1.26. To determine whether a new LIFO layer was added in 2010, we must restate the December 31, 2010 inventory in terms of base-period costs:

| | | |
|---|---|---|
| Ending inventory expressed in base-period costs ($170,100/1.26) | | $135,000 |
| Beginning inventory expressed in base-period costs | | |
| Base-period layer | $100,000 | |
| 2008 layer ($24,640/1.12) | 22,000 | |
| | | 122,000 |
| Inventory increase expressed in base-period costs | | $ 13,000 |

The new 2010 LIFO layer must be added to LIFO inventory using the cost level in effect in 2010. To do this, we must multiply the inventory increase expressed in base-period costs ($13,000) by the December 31, 2010 price index, which is 1.26. Thus, the December 31, 2010 dollar-value LIFO inventory would consist of three layers:

| | Base-Period Costs | Adjustment Factor | Dollar-Value LIFO Carrying Amount |
|---|---|---|---|
| Beginning inventory | $100,000 | 1.00 | $100,000 |
| 2008 layer | 22,000 | 1.12 | 24,640 |
| 2010 layer | 13,000 | 1.26 | 16,380 |
| Ending inventory, dollar-value LIFO | | | $141,020 |

The steps required to compute dollar-value LIFO are summarized as follows:

1. Ending inventory is initially computed in terms of year-end costs. This simplifies recordkeeping.

2. To determine whether a new LIFO layer had been added (or whether an existing layer has been liquidated), the ending inventory must be restated to base-period cost and compared to the beginning inventory at base-period cost. This eliminates the effect of input cost changes. After restatement, any difference between beginning and ending inventory is the inventory change expressed in base-period cost. It indicates whether inventory *quantities* have changed.

3. Any inventory change determined from Step 2 must be costed as follows:

   a. New LIFO layers are valued using costs of the year in which the layer was added.

   b. Decreases in old LIFO layers are removed using costs that were in effect when the layer was originally formed.

> The procedures for costing new dollar-value LIFO layers are technically inconsistent with a strict LIFO flow assumption. For example, notice that the 2010 layer added in the example is costed at 1.26, a figure that represents 2010 *year-end* costs. Under traditional LIFO, new layers are added using beginning-of-year costs, not end-of-year costs. Because dollar-value LIFO is a computational convenience, this inconsistency in costing new layers is usually ignored to simplify the computations.

## EXERCISES

On January 1, 2008, Manuel Company's merchandise inventory was $300,000. During 2008, Manuel purchased $1,900,000 of merchandise and recorded sales of $2,000,000. The gross profit margin on these sales was 20%.

**Required:**
What is Manuel's merchandise inventory at December 31, 2008?

**E9-1**

Account analysis

**AICPA**
ADAPTED

Sperry-New Holland manufactures farm machinery. During 2008, it incurred a variety of costs, several of which appear on the following list.

**Nature of Incurred Cost**

a. Comprehensive liability insurance premium on corporate headquarters

b. Depreciation on production equipment

c. Electricity consumed

d. Property and casualty insurance premiums

e. Raw material used

f. Royalties paid to the designer of one of the company's products

g. Salaries of corporate legal counsel

h. Travel expenses for sales force

**E9-2**

Product versus period costs

i. Wages of plant maintenance personnel

j. Wages of production workers

k. Workers compensation insurance

**Required:**

Classify each listed cost as a product or period cost, or both. For costs that are probably allocable to both classifications, suggest a reasonable allocation approach.

---

**E9-3**

Cost flow computations

AICPA
ADAPTED

City Stationers, Inc. had 200 calculators on hand at January 1, 2008 costing $18 each. Purchases and sales of calculators during the month of January were as follows:

| Date | Purchases | Sales |
|------|-----------|-------|
| January 12 | | 150 @ $28 |
| 14 | 100 @ $20 | |
| 29 | 100 @ 22 | |
| 30 | | 100 @ $32 |

City does not maintain perpetual inventory records. According to a physical count, 150 calculators were on hand at January 31, 2008.

**Required:**

1. What is the cost of the inventory at January 31, 2008 under the FIFO method?

2. What is the cost of the inventory at January 31, 2008 under the LIFO method?

---

**E9-4**

Analyzing accounts

AICPA
ADAPTED

The following information is available for Day Company for 2008:

| | |
|---|---|
| Cash disbursements for purchase of merchandise | $290,000 |
| Increase in trade accounts payable | 25,000 |
| Decrease in merchandise inventory | 10,000 |

**Required:**

What is the cost of goods sold for 2008?

---

**E9-5**

Analyzing accounts

AICPA
ADAPTED

For the year 2008, Dumas Company's gross profit was $96,000; the cost of goods manufactured was $340,000; the beginning inventories of goods in process and finished goods were $28,000 and $45,000, respectively; and the ending inventories of goods in process and finished goods were $38,000 and $52,000, respectively.

**Required:**

What is the dollar amount of Dumas Company sales for 2008?

---

**E9-6**

Analyzing accounts

AICPA
ADAPTED

Hestor Company's records indicate the following information:

| | |
|---|---|
| Merchandise inventory, January 1, 2008 | $ 550,000 |
| Purchases, January 1 through December 31, 2008 | 2,250,000 |
| Sales, January 1 through December 31, 2008 | 3,000,000 |

On December 31, 2008 a physical inventory determined that ending inventory of $600,000 was in the warehouse. Hestor's gross profit on sales has remained constant at 30%. Hestor suspects some of the inventory may have been taken by some new employees.

**Required:**

At December 31, 2008, what is the estimated cost of missing inventory?

---

**E9-7**

Analyzing accounts

AICPA
ADAPTED

On June 30, 2008, a flash flood damaged Padway Corporation's warehouse and factory completely destroying the work-in-process inventory. Neither the raw materials nor finished goods inventories were damaged. A physical inventory taken after the flood revealed the following valuations:

| | |
|---|---|
| Raw materials | $ 62,000 |
| Work in process | –0– |
| Finished goods | 119,000 |

The inventory of January 1, 2008 consisted of the following:

| | |
|---|---|
| Raw materials | $ 30,000 |
| Work in process | 100,000 |
| Finished goods | 140,000 |
| | $270,000 |

A review of the books and records disclosed that the gross profit margin historically approximated 25% of sales. The sales total for the first six months of 2008 was $340,000. Raw material purchases totaled $115,000. Direct labor costs for this period were $80,000, and manufacturing overhead has historically been applied at 50% of direct labor.

**Required:**

Compute the value of the work-in-process inventory lost at June 30, 2008. Show supporting computations.

---

Frate Company was formed on January 1, 2008. The following information is available from Frate's inventory records for Product Ply:

| | Units | Unit Cost |
|---|---|---|
| January 1, 2008 | | |
| Beginning inventory | 800 | $ 9.00 |
| Purchases: | | |
| January 5, 2008 | 1,500 | 10.00 |
| May 25, 2008 | 1,200 | 10.50 |
| July 16, 2008 | 600 | 11.00 |
| November 26, 2008 | 900 | 11.50 |

A physical inventory on December 31, 2008 shows 1,600 units on hand.

**Required:**

Prepare schedules to compute the ending inventory at December 31, 2008 under each of the following inventory methods:

1. FIFO

2. LIFO

3. Weighted average

Show supporting computations in good form.

**E9-8**

Cost flow computations

**AICPA**
ADAPTED

---

Information from Peterson Company's records is available as follows for the year ended December 31, 2008:

| | |
|---|---|
| Net sales | $1,400,000 |
| Cost of goods manufactured: | |
| Variable | $ 630,000 |
| Fixed | $ 315,000 |
| Operating expenses: | |
| Variable | $ 98,000 |
| Fixed | $ 140,000 |
| Units manufactured | 70,000 |
| Units sold | 60,000 |
| Finished goods inventory, 1/1/08 | None |

No work-in-process inventories existed at the beginning or end of 2008.

**Required:**

1. What would be Peterson's finished goods inventory cost under the variable (direct) costing method at December 31, 2008?

2. Under the absorption costing method, what would be Peterson's operating income be?

**E9-9**

Absorption versus variable costing

**AICPA**
ADAPTED

| | |
|---|---|
| **E9-10**<br><br>Absorption versus variable costing<br><br>AICPA<br>ADAPTED | Selected information concerning the operation of Kern Company for the year ended December 31, 2008 is available as follows: |

| | |
|---|---|
| Units produced | 10,000 |
| Units sold | 9,000 |
| Direct materials used | $40,000 |
| Direct labor incurred | $20,000 |
| Fixed factory overhead | $25,000 |
| Variable factory overhead | $12,000 |
| Fixed selling and administrative expenses | $30,000 |
| Variable selling and administrative expenses | $ 4,500 |
| Finished goods inventory, January 1, 2008 | None |

No work-in-process inventories existed at the beginning or end of 2008.

**Required:**
1. What would be Kern's finished goods inventory cost under the variable (direct) costing method at December 31, 2008?

2. Which costing method—absorption or variable costing—would show a higher operating income for 2008, and by what amount?

| | |
|---|---|
| **E9-11**<br><br>Changing to LIFO method<br><br>AICPA<br>ADAPTED | Hastings Company began operations on January 1, 2008 and uses the FIFO method in costing its raw material inventory. Management is contemplating a change to the LIFO method in 2009 and is interested in determining how such a change will affect net income. Accordingly, the following information has been developed: |

| | **2008** | **2009** |
|---|---|---|
| Final inventory | | |
| FIFO | $240,000 | $270,000 |
| LIFO | 200,000 | 210,000 |
| | | |
| Net income | | |
| (Computed under | | |
| the FIFO method) | $120,000 | $170,000 |

**Required:**
Based on this information, what would 2009 net income be after the change to the LIFO method?

| | |
|---|---|
| **E9-12**<br><br>Converting LIFO to FIFO | KW Steel Corp. uses the LIFO method of inventory valuation. Waretown Steel, KW's major competitor, instead uses the FIFO method. The following are excerpts from each company's 2008 financial statements: |

| | **KW Steel Corp.** | | **Waretown Steel** | |
|---|---|---|---|---|
| ($ in millions) | **2008** | **2007** | **2008** | **2007** |
| Total inventories | $ 797.6 | $ 692.7 | $ 708.2 | $ 688.6 |
| LIFO reserve | 378.0 | 334.9 | | |
| | | | | |
| Sale | 4,284.8 | 4,029.7 | 3,584.2 | 3,355.8 |
| Cost of goods sold | 3,427.8 | 3,226.5 | 2,724.0 | 2,617.5 |

**Required:**
1. Compute each company's 2008 gross margin percentage and inventory turnover using cost of goods sold as reported by each company. (Round answers to one decimal place.) For each ratio, how does KW Steel compare to Waretown Steel?

2. Restate KW's cost of goods sold and inventory balances to the FIFO basis. On the basis of its adjusted data, recompute KW's gross margin percentage and inventory turnover. Explain how the revised figures alter your earlier comparisons.

Nathan's Grills, Inc. imports and sells premium-quality gas grills. The company had the following layers in its LIFO inventory at January 1, 2008 at which time the replacement cost of the inventory was $675 per unit.

| Year LIFO Layer Added | Units | Unit Cost |
| --- | --- | --- |
| 2005 | 50 | $450 |
| 2006 | 40 | 500 |
| 2007 | 60 | 600 |

The replacement cost of grills remained constant throughout 2008. Nathan's sold 275 units during 2008. The company established the selling price of each unit by doubling its replacement cost at the time of sale.

**Required:**

1. Determine gross margin and the gross margin percentage for 2008 assuming that Nathan's Grills purchased 280 units during the year.

2. Determine gross margin and the gross margin percentage for 2008 assuming that Nathan's Grills purchased 180 units during the year.

3. Explain why the assumed number of units purchased makes a difference in your answers.

Miller's Snow Blowers, Inc. had the following layers in its LIFO inventory at January 1, 2008:

| Year LIFO Layer Added | Units | Unit Cost |
| --- | --- | --- |
| 2005 | 100 | $750 |
| 2006 | 95 | 780 |
| 2007 | 80 | 800 |

The company sets its selling price at 180% of replacement cost at the time of the sale. Replacement cost as of January 1, 2008 was $825 per unit and remained unchanged throughout 2008. During 2008, the company purchased 475 units and sold 675 units.

**Required:**

Calculate the difference between Miller's current cost operating margin (that is, on a replacement cost basis) and the LIFO operating margin as reported by the company in 2008. What does this difference represent?

Watsontown Yacht Sales has been selling large power cruisers for 25 years. On January 1, 2008, the company had $5,950,000 in inventory (based on a FIFO valuation). While the number of yachts in Watsontown Yacht Sales' inventory remained fairly constant throughout 2008, by December 31, 2008 yacht prices were 7% higher than at the start of the year. The company reported cost of goods sold for 2008 of $23,800,000.

**Required:**

Calculate the amount of realized holding gains in Watsontown Yacht Sales' income for 2008.

The following inventory valuation errors have been discovered for Knox Corporation:

- The 2006 year-end inventory was overstated by $23,000.
- The 2007 year-end inventory was understated by $61,000.
- The 2008 year-end inventory was understated by $17,000.

The reported income before taxes for Knox was:

| Year | Income before Taxes |
|------|---------------------|
| 2006 | $138,000 |
| 2007 | 254,000 |
| 2008 | 168,000 |

**Required:**

Compute what income before taxes for 2006, 2007, and 2008 should have been after correcting for the errors.

---

**E9-17**

Lower of cost or market

AICPA
ADAPTED

Moore Corporation has two products in its ending inventory; each is accounted for at the lower of cost or market. A profit margin of 30% on selling price is considered normal for each product. Specific data with respect to each product follows:

| | Product 1 | Product 2 |
|---|---|---|
| Historical cost | $17 | $ 45 |
| Replacement cost | 15 | 46 |
| Estimated cost to dispose | 5 | 26 |
| Estimated selling price | 30 | 100 |

**Required:**

In pricing its ending inventory using the lower of cost or market rule, what unit values should Moore use for products 1 and 2, respectively?

---

**E9-18**

Computing dollar-value LIFO

AICPA
ADAPTED

Acute Company manufactures a single product. On December 31, 2005, it adopted the dollar-value LIFO inventory method. The inventory on that date using the dollar-value LIFO inventory method was determined to be $300,000. Inventory data for succeeding years follow:

| Year Ended December 31 | Inventory at Respective Year-End Prices | Relevant Price Index (Base Year 2005) |
|---|---|---|
| 2006 | $363,000 | 1.10 |
| 2007 | 420,000 | 1.20 |
| 2008 | 430,000 | 1.25 |

**Required:**

Compute the inventory amounts at December 31, 2006, 2007, and 2008, using the dollar-value LIFO inventory method for each year.

---

**E9-19**

Computing dollar-value LIFO

AICPA
ADAPTED

On December 31, 2007, Fern Company adopted the dollar-value LIFO inventory method. All of Fern's inventories constitute a single pool. The inventory on December 31, 2007 using the dollar-value LIFO inventory method was $600,000. Inventory data for 2008 are as follows:

| | |
|---|---|
| December 31, 2008, inventory at year-end prices | $780,000 |
| Relevant price index at year-end (base year 2007) | 1.20 |

**Required:**

Under the dollar-value LIFO inventory method, what would Fern's inventory be at December 31, 2008?

---

JD Electronics sells sound systems and other consumer electronics through a chain of retail outlets. Joanna Danielle, president of the company, recently read that many companies were adopting the LIFO method of inventory valuation to reduce income taxes and eliminate holding gains from current period income. She wonders whether switching to LIFO from the company's current periodic FIFO inventory method would be beneficial. The following data concerning a popular model of entertainment center were taken from the company's inventory records:

| | **Inventory Purchases** | | |
| --- | --- | --- | --- |
| | **Units** | **Cost per Unit** | **Total** |
| Beginning inventory | 3,100 | $1,875 | $ 5,812,500 |
| March 1, 2008 | 4,000 | 1,825 | 7,300,000 |
| June 15, 2008 | 3,500 | 1,800 | 6,300,000 |
| August 1, 2008 | 3,800 | 1,785 | 6,783,000 |
| October 1, 2008 | 4,500 | 1,760 | 7,920,000 |
| December 15, 2008 | 3,000 | 1,750 | 5,250,000 |
| | 21,900 | | $39,365,500 |

| | **2008 Sales** | | |
| --- | --- | --- | --- |
| | **Units** | **Price per Unit** | **Total** |
| First quarter | 4,100 | $3,400 | $13,940,000 |
| Second quarter | 4,600 | 3,300 | 15,180,000 |
| Third quarter | 3,500 | 3,250 | 11,375,000 |
| Fourth quarter | 5,500 | 3,200 | 17,600,000 |
| | 17,700 | | $58,095,000 |

**Required:**

1. Determine cost of goods sold for the entertainment centers under (a) periodic FIFO and (b) periodic LIFO. Ignore lower of cost or market considerations.

2. Assume that operating expenses of $15,000,000 are related to this product and that the company has a 35% income tax rate. Calculate net income under both inventory valuation methods.

3. Assume that the price trend on the entertainment centers is generally mirrored by the other items in JD Electronics' inventory. Would the company be well advised to switch to the periodic LIFO method to value its inventory?

---

Cost for inventory purposes should be determined by the inventory cost flow method most clearly reflecting periodic income.

**Required:**

1. Describe the fundamental cost flow assumptions for the average cost, FIFO, and LIFO inventory cost flow methods.

2. Discuss the reasons for using LIFO in an inflationary economy.

3. Where there is evidence that the utility of goods in their disposal in the ordinary course of business will be less than cost, what is the proper accounting treatment, and under what concept is that treatment justified?

## PROBLEMS / DISCUSSION QUESTIONS

**P9-1**

LIFO versus FIFO

Keefer, Inc. began business on January 1, 2007. Information on its inventory purchases and sales during 2007 and 2008 follow:

### Inventory Purchases

| Date | Units | Cost per Unit | Total |
|---|---|---|---|
| January 1, 2007 | 85 | $25 | $ 2,125 |
| March 15, 2007 | 100 | 27 | 2,700 |
| May 15, 2007 | 90 | 28 | 2,520 |
| August 1, 2007 | 100 | 30 | 3,000 |
| September 3, 2007 | 125 | 31 | 3,875 |
| December 5, 2007 | 50 | 32 | 1,600 |
| Total purchases—2007 | 550 | | $15,820 |
| February 20, 2008 | 150 | $31 | $ 4,650 |
| March 29, 2008 | 100 | 30 | 3,000 |
| July 1, 2008 | 100 | 29 | 2,900 |
| August 20, 2008 | 100 | 28 | 2,800 |
| November 3, 2008 | 80 | 27 | 2,160 |
| Total purchases—2008 | 530 | | $15,510 |

### Inventory Sales

| | Units | Price per Unit | Total |
|---|---|---|---|
| March 18, 2007 | 65 | $50 | $ 3,250 |
| August 15, 2007 | 200 | 52 | 10,400 |
| October 6, 2007 | 175 | 53 | 9,275 |
| Total sales—2007 | 440 | | $22,925 |
| February 12, 2008 | 100 | $53 | $ 5,300 |
| June 2, 2008 | 200 | 52 | 10,400 |
| September 30, 2008 | 210 | 50 | 10,500 |
| Total sales—2008 | 510 | | $26,200 |

**Required:**

1. Calculate ending inventory, cost of goods sold, and gross margin for 2007 and 2008 under the periodic FIFO inventory valuation method.

2. Calculate ending inventory, cost of goods sold, and gross margin for 2007 and 2008 under the periodic LIFO inventory valuation method.

3. Discuss the difference in reported results under FIFO versus LIFO for each year.

**P9-2**

Account analysis

The following information pertains to Yuji Corporation:

| | January 1, 2008 | December 31, 2008 |
|---|---|---|
| Raw materials inventory | $ 34,000 | $ 38,000 |
| Work-in-process inventory | 126,000 | 145,000 |
| Finished goods inventory | 76,000 | 68,000 |

Costs incurred during the year 2008 were as follows:

| | |
|---|---|
| Raw material purchased | $116,000 |
| Wages to factory workers | 55,000 |
| Salary to factory supervisors | 25,000 |
| Salary to selling and administrative staff | 40,000 |
| Depreciation on factory building and equipment | 10,000 |
| Depreciation on office building | 12,000 |
| Utilities for factory building | 5,000 |
| Utilities for office building | 7,500 |

**Required:**

Sales revenue during 2008 was $300,000. The income tax rate is 40%. Compute the following:

1. Cost of raw materials used.

2. Cost of goods manufactured/completed.

3. Cost of goods sold.

4. Gross margin.

5. Net income.

---

Alex Wholesalers, Inc. began its business on January 1, 2008. Information on its inventory purchases and sales during 2008 follow:

**P 9 - 3**

Inventory accounting— comprehensive

mhhe.com/revsine4e

| | Inventory Purchases | | |
|---|---|---|---|
| | **Units** | **Cost per Unit** | **Total** |
| January 1 | 10,000 | $4.00 | $ 40,000 |
| March 10 | 8,000 | 4.10 | 32,800 |
| April 12 | 12,000 | 4.30 | 51,600 |
| September 15 | 7,500 | 4.45 | 33,375 |
| November 11 | 6,000 | 4.75 | 28,500 |
| December 29 | 6,500 | 5.00 | 32,500 |
| **Units available for sale** | 50,000 | | $218,775 |

| | Inventory Sales | | |
|---|---|---|---|
| | **Units** | **Price per Unit** | **Total** |
| March 1 | 7,000 | $8.00 | $ 56,000 |
| September 1 | 20,000 | 8.50 | 170,000 |
| December 1 | 11,000 | 9.00 | 99,000 |
| **Units sold** | 38,000 | | $325,000 |

Assume a tax rate of 40%.

**Required:**

1. Compute the cost of ending inventory and cost of goods sold under each of the following methods: (1) FIFO, (2) Weighted average cost, and (3) LIFO. Assume that Alex uses the periodic inventory procedure.

2. Assume that Alex uses the periodic LIFO method.

   a. Calculate the replacement cost of the ending inventory and the LIFO reserve as of year-end. You may assume that year-end purchase cost was still $5 per unit.

   b. Estimate Alex's cost of goods sold under the periodic FIFO method based only on the information that will be publicly available to Alex's investors. Explain why your answer differs from FIFO cost of goods sold computed in requirement 1.

   c. Alex's purchasing manager was planning to acquire 10,000 units of inventory on January 5, 2009 at $5 per unit. Its accountant suggests that the company will be better off if it acquires the inventory instead on December 31, 2008. What are the pros and cons of the accountant's suggestion? Wherever possible, show supporting calculations.

3. Calculate cost of goods sold assuming that Alex uses the perpetual FIFO method.

---

The inventory footnote to the 2008 annual report of Ruedy Company reads in part as follows:

**P 9 - 4**

Analyzing a LIFO liquidation

Because of a prolonged strike in one of our supplier's plants, inventories were unavoidably reduced during 2008. Under the LIFO system of accounting, this "eating into LIFO layers" resulted in an increase in *after-tax* net income of $36,000 over what it would have been had inventories been maintained at their physical levels that existed at the start of the year.

The price of Ruedy's merchandise purchases was $22 per unit for 20,000 units during 2008. Prior to 2008, inventory prices had risen steadily for many years. Ruedy uses the periodic inventory method. A summary of its inventory positions at the beginning and end of the year follow. Ruedy's income tax rate is 40%.

| Date | Physical Count of Inventory | LIFO Cost of Inventory |
|---|---|---|
| January 1, 2008 | 30,000 units | $? |
| December 31, 2008 | 20,000 units | $260,000 |

**Required:**

1. Was 2008 cost of goods sold higher or lower as a result of the LIFO liquidation? By how much?

2. Were 2008 income taxes higher or lower as a result of eating into LIFO layers? By how much?

3. What was the average cost per unit of the 10,000 units removed from the January 1, 2008 LIFO inventory?

4. What was the January 1, 2008, LIFO cost of inventory?

5. What was the reported 2008 cost of goods sold for Ruedy Company?

---

**P9-5**

LIFO liquidation and interyear comparisons

Courtney, Inc. began operations in 2000 as a publisher of children's books. From modest beginnings, the company grew steadily with sales reaching $52.3 million in 2008. In late 2006, management began revamping the company's production process to enhance profitability. Streamlining operations permitted the company to effectively operate with lower raw material inventory levels, so these inventories were gradually reduced during 2007 and 2008. Courtney's raw materials consist primarily of ink and paper, with costs of the latter rising steadily since 2000 as a result of curtailed logging operations in the United States and increased transportation costs on imported paper. The following information was excerpted from Courtney's 2008 annual report:

| ($ in thousands) | 2008 | 2007 | 2006 |
|---|---|---|---|
| Net sales | $52,328 | $46,931 | $45,286 |
| Cost of goods sold | 34,746 | 31,538 | 31,157 |
| Gross profit | $17,582 | $15,393 | $14,129 |

## Note 1: Inventories

During 2007 and 2008, the Company streamlined its operations, permitting the liquidation of certain LIFO inventories that were carried at costs lower than current replacement costs. These liquidations increased earnings before income taxes by $892,000 and $2,355,000 in 2007 and 2008, respectively.

**Required:**

1. Calculate Courtney's gross profit as a percentage of sales as reported for 2006 through 2008.

2. Recompute the company's gross profit percentage for 2006 through 2008 adjusting for the LIFO dipping effect.

3. Assume that Courtney's annual report contained a comment in the Management's Discussion and Analysis section citing the company's increased gross profit as evidence that the production process changes were having the desired effect. Would such a statement be justified?

---

**P9-6**

Criteria for choosing a cost flow assumption

Jeanette Corporation's president is in a dilemma regarding which inventory method (LIFO or FIFO) to use. The controller provides the following list of factors that should be considered before making a choice.

a. Jeanette has borrowed money during the current month and has entered into a debt contract. The covenants of this contract require Jeanette to achieve a certain amount of net income and maintain a certain amount of working capital.

b. The Jeanette's board of directors is contemplating a proposal to reward the top corporate management with an incentive bonus based on accounting net income.

c. The vice president of finance suggests using the LIFO method for tax purposes and the FIFO method for financial reporting purposes. With lower taxable income, Jeanette can save on the current tax it pays, and, at the same time, it can show higher income in the financial reports and "look good."

d. The controller cautions that while the LIFO method could reduce the current period tax liability, "it could hit us hard when things are not going so well." This potential problem with the LIFO method could be "avoided if we use FIFO in the first place."

e. However, the president would like to adopt the method that provides both a better application of the matching principle and a more current measure of inventory on the balance sheet.

f. The controller suggests that Jeanette adopt the FIFO method because higher accounting income means a higher stock price.

**Required:**

Jeanette's president has asked you to write a report evaluating the pros and cons of each of the issues raised. Given her busy schedule, she would like the report to be brief. In answering this question, assume that Jeanette Corporation expects an upward trend in inventory prices.

---

Princess Retail Stores started doing business on January 1, 2008. The following data reflect its inventory purchases and sales during the year:

| | | Inventory Purchases | |
| --- | --- | --- | --- |
| | **Units** | **Cost per Unit** | **Total** |
| January 1 | 20,000 | $ 7.00 | $140,000 |
| March 1 | 16,000 | 9.00 | 144,000 |
| June 1 | 14,000 | 11.00 | 154,000 |
| September 1 | 10,000 | 13.00 | 130,000 |
| December 1 | 12,000 | 15.00 | 180,000 |
| | 72,000 | | $748,000 |

| | | Sales | |
| --- | --- | --- | --- |
| | **Units** | **Price per Unit** | **Total** |
| March 2 | 24,000 | $14.00 | $336,000 |
| September 2 | 18,000 | 16.00 | 288,000 |
| December 2 | 20,000 | 18.00 | 360,000 |
| | 62,000 | | $984,000 |

**P9-7**

Choosing between inventory alternatives

mhhe.com/revsine4e

**Required:**

1. Compute gross margin and cost of ending inventory using the periodic FIFO cost flow assumption.

2. Compute gross margin and cost of ending inventory using the periodic LIFO cost flow assumption. Compute the dollar amount of the LIFO reserve. Using this additional disclosure, how might an analyst estimate Princess's cost of goods sold under the FIFO method based only on publicly available information? Show supporting calculations.

3. Under historical cost accounting, gross margin is calculated as current output price minus historical input price. For analytical convenience, we can break the gross margin into two components:

    a. "True" operating margin = Current output price − Current input price.

    b. Inventory profits = Current input price − Historical input price.

Provide an estimate of the "true" operating margin for Princess Retail Stores.

4. The following are excerpts from a recent top management meeting at Princess Retail Stores. Your assignment is to clearly provide guidelines to the top management team on each issue raised in the meeting. Show calculations when necessary.

a. "I am most concerned about appropriately matching revenues and expenses. I suggest that we look for an inventory accounting method that achieves this objective both during inflationary and deflationary times." (Frances Iyer, chairman)

b. "Frances, I think the choice is obvious. What other method can achieve better matching of revenues and expenses than the specific identification method? By choosing this method, we would send a clear signal to the stock market that we are not playing any earnings management games." (Sandra Kang, VP, Investor Relations)

c. "I would like to maximize our current profits. What inventory method might help us achieve this most important goal and why?" (Antonia Iyer, CEO)

d. "Antonia, I know you can't stop thinking about your earnings-based bonus. My primary objective is to minimize the present value of future income tax outflows." (Juanita Kang, CFO)

e. "I would like to have our cake and eat it too. Why don't we follow Juanita's suggestion for income tax accounting and follow Antonia's idea for external financial reporting?" (B. T. Kang, VP, Operations)

---

**P9-8**

Identifying the LIFO reserve effect on various ratios

Dembo, Inc., a manufacturer of office furniture, reported the following data in its 2008 annual report. Dembo uses the LIFO inventory valuation method. Interest is reported as an operating expense and is not material in amount.

## Dembo, Inc.

### Condensed Financial Statements

| Income Statement<br>($ in millions) | Year Ended<br>December 31, 2008 | |
|---|---|---|
| Revenue | $4,800.0 | |
| Cost of sales | 2,880.0 | |
| Operating expenses | 1,056.0 | |
| Income taxes | 480.0 | |
| Net income | $ 384.0 | |

| Balance Sheet | December 31, 2008 | December 31, 2007 |
|---|---|---|
| Current assets | $2,520.0 | |
| Property and equipment, net | 3,148.2 | |
| Intangibles and other assets | 1,001.8 | |
| Total assets | $6,670.0 | $6,130.0 |
| Current liabilities | $1,800.0 | |
| Long-term liabilities | 2,087.2 | |
| Stockholders' equity | 2,782.8 | |
| Total liabilities and shareholders' equity | $6,670.0 | |

| Inventories consist of | December 31, 2008 | December 31, 2007 |
|---|---|---|
| Finished goods | $ 389.4 | $ 381.3 |
| Work in process | 215.4 | 215.1 |
| Raw materials | 907.2 | 823.6 |
| Inventory—FIFO | 1,512.0 | 1,420.0 |
| Less: LIFO reserve | 575.0 | 557.0 |
| Inventory—LIFO | $ 937.0 | $ 863.0 |

**Required:**

1. Compute Dembo's (a) current ratio, (b) return on assets, (c) debt/equity ratio, and (d) inventory turnover using the company's 2008 financial data as originally reported. Round answers to two decimal places.

2. Recompute the ratios in requirement 1 after transforming Dembo's numbers to a FIFO basis. Ignore income tax effects.

3. For each ratio computed in requirements 1 and 2, indicate which computation (LIFO basis or FIFO basis) best captures the underlying economics.

---

The following is excerpted from the financial statements of Baldwin Piano and Organ Company:

**P9-9**

Inventory turnover

### Consolidated Statements of Earnings

| | Years Ended December 31 | | |
| --- | --- | --- | --- |
| | Year 3 | Year 2 | Year I |
| Net sales | $120,657,455 | $110,076,904 | $103,230,431 |
| Cost of goods sold | 89,970,702 | 79,637,060 | 74,038,724 |
| Gross profit | $ 30,686,753 | $ 30,439,844 | $ 29,191,707 |

| Inventories Consist of | Year 3 | Year 2 |
| --- | --- | --- |
| FIFO cost | | |
| Raw materials | $ 9,930,923 | $ 9,500,765 |
| Work in process | 7,081,883 | 5,943,672 |
| Finished goods | 36,149,809 | 39,328,177 |
| | 53,162,615 | 54,772,614 |
| Excess of FIFO cost over | | |
| LIFO inventory value | (8,085,250) | (6,828,615) |
| | $45,077,365 | $47,943,999 |

At December 31, Year 3, approximately 77% of the company's inventories were valued on the LIFO method.

During the past three years, certain inventories were reduced. This reduction resulted in the liquidation of LIFO inventory layers carried at the lower costs prevailing in prior years as compared with the current cost of inventories. The effect of these inventory liquidations was to increase net earnings for Year 3, Year 2, and Year 1 by approximately $694,000 ($.20 per share), $519,000 ($.15 per share), and $265,000 ($.08 per share), respectively.

**Required:**

1. Estimate Baldwin's cost of goods sold and the cost of goods manufactured for Year 3; assume that the company had used FIFO instead of LIFO.

2. On the basis of these FIFO numbers, compute Baldwin's finished goods and work-in-process inventory turnovers (expressed in days) for Year 3. What do these turnovers tell you about Baldwin's operating cycle?

---

Parque Corporation applied to Fairview Bank early in 2008 for a $400,000 five-year loan to finance plant modernization. The company proposes that the loan be unsecured and repaid from future operating cash flows. In support of the loan application, Parque submitted an income statement for 2007. Prepared using the FIFO inventory cost flow approach, this income statement reflected annual profit that was approximately 50% of the principal amount of the loan. It was offered as evidence that the loan could easily be repaid within the five-year term.

Parque is in the business of recycling yelpin, an industrial lubricant. The company buys used yelpin from large salvage companies and, after cleaning and reconditioning it, sells it to

**P9-10**

Analyzing gross margins and cash flow sustainability

manufacturing companies. The recycling business is very competitive and has typically generated small gross margins. The salvage companies set yelpin prices on the first day of each quarter, and Parque purchases it at the established price for the entire quarter. Yelpin prices fluctuate with business conditions. Prices paid to salvage companies have risen in recent years but tend to fall during economic downturns.

Parque sells the recycled yelpin at $1 per pound above the currently prevailing price that it pays to acquire the used yelpin from salvage companies. December 31, 2006, inventory was 300,000 pounds at a cost of $7.00 per pound. Purchases and sales in 2007 were:

|  | **Purchases** | **Sales** |
| --- | --- | --- |
| First quarter 2007 | 600,000 lbs. @ $7.20/lb. | 700,000 lbs. @ $8.20/lb. |
| Second quarter 2007 | 700,000 lbs. @ $7.40/lb. | 600,000 lbs. @ $8.40/lb. |
| Third quarter 2007 | 800,000 lbs. @ $7.80/lb. | 700,000 lbs. @ $8.80/lb. |
| Fourth quarter 2007 | 600,000 lbs. @ $8.10/lb. | 650,000 lbs. @ $9.10/lb. |

Cash operating costs during 2007 totaled $2,800,000.

**Required:**

1. Compute 2007 income for Parque Corporation using the FIFO inventory flow assumption. Ignore income taxes.

2. Did Parque really earn a profit from its *operating* activities in 2007?

3. Given the circumstances described, what risks exist that could threaten ultimate repayment of the loan?

---

**P9-11**

Evaluating inventory cost flow changes

The following is an excerpt from the financial statements of Trinity Industries:

Effective September 30, 2007, the Company changed its method of accounting for inventories from the LIFO method principally to the Specific Identification method, because, in the opinion of management, there is a better matching of revenues and expenses, better correlation of accounting and financial information with the method by which the Company is managed, and better presentation of inventories at values that more fairly present the inventories' cost.

During 2008, SPS Technologies changed its inventory cost flow assumption from LIFO to the average cost method. The following is an excerpt from SPS Technologies financial statements.

The change to the average cost method will conform all inventories of the Company to the same method of valuation. The Company believes that the average cost method of inventory valuation provides a more meaningful presentation of the financial position of the Company since it reflects more recent costs in the balance sheet. Under the current economic environment of low inflation and an expected reduction in inventories and low production costs, the Company believes that the average cost method also results in a better matching of current costs with current revenues.

**Required:**

1. Evaluate each of the justifications provided by Trinity for changing its inventory cost flow assumption.

2. Evaluate each of the justifications provided by SPS Technologies for changing its inventory cost flow assumption.

---

**P9-12**

Assessing managerial opportunism

JKW Corporation has been selling plumbing supplies since 1981. In 2000, the company adopted the LIFO method of valuing its inventory. The company has grown steadily over the years and a layer has been added to its LIFO inventory in each of the years the method has been used. The company's inventory turnover ratio has averaged 4.5 in recent years. Management attempts to maintain a stable level of inventory at each store; the growth in inventory has been due to new stores being opened each year. In 2007, the board of directors approved an incentive program that pays managers a sizable bonus in each year that certain performance targets are met. For

2008, targeted earnings per share are $2.75. In an effort to track progress toward meeting this target, management produced the following income statement for the first nine months of 2008.

## JKW Corporation

### Income Statement
### January 1–September 30, 2008

| | |
|---|---:|
| Sales | $13,284,000 |
| Cost of goods sold | 7,970,400 |
| Gross margin | 5,313,600 |
| Operating expenses | 2,391,120 |
| Income before taxes | 2,922,480 |
| Income tax expense | 1,022,868 |
| Net income | $ 1,899,612 |
| Earnings per share (1,000,000 shares outstanding) | $ 1.90 |

Based on past history, management expects 30% of the company's annual sales to take place in the fourth quarter. Operating expenses and gross margin are expected to remain at 18% and 40% of sales, respectively, for the remainder of the year. The company's tax rate is 35%.

**Required:**

1. Assuming that management maintains a stable level of inventory, project earnings per share for 2008 based on the data provided.

2. Assume that you are JKW's independent auditor, and your analysis indicates that projected earnings per share will fall short of the bonus target. In the past, JKW's managers have used aggressive (and possibly unethical) behavior to achieve salary bonus targets. You suspect that the managers intend to deplete old LIFO layers deliberately in the fourth quarter. To help you detect such behavior, calculate the amount of the LIFO dip that would be needed in the fourth quarter to hit the EPS target in 2008.

---

Fraser Corporation uses the LIFO method of inventory valuation and is preparing its financial statements for the year 2008. Its controller provided the following income statement for the year ended December 31, 2008 to top management for review:

**P9-13**

Making interfirm comparisons

| | | |
|---|---:|---:|
| **Sales revenue** | | $1,000,000 |
| Cost of goods sold: | | |
| Beginning Inventory | 150,000 | |
| Add: Purchases | 650,000 | |
| Less: Ending Inventory | (200,000) | |
| | | (600,000) |
| **Gross profit** | | 400,000 |
| Selling and administrative expenses | | (150,000) |
| Net income before taxes | | 250,000 |
| Income taxes | | (75,000) |
| Net income | | $ 175,000 |

Fraser's CEO had mixed emotions after examining the income statement. He wanted to know how Fraser compares with its closest rival, KAS Corporation, and he instructed the controller to "compute some ratios for both companies." KAS uses the FIFO method of inventory valuation. The following are excerpts from the controller's report:

| | Fraser | KAS |
|---|:---:|:---:|
| Gross margin percentage (Gross margin/Sales) | ? | 49% |
| Return on sales (Net income/Sales) | ? | 21% |
| Inventory turnover (COGS/Average inventory) | ? | 1.8 |

**Required:**

1. Complete the controller's report by computing the ratios for Fraser based on the information given in the preceding income statement. For each ratio, how does Fraser compare with KAS? Explain how the choice of inventory methods biases the comparisons in favor of either Fraser or KAS.

2. After reviewing the controller's report, the CEO was concerned about Fraser's performance relative to KAS on two of the three ratios. However, the controller pointed out to the CEO that Fraser's "perceived underperformance" is primarily driven by differences in accounting methods. In addition, the controller added that if one takes into account "our current period LIFO tax savings, Fraser has outperformed KAS." The CEO asked the controller, "Why don't you show me how an analyst might adjust our income statement to make it comparable to that of KAS?" Your task is to help the controller by preparing a pro forma income statement for Fraser that is comparable to that of KAS. Assume that if Fraser had used the FIFO method, the beginning and ending inventories would have been higher by $50,000 and $150,000, respectively. On the basis of the "adjusted" income statement, recompute the three ratios given in the controller's report, and explain how and why the revised figures alter the CEO's earlier conclusions.

---

**P9-14**

LIFO and ratio effects

Don Facundo Bacardy Maso founded the original Bacardi® rum business in Cuba in 1862. The following information is excerpted from Bacardi Corporation's annual report for the year ended December 31, Year 2. Bacardi's effective tax rate was 17% in Year 2.

The company follows the last-in, first-out (LIFO) method of determining inventory cost. The LIFO method is considered by management to be preferable because it more closely matches current costs with current revenues in periods of price level changes. Under this method, current costs are charged to costs of sales for the year.

In Year 2, LIFO liquidation was caused primarily by a substantial reduction during the year in [the inventory of] molasses (the major raw material). This LIFO liquidation, which resulted in cost of products sold being charged with higher inventory costs from prior years, caused a decrease in Year 2 net income of approximately $1,400,000 or $0.14 per share.

LIFO inventories at December 31, Year 2 and Year 1 were $51,892,000 and $53,812,000 respectively, which is approximately $700,000 and $20,800,000 less than replacement cost at those dates.

In accordance with generally recognized trade practices, inventories of distilled spirits in bonded aging warehouses have been included in current assets, although the normal aging period is usually from one to three years.

Ending inventories consist of the following:

| ($ in thousands) | Year 2 | Year 1 |
|---|---|---|
| Finished goods | $ 2,684 | $ 2,420 |
| Aging rum in bond | 40,285 | 39,921 |
| Raw materials and supplies | 8,923 | 11,471 |
| | $51,892 | $53,812 |

Cost of goods sold and net income (after tax) during Year 2 were $65,374,000 and $45,568,000, respectively.

**Required:**

1. Compute the cost of goods manufactured (fully aged rum) during Year 2. Without using the LIFO reserve information, compute the finished goods inventory turnover (the number of days from inventory completion until its sale) and the work-in-process inventory turnover (the number of days the inventory is in the production cycle). Is the difference between the two inventory turnover ratios consistent with the nature of Bacardi's business? Explain.

2. On the basis of available information, estimate Bacardi's net income if the company had used FIFO during Year 2. By comparing the reported LIFO income with your estimate of FIFO income, what do you learn about the business conditions Bacardi faced during Year 2?

3. Using all available information, compute a total inventory turnover measure (expressed in number of days). Does your estimate of inventory turnover capture Bacardi's "true" physical turnover (based on what you know about the business)? Explain. If it does not capture the true physical turnover, provide possible reasons. Be specific.

The comparative income statements and edited inventory footnote for Oxford Industries, Inc. for Year 3 follow. Located in Atlanta, Oxford designs, manufactures, markets, and sells consumer apparel products for both men and women. Its ticker symbol is OXM.

**P9-15**

LIFO inventory:
Comprehensive

## Oxford Industries, Inc. and Subsidiaries

### Consolidated Statements of Earnings

|  | Years Ended | | |
| --- | --- | --- | --- |
| ($ in thousands, except per share amounts) | June 2, Year 3 | May 28, Year 2 | May 29, Year 1 |
| Net sales | $839,533 | $862,435 | $774,518 |
| Costs and expenses | | | |
| Cost of goods sold | 685,841 | 698,170 | 619,690 |
| Selling, general and administrative | 112,056 | 116,284 | 111,041 |
| Interest, net | 3,827 | 4,713 | 3,421 |
|  | 801,724 | 819,167 | 734,152 |
| Earnings before income taxes | 37,809 | 43,268 | 40,366 |
| Income taxes | 14,368 | 16,875 | 15,743 |
| Net earnings | $ 23,441 | $ 26,393 | $ 24,623 |
| Basic earnings per common share | $3.04 | $3.15 | $2.79 |
| Diluted earnings per common share | $3.02 | $3.11 | $2.75 |

### Edited Inventory Footnote*

The components of inventories are summarized as follows:

| ($ in thousands) | June 2, Year 3 | May 28, Year 2 |
| --- | --- | --- |
| Finished goods | $ 90,961 | $ 92,195 |
| Work in process | 25,903 | 24,579 |
| Fabric | 28,255 | 23,280 |
| Trim and supplies | 8,118 | 6,874 |
|  | $153,237 | $146,928 |

The excess of replacement cost over the value of inventories based on the LIFO method was $37,154 at June 2, Year 3; $37,367 at May 28, Year 2; and $39,205 at May 29, Year 1. Changes in the LIFO reserve increased earnings $0.02 per share basic in Year 3, $0.13 per share basic in Year 2, and decreased earnings $0.06 per share basic in Year 1.

During fiscal Year 3, inventory quantities were reduced, which resulted in a liquidation of LIFO inventory layers carried at lower costs that had prevailed in prior years. The effect of the liquidation was to decrease cost of goods sold by approximately $147 and to increase net earnings by $91 or $0.01 per share basic. During fiscal Year 2, the effect of [the Year 2] liquidation was to decrease cost of goods sold by approximately $1,174 and to increase net earnings by $716 or $0.09 per share basic. During fiscal Year 1, the effect of [the Year 1] liquidation was to decrease cost of goods sold by approximately $591 and to increase net earnings by $361 or $0.04 per share basic.

---

* The footnote was edited to include selected Year 1 data. Dollar amounts in the footnote are in thousands, except per share figures. Assume that the effective tax rate is 35%.

**Required:**

1. Based on the available information, provide an estimate of Oxford Industries earnings before income taxes for Year 3 and Year 2 if the company had used FIFO accounting.

2. Using the available data, provide estimates of the amount of realized holding gains (inventory profits) that were included in Year 3, Year 2, and Year 1 earnings before income taxes under the LIFO method.

3. Explain why the estimated FIFO income numbers (see requirement 1) are higher or lower than those under the LIFO method. (*Hint:* To do this prepare a reconciliation of changes in the LIFO reserve for Year 3 and Year 2 as illustrated on page 496 of the text.)

4. As of the end of Year 3 and Year 2, compute the total amount of income tax saved by Oxford from the time of its initial adoption of LIFO. Ignore present value effects in your calculations. For the fiscal Year 3 alone, did Oxford pay higher or lower income tax under LIFO compared to what it would have paid under FIFO? How much?

5. Compute Oxford's inventory turnover ratio (without making any adjustments) for Year 3 under the LIFO cost flow assumption. (Express it in number of days.) Does this number provide a good estimate of the number of days inventory is held by Oxford Industries? If not, propose (and defend) an alternative approach to calculating inventory turnover. Show supporting calculations.

---

**P9-16**

**LIFO reporting: Comprehensive**

Maple Company has used the LIFO method of inventory accounting since its inception in 2000. At December 31, 2006, the ending inventory was:

| | | | |
|---|---|---|---|
| Base layer | 5,000 units @ $1.00 | = | $5,000 |
| 2002 layer | 2,000 units @ $1.30 | = | 2,600 |
| | | | $7,600 |

The company uses the periodic inventory system that assumes sales have been made from the last inventory units acquired during the year. Purchase prices for Maple Company's inventory are adjusted twice a year by its supplier on January 1 and July 1.

Purchase and sales transactions for 2007 and 2008 were:

| | **Units Purchased** | **Units Sold** |
|---|---|---|
| 2007 | | |
| January–June | 40,000 units @ $2.50 | 30,000 units @ $3.80 |
| July–December | 40,000 units @ 2.70 | 50,000 units @ 3.90 |
| 2008 | | |
| January–June | 40,000 units @ 2.75 | 43,000 units @ 4.00 |
| July–December | 40,000 units @ 3.00 | 43,000 units @ 4.30 |

Other expenses totaled $60,000 in 2007 and $66,000 in 2008. Inventory purchase prices in effect during the last half of 2006 were $2.40 per unit.

**Required:**

1. Compute Maple Company's operating income on the LIFO historical cost basis for 2007 and 2008.

2. Compute Maple's current cost income from continuing operations for 2007 and 2008.

3. Determine the total increases in current cost amounts (that is, unrealized cost savings or holding gains) occurring in 2007 and 2008.

4. What portion of the reported 2007 and 2008 LIFO income consisted of realized holding gains (that is, "inventory profits")?

5. What was the dollar amount of Maple's LIFO reserve at December 31, 2006? Compute the increases and decreases to the LIFO reserve in 2007 and 2008. Identify the cause for each increase and decrease.

6. LIFO, a method that supposedly is designed to keep inventory profits out of income, does not accomplish this result for Maple Company in either 2007 or 2008. Why?

---

Sirotka Retail Company began doing business in 2006. The following information pertains to its first three years of operation:

**P9-17**

LIFO: Comprehensive

| Year | Operating Expenses | Purchases | | Sales | |
|------|--------------------|-----------|-----------|--------|-----------|
|      |                    | Units | Unit Cost | Units | Unit Price |
| 2006 | $60,000 | 15,000 | $20.00 | 12,000 | $35 |
| 2007 | 90,000  | 20,000 | 25.00  | 18,000 | 40 |
| 2008 | 65,000  | 5,000  | 30.00  | 10,000 | 40 |

Assume the following:

- The income tax rate is 40%.
- Purchase and sale prices change only at the beginning of the year.
- Sirotka uses the LIFO cost flow assumption.
- Operating expenses are primarily selling and administrative expenses.

**Required:**

1. Compute cost of goods sold and the cost of ending inventory for each of the three years. (Identify the number of units and the cost per unit for each LIFO layer in the ending inventory.)

2. Prepare income statements for each of the three years.

3. Compute the LIFO reserve at the end of 2006, 2007, and 2008.

4. Compute the effect of LIFO liquidation on the net income of the company for the years 2007 and 2008.

5. Compute the inventory turnover ratio for the years 2007 and 2008. Do not make adjustments for any potential biases in LIFO accounting. Comment on the direction of the bias (that is, understated/overstated) in the inventory turnover ratio under LIFO. Is the ratio in one year more biased than in the other? Explain.

6. How can the physical turnover of inventory (that is, true inventory turnover) best be approximated using *all* of the information available in a LIFO financial statement? Illustrate your approach by recomputing Sirotka's inventory turnover ratios for 2007 and 2008.

7. Compute the gross margin percentages for the years 2007 and 2008. Explain whether the difference in the gross margin percentages between 2007 and 2008 reflect the change in Sirotka's economic condition from 2007 to 2008.

8. Provide an *estimate* of the FIFO cost of goods sold for the years 2006, 2007, and 2008 using the information available in the financial statements.

9. Based on your answers to requirements 1 and 8, estimate Sirotka's tax savings for 2006, 2007, and 2008.

10. Assuming a discount rate of 10%, compute the December 31, 2005 present value of the tax savings over the period 2006–2008 (that is, discount the 2006 tax savings one period, and so on).

Caldwell Corporation operates an ice cream processing plant and uses the FIFO inventory cost flow assumption. A partial income statement for the year ended December 31, 2008 follows:

## Caldwell Corporation

### Statement of Income
### For the Year Ended December 31, 2008

| | |
|---|---|
| Sales revenues | $680,000,000 |
| Cost of goods sold | 360,000,000 |
| Gross margin | 320,000,000 |
| SG&A expenses | 200,000,000 |
| Income before taxes | $120,000,000 |

Caldwell's physical inventory levels were virtually constant throughout 2008. The FIFO dollar amount of inventory at January 1, 2008 was $60,000,000. During 2008, the Consumer Price Index (an index of overall average purchasing power for typical urban-dwelling consumers) increased by 4%.

Caldwell Corporation's largest competitor, Cohen Confections, uses LIFO for inventory accounting. Excerpts from its December 31, 2008 inventory footnote were:

## Cohen Confections

### Inventory Footnote

Inventories are computed using the LIFO cost flow assumption. Comparative amounts were:

| | December 31 | |
|---|---|---|
| | **2008** | **2007** |
| Raw materials | $ 8,100,000 | $ 8,000,000 |
| Finished goods | 76,000,000 | 80,000,000 |
| | $84,100,000 | $88,000,000 |

The difference between the LIFO inventory amounts and the replacement cost of the inventory at December 31, 2008 and 2007, respectively, was $18,000,000 and $12,000,000. A LIFO liquidation occurred in 2008, which increased the reported gross margin by $1,000,000.

### Required:

Using the preceding information, what is the *best* estimate of the amount of realized holding gains (or inventory profits) included in Caldwell Corporation's income before taxes?

Ramps by Andy, Inc. manufactures skateboard ramps. The company uses independent sales representatives to market its products and pays a commission of 10% on each sale. Data regarding the five styles of ramps in the company's inventory at December 31, 2008, follow. The normal profit margin on each style is expressed as a percentage of the item's selling price.

| Inventory Item | Original Cost | Replacement Cost | Selling Price | Normal Profit Margin % |
|---|---|---|---|---|
| Style 1 | $125 | $130 | $260 | 35% |
| Style 2 | 210 | 190 | 350 | 40 |
| Style 3 | 95 | 90 | 130 | 20 |
| Style 4 | 460 | 455 | 500 | 30 |
| Style 5 | 390 | 390 | 650 | 20 |

**Required:**

Determine the appropriate inventory value to use for each item in the company's December 31, 2008, inventory.

**C9-1**

Barbara Trading Company:
Understanding LIFO
distortions

Barbara Trading Company has used the LIFO method of inventory accounting since its inception in 1990. At December 31, 2006, the ending inventory was:

| | | |
|---|---|---|
| Base layer | 10,000 units @ $ 7 | $ 70,000 |
| 2000 layer | 5,000 units @  12 | 60,000 |
| | | $130,000 |

The company uses the periodic inventory method that assumes sales were made from the last inventory units acquired during the year (periodic LIFO). The purchase and sales prices change only once a year on January 1. Operating expenses are $600,000 per year, and the income tax rate is 40%.

| Year | Units Purchased | Units Sold |
|---|---|---|
| 2007 | 100,000 units @ $25 | 100,000 units @ $35 |
| 2008 | 90,000 units @  30 | 100,000 units @  40 |

During 2008, the company implemented a new inventory management program to reduce the level of inventory carried.

**Required:**

1. Prepare Barbara's income statements for the years 2007 and 2008.

2. Barbara's CEO, I. M. Greedy, examined the effect of the new inventory management program on the company's inventory turnover. After doing some quick calculations, she was overjoyed. "When our competitors are turning their inventory over 12 to 15 times a year, our inventory turnover for 2008 has exceeded 30!" How did the CEO estimate the inventory turnover ratio for 2008? Based on all available information, provide an estimate of Barbara's true inventory turnover during 2008. Assume that the competitors' turnovers were based on data from their financial statements. What might be the potential limitations of comparing Barbara's inventory turnover with its competitors'? Show supporting figures where necessary.

3. Greedy was also quite ecstatic about the company's overall performance during 2008. "I am extremely pleased with the growth in our bottom line. Although some of the growth is probably due to the increase in selling price, most of it appears to be the result of our new inventory management program." Prepare a memo to her explaining the true reasons behind the change in net income from 2007 to 2008. Show supporting figures when necessary. Also critically evaluate the CEO's rationale for the growth in earnings.

4. Barbara Trading Company's CFO, I. M. Taxed, was rather concerned about the tax implications of reducing inventory levels. He was lamenting, "I told you all about the LIFO boomerang. We could have avoided paying a lot of taxes that resulted from our inventory liquidations had we adopted FIFO in the first place." Evaluate the CFO's analysis of the LIFO tax effects.

| C 9 - 2 |
|---|

**General Electric: Interpreting a LIFO footnote**

The following inventory footnote appears in General Electric's Year 3 annual report.

### General Electric Company

### Edited Inventory Footnote

|  | December 31 | |
|---|---|---|
| ($ in millions) | Year 3 | Year 2 |
| **GE** | | |
| Raw materials and work in process | $4,894 | $4,708 |
| Finished goods | 4,379 | 3,951 |
| Unbilled shipments | 372 | 312 |
|  | 9,645 | 8,971 |
| Less revaluation to LIFO | (606) | (676) |
|  | 9,039 | 8,295 |
| **GE Capital Services** | | |
| Finished goods | 208 | 270 |
|  | $9,247 | $8,565 |

LIFO revaluations decreased $70 million in Year 3, compared with decreases of $169 million in Year 2 and $82 million in Year 1. Included in these changes were decreases of $21 million, $8 million and $6 million in Year 3, Year 2 and Year 1, respectively, that resulted from lower LIFO inventory levels. There were net cost decreases in each of the last three years.

GE's earnings before income taxes were $18.891 billion in Year 3. Assume a 35% marginal tax rate.

**Required:**

1. What are the total cumulative tax savings as of December 31, Year 3 that GE has realized as a result of using the LIFO inventory method?

2. What would GE's pre-tax earnings have been in Year 3 if it had been using FIFO?

3. What December 31, Year 3 balance sheet figures would be different—and by how much— if GE had used FIFO to account for its inventories?

4. What were the LIFO liquidation profits reported in Year 3 both pre-tax and after-tax?

5. Explain what factors cause the difference between the LIFO pre-tax income number and the FIFO pre-tax income number you estimated in requirement 2. (*Hint:* Reconcile the change in the LIFO reserve for Year 3).

| C 9 - 3 |
|---|

**Gardner Denver, Inc.: Interpreting a LIFO footnote**

The following inventory footnote is taken from Gardner Denver's Year 3 annual report. You are to use this information in answering the questions that follow.

### Gardner Denver, Inc.

### Edited Inventory Footnote

|  | December 31 | |
|---|---|---|
| ($ in thousands) | Year 3 | Year 2 |
| Raw materials | $33,400 | $33,156 |
| Work-in-process | 9,077 | 15,908 |
| Finished goods | 27,630 | 30,942 |
| Perishable tooling and supplies | 2,456 | 2,328 |
|  | 72,563 | 82,334 |
| Excess of FIFO costs over LIFO costs | (5,115) | (5,684) |
| Inventories net | $67,448 | $76,650 |

During Year 3, Year 2 and Year 1, reductions in inventory quantities (net of acquisitions) resulted in liquidations of LIFO inventory layers carried at lower costs prevailing in prior years. The effect was to increase net income in Year 3, Year 2 and Year 1 by $268, $319 and $427, respectively.

**Required:**

1. By how much would net income for Year 3 have differed had Gardner Denver used FIFO to value those inventory items valued under LIFO? Assume a 35% marginal tax rate. Be sure to indicate whether FIFO income would be higher or lower than LIFO income.

2. What would the LIFO reserve have been on December 31, Year 3 if no LIFO liquidation had occurred in Year 3?

3. What was the net difference in Year 3 income taxes that Gardner Denver experienced as a result of using LIFO rather than FIFO? Assume a 35% tax rate and indicate whether FIFO or LIFO would yield the higher tax and by how much.

4. What was the approximate rate of change in input costs in Year 3 for Gardner Denver's inventory?

---

Baines Corporation manufactures fireplace tools and accessories. It has been prosperous since its incorporation in 1980, largely due to a small, exceptionally skilled, and highly motivated managerial staff. Baines has been able to attract and retain its excellent management team because of a very attractive managerial incentive plan. The plan allocates 23% of total pre-tax FIFO-absorption cost profits into a pool that is distributed to managers as a year-end bonus. The bonus pool is allocated to individual managers using a point system based on each manager's performance relative to a budgeted goal.

**C9-4**

Baines Corporation: Using absorption versus variable costing

mhhe.com/revsine4e

Data relating to 2007 operations follow:

| | |
|---|---|
| Beginning inventory | 1,500,000 units @ $2.95 |
| Ending inventory | 1,500,000 units @ $2.95 |
| Production | 4,000,000 units |
| Sales | 4,000,000 units @ $3.50 |
| Variable production costs | $1.45/unit |
| Fixed production costs | $6,000,000/year |

Reported pre-tax profit for 2007 was:

| | | | |
|---|---|---|---|
| Sales revenues | (4,000,000 @ $3.50) | | $14,000,000 |
| Costs of goods sold | | | |
|   Variable production costs | (4,000,000 @ $1.45) | $5,800,000 | |
|   Fixed production costs | (4,000,000 @ $1.50) | 6,000,000 | |
| | | | 11,800,000 |
| Operating profit | | | 2,200,000 |
| Interest expense | | | 200,000 |
| Pre-tax profit | | | $ 2,000,000 |

Early in 2008, interest rates increased, and the company's president, Ross Eldred, was concerned about the rising cost of financing the inventory. After a careful study of the situation, he became convinced that inventory levels could be reduced considerably without adversely affecting sales or delivery performance provided certain changes in purchasing, production, and sales procedures were adopted. Accordingly, Eldred called a meeting of the management group in February 2008 and outlined his multifaceted plan for reducing inventories.

His basic strategy was immediately accepted, and several participants suggested various additional efficiencies and other inventory management improvements. The meeting adjourned with each manager resolving to do all that was possible to decrease inventory levels and thereby reduce interest expense.

As the year progressed, Eldred's proposals and the refinements suggested by the other managers were put into practice; as a result, inventory levels were significantly reduced by December 31, 2008. The managers were quite pleased with their successful implementation of the new strategy, and morale was quite high.

Basic facts concerning 2008 performance were as follows:

| | |
|---|---|
| Beginning inventory | 1,500,000 units @ $2.95 |
| Ending inventory | 700,000 units @ $3.325 |
| Production | 3,200,000 units |
| Sales | 4,000,000 units @ $3.50 |
| Variable production costs | $1.45/unit |
| Fixed production costs | $6,000,000/year |
| Interest expense | $100,000/year |

Shortly after the final 2008 profit figures were reported early in 2009, a general management meeting was held. As he walked into the room, Eldred was somewhat surprised to see a rather sullen and dispirited group of managers confronting him. One was heard to mumble, "Well, I wonder what this year's double cross will be!"

**Required:**

1. What do you think caused the abrupt change in the mood of the management team at Baines Corporation? Cite figures to support your explanation.

2. How might this problem have been prevented? Cite figures to support your explanation.

# COLLABORATIVE LEARNING CASE

**C9-5**

Weldotron Corporation: Strategic choice of accounting methods

 **Collaborative**

The following excerpts are taken from Weldotron's financial statements.

## Weldotron Corporation and Subsidiaries

### Condensed Consolidated Balance Sheets
### February 28, Year 4, and February 28, Year 3

| ($ in thousands) | Year 4 | Year 3 |
|---|---|---|
| **Assets** | | |
| Total current assets | $15,449 | $16,162 |
| Net property, plant, and equipment | 3,417 | 3,725 |
| Other assets | 220 | 170 |
| Total assets | $19,086 | $20,057 |
| **Liabilities and Stockholders' Equity** | | |
| Total current liabilities | $ 7,144 | $ 7,021 |
| Long-term debt less current portion | 1,527 | 1,585 |
| Other long-term liabilities | 683 | 637 |
| Total liabilities | 9,354 | 9,243 |
| Minority interest | 722 | 700 |
| Stockholders' equity | | |
| Common stock, par value $0.05 per share; issued 2,352,720 in Year 4 and | | |
| 1,882,720 in Year 3 | 118 | 94 |
| Additional paid-in capital | 9,798 | 8,715 |
| (Deficit) Retained earnings | (783) | 1,428 |
| | 9,133 | 10,237 |
| Less: Common stock in treasury | (123) | (123) |
| Total stockholders' equity | 9,010 | 10,114 |
| Total liabilities & stockholders' equity | $19,086 | $20,057 |

## Weldotron Corporation and Subsidiaries

### Condensed Consolidated Statements of Operations
### For the Years Ended February 28, Year 4, February 28, Year 3, and February 29, Year 2

| ($ in thousands) | Year 4 | Year 3 | Year 2 |
|---|---|---|---|
| Net sales | $30,440 | $26,400 | $29,061 |
| Costs and expenses | | | |
| Cost of sales | 22,375 | 19,322 | 21,372 |
| Selling, general, and administrative | 9,258 | 9,471 | 8,902 |
| Depreciation and amortization | 558 | 612 | 678 |
| Restructuring charges | 625 | –0– | –0– |
| | 32,816 | 29,405 | 30,952 |
| Loss from operations | (2,376) | (3,005) | (1,891) |
| Other income (expenses) | 128 | (33) | 606 |
| Income tax (benefit) provision | (59) | 26 | –0– |
| Minority interest share of (income) loss | (22) | (57) | 123 |
| Loss from continuing operations | (2,211) | (3,121) | (1,162) |
| Discontinued operations | –0– | –0– | (1,059) |
| Net loss | $(2,211) | $(3,121) | $(2,221) |

Excerpts from footnotes *($ in thousands)*:

1. Summary of Significant Account Policies

    Inventories: Substantially all inventories are valued at the lower of cost, determined by the use of the first in, first out method (FIFO) or market (see Note 2).

    Income Taxes: Weldotron Corporation and its subsidiaries file a consolidated federal income tax return. Accumulated undistributed earnings of the Company's foreign subsidiary were approximately $352 at February 28, Year 4. No provision has been made for U.S. income taxes on these earnings as the Company has reinvested or plans to reinvest overseas.

2. Change in Accounting Principle for Inventories

    Effective February 28, Year 4, the Company changed its basis of valuing inventories from the last in, first out (LIFO) method to the first in, first out (FIFO) method.

    In previous years, the Company experienced significant operating losses and has addressed these problems by discontinuing certain products and related parts. The results of inventory reductions in previous years resulted in the liquidation of LIFO layers which resulted in a mismatching of older costs with current revenues, which defeats the primary objective of LIFO. Further reductions of inventory levels are expected from the discontinuance of products and parts as well as better manufacturing methods which will reduce production lead times. Under these circumstances, the FIFO method of inventory valuation is the preferable method due to the improved matching of revenues and expenses and the current industry practice.

    The change has been applied retroactively by restating prior years' financial statements. The effects of the reversal of the previous LIFO reserve were partially offset by the appropriate application of FIFO costing requirements. The effects of this change in the method of valuing inventory were to increase the net loss previously reported in Year 3 by $128 and to decrease the net loss previously reported in Year 2 by $97. The effects on Year 4 were not material. The effects of this restatement were also to increase retained earnings as of March 1, Year 1, by $2,356.

7. Long Term Debt and Short Term Borrowings

    On June 25, Year 1, the Company entered into a credit facility (the "Credit Facility") with Congress Financial Corporation ("Congress"), a CoreStates Company, to provide a revolving line of credit and term loan for working capital purposes not to exceed $5,000, which replaced the Company's existing credit facility. The interest rate is 3.75% over the CoreStates floating base rate, which was 6% at February 28, Year 4. The Credit Facility further requires that the Company pay fees on the unused line of credit, for administration and on early termination of the Credit Facility. On April 13, Year 4, the Credit Facility was extended for one year. It expires and is due and payable on or before June 25, Year 5.

The Credit Facility is collateralized by substantially all of the assets of the Company and its domestic subsidiaries. Borrowings under the Credit Facility are limited to certain percentages of eligible inventory and accounts receivable including stipulations as to the ratio of advances collateralized by receivables compared to advances collateralized by inventory.

The Credit Facility's covenants stipulate that tangible domestic net worth of greater than $8,200 and consolidated working capital greater than $9,500 be maintained. In addition the Credit Facility restricts the payment of dividends, limits the amount of the advances to and guarantees for the Company's foreign subsidiary and limits annual capital expenditures to $500. At February 28, Year 4, the Company was in compliance with the covenants of the Credit Facility.

Borrowings under the Credit Facility aggregated $3,215, including a $1,500 long-term loan at February 28, Year 4. The remaining borrowing under the Credit Facility is included in current liabilities.

**Tax Note**

At February 28, Year 4, $8,400 of Federal tax loss carryforwards are available for regular income tax purposes.

Note 2 states that Weldotron changed its inventory method from LIFO to FIFO effective February 28, Year 4. In the same note, the Company has provided justifications for the change in the inventory cost flow assumption. Note 7 discloses details of the Company's credit facility and covenants. This note states that the Company was in compliance with the covenants on February 28, Year 4.

**Required:**

Financial reporting choices can sometimes allow companies to achieve strategic objectives and benefit shareholders. Using this perspective, evaluate the effect of Weldotron's inventory accounting change on its debt covenants, specifically on the tangible domestic net worth constraint of $8,200 and the consolidated working capital constraint of $9,500. (*Note:* In answering this question, you should keep in mind that when applying the working capital constraint, lenders often ignore current liabilities related to the borrowing itself.)

**Remember to check the book's companion Web site for additional study material.**

# Long-Lived Assets and Depreciation

| ($ in millions) | | $22,011.9 |
|---|---|---|
| Sales | | |
| Costs, Expenses and Other | 001.1 | 5,149.6 |
| Materials and production | 665.4 | 7,155.5 |
| Marketing and administrative | 92.9 | 3,848.0 |
| Research and development | | |
| Restructuring costs | 2.3 | 322.2 |
| Equity income | 4) | (1,717.1) |
| | | (110.2) |
| | | 14,648.0 |
| Net income | | 7,363 |

A n asset is something that generates future economic benefits and is under the exclusive control of a single entity. Assets can be tangible items such as inventories and buildings or intangible items such as patents and trademarks.

The previous two chapters—on receivables and inventories—examined current assets. Current assets represent a large part of total assets for many companies. Recall that a current asset is expected to be converted into cash within one year or within the operating cycle, whichever is longer.

This chapter concentrates on operating assets expected to yield their economic benefits (or service potential) over a period longer than one year. Such assets are called **long-lived assets.**

Long-lived assets represent a significant percentage of total assets in industries such as oil exploration and refining, automobile manufacturing, and steel. Exhibit 10.1 shows the asset portion of Sunoco, Inc.'s balance sheet in both dollar and common-size terms at December 31, 2005. Notice that long-lived assets (Properties, plants, and equipment) comprises 57.0% of total assets. Firms have latitude in how much detail they provide about separate long-lived asset components. Sunoco chose to provide a footnote breakdown of the total properties by industry segment (see Exhibit 10.2). Notice that the highlighted net properties total from Exhibit 10.1 ($5,658 million) appears again in Exhibit 10.2. Statement readers can then see the breakdown of gross and net property, plant and equipment across industry segments.

> The *operating cycle* for a manufacturer begins with the receipt of raw materials inventory and ends when cash is received for the completed product that has been sold. If inventory turns over every 90 days and if the average receivables collection period is 50 days, then the operating cycle is 140 days (that is, 90 + 50).

Clearly, there's a high proportion of long-lived assets in some industries. However, the GAAP rules used to measure the carrying amounts of long-lived assets are frequently criticized, and we'll see why next.

## LEARNING OBJECTIVES

**After studying this chapter, you will understand:**

1. What measurement base is used in accounting for long-lived assets and why this base is used.

2. What specific costs can be capitalized and how joint costs are allocated among assets.

3. How generally accepted accounting principles (GAAP) measurement rules complicate both trend analysis and cross-company analysis and how to avoid misinterpretations.

4. Why balance sheet carrying amounts for internally developed intangibles usually differ from their real values.

5. When long-lived asset impairment exists and how it is recorded.

6. How different depreciation methods are computed.

7. How analysts can adjust for different depreciation assumptions and improve interfirm comparisons.

8. How long-lived asset accounting and depreciation practices differ internationally.

*Chapter*

**EXHIBIT 10.1**    Sunoco, Inc.

**Partial Consolidated Statement of Financial Position
December 31, 2005**

| ($ in millions) | | Percentage |
|---|---:|---:|
| Assets | | |
| Cash and cash equivalents | $ 919 | |
| Accounts and notes receivable, net | 1,754 | |
| Inventories | 799 | |
| Deferred income taxes | 215 | |
| Total current assets | 3,687 | 37.1% |
| Investments and long-term receivables | 143 | 1.4 |
| Properties, plants, and equipment (net) | 5,658 | 57.0 |
| Deferred charges and other assets | 443 | 4.5 |
| Total | $9,931 | 100.0% |

*Source:* Sunoco, Inc. 2005 annual report.

**EXHIBIT 10.2**    Sunoco, Inc.

**Condensed Footnote Breakdown of Property, Plant and Equipment
December 31, 2005**

| ($ in millions) | Gross Investments at Cost | Accumulated Depreciation, Depletion and Amortization | Net Investment |
|---|---:|---:|---:|
| Refining and supply | $4,872 | $2,289 | $2,583 |
| Retail marketing | 1,504 | 624 | 880 |
| Chemicals | 1,317 | 301 | 1,016 |
| Logistics | 1,327 | 495 | 832 |
| Coke | 556 | 209 | 347 |
| | $9,576 | $3,918 | $5,658 |

*Source:* Sunoco, Inc. 2005 annual report.

# MEASUREMENT OF THE CARRYING AMOUNT OF LONG-LIVED ASSETS

Long-lived assets could potentially be measured on balance sheets in two ways:

1. Assets could be measured at their estimated value in an *output* market—a market where assets are *sold.* We call measures that use output market numbers **expected benefit approaches.**

2. Assets could be measured at their estimated cost in an *input* market—a market where assets are *purchased.* Measures that use input market costs are called **economic sacrifice approaches.**

Expected benefit approaches recognize that assets are valuable because of the *future cash inflows* they are expected to generate. Consequently, these approaches measure various definitions of future cash inflows that are expected to be generated by the asset. One example of an expected benefit approach is **discounted present value.** Under it, the value of an item of manufacturing equipment is measured by estimating the discounted present value of the stream of future net operating cash inflows it's expected to generate over its operating life. Another example of an expected benefit approach is the cash inflow that the asset would bring if it were sold instead of being used in operations. Under this variant of the expected benefit approach, long-lived assets are reported at their **net realizable value**—the amount that would be received if the assets were sold in the used asset market.

Economic sacrifice approaches to asset measurement focus on the amount of resource expenditure necessary to acquire it. One example of an economic sacrifice approach is **historical cost** (the dominant GAAP measurement method)—that is, the historical amount spent to buy the asset constitutes the *past* sacrifice incurred to bring the asset into the firm. Another example of an economic sacrifice approach involves measuring the current (or replacement) cost of the asset. Under a **replacement cost** approach, assets are carried at their current purchase cost—the expenditure (sacrifice) needed *today* to buy the asset.

## The Approach Used by GAAP

Exhibit 10.3 shows a hypothetical range of long-lived asset carrying amounts as measured under each approach—expected benefit versus economic sacrifice. Assume that the fixed asset is a truck used by a freight hauler to transport heavy industrial equipment. Let's say the truck originally cost $100,000, is two years old, has a remaining useful life of eight years, is being depreciated straight-line, and is expected to have no salvage value (market value) at the end of its useful life.

---

| **EXHIBIT 10.3** | Hypothetical Long-Lived Asset Carrying Amounts |
| --- | --- |

### Expected Benefit Approach Examples

1. Discounted present value:

    Expected net operating cash inflows = $18,000 per year (assumed) for eight remaining years, discounted at a 10% (assumed) rate

    $$5.33493^* \times \$18,000 = \$96,029$$

2. Net realizable value:

    Current resale price from an over-the-road equipment listing (Purple Book) for the specific vehicle model

    $$\$85,000 \text{ (assumed)}$$

### Economic Sacrifice Approach Examples

3. Replacement cost:

    Replacement cost of a two-year-old vehicle in equivalent condition

    $$\$90,000 \text{ (assumed)}$$

4. Historical cost less accumulated depreciation:

    $$\$100,000 - \left( \frac{\$100,000}{10 \text{ years}} \times 2 \text{ years} \right) = \$80,000$$

---

* Discount factor for an ordinary annuity for eight years at 10%. See "Present Value of an Ordinary Annuity of $1" table in end-of-book Appendix.

**Contracting**

GAAP uses historical cost—an economic sacrifice approach—to measure long-lived assets in almost all circumstances. The choice of historical cost is not an accident. It results from several pragmatic aspects of the existing financial reporting environment.

As discussed in Chapter 1, financial reports play a critical role in resource allocation decisions such as equity investing and lending. Accounting numbers are widely used in contracts such as loan agreements, incentive compensation plans, and union contracts (see Chapter 7). Because of these uses, ***parties whose transactions are explicitly or implicitly tied to accounting numbers expect them to be reliable numbers.*** By **reliable,** we mean the numbers must not be prone to manipulation. If the numbers were not reliable—for example, if they could be easily manipulated by one party to the contract—then cautious decision makers would be reluctant to enter into contracts using such "soft" numbers. The reason is that manipulation by one party could circumvent the contract terms.

Auditors also prefer that financial statement numbers have certain characteristics. One is that the numbers be verifiable. **Verifiability** means the numbers should arise from readily observable, corroborable facts rather than from subjective beliefs. Verifiable numbers are important to auditors because of the many legal suits arising from audited financial statements. Auditors believe that verifiable data help provide a defense in court, reducing potential litigation losses.

As modern financial reporting evolved, reliability and verifiability were used as qualitative criteria, or guidelines, for selecting acceptable long-lived asset measurement rules. Expected benefit approaches, such as discounted present value reporting, were discarded because the resulting numbers were deemed to be neither reliable nor verifiable. That's because present value computations require inherently subjective forecasts of future net cash flows as well as an assumed discount rate. This is illustrated in Exhibit 10.3 where alternative 1—the discounted present value/expected benefit approach—requires an estimate of expected net operating cash inflows ($18,000) and a choice of discount rate (10%). Most decision makers won't tie contracts to such numbers because the other party to the contract could easily evade certain contract terms by simply altering the cash flow forecast amounts or the discount rate.

**International**

Depreciation is an allocation of historical cost to time periods. Except by coincidence, the net book value number at a point in time—original cost less accumulated depreciation—does not reflect the economic worth of the asset at that time.

In contrast to U.S. GAAP, IAS 16, *Property, Plant and Equipment,* allows firms to revalue fixed assets upward periodically. Assets are reported at the revalued amount less subsequent depreciation of the revalued amount.

Another expected benefit approach—the net realizable value from selling the asset (alternative 2)—has also been rejected as a measurement base because of its frequent lack of verifiability. Our example in Exhibit 10.3 assumed that the long-lived asset had a readily determinable market price, as some do. However, many long-lived assets such as buildings are immobile, and others are highly specialized and therefore traded in thin markets; consequently, selling prices are often not readily determinable. The current selling price for these long-lived assets needs to be estimated using past transaction prices or transactions involving similar (but not necessarily identical) assets. Numbers obtained from such procedures often fail the verifiability test.

The economic sacrifice approach that uses replacement cost—that is, the estimated current cost of *replacing* the asset (alternative 3)—has also been disqualified on the basis of similar assertions that the numbers lack verifiability.

The only long-lived asset measurement method that survives the dual screens of reliability and verifiability is the economic sacrifice approach called *historical cost* (alternative 4). Consequently, long-lived assets are generally reflected in U.S. financial statements at the original historical cost of acquiring the asset (minus accumulated depreciation). Long-lived assets typically last for many years, and their replacement cost tends to increase. But GAAP prohibits adjustment for upward revisions in the replacement cost of the asset. However, when asset values are impaired, GAAP mandates write-downs, as you'll see later.

**Because long-lived assets are predominantly carried at depreciated historical cost, statement users should not expect balance sheet numbers for such assets to necessarily approximate their real economic worth. This is a serious limitation (with important implications for statement users) that we explore later in this chapter.**

# LONG-LIVED ASSET MEASUREMENT RULES ILLUSTRATED

The initial balance sheet carrying amount of a long-lived asset is governed by two rules:

1. All costs necessary to acquire the asset and make it ready for use are included in the asset account. Costs included in the asset account are called **capitalized costs.** (Expenditures excluded from asset categories are "charged-off" to income—that is, expensed.)

2. **Joint costs** incurred in acquiring more than one asset are apportioned among the acquired assets on a relative fair (market) value basis or some proxy thereof.

Both rules are illustrated in the Canyon Corporation example that follows in Exhibit 10.4.

Capitalized land costs include many items in addition to the $6,000,000 cash payment. For example, the cost of demolishing the existing structure (net of salvaged materials) is added to the land account because the land had to be cleared before the new building could be erected. This illustrates initial carrying amount Rule 1—all costs necessary to prepare the asset for its

| EXHIBIT 10.4 | Canyon Corporation |
|---|---|

### Joint Cost Allocation, Fixed Asset Purchase

Canyon Corporation acquired a tract of land on June 1, 2008 by paying $6,000,000 and by assuming an existing mortgage of $1,000,000 on the land. Canyon demolished an empty structure on the property at a cost of $650,000. Bricks and other materials from the demolished building were sold for $10,000. Regrading and clearing the land cost $35,000. Canyon then began constructing a new factory on the site. Architectural fees were $800,000, and the payments to contractors for building the factory totaled $12,000,000. Canyon negotiated a bank loan to help ease the cash flow crunch during construction. Interest payments over the construction period totaled $715,000. Legal fees incurred in the transaction totaled $57,000, of which $17,000 was attributable to both examination of title covering the land purchase and legal issues linked to the assumption of the existing mortgage. The remaining $40,000 of legal fees related to contracts with the architect and the construction companies. The construction project was completed on December 31, 2008.

The amounts allocated to the land and building accounts, respectively, are:

**Land**

| | | |
|---|---:|---:|
| Cash payment | | $ 6,000,000 |
| Mortgage assumed | | 1,000,000 |
| Demolition of existing structure | $650,000 | |
| Less: Salvage value of material | (10,000) | |
| | | 640,000 |
| Regrading and clearing land | | 35,000 |
| Legal fees allocated | | 17,000 |
| **Capitalized land costs** | | **$ 7,692,000** |

**Building**

| | |
|---|---:|
| Architectural fees | $    800,000 |
| Building costs | 12,000,000 |
| Interest capitalized | 715,000 |
| Legal fees allocated | 40,000 |
| **Capitalized building costs** | **$13,555,000** |

intended use are capitalized—here as land costs. The legal fees illustrate Rule 2—joint costs are apportioned among assets to both the land and building in this case.

The costs allocated to the building include the interest arising from the loan that Canyon negotiated to finance construction. GAAP requires capitalizing what are called **avoidable interest** payments. *Statement of Financial Accounting Standards (SFAS) No. 34* (para. 12) defines this as interest that "could have been avoided . . . if expenditures for the assets had not been made."[1] To qualify as avoidable interest, the interest doesn't have to arise from borrowing that is directly linked to a construction loan. So long as some debt was outstanding during the construction period, a portion of the interest was avoidable and qualifies for capitalization. Here's why. Building the asset required spending cash. *If the asset had not been built, that cash could have been used to retire debt, thereby lowering interest costs.* This is why the interest is *avoidable*, and this is why the capitalized interest doesn't have to arise from a dedicated construction loan. Capitalizing interest is another application of Rule 1—interest paid to lenders during the construction period is considered to be a cost necessary to prepare the asset for its intended use.

Interest can also be capitalized for borrowings that are outstanding when the assets are being constructed for others—that is, for inventory intended for sale or lease. To qualify for interest capitalization, the inventory being constructed must be an identifiable, discrete project (a three-year contract to construct two aircraft carriers for the Navy is an example).

Apportionment is also necessary when more than one asset is acquired for a lump-sum price. Assume that two tracts of land are acquired for $1,000,000. For property tax purposes, the land tracts are assessed as follows:

| | Assessment | Percentage |
|---|---|---|
| Tract 1 | $240,000 | 40% |
| Tract 2 | 360,000 | 60% |
| Total | $600,000 | 100% |

The $1,000,000 purchase price is then apportioned between the tracts in proportion to their assessed value—40% to Tract 1 and 60% to Tract 2.

Present international financial reporting standards (IFRS) allow more latitude than FASB standards for interest capitalization. Firms may expense all borrowing costs in the period incurred or they may capitalize these costs. The guidelines for allowable capitalization are similar to those in *SFAS No. 34*. After January 1, 2009, interest costs incurred during construction are required to be capitalized. See "Borrowing Costs," *IAS 23* (revised 2007) (London: International Accounting Standards Committee [IASC], 2007).

**International**

## Computing Avoidable Interest

Avoidable interest is the product of cumulative weighted average expenditures on the constructed asset times the interest rate. Let's first illustrate the computation of cumulative weighted average expenditures. The computation measures the timing of the dollar expenditures over the construction period. The earlier in the period the expenditure takes place, the more days that the expenditure needs to be financed—and the more interest is incurred. For example, assume that expenditures of $1,000,000 are incurred evenly over the 2008 year that construction took place. Here, cumulative weighted average expenditures are simply $1,000,000/2 = $500,000.

To illustrate the computation when construction expenditures do not take place evenly, assume the following timing of expenditures in Exhibit 10.4 on Canyon's construction project completed on December 31:

| Date and Amount | | | Portion of Year | | Cumulative Weighted Average Expenditures |
|---|---|---|---|---|---|
| June 1 | $10,000,000 | × | 58.630%* | = | $5,863,000 |
| August 22 | 3,555,000 | × | 36.203%† | = | 1,287,000 |
| | | | | | $7,150,000 |

* June 1 through December 31 = 214 days, and 214/365 = 58.630% of a year.

† August 22 through December 31 = 132 days, and 132/365 = 36.203% of a year (rounded).

Assuming a 10% interest rate on the outstanding debt, avoidable interest is $715,000 (10% × $7,150,000). GAAP limits the amount of interest that can be capitalized to the *lower* of

[1] "Capitalization of Interest Cost," *Statement of Financial Accounting Standards (SFAS) No. 34* (Stamford, CT: Financial Accounting Standards Board [FASB], 1979).

(1) interest actually incurred or (2) avoidable interest. If Canyon's interest actually incurred had been $800,000, the capitalized amount would be limited to avoidable interest, $715,000. If interest actually incurred was only $600,000, then just $600,000 would be capitalized.

However, **capitalization is restricted to interest arising from actual borrowings from outsiders.** To see the financial statement effect of this restriction, let's assume that Canyon had not borrowed from a bank but had instead issued more common stock and used the proceeds to finance construction. Also assume that Canyon had absolutely no interest-bearing debt outstanding. Equity funds are not "free"—stockholders expect to earn a return, and they get angry when it doesn't materialize! Despite this, GAAP does not allow Canyon to calculate an artificial interest charge on the equity financing and capitalize this "imputed interest" as a part of the cost of the building. **So, the way the construction is financed can alter the cost capitalized under GAAP when a company initially has no outstanding debt.**

Treating equity that is issued to finance construction as "free" (when there is no interest-bearing debt outstanding) is consistent with the traditional accounting model. That is, GAAP does not recognize the imputed cost associated with capital provided by stockholders. These funds are treated as if they are free. So, the cost of equity capital is ignored under GAAP in both income determination and asset costing.

Interest capitalization can complicate the analysis of firm performance over time. Because of interest capitalization, an increase in capital expenditures can temporarily decrease the amount of interest *expense* shown on the income statement and—all other factors being equal—increase income (or partially offset an income decrease). But this change in the income pattern does not result from increased sales, lower costs, or other operating efficiencies. Consequently, the year-to-year profit change is partially unrelated to operating activities and may not be sustainable. Exhibit 10.5 shows an excerpt from the 2006 annual report of Pogo Producing Company, a New York Stock Exchange company engaged in the exploration, development, and production of oil and natural gas. This disclosure will help us see how interest capitalization can alter year-to-year profit assessments.

> As discussed in Chapter 15, GAAP utilizes what is called the *proprietary view of the firm*. The proprietary view deems the firm and its owners to be indistinguishable. Consequently, funds contributed by owners do not come from "outsiders." **The firm can't charge itself interest on contributed ownership capital.**

---

## EXHIBIT 10.5    Pogo Producing Company

### Panel (a)

### Effect of Capitalized Interest on Year-to-Year Income Changes

**Capitalized Interest.** Interest costs related to financing major oil and gas projects in progress are required to be capitalized until the projects are substantially complete and ready for their intended use if projects are evaluated as successful. The increase in capitalized interest for 2006 compared to 2005, and for 2005 compared to 2004, resulted from an increase in the average amount of capital expenditures subject to interest capitalization, as well as the increase in interest charges discussed above. The average amount of capital expenditures subject to interest capitalization was $1.1 billion, $358 million, and $210 million for the years 2006, 2005, and 2004, respectively.

### Panel (b)

| ($ in millions) | Year Ended December 31 | | Year-to-Year Change |
| --- | --- | --- | --- |
| | **2006** | **2005** | |
| Income from continuing operations before taxes | $499.3 | $458.0 | +9.0% |
| Minus: Capitalized interest | 230.4 | 139.2 | +65.5% |
| Income from continuing operations before taxes and *without* interest capitalization | $268.9 | $318.8 | −15.7% |

The financial statement footnote on capitalized interest is shown in Panel (a) of Exhibit 10.5. The highlighted portion discloses a large increase in capital expenditures, which increased interest capitalization in 2006. In the highlighted portion of Panel (b), we see that capitalized interest increased from $139.2 million in 2005 to $230.4 million in 2006, a jump of 65.5%. Pre-tax reported income increased 9.0%. But without the capitalized interest, pre-tax income would have actually *decreased* by 15.7% from 2005 to 2006. By capitalizing interest, GAAP makes year-to-year income changes a function of changes in *both* operating performance and levels of capital expenditures. This complicates the analysis of earnings sustainability.

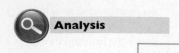

This adjustment is only an approximation of the effect of capitalized interest on 2006 income. It's an approximation because some portion of interest capitalized in previous years was amortized in 2006. So, the 2006 "income cushion" is smaller than $230.4 million by the amount of this amortization. GAAP does not require disclosure of the dollar amount of prior years' capitalized interest that has been amortized in the current year.

### Tax versus Financial Reporting Incentives

The way incurred costs are allocated between land and building affects the amount of income that will be reported in future periods. Land is a permanent or non-wasting asset, so it's not depreciated. A factory building has a finite life and *is* depreciated over future years. For *financial reporting purposes,* the manner in which costs are allocated between, say, land and building, is guided by which one (land or building) generated the cost.

For *tax purposes,* the incentives for allocating costs between land and building asset categories are completely different because the objective of most firms is to minimize tax payments, not to "correctly" allocate costs. The higher the costs allocated to land for tax purposes, the *higher* the future taxable income becomes because land cannot be depreciated. Aggressive taxpayers seek to minimize the amount of joint expenditures allocated to nondepreciable assets such as land. Similarly, taxpayers would prefer not to capitalize interest payments for tax purposes because the benefits of the deduction would be spread over the depreciable life of the asset rather than being deductible immediately. However, U.S. income tax rules generally parallel financial reporting rules and *require* cost allocations between land and buildings that are similar to U.S. GAAP rules. The same is true for interest capitalization—U.S. tax rules closely parallel GAAP rules and therefore require avoidable interest to be capitalized for tax purposes.

### Capitalization Criteria—An Extension

Businesses frequently upgrade their long-lived assets to increase their usefulness. For example, a trucking company might install new motors in its older vehicles. GAAP capitalizes such expenditures—that is, increases the carrying amount of a long-lived asset—when the expenditure causes *any* of the following conditions:

- The useful life of the asset is extended.
- The capacity of the asset is increased (that is, when attainable units of output increases).
- The efficiency of the asset is increased (that is, when fewer labor hours or raw material inputs are required).
- There is any other type of increase in the economic benefits (or future service potential) of the asset that results as a consequence of the expenditure.

When the expenditure does not meet any of these conditions, it must be treated as a period expense and be charged to income. Routine equipment maintenance is one example.

To illustrate how these capitalization criteria work, consider the example in Exhibit 10.6. In it, total expenditures that are capitalized—that is, those that are included in the carrying

**EXHIBIT 10.6**     Winger Enterprises

**Determination of Capitalized Costs**

On January 1, 2008, Winger Enterprises purchased a machine that will be used in operations. Its cash purchase price was $80,000. The freight cost to transport the machine to Winger's factory was $1,200. During the month of January 2008, Winger's employees spent considerable time calibrating the machine and making adjustments and test runs to get it ready for use. Costs incurred in doing this were:

| | |
|---|---|
| Allocated portion of production manager's salary for coordinating machine adjustments | $2,200 |
| Hourly wages of production workers engaged in test runs of the machine | 3,600 |
| Cost of raw materials that were used in test runs (the output was not salable) | 1,500 |

Given these facts, the capitalized amount of the machine on January 1, 2008 would be the total of all of the costs ($80,000 + $1,200 + $2,200 + $3,600 + $1,500 = $88,500).

amount of the machine—include *all* of the highlighted costs ($88,500) associated with getting the machine ready for production use, not just the invoice cost of $80,000.

To further illustrate the capitalization criteria, lets jump forward in time. Suppose that in January 2011, Winger spends an additional $8,000 on the machine. The total expenditure consisted of:

- $2,000 for ordinary repairs and maintenance, required every several years.
- $6,000 for the installation of a new component that allowed the machine to consume less raw material and operate more efficiently.

In this example, the $2,000 would be treated as a period expense while the $6,000 would be capitalized in 2011 and added to the carrying amount of the machine because it increases the asset's efficiency.

Executives of WorldCom, once the leading telecommunications company in the United States, were convicted of deliberately misapplying the asset capitalization rules to boost reported pre-tax income by approximately $3.8 billion over five quarters in 2001 and 2002.[2] WorldCom's method was simple. Normal operating costs of connecting to other firm's telecommunications lines—clearly period expenses—were instead capitalized. Because these items (called *line costs*) were debited to balance sheet asset accounts rather than charged to income statement expenses, income was overstated. The motive for this misrepresentation was to hide WorldCom's inherent unprofitability due to excess industry capacity. So, a failure to correctly apply the capitalization criteria resulted in an enormous income misstatement (see Figure 10.1).

---

[2] See J. Sandberg, D. Solomon, and R. Blumenstein, "Inside WorldCom's Unearthing of a Vast Accounting Scandal," *The Wall Street Journal,* June 27, 2002, and K. Eichenwald and S. Romero, "Inquiry Finds Effort at Delay at WorldCom." *The New York Times,* July 4, 2002.

## Figure 10.1

IMPACT OF WORLDCOM'S
MISAPPLICATION OF ASSET
CAPITALIZATION RULES

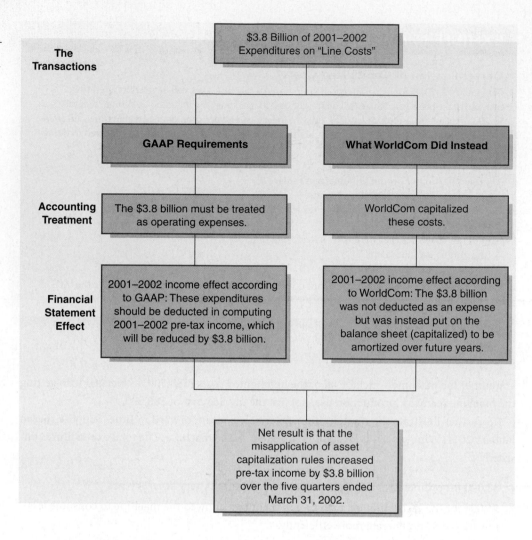

**The Transactions**

$3.8 Billion of 2001–2002 Expenditures on "Line Costs"

**GAAP Requirements**

**What WorldCom Did Instead**

**Accounting Treatment**

The $3.8 billion must be treated as operating expenses.

WorldCom capitalized these costs.

**Financial Statement Effect**

2001–2002 income effect according to GAAP: These expenditures should be deducted in computing 2001–2002 pre-tax income, which will be reduced by $3.8 billion.

2001–2002 income effect according to WorldCom: The $3.8 billion was not deducted as an expense but was instead put on the balance sheet (capitalized) to be amortized over future years.

Net result is that the misapplication of asset capitalization rules increased pre-tax income by $3.8 billion over the five quarters ended March 31, 2002.

# FINANCIAL ANALYSIS AND FIXED ASSET REPORTING

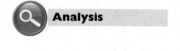

**Analysis**

Using depreciated historical cost as the measure of fixed asset values introduces many potential pitfalls for unwary statement readers. Here's a simple example.

Chen Corporation purchases long-lived assets and begins operations on January 1, 2008. The assets cost $1,000,000, have a 10-year expected life, no salvage value, and will be depreciated using the straight-line method. Assume that net operating cash flows (that is, revenues minus variable operating expenses) for 2008 are $220,000. Chen's reported pre-tax return on beginning assets for 2008 is 12%, computed as:

| | |
|---|---|
| Pre-tax net operating cash flow | $220,000 |
| Depreciation ($1,000,000/10 years) | 100,000 |
| Pre-tax profit | $120,000 |

The pre-tax return on beginning net assets is calculated as:

$$\frac{\text{Pre-tax profit}}{\text{Beginning net assets}} = \frac{\$120,000}{\$1,000,000} = 12\%$$

| EXHIBIT 10.7 | Chen Corporation |
|---|---|

**Time-Series Distortions from Aging Assets and Inflation**

| | January 1, 2008 | December 31, | | | | |
|---|---|---|---|---|---|---|
| | | **2008** | **2009** | **2010** | **2011** | **2012** |
| Asset net book value | $1,000,000 | $900,000 | $800,000 | $700,000 | $600,000 | $500,000 |
| Net operating cash flow (increasing by 3% per year) | | $220,000 | $226,600 | $233,398 | $240,400 | $247,612 |
| Depreciation | | 100,000 | 100,000 | 100,000 | 100,000 | 100,000 |
| Pre-tax profit | | $120,000 | $126,600 | $133,398 | $140,400 | $147,612 |
| Return on beginning of year net assets* | | 12% | 14.1% | 16.7% | 20.1% | 24.6% |
| Average age of assets | | 1 year | 2 years | 3 years | 4 years | 5 years |

\* 2009 calculation is $126,600/$900,000 = 14.1%. Other years' returns are computed similarly.

Let's assume that Chen makes no additional capital expenditures over the ensuing four years. Consequently, the average age of its operating assets increases over this period. Also assume that, on average, prices in the economy are increasing at 3% per year and that Chen is able to keep pace by increasing its net operating cash flow by 3%. Our example incorporates two features—aging assets and inflation—that complicate statement analysis. Exhibit 10.7 shows why.

Notice that the return on beginning assets rises from 12% to 24.6% over the five years, highlighted in Exhibit 10.7. As we are about to explain, this increase is caused by two factors:

1. An aging asset base.
2. Increasing costs and prices.

Our example is contrived, but it does help us understand how historical cost reporting for fixed assets may make trend analyses misleading. Specifically, how should the increasing return be interpreted? Is Chen's year-to-year performance really improving? Is the 2012 rate of return sustainable?

Is year-to-year performance improving? Probably not. The upward drift in reported return on assets is caused by operating cash flows that just keep pace with inflation while depreciation and the asset's original cost do not change under historical cost reporting. To know whether the rate of return increase is "real," we need each year's numbers expressed in terms of current year's prices. That is, to determine whether the return increase from 12% to 14.1% (in 2009) represents real improvement, we would need to know the replacement cost of the assets, and we would need to recompute the rate of return using replacement cost depreciation and asset value. Only then could we assess whether some portion of the year-to-year "improvement" is real—as opposed to being an artifact of the historical cost basis of accounting for fixed assets.

Is the 2012 return sustainable? No, it's not. If the rate of return for 2012 were recomputed on a replacement cost basis, it would be lower than 24.6%. Statement readers seldom have enough information to adjust for year-to-year distortions such as those in Exhibit 10.7. However, they must understand that *when asset reinvestment is not continuous, the increasing age of the asset base in conjunction with rising prices introduces distortions* such as those in Exhibit 10.7—and thus, projections must be made with caution.

Historical cost accounting for long-lived assets also creates problems for statement readers who try to make comparisons between companies such as Chen Corporation and its competitors. To see why, suppose Chen's biggest competitor is Rizzo Corporation. As of January 1, 2008, Rizzo had assets with a net book value of $1,000,000. Recall that Chen also had an asset net book value of $1,000,000 on that same date. While Chen's assets were new, let's assume that Rizzo's were, on average, slightly less than 5 years old and had a 10-year expected life. Rizzo also uses straight-line depreciation with no salvage value. Rizzo's policy is to replace 10% of its assets each year at the end of their useful lives. Also assume that the cost of replacing the assets retired each year has consistently increased by 3% annually in past years. Given these assumptions, Rizzo's asset net book value consists of:[3]

| | |
|---|---|
| Long-lived assets at original cost | $1,741,098 |
| Less: Accumulated depreciation | 741,098 |
| Net asset book value | $1,000,000 |

Assume that Rizzo's pre-tax net operating cash flow for 2008 is $294,110 and that its pre-tax return on beginning net assets is 12%, as shown here:

| | |
|---|---|
| Pre-tax net operating cash flow | $294,110 |
| Depreciation ($1,741,098/10 years) | 174,110 |
| Pre-tax profit | $120,000 |

The pre-tax return on beginning net assets is calculated as:

$$\frac{\text{Pre-tax profit}}{\text{Beginning net assets}} = \frac{\$120,000}{(\$1,741,098 - \$741,098)} = 12\%$$

Rizzo's 2008 pre-tax return on assets is 12%, the same as Chen's. Rizzo is also able to keep pace with inflation by increasing its net operating cash flow by 3% each year. We assume that its annual capital expenditures to replace 10% of its assets each year also continue to increase at 3%, just as in past years, and that the new assets are purchased on the last day of each year. These assumptions yield the performance data for 2008–2012 in Exhibit 10.8.

Here's what our Chen (Exhibit 10.7) versus Rizzo Corporation (Exhibit 10.8) comparison illustrates. Both firms start in identical financial reporting positions on January 1, 2008. Each has assets with a *net* book value of $1,000,000. The *only* difference is that Chen's assets are new

---

[3] These numbers were determined as follows. Because Rizzo replaces 10% of its assets each year, there are 10 asset layers. Furthermore, each year's layer cost 3% more than the previous layer. With these assumptions, the January 1, 2008 figures for original cost and accumulated depreciation—layer by layer—are:

| Asset Purchased on Dec. 31 | Cost | Accumulated Depreciation | Asset Purchased on Dec. 31 | Cost | Accumulated Depreciation |
|---|---|---|---|---|---|
| 1998 | $151,877 | $136,689 | 2003 | $176,067 | $ 70,427 |
| 1999 | 156,433 | 125,146 | 2004 | 181,349 | 54,405 |
| 2000 | 161,126 | 112,788 | 2005 | 186,789 | 37,358 |
| 2001 | 165,960 | 99,576 | 2006 | 192,393 | 19,239 |
| 2002 | 170,939 | 85,470 | 2007 | 198,165 | — |
| | | | | $1,741,098 | $741,098 |

Average age equals 4.5 years.

*Source:* We are grateful to Meredith Maher for formulating this example.

| EXHIBIT 10.8 | Rizzo Corporation |
| --- | --- |

**Time-Series Without Distortion from Aging Assets**

| | January 1, 2008 | Year Ended December 31, | | | | |
| --- | --- | --- | --- | --- | --- | --- |
| | | 2008 | 2009 | 2010 | 2011 | 2012 |
| Asset net book value | $1,000,000 | $1,030,000* | $1,060,900 | $1,092,727 | $1,125,508 | $1,159,274 |
| Capital expenditures (increasing by 3% per year) | | 204,110 | 210,233 | 216,540 | 223,036 | 229,727 |
| Net operating cash flow (increasing by 3% per year) | | 294,110 | 302,933 | 312,021 | 321,382 | 331,023 |
| Depreciation (see details below) | | 174,110 | 179,333 | 184,713 | 190,255 | 195,962 |
| Pre-tax profit | | $ 120,000 | $ 123,600 | $ 127,308 | $ 131,127 | $ 135,061 |
| Return on beginning of year net assets | | 12.0% | 12.0% | 12.0% | 12.0% | 12.0% |
| Average age of assets | | 4.5 years | 4.5 years | 4.5 years | 4.5 years | 4.5 years |

| Depreciation Details Explained | 2008 | 2009 | 2010 | 2011 | 2012 |
| --- | --- | --- | --- | --- | --- |
| 1. Beginning-of-year gross original cost of assets | $1,741,098 | $1,793,331 | $1,847,131 | $1,902,545 | $1,959,621 |
| 2. Gross cost of assets retired at year-end | (151,877) | (156,433) | (161,126) | (165,960) | (170,939) |
| 3. Capital expenditure on new assets (increases by 3%) | 204,110 | 210,233 | 216,540 | 223,036 | 229,727 |
| 4. Year-end gross original cost of assets | $1,793,331 | $1,847,131 | $1,902,545 | $1,959,621 | $2,018,409 |
| Depreciation for year: Item 1 × 10% | $ 174,110 | $ 179,333 | $ 184,713 | $ 190,255 | $ 195,962 |

*\* Computed as: Beginning net book value ($1,000,000) + Capital expenditure ($204,110) − Depreciation ($174,110) = $1,030,000. All other years are computed similarly. This item is increasing by 3% per year.*

while Rizzo's are 4.5 years old on average. Rizzo constantly replaces a portion of its assets and maintains an average asset age of 4.5 years as highlighted in Exhibit 10.8, while the average age of Chen's assets is increasing, as highlighted in Exhibit 10.7. Rizzo's reported return on beginning assets at the end of 2012 is 12.0%; Chen's is 24.6%. Both firms experienced identical economic conditions and were able to respond identically. The only difference is that over this period, Rizzo constantly maintained a long-lived asset age of 4.5 years while the average age of Chen's assets increased from one year to five years. An analyst who is unaware of the asset age differential might erroneously conclude that Chen is more profitable than Rizzo in 2012 (a return on assets of 24.6% versus 12.0%) and that Chen's dramatic upward trend implies a rosier future. As we have just seen, such inferences are unwarranted because the difference across firms is driven by the way that historical-cost, fixed-asset accounting rules affect firms with aging assets.

Exhibit 10.7 is intended to convey the problems analysts face in doing a trend analysis for a single firm. These problems exist because of the GAAP rules used in long-lived asset financial reporting. Exhibit 10.8 extends this critique of GAAP rules by showing how firms such as Rizzo whose assets are continually being replaced cannot easily be compared to firms with aging assets such as Chen.

Although the issues raised in Exhibits 10.7 and 10.8 are real, the problems confronting analysts in practice are not usually as extreme. To understand why, let's focus on year-to-year (time-series) analyses such as those in Exhibit 10.7. Unlike Chen, most firms replace some assets each year. Established firms with continuous capital expenditures do not experience the increasing average asset age shown in Exhibit 10.7. Instead, with regular replacement, the average age of long-lived assets remains fairly constant from year to year. For these firms, the year-to-year pattern of returns do not display an artificial upward drift such as that of Chen. That is why we introduced an example of a firm whose average asset age remained constant like Rizzo's. Of course, in those rare instances in which capital expenditures are "lumpy," statement readers must recognize the possibility that an aging asset base can lead to distorted returns on assets, such as those of Exhibit 10.7. Also, the higher the rate of input cost and output price increases, the greater is the trend distortion.

GAAP for long-lived assets does significantly impede rate-of-return comparisons across companies in certain situations. Within the same industry, differences similar to those between Chen and Rizzo would be unusual because competition often leads firms to pursue similar investment and operating strategies. Firms that don't modernize or innovate are ultimately left behind. Consequently, market forces lead to commonalities that usually make comparisons across firms *within the same industry* meaningful.

The historical cost basis used for long-lived assets does create potentially significant problems for those comparing firms in *different industries*. Operating conditions, capital expenditure policies, and the rate of input cost change can vary significantly across industries. For example, if one industry has little technological change, firms have little incentive to replace old—but still functional—assets. In stagnated industries, the average age of assets can increase, and this tendency contrasts with industries in which technological advancements have proliferated. This average age differential can lead to misleading comparisons such as those illustrated in Exhibit 10.7 (where Chen experienced an increase in asset age) as compared to Exhibit 10.8 (where Rizzo's asset age remained stable).

## RECAP

**GAAP rules for fixed asset accounting complicate financial analysis. Statement readers need to understand what factors might cause trend and across-firm distortions and adjust for them. Often, information to make the adjustment is unavailable. In these circumstances, knowing the approximate direction of any biases may help the statement reader avoid unwarranted inferences.**

## INTANGIBLE ASSETS

Intangible assets such as patents, trademarks, and copyrights convey future benefits to their owners. When one firm purchases an intangible asset from another—for example, a valuable trademark—few new accounting or reporting issues arise. The acquired intangible asset is recorded at the arm's-length transaction price and is amortized over its expected useful life, as described later in the chapter. (Another category of acquired intangible assets, called *goodwill*, arises as a consequence of certain types of corporate takeovers. This category of intangible assets is discussed in Chapter 16.)

Difficult financial reporting issues exist when the intangible asset is developed internally instead of being purchased from another company. These difficulties arise because the expenditures that ultimately create valuable intangibles such as patents or trademarks are expensed as incurred.

A patent, for example, is the result of successful research and development expenditures; a valuable trademark is the result of successful advertising, a great product, clever packaging, or brand loyalty. The recoverability of research and development (R&D) expenditures is highly uncertain at the start of a project. Consequently, the FASB requires that virtually all R&D expenditures be charged to expense immediately.[4] This mandated financial reporting uniformity is viewed as a practical way to deal with the risk of nonrecoverability of R&D expenditures. Similarly, prevailing accounting principles have long required companies to treat advertising and creative product development expenditures as period costs, again because of the highly uncertain, difficult-to-predict, future benefits.

The major types of cash outflows most likely to result in intangibles creation (R&D, advertising costs, and so forth) are immediately expensed. ***When past outflows successfully create intangible assets, these outflows have already been expensed and there are usually few remaining future outflows to capitalize!*** Consequently, the balance sheet carrying amount for intangible assets is often far below the value of the property right. For example, Polaroid Corporation's 1991 annual report indicated that "Patents and trademarks" were valued at $1. However, a footnote in that same annual report discloses that Polaroid was awarded a court judgment arising from a suit alleging that Eastman Kodak Company's instant cameras and film infringed on Polaroid patents. The judgment was ultimately settled for $924.5 million. The size of the judgment and settlement indicated that the Polaroid patents were extremely valuable. Nevertheless, the real economic value of these internally developed intangible assets did not appear on Polaroid's balance sheet because the costs incurred in developing the valuable patents were expensed as incurred. This situation is not unusual.

As software development companies proliferated in the 1980s, the FASB ultimately provided guidance in accounting for software development costs.[5] *SFAS No. 86* applies the previously described R&D rules to the particular circumstances faced by companies developing computer software products. Specifically, *prior to* establishing the **technological feasibility** of a computer software product, a company expenses *all* R&D costs incurred to develop it. After technological feasibility is established, additional costs incurred to ready the product for general release to customers are supposed to be capitalized. Capitalization of additional costs ceases when the final product is available for sale. The costs incurred before technological feasibility is established can be considerable; because feasibility may not be ensured until late in the expenditure cycle, there may be few costs left to capitalize. Accordingly, the intangible software asset may be recorded at an amount far lower than its value to the software development firm, just as in other (non-software) R&D settings.

> *SFAS No. 86* states that technological feasibility is established "when the enterprise has completed all planning, designing, coding and testing activities that are necessary to establish that the product can be produced to meet its design specifications including functions, features, and technical performance requirements" (para. 4).

The GAAP bias that leads to an understatement of internally developed intangible assets has hindered financial analysis for many years, and the problem has worsened as economic activity shifted in the 1980s from heavy manufacturing to high technology. In high-technology industries such as software development and biotechnology, research has contributed to large increases in the value of intellectual property rights such as patents and trademarks, yet accounting rules for internally developed intangibles have not kept pace.

---

[4] "Accounting for Research and Development Costs," *SFAS No. 2* (Stamford, CT: FASB, 1974). The only exception to immediate expensing is when the R&D expenditures will be reimbursed by some outside group.

[5] "Accounting for the Costs of Computer Software to Be Sold, Leased, or Otherwise Marketed," *SFAS No. 86* (Stamford, CT: FASB, 1985).

## Figure 10.2

SOFTWARE
CAPITALIZATION RATES

*Source:* Elizabeth A. Eccher, "Managerial Discretion in Financial Reporting," Working Paper, Massachusetts Institute of Technology, August 1998. Reprinted with permission.

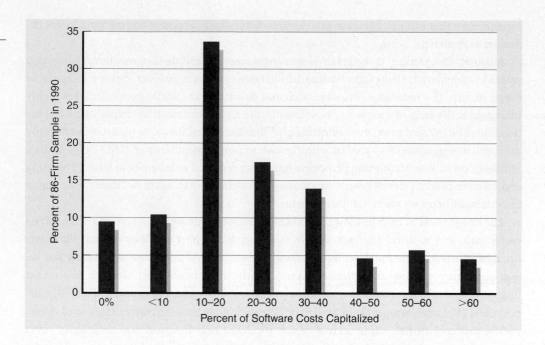

The FASB justified expensing all R&D for three reasons:

1. The future benefits accruing from these expenditures are highly uncertain.
2. A causal relationship between current R&D and future revenue has not been demonstrated.
3. Whatever benefits may arise cannot be objectively measured.[6]

But recent research indicates that these assertions are probably incorrect. One study examined the relationship between R&D expenditures and both future earnings and share values.[7] The study found that a $1 increase in R&D expenditures results in a cumulative $2 profit increase over a seven-year period. Furthermore, a $1 increase in R&D expenditures leads to a $5 increase in the market value of a firm's shares, on average. So, R&D expenditures *are* related to future benefits, and logic suggests that a causal relationship exists. Another study developed statistically reliable estimates of unrecorded R&D asset costs.[8] These estimates were then used to adjust reported earnings and book values to reflect capitalization of R&D. The adjusted numbers that reflected R&D capitalization (and subsequent amortization) were strongly associated with stock prices and returns and, thus, were value-relevant to investors. So, investors' behavior suggests that the adjusted numbers are measuring R&D benefits. Together, the results of these two studies contradict the three reasons the FASB used to justify expensing R&D.

Some (often small) portion of total software development costs is capitalized once technological feasibility is established. But the proportion of total software development costs that is capitalized is subjectively determined and varies across firms, (see Figure 10.2). More than 50% of the firms included in the Figure 10.2 sample capitalized between 0 to 20% of software development costs while about 5% capitalized more than 60%. So, one question that arises is whether a GAAP standard that conveys such latitude also provides information that is relevant to investors. One study found that it does because the capitalization-related variables

**Valuation**

---

[6] *SFAS No. 2,* paras. 39–46.

[7] T. Sougiannis, "The Accounting Based Valuation of Corporate R&D," *The Accounting Review,* January 1994, pp. 44–68.

[8] B. Lev and T. Sougiannis, "The Capitalization, Amortization, and Value-Relevance of R&D," *Journal of Accounting and Economics,* February 1996, pp. 107–38.

(annual amount capitalized, amount of the software asset, and annual amortization) were significantly associated with stock prices, returns, and future earnings.[9] But the next question is whether value relevance would *increase* if GAAP permitted even larger amounts of software development costs to be capitalized. Another study explored this.[10] The author found that capitalizing 100% of software development costs and amortizing them over three years produced accounting numbers that are more consistent with observed market prices than are *SFAS No. 86* partial capitalization numbers. So, ***relaxing the expense charge-off criteria improved value relevance.***

To summarize, research findings almost uniformly indicate that existing GAAP for both R&D and software development is too conservative. The expenditures create assets that do not appear on balance sheets, and income for current as well as future years is misstated. Fortunately, analysts can adjust for these problems using required GAAP disclosures. For example, firms are required to disclose separately total expensed R&D costs.[11] Similarly, *SFAS No. 86* requires disclosure of unamortized software assets, amortization and write-downs of the assets in each period, and all costs that are expensed prior to technological feasibility.[12] ***Analysts can use these disclosures to reconstruct what asset and amortization amounts would be if GAAP allowed full capitalization.*** (Analysts can create their own estimation procedures or use the methods in the articles cited in footnotes 8 and 10.) Unhappily, disclosures of marketing and advertising expenditures are too cryptic to permit a similar adjustment approach for trademarks or brands. So, it's harder to undo the deficiencies of GAAP for these unrecorded intangible assets.

 **Valuation**

### Intangibles and Mergers

The merger boom of the late 1990s increased the understatement of R&D assets. Here's why. When one firm acquires another and uses the **purchase method** to account for the acquisition (discussed in Chapter 16), the total purchase price must be apportioned to the individual assets acquired. The firms that were taken over often had ongoing R&D projects. Managers of the acquiring firm have strong incentives to allocate a large portion of the acquisition cost to this **purchased in-process R&D.** Why? Well, GAAP requires R&D to be written off as incurred. Allocating a large portion of the purchase price to in-process R&D provides a justification for immediately charging the *acquired* R&D to expense. Some managers of acquiring companies believe that large income statement charges arising from acquisitions are treated as transitory (or even valuation irrelevant) events by analysts. So, their impact on firm valuation is presumed to be minimal. They feel that aggressively allocating much of the purchase price to in-process R&D reduces both consolidated assets and acquisition period income without reducing firm value. But the write-off will *increase* future periods' income because there are fewer dollars of asset cost to amortize later. So, managers get to write off a (potentially large) portion of the acquisition price to the acquisition period income statement—presumably without penalty—and, by reducing assets, also reduce future periods' amortization expenses. From the managers' perspective, it's a win-win situation!

The FASB has recently changed the accounting for purchased in-process R&D.[13] Under the new rules, the acquiring company must recognize the acquiree's intangible assets that are

---

[9] D. Aboody and B. Lev, "The Value Relevance of Intangibles: The Case of Software Capitalization," *Journal of Accounting Research,* Supplement 1998, pp. 161–91.

[10] K. Den Adel, "The Value-Relevance of Alternative Accounting Treatments of Software Development Costs," Unpublished Manuscript, Purdue University, May 2000.

[11] *SFAS No. 2,* para. 13.

[12] *SFAS No. 86,* paras. 11–12.

[13] "Business Combinations," *SFAS No. 141* (revised 2007) (Norwalk, CT: FASB, 2007).

identifiable (that is, arise from contractual-legal rights or are separable), including research and development assets acquired in a business combination at acquisition-date fair values, and record them as intangible assets on the consolidated balance sheet.[14]

With the issuance of *SFAS No. 141* (revised 2007), it seems likely that aggressive write-offs of purchased in-process R&D will be much less frequent, thereby reducing the understatement of intangibles in future years.

## Intangibles Accounting under U.S. GAAP and IFRS: Similarities and Differences

The financial reporting rules for research and development costs under International Financial Reporting Standards (IFRS) are generally similar to those under U.S. GAAP. Under both U.S. GAAP and IFRS rules, marketing and advertising expenditures are treated as period costs. As a result, IFRS balance sheet numbers for patents, trademarks, and similar intangibles are subject to the same type of understatement as those in the United States.

However, the application of the historical cost accounting principle under IFRS differs from that under U.S. GAAP. IFRS accounting rules allow companies to write intangible assets up to new higher carrying values when market value exceeds cost—making adherence to the cost principle more flexible under IFRS rules. The understatement of intangibles on firms' books prompted a few British companies to abandon the historical cost treatment of trademarks (called *brands* in British English) and to write these intangible assets up to their estimated **fair value.** One author summarizes the treatment of brands in the United Kingdom (U.K.) as follows:

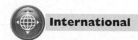

The FASB defines fair value as "the price that would be received to sell an asset or paid to transfer a liability in an orderly transaction between market participants at the measurement date."* The fair value measurement is to consider attributes specific to the asset or liability including the condition and/or location of the asset or liability and restrictions, if any, on the sale or use of the asset on the measurement date.†

* "Fair Value Measurement," *SFAS No. 157* (Norwalk, CT: FASB, 2006), para. 5.
† Ibid., para. 6.

A case can be made that the brand value should be placed on the balance sheet or at least reported to shareholders as part of a firm's financial report. In fact, several British firms have added brand equity to the balance sheet. For example, in 1988 Ranks Hovis McDougall decided to put a balance sheet value of $1.2 billion on its 60 brands. First, such an intangible asset can easily exceed in value that of tangible assets which are scrupulously reported and affect shareholders' valuation of firms. Second, reported brand equity can focus attention upon intangible assets and thus make it easier to justify brand building activities that are likely to pay off in the long term. Without such information, shareholders must rely upon short-term financials.

The major difficulty involves a question of whether any valuation of brand equity can be both objective and verifiable. Unless brand valuation can be defended, it will not be helpful and can result in legal liability. It is no coincidence that in England, where brand value has been placed upon the balance sheet, there is a less litigious environment.[15]

While only a few U.K. firms have actually written brands up to fair value, the fact that some have chosen to do so indicates the perceived limitations of existing accounting for intangibles. However, the latitude for recognizing internally developed intangibles under IFRS rules is restricted.

Revaluation of internally developed intangibles is allowed but only when the amount of the revaluation can be "determined by reference to an active market."[16] Specifically identifiable intangible assets acquired in an acquisition can be capitalized, as is true also under U.S. GAAP. But it should be emphasized that U.S. GAAP has no provision for revaluing intangibles upward even when an active market for these intangibles exists. This increases the potential divergence

---

[14] Ibid., paras. 20 and A59.

[15] D. A. Aaker, *Managing Brand Equity* (New York: Free Press, 1991), p. 28.

[16] "Intangible Assets," *IAS No. 38* (London: International Accounting Standards Board [IASB], 2004). para. 75.

between book amounts and economic values for internally developed intangibles on U.S. firms' financial statements.

**RECAP**

**Balance sheet carrying amounts for internally developed intangible assets such as patents or trademarks are not dependable indicators of their value to the firm. Because the assets are understated, so too is income statement amortization in later years.**

## ASSET IMPAIRMENT

Here we review guidelines for determining when and how assets that have already been capitalized should be treated once their value subsequently becomes impaired.

The notion of **asset impairment** is straightforward. A firm acquires an asset because the future benefits that asset is expected to generate exceed its cost. Subsequently, if the asset's remaining expected future benefits fall below its net book value, that asset is considered to have become impaired.

> Assets are often used in combination with other assets, not just singly. When applying the impairment guidelines to groups of assets, the group should consist of the "lowest [asset] level for which identifiable cash flows are largely independent of the cash flow of other groups of assets . . ." (para. 4).

Measuring impairment encompasses two stages. First, some threshold loss level must be established to determine *when* a write-down must be made. Second, once the threshold is triggered, the *amount* of the write-down must be determined and recorded.

The standards for determining when assets are impaired and the guidelines for reporting impairment amounts are contained in *SFAS No. 144* and summarized in Figure 10.3 on the following page.[17]

We now explain the impairment guidelines step-by-step using the lettered stages in Figure 10.3.

**Stage A.** *SFAS No. 144* states that an impairment review should be made whenever external events raise the possibility that an asset's carrying amount (book value) may not be recoverable. Examples of such external events include a significant decrease in the asset's market value, deterioration in the business climate, or forecasted future losses from using the asset.

**Stage B.** *This stage defines the threshold loss level that triggers the write-down.*

**Stage C.** The threshold is triggered whenever the expected future *net* cash inflow—undiscounted total future inflows minus future outflows—is *lower* than the current carrying amount of the asset.

**Stage D.** When an impairment loss is recognized, the long-lived asset is written down. The income statement charge is included "above the line"—that is, as a component of income from continuing operations before income taxes.

**Stage E.** *This stage defines the amount of the write-down that must be recognized.* The write-down loss is measured as the difference between the fair value of the asset and the current carrying amount of the asset.

The FASB defines the fair value of an asset as "the amount at which that asset . . . could be bought . . . or sold . . . in a current transaction between willing parties. . . ."[18] When market prices are not available, fair value must be estimated using techniques such as discounted present values, the price of similar assets, and other information.[19]

---

[17] "Accounting for the Impairment or Disposal of Long-Lived Assets," *SFAS No. 144* (Norwalk, CT: FASB, 2001).

[18] Ibid., para. 22.

[19] Ibid.

**Figure 10.3**

LONG-LIVED ASSET
IMPAIRMENT GUIDELINES

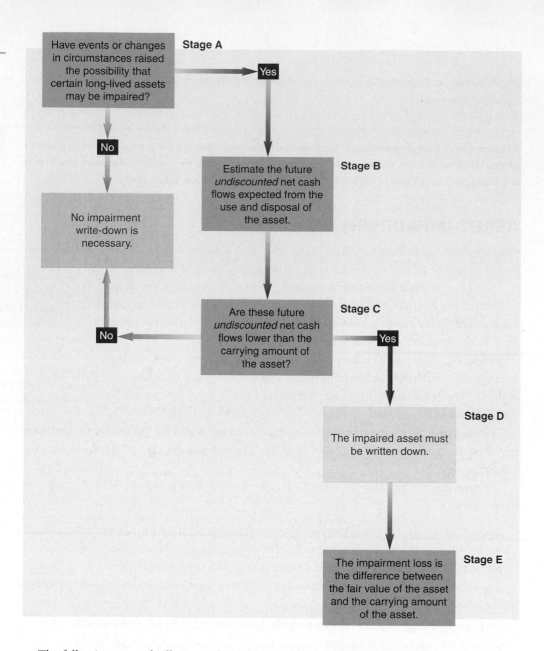

The following example illustrates how the impairment rules are applied.

Solomon Corporation manufactures a variety of consumer electronics products. The growing popularity of DVD players is expected to reduce the demand for Solomon's videocassettes. The videocassettes are produced on an assembly line consisting of five special purpose assets with a carrying amount (net book value) of $2,000,000. Solomon's management believes that this change in the business climate threatens the recoverability of these assets' carrying amount; accordingly, their answer to the question in **Stage A** of Figure 10.3 is yes. Consequently, to apply **Stage B,** they prepare the following estimate of future undiscounted cash flows over the expected three-year remaining life of the videocassette assembly line:

| | |
|---|---:|
| Net operating cash flows | |
| 2008 | $ 800,000 |
| 2009 | 400,000 |
| 2010 | 200,000 |
| Expected salvage value | 100,000 |
| Total undiscounted cash flows | $1,500,000 |

*(continued)*

*(continued from previous page)*

A comparison of the $2,000,000 carrying amount to the $1,500,000 undiscounted flows (**Stage C**) indicates that the asset must be written down (**Stage D**). By reference to used asset price lists, Solomon determines that the entire assembly line can be sold for $750,000. So, the amount of the impairment loss (**Stage E**) is $1,250,000 (that is, $2,000,000 − $750,000).

The threshold for determining whether an impairment exists (**Stage B** in Figure 10.3) is the *undiscounted* future net cash flows the asset is expected to generate. When these undiscounted net cash flows are smaller than the asset's carrying amount, the FASB rule says the asset is impaired. By *not* discounting the future net cash flows, the threshold is higher than it would be if the flows were discounted. Obviously, the higher the threshold, the smaller is the likelihood that the impairment threshold will be triggered. So, the high threshold lessens the probability of recognizing an impairment when none exists.

Impairment write-downs present managers another set of potential earnings management opportunities. For example, in a very good earnings year, managers might be tempted to take an impairment write-down and then write the asset back up (through earnings) in some subsequent year when earnings are down. *SFAS No. 144* eliminates this opportunity for earnings management across years. The FASB prohibits firms from "restoration of a previously recognized impairment loss."[20] Once an asset is written down, it cannot later be written back up to the original higher carrying amount. However, IFRS rules permit reversals of previously recognized impairment losses when there has been a change in the estimates that were previously used to measure the loss.[21] The amount of the reversal increases income.[22] The IASB's greater flexibility in permitting impairment reversals represents a specific illustration of a recurring difference between IAS and U.S. GAAP: IAS typically provide more latitude than do U.S. standards. Some observers view the extra latitude favorably because it provides an opportunity for managers to convey private information about the firm's expected future performance to the investment community. Others object to the extra latitude because it also provides managers opportunities to manage earnings and potentially mislead analysts.

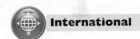

There is also research evidence regarding the timing of impairment write-offs, evidence that predates *SFAS No. 144*.[23] This research was conducted when *SFAS No. 121* constituted U.S. GAAP for impairment write-offs.[24] The impairment guidelines under *SFAS No. 121* are similar to the *SFAS No. 144* guidelines. The study found that impairment write-offs occurring after the issuance of *SFAS No. 121* have a weaker association with economic factors that presumably drive impairments than was the case prior to *SFAS No. 121*. In other words, the relationship between write-offs and the firm's underlying economic condition was smaller. The author concluded that

> the results further indicate that managers are applying greater flexibility in the reporting decisions relating to write-offs after adoption of the standard, contrary to the intentions of the FASB. . . . Overall, the evidence suggests that the reporting of write-offs under SFAS No. 121 has decreased in quality relative to before the standard.[25]

---

[20] Ibid., para. 15.

[21] "Impairment of Assets," *IAS 36* (London: IASB, 2004), paras. 109–123. But the new carrying amount of the asset cannot exceed the carrying amount (net of depreciation) had no impairment loss been recognized in prior years. (para. 117)

[22] This assumes that the originally impaired asset was carried at historical cost. But as you will see later in the chapter, IFRS rules allow firms to revalue assets to an amount *above* their historical cost. When the impairment reversal applies to an asset that was originally revalued and subsequently deemed to be impaired, the reversal "gain" is credited directly to owners' equity. (Ibid., para. 119.)

[23] E. J. Riedl, "An Examination of Long-Lived Asset Impairments," *The Accounting Review*, July 2004, pp. 823–52.

[24] "Accounting for the Impairment of Long-Lived Assets and for Long-Lived Assets to Be Disposed of," *SFAS No. 121* (Norwalk, CT: FASB, 1995).

[25] Riedl, op. cit., p. 849.

Because *SFAS No. 121* is so similar to *SFAS No. 144,* it seems reasonable to tentatively extend these findings to existing GAAP impairment guidelines. This suggests that auditors and other financial statement analysts should be alert to the potential use of write-offs opportunistically by managers. The author cites "big bath" bunching of impairment write-off as an example.

Sometimes the liability arises *after* the asset is placed into service. For example, suppose a new law is passed requiring removal of gasoline storage tanks at the end of their useful lives. For firms utilizing these tanks, the liability arises when the law is passed, not when the tank was first placed into service. Also, liabilities may arise over time as the asset is used. If a coal strip mine must be reclaimed, the liability arises proportionately as mining occurs.

This is the risk-free rate of interest on U.S. Treasury instruments plus an adjustment for the credit standing of the firm. So, if the risk-free rate is 5% and the firm's credit standing allows it to borrow at 3% over the risk-free rate, the credit adjusted risk-free rate is 8%.

The present value factor for a payment five years away at 8% is 0.68058. So rounded to the nearest thousand, the present value is $12 million $\times$ 0.68058 = $8,167,000.

## Obligations Arising from Retiring Long-Lived Assets

When an electric utility builds a nuclear plant or an oil company constructs an offshore drilling rig, regulatory authorities require public welfare and safety expenditures at the end of the asset's life. Nuclear plants must be decontaminated and drilling rigs must be disassembled. This costs money. And by law, these expenditures must take place. *So, when certain assets types are built, a liability simultaneously arises.* Until recently, GAAP often ignored these required outflows at the end of an asset's life, so no liability appeared on firms' books. But this changed when the FASB issued *SFAS No. 143*. This pronouncement requires firms to record a liability when certain assets are placed into service.[26]

Here's how the rules work. Firms are required to estimate the expected present value of the outflows that will occur when assets are eventually retired. These outflows are discounted using what the FASB terms a **credit-adjusted risk-free rate.** The liability's discounted present value is recorded along with an increase in the carrying amount of the related long-lived asset. Consider the following example.

Kalai Oil Corporation constructs on oil drilling rig off the Texas coast, which is placed into service on January 1, 2008. The rig cost $300 million to build. Texas law requires that the rig be removed at the end of its estimated useful life of five years. Kalai estimates that the cost of dismantling the rig will be $12 million and its credit-adjusted risk-free rate is 8%. The liability's discounted present value is $8,167,000. Assume that Kalai has already capitalized the $300 million cost of the rig in the account Drilling rig.

When the asset is placed into service, Kalai records the asset retirement obligation (ARO) as:

| | | | |
|---|---|---|---|
| **DR** | Drilling rig (asset retirement cost)......................... | $8,167,000 | |
| **CR** | ARO liability...................................... | | $8,167,000 |

The $8,167,000 debit to the asset account is allocated to expense using some systematic method. Assuming straight-line depreciation over the expected useful life of five years, the entry is:

| | | | |
|---|---|---|---|
| **DR** | Depreciation expense.................................... | $1,633,400* | |
| **CR** | Accumulated depreciation—drilling rig.................... | | $1,633,400 |

* $8,167,000/5 yrs. = $1,633,400.

---

[26] "Accounting for Asset Retirement Obligations," *SFAS No.143* (Norwalk, CT: FASB, 2001).

The liability is initially recorded at its present value but increases over time as retirement nears. The liability's present value will increase by 8% per year, as the following schedule shows.

| | (a) Present Value of the Liability at Start of Year | (b) Accretion Expense [8% × Column (a) Amount] | (c) Present Value of the Liability at Year-End [Column (a) + Column (b)] |
|---|---|---|---|
| 2008 | $ 8,167,000 | $653,360 | $ 8,820,360 |
| 2009 | 8,820,360 | 705,629 | 9,525,989 |
| 2010 | 9,525,989 | 762,079 | 10,288,068 |
| 2011 | 10,288,068 | 823,045 | 11,111,113 |
| 2012 | 11,111,113 | 888,887* | 12,000,000 |

\* Rounded

The entry to record the increase in the liability in 2008 is:

| DR | Accretion expense | $653,360 | |
|---|---|---|---|
| | CR | ARO liability | $653,360 |

Accretion expense is classified above the line (as part of income from continuing operations) in the income statement as an operating expense. It reflects the current period's increase, or *accretion,* of the liability. The FASB says that account titles other than Accretion expense can be used so long as the nature of the expense is clearly conveyed.[27]

To complete the illustration, assume that an outside contractor dismantles the rig early in January 2013 at a cost of $11,750,000. The journal entry is:

| DR | ARO liability | $12,000,000 | |
|---|---|---|---|
| | CR | Cash | $11,750,000 |
| | CR | Gain on settlement of ARO liability | 250,000 |

## Assets Held for Sale

Firms constantly experience changing market conditions such as the emergence of new competing products or the development of more efficient distribution systems. In responding to these innovations, firms often seek to dispose of groups of assets that are no longer suited to the new environment they face. When firms actively try to sell some of the assets they currently own, these asset groups should be classified in the balance sheet as "held for sale" if they are expected to be sold within one year.[28] When assets are held for sale, they are reported at the lower of book value or fair value **less costs to sell.**[29] To illustrate, assume the following facts regarding Nebozenko Corporation's assets held for sale:

- Book value of assets (cost minus accumulated depreciation)  $2,500,000
- Fair value of assets  2,350,000
- Expected legal fees associated with sale  46,000

So, these assets would be shown on the balance sheet at $2,304,000, that is, at fair value minus expected legal fees ($2,350,000 − $46,000). The operating results of asset components classified

Assets that are eligible to be separately classified must comprise "operations and cash flows that can be clearly distinguished, operationally and for financial reporting purposes, from the rest of the entity" (*SFAS No. 144,* para. 41). This is the same criterion that was used in Chapter 2 to identify elements that must be reflected in the discontinued operations section of the income statement.

[27] Ibid., para. 14 and footnote 13.
[28] *SFAS No. 144,* paras. 30–33.
[29] Ibid., para. 34.

as "held for sale" are reported in the discontinued operations section of the income statement in the period(s) in which they occur even if the assets have not yet been sold as of the financial statement date.[30] Once the asset group has been sold, the assets are removed from the balance sheet and the income statement disclosure policies for discontinued operations discussed in Chapter 2 are applied. That is, the firm will separately disclose "below the line" the gain or loss (net of taxes) from utilizing these assets during the period covered as well as any gain or loss on disposal of the assets themselves.

Segregating the assets held for sale on the balance sheet and separately disclosing their operating results on the income statement are designed to help analysts better understand past firm performance and assess future prospects. For example, in evaluating the efficiency of past asset utilization using the return-on-assets ratio, assets that are destined for sale should be excluded from the rate-of-return denominator and their profit or loss contribution should be excluded from the numerator. This exclusion provides a better measure of expected *future* performance based on assets expected to remain in the firm. The *SFAS No. 144* disclosure rules provide guidance on when certain assets should be segregated on the balance sheet, which alerts analysts to items that should be omitted from rate-of-return calculations. Similarly, income forecasts are enhanced insofar as the income or loss from the asset groups that have been or are about to be sold are isolated "below the line" and are no longer factored into the analysts' forecast.

## DEPRECIATION

Productive assets such as buildings, equipment, and machinery eventually wear out. Assets including patents, which have a finite economic life, ultimately expire. Consequently, the cost of these assets must be apportioned to the periods in which they provide benefits. This is the application of the matching principle (Chapter 2) to long-lived assets. This matching process is called **depreciation.** For intangible assets, the allocation of costs to periods is referred to as **amortization.** For mineral deposits and other wasting assets, the assignment of expired costs to periods is called **depletion.** For simplicity, we refer collectively to any of these allocations of costs to periods as the **depreciation process.**

In financial reporting, the cost to be allocated to periods through the depreciation process is the asset's original historical cost minus its expected salvage value. The objective is to spread the original cost over the period of asset use; *depreciation is not intended to track the asset's declining market value.* Realistically, the asset's end-of-period book value (its original cost minus cumulative depreciation) would approximate its market value only by sheer coincidence. We stress this *absence of correspondence* between accounting measures of depreciation and value decrement because GAAP accounting depreciation, as we have said, is a process of cost allocation, *not* asset valuation.

When applied to long-lived assets, the matching process requires the reporting entity to estimate three things:

1. The expected useful life of the asset.
2. The depreciation pattern that will reflect the asset's declining service potential.
3. The expected salvage value that will exist at the time the asset is retired.

Each requires estimates of future events, especially the pace of technological change and shifts in consumer tastes and preferences. Assets whose economic benefits expire evenly over time are depreciated on a straight-line basis while those that provide more valuable services in the early years are depreciated on an accelerated basis. The example in Exhibit 10.9 illustrates the procedures.

---

[30] Ibid., para. 43.

**EXHIBIT 10.9**  **Depreciation Example**

### Facts

| | |
|---|---|
| Cost of the asset | $10,500 |
| Expected salvage value | $ 500 |
| Expected useful life | 5 years |

### Straight-Line Depreciation (SL)

$$(\text{Constant rate} \times \text{Constant base}) = \frac{\text{Cost} - \text{Salvage value}}{\text{Estimated life}}$$

$$\left(\frac{1}{5}\right) \times (\$10,500 - \$500) = \$2,000 \text{ per year for all 5 years}$$

### Double-Declining Balance Depreciation (DDB)

$$(\text{Constant rate} \times \text{Changing base}) = \begin{array}{l}\text{Double the straight-line} \\ \text{rate} \times \text{Book value at beginning} \\ \text{of each period}\end{array}$$

$$\text{Straight-line rate} = 20\% \text{ (that is, 5-year life)}$$

$$\text{Double straight-line rate} = 20\% \times 2 = 40\%$$

| Year | Beginning-of-Year Book Value | Depreciation (40% of Beginning-of-Year Book Value) | Year-End Book Value |
|---|---|---|---|
| 1 | $10,500.00 | $4,200.00 | $6,300.00 |
| 2 | 6,300.00 | 2,520.00 | 3,780.00 |
| 3 | 3,780.00 | 1,093.33* | 2,686.67 |
| 4 | 2,686.67 | 1,093.33 | 1,593.34 |
| 5 | 1,593.34 | 1,093.34 | 500.00 |

\* Year 3: Switch to straight-line method (as explained in the text).
$3,780 − $500 = $3,280; $3,280/3 = $1,093.33

### Sum-of-the-Years' Digits Depreciation (SYD)

$$\left(\begin{array}{c}\text{Changing} \\ \text{rate}\end{array} \times \begin{array}{c}\text{Constant} \\ \text{base}\end{array}\right) = \frac{\text{Years remaining in life}}{\text{Sum-of-the-years' digits}^\dagger} \times (\text{Cost} - \text{Salvage})$$

$$\text{Sum-of-the-years' digits} = 5 + 4 + 3 + 2 + 1 = 15$$

| Year | Depreciable Basis ($10,500 − $500) | Applicable Fraction | Depreciation |
|---|---|---|---|
| 1 | $10,000 | 5/15 | $ 3,333.33 |
| 2 | 10,000 | 4/15 | 2,666.67 |
| 3 | 10,000 | 3/15 | 2,000.00 |
| 4 | 10,000 | 2/15 | 1,333.33 |
| 5 | 10,000 | 1/15 | 666.67 |
| Total | | 15/15 | $10,000.00 |

$^\dagger$ The formula for determining the sum-of-the-years' digits is $n(n + 1)/2$ where $n$ equals the estimated life of the asset. In our example: $5(5 + 1)/2 = 15$. This, of course, is the answer we get by tediously summing the years' digits—that is, $5 + 4 + 3 + 2 + 1 = 15$.

The **straight-line** (SL) depreciation method simply allocates cost minus salvage value evenly over the asset's expected useful life.

The depreciation rate for the **double-declining balance** (DDB) method is double the straight-line rate (in Exhibit 10.9, 20% per year for SL, 40% per year for DDB). Applying a constant DDB depreciation percentage to a declining balance will never depreciate book value down to salvage value. To depreciate down to an asset's expected salvage value using DDB, two steps must be employed. First, in Years 1 and 2, apply the 40% rate to the book value of the assets without subtracting the salvage value. Second, once the DDB depreciation amount falls below what it would be with straight-line depreciation, a switch to the straight-line method is made. This happens in Year 3 when DDB depreciation would have been $1,512 ($3,780 × 40%), which is less than the straight-line depreciation of $2,000. Therefore, straight-line depreciation is used beginning in Year 3. The $1,093.33 SL amount is determined by taking the end of Year 2 remaining DDB book value of $3,780, subtracting the salvage value of $500, and dividing the result, $3,280, by 3.

**Sum-of-the-years' digits** (SYD) is another accelerated depreciation method. It depreciates an asset to precisely its salvage value, so a switch to SL is unnecessary.

Figure 10.4(a) shows the annual depreciation charges under the alternative depreciation methods; Figure 10.4(b) shows the resulting net book value at each year-end.

In preparing external financial reports, companies are free to select the depreciation method they believe best reflects both the pattern of an asset's use and the services it provides. Within the same industry, different companies may use different methods. Even within the same company, different types of assets may be depreciated using different methods. For example, buildings might be depreciated using the SL method while trucks might be depreciated using the SYD method. Exhibit 10.10 illustrates an annual survey of book depreciation choices used by 600 companies.

This annual AICPA survey shows that straight-line depreciation predominates for financial reporting purposes. However, accelerated depreciation is almost universally used for tax purposes. While some evidence indicates that the market adjusts for differences in depreciation methods when establishing securities prices,[31] the diversity of depreciation methods across firms complicates security analysis.

> Firms that are not currently paying taxes because of losses or operating loss carryforwards have an incentive not to use accelerated depreciation. But even here, tax rules require certain depreciation methods. Consequently, companies are constrained in efforts to abandon accelerated tax depreciation methods when losses materialize.

| EXHIBIT 10.10 | Depreciation Choices | | | |
|---|---|---|---|---|
| | **Number of Companies** | | | |
| | **2005** | **2004** | **2003** | **2002** |
| Straight-line | 592 | 586 | 580 | 579 |
| Declining balance | 14 | 16 | 22 | 22 |
| Sum-of-the-years' digits | 4 | 6 | 5 | 5 |
| Accelerated method—not specified | 30 | 32 | 41 | 44 |
| Units-of-production | 24 | 22 | 30 | 32 |
| Group/composite | 10 | 8 | 4 | — |
| Other | — | — | — | 7 |

*Source:* Reprinted with permission from Y. Iofe and M. C. Calderisi (eds.), *Accounting Trends and Techniques*, 2006, page 366. Copyright © 2006 by the American Institute of Certified Public Accountants (AICPA), Inc. The numbers for each year do not total 600 because companies use more than one depreciation method (for example, straight-line for buildings and accelerated for automobiles).

## Disposition of Long-Lived Assets

When individual long-lived assets are disposed of before their useful lives are completed, any difference between the net book value of the asset and the disposition proceeds is treated as a

[31] W. H. Beaver and R. E. Dukes, "Interperiod Tax Allocation and δ-Depreciation Methods: Some Empirical Results," *The Accounting Review*, July 1973, pp. 549–59.

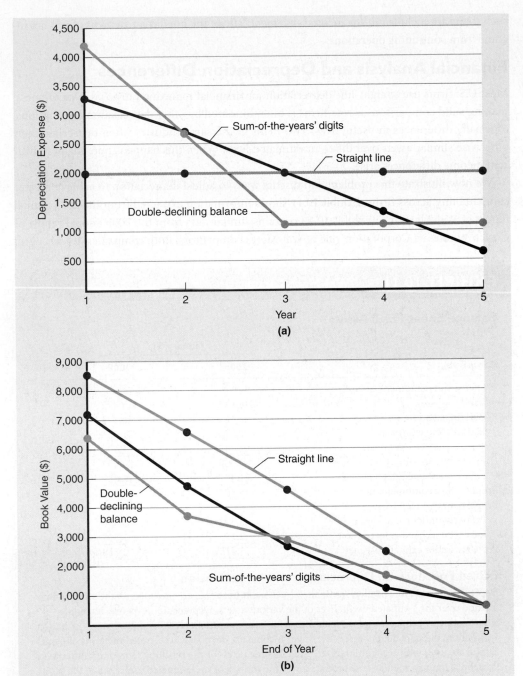

## Figure 10.4

ALTERNATIVE DEPRECIA-
TION METHODS

(a) Annual Depreciation
Charges and (b) Net Book
Value

gain or loss. Assume that the asset in the Exhibit 10.9 example is being depreciated using the DDB method and is sold at the end of Year 2 for $5,000 when its book value is $3,780. The following entry is made:

| | | | | |
|---|---|---|---|---|
| **DR** | Cash | | $5,000 | |
| **DR** | Accumulated depreciation | | 6,720 | |
| | **CR** | Long-lived asset | | $10,500 |
| | **CR** | Gain on sale of asset | | 1,220 |

Dispositions of individual assets occur frequently as firms respond to changing production and consumer-demand conditions. For this reason, gains and losses from asset sales do not satisfy the criteria for the extraordinary item treatment described in Chapter 2. Accordingly,

Gains or losses on sales of assets comprising a clearly distinguishable component of an entity, as described in the earlier section "Assets Held for Sale," are shown in the discontinued operations section.

 **Analysis**

such items are included in the income statement "above the line" as an element of pre-tax income from continuing operations.

## Financial Analysis and Depreciation Differences

Most U.S. firms use straight-line depreciation for financial reporting purposes. Nevertheless, making valid comparisons across firms is often hindered by other depreciation assumptions, especially differences in useful lives. Two firms in the same industry often depreciate their otherwise similar assets over different estimated lives. When this happens potentially significant income differences arise.

We now illustrate this problem and discuss ways to adjust depreciation to achieve greater comparability across firms. Exhibit 10.11 shows information extracted from the 2005 annual report of Wal-Mart, Inc.; Exhibit 10.12 contains similar data from the 2005 annual report of Costco Wholesale Corporation, one of Wal-Mart's competitors. Both companies depreciate all

---

### EXHIBIT 10.11     Wal-Mart Corporation

#### Balance Sheet Fixed Assets

| ($ in millions) | January 31 | |
| --- | --- | --- |
| | **2006** | **2005** |
| Property and equipment, at cost: | | |
| Land | $16,643 | $14,472 |
| Buildings and improvements | 56,163 | 46,574 |
| Fixtures and equipment | 22,750 | 21,461 |
| Transportation equipment | 1,746 | 1,530 |
| Property and equipment, at cost | 97,302 | 84,037 |
| Less accumulated depreciation | 21,427 | 18,637 |
| Property and equipment, net | 75,875 | 65,400 |
| Property under capital lease: | | |
| Property under capital lease | 5,578 | 4,556 |
| Less accumulated amortization | 2,163 | 1,838 |
| Property under capital lease, net | 3,415 | 2,718 |

#### Edited Footnote on Depreciation and Amortization

Depreciation and amortization for financial statement purposes are provided on the straight-line method over the estimated useful lives of the various assets. Depreciation expense, including amortization of property under capital leases for fiscal years 2006, 2005 and 2004 was $4.8 billion, $4.3 billion and $3.9 billion, respectively. For income tax purposes, accelerated methods of depreciation are used with recognition of deferred income taxes for the resulting temporary differences. Leasehold improvements are depreciated over the shorter of the estimated useful life of the asset or the remaining lease term. Estimated useful lives for financial statement purposes are as follows:

| | |
| --- | --- |
| Buildings and improvements | 5–50 years |
| Fixtures and equipment | 3–12 years |
| Transportation equipment | 3–15 years |

#### Selected Income Statement Information

| ($ in millions) | Year Ended January 31 | |
| --- | --- | --- |
| | **2006** | **2005** |
| Depreciation (rounded) | $ 4,800 | $ 4,300 |
| Income before income taxes and minority interest | $17,358 | $16,105 |

*Source:* Wal-Mart Corporation 2005 annual report.

---

Notice that Wal-Mart rounded its depreciation expense disclosure to the nearest $100 million. As a result, all of our computations in Exhibit 10.13 and the text adjustments that follow it must unavoidably also be rounded to the nearest $100 million. This rounding reduces the precision of the resulting adjustments.

**EXHIBIT 10.12**  **Costco Wholesale Corporation**

### Balance Sheet Fixed Assets

| ($ in thousands) | August 28 2005 | August 29 2004 |
|---|---|---|
| Property and Equipment | | |
| Land | $ 2,502,247 | $ 2,269,543 |
| Buildings, leaseholds and land improvements | 5,622,439 | 5,164,658 |
| Equipment and fixtures | 2,181,740 | 1,974,995 |
| Construction in progress | 180,604 | 132,180 |
| | 10,487,030 | 9,541,376 |
| Less accumulated depreciation and amortization | (2,696,838) | (2,321,547) |
| Net property and equipment | 7,790,192 | 7,219,829 |

### Edited Footnote on Property and Equipment Accounting Policy

Property and equipment are stated at cost. Depreciation and amortization expenses are computed using the straight-line method for financial reporting purposes. Buildings are generally depreciated over twenty-five to thirty-five years; equipment and fixtures are depreciated over three to ten years; leasehold improvements are amortized over the initial term of the lease or the useful lives of the assets if shorter. The Company capitalizes certain costs related to the acquisition and development of software and amortizes those costs using the straight-line method over their estimated useful lives, which range from three to five years.

### Selected Income Statement Information

| ($ in thousands) | Years Ended | |
|---|---|---|
| | Aug. 28, 2005 | Aug. 29, 2004 |
| Depreciation and amortization | $477,868 | $440,721 |
| Income before income taxes | $1,548,962 | $1,400,624 |

*Source:* Costco Wholesale Corporation 2005 annual report.

of their long-lived assets using the straight-line method. However, Wal-Mart depreciates buildings and improvements over useful lives of 5 to 50 years; for Costco useful lives range from 25 to 35 years. A difference in useful life assumptions also exists for equipment and fixtures; Wal-Mart's estimated lives range from 3 to 12 years while Costco's are from 3 to 10 years. (See highlighted sections in Exhibits 10.11 and 10.12.)

Clear differences exist but the level of disclosure is too cryptic to allow analysts to compute precise adjustments. Despite this drawback, by making reasonable assumptions, we can estimate the effect on income arising from the differences in asset lives for Wal-Mart and Costco. Let's see how.

Because both companies use straight-line depreciation, the ratio of average gross property, plant, and equipment divided by depreciation expense gives us a rough approximation of the estimated useful (depreciable) life of the average asset. Here's why. Straight-line depreciation expense (SL) is computed as:

$$SL = \frac{\text{Gross property, plant, and equipment (minus salvage value)}}{\text{Average useful life}} \qquad (10.1)$$

Rearranging terms:

$$SL \times (\text{Average useful life}) = \text{Gross property, plant, and equipment (minus salvage value)} \qquad (10.2)$$

**EXHIBIT 10.13**    Computing Approximate Average Useful Lives

| ($ in billions) | Wal-Mart | Costco |
|---|---|---|
| Average gross property, plant and equipment* | ($86.3 + $74.2)/2 | ($7.8 + $7.2)/2 |
| Depreciation expense | $4.8 | $0.5 |
| | $\dfrac{\$80.2}{\$4.8} = 16.7$ years | $\dfrac{\$7.5}{\$0.5} = 15.0$ years |

* Excludes land and construction in progress. For example, January 31, 2006 numbers were computed as follows using Exhibit 10.11 data for Wal-Mart (rounded to the nearest $100 million): $56.2 + $22.8 + $1.7 + $5.6 = $86.3. For Costco at August 28, 2005, the computation is: $5.6 + $2.2 = $7.8.

Further rearranging yields:

$$\text{Average useful life} = \frac{\text{Gross property, plant, and equipment (minus salvage value)}}{\text{SL}} \quad (10.3)$$

The ratio in equation (10.3) is only a rough approximation for many reasons. One is that we cannot estimate the salvage values assumed by Wal-Mart and Costco. Other factors that make the computation approximate are discussed later. The computation of average useful lives using the equation (10.3) approximation is shown in Exhibit 10.13. Each company's end-of-year and start-of-year gross property are summed in Exhibit 10.13 and then divided by 2 to estimate its average gross property for 2005. Applying the equation (10.3) approach suggests that, *on average,* Wal-Mart is using longer estimated lives (16.7 years) than Costco (15.0 years).[32]

To improve comparisons of profitability between Wal-Mart and Costco, the analyst would like to undo these differences in depreciation lives. One way to undo them is to divide Wal-Mart's average gross property number by Costco's estimated depreciable life—that is,

$$\frac{\$80.2}{15.0 \text{ years}} = \$5.3$$

The quotient, $5.3 billion, is the approximate annual Wal-Mart depreciation expense number that would result from using Costco's longer estimated useful life assumption. If these rough approximations are correct, Wal-Mart's fiscal year 2006 depreciation would rise by $500 million—that is, the $5.3 billion just computed minus the $4.8 billion reported in Exhibit 10.11—and earnings before taxes and minority interest would rise by the same

---

[32] To understand why the Exhibit 10.13 answer is in years (that is, 16.7 years and 15.0 years), let's express average gross property divided by depreciation expense in terms of the underlying measurement dimensions:

$$\frac{\text{Average gross property, plant, and equipment}}{\text{Depreciation expense}} \quad \begin{array}{l} \leftarrow \text{The underlying measurement dimension is } \$s \\ \leftarrow \text{The underlying measurement dimension is } \$s \text{ per year} \end{array}$$

Expressing the computation in underlying measurement dimensions, the division in Exhibit 10.13 becomes:

$$\frac{\$s}{\$s/\text{Year}}$$

Following algebraic rules for division by fractions, we invert the denominator and multiply it by the numerator:

$$\$s \times \frac{\text{Year}}{\$s}$$

The $s cancel, and the answer is expressed dimensionally in years (for example, 16.7 years and 15.0 years).

amount. This represents a pre-tax earnings decrease of approximately 2.9%. However, Costco combines depreciation and amortization and does not give a separate disclosure for only depreciation as Wal-Mart does. Because Costco capitalizes and amortizes software development costs (see Exhibit 10.12), this could distort the computation of average depreciation lives from Exhibit 10.13.[33]

This adjustment process is crude and relies on assumptions. The adjustment assumes that the useful life differences are artificial and do not reflect real differences in expected asset longevity. It also assumes that the salvage value proportions are roughly equivalent for both firms and that the dollar breakdown within asset categories is similar for both Wal-Mart and Costco—that is, the computation assumes that Wal-Mart and Costco both have roughly the same proportionate dollar amount of transportation equipment, store fixtures, and so on. If these assumptions are incorrect, the average age computation for one firm cannot legitimately be applied to the other's asset base to estimate "adjusted" depreciation. However, if these assumptions hold, the adjusted numbers should make a comparison between Wal-Mart and Costco more accurate.

> It is possible that the useful life differences reflect real economic differences rather than accounting choices. For example, Wal-Mart's gross property, plant, and equipment might be more durable and, on average, have longer useful lives. If the useful lives differences are "real," then analysts' attempts to "undo" the differences may impede, rather than improve, profit comparisons.

In Chapter 13, we illustrate another adjustment approach for depreciation differences that uses data from the deferred income tax footnote.

> Also, the two companies' fiscal years-end do not coincide. The effect of this slight deviation is probably very small.

## INTERNATIONAL PERSPECTIVE

IFRS rules are generally similar to U.S. GAAP. However, very significant differences between the two exist in accounting for long-lived assets. Throughout the chapter, we have seen that U.S. GAAP requires historical cost measurement—a specific, narrow application of the economic sacrifice approach introduced on p. 546. In contrast, *IAS 16*[34] permits two different methods for long-lived assets accounting:

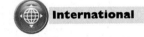
**International**

- **Cost method:** The asset is carried at cost less accumulated depreciation (and any impairment charge that has been recognized)[35] as under U.S. GAAP.

- **Revaluation method:** The asset is carried at a revalued amount reflecting its fair value at the revaluation date. Subsequent depreciation should be based on the fair value, not original cost.[36] The difference between depreciation based on the revalued carrying amount of the asset and depreciation based on the asset's original cost is transferred from the Revaluation surplus to Retained earnings as the asset is depreciated.[37]

So, under IFRS, companies are permitted to periodically revalue land and buildings and thereby abandon historical cost accounting for long-lived assets. When this is done, the accumulated depreciation account is removed and the revalued amount becomes the new book value. The amount of the write-up is credited to an owners' equity account called **Revaluation surplus.** Write-downs are debited to this surplus account.

---

[33] The distortion arises because the amount of undisclosed capitalized software costs is omitted from the numerator but the amortization is included in the denominator. These omissions do not offset. Instead, they downwardly bias (understate) the average depreciation life computed for Costco in Exhibit 10.13.

[34] "Property, Plant and Equipment," *IAS 16* (London: IASB, revised 2003), paras. 30–31.

[35] Ibid., para. 30.

[36] Ibid., para. 31.

[37] Ibid., para. 41.

Assume that a building that originally cost €20,000,000 and has an accumulated depreciation balance of €10,000,000 is appraised at €35,000,000 and accordingly written up, as permitted by *IAS 16*. The accounting entry is:

| | | | |
|---|---|---|---|
| **DR** | Building............................................... | €15,000,000 | |
| **DR** | Accumulated depreciation ............................ | 10,000,000 | |
| | **CR** Revaluation surplus ............................ | | €25,000,000 |

The new net book value becomes €35,000,000 after this entry is made, as follows:

| | Net Book Value prior to Revaluation | Revaluation | | Net Book Value after Revaluation |
|---|---|---|---|---|
| Building | €20,000,000 | **DR** | €15,000,000 | €35,000,000 |
| Less: Accumulated depreciation | (10,000,000) | **DR** | €10,000,000 | — |
| Net book value | €10,000,000 | | | €35,000,000 |

The Revaluation surplus account that is credited in the previous entry is an owners' equity account. Under IAS, this amount would be disclosed as a separate line item in the owners' equity section of the balance sheet.

Depreciation in subsequent periods is based on the revaluation net book value (€35,000,000). If the building has an expected remaining useful life of 20 years at the time of the revaluation, annual depreciation on the income statement will be €1,750,000 (that is, €35,000,000/20).

While revaluations are not mandatory, if a company does voluntarily revalue assets, all assets of a similar class (nature or function) must be revalued.[38] Furthermore, once assets are revalued, regular reassessments are required to keep the valuations up to date.[39] However, firms are not *required* to revalue fixed assets. This complicates comparisons across companies using IFRS because some firms' fixed assets are carried at historical costs incurred years earlier while others carry these assets at more recent revalued amounts.

This example illustrates that despite the general similarities between U.S. GAAP and IFRS reporting rules, important differences do exist. Writing up fixed assets to reflect reappraisal increases is forbidden in the United States. Differences of this type make financial analyses of foreign companies—even companies in "similar" reporting environments—a perilous activity.

---

The amount in the owners' equity Revaluation surplus account would be transferred year-by-year to Retained earnings as the revalued asset is depreciated. For example, if we assume that the asset is not subsequently revalued over the ensuing 20 years, €1,250,000 (that is, €25,000,000/20) would be reclassified each year. The entry is:

| | | | |
|---|---|---|---|
| **DR** | Revaluation surplus ........... | €1,250,000 | |
| | **CR** Retained earnings ....... | | €1,250,000 |

This reclassification entry is made to reduce the Revaluation surplus as the asset ages. If no entry were made, there would still be a Revaluation surplus amount on the books even after the asset is removed from service. The year-by-year transfer ultimately reduces the surplus to zero.

## Investment Property

Another area in which U.S. GAAP and IFRS rules for long-lived assets potentially diverge is accounting for **investment property**.[40] Long-lived investment property consists of assets such as land, buildings, and equipment that are held to earn rentals, for capital appreciation, or for both. To understand how these differ from other long-lived assets under IFRS, investment properties are assets that are *not* used to produce or supply goods or services, nor are they held for sale in

 **International**

---

[38] Para. 36.

[39] Para. 31.

[40] "Investment Property," *IAS 40* (London: IASB, 2003).

the ordinary course of business (as inventories are). They are distinct from the company's operating assets.[41]

When investment properties are initially acquired, they are measured at cost. Subsequently, however, firms have the choice under *IAS 40* to carry investment properties at either amortized historical cost or fair value. The method selected must be applied to all investment properties. So, a firm would not be allowed to use the fair value method for investment land while simultaneously measuring buildings held for investment at cost.

If the fair value method is chosen, any gain or loss arising from a change in fair value is recognized in income in the period of the change.[42] Notice that this differs from the treatment accorded revaluations of operating assets under *IAS 16*, as discussed earlier. Revaluations of operating long-lived assets are debited or credited to Revaluation surplus (a balance sheet owners' equity account), and not run through income. The reason for the different treatment is straightforward. Firms hold investment properties for the express purpose of generating market-driven gains or losses. So, it is appropriate that these gains or losses be recognized in income as they occur. In contrast, operating assets are held to generate future returns, not for short-term liquidation. Accordingly, revaluation increases or decreases go directly to the Revaluation surplus account.

## EXCHANGES OF NONMONETARY ASSETS

Occasionally firms will exchange one nonmonetary asset such as inventory or equipment for another nonmonetary asset. Unless certain exceptions in the following discussion apply, the recorded cost of a nonmonetary asset acquired in exchange for some other nonmonetary asset is the fair value of the asset that was given up. Any resulting gain or loss on the transaction is recognized.[43] To illustrate how the cost of a nonmonetary asset acquired in an exchange is determined, consider the following example.

Rohan Department Store exchanges a delivery truck with a fair value of $70,000 for 10 checkout scanners from Electronic Giant Warehouse, Inc. The truck's book value is $60,000—original cost of $80,000 minus accumulated depreciation of $20,000. In addition to the truck, Rohan pays Electronic Giant $15,000.

The cost of the acquired assets (scanners) is the fair value of the assets (truck and cash) that were exchanged to obtain it. So, in this example, the cost of the scanners is:

| | |
|---|---|
| Fair value of the truck | $70,000 |
| Cash payment | 15,000 |
| Cost of acquired assets | $85,000 |

Rohan's entry is

| | | | |
|---|---|---|---|
| **DR** | Store equipment | $85,000 | |
| **DR** | Accumulated depreciation—delivery truck | 20,000 | |
| | **CR** Delivery truck | | $80,000 |
| | **CR** Cash | | 15,000 |
| | **CR** Gain on exchange | | 10,000 |

> When the fair value of the asset *received* is more clearly evident than the fair value of the asset *given up,* the fair value of the asset received is used as the new cost base. See *APB Opinion No. 29,* para. 18.

---

[41] For example, *IAS 40* treats assets held under capital leases by lessees and used exclusively for rental to others under operating leases as investment properties.

[42] Ibid., para. 35.

[43] Accounting for Nonmonetary Transaction," *Accounting Principles Board (APB) Opinion No. 29* (New York: AICPA, 1973).

Notice that the amount in the Gain on exchange account is simply the difference between the truck's fair value ($70,000) and its book value ($60,000).

For many years, asset exchanges occurred infrequently, so the rule we just illustrated was seldom an important part of firms' financial statements. But that all changed during the boom years of the 1990s and beyond. Asset exchanges—or swaps—proliferated. One article stated:

> When the business history of the past decade is written, perhaps nothing will sum up the outrageous financial scheming of the era as well as the frenzied swapping that marked its final years. Internet companies . . . milked revenue from complex advertising exchanges with other dot-coms in ultimately worthless deals. In Houston, equal amounts of energy were pushed back and forth between companies. . . .
>
> But the swaps rage turned out to be no bargain for investors. The bad deals contributed to an epidemic of artificially inflated revenue. In many cases, swaps slipped through legal loopholes left in place by regulators who had failed to keep pace with the ever-changing deal-making of ever-changing industries. The unraveling of those back-scratching arrangements helped usher in the market collapse and led to the realization by investors that the highest-flying industries of the boom era—telecom, energy, the Internet—were built in part on a combustible mix of wishful thinking and deceit.[44]

Here's an example of the manipulation of these asset exchange rules to overstate revenues and income. Telecom companies would sign agreements with other telecom companies to exchange access to each other's fiber-optic network. These deals were termed "capacity swaps"[45] and were generally structured as leases. That is, Company One would agree to lease capacity to Asia on Company Two's network for 20 years and *simultaneously* Company Two would agree to lease capacity to Europe on Company One's network for 20 years. Each company would promise to pay the other $5 million per year under the two separate leases.

| For a further discussion of this earnings management scheme, see Chapter 3. |

Each company received cash, and the stage was therefore set for potentially recognizing revenues and income on these deals. Furthermore, Company One would structure the lease that *provided* access to its network as an operating lease while the lease in which it *obtained* access to Company Two's network was treated as a capital lease (leases are discussed in Chapter 12). What this means is that the network access (that is, the "asset") Company One "sold" in the swap was treated in part as current period's revenue while the access it bought in the swap was capitalized and expensed over future periods. So, these deals sometimes generated upfront income. Even if they didn't generate income, they did increase revenues—an important factor "since investors focused on revenue in new industries that often had little earnings to show for themselves."[46]

To prevent a repeat of these abuses, the FASB issued rules that now require companies to record certain exchanges of nonmonetary assets at the existing ***book value*** of the relinquished asset if any of the following conditions apply:[47]

1. The fair value of neither the asset(s) received nor the asset(s) relinquished is determinable within reasonable limits.

2. The transaction lacks commercial substance.

3. The exchange transaction is made to facilitate sales to customers. Specifically, the transaction is an exchange of inventory or property held for sale in the ordinary course of business for other inventory or property to be sold in the same line of business.

---

[44] D. K. Berman, J. Angwin, and C. Cummins, "As the Bubble Neared Its End, Bogus Swaps Padded the Books," *The Wall Street Journal,* December 23, 2002. Copyright © 2002 Dow Jones & Company, Inc. All rights reserved worldwide. Reprinted with permission.

[45] Ibid. Also see K. Brown, "Creative Accounting: How to Buff a Company," *The Wall Street Journal,* February 21, 2002.

[46] Op. cit.

[47] "Exchanges of Nonmonetary Assets: An Amendment of APB No. 29," *SFAS No. 153* (Norwalk, CT: FASB, 2004).

In the next section, we illustrate these three circumstances under which exchanges of non-monetary assets must be recorded at book value.

## Exchanges Recorded at Book Value

**Fair Value Not Determinable**  To illustrate the accounting for exchanges of non-monetary assets when the fair value of the exchanged assets cannot be determined, consider the following example.

> Denver Construction Corporation agrees to swap with Cody Company one type of crane in exchange for a slightly different model whose features are better suited for a highway bridge project it is currently engaged in. The old crane Denver is exchanging has a book value of $600,000 at the time of the transaction. Its original cost was $700,000, and accumulated depreciation is $100,000. Denver also pays Cody $40,000 to complete the transaction. It is not possible to measure the fair value of either crane within reasonable limits.

Because neither crane's fair value is known, the new crane is recorded at the sum of the *book value* of the old crane ($600,000) plus the cash given ($40,000). The entry is:

| | | | |
|---|---|---|---|
| **DR** | Construction crane (new) | $640,000 | |
| **DR** | Accumulated depreciation—construction crane (old) | 100,000 | |
| | **CR**  Construction crane (old) | | $700,000 |
| | **CR**  Cash | | 40,000 |

**The Commercial Substance Criterion**  Booking exchange transactions at fair value introduces the possibility of gains (or losses) on the transaction. To preclude firms from engaging in "sham" exchanges to generate artificial gains, the FASB requires that the transaction must possess **commercial substance.** An exchange transaction has commercial substance when the firm's future cash flows are expected to change significantly as a result of the exchange.

A significant cash flow change exists if either:

1. The configuration (risk, timing, and amount) of the future cash flows of the asset(s) received differs significantly from the configuration of the future cash flows of the asset(s) transferred.
2. The entity-specific value of the asset(s) received differs from the entity-specific value of the asset(s) transferred, and the difference is significant in relation to the fair values of the assets exchanged.[48]

If both conditions are *not* met, the transaction must be recorded using the book value of the asset(s) relinquished, using the procedure in the previous illustration. This precludes any gain recognition.

**Exchange Transaction to Facilitate Sales to Customers**  Sometimes firms exchange assets with other firms—even competitors—to balance inventories, as in the following example.

> Lee Electronics faces a shortage of plasma television sets but has an excess of liquid crystal display (LCD) sets. It agrees to swap LCDs with a fair value of $50,000 and a book value of $40,000 for plasma sets with a fair value of $52,000 from Bonnie Enterprises.

---

[48] Ibid., para. 21.

Here, the assets being exchanged (plasma and LCD sets) are both stocked for sale to customers. The exchange does not culminate an earning process. One asset is merely traded for another that serves a similar purpose. For this reason, Lee Electronics does not report a gain but instead records the plasma sets at $40,000—the book value of the LCDs that were relinquished in the transaction. The entry is simply:

| | | | |
|---|---|---|---|
| **DR** | Inventory—plasma sets | $40,000 | |
| | **CR**  Inventory—LCDs | | $40,000 |

The apparent $12,000 gain on the swap ($52,000 fair value minus $40,000 book value) will be recognized only when the plasma sets are ultimately sold to customers.

### Cash Received—A Special Case

Let's continue the previous example with one difference. We still assume that the fair value of the plasma sets is $52,000, but we now assume that Lee Electronics also receives $5,778 from Bonnie Enterprises.

This transaction is more complicated because Lee received both cash and the plasma television sets. Indeed, cash represents 10% of the total proceeds:

This gain is determined as follows:

| | |
|---|---|
| Fair value of plasma television sets | $52,000 |
| + Cash received | 5,778 |
| Total consideration received | $57,778 |
| − Book value of LCDs relinquished | (40,000) |
| Gain on transaction | $17,778 |

$$\frac{\text{Cash received}}{\text{Total proceeds}} = \frac{\$5,778}{\$5,778 + \$52,000} = 0.10$$

Because 10% of the proceeds were received in cash, 10% of the LCD assets are considered to be sold, and that portion of the earning process is complete. So, 10% of the $17,778 gain on the transaction will be recognized.[49] The entry is:

| | | | |
|---|---|---|---|
| **DR** | Cash | $ 5,778 | |
| **DR** | Inventory—plasma sets | 36,000 | |
| | **CR**  Inventory—LCDs | | $40,000 |
| | **CR**  Recognized gain on exchange | | 1,778 |

The carrying amount of the inventory of plasma sets is computed as follows:

| | | |
|---|---|---|
| Fair value of plasma sets | | $52,000 |
| Less: Portion of gain deferred: | | |
| Total gain | $17,778 | |
| Gain recognized | (1,778) | |
| Gain deferred | | (16,000) |
| Inventory—plasma sets | | $36,000 |

Notice that the $16,000 deferred gain will ultimately be recognized when the plasma sets are sold because the inventory carrying amount has been reduced by the amount of the deferred gain.

---

[49] *APB Opinion No. 29*, para. 22.

- GAAP for long-lived assets is far from perfect. The need for reliable and verifiable numbers causes these assets to be measured in terms of the economic sacrifice incurred to obtain them—their historical cost—rather than in terms of their current expected benefit—or worth—to the firm.

- Because it is uncertain whether future benefits result from research and brand development costs, these costs are generally expensed in the period incurred. Consequently, balance sheet carrying amounts for intangible assets often differ from their real value to the firm. Analysts must scrutinize disclosures of R&D expenses to undo the overly conservative accounting.

- Prior to 2009, managers could deliberately allocate an excessive portion of the total purchase price in a business combination to in-process R&D to increase postacquisition earnings.

- Changes in the amount of capitalized interest from one period to the next can distort earnings trends. A thorough understanding of how the GAAP measurement rules are applied allows statement readers to avoid pitfalls in trend analysis when investment in new assets is sporadic.

- When comparing return on assets (ROA) ratios across firms, one must remember that—all other factors being equal—there is an upward drift in reported ROA as assets age. So, analysts must determine whether the average age of the long-lived assets for firms being analyzed is stable or rising. Inflation also injects an upward bias into reported ROA.

- Asset impairment write-downs depend on subjective forecasts and could be used to manage earnings, especially under IFRS rules.

- An understanding of differences in depreciation choices across firms permits better interfirm comparisons. When making interfirm comparisons, analysts should use footnote disclosures to overcome differences in the long-lived asset useful lives chosen by each firm and, when possible, in their depreciation patterns.

- International practices for long-lived assets and book depreciation charges are sometimes very different from those in the United States. Statement users who make cross-country comparisons must exercise caution.

## EXERCISES

Phoenix Co. acquired a large piece of specialized machinery used in its manufacturing process. The following costs were incurred in connection with the acquisition:

| | |
|---|---:|
| Finder's fee | $ 2,000 |
| List price | 230,000 |
| Transportation fee | 4,000 |
| Speeding ticket during transportation | 65 |
| Installation fee | 2,500 |
| Cost to repair a door damaged during installation | 1,200 |

**E10-1**

Capitalizing costs

**Required:**

Which of the costs incurred by Phoenix Co. should be capitalized to the machinery account?

In January 2008, Action Corporation entered into a contract to acquire a new machine for its factory. The machine, which had a cash price of $150,000, was paid for as follows:

| | |
|---|---:|
| Down payment | $ 15,000 |
| Note payable due June 1, 2008 | 120,000 |
| 500 shares of Action common stock with a value of $50 per share | 25,000 |
| Total | $160,000 |

**E10-2**

Determining asset cost and depreciation expense

**AICPA**
ADAPTED

Prior to the machine's use, installation costs of $4,000 were incurred. The machine has an estimated useful life of 10 years and an estimated salvage value of $5,000.

**Required:**

What should Action record as depreciation expense for 2008 under the straight-line method?

---

**E10-3**

Capitalizing costs subsequent to acquisition

Gonzo Co. owns a building in Georgia. The building's historical cost is $970,000, and $440,000 of accumulated depreciation has been recorded to date. During 2008, Gonzo incurred the following expenses related to the building:

| | |
|---|---|
| Repainted the building | $ 48,000 |
| Major improvement to the plumbing | 109,000 |
| Replaced carpet in the plant's accounting offices | 47,600 |
| Added a 7,000 square foot lobby | 234,600 |
| Repaired a broken water main | 155,800 |

**Required:**

1. Which of the costs incurred by Gonzo Co. should be capitalized to the building account?

2. What is the subsequent carrying amount of the building?

---

**E10-4**

Determining depreciation expense

**AICPA**
ADAPTED

Turtle Company purchased equipment on January 2, 2006 for $50,000. The equipment had an estimated five-year service life. Turtle's policy for five-year assets is to use double-declining balance depreciation for the first two years of the asset's life and then to switch to the straight-line depreciation method.

**Required:**

In its December 31, 2008 balance sheet, what amount should Turtle report as accumulated depreciation for equipment?

---

**E10-5**

Determining depreciation base

**AICPA**
ADAPTED

Apex Company purchased a tooling machine on January 3, 1998 for $30,000. The machine was being depreciated on the straight-line method over an estimated useful life of 20 years, with no salvage value.

At the beginning of 2008, when the machine had been in use for 10 years, the company paid $5,000 to overhaul it. As a result of this improvement, the company estimated that the remaining useful life of the machine was now 15 years.

**Required:**

What should be the depreciation expense recorded for this machine in 2008?

---

**E10-6**

Determining what amount to capitalize

**AICPA**
ADAPTED

On June 18, 2008, Dell Printing Company incurred the following costs for one of its printing presses:

| | |
|---|---|
| Purchase of collating and stapling attachment | $84,000 |
| Installation of attachment | 36,000 |
| Replacement parts for overhaul of press | 26,000 |
| Labor and overhead in connection with overhaul | 14,000 |

The overhaul resulted in a significant increase in production capability. Neither the attachment nor the overhaul increased the estimated useful life of the press.

**Required:**

What total amount of the preceding costs should be capitalized?

---

**E10-7**

Analyzing various costs

**AICPA**
ADAPTED

Samson Manufacturing Company, a calendar-year company, purchased a machine for $65,000 on January 1, 2006. At the date of purchase, Samson incurred the following additional costs:

| | |
|---|---|
| Loss on sale of old machinery | $1,000 |
| Freight-in | 500 |
| Installation cost | 2,000 |
| Testing costs prior to regular operation | 300 |

The machine's estimated salvage value was $5,000, and Samson estimated it would have a useful life of 20 years with depreciation being computed on the straight-line method. In January 2008, accessories costing $3,600 were added to the machine to reduce its operating costs. These accessories neither prolonged the machine's life nor provided any additional salvage value.

**Required:**

What should Samson record as depreciation expense for 2008?

---

On January 1, 2008, Hardy, Inc. purchased certain plant assets under a deferred payment contract. The agreement called for making annual payments of $10,000 for five years. The first payment is due on January 1, 2008, and the remaining payments are due on January 1 of each of the next four years. Assume an imputed interest rate of 10%.

**E10-8**

Deferred payment contract

**Required:**

What entry should be made to record the purchase of these plant assets on January 1, 2008?

---

On February 1, 2008, Reflection Corporation purchased a parcel of land as a factory site for $50,000. An old building on the property was demolished, and construction began on a new building, completed on November 1, 2008. Costs incurred were:

**E10-9**

Classifying costs

**AICPA**
ADAPTED

| | |
|---|---:|
| Demolition of old building | $ 4,000 |
| Architect's fees | 10,000 |
| Legal fees for title investigation and purchase contract | 2,000 |
| Construction costs | 500,000 |

Salvaged materials resulting from demolition were sold for $1,000.

**Required:**

What cost should be recorded for the land and new building, respectively?

---

On July 1, 2008, Town Company purchased for $540,000 a warehouse building and the land on which it is located. The following data were available concerning the property:

**E10-10**

Classifying costs

**AICPA**
ADAPTED

| | Current Appraised Value | Seller's Original Cost |
|---|---:|---:|
| Land | $200,000 | $140,000 |
| Warehouse building | 300,000 | 280,000 |
| | $500,000 | $420,000 |

**Required:**

At what amount should Town record the land?

---

Clay Company started construction on a new office building on January 1, 2007, and it moved into the finished building on July 1, 2008. Of the building's $2,500,000 total cost, $2,000,000 was incurred in 2007 evenly throughout the year. Clay's incremental borrowing rate was 12% throughout 2007, and the total amount of interest incurred by Clay during 2007 was $102,000.

**E10-11**

Capitalizing interest

**AICPA**
ADAPTED

**Required:**

What amount should Clay report as capitalized interest at December 31, 2007?

---

Cole Company began constructing a building for its own use in January 2008. During 2008, Cole incurred interest of $50,000 on specific construction debt and $20,000 on other borrowings. Interest computed on the weighted-average amount of accumulated expenditures for the building during 2008 was $40,000.

**E10-12**

Capitalizing interest

**AICPA**
ADAPTED

**Required:**

What amount of interest cost should Cole capitalize? Prepare the journal entry to record payment of the interest.

**E10-13**

Analyzing accounts

AICPA
ADAPTED

Weir Company uses straight-line depreciation for its property, plant, and equipment, which, stated at cost, consisted of the following:

| | December 31 | |
| --- | --- | --- |
| | **2008** | **2007** |
| Land | $ 25,000 | $ 25,000 |
| Buildings | 195,000 | 195,000 |
| Machinery and equipment | 695,000 | 650,000 |
| | 915,000 | 870,000 |
| Less accumulated depreciation | (400,000) | (370,000) |
| | $515,000 | $500,000 |

Weir's depreciation expense for 2008 and 2007 was $55,000 and $50,000, respectively.

**Required:**

What amount was debited to accumulated depreciation during 2008 because of property, plant, and equipment retirements?

**E10-14**

Identifying depreciation expense patterns

AICPA
ADAPTED

The following graph depicts three depreciation expense patterns over time.

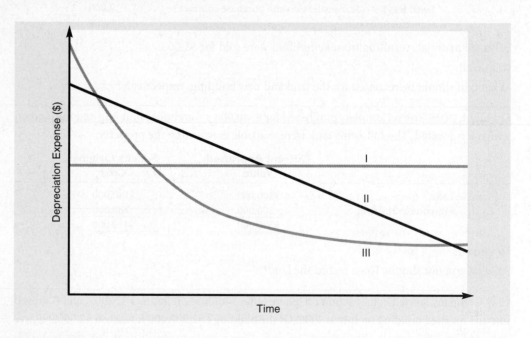

**Required:**

Pattern I, of course, is straight-line depreciation. Which depreciation expense pattern corresponds to the sum-of-the-years' digits method and which corresponds to the double-declining balance method? Explain why the shape of the Pattern II and Pattern III lines differs.

**E10-15**

Amortizing intangibles

AICPA
ADAPTED

On January 1, 2004, Vick Company purchased a trademark for $400,000, which had an estimated useful life of 16 years. In January 2008, Vick paid $60,000 for legal fees in a successful defense of the trademark.

**Required:**

How much should Vick record as trademark amortization expense for 2008?

On January 2, 2005, Lava, Inc. purchased a patent for a new consumer product for $90,000. At the time of purchase, the patent was valid for 15 years; however, its useful life was estimated to be only 10 years due to the product's competitive nature. On December 31, 2008, the product was permanently withdrawn from sale under governmental order because of a potential health hazard in the product.

**Required:**
What should the total charge against income on this patent be in 2008?

**E10-16**

Determining amount of intangibles expensed

**AICPA**
ADAPTED

---

During 2008, Orr Company incurred the following costs:

| | |
|---|---|
| Research and development services performed by Key Corporation for Orr | $150,000 |
| Design, construction, and testing of preproduction prototypes and models | 200,000 |
| Testing in search for new products or process alternatives | 175,000 |

**Required:**
How much research and development expense should Orr report in 2008?

**E10-17**

Treating R&D cost

**AICPA**
ADAPTED

---

In 2008, Ball Labs incurred the following costs:

| | |
|---|---|
| Direct costs of doing contract research and development work for the government to be reimbursed by a governmental unit | $400,000 |

Research and development costs not included above were:

| | |
|---|---|
| Depreciation | $300,000 |
| Salaries | 700,000 |
| Indirect costs appropriately allocated | 200,000 |
| Materials | 180,000 |

**Required:**
What was Ball's total research and development expense in 2008?

**E10-18**

Treating R&D cost

**AICPA**
ADAPTED

---

Pearl Inc. develops and markets computer software. During 2007, one of Pearl's engineers began developing a new and very innovative software product. On July 1, 2008, a team of Pearl engineers determined that the software product was technologically feasible. Pearl engineers continued to ready the software for general release and in January 2009, the first product sales were made. Total costs incurred follow:

| | |
|---|---|
| 2007 | $3,200,000 |
| 2008 | $3,600,000 (evenly throughout the year) |

**Required:**
1. How should Pearl account for the costs incurred during 2007, and what is the rationale for your answer?
2. How should Pearl account for the costs incurred during 2008? If your answer differs from your answer in requirement 1, explain why.

**E10-19**

Accounting for software development costs

---

In January 2008, Vorst Company purchased a mineral mine for $2,640,000. Removable ore was estimated at 1,200,000 tons. After it has extracted all the ore, Vorst will be required by law to restore the land to its original condition at an estimated cost of $180,000. Vorst believes it will be able to sell the property for $300,000. During 2008, Vorst incurred $360,000 of development costs to prepare the mine for production, and it removed and sold 60,000 tons of ore.

**Required:**
In its 2008 income statement, what amount should Vorst report as depletion expense?

**E10-20**

Determining depletion expense

**AICPA**
ADAPTED

# PROBLEMS / DISCUSSION QUESTIONS

**P10-1**

Computing depreciation expense

AICPA
ADAPTED

On January 2, 2007, Half, Inc. purchased a manufacturing machine for $864,000. The machine has an eight-year estimated life and a $144,000 estimated salvage value. Half expects to manufacture 1,800,000 units over the machine's life. During 2008, Half manufactured 300,000 units.

**Required:**

For each item, calculate depreciation expense for 2008 (the second year of ownership) for the machine just described under the method listed:

1. Straight-line

2. Double-declining balance

3. Sum-of-the-years' digits

4. Units-of-production

(*Hint:* The units-of-production method was not discussed in the text but is easy to understand. Depreciation is based on a ratio; the ratio numerator is production during the period and the denominator is estimated total production over the life of the machine. This ratio is then multiplied by the machine's cost minus salvage value to determine depreciation expense.)

**P10-2**

Recording lump-sum purchases

On June 30, 2008, Macrosoft Company acquired a 10-acre tract of land. On the tract was a warehouse that Macrosoft intended to use as a distribution center. At the time of purchase, the land had an assessed tax value of $6,300,000, and the building had an assessed tax value of $11,200,000. Macrosoft paid $15,000,000 for the land and building. After the purchase, the company paid $1,000,000 to have various modifications made to the building.

**Required:**

1. At what amount should Macrosoft record the land and building?

2. For financial reporting purposes, why might Macrosoft managers prefer to assign a larger portion of the $15,000,000 to the land rather than to the building?

**P10-3**

Determining asset cost under a deferred payment plan

Cayman Diving Inc. needs to acquire a new dive boat. The seller will accept a noninterest-bearing note for $400,000 due in four years or $250,000 in cash. The company's incremental cost of borrowing is 10%.

**Required:**

Which option should Cayman Diving select? Would your answer change if Cayman's incremental borrowing rate was 13%? Why?

**P10-4**

Allocating acquisition costs among asset accounts

On April 23, 2008, Starlight Department Stores Inc. acquired a 75-acre tract of land by paying $25,000,000 in cash and by issuing a six-month note payable for $5,000,000 and 1,000,000 shares of its common stock. On April 23, 2008, Starlight's common stock was selling for $80.00 a share and had a $2.50 par value. The land had two existing buildings, one that Starlight intended to renovate and use as a warehouse, and another that Starlight intended to demolish to make way for the construction of a new department store. At the time of the purchase, the assessed values for property tax purposes of the land and the building to be renovated were $105,000,000 and $20,000,000, respectively. To complete the purchase, Starlight incurred legal fees of $25,000. The cost of demolishing the unneeded building was $50,000. Starlight paid $250,000 to have the land graded so that the new store could be built. Starlight paid a total of $100,000,000 to have the new department store built and another $25,000,000 to renovate the old building. To fund the work on the renovation and the new store, Starlight obtained a loan from Gotham City Bank. Starlight made total interest payments of $10,000,000 during the period the buildings were being completed. (Assume that all of the interest payments qualify for capitalization.) Because parking would be needed for both the new department store and the warehouse, Starlight had a portion of the land covered with asphalt at a cost of $450,000. Starlight also paid $200,000 to install lighting for the parking lots and $75,000 to install decorative fencing and a parking access gate. During 2008, Starlight paid property taxes of $150,000 on the new property. All work was completed by December 31, 2008, and the new store and warehouse were placed in service on January 1, 2009.

**Required:**

Determine what costs should be assigned to the (1) land, (2) building, and (3) land improvements asset accounts. (*Hint:* The allocation of the original purchase price between the land and building should be made in proportion to the relative assessed values of the land and building at the time of the purchase.)

---

Formidable Express provides overnight delivery of letters and small parcels to numerous locations throughout the United States. As part of its operations, the company maintains a sizable fleet of delivery trucks. Assume that Formidable made the following expenditures related to the fleet during 2008:

**P10-5**

Capitalizing or expensing various costs

1. The company has the engines in its trucks serviced (that is, "tuned-up") once every two years. The cost of the servicing in 2008 was $11.0 million.

2. Due to the high mileage put on the delivery vehicles, the company normally replaces 20% of its fleet's engines every year. In 2008, the cost incurred to replace engines amounted to $7.8 million.

3. The tires on each vehicle are replaced once every three years. The cost of the new tires installed in 2008 amounted to $1.0 million.

4. In 2008, the company paid $3.5 million to have the trucks in the fleet rustproofed. Management expects that the trucks will now last an extra three years.

5. Because each truck was out of service for about a week due to the rustproofing in (4), the company estimates that it lost $12.0 million in revenue during the course of the year.

**Required:**

Which expenditures should Formidable capitalize and which should be expensed?

---

Fly-by-Night is an international airline company. Its fleet includes Boeing 757s, 747s, 727s, Lockheed L-1011s, and McDonnell Douglas MD-83s, MD-80s, and DC-9s. Assume that Fly-by-Night made the following expenditures related to these aircraft in 2008:

**P10-6**

Capitalizing or expensing various costs

1. New jet engines were installed on some of the MD-80s and MD-83s at a cost of $25.0 million.

2. The company paid $2.0 million to paint one-eighth of the fleet with the firm's new colors to create a new public image. It intends to paint the remainder of the fleet over the next seven years.

3. Routine maintenance and repairs on various aircraft cost $8.0 million.

4. Noise abatement equipment ("hush kits") was installed on the fleet of DC-9s to meet FAA maximum allowable noise levels on takeoff. Equipment and installation cost $7.5 million.

5. The avionics systems were replaced on the Lockheed L-1011s. This will allow the aircraft to be used four more years than originally expected.

6. The existing seats on all 747s were replaced with new, more comfortable seats at a cost of $0.5 million.

7. The jet engines on 50% of the Boeing 727s received a major overhaul at a cost of $5.0 million. As a result, the aircraft should be more fuel efficient.

**Required:**

1. Which of these expenditures should Fly-by-Night capitalize? Why?

2. How might Fly-by-Night use expenditures like these to manage its earnings?

---

**P10-7**

Determining an asset's cost

On July 23, 2008, Consolidated Parcel Service (CPS) acquired a new de-icing machine for use at its facility at Chicago's O'Hare airport. The machine is used to de-ice the wings of the firm's aircraft in winter months. The machine's invoice price was $15,000,000. The seller offered CPS a 2% cash discount on the gross invoice price if CPS paid for the machine by August 1, 2008. The cost to ship the machine from the seller's warehouse was $15,000 and was paid by CPS. Insurance during transport amounted to $5,000, also paid by CPS. Many CPS employees were involved with the assembly and testing of the machine. Their wages totaled $20,000. As part of testing the machine, $35,000 worth of de-icing fluid was used to ensure that the machine operated properly. During testing, one of CPS's cargo planes was inadvertently damaged. The cost to repair the aircraft (not covered by insurance) amounted to $250,000. As a result of the damaged aircraft being out of service while it was being repaired, CPS lost $750,000 in revenue. Finally, because the machine was larger than the previous one, CPS had to erect a new storage facility. The cost of doing so was $75,000 for materials, $25,000 for labor, and $5,000 for salaries of the supervisory personnel who directed the construction.

**Required:**

Assuming that CPS paid for the machine on July 29, 2008, determine the capitalizable cost of the machine to CPS.

---

**P10-8**

Determining asset impairment

Four years ago Omega Technology Inc. acquired a machine to use in its computer chip manufacturing operations at a cost of $35,000,000. The firm expected the machine to have a seven-year useful life and a zero salvage value. The company has been using straight-line depreciation for the asset. Due to the rapid rate of technological change in the industry, at the end of Year 4, Omega estimates that the machine is capable of generating (undiscounted) future cash flows of $11,000,000. Based on the quoted market prices of similar assets, Omega estimates the machine to have a fair value of $9,500,000.

**Required:**

1. What is the machine's book value at the end of Year 4?

2. Should Omega recognize an impairment of this asset? Why or why not? If so, what amount of the impairment loss should be recognized?

3. At the end of Year 4, at what amount should the machine appear in Omega's balance sheet?

---

**P10-9**

Testing for asset impairment

Norway Co. manufactures and sells television receivers. Due to recent innovations (plasma screens), Norway suspects that some of its equipment may be impaired. The equipment's historical cost is $4,000,000, but it has been owned, used, and depreciated for three years. When the equipment was purchased, Norway anticipated a 10-year useful life with no residual value. Norway anticipates that the equipment will generate cash sales of $1,000,000 per year for the next three years and will require operating cash expenditures of $250,000 per year during that same time period. At the end of three years, the equipment will be scrapped. Similar equipment sells for $1,950,000 on the used asset market.

**Required:**

1. What circumstances should prompt Norway Co. to perform an asset impairment test?

2. Is Norway's manufacturing equipment impaired? Why or why not?

3. Prepare any journal entry necessary based on your answer in requirement 2.

4. If two years from now there is an unexpected resurgence of demand for ordinary television receivers, will this impact any entry made in requirement 3?

In its Year 2 balance sheet, IBM reported the following account:

| ($ in millions) | Year 2 | Year 1 |
|---|---|---|
| Software, less accumulated amortization (Year 2: $11,276; Year 1: $10,793) | $2,419 | $2,963 |

In the footnotes to its financial statements, IBM reported that it spent $2,997 million on computer software–related activities. Assume that these expenditures were related to projects in which technological feasibility has been proved.

**Required:**

1. How is IBM required to account for computer software–related expenditures?

2. As of the end of Year 2, how much has IBM spent on existing computer software–related activities in past years?

3. As of the end of Year 2, how much of its computer software–related expenditures has IBM capitalized?

4. Based on the information given, estimate IBM's amortization of computer software costs in Year 2.

5. Assume that IBM amortizes its capitalized software costs using the straight-line method. Estimate the average useful life of the software products developed as of the end of Year 2.

6. How might firms use the accounting for computer software costs to manage their earnings?

National Sweetener Company owns the patent to the artificial sweetener known as Supersweet. Assume that National Sweetener acquired the patent on January 1, 2002 at a cost of $300 million dollars, expected the patent to have an economic useful life of 12 years, and has been amortizing the patent on a straight-line basis. Assume that when the patent was acquired, National Sweetener expected that the process would generate future net cash flows of $30 million the first year of its useful life and that the cash flows would increase at a 10% rate each year over the remainder of its useful life. By the year 2014 that is, after 12 years, National Sweetener expected that several other artificial sweeteners would be on the market and therefore that it would sell the Supersweet patent then for about $60.0 million.

| Year | Expected Future Cash Flows ($ in millions) | Year | Expected Future Cash Flows ($ in millions) |
|---|---|---|---|
| 2002 | $30.0 | 2009 | $ 58.7 |
| 2003 | 33.0 | 2010 | 64.3 |
| 2004 | 36.3 | 2011 | 70.7 |
| 2005 | 39.9 | 2012 | 77.8 |
| 2006 | 43.9 | 2013 | 85.6 |
| 2007 | 48.3 | Total | $641.6 |
| 2008 | 53.1 | | |

On December 31, 2008 when the patent's book value was $160.0 million ($300.0 − $140.0), National Sweetener learned that one of its competitors had developed a revolutionary new sweetener that could be produced much more economically than Supersweet. National Sweetener expects that the introduction of this product on January 1, 2009 will substantially reduce the cash flows from its Supersweet patent process.

Consider the following two independent scenarios:

***Scenario I:*** National Sweetener expects that the cash flows from Supersweet over the period 2009–2013 will be only 50% of those originally projected and that the sale of the Supersweet patent will bring only $25 million when sold. When discounted at a rate of 15% (which National Sweetener feels is appropriate), these amounts yield a present value of $129.0 million. National Sweetener estimates that the market value of the Supersweet patent on December 31, 2008 is $160.0 million.

*Scenario II:* National Sweetener expects that the cash flows from Supersweet over the period 2009–2013 will be only 25% of those originally projected and that the sale of the Supersweet patent will bring only $25 million when sold. When discounted at a rate of 15%, these amounts yield a present value of $70.7 million. National Sweetener estimates that the market value of the Supersweet patent on December 31, 2008 is $68.0 million.

**Required:**

1. Should National Sweetener recognize an impairment of its Supersweet patent in Scenario I? If so, what is the amount of the loss and at what amount should the patent be reported in National Sweetener's 2008 ending balance sheet?

2. Repeat requirement 1 for the second scenario.

---

**P10-12**

Capitalizing interest

To meet the increasing demand for its microprocessors, Intelligent Micro Devices began construction of a new manufacturing facility on January 1, 2008. Construction costs were incurred uniformly throughout 2008 and were recorded in the firm's Construction-in-progress account. The average balance in the Construction-in-progress account during 2008 was $150,000,000.

To facilitate the facility's construction, the firm arranged for an $80,000,000 construction loan on January 1 at a rate of 13%. The firm also issued $40,000,000 of common stock to help finance the project. Management estimates that the firm's cost of equity capital is 16%. On January 1, 2008, the firm also issued bonds in the amount of $200,000,000, carrying a weighted-average interest rate of 11.5%. Earnings before interest and taxes for 2008 is $50,000,000.

**Required:**

1. What is the total amount of interest the firm incurred in 2008?

2. Assume that the firm bases the amount of capitalized interest on the average balance in the Construction-in-progress account. How much of the interest in requirement 1 should be capitalized?

3. How much of the amount in requirement 2 will be related to the firm's common stock issue? Why?

4. Where will the amount in requirement 2 appear in the firm's 2008 financial statements?

5. What amount of interest expense will appear in the firm's 2008 income statement?

6. Assume that the facility is completed on December 31, 2008 and that it is placed in service on January 1, 2009. How, if at all, will the amount in requirement 2 affect the future income of the firm?

7. Calculate the firm's interest coverage ratio (income before interest and taxes divided by interest expense) with and without the interest capitalization. Which coverage ratio would be more useful to a creditor in the evaluation of the firm's risk of insolvency?

---

**P10-13**

Accounting for internally developed patents versus purchased patents

mhhe.com/revsine4e

Consider the following two scenarios;

*Scenario I:* Over the 2005–2008 period, Micro Systems, Inc. spends $10,000,000 a year to develop patents on new computer hardware manufacturing technology. While some of its projects failed, the firm did develop several new patents each year during the period.

*Scenario II:* Over the 2005–2008 period, Macro Systems, Inc., a competitor of Micro Systems, Inc., paid $10,000,000 each year to acquire patent rights from other firms. The firm assigned a five-year useful life to all of the patents.

1. Each firm had sales of $200,000,000, $242,000,000, $290,000,000, and $350,000,000, respectively, over the 2005–2008 period.

2. Each firm's operating expenses (excluding the preceding patent-related information) were $140,000,000, $170,000,000, $205,000,000, and $245,000,000, respectively, over the 2005–2008 period.

3. Assume that a 34% income tax rate applies to both firms.

**Required:**

1. How would the two firms account for their patent-related expenditure?

2. Calculate each firm's net income and net income as a percent of sales (that is, profit margin) for the 2005–2008 period. Contrast the reported profitability of the two firms.

3. Assume that the firms continue to spend $10,000,000 per year in the way just described. How would the comparability of their income statements be affected?

---

Assume that Major Motors Corporation, a large automobile manufacturer, reported in a recent annual report to shareholders that its buildings had an original cost of $4,694,000,000.

1. Major Motors uses the straight-line depreciation method to depreciate the buildings over a useful life of 34 years.

2. Assume that the ratio of end-of-year accumulated depreciation on the buildings to their depreciable cost is 35.3%. This implies that the buildings, on average, are about 12 years old. Assume that Major Motors depreciates them to a salvage value of 5% of their original cost.

3. Assume that Major Motors' management is considering both extending the original useful lives of the buildings to 40 years from 34 years and increasing the salvage value to 10% of the buildings' original cost.

4. Assume a tax rate of 34%.

**Required:**

1. What is the book value of the buildings at the end of the current year (that is, before adjusting for any change in useful lives or salvage values)?

2. What would be the dollar amount and direction of the effect on Major Motors' net income if the proposed changes to the useful lives and salvage values were implemented at the start of the next fiscal year?

**P10-14**

Determining earnings effects of changes in useful lives and salvage values

---

The 2007 income statement and other information for Mallard Corporation, which is about to purchase a new machine at a cost of $500 and a new computer system at a cost of $300, follows.

| | |
|---|---|
| Sales | $1,000 |
| Cost of goods sold | 600 |
| Gross profit | 400 |
| Operating expenses | 150 |
| Income before tax | 250 |
| Income taxes | 85 |
| Net income | $ 165 |

**P10-15**

Identifying straight-line versus accelerated depreciation ratio effects

mhhe.com/revsine4e

**Additional Information:**

- The two new assets are expected to generate a 25% annual rate of growth in the firm's sales.

- The firm will include the machine's depreciation expense as part of cost of goods sold and the depreciation expense on the computer system as part of operating expenses.

- *Excluding* the new machine's depreciation, the firm's cost of goods sold is expected to increase at an annual rate of 7.5%.

- *Excluding* the new computer system's depreciation, the firm's operating expenses are expected to increase at an annual rate of 4.0%.

- The firm's gross total assets (net of asset retirements) are expected to increase at a rate of 20% per year. Average gross total assets in 2007 were $1,000. Assume that asset retirements generate no gains or losses.

- Both the machine and the computer system have a three-year useful life and a zero salvage value.

- Assume an income tax rate of 34%.

**Required:**

1. Assume that the assets are purchased on January 1, 2008. Prepare pro forma income statements for 2008 through 2010. Assume the firm elects to use the straight-line depreciation method for depreciating the new assets.

2. Repeat requirement 1 assuming instead that the firm elects to use the sum-of-the-years' digits method for depreciating the new assets.

3. For both requirements 1 and 2, calculate the firm's gross profit rate (gross profit divided by sales), NOPAT margin (net operating profit after tax divided by sales), and return on assets (NOPAT divided by average total assets). How does the use of the different depreciation methods affect the behavior of the ratios over the 2008–2010 period?

---

**P10-16**

Making asset age and intercompany comparisons

mhhe.com/revsine4e

Gardenia Co. and Lantana Co. both operate in the same industry. Gardenia began its operations in 2008 with a $20 million initial investment in plant and equipment with an expected life of 10 years. Lantana's net asset base is also $20 million, but its assets are, on average, 5 years old with 10-year expected useful lives on January 1, 2008. Lantana replaces 10% of its assets each year at year-end, while Gardenia, having just entered the industry, does not have immediate plans to replace any assets.

Per year pre-tax net operating cash flow generated $3,000,000 for Gardenia, and $5,000,000 for Lantana. Inflation is expected to be 2% per year, and each company expects to keep pace by increasing its pre-tax net operating cash flow by 2% per year. The cost of Lantana's planned asset replacements will also increase at 2% per year. (*Note:* For simplicity, assume that prior to 2008, the replacement cost of Lantana's assets remained constant.)

**Required:**

1. Compute return on assets for Gardenia Co. for 2008 through 2012.

2. Compute return on assets for Lantana Co. for 2008 through 2012.

3. Discuss the differences between your answers to requirement 1 and requirement 2.

---

**P10-17**

Accounting for asset retirement obligations

Coyote Co. is building a waste landfill in the desert between Arizona and California. Coyote estimates that this landfill will be in operation for five years, will cost $250 million to build, and will generate $800 million in revenues during its useful life. Federal law requires that Coyote decommission and decontaminate the site at the end of its useful life. A team of engineers has studied the decontamination procedure and has estimated that Coyote will have to spend $15 million on the decommissioning process when the landfill is shut down in five years. Coyote's credit-adjusted rate of interest is 10%.

**Required:**

1. In accordance with *SFAS No. 143*, how should Coyote Co. account for the costs associated with the decommissioning process? Prepare the journal entry required and prepare an amortization table.

2. How are the costs associated with the decommissioning process reflected on the income statement? Explain how this accounting treatment improves the matching process.

Prescott Co. management has committed to a plan to dispose of a group of assets associated with the manufacture of railroad cars. This group of assets qualifies as a component of an entity for financial reporting purposes. As of December 31, 2008, management has located a likely purchaser and is in negotiations to complete the sale. It's expected that the component will be sold in late 2009 for $5,900,000 and that the following costs will be incurred in conjunction with the sale:

| Brokers' fees | $360,000 |
| Legal fees | 246,000 |
| Closing costs | 67,000 |

The railroad manufacturing assets have an historical cost of $12,000,000 and accumulated depreciation of $5,500,000 computed using the straight-line method. These assets generated a net loss during 2008 of $475,000 on sales of $1,800,000 and are expected to generate a loss of $525,000 during 2009.

During 2008, Prescott had operating income, including the railroad component, of $7,400,000 and total productive assets, including the railroad component, of $94,500,000 (net of cumulative straight-line depreciation). Sales for the company as a whole for the year ended December 31, 2008 were $20,000,000.

**Required:**

1. Compute the carrying value at December 31, 2008 of the railroad assets held for sale. How are these assets reported on the December 31, 2008 balance sheet?

2. Prepare a partial income statement including the discontinued operations section for Prescott Co. for the year ended December 31, 2008. Ignore income taxes.

3. Ignoring income taxes, compute return on continuing operating assets and operating margin for Prescott Co. for 2008. Now, assuming that the provisions of *SFAS No. 144* did **not** apply to assets held for sale, compute ROA and operating margin for Prescott for 2008. Contrast the two sets of ratios and comment on your results.

4. How will the group of railroad assets be accounted for during 2009?

**Required:**

1. Contrast the economic sacrifice and expected benefit approaches to long-lived asset valuation.

2. GAAP requires firms to use historical cost (in most cases) to report the value of long-lived assets. As a statement reader, do you think that firms should be encouraged to voluntarily report their asset values under alternative valuation approaches? Why or why not?

3. As the manager of a publicly held company, what costs and benefits do you see associated with the voluntary disclosure of asset values using approaches other than historical cost?

# CASES

Target Corporation is a general merchandise retailer. Its Target and Supertarget stores are part of the upscale discount chain.

Wal-Mart Stores, Inc. operates retail stores in various retailing formats in all 50 states in the United States. The company's merchandising operations serve its customers primarily through the operation of three segments: the Wal-Mart stores segment includes its discount stores, Supercenters, and Neighborhood Markets in the United States; the Sam's Club segment includes the warehouse membership clubs in the United States; the international segment includes all of its operations in Argentina, Brazil, Canada, China, Japan, Germany, Korea, Mexico, Puerto Rico, and the United Kingdom.

**C10-1**

Target Corporation and Wal-Mart Stores: Identifying depreciation differences and performing financial statement analysis

Information taken from both firms' 2003 annual reports to shareholders follows.

## Target Corporation

### Property and Equipment

| ($ in millions) | February 1 2003 | February 2 2002 |
|---|---|---|
| Land | $ 3,236 | $ 2,833 |
| Buildings and improvements | 11,527 | 10,103 |
| Fixtures and equipment | 4,983 | 4,290 |
| Construction in progress | 1,190 | 1,216 |
| Accumulated depreciation | (5,629) | (4,909) |
| Property and equipment—net | $15,307 | $13,533 |

Property and equipment are recorded at cost, less accumulated depreciation. Depreciation is computed using the straight-line method over estimated useful lives. Accelerated depreciation methods are generally used for income tax purposes.

Estimated useful lives by major asset category are as follows:

| Asset | Life (in Years) |
|---|---|
| Buildings and improvements | 8–50 |
| Fixtures and equipment | 4–8 |
| Computer hardware and software | 4 |

### Selected Income Statement Information

| ($ in millions) | Years Ended | |
|---|---|---|
| | February 1 2003 | February 2 2002 |
| Depreciation and amortization | $1,212 | $1,079 |
| Earnings before income taxes and extraordinary charge | 2,676 | 2,207 |
| Net earnings | $1,654 | $1,368 |

## Wal-Mart Corporation

### Property and Equipment

| ($ in millions) | January 31 2003 | January 31 2002 |
|---|---|---|
| Land | $11,228 | $10,241 |
| Buildings and improvements | 33,750 | 28,527 |
| Fixtures and equipment | 15,946 | 14,135 |
| Transportation equipment | 1,313 | 1,089 |
| Property under capital lease | 4,814 | 4,626 |
| Less-accumulated depreciation and amortization: | | |
| Property owned | (13,537) | (11,436) |
| Property under capital leases | (1,610) | (1,432) |
| Total | $51,904 | $45,750 |

Depreciation and amortization for financial statement purposes are provided on the straight-line method over the estimated useful lives of the various assets. For income tax purposes, accelerated methods are used with recognition of deferred income taxes for the resulting temporary differences.

Estimated useful lives for financial statements purposes are as follows.

| Asset | Life (in Years) |
|---|---|
| Buildings and improvements | 5–50 |
| Fixtures and equipment | 5–12 |
| Transportation equipment | 2–5 |
| Internally developed software | 3 |

## Selected Income Statement Information

| ($ in millions) | January 31 2003 | January 31 2002 |
|---|---|---|
| Depreciation and amortization | $ 3,432 | $ 3,290 |
| Earnings before income taxes and minority interests | 12,719 | 10,751 |
| Net income | $ 8,039 | $ 6,671 |

**Required:**

Assume a 35% tax rate.

1. Estimate the average useful life of each firm's long-lived assets.

2. Calculate a revised estimate of Wal-Mart's 2003 depreciation expense using the estimated average useful life of Target's assets. Use this amount to recalculate Wal-Mart's 2003 income before taxes and net income.

3. Calculate a revised estimate of Target's 2003 depreciation expense using the estimated average useful life of Wal-Mart's assets. Use this amount to recalculate Target's 2003 income before taxes and net income.

4. Why might a financial analyst want to make the adjustments in requirements 2 and 3?

5. What factors will affect the reliability and accuracy of the adjustments performed in requirements 2 and 3?

---

Granite Construction is one of the largest heavy civil construction contractors in the United States. Granite operates nationwide, serving both public and private sector clients. Within the public sector, the company primarily concentrates on infrastructure projects, including the construction of roads, highways, bridges, dams, tunnels, canals, mass transit facilities, and airport infrastructure.

    The following information was taken from Granite's annual report to shareholders.

**C10-2**

Granite Construction: Analyzing financial statement effects of capitalized interest

## Granite Construction Incorporated

### Consolidated Statement of Income

| ($ in thousands) | Years Ended December 31, 2006 | 2005 | 2004 |
|---|---|---|---|
| Interest expense | $ 4,492 | $ 6,932 | $ 7,191 |
| Capitalized interest | (4,800) | (3,300) | (1,900) |
| Income before income taxes | 113,017 | 142,311 | 94,924 |
| Net income | $ 80,509 | $ 83,150 | $ 57,007 |

### Consolidated Statement of Cash Flows

| | | | |
|---|---|---|---|
| Cash paid during the year for interest | $ 5,009 | $ 6,801 | $ 7,000 |

**Required:**

Assume a 35% income tax rate.

1. What is the underlying rationale for the capitalization of interest?

2. Assume that none of the assets to which 2006 capitalized interest applies have been completed and placed into service. Calculate the firm's 2006 income before income taxes,

assuming that no interest was capitalized in 2006. What is the percentage change from the reported amount?

3. Starting with net income of $80,509 as reported in 2006, assume the same facts as in requirement 2 and recalculate Granite's *net* income.

4. Briefly discuss the impact of capitalized interest on a firm's future reported earnings.

---

**C10-3**

Microsoft Corporation: Capitalizing versus expensing R&D

mhhe.com/revsine4e

Microsoft Corporation develops, manufactures, licenses, and supports a wide range of software products for many computing devices. The company's software products include operating systems for servers, personal computers, and intelligent devices; server applications for distributed computing environments; information worker productivity applications; business solution applications; high-performance computing applications; and software development tools. Microsoft provides consulting and product support services and trains and certifies computer system integrators and developers. The company also sells the Xbox 360 video game console and games, PC games, and peripherals. Online offerings and information are delivered through Windows Live, Office Live, and MSN portals and channels. Microsoft also researches and develops advanced technologies for future software products.

Income statement and balance sheet information from Microsoft's recent annual reports to shareholders follows. Assume an income tax rate of 35%.

| Microsoft: Selected Financial Information | | | | | |
| --- | --- | --- | --- | --- | --- |
| (*$ in millions*) | **2002** | **2003** | **2004** | **2005** | **2006** |
| Sales | $28,365 | $32,187 | $36,835 | $39,788 | $44,282 |
| Net income (NOPAT) | 5,355 | 7,531 | 8,168 | 12,254 | 12,599 |
| Total assets | 67,646 | 81,732 | 92,389 | 70,815 | 69,597 |
| Total shareholders' equity | 52,180 | 64,912 | 74,825 | 48,115 | 40,104 |
| Research and development | 6,299 | 6,595 | 7,779 | 6,097 | 6,584 |

**Required:**

1. How does current GAAP require firms to account for their research and development expenditures?

2. Use the reported information to calculate Microsoft's net operating profit after taxes divided by sales margin (NOPAT), asset turnover (sales divided by average total assets), return on assets (NOPAT divided by average total assets), and return on shareholders' equity (NOPAT divided by average shareholders' equity) for 2004, 2005, and 2006.

3. Assume that Microsoft expects its research and development expenditures to benefit the current accounting period as well as the next two accounting periods. Briefly describe how Microsoft's 2004 income statement and balance sheet would be different if it had capitalized rather than expensed its research and development (R&D) expenditures.

4. Repeat requirement 2 after capitalizing R&D expenditures and amortizing them as described in requirement 3. As a statement reader, would you find the differences in the ratios in requirements 2 and 4 to be significant? Why?

---

**C10-4**

Dallas versus Houston: Performing financial analysis and fixed asset reporting

mhhe.com/revsine4e

Dallas Inc. began operations on January 1, 2008 when it purchased some long-lived assets at a cost of $120,000. The assets have a 12-year useful life and no salvage value; Dallas intends to use the straight-line depreciation method. Assume that the firm will generate net operating cash flows of $33,000 in 2008 and that its net operating cash flows will grow at an annual rate of 10%. Assume that Dallas does not intend to make any capital expenditures over the next five years.

Houston Inc. is a competitor of Dallas Inc. On January 1, 2008, the book value of Houston's assets is $120,000 (original cost of $240,000). Houston's assets, like those of Dallas, have a 12-year useful life, no salvage value, and are depreciated on a straight-line basis. However, they are 6 years old and are halfway through their useful life of 12 years. Houston's policy is to replace one-twelfth of its assets each year at the end of the assets' useful lives. Assume that Houston will generate net operating cash flows of $43,000 in 2008 and that the firm's net operating cash flows will increase at an annual rate of 10%. To keep pace with inflation, Houston's management will increase the capital expenditures of the firm by 10% per year. (*Note:* For simplicity, assume that prior to 2008, the replacement cost of Houston's assets remained constant.)

**Required:**

1. Prepare a schedule of Dallas Inc.'s net book value of assets, net operating cash flow, depreciation expense, income before tax, income taxes, net income, average asset age, and return on net assets (net income divided by beginning book value of net assets) for the 2008–2012 period. Assume an income tax rate of 34%.
2. Repeat requirement 1 for Houston Inc.
3. Compare the return on net assets of the firms over the 2008–2012 period.
4. Which firm's 2012 income is more sustainable? Why?

---

On the following page is information pertaining to the Property, plant, and equipment accounts of Intel Corporation. This information was taken from Intel's Year 2 10-K report. A 10-K is an annual report that firms must file with the SEC within 90 days of the end of their fiscal year. (All figures are in thousands.)

**C10-5**

Intel Corporation: Reporting long-lived assets

**Additional Information:**

All amounts under the heading Retirements and Sales are retirements.

**Required:**

1. Solve for the unknowns in Intel's Property, Plant, and Equipment and Accumulated Depreciation schedules for Year 2.
2. What was the total amount expended on the acquisition of new property, plant, and equipment in Year 2? Where would this amount appear in the financial statements?
3. What was the net gain (or net loss) reported in Year 2 on the retirement of property, plant, and equipment? Where would this amount appear in the financial statements?
4. Make all the journal entries related to the Property, plant, and equipment and Accumulated depreciation accounts for Year 2.
5. Prepare a schedule of the depreciation expense to be taken for financial reporting purposes on the new machinery and equipment acquired in Year 2. Prepare separate schedules assuming straight-line, sum-of-the-years' digits, and double-declining balance. Assume a zero salvage value for all assets and a three-year useful life; also assume that Intel takes a full year of depreciation in the year an asset is purchased.
6. Assume that one of Intel's long-term debt contracts requires Intel to maintain a minimum interest coverage ratio of 5.0. If Intel's interest coverage ratio falls below 5.0, the lenders have the option to require immediate payment of their debt or renegotiate the interest rate. Assume that Intel's interest coverage ratio at the end of Year 1 was 4.9. Briefly describe how the restriction on the firm's interest coverage ratio could affect management's choice of depreciation policy for all or some of the new long-term assets acquired in Year 2.
7. What other settings in which management may be tempted to use depreciation policy strategically to influence the numbers reported in the financial statements can you identify?

8. Identify other items in the financial statements (in addition to depreciation expense) that management is capable of "managing." Are some easier for outside parties to observe?

9. Several years ago, the SEC decided to stop requiring firms to report the detailed information about the underlying changes in the long-term asset and accumulated depreciation accounts that appear in the following two schedules. As a financial analyst, do you approve or disapprove? Explain why.

## Intel Corporation

### Property, Plant and Equipment

| ($ in thousands) | Balance at Beginning of Year 2 | Additions at Cost | Retirements and Sales | Transfers, Reclassifications and Other In (Out) | Balance at End of Year 2 |
|---|---|---|---|---|---|
| Land and buildings | $   (a) | $  24,612 | $12,455 | $124,001 | $1,097,526 |
| Machinery and equipment | 1,764,623 | 596,068 | (b) | 30,322 | 2,288,200 |
| Construction in progress | 87,614 | (c) | 2,470 | (d) | 258,430 |

### Accumulated Depreciation, Property, Plant and Equipment

| ($ in thousands) | Balance at Beginning of Year 2 | Additions at Cost | Retirements and Sales | Transfers, Reclassifications and Other In (Out) | Balance at End of Year 2 |
|---|---|---|---|---|---|
| Buildings and improvements | $226,533 | $   (e) | $  1,812 | $(116) | $  283,954 |
| Machinery and equipment | (f) | 358,903 | 91,044 | 116 | 1,197,479 |

---

**C10-6**

National Coal Corporation: Analyzing financial statement effects of depreciation policy changes

National Coal Corporation mines, processes, and sells high-quality bituminous steam coal from mines located in Tennessee and southeastern Kentucky. The company owns the coal mineral rights to approximately 74,600 acres of land and leases the rights to approximately 40,900 additional acres. National Coal has expanded its operations considerably since commencing operations at a single surface mine in Tennessee in July 2003.

The following information is excerpted from National Coal Corporation's 2005 annual report to shareholders.

## National Coal Corporation

### Consolidated Statements of Operations

| | Year Ended December 31, | | Eleven Months Ended December 31, |
|---|---|---|---|
| | 2005 | 2004 | 2003 |
| Total revenues | $65,872,634 | $ 16,998,912 | $ 1,190,643 |
| Expenses: | | | |
| Cost of sales | 51,115,116 | 16,322,632 | 1,737,937 |
| Depreciation, depletion, and amortization | 10,107,723 | 2,473,369 | 617,155 |
| General and administrative | 7,213,346 | 5,242,437 | 1,871,414 |
| Total operating expenses | 68,436,185 | 24,038,438 | 4,226,506 |
| Operating loss | (2,563,551) | (7,039,526) | (3,035,863) |
| Total other income (expense) | (4,227,620) | (3,389,604) | (297,022) |
| Net (loss) | $(6,791,171) | $(10,429,130) | $(3,332,885) |

### Property, Plant, Equipment and Mine Development

Property and equipment are stated at cost. Maintenance and repairs that do not improve efficiency or extend economic life are expensed as incurred. Plant and equipment are depreciated using the straight-line method over the estimated useful lives of assets which generally range from seven to thirty years for building and plant and one to five years for equipment. On sale or retirement, asset cost and related accumulated depreciation are removed from the accounts and any related gain or loss is reflected in income.

The Company periodically reviews the estimated useful lives of its fixed assets. During the second quarter of 2005, this review indicated that the estimated useful lives for certain asset categories were generally determined to be less than those employed in calculating depreciation expense. As a result, the Company revised the estimated useful lives of mining equipment as of the beginning of the second quarter.

### Depreciation, Depletion, Accretion and Amortization Expense

The increase in depreciation, depletion, accretion and amortization expense in the twelve-month period ended December 31, 2005 compared to the twelve-month period ended December 31, 2004 is primarily attributable to a 493.3% increase in depreciation. This change was due to the acquisition of $19.3 million of fixed assets, primarily mining equipment, and a change in the estimated useful lives of our mining equipment. On April 1, 2005, we changed our policy for the depreciable life of mining equipment to three to five years from seven years. Subsequently, most of our equipment was estimated to have a three-year useful life. This had the impact of increasing depreciation on mining equipment by approximately $3.6 million during 2005. This adjustment was treated as a change in accounting estimate and depreciation expense was adjusted on a prospective basis.

### Required:
1. Calculate the impact of the depreciation policy change on National Coal's 2005 net income (loss). Consider the effects of income taxes in your answer.
2. How will the change affect National Coal's reported earnings over the next few years?
3. How might a financial analyst determine whether the change National Coal made is reasonable in light of industry conditions?
4. How might firms use depreciation policy changes to manage their earnings? Is there anything to prevent rampant use of depreciation policy changes as a tool to manage reported earnings?
5. In light of contracting issues discussed in Chapter 7, speculate as to the possible reasons National Coal made the change in its depreciation policy.

**Remember to check the book's companion Web site for additional study material.**

# Financial Instruments as Liabilities | 11

## LEARNING OBJECTIVES

**After studying this chapter, you will understand:**

1. How to compute a bond's issue price from its effective yield to investors.

2. How to construct an amortization table for calculating bond interest expense and net carrying value.

3. Why and how bond interest expense and net carrying value change over time.

4. How and when floating-rate debt protects lenders.

5. How the fair value option in *SFAS No. 159* can reduce earnings volatility.

6. How debt extinguishment gains and losses arise, and what they mean.

7. How to find the future cash payments for a company's debt.

8. Why statement readers need to beware of off-balance-sheet financing and loss contingencies.

9. How futures, swaps, and options contracts are used to hedge financial risk.

10. When hedge accounting can be used, and how it reduces earnings volatility.

T

he Financial Accounting Standards Board (FASB) says:

> Liabilities are probable future sacrifices of economic benefits arising from present obligations of a particular entity to transfer assets or to provide services to other entities in the future as a result of past transactions or events.[1]

Simply, this means that a financial statement liability is

1. An existing obligation arising from past events, which calls for
2. Payment of cash or provision of goods and services (say, delivery of a product for which a deposit has already been received) to some other entity at some future date.

**Liabilities** help businesses conduct their affairs by permitting delay—delay in payment or performance. But because "time is money," interest is a common feature of delayed payment liabilities. **Interest** is the price charged for delaying payment.

Most liabilities are **monetary liabilities** because they are payable in a fixed future amount of cash. There are **nonmonetary liabilities** that are satisfied by the delivery of items other than cash, such as goods or services. An example of a nonmonetary liability is a product warranty. If the product fails during the warranty period, the warranty liability is satisfied by either repairing or replacing the product. The liability is paid by providing nonmonetary assets—labor and replacement parts from inventory or a new product—but not cash.

Conceptually, monetary liabilities should be shown in the financial statements at the *discounted present value* of the future cash outflows required to satisfy the obligation. This discounted present value approach allows interest to accumulate over time through accounting entries that assign interest expense—the cost of delay—to the time period(s) over which payment is delayed. In practice, this is what is done with long-term monetary liabilities.

However, **current liabilities**—obligations due within a year or within the company's operating cycle, whichever is longer—are rarely discounted. Current liabilities are rarely

---

[1] "Elements of Financial Statements," *Statement of Financial Accounting Concepts No. 6* (Stamford, CT: FASB, 1985), para. 35. In October 2000, the FASB proposed broadening this definition to include as liabilities certain obligations settled by the issuance of equity shares (see "Proposed Amendment to FASB Concepts Statement No. 6 to Revise the Definition of Liabilities," *Financial Accounting Series Exposure Draft* [Norwalk, CT: FASB, 2000]). Certain issues raised in the *Exposure Draft* were resolved in 2002 and are discussed later in the chapter. Other issues continue to be deliberated as part of the FASB's Liabilities and Equity Project. Among other things, the goal of this project is to provide improved guidance for determining when a financial instrument should be classified as a liability or as equity.

*Chapter*

**601**

## EXHIBIT 11.1 · Oracle Corporation

### Liabilities Section of Consolidated Balance Sheets

| ($ in millions) | 2007 | 2006 |
|---|---|---|
| Current liabilities: | | |
| Short-term borrowings and current portion of long-term debt | $1,358 | $ 159 |
| Accounts payable | 315 | 268 |
| Income taxes payable | 1,237 | 810 |
| Accrued compensation and related benefits | 1,349 | 1,172 |
| Accrued restructuring | 201 | 412 |
| Deferred revenues | 3,492 | 2,830 |
| Other current liabilities | 1,435 | 1,279 |
| Total current liabilities | $9,387 | $6,930 |
| Non-current liabilities: | | |
| Notes payable and long-term debt, net of current portion | 6,235 | 5,735 |
| Deferred tax liabilities | 1,121 | 564 |
| Accrued restructuring | 258 | 273 |
| Deferred revenues | 93 | 114 |
| Other long-term liabilities | 559 | 401 |
| Total non-current liabilities | $8,266 | $7,087 |

discounted because their short maturity makes immaterial the difference between the amount due at maturity and the present value of that maturity amount. So, current liabilities are shown at the undiscounted amount due.[2] This treatment of current liabilities departs from the conceptual "ideal" solely on pragmatic grounds—the dollar difference between maturity amount and present value amount is quite small.

***Noncurrent monetary liabilities are initially recorded at their present value when incurred.*** There are occasional exceptions, which we will discuss in Chapter 13, but the general rule is that noncurrent monetary liabilities are first recorded at their present value.

To help you visualize how these liability valuation concepts apply in practice, refer to Exhibit 11.1, which reproduces the liabilities section of Oracle Corporation's balance sheet. Oracle is one of the world's leading suppliers of software for information management.

Listed among the company's current liabilities you will find:

- Accounts payable that represent amounts owed to suppliers,

- Income taxes payable that represent amounts owed to state and federal income tax agencies, and

- Accrued restructuring costs that represent estimated future outlays from restructuring the business activities of Hyperion, a company recently acquired by Oracle.

Because these accounts are shown as current liabilities, you can be sure of two things;

1. The obligations are due within a year or within the company's operating cycle, whichever is longer—at Oracle, "current" means "due within one year."

2. These current liabilities are shown at the undiscounted amount due even though some may remain unpaid for a full year.

---

[2] An exception is the current portion of long-term debt.

Oracle's current liabilities also include Deferred revenues that arise when customers pay for the company's software upgrades or consulting services in advance of actual delivery. Because Oracle is obligated to provide software products or consulting services—but not cash—in the future, this account is a nonmonetary liability and the amount shown represents the cash payments received from these customers.

Accrued compensation and related benefits represents cash owed to the company's employees, and this monetary liability is shown at the undiscounted amount due.

Oracle's long-term debt is shown in two places on the balance sheet:

- The amount due within one year is listed among current liabilities as Short-term borrowings and current portion of long-term debt.

- Amounts due after one year are shown separately as Notes payable and long-term debt.

> The Deferred tax liabilities listed among noncurrent liabilities on Oracle's balance sheet are described in Chapter 13. Other long-term liabilities, which arise primarily from employee pension and health care benefits, are described in Chapter 14.

This classification helps analysts and investors spot any large debt payments that may come due next year—for Oracle, the amount of short-term borrowings and long-term debt due in 2008 (that is, the next year) is $1,358 million. Long-term debt is a noncurrent monetary liability and is shown at the discounted present value of the amount due.

## Debt or Equity?

Suppose a start-up Internet company, Yellowbird.com, buys $100,000 of computers from a manufacturer, say Dell Inc. Instead of paying cash, Yellowbird promises to pay Dell $100,000 worth of Yellowbird stock when the company goes public (in about six months). Yellowbird is using its stock as "currency" for the transaction because it lacks cash. Should the promised payment be classified as a liability or as equity on Yellowbird's books?

Financial instruments with characteristics of both liabilities and equity are not easily assigned to either balance sheet category. In this example, the financial instrument is Yellowbird's payment promise. The promise does indeed constitute an *existing obligation* (to pay Dell $100,000) *arising from past events*, and these two characteristics meet the definition of an accounting liability as described on page 601. However, cash is not the form of payment. Dell will instead receive shares of Yellowbird stock. This characteristic fails to meet the definition of an accounting liability and makes the transaction appear to be an equity investment by Dell. How then should Yellowbird classify its obligation to Dell?

Recent guidance from the FASB resolves the dilemma.[3] Notice that a fixed amount of value ($100,000), not a fixed number of Yellowbird shares, must be conveyed to Dell. The FASB says that this feature of the promise makes the relationship more like that of a debtor–creditor. Unlike an owner, Dell cannot benefit from increases or suffer from decreases in share value because Yellowbird is obligated to deliver stock worth exactly $100,000. So, Yellowbird must record the payment obligation as a $100,000 liability.

Here is another financial instrument with characteristics of both debt and equity. Wilbourne Corporation issues $250,000 of 10% preferred stock to investors who pay cash for the shares. The "10%" means that stockholders can expect to receive a preferred dividend payment of $25,000 (or 10% of the $250,000 issue price) each year. Under normal circumstances, Wilbourne classifies the financial instrument (preferred stock) as equity on its balance sheet. But

---

[3] "Accounting for Certain Financial Instruments with Characteristics of Both Liabilities and Equity," *Statement of Financial Accounting Standards (SFAS) No. 150* (Norwalk, CT: FASB, 2003).

suppose the preferred shares are issued with a **mandatory redemption** feature that requires Wilbourne to buy back the stock in five years for $250,000. This unconditional obligation to repurchase makes the instrument much more like debt than equity. Notice that the preferred stock cash flow stream is identical to that for a five-year loan of $250,000 with annual interest payments set at 10% of the loan balance. So, even though the instrument's legal form is preferred stock, *SFAS No. 150* says Wilbourne must classify the payment obligation as a liability.

Financial instruments with both liability and equity characteristics are common today, and new instruments are created every year. They pose significant challenges for accountants, who must determine the proper balance sheet classification for each instrument, and for analysts, who must unravel its implications for enterprise valuation and credit risk.

## BONDS PAYABLE

Firms issue bonds to raise cash. A **bond** is a financial instrument that represents a formal promise to repay both the amount borrowed as well as the interest on the amount borrowed. **Debentures,** the most common type of corporate bond, are backed only by the company's general credit. **Mortgage bonds** use real estate as collateral for repayment of the loan. **Serial bonds** require periodic payment of interest and a portion of the principal (for example, an equal amount each year to maturity). Despite these and other differences, the accounting for these debt instruments follows the general approach described here.

The precise terms of the borrowing are specified in the **bond indenture agreement**—the contract between the bond's issuer (that is, the borrower) and the bond's investors (lenders). In this section, we look at how companies account for this debt instrument and how to interpret debt disclosures in financial statements.

### Characteristics of Bond Cash Flows

Bond certificates are usually issued with a **principal amount** of $1,000. The principal amount—also called the **par value, maturity value,** and **face value**—represents the amount that will be repaid to the investor at the maturity date specified in the indenture agreement. The bond certificate also displays the **stated interest rate**—sometimes called the **coupon** or **nominal rate.**

*The annual cash interest payments on the bond are computed by multiplying the principal (face) amount by the stated interest rate.* A bond with $1,000 principal and a 9% per year stated interest rate will have annual cash interest payments of $90. Typically, the total annual cash interest is paid in installments, either quarterly or semiannually.

Investors must be careful to read the details of a bond's interest payment terms. For example, investors who put money into a bond that pays "9% interest annually" receive a single payment of $90 (per $1,000 of face value) each year. A bond that pays "9% interest semiannually" yields two payments of $45 each year (9%/2 = 4.5% each payment period). Although the total dollar interest payment is $90 per year in both cases, the semiannual bond is slightly more valuable because investors receive half of the cash earlier each year than in the case of the annual payment bond.

While the face value is typically $1,000 per bond, the price at which it is issued can be equal to or less or more than the face value.

- When the issue price exactly equals the face value, the bond is sold at **par.**
- If the issue price is less than face value, the bond is sold at a **discount.**
- If the issue price is more than the face value, the bond is sold at a **premium.**

Market conditions and the borrower's credit risk dictate the relationship between what investors are willing to pay—the issue price—and the bond's face value.

# Bonds Issued at Par

A bond's issue price determines its **effective yield**—or true rate of return. When the bond's issue price equals its par value, the effective yield to investors exactly equals the coupon (or stated) rate. Consider this example:

> On January 1, 2008, Huff Corporation issued $1,000,000 face value of 10% per year bonds at par—that is, Huff obtained $1,000,000 cash from investors and promised to make interest and principal payments in the future. Because the cash interest payments on the bonds always equal the stated interest rate (10%) times the bond principal amount ($1,000,000), cash interest will total $100,000 per year. The bonds mature in 10 years (on December 31, 2017), and interest is paid annually on December 31 of each year.

The accounting entry to record issuance of these bonds on Huff's books is:

| **DR** Cash | $1,000,000 | |
|---|---|---|
| **CR** Bonds payable | | $1,000,000 |

The bond is recorded at its issue price—the $1,000,000 cash Huff received.

When bonds are sold at par (or face value), their effective yield to the investor exactly equals the coupon interest rate, which is 10% in this example. To show that the effective yield equals 10% in this example, we list the cash payments and compute their present value as of the issue date—January 1, 2008—in Exhibit 11.2. The effective yield is precisely 10% because the present value of the 10 annual interest payments ($614,456) plus the present value of the principal repayment ($385,544) equals the issue proceeds received on January 1, 2008 ($1,000,000) when discounted at a 10% rate.

> The cash interest payments on the Huff bonds are an **annuity,** which means a series of payments in the same amount made at equally spaced time intervals. If the first payment is made at the start of Period 1, then it's an **annuity due.** Apartment leases often have this feature—the first month's payment is due when the lease is signed. The cash interest payments on Huff's bonds are an **ordinary annuity** (in arrears) because the first payment is due at the end of period 1 (December 31, 2008).

*For bonds issued at par, the coupon interest rate on the bond equals the effective yield earned by bond investors. Furthermore, recording the bonds at par on the issuer's books automatically records them at their discounted present value.*

| **EXHIBIT 11.2** | **Huff Corporation** |
|---|---|

**Demonstration That the Yield on Bonds Issued at Par Equals the Coupon Interest Rate (here 10%)**

| Date of Payment | Type of Payment | Amount of Payment | 10% Present Value Factor | Discounted Present Value |
|---|---|---|---|---|
| 12/31/08 | Interest | $ 100,000 | 0.90909 | $ 90,909 |
| 12/31/09 | Interest | 100,000 | 0.82645 | 82,645 |
| 12/31/10 | Interest | 100,000 | 0.75131 | 75,131 |
| 12/31/11 | Interest | 100,000 | 0.68301 | 68,301 |
| 12/31/12 | Interest | 100,000 | 0.62092 | 62,092 |
| 12/31/13 | Interest | 100,000 | 0.56447 | 56,447 |
| 12/31/14 | Interest | 100,000 | 0.51316 | 51,316 |
| 12/31/15 | Interest | 100,000 | 0.46651 | 46,651 |
| 12/31/16 | Interest | 100,000 | 0.42410 | 42,410 |
| 12/31/17 | Interest | 100,000 | 0.38554 | 38,554 |
| Total present value of interest payments | | | | $ 614,456 |
| 12/31/17 | Principal | $1,000,000 | 0.385544 | 385,544 |
| Total issue price on January 1, 2008 | | | | $1,000,000 |

In the example, the amount received for the bonds ($1,000,000) exactly equals the present value of the future debt-related cash outflows (interest and principal payments) discounted at the 10% effective yield on the bonds.

Subsequent accounting for bonds issued at par is straightforward. Let's say that Huff prepares monthly financial statements; the *monthly* journal entry to record interest expense and Huff's liability for unpaid ("accrued") interest is:

| | | |
|---|---|---|
| **DR** Interest expense ........................................... | $8,333.33 | |
| **CR** Accrued interest payable ............................. | | $8,333.33 |

This (rounded) amount represents $1/12$ of the $100,000 annual interest. At the end of the year, the accrued (unpaid) interest will be $100,000; upon Huff's payment of the interest, the entry is:

| | | |
|---|---|---|
| **DR** Accrued interest payable ................................. | $100,000.00 | |
| **CR** Cash ........................................... | | $100,000.00 |

## Bonds Issued at a Discount

Arranging for the sale of bonds can take considerable time. The terms of the indenture—the bond contract—must be drafted, the bond certificates themselves must be engraved and printed, and an investment banker must be found. Time is also consumed in waiting for the Securities and Exchange Commission (SEC) to review and accept the security-offering prospectus. Market interest rates may change during the time it takes to do this and before the bonds are ready to be issued.

> The issuing company seldom sells bonds directly to investors. Instead, the bonds are sold through a financial intermediary—an **investment bank.** In most cases, the investment bank purchases the bonds and resells them to institutional investors (for example, pension funds) at whatever price the market will bear. The investment bank's profit (or loss) is the difference between the price it pays to buy the bonds from the issuing company and the price at which it sells them to investors, plus any fees paid by the company.

Assume that the Huff bonds are printed during late 2007 and carry a 10% coupon interest rate. The coupon rate immediately establishes the yearly cash interest payout of $100,000 (10% multiplied by the $1,000,000 face amount of the bonds).

But let's say there's a sudden increase in the anticipated rate of inflation, causing investors to demand an 11% return on the Huff bonds as of the January 1, 2008 issue date. To provide the 11% return that investors now demand, Huff must sell the bonds at a *discount* relative to face value. Here's why. The annual cash interest and maturity payments are fixed by the indenture agreement at $100,000 and $1,000,000, respectively. If investors pay the full face amount ($1,000,000) for the bonds, they will just earn a 10% return on their investment. To attract investors who expect to earn an 11% return, Huff must be willing to issue the bonds at a price lower than the $1,000,000 face amount. How much lower than $1,000,000 must the issue price be? It must be reduced to a level that gives prospective investors exactly the 11% return they require. ***The bond's price is determined by discounting the contractual cash flows at 11%,*** as shown in Exhibit 11.3. Lowering the issue price gives investors the higher return they demand.

The price that yields the required 11% return, given the stipulated $100,000 annual contractual interest payments, is $941,108 (Exhibit 11.3). Investors seeking an 11% return will not be willing to pay more than $941,108 for 10-year bonds that have a $1,000,000 face value and a 10% coupon interest rate. Why? Because if they pay more than $941,108, they will earn less than 11% on the bond's fixed cash flow stream. And Huff will not be willing to issue the bonds for less than $941,108 because to do so would mean paying more than 11% to investors. Thus, market forces will set the issue price at $941,108.

## EXHIBIT 11.3      Huff Corporation

### Determining the Issue Price for 10% Coupon Bonds When the Market Rate Is 11%

| Date of Payment | Type of Payment | Amount of Payment | 11% Present Value Factor | Discounted Present Value |
|---|---|---|---|---|
| 12/31/08 | Interest | $ 100,000 | 0.90090 | $ 90,090 |
| 12/31/09 | Interest | 100,000 | 0.81162 | 81,162 |
| 12/31/10 | Interest | 100,000 | 0.73119 | 73,119 |
| 12/31/11 | Interest | 100,000 | 0.65873 | 65,873 |
| 12/31/12 | Interest | 100,000 | 0.59345 | 59,345 |
| 12/31/13 | Interest | 100,000 | 0.53464 | 53,464 |
| 12/31/14 | Interest | 100,000 | 0.48166 | 48,166 |
| 12/31/15 | Interest | 100,000 | 0.43393 | 43,393 |
| 12/31/16 | Interest | 100,000 | 0.39093 | 39,093 |
| 12/31/17 | Interest | 100,000 | 0.35218 | 35,218 |
| Total present value of interest payments | | | 5.88923 | $588,923 |
| 12/31/17 | Principal | $1,000,000 | 0.352185 | 352,185 |
| Total issue price on January 1, 2008 | | | | $941,108 |

Equivalently

| December 31 | 2007 | 2008 | 2009 | 2010 | 2011 | 2012 | 2013 | 2014 | 2015 | 2016 | 2017 |
|---|---|---|---|---|---|---|---|---|---|---|---|
| Cash interest payments | | $100k | $100k | $100k | $100k | $100k | $100k | $100k | $100k | $100k | $100k |
| Cash principal payment | | | | | | | | | | | $1 m |

Present value of single payment at 11%: $1 million × 0.352185 = $352,185

Present value of 10-period ordinary annuity at 11%: $100,000 × 5.88923 = $588,923

The accounting entry made on issuance of the 10% coupon bonds at a price that yields an 11% return to investors is:

| | | |
|---|---|---|
| **DR** | Cash .................................................... | $941,108 |
| **DR** | Bond discount ............................................ | 58,892 |
| | **CR**  Bonds payable—par..................................... | $1,000,000 |

The Bond discount is a **liability valuation account** that is deducted from the Bonds payable account for financial reporting purposes. The net balance sheet (or carrying) value of the bonds when they are issued will be $941,108 ($1,000,000 minus $58,892)—the amount of cash Huff received. This again illustrates the basic principle that newly issued bonds are recorded at the present value of the contractual cash outflows for interest and principal repayment—where *the discount rate is the effective yield on the bonds at the issuance date* (here 11%).

When bonds are not sold at par, the calculation of annual interest expense and the accounting entry that records that expense are slightly more complicated. Consider the nature of the bond discount of $58,892. The discount amount is the difference between the cash Huff received from investors and the amount Huff promised to repay them on December 31, 2017. This $58,892 is really just additional interest—over and above the contractual cash interest of $100,000 per year—that will be *earned* over the term of the loan, but it will not be *paid* until maturity. Cumulative interest expense over the 10 years will total $1,058,892—the coupon interest of $1,000,000 paid out over the life of the bond plus the issue discount of $58,892 paid at maturity.

**Cumulative interest expense** can also be thought of as follows. Investors will ultimately be paid total cash flows of $2,000,000 in principal plus cash interest; that is, $1,000,000 paid at maturity, and 10 annual payments of $100,000. Huff received only $941,108 when the bonds were issued. The difference ($2,000,000 − $941,108) is $1,058,892, which must be the cumulative total interest expense over the life of the bond.

**EXHIBIT 11.4** **Huff Corporation**

**Bond Discount Amortization Schedule**

| Year | (a)<br>Bond Net Carrying<br>Amount at<br>Start of Year | (b)<br>Interest<br>Expense<br>(Column [a] × 11%) | (c)<br>Bond Discount<br>Amortized<br>(Column [b] − $100,000) | (d)<br>Bond Discount<br>Balance<br>at End of Year | (e)<br>Bond Net Carrying Amount<br>at End of Year<br>(Column [a] + Column [c]) |
|---|---|---|---|---|---|
| 2008 | $941,108 | $ 103,522 | $ 3,522 | $55,370 | $ 944,630 |
| 2009 | 944,630 | 103,909 | 3,909 | 51,461 | 948,539 |
| 2010 | 948,539 | 104,339 | 4,339 | 47,122 | 952,878 |
| 2011 | 952,878 | 104,817 | 4,817 | 42,305 | 957,695 |
| 2012 | 957,695 | 105,346 | 5,346 | 36,959 | 963,041 |
| 2013 | 963,041 | 105,935 | 5,935 | 31,024 | 968,976 |
| 2014 | 968,976 | 106,587 | 6,587 | 24,437 | 975,563 |
| 2015 | 975,563 | 107,312 | 7,312 | 17,125 | 982,875 |
| 2016 | 982,875 | 108,116 | 8,116 | 9,009 | 990,991 |
| 2017 | 990,991 | 109,009 | 9,009 | — | $1,000,000 |
| | | $1,058,892 | $58,892 | | |

Amounts rounded to nearest dollar.

How should this "extra" interest of $58,892 be allocated across the 10 years? Generally accepted accounting principles (GAAP) recommend that the bond discount be allocated to interest expense on an **effective interest basis.** This requires the use of an amortization schedule, as shown in Exhibit 11.4. In Column (a), Huff received $941,108 on January 1, 2008 in exchange for issuing the bond certificates. Bondholders require an 11% return on the amount invested. Therefore, their interest income—and Huff's interest expense—in 2008 must be 11% of $941,108 or $103,522, as shown in Column (b). The difference between Huff's $103,522 interest expense and the cash interest of $100,000 is the portion of "extra" interest allocated to 2008. This "extra" interest reduces the bond discount amount. If interest is recorded annually, the 2008 entry is:

> But it's an unusual "recommendation" because GAAP allows other methods only if their results are not much different.

| | | |
|---|---|---|
| **DR** | Interest expense........................................... | $103,522 |
| **CR** | Accrued interest payable............................... | $100,000 |
| **CR** | Bond discount........................................... | 3,522 |

The process of "spreading" the discount on bonds to increase interest expense over the life of the bonds is called **discount amortization.** The yearly amortization amount is shown in Column (c) of Exhibit 11.4. After the amortization is recorded, the year-end balance in the bond discount account—shown in Column (d)—will be $55,370 (the original discount of $58,892 minus the 2008 amortization of $3,522). Notice that the smaller the balance in the Bond discount account, shown in Column (d), the higher the **net carrying value** of the bond liability in Column (e). The bond's balance sheet value increases as the discount is amortized.

The bond amortization schedule illustrates that annual interest expense, Column (b), always equals the effective interest rate (here 11%) multiplied by the start-of-the-year borrowing balance, Column (a). The difference between the accrual accounting interest expense, Column (b), and the $100,000 cash interest paid each year is the discount amortization, Column (c). This effective interest amortization process is represented in Exhibit 11.5.

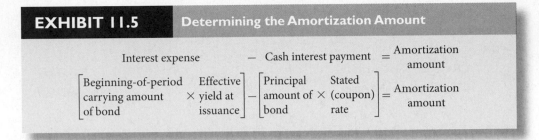

**EXHIBIT 11.5** — Determining the Amortization Amount

$$\text{Interest expense} \quad - \quad \text{Cash interest payment} \quad = \quad \text{Amortization amount}$$

$$\begin{bmatrix} \text{Beginning-of-period} & \text{Effective} \\ \text{carrying amount} & \times \text{ yield at} \\ \text{of bond} & \text{issuance} \end{bmatrix} - \begin{bmatrix} \text{Principal} & \text{Stated} \\ \text{amount of} \times \text{(coupon)} \\ \text{bond} & \text{rate} \end{bmatrix} = \begin{array}{c} \text{Amortization} \\ \text{amount} \end{array}$$

## Bonds Issued at a Premium

Recording bonds issued at a premium is similar to accounting for bonds issued at a discount. Assume that immediately after Huff Corporation bonds were printed late in 2007, interest rates *fell* to 9%. If these newly issued bonds were sold at par, Huff would be paying investors 10%—the coupon interest rate as printed. But why should Huff pay 10% when investors are willing to accept 9% interest? Here's how Huff pays 9% instead of 10% despite the contractual 10% specified. Rather than selling the bonds at par, Huff will issue the bonds at a *premium*—that is, at an amount sufficiently higher than the $1,000,000 face value so that investors will receive only a 9% return. The exact amount is determined, as in the previous discount example, by taking the bond-related cash flows and discounting them at the effective yield rate (here 9%), as shown in Exhibit 11.6.

The bonds would be issued for $1,064,177—the present value of the contractual principal and interest payments at a discount rate of 9% as shown in Exhibit 11.6. Buying the bonds at this price will give investors a 9% effective yield.

**EXHIBIT 11.6** — Huff Corporation

### Determining the Issue Price for 10% Coupon Bonds When the Market Rate Is 9%

| Date of Payment | Type of Payment | Amount of Payment | 9% Present Value Factor | Discounted Present Value |
|---|---|---|---|---|
| 12/31/08 | Interest | $ 100,000 | 0.91743 | $ 91,743 |
| 12/31/09 | Interest | 100,000 | 0.84168 | 84,168 |
| 12/31/10 | Interest | 100,000 | 0.77218 | 77,218 |
| 12/31/11 | Interest | 100,000 | 0.70843 | 70,843 |
| 12/31/12 | Interest | 100,000 | 0.64993 | 64,993 |
| 12/31/13 | Interest | 100,000 | 0.59627 | 59,627 |
| 12/31/14 | Interest | 100,000 | 0.54703 | 54,703 |
| 12/31/15 | Interest | 100,000 | 0.50187 | 50,187 |
| 12/31/16 | Interest | 100,000 | 0.46043 | 46,043 |
| 12/31/17 | Interest | 100,000 | 0.42241 | 42,241 |
| Total present value of interest payments | | | 6.41766 | $ 641,766 |
| 12/31/17 | Principal | $1,000,000 | 0.422411 | 422,411 |
| Total issue price on January 1, 2008 | | | | $1,064,177 |

Equivalently

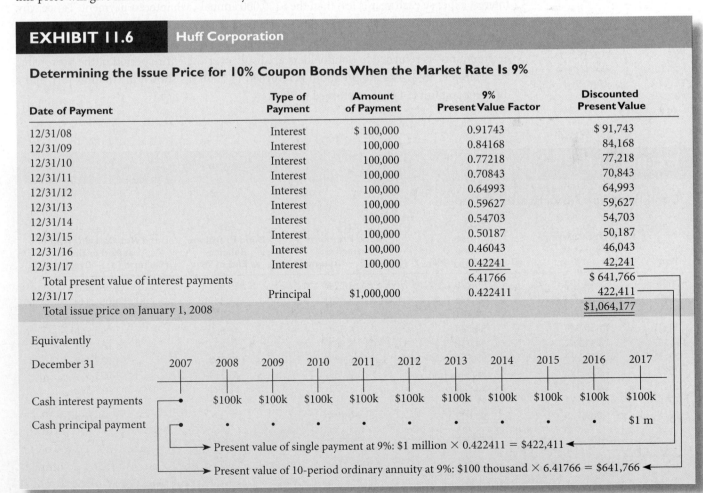

| December 31 | 2007 | 2008 | 2009 | 2010 | 2011 | 2012 | 2013 | 2014 | 2015 | 2016 | 2017 |
|---|---|---|---|---|---|---|---|---|---|---|---|
| Cash interest payments | | $100k | $100k | $100k | $100k | $100k | $100k | $100k | $100k | $100k | $100k |
| Cash principal payment | | | | | | | | | | | $1 m |

Present value of single payment at 9%: $1 million × 0.422411 = $422,411

Present value of 10-period ordinary annuity at 9%: $100 thousand × 6.41766 = $641,766

The entry to record the bond issuance is:

| | | | |
|---|---|---|---|
| **DR** | Cash ................................................. | $1,064,177 | |
| | **CR** Bond premium....................................... | | $ 64,177 |
| | **CR** Bonds payable—par ................................ | | 1,000,000 |

The Bond premium (like the Bond discount) is also a liability valuation account; the premium balance, $64,177 in this example, is added to the Bonds payable account to increase the balance sheet carrying value of the bonds. The Huff bonds will initially have a carrying value of $1,064,177. **When bonds are sold at a premium, interest expense will always be less than the cash interest payment.** The extra cash paid represents the amount of the premium being returned to bondholders. Exhibit 11.7 shows the amortization schedule. For example, the 2008 interest expense entry shows interest expense (from Column [b]) equal to $95,776, or the $100,000 cash interest payment minus the $4,224 premium amortization (from Column [c])— that is:

| | | | |
|---|---|---|---|
| **DR** | Interest expense ............................................. | $95,776 | |
| **DR** | Bond premium ............................................. | 4,224 | |
| | **CR** Cash ................................................. | | $100,000 |

Interest expense each year is less than the $100,000 annual cash interest payment. To see why, notice that Huff initially received more cash than it promised to pay back at the end of 10 years—that is, Huff received $1,064,177 but agreed to pay back $1,000,000. The difference— or premium—is returned to bondholders gradually over the entire period of the borrowing. For example, $4,224 of the premium is returned in 2008 (as shown in Column [c]), and a different amount ($4,604) is returned in 2009.

| EXHIBIT 11.7 | Huff Corporation |
|---|---|

**Bond Premium Amortization Schedule**

| Year | (a) Bond Net Carrying Amount at Start of Year | (b) Interest Expense (Column [a] × 9%) | (c) Bond Premium Amortized ($100,000 − Column [b]) | (d) Bond Premium Balance at End of Year | (e) Bond Net Carrying Amount at End of Year (Column [a] − Column [c]) |
|---|---|---|---|---|---|
| 2008 | $1,064,177 | $ 95,776 | $ 4,224 | $59,953 | $1,059,953 |
| 2009 | 1,059,953 | 95,396 | 4,604 | 55,349 | 1,055,349 |
| 2010 | 1,055,349 | 94,981 | 5,019 | 50,330 | 1,050,330 |
| 2011 | 1,050,330 | 94,530 | 5,470 | 44,860 | 1,044,860 |
| 2012 | 1,044,860 | 94,037 | 5,963 | 38,897 | 1,038,897 |
| 2013 | 1,038,897 | 93,501 | 6,499 | 32,398 | 1,032,398 |
| 2014 | 1,032,398 | 92,916 | 7,084 | 25,314 | 1,025,314 |
| 2015 | 1,025,314 | 92,278 | 7,722 | 17,592 | 1,017,592 |
| 2016 | 1,017,592 | 91,583 | 8,417 | 9,175 | 1,009,175 |
| 2017 | 1,009,175 | 90,825 | 9,175 | — | 1,000,000 |
| | | $935,823 | $64,177 | | |

Amounts rounded to nearest dollar.

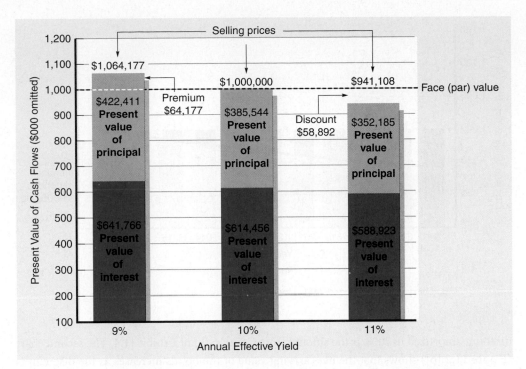

**Figure 11.1**

SELLING PRICES OF 10% COUPON BONDS AT DIFFERENT MARKET (EFFECTIVE) YIELDS

## Graphic Look at Bonds

The bar graphs in Figure 11.1 depict the components of issue price for Huff bonds when the interest rate is 10% (from Exhibit 11.2), 11% (from Exhibit 11.3), and 9% (from Exhibit 11.6). These bar graphs illustrate that *the issue price is determined by discounting the contractual principal and interest flows at the market yield rate.*

Figure 11.2 is based on the amortization schedule numbers from Exhibit 11.4, where the Huff bonds sold at a discount because the market interest rate was 11%. Figure 11.2(a) shows the interest expense and cash interest payments for each year of the term of the bond, and the difference between the two amounts is the discount amortization. For example, $3,522, the

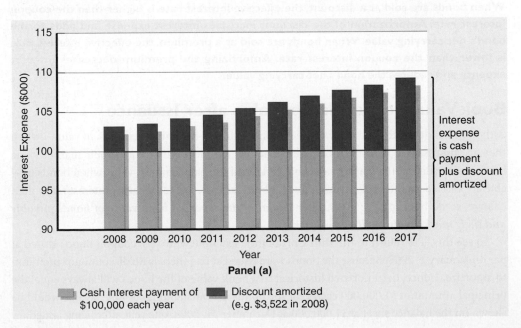

**Figure 11.2(a)**

CASH INTEREST PAYMENT AND INTEREST EXPENSE

Market yield 11%

### Figure 11.2(b)

CARRYING VALUE FOR
10% BONDS SOLD AT
DISCOUNT

Market yield 11%

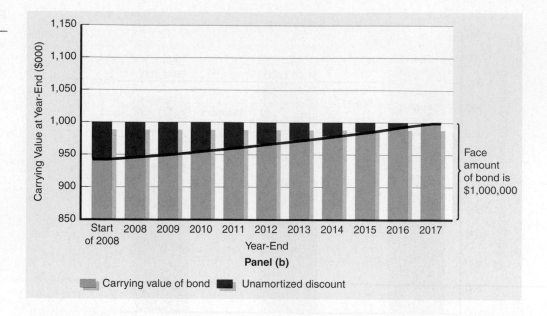

**Panel (b)**

Carrying value of bond    Unamortized discount

discount amortized in 2008, is the amount from Column (c) of Exhibit 11.4. The second chart (Figure 11.2 [b]) shows that the net carrying value of the bonds increases as the discount is amortized each year.

Figure 11.3 depicts the bond sold at a premium due to a 9% market interest rate. Panel (a) of Figure 11.3 shows that interest expense each year is less than the coupon cash payment of $100,000. Panel (b) shows that the carrying value of the bond falls as the premium is amortized.

---

## RECAP

**The cash interest and principal payments on a bond are set before the bond is issued, but market forces determine the issue price and thus the effective yield to investors. All bonds are first recorded on the borrower's books at the issue price. The issue price exactly equals the present value of the cash payment obligation (interest payments plus principal payment) discounted at the effective interest rate. The effective interest rate is then used to compute interest expense and the net carrying value of the bond in subsequent periods. When bonds are sold at a discount, the effective interest rate is higher than the coupon interest rate. Amortization of the discount increases interest expense and adds to the bond's net carrying value. When bonds are sold at a premium, the effective interest rate is lower than the coupon interest rate. Amortizing the premium decreases interest expense and reduces the bond's net carrying value.**

## Book Value versus Market Value after Issuance

Although bonds payable are shown at their market value—meaning their present value—when they are first issued, their balance sheet value will not necessarily equal their market value later. After issuance, the market value may not equal the balance sheet value when bonds payable are carried on the books at **amortized historical cost**. Because market interest rates often change, so do bond prices. *Thus, after issuance, the reported book value of bonds payable and their market value will likely differ.*

To see this, let's return to the Huff Corporation example with 10% coupon bonds issued at par on January 1, 2008. Because the bonds were issued at par, there is no discount nor premium to amortize. Hence, the amortized historical cost book value of the bonds will always equal the principal amount of $1,000,000 each year the bonds are outstanding. Bonds payable would be shown on the balance sheet at $1,000,000 at December 31, 2008, one year after being issued.

> Market interest rates change up or down almost on a daily basis and, thus, so do bond prices. Changes in a company's credit risk also influence bond prices. These changes are less frequent but no less important.

## Figure 11.3

PANEL (a) CASH INTEREST PAYMENT AND INTEREST EXPENSE AND PANEL (b) CARRYING VALUE FOR 10% BONDS SOLD AT PREMIUM

Market yield 9%

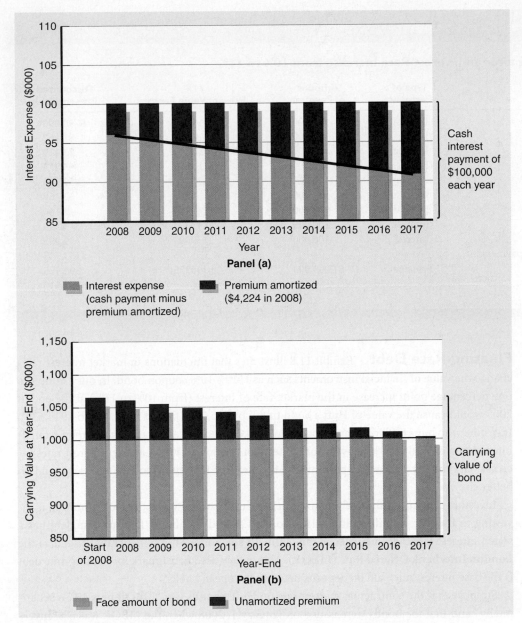

Now it's January 1, 2009, one year after the bonds were first issued, and the market interest rate suddenly jumps to 11%. Remember that prevailing interest rates last year "set" the price at which the bonds were originally issued. It's no different after the bonds have been issued—prevailing interest rates still set the market price. So, the market price of Huff bonds after interest rates jump on January 1, 2009 equals the remaining cash interest and principal payments discounted at the new 11% effective yield that investors now require. The market price on January 1, 2009 would be $944,630 (see Exhibit 11.8). However, under GAAP, the bond payable would still be shown on Huff's books at the original $1,000,000 amount. In general then, ***reported book values after issuance will not necessarily equal the market value of the bonds because market interest rates fluctuate over time.***[4]

---

[4] As we describe later in the chapter, firms now have the option to use fair value accounting rather than amortized historical cost accounting for bonds payable.

| EXHIBIT II.8 | Huff Corporation |
|---|---|

**Calculation of Bond Price after an Interest Rate Increase from 10% to 11%**

| Date of Payment | Type of Payment | Amount of Payment | 11% Present Value Factor | Discounted Present Value |
|---|---|---|---|---|
| 12/31/09 | Interest | $ 100,000 | 0.90090 | $ 90,090 |
| 12/31/10 | Interest | 100,000 | 0.81162 | 81,162 |
| 12/31/11 | Interest | 100,000 | 0.73119 | 73,119 |
| 12/31/12 | Interest | 100,000 | 0.65873 | 65,873 |
| 12/31/13 | Interest | 100,000 | 0.59345 | 59,345 |
| 12/31/14 | Interest | 100,000 | 0.53464 | 53,464 |
| 12/31/15 | Interest | 100,000 | 0.48166 | 48,166 |
| 12/31/16 | Interest | 100,000 | 0.43393 | 43,393 |
| 12/31/17 | Interest | 100,000 | 0.39093 | 39,093 |
| Total present value of interest payments | | | 5.53705 | $553,705 |
| 12/31/17 | Principal | $1,000,000 | 0.390925 | 390,925 |
| Total market price on January 1, 2009 | | | | $944,630 |

**Floating-Rate Debt**   Exhibit 11.8 illustrates that fluctuations in market interest rates change the value of financial instruments such as Huff's 10% coupon bond. In our example, a one percentage point increase in the market rate of interest (from 10% to 11%) at the end of 2008 would cause the value of Huff's bond to fall by $55,370 (from $1,000,000 to $944,630). Investors who buy Huff bonds are exposed to market value losses because the coupon (stated) interest rate is fixed at 10% per year for the term of the bonds. When market interest rates increase, Huff bonds continue to pay only the fixed rate of 10% even though investors could do better elsewhere.

Investors can protect themselves from such losses in several ways; the most common is investing in **floating-rate debt.** In contrast to Huff's fixed-rate bond, floating-rate debt has a stated interest rate that fluctuates in tandem with some interest rate benchmark such as the **London Interbank Offered Rate (LIBOR).** This widely used benchmark for floating-rate debt is the base interest rate paid on deposits between European banks.

Suppose that the contractual interest rate on Huff's bonds was "LIBOR plus 4%, reset annually" and that the bonds were issued on January 1, 2008 when the LIBOR was 6%. Investors would receive a cash interest payment of $100,000 during 2008 because the contractual interest rate is 10% (LIBOR of 6% plus another 4%). If the LIBOR had increased to 7% by January 1, 2009, investors would receive a cash interest payment of $110,000 (or 11%) that year because of the annual "reset" provision. The new rate equals the LIBOR of 7% plus 4% by contract. The additional $10,000 cash payment, if maintained over the bond's life, would exactly offset in present value terms the $55,370 value decline ($1,000,000 − $944,630) we computed in Exhibit 11.8. *The market value of Huff's floating-rate debt would remain $1,000,000, and investors would be protected from losses such as those associated with Huff's fixed-rate debt.*

Floating-rate debt can also benefit the issuing company. If the LIBOR falls to 5%, Huff would be able to reduce its cash interest payments to $90,000 because the contractual interest rate would be reset to 9% (LIBOR of 5% plus another 4% by contract).

Investors benefit from floating-rate debt when market interest rates increase, and issuing corporations benefit when market rates fall. Floating-rate debt allows investors and issuing companies to share in the risks and rewards of changing market interest rates. Risk sharing lowers the company's overall borrowing costs, and this translates into floating-rate debt that has a lower (expected) interest rate than would be charged on comparable fixed-rate debt.

Because virtually all floating-rate debt is issued at par, the accounting entries required are simple. Interest expense and accrued interest payable are recorded using the contractual interest rate in effect during the period. Huff would make these entries if it had issued the "LIBOR plus 4%, reset annually" bonds on January 1, 2008:

| | | | | |
|---|---|---|---|---|
| 1/1/08: | **DR** | Cash | $1,000,000 | |
| | **CR** | Bonds payable | | $1,000,000 |
| 12/31/08: | **DR** | Interest expense | $100,000 | |
| | **CR** | Accrued interest payable | | $100,000 |
| | 2008 interest rate set at 10% (LIBOR of 6% plus 4%). | | | |
| 12/31/09: | **DR** | Interest expense | $110,000 | |
| | **CR** | Accrued interest payable | | $110,000 |
| | 2009 interest rate reset to 11% (LIBOR of 7% plus 4%). | | | |

The balance sheet would continue to show bonds payable at $1,000,000, which also equals the market value of the floating-rate debt.

## Extinguishment of Debt

Interest rates constantly adjust to changes in levels of economic activity and changes in expected inflation rates among many other factors. When interest rates change, the market price of fixed-rate debt changes but in the opposite direction—as interest rates rise, the market price of debt falls; as interest rates fall, the market price of debt rises. However, as you just saw, most GAAP accounting for debt is at the original transaction price using the original effective interest rate. Subsequent market price changes are not recorded on the financial statements. Because market price changes of debt are not recorded, the balance sheet value of debt and its market value will differ (nearly always—unless the firm elects the fair value option described later). This divergence creates no accounting gain or loss for debt that is not retired before maturity—remember that book value and debt market value are always equal on the maturity date.

> **Book value** equals **market value** on the maturity date because the principal payment is then due immediately and, consequently, is not discounted for time or risk.

> *However, when debt is retired before maturity, amortized historical cost book value and market value are not typically equal at the retirement date, generating an accounting gain or loss.*

To see this, let's go back to Huff's $1,000,000 of 10% fixed-rate debt. On January 1, 2009, immediately after interest rates jump to 11%, Huff repurchases the 10% coupon bonds issued one year earlier. At the repurchase date, the bonds' market value is $944,630, as in Exhibit 11.8. The book value is $1,000,000. The entry to record the repurchase (ignoring possible income taxes) is:

> When bonds are sold at a premium or discount, the initial book value equals the face value plus the premium or minus the discount. The premium or discount account must also be brought to zero when debt is retired if amortized historical cost accounting is used. Remember that interest expense and accrued interest payable may need to be brought up to date before recording the extinguishment itself.

| | | | |
|---|---|---|---|
| **DR** | Bonds payable | $1,000,000 | |
| **CR** | Cash | | $944,630 |
| **CR** | Gain on debt extinguishment | | 55,370 |

The accounting gain (or loss) at retirement—more commonly called **extinguishment**—is the difference between the cash paid to extinguish the debt and the debt's book value. Until recently, the FASB required companies to report any extinguishment gain or loss as an *extraordinary* item on the income statement,[5] but no longer. Now gains and losses from debt extinguishment are subject to the same criteria used to determine whether other gains and losses qualify for extraordinary item treatment.[6] From Chapter 2, remember that to qualify as an extraordinary item under GAAP, the event must be both *unusual* and *infrequent*. For many firms, debt extinguishment is neither unusual nor infrequent because early retirement is part of an ongoing interest rate risk management strategy.

One more thing! Where did Huff obtain the $944,630 cash needed to retire the old 10% fixed-rate bonds on January 1, 2009? The cash may have come from selling assets such as marketable securities, from operating cash flows, or a combination of the two, or Huff may have borrowed the money by issuing new nine-year, 10% fixed-rate bonds with a face value of $1,000,000. Per Exhibit 11.8, Huff would have received cash proceeds of $944,630 by issuing the new 10% bonds at a price that yields an 11% return to investors. The cash raised from selling the new bonds could then be used to retire the old 10% fixed-rate debt. The entries to record this two-step process for retiring the 10% bonds are:

| | | |
|---|---|---|
| **DR** Cash ........................................................... | $944,630 | |
|    **CR** Bonds Payable (new 10%) ............................ | | $944,630 |

To record the issuance of nine-year, 10% fixed-rate bonds with a face value of $1,000,000.

| | | |
|---|---|---|
| **DR** Bonds Payable (old 10%)................................. | $1,000,000 | |
|    **CR** Cash ............................................... | | $944,630 |
|    **CR** Gain on debt extinguishment ......................... | | 55,370 |

To record the retirement of the 10% fixed-rate bonds.

The two-step process removes a $1,000,000 liability from Huff's balance sheet but ads another $944,630 liability. Huff still reports a gain on debt retirement even though the company just replaced one debt instrument (the old 10% bonds) with another debt instrument (the new 10% bonds) of equal market value and the contractual cash flows for both bonds are the same.

## Fair Value Option

During 2007 and 2008, some firms had a rare opportunity to recognize as profit the falling value of their own debt without going through the effort and expense of an actual debt retirement. The reason why is that the new *SFAS No. 159* allows firms to elect the **fair value option** for debt.[7]

The fair value accounting option works this way. Suppose that Huff Corporation issued $1,000,000 of bonds at par several years ago, say in 2004. By December 2007, the bonds had fallen in value to $950,000 because market interest rates had increased, Huff's creditworthiness had deteriorated, or both. Yet the bonds are carried on the balance sheet at $1,000,000 amortized historical cost. Under *SFAS No. 159*, Huff can elect in 2007 to use fair value rather than amortized historical cost as this liability's carrying value. Doing so would reduce the

---

[5] "Reporting Gains and Losses from Extinguishment of Debt," *SFAS No. 4* (Stamford, CT: FASB, 1975).

[6] "Recision of FASB Statements No. 4, 44, and 64, Amendment of FASB Statement No. 13, and Technical Corrections," *SFAS No. 145* (Norwalk, CT: FASB, 2002).

[7] "The Fair Value Option for Financial Assets and Financial Liabilities, Including an Amendment of FASB Statement 115," *SFAS No. 159* (Norwalk, CT: FASB, 2007). *SFAS No. 159* is effective for fiscal years beginning after November 15, 2007. Early adoption is permitted as of the beginning of the previous fiscal year provided that the company also elects to apply the provisions of "Fair Value Measurements," *SFAS No. 157* (Norwalk, CT: FASB 2007), described in Chapter 6.

reported book value of Huff's balance sheet liability by $50,000, the difference between the bonds' fair value ($950,000) and this original carrying value ($1,000,000). The $50,000 difference also appears on the 2007 income statement as a gain that boosts reported profits.

Is this 2007 profit boost real or just illusory? Suppose that Huff doesn't plan to retire the bonds until they mature in 2013—10 years after they were first issued. As you already know from our previous discussion, the bonds will have a fair value of $1,000,000 at maturity. This means that any profit boost from temporary value declines in the early years will be offset by losses in later years when bond value recovers. In other words, Huff's $50,000 gain in 2007 is an illusion because fair value losses of $50,000 will eventually be booked in later periods as the bonds approach maturity.

> What if the bonds had gained in value? In that case, fair value option election would trigger an increase to Huff's reported balance sheet liabilities and an income statement loss.

This feature of *SFAS No. 159*—that firms can record a profit when their own liabilities fall in value—is controversial. Critics claim it opens a new door for firms to dress up their balance sheets and massage earnings. Proponents, on the other hand, say that *SFAS No. 159* eliminates accounting-induced volatility and improves financial statement transparency. Before we evaluate these opposing viewpoints, let's take a closer look at the *SFAS No. 159* guidelines.

### SFAS No. 159 Guidelines

Under *SFAS No. 159*, firms may choose to measure eligible financial instruments at fair value rather than historical cost. This fair value option is available for most basic *financial assets*—accounts and notes receivable, investments in debt and equity securities—as well as most *financial liabilities* including accounts and notes payable plus long-term debt such as bonds payable.[8] In addition, firms may elect to use the fair value option on equity method investments (discussed in Chapter 16), debt and equity investments not traded in organized markets, and certain other obligations.

Firms may elect the fair value option for a single eligible instrument without electing it for other identical instruments even if the instruments are part of a single transaction. For example, suppose that Bluff, Inc. purchases for investment purposes 1,000 bonds issued by Apex Corp. Bluff may elect the fair value option for 500 bonds and not elect it for the other 500 bonds because each individual bond is considered the minimum denomination of that security. However, a financial instrument that is legally a single contract (e.g., one share of Berkshire Hathaway stock that trades at $140,900 as this book goes to press) may not be separated into parts.

When must firms elect the fair value option? For existing financial instruments, its choice is made when *SFAS No. 159* is first adopted in either 2007 or 2008. After adoption, the election is made when the new financial asset or liability is first recognized on the company's books or later when some event (e.g., a business acquisition) triggers a new basis of accounting for that instrument. Once the choice has been made, it is irrevocable. If a firm elects the fair value option for a particular financial instrument, it must continue to use fair value measurement for that instrument until the asset is sold or liability extinguished. Similarly, once a firm elects to forgo the fair value option for an instrument, it may not later use fair value measurement on that specific instrument (unless a triggering event occurs). Special financial statement disclosures are required so that investors and analysts can understand:

- Management's rationale for electing the fair value option.
- The impact of changes in fair values on earnings for the period.
- The difference between fair values and contractual cash flows for certain items.

---

[8] There are exceptions. The fair value option is not available for leasing assets and liabilities (Chapter 12), deferred income tax assets and liabilities (Chapter 13), pension assets and liabilities (Chapter 14), and items eliminated upon consolidation (Chapter 16). Nor does *SFAS No. 159* apply to nonfinancial assets and liabilities such as inventory; property, plant, and equipment; intangible assets; warranty service obligations; and deferred revenues.

## How the Fair Value Option Mutes Earnings Volatility

The chief benefit of *SFAS No. 159* is that it reduces the volatility in reported earnings caused when certain financial instruments are measured using fair value while others are measured at cost. For some firms, this mismatch in measurement bases produces artificial earnings volatility. Before we illustrate how *SFAS No. 159* dampens this artificial volatility, let's take a closer look at fair value accounting for the financial assets purchased by Bluff Inc.

As you may recall, Bluff bought for investment purposes some bonds issued by Apex Corp. Suppose that the borrower (Apex) issued the bonds, and the investor (Bluff) purchased them on January 1, 2008. Assume further that the bonds have a $1 million face value, pay 10% interest annually, and mature in 10 years on December 31, 2017. If the effective yield on the bonds at issuance is also 10%, Bluff pays Apex $1,000,000 and records the January 1, 2008 investment at cost:

> There are other benefits. *SFAS No. 159* reduces the need for companies to comply with the complex and voluminous rules for hedge accounting rules described later in this chapter. It also contributes to the convergence of U.S. GAAP with international financial reporting standards by providing a fair value option that is similar, but not identical, to that found in *IAS No. 39*.[9]

| | | | |
|---|---|---|---|
| **DR** | Investment in Apex Bonds | $1,000,000 | |
| | **CR** Cash | | $1,000,000 |

Bluff elects to use *SFAS No. 159* fair value accounting for its Apex investment.

At year-end, the market interest rate suddenly jumps to 11%, and the fair value of Apex bonds falls to $944,630. (The details are in Exhibit 11.8 because the Apex bonds are identical to those issued by Huff Corporation in our earlier example.) Bluff has a $55,370 **unrealized holding loss** on the investment. This unrealized loss is the difference between the initial fair value ($1,000,000) of the bonds and their fair value ($944,630) as of December 31, 2008. Having opted for *SFAS No. 159* fair value accounting, Bluff must recognize the unrealized loss and reduce the carrying value of its Apex investment:

| | | | |
|---|---|---|---|
| **DR** | Unrealized holding loss on Apex bonds | $55,370 | |
| | **CR** Fair value adjustment—Apex bonds | | $55,370 |

The unrealized holding loss flows to the 2008 income statement. Bluff deducts the fair value adjustment (a credit amount) from the original $1,000,000 cost of the Apex bonds to arrive at the $944,630 fair value to be reported on the year-end balance sheet.

> If Bluff elects not to use the fair value option, it would record no unrealized holding loss in 2008, and the year-end carrying value of the Apex investment would remain at $1,000,000 (historical cost).

What if the investment's fair value changes again next year? In that case, Bluff would recognize an unrealized holding loss (if fair value declines in 2009) or gain (if fair value increases) equal to the fair value change that year. A corresponding dollar amount would be added to (if a loss) or subtracted from (if a gain) the Fair value adjustment account so that the year-end balance sheet would report Bluff's investment in Apex bonds at the new fair value.

Now that you understand how the *SFAS No. 159* fair value option works, let's see how it can reduce artificial earnings volatility. We need to make two important changes to our example. First, suppose that existing GAAP rules already require Bluff to use fair value accounting for its Apex investment. That would be the case if the investment qualifies for required fair value accounting under *SFAS No. 115* (described in Chapter 16).[10] Second, suppose that instead of using cash on hand, Bluff borrows the

---

[9] "Financial Instruments: Recognition and Measurement," *International Accounting Standards (IAS) No. 39* (London: International Accounting Standards Board (IASB), 1998) as later revised.

[10] "Accounting for Certain Investments in Debt and Equity Securities," *SFAS No. 115* (Norwalk, CT: FASB, 1993).

---

**EXHIBIT 11.9** | **Bluff Corporation**

### How *SFAS No. 159* Reduces Earnings Volatility

**Panel (a) Prior GAAP with the Fair Value Option Not Available**

January 1, 2008: To record Bluff's bond issuance and the purchase of Apex debt securities.

| | | | |
|---|---|---|---|
| **DR** | Cash ................................... | $1,000,000 | |
| | **CR** Bonds payable ...................... | | $1,000,000 |
| **DR** | Investment in Apex bonds ................ | $1,000,000 | |
| | **CR** Cash ............................. | | $1,000,000 |

December 31, 2008: To record the year-end fair value adjustment required by GAAP.

| | | | |
|---|---|---|---|
| **DR** | Unrealized holding loss—Apex investment ... | $ 55,370 | |
| | **CR** Fair value adjustment—Apex bonds .... | | $ 55,370 |

**Panel (b) *SFAS No. 159* and the Fair Value Option**

January 1, 2008: To record Bluff's bond issuance and the purchase of Apex debt securities. Bluff also elects to use the fair value option for bonds payable

| | | | |
|---|---|---|---|
| **DR** | Cash ................................... | $1,000,000 | |
| | **CR** Bonds payable ...................... | | $1,000,000 |
| **DR** | Investment in Apex bonds ................ | $1,000,000 | |
| | **CR** Cash ............................. | | $1,000,000 |

December 31, 2008: To record the year-end fair value adjustments required by GAAP.

| | | | |
|---|---|---|---|
| **DR** | Unrealized holding loss—Apex investment ... | $ 55,370 ◄ | |
| | **CR** Fair value adjustment—Apex bonds .... | | $ 55,370 |
| **DR** | Fair value adjustment—Bonds payable ....... | $ 55,370 | |
| | **CR** Unrealized holding gain—Bonds payable . | | $ 55,370 ◄ |

Gain offsets the loss.

---

money it needs to buy Apex bonds by issuing at par $1,000,000 of 10-year, 10% bonds on January 1, 2008. Exhibit 11.9 illustrates the journal entries needed to record the borrowing and subsequent purchase of Apex bonds.

When the market interest rate suddenly jumps to 11% at year-end, the fair value of the Apex investments falls to $944,630. So does the fair value of the bonds payable liability. As proponents of *SFAS No. 159* are quick to point out, one fair value change offsets the other in real terms. But this is not what happens under GAAP before *SFAS No. 159*! Without the fair value option, Bluff must recognize the unrealized holding loss on the Apex investment as required but not the offsetting unrealized gain from its own bonds payable. No gain is recognized because GAAP before *SFAS No. 159* does not allow fair value accounting for financial liabilities. Instead, bonds payable are carried on the books at amortized historical cost ($1,000,000 in this example). The resulting mismatch of measurement bases—fair value for the financial asset (Investment in Apex bonds) but amortized historical cost for the financial liability (Bonds payable)—induces artificial earnings volatility as shown in Panel (a) of Exhibit 11.9.

The fair value option of *SFAS No. 159* eliminates this artificial volatility. Panel (b) of Exhibit 11.9 illustrates how. In this case, Bluff elects to use fair value accounting for the bond liability and, therefore, must also record an unrealized holding gain at year-end. This gain just offsets the unrealized

> To see this economic offset, notice that Bluff could unwind the investment by selling Apex bonds for $944,630 and then using the cash to extinguish its own bonds payable. The resulting realized loss ($55,370) on the sale of the Apex investment would then be offset by a corresponding realized gain (also $55,370) on early debt retirement.

loss on the Apex investment. Earnings volatility is eliminated when fair value measurement is used for both the financial asset and its related financial liability.

### Opposing Views on the Fair Value Option

*SFAS No. 159* allows companies to adopt fair value measurement selectively so that they can report financial assets and financial liabilities that are related to one another using the same method. Previously, companies suffered accounting-induced earnings volatility because they were required to report these related financial assets and financial liabilities using different measurement methods. But *SFAS No. 159* does not limit the use of the fair value option to situations in which the financial assets and liabilities are related. For example, Bluff Corporation could elect the fair value option for its bonds payable liability—and boost 2008 earnings by $55,370—even though it uses the cash for general business purposes rather than to invest in Apex bonds. Critics assert that this creates the worrisome opportunity for companies to use *SFAS No. 159* to dress up their balance sheets and manage reported earnings.

It is easy to see why critics are concerned. Suppose that 2009 is an extremely difficult year for Bluff: Customers begin shopping elsewhere in large numbers, the company incurs a $200,000 operating loss, and its credit rating falls precipitously. The fair value of Bluff's debt goes down as well, say to $600,000, because creditors now fear that Bluff will be unable to make the bond interest and principal payments as required. Despite the company's obvious financial distress, Bluff would record a $344,630 ($944,630 − $600,000) unrealized holding gain that year and reduce its balance sheet debt by the same amount. *SFAS No. 159* thus transforms an otherwise disastrous year into a profitable one—the unrealized holding gain more than offsets the operating loss—and less debt is reported on the balance sheet. The financial statement effects are counterintuitive and misleading. The earnings boost is not sustainable, and Bluff remains contractually obligated to repay the full amount borrowed ($1,000,000 plus interest), not just debt carrying value ($600,000).

*SFAS No. 159* also requires analysts and investors to rethink how they evaluate a company's debt-to-equity ratio. Conventional wisdom holds that firms in financial distress have higher debt-to-equity ratios than do healthy firms (recall the discussion in Chapter 5). But fair value accounting for debt can produce the opposite result. Bluff Corporation's debt-to-equity ratio might actually decline rather than increase as the company slides into financial distress. Here is why. Under *SFAS No. 159*, Bluff's debt-to-equity ratio numerator (debt) is reduced by $344,630 and the denominator (equity) is increased by this same amount. The combined effect is a smaller, not larger, debt-to-equity ratio in 2009.

 **Analysis**

---

## RECAP

When interest rates change after a bond has been issued, the bond's reported book value and market value are no longer the same. That's because GAAP requires bonds to be carried on the issuer's books at amortized historical cost (unless the fair value option of *SFAS No. 159* has been chosen) using the effective yield to investors when the bonds were first issued. So, when interest rates have increased and bonds have been retired before maturity, market value will be less than book value, generating an accounting gain. If interest rates have fallen, market value would be lower than book value, resulting in an accounting loss. Gains and losses from early debt retirement are sometimes treated as extraordinary items on the income statement if they qualify as such under GAAP.

*SFAS No. 159* allows firms to use fair value accounting for debt rather than amortized historical cost. This fair value option can dampen artificial earnings volatility, but it may also open new doors for firms to dress up their balance sheets.

# MANAGERIAL INCENTIVES AND FINANCIAL REPORTING FOR DEBT

In Chapters 1 and 7, we explained that accounting numbers are widely used to enforce contracts. One example involves debt covenants, which could motivate managers to manipulate accounting numbers to evade contract restrictions. Critics suggest that GAAP accounting for long-term debt makes it possible to "manage" accounting numbers to achieve this evasion.

## Debt Carried at Amortized Historical Cost

Some analysts contend that reporting debt at amortized historical cost (the $1,000,000 bond shown on Huff Corporation's books)—rather than at current market value (or $944,630 in the Huff example)—makes it easier to manipulate accounting numbers. **Debt-for-debt swaps** and **debt-for-equity swaps** illustrate the types of transactions that may be driven more by the financial statement effects they elicit than by any underlying economic benefits. In a debt-for-debt swap, the company offers investors the opportunity to exchange existing (old) debt for new debt issued by the company. Debt-for-equity swaps give investors the opportunity to exchange old debt for the company's common stock.

This $982,146 market value corresponds exactly to the present value of the principal payment ($1,000,000/1.12 = $892,860 rounded) plus the present value of the final interest payment ($100,000/1.12 = $89,286 rounded), both discounted at the market rate of 12%.

To illustrate, suppose that Shifty Corporation has $1 million of outstanding 10% fixed-rate debt originally issued at par. This debt matures in exactly one year. Because the debt was sold at par, its book value is $1 million. Assume that the current market rate for bonds of similar risk is 12%, which means that Shifty's bonds have a market value of $982,146. Shifty offers bondholders the opportunity to swap their old 10% bonds for new 12% bonds that also mature in exactly one year. Just to keep things simple, let's assume that bondholders are willing to swap as long as they receive 12% bonds worth $982,146, or the market value of the old 10% bonds that will be given back to the company. If the market interest rate is 12%, the new 12% bonds will be issued at par, and the face value will be $982,146. This debt-for-debt swap is illustrated in Figure 11.4.

Bondholders will be presumably indifferent between the old 10% bonds and the new 12% bonds because the market values are identical. (To induce real-world bondholders to exchange

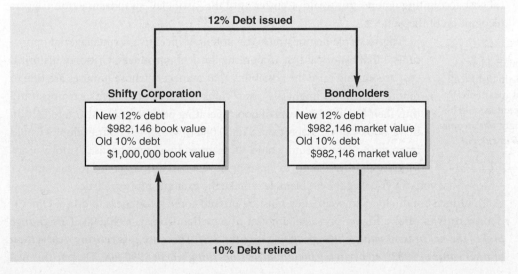

**Figure 11.4**

SHIFTY CORPORATION

Debt-for-Debt Swap

the 10% bonds for 12% bonds, some "sweetener"—a slightly higher interest rate or a slightly higher face value—would have to be included.) The market values are identical precisely because the present values of the two cash flow streams are identical when discounted at the prevailing 12% market interest rate:

| Old 10% Bonds at 12% Market Interest Rate | New 12% Bonds at 12% Market Interest Rate |
|---|---|
| **Principal Repayment** | **Principal Repayment** |
| $1,000,000 × 0.89286 = $892,860 | $ 982,146 × 0.89286 = $876,919* |
| **Interest Payment** | **Interest Payment** |
| $ 100,000 × 0.89286 = 89,286 | $ 117,854* × 0.89286 = 105,227* |
| $1,100,000 $982,146 | $1,100,000 $982,146 |
| **Interest Computation** | **Interest Computation** |
| $1,000,000 × 10% = $100,000 | $ 982,146 × 12% = $117,854* |

*Note:* The present value of $1 due in one year at 12% is 0.89286.

\* Rounded

As the computation reveals, even the *undiscounted* cash flows are identical because the principal payment plus interest payment is $1,100,000 in both cases. A debt-for-debt swap such as this has no real economic benefit to Shifty (there may be income tax effects). However, if the swap was consummated, the entry on Shifty's books would be:

| | | | |
|---|---|---|---|
| **DR** | Bonds payable (old 10%) | $1,000,000 | |
| | **CR** Bonds payable (new 12%) | | $982,146 |
| | **CR** Gain on debt extinguishment | | 17,854 |

Despite the absence of real economic substance, an accounting "gain" would still be reported. The gain really arose in prior periods as unanticipated inflation or other factors caused the market rate on the bonds to rise above the coupon interest rate. Because Shifty was paying interest at 10% when prevailing rates were higher, a year-by-year wealth transfer from the pockets of the original bondholders into the pockets of Shifty's shareholders was taking place. Historical cost accounting ignores this wealth transfer until the "artificial" swap transaction triggers recognition of the gain.

> This same financial statement result would occur if Shifty first issued the new 12% bonds for cash and then used the cash proceeds to retire old 10% bonds. (See the Huff Corporation two-step debt retirement on page 616.) Income tax considerations and transaction costs may favor a debt-for-debt swap rather than a two-step debt extinguishment.

> The wealth transfer gain from bondholders to stockholders is reflected obliquely in historical cost statements because historical cost interest expense is lower than interest expense would be at current market rates. Accordingly, *net income is higher than it would have been at current interest rates.*

This example demonstrates the potential incentive for managerial opportunism that historical cost accounting for debt introduces. Critics of historical cost accounting raise the possibility that managers whose bonuses are tied to reported earnings might use swap gains to boost their firm's earnings (and thus their bonuses) in years of poor operating performance. Also, a reduction in the book value of debt (from $1,000,000 to $982,146 in our example) would improve the debt-to-equity ratio—thus providing "opportunistic" motivations for companies in danger of violating covenant restrictions tied to this ratio.

Now that you can visualize the problem, let's make the example more realistic.

To induce bondholders to swap, they must be offered some sweeteners to do so. One inducement is to offer a higher principal amount of new bonds—say, $990,000. **This change makes the net present value of the swap negative for Shifty because it is retiring debt with a market value of $982,146 by giving bondholders something worth $990,000.** Despite this real economic loss to Shifty, if the swap went through on these altered terms, Shifty would still report an accounting *gain* of $10,000—the difference between the $1 million book value of the old bonds and the $990,000 market value of the new bonds. Extinguishment gains are generally taxable, and fees must be paid to investment bankers who orchestrate the transaction. These added costs further increase the potential disparity between the reported accounting gain and the economic effects of the swap.

On the other hand, sometimes real economic benefits are associated with debt-for-debt exchanges. In the real world, debt-for-debt swaps are rarely designed to be a "wash" in which debt instruments with identical maturities and market values are exchanged. Typical swaps are structured to extend debt maturity, postpone cash outflows by altering the mix of interest and principal payments, or take advantage of expiring operating loss carryforwards, thus making the swap tax free. On balance, therefore, it is entirely possible that some debt-for-debt exchanges generate real economic benefits even after factoring in transaction costs.

This is precisely what a study of debt swaps in the airline industry found. Analyzing the economic effects of swaps structured by American Airlines, Eastern Airlines, and TWA revealed economic benefits for each company in the range of $4.6 million to $5.0 million.[11] However, *the reported book gain (net of tax) for each airline was substantially higher*—for example, it was $24.65 million for Eastern, $47.1 million for TWA, and $48.4 million for American. Therefore, a large disparity exists between the reported historical cost book gains and the estimated real economic benefits. If the economic benefits of debt-for-debt exchanges are small on average, stock prices should change little when swaps are announced. In fact, that is the case.[12]

Differences between book profits and real profits have aroused curiosity about the motives underlying another—somewhat similar—debt extinguishment transaction: debt-for-equity swaps.

The conditions for a debt-for-equity swap exist when a company has low coupon interest rate (say, 4½%) debt outstanding and market rates are much higher (say, 12%). *The market value of that debt is much lower than its book value.* As Figure 11.5 shows, Company X retires its low coupon debt by issuing common stock of equal market value. The difference between the book value of the debt and the market value of the stock that is issued is recorded as an accounting gain. The convoluted nature of the transaction, as well as the investment bank's involvement, is required to make the gain on debt extinguishment tax free.

The accounting entry on the books of Company X is:

| | | |
|---|---|---|
| **DR** | Bonds payable ..................................... | $ Book value |
| **CR** | Common stock ............................... | $ Market value |
| **CR** | Gain on debt extinguishment .................. | $ Difference |

Debt book value is higher than the market value of stock issued because the debt has a low coupon interest rate but the market interest rate is high.

Debt-for-equity swaps alter the company's capital structure and undoubtedly precipitate real economic effects. One study found that debt-for-equity swaps were associated with a 9.9%

---

[11] J. R. Dietrich and J. W. Deitrick, "Bond Exchanges in the Airline Industry: Analyzing Public Disclosures," *The Accounting Review,* January 1985, pp. 109–26.

[12] See J. R. Dietrich, "Effects of Early Bond Refundings: An Empirical Investigation of Security Returns," *Journal of Accounting and Economics,* April 1984, pp. 67–96; and W. B. Johnson, "Debt Refunding and Shareholder Wealth: The Price Effects of Debt-for-Debt Exchange Offer Announcements," *The Financial Review,* February 1988, pp. 1–23.

## Figure 11.5

THE SEQUENCE OF EVENTS IN A DEBT-FOR-EQUITY SWAP

*Source:* From J. R. M. Hand, "Did Firms Undertake Debt–Equity Swaps for an Accounting Paper Profit or True Financial Gain?" *The Accounting Review,* October 1989, pp. 587–623. Reprinted with permission.

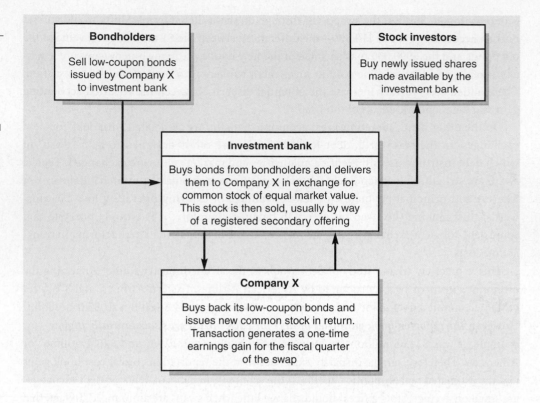

share price decline (on average) at the transaction's announcement.[13] That price decline is especially interesting because most debt-for-equity transactions result in extinguishment gains rather than losses. This prevalence of gains (and negative market reaction) raises the suspicion that earnings enhancement—rather than capital structure alternation—may be the motivation behind these transactions. Companies can use debt-for-equity swaps to smooth otherwise unexpected and transitory decreases in quarterly earnings per share or to relax otherwise binding covenant constraints.[14]

Debt-for-debt swaps, debt-for-equity swaps, and other similar transactions may serve valid economic purposes in certain instances. Nevertheless, some analysts still believe that the dominant motivation for these transactions is to increase reported income. But no matter what motivates management to swap old debt, the result is the same: an earnings boost that may not reflect economic reality but instead represents the difference between the book value and market value of the liabilities.

In response to this and other criticisms of accounting for liabilities, the FASB issued *SFAS No. 107,* which requires footnote disclosure of the market value of all financial instruments—both financial liabilities and assets.[15] However, the FASB response is unlikely to eliminate "accounting-driven" liability transactions. Because the *SFAS No. 107* market value disclosures appear in a footnote to the financial statements, the carrying amount of liabilities on the balance sheet itself is not altered. Consequently, the swap transactions described here still

---

[13] See R. Masulis, "The Impact of Capital Structure Changes on Firm Value: Some Estimates," *Journal of Finance,* March 1983, pp. 107–26. Interestingly, this same study found that share prices *increase* by 14% (on average) when firms announce their willingness to retire common stock in exchange for new debt.

[14] J. R. M. Hand, "Did Firms Undertake Debt–Equity Swaps for an Accounting Paper Profit or True Financial Gain?" *The Accounting Review,* October 1989, pp. 587–623.

[15] "Disclosures about Fair Value of Financial Instruments," *SFAS No. 107* (Norwalk, CT: FASB, 1991).

generate income statement gains and favorable financial ratio effects. Managers can still use these transactions as mechanisms for altering bonus payouts as well as for evading loan covenant restrictions or other contracting effects when the contracts are tied to the financial numbers reported in the body of the statement. Only if the contract ratios and income measures are computed using the fair value footnote data would *SFAS No. 107* be effective in reducing this avenue for managerial opportunism.

RECAP

**GAAP for long-term debt creates opportunities for managing reported earnings and balance sheet numbers using debt-for-debt or debt-for-equity swaps. So, statement readers must be alert to the possibility that reported swap gains (and losses) are just window dressing. How can you tell? Look behind the accounting numbers and see whether the swap offers real economic benefits.**

## IMPUTED INTEREST ON NOTES PAYABLE

Salton, Inc. designs and markets a variety of popular household appliances including the George Foreman Grill, the BreadMan bread machine, and Toastmaster toaster ovens. In the past, the company paid Foreman a royalty equal to 60% of the gross profit on sales of George Foreman Grills. (It's a hefty sum, but then Foreman—a past heavy-weight boxing champion—is probably a tough negotiator.) At the beginning of 2000, the company purchased the rights to use the George Foreman name in perpetuity in exchange for shares of Salton stock valued at $23.750 million and a $113.750 million note payable in five annual installments of $22.750 million each. Foreman received a check for the first installment the same day the deal was inked. Here is how Salton recorded its purchase of the George Foreman name (amounts in millions):

| | | | |
|---|---|---|---|
| **DR** | Intangible asset (George Foreman name) | $121.020 | |
| | **CR** Common stock | | $23.750 |
| | **CR** Note payable | | $97.270 |

To record the purchase of the rights to use the George Foreman name in perpetuity.

| | | | |
|---|---|---|---|
| **DR** | Note payable | $ 22.750 | |
| | **CR** Cash | | $22.750 |

To record the immediate payment to Mr. Foreman of the first installment on the note.

> Imputed interest on notes receivable is discussed in Chapter 8.

And here's what Salton had to say about the transaction in its 2000 financial statements: "The effect of the acquisition of the George Foreman name related to fiscal 2000 was the elimination of royalty payments partially offset by amortization of $8.1 million and **imputed interest** of $6.3 million."

Several aspects of this accounting treatment may at first seem perplexing. For example, why did Salton record the $113.750 million note payable at a value of only $97.270 million? What is "imputed interest," how is it calculated, and when is it recorded? The answers to these questions illustrate once again that noncurrent monetary liabilities are recorded initially at their present value. Salton amortizes the intangible asset over 15 years, so the $8.1 million of amortization is computed as $121.020/15 with slight rounding.

Let's start with the value assigned to the note itself and assume that both Salton and Foreman agree that the note is worth $97.270 million at the signing date. Why isn't the note worth the full $113.750 million? Because the installment payments are spread over five years, and the extra $16.480 million is interest that Foreman will receive as compensation for delayed payment.

What is the rate of interest on the note payable? To answer that question, we need to find an interest rate that makes the value of the note ($97.270 million) equal to the present value of the installment payments. The actual calculation can be cumbersome, although a financial calculator or computer spreadsheet can make the solution easy. The following diagram illustrates how to find a note's imputed rate of interest.

| | Payment in Millions at the Beginning of the Year | | | | | |
| | 2000 | 2001 | 2002 | 2003 | 2004 | Total payments |
|---|---|---|---|---|---|---|
| | $22.750 | $22.750 | $22.750 | $22.750 | $22.750 | $113.750 |
| Present value of 2001 payment | 20.968 ◄———— | 0.92166 | | | | |
| Present value of 2002 payment | 19.325 ◄———————— | | 0.84946 | | | |
| Present value of 2003 payment | 17.811 ◄———————————— | | | 0.78291 | | |
| Present value of 2004 payment | 16.416 ◄———————————————— | | | | 0.72157 = Present value factor for 4 years at 8.5% | |
| Present value of note | $97.270 | | | | | |
| Imputed rate of interest | 8.50% | | | | | |

Notice that all installment payments occur at the beginning of the year. As a result, the present value of the first $22.750 million installment payment is exactly $22.750 million. However, the present value of the second installment payment—which occurs at the beginning of 2001—is smaller than $22.750 million. How much smaller depends on the interest rate. Let's take a guess that the correct imputed interest rate is 8.50%. (In a moment, we will show you why 8.50% is a reasonable "guestimate" for the imputed interest rate.) In this case, the second installment payment needs to be discounted for one year at 8.50% and the discount factor is 0.92166 (or $1/[1 + 0.085]$). The present value of the 2001 payment is $20.968 million, which equals the $22.750 million cash payment multiplied by the 0.92166 discount factor. A similar process is used to compute the present value for each remaining installment payment. When all five present value amounts are summed, they total $97.270 million. And that's the key step: 8.50% is the imputed rate of interest on the note precisely because it is the interest rate that makes the value of the note ($97.270) equal to the present value of the installment payments (also $97.270 million).

Was our 8.50% interest rate estimate just a lucky guess? Not exactly. Salton's financial statement indicates that interest expense on the note payable was $6.3 million in 2000. Because interest is a charge for delayed payment and the first installment payment was made immediately, the $6.3 million in interest must represent a charge for the $74.520 million unpaid balance of the note ($74.520 = $97.270 initial note value − $22.750 first payment). We can now derive an estimate of the note's true imputed interest rate using the ratio of interest expense to the unpaid balance of the note. The result is ($6.3/$74.520) = 0.08454, or 8.45%. Why doesn't this process yield the correct 8.50% imputed interest rate? Because the $6.3 million interest expense figure Salton mentions is rounded slightly. The actual interest expense on the note that year was $6.3342 million (or $74.520 × 8.50%).

If Salton records interest expense only once a year, it makes the following entry at the end of 2000 (dollars in millions):

| **DR** | Interest Expense ........................................... | $6.3342 | |
|---|---|---|---|
| | **CR** Note payable ....................................... | | $6.3342 |

To record interest expense on the unpaid balance of the Foreman note payable.

The unpaid interest is added to the note payable balance. This means that the note payable, a noncurrent monetary liability, will be shown on the 2000 year-end balance sheet at an amount ($80.8542) that corresponds to its present value (using the 8.5% imputed interest rate) as of the balance sheet date. We leave the task of verifying this fact to you.

RECAP

**Noncurrent monetary liabilities are initially recorded at their present value when incurred. This is true even for installment notes that make no mention of an interest rate. In such cases, an interest rate must be imputed.**

# ANALYTICAL INSIGHTS: FUTURE CASH FLOW EFFECTS OF DEBT

Analysis

See Exhibit 11.10 for excerpts from Dentsply International's financial statement footnote for long-term debt. Dentsply develops, manufactures, and markets medical instruments and supplies for the dental market. This example illustrates the type of information about a company's long-term debt that is available in corporate annual reports.

| **EXHIBIT 11.10** | Dentsply International | | |
|---|---|---|---|
| **Long-Term Debt** | | | |
| ($ in millions) | | **2006** | **2005** |
| Multi-currency revolving credit agreement expiring May 2010 | | | |
|   U.S. dollar 50 million at 5.73% | | $ 50.000 | $ — |
|   Japanese yen 12.6 billion at 0.89% | | 105.417 | 106.359 |
|   Swiss francs 65 million at 2.29% | | 53.287 | — |
| Prudential private placement notes, Swiss franc denominated, 28.1 million (56.3 million at December 2005) at 4.56% and . . . | | 45.595 | 145.662 |
| Eurobonds, 350.0 million Euros at 5.75% matured December 2006 | | — | ① 419.348 |
| U.S. dollar commercial paper facility at 5.45% | | 55.000 | 6.700 |
| Euro multi-currency commercial paper facility, 38 million Euro at 3.71% | | 50.122 | — |
| Other borrowings, various currencies and rates | | 7.961 | 2.814 |
| | | $367.382 | $680.883 |
| Less: Current portion | | ③ 0.221 | 410.779 |
| | | $367.161 | $270.104 |

② The Company has a $500 million revolving credit agreement with participation from thirteen banks. The revolving credit agreements contain a number of covenants and two financial ratios which the Company is required to satisfy. The most restrictive of these covenants pertain to asset dispositions and prescribed ratios of indebtedness to total capital and operating income plus depreciation and amortization to interest expense. Any breach of any such covenant would result in a default . . . [and] permit the lenders to declare all borrowings . . . immediately due and payable. At December 31, 2006, the Company was in compliance with these covenants.

  At December 31, 2006, the Company had total unused lines of credit . . . of $212.5 million.

  ④ [T]he contractual maturity dates of the various long-term debt at December 31, 2006 (in thousands) are: 2007—$221; 2008—$1,527; 2009—$111; 2010—$364,922; 2011—$69; 2012 and beyond—$532. The individual borrowings under the revolving credit agreement are structured to mature on a quarterly basis but because the Company has the intent and ability to extend them until the expiration date of the agreement, these borrowings are considered contractually due in May 2010.

Among the company's long-term debt items, notice the roughly $420 million in Euro-bonds that matured in December 2006 and were retired (see ① in the table). Where did Dentsply get the cash needed to pay off this loan? By comparing the 2006 and 2005 amounts in the table for each major class of long-term debt, we can see that Dentsply tapped its multicurrency revolving credit line for more than $100 million in 2006 and raised another $100 million that year by issuing commercial paper. It is reasonable to presume that the cash raised from these new loans combined with cash on hand was used to retire the maturing Eurobonds.

Dentsply provides details about interest rates and maturity dates for each major class of long-term debt. However, the company provides only general information about the covenants contained in its various borrowing agreements (see the paragraph next to ②). This nondisclosure is typical and imposes a burden on the financial analyst who must search through the lending agreements themselves to discover covenant details.

Dentsply's footnote disclosure provides a wealth of information useful for determining the future cash flow implications of the company's long-term debt. For example, the table reveals current maturities (that is, the "current portion of long-term debt") of $221 thousand at the end of 2006 (see highlighted figure next to ③). This is the debt principal amount that Dentsply must repay in 2006.

Like all U.S. companies today, Dentsply is required to disclose scheduled debt repayments for each of the five years after the balance sheet date. From the paragraph adjacent to ④, we can see that these repayments are particularly large in 2010 ($364.922 million). Analysts studying the company will want to estimate whether Dentsply's operating cash flows that year will be sufficient when combined with cash on hand to meet this scheduled debt principal repayment. Any anticipated shortfall could necessitate asset sales or additional financing.

To ease analysts' concerns, Dentsply says that the 2010 repayment comes about because a large revolving credit agreement expires that year. Rather than pay out cash, Dentsply is likely to renew the agreement when it comes due.

Elsewhere in the annual report, we learn that Dentsply paid $11.2 million in interest during 2006. This amount represents interest Dentsply paid on the long-term debt shown in Exhibit 11.10 plus any short-term interest-bearing debt shown on the company's balance sheet. Dividing this cash interest payment by the average book value of outstanding long-term debt—($367.161 + $270.104)/2 = $318.632—plus average short-term debt from the balance sheet—($2.995 + $412.212)/2 = $207.604—not shown in Exhibit 11.10 suggests that the company's "cash" interest rate for 2006 was about 2.1%, or $11.2/($318.632 + $207.604). Using this rate as the basis for forecasting 2007 interest payments, we discover that Dentsply will spend about $7.8 million (2.1% × $370.156 million of interest-bearing debt outstanding—comprised of $367.161 million of long-term debt plus $2.995 million of short-term debt) for 2007 interest. This cash outflow is in addition to the $221,000 scheduled principal repayment for 2007. Cash flow forecasts of this type can be constructed for each year from 2007 through 2011.

Dentsply also tells us about the fair value of its long-term debt and other financial instruments, including financial assets. The fair value of Dentsply's debt roughly equals its balance sheet carrying value. Why? As the company points out, most of Dentsply's debt has floating (not fixed) interest rates that approximate current market rates. As we have already discussed, this loan feature insulates debt fair values from changes in market interest rates, and so it is not at all surprising to learn that debt fair value and carrying value are the same.

Dentsply does have fixed-rate notes whose fair value and carrying value are not the same amount. The reason is explained in the last sentence in Exhibit 11.11—market interest rates

| EXHIBIT 11.11 | Dentsply International |
| --- | --- |

**Financial Instruments**

The fair value of financial instruments is determined by reference to various market data and other valuation techniques as appropriate. The Company believes that the carrying amounts of cash and cash equivalents, short-term investments, accounts receivable (net of allowance for doubtful accounts), . . . accounts payable, . . . and notes payable approximate fair value due to the short-term nature of these instruments. The Company estimates the fair value of its long-term debt was $367.5 million versus its carrying value of $367.4 million as of December 31, 2006. The fair value approximated the carrying value since much of the Company's debt is variable rate and reflects current market rates. The Company has fixed rate Swiss franc denominated notes with estimated fair value that differ from their carrying values. . . . The fair values differ from the carrying value due to lower market interest rates at December 31, 2006 versus the rates at issuance of the [Swiss franc] notes.

have fallen since the notes were first issued. A market interest rate decline causes the fair value of fixed-rate debt to increase. So, now we know that Dentsply's long-term debt has a fair value ($367.5 million) that exceeds its carrying value ($367.4 million). This increased fair value is traceable to the fixed-rate notes.

Suppose instead that a company, say Brownlee Inc., tells us that the fair value of its long-term debt is less than the balance sheet carrying value of the debt. There are two reasons why this might happen:

- Brownlee is a worse credit risk today than it was several years ago when it first issued the debt. As a company's creditworthiness deteriorates, the fair value of its debt decreases even though the book value of the debt is unchanged.

- Interest rates have increased for reasons unrelated to the company itself (for example, higher expected inflation or a weakening economy). From our earlier discussion, you know that an increase in interest rates—whether due to company-specific factors or to macroeconomic forces—will cause the market value of fixed-rate debt to increase.

# INCENTIVES FOR OFF-BALANCE-SHEET LIABILITIES

In Chapters 1 and 7, we described business contracts linked to (among other things) the amount of liabilities on a company's balance sheet. Examples include loan covenants and bond indentures. These contracts usually contain terms and conditions designed to protect the lender against loss. The protection is in the form of contract terms (covenant triggers) tied to the borrower's debt-to-equity ratio, debt-to-tangible-asset ratio, or some other financial ratio that includes reported liabilities. Accounting-related covenants typically contain language such as "the debt-to-equity ratio may not exceed 1.7 in any quarter." The intent of these covenants is to provide an early warning signal regarding deteriorating creditworthiness. In principle, the early warning allows the lender to require repayment of the loan before the borrower's condition worsens further.

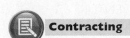 **Contracting**

Such loan contract terms create incentives for managers of borrowing companies to minimize *reported* financial statement liabilities. Reducing the total amount of reportable liabilities in the contractual ratio makes covenant violations less likely.

As will be explained in Chapter 16, **consolidation** essentially means that the separate financial statements of the parent and subsidiary are added together line-by-line to form a single combined ("consolidated") set of financial statements. For example, the consolidated balance sheet would report as Cash the sum of the parent's cash plus the subsidiary's cash. Similarly, total consolidated liabilities would consist of the sum of the parent's liabilities plus those of the subsidiary. Chapter 16 provides the details and describes the accounting rules for unconsolidated subsidiaries.

Consider one example of the way these incentives influence business behavior: **Unconsolidated subsidiaries** are sometimes established to finance specialized projects or **joint ventures.** Critics say these separately incorporated entities have sometimes been used to evade loan covenants linked to reported liabilities and to misrepresent he firm's total liabilities. This strategy exploits a loophole in the rules governing when subsidiaries need to be consolidated.

When one company owns *more* than 50% of the stock of another affiliated company, the owner (parent) is deemed to "control" the other company (subsidiary). The financial statements of subsidiaries that are under the control of a parent must be consolidated with these of the parent. But when one company owns 50% or *less* of another company's stock, consolidation is not required except under special circumstances described in Chapter 16. Instead, the owner's *net investment* in the subsidiary is reported as an asset in the owner's balance sheet using what is called the **equity method** of accounting.

The equity method is described in Chapter 16. Here's an example illustrating all you need to know about it now.

In real-world joint ventures, the debt is often guaranteed by the parent companies because the joint venture (for example, Gray Company) is usually thinly capitalized and lenders accordingly look to the parents (Blue Company and Black Company) for added assurance that the loan will be repaid.

Assume that Blue Company and Black Company both use an identically manufactured input, T-spanners, in their respective production processes. Manufacturing T-spanners requires a large investment in plant and equipment that must be financed by borrowing. Both Blue Company and Black Company wish to avoid adding more debt to their balance sheets, so they agree to form a separate jointly owned venture called Gray Company.

Each venture partner contributes $25 million cash to establish Gray Company and receives common stock representing a 50% ownership interest in it. A bank then loans Gray $300 million to purchase the plant and equipment needed to produce T-spanners. This loan is collateralized by Gray's factory and guaranteed by both Blue Company and Black Company. Immediately after these transactions take place, Gray Company's balance sheet would appear as shown in Figure 11.6.

The balance sheets of Blue Company and Black Company would each show that company's $25 million investment in the asset account Investment in joint venture. Under the equity method, this account balance would increase if further investments were made in the joint venture or if Gray earned a profit. Because Blue and Black own Gray equally, each would add 50% of Gray's profit to the balance in its Investment in joint venture account.

***The partners' balance sheets do not report any of the joint venture's $300 million bank loan!*** Neither Blue nor Black owns more than 50% of Gray, so neither needs to consolidate it.

## Figure 11.6

JOINT VENTURE
FINANCING

($ in millions)

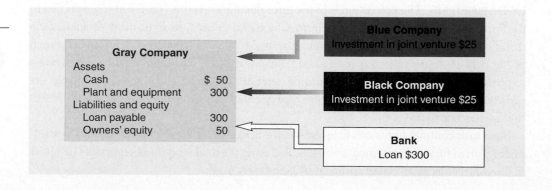

| Gray Company | |
|---|---|
| Assets | |
|   Cash | $ 50 |
|   Plant and equipment | 300 |
| Liabilities and equity | |
|   Loan payable | 300 |
|   Owners' equity | 50 |

**Blue Company**
Investment in joint venture $25

**Black Company**
Investment in joint venture $25

**Bank**
Loan $300

Consequently, the borrowing necessary to fund the venture appears on neither partner's financial statements under the equity method. The Investment in joint venture account on each company's books would continue to show $25 million, yet Blue and Black have effectively each borrowed $150 million "off balance sheet"![16] Proportionate consolidation, the benchmark accounting treatment under IFRS and required by Canadian GAAP, would solve this problem (see Chapter 18).

> The Investment in joint venture account is unchanged because each partner's investment in the net assets (that is, assets minus liabilities) of the joint venture is unchanged by the borrowing. Gray Company's assets increased by $300 million but so did liabilities. Consequently. Gray's *net* assets remained at $50 million after the borrowing.

So-called **special purpose entities** (SPEs) represent a variation of the simple joint venture arrangement between Blue Company and Black Company. One common type of SPE involves assets with more or less predictable cash flows such as credit card receivables. Without going into all of the details, suppose a retailer such as Sears needs to borrow money and wants to do so at the best available interest rate. Instead of obtaining a traditional bank loan, Sears decides to create an SPE and then transfers a portion of its customer credit card receivables to the new entity. The SPE next obtains a low-interest loan to be repaid from the future cash flows associated with the credit card receivables, sending the money to Sears as payment for the transferred receivables. Although the transaction may seem unduly complex, the SPE structure allows Sears to isolate assets with predictable cash flows (in this case, the credit card receivables) from its other assets with less predictable cash flows. Isolating the credit card receivables in this way reduces the lender's credit risk, which in turn reduces the interest rate that Sears must pay on the loan. SPEs of this type were often not required to be consolidated on the financial statements of the parent company (that is, Sears), so the loan was another example of "off-balance-sheet" debt.

Special purpose entities became notorious following the collapse of Enron. In November 2001, Enron announced that it would restate earnings for 1997 through 2001 downward by $1.2 billion because the company and its auditors had determined that three unconsolidated SPEs should have been consolidated. As part of the restatement, Enron increased its balance sheet debt by $628 million in 2000. Over the course of the next several months, investors and creditors learned that Enron's off-balance-sheet SPEs were used to hide the company's mounting losses and cash flow problems. Several former Enron senior officials were later charged with violating the antifraud provisions of the federal securities laws.

The FASB recently tightened the rules governing the consolidation of special purpose entities, which are now called **variable interest entities** (VIEs), in an effort to avoid future Enron debacles. Chapter 16 tells you more.

---

**The motivation for off-balance-sheet financing transactions is strong. Managers continue to develop innovative strategies to understate reported liabilities and to ensure that certain items remain "off the balance sheet." Financial analysts and auditors must remember the motivations behind off-balance-sheet financing, know how to identify peculiar and contorted borrowing arrangements, and adjust the reported financial statement numbers to better reflect economic reality.**

**RE**CAP

---

[16] Prior to the issuance of "Consolidation of All Majority-Owned Subsidiaries," *SFAS No. 94* (Stamford, CT: FASB, 1987), even 100% wholly owned subsidiaries were accounted for in many cases under the equity method. This kept the subsidiaries' debt off the balance sheet in much the same manner as joint-venture debt. Here's how: In many industries, companies help customers finance the purchase of their products. One example is the automobile industry. If no financing subsidiary were formed, the cash necessary to finance the credit extended to dealers and consumers would come from bank loans or other borrowing by the parent. As a consequence, the parent's debt-to-equity ratio would be worsened. However, if a separate finance subsidiary were formed and this subsidiary borrowed the funds directly in its own name, the borrowing would be effectively kept off the parent's balance sheet. The trick here was accomplished by using the equity method of accounting for subsidiaries, as will be discussed in Chapter 16. This is no longer permitted.

# HEDGES

Businesses are exposed to **market risks** from many sources—changes in interest rates, foreign currency exchange rates, and commodity prices.[17] Suppose a bank makes numerous five-year term loans at an annual interest rate of 8%. The earnings from those loans generate the cash needed to pay interest to "money market" account depositors. The loans expose the bank to interest rate risk: If money market interest rates rise, the 8% fixed return from the loans may not be adequate to pay the new higher rates promised to depositors.

Similar risks confront manufacturers. Consider Ridge Development, a real estate company that simultaneously constructs many single-family homes. Buyers make a down payment and agree to a fixed contract price to be paid when the home is completed. The typical home is completed in four months or less, and lumber comprises the bulk of construction costs. Because lumber prices are volatile, the developer is at risk that profits could erode (or disappear entirely) if lumber prices were to soar during the four-month construction cycle.

Or consider Southwest Airlines. It sells airline transportation services to passengers, many of whom pay a month or more in advance of the actual flight. Fuel is a major cost component in the airline industry, and fuel prices fluctuate on almost a daily basis. Because the passenger ticket price is set prior to the flight, Southwest Airlines is at risk that escalating fuel prices could turn an otherwise profitable flight into a loss.

Managing market risk is essential to the overall business strategies of most companies today. This trend has been driven by the need to reduce cash flow volatility that arises from factors beyond management's control—the exchange rate of U.S. dollars to Japanese yen, the LIBOR interest rate (the benchmark interbank interest rate for European banks), or the price of natural gas to run a factory. In response to these and other market risks, many companies today engage in **hedging**—business transactions designed to insulate them from commodity price, interest rate, or exchange rate risk. **Derivative securities,** which we explain next, are often used to accomplish this insulation.

> Commodities are bulk goods such as wheat, corn, lumber, jet fuel, and copper.

> Businesses are also exposed to **operating risks** from severe weather conditions, industrial accidents, raw material shortages, labor strikes, and so on. Insurance contracts, financial guarantees, and other business arrangements are used to hedge operating risks—but these risks do not qualify for the special hedge accounting rules described later in this section. Only certain financial risks qualify for hedge accounting.

## Typical Derivative Securities and the Benefits of Hedging

Derivative securities are so named because they are securities that have no inherent value but represent a claim against some other asset—their value is *derived* from the value of the asset underlying that claim.[18]

A **forward contract** is one example of a derivative security. In a forward contract, two parties agree to the sale of some asset or commodity on some *future* date—called the *settlement date*—at a price specified today. You have been dealing with forward contracts your whole life, perhaps without knowing it. Suppose you walk into a bookstore on October 5 to buy the best-selling *Seven Unbeatable Strategies for e-Commerce.* The book is sold out, but the clerk offers to reorder it for you and call you when it arrives. The clerk says that the book should arrive in about 15 days and will cost $39.95. If you agree on October 5 to pick up and pay for

---

[17] We gratefully acknowledge the substantial contribution of Professor Thomas Linsmeier, now serving as an FASB member, to the material in this section.

[18] For an overview of the characteristics and uses of derivative securities, see S.A. Ross, R. W. Westerfield, and B. D. Jordan, *Fundamentals of Corporate Finance,* 8th ed. (New York: McGraw-Hill, 2008); S. Ryan, *Financial Instruments and Institutions* (Hoboken, NJ: Wiley & Sons, 2007); and C. W. Smithson, C. W. Smith, and D. S. Wilford, *Managing Financial Risk* (Homewood, IL; Irwin, 1995).

the book when called, you and the clerk have agreed to a forward contract. Three elements of this contract are key: the agreed upon price ($39.95) to be paid in the future; the delivery date ("in about 15 days"); and that you will "take delivery" by paying for the book and picking it up when notified. The clerk has "sold" you a forward contract for the best seller.

**Futures Contracts**    A variation of a forward contract takes place on financial exchanges such as the New York Mercantile Exchange where **futures contracts** are traded daily in a market with many buyers and sellers. Futures contracts exist for commodities such as corn, wheat, live hogs and cattle, cotton, copper, crude oil, lumber, and even electricity. Here is how they work.

Suppose on October 5 you "write" (meaning sell) a futures contract for 10 million pounds of February copper at 95 cents per pound—we'll show why you might want to do so in just a moment. By selling the contract, you are obligated to deliver the copper at the agreed-upon price in February. The buyer (or contract counterparty) is obliged to pay the fixed price per pound and take delivery of the copper. So far this looks like a forward contract because both parties have an obligation to perform in the future (February).

But there's more! Futures contracts do not have a predetermined settlement date—you (the seller) can choose to deliver the copper on any day during the delivery month (February). This gives sellers additional flexibility in settling the contract. When you decide to deliver the copper, you notify the exchange clearinghouse, which then notifies an individual—let's call her Anne Smythe—who bought February copper contracts. (The clearinghouse selected Smythe at random from all individuals who hold February copper contracts.) Smythe is then told to be ready to accept delivery within the next several days. But what if she bought the contract as a speculative investment, has no real use for the copper, and doesn't want delivery? Futures contracts have an added advantage over forward contracts because futures are actively traded on an exchange. This means Smythe can avoid delivery by immediately selling a February copper contract for 10 million pounds, thus creating a zero net position. The first contract obligates Smythe to accept delivery of 10 million pounds of copper, but the second contract obligates her to turn over 10 million pounds to someone else. One contract cancels the other, and Smythe avoids the embarrassment of having all of that copper dumped on her garage floor.

Now that you understand how futures contracts work, let's see how they can be used to hedge financial risk.

Consider the opportunities confronting Rombaurer Metals, a copper mining company. On October 1, 2008, Rombaurer has 10 million pounds of copper inventory on hand at an average cost of 65 cents per pound. The "spot" (current delivery) price for copper on October 1 is 90 cents a pound. Rombaurer could receive $9 million (10 million pounds × $0.90 per pound) by selling its entire copper inventory today. This would yield a $2.5 million gross profit ($0.90 selling price − $0.65 average cost per pound × 10 million pounds). However, Rombaurer has decided to hold on to its copper until February 2009 when management believes the price will return to a normal level of 95 cents a pound. The commodities market seems to agree because February copper futures are priced as though copper will sell for 95 cents in February. The decision not to sell copper in October exposes Rombaurer to **commodity price risk** from a possible future decline in copper prices.

Figure 11.7(a) illustrates the company's commodity price risk exposure. If copper prices increase to 95 cents by February as expected, Rombaurer will receive $9.5 million for its copper and earn a gross profit of $3 million ($0.95 selling price − $0.65 average cost per pound × 10 million pounds). That's $0.5 million more gross profit than Rombaurer would earn by selling the copper on October 1. But what if the February price of copper falls to 85 cents? The cash received from

---

What happens if you pay for the book on October 5? Then it's a simple cash sales transaction (with a promised future delivery date). As long as both parties are *obligated* to perform at some future date under the agreement, it's a forward contract. Here that means the clerk is required to obtain a copy of the best seller and deliver it to you within the specified time. And you are required to pay the agreed upon price and to take delivery when the book arrives.

How can you (the seller) avoid having to deliver the copper? Form a zero net position of your own by purchasing a February copper contract from someone else—perhaps even from Anne Smythe.

## Figure 11.7a

ROMBAURER METALS

Using Futures Contracts to Hedge Copper Inventory: Before the Hedge

*Potential gross profit and loss from the sale of copper in February*

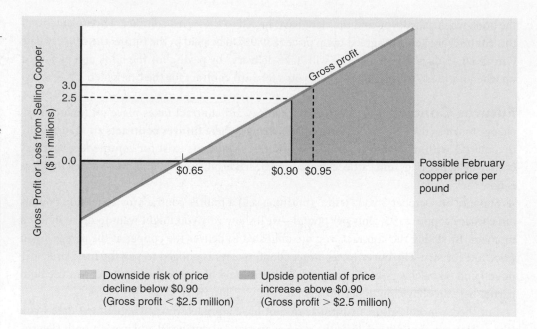

Downside risk of price decline below $0.90 (Gross profit < $2.5 million)

Upside potential of price increase above $0.90 (Gross profit > $2.5 million)

selling copper would then be only $8.5 million, and the gross profit would be only $2 million. Each 10-cent decline in the February copper price lowers the company's cash flows and expected gross profits by $1 million. At 65 cents per pound, Rombaurer just breaks even (zero gross profit) and, at any price below 65 cents, the company has a loss. These potential cash flow and gross profit declines represent the *downside risk* associated with the February price of copper.

There is *upside potential* as well. Each 10-cent increase in the February copper price will produce a $1 million increase in the company's cash flows and gross profits.

***One way Rombaurer can protect itself from a decline in the price of copper is to hedge its position with futures contracts.*** Suppose that Rombaurer sells 400 copper contracts—each contract is for 25,000 pounds—at 95 cents a pound for February delivery. The delivery month is chosen to coincide with the company's expected physical sale of the copper. The ultimate value of these contracts depends on the February price of copper as shown in Figure 11.7(b).

For example, if the February copper price is 85 cents, the contracts will have provided $1 million of cash flow and profit protection ($0.95 contract price − $0.85 February spot market price × the 10 million pounds of copper). If the February spot price is 65 cents, the contracts will have provided $3 million of protection.

The futures contracts "lock in" a February price of 95 cents and eliminate the company's downside exposure to a decline in copper prices. February cash receipts will be $9.5 million, and profits will total $3.0 million, no matter what the February spot price for copper turns out to be.

Of course, there is another side to the story. By hedging its original exposure to commodity price risk with futures contracts, Rombaurer has given up the cash flow and gross profit increases that could result if the February spot price is above $0.95. Figure 11.7(c) shows how the company's hedging strategy eliminates downside risk (and upside potential) and results in predictable cash flows and gross profits.

> Indeed, the futures contracts provide an immediate 5 cent per pound benefit (ignoring present value considerations, inventory holding costs, and fees and commissions of the contracts) because the October 1 price of copper is only 90 cents.

**Swap Contracts**   Another common derivative security is a **swap contract.** This contract is a popular way to hedge interest rate or foreign currency exchange rate risk. Let's say that Kistler Manufacturing has issued $100 million of long-term 8% fixed-rate debt and wants to protect itself against a *decline* in market interest rates. The company could

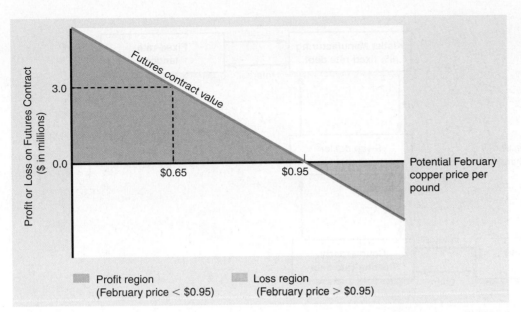

**Figure 11.7b**

ROMBAURER METALS

Using Futures Contracts to
Hedge Copper Inventory:
The Hedging Instrument

*Potential value of futures contract for
February copper*

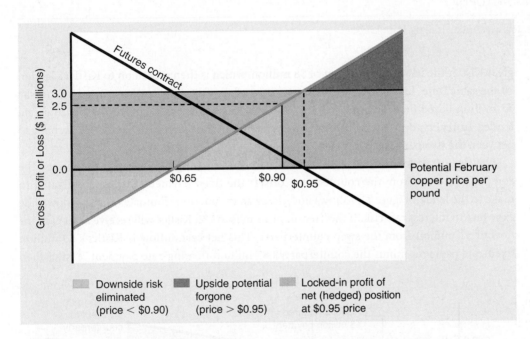

**Figure 11.7c**

ROMBAURER METALS

Using Futures Contracts to
Hedge Copper Inventory:
After the Hedge

*Gross profit from hedged position:
Combination of unhedged copper
inventory and futures contract*

reduce its exposure in several ways. We discussed one earlier in this chapter, using a debt-for-debt exchange offer to replace fixed-rate debt with a floating-rate loan. A second and perhaps less costly way that Kistler can reduce its interest rate risk exposure is to create *synthetic* floating-rate debt using an **interest rate swap.**

This form of hedging is accomplished with a "swap dealer." Swap dealers are typically banks that locate another company—called a *counterparty*—who is willing to make fixed-rate interest *payments* in exchange for floating-rate interest *receipts.* (Recall that Kistler wants to make floating-rate interest payments.) The swap transaction in Figure 11.8 includes Kistler with fixed-rate debt outstanding, the swap dealer, and the counterparty company with outstanding floating-rate debt with interest payments linked to the one-year U.S. Treasury bill rate. This is exactly the type of interest payment Kistler seeks.

Kistler and the counterparty agree to swap interest payments on $100 million of debt for the next three years with settlement every year. At the settlement date, the counterparty

> One reason protection might be needed is that Kistler's operating cash flows are positively correlated with interest rates. A decline in market rates would then be accompanied by a decrease in operating cash flows, and the company might lack the cash flow needed to meet its fixed-rate payment.

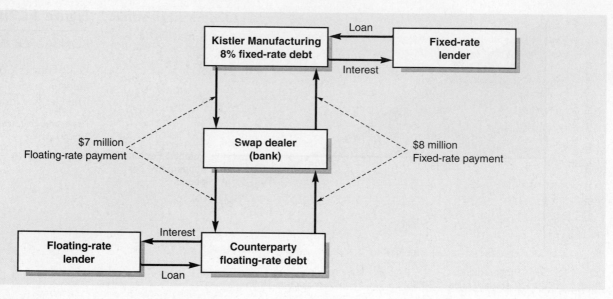

**Figure 11.8** KISTLER MANUFACTURING

An Interest Rate Swap That Creates Synthetic Floating-Rate Debt

---

> What does the counterparty gain? By replacing floating-rate interest payments with synthetic fixed-rate payments, the counterparty has reduced its exposure to cash flow volatility from interest rate changes.

gives Kistler the fixed-rate payment of $8 million, which is then passed on to Kistler's lender. At the same time, Kistler gives the counterparty cash equal to the floating-rate payment (say $7 million based on a Treasury rate of 7%), and this too is passed on to the floating-rate lender. In reality, only the $1 million difference in interest payments would be exchanged between the two parties to the swap.

The swap transforms Kistler's fixed-rate debt into floating rate because the money the company receives from the counterparty offsets the fixed payment Kistler is obligated to make to the lender. Figure 11.9 shows how the swap transaction eliminates Kistler's downside exposure to interest rate risk. If the Treasury rate falls to 7%, Kistler will receive a net cash inflow of $1 million from the swap counterparty. This net cash inflow is Kistler's $8 million fixed-rate payment minus the counterparty's $7 million floating-rate payment. Kistler then

**Figure 11.9**

KISTLER MANUFACTURING

Using a Swap to Hedge Interest Rate Risk

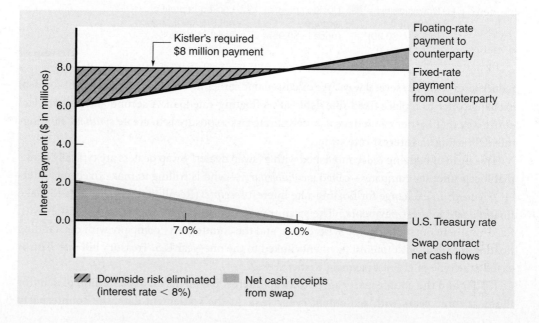

pays its lender $8 million as required with $1 million of the payment coming from the swap counterparty. Kistler's out-of-pocket interest cost is just $7 million, the amount it would have been required to pay if it had issued floating-rate debt in the first place.[19]

Kistler ends up with floating-rate debt that it could perhaps not otherwise obtain at attractive rates. The result is that the counterparty has fixed interest payments, and the bank earns a fee for arranging the swap transaction. Everybody wins—as long as all parties fulfill their payment obligations.

A foreign exchange (currency) swap has the same structural features as those outlined in Exhibits 11.8 and 11.9 except that the loans are denominated in different currencies. Suppose that St. Jean Inc. manufactures products in France but sells them exclusively in the United States. The company borrows euros to finance construction of a manufacturing plant in France, and it wants to hedge its foreign exchange exposure on the loan. The company's exposure arises because its operating cash flows are in U.S. dollars but its loan payments are in euros. With the aid of a swap dealer, the company can identify a counterparty willing to exchange euro-denominated payments for dollar-denominated payments. The pattern of swapped cash flows is identical to the flows depicted in Figure 11.8. St. Jean ends up with *synthetic* U.S. dollar-denominated debt and eliminates its exposure to fluctuations in the euro-dollar exchange rate.

**Options Contract**   Futures and swaps are derivatives that require each party to the contract to complete the agreed-upon transaction. But other types of derivative securities exist. One is an *option contract,* which gives the holder an "option"—the right but not the obligation—to do something. To illustrate how options work, let's revisit our homebuilder discussed at the beginning of this section.

Suppose it's now January and Ridge Development needs 10 million board feet of lumber on hand in three months (April) to construct homes that have been presold to residential homebuyers. Lumber currently sells for $250 per 1,000 board feet (kbf), so Ridge must purchase $2.5 million of lumber at the current (January) price to meet its April construction commitment. But Ridge has no place to store the lumber, and lumber prices are expected to increase over the next few months. How can the company eliminate its commodity price risk from its *anticipated* lumber purchase three months from now?

One approach is to buy a futures contract for April lumber. Ridge can "lock in" the profit margin on unbuilt homes it has sold by agreeing to pay a set price now (in January) for lumber delivered in April. But if lumber prices fall over the next three months, the builder—now locked into higher lumber prices by the futures contract—would forgo the increased profits from lower lumber prices.

***By using options instead of futures, Ridge can protect against lumber cost increases without sacrificing potential gains if lumber prices decline.*** This can be done by purchasing a call option on lumber—an option to buy lumber at a specified price over the option period. The call option protects the builder against lumber cost increases. But because it is an option, Ridge is not obligated to exercise the option should lumber prices fall. Options enable Ridge to hedge unfavorable price movements and still participate in the upside possibility of increased profit margins if lumber prices fall. Figure 11.10 shows how.

Without hedging its anticipated lumber purchase, Ridge is exposed to commodity price risk if lumber prices rise above the current $250 level over the next three months. To eliminate this exposure, Ridge buys a call option for 10 million board feet of April lumber at $250 per 1,000 board feet. If the April price of lumber is more than $250 per 1,000 board feet, Ridge will exercise the option and pay just the $250 contract price. But if the April price is, say, $200,

> Some option contracts give the holder the right to *buy* a specific underlying asset at a specified price during a specified time. These are known as **call options.** Other option contracts give the holder the option to *sell* an asset at a specified price during a specified time period. These are **put options.**

---

[19] An **interest rate "collar"** may be part of the swap agreement as well—for example, the two parties could agree that the swap remains in force as long as the Treasury rate is less than 8.5% and more than 6%.

## Figure 11.10

RIDGE DEVELOPMENT
COMPANY

Using an Option to Hedge
Commodity Price Risk

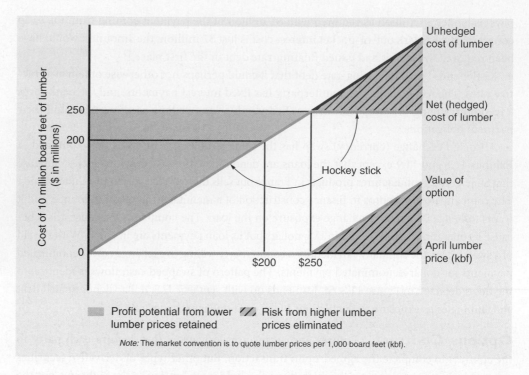

Note: The market convention is to quote lumber prices per 1,000 board feet (kbf).

Ridge will let the option expire and instead buy lumber in the open market—saving $500,000 in lumber costs ($50 per 1,000 board feet). The net result of the option hedge is a "hockey stick" shape (see Figure 11.10)—the *downside risk* of a lumber price increase is eliminated but the *upside potential* of a lumber price decrease is retained.

When options are used in this way, they do not necessarily "lock in" a specified profit margin or price. Instead, they provide a hedge that resembles insurance. Options allow companies to hedge against downside risk—value losses—while retaining the opportunity to benefit from favorable price movements. Insurance does the same thing. It provides protection against losses.

 RECAP

**Derivative securities are extremely useful tools for managing financial risk. New and more complicated hedging instruments and transactions are created each year, and they sometimes have unintended consequences. That is what the soap company Procter & Gamble learned in 1994 when it had to liquidate two contracts for interest rate swaps. The lesson cost the company $157 million, one of the largest derivative losses suffered by a U.S. company at the time. William J. McDonough, president of the Federal Reserve Bank of New York, said at the time, "People of my generation who are not astrophysicists have to strain to understand these products [hedging instruments and transactions]. To put it simply and directly, if the bosses do not or cannot understand both the risks and the rewards in their products, their firm should not be in the business."[20]**

## Financial Reporting for Derivative Securities

Before we turn our attention to hedge accounting, let's consider how GAAP treats stand-alone derivative securities in the absence of a hedging transaction. Here's a quick synopsis:

- All derivatives must be carried on the balance sheet at fair value—no exceptions. Fair value is the derivative's market price at the balance sheet date.
- Generally, changes in the fair value of derivatives must be recognized in income when they occur. The only GAAP exception is for derivatives that qualify as hedges (explained later).

---

[20] Quoted in L. Malkin, "Procter & Gamble's Tale of Derivatives Woe," *International Herald Tribune*, April 14, 1994.

This example illustrates the basic accounting treatment for derivatives that do *not* qualify for special hedge accounting rules:

> On March 1, 2008, Heitz Metals buys call options (that is, options to purchase) for 10 million board feet of June lumber. Each call option gives Heitz the opportunity to purchase 1,000 board feet of lumber, so the firm bought a total of 10,000 option contracts (10 million board feet divided by 1,000 per contract). Heitz has no use for the lumber, nor is the company hedging a financial risk. ***Instead, Heitz is just speculating that lumber prices will increase during the next several months.*** The settlement price is $240 per 1,000 board feet, the current spot price is $240, and Heitz pays $50,000 for the contracts.
>
> Over the next 30 days, a series of winter storms dump several feet of snow in the mountains of the Pacific Northwest. This late snowfall delays the timber-harvesting season and creates a lumber shortage. By March 31, the spot price for lumber is $245, and June contracts for 10 million board feet are trading for $75,000 at the commodities exchange. Lumber prices have increased to $245, but Heitz owns an option to buy lumber at $240, so the value of the option has increased along with lumber prices. On April 15, Heitz decides to liquidate its position. It sells the June lumber contracts for $13 each (or $130,000 in total) when the spot price for lumber is $252.

The value of an option contract can be broken into two components: intrinsic value and timing value. The option contract's *intrinsic value* is the difference between the settlement price, which is specified in the contract and does not change over time, and the spot price, which can change on a daily basis. The Heitz option has an intrinsic value of zero on March 1 because the settlement price ($240) equals the spot price ($240) that day. Why is Heitz willing to pay $5 per contract on March 1 for an option that has zero intrinsic value? It is because of the option's *timing value*. This $5 timing value reflects the possibility that lumber spot prices (and thus, intrinsic value) may rise above the current $240 level between March 1 and the option's expiration date. Timing value is zero at the option expiration date.

The accounting entry to record Heitz Metals' *speculative* purchase—remember that Heitz has no real use for the lumber—of June lumber contracts is:

| | | | |
|---|---|---|---|
| **DR** | Marketable securities—lumber options | $50,000 | |
| **CR** | Cash | | $50,000 |

The derivative securities (call options) are recorded as an asset at fair value—the purchase price paid. At the end of March, the call option price has increased to $7.50 per contract. Heitz records the derivative's *change* in fair value for the month ($75,000 fair value at the end of March − $50,000 fair value at the start of March, or $25,000):

| | | | |
|---|---|---|---|
| **DR** | Market adjustment—lumber options | $25,000 | |
| **CR** | Unrealized holding gain on lumber options (to income) | | $25,000 |

The $25,000 Market adjustment is added to the $50,000 balance in Marketable securities. The contracts are now carried on the balance sheet at $75,000—which is their fair value as of the end of March—and a $25,000 unrealized gain has been recorded in income for March. (If the options had declined in value, Heitz would have recorded an unrealized holding loss along with a downward adjustment in the carrying value of the options.) Heitz then liquidates the options contracts on April 15:

> The unrealized gain (or loss) would be included in Income from continuing operations on the Heitz income statement.

| | | | |
|---|---|---|---|
| **DR** | Cash | $130,000 | |
| **CR** | Marketable securities—lumber options | | $50,000 |
| **CR** | Market adjustment—lumber options | | 25,000 |
| **CR** | Realized holding gain on lumber options (to income) | | 55,000 |

These accounting entries are used for all types of derivatives—forwards, futures, swaps, and options—unless the special hedge accounting rules described next apply. Three key points about derivatives that do not qualify for special hedge accounting treatment should be remembered:

1. Derivative contracts represent balance sheet assets and liabilities.

2. The carrying value of the derivative is adjusted to fair value at each balance sheet date.

3. The amount of the adjustment—the change in fair value—flows to the income statement as a holding gain (or loss).

As a result of these GAAP rules, speculative investments in derivative contracts can increase the volatility of reported earnings. But the earnings volatility that results from this accounting treatment perfectly reflects the derivative's inherent economic risk.

## Hedge Accounting

When a company successfully hedges its exposure to market risk, any economic loss on the hedged item (for example, copper inventory) will be offset by an economic gain on the derivative securities (for example, copper futures contracts). ***To accurately reflect the underlying economics of the hedge, the company should match the loss on the hedged item with the derivative's offsetting gain in the income statement of the same period.*** This matching is what the GAAP rules governing hedge accounting try to accomplish.[21] The special hedge accounting rules eliminate or reduce the earnings volatility that would otherwise result from reporting the change in the derivative's fair value in income each period.

The type of special hedge accounting to be applied varies depending on the nature of the exposure being hedged. In some cases, changes in the derivative's fair value are reported in income as they occur, but the earnings impact is then offset by a corresponding charge (or credit) from adjusting the carrying value of the asset or liability being hedged. In other cases, earnings volatility is avoided by recording changes in the fair value of the derivative directly in Other comprehensive income.

When can hedge accounting be used? The answer depends on four considerations:

- Hedged item
- Hedging instrument
- Risk being hedged
- Effectiveness of hedge

Stringent GAAP criteria must be met to qualify for hedge accounting. To fulfill the criteria, management must do three things: designate the derivative security as a hedging instrument; describe the hedging strategy; and document its effectiveness in eliminating a specific market risk for a specific hedged item. The details are voluminous and complex, so we cannot possibly cover all bases here. What we can do is provide an overview of the most common hedging situations and how hedge accounting works. The basics are outlined in Figure 11.11.

The **hedged item** can be either (1) an existing asset or liability on the company's books, (2) a firm commitment, or (3) an anticipated (forecasted) future transaction. Inventories of

---

The matching process works like this. If an economic gain (or loss) on the *hedged item* flows to accounting income in the current period, so does the offsetting loss (or gain) on the derivative. But if the hedged item's economic gain (or loss) flows to accounting income some time later, then income statement recognition of the derivative's offsetting loss (or gain) is also postponed to that later period.

You may want to review Chapter 2 for a discussion of **other comprehensive income** and the income statement.

---

[21] "Accounting for Derivative Instruments and Hedging Activities," *SFAS No. 133* (Norwalk, CT: FASB, 1998) and "Accounting for Certain Derivative Instruments and Certain Hedging Activities," *SFAS No. 138* (Norwalk, CT: FASB, 2000). These statements are summarized and interpreted in the 540-page implementation guide *Accounting for Derivative Instruments and Hedging Activities* (Norwalk, CT: FASB, 2000). To learn more about hedge accounting, see S. Ryan, *Financial Instruments and Institutions* (Hoboken, NJ: Wiley & Sons, 2007) and M. Trombley, *Accounting for Derivatives and Hedging* (New York: McGraw-Hill, 2003).

commodities such as copper and lumber, receivables and loans, and debt obligations are examples of *existing assets and liabilities* that qualify as hedged items. If Hess Company agrees in June to buy network storage equipment from another company at a specific price with delivery in the future (say, August), that's a *firm commitment*. If, on the other hand, Hess just knows in June that it must buy the equipment by August but has signed no purchase agreement, it's an *anticipated transaction*.

The **hedging instrument** is commonly a derivative security, although not all derivatives meet the strict GAAP rules and some qualifying hedges (for example, the call provision of a callable bond) do not involve derivatives as the term is commonly used. Qualifying hedging instruments include options to purchase or sell an exchange-traded security, futures and forward contracts, and interest rate and currency swaps. ***Insurance contracts, options to purchase real estate, traditional equity and debt securities, and financial guarantee contracts do not qualify as hedging instruments.***

The **risk being hedged** must meet certain GAAP criteria. The eligible market risks are limited to risks arising from overall changes in the fair value or cash flow of the hedged item or risks from changes in benchmark interest rates (for example, LIBOR), commodity prices (such as copper), foreign currency exchange rates (for example, Japanese yen to U.S. dollar), and the creditworthiness of the party (a company, institution, or government agency) that issued a financial security. Other financial and operating risks (such as risks from weather conditions, industrial accidents, or labor strikes) do not qualify for hedge accounting. (We will discuss hedge effectiveness later.)

GAAP groups the risks being hedged into three categories:

1. A **fair value hedge** is a hedge of the exposure to changes in the *fair value* of an *existing* asset or liability, or a *firm commitment*. Common examples of a fair value hedge include:
   - An interest rate swap that synthetically converts fixed-rate debt into floating rate debt (interest rate risk exposure of an existing liability).
   - A gold futures contract that "unlocks" a gold mining company's agreement to sell refined gold to a jewelry manufacturer next year at a fixed price (commodity price risk exposure of a firm commitment).

2. A **cash flow hedge** is a hedge of the exposure to changes in *cash flows* of an *existing* asset or liability, or an *anticipated transaction*. Common examples of a cash flow hedge include:
   - An interest rate swap that synthetically converts floating-rate debt into fixed-rate debt (interest rate risk exposure of an existing liability.
   - A lumber futures contract that "locks in" the price a building contractor will pay in two months for lumber (commodity price risk exposure for an anticipated transaction).

3. A **foreign currency exposure hedge** is a hedge of the exposure to changes in currency exchange rates of an existing asset or liability, a firm commitment, a forecasted transaction, or a multinational company's net investment in a foreign operation. Here GAAP applies the fair value and cash flow hedge accounting rules to foreign currency exchange exposure. The unique element of this exposure is a net investment in foreign operations. In Chapter 16, we describe the accounting and reporting issues unique to foreign subsidiaries.

Figure 11.11 describes the accounting procedures for (Panel [a]) derivatives that qualify for hedge accounting and

Derivatives that fail to meet the GAAP rules for hedge accounting—because either the hedged item, the derivative itself, or the hedged risk doesn't qualify—are treated as though they were speculative investments.

How can an interest rate swap qualify as both a fair value hedge and a cash flow hedge? The answer lies in understanding how interest rate changes affect the market values and cash flows of debt obligations. For fixed-rate debt, interest rate changes produce market value changes in the opposite direction but debt cash flows are "fixed" (meaning unchanged). So, an interest rate swap that converts fixed-rate debt into floating-rate debt eliminates fluctuations in market values and thus is a fair value hedge. For floating-rate debt, interest rate changes produce changes in debt cash flows—if rates increase, the borrower must pay additional interest—but debt market value is unaffected. So, an interest rate swap that converts floating-rate debt into fixed-rate debt eliminates fluctuations in cash flows and thus is a cash flow hedge.

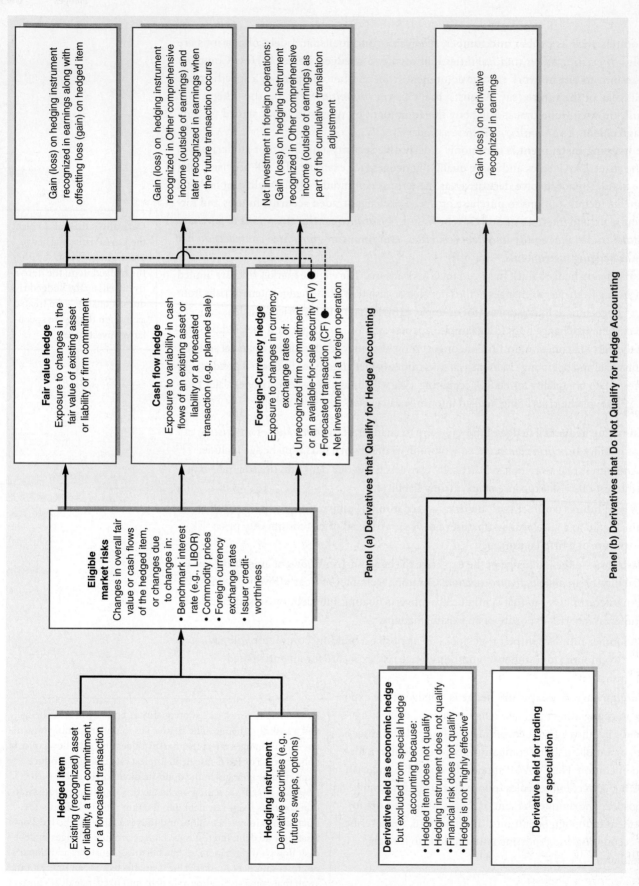

**Figure 11.11** FINANCIAL REPORTING FOR DERIVATIVE SECURITIES

(Panel [b]) derivatives that do not qualify for hedge accounting. GAAP requires all derivative securities—whether held for trading and speculation or as financial hedges—to be **marked-to-market,** meaning that they are carried at fair value on the balance sheet as assets or liabilities. The offsetting debit or credit that results from marked-to-market accounting then flows either to current income (for fair value hedges, certain foreign currency hedges and derivatives that do not qualify for hedge accounting) or to Other comprehensive income (for cash flow hedges and most other foreign currency hedges).

## Fair Value Hedge Accounting

*Hedge accounting makes it possible for companies engaged in financial risk management to recognize the gain (or loss) on the hedged item in the same period as the offsetting loss (or gain) on the derivative security.* To see how this is done, let's return to Rombaurer Metals and its copper inventory hedge:

On October 1, 2008, Rombaurer has 10 million pounds of copper inventory on hand at an average cost of $0.65 a pound. The spot price for copper is $0.90 a pound. Instead of selling copper now, Rombaurer decides to hold the inventory until February 2009 when management believes the price will return to a normal level of $0.95 a pound. To hedge its position, Rombaurer sells futures contracts for 10 million pounds at $0.95 for February delivery. The margin deposit on the contracts is $280,000—the amount the commodities broker requires as a good-faith cash deposit on the contracts. The market's spot and futures prices over the next several months are:

| | NYMEX Copper Prices | |
|---|---|---|
| | Spot Price | February 2009 Futures Price |
| October 1, 2008 | $0.90 | $0.95 |
| December 31, 2008 | 0.85 | 0.91 |
| February 26, 2009 | 0.94 | 0.94 |

Rombaurer has successfully hedged its exposure to commodity price risk—and the fair value of its existing copper inventory—by selling futures contracts. Rombaurer then designates the futures contracts (the hedging instrument) as a **fair value hedge** of its exposure to market price fluctuations (the hedged risk) for existing copper inventory (the hedged item). As long as the futures contracts pass the GAAP test for hedge effectiveness—and they do, as you will later see—Rombaurer can use the special **fair value hedge accounting** rules. Here are the accounting entries.

On October 1, 2008, Rombaurer records the initial margin deposit on its fair value hedge:

| **DR** | Amount due from broker (a receivable) | $280,000 | |
|---|---|---|---|
| **CR** | Cash | | $280,000 |

No entry is made that day for the futures contracts themselves because they have zero value at inception—the February contract price ($0.95) equals the current $0.95 market price of February copper (and we are ignoring any timing value).

The spot price and the February futures price of copper both decline over the next several months. Rombaurer makes two journal entries at year-end, December 31. The first entry records the fair value increase for the hedging instrument:

| **DR** | Amount due from broker | $400,000 | |
|---|---|---|---|
| **CR** | Gain on hedge activity (to income) | | $400,000 |

The futures contracts are worth $400,000 on December 31, 2008. This amount is the difference between the copper price guaranteed by the contracts ($0.95) and the current futures price of February copper ($0.91) multiplied by the 10 million pounds of copper being hedged. Copper prices have fallen, but the hedge has provided $400,000 of commodity price protection. Notice too that the broker receivable now has a balance of $680,000 representing the initial margin deposit ($280,000) *plus* the fair value of the futures contracts ($400,000).

The second year-end entry adjusts the carrying value of the hedged item—copper inventory—for the change in fair value ($0.91 − $0.95, a $0.04 loss, ×10 million pounds):

| | | | |
|---|---|---|---|
| **DR** | Loss on hedge activity (to income) | $400,000 | |
| **CR** | Copper inventory | | $400,000 |

The carrying value of the copper inventory is now $6.1 million; that's the inventory's $6.5 million historical cost minus the $400,000 decline in the February fair value since October 1, 2008. (Note that GAAP measures this fair value decline using the October 1 $0.95 *futures* contract price as the benchmark. The October 1 *spot* price of $0.90 does not enter into the GAAP calculation of the fair value decline.)

In the first December 31 entry, the derivative is marked-to-market and Rombaurer records a gain on the hedging instrument to income. But the gain from the futures contracts is fully offset by the loss on copper inventory in the second entry. (In practice, only one Gain or loss on hedge activity account is used to record the gain and the loss.) These offsetting gains and losses eliminate earnings volatility.

On February 26, 2009, Rombaurer sells the copper on the spot market for $0.94 a pound and cancels the futures contracts. It makes three journal entries at this time.

The first entry records the fair value change for the hedging instrument ($0.91 − $0.94, a $0.03 loss, ×10 million pounds), the cash returned by the broker, and eliminates the broker receivable:

| | | | |
|---|---|---|---|
| **DR** | Cash | $380,000 | |
| **DR** | Loss on hedge activity (to income) | 300,000 | |
| **CR** | Amount due from broker | | $680,000 |

February copper prices have increased $0.03 a pound since December, and the futures contracts are now worth only $100,000 ($0.95 − $0.94 × 10 million pounds), so Rombaurer records a $300,000 loss. This $300,000 loss is fair value change in the futures contracts since December 31. Rombaurer also receives $380,000 from the broker. This amount is the sum of the returned margin deposit ($280,000) and the settlement value of the contracts ($100,000).

The second entry adjusts the carrying value of the hedged copper inventory for the fair value change ($0.94 − $0.91 × 10 million pounds):

| | | | |
|---|---|---|---|
| **DR** | Copper inventory | $300,000 | |
| **CR** | Gain on hedge activity (to income) | | $300,000 |

In this case, the loss from the futures contracts (the first entry) is offset by a gain on copper inventory (the second entry).

The third and final entry records the credit sale of copper inventory at the spot market price:

| | | | |
|---|---|---|---|
| **DR** | Accounts receivable | $9,400,000 | |
| **DR** | Cost of goods sold | 6,400,000 | |
| **CR** | Sales revenue | | $9,400,000 |
| **CR** | Copper inventory | | 6,400,000 |

Rombaurer's gross profit from selling copper is $3 million (the $9.4 million selling price – the $6.4 million adjusted carrying value of the inventory sold). This is exactly the gross profit Rombaurer would have reported if it had sold the inventory—originally carried on the books at $6.5 million—at the anticipated February price of $0.95 a pound, or $9.5 million. By selling futures contracts, Rombaurer "locked in" the February price of $0.95 a pound and eliminated its exposure to commodity price risk.

| The $6.4 million adjusted carrying value ($0.64 per pound) is determined as: | | |
|---|---|---|
| 10/1/08 | cost at $0.65 per pound | $6.5 million |
| 12/31/08 | adjustment for $0.04 decline | (0.4) million |
| 2/26/09 | adjustment for $0.03 increase | 0.3 million |
| 2/26/09 | adjusted carrying value | $6.4 million |

That's the economics behind Rombaurer's hedging activities, and that's what the accounting statements report.

What if Rombaurer did not (or could not) use hedge accounting rules for the copper futures contracts? In that case, GAAP still requires the derivative security to be marked-to-market. So, Rombaurer would record a $400,000 gain on December 31, 2008 followed by a $300,000 loss on February 26, 2009—the change in fair value of the futures contracts. But GAAP would not allow an offsetting loss (on December 31, 2008) or gain (on February 26, 2009) to be recorded on the copper inventory itself. Instead, the inventory would continue to be carried at its historical cost of $6,500,000 until sold. The net result is increased earnings volatility: Net income for 2008 would include a $400,000 gain, while net income for 2009 would include a $300,000 loss and a $100,000 gross margin reduction due to the higher carrying value of inventory ($0.65 per pound original cost rather than $0.64 per pound adjusted carrying value).

## Cash Flow Hedge Accounting

Exhibit 11.12 illustrates the accounting for a **cash flow hedge.** Chalk Hill Inc. issues a $10 million, three-year floating-rate note with interest equal to the LIBOR rate, reset annually. To hedge its exposure to cash flow variability from changes in the LIBOR, Chalk Hill enters into an interest rate swap with a bank. The bank agrees to make the required floating-rate interest payments, and Chalk Hill agrees to pay the bank 7.5% fixed-rate interest annually for the entire three years. The interest rate swap allows Chalk Hill to "lock in" the 7.5% fixed-rate cash payment for interest even though the actual interest rate charged on the note will rise or fall with changes in the LIBOR rate.

As you work through the journal entries in Exhibit 11.12, notice that the hedging instrument (swap contract) shows up as a balance sheet asset or liability. (If the account has a debit balance, it's an asset; if the balance is a credit, it's a liability.) The swap's carrying value is its fair value at each balance sheet date. This means that changes in the swap's fair value are recorded when they occur—**but they do not flow directly to the income statement.** Instead, gains and losses on the swap contract flow to Other comprehensive income and shareholders' equity as in Figure 11.11. What's the reason for this accounting treatment? Changes in the LIBOR rate do not affect the underlying economic value of the floating-rate note—as interest rates on a floating-rate liability change, the liability's market price remains constant. So, we are unable to offset fair value changes in the hedging instrument with changes in the hedged item's fair value. The only way earnings volatility can be avoided is to keep swap gains and losses off the income statement by allowing them to flow to Other comprehensive income.

You need to observe one more feature of the Chalk Hill example. Interest expense is $750,000 each year, or the 7.5% fixed-rate of interest multiplied by the $10 million note principal amount. This may at first seem surprising because Chalk Hill makes a floating-rate interest payment each year, and the amount paid varies from $700,000 to $850,000 over the three years. But the interest rate swap insulates Chalk Hill from this cash flow volatility. For example, in 2009, Chalk Hill pays $850,000 in interest on the note but receives $100,000 from the swap counterparty. Chalk Hill's net cash payment for interest that year is $750,000, which is also the amount of interest expense reported.

> Problem 11-9 considers the accounting for Chalk Hill's swap when it does not qualify for hedge accounting.

| EXHIBIT 11.12 | Chalk Hill's Cash Flow Hedge |
|---|---|

## Using an Interest Rate Swap to Hedge Variable Rate Debt

On January 1, 2008, Chalk Hill borrows $10 million by signing a three-year note with interest equal to the LIBOR (currently at 7.5%), reset annually on December 31. To hedge its exposure to the variability in cash flows associated with the floating-rate note, Chalk Hill enters into a three-year interest rate swap with Beringer Bank. Under the swap contract, Chalk Hill pays interest to the bank at the fixed 7.5% rate and receives interest payments from the bank at a variable rate equal to the LIBOR, based on a notional amount of $10 million. Both the note and swap require that payments be made or received annually on December 31 of each year.

Chalk Hill designates the swap (hedging instrument) as a ***cash flow hedge*** of its exposure to variability in the cash flows of the floating-rate note (hedged item) with the specific risk being changes in cash flows due to changes in the LIBOR rate. This hedge is fully effective because the key terms of the note and swap are identical. The LIBOR rates, cash payments made and received, and the fair value of the swap contract (based on dealer quotes) are:

| | | Gross Cash Flow | | | |
|---|---|---|---|---|---|
| | LIBOR Rate | To Beringer Bank | From Beringer Bank | Net Cash Flow | Swap Fair Value Asset (Liability) from Dealer Quotes |
| January 1, 2008 | 7.50% | $750,000 | $750,000 | — | — |
| December 31, 2008 | 8.50 | 750,000 | 850,000 | $100,000 | $323,000 |
| December 31, 2009 | 7.00 | 750,000 | 700,000 | (50,000) | (55,000) |

Swap contracts are not traded in an organized exchange (such as the NYMEX where copper futures contracts are traded), so contract fair values can be difficult to determine. Chalk Hill's fair value estimates ("quotes") are from knowledgeable "dealers" (usually investment banks) who are actively involved in structuring swap transactions.*

Chalk Hill makes the following entries over the life of the swap contract and note:

### January 1, 2008

| **DR** Cash | $10,000,000 | |
|---|---|---|
| **CR** Note payable | | $10,000,000 |

To record the company's initial borrowing. There is no entry for the swap contract because it has no initial value—the "pay" and "receive" rates for both parties are the same, 7.5% times $10 million.

### December 31, 2008

| **DR** Interest expense | $750,000 | |
|---|---|---|
| **CR** Interest payable | | $750,000 |

To accrue annual interest at a 7.5% variable rate—the LIBOR rate on January 1, 2008.

| **DR** Interest payable | $750,000 | |
|---|---|---|
| **CR** Cash | | $750,000 |

To record the annual interest payment on the note. There is no entry for the swap settlement this year because the "pay" and "receive" amounts are the same, $750,000.

| **DR** Swap contract | $323,000 | |
|---|---|---|
| **CR** Other comprehensive income | | $323,000 |

To record the change in fair value of the swap based on dealer quotes.

### December 31, 2009

| **DR** Interest expense | $850,000 | |
|---|---|---|
| **CR** Interest payable | | $850,000 |

To accrue annual interest at an 8.5% variable rate—the LIBOR rate on December 31, 2008.

| **DR** Interest payable | $850,000 | |
|---|---|---|
| **CR** Cash | | $850,000 |

To record the annual interest payment on the note.

*(continued)*

---

* To learn more about how practitioners value swaps and other derivatives, see C. W. Smithson, C. W. Smith, and D. S. Wilford, *Managing Financial Risk* (Homewood, IL: Irwin, 1995).

| EXHIBIT 11.12 | Chalk Hill's Cash Flow Hedge (*continued*) |
|---|---|

**DR** Cash .................................................... $100,000
    **CR** Interest expense ......................................                          $100,000
To record the swap settlement net receipt from Beringer Bank.

**DR** Other comprehensive income............................. $378,000
    **CR** Swap contract .......................................                          $378,000
To record the change in fair value of the swap based on dealer quotes. The Swap contract account now has a $55,000 credit balance.

**December 31, 2010**

**DR** Interest expense.......................................... $700,000
    **CR** Interest payable......................................                          $700,000
To accrue annual interest at a 7.0% variable rate—the LIBOR rate on December 31, 2009.

**DR** Interest payable ......................................... $700,000
    **CR** Cash...............................................                          $700,000
To record the annual interest payment on the note.

**DR** Interest expense.......................................... $50,000
    **CR** Cash...............................................                          $50,000
To record the swap settlement net payment to Beringer Bank.

**DR** Swap contract ........................................... $55,000
    **CR** Other comprehensive income .........................                          $55,000
To record the change in fair value of the swap. The swap agreement has now been concluded, and the contract has no further value to either party.

**DR** Note payable ........................................... $10,000,000
    **CR** Cash..............................................                          $10,000,000
To record payment of the note principal.

## Hedge Accounting for a Forecasted Transaction

Now let's see how hedge accounting for a **forecasted transaction** works. In this example, Vintage Construction uses lumber options contracts as a *cash flow* hedge for its projected lumber needs during the year:

> Vintage Construction Corporation builds residential homes in the far northern United States from April through November. It builds no homes on speculation. Building begins only after the home buyer and Vintage sign a firm contract. Construction takes about four months. Because contract prices with home purchasers are fixed, Vintage is vulnerable to lumber price increases during construction. To protect its margins, Vintage buys 20 lumber futures contracts on April 1, 2008. The expiration dates on these contracts are staggered over the April–November building season to approximate the monthly level of construction activity.
>
> Lumber prices rise during the 2008 season. These unanticipated higher costs reduce gross profits from home construction by $600,000. However, Vintage realized a $580,000 gain on the futures contracts due to the lumber price increase. How did the company's financial statements reflect this gain?

Vintage designates the lumber contracts as a ***cash flow hedge*** of forecasted lumber purchases with commodity price volatility being the source of market risk. At inception, it records the futures contracts as an asset at the purchase price. At each monthly balance sheet date, the contracts are marked-to-market with the change in fair value flowing to Other comprehensive income and then shareholders' equity. As homes are completed each month, Vintage records the revenues and expenses from the construction business. At the same time, the cumulative gain and loss on the lumber contracts for completed homes is transferred out of Other comprehensive income to the income statement.

> Because Vintage doesn't yet own the lumber, the futures contracts cannot qualify as a fair value hedge of an *existing* asset.

*This accounting treatment offsets changes in the gross profit from construction due to lumber price fluctuations (the hedged item) with realized gains and losses from lumber futures contracts (the hedging instrument).* Earnings volatility is avoided by allowing the futures contracts gains and losses to initially flow to shareholders' equity. These gains and losses eventually flow to earnings, but only when the forecasted transaction is completed and affects earnings. For Vintage Construction, that means when the homes are finished and the buyer takes possession—not earlier when lumber is purchased.

Because all of the options contracts were realized in 2008, the $580,000 gain is included in income and largely offsets the $600,000 gross margin reduction reflected in income that same period. This income statement result corresponds to the almost perfect hedging strategy followed by Vintage Construction. A "perfect" hedge would have exactly offset the $600,000 margin shortfall.

## Hedge Effectiveness

Few hedges are perfect. When they are not—as here—notice that reported income corresponds to the underlying economics. That is, while Vintage insulated itself from most of the lumber price increase, it did experience a $20,000 earnings reduction. This is precisely the reported income statement effect (that is, a $580,000 gain on the options contracts and a $600,000 gross margin reduction).

**Hedge effectiveness**—the derivative's ability to generate offsetting changes in the fair value or cash flows of the hedged item—is a key qualifying criterion for hedge accounting. If critical terms of the hedging instrument and hedged item are the same, changes in the derivative's fair value or cash flow (for example, a $1 gain) completely offset changes in the fair value or cash flow of the hedged item (a $1 loss). In this case, the hedge is "fully effective." Except for Vintage Construction, all of our examples have involved fully effective hedges.

> For interest rate swaps such as the one described in Exhibit 11.12, the critical terms include the notional (that is, principal) amount, contract term and loan maturity date, "pay" and "receive" rates on the benchmark interest rate, and the interest rate reset dates.

But what if the hedge is not fully effective? Does that disqualify the derivative from special hedge accounting rules? It does not necessarily because GAAP requires only that the hedge be "highly effective"—as defined by GAAP—in offsetting changes in those fair values or cash flows that are due to the hedged risk. This requirement must be met both at the inception of the hedge and on an ongoing basis. *SFAS No. 133* provides general guidelines but does not say exactly how effectiveness should be determined.

How effective is "highly effective"? The hedging instrument should offset somewhere between 80% and 125% of the hedged item's fair value or cash flow changes attributable to the hedged risk. For Vintage Construction, this means that the company must purchase enough staggered lumber futures contracts to hedge at least 80% of its exposure to lumber price fluctuations. Purchase less than this amount and the futures contracts are an "ineffective" hedge according to GAAP. On the other hand, if Vintage buys too many contracts, the hedge is also considered ineffective. That's because the futures contracts are excessive and more like a speculative investment than a true hedge of underlying market risk.

> *SFAS Nos. 133* and *No. 138* do not provide a bright line that defines "highly effective," so interpretation of this phrase is a matter of professional judgment. The range of 80% to 125% is becoming an accepted threshold for high effectiveness, but the FASB has not sanctioned it. You should know about one more feature of hedge effectiveness. Vintage Construction can instead purchase 10 lumber futures contracts and still have a "highly effective" hedge if (1) it designates the contracts as a "partial hedge" of its risk exposure (for example, 50% of its lumber purchases) and (2) the contracts are "highly effective" in hedging that partial exposure.

The GAAP distinction between *highly effective* and *ineffective* hedges determines when gains and losses on the hedging instrument flow to current income. A highly effective hedge qualifies for special hedge accounting treatment; an ineffective hedge does not. Even if the highly effective test is met, some ineffectiveness may occur. And when it does, the ineffective portion of the hedge must flow directly to income. So, if Vintage Construction buys futures contracts that hedge just 50% of its full exposure, all of the gains and losses from this *ineffective* hedge flow directly to current income. That's because the contracts are ineffective and do not qualify for hedge accounting. And if the company buys futures contracts to hedge 110% of its exposure, the gains and losses on the *ineffective* portion of the hedge (the portion over 100% coverage) also flow directly to current income. Gains and losses on the remaining effective portion (equal to 100% coverage) of the hedge flow to Other comprehensive income because the contracts qualify as a "highly effective" hedge and hedge accounting rules apply.

In a letter to the FASB, Al Wargo of Eastman Chemical said that hedge accounting could cause his company's quarterly earnings per share (EPS) to fluctuate by roughly 100% in either direction—from a $0.12 loss to a $2.24 profit based on Eastman's $1.12 EPS for the second quarter of 2000. The only way Eastman can eliminate this EPS volatility is to change how it hedges financial risk. But this means replacing a sound economic hedging trasaction with a less effective hedge. EPS would then be less volatile, but the company may be more exposed to financial risks.

*Source: P. A. McKay and J. Niedzielski, "New Accounting Standard Gets Mixed Reviews," The Wall Street Journal, October 23, 2000.*

Critics of hedge accounting claim that additional income statement and balance sheet volatility is created when the gains and losses on the hedging instrument exceed the losses and gains on the hedged item. ***This added volatility may force managers to choose between achieving sound economic results—meaning hedges that effectively address real financial risks—or minimizing accounting volatility using risk management approaches that are less efficient or simply not prudent.***

**RE**CAP

**Derivatives, when used properly, allow companies to stabilize their operating cash flows by eliminating specific sources of volatility such as fluctuations in interest rates, exchange rates, and commodity prices. The GAAP rules for derivatives are detailed and complex, but the essential points are simple. Derivative contracts represent balance sheet assets and liabilities that must be marked-to-market at each balance sheet date. The resulting mark-to-market adjustment—the change in fair value—then flows either to current earnings (for fair value hedges, certain foreign currency hedges, and derivatives held for trading and speculation) or to Other comprehensive income (for cash flow hedges and most other foreign currency hedges). Other aspects of hedge accounting then match gains (or losses) on the derivative with offsetting losses (or gains) on the hedged item. This allows the financial statements to reflect accurately the underlying economics of the hedge.**

## CONTINGENT LIABILITIES

**Contingent liabilities** differ in one important way from the liabilities described elsewhere in this chapter—contingent liabilities are shrouded in uncertainty as to whether or not an obligation really exists. And the uncertainty will be resolved only at some future date when an event does or does not occur. For example, suppose that Whiffle Toy is being sued for $10 million in alleged damages related to its Whamo lawn dart game. If the court rules against Whiffle, an obligation exists because the company then owes plaintiffs the $10 million in damages. But if the court rules for Whiffle, no obligation exists. Loss contingencies of this type arise from factors such as litigation, industrial accidents, debt guarantees, and product warranties. For financial reporting purposes, two questions about contingent liabilities must be resolved: (1) When do loss contingencies need to be measured and recognized in the financial statements? (2) Under what circumstances do these contingencies need to be disclosed in footnotes, even when no liability is recorded on the balance sheet itself?

# Measuring and Recognizing Loss Contingencies

The rules for measuring and recognizing loss contingencies in the financial statements are virtually identical to the rules governing revenue recognition. *SFAS No. 5* states that a loss contingency shall be accrued by a charge to income if *both* of the following conditions exist:

1. It is *probable* that an asset has been impaired or a liability has been incurred at the date of the financial statements.
2. The amount of loss can be *reasonably estimated.*[22]

Here's an example of an accrued loss contingency disclosure taken from the financial statements of Stanley Inc.:

> In the normal course of business, . . . the company is party to a number of proceedings before federal and state regulatory agencies relating to environmental matters. . . . The company's policy is to accrue environmental investigatory and remediation costs for identified sites when it is probable that a liability has been incurred and the amount of loss can be reasonably estimated. . . . As of December 29, 2001, the company had reserves of $14.6 million, primarily for remediation activities associated with company-owned properties as well as for Superfund sites.
>
> *Source:* Stanley Inc., 2001 annual report.

Stanley has recorded a $14.6 million loss contingency for environmental cleanup at some of its current and former manufacturing sites. And a corresponding $14.6 million contingent liability is shown on the company's balance sheet. Stanley also explains why it has already accrued the loss: The company believes that it is probable that an obligation to clean up these sites exists, and the amounts involved can be reasonably estimated. Under these circumstances, *SFAS No. 5* requires that a contingent loss and corresponding liability be recorded.

Loss contingency disclosures are also sometimes made even when no loss has been recognized in the income statement itself. For example, if the loss probability is only "reasonably possible" or "remote" (refer to Figure 11.12), then no loss accrual needs to be made in the financial statements. ***Nevertheless, footnote disclosure of loss contingencies is necessary when the loss is both reasonably possible and can be estimated.*** Furthermore, even contingencies arising from remote possibilities must be disclosed in certain circumstances, such as when one company guarantees another company's debt—that is, it agrees to repay a loan if the borrower cannot.

Here's an example of a loss contingency disclosure when no loss has been recognized on the income statement. As you will notice, current and former shareholders are suing Mattel, Inc. for reasons described in the financial statement footnote.

> Following Mattel's announcement in October 1999 of the expected results of its Learning Company division for the third quarter of 1999, several of Mattel's stockholders filed purported class action complaints naming Mattel and certain of its present and former officers and directors as defendants. The complaints generally allege, among other things, that the defendants made false or misleading statements, in the joint proxy statement for the merger of Mattel and Learning Company and elsewhere, that artificially inflated the price of Mattel's common stock. . . . Mattel believes that the actions are without merit and intends to defend them vigorously.
>
> *Source:* Mattel Inc., 2001 annual report.

Mattel does not specifically mention a dollar amount for its contingent obligation (perhaps because it cannot be reasonably estimated), nor does the company reveal its internal assesment

---

[22] "Accounting for Contingencies," *SFAS No. 5* (Stamford, CT: FASB, 1975), para. 8.

**Figure 11.12**

*SFAS NO. 5* LOSS
PROBABILITY CONTINUUM

| *Less likely* | | *More likely* |
|---|---|---|
| Remote | Reasonably Possible | Probable |
| The chance of the future event is slight | The chance of occurrence is more than remote but less than likely | The future event is likely to occur |

of the probability that the court will uphold the shareholders' claims. But the language Mattel uses—"actions are without merit" and "defend them vigorously"—suggests that management believes the court will decide the matter in Mattel's favor. Accordingly, Mattel has not yet accrued a contingent loss for the ongoing litigation.

The FASB established a range representing the likelihood of losses occurring, which is depicted in Figure 11.12, where "probable" indicates the highest likelihood. Notice that the two loss contingency recognition conditions correspond to the two income recognition conditions—"critical event" and "measurability"—discussed in Chapter 2. Specifically, the critical event for loss recognition is that it is probable that a loss has occurred or will occur; similarly, the measurability criterion corresponds closely to how well the loss can be estimated. In this sense, the criteria that trigger income and loss recognition are roughly parallel.

For certain categories of events, applying the loss contingency rules has become routine. One example of a routine loss contingency is the expense for **estimated uncollectible receivables** described in Chapter 8. Uncollectibles represent a normal cost of business when companies sell goods or services on credit, but the amount of the uncollectible loss is unknown at the time of sale. Because some loss is probable and the amount can be estimated, an expense (estimated uncollectible loss) is recorded in the same period that the sale occurs.

In other situations, the issue of whether to recognize a loss contingency is highly subjective and complicated by the fact that recognizing and disclosing the loss could itself cause further harm. Consider a company that is being sued for actions that allegedly harmed others.

> Wren Corporation manufactures a wide range of chemical food additives sold to numerous food processors throughout the country. Due to a serious production error, Wren produced and sold a highly toxic batch of a flavor enhancer in October 2005. Thousands of consumers were made seriously ill; some died. A class action lawsuit seeking $10 billion in damages has been filed.

The fictitious Wren scenario illustrates a setting in which a straightforward application of the *SFAS No. 5* loss contingency rules could prove harmful to the company. Let's say that Wren's management was indeed negligent and expects to negotiate an approximately $2 billion out-of-court settlement. If Wren accrued a charge for this expected payout, its negotiating position could be seriously weakened by a disclosure to the plaintiffs that it is prepared to pay at least $2 billion. Because the plaintiffs might be willing to settle for less than $2 billion, candid disclosure of the minimum estimated loss by Wren could raise the ultimate loss payout. Companies like Wren have strong incentives to either:

1. Accrue a loss that is significantly *smaller* than the real estimated loss.
2. Disclose that while a loss may have occurred, its amount is not yet measurable.

Consequently, the *SFAS No. 5* rules for loss contingencies arising from litigation are difficult to enforce. ***Statement readers must be aware of the potential understatement of litigation losses and liabilities.***

**Loss Contingency Disclosures**   When companies accrue a loss contingency, they also usually disclose other information regarding the loss separately in footnotes to the financial statements. *SFAS No. 5* requires this disclosure when a failure to provide additional supplemental data could lead to misleading inferences.

## Recording Gain Contingencies

> When they are recorded, the gain flows to income, and a corresponding contingent receivable is shown on the balance sheet.

While the defendant in a lawsuit (for example, Mattel Corporation) faces a contingent loss, the other side—the plaintiff—has a contingent gain reflecting the possibility that the court will decide that monetary damages must be paid to the plaintiff. As you now know, loss contingencies are accrued when the event confirming the obligation is probable and the amount can be reasonably estimated. **Gain contingencies,** on the other hand, are not recorded until the event actually occurs and the obligation is confirmed. This differing treatment of loss contingencies and gain contingencies illustrates **accounting conservatism**—the notion that it's desirable to anticipate losses, but recognizing gains should wait until their confirmation and realization.

## SUMMARY

- An astounding variety of financial instruments, derivatives, and nontraditional financing arrangements is now used to fund corporate activities and to manage risk. Statement readers face a daunting task when trying to grasp the economic implications of some financial innovations.

- Off-balance-sheet obligations and loss contingencies are difficult to evaluate because the information needed for that evaluation is often not disclosed.

- Derivatives—whether used for hedging or speculation—pose special problems because of both their complexity and the involved details of hedge accounting.

- For many companies, the most important long-term obligation is still traditional debt financing. GAAP in this area is quite clear. Noncurrent monetary liabilities are initially recorded at the discounted present value of the contractual cash flows—that is, the issue price. The effective interest method is then used to compute interest expense and net carrying value in each period. Interest rate changes occurring after the debt has been issued are ignored.

- GAAP accounting for long-term debt makes it possible to "manage" reported income statement and balance sheet numbers when debt is retired before maturity. The opportunity to "manage" those numbers comes from the difference between debt book value and market value when interest rates have changed.

- The incentives for "managing" income statement and balance sheet numbers may be related to debt covenants, compensation, regulation, or just the desire to paint a favorable picture of the company's performance and health.

- Extinguishment gains and losses from early debt retirement and swaps require careful scrutiny. Statement readers need to know whether real economic benefits for the company and its shareholders are produced—or if the gains or losses are just window dressing.

- GAAP now allows firms to opt for fair value accounting for long-term debt. Doing so can reduce earnings volatility in some settings.

## MALLARD CORPORATION

Mallard Corporation constructs and operates private waterfowl hunting facilities throughout the western United States. On July 1, 2008, the company issued $5 million of par value, 10-year bonds to finance construction of a guest lodge at its newest site in Klamath, Oregon. The bonds pay interest semiannually (on December 31 and June 30) at an annual rate of 8% and are callable by Mallard at 102% of par value. The bonds were issued at a price that yields 10% annually to maturity.

1. **Compute the issue price of the bonds.** The bond cash flows include a semiannual interest payment of $200,000 (or $5 million at 4%) plus the principal payment of $5 million at maturity. With an effective (market) interest rate of 5% for each six-month interval, the present value factors are:

   20-period ordinary annuity at 5% = 12.46221

   20-period single payment =  0.37689

   Multiplying each factor by the corresponding cash flow gives the issue price as:

   $$\begin{array}{rll} \$\ \ 200{,}000 \times 12.46221 &= \$2{,}492{,}442 \\ +\ 5{,}000{,}000 \times\ \ \ 0.37689 &=\ \underline{1{,}884{,}450} \\ & \ \ \ \$4{,}376{,}892 \end{array}$$

   The bonds were thus issued at a discount of $623,108 (or $5,000,000 − $4,376,892).

2. **Compute the amount of interest expense on the bonds for 2008. Mallard Corporation uses the effective interest method for amortizing bond discounts and premiums.** Because the bonds were issued on July 1, 2008, only six months of interest need be recorded for the year. Interest expense is computed at the effective interest rate of 5%. This rate is multiplied by the amount borrowed (beginning book value) to find interest expense:

   $4,376,892 × 5% = $218,845 (rounded)

   Computed interest expense is more than the required $200,000 cash payment. The $18,845 difference represents amortization of the bond discount—that is, an increase to the bond's book value. Mallard Corporation's year-end financial statements would show the bond at $4,395,737 ($4,376,892 + $18,845).

3. **Mallard uses the indirect method of computing cash flows from operations on its cash flow statement. Indicate how much will be added to (or subtracted from) the 2008 accrual-basis net income figure that is related to the bonds to obtain cash flows from operations.** The accrual income figure contains interest expense of $218,845, but the cash interest payment is only $200,000. The additional $18,845 interest expense does not represent an operating cash outflow for the year, and so it is added back to net income to arrive at cash flows from operations. Notice that this amount equals the discount amortization for the year.

4. **Assume that the market yield on the bonds had fallen to 9% by July 1, 2010 and that Mallard decided to retire the debt on that date either by purchasing the bonds on the open market or by exercising its 102% call option. Which method of debt retirement is the least expensive for Mallard?** Under the terms of the call option, Mallard can retire the debt by paying bond holders 102% of par value, or:

   $5,000,000 × 1.02 = $5,100,000

However, the bonds' current market value at an annual yield of 9% is:

$$
\begin{aligned}
\$\ 200{,}000 \times 11.23402 &= \$2{,}246{,}804 \\
+\ 5{,}000{,}000 \times\ \ 0.49447 &= \underline{\ 2{,}472{,}350} \\
&\ \ \ \ \$4{,}719{,}154
\end{aligned}
$$

The open-market purchase is the least expensive way for Mallard to retire its debt. (Notice that the present value factors used to compute the current market price are based on a 4.5% semiannual yield and 16 six-month periods to July 1, 2018.)

5. **Produce the journal entry that Mallard Corporation recorded on July 1, 2010 when it retired the bonds through an open market purchase.** Assume that all interest expense and cash interest payments have been recorded. Then the bonds' book value on July 1, 2010 is $4,458,115, as shown in the amortization table.

| | Period (six-month interval) | Liability at Start of Period | Effective Interest: 5% per Period | Coupon Rate: 4% of Par | Increase in Recorded Book Value | Liability at End of Period |
|---|---|---|---|---|---|---|
| 7/1/08 | 0 | | | | | $4,376,892 |
| 1/1/09 | 1 | $4,376,892 | $218,845 | $200,000 | $18,845 | 4,395,737 |
| 7/1/09 | 2 | 4,395,737 | 219,787 | 200,000 | 19,787 | 4,415,524 |
| 1/1/10 | 3 | 4,415,523 | 220,776 | 200,000 | 20,776 | 4,436,300 |
| 7/1/10 | 4 | 4,436,300 | 221,815 | 200,000 | 21,815 | 4,458,115 |

Based on our previous calculation, we find that Mallard would pay $4,719,154 to retire the bonds on that date, so the entry is:

| | | | |
|---|---|---|---|
| **DR** | Bonds payable............................................ | $5,000,000 | |
| **DR** | Loss on debt retirement.................................. | 261,039 | |
| | **CR** Discount on bonds ................................ | | $ 541,885 |
| | **CR** Cash............................................. | | 4,719,154 |

where $541,885 represents the remaining (unamortized) balance of the original issue discount ($5,000,000 face value − $4,458,115 book value).

---

## SELF-STUDY PROBLEM

### SNAP-ON INC.

Exhibit 11.13 is taken from the 2002 Shareholder Report of Snap-On Inc., a manufacturer and marketer of high-quality professional automotive and industrial tools. The exhibit typifies the required disclosures for long-term debt, although Snap-On also devotes a portion of this footnote to a discussion of its short-term debt. The exhibit also identifies the various debt categories and describes the major debt instruments' key characteristics—such as covenants tied to financial statement ratios. An enumeration of scheduled principal repayments over the ensuing five years is also provided. The intent of the disclosure is to provide data on future cash outflows and credit risk; these data help analysts and others generate cash flow forecasts.

1. **The first paragraph of the footnote indicates that "notes payable and long-term debt" totaled $360.7 million at the end of 2002. What are the individual components that make up this total amount?** The company's short-term and long-term debt at year-end 2002 consists of notes payable to banks ($22.3 million), commercial paper denominated in U.S. dollars ($25.0 million), commercial paper denominated in Japanese yen ($7.9 million),

# EXHIBIT 11.13   Snap-On Inc.

## 2002 Short-Term and Long-Term Debt Footnote

Notes payable and long-term debt at the end of 2002 totaled $360.7 million, down $113.9 million from the $474.6 million reported at year-end 2001. Notes payable to banks under bank lines of credit totaled $22.3 million and $26.5 million at the end of 2002 and 2001. At the end of 2002, Snap-On had commercial paper outstanding denominated in U.S. dollars of $25.0 million and Japanese yen of $7.9 million compared to commercial paper outstanding denominated in U.S. dollars of $135.0 million and Japanese yen of $7.2 million at year-end 2001. Snap-On classified its outstanding commercial paper as long-term debt at year-end 2001 as it was Snap-On's intent, and it had the ability (supported by its long-term revolving credit facilities), to refinance this debt on a long-term basis. Snap-On's increased cash provided by operating activities in 2002 was used primarily to reduce commercial paper borrowings. The company currently anticipates that it will continue to have positive cash flow and debt reduction for the foreseeable future and, as a result, commercial paper borrowings at December 28, 2002, of $32.9 million are included in "Notes payable and current maturities of long-term debt" on the accompanying Consolidated Balance Sheets.

At December 28, 2002, Snap-On had $408 million of multi-currency revolving credit facilities that also serve to back its commercial paper programs, including a $200 million, 364-day revolving credit facility with a one-year term-out option that terminates on August 8, 2003. The term-out option allows Snap-On to elect to borrow under the credit facility for an additional year after the termination date. In addition, Snap-On has a five-year, $208 million revolving credit facility that terminates on August 20, 2005. At the end of 2002 and 2001, Snap-On was in compliance with all covenants of the revolving credit facilities and there were no borrowings under either revolving credit commitment. The most restrictive financial covenant requires that Snap-On maintain a total debt to total capital (defined as total debt plus shareholders' equity) ratio that does not exceed 60%. Snap-On's total debt to total capital ratio, computed as defined by the financial covenant, was 30.3% at December 28, 2002, and 38.0% at December 29, 2001. At December 28, 2002, Snap-On also had an unused committed $20 million bank line of credit that expires on August 1, 2003. At December 28, 2002, Snap-On had approximately $395 million of unused available debt capacity under the terms of its revolving credit facilities and committed bank line of credit.

Average commercial paper and bank notes outstanding were $189.6 million in 2002 and $389.2 million in 2001. The weighted-average interest rate on these instruments was 1.7% in 2002 and 4.3% in 2001. As of December 28, 2002, and December 29, 2001, commercial paper and bank notes outstanding had a weighted-average interest rate of 1.3% and 2.1%.

In August 2001, Snap-On issued $200 million of unsecured notes pursuant to a $300 million shelf registration statement filed with the Securities and Exchange Commission in 1994. In October 1995, Snap-On issued $100 million of unsecured notes to the public under this shelf registration. The August 2001 notes require semiannual interest payments at the rate of 6.25% and mature in their entirety on August 15, 2011. The October 1995 notes require semiannual interest payments at a rate of 6.625% and mature in their entirety on October 1, 2005. The proceeds from these issuances were used to repay a portion of Snap-On's outstanding commercial paper and for working capital and general corporate purposes.

Snap-On's long-term debt at year-end 2002 and 2001 consisted of the following:

| (Amounts in millions) | 2002 | 2001 |
|---|---|---|
| Senior unsecured indebtedness | $300.0 | $300.0 |
| Borrowings under commercial paper programs | — | 142.2 |
| Other long-term debt | 5.5 | 5.9 |
| | 305.5 | 448.1 |
| Current maturities | (1.2) | (2.6) |
| Total long-term debt | $304.3 | $445.5 |

The annual maturities of Snap-On's long-term debt due in the next five years are $1.2 million in 2003, $.5 million in 2004, and $100.2 million in 2005, with no maturities of long-term debt in 2006 and 2007.

senior unsecured indebtedness ($300 million), and "other" long-term debt ($5.5 million). These amounts total $360.7 million, an amount that includes $1.2 million in current maturities of long-term debt.

2. **Why did the company classify its commercial paper as long-term debt in 2001 but as short-term debt in 2002?** As 2001 ended, Snap-On was planning to replace the commercial paper loans with long-term debt in early 2002. So, the company included commercial paper along with its other long-term debt to alert analysts and investors about the planned refinancing. Apparently, management changed its mind in 2002 and decided not to refinance the debt. Accordingly, the company's commercial paper is shown then as a short-term obligation.

*Commercial paper* refers to short-term debt obligations with maturities ranging from 2 to 270 days issued by banks, corporations (for example, Snap-On), and other borrowers to investors with temporarily idle cash.

3. **The third paragraph of the footnote discloses the "average" commercial paper and bank notes outstanding for 2002, along with the weighted-average interest rate on those instruments. Why might this information be of use to an analyst?** The average outstanding balance of these short-term obligations ($189.6 million) for 2002 is substantially above the year-end amount outstanding ($55.2 million as described in the answer to question 1). Snap-On apparently has seasonal borrowing needs, in which case the average outstanding balance better indicates the company's true debt during the year. Because the weighted average interest rate on commercial paper was 1.7% in 2002, the interest expense for these short-term obligations must have been about $3.2 million (or $189.6 average outstanding balance multiplied by the 1.7% weighted average interest rate).

4. **How much cash did the company receive in 2001 when it issued the $200 million of "Senior unsecured indebtedness"?** The footnote describes two occasions when Snap-On issued (senior) unsecured debt: $200 million issued in 2001 and another $100 million issued in 1995. The amounts described in the footnote represent the face value of the debt. But the footnote table reveals that the debt's book value is also $300 million. Apparently, Snap-On issued the debt at face value and thus received $200 million of cash in 2001 (and $100 million in 1995).

5. **How much interest expense did the company record on the senior unsecured debt in 2002?** The 1995 senior unsecured debt has an interest rate of 6.625%, and the entire $100 million principal amount was outstanding for 2002. So, Snap-On recorded interest expense in the amount of $6.625 million ($100 million × the 6.625% interest rate) for the 1995 debt. The same line of reasoning indicates that Snap-On recorded interest expense of $12.500 million ($200 million × the 6.25% interest rate) for the 2001 debt. Total interest expense for these two long-term obligations in 2002 would thus be $19.125 million.

6. **Does the company face any near-term cash flow problems as a consequence of its current borrowings?** The final paragraph of the footnote describes the company's scheduled debt payments for the next five years. Here we see that Snap-On is required to make a $100.2 million payment in 2005, so this could be a critical cash flow year.

7. **Is Snap-On close to violating any debt covenants?** Apparently not. The second paragraph of the footnote indicates the company was "in compliance" with all covenants of its revolving credit facilities. In fact, the most restrictive covenant requires Snap-On to maintain a total debt-to-capital ratio that does not exceed 60%. But the company seems to have considerable slack in this covenant because its actual total debt-to-capital ratio is only 30.3%. There is no mention of covenants for the company's other debt instruments—and there surely are some—but they may be less restrictive than are those of its revolving credit line.

# EXERCISES

**E11-1**

Finding the issue price

**AICPA**
ADAPTED

mhhe.com/revsine4e

Akers Company sold bonds on July 1, 2008 with a face value of $100,000. These bonds are due in 10 years. The stated annual interest rate is 6% per year, payable semiannually on June 30 and December 31. These bonds were sold to yield 8%.

**Required:**
How much did these bonds sell for on July 1, 2008?

By July 1, 2009, the market yield on the Akers Company bonds described in E11–1 had risen to 10%.

**Required:**

What was the bonds' market price on July 1, 2009?

Determining market price following a change in interest rates

mhhe.com/revsine4e

---

On January 1, 2008 when the market interest rate was 14%, Luba Corporation issued bonds in the face amount of $500,000 with interest at 12% payable semiannually. The bonds mature on December 31, 2017.

**Required:**

Calculate the bond discount at issuance. How much of the discount should be amortized by the effective interest method on July 1, 2008?

Finding the discount at issuance

AICPA
ADAPTED

---

On January 2, 2008, West Company issued 9% bonds in the amount of $500,000 that mature on December 31, 2017. The bonds were issued for $469,500 to yield 10%. Interest is payable annually on December 31. West uses the effective interest method of amortizing bond discounts.

**Required:**

In its June 30, 2008 balance sheet, what net amount should West report as bonds payable?

Determining a bond's balance sheet value

AICPA
ADAPTED

---

On February 1, 2005, Davis Corporation issued 12%, $1,000,000 par, 10-year bonds for $1,117,000. Davis reacquired all of these bonds at 102% of par, plus accrued interest, on May 1, 2008 and retired them. The unamortized bond premium on that date was $78,000.

**Required:**

Before income taxes, what was Davis's gain or loss on the bond retirement?

Calculating gain or loss at early retirement

AICPA
ADAPTED

---

Webb Company has outstanding a 7% annual, 10-year, $100,000 face value bond that it had issued several years ago. It originally sold the bond to yield 6% annual interest. Webb uses the effective interest rate method to amortize the bond premium. On June 30, 2008, the outstanding bond's carrying amount was $105,000.

**Required:**

What amount of unamortized premium on the bond should Webb report in its June 30, 2009 balance sheet?

Amortizing a premium

AICPA
ADAPTED

---

Brower Corporation owns a manufacturing plant in the country of Oust. On December 31, 2008, the plant had a book value of $5,000,000 and an estimated fair value of $8,000,000. Oust's government has clearly indicated that it will expropriate the plant during the coming year and will reimburse Brower for only 40% of the plant's estimated fair value.

**Required:**

What journal entry should Brower make on December 31, 2008 to record the intended expropriation?

Recording loss contingencies

AICPA
ADAPTED

---

On January 1, 2008, Buckingham Corporation issued $10 million of 8% coupon bonds. The bonds pay interest semiannually on June 30 and December 31, and they mature in 10 years. They were issued to yield a market interest rate of 8%.

Computing the price of bonds sold at par

**Required:**

Compute the issue price of the bonds on January 1, 2008. Why is there no discount or premium to record?

---

**E11-9**

Debt-for-equity swap

**eXcel**

mhhe.com/revsine4e

On January 1, 2008, Tusk Corporation issued $100 million of 10% coupon bonds at par value. Interest is paid semiannually on June 30 and December 31 of each year. The bonds mature in 10 years. On January 1, 2011, the market yield on Tusk bonds is 14%.

**Required:**

1. What is the market value of the bonds on January 1, 2011?

2. Suppose that Tusk retired the bonds on January 1, 2011 by exchanging common stock of equal value with bondholders. What journal entry would Tusk record to retire the bonds?

---

**E11-10**

Imputing interest

Greg Miller wants to buy a new automobile. The dealer has the exact car Miller wants and has given him two payment options: pay (1) the full cash price of $19,326 today or (2) only $2,000 down today and then make four more annual payments of $5,000 beginning one year from today. Miller doesn't have the cash needed to pay the car's full price, but he does have enough for the down payment. He can also obtain an automobile loan from his bank at 5% interest per year.

**Required:**

1. Verify that the imputed interest rate on the dealer's loan is 6%. That is, show that the present value of Miller's payments equal $19,326 (rounded to the nearest dollar) when discounted at 6%.

2. Which payment option should Miller accept?

---

**E11-11**

Zero coupon bonds

**eXcel**

mhhe.com/revsine4e

Zero coupon bonds pay no interest—the only cash investors receive is the lump-sum principal payment at maturity. On January 1, 2008, The Ledge Inc. issued $250 million of zero coupon bonds at a market yield rate of 12%. The bonds mature in 20 years.

**Required:**

1. What was the January 1, 2008 issue price of these zero coupon bonds?

2. How much interest expense will The Ledge record on the bonds in 2008?

---

**E11-12**

Floating-rate debt

On January 1, 2008, 3Way Energy issued $200 million of 15-year, floating-rate debentures at par value. The debentures pay interest on June 30 and December 31 of each year. The floating interest rate is set equal to "LIBOR plus 6%" on January 1 of each year. The LIBOR was 6% when the bonds were issued and 8% on January 1, 2009.

**Required:**

1. How much cash interest did 3Way Energy pay on the debentures in 2008? How much will it pay in 2009?

2. How much interest expense did the company record on the debentures in 2008? How much will it record in 2009?

---

**E11-13**

Identifying incentives for early debt retirement

**eXcel**

mhhe.com/revsine4e

On January 1, 2007, Roland Inc. issued $125 million of 8% coupon bonds at par. The bonds pay interest semiannually on June 30 and December 31 of each year, and they mature in 15 years. On December 31, 2008 (one day before the next interest payment is made), the bonds are trading at a market yield of 12% plus accrued interest.

**Required:**

1. Suppose that Roland repurchased the entire $125 million bonds for cash at the market price on December 31, 2008. Using a 40% corporate tax rate, how much gain or loss would the company record on this transaction?

2. Why might the company want to retire the debt early?

Wood Company and Willie Inc. form a joint venture—Woodly Partners—to manufacture and distribute agricultural pesticides. Wood and Willie each contribute $20 million cash and receive 50% of Woodly's common stock. Woodly then borrows $200 million from a consortium of banks and uses the money to build its manufacturing and distribution facilities. The loan is made on December 31, 2008 and is fully guaranteed by both Wood and Willie.

**E11-14**

Off-balance-sheet debt

**Required:**

How much of the $200 million debt shows up on the December 31, 2008 balance sheet of Wood Company? Why?

McClelland Corporation agreed to purchase some landscaping equipment from Agri-Products for a cash price of $500,000. Before accepting delivery of the equipment, McClelland learned that the same equipment could be purchased from another dealer for $460,000. To avoid losing the sale, Agri-Products has offered McClelland a "no interest" payment plan—McClelland would pay $100,000 at delivery, $200,000 one year later, and the final $200,000 in two years.

**E11-15**

Noninterest-bearing loan

**Required:**

1. McClelland would usually pay 9% annual interest on a loan of this type. What is the present value of the Agri-Products loan at the delivery date?

2. What journal entry would McClelland make if it accepts the deal and buys from Agri-Products?

3. What should McClelland do?

**Required:**

1. Which of the following qualifies as a hedged item?

   a. A company's work-in-process inventory of unfinished washers, dryers, and refrigerators.

   b. Credit card receivables at Sears, Roebuck and Company.

   c. Bushels of corn owned by the Farmers' Cooperative.

   d. Salaries payable to employees of Ford Motor Company.

   e. A three-year note issued by General Motors and payable in U.S. dollars.

   f. A three-year note issued by Chrysler and payable in euros.

**E11-16**

Understanding GAAP hedges

2. Which of the following qualifies as a hedging instrument?

   a. An electricity futures contract purchased by Alliant Energy, an electrical power company.

   b. A crop insurance contract purchased by Farmers' Cooperative that pays the co-op for crop losses from drought or flood.

   c. An option to buy shares of common stock in Ford Motor Company.

   d. An option to sell shares of common stock in General Motors.

   e. A four-year lease for office space in downtown Toronto.

3. Which of the following qualifies as an eligible risk for hedge accounting?

   a. Alliant Energy's risk that summer demand for electricity may exceed the company's power-generating capacity.

   b. Ford Motor Company's risk that not enough steel will be available in six months when the company must purchase steel to produce a new sports utility vehicle.

   c. The risk to American Express that its members won't pay their credit card bills.

   d. The risk to Farmers' Cooperative that corn mold will destroy its inventory of corn held in silos for sale next year.

   e. The possibility of changes in the exchange rate of U.S. dollars for Mexican pesos for Coca-Cola Company, which has a major foreign investment in Mexico.

# PROBLEMS / DISCUSSION QUESTIONS

On July 1, 2008, McVay Corporation issued $15 million of 10-year bonds with an 8% coupon interest rate. The bonds pay interest semiannually on June 30 and December 31 of each year. The market rate of interest on July 1, 2008 for bonds of this type was 10%. McVay closes its books on December 31.

**Required:**

1. At what price were the bonds issued?

2. Using the effective interest method, prepare an amortization schedule showing interest expense, discount or premium amortization, and bond carrying value for each of the first four semiannual interest payment periods.

3. Prepare journal entries to record the first four semiannual interest payments.

4. How should the bonds be shown on McVay's December 31, 2008 balance sheet and on its December 31, 2009 balance sheet?

On January 1, 2008, Fleetwood Inc. issued bonds with a face amount of $25 million and a coupon interest rate of 8%. The bonds mature in 10 years and pay interest semiannually on June 30 and December 31 of each year. The market rate of interest on January 1, 2008 for bonds of this type was 6%. Fleetwood closes its books on December 31.

**Required:**

1. At what price were the bonds issued?

2. Using the effective interest method, prepare an amortization schedule showing interest expense, amortization, and bond carrying value for each of the first four semiannual interest payment periods.

3. Prepare journal entries to record the first four semiannual interest payments.

4. How would the bonds be shown on Fleetwood's December 31, 2008 balance sheet and on its December 31, 2009 balance sheet?

On January 1, 2008, Newell Manufacturing purchased a new drill press that had a cash purchase price of $6,340. Newell decided instead to pay on an installment basis. The installment contract calls for four annual payments of $2,000 each beginning in one year. Newell was not required to make an initial down payment for the drill press.

**Required:**

1. Verify that the imputed interest rate on the installment loan is 10%. That is, show that the present value of the payments Newell must make is $6,340 (rounded to the nearest dollar) when discounted at a 10% rate of interest.

2. What journal entry would Newell make on January 1, 2008 to record the drill press purchase?

3. How much interest expense would Newell record in 2008 for the installment loan? What would the loan balance be on January 1, 2009 after Newell made the first loan payment?

4. How much interest expense would Newell record in 2009 for the installment loan? What would the loan balance be on December 31, 2009—one day before Newell makes the second loan payment?

Cory Company needs to raise about $500,000 to finance the expansion of its office building. It is considering three alternative loan arrangements:

- *Alternative A:* Issue a $500,000, 20-year bond with an interest rate of 10%.
- *Alternative B:* Issue a $700,000, 20-year bond with an interest rate of 6%.
- *Alternative C:* Issue a $400,000, 20-year bond with an interest rate of 12%.

Each bond pays interest annually. The market interest rate for bonds of this risk and duration is 9%, and the company needs to raise the money on January 1, 2008.

**Required:**

1. What is the issue price of each bond?

2. How much cash would the company have to pay in 2008 for each bond?

3. For each alternative, how much interest expense would it record in 2009 and in 2014?

4. For each alternative, how much interest expense would Cory Company record over the loan's entire 20-year life?

5. For each alternative, how much cash would Cory Company pay to bondholders over the loan's entire 20-year life?

6. If Cory Company's marginal tax rate is 40%, which alternative do you recommend? Why?

On January 1, 2008, Mason Manufacturing borrows $500,000 and uses the money to purchase corporate bonds for investment purposes. Interest rates were quite volatile that year and so were the fair values of Mason's bond investment (an asset) and loan (a liability):

| | Fair Value | |
|---|---|---|
| **2008** | **Bond Investment** | **Loan** |
| January 1 | $500,000 | $500,000 |
| March 31 | 450,000 | 465,000 |
| June 30 | 480,000 | 493,000 |
| September 30 | 510,000 | 504,000 |
| December 31 | 485,000 | 495,000 |

**Required:**

1. Mason is required to use fair value accounting for the bond investment. Prepare the journal entry to record the investment purchase on January 1, 2008 and the fair value adjustments required at the end of each quarter: March 31, June 30, September 30, and December 31.

2. Suppose that Mason uses conventional amortized historical cost accounting for the loan. The loan principal is due in five years. Ignore interest on the loan to simplify the problem. What will be the loan's carrying value at the end of each quarter?

3. Suppose that instead Mason elects to use the fair value option permitted by *SFAS No. 159* for the loan. What dollar impact will this change have on reported profits each quarter?

4. Which accounting approach—unamortized historical cost or fair value—do you believe Mason should use for the loan? Why?

On July 1, 2008, Stan Getz, Inc. bought call option contracts for 500 shares of Selmer Manufacturing common stock. The contracts cost $200, expire on September 15, and have an exercise price of $40 per share. The market price of Selmer's stock that day was also $40 a share. On July 31, 2008, Selmer stock was trading at $38 a share, and the option contracts' fair value was $125—that is, Getz could buy the identical $40 strike price contracts on July 31 for $125. On August 31, 2008, the market price of Selmer stock was $44 a share, and the fair value of the options contracts was $2,075.

**Required:**

1. Prepare the journal entry to record Getz's purchase of call option contracts on July 1, 2008.

2. Prepare the journal entry to record the change in fair value of the option contracts on July 31, 2008.

3. Prepare the journal entry to record the change in fair value of the option contracts on August 31, 2008.

4. Why are the option contracts worth so much more on August 31 ($2,075) than they were worth on July 31 ($125)?

5. What entry would Getz make to record exercising the options on September 15, 2008 when Selmer's shares were trading at $46?

6. Suppose instead that Getz allowed the option contracts to expire on September 15, 2008 without exercising them. What entry would Getz then make?

---

**P11-7**

Retiring debt early

mhhe.com/revsine4e

On January 1, 2008, Tango-In-The-Night, Inc. issued $75 million of bonds with a 9% coupon interest rate. The bonds mature in 10 years and pay interest semiannually on June 30 and December 31 of each year. The market rate of interest on January 1, 2008 for bonds of this type was 11%. The company closes its books on December 31.

**Required:**

1. At what price were the bonds issued?

2. What is the book value of the bonds on January 1, 2010?

3. On January 1, 2010, the market interest rate for bonds of this type is 10%. What is the market value of the bonds on this date?

4. Suppose that the bonds were repurchased for cash on January 1, 2010 at the market price. If you ignore taxes, what journal entry would the company make to record the debt retirement?

---

**P11-8**

Partial debt retirement

mhhe.com/revsine4e

On July 1, 2009, Mirage Company issued $250 million of bonds with an 8.5% coupon interest rate. The bonds mature in 10 years and pay interest semiannually on June 30 and December 31 of each year. The market rate of interest on July 1, 2009 for bonds of this risk class was 7%. Mirage closes its books on December 31.

**Required:**

1. At what price were the bonds issued?

2. Using the effective interest method, prepare an amortization schedule showing interest expense, amortization, and bond carrying value for each of the first four semiannual payment periods.

3. Prepare journal entries to record the first four semiannual interest payments and related interest accruals.

4. On July 1, 2011, the market interest rate for bonds of this risk class is 8.0%. What is the market value of the bonds on this date?

5. Suppose that 50% of the bonds were repurchased for cash on July 1, 2011 at the market price. If you ignore taxes, what journal entry would the company make to record this partial retirement?

---

**P11-9**

Chalk Hill: Using an interest rate swap as a speculative investment

Exhibit 11.12 describes Chalk Hill's use of an interest rate swap to hedge its cash flow exposure to interest rate risk from variable rate debt. The journal entries in the exhibit illustrate how special "hedge accounting" rules apply to the swap. Suppose instead that the swap *did not qualify* for special hedge accounting—but that all other aspects of the transaction remain as described in the exhibit.

**Required:**

Prepare the journal entries needed to account for the variable rate debt and swap transaction for January 1, 2008 through December 31, 2010.

### SMALL FIRMS LOOK TO DERIVATIVES TRADING TO MANAGE COSTS

Karl Fowler isn't a traditional publisher. His books, which chronicle major sporting events and teams, can weigh more than 90 pounds and go for as much as $4,000. So to control the costs of the raw materials Mr. Fowler needs to produce these hefty tomes, the entrepreneur is using an equally untraditional approach for small businesses: derivatives trading.

These sophisticated financial instruments—which allow investors to hedge risks and bet on fluctuations in anything from the weather to orange-juice prices—might not seem relevant to a small book publisher. But Mr. Fowler cut his teeth as a derivatives trader. So when he left the finance world in 2002 for book publishing, it was only natural for him to apply his specialty to help insulate his British firm, Kraken Group, from rising prices for raw materials like paper, ink, and silk. . . .

*Source:* Excerpt from "Small Firms Look to Derivatives Trading to Manage Costs," *The Wall Street Journal*, May 29, 2007. Copyright ©2007 Dow Jones & Company, Inc. All rights reserved worldwide. Reprinted with permission.

**Required:**

1. One Kraken Group strategy is to buy pulp-paper futures on commodities exchanges. Paper prices can go up and down by more than 10% in a short period. When paper prices increase, Kraken's operating profits fall. Explain how pulp-paper futures can be used to protect Kraken's profits from harmful paper price increases.

2. How will the pulp-paper futures affect profits if paper prices instead decline?

3. Ink prices tend to be even more volatile than paper prices but cannot be hedged by exchange-traded futures. So, Mr. Fowler asked an ink supplier to set up a forward contract for about half of the amount purchased each year. Explain how a forward contract can be used to protect Kraken's profits from harmful ink price increases.

4. How will the forward contract affect profits if ink prices decline instead?

Information taken from a Sears, Roebuck and Company annual report follows.

| | December 31 | |
|---|---|---|
| **Long-Term Debt** (*$ in millions*) | **Year 2** | **Year 1** |
| 7% debentures, $300 million face value, due Year 11, effective rate $14.6% | $    188.6 | $    182.7 |
| Zero coupon bonds, $500 million face value, due Year 8, effective rate 12.0% | 267.9 | 239.2 |
| Participating mortgages, $850 million face value, due Year 5, effective rate 8.7%, collateralized by Sears Tower and related properties | 834.5 | 833.9 |
| Various other long-term debt | 12,444.2 | 16,329.2 |
| Total long-term debt | $13,735.2 | $17,585.0 |

**Required:**

1. How much interest expense did the company record during Year 2 on the 7% debentures? How much of the original issue discount was amortized during Year 2?

2. How much interest expense did the company record during Year 2 on the zero coupon bonds?

3. Suppose that interest payments on the participating mortgages are made on December 31 of each year. What journal entry did the company make in Year 2 to recognize interest expense on this debt?

4. How much cash interest did the company pay out during Year 2 on the 7% debentures and the zero coupon bonds?

---

**P11-12**

Hedging

The following excerpts were taken from a recent annual report of Quaker Oats Company:

### Foreign Currency Swaps

[Several years ago] the Company swapped $15.0 million of long-term debt for 27.9 million in deutsche mark (DM) denominated long-term debt, effectively hedging part of the German net investment. . . . Due to the sale of the European pet food business last year, the net investment in Germany was reduced to the point where the DM swap was no longer effective as a net investment hedge, requiring any subsequent revaluation adjustments to be charged or credited to the consolidated income statement. To offset this charge or credit, the Company entered into a foreign exchange forward contract and the net effect on the consolidated income statements . . . was not material. . . .

### Commodity Options and Futures

The Company uses commodity options and futures contracts to reduce its exposure to commodity price changes. The Company regularly hedges purchases of oats, corn, corn sweetener, wheat, coffee beans, and orange juice concentrate. Of the $2.81 billion in cost of goods sold, approximately $275 million to $325 million is in commodities that may be hedged. The Company's strategy is typically to hedge certain production requirements for various periods up to 12 months. As of December 31, . . . approximately 32% . . . of hedgeable production requirements for the next 12 months were hedged. . . .

### Interest Rate Hedges

The Company actively monitors its interest rate exposure. Last year the Company entered into interest rate swap agreements with a notional value of $150.0 million. The swap agreements were used to hedge fixed interest rate risk related to anticipated issuance of long-term debt. The swap agreements were subsequently terminated at a cost of $11.9 million as long-term debt was issued. Included in the consolidated balance sheets as of December 31, [Years 1 and 2] were $8.9 million and $10.8 million, respectively, of prepaid interest expense as settlement of all the interest rate swap agreements. . . . [Two years ago] the Company entered into interest rate cap agreements with a notional value of $600.0 million to hedge floating interest rate risk. . . .

**Required:**

1. What did Quaker accomplish by swapping $15.0 million of its long-term debt for 27.9 million in deutsche mark (DM)–denominated long-term debt?

2. Why was the DM swap "no longer effective" after Quaker sold its European pet food business?

3. What is a foreign exchange forward contract, and how can it be used to hedge a company's foreign currency exposure?

4. What are commodity options and futures contracts, and how do they reduce Quaker's exposure to commodity price changes?

5. What is an interest rate swap, and how can it reduce a company's exposure to interest rate risk?

6. What is an interest rate cap, and how is it used to reduce a company's exposure to interest rate changes?

---

### TROUBLE LOOMS FOR CHECKPOINT SYSTEMS

Shares of Checkpoint Systems, which makes electronic anti-theft tags used by retailers, have dropped from 18 in April to 12.50 lately, in part because of an unseasonably warm winter, which dampened apparel sales. But don't expect the stock to rebound soon, say some pros: The stock may well keep tumbling because of an antitrust lawsuit that Checkpoint lost. . . .

In late May, a U.S. District Court in Pennsylvania assessed damages of $26 million. . . . The verdict could put Checkpoint in violation of bank covenants on 1999 bank loans.

Even if Checkpoint appeals and puts off paying damages, accountants may require it to acknowledge the potential damages in its financial statement. Therein lies the problem: It had borrowed $273.9 million from banks. Those loans have covenants that might be violated by putting new debt on its balance sheet. The covenants also require Checkpoint to have a net worth of $200 million. Its current net worth is $240 million, and the damages it will have to pay will bring it below required levels.

*Source: "Trouble Looms for Checkpoint Systems," BusinessWeek, June 17, 2002.*

### Required:

1. When must firms record contingent liabilities on their balance sheets?

2. How does the district court decision influence whether Checkpoint's litigation contingency must be recorded?

3. Explain how recognition of the contingent liability will cause Checkpoint to violate its net worth covenant.

4. Is it likely that the banks will just waive the covenant violation if it occurs? (*Hint:* You may want to review the covenant violation discussion in Chapter 7).

---

On January 1, 2008, Merrill Corporation issued $2 million of par value 10-year bonds. The bonds pay interest semiannually on January 1 and July 1 at an annual rate of 10% and are callable at 102% of par. The bonds were issued to yield 8% annually.

### Required:

1. Compute the issue price of the bonds.

2. Compute the amount of interest expense on the bonds for 2008, assuming that the effective interest method is used.

3. Merrill uses the *indirect method* of computing cash flows from operations on its cash flow statement (see Chapter 4). How much will be added to or subtracted from reported net income in 2008 for these bonds to obtain cash flows from operations?

4. On January 1, 2009, the market yield on the bonds increased to 9%, and Merrill decided to retire the debt early. Indicate how much Merrill would save by exercising the call option rather than by purchasing the debt in the open market.

5. What entry would Merrill make on January 1, 2009 to record the bond retirement, assuming that it exercises the call option?

Clovis Company recently issued $500,000 (face value) bonds to finance a new construction project. The company's chief accountant prepared the following bond amortization schedule:

| Date | Interest Expense | Semiannual Payment | Premium Amortization | Net Liability |
|---|---|---|---|---|
| 7/1/08 | | | | $540,554 |
| 12/31/08 | $21,622 | $25,000 | $(3,378) | 537,176 |
| 6/30/09 | 21,487 | 25,000 | (3,513) | 533,663 |
| 12/31/09 | 21,347 | 25,000 | (3,653) | 530,010 |
| 6/30/10 | 21,200 | 25,000 | (3,800) | 526,210 |
| 12/31/10 | 21,048 | 25,000 | (3,952) | 522,258 |
| 6/30/11 | 20,890 | 25,000 | (4,110) | 518,148 |
| 12/31/11 | 20,726 | 25,000 | (4,274) | 513,874 |
| 6/30/12 | 20,555 | 25,000 | (4,445) | 509,429 |
| 12/31/12 | 20,377 | 25,000 | (4,623) | 504,806 |
| 6/30/13 | 20,194 | 25,000 | (4,806) | 500,000 |

**Required:**

1. Compute the discount or premium on the sale of the bonds, the semiannual coupon interest rate, and the semiannual effective interest rate.

2. The company's vice president of finance wants any discount (or premium) at issuance of the bonds to be recorded immediately as a loss (or gain) at the issue date. Do you agree with this approach? Why or why not?

3. On December 31, 2010, the bonds' net carrying value is $522,258. In present value terms, what does this amount represent?

4. Suppose that market interest rates were 6% semiannually on January 1, 2011, or 12.36% annually. (This 12.36% annual rate of interest is equal to the 6% semiannual rate, compounded: $0.1236 = [1.06 \times 1.06] - 1.00$.) What is the bond's market price on that date? Is the company better or worse off because of the interest rate change? Explain.

On January 1, 2008, MyKoo Corporation issued $1 million in five-year, 5% serial bonds to be repaid in the amount of $200,000 on January 1 of 2009, 2010, 2011, 2012, and 2013. Interest on the bonds' unpaid balance is due at the end of each year. The bonds were sold to yield 6%.

**Required:**

1. Prepare a schedule showing the computation of the total amount received from the issuance of the serial bonds.

2. Prepare a schedule of amortization of the bond discount through 2013 using the effective interest rate method.

The following information appeared in the 2008 annual report of Rumours, Inc.:

## Long-Term Debt

[Rumours, Inc. issued] $10 million, 10% coupon bonds on January 1, 2005 due on December 31, 2009. The prevailing market interest rate on January 1, 2005 was 12%, and the bonds pay interest on June 30 and December 31 of each year.

On January 1, 2006, [Rumours issued] $10 million, 10% coupon bonds due on December 31, 2010. The prevailing market interest rate on January 1, 2006 was 8%, and the bonds pay interest on June 30 and December 31 of each year.

**Required:**

1. See the following (incomplete) table for each bond's carrying value. Calculate the missing values.

| | Carrying Value | |
| --- | --- | --- |
| | December 31, 2007 | December 31, 2008 |
| 10% bonds due in 2009 | $9,653,550 | ? |
| 10% bonds due in 2010 | ? | $10,362,950 |

2. How much interest expense did Rumours record in 2008 on the bonds due in 2009?

3. How much interest expense did Rumours record in 2008 on the bonds due in 2010?

---

The following information appeared in the annual reports of Apparel America, Borden, Inc., and Exxon Corporation.

**P11-18**

Loss contingencies

## Apparel America, Inc.

In December 1994 the Company entered into an agreement to pay $460,000 to a former executive in settlement of certain litigation. According to the terms of the agreement, an initial payment of $150,000 was made in December 1994, with the balance payable in five semiannual installments of $50,000 commencing June 30, 1995 and a final payment of $60,000 on December 31, 1997. The settlement has been discounted at an annual effective interest rate of 9% to reflect its present value at July 31, 1996. [Excerpt from the company's 1996 annual report.]

## Borden, Inc.

Accruals for environmental matters are recorded when it is probable that a liability has been incurred and the amount of the liability can be reasonably estimated. Environmental accruals are routinely reviewed on an interim basis as events and developments warrant and are subjected to a comprehensive review annually during the fiscal fourth quarter. The Company and the Combined Companies have each accrued approximately $26 million (including those costs related to legal proceedings) at December 31, 2000 and 1999, for probable environmental remediation and restoration liabilities. This is management's best estimate of these liabilities. Based on currently available information and analysis, the Company believes that it is reasonably possible that costs associated with such liabilities may exceed current reserves by amounts that may prove insignificant, or by amounts, in the aggregate, of up to approximately $16 million. [Excerpt from the company's 2000 annual report.]

## Exxon Corporation

A number of lawsuits, including class actions, have been brought in various courts against Exxon Corporation and certain of its subsidiaries relating to the release of crude oil from the tanker *Exxon Valdez* in 1989. Most of these lawsuits seek unspecified compensatory and punitive damages; several lawsuits seek damages in varying specified amounts. Certain of the lawsuits seek injunctive relief. The claims of many individuals have been dismissed or settled. Most of the remaining actions are scheduled for trial in federal court commencing May 2, 1994. Other actions will likely be tried in state court later in 1994. The cost to the corporation from these lawsuits is not possible to predict; however, it is believed that the final outcome will not have a materially adverse effect upon the corporation's operations or financial condition. [Excerpt from the company's 1993 annual report.]

**Required:**

1. What is a loss contingency, and why is it disclosed in financial statements? Which of the preceding examples represents a loss contingency?

2. What was the December 1994 present value of Apparel America's settlement with its former executive? What is the July 31, 1996 present value, and where is it shown in the financial statements?

3. Borden has a $26 million liability on its 2000 balance sheet for "probable environmental remediation and restoration." But the company says actual remediation and restoration costs could be up to $16 million more than this amount. Why doesn't Borden's balance sheet liability include the additional $16 million?

4. Why doesn't Exxon report a dollar amount for its litigation cases like the one reported by Apparel America?

5. Does the lack of a specific dollar amount in Exxon's cases mean that stock analysts will just ignore the litigation when valuing the company? Why or why not?

6. In its 2002 annual report, Exxon (now ExxonMobil) had more to say about the *Exxon Valdez* incident:

   [O]n September 24, 1996, the United States District Court for the District of Alaska entered a judgment in the amount of $5.058 billion. The District Court awarded approximately $19.6 million in compensatory damages to plaintiffs, $38 million in prejudgment interest on the compensatory damages, and $5 billion in punitive damages.... The District Court stayed execution on the judgment pending appeal.... ExxonMobil appealed the judgment. On November 7, 2001, the United States Court of Appeals for the Ninth Circuit vacated the punitive damage award as being excessive under the Constitution and remanded the case to the District Court for it to determine the amount of the punitive damage award.... On December 6, 2002, the District Court reduced the punitive damages from $5 billion to $4 billion....

   Based on the information provided, when did Exxon first report a balance sheet liability for the *Exxon Valdez* litigation? What was the amount of that liability?

7. In October 2007, the U.S. Supreme Court agreed to decide whether Exxon should be required to pay $2.5 billion in punitive damages to oil spill victims. Explain how the Court's willingness to hear the Exxon appeal affects the company's accounting for this contingent liability.

---

**P11-19**

**Recording floating-rate debt**

On January 1, 2008, Nicks Corporation issued $250 million of floating-rate debt. The debt carries a contractual interest rate of "LIBOR plus 5.5%," which is reset annually on January 1 of each year. The LIBOR rates on January 1, 2008, 2009 and 2010 were 6.5%, 7.0%, and 5.5%, respectively.

**Required:**

1. Prepare a journal entry to record the issuance of the bonds on January 1, 2008 at par. What was the effective (or market) interest rate when the bonds were issued?

2. Prepare a journal entry to record interest expense for 2008, 2009, and 2010. Assume that interest is paid annually on December 31.

3. What is the market value of the debt at December 31, 2010 assuming Nicks Corporation's credit risk has not changed.

---

**P11-20**

**Unconditional purchase obligations**

The following information appeared in the 2002 annual report of Lyondell Petrochemical Company, a manufacturer of petrochemicals and refined petroleum products such as gasoline, heating oil, jet fuel, aromatics, and lubricants:

The Company is party to various unconditional purchase obligation contracts as a purchaser for products and services, principally for steam and power. At December 31, 2002, future minimum payments under these contracts with noncancelable contract terms in excess of one year and fixed minimum payments were as follows ($ in millions):

| | |
|---|---:|
| 2003 | $ 164 |
| 2004 | 168 |
| 2005 | 169 |
| 2006 | 157 |
| 2007 | 151 |
| Thereafter | 1,749 |
| Total minimum payments | $2,558 |

**Required:**

1. Suppose that the company were obligated to purchase $349.8 million per year in 2008 and each of the next four years for a total of $1,749. If Lyondell's normal rate of interest for a 10-year loan is 8%, what is the present value of the company's purchase commitments?

2. The company's 2002 balance sheet shows long-term debt of $3,926 million and shareholders' equity of $1,179 million. The unconditional purchase obligation is not shown on the balance sheet. What impact would including the present value of unconditional purchase obligations as part of long-term debt have on the company's 2002 ratio of long-term debt to shareholders' equity?

3. Why are unconditional purchase obligations an off-balance-sheet liability? Why might some companies prefer to keep the purchase commitment off the balance sheet?

---

On January 1, 1998, Chain Corporation issued $5 million of 7% coupon bonds at par. The bonds mature in 20 years and pay interest semiannually on June 30 and December 31 of each year. On December 31, 2008, the market interest rate for bonds of similar risk was 14%, and the market value of Chain Corporation bonds (after the December 31 interest payment) was $3,146,052.

**P11-21**

**Debt-for-debt swaps**

Although the company's books are not yet closed for the year, a preliminary estimate shows net income to be $500,000. This amount is substantially below the $3 million management had expected the company to earn. The company has long-term debt totaling $7.5 million (including the $5 million bond issue) and shareholders' equity of $12.5 million (including the $500,000 of estimated net income). This means the company's long-term debt-to-equity ratio is 60%.

Unfortunately, a covenant in one of the company's loan agreements requires a long-term debt-to-equity ratio of 55% or less. Violating this covenant gives lenders the right to demand immediate repayment of the loan principal. Worse yet, a "cross default" provision in the $5 million bond makes it immediately due and payable if the company violates any of its lending agreements.

Because the company does not have the cash needed to repurchase the bonds, management is considering a debt-for-debt exchange in which the outstanding 7% bonds would be replaced by new 14% bonds with a face amount of $3.2 million. The interest rate on the new bonds is equal to the market interest rate.

**Required:**

1. Prepare a journal entry to record the swap on December 31, 2008. (Any gain or loss to the company would be taxed at 35%, and the tax should be included in your entry.)

2. What would the company's debt-to-equity ratio be after the swap?

3. What impact would the transaction have on net income for the year?

4. How else could management have avoided violation of the loan covenant?

**P11-22**

Zero coupon bonds

The following information was taken from the financial statements of ALZA Corporation.

### Note 6: Borrowings

On July 28, 2000, ALZA completed a private offering of the 3% Zero Coupon Convertible Subordinated Debentures which were issued at a price of $551.26 per $1,000 principal amount at maturity. At December 29, 2002, the outstanding 3% Debentures had a total principal amount at maturity of $1.0 billion with a yield to maturity of 3% per annum, computed on a semiannual bond equivalent basis. . . . At December 29, 2002, the fair value based on quoted market value of the 3% Debentures was $813 million. . . .

**Required:**

1. ALZA issued zero coupon debentures with a total maturity value of $1.0 billion at a price of $551.26 per $1,000 principal amount at maturity. How much cash did the company receive when it issued these debentures?

2. The debentures mature in 20 years from the date of issuance, but no interest payments are made until maturity. Show that the issue price of $551.26 gives investors a 3% yield to maturity.

3. Suppose that the debentures were issued on January 1, 2000 instead of July 28, 2000. Reproduce the journal entries ALZA would record in 2000 for the debentures. For each *cash entry,* indicate whether the cash increase or decrease represents an operating, investing, or financing activity.

4. Explain why the debentures have a market value of $813 million at the end of 2002, almost $300 million more than the 2000 issue price.

**P11-23**

Comprehensive problem on bond premium

**eXcel**

mhhe.com/revsine4e

On July 1, 2008, LekTech Corporation issued $20 million of 12%, 20-year bonds. Interest on the bonds is paid semiannually on December 31 and June 30 of each year, and the bonds were issued at a market interest rate of 8%.

**Required:**

1. Compute the bonds' issue price on July 1, 2008.

2. Prepare an amortization schedule that shows interest expense, premium or discount amortization, bond carrying value, and cash interest payment for each interest payment period through December 31, 2013.

3. Prepare the journal entries to record all interest expense and all cash interest payments for 2009.

4. A new employee in the accounting group at LekTech has asked you to explain why interest expense on the bonds changes each year. Write a two-paragraph memo that helps the employee understand interest recognition for these bonds.

5. LekTech used the bonds' proceeds to construct a new manufacturing facility near Waterloo, Iowa. The company will make taillight lenses for tractors manufactured by Deere & Company at its Waterloo plant. In fact, Deere has signed a letter guaranteeing payment of the LekTech bonds. How is the guarantee shown in Deere's financial statements?

6. On January 1, 2014, the company exercised a call provision in the debenture agreement and redeemed 40% of the bonds at 105% of par. What journal entry did the company make to record this partial redemption?

7. The market yield for the bonds on January 1, 2014 was 10%. How much less did the company pay to retire bonds using the call provision than it would have paid using an open market purchase?

Silverado Inc. buys titanium from a supplier that requires a six-month firm commitment on all purchases. On January 1, 2008, Silverado signs a contract with the supplier to purchase 10,000 pounds of titanium at the current forward rate of $310 per pound with settlement on June 30, 2008. However, Silverado wants to actually pay the June 30 market price for titanium. To achieve this goal, the company enters into a forward contract to sell 10,000 pounds of titanium at the current forward price of $310 per unit. The firm commitment contract and the forward contract both have zero value at inception. Titanium spot prices and the contract fair values are:

**P11-24**

Hedging a purchase commitment

| | Spot Price | Forward Price (June 30) | Contract Fair Value | |
|---|---|---|---|---|
| | | | Forward | Firm Commitment |
| January 1, 2008 | $300 | $310 | –0– | –0– |
| March 31, 2008 | 292 | 297 | $128,079 | ($128,079) |
| June 30, 2008 | 285 | N.A. | 250,000 | (250,000) |

**Required:**

1. Why did Silverado hedge its firm commitment with the supplier? After the fact, was it a good idea to do so?

2. What journal entries were made when the two contracts are signed on January 1, 2008?

3. Silverado designated the forward contract as a fair value hedge of its future titanium purchase. What journal entries were made on March 31, 2008?

4. What journal entries were made on June 30, 2008 when the contracts are settled and Silverado pays for the titanium?

---

Newton Grains plans to sell 100,000 bushels of corn from its current inventory in March 2009. The company paid $1 million for the corn during the fall 2008 harvest season. On October 1, 2008, Newton writes a forward contract to sell 100,000 bushels of corn on March 15, 2009 for $1,100,000. The forward contract has zero value at inception. On December 31, 2008, the March forward price for corn is $1,050,000 and the forward contract has a fair value of $95,000. On March 15, 2009, Newton sells the corn for $1,075,000 and settles the forward contract (now valued at $25,000).

**P11-25**

Hedging a planned sale

**Required:**

1. Why did Newton hedge its planned sale of corn? Was it a good idea to do so?

2. Newton designated the forward contract as a cash flow hedge of its exposure to corn price fluctuations. What journal entries were made when the forward contract was signed on October 1, 2008?

3. What journal entries were made on December 31, 2008?

4. What journal entries were made on March 15, 2009 when the forward contract was settled and Newton sold the corn?

5. How would your original journal entries change if the forward contract covered only 50,000 bushels of corn? (Contract fair values would then have been $47,500 on December 31, 2008 and $12,500 on March 15, 2009.)

---

Basie Business Forms borrowed $5 million on July 1, 2008 from First Kansas City Bank. The loan required annual interest payments at the LIBOR rate, reset annually each June 30. The loan principal is due in five years. The LIBOR rate for the first year is 6.0%.

 Basie decided to swap its variable interest payments for fixed interest payments of 6.0%. Basie will pay 6.0% interest to the swap counterparty—Quincy Bank & Trust—and receive LIBOR payments based on a $5 million notional amount for the entire five-year term of the original loan. The swap has no value at its inception on July 1, 2008.

**P11-26**

Using interest rate swap as a cash flow hedge

Basie designates the swap as a hedge of its cash flow exposure to interest rate risk on its variable rate debt. The hedge is fully effective because the key terms of the loan and swap are identical. The variable rate was reset to 6.25% on June 30, 2009 and to 5.75% on June 30, 2010. Basie uses a June 30 fiscal year-end and records interest expense annually.

**Required:**

1. How much net cash settlement will Basie pay to (or receive from) Quincy Bank & Trust on July 1, 2009? On July 1, 2010?

2. How much cash will Basie pay to First Kansas City Bank on July 1, 2009? On July 1, 2010?

3. On June 30, 2009, the swap has a fair value of $40,000 based on dealer quotes. Prepare journal entries to record Basie's cash interest payments and receipts as well as interest expense for the year ended June 30, 2009.

4. On June 30, 2010, the swap has a fair value of $(28,000), a negative amount. Prepare journal entries to record Basie's cash interest payments and receipts as well as interest expense for the year ended June 30, 2010.

---

**P11-27**

Using interest rate swap as a fair value hedge

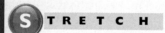

On January 1, 2008, Four Brothers Manufacturing borrowed $10 million from Guiffrie Bank by signing a three-year, 8.0% fixed-rate note. The note calls for interest to be paid annually on December 31. The company then entered into an interest rate swap agreement with Herman Bank. The agreement is that Four Brothers will receive from Herman a fixed-rate interest payment of 8.0% based on a $10 million notional amount each December 31 for three years. Four Brothers will pay Herman a variable LIBOR rate reset every December 31. The LIBOR rate for the first year is 8.0%.

Four Brothers designates the swap as a hedge of its fair value exposure to interest rate risk on its fixed-rate note. The hedge is fully effective because the key terms of the note and swap are identical. The variable rate was reset to 8.25% on December 31, 2008 and to 7.75% on December 31, 2009. Four Brothers uses a December 31 year-end and records interest expense annually.

**Required:**

1. How much net cash settlement will Four Brothers pay to (or receive from) Herman Bank on December 31, 2008? On December 31, 2009?

2. How much cash will Four Brothers pay to Guiffrie Bank on December 31, 2008? On December 31, 2009?

3. On December 31, 2008, the swap has a fair value of $(45,000), a negative amount, and the fair value of the $10 million note was $9,955,000. Prepare journal entries to record Four Brothers' cash interest payments and receipts as well as interest expense for the year ended December 31, 2008.

4. On December 31, 2009, the swap has a fair value of $23,000, and the fair value of the $10 million note was $10,023,000. Prepare journal entries to record Four Brothers' cash interest payments and receipts as well as interest expense for the year ended December 31, 2009.

---

**P11-28**

Determining hedge effectiveness

Recall the Rombaurer Metals example in the chapter: On October 5, 2008, Rombaurer has 10 million pounds of copper inventory on hand at an average cost of $0.65 a pound. The spot price for copper is $0.90 a pound. Instead of selling copper now, Rombaurer decides to hold the inventory until February 2009 when management believes the price will return to a normal level of $0.95 a pound. To hedge its position, Rombaurer sells futures contracts at $0.95 for February delivery. Spot and futures prices over the next several months are as follows:

| | NYMEX Copper Prices | |
|---|---|---|
| | **Spot Price** | **February 2009 Futures Price** |
| October 5, 2008 | $0.90 | $0.95 |
| December 31, 2008 | 0.85 | 0.91 |
| February 26, 2009 | 0.94 | 0.94 |

On February 26, 2009, Rombaurer sells its copper on the spot market for $0.94 a pound and cancels the futures contracts.

The chapter described how "hedge accounting" rules are used when Rombaurer hedges its entire 10 million pounds of copper inventory.

**Required:**

1. Suppose that Rombaurer sells futures contracts for only 5 million pounds of copper. (Management had decided that it is prudent to hedge only half of the company's economic exposure.) The margin requirement on these contracts is $140,000. Because the futures contracts are now "ineffective" in hedging the company's entire fair value exposure to copper price fluctuations, Rombaurer cannot use hedge accounting. Prepare all journal entries needed to account for the futures contracts and sale of copper from October 5, 2008 through February 26, 2009.

2. Now assume that Rombaurer designates these futures contracts as a "fully effective" hedge of its risk exposure for 5 million pounds of copper inventory. (The remaining 5 million pounds of inventory is not being hedged.) Rombaurer can now use hedge accounting for the futures contracts. Prepare all journal entries needed to account for the futures contracts and sale of copper from October 5, 2008 through February 26, 2009.

3. What impact does changing the definition of the hedged item (10 million pounds of copper inventory versus 5 million pounds) have on the company's financial statements for 2008 and 2009?

## CASES

### C11-1

**Analyzing debt covenants**

The 2006 annual report of Tupperware Brands Inc. contained the following note:

During 2006, the Company renegotiated a line of credit with a financial institution in Australia. . . . The Credit Agreement contains covenants of a similar nature to those under the previous agreement and customary for similarly rated companies. While the covenants are restrictive and could inhibit the Company's ability to borrow, to pay dividends, acquire its own stock or make capital investments in its business, this is not currently expected to occur.

The primary financial covenants are a fixed charge coverage ratio, a leverage ratio and an adjusted net worth requirement. The covenant restrictions include adjusted covenant earnings and net worth measures that are non-GAAP measures. The non-GAAP measures may not be comparable to similarly titled measures used by other entities and exclude unusual, non-recurring gains, certain non-cash charges and changes in accumulated other comprehensive income. . . .

The Company's fixed charge ratio is required to be in excess of 1.05 through September 29, 2007 at which point the requirement becomes more difficult to meet as it increases to 1.20 and then increases annually after the end of each fiscal third quarter until it increases to 1.50 after the end of the third quarter of 2010. . . .

**Required:**

1. Why do loan agreements contain financial covenants that use non-GAAP measures?

2. Why are nonrecurring gains excluded from the financial covenant measure?

3. Why are nonrecurring losses included?

4. The fixed coverage charge covenant becomes more difficult to meet over time. How does this covenant feature provide added protection for the lender?

5. Based only on the information in the Tupperware Brands note, would you say that the company is characterized by high or low credit risk? Why?

**C11-2**

**Century and beyond bonds**

As a senior partner at one of the nation's largest public accounting firms, you serve as chairperson of the firm's financial reporting policy committee. You are also the firm's chief spokesperson on financial reporting matters that come before the FASB and the Securities and Exchange Commission. The year is 1997.

Two new debt securities have caught the attention of your committee, the FASB, the SEC, and the Treasury Department. Dresser Industries recently completed a $200 million offering of so-called **century bonds** that mature in 2096, or in 100 years. Safra Republic Holdings announced that in October it will issue $250 million of **millennium bonds** that mature in 2997, or in 1,000 years. Neither company is a client of the firm.

---

### FIRM TO ISSUE $200 MILLION IN BONDS AS 100-YEAR PAPER

Dresser Industries Inc. said it will join the ranks of the small number of companies that have century bonds with the sale of $200 million of debentures due 2096. The oil-field services company said the sale, with Salomon Brothers Inc. as lead underwriter, is expected to occur this week. Proceeds will be used for general corporate purposes, including repayment of commercial paper outstanding and share repurchases.

The issue hasn't been priced, but analysts expect the rate to be about 7.5%. Only nine companies have issued 100-year paper since 1993, when Walt Disney Co. began the modern trend; no such bonds had been sold for more than 20 years. Earlier this year, the U.S. Treasury Department proposed that companies be prohibited from deducting interest on bonds with a maturity of more than 40 years, but Congress hasn't voted on the matter.

*Source: "Firm to Issue $200 Million in Bonds as 100-Year Paper," The Wall Street Journal, August 7, 1996. Copyright ©1996 Dow Jones & Company, Inc. All rights reserved worldwide. Reprinted with permission.*

---

### SAFRA REPUBLIC $250 MILLION 1000-YEAR SUBORDINATED DEBENTURES RATED 'AA-' BY FITCH

Safra Republic Holdings S.A.'s (SRH) $250 million issue of 7.125% subordinated debentures, due October 15, 2997, is rated 'AA-' by Fitch. The rating reflects superior risk-based capital ratios, indicative of the modest amount of assets represented by loans; sizable liquidity; comfortable funding from a growing client base; and a management organization seasoned in relationships with high net worth clients in over 80 countries. SRH's 49% ownership by the Republic National Bank of New York provides important support by a risk averse U.S.

banking institution, whose fundamentals garner a 'AA+' senior debt rating.

SRH is a Luxembourg-based holding company, operated through six wholly owned banking subsidiaries. These units provide international private banking, asset management and other related investment services to over 22,000 high net worth individuals, partnerships and closely held corporations. Client assets at SRH, both on- and off-balance sheet, stood at $29 billion at the end of September, compared to $20.8 billion at the like date in 1996.

*Source: "Safra Republic $250 Million 1000-Year Subordinated Debentures Rated 'AA-' by Fitch," PR Newswire, October 16, 1997.*

---

### IS THE PARTY OVER FOR 100-YEAR BONDS?

In recent months, a number of U.S. companies have been tapping the market for so-called century bonds, taking advantage of low interest rates and a strong appetite among some institutional investors for such long-term debt.

But the days may be numbered for this rather obscure part of the bond market. The Treasury Department is proposing to

eliminate the corporate tax deduction for interest paid on the last 60 years of century bonds, effectively killing the securities. The proposal is included in President Clinton's fiscal 1998 budget, which will be unveiled Thursday.

The Treasury argues that 100-year debt should be treated the same as equity because the bonds are more like permanent capital. Since stock dividend payments can't be deducted

*(continued)*

from taxable earnings, the Treasury says, interest payments on the last 60 years of 100-year debt shouldn't be deductible either.

Corporate treasurers and Wall Street underwriters say they will fight the proposal. They contend that ending the tax break for 100-year bonds will put U.S. companies at a competitive disadvantage to foreign-bond issuers, which aren't subject to U.S. tax.

For now, prospects for the tax change are unclear. When the idea surfaced in December 1995, it cast a pall over century-bond issues. The market recovered only after congressional tax committee chairmen said any changes wouldn't affect bond issues completed before their committees take action. In the meantime, century bonds are likely to remain a popular financing tool for corporate treasurers, especially if interest rates remain low. The reason is clear: The bonds offer really long-term money at a relatively cheap price. Institutional investors, in turn, like the bonds because they offer a predictable rate of return that is better than what companies—or the U.S. Treasury—offer for 30-year debt. . . .

The risk/reward decisions investors are making are crucial to the popularity of the century bonds. One risk with most of the offerings is that interest rates can shoot up, leaving the investor with a stream of payments that are woefully weak in future years and a trading price that would result in a big loss if the bonds are sold in the open market. So too, there is less chance a company will be in business in 100 years than in the next 20 or 30 years.

Most of the railroad companies that issued century bonds in the 1860s and 1870s weren't around when it came to paying back bondholders. Of the companies and institutions recently issuing century bonds, only a few have met the 100-year test already.

Since most century bonds aren't callable (meaning companies can't pay off investors early to get out of obligations), they are more attractive when a drop in rates causes price to rise.

That is why, despite the 100-year maturity, century bond offerings also attract short-term players.

*Source:* "Is the Party Over for 100-Year Bonds?" *The Wall Street Journal,* February 4, 1997. Copyright ©1997 Dow Jones & Company, Inc. All rights reserved worldwide. Reprinted with permission.

**Required:**

1. Suppose that Dresser Industries issued its $200 million century bonds on January 1, 1996 at a market yield of 7.5%, the same as the stated interest rate. To keep things easy, also assume that the bonds pay interest just once a year, on December 31. Compute the bonds' issue price. How much of that price comes from the present value of the interest payments, and how much comes from the promised principal payment?

2. In present value terms, how much of a tax savings does the company get from its century bond? (Use a 40% effective tax rate.) How much of a tax savings would be lost if only the first 40 years of interest deductions were allowed?

3. Suppose that the century bonds were issued with a stated rate of 7.5% when the market yield rate was 8.5%. What would the issue price be? How about if the market yield were 6.5%?

4. Suppose that Safra Republic issued its $250 million of millennium bonds on January 1, 1998 at a market yield of 7.125%, the same as the stated interest rate. Assume that the bonds pay interest just once a year, on December 31. What is the issue price of these bonds, and how much of that price comes from the present value of interest payments?

5. Suppose that Safra Republic were a U.S. company paying taxes at a 40% rate. In present value terms, how much of a tax savings does the company receive from its millennium bonds? How much of a tax savings would be lost if only the first 40 years of interest deductions were allowed?

6. Suppose that the millennium bonds were issued with a 7.125% stated interest rate when the market yield rate was 8.125%. What would the issue price be? How about if the market yield were 6.125%?

7. Why would the Treasury Department be opposed to unlimited interest deductions on century and millennium bonds? According to U.S. GAAP, are these securities debt or equity?

Tuesday Morning Corporation operates a chain of discount retail stores. The company purchases closeout merchandise at prices generally ranging from 10% to 50% of the normal wholesale price and sells the merchandise at prices that are 50% to 80% lower than retail prices generally charged by department and specialty stores.

The following is information taken from a recent Tuesday Morning annual report.

### Note 5: Mortgages on Property, Plant, and Equipment

| ($ in thousands) | Year 2 | Year 1 |
|---|---|---|
| Industrial development bond, payable in quarterly installments of $108 plus interest at 91.656% of prime (not to exceed 15%), maturing March 31, Year 6 | $1,401 | $1,834 |
| Payable to bank, payable in quarterly installments of $104 plus interest at LIBOR plus 2.50%, maturing September 30, Year 5, with remaining principal due at that time | 4,504 | 4,920 |
| Payable to bank, payable in quarterly installments of $112 plus interest at LIBOR plus 2.50% through October 15, Year 2, with the remaining principal and interest due April 30, Year 3 | 1,794 | 2,243 |

In connection with these mortgages, the Company is required to maintain minimum net worth and comply with other financial covenants, including a restriction limiting loans to officers to less than $2,000,000. At December 31, Year 2 the Company is in compliance with these covenants.

The $1,794,000 note payable to bank due on April 30, Year 3 is classified as a current liability at December 31, Year 2. The aggregate maturities of mortgages are as follows ($ in thousands):

| Year | Amount |
|---|---|
| Year 3 | $2,747 |
| Year 4 | 849 |
| Year 5 | 4,003 |
| Year 6 | 100 |

### Consolidated Balance Sheet

| ($ in thousands) | Year 2 | Year 1 |
|---|---|---|
| Current liabilities: | | |
| Current installments on mortgages | $ 2,747 | $ 1,402 |
| Current installments on capital lease obligation | 607 | –0– |
| Accounts payable | 12,916 | 15,859 |
| Accrued sales tax | 1,574 | 1,760 |
| Other accrued expenses | 1,945 | 3,118 |
| Deferred income taxes | 303 | 146 |
| Due to officer | –0– | 599 |
| Income taxes payable | 988 | –0– |
| Total current liabilities | $21,080 | $22,884 |

### Consolidated Statement of Cash Flows

| ($ in thousands) | Year 2 | Year 1 |
|---|---|---|
| Cash flows from financing activities: | | |
| Net increase (decrease) in notes payable | $  –0– | $ (3,500) |
| Principal payments on mortgages | (1,298) | (1,194) |
| Principal payments under capital lease obligation | (214) | –0– |
| Proceeds from common stock offering | –0– | –0– |
| Proceeds from exercise of common stock options | 255 | 145 |
| Repurchase of common stock | –0– | (3,383) |
| Net cash provided by (used in) financing activities | $ (1,257) | $ (7,932) |

**Required:**

1. What was the *current portion* of Tuesday Morning's mortgage payable at the end of Year 1?

2. How much did Tuesday Morning pay in cash to reduce its mortgage payable during Year 2?

3. Explain the difference between your answer to requirement 1 and your answer to requirement 2.

4. What are the components of the current portion of the mortgage payable as of the end of Year 2?

5. Assume that the next quarterly installment on the industrial development bond is due on March 31, Year 3. Prepare a journal entry to record the installment payment and any interest. Assume that the effective interest rate for the bond is 14% per year.

6. The company has a mortgage note payable for $1,794,000 that comes due on April 30, Year 3. Suppose that this note is paid by the signing of a new 14% note for the amount due. Prepare the April 30, Year 3 journal entry to record this refinancing of the old note.

7. Instead of refinancing the note, suppose the company pays the principal along with any remaining interest on April 30, Year 3. Prepare a journal entry to record this cash payment.

---

Groupe Casino is a French multinational company that operates more than 9,000 multiformat retail stores—hypermarkets, supermarkets, discount stores, convenience stores, and restaurants—throughout the world. In January 2005, Casino issued €600 million of undated deeply subordinated fixed-to-CMS-floating-rate notes at a price of 101. The offering circular described certain aspects of the notes as follows:

**C11-4**

**Groupe Casino: Determining whether it is debt or equity**

**Deeply Subordinated Obligations**

The Notes are deeply subordinated obligations of the Issuer and are the most junior debt instruments of the Issuer, subordinated to and ranking behind the claims of all other unsubordinated and subordinated creditors of the Issuer.

**Undated Securities**

The Notes are undated securities, with no specified maturity date. The Issuer is under no obligation to redeem the Notes at any time.

The Noteholders have no right to require redemption of the Notes, except if a judgment is issued for the judicial liquidation (*liquidation judiciaire*) of the Issuer or, following an order of *redressement judiciaire*, the sale of the whole of the business (*cession totale de l'enterprise*) of the Issuer, or in the event of the voluntary dissolution of the Issuer or if the Issuer is liquidated for any other reason.

**Interest Interruption**

The Issuer has the option to decide not to pay interest on the Notes on any Interest Payment Date if, during the 12-months period preceding such Interest Payment Date, it has not paid or declared any dividend on its Equity Securities and provided it has not made, during any such period, any payments on (including *inter alia* by way of redemption, purchase or redemption of) any Equity Securities. The interest payment provisions of the Notes are non-cumulative. Accordingly, any interest not paid on the Notes as a result of the valid exercise by the Issuer of such option will be forfeited and accordingly will no longer be due and payable by the Issuer.

**No Voting Rights**

The Notes are nonvoting.

**No Prior Market for the Notes; Resale Restrictions**

There is no existing market for the Notes, and there can be no assurance that any market will develop for the Notes or that holders of the Notes will be able to sell their Notes in the secondary market.

**Interest Rate**

The coupon on the Notes for each Floating Rate Interest Period is linked to the 10-year Constant Maturity Swap (CMS 10), the annual rate for euro interest rate swap transactions with a maturity of 10 years.

The CMS 10 is a variable rate and as such is not pre-defined for the lifespan of the Notes; conversely it allows investors to follow market changes with an instrument reflecting changes in the levels of yields. Higher rates mean a higher coupon and lower rates mean a lower coupon.

In summary, the notes:

- Are Casino's undated perpetual obligations in that they have no maturity date and the lender (investor) cannot force redemption.

- Pay interest at fixed and floating rates, but Casino may "interrupt" interest payments at any time and for any reason and the lender has no claim to interrupted interest payments.

- Do not confer voting rights to the investor, nor are they convertible into shares of common or preferred stock of Casino or any other company.

**Required:**

1. Casino management intends to treat the notes as equity instruments for financial reporting purposes in accordance with International Financial Reporting Standards (IFRS). What specific guidance do IFRS provide that helps accountants and auditors distinguish between liabilities and equities?

2. Do you concur with management's decision to treat the notes as equity instruments? Why?

3. Suppose the notes are issued on January 1, 2005, that the first year's interest rate is 5%, and that interest is paid on December 31 of each year. Prepare the journal entries Casino would use to record (a) issuance of the notes on January 1, 2005, (b) interest expense for the year, and (c) the cash interest payment on December 31, 2005. Income tax considerations may be ignored. Use an 8% interest rate for these journal entries.

4. The notes were issued at a price of 101, which is a slight premium over the face value. What "red flags" does this issue price raise?

---

| | |
|---|---|
| **C11-5** | |
| Coca-Cola Company: Using long-term debt footnotes | |

The following information is from Coca-Cola Company's 2006 annual report:

**9. Long-term Debt**

| ($ in millions) | 2006 | 2005 |
|---|---|---|
| 5¾% U.S. dollar notes due 2009 | $   399 | $   399 |
| 5¾% U.S. dollar notes due 2011 | 499 | 499 |
| 7⅜% U.S. dollar notes due 2093 | 116 | 116 |
| Other, due 2002 to 2013 | 333 | 168 |
| | $1,347 | $1,182 |
| Less current portion | 33 | 28 |
| | $1,314 | $1,154 |

The principal amount of our long-term debt that had fixed and variable interest rates, respectively, was $1,346 million and $1 million on December 31, 2006 . . . [and] $1,181 million and $1 million on December 31, 2005. The weighted-average interest rate on long-term debt was 6 percent for both years ended December 31, 2006 and 2005, respectively. Total interest paid was approximately $212 million, $233 million, and $188 million in 2006, 2005, 2004, respectively. Maturities of long-term debt for the five years succeeding December 31, 2006, are as follows (in millions): 2007—$33; 2008—$175; 2009—$436; 2010—$55; and 2011—$522.

**Required:**

1. How much of Coca-Cola's long-term debt is due in 2007?

2. How much of Coca-Cola's long-term debt is due in each of the next 4 years (2008–2011)?

3. Why might financial analysts be interested in these scheduled debt payments? What options does the company have with regard to making its payments?

4. Compute the company's effective interest rate for 2006 using the reported cash interest payments and the average amount of debt outstanding during the year. In addition to long-term debt stated in the report, the company had $3,877 million in average short-term debt outstanding.

5. What will the company's interest expense be for 2007?

6. Why might the effective interest rate calculation described in requirement 4 misstate a company's true interest cost when debt is issued at a premium or discount?

7. Approximately $436 million of long-term debt is due in 2009. Describe how the company might obtain the cash needed to make this payment.

8. Approximately $116 million of long-term debt is due in 2093 because Coca-Cola is one of those companies that has issued "century bonds" (see Case C11–2). Describe the accounting and income tax issues raised by this maturity date.

---

The following article raises questions about Cardinal Health's accounting for an expected legal settlement. Management responded to the accusations by sending a letter to all shareholders and to analysts who covered the firm.

**C11-6**

**Cardinal Health: Contingent receivables**

## CARDINAL HEALTH'S ACCOUNTING RAISES SOME QUESTIONS

It's a cardinal rule of accounting: Don't count your chickens before they hatch. Yet new disclosures in Cardinal Health Inc.'s latest annual report suggest that is what the drug wholesaler has done not just once, but twice, independent accounting specialists say.

As the disclosures show, Cardinal recorded $22 million of an expected legal settlement with certain vitamin manufacturers that it had accused of overcharging for products—in advance of an actual settlement. Specifically, Cardinal recorded a $10 million pre-tax gain, as well as a corresponding receivable on its balance sheet, during its December 2000 quarter. It recorded a further $12 million gain during the quarter ended Sept. 30, 2001, after concluding that its minimum future recovery would be that much bigger.

Cardinal, which says it has done nothing improper, did reach a $35.3 million settlement in the vitamin antitrust litigation last spring. The company recorded the remaining $13.3 million during the final quarter of its past fiscal year, ended June 30.

To those unfamiliar with accounting rules, the posting of the two initial sums might not raise obvious questions. Yet even first-year accounting students are taught this: Under generally accepted accounting principles, companies aren't supposed to record expected gains as current income until they are certain the gains will be realized. When it comes to litigation settlements, that means waiting until an actual settlement agreement has been reached with a party that is able to pay, independent accounting specialists say.

Now consider this twist: Had Cardinal not recorded the two initial gains when it did, it would have fallen short of Wall Street analysts' earnings targets by two cents a share for both the December 2000 and September 2001 quarters; Cardinal's earnings met analysts' targets for each of the quarters. Cardinal didn't disclose the size of the gains until September 2002, when it filed its latest annual report.

"That's abracadabra accounting," says Walter Schuetze, a former chief accountant for the Securities and Exchange Commission. "Cardinal should not have recognized a receivable and a gain until June 2002." Before then, "it was all a matter of speculation," he says, adding, "Cardinal's actions explain what is meant by the term earnings management. This is diddling the numbers." . . .

"Cardinal Health is absolutely confident in our accounting and report practices and our adherence to high ethical standards," Mr. Miller [Cardinal's chief financial officer] says. "With regard to GAAP and SEC regulations, we are in full compliance in all material respects." . . .

## CARDINAL HEALTH

**A Note from Steve Fischbach, VP Investor Relations**

I wanted to make sure all of our investors and analysts received some information that responds to today's *Wall Street Journal* Heard on the Street article titled "Cardinal Health's Accounting Raises a Number of Questions." . . .

**Here are the facts:**

**As we have explained to the reporter, this item was not a recording of a contingent gain under *SFAS 5*.** The recoveries that Cardinal Health recorded related to vendor overcharges in our vitamin business were based on the virtual certainty of the recovery as supported by numerous external factors.

The reporter questioned the timing of two items recorded by the company ($10 million in the second quarter of fiscal year 2001 and $12 million in the first quarter of fiscal year 2002) related to the vitamin overcharge situation. This event was the recognition of an asset related to recoveries for vendor overcharges, based on the following five factors:

1. Vendors had admitted overcharging and plead guilty in a criminal proceeding. In prior periods Cardinal Health was in fact overcharged by those vendors and those charges were reflected in prior periods as higher cost of sales.

2. Vendors had settled with a number of plaintiffs, based on their admission of guilt.

3. Vendors were all major pharmaceutical companies with a clear ability to pay.

4. Issue was not "if" we would recover, but "how much."

5. Quantification of the amount of recovery that was virtually certain was supported by written legal opinions from independent outside legal counsel that served as substantial audit evidence.

As it turned out, Cardinal Health received over $120 million from the defendants in the case which exceeded what was actually recorded by over $100 million. That is a very important point because it demonstrates the conservatism with which Cardinal Health dealt with the issue. . . .

*Source:* Cardinal Health Letter to Shareholders (April 2, 2003).

**Required:**

1. Consult *SFAS No. 5,* "Accounting for Contingencies." Are the GAAP rules for recognizing contingent gains (and a corresponding receivable) the same or different from those for recognizing contingent losses (and a corresponding liability)?

2. In view of the details outlined in Cardinal Health's letter to analysts and investors, do you believe the company fully complied with *SFAS No. 5* as it pertains to recognizing contingent gains? Why or why not?

3. If asked, how might management respond to questions about the timing of the gain recognition in 2001 and 2002?

4. Suppose that management was intent on informing analysts and investors about an expected litigation settlement amount. How might this be done in situations where *SFAS No. 5* precluded recognizing the gain on the financial statements?

**.mhhe.com/revsine4e**

**Remember to check the book's companion Web site for additional study material.**

# Financial Reporting for Leases | 12

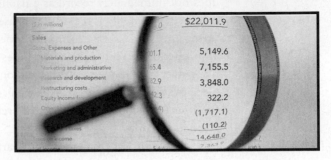

| (in millions) | | $22,011.9 |
|---|---|---|
| Sales | | |
| Costs, Expenses and Other | | |
| Materials and production | 01.1 | 5,149.6 |
| Marketing and administrative | 65.4 | 7,155.5 |
| Research and development | 82.9 | 3,848.0 |
| Restructuring costs | 12.3 | 322.2 |
| Equity income fr... | 4) | (1,717.1) |
| ...es | | (110.2) |
| ...on income | | 14,648.0 |

*"Humans have three basic needs: food, shelter, and . . . keeping debt off the balance sheet."*

—Author unknown

A lease is a contract in which the owner of an asset—the **lessor**—conveys to another party—the **lessee**—the right to use that asset. This right is granted in exchange for a fee—the **lease payment**—that is usually paid in installments. The lessor typically retains legal title to the asset. The duration of a lease may be short, such as a one-week car rental agreement, or long, such as a 20-year lease for retail space in a shopping center.

At its inception, a lease is a **mutually unperformed contract.** This means that neither party to the lease arrangement has yet performed all of the duties called for in the contract. For example, the lessor has an obligation to provide the lessee with the right to use the asset for the entire duration of the lease; in exchange, the lessee has an obligation to pay the stipulated periodic fee to the lessor during the lease term. When the lease contract is first signed, the right to use the asset has not been provided, nor have the required periodic contract payments been made. As you will see, the accounting for these unperformed contracts is controversial.

## EVOLUTION OF LEASE ACCOUNTING

*Statement of Financial Accounting Standards (SFAS) No. 13* spells out the current generally accepted accounting principles (GAAP) for leases.[1] Before it was issued in 1976, virtually all leases were accounted for using the **operating lease approach.**

The following example illustrates the operating lease approach.

> Crest Company owns a building with a $200,000 book value. It leases this building to Iris Company under a five-year lease for a monthly rental of $2,000, which is to be paid at the end of each month.

Upon signing the lease, Iris Company, the lessee, makes no entry on its books. The accounting here conforms to the legal structure of lease arrangements. Because lease

### LEARNING OBJECTIVES

**After studying this chapter, you will understand:**

1. The difference between capital leases and operating leases.

2. Lessees' incentives to keep leases off the balance sheet.

3. The criteria used to classify leases on the lessee's books.

4. The treatment of executory costs, residual values, and other aspects of lease contracts.

5. The effects of capital lease versus operating lease treatment on lessees' financial statements.

6. How analysts can adjust for ratio distortions from off-balance-sheet leases when comparing firms.

7. That lessors also classify leases either as capital leases or as operating leases but that their reporting incentives are very different from those of lessees.

8. The difference among sales-type, direct financing, and operating lease treatment by lessors and the criteria for choosing the accounting treatment.

9. How the different lessor accounting treatments can affect income and net asset balances.

10. Sale/leaseback arrangements and other special leasing situations.

11. How to use footnote disclosures to estimate the increase in assets and liabilities that would ensue if operating leases had been capitalized instead.

---

[1] "Accounting for Leases," *SFAS No. 13* (Stamford, CT: Financial Accounting Standards Board [FASB], 1976).

contracts typically do not convey title, the asset remains on the lessor's books and no asset is reflected on the lessee's books. Furthermore, under the operating lease approach, the lessee does not immediately record as a liability the stream of future payments specified in the contract. No liability is recorded because the lessee is not legally obligated to make the payments until the lessor performs the duties specified in the contract. Because these are mutually unperformed contracts—sometimes called **executory** contracts—accounting entries are made over time in piecemeal fashion only as partial performance under the contract takes place. *As each party performs its respective duties, that portion of the contract that has been performed is no longer considered executory and is accordingly recognized in the financial records.*

Each month, as Crest performs its part of the agreement by making the premises available to Iris Company, Iris accrues a liability for that portion of the contract that has been performed:

| | | |
|---|---|---|
| **DR** Rent expense | $2,000 | |
| **CR** Lease liability | | $2,000 |

Upon payment of the stipulated rental fee at month-end, Iris makes the following entry:

| | | |
|---|---|---|
| **DR** Lease liability | $2,000 | |
| **CR** Cash | | $2,000 |

Iris records no liability on its books for *future* rental payments—neither at the signing of the lease nor afterward. The reason is that these future rental payments are contingent upon future performance by Crest, the lessor. The stipulated payments do not become a liability to Iris under the operating lease approach until time passes and performance takes place. As each party to the mutually unperformed contract performs its duties specified in the contract, the "performed" portion is no longer considered executory. So, as you just saw, the stipulated rental for the month over which performance took place is recorded as an expense and accrued as a liability; the liability is reduced when payment is made.

> In practice, the accrual for the lease liability is seldom made. Instead, only one entry is made at the time of cash payment:
>
> **DR** Rent expense .. $2,000
> **CR** Cash .... $2,000

Similarly, Crest, the lessor, would make no entry on its books at the time this operating lease was signed. However, as piecemeal performance takes place month-by-month and it receives payment, Crest makes the following entry on its books:

| | | |
|---|---|---|
| **DR** Cash | $2,000 | |
| **CR** Rental revenue | | $2,000 |

Because the building remains an asset on Crest's books, periodic depreciation is also recorded:

| | | |
|---|---|---|
| **DR** Depreciation expense—leased building | $XXX | |
| **CR** Accumulated depreciation—leased building | | $XXX |

**RECAP**

**The operating lease approach conforms to the legal structure of lease arrangements. Journal entries are made piecemeal over time as partial performance takes place.**

# Why Lessees Like the Operating Lease Method

Lessees prefer the operating lease method for lease accounting. One obvious reason is that the operating lease method doesn't reflect the cumulative liability for all future lease payments on the lessee's balance sheet. Instead, only a portion of the obligation gets accrued piecemeal as partial performance takes place under the lease. The phrase **off-balance sheet financing** is used to reflect the fact that the lessee has financed the acquisition of asset services without recognizing a liability on the financial statement.

As we will show you, GAAP requires *footnote* disclosure of the lessee's future cash outflows arising from operating leases. And because reasonably informed financial decision makers do read statement footnotes, the liability isn't really "hidden." Nevertheless, it is easy to envision circumstances in which lessees would be better off by using the operating lease method. To see

> Operating leases for office or retail store space often have noncancelable terms such as 12 or 15 years. But if the lessee experiences a decrease in demand during the noncancelable lease term, the leased facility may become unneeded. Periodic lease payments continue without any corresponding economic benefits to the lessee. Once the leased item becomes superfluous, the lessee should recognize a liability at its fair value as well as an offsetting debit to expense. The fair value of the liability is the discounted present value of the remaining lease rentals. As time passes, the liability is increased (and an expense is recognized) using accretion procedures such as those described for asset retirement obligations in Chapter 10, pp. 566–567.
>
> *Source:* "Accounting for Costs Associated with Exit or Disposal Activities," *SFAS No. 146* (Norwalk, CT: FASB, 2002), paras. 14–16.

how they are made better off, recall that many contracts are linked to financial statement numbers. One example is bank lending agreements that contain **covenants**—safety measures to protect banks against the borrower's financial deterioration. Because most covenants are based on financial statement numbers—not on footnote numbers—keeping liabilities off the balance sheet may convey benefits to borrowers even if the liabilities aren't hidden in a real sense. For example, the numerator of the lessee's debt-to-equity ratio is unaffected at the inception of an operating lease because no liability is recorded on signing. Keeping the liability off the balance sheet strengthens the debt-to-equity ratio. The off-balance sheet liability reduces the likelihood that the lessee-borrower will violate a debt-to-equity loan covenant.

Furthermore, some lessees believe that omitting the lease liability improves their ability to obtain *future* credit. Here's why. Lenders use leverage ratios as a rule of thumb in assessing borrowing capacity—that means the amount that can safely be borrowed. Keeping the lease liability off the books lowers reported leverage. Supposedly, the lower the firm's reported leverage, the greater is that firm's perceived borrowing capacity.

Lessees also like the operating lease accounting method because it keeps the leased *asset* off the balance sheet. Certain long-term leases give lessees the *exclusive* right to use assets for most of their economic life. Nevertheless, despite the "ownershiplike" property rights conveyed to the lessee, no balance sheet asset is recorded with operating leases.

Keeping leased assets off the books produces a favorable impact on lessee's financial statements that is just as substantial as the benefit that arises from omitting lease liabilities. Consider an airline that leases a portion of its aircraft fleet and accounts for the leases using the operating lease method. The leased aircraft generate gross revenues and net profits just as the owned aircraft do. However, not reporting the leased aircraft as assets under the operating lease approach raises the return on assets (ROA) ratio:

$$\text{ROA} = \frac{\text{NOPAT}}{\text{Average assets}}$$

Income generated by the leased assets will appear in the numerator, NOPAT, net operating profit after taxes (see Chapter 5); however, the leased assets will not appear in the denominator. The net effect increases the return on *reported* average assets.

Investors and others use ratios such as return on assets to evaluate a firm's performance. The operating lease method makes the ROA for companies that lease a significant portion of their assets *appear* to be higher than the corresponding return for companies that own their assets outright. (See the example illustrated in the appendix to this chapter.)

## The Securities and Exchange Commission's Initiative

Throughout the 1960s and early 1970s, leasing became an important financing vehicle for two reasons. First, leasing provided firms the opportunity to use assets without expending the entire cash purchase price. Second, if the leased asset became technologically obsolete, the lessee could simply lease a newer model. But the virtually exclusive use of the operating lease approach was criticized, especially by the Securities and Exchange Commission (SEC) because it believed that this accounting approach did not portray the economics of many leasing transactions.

The SEC issued *Accounting Series Release (ASR) No. 147* in 1973 to improve financial reporting for leases.[2] The SEC took what is called a **property rights** approach to lease accounting. This approach views leases as conveying property rights in the asset to the lessee and the payment stream as representing the lessee's liability. Following this accounting method, the lessee records both an asset and a liability on its books equal to the present value of future lease payments when a lease is signed:

| | | |
|---|---|---|
| **DR** | Leased asset (to reflect the property right the lessee now has in the asset) . . . . . . . . . . . . . . . . . . . . . . . . . . . . . . . . . . . . . . . . . . . . . . . . . . . . . . | \$XXX |
| | **CR** | Lease obligation (to reflect the liability arising from the future lease payments) . . . . . . . . . . . . . . . . . . . . . . . . . . . . . . . . . . . . |
| | | \$XXX |

This is called the **capital lease** approach because the lessee capitalizes (puts it on its books) the lease.[3] The FASB soon extended and embellished the SEC property rights approach, as we discuss next.

Figure 12.1 provides an overview of the two different lease accounting approaches.

## LESSEE ACCOUNTING

Under *SFAS No. 13,* leases meeting certain specified criteria *must* be treated as capital leases. So, a lease asset and lease liability appear on the lessee's balance sheet. Leases not meeting the *SFAS No. 13* criteria *cannot* be capitalized. Noncapitalized leases are called **operating leases** and are accounted for using the procedures we just described.

### *SFAS No. 13* Criteria for Capital Lease Treatment

If, at its inception, a lease satisfies *any one or more* of the following criteria, it must be treated as a capital lease on the lessee's books.

1. The lease transfers ownership of the asset to the lessee by the end of the lease term.

2. The lease contains a bargain purchase option.

3. The noncancelable lease term is 75% or more of the estimated economic life of the leased asset.

4. The present value of the minimum lease payments equals or exceeds 90% of the current fair market value of the leased asset.

---

[2] "Notice of Adoption of Amendments to Regulations S-X Requiring Improved Disclosure of Leases," *ASR No. 147* (Washington, DC: SEC, 1973).

[3] However, *ASR No. 147* emphasized footnote *disclosure* and thus stopped short of requiring balance sheet *recognition* of leases that conveyed property rights.

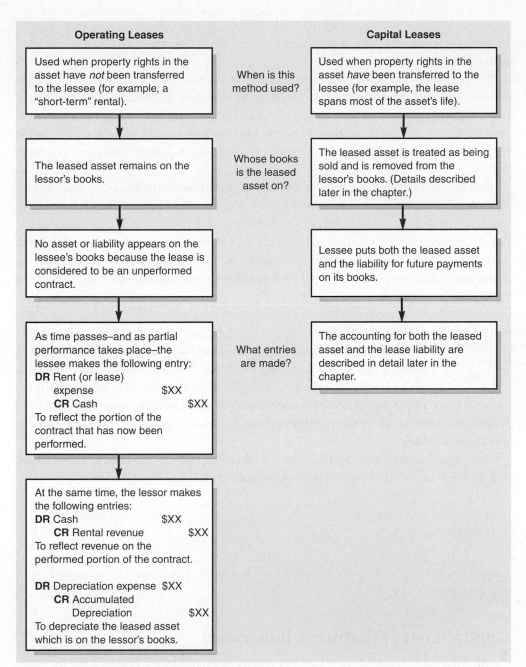

| | Operating Leases | | Capital Leases |
|---|---|---|---|
| **When is this method used?** | Used when property rights in the asset have *not* been transferred to the lessee (for example, a "short-term" rental). | | Used when property rights in the asset *have* been transferred to the lessee (for example, the lease spans most of the asset's life). |
| **Whose books is the leased asset on?** | The leased asset remains on the lessor's books. | | The leased asset is treated as being sold and is removed from the lessor's books. (Details described later in the chapter.) |
| | No asset or liability appears on the lessee's books because the lease is considered to be an unperformed contract. | | Lessee puts both the leased asset and the liability for future payments on its books. |
| **What entries are made?** | As time passes–and as partial performance takes place–the lessee makes the following entry:<br>**DR** Rent (or lease)<br> expense $XX<br> **CR** Cash $XX<br>To reflect the portion of the contract that has now been performed. | | The accounting for both the leased asset and the lease liability are described in detail later in the chapter. |
| | At the same time, the lessor makes the following entries:<br>**DR** Cash $XX<br> **CR** Rental revenue $XX<br>To reflect revenue on the performed portion of the contract.<br><br>**DR** Depreciation expense $XX<br> **CR** Accumulated<br> Depreciation $XX<br>To depreciate the leased asset which is on the lessor's books. | | |

**Figure 12.1**

DIFFERENCES BETWEEN OPERATING AND CAPITAL LEASES

International Financial Reporting Standards (IFRS) also differentiate between operating leases and capital leases. (The latter are called *finance leases*.) Classification is based on which party has the risks and rewards of ownership. Criteria that are similar to (but less precise than) the four *SFAS No. 13* criteria are cited as examples of situations in which a lease should be classified as a finance lease. In addition, IFRS identify other potential capitalization criteria. For example, if the leased asset is so specialized that only the lessee can use it, or if the lessee must compensate the lessor for losses from canceling the lease, capital lease treatment may be needed.

*Source:* "Accounting for Leases," *IAS 17* (London: International Accounting Standards Board [IASB], 2003), paras. 10–11.

*Each criterion represents a situation under which property rights in the leased asset have been transferred to the lessee.* The transfer of property rights is easily seen in criterion (1). If a lease transfers ownership, title to the asset will eventually pass to the lessee, and the FASB requires that the accounting method conform to the substance of the transaction—an installment purchase—rather than to its legal form—a long-term rental agreement. Similarly, in lease arrangements in which a **bargain purchase option**[4] exists—criterion (2)—there is a strong probability the lessee will exercise the option and obtain ownership. These two criteria

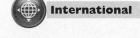

**International**

---

[4] *SFAS No. 13,* para. 5(d) defines "bargain" as a price that is low enough that the purchase is "reasonably assured." For example, the lessee may have a purchase option of $1,000 for an asset that is expected to be worth $10,000 at the end of the lease term. The lessor and the lessee determine whether a purchase option is a bargain at the beginning of the lease. Subsequent price changes would not change the initial determination.

represent instances in which ownership will likely transfer, thus conveying significant property rights in the leased asset. This is the reason *SFAS No. 13* requires that such leases be treated as capital leases.

The philosophy underlying the third criterion—economic life—is different because legal ownership of the asset does not pass to the lessee. Nevertheless, *SFAS No. 13* indicates that criterion (3) also conveys significant property rights. The reason is that the *right to use* a leased asset for 75% or more of its expected economic life is *itself* an asset—a valuable property right representing an exclusive claim to the asset's services for the preponderance of its benefit period.

Criterion (4), sometimes called the **recovery of investment criterion,** is the most technically complicated but easy to understand in principle. A good indication that the lessor is recovering virtually all of the investment in the asset occurs when the present value of the minimum lease payments is equal to or greater than 90% of the fair value of the asset itself. The relative magnitude of the payment schedule and the willingness of the lessee to engage in the transaction are both considered evidence that substantial property rights have been transferred to the lessee.

> For example, criterion (4) is triggered if a lessee leases an asset with a fair value of $100,000 and agrees to a payment stream whose present value is $93,000 because $93,000 is more than 90% of $100,000.

These four criteria for capital leases suggest that the FASB has moved part of the way toward the property rights approach. But it's not a "pure" property rights approach because these criteria do not consider *all* leases to convey property rights. Only leases that satisfy certain arbitrary conditions (for example, the 75% rule or the 90% rule) qualify. *So SFAS No. 13 is a compromise between the operating lease approach, for which no leases appear on the lessee's balance sheet, and a strict property rights approach, for which all leases would be shown as assets and liabilities.*

To summarize, leases that satisfy at least one of the four criteria are treated as capital leases, and the following entry is made on the lessee's books at the inception of the lease:

| | | |
|---|---|---|
| **DR** | Leased asset—capital lease ........................................ | $XXX |
| **CR** | Obligation under capital lease ............................... | $XXX |

Leases that do not satisfy *any* of the previously discussed criteria must be accounted for as operating leases.

## Capital Lease Treatment Illustrated

To illustrate the accounting for leases that qualify as capital leases, consider the following example.

> Lessee Company signs a five-year noncancelable lease with Lessor Company on January 1, 2008 when the lease begins. Several other facts pertain to the lease:
>
> 1. The lease calls for five payments of $79,139.18 to be made at the end of each year.
> 2. The leased asset has a fair value of $315,000 on January 1, 2008.
> 3. The lease has no renewal option, and possession of the asset reverts to the lessor on January 1, 2013.
> 4. Lessee Company regularly uses the straight-line method to depreciate assets of this type that it owns.
> 5. The leased asset has an expected economic life of six years.

Because the five-year lease term covers more than 75% of the asset's six-year expected economic life (5/6 = 83.3%), this lease must be treated as a capital lease, following criterion (3). Thus, Lessee Company must recognize both an asset and a liability on its books.

But what is the asset and liability dollar amount that should be recorded? *SFAS No. 13* requires that the dollar amount be equal to the discounted present value of the **minimum lease payments** specified in the lease. Contingent payments are ignored. The discount rate used to determine the present value is the *lower* of the lessee's incremental borrowing rate[5] or the lessor's rate of return implicit in the lease.[6] If the lessee can't determine the lessor's rate of return, the lessee uses the incremental borrowing rate.

> *Minimum lease payments* are defined as the noncontingent, fixed payments specified in the lease agreement. For example, if the payment schedule called for a fixed fee of $79,139.18 per year plus an additional fee of five cents per unit for each unit manufactured using the leased asset, only the $79,139.18 would be included in the computation of minimum lease payments. The five cents per unit for each unit manufactured is *a contingency that is ignored in the calculation.* In more complicated leases, the minimum lease payments also include:
>
> 1. The amount of any **residual value guarantee** by the lessee (as discussed later).
> 2. Any penalties that must be paid if the lessee chooses not to renew the lease.
> 3. The amount of any bargain purchase option payment if the lease contains a bargain purchase option.

Assume that Lessee Company's incremental borrowing rate is 10% and the lessee can't determine the lessor's implicit rate of return on the lease. The discount rate is accordingly 10%, and the present value of the minimum lease payments in our example is:

> International standards differ here. The interest rate implicit to the lease should be used, if known; if not, the incremental borrowing rate is used. See *IAS 17*, para. 20.

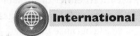

| Present value of minimum lease payments | = | Minimum lease payment | × | Present value factor for an ordinary annuity for five years at 10% |
|---|---|---|---|---|
| $300,000 | = | $79,139.18 | × | 3.79079 (from Appendix I, Present Value Tables, Table 2) |

Lessee Company makes the following entry on January 1, 2008 at the inception of the lease:

| | | |
|---|---|---|
| **DR** | Leased asset—capital lease ................................... | $300,000 |
| **CR** | Obligation under capital lease ......................... | $300,000 |

It is important to understand that the amount shown for the asset and the amount shown for the related liability ($300,000) are equal only at the inception of the lease. Thereafter, as the term of the lease progresses, the amount in the asset account will equal the amount in the liability account only by sheer coincidence. The reason that the two amounts will differ subsequently is that the asset account will be reduced in accordance with Lessee Company's depreciation schedule for assets of this type, whereas the liability account is reduced in accordance with the payment schedule contained in the lease. The asset account and liability account are reduced at independent—and usually different—rates over the life of the lease. (The appendix to this chapter illustrates the effect of these different reduction rates on the carrying value of the lease asset and liability.)

> The lease also meets criterion (4) because 90% of the asset's $315,000 fair value equals $283,500, and the present value of the minimum lease payments ($300,000) is greater than $283,500.

---

[5] The FASB defines the **lessee's incremental borrowing rate** as the rate that the lessee "would have incurred to borrow the funds necessary to buy the leased asset on a secured loan with repayment terms similar to the payment schedule called for in the lease" (*SFAS No. 13*, para. 5 [1]).

[6] The **lessor's rate of return** is the pre-tax internal yield on the lease contract (that is, the rate that equates the fair value of the asset and the present value of the payments accruing the lessor). Ibid., para. 5(k).

Each lease payment of $79,139.18 is composed of two elements. One represents interest on the present value of the obligation that was outstanding during the year. The other represents a repayment of a portion of the principal amount of the obligation. *SFAS No. 13* requires that the interest and principal repayment portions of each $79,139.18 outflow be measured using the **effective interest method.** The amortization schedule in Exhibit 12.1 shows this break-down in Column (b), Interest Expense, and Column (c), Principal Payment. For example, the $79,139.18 payment made on December 31, 2008 consists of a $30,000 interest component and a $49,139.18 principal payment component.

On December 31, 2008, Lessee Company records both the $79,139.18 cash payment (Column [a]) and the amortization of the capitalized leased asset (Column [e]). Based on the figures in Exhibit 12.1, the entries are:

| | | | |
|---|---|---|---|
| **DR** | Obligation under capital lease | $49,139.18 | |
| **DR** | Interest expense | 30,000.00 | |
| | **CR**  Cash | | $79,139.18 |
| | | | |
| **DR** | Depreciation expense—capital lease | $60,000.00 | |
| | **CR**  Accumulated depreciation—capital lease | | $60,000.00 |

If a lease meets either the first or second capital lease criterion on p. 684, the leased asset is depreciated over the *asset's* life because the asset's legal title ultimately passes to the lessee. If the lease is a capital lease because it meets either the third or fourth criterion but not the first or second criterion, it is depreciated over the *lease's* life because the asset reverts to the lessor at lease-end. In Exhibit 12.1, the asset is depreciated over five years because it qualified under both the third and fourth criteria but not the first or second criterion.

The amount of interest expense recognized each year equals 10% (the discount rate) times the present value of the obligation outstanding at the start of the year. Because the present value of the lease obligation at the start of the lease on January 1, 2008 was $300,000 (Column [d]), the interest expense for 2008 is $300,000 times 10%, or $30,000. The difference between the $79,139.18 cash payment and the $30,000 interest expense represents repayment of principal. This 2008 difference—$49,139.18 (Column [c])—reduces the remaining principal balance of the lease at December 31, 2008 to $250,860.82 ($300,000 − $49,139.18) as shown in

**EXHIBIT 12.1**    Lessee Company

**Amortization Schedule—Effective Interest Method**

| Date | (a) Total Payment | (b) Interest Expense* | (c) Principal Payment† | (d) Lease Obligation Balance | (e) Amortization of Asset | (f) Total Annual Capital Lease Expense (Col. [b] + Col. [e]) |
|---|---|---|---|---|---|---|
| 1/1/08 | | | | $300,000.00 | | |
| 12/31/08 | $ 79,139.18 | $30,000.00 | $ 49,139.18 | 250,860.82 | $ 60,000.00 | $ 90,000.00 |
| 12/31/09 | 79,139.18 | 25,086.08 | 54,053.10 | 196,807.72 | 60,000.00 | 85,086.08 |
| 12/31/10 | 79,139.18 | 19,680.77 | 59,458.41 | 137,349.31 | 60,000.00 | 79,680.77 |
| 12/31/11 | 79,139.18 | 13,734.93 | 65,404.25 | 71,945.06 | 60,000.00 | 73,734.93 |
| 12/31/12 | 79,139.18 | 7,194.12‡ | 71,945.06 | — | 60,000.00 | 67,194.12 |
| | $395,695.90 | $95,695.90 | $300,000.00 | $   −0− | $300,000.00 | $395,695.90 |

* Column (d) for preceding year times 10%.

† Column (a) minus Column (b).

‡ Rounded.

Column (d). Interest expense for 2009 would then be $250,860.82 times 10%, or $25,086.08. The 2009 journal entry for the cash payment is:

> **DR** Obligation under capital lease .......................... $54,053.10
> **DR** Interest expense ........................................ 25,086.08
>     **CR** Cash............................................ $79,139.18

The depreciation expense is based on the $300,000 capitalized amount, not the $315,000 fair value. Notice that the entry to record depreciation expense is the same in all years of the lease because Lessee Company uses the straight-line depreciation method.

Figure 12.2 summarizes lessees' accounting for capital leases.

## Executory Costs

**Executory costs** represent costs of *using* assets, such as maintenance, taxes, and insurance. Often the lessee pays these costs directly. Sometimes the lessor pays them and passes them along to the lessee as an additional lease payment. For example, if executory costs paid by Lessor Company total $2,000 per year, Lessor would include an added yearly charge of $2,000 in the lease in addition to the basic $79,139.18 rental fee.

Because executory costs represent a cost of using assets—rather than a cost of the assets themselves—these costs are omitted when determining minimum lease payments, and thus they are not a component of the capitalized amount shown in the Leased asset—capital lease account. Consider this extension of the previous example. If Lessee Company's annual rental fee totals $81,139.18, which includes a $2,000 per year maintenance contract with the lessor,

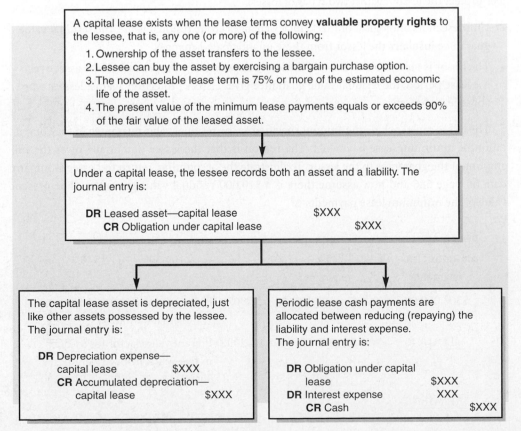

**Figure 12.2**

LESSEES' ACCOUNTING FOR CAPITAL LEASES

the minimum lease payments to be capitalized would be $79,139.18 (that is, $81,139.18 − $2,000). Under this assumption, the capitalized amount would still total $300,000 and the amortization schedule would be identical to that in Exhibit 12.1. Lessee Company would treat the $2,000 of executory costs from the maintenance contract as a period cost and charge it to expense when paid. For example, the $81,139.18 payment on December 31, 2008 would trigger this entry:

| | | |
|---|---|---|
| **DR** | Obligation under capital lease . . . . . . . . . . . . . . . . . . . . . . . . . . . . . | $49,139.18 |
| **DR** | Interest expense . . . . . . . . . . . . . . . . . . . . . . . . . . . . . . . . . . . . . . . | 30,000.00 |
| **DR** | Miscellaneous lease expense . . . . . . . . . . . . . . . . . . . . . . . . . . . . . | 2,000.00 |
| **CR** | Cash . . . . . . . . . . . . . . . . . . . . . . . . . . . . . . . . . . . . . . . . . . . . . . . | $81,139.18 |

## Residual Value Guarantees

Lease contracts sometimes contain a provision under which the lessee guarantees that the leased asset will have a certain value at the end of the lease. If the actual market value of the asset is less than this **residual value guarantee,** the lessee must pay the difference to the lessor. Continuing the previous example, assume that the lease required Lessee Company to guarantee that the asset's residual value would be no lower than $20,000 when the lease ends on January 1, 2013. If the asset's fair value on that date is $20,000 or higher, Lessee would simply return it to the lessor because the residual value guarantee is satisfied. But if the fair value is only $15,000 on January 1, 2013, Lessee would return the asset and pay Lessor Company $5,000 cash.

Leased assets often revert to the lessor at the end of the lease term. Residual value guarantees protect the lessor against two types of losses:

- Unforeseen technological or marketplace changes erode residual value; the residual value guarantee insulates the lessor from these unanticipated changes.

- The lessor is vulnerable to losses if the lessee does not take proper care of the asset over the lease period; the residual value guarantee gives lessors protection against lessees who abuse leased assets.

The lessee must include the amount specified as the residual value guarantee in the computation of minimum lease payments. The reason is that the lessee potentially owes the full amount of the guarantee to the lessor. To illustrate the accounting, return to Lessee Company data on page 686 and now assume there is a $20,000 residual value guarantee. The present value of the minimum lease payments is:

| Present value of minimum lease payments | | Minimum lease payment | | Present value factor at 10% |
|---|---|---|---|---|
| $300,000.00 | = | $79,139.18 | × | 3.79079 (Present value factor for five-year ordinary annuity) |
| 12,418.40 | = | $20,000.00 | × | 0.62092 (Present value factor for $1 due in five years, from Appendix I, Table 1) |
| $312,418.40 | | | | |

| EXHIBIT 12.2 | Lessee Company |
|---|---|

**Amortization Schedule—Effective Interest Method
With Guaranteed Residual Value**

| Date | (a) Total Cash Payment | (b) Interest Expense* | (c) Principal Payment† | (d) Lease Obligation Balance | (e) Amortization of Asset; Residual Value Return | (f) Lease Asset Balance | (g) Total Annual Capital Lease Expense (b) + (e) |
|---|---|---|---|---|---|---|---|
| 1/1/08 | — | — | — | $312,418.40 | — | $312,418.40 | — |
| 12/31/08 | $ 79,139.18 | $ 31,241.84 | $ 47,897.34 | 264,521.06 | $ 58,483.68‡ | 253,934.72 | $ 89,725.52 |
| 12/31/09 | 79,139.18 | 26,452.11 | 52,687.07 | 211,833.99 | 58,483.68 | 195,451.04 | 84,935.79 |
| 12/31/10 | 79,139.18 | 21,183.40 | 57,955.78 | 153,878.21 | 58,483.68 | 136,967.36 | 79,667.08 |
| 12/31/11 | 79,139.18 | 15,387.82 | 63,751.36 | 90,126.85 | 58,483.68 | 78,483.68 | 73,871.50 |
| 12/31/12 | 79,139.18 | 9,012.33$ | 70,126.85 | 20,000.00 | 58,483.68 | 20,000.00 | 67,496.01 |
| 1/1/13# | — | — | 20,000.00 | — | 20,000.00 | — | — |
| | $395,695.90 | $103,277.50 | $312,418.40 | $ –0– | $312,418.40 | $ –0– | $395,695.90 |

* Column (d) for preceding year times 10%.

† Column (a) minus Column (b).

‡ ($312,418.40 − $20,000) ÷ 5.

$ Rounded.

# Asset returned.

With the residual value guarantee, Lessee makes the following entry on January 1, 2008 at the inception of the lease:

| **DR** Leased asset—capital lease | $312,418.40 | |
|---|---|---|
| **CR** Obligation under capital lease | | $312,418.40 |

Exhibit 12.2 shows the amortization schedule that Lessee uses when this residual value guarantee is included in the lease. After making the December 31, 2012 cash payment of $79,139.18, the lease obligation balance (Column [d]) and the lease asset balance (Column [f]) both are $20,000 (see the highlighted numbers). We're assuming that the asset's value at the end of the lease on January 1, 2013 equals or exceeds $20,000—the amount of the residual value guarantee. When Lessee returns the asset on that date, it satisfies its obligation to Lessor Company, and the follwing entry results:

| **DR** Obligation under capital lease | $20,000.00 | |
|---|---|---|
| **CR** Leased asset—capital lease | | $20,000.00 |

Now let's alter the example and assume that the asset has a fair value of only $15,000 at December 31, 2012. Lessee Company would have to pay $5,000 in addition to relinquishing the asset. The entry is:

| **DR** Obligation under capital lease | $20,000.00 | |
|---|---|---|
| **DR** Loss on residual value guarantee | 5,000.00 | |
| **CR** Leased asset—capital lease | | $20,000.00 |
| **CR** Cash | | 5,000.00 |

Columns (a) through (d) would be similar for a lease with a bargain purchase option. However, a bargain purchase would have required the lessee to depreciate the asset over the economic life of six years, resulting in annual depreciation expense of $52,069.73 ($312,418.40/6), thereby making columns (e) through (g) different.

## Payments in Advance

When lease payments are due at the *start* of each lease period, the journal entries and amortization tables differ slightly. We'll use the original Lessee Company example on page 686 to illustrate this. Assume that the annual payment is due at the start of each year and, because the payments are received earlier, the lessor lowers the required annual payment to $71,945. Under these slightly altered conditions, the present value of the minimum lease payments is:

| Present value of minimum lease payments | | Minimum lease payment | × | Present value factor for an annuity in advance for five years at 10% |
|---|---|---|---|---|
| $300,000 | = | $71,945 | × | 4.16987 (from Appendix I, Table 3) |

Exhibit 12.3 shows the amortization schedule for this lease with up-front payments. Lessee records the following two entries on January 1, 2008 upon signing the lease and making the required lease payment:

| | | | |
|---|---|---|---|
| **DR** | Leased asset—capital lease . . . . . . . . . . . . . . . . . . . . . . . . . . . . . . . | $300,000 | |
| | **CR**   Obligation under capital lease . . . . . . . . . . . . . . . . . . . . . . . . . | | $300,000 |
| **DR** | Obligation under capital lease . . . . . . . . . . . . . . . . . . . . . . . . . . . . . | $ 71,945 | |
| | **CR**   Cash . . . . . . . . . . . . . . . . . . . . . . . . . . . . . . . . . . . . . . . . . . . . . | | $ 71,945 |

Notice in both the second journal entry and Exhibit 12.3 that no portion of the January 1, 2008 payment represents interest expense; instead, all of the $71,945 payment reduces the principal balance. The reason is that interest expense ensues only as time passes, not at the lease's inception.

---

| **EXHIBIT 12.3** | **Lessee Company** |
|---|---|

### Amortization Schedule—Effective Interest Method With Payments at the Start of Each Period

| Date | (a) Total Payment | (b) Interest Expense* | (c) Principal Payment† | (d) Lease Obligation Balance | (e) Amortization of Asset | (f) Total Annual Capital Lease Expense (b) + (e) |
|---|---|---|---|---|---|---|
| 1/1/08 | | | | $300,000.00 | | |
| 1/1/08 | $ 71,945.00 | — | $ 71,945.00 | 228,055.00 | $ 60,000.00 | $ 60,000.00 |
| 1/1/09 | 71,945.00 | $22,805.50 | 49,139.50 | 178,915.50 | 60,000.00 | 82,805.50 |
| 1/1/10 | 71,945.00 | 17,891.55 | 54,053.45 | 124,862.05 | 60,000.00 | 77,891.55 |
| 1/1/11 | 71,945.00 | 12,486.21 | 59,458.79 | 65,403.26 | 60,000.00 | 72,486.21 |
| 1/1/12 | 71,945.00 | 6,541.74‡ | 65,403.26 | — | 60,000.00 | 66,541.74 |
| | $359,725.00 | $59,725.00 | $300,000.00 | $   –0– | $300,000.00 | $359,725.00 |

\* Column (d) for preceding year times 10%.

† Column (a) minus Column (b).

‡ Rounded.

## Financial Statement Effects of Treating a Lease as a Capital Lease versus Treating It as an Operating Lease

To understand the financial statement effects of lease capitalization, we need to compare the numbers that result from the capital lease approach with the numbers that would have resulted had the operating lease method been used instead.

To make that comparison, return to the beginning of Lessee Company example (p. 686) in which we assumed that lease payments were due at year-end, executory costs were zero, and there was no residual value guarantee. If that lease had been accounted for as an operating lease, the following journal entry would have been made in each of the five years of the lease:

> Assuming that zero executory costs is equivalent to assuming that the executory costs are paid directly by the lessee and are not included in the payments due to the lessor.

| **DR** | Lease expense | $79,139.18 | |
|---|---|---|---|
| **CR** | Cash | | $79,139.18 |

Under the operating lease method, the total lease expense over the life of the lease equals the total cash outflow. This total expense number under the operating lease method is $395,695.90 and is shown at the bottom of Column (a) of Exhibit 12.1.

Under the capital lease method, the total lease expense over the life of the lease comprises both (1) the interest payments and (2) the amortization of the capitalized asset amount. The sum of these two elements is shown at the bottom of Column (f) of the amortization schedule in Exhibit 12.1. This total is also $395,695.90.

A comparison of the Exhibit 12.1 Column (a) total (lifetime expense under the operating lease method) and the Column (f) total (lifetime expense under the capital lease method) demonstrates that **the two methods give rise to identical cumulative total lifetime charges to expense.** Over the life of a lease, total expense is unaffected by the choice of lease accounting method. However, a comparison of the year-by-year numbers in Columns (a) and (f) demonstrates that the *timing* of the expense charge for the two methods differs. The capital lease approach leads to higher expense in the earlier years of the lease and lower lease expense in the later years, as shown in Figure 12.3. You can see in the graphical representation that in the early lease years, expenses under the capital lease approach exceed lease expenses that would be recognized under the operating lease approach. Ultimately, capital lease expense drops below operating lease expense.

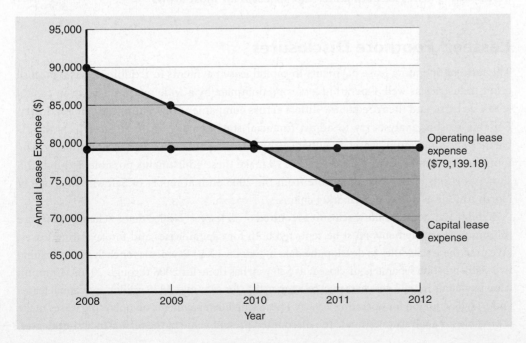

**Figure 12.3**

LESSEE COMPANY PATTERN OF EXPENSE RECOGNITION: CAPITAL VERSUS OPERATING LEASE METHOD

This accelerated recognition of lease expenses under the capital lease approach provides another reason why many lessees prefer the operating lease method. Consider the incentives of a manager whose performance evaluations and bonuses are tied to financial numbers. Because the capital lease accounting method loads the lease expenses at the front end of the lease term, it lowers income during that front-end period and thus reduces the discounted present value of expected bonuses. Worse yet, if managers' accomplishments are evaluated "strictly by the numbers," the higher expenses and lower profitability could jeopardize their continuing employment and advancement. So, managers have a strong incentive to structure lease contracts in ways that circumvent the capitalization rules.

Exhibit 12.4 shows the total amount of scheduled capital lease payments versus operating lease payments for the five largest firms in each of five industries that use leases extensively. Notice that the dollar amount of the minimum lease payments arising from operating leases is, on average, almost 100 times more than the capital lease payments for airlines and almost 72 times more for railroads. This demonstrates that capital leases arise infrequently even in industries that utilize leasing heavily.

One possible explanation for the preponderance of operating leases in Exhibit 12.4 is that the criteria for capitalizing lease commitments in *SFAS No. 13* can be readily circumvented. For example, a lessee can simply refuse to sign a lease contract that transfers legal title or contains a bargain purchase option. This avoids triggering the first and second capitalization criteria. Criterion (3)—the 75% rule—can also be circumvented by bargaining with the lessor to shorten the lease term until it is less than 75% of the asset's expected economic life. However, criterion (4)—the 90% rule (or recovery of investment criterion)—is the most difficult to circumvent and undoubtedly accounts for many capital leases that ultimately appear on financial statements.

We can only infer why companies in these five industries that extensively use leases have so few capital leases. A reasonable conjecture is that they have chosen to keep these leases "off the balance sheet" to improve ratios such as debt to equity and return on assets.

## RECAP

**Lessees have incentives to keep leases off the balance sheet. Criteria exist for identifying capital leases. However, the terms of a lease can easily be designed to evade these criteria. So, operating leases far outnumber capital leases for most firms.**

## Lessees' Footnote Disclosures

The ratio of operating lease payments to capital lease payments in Exhibit 12.4 is typical of other industries as well. Operating leases predominate by a wide margin. However, capital leases *do* exist, and their frequency differs across companies even within the same industry. For this reason, analysts try to adjust financial statements to include the effects of off-balance sheet operating leases to enhance comparisons between firms in an industry. The footnote disclosures required by *SFAS No. 13* make these adjustments possible. Exhibit 12.5 shows portions of the leases footnote from the 2005 annual report of Safeway Inc., one of North America's largest supermarket chains.

Exhibit 12.5 contains the disclosures required of all lessees. Notice that a schedule of future minimum lease payments must be reported both for capital leases and for operating leases. (We used these schedules to develop the data in Exhibit 12.4.) Payments for each of the ensuing five years must be separately disclosed, as Safeway has done for 2006 through 2010. Minimum lease payments for all later years may be aggregated (for example, $875 million for capital leases and $2,645.9 million for operating leases). These scheduled payments on operating leases make it possible for analysts to estimate the discounted present value of the off-balance sheet leases.

| EXHIBIT 12.4 | Comparison of Undiscounted Dollar Magnitudes of Capital and Operating Lease Payments |

**2005 Fiscal Year**

| ($ in millions) | Total Scheduled Minimum Lease Pyaments | | Ratio of Operating to Capital Lease Payments |
|---|---|---|---|
| | Operating Leases | Capital Leases | |
| **Department/Variety Stores** | | | |
| Wal-Mart | $ 9,683 | $6,341 | $ 1.53 |
| Target | 3,097 | 223 | 13.89 |
| Costco Wholesale | 1,562 | — | * |
| Sears | 7,275 | 1,503 | 4.84 |
| Federated Department Stores | 3,362 | 169 | 19.89 |
| Average | | | 10.04 |
| **Supermarkets** | | | |
| Kroger | 7,067 | 616 | 11.47 |
| Safeway | 4,570 | 1,370 | 3.34 |
| Supervalu | 930 | 788 | 1.18 |
| Publix Super Markets | 4,086 | — | * |
| Delhaize America | 2,077 | 1,580 | 1.31 |
| Average | | | 4.33 |
| **Railroads** | | | |
| Union Pacific Corporation | 4,934 | 2,100 | 2.35 |
| Burlington Northern Santa Fe | 6,143 | 720 | 8.53 |
| CSX Corp | 196 | 42 | 4.67 |
| Norfolk Southern Corporation | 1,067 | 318 | 3.36 |
| Kansas City Southern | 916 | 3 | 305.33 |
| Average | | | 71.63 |
| **Airlines** | | | |
| AMR | 12,217 | 1,804 | 6.77 |
| UAL | 12,122 | 2,016 | 6.01 |
| Delta Airlines | 13,040 | 996 | 13.09 |
| Northwest Airlines | 4,929 | 11 | 448.09 |
| Continental Airlines | 14,999 | 614 | 24.43 |
| Average | | | 99.68 |
| **Communications** | | | |
| Verizon Communications Inc. | 4,451 | 165 | 26.98 |
| AT&T Inc. | 10,089 | 2,660 | 3.79 |
| Sprint Nextel Corporation | 16,379 | 207 | 79.13 |
| BellSouth | 582 | — | * |
| Qwest Communications | 2,106 | 172 | 12.24 |
| Average | | | 30.53 |

* Ratio cannot be calculated due to lack of capitalized leases.

*Source:* Company SEC filings and annual reports.

In the appendix to this chapter, we use the Safeway disclosures to illustrate this computation step-by-step. Once the present value of the off-balance sheet leases is determined, the computed dollar amount can be added to both the asset account (Leased asset—capital lease) and the liability account (Obligation under capital lease). This adjustment allows analysts to compensate for distortions that can arise from off-balance sheet leases when making interfirm comparisons.

**EXHIBIT 12.5**     Safeway Inc. and Subsidiaries

**Edited Excerpts from Leases Footnote December 31, 2005**
As of year-end 2005, future minimum rental payments applicable to non-cancelable capital and operating leases with remaining terms in excess of one year were as follows (in millions):

|  | Capital Leases | Operating Leases |
|---|---|---|
| 2006 | $ 105.7 | $ 426.1 |
| 2007 | 104.3 | 410.6 |
| 2008 | 103.9 | 397.3 |
| 2009 | 94.7 | 359.9 |
| 2010 | 86.1 | 330.2 |
| Thereafter | 875.0 | 2,645.9 |
| Total minimum lease payments | 1,369.7 | $4,570.0 |
| Less amounts representing interest | (686.5) | |
| Present value of net minimum lease payments | 683.2 | |
| Less current obligations | (39.1) | |
| Long-term obligations | $ 644.1 | |

Future minimum lease payments under non-cancelable capital and operating lease agreements have not been reduced by minimum sublease rental income of $176.9 million.

Our discussion for operating leases so far has assumed that payments are constant. Under this scenario, the entire operating lease obligation is generally off-balance sheet. However, *SFAS No. 13,* para. 15 requires that rent expense be recognized on a straight-line basis even if payments are not the same over time. For example, to make a lease more attractive, the lessor may offer a "rent holiday" by suspending rent payments for the first year. Under *SFAS No. 13,* firms must determine total rent to be paid over the life of the lease and accrue it evenly over the lease term. The form of the accrual and payment entry is:

| **DR** | Rent expense............................................... | $XXX | |
|---|---|---|---|
| | **CR** Accrued rent expense ..................................... | | $XXX |
| | **CR** Cash..................................................... | | XXX |

As a result of this entry, the balance sheet has a liability. This liability is reduced as the rental payment amounts increase during the lease term. Between 2004 and 2006, more than 250 firms had to restate their financial statements because of this and other issues related to operating lease accounting.[7]

## Income Adjustment

**Analysis**

If one company has structured its lease contracts to keep these commitments off the balance sheet while a competitor has not, how do analysts make the two companies' income numbers comparable? It is not difficult to make such adjustments for companies whose average lease is approximately 50% expired. Refer to Figure 12.3, which shows that halfway through the life of the lease (December 31, 2010), Lessee Company's lease expense under the operating lease approach is very close to lease expense under the capital lease approach. Exhibit 12.1 indicates that operating lease expense in 2010 is $79,139.18 while capital lease expense is $79,680.77—virtually the same.

---

[7] For more information on the restatements, see A. A. Acito, J. J. Burks, and W. B. Johnson, "Materiality Decisions and the Correction of Accounting Errors," Working paper, Tippie College of Business, University of Iowa (2007).

**EXHIBIT 12.6**　　Kmart Corporation

**Excerpts from Leases Footnote January 25, 1995**

Reconciliation of capital lease information: The impact of recording amortization and interest expense versus rent expense on capital leases follows:

| ($ in millions) | 1994 | 1993 | 1992 |
|---|---|---|---|
| Amortization of capital lease property | $119 | $117 | $113 |
| Interest expense related to obligations under capital leases | 196 | 192 | 185 |
| Amounts charged to earnings | 315 | 309 | 298 |
| Related minimum lease payments net of executory costs | (312) | (306) | (294) |
| Excess of amounts charged over related minimum lease payments | $ 3 | $ 3 | $ 4 |

Related minimum lease payments in the table exclude executory costs for 1994, 1993, and 1992 in the amounts of $97, $91, and $96, respectively.

The intuition behind the intersecting operating lease and capital lease curves in Figure 12.3 can be extended to financial analysis by reference to Exhibit 12.6, an excerpt from Kmart's 1995 annual report lease footnote. In it, Kmart voluntarily disclosed the difference between its *reported* capital lease expense and the lease expense that *would have been reported* if those capital leases had, instead, been treated as operating leases.[8] These expense differences for 1992 through 1994 (highlighted in Exhibit 12.6) are $4 million in 1992 and $3 million in 1993 and 1994. What is important to see is that the $3 million expense difference is less than 1% of the 1994 capital lease expense of $315 million. This small difference reflects the fact that Kmart was a mature company with a stable portfolio of leases that were, on average, close to the midpoint of their contractual life. So, the income statement lease expense charge would be virtually the same under either the capital lease approach or operating lease approach.

We can extend this intuition to comparisons of companies. Assume that two competitors in the same industry have capitalized different percentages of their leases and that both companies have a stable portfolio of leases. Then, generalizing from the Kmart illustration, despite these different capitalization policies, the two firms will, nevertheless, have comparable lease expense numbers. *For mature firms, the income statement effects of capital lease versus operating lease treatment is often not significantly different.*

We show in the next subsection that this is not true for balance sheet effects. On the contrary, capital lease versus operating lease treatment can significantly alter balance sheet numbers and resulting ratios.

## Balance Sheet and Ratio Effects: Capital Lease versus Operating Lease Approach

Accounting for leases using the capital lease approach invariably worsens certain key ratios on the lessee's balance sheet—thus providing another explanation for lessees' resistance to lease capitalization.[9]

---

[8] Kmart abandoned this disclosure in its 1996 annual report. This information was useful and explains why we continue to use the 1995 report even though more recent reports are now available.

[9] See E. A. Imhoff Jr., R. C. Lipe, and D. W. Wright, "Operating Leases: Impact of Constructive Capitalization," *Accounting Horizons,* March 1991, pp. 51–63.

You may wonder why the current portion at January 1, 2008 is only $49,139.18, not the entire $79,139.18 cash payment due on December 31, 2008. The difference between the two numbers is 2008 interest expense of $30,000. Interest is an expense that *accrues* as time passes. Because we are computing the current ratio at January 1, 2008, none of this 2008 interest expense nor the associated liability has yet accrued. So, the current portion is limited to $49,139.18. If we were to recompute the current ratio one month later on February 1, 2008, the current liability would then be the sum of $49,139.18 plus the dollar interest that had accrued during January, 2008.

 **Contracting**

When lease payments must be paid in *advance*, there is also a current ratio *numerator* effect under the capital lease approach. The advance payment reduces cash as well as the liability account Obligation under capital lease, as shown in the journal entry on page 692. The net effect is to lower the numerator of the current ratio. By contrast, if the same lease were treated as an operating lease, when cash is credited, the offsetting debit is to Prepaid expense—a current asset account. Accordingly, the current ratio numerator is unchanged.

In the recent past, several telecom firms artificially increased reported revenues by simultaneously leasing line capacity *to* a competitor (thereby generating revenue) while at the same time leasing an equivalent amount of capacity *from* that same competitor. The cash inflows from one lease were exactly equal to the cash outflows on the other. These transactions were designed to overstate not just revenues but *operating* cash flows too. Here's how it worked. The lease of line capacity *to* the competitor was treated as an operating lease. So, these cash inflows were classified as operating cash inflows on the cash flow statement. But the lease of line capacity *from* the competitor was treated as a capital lease. As you just saw, the principal payment component of the cash outflow is a *financing flow* on the cash flow statement. So, from a cash flow statement perspective, this "round-trip" pair of leases with equal cash inflows and outflows nevertheless increased reported operating cash inflows.

*Source:* K. Brown, "Creative Accounting: How to Buff a Company," *The Wall Street Journal,* February 21, 2002.

One ratio that deteriorates under capital lease accounting is the current ratio. Using numbers in the Lessee Company example from Exhibit 12.1, *we will demonstrate that the current ratio over the lease term will be lower under the capital lease approach than it would be under the operating lease approach.* To see this, assume that Lessee is preparing a balance sheet on January 1, 2008 immediately after signing the lease. Under the operating lease approach, the first cash payment of $79,139.18 due on December 31, 2008 is not considered to be a liability; it will accrue as a liability only as time passes and as the lessor performs its duties under the lease. Because no part of the year-end 2008 payment of $79,139.18 is recognized as a liability at January 1, 2008 under the operating lease approach, the current ratio would be unaffected on signing if Lessee were somehow able to avoid capitalization and were allowed to treat this as an operating lease.

By contrast, at the inception of the lease, the capital lease approach *does* recognize a liability—called Obligation under capital lease. As shown in Exhibit 12.1, the balance in this liability account at January 1, 2008 is $300,000.00. Furthermore, *SFAS No. 13* requires that a portion of this $300,000.00 balance be classified as a current liability. The current portion of the Obligation under capital lease is the reduction in the principal balance that will take place over the ensuing 12 months of 2008. Exhibit 12.1 shows the current portion to be $49,139.18, the expected 2008 reduction in the principal balance. Thus, treating the lease as a capital lease rather than as an operating lease will increase Lessee's current liabilities by $49,139.18 and thereby lower its January 1, 2008 current ratio. Exhibit 12.1 illustrates that this negative effect on the current ratio *increases* as the lease ages because the portion of each $79,139.18 cash outflow that represents principal repayment increases over time.

To protect the lender, many loan agreements require borrowers to maintain a certain prespecified current ratio level. It is not surprising, therefore, that lessees resist lease capitalization. As the preceding discussion illustrates, treating a lease as a capital lease lowers the current ratio; therefore, capitalization could push financially struggling lessees into technical violation of their existing loan agreements by lowering their current ratio below the prespecified limit.

Two far more obvious cases of ratio deterioration under capital lease accounting relate to the leverage ratio and the return on assets ratio. These effects were discussed at the beginning the chapter and will not be repeated here.

Lease treatment also has cash flow statement implications. To see this, refer back to Exhibit 12.1, which shows the amortization schedule for a capital lease. On the cash flow statement, the interest expense component—Column (b)—of each yearly payment would be classified as an *operating* cash flow while the principal payment component—Column (c)—would be classified as a *financing* cash flow. In contrast, if the lease had been treated as an operating lease, the entire $79,139.18 annual payment would be classified as an operating cash flow. So, when lessees successfully keep leases off the balance sheet, reported cash flow from operations is lower than it would be under the capital lease approach. This is the only adverse financial statement effect lessees experience under the operating lease approach.

We have shown that lease capitalization affects balance sheet ratios and that the *SFAS No. 13* capitalization criteria can be circumvented. Because different firms can conceivably treat virtually identical leases dissimilarly, financial statements may not be immediately comparable across firms. To make comparisons, statement users need to adjust for these differences. The appendix to this chapter outlines procedures for capitalizing off-balance-sheet (operating) leases and thereby increasing interfirm statement comparability.

# LESSOR ACCOUNTING

In addition to outlining rules for lessees, *SFAS No. 13* specifies the treatment of leases on lessors' books. While lessees have been reluctant to treat leases as capital leases, lessors have not. Treating a lease as a capital lease on the lessor's books accelerates the timing of the recognition of leasing income—thus creating favorable financial statement effects for the lessor, as we'll show in the following sections.

## Sales-Type and Direct Financing Leases

From the perspective of the lessor, if a lease arrangement

1. Transfers property rights in the leased asset to the lessee *and*
2. Allows reasonably accurate estimates regarding the amount and collectibility of the eventual net cash flows to the lessor,

the lessor treats the lease as a capital lease. In a lessor's capital lease, the leased asset is considered to be "sold" and is removed from the lessor's books. Lessors, use two types of capital leases:

1. A **sales-type lease,** which exists when the lessor is a manufacturer or dealer.
2. A **direct financing lease,** which exists when the lessor is a financial institution (for example, an insurance firm, bank, or financing company).

When both conditions—the transfer of property rights *and* reasonably accurate estimates of net cash flows—are *not simultaneously* met, the lease must be treated as an operating lease.

Figure 12.4 diagrams the various possibilities for lessor accounting, which we are about to explain in detail.

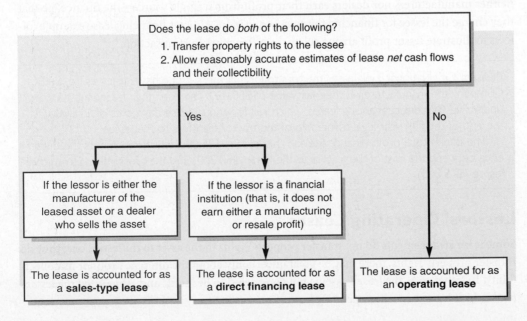

## Figure 12.4

DECISION TREE FOR LESSOR'S TREATMENT OF LEASES

**Sales-Type Leases**    For manufacturers or dealers, leases can serve as a marketing vehicle because leasing arrangements generate "sales" from potential customers who are unwilling or unable to buy the assets outright for cash. For example, Deere & Company manufactures farm equipment for sale and leases farm equipment through its wholly owned subsidiary, John Deere Credit. A lessor who uses leasing as a means for marketing products earns a profit from two sources:

1. One component of the total return on the lease is the **manufacturer's or dealer's profit**— the difference between the fair value (*cash* sales price) of the asset and its cost to the manufacturer or dealer.

2. Another component of the lessor's return is **financing profit**—the difference between the total (undiscounted) minimum lease payments plus unguaranteed residual value and the fair value of the leased asset.

The following sales-type lease example illustrates these components.

---

ABC Company manufactures tractors. Each tractor has a total production cost of $36,000 and a cash sales price of $50,000. ABC Company "sells" some of these tractors under five-year sales-type leases, which call for annual lease payments of $15,000. At the end of the fifth year, legal ownership of the tractor transfers to the lessee.

ABC Company's total profit over the five years of the lease is $39,000—that is, the lessee's payments of $75,000 ($15,000 per year times five years) minus the production cost of $36,000. This total profit comprises two components:

| | |
|---|---:|
| **Manufacturer's profit:** Cash sales price of $50,000 minus production cost of $36,000 | $14,000 |
| **Financing profit:** The difference between the cash sales price of the tractor ($50,000) and the gross inflows from the lessee ($15,000 × 5 years = $75,000) | 25,000 |
| **Total profit** | $39,000 |

---

**Direct Financing Leases**    Some lessors are not manufacturers or dealers; they are organizations such as banks, insurance firms, or financing companies that provide lessees with a means to finance asset acquisitions. These banks and other organizations acquire assets from manufacturers by paying the fair value and then leasing the asset to lessees. Lessors who are neither manufacturers nor dealers earn their profit from a single source—the finance fee that they charge the lessee for financing the asset acquisition. A direct financing lease example follows to illustrate lessor profit arising solely from financing the transaction.

---

Pleasant City National Bank leases tractors to local farmers. It purchases tractors from ABC Company, the manufacturer, at their fair value of $50,000. The Bank then leases the tractors under five-year direct financing leases, which call for annual lease payments of $15,000. At the end of the fifth year, legal ownership of the tractor transfers to the lessee.

The Bank's total profit (finance fee) on this lease is $25,000, which represents the difference between the cost of the tractor to the bank ($50,000) and the gross inflows from the lessee ($75,000).

---

## Lessors' Operating Leases

Some lease arrangements do not transfer property rights in the asset to the lessee, or if they do transfer property rights, there may be great uncertainty about the ultimate profit or its collectibility. In either case, the leased asset is not considered to be "sold" and *remains on the lessor's books.* Such leases are called *operating leases.*

# Distinction between Capital and Operating Leases

*SFAS No. 13* identifies two types of characteristics that must be met for a lease to be treated as a capital lease—either a sales-type lease or a direct financing lease—on the lessor's books. For ease of reference, these will be called Type I and Type II characteristics. A lease meeting *at least one* of the Type I characteristics and *both* of the Type II characteristics is a capital lease. The Type I characteristics are identical to the lessee's criteria for capital lease treatment.

### Type I Characteristics

1. The lease transfers ownership of the asset to the lessee by the end of the lease term.

2. The lease contains a bargain purchase option.

3. The noncancelable lease term is 75% or more of the estimated economic life of the leased asset.

4. The present value of the minimum lease payments equals or exceeds 90% of the leased asset's fair value.

### Type II Characteristics

1. The collectibility of the minimum lease payments is reasonably predictable.

2. No important uncertainties surround the amount of unreimbursable costs yet to be incurred by the lessor under the lease.

The purpose of these Type I and Type II characteristics is to establish the appropriate time for recognizing revenue and income on the lessor's books. We already know from Chapter 2 that revenue should be recognized when both of the following conditions exist:

1. The "critical event" in the process of earning the revenue has taken place.

2. The amount of the revenue that has been earned is measurable with a reasonable degree of assurance.

Accounting rules for the lessor in *SFAS No. 13* are directly linked to these two revenue recognition criteria. The Type I characteristics dealing with transfer of property rights identify the critical event in determining whether a lease is in substance a "sale of assets." That is, if any one of the four Type I characteristics is met, valuable property rights have been transferred to the lessee. This transfer of property rights constitutes the "critical event." The Type II characteristics in *SFAS No. 13* relate to the predictability and risk of cash flows and thus to the measurability of revenue.

> Under the operating lease treatment, the recognition of financing profit is related to performance (that is, passage of time). As we will see, the recognition of financing profit is accelerated when it is recognized using an effective interest approach rather than as a function of performance.

*When at least one of the Type I characteristics and both of the Type II characteristics are satisfied by a lease, the criteria for revenue recognition are met. This means that manufacturers or dealers can immediately recognize the sale, match costs, and reflect manufacturer's or dealer's profit.* (By contrast, under the operating lease treatment, this profit recognition occurs over the life of the lease as each party performs its duties.) Furthermore, lessors can begin to recognize financing profit using an effective interest approach when the Type I and Type II characteristics exist in a lease.

When a lease does not meet *any* of the Type I characteristics, or when it meets at least one of the Type I characteristics but not *both* of the Type II characteristics, that lease must be accounted for on the lessor's books as an operating lease. Under the operating lease approach,

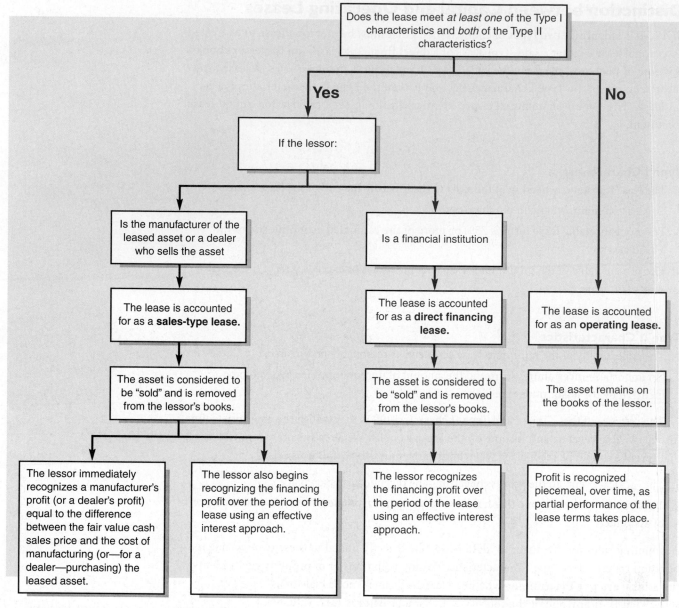

**Figure 12.5**

DETAILED EXPANSION OF FIGURE 12.4—DECISION TREE FOR LESSOR'S TREATMENT OF LEASES

the lessor's recognition of income takes place piecemeal as contractual performance progresses, as we illustrate later.

Figure 12.5 summarizes the rules for how to classify and record leases on the lessor's books. This figure is a more detailed expansion of Figure 12.4.

*SFAS No. 13* tries to establish symmetry in the accounting for leases by lessors and lessees. If a lease qualifies as a "sale" from the lessor's perspective, the property rights inherent in the lease require asset recognition by the lessee. Of course, this symmetry is not perfect because a particular lease may meet at least one of the Type I characteristics but not both of the Type II characteristics. In such cases, the asset appears on *both* the lessor's and the lessee's books. Another factor that inhibits symmetry is that the discount rate used by the lessor and the lessee could differ. ***The lessor is required to use the rate of return that is implicit to the lease.***

If this rate is *higher* than the lessee's incremental borrowing rate, the lessor and the lessee use different discount rates when accounting for the lease.

## Direct Financing Lease Treatment Illustrated

To illustrate the accounting for leases that qualify as direct financing leases, we use a variation of our earlier lease example.

---

Assume that Lessee Company signs a noncancelable five-year lease on January 1, 2008 with Lessor Company. The lease begins on January 1, 2008 and has the following terms:

1. It calls for five payments of $79,139.18 to be made at the end of each year.
2. The leased asset has a fair value of $304,359.49 on January 1, 2008.[10]
3. The lease has no renewal option, and possession of the asset reverts to Lessor Company on January 1, 2013.
4. The leased asset has an expected economic life of six years.
5. The collectibility of the lease payments is reasonably predictable.
6. No important uncertainties regarding unreimbursable costs yet to be incurred by Lessor Company exist.
7. The lease contract requires the lessee to guarantee a residual value of $20,000 at the end of the fifth year of the lease.

---

These lease terms satisfy both the third and the fourth Type I characteristics. We'll assume that the lease also satisfies both Type II characteristics. Therefore, this is a capital lease. Assume that Lessor Company is not a manufacturer or dealer, so this lease is a direct financing capital lease. *SFAS No. 13* (para. 17b) specifies that the discount rate that the lessor uses to record the lease is the lessor's implicit rate to return on the lease. Exhibit 12.7 shows how the 11% rate is used to compute the lease payment. Therefore, Lessor must use an 11% interest factor in accounting for this lease.

| **EXHIBIT 12.7** | **Lessor Company** |
| --- | --- |

**Computation of Lease Payment**

| | | |
| --- | --- | ---: |
| Fair value of leased asset at 1/1/08 | | $304,359.49 |
| Less : | Present value of the guaranteed residual value $20,000 × .59345* | 11,869.00 |
| Amount to be recovered through lease payments | | $292,490.49 |
| Divided by : | Present value factor for a five-year ordinary annuity at 11% | 3.69590 |
| Equals : | Lease payment | $ 79,139.18 |

\* Present value factor of $1 due in five years at 11%.

---

[10] This unusual amount was chosen to arrive at a round number (exactly 11%) for the rate of return implicit to the lease. In the previous residual value guarantee example on pages 690–691, Lessee Company capitalized $312,418.40 using a discount rate of 10%. In the altered example here, we see that the asset's fair value is only $304,359.49. If this fair value also applied to the example on pages 690–691. Lessee would capitalize only $304,359.49 and use an 11% amortization rate.

**EXHIBIT 12.8**   Lessor Company

### Amortization Schedule—Effective Interest Method

| Date | (a) Total Receipts | (b) Interest (Financing) Income* | (c) Principal Reduction† | (d) Remaining Principal Amount |
|------|------|------|------|------|
| 1/1/08 | | | | $304,359.49 |
| 12/31/08 | $ 79,139.18 | $ 33,479.54 | $ 45,659.64 | 258,699.85 |
| 12/31/09 | 79,139.18 | 28,456.98 | 50,682.20 | 208,017.65 |
| 12/31/10 | 79,139.18 | 22,881.94 | 56,257.24 | 151,760.41 |
| 12/31/11 | 79,139.18 | 16,693.65 | 62,445.53 | 89,314.88 |
| 12/31/12 | 79,139.18 | 9,824.30‡ | 69,314.88 | 20,000.00 |
| | $395,695.90 | $111,336.41 | $284,359.49 | |

---

\* Column (d) for preceding year times 11%.

† Column (a) minus Column (b).

‡ Rounded.

Lessor Company's amortization schedule for this lease is shown in Exhibit 12.8. Notice that the initial amount in Column (d), Remaining Principal Amount, equals the asset's fair value. The lessor's table always begins with the fair value and uses the implicit rate.

At the lease's inception, Lessor creates the account Gross investment in leased asset—the sum of the minimum rental payments plus the guaranteed residual value of the asset at the end of the lease term.

| | |
|---|---|
| Minimum rental payments over the life of the lease ($79,139.18 × 5) | $395,695.90 |
| Guaranteed residual value at 12/31/12 | 20,000.00 |
| Gross investment in leased asset | $415,695.90 |

The journal entry on January 1, 2008 is:

| | | | |
|---|---|---|---|
| **DR** | Gross investment in leased asset ........................ | $415,695.90 | |
| | **CR** Equipment ...................................... | | $304,359.49 |
| | **CR** Unearned financing income—leases ............... | | 111,336.41 |

The credit to unearned financing income is the difference between the gross investment in leased asset and the $304,359.49 Lessor paid to purchase the asset. Unearned financing income—leases, a contra-account to Gross investment in leased asset, is used to arrive at Net investment in leased asset. Only the Net investment in leased asset appears on the balance sheet, but the lessor's footnote disclosure for leases shows:

| | |
|---|---|
| Gross investment in leased asset | $415,695.90 |
| Less: Unearned financing income—leases | (111,336.41) |
| Net investment in leased asset | $304,359.49 |

This entry removes the asset account representing the equipment being leased and replaces it with two accounts that together reflect the net investment in the lease. The dollar amount for the equipment removed ($304,359.49) equals the dollar amount for the net investment in leased asset ($415,695.90 − $111,336.41).

At December 31, 2008, when the first cash payment is received from the lessee, Lessor Company makes the following journal entries:

| | | | |
|---|---|---|---|
| **DR** | Cash ................................................ | $79,139.18 | |
| | **CR** Gross investment in leased asset ..................... | | $79,139.18 |
| **DR** | Unearned financing income—leases ....................... | $33,479.54 | |
| | **CR** Financing income—leases .......................... | | $33,479.54 |

The amount of financing income recognized in each year equals the amounts shown in Column (b) of Exhibit 12.8, Lessor's amortization schedule. For example, the $33,479.54 is the product of the January 1, 2008 net investment in leased asset ($304,359.49 from Column [d]) multiplied by 11%, Lessor's rate of return on the lease. Lessor records no depreciation because the equipment itself was removed from its books (see the preceding January 1, 2008 journal entry).

After the last payment is received at the end of the lease term on December 31, 2012, the balance in the Gross investment in leased asset account will be $20,000.00 (Column [d] of the amortization schedule). This amount represents the guaranteed residual value of the asset on the date that possession of the asset reverts to Lessor Company. Assume that the asset's fair value equals or exceeds $20,000; then the following entry will be made on December 31, 2012 to reflect the end of the lease and physical repossession of the asset.

| | | | |
|---|---|---|---|
| **DR** | Equipment—residual value.............................. | $20,000.00 | |
| | **CR** Gross investment in leased asset ..................... | | $20,000.00 |

If the equipment's residual value is less than $20,000, the lessee must remit the deficiency in cash when it returns the asset to Lessor Company. So, if the asset's residual value is only $15,000 on December 31, 2012, the entry is:

| | | | |
|---|---|---|---|
| **DR** | Cash ................................................ | $ 5,000 | |
| **DR** | Equipment—residual value.............................. | 15,000 | |
| | **CR** Gross investment in leased asset ..................... | | $20,000 |

## Guaranteed versus Unguaranteed Residual Values

Lease contracts do not usually require the lessee to guarantee that the residual value will exceed a certain dollar amount. When no such contract clause exists, the residual value is **unguaranteed.**

If the asset reverts to the lessor at the end of the lease term, the initial entry to record the lease is identical regardless of whether the residual value is guaranteed or unguaranteed. To see why, return to the example in Exhibit 12.7. It assumed that the residual value would be $20,000 and that the lessee would make up any deficiency if the December 31, 2012 value were less than $20,000. So, the discounted present value at 11% of the $20,000 residual value ($11,869) belongs to the lessor and is subtracted from the fair value of $304,359.49. If we alter the example and assume that the expected asset residual value of $20,000

> Of course, with an unguaranteed residual value, the lessor bears higher risk. If the December 31, 2012 residual value is less than $20,000, the lessor loses because the lessee does not make up the difference. So, the actually achieved rate of return to the lessor will be less than the Exhibit 12.7 expected return of 11%.

is *un*guaranteed, the asset still reverts to the lessor at December 31, 2012 and the expected (but now unguaranteed) net present value of the residual value ($11,869) still belongs to the lessor. So, the $11,869 is still subtracted from the fair value just as it would be if it were guaranteed.

From the lessee's perspective, the initial entry to record the lease *is* different if the residual value is unguaranteed. Only *guaranteed* residual values are obligations to the lessee and thereby included in the computation of minimum lease payments, as discussed on page 690.

## Financial Statement Effects of Direct Financing versus Operating Leases

Comparing the financial statement effects of direct financing versus operating lease treatment allows a more complete understanding of lessor accounting.

Had Lessor Company accounted for the previous lease as an operating lease, it would make the following journal entry each year:

| | | | |
|---|---|---|---|
| **DR** | Cash | $79,139.18 | |
| | **CR** | Rental revenue | $79,139.18 |

Because the leased asset remains on the lessor's books under the operating method, annual depreciation must be recognized. Assume that the asset is depreciated down to a $20,000 residual value on a straight-line basis; then the annual depreciation expense is $56,871.90 ([$304,359.49 − $20,000.00]/5), and the entry each year is:

| | | | |
|---|---|---|---|
| **DR** | Depreciation expense | $56,871.90 | |
| | **CR** | Accumulated depreciation | $56,871.90 |

Exhibit 12.9 shows operating method amounts in Columns (a), (b), (c) and (f) and contrasts these numbers with direct financing amounts in Columns (d) and (g). Income for the operating method totals $111,336.41 over the life of the lease, as shown in Column (c). This total is identical to the income recognized under the direct financing method, as the total in Column (d) reflects. *So, income over the life of the lease is unaffected by which accounting method—the operating lease method or the direct financing method—is used. However, the timing of income does differ for the two methods,* as indicated in the highlighted Column (e) of Exhibit 12.9. The direct financing method recognizes income sooner. Notice that the income timing difference would widen if an accelerated depreciation method were used in conjunction with the operating method as opposed to the straight-line method employed in the example.

---

**EXHIBIT 12.9**     Lessor Company

### Operating Method versus Direct Financing Method Income and Asset Balance Comparison

| | Operating Method | | | | | Net Asset Balance at End of Year | | |
|---|---|---|---|---|---|---|---|---|
| Year | (a) Lease Payment Received | (b) Depreciation | (c) Operating Method Income* | (d) Direct Financing Method Income† | (e) Income Difference Between Methods | (f) Operating Method‡ | (g) Direct Financing Method§ | (h) Asset Balance Difference Between Methods |
| 2008 | $ 79,139.18 | $ 56,871.90 | $ 22,267.28 | $ 33,479.54 | +$11,212.26 | $247,487.59 | $258,699.85 | +$11,212.26 |
| 2009 | 79,139.18 | 56,871.90 | 22,267.28 | 28,456.98 | + 6,189.70 | 190,615.69 | 208,017.65 | + 17,401.96 |
| 2010 | 79,139.18 | 56,871.90 | 22,267.28 | 22,881.94 | + 614.66 | 133,743.79 | 151,760.41 | + 18,016.62 |
| 2011 | 79,139.18 | 56,871.90 | 22,267.28 | 16,693.65 | − 5,573.63 | 76,871.89 | 89,314.88 | + 12,442.99 |
| 2012 | 79,139.18 | 56,871.89 | 22,267.29 | 9,824.30 | − 12,442.99 | 20,000.00 | 20,000.00 | $ −0− |
| | $395,695.90 | $284,359.49 | $111,336.41 | $111,336.41 | $ −0− | | | |

\* Column (a) minus Column (b).

† From Column (b) of Exhibit 12.8.

‡ $304,359.49 minus the period-to-date cumulative depreciation amount from Column (b).

§ From Column (d) of Exhibit 12.8.

The "front ending" of income under the direct financing method may explain why lessors—unlike lessees—have never seriously opposed the capital lease approach to lease accounting. Furthermore, the direct financing method results in other favorable financial statement effects. For example, the lessor's rate of return on assets ratio usually improves under the direct financing method in the early years of a lease. Highlighted Columns (e) and (h) in Exhibit 12.9 illustrate this effect. Income and the end-of-year asset balance are both $11,212.26 more under the direct financing method in 2008. An equal dollar increase in the numerator and denominator of a ratio increases the ratio value as long as the ratio of initial value is less than 100%. Because reported rates of return on assets are almost always far less than 100%, the adoption of the direct financing method almost always increases the lessor's reported rate of return in the lease's early years.

Of course, Exhibit 12.9 also illustrates that this effect reverses as the lease ages. In 2012, for example, income is $12,442.99 less under the direct financing method while the end-of-year asset value equals what it would have been under the operating lease treatment. This would make the 2012 return on the direct financing method less than the return that would have been reported on the operating lease approach.[11]

The current ratio of a lessor that uses the direct financing method will also be improved. Consider the current ratio at December 31, 2008. Under the operating lease method, the December 31, 2009 expected lease cash receipt of $79,139.18 would not be shown as an asset on Lessor's books on December 31, 2008 because performance under the lease contract has not yet taken place and will not take place until 2009. Under the direct financing method, however, the 2009 lease payment would be included as a component of the Net investment in leased assets account. Returning to Exhibit 12.8, look at the December 31, 2008 balance in this account (Column [d]), which is $258,699.85; of this amount, $50,682.20 (the principal reduction in the next 12 months) is classified as a current asset. This amount shown in Column (c) of Exhibit 12.8 represents the difference between the gross December 31, 2009 cash receipt of $79,139.18 from the lessee and the interest income of $28,456.98 that will be recognized in 2009. Thus, current assets on the direct financing basis would be higher than they would have been under the operating lease approach—and the current ratio is accordingly improved.

## Sales-Type Lease Treatment Illustrated

Accounting for sales-type leases is a simple extension of the direct financing method. A sales-type lease includes a manufacturer's or dealer's profit *in addition to* financing profit; a direct financing lease has only the financing profit component.

To illustrate the accounting for sales-type leases, we now assume that Lessor Company *manufactures* the leased equipment. Prior to the start of the lease on January 1, 2008, the equipment was carried on Lessor's books at its manufactured cost of $240,000. All other facts in the original example (page 703) remain unchanged.

---

[11] The ratio effect described here holds for each lease in isolation. However, most lessors have many leases of various ages outstanding. In these situations, the number of leases outstanding over time determines the effect on the return ratio. Assume that Lessor Company's total number of leases is constant over time. Initially, when Lessor uses the direct financing method for new leases, its reported rate of return will increase. However, with a constant volume of leases, the average age of the leases accounted for on the direct financing method will eventually stabilize. When this happens, the return on assets ratio under the direct financing method will essentially equal what it would have been under the operating approach. If Lessor's leasing business expands over time, there will be a constant infusion of new leases, and the average age of the leases in place will be falling. When this situation exists, the rate of return on assets will be higher under the direct financing method.

Lessor records the transaction on January 1, 2008 as:

| | | | |
|---|---|---|---|
| **DR** | Gross investment in leased asset | $415,695.90 | |
| **DR** | Cost of goods sold | $240,000.00 | |
| | **CR** Sales revenue | | $304,359.49 |
| | **CR** Unearned financing income—leases | | 111,336.41 |
| | **CR** Inventory | | 240,000.00 |

This entry assumes that the residual value is guaranteed. If it is not, the discounted present value of the residual value—which at 11% is 0.59345 × $20,000 = $11,869—is deducted from both sales revenue and cost of goods sold. The reason $11,869 is deducted is that if the residual value is unguaranteed, the "critical event" in recognizing revenue on the residual value has not yet occurred. There is no assurance that the residual value will ultimately be realized. Only a portion of the asset has been "sold." So, both Sales revenue and Cost of goods sold are reduced by $11,869. The entries with an unguaranteed residual value are:

| | | | |
|---|---|---|---|
| **DR** | Gross investment in leased asset | $415,695.90 | |
| **DR** | Cost of goods sold | 228,131.00* | |
| | **CR** Sales revenue | | $292,490.49† |
| | **CR** Unearned financing income—leases | | 111,336.41 |
| | **CR** Inventory | | 240,000.00 |

Notice that the amount of Gross investment in leased asset is $415,695.90 regardless of whether the residual value is unguaranteed or guaranteed. Similarly, the amount of manufacturing profit is $64,359.49 (that is, $292,490.49 − $228,131.00), the same net amount when the residual value is guaranteed (that is, $304,359.49 − $240,000.00 = $64,359.49).

* $240,000 − $11,869 = $228,131.00
† $304,359.49 − $11,869 = $292,490.49

The net effect of these entries is to recognize $64,359.49 of manufacturing profit ($304,359.49 − $240,000.00) immediately. The $111,336.41 of financing profit will be recognized over the life of the lease, as shown in Column (b) of the amortization schedule in Exhibit 12.8. The entries for recording this financing profit are absolutely identical to the entries for the direct financing method on page 705.

Let's extend the example by assuming that Lessor also promises to provide maintenance services on the leased asset for an additional annual fee of $2,000. So, Lessee Company's annual payments now total $81,139.18—that is, the $79,139.18 basic fee plus the $2,000 executory maintenance costs. But the amount recorded by Lessor as Gross investment in leased asset is still $415,695.90; that is:

| | |
|---|---|
| Annual total payments | $ 81,139.18 |
| Less: Executory cost | (2,000.00) |
| Payments net of executory cost | 79,139.18 |
| Number of years | × 5 |
| | $395,695.90 |
| Plus: Residual value | 20,000.00 |
| Gross investment in leased assets | $415,695.90 |

Notice that the executory costs are subtracted in computing the capitalized amount.

At December 31, 2008, when the first cash payment is received from Lessee Company, Lessor Company makes the following journal entries:

| | | | |
|---|---|---|---|
| **DR** | Cash | $81,139.18 | |
| | **CR** Gross investment in leased asset | | $79,139.18 |
| | **CR** Maintenance revenue | | 2,000.00 |
| **DR** | Unearned financing income—leases | $33,479.54 | |
| | **CR** Financing income—leases | | $33,479.54 |

The costs incurred over the year in fulfilling the maintenance contract (not shown) will be expensed and deducted from the Maintenance revenue of $2,000.

The capital lease versus operating lease dichotomy also exists for lessors. The criteria for classifying these leases include the same four criteria that apply to lessees plus two additional criteria. Lessors' incentives regarding how to classify leases are different from lessees' incentives because capital lease treatment accelerates the timing of income recognition for lessors. In addition, capital lease treatment improves many ratios for lessors in comparison to the level of these ratios under the operating lease approach.

# ADDITIONAL LEASING ASPECTS

## Sale and Leaseback

A sale and leaseback occurs when one company sells an asset to another company and immediately leases it back. This is done as a way to finance asset acquisition and/or for tax reasons. For example:

> First Company sells a manufacturing plant (excluding land) with a book value of $800,000 to Second Company for $1,000,000. First Company immediately leases the plant from Second Company for 20 years at an annual rental of $120,000.

First Company (the seller-lessee) can treat the entire annual rental of $120,000 as a deductible expense for tax purposes; if it had continued to own the asset, it could deduct depreciation only for the building itself but not for the land on which the building is located. Thus, total tax deductions could be higher under sale and leaseback arrangements. Also, the cash infusion of $1,000,000 could help meet cash flow needs.

No new *lease* accounting issues arise in sale and leaseback transactions. If the lease satisfies any of the four lessees' criteria on page 684, First Company must account for the lease as a capital lease; if none of the criteria is met, it must be treated as an operating lease. If the lease satisfies at least one of the lessor's Type I characteristics and both of the Type II characteristics (page 701), Second Company (the buyer-lessor) treats the lease as a direct financing lease; otherwise, it is an operating lease on Second Company's books.

The only complication in sale and leaseback arrangements is the treatment of the difference between the $1,000,000 sale price and the $800,000 carrying value of the manufacturing plant on First Company's books. Typically, when the assets are sold, this $200,000 will be recognized immediately on First Company's books as a gain on sale.

But this is not the way gains are treated in sale and leaseback transactions. Instead, First Company must record the $200,000 as a balance sheet credit, called a **deferred gain.** If the lease is a capital lease to First Company, this gain is then amortized into income using the same rate and life used to amortize the asset itself. If the lease is an operating lease to First Company, the gain is amortized in proportion to rental expense.

Assume that the lease qualifies as a capital lease; then First Company's entries are initially:

| | | | |
|---|---|---|---|
| **DR** | Cash (or receivable) | $1,000,000 | |
| | **CR** Property | | $ 800,000 |
| | **CR** Deferred gain | | 200,000 |
| **DR** | Leased asset—capital lease | $1,000,000 | |
| | **CR** Obligation under capital lease | | $1,000,000 |

[This assumes that the discounted present value of the minimum lease payments equals $1,000,000.]

The rationale for deferring the gain is simple. Notice that at the time of "sale," the $1,000,000 sales price and the $120,000 annual lease payment schedule are simultaneously set, and the transaction will continue for 20 years. It may be that the property is "worth" only $800,000 and that Second Company is effectively loaning $200,000 to First Company, which will be recovered over time through the $120,000 annual payments on the lease. Recognizing a gain in such circumstances allows First Company to initially overstate its income by $200,000; this will be offset in later years by overstating its expenses by an identical amount. Thus, the U.S. GAAP requirement of deferring the gain protects against income manipulation possibilities such as creating artificial "gains on sale" by overstating the asset's "sale" price. However, the conservatism inherent to GAAP requires that losses in sale and leaseback transactions be recognized immediately on the seller's books.

Notice that if the sale and leaseback terms do not trigger any of the four lessees' criteria (p. 684), the transaction is an operating lease to First Company (the lessee). So, carefully structured transactions allow firms to:

1. Remove *existing* assets from their books using sale and leaseback accounting.
2. Keep the asset and associated liability from reappearing by treating the lease as an operating lease.

Sale and leaseback accounting cannot be used when the seller-lessee (First Company in our example) retains some of the risks and rewards of ownership, such as the right to participate in any future appreciation in the value of the leased property. Such **continuing involvement** with ownershiplike characteristics is inconsistent with a "sale." That's why the existence of any such features disqualifies a transaction from sale and leaseback treatment.[12]

## Other Special Lease Accounting Rules

*SFAS No. 13* also covers a number of highly specialized leasing situations and outlines in detail the rules for handling these situations. A real estate lease is an example of a situation requiring specialized rules in *SFAS No. 13*.[13] A leveraged lease represents another example. In a **leveraged lease,** the lessor obtains nonrecourse financing for the leased asset from a third party, such as a bank. The lease is "leveraged" because the lessor borrows to finance the transaction. A leveraged lease does not affect the lessee's accounting. For these leases, lessees use the standard lease classification procedures outlined earlier. However, the lessor must account for leveraged leases using the direct financing approach, and special details—outlined at length in *SFAS No. 13*—apply.

## Financial Reporting versus Tax Accounting for Leases

The U.S. income tax rules also distinguish between operating leases and capital leases. However, the tax criteria for differentiating between them are not the same as the *SFAS No. 13* criteria. Further, the lessor's and the lessee's incentives are reversed for tax purposes. *Lessees* prefer the capital lease approach because it accelerates recognition of expenses and thereby lowers

---

[12] "Accounting for Leases," *SFAS No. 98* (Norwalk, CT: FASB, 1988), paras. 7–13.
[13] Op. cit., para. 24–27.

the discounted present value of their tax liability. *Lessors* prefer the operating lease approach on the tax return because it delays recognition of revenue and lowers the present value of the tax liability. So, book-versus-tax differences are frequent for both lessors and lessees.

The divergence between book accounting and tax accounting for lessees widened in recent years with the creation of **synthetic leases.** Synthetic leases result from complicated arrangements that include a lender, outside investors, a SPE, and the lessee. We'll skip the gory details of the legal arrangement and give you the punchline. A synthetic lease was structured to achieve the best of both worlds from the lessee's perspective: operating lease treatment on the books and capital lease treatment on the tax return. The lease contract carefully avoided triggering any of the four *SFAS No. 13* criteria, so it was an operating lease for financial reporting purposes. But for tax purposes, the lessee is considered the asset's owner because the contractual arrangement gives the lessee the proceeds of any appreciation in the asset's value at the end of the lease term.

The SPE played a crucial role in keeping the asset and liability off the lessee's books. However, after the Enron scandal, the FASB tightened the rules for consolidating SPEs.[14] Under these new rules, when the lessee is the potential beneficiary of the appreciation rights, the SPE must be consolidated. This effectively puts the lease asset and liability on the lessee's books, thereby negating the off-balance sheet treatment of synthetic leases. While these FASB rules have limited the off-balance sheet treatment of synthetic leases, they have not eliminated it completely.[15]

## Lessors' Disclosures

Exhibit 12.10 is taken from the notes to the December 31, 2005 financial statements of Boeing Corporation, the aircraft manufacturer. The exhibit illustrates *SFAS No. 13* disclosure requirements for lessors. Capital and operating leases must be disclosed separately, and lessors must provide a minimum lease payment schedule—just as lessees must do. Furthermore, the components of the net investment in capital leases (minimum lease payments, estimated residual values, etc.) are delineated, as are the cost and accumulated depreciation of assets under operating leases. The proportion of operating leases to capital leases for lessors is frequently less than 1—a stark contrast with lessees. The ratio for Boeing in Exhibit 12.10 is $3,144 ÷ $4,778 (see highlighted numbers), which equals 0.66. If we contrast this value with those in Exhibit 12.4 we see that—unlike the ratio values for lessees—it is below 1.00. This is consistent with the fact that lessors like capital lease treatment because it accelerates income recognition and improves certain financial statement ratios in comparison to the operating lease approach.

---

[14] See *FASB Interpretation No. 46* cited earlier.

[15] One example of a synthetic lease that remains off-balance sheet even after the issuance of *FASB Interpretation No. 46* (*FIN No. 46*) is disclosed in Citrix Systems Inc.'s 2005 annual report:

> FIN No. 46 (revised) was effective immediately for certain disclosure requirements and variable interest entities referred to as special-purpose entities for periods ending after December 15, 2003 and for other types of entities for financial statements for periods ending after March 15, 2004. We determined that we are not required to consolidate the lessor, the leased facility or the related debt associated with our synthetic lease in accordance with FIN No. 46 (revised). Accordingly, there was no impact on our financial position, results of operations or cash flows from adoption. However, if the lessor were to change its ownership of the property or significantly change its ownership of other properties that it currently holds, we could be required to consolidate the entity, the leased facility and the debt in a future period.

Another off-balance sheet synthetic lease is disclosed in the 2005 annual report of O'Reilly Automotive, Inc. and Subsidiaries:

> The Synthetic Lease has been accounted for as an operating lease under the provisions of Financial Accounting Standards Board ("FASB") SFAS No. 13 and related interpretations, including FASB Interpretation No. 46.

These are representative disclosures. There are many others.

**EXHIBIT 12.10** Boeing Corporation

**Illustration of Lessor's Financial Statement Note Disclosures**
**December 31, 2005 (amounts in millions)**

Customer financing at December 31 consisted of the following:

|  | 2005 |  | 2004 |
|---|---|---|---|
| Investment in Sales-type/Finance Leases |  |  |  |
| Aircraft financing | $3,036 |  | $3,799 |
| Operating Leases |  |  |  |
| Operating lease equipment cost: |  |  |  |
| Aircraft financing | $5,498 | $5,935 |  |
| Other equipment financing | 408 | 366 |  |
|  | $5,906 |  | $6,301 |
| Less: Accumulated depreciation: |  |  |  |
| Aircraft financing | (881) | (823) |  |
| Other equipment financing | (106) | (72) |  |
|  | (987) |  | (895) |
| Net investment | $4,919 |  | $5,406 |

Scheduled payments on customer financing are as follows:

| Year | Sales-Type/ Financing Lease Payments Receivable | Operating Lease Equipment Payments Receivable |
|---|---|---|
| 2006 | $ 367 | $ 500 |
| 2007 | 429 | 433 |
| 2008 | 317 | 373 |
| 2009 | 297 | 308 |
| 2010 | 284 | 263 |
| Beyond 2010 | 3,084 | 1,267 |
|  | $4,778 | $3,144 |

The components of investment in sales-type/financing leases at December 31 were as follows:

|  | 2005 | 2004 |
|---|---|---|
| Minimum lease payments receivable | $4,778 | $5,998 |
| Estimated residual value of leased assets | 690 | 833 |
| Unearned income | (2,432) | (3,032) |
| Total | $3,036 | $3,799 |

*Authors' note:* This financial statement note has been edited and a portion of the disclosure format has been modified slightly. The unedited footnote also includes notes receivable from customers.

# RECONSIDERATION OF GAAP FOR LEASES

The Sarbanes-Oxley Act of 2002 required the SEC to examine "whether current financial statements of issues transparently reflect the economics of off-balance sheet arrangements."[16] This was a Congressional reaction to the financial statement distortions that were widespread in the period around Enron's failure. As illustrated in this chapter, operating leases are a prevalent

[16] Staff of the U.S. Securities and Exchange Commission, "Report and Recommendations Pursuant to Section 401(c) of the Sarbanes-Oxley Act of 2002 on Arrangements with Off-Balance Sheet Implications, Special Purpose Entities, and Transparency of Filings by Issuers," June, 2005.

off-balance sheet vehicle, and the accounting for leases received considerable criticism in the SEC report. One section of the report stated:

> The "all-or-nothing" nature of the guidance means that economically similar arrangements may receive different accounting—if they are just to one side or the other of the bright line test. For example, most would agree that there is little economic difference between a lease that commits an issuer to payments equaling 89% of an asset's fair value vs. 90% of an asset's fair value. Nonetheless, because of the bright-line nature of the lease classification tests, this small difference in economics can completely change the accounting. Conversely, economically different transactions may be treated similarly. For example, most would agree that there is a significant economic difference between a one-month lease of a building and a 10-year lease of that building. However, if both leases qualified for operating lease treatment, they would likely both have little to no effect on the balance sheet. The extensive disclosures required for leases do provide some information about the rights and obligations inherent in operating leases.
>
> Problems with the all-or-nothing character of the accounting have been magnified because many issuers involved in leases, taking advantage of the bright-line nature of the lease classification guidance, structure their lease arrangements to achieve whatever accounting (sales-type/capital or operating) is desired.[17]

The SEC report also stated that "[l]ease accounting has been identified repeatedly as an area that should be reexamined by the FASB."[18]

Because of the repeated criticisms of lease accounting such as those in the SEC report, the FASB has added a project to its agenda to reconsider the existing accounting for leases. The Board stated that the review will be comprehensive and will be a joint project with the IASB. It will take several years for this project to be completed. But considering the specific criticisms of *SFAS No. 13*, most observers believe that the rules will be rewritten in a way that will force more leases to be reflected on lessees' balance sheets. Indeed, the constructive capitalization approach described in the appendix to this chapter may reflect revised and improved GAAP in the next decade.

## SUMMARY

- The treatment of leases in *SFAS No. 13* represents a compromise between the unperformed-contracts and property-rights approaches.

- *SFAS No. 13* adopted a middle-of-the-road position that neither capitalized all leases nor prohibited capitalization.

- The FASB developed criteria for determining the precise intermediate circumstances under which leases are capitalized.

- Several of the lease capitalization criteria that the FASB decided on are arbitrary; examples are the 75% economic life rule and the 90% recovery of investment rule. Because lease capitalization adversely affects lessees' financial statements, many lessees circumvent the *SFAS No. 13* rules and thus avoid lease capitalization.

- The proportion of operating lease commitments to capital lease commitments can vary greatly even between firms in the same industry. This complicates financial analysis because keeping leases off the balance sheet improves various ratios (e.g., return on assets, debt-to-equity, and the current ratio). Consequently, analysts must constructively capitalize operating leases to make valid comparisons between firms with different proportions of capitalized leases.

---

[17] Ibid., pp. 62–63.
[18] Ibid., p. 105.

- Lessors' use of the capital lease approach accelerates income recognition in contrast to the timing of income recognition under the operating lease approach. Lessors' financial statement ratios are also improved. It is perhaps not surprising, therefore, that capital leases appear frequently on lessors' financial statements.

- The FASB has been compelled to issue 10 statements on leases subsequent to *SFAS No. 13* and numerous interpretations of the original statement in an effort to close loopholes for keeping leases off the balance sheet as soon as those loopholes are perceived. But this process demonstrates the inherent weakness of a compromise approach that must rely on essentially arbitrary criteria for implementation.

- The FASB and IASB are working on a joint project to improve lease accounting. The revised accounting will probably require many more leases to be treated as capital leases.

## APPENDIX

**Analysis**

# MAKING BALANCE SHEET DATA COMPARABLE BY ADJUSTING FOR OFF-BALANCE SHEET LEASES

To make their debt burden appear lower, some lessees carefully design their lease contracts to evade capital lease criteria, thereby keeping most of their leases off the balance sheet. Other companies structure their leases and apply the lease accounting rules less aggressively and have a higher proportion of capital leases. This complicates comparisons between companies because each may have similar lease contract terms but very dissimilar lease balance sheet numbers. Despite this complication, comparisons can still be made.

The most straightforward method for making lessees' balance sheet data comparable is to treat *all* leases as if they were capital leases. That is, analysts should use the disclosed minimum *operating* lease payment schedule as a basis for approximating what the balance sheet numbers would have been had those operating leases been treated instead as capital leases. This is **constructive capitalization.** We use the Safeway, Inc. 2005 data from Exhibit 12.5 to illustrate how this is done. For convenience, these numbers for Safeway are reproduced in the following table.

The liability that would appear on the balance sheet if these operating leases were instead treated as capital leases is the *discounted present value* of the stream of minimum operating lease payments. This payment stream (undiscounted) totals $4,570 million. Two items must be estimated to compute this present value. First, an appropriate discount rate must be determined. Second, each year's payments beyond 2010 must be estimated because lease payments for all years after 2010 are aggregated under the caption "Thereafter."

### Safeway Inc. and Subsidiaries

**Operating Lease Payments from Lease Footnote, 2005 Annual Report**

| ($ in millions)<br>Fiscal Year | Minimum Operating<br>Lease Payments |
|---|---|
| 2006 | $ 426.1 |
| 2007 | 410.6 |
| 2008 | 397.3 |
| 2009 | 359.9 |
| 2010 | 330.2 |
| Thereafter | 2,645.9 |
| Total minimum lease payments | $4,570.0 |

**Determining the Discount Rate**  Two alternatives for determining the discount rate for computing the present value of operating lease payments exist:

- The weighted average discount rate implicit in capital leases.
- The weighted average discount rate on long-term debt (including capital lease commitments).

In some cases, a company discloses the weighted average discount rate used for capital leases in its lease footnote. If this rate is not disclosed, it can be estimated provided the current portion of capital leases (that is, that portion that represents a current liability) is disclosed. This information is often provided either on the balance sheet or in the lease footnote.

Here's how the calculation is made. Recall from the discussion in the chapter that each periodic lease payment comprises two elements: (1) interest based on the present value of the lease obligation at the beginning of the period and (2) the principal payment on the unpaid lease obligation. The current portion of the capital lease obligation represents the second component—that is, the amount of next year's lease payment that reduces the principal balance of the lease obligation. Therefore, subtracting this principal reduction amount from the total scheduled lease payment for the coming year leaves the interest expense component. Dividing the interest expense *component* by the present value of the capital lease obligation shown in the footnote on the current balance sheet date (which is also the present value of the lease obligation at the beginning of the next fiscal year) yields the average implicit interest rate for capital leases. To summarize:

> For example, Target Corporation disclosed in its fiscal year 2002 lease footnote that the present value of minimum lease payments was "calculated using the interest rate at inception for each lease (the weighted average interest rate was 8.7 percent)."
>
> *Source:* Target Corporation February 1, 2003 annual report.

$$\frac{\text{Interest expense on}}{\text{capital leases}} = \frac{\text{Implicit interest rate}}{\text{in capital lease contracts}} \times \frac{\text{Present value of lease obligation}}{\text{at beginning of year}}$$

Rearranging we get:

$$\frac{\text{Interest expense on capital leases}}{\text{Present value of lease obligation}} = \frac{\text{Implicit interest rate in}}{\text{capital lease contracts}}$$
$$\text{at beginning of year}$$

> The schedule of lease payments found in the lease footnote always provides the amount of next year's lease payment. The current portion may be found in the lease footnote, the debt footnote, or the balance sheet.

Safeway's lease footnote in Exhibit 12.5 reveals that the current portion of capital leases is $39.1 million. Subtracting this from the $105.7 million scheduled capital lease payment in 2006 leaves $66.6 million as the interest expense component of the 2006 lease payment. Dividing this number by the $683.2 million present value of total capital lease commitments as of December 31, 2005 yields an average implicit interest rate of 9.75%. This rate can then be used to compute the present value of the scheduled operating lease payments (see page 714).

A second estimate of the discount rate can be derived from the lessee's financial statement footnote for long-term debt. This footnote discloses the interest rate on each debt issue. The weighted average rate on long-term debt provides an alternative rate for discounting the operating lease payments. Another, and somewhat easier, way to approximate the weighted average interest rate on long-term debt is to compute the ratio of total interest expense (often shown on the income statement or in statement footnotes) by the average of beginning and end-of-year long-term debt outstanding (including the long-term portion of capital leases). Doing this using data from Safeway's 2005 debt footnote yields an estimated rate of 6.9%.

> Safeway discloses interest expense in its 2005 annual report of $.403 billion. Long-term debt (including capitalized lease obligations) at the beginning of 2005 was $6.124 billion and at the end of 2005 was $5.605 billion. So, a simple estimate of average debt outstanding is $5.864 billion. The estimate of the long-term debt rate is:
>
> $$\frac{\$.403 \text{ billion}}{\$5.864 \text{ billion}} \cong 6.9\%$$

Because the first discount estimation approach is more accurate, we round the 9.75% figure to 10% and use this rate for capitalizing the operating leases of Safeway as follows.

**Estimating Payments beyond Five Years**   Procedures for estimating annual operating lease payments for periods after 2010 can also be developed. One approach is as follows. Notice from page 714 that the annual *decline* in minimum operating lease payments between 2008 and 2009 is $37.4 million (that is, $397.3 − $359.9); between 2009 and 2010, the decline is $29.7 million (that is, $359.9 − $330.2). So, the average annual decline over the three-year period is $33.6 million (that is [$37.4 + $29.7]/2). This suggests that the undisclosed minimum operating lease payment for 2011 is probably in the vicinity of $296.6 million—the $330.2 million 2010 payment minus approximately $33.6 million of estimated yearly decline. The simplest approach for estimating a schedule of annual payments for 2011 and beyond is to assume that all subsequent payments are also somewhere near $296.6 million per year. Dividing the total later years' minimum operating lease payments ($2,645.9 million, the highlighted amount) by $296.6 million yields an *initial* estimate of how many years beyond 2010 the existing operating leases run. The computation is:

> Because the payments after 2010 are assumed to be spread evenly over a 9-year period, we adjust our estimated yearly lease payment to be $2,645.9/9 years = $294 million per year in Exhibit 12.11.

$$\frac{\text{Minimum operating lease payments for years after 2010}}{\text{Estimated yearly lease payment (assumed to be the same for all years)}} = \frac{\$2,645.9 \text{ million}}{\$296.6 \text{ million per year}} = 8.92 \text{ years}$$

The initial estimate is 8.92 years, which we round to 9 years. Based on this estimate, the net minimum lease payments will be discounted over a 14-year period—that is, 2006 through 2010 (5 years) plus the estimated 9 years we just computed.

Our estimate of the amount of additional liability on Safeway's balance sheet at December 31, 2005 if all operating leases were capitalized is the highlighted amount of $2,527.3 million shown in Exhibit 12.11. A small portion ($173.4 million) would be a current liability and $2,527.3 million − $173.4 million, or $2,353.9 million, would be a long-term liability.

> The $173.4 million current liability is determined as follows. Interest expense in 2006 on these capitalized operating leases would be $2,527.3 × 10%, or approximately $252.7 million. The 2006 minimum operating lease payment is $426.1 million in Exhibit 12.11. Because interest is a liability that accrues over time, only the difference between the total 2006 payment of $426.1 million and the as yet unaccrued interest of $252.7 million (that is, $173.4 million) is a current liability as of January 1, 2006.

| EXHIBIT 12.11 | Safeway Inc. and Subsidiaries |
| --- | --- |

**Estimate of Capitalized Operating Lease Liability as of December 31, 2005**

| ($ in millions)<br>Fiscal Year | Minimum Operating<br>Lease Payment | Present<br>Value Factor*<br>at 10% | Discounted<br>Present<br>Value |
| --- | --- | --- | --- |
| 2006 | $426.1 | .90909 | $ 387.4 |
| 2007 | 410.6 | .82645 | 339.3 |
| 2008 | 397.3 | .75132 | 298.5 |
| 2009 | 359.9 | .68301 | 245.8 |
| 2010 | 330.2 | .62092 | 205.0 |
| 2011⎱<br>2019⎰ | 294.0 | 3.5759† | 1,051.3 |
| Total | | | $2,527.3 |

* Present value factors for interest rates not included in Appendix I can be found at the text Web site: www.mhhe.com/revsine4e.

† Present value of an ordinary annuity for 14 years at 10% minus present value of an ordinary annuity for five years at 10%, or 7.36669 minus 3.79079.

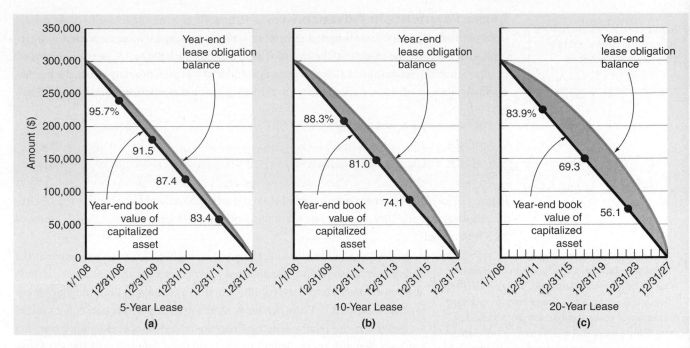

**Figure 12.6** LESSEE COMPANY

General Relationship between Capital Lease Asset and Liability When Payments Are at *End* of Period (a) 5-Year Lease, (b) 10-Year Lease, and (c) 20-Year Lease

---

When the capitalized operating lease liability has been estimated, the next task is to estimate the capitalized operating lease *asset* amount. One approach is to assume that the asset amount equals the amount of the computed operating lease liability. Because the asset and liability amounts are equal at the inception of a capital lease, this approach assumes that this initial equality is maintained over the lease's entire life. But a more precise estimate can easily be made (see Figure 12.6).

Figure 12.6(a) graphically represents data from the Lessee Company illustration in Exhibit 12.1 where lease payments are due at the end of each period. The year-end book value of the capitalized asset (the black line in the graph) starts at $300,000 and declines yearly by $60,000—the straight-line amortization amount from Column (e) in Exhibit 12.1—until it reaches zero at the end of 2012. The blue line depicts the year-end lease obligation balance from Column (d) in Exhibit 12.1. While the two balances are obviously equal at the beginning and end of the lease, for all intermediate periods, the asset amount is lower than the liability. This relationship holds in general because early year payments do not reduce the liability by as much as later year payments do (compare Columns [c] and [e] of Exhibit 12.1). Notice that Figure 12.6(a) includes the percentage relationship between the capitalized asset and liability balances for all intermediate lease years. For example, at December 31, 2008, the asset balance is 95.7% of the obligation balance for the five-year lease.

Parts (b) and (c) in the figure show the relationship between the lease asset and lease liability balances for the same basic facts as in (a), but in (b) and (c), the lease period is for 10 years and 20 years, respectively. The *difference* between the asset and liability balances *increases* the longer the life of the lease. The reason is that the lease liability balance decreases at a lower rate when lease payments are spread over longer periods—that is, a larger portion of each early lease payment is for interest and a correspondingly smaller portion goes toward reducing the lease obligation the longer the term of the lease.

> Lessee Company's interest expense for 2009 would be 10% times $228,055, or $22,805.50.

**Lease Payments in Advance** Leases frequently require the lessee to make an up-front payment when the lease is signed. Advance payments in a capital lease mean that at the inception of the lease the amount of the recorded asset exceeds the liability. Using the Exhibit 12.3 example (p. 692), we assume a 10% discount rate and that Lessee Company makes its five annual payments in advance. Each payment is $71,945. The journal entry on January 1, 2008 is:

| | | | |
|---|---|---|---|
| **DR** | Capital lease asset | $300,000 | |
| | **CR** Cash | | $ 71,945 |
| | **CR** Obligation under capital lease | | 228,055 |

Figure 12.7 depicts the general relationship between the lease asset and lease liability for a 5-, 10- and 20-year lease at a 10% discount rate when the contract calls for payments at the beginning of each lease period.

> The relationship also will depend on the discount rate. With higher discount rates, the lease liability balance will decrease at a slower rate. Accordingly, the curvature of the lease liability book value line depicted in Figure 12.7 will be more pronounced.

In contrast to the situation depicted in Figure 12.6 with payments at the end of each lease period, the up-front payment means that the asset carrying amount initially *exceeds* the liability amount, as shown in both the journal entry and Figure 12.7. With payments in advance in periods subsequent to the lease signing, the relationship between the leased asset and liability carrying amounts depends on the length of the lease term. With 5- and 10-year leases and a 10% discount rate, the carrying value of the lease liability is always less than the asset book value throughout the lease term. However, as shown for a 20-year lease, the liability

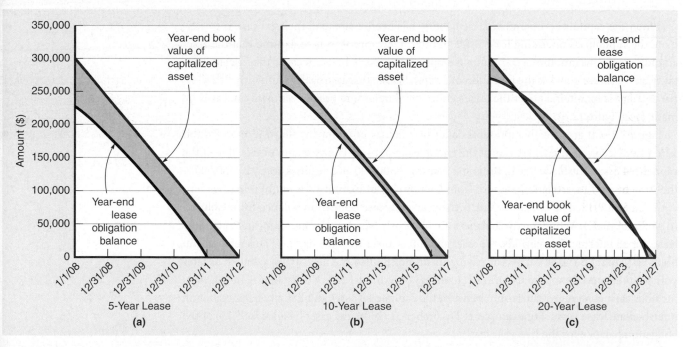

**Figure 12.7** LESSEE COMPANY

General Relationship between Capital Lease Asset and Liability When *Up-Front* Payments Are Made for a (a) 5-Year Lease, (b) 10-Year Lease, and (c) 20-Year Lease.

With a $300,000 present value at 10%, the annual payments for a 5-year, 10-year, and 20-year lease are $71,945.00, $44,385.11, and $32,034.44, respectively. The vertical distance between the lease asset and obligation lines on 1/1/08 represent these initial payments.

amount quickly exceeds the asset amount, and this relationship is maintained until the last two years of the lease. This excess is the blue shaded area in Figure 12.7(c). The liability quickly "overtakes" the asset because early year payments on an amortization schedule do not reduce the liability by as much as later year payments do. For a given lease length, the higher the interest rate, the quicker the liability exceeds the asset.

Most companies have a portfolio of operating leases with different ages, interest rates, and payment timing. Therefore, on average across the entire portfolio, the asset-to-liability ratio for many companies will be somewhere in the blue shaded area of Figure 12.7(c). Additionally, many leases are based on monthly rather than annual payments. Consequently, *the capital lease liability will often exceed the asset as illustrated in both Figure 12.6 and 12.7(c).* However, exceptions exist. When most of a firm's leases have up-front payments, the interest rate is low, and/or the life of the average lease is relatively short, the asset amount *can* exceed the liability amount.

The percentage relationship between the asset and the liability is a function of payment timing, the interest rate, and the length of the lease.[19] Furthermore, the precise relationship *at any specific date* depends on the average age of existing leases. Rather than attempting to estimate the percentage relationship between the asset and liability for capitalized operating leases, we can use the disclosure the company makes for capital leases. For example, at December 31, 2005 Safeway disclosed that its net capital lease assets totaled $522.4 million and its net capital lease obligations were $683.2 million. This results in a 76.5% asset-to-liability ratio for capital leases. It may be reasonable to use this same percentage to estimate the operating lease asset to be capitalized. Our estimate of the balance sheet asset that would arise from capitalized operating leases is therefore the computed liability from Exhibit 12.11—$2,527.3 million—times 76.5%, or $1,932.5 million.

> *SFAS No. 13* (para. 16) requires that lessees disclose the net capital lease asset and liability.

> Of course, this is only a rough approximation. The higher the proportion of leases with up-front payments, the shorter the lease life, and/or the lower the interest rate, the higher the asset-to-liability ratio. So, if operating leases differ along these dimensions from capital leases, using the disclosed capital leases asset-to-liability ratio tends to misstate the asset carrying value after capitalizing operating leases.

Exhibit 12.12 illustrates the estimated ratio effects for 2005 that result from capitalizing operating leases for Safeway. Exhibit 12.12(a) Column (a) shows financial statement numbers as reported in Safeway's December 31, 2005 statements. Column (b) shows the adjustments for operating lease capitalization. Notice, in addition to the capital lease asset and liability adjustments, there is a "net debit to balance" of $594.8 million—simply the difference between the $1,932.5 million estimated asset amount minus the $2,527.3 million liability amount. The $594.8 million debit comprises two items: (1) a debit to a deferred tax asset and (2) a debit to owners' equity.

A deferred tax asset arises because capitalization accelerates expense recognition. Accordingly, constructively capitalizing these leases means that expenses are recognized earlier on the books than on the tax return and a deferred tax asset consequently results. The amount of the deferred tax asset is determined by the cumulative capital versus operating lease expense difference. Unfortunately, this cumulative difference cannot be estimated easily or accurately. As a result, we cannot subdivide the $594.8 between the deferred tax asset and the owners' equity debit.

As discussed in the chapter, the income statement effects of capital lease treatment versus operating lease treatment often do not significantly differ for mature firms. Consequently, we do not adjust income in Exhibit 12.12(a).

> This paragraph assumes that you are comfortable with deferred tax concepts. If you are not, you can safely skip this paragraph and return to Exhibit 12.12 after reading Chapter 13.

---

[19] See Imhoff, Lipe, and Wright, op. cit., pp. 51–63. A table (based on end-of-year payments) in this article computes the asset-to-liability ratio for leases of various duration and interest rates. Based on this analysis, the authors suggest that a good rule of thumb for the asset-to-liability ratio is 70%.

| EXHIBIT 12.12 | Safeway Inc. and Subsidiaries |
|---|---|

**Effect on Selected Ratios of Capitalizing Operating Leases**
**December 31, 2005**

### Panel (a): Financial Statement Data

| ($ in millions)<br>Statement Item | (a)<br>December 31, 2005<br>Financial<br>Statements | (b)<br>Adjustments for<br>Constructive<br>Capitalization | | (c)<br>Total after<br>Constructive<br>Capitalization |
|---|---|---|---|---|
| Total assets | $15,756.9 | Capital lease asset | + $1,932.5 | $17,689.4 |
| Current portion lease obligation | 39.1 | Current portion lease obligation | + 173.4 | 212.5 |
| Total long-term obligations | 5,605.3 | Long-term lease obligation | + 2,353.9 | 7,959.2 |
| Owners' equity | 4,919.7 | Net debit to balance | − 594.8 | 4,324.9 |
| NOPAT* | 822.8 | | −0− | $ 822.8 |

### Panel (b): Adjusted Ratios after Capitalization

| Ratio | As Reported in<br>12/31/05 Financial Statements | Ratio after<br>Constructive Capitalization<br>of Operating Leases |
|---|---|---|
| Total long-term obligations to equity ratio | 1.14 | 1.84[†] |
| ROA | 5.22% | 4.65%[‡] |

---

* NOPAT refers to the company's net operating profit after taxes. To compute NOPAT, you (1) eliminate nonoperating or nonrecurring items from reported income and (2) add back after-tax interest expense. (See Panel [b].)

[†] Computed by adding $2,353.9 to Column (e) obligations and subtracting $594.8 from Column (a) equity. This ignores the unknown deferred tax effect and distorts the adjusted ratio slightly. If Safeway had an accrual on its balance sheet for "rent holidays" (see p. 696), the lease obligation would be decreased and owners' equity would be increased for the accrual amount.

[‡] Computed by adding $1,932.5 to Column (a) total assets. This ignores the unknown deferred tax effect and distorts the adjusted ratio slightly. The ending balance of adjusted total assets was used to compute ROA as follows. The tax rate was assumed to be 35%.

$$ROA = \frac{NOPAT}{Total\ assets} = \frac{Net\ income\ +\ Charges\ and\ gains\ \times\ (1\ -\ Tax\ rate)\ +\ Interest\ \times\ (1\ -\ Tax\ rate)}{Total\ assets}$$

---

Exhibit 12.4 shows that two of the other firms in the supermarkets industry have a higher ratio of operating to capital lease payments than Safeway. This difference underscores the importance of making adjustments to Safeway's competitors before undertaking financial comparisons.

The adjusted ratios after capitalization are shown in Exhibit 12.12(b). Notice that the adjustments from capitalizing operating leases alter Safeway's ratios. Return on assets (ROA) is lowered from 5.22% to 4.65%, a decrease of approximately 10.9%. The total long-term obligations to equity ratio increases from 1.14 to 1.84, an increase of approximately 62%. It is important to make such adjustments if you're making financial comparisons *across* firms. While the effect on Safeway is not trivial, some of its competitors could be even more aggressive in keeping leases off the balance sheet. So, interfirm comparisons may be misleading unless adjustments are also made to the competitors' statements. The underlying real economic differences are revealed only by comparing the adjusted statements for all firms. The easiest way to overcome these capitalization differences between firms is to treat all leases that convey significant property rights as though they were capital leases.

A movement to do this in the financial statements themselves is emerging as discussed in the chapter.

Fox Company, a dealer in machinery and equipment, leased equipment to Tiger, Inc. on July 1, 2008. The lease is appropriately accounted for as a sale by Fox and as a purchase by Tiger. The lease is for a 10-year period (the asset's useful life), expiring June 30, 2018. The first of 10 equal payments of $500,000 was made on July 1, 2008. Fox had purchased the equipment for $2,675,000 on January 1, 2008 and established a list selling price of $3,375,000 on the equipment. Assume that at July 1, 2008 the present value of the rent payments over the lease term discounted at 12% (the appropriate interest rate) was $3,165,000.

**E12-1**

Accounting for lessee and lessor

AICPA
ADAPTED

**Required:**

1. What is the amount of profit on the sale and the amount of interest income that Fox should record for the year ended December 31, 2008? How much interest income should Fox record in 2009?

2. Assume that Tiger uses straight-line depreciation and a 12% discount rate. What is the amount of depreciation and interest expense that Tiger should record for the year ended December 31, 2008 and for the year ended December 31, 2009?

On January 2, 2008, Lafayette Machine Shops, Inc. signed a 10-year noncancelable lease for a heavy-duty drill press, stipulating annual payments of $15,000 starting at the end of the first year, with title passing to Lafayette at the expiration of the lease. Lafayette treated this transaction as a capital lease. The drill press has an estimated useful life of 15 years with no salvage value. Lafayette uses straight-line depreciation for all of its fixed assets. Aggregate lease payments were determined to have a present value of $92,170 based on an implicit interest rate of 10%.

**E12-2**

Accounting for lessee

AICPA
ADAPTED

**Required:**

What amount should Lafayette record for interest expense and depreciation expense for 2008?

East Company leased a new machine from North Company on May 1, 2008 under a lease with the following information:

**E12-3**

Accounting for lessee: Purchase option

AICPA
ADAPTED

| | |
|---|---|
| Lease term | 10 years |
| Annual rental payable at beginning of each lease year | $40,000 |
| Useful life of machine | 12 years |
| Implicit interest rate | 14% |
| Present value of an annuity of $1 paid at the beginning of each of 10 periods at 14% | 5.95 |
| Present value of $1 due at the end of 10 periods at 14% | 0.27 |

East has the option to purchase the machine on May 1, 2018 by paying $50,000, which approximates the expected fair value of the machine on the option exercise date.

**Required:**

What is the amount of the capitalized leased asset on May 1, 2008?

On December 31, 2008, Ball Company leased a machine from Cook for a 10-year period, expiring December 30, 2018. Annual payments of $100,000 are due on December 31. The first payment was made on December 31, 2008, and the second payment was made on December 31, 2009. The present value at the inception of the lease for the 10 lease payments discounted at 10% was $676,000. The lease is appropriately accounted for as a capital lease by Ball.

**E12-4**

Accounting and reporting for lessee

AICPA
ADAPTED

**Required:**

1. Compute the December 31, 2009 amount that Ball should report as a lease liability.

2. What portion of this total liability should be classified as a current liability?

| | |
|---|---|
| **E12-5**<br><br>Accounting for lessor<br><br>**AICPA**<br>ADAPTED | Grady Company purchased a machine on January 1, 2008 for $720,000. The machine is expected to have a 10-year life, no residual value, and will be depreciated by the straight-line method. On January 1, 2008, it leased the machine to Lesch Company for a three-year period at an annual rental of $125,000. Grady could have sold the machine for $860,000 instead of leasing it. Grady incurred maintenance and other executory costs of $15,000 in 2008 under the terms of the lease.<br><br>**Required:**<br>What amount should Grady report as operating profit on this leased asset for the year ended December 31, 2008. |
| **E12-6**<br><br>Recording lessor's sales-type lease<br><br>**AICPA**<br>ADAPTED | Benedict Company leased equipment to Mark Inc. on January 1, 2008. The lease is for an eight-year period, expiring December 31, 2015. The first of eight equal annual payments of $600,000 was made on January 1, 2008. Benedict had purchased the equipment on December 29, 2007 for $3,200,000. The lease is appropriately accounted for as a sales-type lease by Benedict. Assume that at January 1, 2008, the present value of all rental payments over the lease term discounted at a 10% interest rate was $3,520,000.<br><br>**Required:**<br>What amount of interest income should Benedict record in 2009 (the second year of the lease period) as a result of the lease? |
| **E12-7**<br><br>Accounting for lessor's direct financing leases<br><br>**AICPA**<br>ADAPTED | Glade Company leases computer equipment to customers under direct financing leases. The equipment has no residual value at the end of the lease term, and the leases do not contain bargain purchase options. Glade wishes to earn 8% interest on a five-year lease of equipment with a fair value of $323,400. The present value of an annuity of $1 paid at the start of each period for five years at 8% is 4.312.<br><br>**Required:**<br>Compute the total amount of interest revenue that Glade will earn over the life of the lease. |
| **E12-8**<br><br>Accounting for lessor's sales-type lease<br><br>**AICPA**<br>ADAPTED | Peg Company leased equipment from Howe Corporation on July 1, 2008 for an eight-year period expiring June 30, 2016. Equal payments under the lease are $600,000 and are due on July 1 of each year. The first payment was made on July 1, 2008. Peg and Howe contemplate the rate of interest at 10%. The equipment's cash selling price is $3,520,000, and the cost of the equipment on Howe's accounting records is $2,800,000. The lease is appropriately recorded as a sales-type lease.<br><br>**Required:**<br>Determine the amount of profit on the sale and interest revenue that Howe should record for the year ended December 31, 2008. |

| | |
|---|---|
| **E12-9**<br><br>Accounting for lessee: Discount rate<br><br>**AICPA**<br>ADAPTED | On December 31, 2008, Day Company leased a new machine from Parr with the following pertinent information: |

| | |
|---|---|
| Lease term | 6 years |
| Annual rental payable at beginning of each year | $50,000 |
| Useful life of machine | 8 years |
| Day's incremental borrowing rate | 15% |
| Implicit interest rate in lease (known by Day) | 12% |
| Present value of annuity of $1 paid at the start of each of six periods at | |
| 12% | 4.61 |
| 15% | 4.35 |

The lease is not renewable, and the machine reverts to Parr at the termination of the lease. The cost of the machine on Parr's accounting records is $375,500.

**Required:**
Compute the amount of Day's lease liability at the beginning of the lease term.

Robbins, Inc. leased a machine from Ready Leasing Company. The lease qualifies as a capital lease and requires 10 annual payments of $10,000 beginning immediately. The lease specifies an interest rate of 12% (the lessor's return) and a purchase option of $10,000 at the end of the 10th year even though the machine's estimated value on that date is $20,000. Robbins' incremental borrowing rate is 14%. The present value of an annuity paid at the start of each period is:

> 12% for 10 years is 6.328
> 14% for 10 years is 5.946

The present value of $1 is:

> 12% for 10 years is 0.322
> 14% for 10 years is 0.270

**Required:**
Compute the amount that Robbins should record as the lease liability at the beginning of the lease term.

**E12-10**
Accounting for lessee's purchase option

**AICPA**
ADAPTED

---

On January 1, 2008, Babson, Inc. leased two automobiles for executive use. The lease requires Babson to make five annual payments of $13,000, beginning January 1, 2008. At the end of the lease term on December 31, 2012, Babson guarantees that the residual value of the automobiles will total $10,000. The lease qualifies as a capital lease. The interest rate implicit in the lease is 9%. Present value factors for the 9% rate implicit in the lease follow:

| | |
|---|---|
| For a five-period annuity paid at the start of each period | 4.240 |
| For a five-period annuity paid at the end of each period | 3.890 |
| Present value of $1 due in five periods | 0.650 |

**Required:**
Compute Babson's recorded capital lease liability immediately after the first required payment.

**E12-11**
Accounting for lessee

**AICPA**
ADAPTED

---

On December 31, 2008, Roe Company leased a machine from Colt for a five-year period. Equal annual payments under the lease are $105,000 (including $5,000 annual executory costs) and are due on December 31 of each year. The first payment was made on December 31, 2008, and the second payment was made on December 31, 2009. The five lease payments are discounted at 10% over the lease term. The present value of minimum lease payments at the inception of the lease and before the first annual payment was $417,000. Roe appropriately accounts for the lease as a capital lease.

**Required:**
What is the lease liability that Roe should report in its December 31, 2009 balance sheet?

**E12-12**
Accounting for executory costs

**AICPA**
ADAPTED

---

On December 31, 2008, Lane, Inc. sold equipment to Noll and simultaneously leased it back for 12 years. Pertinent information at this date is as follows:

| | |
|---|---|
| Sales price | $480,000 |
| Carrying amount | $360,000 |
| Estimated remaining economic life | 15 years |

**Required:**
1. At December 31, 2008, should Lane report a gain from the sale of the equipment?
2. If not, how should it account for the sale and leaseback?

**E12-13**
Accounting for sale and leaseback

**AICPA**
ADAPTED

---

Coates Corporation is planning to enter into a three-year lease with annual payments of $30,000 due at the beginning of each year. If the lease qualified as a capital lease, the breakdown of the payments would be as follows:

| | |
|---|---|
| Present value of an annuity due factor for 3 years at 8% | 2.78326 |
| Annual lease payment | × $30,000 |
| Present value of lease payments | $83,498 |

**E12-14**
Determining cash flow statement effects of capital versus operating leases

Amortization Table

| Date | Total Payment | Interest Expense | Principal Payment | Lease Obligation Balance |
|------|--------------|------------------|-------------------|--------------------------|
| Inception | | | | $83,498 |
| Year 1 | $30,000 | $ –0– | $30,000 | 53,498 |
| Year 2 | 30,000 | 4,280 | 25,720 | 27,778 |
| Year 3 | 30,000 | 2,222 | 27,778 | –0– |

**Required:**

1. If the lease were an operating lease, what would be the year-by-year effects on operating and financing cash flows?

2. If the lease were a capital lease, what would be the year-by-year effects on operating and financing cash flows?

---

**E12-15**

Determining ratio effects of capital versus operating leases

Sandra Company and Nova Inc. each signed lease agreements on January 1, 2008. Nova's lease qualified for capital lease treatment, but Sandra's lease did not. All other information for both companies is identical. Payments on each lease were due at the end of each year. The following information is from each company's December 31, 2007 financial statements:

| | Sandra | Nova |
|---|--------|------|
| Current assets | $2,000 | $2,000 |
| Total assets | 5,000 | 5,000 |
| Current liabilities | 2,000 | 2,000 |
| Total liabilities | 2,500 | 2,500 |
| Net income | 500 | 500 |

**Required:**

1. Based on this information, what will be the impact of the lease transaction on Nova's current ratio and debt-to-equity ratio on January 1, 2008 immediately after signing the lease?

2. What will be the impact on the return on assets ratio for 2008?

3. How would Sandra's ratio effects differ from Nova's? (*Hint:* Compute Nova's ratios before and after the capital lease transaction and assume that the lease liability and asset were recorded at $1,000.)

---

# PROBLEMS / DISCUSSION QUESTIONS

**P12-1**

Making computations and journal entries: Lessee accounting

Bunker Company negotiated a lease with Gilbreth Company that begins on January 1, 2008. The lease term is three years, and the asset's economic life is four years. The annual lease payments are $7,500, payable at the end of the year. The cost and fair value of the asset are $21,000. The asset will have no residual value at the end of the lease term. The lessee's cost of borrowing is 9%.

**Required:**

1. Determine whether Bunker must treat this lease as an operating lease or a capital lease.

2. Prepare an amortization table for the lease.

3. Prepare Bunker's journal entries for the life of the lease.

4. Assume that all facts remain the same except that the asset's useful life is six years. Is this an operating lease or a capital lease? Prepare journal entries for the life of the lease.

5. Compare the financial statement effects of the lease treatment you selected in requirement 3 with the financial statement effects of the treatment you selected in requirement 4. Specifically, compare the effects on assets, liabilities, and equity under the two alternative sets of assumptions as of December 31, 2008 immediately *after* the first lease payment is made.

Lessor Company has a machine with a cost and fair value of $100,000 that it leases for a 10-year period to Lessee Company. The machine has a 12-year expected economic life. Payments are received at the beginning of each year. The machine is expected to have a $10,000 residual value at the end of the lease term. (Lessee is not guaranteeing the residual value.)

**Required:**

1. What would the lease payments be if Lessor wants to earn a 10% return on its net investment?

2. What lease obligation would Lessee report when the lease is signed?

3. What would be the interest revenue reported by Lessor and the interest expense reported by Lessee in the first year, assuming they both use the 10% discount rate?

4. How would the answers to requirements 2 and 3 change for Lessee if it guaranteed the residual value?

**P12-2**

Reporting overview: Lessors and lessees

---

On January 1, 2008, Seven Wonders Inc. signed a five-year noncancelable lease with Moss Company. The lease calls for five payments of $277,409.44 to be made at the end of each year. The leased asset has a fair value of $1,200,000 on January 1, 2008. Seven Wonders cannot renew the lease, there is no bargain purchase option, and ownership of the leased asset reverts to Moss at the lease end. The leased asset has an expected useful life of six years, and Seven Wonders uses straight-line depreciation for financial reporting purposes. Its incremental borrowing rate is 12%. Moss's implicit rate of return on the lease is unknown. Seven Wonders uses a calendar year for financial reporting purposes.

**Required:**

1. Why must Seven Wonders account for the lease as a capital lease?

2. Prepare an amortization schedule for the lease liability. Round the amount of the initial lease liability at January 1, 2008 to the nearest dollar. Round all amounts in the amortization table to the nearest cent.

3. Make the journal entry to record (a) the lease as a capital lease on January 1, 2008; (b) the lease payments on December 31, 2008 and 2009; and (c) the leased asset's depreciation in 2008 and 2009.

4. What is the total amount of expense reported on Seven Wonders' 2008 income statement from the lease? Is this amount the same as, more than, or less than the amount that would have been reported if the lease had been classified as an operating lease? Why?

**P12-3**

Accounting for lessees' capital leases

mhhe.com/revsine4e

---

**Required:**

1. Repeat requirement 2 of P12–3. Assume that the lease payments are due at the beginning rather than at the end of the year. In this case, the first $277,409.44 payment would be made on January 1, 2008. Round the amount of the initial lease liability at January 1, 2008 to the nearest dollar. Round all amounts in the amortization table to the nearest cent.

2. Make the journal entry to record the lease as a capital lease on January 1, 2008. Also prepare the lessee's adjusting entries for December 31, 2008 and 2009 as well as the entries to record the lease payments on January 1, 2009 and 2010, and the leased asset's depreciation in 2008 and 2009.

**P12-4**

Accounting for lessees' capital leases

mhhe.com/revsine4e

---

On January 1, 2008, Bare Trees Company signed a three-year noncancelable lease with Dreams Inc. The lease calls for three payments of $62,258.09 to be made at each year-end. The lease payments include $3,000 of executory costs. The lease is nonrenewable and has no bargain purchase option. Ownership of the leased asset reverts to Dreams at the end of the lease period, at which time Bare Trees has guaranteed that the leased asset will be worth at least $15,000. The leased asset has an expected useful life of four years, and Bare Trees uses

**P12-5**

Accounting for lessees' capital leases including executory costs and residual value guarantee straight-line depreciation for financial reporting purposes. Bare Trees' incremental borrowing rate is 9%, which is less than Dreams' implicit rate of return on the lease.

**Required:**

1. Prepare an amortization schedule for the lease liability. Round the amount of the initial lease liability at January 1, 2008 to the nearest dollar. Round all amounts in the amortization table to the nearest cent.

2. Make the journal entry to record (a) the lease on January 1, 2008; (b) the lease payments on December 31, 2008 and 2009; and (c) the leased asset's depreciation in 2008 and 2009.

3. Assume that at the end of the lease term, the leased asset will be worth $16,000. Make the journal entry to account for the residual value guarantee.

4. Repeat requirement 3, but assume that the leased asset will be worth only $12,000 at the end of the lease term.

| | |
|---|---|
| **P 1 2 - 6**<br><br>Assessing guaranteed versus unguaranteed residual value: Lessee's perspective | On January 1, 2008, Task Co. signs an agreement to lease office equipment from Coleman, Inc. for three years with payments of $193,357 beginning December 31, 2008. The equipment's fair value is $500,000 with an expected useful life of four years. At the end of three years, the equipment is expected to have a $50,000 residual value, which Task does not guarantee. Both Task and Coleman use a 12% rate of return in evaluating this transaction. Task uses straight-line depreciation. |

**Required:**

1. What type of a lease is this for Task and why?

2. Prepare a schedule to amortize the lease liability. Round the amount of the initial lease liability to the nearest dollar and all amounts in the schedule to the nearest cent.

3. Prepare the journal entries required on Task's books for 2008 and 2010.

4. Assume now that Task guarantees the residual value. Prepare an amortization table and the journal entries necessary on Task's books for 2008 and 2010. Further assume that the equipment's residual value on December 31, 2010 is $40,000.

| | |
|---|---|
| **P 1 2 - 7**<br><br>Assessing guaranteed versus unguaranteed residual value: Lessor's perspective | **Required:**<br>Using the data in P12–6, prepare the journal entries required by Coleman, Inc. on January 1, 2008 assuming that (a) Task does not guarantee the residual value and (b) Task does guarantee it. Coleman paid $500,000 to acquire the office equipment several weeks prior to the leasing transaction. |

| | |
|---|---|
| **P 1 2 - 8**<br><br>Determining capital lease effects on ratios and income | On December 31, 2008, Thomas Henley, financial vice president of Kingston Corporation, signed a noncancelable three-year lease for an item of manufacturing equipment. The lease called for annual payments of $41,635 per year due at the *end* of each of the next three years. The leased equipment's expected economic life was four years. No cash changed hands because the first payment wasn't due until December 31, 2009.<br><br>Henley was talking with his auditor that afternoon and was surprised to learn that the lease qualified as a capital lease and would have to be put on the balance sheet. Although his intuition told him that capitalization adversely affected certain ratios, the size of these adverse effects was unclear to him. Because similar leases on other equipment were up for renewal in 2009, he wanted a precise measure of the ratio deterioration. "If these effects are excessive," he said, "I'll try to get similar leases on the other machinery to qualify as operating leases when they come up for renewal next year."<br><br>Assume that the appropriate rate for discounting the minimum lease payments is 12%. (The present value of an ordinary annuity of $1 per period for three periods at 12% is 2.40183.) Also assume that the asset Leased equipment under capital leases will be depreciated on a straight-line basis. |

**Required:**

1. Prepare an amortization schedule for the lease.

2. The effect of lease capitalization on the current ratio worried Henley. *Before factoring in the capital lease signed on December 31, 2008,* Kingston Corporation's current ratio at December 31, 2008 was:

$$\frac{\text{Current assets \$500,000}}{\text{Current liabilities \$294,118}} = 1.7$$

Once this lease is capitalized on December 31, 2008, what is the adjusted December 31, 2008 current ratio?

3. Henley was also concerned about the effect that lease capitalization would have on net income. He estimated that if the lease previously described were treated as an *operating* lease, 2009 pre-tax income would be $225,000. Determine the 2009 pre-tax income on a capital lease basis if this lease were treated as a capital lease and if the leased equipment were depreciated on a straight-line basis over the life of the lease.

---

On December 31, 2008, Rankin Corporation, a lessor of office machines, purchased a new machine for $725,000. It was delivered the same day (by prior arrangement) to Liska Company, the lessee. The following information relating to the lease transaction is available:

- The leased asset has an estimated useful life of five years, which coincides with the lease term.
- At the end of the lease term, the machine will revert to Rankin, at which time it is expected to have a salvage value of $60,000 (not guaranteed by Liska).
- Rankin's implicit rate of return on its net lease investment is 8% (known by Liska).
- Liska's incremental borrowing rate is 12% at December 31, 2008.
- Lease rentals consist of five equal annual payments, the first of which was paid on December 31, 2008.
- The lease is appropriately accounted for as a direct financing lease by Rankin and as a capital lease by Liska. Both lessor and lessee are calendar-year corporations and depreciate all fixed assets on the straight-line basis.

**P12-9**

Recording lessors' direct financing lease

**AICPA**
ADAPTED

**Required:**
Round all amounts to the nearest dollar.

1. Compute the annual rental under the lease.

2. Compute the amounts of the Gross lease receivable and the Unearned interest revenue that Rankin should disclose at the inception of the lease on December 31, 2008.

3. What expense should Liska record for the year ended December 31, 2009?

---

On January 1, 2008, Railcar Leasing Inc. (the lessor) purchased 10 used boxcars from Railroad Equipment Consolidators at a price of $8,345,640. Railcar leased the boxcars to the Reading Railroad Company (the lessee) on the same date. The lease calls for eight annual payments of $1,500,000 to be made at the beginning of each year (that is, the first payment is due at the inception of the lease on January 1, 2008). The boxcars have an eight-year remaining useful life, the lease contains no renewal or bargain purchase option, and possession of the boxcars reverts to the lessor at the lease's end. The lease does not require the lessee to guarantee any residual value for the boxcars. The payment's collectibility is reasonably certain with no important uncertainties regarding unreimbursable costs to be incurred by the lessor. The lessor has structured the lease to earn a rate of return of 12.0%.

**P12-10**

Recording lessors' direct financing lease

mhhe.com/revsine4e

**Required:**

1. What method must Railcar Leasing Inc. use to account for the lease?

2. Prepare an amortization schedule for the lease for Railcar. (Round all amounts to the nearest cent.)

3. Make all journal entries for Railcar for 2008 and 2009. Assume that it reports on a calendar-year basis.

---

**P12-11**

Recording lessors' direct financing lease

Refer to the information in P12–10. Assume that collectibility of the payments is *not* reasonably certain and that the lessor uses the straight-line depreciation method.

**Required:**

1. Make the necessary journal entries for Railcar for 2008 and 2009 under the lease.

2. How much total income before tax does the firm expect to recognize over the life of the lease in these altered circumstances?

3. Is the amount in requirement 2 the same as, more than, or less than the total amount of income before tax that is recognized in P12–10?

---

**P12-12**

Accounting for lessor's sales-type leases

mhhe.com/revsine4e

On January 1, 2008, ABC Builders Inc. (the lessor) entered into a lease with Winged Foot Company (the lessee) for an asset that ABC had manufactured at a cost of $15,000,000. The asset's fair value on January 1, 2008 is $19,354,730. The lease calls for six annual payments of $5,000,000 to be made at each year-end. The asset has a useful life of six years. The lease contains no renewal or bargain purchase option, and possession of the asset reverts to ABC at the end of the lease. The lease requires that Winged Foot guarantee that the asset's residual value will be at least $1,000,000 at the lease's end. The collectibility of the payments is reasonably certain, and no important uncertainties regarding unreimbursable costs to be incurred by the lessor exist. ABC has structured the lease so as to earn a rate of return of 15.0%.

**Required:**

1. Why must ABC Builders account for the lease as a sales-type lease?

2. Prepare an amortization schedule for the lease for ABC. (Round all amounts to the nearest cent.)

3. Make the journal entries for ABC at the inception of the lease and for the payments received in 2008 and 2009.

4. Make the journal entry for ABC at the expiration of the lease. Assume that the leased asset's residual value is $0.

---

**P12-13**

Identifying financial statement effects for lessees: Capital versus operating leases

mhhe.com/revsine4e

Assume that on January 1, 2008, Trans Global Airlines leases two used Boeing 727s from Aircraft Lessors Inc. The eight-year lease calls for payments of $10,000,000 at each year-end. On January 1, 2008, the Boeing 727s have a total fair value of $55,000,000 and a remaining useful life of 10 years. Assume that Trans Global's incremental borrowing rate is 12% and that it uses straight-line depreciation for financial reporting purposes. The lease is noncancelable, and Trans Global cannot renew it. In addition, there is no bargain purchase option, and ownership of the leased asset reverts to Aircraft Lessors at the end of the lease. Aircraft Lessors' implicit rate of return on the lease is unknown.

**Required:**

1. Should Trans Global account for the lease as a capital or an operating lease? Why?

2. Based on your answer to requirement 1, make all journal entries that Trans Global would make related to the lease for 2008, 2009, 2010, and 2015. Round all amounts to the nearest cent.

3. Assume that Trans Global accounts for the lease using whichever method (capital or operating) that you did not select in requirement 1. Make all journal entries related to the lease for 2008, 2009, 2010, and 2015.

4. Prepare a schedule of the year-to-year and total (before-tax) income differences that would result from accounting for the lease as a capital lease versus an operating lease. Round all amounts to the nearest cent.

5. Why might Trans Global's managers prefer the lease to be accounted for as an operating lease rather than as a capital lease?

---

On January 1, 2008, Overseas Leasing Inc. (the lessor) purchased five used oil tankers from Seven Seas Shipping Company at a price of $99,817,750. Overseas immediately leased the oil tankers to Pacific Ocean Oil Company (the lessee) on the same date. The lease calls for five annual payments of $25,000,000 to be made at each year-end. The tankers have a remaining useful life of five years with no salvage value, and the lease does not require the lessee to guarantee any residual value for the tankers. The lessor has structured the lease to earn a rate of return of 8.0%.

**Required:**

Prepare a schedule like the one appearing in Exhibit 12.9 of the text. This schedule should contain the year-to-year income statement and balance sheet differences that would arise depending on whether this lease is accounted for as a direct financing lease or as an operating lease.

**P12-14**

Comparing direct financing versus operating leases: Lessors' income statement and balance sheet effects

mhhe.com/revsine4e

---

As a loan officer for First Bank, you're evaluating Newton Co.'s financial statements. Your evaluation reveals that Newton has no capital leases recorded on its financial statements while most other companies in its industry do have such leases. To effectively evaluate Newton's financial position and compare it to industry standards, you've decided to constructively capitalize Newton's operating leases. The following information is available from Newton's financial statements for the year ended December 31, 2008:

**P12-15**

Constructively capitalizing operating leases

| Operating Lease Payments | |
|---|---|
| **Year** | **Minimum Operating Lease Payments** |
| 2009 | $  500 |
| 2010 | 450 |
| 2011 | 410 |
| 2012 | 380 |
| 2013 | 350 |
| After 2013 | 2,880 |
| Total | $4,970 |

**Required:**

1. Assuming that Newton's long-term debt rate is 10%, estimate its constructively capitalized operating lease liability.

2. How might you estimate the capitalized operating lease asset amount?

---

On January 1, 2008, Merchant Co. sold a tractor to Swanson, Inc. and simultaneously leased it back for five years. The tractor's fair value is $250,000, but its carrying value on Merchant's books prior to the transaction was $200,000. The tractor has a six-year remaining estimated useful life, and Merchant and Swanson both used 8% interest in evaluating the transaction. Merchant has agreed to make five payments of $57,976 beginning January 1, 2008.

**P12-16**

Evaluating sale and leaseback

**Required:**

1. What type of a lease is this for Merchant and why?

2. Compute the amount of Merchant's gain on the transaction and explain how Merchant will account for it.

3. Prepare the January 1, 2008 entries on Merchant's books to account for the sale and leaseback.

4. Assume that the tractor's carrying value on Merchant's books was $260,000. Explain how Merchant would account for the loss.

---

**P12-17**

Visualizing the asset–liability relationship over time: Capital leases

mhhe.com/revsine4e

This problem is designed to allow you to see how different lease durations and interest rates affect the relationship between the capitalized lease asset and lease liability. Of course, these same asset–liability relationships apply if you wish to constructively capitalize a lease that the lessee has treated as an operating lease.

Assume that Cambria Corporation signs a noncancelable lease that obliges it to make annual payments of $10,000. This amount excludes all executory costs, and the lease term includes no residual value guarantee. The lease will be treated as a capital lease. Cambria uses straight-line depreciation for the leased asset.

**Required:**

1. Assume that the lease payments are made at the *beginning* of each period.

   a. If the discount rate is 8% and the lease runs for 20 years, approximately when—if at all—does the capitalized lease liability first exceed the depreciated net carrying value of the leased asset?

   b. Repeat this calculation using a 12% discount rate for 20 years.

   c. Repeat this calculation using a 12% discount rate for 12 years.

2. Assume that the lease payments are made at the *end* of each period.

   a. If the discount rate is 8% and the lease runs for 20 years, does the depreciated carrying value of the leased asset ever exceed the capitalized lease liability?

   b. Will this result change if you raise the interest rate and/or shorten the duration of the lease?

---

# CASES

**C12-1**

AMR Corporation: Constructively capitalizing operating leases

mhhe.com/revsine4e

AMR Corporation is the parent of American Airlines, one of the largest airline companies in the world. Excerpts from its 2006 annual report follow.

### AMR Corporation Consolidated Balance Sheets

| | December 31, | |
| --- | --- | --- |
| *(in millions, except shares and par value)* | **2006** | **2005** |
| **Assets** | | |
| **Current Assets** | | |
| Cash | $ 121 | $ 138 |
| Short-term investments | 4,594 | 3,676 |
| Restricted cash and short-term investments | 468 | 510 |
| Receivables, less allowance for uncollectible accounts (2006—$45; 2005—$60) | 988 | 991 |
| Inventories, less allowance for obsolescence (2006—$411; 2005—$410) | 506 | 515 |
| Other current assets | 225 | 334 |
| Total current assets | 6,902 | 6,164 |

*(continued)*

| (in millions, except shares and par value) | December 31, | |
| --- | --- | --- |
| | 2006 | 2005 |
| **Equipment and Property** | | |
| Flight equipment, at cost | 22,913 | 22,491 |
| Less accumulated depreciation | 8,406 | 7,648 |
| | 14,507 | 14,843 |
| Purchase deposits for flight equipment | 178 | 278 |
| Other equipment and property, at cost | 5,097 | 5,156 |
| Less accumulated depreciation | 2,706 | 2,750 |
| | 2,391 | 2,406 |
| | 17,076 | 17,527 |
| **Equipment and Property under Capital Leases** | | |
| Flight equipment | 1,744 | 1,881 |
| Other equipment and property | 217 | 199 |
| | 1,961 | 2,080 |
| Less accumulated amortization | 1,096 | 1,061 |
| | 865 | 1,019 |
| **Other Assets** | | |
| Route acquisition costs and airport operating and gate lease rights, less accumulated amortization (2006—$361; 2005—$331) | 1,167 | 1,194 |
| Other assets | 3,135 | 3,591 |
| | 4,302 | 4,785 |
| **Total Assets** | $29,145 | $29,495 |

The accompanying notes are an integral part of these financial statements.

| **Liabilities and Stockholders' Equity (Deficit)** | | |
| --- | --- | --- |
| **Current Liabilities** | | |
| Accounts payable | $ 1,073 | $ 1,078 |
| Accrued salaries and wages | 551 | 635 |
| Accrued liabilities | 1,750 | 1,705 |
| Air traffic liability | 3,782 | 3,615 |
| Current maturities of long-term debt | 1,246 | 1,077 |
| Current obligations under capital leases | 103 | 162 |
| Total current liabilities | 8,505 | 8,272 |
| **Long-Term Debt, Less Current Maturities** | 11,217 | 12,530 |
| **Obligations under Capital Leases, Less Current Obligations** | 824 | 926 |
| **Other Liabilities and Credits** | | |
| Deferred gains | 372 | 421 |
| Pension and postretirement benefits | 5,341 | 4,998 |
| Other liabilities and deferred credits | 3,492 | 3,778 |
| | 9,205 | 9,197 |
| **Commitments and Contingencies** | | |
| **Stockholders' Equity (Deficit)** | | |
| Preferred stock—20,000,000 shares authorized; None issued | — | — |
| Common stock—$1 par value; 750,000,000 shares authorized; shares issued: 2006—228,164,821; 2005—195,350,259 | 228 | 195 |
| Additional paid-in capital | 2,718 | 2,258 |
| Treasury shares at cost: 2006—5,940,399; 2005—12,617,908 | (367) | (779) |
| Accumulated other comprehensive loss | (1,291) | (979) |
| Accumulated deficit | (1,894) | (2,125) |
| | (606) | (1,430) |
| **Total Liabilities and Stockholders' Equity (Deficit)** | $29,145 | $29,495 |

The accompanying notes are an integral part of these financial statements.

## 5. Leases

AMR's subsidiaries lease various types of equipment and property, primarily aircraft and airport facilities. The future minimum lease payments required under capital leases, together with the present value of such payments, and future minimum lease payments required under operating leases that have initial or remaining non-cancelable lease terms in excess of one year as of December 31, 2006, were (in millions):

| Year Ending December 31, | Capital Leases | Operating Leases |
|---|---|---|
| 2007 | $ 197 | $ 1,098 |
| 2008 | 236 | 1,032 |
| 2009 | 175 | 929 |
| 2010 | 140 | 860 |
| 2011 | 142 | 855 |
| 2012 and thereafter | 651 | 6,710 |
| | 1,541 | $11,484(1) |
| Less amount representing interest | 614 | |
| Present value of net minimum lease payments | $ 927 | |

(1) As of December 31, 2006, included in Accrued liabilities and Other liabilities and deferred credits on the accompanying consolidated balance sheet is approximately $1.4 billion relating to rent expense being recorded in advance of future operating lease payments.

At December 31, 2006, the Company was operating 210 jet aircraft and 21 turboprop aircraft under operating leases and 89 jet aircraft and one turboprop aircraft under capital leases. The aircraft leases can generally be renewed at rates based on fair market value at the end of the lease term for one to five years. Some aircraft leases have purchase options at or near the end of the lease term at fair market value, but generally not to exceed a stated percentage of the defined lessor's cost of the aircraft or a predetermined fixed amount.

Rent expense, excluding landing fees, was $1.4 billion, $1.3 billion and $1.3 billion in 2006, 2005 and 2004, respectively.

**Required:**

All questions relate to 2006 unless stated otherwise.

1. What is the net amount of capital lease assets on the balance sheet?
2. What is the total amount of capital lease obligations on the balance sheet?
3. Why are the amounts in questions 1 and 2 different?
4. Compute AMR's total debt to total assets.
5. What entry would AMR make in 2007 to record the effects of capital leases existing at December 31, 2006? You may omit the depreciation entry.
6. What is the amount of operating lease obligations on the balance sheet?
7. What is the present value of operating lease payments? Assume a 10% discount rate.
8. What entry would be made to constructively capitalize the leases. (Ignore the effects of taxes.)
9. Recompute the total debt to total assets ratio after making the entry in requirement 8. What is the percentage change from the ratio computed in requirement 4?

---

| C12-2 |
|---|

**Wal-Mart: Lessee reporting— Capital versus operating treatment—Comprehensive**

Wal-Mart Stores, Inc. operates retail stores in various retailing formats in all 50 states in the United States. The company's mass merchandising operations serve its customers primarily through the operation of three segments. The Wal-Mart Stores segment includes its discount stores, Supercenters, and Neighborhood Markets in the United States. The SAM's Clubs segment includes the warehouse membership clubs in the United States. The International segment includes all of its operations in Argentina, Brazil, Canada, China, Japan, Germany, Korea, Mexico, Puerto Rico, and the United Kingdom. The company's subsidiary, McLane Company, Inc. provides products and distribution services to retail industry and institutional foodservice customers.

Information taken from Wal-Mart's fiscal year 2003 annual report follows:

## Note 9: Commitments

The Company and certain of its subsidiaries have long-term leases for stores and equipment. Rentals (including, for certain leases, amounts applicable to taxes, insurance, maintenance, other operating expenses and contingent rentals) under all operating leases were $1,091 million, $1,043 million, and $893 million in 2003, 2002, and 2001, respectively. Aggregate minimum annual rentals at January 31, 2003, under noncancelable leases are as follows (in millions):

| Fiscal Year | Operating Leases | Capital Leases |
|---|---|---|
| 2004 | $ 589 | $ 440 |
| 2005 | 576 | 431 |
| 2006 | 560 | 428 |
| 2007 | 546 | 419 |
| 2008 | 515 | 412 |
| Thereafter | 5,202 | 3,152 |
| Total minimum rentals | $7,988 | A |
| Less estimated executory costs | | $ 57 |
| Net minimum lease payments | | B |
| Less imputed interest at rates ranging from 6.1% to 14.0% | | C |
| Present value of minimum lease payments | | D |

## Excerpts from Wal-Mart's 2003 consolidated balance sheets follow:

| ($ in millions) | 1/31/2003 |
|---|---|
| **Liabilities and Shareholders' Equity:** | |
| Current Liabilities | |
| Commercial paper | $ 1,079 |
| Accounts payable | 17,140 |
| Accrued liabilities | 8,945 |
| Accrued income taxes | 739 |
| Long-term debt due within one year | 4,538 |
| Obligations under capital leases due within one year | 176 |
| Total Current Liabilities | $32,617 |
| Long-term debt | $16,607 |
| Long-term obligations under capital leases | 3,001 |
| Deferred income taxes and other | 1,761 |
| Total Long-term Liabilities | $21,369 |

**Required:**

1. Solve for the unknowns (A, B, C, and D) in Note 9.

2. Make the journal entry to account for Wal-Mart's fiscal year 2004 capital lease payment. (Ignore allocating the executory cost portion because there is insufficient information to do so.)

3. Assume that the amount of Wal-Mart's operating lease payment due each year after 2008 is equal and is paid at the end of each fiscal year. Assume that all of these leases terminate at the end of 2019. Using an interest rate of 8%, calculate the present value of the operating lease payments at January 31, 2003.

4. Make the journal entry that would be necessary at January 31, 2003 to account for the operating leases as if they were being treated as capital leases. (Ignore income taxes and assume that the amount of the capitalized asset equals the capitalized liability.)

5. Based on your answer to requirement 3, make the necessary journal entries for the fiscal year ended January 31, 2004 assuming operating leases are being accounted for as capital leases. Assume a 16-year useful life, zero salvage value, and straight-line depreciation for all capitalized leased assets.

6. Wal-Mart's total shareholders' equity listed on its January 31, 2003 consolidated balance sheet was $39,337 million. This gives a long-term debt-to-shareholders' equity ratio of 54.3%. Calculate Wal-Mart's total long-term debt-to-shareholders' equity ratio after treating its operating leases as if they were capital leases. (Ignore tax effects.)

7. Comment on the differences between the unadjusted and adjusted ratios.

---

**C12-3**

Guaraldi Bank, Inc.:
Determining lease
classification and the times
interest earned ratio

The following information is based on an actual annual report. In a recent lending agreement (dated March 3, 2008), Guaraldi Bank, Inc., included the following definitions for terms used in its loan covenants with a borrower:

Fixed Charges means the sum of, for Borrower and its Subsidiaries, determined in accordance with GAAP on a consolidated basis, (a) interest expense (including interest expense pursuant to Capital Leases), plus (b) lease expense payable for Operating Leases, determined for the four fiscal quarters preceding the date of calculation.

Net Earning Available for Fixed Charges means, for Borrower and its Subsidiaries, determined in accordance with GAAP on a consolidated basis, (a) Net Income before Taxes, plus (b) extraordinary noncash charges, plus (c) interest expense (including interest expense pursuant to Capital Leases), plus (d) lease expense pursuant to Operating Leases, determined for the fiscal quarter preceding the date of calculation.

Fixed Charges Coverage Ratio means the ratio of Net Earnings Available for Fixed Charges to Fixed Charges.

Borrower shall not permit the Fixed Charges Coverage Ratio to be less than the following ratios for the fiscal quarters ending as follows:

| December 31, 2007 | 0.70 to 1.00 |
| March 31, 2008 | 1.00 to 1.00 |
| June 30, 2008 | 1.20 to 1.00 |
| September 30, 2008 | 1.50 to 1.00 |
| December 31, 2008 | 1.75 to 1.00 |

Notice that the definitions of Fixed charges and Net earnings available for fixed charges *both* add back lease expenses under operating leases. The objective of this case is to allow you to see why astute lenders carefully design covenants to protect themselves against borrowers who might use the latitude in GAAP lease accounting rules to circumvent covenant restrictions.

Assume the following initial conditions for the borrower on June 30, 2008:

| Income before interest and taxes | $120,000 |
| Interest on capital lease | $ 60,000 |
| Interest on other borrowings | 40,000 |
| Fixed charges | $100,000 |
| Fixed charges coverage ratio | 1.20 |

Notice that the fixed charges coverage ratio equals the covenant constraint at June 30, 2008; even minor adversity might cause a covenant violation in the next quarter. In addition, the borrower is required to increase the ratio to 1.50 by September 30, 2008.

**Required:**

1. Assume that the borrower "somehow" restructures the existing lease to have it qualify as an operating lease. What effect will this change in lease classification have on the times-interest-earned ratio as typically defined? (See Chapter 5.) What effect will this change have on the fixed charges coverage ratio as defined in the lending agreement? What does your answer to this part tell you about the vigilance that credit analysts must exert in designing and monitoring financial contractual restrictions?

2. Now assume that the initial times-interest-earned ratio was less than 1.00 to 1.00. Would changing the capital lease to an operating lease benefit the borrower's compliance with lending covenants?

   (*Note:* In answering both parts, make assumptions when sufficient information is not available.)

## COLLABORATIVE LEARNING CASE

The following information is drawn from recent annual reports of three firms in the retail industry: JC Penney Company, Inc., Dillard Department Stores, Inc., and Macy's Inc.

**A.** JC Penney is a major retailer operating 1,049 department stores in 49 states, Puerto Rico, and Mexico. In addition, it operates 54 Renner department stores in Brazil. A major portion of JC Penney Company's business consists of providing merchandise and services to consumers through department stores, catalog departments, and the Internet. Selected financial information follows:

**C12-4**

The retail industry: Comparing the effects of constructive capitalization

mhhe.com/revsine4e

| ($ in millions) | January 25, 2003 | January 26, 2002 |
| --- | --- | --- |
| Long-term debt | $ 4,940 | $ 5,179 |
| Total shareholders' equity | 6,370 | 6,129 |
| Total liabilities and shareholders' equity | 17,867 | 18,048 |

An excerpt from its lease footnote follows:

The Company conducts the major parts of its operations from leased premises that include retail stores, catalog fulfillment centers, warehouses, offices, and other facilities. Future minimum lease obligations as of January 25, 2003, were:

| ($ in millions) | Operating Leases | Capital Leases |
| --- | --- | --- |
| 2003 | $ 671 | $17 |
| 2004 | 611 | 16 |
| 2005 | 544 | 12 |
| 2006 | 494 | 4 |
| 2007 | 455 | 2 |
| Thereafter | 4,128 | — |
| Minimum payments | $6,903 | $51 |
| Present value of minimum payments | | $43 |

**B.** Dillard Department Stores Inc. operates retail department stores located primarily in the Southwest, Southeast, and Midwest. Selected financial information follows:

| ($ in thousands) | February 1, 2003 | February 2, 2002 |
| --- | --- | --- |
| Long-term debt | $2,193,006 | $2,124,577 |
| Total shareholders' equity | 2,264,196 | 2,668,397 |
| Total liabilities and shareholders' equity | 6,675,932 | 7,074,559 |

An excerpt from its lease footnote follows:

Future minimum payments under capital leases and the future minimum rental commitments for all noncancelable operating leases as of February 1, 2003 are as follows ($ in thousands):

| Fiscal Year | Capital Leases Amount | Operating Leases Amount |
|---|---|---|
| 2003 | $ 3,806 | $ 59,299 |
| 2004 | 3,622 | 50,479 |
| 2005 | 3,339 | 41,797 |
| 2006 | 3,232 | 38,588 |
| 2007 | 2,578 | 29,482 |
| After 2007 | 21,595 | 105,323 |
| Total minimum lease payments | 38,172 | |
| Less amount representing interest | (17,716) | |
| Present value of net minimum payments | $20,456 | |

**C.** Macy's, Inc. (formerly, Federated Department Stores Inc.) is one of the leading operators of full-line department stores in the United States with more than 850 department stores in 45 states. The company's department stores are located at urban or suburban sites, principally in densely populated areas across the United States. Selected financial information follows:

| ($ in millions) | February 1, 2003 | February 2, 2002 |
|---|---|---|
| Long-term debt | $ 3,408 | $ 3,859 |
| Total shareholders' equity | 5,762 | 5,564 |
| Total liabilities and shareholders' equity | 14,441 | 16,112 |

An excerpt from its lease footnote follows:

Minimum rental commitments as of February 1, 2003 for noncancelable leases are:

| ($ in millions) | Operating Leases | Capital Leases |
|---|---|---|
| 2003 | $ 162 | $ 11 |
| 2004 | 159 | 11 |
| 2005 | 149 | 9 |
| 2006 | 151 | 8 |
| 2007 | 145 | 8 |
| Thereafter | 1,943 | 69 |
| Minimum payments | $2,709 | 116 |
| Less amount representing interest | | 56 |
| Present value of minimum payments | | $ 60 |

### Additional Information:

1. For JC Penney, assume that the operating lease payments due after 2007 are equal and will be made over a 10-year period.

2. For Dillard's, assume that the operating lease payments due after 2007 are equal and will be made over a five-year period.

3. For Macy's, assume that the operating lease payments due after 2007 are equal and will be made over a 14-year period.

### Required:

1. Show that the interest rate implicit in the capital lease obligations of JC Penney is closer to 8.5% than to 10%.

2. Using the 8.5% rate from requirement 1, calculate the present value of JC Penney's operating lease obligations.

3. Using the approach followed in requirement 1, we can determine that the interest rate implicit in Dillard's capital lease obligations is close to 10%. Use this rate to calculate the present value of the firm's operating lease payments.

4. The approach in requirement 1 allows us to determine that the interest rate implicit in Macy's capital lease obligations Macy's is close to 11.5%. Use this rate to calculate the present value of the firm's operating lease payments.

5. Using the balance sheet information reported earlier, calculate the long-term debt to shareholders' equity ratio and the long-term debt to total assets ratio of the three firms for their most recent fiscal year.

6. Repeat requirement 5 after treating the operating leases as if they are being accounted for as capital leases. How do the results compare with those in requirement 5? (Ignore taxes and assume that the capitalized asset equals the capitalized liability.)

**Remember to check the book's companion Web site for additional study material.**

# Income Tax Reporting | 13

| (Sin millions) | | $22,011.9 |
|---|---|---|
| Sales | | |
| Costs. Expenses and Other | 01.1 | 5,149.6 |
| Materials and production | 65.4 | 7,155.5 |
| Marketing and administrative | 82.9 | 3,848.0 |
| Research and development | 2.3 | 322.2 |
| Restructuring costs | | (1,717.1) |
| Equity income fr | | (110.2) |
| | | 14,648.0 |

*"I'm proud to be paying taxes to the United States. The only thing is . . . I could be just as proud for half the money."*

—Arthur Godfrey, television host
1940s–1970s

I n the United States and many other industrialized countries, the rules for computing income for financial reporting purposes—known as **book income**—do not correspond to the rules for computing income for taxation purposes—referred to as
**taxable income.** This divergence is allowable and makes sense because of the different
objectives underlying book income versus taxable income.[1] Book income is intended to
reflect increases in a firm's "well-offness"; it includes all changes in net assets that meet
the GAAP criteria for revenue recognition (critical event and measurable) and for costs
that have expired according to the expense matching principle (Chapters 2 and 3). ***Book
income includes all earned inflows of net assets, even inflows not immediately convertible into cash, and it reflects expenses as they accrue, not just when they are paid.***

Determining income for tax purposes does not always focus on changes in well-
offness. Instead, taxable income is governed by the "constructive receipt/ability to pay"
doctrine. According to this doctrine, when liquid assets enter the firm, they are frequently taxed because it is easiest to collect money at that time. For example, rent
received in advance is taxed when received even though it is not yet earned from an
accounting standpoint. Similarly, tax deductions generally are allowed only when expenditures are made or when a loss occurs. ***Because of different underlying objectives, the
rules for determining book income—according to generally accepted accounting principles (GAAP)—diverge from the rules for determining taxable income (according to
the Internal Revenue Service or IRS). This divergence complicates the way that income
taxes are reflected in financial reports.***

This chapter describes the major differences between U.S. book income and taxable
income and how these differences complicate the reporting of tax expense and tax obligations. First we outline the major categories of differences between book income and
taxable income, and we illustrate the distortions that would result on GAAP income
statements if tax expense were to be set equal to taxes owed the IRS. Next we explain and

## LEARNING OBJECTIVES

**After studying this chapter, you
will understand:**

1. The different objectives underlying
income determination for financial
reporting (book) purposes versus
tax purposes.

2. The distinction between temporary
(timing) and permanent book/tax
differences, the items that cause each
of these differences, and how each
affects book income versus taxable
income.

3. The distortions created when the
deferred tax effects of temporary
differences are ignored.

4. How tax expense is determined with
interperiod tax allocation.

5. How tax rate changes are
recognized.

6. The reporting rules for net operating
loss carrybacks and carryforwards.

7. How to read and interpret tax
footnote disclosures and how these
footnotes can be used to enhance
interfirm comparability.

8. How *FASB Interpretation No. 48
(FIN 48)* disclosures reveal information about firms' uncertain tax
positions.

9. How tax footnotes can be used to
evaluate the degree of conservatism
in firms' book (GAAP) accounting
choices.

*Chapter*

---

[1] Countries in which the rules for determining accounting (book) income and taxable income for parent companies
are essentially the same include, for example, Germany, Japan, and Switzerland.

illustrate the GAAP solution for avoiding these distortions—referred to as **deferred income tax accounting** or **interperiod tax allocation.** We also explore what happens when Congress changes income tax rates, and we discuss how the accounting works for special U.S. tax laws that apply to unprofitable firms.

The second part of the chapter guides you through an analysis of typical income tax footnote disclosures. Our purpose is to explain the wealth of information that can be extracted from these disclosures. We demonstrate how analysts can use tax footnotes to glean information not provided elsewhere in the financial statements to better understand a firm's performance and future prospects.

> *Interperiod tax allocation* refers to the allocation of income tax expense *across periods* when book and tax income differ. **Intraperiod tax allocation,** introduced in Chapter 2, refers to the allocation of the tax cost (benefit) across various components of book income *within a given period.* For example, the current tax provision (expense) is related to (pre-tax) income from continuing operations while gains and losses from discontinued operations and extraordinary items are reported *net of tax* on the income statement.

> In this chapter, we use the terms *temporary* and *timing* differences interchangeably. They mean the same thing. *Accounting Principles Board (APB) Opinion No. 11,* "Accounting for Income Taxes," used the term "timing difference," while *Statement of Financial Accounting Standards (SFAS) No. 109,* "Accounting for Income Taxes," which superseded *APB Opinion No. 11,* uses the term "temporary differences." The same term should have been used in both standards but, unfortunately, it wasn't.

# UNDERSTANDING INCOME TAX REPORTING
## Temporary and Permanent Differences between Book Income and Taxable Income

The differences that result from determining income reported in external financial statements on the one hand and determining taxable income for tax purposes on the other fall into two broad categories:

1. **Temporary** or **timing differences**
2. **Permanent differences**

A timing difference results when a revenue (gain) or expense (loss) enters into the determination of book income in one period but affects taxable income in a different (earlier or later) period. A brief summary of common temporary differences is provided in Exhibit 13.1. Timing differences are considered "temporary" because they eventually reverse. That is, a revenue (or expense) item that causes book income to be more (less) than taxable income when it is initially recorded—called an *originating* **timing difference**—will eventually reverse. These reversals cause book income to be less (more) than taxable income in future periods and are called *reversing* **timing differences.**

Temporary differences that will cause taxable income to be *higher* than book income in future periods give rise to a **deferred tax liability.** Conversely, temporary differences that will cause taxable income to be *lower* than book income in future periods give rise to a **deferred tax asset.** Deferred tax liabilities and assets are explained in the following sections.

A **permanent difference** between taxable income and book income is caused by items that:

1. Enter into the determination of accounting income but *never* affect taxable income. For example, interest income received on municipal bonds is included in accounting income but not in taxable income under current U.S. tax rules.
2. Enter into the determination of taxable income but *never* affect accounting income. For example, the **dividends-received deduction** in the U.S. tax laws allows one U.S. corporation to deduct from taxable income a portion of the dividends received from another U.S. corporation. The details are described later.

Because permanent differences between book income and taxable income do not reverse and are not offset by corresponding differences in later periods, they do *not* give rise to deferred tax assets or liabilities. Refer to Exhibit 13.2 for examples of permanent differences.

| EXHIBIT 13.1 | Examples of Temporary (Timing) Differences between Book Income and Taxable Income |
| --- | --- |

### Depreciation Expense

Accelerated depreciation is used for taxable income but straight-line is typically used for book income. **Modified Accelerated Cost Recovery System** (MACRS) useful lives are employed for taxable income whereas useful economic lives are employed for book income. Both of these items result in larger depreciation deductions for tax purposes than for book purposes in the early years of an asset's life, and the opposite effect occurs in later years.

### Bad Debts Expense

Bad debts are accrued and recognized under the allowance method for book purposes, but tax rules follow the direct write-off method, allowing a deduction only when a particular account is deemed to be uncollectible and written off.

### Warranty Expense

Warranty expenses are accrued and recorded in the year the product is sold for book purposes, but for tax purposes, the deduction is allowed when the actual warranty expenditures are made to correct the defect.

### Prepaid Expenses

Some business expenses, such as insurance premiums and rent, are paid in advance. For book purposes, these expenditures are initially recorded as assets—Prepaid insurance or Prepaid rent—but later are expensed over the periods when the benefits are received. Tax rules allow the deduction in the period the payment is made.

### Pension and Other Post-Retirement Benefits (OPEB) Expenses

For book purposes, the deduction is based on the amount of pension or OPEB expense accrued. For pensions, a tax deduction is allowed for the amounts funded (that is, contributed to the pension fund) each period, and for OPEB costs, a deduction is allowed for amounts actually paid during the period.

### Purchased Goodwill

The Revenue Reconciliation Act of 1993 allows firms a deduction for goodwill amortization on a 15-year straight-line basis under certain special conditions. But in most situations, goodwill is *not* deductible. For book purposes, purchased goodwill is subject to periodic impairment tests (see Chapter 16). If impaired, goodwill is written down to fair value with an offsetting charge to earnings.

### Installment Sales

Sales are generally recognized for book purposes when the goods are delivered to the customer regardless of when collections are made. If collections are made over an extended period, tax rules record the sales revenue as payments are received.

### Long-Term Construction Contracts

For long-term construction contracts (Chapter 3), firms may elect to use either the percentage-of-completion or the completed-contract method of revenue recognition for book purposes. In general, taxpayers may only use the percentage-of-completion method to account for long-term contracts entered into after July 11, 1989.

> A great deal of confusion surrounds the tax deductibility of goodwill. The financial press and even financial analysts often assume that recorded goodwill is deductible for tax purposes, but in most cases, it is not.
>
> When is goodwill tax deductible? Goodwill is tax deductible when the *tax basis* of the acquired firm's assets are stepped-up (that is, recorded at fair value at date of acquisition). Whether goodwill is deductible for tax purposes hinges on whether the acquiring entity is buying the assets of another entity directly (for example, ABC Company buys a division of XYZ Company) or whether the acquiring entity gains control over the assets of another entity by buying the voting stock of that entity (for example, ABC Company acquires 80% of the common stock of XYZ Company). Goodwill that arises from direct asset purchases is deductible for tax purposes, while it is not deductible for the indirect stock purchase. Because most goodwill on consolidated balance sheets arises from stock transactions rather than outright asset purchases, it is not deductible for tax purposes.
>
> See M. Scholes, M. Wolfson, M. Erickson, E. Maydew, and T. Shevlin, *Taxes and Business Strategy: A Planning Approach* (Upper Saddle River, NJ: Prentice Hall, 2002).

### Revenues Received in Advance

Revenues received in advance (for example, rent revenue or subscription revenue) are initially recorded as a liability for book purposes and are transferred to income as those revenues are "earned." For tax purposes, these amounts are taxed when received.

### Equity in Undistributed Earnings of Investees

If a company (Investor) owns 20% or more of the outstanding voting stock of another corporation (Investee), the equity method of accounting is used for book purposes (Chapter 16). Under the equity method, the Investor records as income its share of Investee profits for the period. For tax purposes, income is recognized when Investee dividends are received, but this recognition is subject to special dividends-received deduction rules discussed below under permanent differences.

| **EXHIBIT 13.2** | **Examples of Permanent Differences between Book Income and Taxable Income** |

### Items Recognized for Book Purposes but *Not* for Tax Purposes

- Interest received on state and municipal bonds is not subject to federal or state tax but is included in book income.
- If a company pays fines or expenses resulting from violations of the law (for example, environmental damages), these payments are not deductible for tax purposes but would be deducted from book income.
- Goodwill write-offs generally are not deductible for tax purposes unless they meet certain special conditions.* Goodwill writedown as a result of impairment is subtracted in determining book income (see Chapter 16).
- Premiums for life insurance on executives paid for by a company that is the designated beneficiary are not deductible for tax purposes. Similarly, any benefits collected are not taxed. For book purposes, both the premiums paid and benefits received are used in determining income.
- Compensation expense associated with certain ("nonqualified") employee stock options is not deductible for tax purposes but is deductible in determining book income.

> Unless otherwise specified, you should assume for purposes of working problems in this chapter that goodwill write-off is treated as a permanent difference item—that is, it is *not* deductible for tax purposes.

### Items Recognized for Tax Purposes but *Not* for Book Purposes

- Tax laws allow a statutory depletion deduction on certain natural resources that may be in excess of the cost-based depletion recorded for book purposes. This excess statutory depletion is a permanent difference between book and taxable income.
- U.S. corporations that own stock in other U.S. companies are allowed to deduct a portion of the dividends received from these investees from taxable income according to the following schedule:

| Ownership Portion | Deductible Portion of Dividends |
| --- | --- |
| Less than 20% | 70% |
| Equal to or greater than 20%, but less than 80% | 80 |
| Equal to or greater than 80% | 100 |

* See P. McConnell, "Goodwill: The Facts," *Accounting Issues* (New York: Bear Stearns & Co., August 26, 1994); and Sections 1060 and 338 of the Internal Revenue Code.

---

## RECAP

**Temporary differences occur when a revenue (gain) or expense (loss) enters into the determination of book (GAAP) income and taxable income in different periods. Temporary differences that cause taxable income to be higher (lower) than book income in future periods give rise to a deferred tax liability (asset). Permanent differences are revenue or expense items that are recognized as part of book income but are *never* recognized as part of taxable income, or vice versa. Permanent differences do *not* give rise to deferred tax assets or liabilities.**

## Problems Caused by Temporary Differences

> Technically, firms are required to use MACRS depreciation schedules for tax purposes, and these differ by type of asset and useful life. We use SOYD here to simplify the illustration of depreciation-induced temporary differences.

To illustrate the issues related to interperiod tax allocation, consider the most prevalent temporary book/tax timing difference: depreciation expense. For tax purposes, profit-maximizing firms try to *minimize* the discounted present value of their future tax payments. Each dollar of tax deduction today is more valuable than a dollar of tax deduction in the future. This time-value-of-money principle is the reason that most firms use accelerated depreciation for tax purposes. But many of these same firms use straight-line depreciation for financial reporting purposes. This creates a temporary difference between book income and taxable income.

Consider this illustration. Assume that Mitchell Corporation buys new equipment for $10,000 on January 1, 2008. The asset has a five-year life and no salvage value. It will be depreciated using the straight-line method for book purposes, but for tax purposes the sum-of-the-years'-digits (SOYD) method will be used. Refer to Exhibit 13.3 and Figure 13.1(a) for the two depreciation schedules.

## ∘EXHIBIT 13.3   Mitchell Corporation

### Book-versus-Tax Depreciation

| Year | (a) Book Depreciation | (b) Tax Return Depreciation | (c) Excess of Tax over Book Depreciation | |
|------|----------------------|------------------------------|-------------------------------------------|--|
| 2008 | $ 2,000 | $ 3,333 | $ 1,333 | ⎫ Originating timing |
| 2009 | 2,000 | 2,667 | 667 | ⎬ differences |
| 2010 | 2,000 | 2,000 | — | |
| 2011 | 2,000 | 1,333 | (667) | ⎫ Reversing timing |
| 2012 | 2,000 | 667 | (1,333) | ⎬ differences |
| | $10,000 | $10,000 | –0– | |

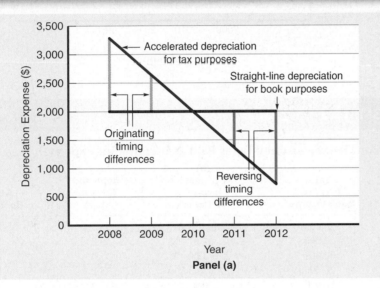

**Panel (a)**

### Figure 13.1(a)

MITCHELL CORPORATION

Comparison of Book-versus-Tax Depreciation Expense

Let's assume for Mitchell Corporation that depreciation constitutes the only book-versus-tax difference. Income before depreciation is expected to be $22,000 each year over the next five years and the statutory tax rate is 35%. Pre-tax book income, taxable income per Mitchell's tax return, and taxes payable are reflected in Exhibit 13.4. Figure 13.1(b) displays graphically the relation between taxable income and pre-tax book income over the five-year period.

> The **statutory tax rate** for corporations is the rate set by law—in this case, 35%.

## EXHIBIT 13.4   Mitchell Corporation

### Income and Income Tax Payable

| Year | (a) Pre-Tax Book Income ($22,000 – Book Depreciation) | (b) Taxable Income per Tax Return ($22,000 – Tax Depreciation) | (c) Income Tax Payable (35% of Col. [b]) |
|------|------------------------------------------------------|----------------------------------------------------------------|-------------------------------------------|
| 2008 | $ 20,000 | $ 18,667* | $ 6,533 |
| 2009 | 20,000 | 19,333 | 6,767 |
| 2010 | 20,000 | 20,000 | 7,000 |
| 2011 | 20,000 | 20,667 | 7,233 |
| 2012 | 20,000 | 21,333 | 7,467 |
| Total | $100,000 | $100,000 | $35,000 |

* For example, in 2008, $22,000 − $3,333 (Exhibit 13.3, column [b]) = $18,667.

# Figure 13.1(b)

MITCHELL CORPORATION

Pre-tax Book Income and
Taxable Income

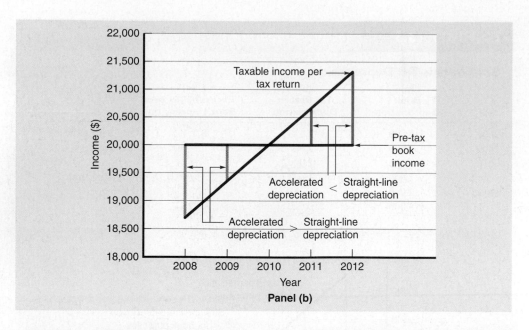

Panel (b)

| EXHIBIT 13.5 | Mitchell Corporation |
| --- | --- |

**Result from Treating Actual Taxes Paid as Income Tax Expense**

| Year | (a) Pre-Tax Book Income | (b) Tax Expense = Income Tax Payable | (c) Reported Tax Rate (b/a) | (d) After-Tax Book Income |
| --- | --- | --- | --- | --- |
| 2008 | $20,000 | $6,533 | 32.7% | $13,467 |
| 2009 | 20,000 | 6,767 | 33.8 | 13,233 |
| 2010 | 20,000 | 7,000 | 35.0 | 13,000 |
| 2011 | 20,000 | 7,233 | 36.2 | 12,767 |
| 2012 | 20,000 | 7,467 | 37.3 | 12,533 |

The easiest way to reflect book income tax expense here would be to simply treat the actual taxes payable each year (Column [c] of Exhibit 13.4) as the reported *book* income tax expense. Exhibit 13.5 and Figure 13.2 on the next page show you what would happen if this were done.

As you can readily see in the exhibit and figure, this approach *mismatches* tax expense with pre-tax book income. This mismatch causes the effective (book) tax rate to increase over time even though the pre-tax book income ($20,000) and the statutory tax rate (35%) are stable over the five-year period. Treating actual cash taxes paid as income tax expense would *not* reflect the true economics of the situation. Without adjusting tax expense for the temporary differences between book and tax depreciation expense, the results show an *increasing* effective (book) tax rate—and *declining* after-tax income—over the five-year period. The effective (book) tax rate would range from 32.7% in 2008 to 37.3% in 2012 (Figure 13.2), and the after-tax earnings would decline from $13,467 in 2008 to $12,533 in 2012 (Column [d] of Exhibit 13.5). Clearly, this approach leads to an inappropriate matching between pre-tax book income and income tax expense.

Besides the income statement mismatch, treating actual cash taxes paid as income tax expense introduces a reporting distortion on the balance sheet. This distortion occurs because total tax depreciation deductions on an asset cannot exceed the asset's cost minus its salvage value. Accordingly, "extra" tax depreciation in early years will be offset by lower allowable tax depreciation in later years. As shown in Column (c) of Exhibit 13.3, during 2008 tax depreciation ($3,333) exceeds book depreciation ($2,000). The "extra" tax depreciation of $1,333 means

The **effective** (book) **tax rate** is the tax expense divided by pre-tax income that is reported on the GAAP income statement.

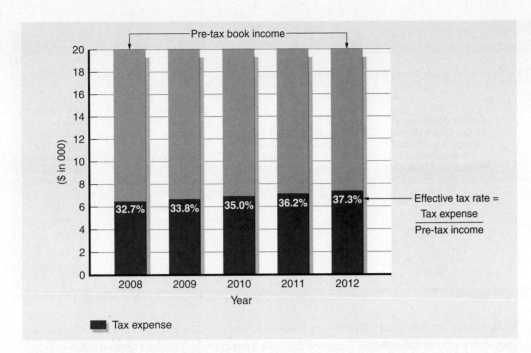

**Figure 13.2**

MITCHELL CORPORATION

Tax Expense *without* Interperiod Tax Allocation

that future years' *tax* depreciation must be $1,333 lower than future years' *book* depreciation. Thus, the extra tax depreciation taken in 2008 generates a "liability" for future taxes of $1,333 times 35%, or $467, but this "liability" goes unrecorded when the tax expense is set equal to actual cash taxes paid or payable.

There is another way to visualize how the extra tax depreciation creates a liability for future taxes. The Financial Accounting Standards Board (FASB) states that GAAP assumes "the reported amounts of assets . . . will be recovered. . . . Based on that assumption, a difference between the tax basis of an asset . . . and its reported amount . . . will result in taxable . . . amounts . . . when the reported amounts . . . are recovered. . . ."[2] In our example, at the end of 2008, the reported (book) amount of the asset is $8,000 (that is, $10,000 − $2,000 book depreciation), while the tax basis is $6,667 (that is, $10,000 − $3,333 tax depreciation). Notice that if the asset was sold for its $8,000 GAAP net book value, a taxable IRS gain of $1,333 would ensue, measured as the difference between the $8,000 cash received and the asset's $6,667 *tax* basis. Thus, given the GAAP assumption that reported amounts of assets will be recovered, the extra depreciation in 2008 would generate a liability for future taxes of $1,333 times 35%, or $467.

---

**RECAP**

**Setting tax expense equal to current taxes payable (as in Column [b] of Exhibit 13.5) ignores the future tax liability that results from temporary (timing) differences between book and taxable income, and it results in a mismatching of tax expense with the related revenue and expense items reported on the GAAP income statement.**

## Deferred Income Tax Accounting: Interperiod Tax Allocation

To avoid the drawbacks just illustrated, income tax accounting does not simply equate tax expense with current taxes paid (or payable). Instead, the journal entry for income taxes reflects both taxes currently due as well as any liability for future taxes arising from current period

---

[2] "Accounting for Income Taxes," *Statement of Financial Accounting Standards No. 109* (Norwalk, CT: FASB, 1992), para. 11.

| EXHIBIT 13.6 | Mitchell Corporation |
|---|---|

**Computation of Income Tax Expense with Interperiod Tax Allocation**

| Year | (a) Current Income Tax Payable (Exhibit 13.4, Col. [c]) | (b) Excess (Deficiency) of Tax Depreciation Relative to Book Depreciation (Exhibit 13.3, Col. [c]) | (c) Increase (Decrease) in Deferred Income Tax Liability (Col. [b] × 35%) | (d) Total Income Tax Expense (Col. [a] + Col. [c]) | (e) Cumulative Balance in Deferred Income Tax Payable at Year-End |
|---|---|---|---|---|---|
| 2008 | $ 6,533 | $1,333 | $467 | $ 7,000 | $467 |
| 2009 | 6,767 | 667 | 233 | 7,000 | 700 |
| 2010 | 7,000 | –0– | –0– | 7,000 | 700 |
| 2011 | 7,233 | (667) | (233) | 7,000 | 467 |
| 2012 | 7,467 | (1,333) | (467) | 7,000 | –0– |
|  | $35,000 | –0– | –0– | $35,000 |  |

book-versus-tax temporary differences that will reverse in later periods. The GAAP rules are specified in *SFAS No. 109*.[3] To illustrate them we continue the Mitchell Corporation example in Exhibit 13.6.

Column (c) shows that for 2008, the *change* in the liability for future taxes is an increase of $467 (35% tax rate × $1,333 depreciation timing difference). Income tax currently payable is 35% of tax return income of $18,667, or $6,533. Under *SFAS No. 109*, income tax expense equals the total of the current taxes owed (that is, income taxes payable) and the *change* in the deferred tax liability. The computation is:

| Computation of Income Tax Expense for 2008 | |
|---|---|

1. Current income tax payable (35% × $18,667)                                    $6,533

**plus**

2. *Increase* in liability for future taxes arising during the year ($1,333 × 35%)        467

   **Total income tax expense for 2008 = Sum of steps (1) and (2)**           **$7,000**

The accounting entry for 2008 income taxes is:

| **DR** Income tax expense .......................................... | $7,000 | |
|---|---|---|
| **CR** Income tax payable ..................................... | | $6,533 |
| **CR** Deferred income taxes payable .......................... | | 467 |

In any year Congress changes U.S. tax rates, this matching disappears under *SFAS No. 109*. The reason is that *SFAS No. 109* focuses on the liability for future taxes, which changes as tax rates change.

When tax rates do not change from year to year, this entry simultaneously overcomes both of the drawbacks that would exist if we simply measured tax expense as cash taxes paid—the liability for future taxes is explicitly recognized, and the reported tax expense is exactly 35% of pre-tax book income of $20,000 (that is, $7,000/$20,000 = 35%). Thus, tax expense is also "matched" with book income. (This is true provided no permanent book/tax differences exist. When permanent differences between book and taxable income occur, tax expense will *not* equal the tax rate times the pre-tax book income—a point demonstrated later in the chapter.)

You can readily see what this entry simultaneously accomplishes by carefully analyzing how each debit and credit is computed:

---

[3] Ibid.

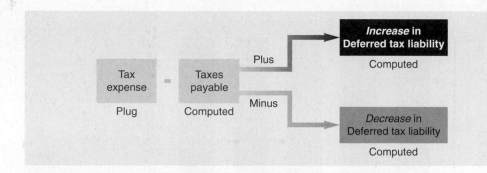

**Figure 13.3**

RELATION BETWEEN TAX EXPENSE, TAXES PAYABLE, AND CHANGES IN DEFERRED TAX LIABILITIES

| | | |
|---|---|---|
| **DR** | Income tax expense (plug figure) ............................... | $7,000 |
| | **CR**    Income tax payable ...................................... |        $6,533 |
| |         (35% times taxable income per tax return of $18,667) | |
| | **CR**    Deferred income taxes payable ........................... |        467 |
| |         (35% times the "excess" depreciation temporary difference of $1,333 in 2008—Exhibit 13.6 Column [b]) | |

As illustrated here, the debit to income tax expense is a "plug" number that represents the combination of current taxes payable and any *change* in the deferred tax liability balance that arises from timing differences during the year. When the deferred income tax liability increases, the increase is *added* to current income tax payable to arrive at income tax expense. When the deferred income tax liability decreases, the decrease is *subtracted* from current income tax payable to determine income tax expense. Figure 13.3 summarizes these important relationships.

The 2008 accounting entry we have just described records an originating book/tax timing difference for depreciation expense that results in an increase in the liability for future (deferred) taxes. A similar entry would be made in 2009. Tax expense in that year would be $7,000, or the current tax payable amount ($6,767) plus the increase in the deferred tax liability ($233) shown in Exhibit 13.6.

To see what happens when book-versus-tax temporary differences reverse, let's consider the income tax entry in 2011. From Figure 13.3, the formula for computing income tax expense is as follows.

1. Current income tax payable

     **minus**

2. *Decrease* in liability for future taxes arising during the year
   = Income tax expense

Because book depreciation exceeds tax depreciation in 2011 by $667, the liability for future taxes *decreases* by $667 times 35%, or $233. Therefore, tax expense for 2011 is:

> Sometimes the originating book/tax timing differences generate deferred income tax *assets*. This asset (future benefit) arises because taxable income will be lower than book income in future periods when those differences reverse. In such circumstances, the debit to income tax expense represents the sum of current taxes payable *plus* the decrease (*minus* the increase) in the deferred tax *asset* account for the period. This is discussed more fully on pages 748–750.

## Computation of Income Tax Expense for 2011

| | | |
|---|---|---|
| 1. | Current income tax payable: | |
| |     $20,667 × 35% | $7,233 |
| |             **minus** | |
| 2. | *Decrease* in liability for future taxes: | |
| |     $667 × 35% | (233) |
| | **Total income tax expense for 2011** | **$7,000** |

## Figure 13.4

MITCHELL CORPORATION

Tax Expense *with* Interperiod
Tax Allocation

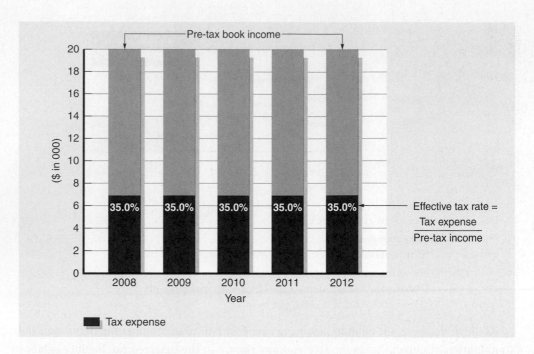

The journal entry for 2011 taxes is:

| | | | |
|---|---|---|---|
| **DR** | Income tax expense | $7,000 | |
| **DR** | Deferred income taxes payable | 233 | |
| | **CR**   Income tax payable | | $7,233 |

Mitchell Corporation's computation of income tax expense for each year using interperiod tax allocation is illustrated Exhibit 13.6. Notice that in 2008 and 2009, the deferred tax liability *increases* and these increases are *added* to taxes payable to arrive at the tax expense reported on the income statement for those years. In 2011 and 2012, the depreciation timing differences reverse, resulting in *decreases* in the deferred tax liability (because the additional taxes are now being paid), and these decreases are *subtracted* from taxes payable to arrive at tax expense for those years. By the end of 2012, the depreciation book-versus-tax timing differences have totally reversed, and the balance in deferred income tax payable is zero. With constant tax rates of 35% over the entire period, income tax expense (Column [d] in Exhibit 13.6) is always 35% times pre-tax book income of $20,000, and the pattern of tax expense matches the pattern of pre-tax book income.

**With interperiod tax allocation, tax expense equals current taxes payable to the IRS plus the increase (minus the decrease) in deferred tax liabilities. This results in a GAAP tax expense number that is matched with the revenue and expense amounts that are recognized for book purposes as shown in Figure 13.4.**

*SFAS No. 109* calls temporary differences that result in deferred tax liabilities **future taxable amounts** because future tax return income will be higher than future book income. Temporary differences that result in deferred tax assets are called **future deductible amounts** because future tax return income—all other factors being equal—will be lower than future book income.

## Deferred Income Tax Assets

The Mitchell Corporation example illustrates a situation in which pre-tax book income initially exceeds taxable income, creating a deferred income tax liability. Because this temporary difference later reverses, the liability ultimately is eliminated. But temporary differences can go in the opposite direction as well. In certain circumstances, taxable income can initially exceed pre-tax book income, thereby giving rise to deferred income tax assets.

| EXHIBIT 13.7 | Paul Corporation |
| --- | --- |

**Book versus Tax Timing Differences That Give Rise to a Deferred Tax Asset**

| | | 2008 Lease Receipt of $100,000 | | |
| --- | --- | --- | --- | --- |
| | Book Income | Included in Book Income? | Included in Tax Return Income? | Tax Return Income |
| 2008 | $1,500,000 | No | Yes | $1,600,000 |
| 2009 | 1,500,000 | Yes | No | 1,400,000 |

To illustrate how a deferred income tax asset comes about, let's assume that in December 2008 Paul Corporation owns an office building that it leases to another company for $100,000. The lease covers all of 2009 and specifies that the tenant pay the $100,000 to Paul Corporation immediately on signing the lease in 2008. On an accrual basis, rental income will be earned only in 2009. Accordingly, Paul Corporation makes the following entry on receiving the cash:

| **DR** Cash | $100,000 | |
| --- | --- | --- |
| **CR** Rent received in advance | | $100,000 |

The account Rent received in advance is a liability account. For GAAP reporting purposes this amount will be reduced monthly by $8,333 (with an offsetting credit to a revenue account) in 2009 as Paul provides the tenant with the use of the facility and earns the lease revenue. For tax purposes, the entire $100,000 rent prepayment is included in Paul Corporation's taxable income in 2008 when it is received (consistent with the "constructive receipt/ability to pay" doctrine).

Assume that the lease receipt represents the only book/tax temporary difference for Paul and that 2008 pre-tax book income totals $1,500,000. Taxable income on the tax return will accordingly total $1,600,000 in 2008—$1,500,000 plus the immediately taxable advance rental payment of $100,000. In 2009, the $100,000 lease payment received in 2008 will be "earned" for book purposes and will be included in book income. However, because this amount was already included in 2008 taxable income, it will *not* be included in Paul's 2009 taxable income. The temporary difference that originated in 2008 reverses in 2009. If book income is once again $1,500,000 in 2009, it will exceed taxable income by $100,000 due to the temporary difference reversal. Taxable income will therefore be $1,400,000 in 2009. These relationships are summarized in Exhibit 13.7.

When the rent is earned in 2009 for book purposes, accounting income will exceed taxable income by $100,000—but no tax will be due on this difference because the tax has already been paid in 2008. Thus, the temporary difference ($100,000) that originates in 2008 because of book/tax differences in lease revenue represents a deferred income tax asset at the end of 2008. If we assume that the income tax rate is 35%, 2008 tax expense is composed of the current taxes payable *minus* the deferred tax asset increase computed as follows:

## Computation of Income Tax Expense for 2008

1. Current income tax payable
   (Taxable income × 35% = $1,600,000 × 35%)       $560,000

   **minus**

2. *Increase* in deferred tax asset ($100,000 × 35%)       (35,000)

   **Total income tax expense for 2008**       **$525,000**

| EXHIBIT 13.8 | Paul Corporation |
| --- | --- |

**Computation of Tax Expense *with* Interperiod Tax Allocation**

| Year | (a) Taxable Income per Tax Return | (b) Book Income | (c) Excess (Deficiency) of Tax Lease Revenue over Book Lease Revenue | (d) Taxes Payable (35% of Col. [a]) | (e) Increase (Decrease) in Deferred Tax Asset (Col. [c] × 35%) | (f) Total Income Tax Expense (Col. [d] − Col. [e]) |
| --- | --- | --- | --- | --- | --- | --- |
| 2008 | $1,600,000 | $1,500,000 | $100,000 | $560,000 | $35,000 | $525,000 |
| 2009 | 1,400,000 | 1,500,000 | (100,000) | 490,000 | (35,000) | 525,000 |

Paul Corporation makes the following 2008 entry for income taxes:

| DR | Income tax expense | $525,000 | |
| --- | --- | --- | --- |
| DR | Deferred income tax asset | 35,000 | |
| | CR   Income tax payable | | $560,000 |

> Notice that income tax expense in both 2008 and 2009 is 35% of each year's book income (that is, $525,000/ $1,500,000). Thus, income tax expense is properly matched with pre-tax income.

Book income is $1,500,000 in 2009 after including the $100,000 of rent revenue *earned* that year. If we again assume that no other book/tax temporary differences exist, then taxable income will be $1,400,000, because the $100,000 advance rental receipt was included in taxable income in 2008— the previous year—when the rent was *collected*. The $100,000 temporary difference in lease revenue that originated in 2008 reverses in 2009. The related deferred tax asset of $35,000 created in 2008 (Column [e]) is eliminated in 2009. As shown in Column (f), the $35,000 decrease in deferred tax assets is added to the taxes payable of $490,000 to arrive at the tax expense amount of $525,000. Paul makes the following income tax expense entry in 2009 when the timing difference reverses:

| DR | Income tax expense | $525,000 | |
| --- | --- | --- | --- |
| | CR   Deferred income tax asset | | $ 35,000 |
| | CR   Income tax payable | | 490,000 |

Exhibit 13.8 illustrates the tax expense computations for 2008 and 2009. Figure 13.5 depicts the relationships for computing *SFAS No. 109* income tax expense by adjusting taxes payable for changes in deferred income tax assets and liabilities.[4]

## Deferred Income Tax Asset Valuation Allowances

> Later in this chapter, you'll see that the U.S. Income Tax Code allows unprofitable companies to recapture previously paid taxes. We temporarily ignore this provision in the tax code to sharpen your understanding of the possibility that deferred income tax assets may not generate future benefits.

If Paul Corporation experienced adversity in 2009 and had no taxable income in that year, the $35,000 deferred income tax asset would generate no benefit—that is, if 2009 taxes were zero, the "benefits" arising from the $35,000 tax payment on the 2008 advance rental receipt would be lost. It is always possible that a firm that has recognized deferred income tax assets may not receive tax payment reductions in future years. For this reason, the FASB requires firms to assess the likelihood that deferred income tax assets may not be fully realized in future periods.

The realization of tax benefits from existing deferred income tax assets depends on whether the firm has future taxable income. If management believes that the probability of future taxable income being sufficient to fully realize the deferred tax asset is more than 50%, deferred income tax assets can be recognized in their entirety. However, if management's assessment indicates that *it is more likely than not* that some portion of the benefit will *not* be realized in

---

[4] Later in the chapter, we describe how changes in a tax contingency reserve for uncertain tax positions also affect the determination of tax expense reported on a firm's income statement.

**Figure 13.5**

RELATION BETWEEN TAX
EXPENSE, TAXES PAYABLE,
AND CHANGES IN
DEFERRED TAX ASSETS
AND LIABILITIES

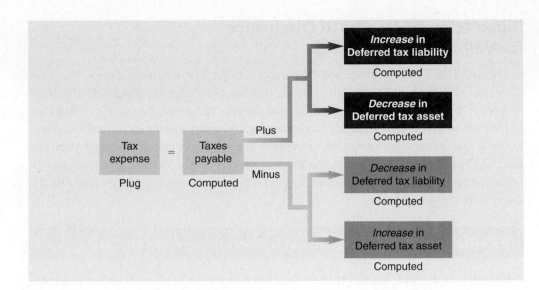

its entirely, a **deferred tax asset valuation allowance** is required. The FASB states that this valuation allowance *"should be sufficient to reduce the deferred tax asset to the amount that is more likely than not to be realized."*[5]

To illustrate the procedure for establishing a deferred tax asset valuation allowance, let's assume that (1) for book purposes, Norman Corporation accrued $900,000 of estimated warranty expenses associated with product sales in 2008 and (2) the actual warranty parts and services from these sales are provided in 2009 and beyond. Because the U.S. Income Tax Code allows companies to deduct warranty expense only when the warranty services are provided, this timing difference gives rise to a deferred tax asset of $315,000 (35% tax rate × $900,000 timing difference) that would be recorded in 2008. If we assume that Norman's pre-tax book income is $600,000, taxable income is $1,500,000, and the 2008 tax expense entry is:

| | | | |
|---|---|---|---|
| **DR** | Income tax expense (plug) .................................. | $210,000 | |
| **DR** | Deferred income tax asset ($900,000 × 0.35) ................. | 315,000 | |
| | **CR**   Income tax payable ($1,500,000 × 0.35) ................. | | $525,000 |

Now assume that early in 2009, Norman Corporation determines that it is unlikely to earn enough taxable income in future years to realize more than $200,000 of the deferred tax asset. The entry made in 2009 is:

| | | | |
|---|---|---|---|
| **DR** | Income tax expense ($315,000 − $200,000) ................... | $115,000 | |
| | **CR**   Allowance to reduce deferred tax | | |
| | asset to expected realizable value ....................... | | $115,000 |

The credit to the allowance account reduces the net carrying amount of the deferred tax asset from $315,000 to $200,000—its estimated realizable value. This occurs because the allowance account is shown on the balance sheet as a contra-account to the deferred tax asset. Notice that income tax expense is increased in the year during which it is determined that a portion of the income tax asset is unlikely to be recovered. If Norman Corporation's future prospects improve and if in 2010 it is determined that an allowance account is no longer needed, the allowance account is reduced to zero and a *credit* to Income tax expense is made.

---

[5] SFAS No. 109, para. 17. Operationally, "more likely than not" means the probability of occurrence is more than 50%.

## Illustration of Footnote Disclosure for Valuation Allowances

See Exhibit 13.9 for an excerpt from the tax footnote for International Business Machines (IBM) 2005 10-K report. The 2005 deferred tax asset valuation allowance (highlighted) is $562 million, or 4.6% of the total recognized deferred tax asset. As noted, the valuation allowance relates primarily to foreign, state, and local operating loss carryforwards and capital loss carryforwards that, in management's opinion, are more likely than not to expire unutilized. Notice that this disclosure provides information about IBM's expected profitability in certain foreign tax jurisdictions. Consequently, analysts may use it to refine estimates of IBM's future profitability from foreign operations.

| EXHIBIT 13.9 | International Business Machines (IBM) Corporation |
| --- | --- |

**Excerpt from 2005 Tax Footnote Valuation Allowance on Deferred Tax Assets**

The significant components of deferred tax assets and liabilities that are recorded in the consolidated statement of financial position were as follows:

| | At December 31 | |
| --- | --- | --- |
| ($ in millions) | 2005 | 2004 |
| **Deferred tax assets:** | | |
| Retirement-related benefits | $ 3,039 | $ 3,908 |
| Stock-based and other compensation | 3,022 | 3,122 |
| Capitalized research and development | 1,728 | 1,794 |
| Bad debt, inventory and warranty reserves | 937 | 1,050 |
| Deferred income | 611 | 612 |
| Foreign tax loss carryforwards | 355 | 298 |
| Infrastructure reduction charges | 335 | 333 |
| Capital loss carryforwards | 220 | 220 |
| Alternative minimum tax credits | 214 | 1,032 |
| State and local tax loss carryforwards | 87 | 95 |
| Other | 1,649 | 2,265 |
| Gross deferred tax assets | 12,197 | 14,729 |
| Less: valuation allowance | 562 | 603 |
| Net deferred tax assets | $11,635 | $14,126 |
| **Deferred tax liabilities:** | | |
| Retirement-related benefits | $ 7,267 | $ 7,057 |
| Leases | 964 | 622 |
| Software development costs | 348 | 381 |
| Other | 1,502 | 1,324 |
| Gross deferred tax liabilities | $10,081 | $ 9,384 |

**Notes to Consolidated Financial Statements**

The valuation allowance at December 31, 2005, principally applies to certain foreign, state and local, and capital loss carryforwards that, in the opinion of management, are more likely than not to expire unutilized. However, to the extent that tax benefits related to these carryforwards are realized in the future, the reduction in the valuation allowance will reduce income tax expense.

For income tax return purposes, the company has foreign, state and local, and capital loss carryforwards, the tax effect of which is $662 million. Substantially all of these carryforwards are available for at least three years or have an indefinite carryforward period. The company also has available alternative minimum tax credit carryforwards of approximately $214 million which have an indefinite carryforward period.

See pp. 756–758 for a discussion of operating loss carryforwards.

The decisions to establish a deferred tax asset valuation allowance and, if so, what amount to record are subjective assessments. Readily observable criteria do not exist, so the potential for abuse is clear. Reported earnings are decreased when the valuation allowance is first established, and decreased again if management later decides to increase the allowance. But suppose management decides to shrink the valuation allowance. In this case, reported earnings will increase. The inherent subjectivity of the valuation allowance means that it can be used to "smooth" year-to year earnings fluctuations. For example, management might decide to establish an allowance account in a "good" earnings year when the offsetting charge to earnings is relatively small. Once the allowance is established, it can be diminished or even eliminated in subsequent "bad" earnings years. Doing so decreases tax expense, thereby partially offsetting the lower earnings. The result is that income fluctuations are smoothed across years.

Two recent studies investigate whether managers use the deferred tax asset valuation allowance to manage earnings. One study finds that bank managers appear to use the valuation allowance to manage earnings toward consensus analysts' forecasts and toward average historical earnings.[6] Another study using a broader sample of manufacturing firms finds that managers use the valuation allowance to manage earnings up (down) when analysts' earnings forecasts are above (below) the premanaged earnings number.[7] Taken together, these two studies provide compelling evidence that managers take advantage of the discretion associated with setting the deferred tax asset valuation allowance to manage earnings in both a positive and a negative direction.

**When circumstances indicate that it is "more likely than not" that some portion of the future tax benefit from a deferred tax asset will not be realized, a deferred tax asset valuation allowance must be established to reduce the deferred tax asset book value to the amount expected to be realized. Because the determination of "more likely than not" is subjective, the valuation account can be used to manage earnings up or down.**

## Deferred Income Tax Accounting When Tax Rates Change

Congress periodically changes tax rates. When this happens, the tax effects of the reversals change as well. To measure deferred income taxes, *SFAS No. 109* adopts the so-called **liability approach**: *in any year current or future tax rates are changed, the income tax expense number absorbs the full effect of the change, and the relationship between that year's tax expense and book income is destroyed.*

Returning to the Mitchell Corporation example in Exhibit 13.6, let's assume that on December 31, 2010, a new income tax law raises the income tax rate from 35% to 38% beginning January 1, 2011. Just prior to the tax law change on December 31, 2010, the amount of deferred income tax payable for Mitchell was $700 (Column [e] of Exhibit 13.6). That number represents the cumulative excess of tax over book depreciation in 2008 and 2009 (the dollar amount of temporary depreciation differences = $1,333 + $667, or $2,000) times the initial tax rate of 35%. But because future tax rates have now increased, the liability for future taxes

[6] C. Schrand and F. Wong, "Earnings Management Using the Valuation Allowance for Deferred Tax Assets under *SFAS No. 109*," *Contemporary Accounting Research*, Fall 2003, pp. 579–611.

[7] S. Rego and M. Frank, "Do Managers Use the Valuation Allowance Account to Manage Earnings around Certain Earnings Targets?" Working Paper, University of Iowa, July 2003.

is actually more than the $700 amount currently reported. At the new, higher income tax rate that will be in effect in 2011 and 2012, the liability for future taxes becomes $760, not $700. This future liability represents the cumulative excess of tax over book depreciation ($2,000) multiplied by the new 38% tax rate that will be in effect beginning January 1, 2011.

*Under the liability approach of* **SFAS No. 109,** *the full change in the amount of future liability for income taxes (in this case, $60) is recognized as an increase or decrease in income tax expense in the year that the tax rate change becomes known.* Accordingly, income tax expense for 2010 is computed as:

1. Current 2010 income tax payable (35% × $20,000 [see Exhibit 13.4])         $7,000

plus

2. *Increase* in the liability for future taxes arising during 2010
   ($1,333 + $667) × (0.38 − 0.35)                                              60

   **Total income tax expense for 2010**                                      **$7,060**

The accounting entry for 2010 income taxes is:

| | | | |
|---|---|---|---|
| **DR** | Income tax expense | $7,060 | |
| | **CR** Income tax payable | | $7,000 |
| | **CR** Deferred income taxes payable | | 60 |

After this entry is made, the balance in Deferred income taxes payable will total $760, which is the liability for future taxes at the new 38% rate. Also, because tax rates for future years were changed in 2010 the debit to Income tax expense does not equal the $20,000 pre-tax book income times the 2010 tax rate of 35%.

Exhibit 13.10 shows the revised computation of income tax expense and deferred taxes payable for Mitchell Corporation for 2010 through 2012 after reflecting the income tax rate increase. The journal entry for income taxes in 2011 is:

| | | | |
|---|---|---|---|
| **DR** | Income tax expense | $7,600 | |
| **DR** | Deferred income tax payable | 253 | |
| | **CR** Income tax payable | | $7,853 |

---

**EXHIBIT 13.10**   **Mitchell Corporation**

**Revised Computation of Income Tax Expense**

| Year | (a) Taxable Income (Exhibit 13.4, Col. [b]) | (b) Current Income Tax Payable = 38% of Col. (a) | (c) Difference between Tax and Book Depreciation (Exhibit 13.3, Col. [c]) | (d) Increase (Decrease) in Liability for Future Taxes = Col. (c) × 38% | (e) Total Income Tax Expense = Col. (b) + Col. (d) | (f) Cumulative Balance in Deferred Income Tax Payable at Year-End |
|---|---|---|---|---|---|---|
| 2010 | $20,000 | $7,000* | — | $ 60† | $7,060 | $760 |
| 2011 | 20,667 | 7,853 | $ (667) | (253) | 7,600 | 507 |
| 2012 | 21,333 | 8,107 | (1,333) | (507) | 7,600 | −0− |

---

* Tax rate is still 35% in 2010 so this is $20,000 × 35%.

† This is the increase that arose in 2010 when the rate went from 35% to 38% (that is, 3% × $2,000 cumulative depreciation differences in Column [b] of Exhibit 13.6).

Similarly, the 2012 entry is:

| | | |
|---|---|---|
| **DR** | Income tax expense . . . . . . . . . . . . . . . . . . . . . . . . . . . . . . . . . . . . . . . . . . | $7,600 |
| **DR** | Deferred income tax payable . . . . . . . . . . . . . . . . . . . . . . . . . . . . . | 507 |
| **CR** | Income tax payable . . . . . . . . . . . . . . . . . . . . . . . . . . . . . . . . . . | $8,107 |

As shown in Column (f) of Exhibit 13.10, the balance in the Deferred income tax payable account will be zero after the year 2012 entry is made.

Because of the oblique way accounting rules recognize the effects of tax rate changes—through an adjustment to the tax expense number—analysts must be alert to recognize how these tax changes can inject one-shot (transitory) adjustments to earnings in the year Congress passes the new tax rates. Moreover, it is important to recognize that the effect of a tax rate change on bottom-line earnings can vary considerably across companies depending on three factors:

> A change in tax rates of this magnitude is not that uncommon. For example, the 1986 Tax Reform Act lowered the marginal corporate tax rate for large firms from 46% to 34%.

1. Whether the tax rates are increased or decreased.
2. Whether the firm has net deferred tax assets or net deferred tax liabilities.
3. The magnitude of the deferred tax balance.

Consider how differently a tax rate change can affect firms' bottom-line earnings: Suppose Congress passes a new tax law in 2008 that raises the marginal statutory corporate tax rate from 35% to 45% effective in 2010. Also assume that Companies A, B, and C have the following net deferred tax asset (liability) balances on their books when the new tax law is passed:

| ($ in millions) | Company A | Company B | Company C |
|---|---|---|---|
| Net deferred tax asset (liability) balance in year 2008 | $100 | $0 | ($100) |

The effect of the change in tax rate on the after-tax earnings of these three companies in 2008—the year the new tax rate is passed—is shown in Exhibit 13.11. We first divide the net deferred tax asset (liability) balance by the old marginal tax rate to get the dollar magnitude of the timing differences that gave rise to these account balances. Recall that the deferred tax asset (liability) account balances equal the cumulative dollar amount of the timing differences giving rise to future deductible (taxable) amounts times the marginal corporate tax rate when those timing differences originated. Therefore, to derive the dollar amount of

| **EXHIBIT 13.11** | **Computation of How Change in Tax Rate Affects Earnings in Year That Rate Change Is Passed** | | |
|---|---|---|---|
| ($ in millions) | Company A | Company B | Company C |
| Net deferred tax asset (liability) balance in 2008 | $ 100 | $ 0 | $ (100) |
| Divide by old marginal tax rate | ÷35% | ÷35% | ÷35% |
| Dollar amount of timing difference | $285.710 ← Future deductible amount | $ 0 | $(285.710) ← Future taxable amount |
| Multiply by difference between old and new tax rates (45% − 35%) | ×10% | ×10% | ×10% |
| Increase (decrease) to after-tax earnings in year of rate change | $ 28.571 | $ 0 | $ (28.571) |

the timing differences, we simply divide the deferred tax asset or liability balance by the relevant tax rate.

In Exhibit 13.11, Company A has $285.71 ($100/0.35) million of future *deductible* amounts, Company C has $285.71 of future *taxable* amounts, and Company B has neither future deductible nor taxable amounts. These timing differences are then multiplied by the *difference* between the new tax rate and the old tax rate (that is, 10%) to obtain the increase in the deferred tax asset (liability) balance and the corresponding increase (decrease) in reported after-tax earnings.

As shown, Company A's 2008 earnings will *increase* by $28.571 million. This is because each dollar of future deductible amounts will yield an additional $0.10 in tax savings under the newly enacted tax rates (that is, when these timing differences reverse). Company C, on the other hand, will report a $28.571 million *decrease* to its after-tax earnings number because each dollar of future taxable amounts will generate $0.10 of additional taxes as these timing differences reverse in future years (when the tax rates will be higher). Company B's 2008 after-tax earnings are unaffected by the tax rate change because no temporary differences exist.

If the tax rates had been reduced from 35% to 25%, the earnings impacts reported for Companies A and C would be reversed. As this example demonstrates, tax rate changes can have very different effects on firms' reported earnings depending on their deferred tax status and the direction of the tax rate change.

## RECAP

**Under *SFAS No. 109*, when tax rates change, the additional tax benefits or costs are recognized as an adjustment to tax expense in the year that the tax rate changes are *passed*, not when they *become effective*. These one-shot earnings effects are often difficult to detect because they are reported as part of the tax expense line on the income statement. However, a careful reading of the tax footnote that reconciles the book-effective tax rate with the marginal statutory tax rate (described in greater detail later in this chapter) can reveal the magnitude of earnings increases or decreases due to tax rate changes.**

## Net Operating Losses: Carrybacks and Carryforwards

Because firms pay taxes during profitable years, denying them some form of tax relief in unprofitable years would be inequitable. That is why the U.S. Income Tax Code provides an opportunity for firms reporting operating losses to offset those losses against either past or future tax payments. When deductible expenses exceed taxable revenues and an operating loss occurs, firms can elect one of two options described in the following sections:

1. *Both* carry back and carry forward the incurred loss.
2. *Only* carry forward the incurred loss.

> Prior to 1998, the loss carryback period was 3 years and the carryforward period was 15 years.

**Carryback and Carryforward**    Assume that Unfortunato Corporation experienced a $1,000,000 pre-tax operating loss in 2008. Under the U.S. Income Tax Code, Unfortunato can elect to carry back the operating loss and offset it against taxable income in the previous two years, 2006 and 2007. The loss must be offset against the earliest year first—in this case, 2006. If the loss exceeds the total taxable income for the 2006–2007 period, the remaining portion of the loss can be carried forward and offset against *future* taxable income in the ensuing 20 years—2009 through 2028—as shown in Figure 13.6, Panel (a).

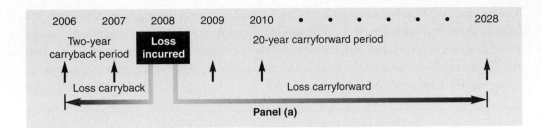

**Panel (a)**

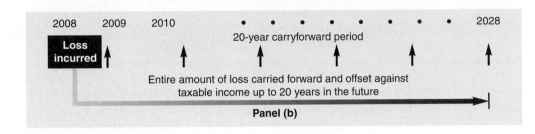

**Panel (b)**

**Figure 13.6**

UNFORTUNATO
CORPORATION

Panel (a): Illustration of Tax
Loss Carryback/Carryforward
Provision

Panel (b): Illustration of Tax
Loss Carryforward

**Carryforward Only**   Another option is available to Unfortunato Corporation. Rather than first carrying the loss back and then carrying forward any unused amounts, Unfortunato could elect *only* to carry the loss forward to reduce taxable profits in the next 20 years (see Figure 13.6, Panel [b]). ————————————————

To illustrate how the two options work, let's assume that the tax rate in effect from 2005 to 2008 was 35% and that Unfortunato had the following operating profits in those years:

> Why would firms elect the carryforward-only option, thereby forgoing an immediate income tax refund? Most companies *do* elect to carryback first because this strategy usually maximizes the discounted present value of the benefit. In unusual situations—for example, a firm expects to be profitable in the future and expects future tax rates to be much higher than past rates—the carryforward-only option may be preferred.

| Year | Taxable Profit (Loss) | Tax (at 35%) |
|---|---|---|
| 2005 | $ 300,000 | $105,000 |
| 2006 | 400,000 | 140,000 |
| 2007 | 350,000 | 122,500 |
| 2008 | (1,000,000) | — |

If Unfortunato Corporation elects to use the combined carryback/carryforward option, 2008 losses must first be offset against 2006 income ($400,000), the earliest year in the two-year carryback period, and then against 2007 income ($350,000). This uses $750,000 of the 2008 loss and generates a tax refund of $262,500 ($750,000 × 35%). Unfortunato makes the following entry in 2008 to reflect the refund due:

| | | |
|---|---|---|
| **DR** Income tax refund receivable | $262,500 | |
| **CR** Income tax expense (*carryback* benefit) | | $262,500 |

The unused loss ($1,000,000 − $400,000 − $350,000 = $250,000) will result in future tax benefits—if Unfortunato becomes profitable again before 2028. If we assume that future tax rates remained at 35%, these potential future benefits would total $87,500 ($250,000 × 35%). If Unfortunato expects that pre-tax income in the ensuing 20 years will exceed $250,000, an additional entry would be made in 2008:

| | | |
|---|---|---|
| **DR** Deferred income tax asset | $87,500 | |
| **CR** Income tax expense (*carryforward* benefit) | | $87,500 |

The Income tax refund receivable asset account would be shown among current assets on the balance sheet, and the deferred tax asset would be apportioned between current and noncurrent categories in accordance with the expected timing of the future income. If we assume that the pre-tax book loss equaled the taxable loss, the credits would be reflected on the accompanying income statement for 2006 as:

| | |
|---|---|
| Pre-tax operating loss | $(1,000,000) |
| Income tax benefit due to operating loss *carryback* | 262,500 |
| Income tax benefit due to operating loss *carryforward* | 87,500 |
| After-tax operating loss | $  (650,000) |

Deferred income tax assets that result from operating loss carryforwards will generate future benefits only if the firm earns profits in the ensuing 20 years. Because future profits are never assured, the probability of realizing deferred income tax assets arising from operating loss carryforwards must be carefully evaluated. The criterion here for deciding whether a valuation allowance is needed is identical to the criterion applied to deferred tax assets arising from book-versus-tax timing differences—if ***it is more likely than not*** that the benefit will not be realized in its entirety, a valuation allowance is required. This allowance should reduce the asset to a net amount that is more likely than not to be realized.

**RECAP**

**U.S. tax rules allow firms to offset operating losses against taxable income. Firms can elect to carry back losses up to two years with any unused loss carried forward up to 20 years; or they can elect only to carry forward the loss up to 20 years. The tax benefit associated with the loss carryback or carryforward is recorded as an adjustment to tax expense in the year of the loss.**

## USING FOOTNOTE DISCLOSURES TO IMPROVE FINANCIAL ANALYSIS
### Understanding Footnote Disclosures

Typical income tax footnote disclosures provide financial statement users a wealth of data. If you understand these disclosures, you'll be able to extract useful insights about a firm's performance and prospects. To illustrate, let's look at the income tax footnote from the 2006 annual report of Merck & Co., Inc., shown in Exhibit 13.12 on the next two pages. To make the discussion easier to follow, we have subdivided the footnote into Panels (a) through (d) and numbered key lines or sections in these panels.

Merck's tax expense provision is described in Panel (a) of Exhibit 13.12. Notice how Merck differentiates between the portion of tax expense that is currently payable (denoted Item ①) and the portion that is deferred taxes (Item ②). Within each category, separate amounts for U.S. federal, foreign, and state taxes are disclosed. In the aggregate, the 2006 entry for taxes ($ in millions) was:

| | | |
|---|---|---|
| **DR** Income tax expense (Item ③) .............................. | $1,787.6 | |
| **DR** Deferred tax liability or asset (Item ②) ...................... | 530.2 | |
| **CR** Income tax currently payable (Item ①) ................. | | $2,317.8 |

| **EXHIBIT 13.12** | Merck & Co., Inc. 2006 Annual Report Footnote on Income Taxes |
|---|---|

### Panel (a)

Taxes on income consist of:

| | | **Years Ended December 31** | |
|---|---|---|---|
| ($ in millions) | **2006** | **2005** | **2004** |
| **Current Provision** | | | |
| Federal | $1,618.4 | $1,688.1 | $1,429.1 |
| Foreign          ① | 458.3 | 739.6 | 530.9 |
| State | 241.1 | 295.9 | 163.8 |
| | 2,317.8 | 2,723.6 | 2,123.8 |
| **Deferred Provision** | | | |
| Federal | (374.1) | 97.0 | 95.6 |
| Foreign          ② | (130.3) | (134.0) | (32.3) |
| State | (25.8) | 46.0 | (14.4) |
| | (530.2) | 9.0 | 48.9 |
| [Current period tax provision*]  ◄——③——►$1,787.6 | | $2,732.6 | $2,172.7 |

### Panel (b)

A reconciliation between the Company's effective tax rate and the U.S. statutory rate is as follows:

| | **2006 Amount** | | **Tax Rate** | |
|---|---|---|---|---|
| | | **2006** | **2005** | **2004** |
| U.S. statutory rate applied to pre-tax income | $2,177.5 | 35.0% | 35.0% | 35.0% |
| Differential arising from | | | | |
| Foreign earnings | (1,024.1) | (16.5) | (12.8) | (10.0) |
| Tax exemption for Puerto Rico operations | (87.6) | (1.4) | (1.3) | (1.6) |
| Acquired research          ④ | 266.9 | 4.3      ⑤ | — | 0.5 |
| State taxes | 129.6 | 2.1 | 2.5 | 1.3 |
| AJCA | — | — | 10.4 | — |
| Other | 325.3 | 5.2 | 3.3 | 1.9 |
| [Reported tax expense*] | $1,787.6 | 28.7%† | 37.1% | 27.1% |

### Panel (c)

Deferred income taxes at December 31 consisted of:

| | **2006** | | **2005** | |
|---|---|---|---|---|
| | **Assets** | **Liabilities** | **Assets** | **Liabilities** |
| Other intangibles | $   27.3 | $   344.1 | $   36.0 | $   158.2 |
| Inventory related | 455.2 | 177.7 | 628.1 | 266.9 |
| Accelerated depreciation | — | 1,262.2 | — | 1,539.1 |
| Advanced payment | 338.6 | — | 338.6 | — |
| Equity investments          ⑥ | 142.4 | 863.8      ⑦ | 104.5 | 676.1 |
| Pensions and OPEB | 281.9 | 188.9 | 151.3 | 789.9 |
| Accrued rebates | 249.1 | — | 151.9 | — |
| Compensation related | 306.8 | — | 241.1 | — |
| Environmental related | 448.4 | — | 314.9 | — |
| Other | 1,404.0 | 269.2 | 1,208.9 | 426.3 |
| Subtotal | 3,653.7 | 3,105.9 | 3,175.3 | 3,856.5 |
| Valuation allowance  ◄——⑧——► (101.8) | | — | (17.6) | — |
| Total deferred taxes | $3,551.9 | $3,105.9 | $3,157.7 | $3,856.5 |
| Net deferred tax assets (liabilities) ◄⑨► $   446.0 | | | | $ (698.8) |

*(continued)*

**EXHIBIT 13.12** Merck & Co., Inc. 2006 Annual Report Footnote on Income Taxes (*continued*)

Panel (d)

| | | | |
|---|---|---|---|
| Recognized as: | | | |
| Prepaid expenses and taxes | | $1,177.7 | $ 662.2 |
| Other assets | ⑩ | 183.7 | 68.5 |
| Income taxes payable | | (62.8) | (159.7) |
| Deferred income taxes and | | (852.6) | (1,269.8) |
| non-current liabilities | | $ 446.0 | $ (698.8) |

\* Description added by authors for clarity.

† Merck's reported pre-tax income was $6,221.4 million, so $1,787.6/$6,221.4 = 28.7%

The $530.2 million debit to deferred taxes arises because of temporary differences in revenue and expense items reported on Merck's 2006 GAAP income statement versus what was reported on its 2006 tax return. In aggregate, these temporary differences caused book income to be less than taxable income in 2006. The result was either a decrease in deferred tax liabilities or an increase in deferred tax assets (both debits).

Exhibit 13.12(b) shows why the debit to tax expense in the 2004–2006 period was different from the U.S. statutory corporate tax rate of 35% times pre-tax book income. For example, the $1,787.6 million debit to tax expense in the previous entry is 28.7% of $6,221.4 million, Merck's reported 2006 pre-tax income. The reconciliation [Item ④ in Exhibit 13.12(b)] explains what caused the divergence between Merck's effective tax rate of 28.7% and the 35% statutory rate (Item ⑤).

The reconciliation in Exhibit 13.12(b) is required under *SFAS 109*.[8] It is potentially useful to analysts because it provides information about the firm's tax policy. Specifically, the divergence between the **statutory tax rate** (the tax rate set forth in federal tax laws) and the **effective tax rate** (measured by book tax expense divided by book pre-tax income) arises from two general sources.

> Exhibit 13.12(b) reveals that Merck saved $87.6 million in taxes for 2006 because it had earnings from Puerto Rico operations that were tax exempt. We can determine the dollar amount of these tax-exempt earnings by dividing the tax savings by the U.S. statutory tax rate ($87.6 million ÷ .35 = $250.3 million).

1. The tax jurisdictions in which the firm chooses to operate.

2. Permanent difference items that are not taxed or are not tax deductible but are included in book income.

One frequent cause for differences between effective and statutory rates is that tax rates differ across countries. For example, certain countries levy extremely low (or no) taxes on income earned within their boundaries to attract investment. Other countries' tax rates may exceed U.S. rates. Furthermore, many U.S. states impose income taxes on income earned within the state, which causes a firm's effective tax rate to exceed the 35% federal statutory rate. One important element of a firm's tax planning strategy is choosing to operate subsidiaries within lower marginal tax rate jurisdictions. This lowers the firm's overall tax burden, thereby increasing after-tax returns to shareholders.[9] Merck apparently did this in 2006.

Another reason for differences between effective and statutory rates is due to special tax law characteristics that treat certain GAAP revenue items as nontaxable and certain GAAP expenses as nondeductible for tax purposes. Remember, book-versus-tax differences that never

---

[8] *SFAS 109,* para. 47.

[9] For an expanded discussion of this point, see M. Scholes, M. Wolfson, M. Erickson, E. Maydew, and T. Shevlin, *Tax and Corporate Financial Strategy: A Global Planning Approach* (Upper Saddle River, NJ: Prentice Hall, 2002).

reverse are referred to as *permanent differences.* Permanent difference items that cause book income to be *higher* but are not taxed (such as interest on municipal bonds) cause the effective tax rate per books to be *lower* than the statutory tax rate. Conversely, permanent differences that cause book income to be *lower* but that are not deductible for tax purposes cause the effective tax rate per books to be *higher* than the statutory rate (examples include fines levied for law violations and most types of goodwill amortization).

The reconciliation between effective and statutory tax rates, such as that shown in Exhibit 13.12(b) (Item ④), can reflect important elements of a firm's tax policy decisions. Effective tax rates that are far lower than statutory tax rates might indicate aggressive tax postures. This could benefit shareholders. But aggressive tax positions might also generate future tax audits and additional tax assessments.[10]

> In the next section, we consider disclosures required under *FASB Interpretation No. 48 (FIN48)* on uncertain tax positions taken by companies for which the taxing authorities may disallow a deduction (or income exclusion) in whole or in part.

Items ⑥ and ⑦ of Exhibit 13.12(c) show year-end balances in deferred tax asset and deferred tax liability accounts and the source of those amounts. After deducting the valuation allowance of $101.8 million on deferred tax assets (Item ⑧), Merck had a *net* deferred tax asset balance at December 31, 2006 of $446.0 million (Item ⑨), or $3,551.9 million of deferred tax assets minus $3,105.9 million of deferred tax liabilities. One year earlier, Merck had a *net* deferred tax liability balance (after allowance) of $698.8 million. Thus, the year-to-year change in *net* deferred tax liabilities was a decrease of $698.8 + $446.0 = $1,144.8 million.

Notice that the $1,144.8 million decrease in Merck's net deferred tax liabilities in Exhibit 13.12(c) does *not* equal the $530.2 million journal entry debit to deferred taxes shown on p. 758. The $614.6 million difference is partially explained by reference to **intraperiod income tax allocation,** discussed briefly in Chapter 2. Recall that all income statement items shown below Income from continuing operations and direct charges or credits to stockholders' equity *are shown net of any related income tax effects.* Accordingly, tax effects (including deferred tax effects) that arise from discontinued operations, extraordinary items, direct charges or credits to stockholders' equity for prior period adjustments, or other comprehensive income items are not included in Merck's tax journal entry on page 758. This journal entry is limited to income tax effects that relate to income from continuing operations.

> This amount is determined in two steps. First, we divide the after-tax amount of $16.6 million by 1 minus the statutory tax rate ($16.6/[1 − 0.35] = $25.5 million). This gives the before-tax amount of net other comprehensive income components. Next, we take the difference between the before-tax amount of $25.5 million and the after-tax amount of $16.6 million, which gives the increase in net deferred tax liabilities ($8.9 million) related to other comprehensive income components.

Merck reported no discontinued operations and no extraordinary items in its 2006 income statement. Therefore, these items do not explain any of the $614.6 million difference noted earlier. However, Merck's statement of comprehensive income (not shown) reveals four items in Other comprehensive income—net unrealized losses on derivatives, net unrealized gains on investment securities, minimum pension liability, and cumulative translation adjustment relating to equity investees—shown net of tax effects. The net of these Other comprehensive income components increased Merck's stockholders' equity by $16.6 million. These items, on a net basis, would have *decreased* deferred tax assets (or *increased* deferred tax liabilities) by $8.94 million, which is in the opposite direction of the change in Merck's net deferred tax liabilities on its balance sheet from 2005 to 2006. Because the deferred tax effects of these Other comprehensive income items move in the opposite direction, they do not help to reconcile the $614.6 million difference noted above.

The most likely sources of the $614.6 million difference are various acquisitions and divestitures made during the year, which are discussed elsewhere in Merck's 2006 annual report. When the acquired or divested subsidiary holds assets having a tax basis that differs from their financial accounting basis, changes occur in deferred tax accounts on the consolidated balance sheet. These deferred tax changes are not reflected in the deferred portion of the current period's tax provision. Unfortunately, Merck's disclosures do not allow us to determine this

---

[10] For an analysis of tax footnote disclosures from the perspective of tax aggressiveness and future tax audit risk, see R. Weber and J. Wheeler, "Using Income Tax Disclosures to Explore Significant Economic Transactions," *Accounting Horizons,* September 1992, pp. 14–29.

amount directly. The lesson here is that certain events such as acquisitions or divestitures of subsidiaries can complicate full reconciliation of the deferred tax accounts.

Exhibit 13.12(c) also shows the specific items that collectively comprise the deferred tax asset (Item ⑥) and deferred tax liability (Item ⑦) balances at December 31, 2006. The major items giving rise to deferred tax assets are inventory, advance payments, and environmental related items, while the major items giving rise to deferred tax liabilities are depreciation differences and equity investments. Finally, Exhibit 13.12(d) shows in which specific accounts the net deferred tax asset and liability amounts of $446.0 million are reported on Merck's December 31, 2006 balance sheet (Item ⑩).

# MEASURING AND REPORTING UNCERTAIN TAX POSITIONS[11]

*FASB Interpretation No. 48 (FIN48)*, effective for fiscal years beginning after December 15, 2006, sets forth the measurement and reporting of uncertain tax positions in firms' financial statements.[12] The term **tax position** refers to a position in a previously filed tax return or a position expected to be taken in a future tax return that is reflected in measuring current taxes payable or deferred income tax assets and liabilities for interim or annual periods.[13] Uncertain tax positions arise, for example, when the firm claims a deduction for an expense that the IRS auditors may later disallow. When it comes to complex business transactions, tax rules are often open to interpretation and management's reading of the rules may differ from that of the IRS.

A tax position can result in a permanent reduction of income taxes payable, a deferral of income taxes otherwise currently payable to future years (creating a temporary difference), or a change in the expected realizability of a deferred tax asset.[14] Uncertainty about whether a firm will realize a tax benefit arises because of ambiguity in the tax law that makes it unclear whether a position taken by a firm on its tax return will eventually be sustained upon review by the taxing authority (e.g., IRS). The FASB issued *FIN48* because it observed inconsistency across firms in criteria used to recognize, derecognize, and measure benefits related to uncertain tax positions. Thus, the objective of *FIN48* is to enhance interfirm comparability of the financial reporting of income taxes and to provide more information about the uncertainty in firms' income tax asset and liability positions.[15]

*FIN48* adopts a two-step process to determine how much benefit to recognize from an uncertain tax position and correspondingly how much a firm should report in its tax contingency reserve as a liability for unrecognized tax benefits. Step 1 involves a recognition threshold. A firm must determine whether the uncertain tax position meets the threshold test of "more likely than not" that it will be able to sustain the tax return position based solely on technical merits.[16] The term "more likely than not" means a likelihood of more than 50%.

---

[11] The authors thank Amy Dunbar, John Phillips, and Ryan Wilson for their comments and suggestions on this section.

[12] "Accounting for Uncertainty in Income Taxes—An Interpretation of FASB Statement No. 109," *FASB Interpretation No. 48*, (Norwalk, CT: FASB, 2006).

[13] Ibid., para. 4.

[14] Paragraph 11 of *FIN 48* states: "An enterprise shall derecognize a previously recognized tax position in the first period in which it is no longer more likely than not that the tax position would be sustained upon examination. Use of a valuation allowance is *not* a permitted substitute for derecognizing the benefit of a tax position when the more-likely-than-not recognition threshold is no longer met." [Emphasis added.]

[15] *FIN48*, Summary.

[16] Factors to be considered in assessing the more-likely-than-not criterion include (1) a presumption that the tax position will be examined by the relevant taxing authority that has full knowledge of all relevant information, (2) technical merits of the tax position are to be based on relevant tax law (legislation, statutes, regulations, tax rulings and case law), and (3) each tax position must be evaluated without consideration of the possibility of offset or aggregation with other positions. See *FIN48*, para. 7.

The more-likely-than-not recognition threshold is a positive assertion by management of the belief that the firm is entitled to the economic benefits associated with the tax position (e.g., the firm is entitled to a deduction taken on its tax return).

If the tax benefit meets the recognition threshold, the firm then moves to Step 2 of the process and measures the tax benefit as the largest amount of benefit that is cumulatively greater than 50 percent likely of being realized (explained subsequently). The difference between the tax benefit as shown on the tax return and the tax benefit as determined using the two-step recognition/measurement process is recorded as an increase in the Tax contingency reserve account, sometimes referred to as Liability for unrecognized tax benefits. We illustrate the recognition and measurement of an uncertain tax position with the following example.

## Assessing Uncertain Tax Position Related to a Permanent Difference

> This is an example of a permanent difference uncertain tax position because the tax rules are unclear as to whether this expense will ever be deductible.

Doyle Company reports pre-tax book income of $10,000 that includes a $1,000 expense that is also deducted on its tax return. The tax law is unclear as to whether this expense is deductible now or at any point in the future, so this deduction leads to an uncertain tax position. Management's assessment is that it is 65% likely that the deduction will be sustained based on technical merits. Assuming that Doyle has no other uncertain tax positions and no book-tax temporary differences or permanent differences and a tax rate of 40%, this deduction results in a $400 uncertain tax benefit. The amounts and related individual probabilities of estimated outcomes are as follows:

| Possible Estimated Outcome ($ amount of benefit) | Individual Probability of Estimated Outcomes | Cumulative Probability of Estimated Outcomes |
|---|---|---|
| $400 | 10% | 10% |
| 300 | 30 | 40 |
| 250 | 20 | 60 |
| –0– | 40 | 100 |

Because Doyle's management assesses the likelihood of this uncertain tax position being sustained to be 65%, the more-likely-than-not recognition condition is satisfied. Doyle next moves to the measurement step. The largest amount of benefit that is cumulatively greater than 50 percent likely of being realized is $250 (see shaded items in the preceding table). So, $250 is the benefit that Doyle will recognize in its financial statements in the current period. The difference between the tax benefit recorded on the tax return due to this deduction ($400) and the $250 determined from the two-step process as described represents the amount that Doyle must add to its tax contingency reserve. Accordingly, the entry that Doyle would make to record tax expense, taxes payable, and the tax contingency for the unrecognized tax benefit associated with this uncertain tax position would be as follows:

> Management's assessment of the likelihood of the uncertain tax position being sustained is *not* directly related to the individual or cumulative probabilities in the schedule above.

| DR | Tax expense | $4,150[a] | |
|---|---|---|---|
| | CR  Income taxes payable | | $4,000[b] |
| | CR  Tax contingency reserve | | 150[c] |

[a] $10,000 × 40% + ($400 − $250)

[b] $10,000 × 40%

[c] $400 − $250

It may be difficult for you to immediately see in this entry how $250 of this uncertain tax benefit has been recognized in the current period's financial statements. But, in fact, it is recognized through lower income taxes payable and lower current tax expense. Here's how. You learned earlier in this chapter (see Figure 13.5) that the Tax expense reported on a firm's income statement is set equal to Income taxes payable (based on taxable income per the tax return) plus or minus the change in Deferred tax assets and Deferred tax liabilities. The $1,000 deduction taken on the current period's tax return lowered Doyle's Income taxes payable by $400 and correspondingly lowered current period Tax expense by $400. Notice that when the Tax contingency reserve account (a contingent liability) is credited for $150 in the preceding entry, the offsetting debit is to Tax expense. So, the net effect of this uncertain tax position has been to lower Doyle's current Tax expense by $250 ($400 − $150). Therefore, $250 of the uncertain tax benefit has been recognized. It is also important to note that increases or decreases to the tax contingency reserve resulting from permanent differences affect the current period's tax provision for the firm. So, the procedure for calculating Tax expense reported on a firm's GAAP income statement as summarized in Figure 13.5 must be adjusted to include changes in the Tax contingency reserve account due to permanent differences.

## Recording Uncertain Tax Position Related to Timing of Deductibility

Uncertain tax positions can sometimes arise because of uncertainty about the timing of the deductibility of an expense under the tax code. Assume from the Doyle Company example that the $1,000 deduction taken on the books and tax return in the current period fails to meet the more-likely-than-not condition. That is, the full deduction taken in the current period's tax return is unlikely to be sustained upon review. However, it is certain based on current tax law that this expenditure would be amortizable (and, therefore, deductible) for tax purposes over a five-year period. Under *FIN48,* Doyle would deduct only $200 of this expenditure (or $1/5$ of $1,000) in computing current tax expense on its income statement. The $800 difference is treated as a temporary difference that gives rise to a tax contingency reserve. The journal entry to record current Tax expense, Income taxes payable, and the Tax contingency reserve would be as follows:

| | | |
|---|---|---|
| **DR** Tax expense .............................................. | $4,320[a] | |
| **CR** Income taxes payable .................................... | | $4,000[b] |
| **CR** Tax contingency reserve .................................. | | 320[c] |

[a] $10,800 × 40%
[b] $10,000 × 40%
[c] $800 × 40%

Notice that the net reduction in tax expense due to uncertainty about the timing of deductibility of this item is $400 − $320 = $80, which is 40% × $200.[17]

---

[17] The logic of how $80 of tax benefit is effectively recognized on Doyle's income statement in the current year is the same as that used in the permanent difference example described above. The $1,000 deduction taken on the current period's tax return lowered Doyle's taxes payable by $400 and correspondingly lowered current tax expense. When the Tax contingency reserve account is credited for $320 in the entry here, the offsetting debit is to Tax expense. So, the net effect of recognizing this uncertain tax position has been to lower Doyle's current tax expense by $80 ($400 − $320). Therefore, Doyle has recognized this amount of the uncertain tax benefit in its income statement in the current period.

An uncertain tax position relating to a temporary difference also gives rise to book–tax basis differences that creates a deferred tax asset or deferred tax liability. In the preceding example, *FIN48* requires the tax basis of the expenditure to be determined according to what is clearly allowed under current tax law (i.e., 1/5 of $1,000 = $200). So, the *FIN48* tax basis of this item at the end of the first year is $800 ($1,000 expenditure minus the $200 deduction allowed under current tax law). The $800 book–tax basis difference gives rise to a deferred tax asset of $320 (40% × $800). The entry to recognize this deferred tax asset under the provisions of *FIN48*'s would be:

| | | | |
|---|---|---|---|
| **DR** | Deferred tax asset | $320 | |
| | **CR** Tax expense (deferred portion) | | $320 |

The net effect of this entry and the one immediately preceding it is to increase the Deferred tax asset account by $320 and to increase the Tax contingency reserve account by a like amount. It is important to note that the net effect of this uncertain tax position on book tax expense is zero. Thus, the only effect on book net income from uncertain tax positions that relate to timing (temporary) differences results from accrual of tax penalties and interest.

The firm records a reclassification entry in each of the subsequent years in which the tax position remains uncertain as a ratable portion ($200) of the original $1,000 expenditure becomes deductible with certainty under current tax law. Note that this entry reverses the Deferred tax asset and Tax contingency reserve accounts over the remaining four-year amortization period of the capitalized expenditure.

| | | | |
|---|---|---|---|
| **DR** | Tax contingency reserve | $80 | |
| | **CR** Deferred tax asset | | $80 |

## Making Changes or Resolving Uncertain Tax Positions

If the original assessed probabilities of outcomes for uncertain tax positions later change or if the uncertain tax position is settled with the taxing authority, appropriate adjustments are made to the Tax contingency reserve account with offsetting adjustments to the Tax expense or Cash account. To illustrate these adjustments, we return to the first example in which Doyle recorded $150 in the Tax contingency reserve account on the $1,000 deduction taken in Year 1. As you may recall, management assessed the likelihood to be 65% that the uncertain tax position would be sustained. A $250 tax benefit associated with this uncertain tax position was recognized as a reduction of the Tax expense account in Year 1 because this was the largest amount of benefit that management judged to be cumulatively greater than 50 percent likely to be realized.

Assume that in Year 2 management is now more optimistic about the uncertain tax position. Management now believes that the largest benefit amount that is cumulatively greater than 50 percent likely to be realized is $300. As the amount of the tax benefit likely to be realized increases, the tax contingency for unrecognized tax benefits is reduced with a corresponding reduction in the Tax expense account (thereby recognizing a portion of the uncertain benefit). To reflect this change, the Tax contingency reserve is debited with an offsetting adjustment to Tax expense in Year 2:

| | | | |
|---|---|---|---|
| **DR** | Tax contingency reserve | $50 | |
| | **CR** Tax expense | | $50 |
| To reduce the Tax contingency reserve from $150 ($400 − $250) to $100 ($400 − $300) and to recognize the increased tax benefit associated with this uncertain deduction. | | | |

If in Year 3 Doyle settles this issue with the taxing authority and pays $130, the entry to close out the Tax contingency reserve account and to pay the settlement is:

| | | |
|---|---|---:|
| **DR** | Tax contingency reserve ........................................ | $100 |
| **DR** | Tax expense ................................................... | 30 |
| | **CR** Cash ...................................................... | $130 |

Tax expense is debited for $30 in this final entry because the settlement with the taxing authority is $30 more than the $100 contingency reserve that previously existed for this uncertain tax position.

## Assessing *FIN48* Disclosures and Adoption Effects

*FIN48* became effective for 2007 fiscal year reporting. It requires that all uncertain tax positions at time of adoption be evaluated using the *FIN48* two-step recognition and measurement approach outlined here. The cumulative effect of applying *FIN48* is reported as an adjustment to the opening balance of the Retained earnings account or other appropriate components of stockholders' equity (Accumulated other comprehensive income) or net assets in the firm's balance sheet. The cumulative effect adjustment to Retained earnings is the difference between the net amount of assets and liabilities recognized in the firm's balance sheet prior to adoption of *FIN48* and the net amount of assets and liabilities recognized as a result of applying *FIN48*. Thus, the increase (decrease) to the Retained earnings account equals the total decrease (increase) in the firm's tax contingency reserve net of increases/decreases to deferred tax assets/liabilities and charges to other accounts. ***The initial* FIN48** *adjustment to Retained earnings provides some indication of how aggressive or conservative a firm has been in recognizing tax benefits associated with uncertain tax positions in prior years.*

Exhibit 13.13 presents the *FIN48* disclosure provided by Merck in its 2007 first quarter report. Several aspects of Merck's *FIN48* disclosure are noteworthy. As of January 1, 2007 when *FIN48* was adopted, Merck's liability for unrecognized tax benefits—Tax contingency reserve account—totaled $5.01 billion exclusive of $2.40 billion of liabilities for accrued interest and penalties related to unrecognized tax benefits. Adding these two amounts together gives a total of $7.41 billion and provides a more complete picture of Merck's total contingent liability for uncertain tax positions.

Merck indicates in this footnote that if it were to fully recognize the benefits associated with uncertain tax positions, its effective tax rate would be favorably impacted by $3.95 billion. This amount reflects the portion of the $5.01 billion contingent tax liability due to permanent differences that, if resolved in Merck's favor, would lower tax expense and raise income by this amount.[18] The difference of $1.06 billion ($5.01 − $3.95) reflects the portion of the tax contingency reserve relating to temporary differences that would be recorded as deferred tax assets on Merck's balance sheet.

The $3.95 billion plus the $2.40 billion liability for interest and penalties ($6.35 billion) reflects Merck's estimate of the additional obligation that would be payable to taxing authorities if the uncertain tax positions were not upheld (i.e., not resolved in Merck's favor). The book value of

---

[18] Only permanent book/tax differences affect a firm's effective tax rates. Temporary differences affect the deferred portion of the current period's tax provision but do not cause a divergence between statutory tax rates and effective tax rates.

**EXHIBIT 13.13**  **Merck 1Q 2007 Report—*FIN48* Disclosures**

### Footnote 10. Taxes on Income

On January 1, 2007, the Company adopted the provisions of FASB Interpretation No. 48, *Accounting for Uncertainty in Income Taxes—an interpretation of FASB Statement No. 109* ("FIN 48"). FIN 48 prescribes a recognition threshold and measurement attribute for the financial statement recognition and measurement of a tax position taken or expected to be taken in a tax return. FIN 48 requires that the Company determine whether the benefits of tax positions are more likely than not of being sustained upon audit based on the technical merits of the tax position. For tax positions that are more likely than not of being sustained upon audit, the Company recognizes the largest amount of the benefit that is more likely than not of being sustained in the financial statements. For tax positions that are not more likely than not of being sustained upon audit, the Company does not recognize any portion of the benefit in the financial statements. As a result of the implementation of FIN 48, the Company recognized an $81 million decrease in its existing liability for unrecognized tax benefits, with a corresponding increase to the January 1, 2007 Retained earnings balance.

As of January 1, 2007, after the implementation of FIN 48, the Company's liability for unrecognized tax benefits was $5.01 billion, excluding liabilities for interest and penalties. If the Company were to recognize these benefits, the effective tax rate would reflect a favorable net impact of $3.95 billion. In addition, at January 1, 2007, liabilities for accrued interest and penalties relating to the unrecognized tax benefits totaled $2.40 billion. As of March 31, 2007, the Company's Consolidated Balance Sheet reflects a liability for unrecognized tax benefits of $3.44 billion. If the Company were to recognize these benefits, the effective tax rate would reflect a favorable net impact of $2.38 billion. Accrued interest and penalties included in the Consolidated Balance Sheet were $1.50 billion as of March 31, 2007. The declines from January 1, 2007 were primarily due to the settlement with the Internal Revenue Service ("IRS") discussed below.

The Company recognizes interest and penalties associated with uncertain tax positions as a component of Taxes on Income in the Consolidated Statement of Income.

---

Merck's total assets on December 31, 2006 was $44.57 billion. So, the estimated additional outflow of cash to taxing authorities due to uncertain tax positions represents roughly 14.2% of Merck's reported assets. On the other hand, resolution of all of these uncertain tax positions in Merck's favor would increase its December 31, 2006 Retained earnings balance ($39.095 billion) by nearly 16.2% ($6.35/$39.095). While neither of these extreme outcomes is likely to hold, the analysis yields an upper and lower bound for how resolution of uncertain tax positions could affect Merck's balance sheet.

Finally, Merck indicates that as a result of implementing *FIN48*, it recognized an $81 million *decrease* in its existing liability for unrecognized tax benefits with a corresponding *increase* to the January 1, 2007 Retained earnings balance. This indicates that prior to *FIN48*, Merck had adopted a relatively conservative approach to recognizing tax benefits associated with uncertain tax positions. Note also that as of March 31, 2007, the liability for unrecognized tax benefits totaled $3.44 billion and accrued interest and penalties related to these unrecognized tax benefits totaled $1.50 billion for a $4.94 billion total contingent liability. The decrease in this total contingent liability from $7.41 billion to $4.94 billion indicates that Merck was able to resolve a significant amount of uncertain tax positions in its favor during the first quarter of 2007. These resolutions are described elsewhere in its *FIN48* footnote, but are not reproduced here.

---

*FIN48* adopts a two-step process to determine how much benefit that a firm can recognize from an uncertain tax position and correspondingly how much a firm should report in its tax contingency reserve for unrecognized tax benefits. The recognition threshold requires that management assess whether the uncertain tax position is "more likely than not" (greater than 50 percent) to be sustained based on the technical merits of the position. If the recognition threshold is met, the firm then measures the amount of the tax benefit to recognize as the largest amount of benefit that is cumulatively greater than 50 percent likely of being realized. The difference between the tax benefit reported on the

tax return and the tax benefit recognized using the two-step recognition/measurement process of *FIN48* is recorded as an increase in the Tax contingency reserve, sometimes referred to as Liability for unrecognized tax benefits.

## Extracting Analytical Insights from Footnote Disclosures

Q **Analysis**

Companies are required to disclose details about individual temporary differences that give rise to the deferred tax asset and deferred tax liability balances on the balance sheet. Scrutiny of the details comprising deferred taxes can reveal important analytical insights about the actions management has taken to boost short-term earnings. To illustrate, refer to Exhibit 13.14 on this page, which contains excerpts from the Year 2 income tax footnote for ChipPAC Company, one of the world's largest independent providers of semiconductor packaging, testing, and distribution services. This excerpt identifies major elements of the deferred tax asset and liability balances. Notice that the deferred income taxes attributable to book-versus-tax depreciation differences (highlighted area) went from a $92 thousand *debit* balance (asset) in Year 1 to $10.870 million *credit* balance (liability) in Year 2, an increase of $10.962 million. Some portion of this increase is likely due to acquisitions of new property, plant and equipment during the year that were depreciated at a faster rate for tax purposes than for book purposes. (ChipPAC's cash flow statement reveals that $93.174 million was spent in Year 2 for acquisition of property and equipment.) However, fixed asset growth explains only a small part of the increase in this segment of deferred tax liabilities. What else might explain the rather large increase in this component of deferred tax liabilities? In another note in its Year 2 annual report, ChipPAC states:

> Effective January 1, Year 2, the Company re-evaluated the estimated useful lives of equipment. Based on an independent appraisal to evaluate the useful lives of such equipment and the Company's internal assessment, the Company changed the estimated useful lives of assembly and test product equipment and furniture and fixtures from five to eight years. Previously, such equipment was depreciated on a straight-line basis over an estimated useful life of five years.

### EXHIBIT 13.14    ChipPAC Inc.

**Excerpt from Year 2 Annual Report**
**Income Tax Footnote**

The tax effects of temporary differences that give rise to significant portions of the deferred tax assets and deferred liabilities at December 31, Year 2 and December 31, Year 1 follow:

| ($ in thousands) | Year 2 | Year 1 |
|---|---|---|
| **Deferred tax assets:** | | |
| Income recognized for tax but not for books | $ 7,598 | — |
| Tax credits | 2,663 | — |
| NOL carryforward | 3,490 | — |
| Other | 3,381 | $6,270 |
| Total gross deferred assets | 17,132 | 6,270 |
| Less: Valuation allowance | (6,122) | |
| Net deferred tax assets | 11,010 | 6,270 |
| **Deferred tax liabilities:** | | |
| Depreciation | (10,870) | 92 |
| Reserves deducted for tax and not for books | (570) | (621) |
| Total deferred tax liabilities | (11,440) | (529) |
| Net deferred tax liabilities | $  (430) | $5,741 |

The net book values of assembly and test product equipment and furniture and fixtures, as of January 1, Year 2, are now being depreciated over the remaining useful life, based on eight years from the date such assets were originally placed into service. This change resulted in a decrease in depreciation expense for the year ended December 31, Year 2 being $29.0 million lower than would have been recorded using five years.

By extending the useful lives of fixed assets, ChipPAC lowered book depreciation and widened the excess of Year 2 book income over tax return income. This increased the deferred tax liability related to depreciation timing differences by $0.35 \times \$29$ million = $10.15 million, or 92.6% of the $10.962 million increase from the prior year. Interestingly, ChipPAC reported a pre-tax *profit* of $18 million in Year 2. Therefore, without the $29 million earnings boost that resulted from lengthening the useful lives, ChipPAC would have reported an $11 million ($18 − $29) pre-tax *loss*.

> This calculation assumes the statutory tax rate of 35% was used to calculate the change in deferred taxes.

A financial statement reader can glean important information from changes in deferred tax balances, as demonstrated in Exhibit 13.14. It was possible to infer that depreciable lives were extended because of the relatively large increase in deferred taxes arising from book-versus-tax depreciation differences. As we saw, ChipPAC clearly disclosed this change in estimated useful lives. *APB Opinion No. 20* requires disclosure of a change in an accounting estimate only if the impact of the change is material.[19]

Regrettably, widely accepted guidelines for assessing materiality do not exist. Consequently, firms that are not as candid as ChipPAC could conceivably decide to extend asset lives and not disclose the change. Their motive could be to manipulate or smooth income, and they would justify nondisclosure by contending that the impact of the change is immaterial. Because materiality guidelines are subjective, careful scrutiny of the income tax footnote provides analysts a way to detect subtle changes in accounting estimates that affect bottom-line earnings but are not separately disclosed. This avenue is especially useful to auditors. A detailed examination of deferred income tax balances provides auditors evidence for evaluating management's candor.[20]

**RECAP**

**Increases in deferred income tax liability balances result from a widening excess of book income over taxable income. These increases represent a potential danger signal that should be investigated because an increase in a deferred tax liability might indicate deteriorating earnings quality. One way to uncover such subtle deterioration in earnings quality is to investigate all large, sudden changes in deferred tax balances. The analyst should try to understand *why* the deferred tax liability balance increased.**

## Using Deferred Tax Footnotes to Assess Earnings Quality

To illustrate how deferred tax footnotes can be used to assess earnings quality, consider the relatively large increase in the deferred tax liability related to depreciation—$10.962 million—highlighted in Exhibit 13.14. We know that if a company lengthens the estimated useful

---

[19] "Accounting Changes," *APB Opinion No. 20* (New York: American Institute of CPAs [AICPA], 1971), para. 38.

[20] For readers who are neither auditors nor studying to be auditors, some elaboration is necessary. At the start of an audit, the auditor discusses significant issues with the client's managers to identify potential problem areas. When managers do not voluntarily disclose things such as income-increasing changes in accounting estimates, auditors consider this to be a potential danger signal that warrants an expansion in the scope of the audit. Scrutiny of the tax footnote provides auditors another tool for identifying problem areas.

lives of its fixed assets, book depreciation will be lowered and the excess of book income over taxable income will be widened, causing an increase in deferred tax liabilities. Other depreciation-related explanations for the increase in the deferred tax liability include growth in capital expenditures and tax law changes that permit more accelerated depreciation. If investigation reveals that the deferral increased without either a corresponding increase in capital expenditures or a change in tax depreciation schedules, the analyst should try to determine whether an undisclosed change in useful lives has been made to raise income. Similar investigations should be undertaken for any sudden increase in other types of deferred income tax liabilities.

Sudden decreases in deferred income tax assets are also a potential sign of deteriorating earnings quality. Using warranty expense as an example, we next explain why a sudden decrease in a deferred tax asset may be a danger signal.

We saw earlier that accruals for product warranties generate deferred tax assets. The reason is that GAAP requires warranty expenses to be matched against the revenues of the products to which the warranty applies. But income tax rules do not allow deductions for warranty expenses until the costs of providing the warranty services are actually incurred. This is often later than the period in which the revenues have been recognized. Accordingly, for growing companies, GAAP warranty expenses exceed tax return warranty expenses, giving rise to a deferred tax asset.

Assume that on January 1, 2008, Carson Company begins offering a one-year warranty on all sales. Its 2008 sales were $20,000,000, and Carson estimates that warranty expenses will be 1% of sales; so, $200,000 of warranty expense is deducted on Carson's books in 2008.

Assume that tax deductions for warranties in 2008 are zero. If tax rates in 2008 are 35%, Carson will have a deferred tax asset of $70,000 for warranties at December 31, 2008—the $200,000 book-versus-tax warranty difference times 35%. If *actual* warranty costs incurred in 2009 but associated with 2008 sales are precisely $200,000, this would mean that Carson's 2008 warranty estimate was accurate and should be maintained in 2009.

Exhibit 13.15(a) shows what will happen if Carson Company uses the same warranty expense estimate of 1% of sales in 2009. It is assumed that sales in 2009 again will be $20,000,000 and that actual warranty costs on 2009 sales will not be incurred until 2010. Using these assumptions, notice that Carson's December 31, 2009 deferred tax asset balance will still be $70,000. That is, the 2008 book-versus-tax timing difference reversed in 2009 (see arrow in Exhibit 13.15[a]), but a new $200,000 timing difference on warranties associated with 2009 sales originated. *The example in Exhibit 13.15(a) is designed to demonstrate that the deferred income tax asset balance will remain stable if the warranty estimate is accurate and if sales volume is unchanged.*

To illustrate why it is also important to scrutinize deferred tax asset balances, let's now assume that instead of maintaining the warranty expense estimate at 1% of sales, Carson lowers the estimate to 0.5% of sales in 2009. Carson does this because management wishes to increase 2009 income despite the fact that the 1% number reflects actual warranty experience. Notice that because the 1% estimate accurately reflects estimated warranty costs in 2008, this change of an accounting estimate in 2009 represents a deterioration in earnings quality.

Exhibit 13.15(b) on the following page shows that the deferred tax asset balance will decrease from $70,000 to $35,000 under these circumstances. The reason for the decrease in the deferred income tax asset balance is that the book-versus-tax difference narrowed from $200,000 in 2008 to $100,000 in 2009 as a consequence of the reduction in estimated warranty expense from 1% to 0.5% of sales.

---

**EXHIBIT 13.15**    Carson Company

### Illustration of Decline in Deferred Tax Assets

#### Panel (a) Warranty Percentage Unchanged

|  | 2009 | 2008 |
|---|---|---|
| Sales revenues | $20,000,000 | $20,000,000 |
| Estimated warranty cost percentage | 0.01 | 0.01 |
| Warranty expense per books | 200,000 | 200,000 |
| Warranty expense per tax return | | |
|    Attributable to 2008 sales | 200,000 | — |
|    Attributable to 2009 sales | — | — |
| Excess of book over tax expense | | |
|    Arising from 2008 sales | — | 200,000 |
|    Arising from 2009 sales | 200,000 | — |
| Tax rate | 0.35 | 0.35 |
| December 31 deferred tax asset balance | $   70,000 | $   70,000 |

*2009 Reversal*

#### Panel (b) Warranty Percentage Lowered in 2009

|  | 2009 | 2008 |
|---|---|---|
| Sales revenues | $20,000,000 | $20,000,000 |
| Estimated warranty cost percentage | 0.005 | 0.01 |
| Warranty expense per books | 100,000 | 200,000 |
| Warranty expense per tax return | | |
|    Attributable to 2008 sales | 200,000 | — |
|    Attributable to 2009 sales | — | — |
| Excess of book over tax expense | | |
|    Arising from 2008 sales | — | 200,000 |
|    Arising from 2009 sales | 100,000 | — |
| Tax rate | 0.35 | 0.35 |
| December 31 deferred tax asset balance | $   35,000 | $   70,000 |

*2009 Reversal*

---

**RECAP**

**This example demonstrates why shrinkage in a deferred tax asset balance should be investigated. Year-to-year changes in warranty expense estimates are just like other changes in accounting estimates in that they need to be disclosed only if they are material. Because materiality guidelines are subjective, companies can conceivably use undisclosed estimate changes as a way to artificially increase earnings. Decreases in deferred tax asset balances can provide clues about such possibilities to statement readers.**

## Using Tax Footnotes to Improve Interfirm Comparability

The deferred tax portion of the income tax footnote can be used to undo differences in financial reporting choices across firms and thus to improve interfirm comparisons.

 **Analysis**

Here's a specific illustration. Lubrizol and Cambrex are both classified in the same Standard Industrial Classification (SIC) code and compete in many product categories. But each uses different depreciation methods. A recent Lubrizol 10-K states the following:

> Accelerated depreciation methods are used in computing depreciation on certain machinery and equipment, which comprise approximately 21% of the depreciable assets. The remaining assets are depreciated using the straight-line method. The estimated useful lives are 10 to 40 years for buildings and land improvements and range from 3 to 20 years for machinery and equipment.

SIC is a system maintained by the Office of Federal Statistical Policy and Standards in the Department of Commerce to classify firms by the nature of their operations. Lubrizol and Cambrex are both in SIC Code 2860—Industrial Organic Chemicals.

So, Lubrizol is using accelerated depreciation for some of its assets. By contrast, Cambrex's annual report for the same year says:

> Property, plant and equipment is stated at cost, net of accumulated depreciation. Plant and equipment are depreciated on a straight-line basis over the estimated useful lives for each applicable asset group as follows:

| | |
|---|---|
| Buildings and improvements | 15 to 20 years |
| Machinery and equipment | 5 to 10 years |
| Furniture and fixtures | 3 to 5 years |

Exhibit 13.16 contains several key financial statement figures for each company from their respective 10-Ks along with excerpts from their income tax footnotes. It's possible that the different depreciation choices of each firm conform perfectly to differences in the service-potential of each firm's assets. But what if they don't? How can an analyst adjust the numbers to improve interfirm comparisons?

Let's begin by looking at Exhibit 13.16(a), which shows the balances in the subcomponents of the Deferred tax liability account for Lubrizol. The highlighted depreciation item reflects the $99.9 million cumulative deferred tax liability arising from book-versus-tax depreciation expense at year-end.

Companies such as Lubrizol have an incentive to use the most accelerated depreciation method that the tax law allows and to depreciate the assets over the shortest allowable tax life.

| EXHIBIT 13.16 | Selected Financial Statement Disclosures from Recent 10-K Reports of Lubrizol and Cambrex |
|---|---|

| | December 31 | |
|---|---|---|
| ($ in thousands) | Year 2 | Year 1 |
| **Panel (a) Lubrizol** | | |
| Book depreciation | $ 88,300 | $ 79,700 |
| Income before income taxes | 195,350 | 118,814 |
| Property, plant and equipment, net of accumulated depreciation (at year-end) | 670,512 | 718,850 |
| **Significant deferred tax liabilities** | | |
| Depreciation and other basis differences | $ 99,938 | $101,658 |
| Undistributed foreign equity income | 5,566 | 3,894 |
| Inventory basis difference | 1,497 | 3,706 |
| Other | 3,977 | 2,986 |
| **Panel (b) Cambrex** | | |
| Book depreciation | $ 33,118 | $ 30,547 |
| Income before income taxes | 58,901 | 61,695 |
| Property, plant and equipment, net of accumulated depreciation (at year-end) | 280,163 | 255,016 |
| **Significant deferred tax liabilities** | | |
| Depreciation | $ 30,967 | $ 29,591 |
| Environmental reserves | 796 | — |
| Intangibles | 14,963 | 14,839 |
| Italian intangibles | 4,581 | 6,086 |
| Other benefits | 2,143 | — |
| Other | 1,722 | 1,667 |

This minimizes the discounted present value of their tax liability by accelerating deductions to the fullest legal extent. These *tax* depreciation rate and useful life deductions exceed the *book* accelerated method and useful lives chosen by Lubrizol, so a deferred liability results. The liability declined by $1.7 million going from $101.6 million in the previous year (labeled Year 1) to $99.9 million in the current year (labeled Year 2).

> A reduction in the deferred tax liability related to depreciation timing differences probably arises because either (1) accelerated methods used for books give higher depreciation than allowed for tax purposes or (2) assets for which Lubrizol uses straight-line depreciation for books have reached a point in their useful lives at which the straight-line depreciation exceeds the accelerated depreciation per tax return (see again Figure 13.1).

The change in the deferred income tax liability arising from depreciation is:

$$\text{Change} = (\text{Tax depreciation} - \text{Book depreciation}) \times \text{Statutory tax rate}$$

Lubrizol's statutory tax rate is 35%, and the depreciation deferred tax *change* was −$1.7 million (a decrease), as shown in Exhibit 13.16(a). Substituting these values into the preceding equation, we get:

$$-\$1.7 \text{ million} = (\text{Tax depreciation} - \text{Book depreciation}) \times 0.35$$

Dividing both sides by 0.35 yields:

$$-\$4.9 \text{ million} = (\text{Tax depreciation} - \text{Book depreciation})$$

Because Exhibit 13.16(a) shows that Lubrizol's book depreciation was $88.3 million, tax depreciation must have been $83.4 million ($88.3 million − $4.9 million), which was 5.5% lower.

We can now perform the same analysis on Cambrex to determine what its tax depreciation was in Year 2. The highlighted portion of Exhibit 13.16(b) shows that Cambrex's depreciation-related deferred income tax liability was slightly less than $31.0 million in Year 2—an increase of $1.4 million over the previous year. Repeating the analytical approach we used for Lubrizol yields:

$$\text{Change} = (\text{Tax depreciation} - \text{Book depreciation}) \times \text{Statutory tax rate}$$

or:

$$\$1.4 \text{ million} = (\text{Tax depreciation} - \text{Book depreciation}) \times 0.35$$

or:

$$\$4 \text{ million} = (\text{Tax depreciation} - \text{Book depreciation})$$

Cambrex's book depreciation was $33.1 million (Exhibit 13.16[b]), so tax depreciation must have been $33.1 million + $4 million = $37.1 million, an increase of 12.1%.

We have now approximated the tax return depreciation taken by each firm and established a "common denominator" for interfirm analysis. While we do not have enough information to put Cambrex on Lubrizol's book depreciation basis, we do have enough information to put each firm on an identical tax depreciation basis, thereby facilitating comparisons.

Adjusting each firm's financial reporting to the same rate as well as the useful lives used for tax purposes increases Lubrizol's pre-tax income by 2.5% ($4.9 million/$195.4 million). Cambrex's pre-tax income decreases by 6.8% ($4 million/$58.9 million). In any setting, the difference may—or may not—be significant. But making interfirm comparisons using comparable data is better than basing the analysis on diverse financial reporting choices.

It is important to note that the preceding analysis works only in those situations where firms have not had major asset disposals during the year. When depreciable assets are sold, the deferred tax amounts for these assets are eliminated from the Deferred tax liability account. Moreover, the amount eliminated due to asset sales is rarely disclosed. So, the year-to-year change in the deferred tax liability balance for depreciation no longer reflects only current period book-versus-tax depreciation differences. We can determine whether the firm sold assets during the period by looking in the Investing Activity section of the cash flow statement to see whether cash was generated from asset sales. In this illustration, neither Lubrizol nor Cambrex reported major asset sales in their Year 2 cash flow statement.

## Using Income Tax Footnotes to Assess the Degree of Conservatism in Firms' Accounting Choices

Determining the degree of conservatism in a firm's set of accounting choices is an important part of assessing the earnings quality for that company. Conservative choices, as with accelerated depreciation, decrease earnings and asset values relative to more liberal techniques, such as straight-line depreciation. All else equal, the more conservative the set of accounting choices, the higher the quality of earnings.

Useful information for assessing the degree of conservatism in a firm's portfolio of accounting choices can be extracted from the income tax footnote by comparing the ratio of pre-tax book income to taxable income. While this is admittedly a relatively coarse way to assess accounting conservatism, it can be useful in selected settings. The ratio is computed as

$$EC = \frac{\text{Pre-tax book income (adjusted for permanent differences)}}{\text{Taxable income per tax return}}$$

where EC is the current period's **earnings conservatism** ratio.

Consider the denominator, Taxable income per tax return. In most instances firms seek to minimize tax return income. Because of this income minimization incentive, the denominator represents a very conservative income benchmark. Usually, it is the lowest permissible—meaning "legal"—taxable income number for the period.

> The only exceptions will arise when firms either (1) have unused operating loss carryforwards that are about to expire or (2) expect future tax rates to rise sharply.

The numerator—pre-tax GAAP income—incorporates the latitude available to firms in selecting accounting method choices, accounting estimates for things such as bad debts expense and asset useful lives, and discretionary expenses such as advertising or research and development (R&D) that we have outlined elsewhere in the book. Consequently, the numerator can range from a highly aggressive (income-increasing) number to a highly conservative (income-decreasing) number.

To illustrate how this ratio is used, we will compute the EC ratio for Merck & Co. for 2006 ($EC_{06}$). Exhibit 13.12(b) on page 759 indicates that 2006 income before income taxes was $6,221.4 million. ***This number needs adjustment for net permanent difference items that do not enter into the computation of taxable income and, therefore, would distort the following comparison between book and taxable income.*** From Exhibit 13.12(b), Merck reported the tax effects of net permanent

> This is the difference between the tax expense based on applying the statutory tax rate to pre-tax earnings versus the tax expense actually reported on the income statement.

difference items to be $389.9 million ($2,177.5 − $1,787.6). We divide this amount by the 35% statutory tax rate to get the before-tax amount of permanent differences ($389.9/0.35 = $1,114.0).

Because Merck's effective tax rate of 28.7% is lower than the statutory rate, this $1,114.0 million of permanent differences represents income reported on Merck's books that will never be taxed. For comparability, we need to subtract this amount from Merck's reported pre-tax book income of $6,221.4 million. This yields $5,107.4 million as the company's adjusted pre-tax book income. This is the numerator of $EC_{06}$.

Because most companies do not disclose details of their income tax returns, we need to estimate the denominator, Taxable income per tax return. We do this by "grossing up" the current portion of tax expense ($2,317.8 million) shown in Exhibit 13.12(a) for Merck. That is, we approximate taxable income per tax return by dividing the current portion of the current period's tax provision by the statutory marginal federal tax rate. We saw in Exhibit 13.12(a) that income taxes currently payable in 2006 totaled $2,317.8 million. Taxable income can then be estimated as:

There are three reasons why this simple procedure for estimating taxable income may not fully capture the taxes paid in that period by the reporting entity.

- Certain items may cause the current portion of tax expense to over- or understate the firm's actual tax liabilities. For example, items such as profits or losses from discontinued operations or extraordinary gains or losses, which are reported below net income from continuing operations, are shown net of tax. While these items affect the entity's taxable income (and thus, taxes paid) in the current period, they are not reported as part of pre-tax income per books under intraperiod tax allocation.

- The current portion of tax expense is reported after tax credits such as research and development credits and foreign tax credits. In the presence of credits, the estimate of taxable income from grossing-up the current tax expense will be measured with error.

- Differing consolidation rules for book and tax purposes can cause the financial statements to include a different group of related corporations than the tax return includes.

See M. Hanlon, "What Can We Infer about a Firm's Taxable Income from Its Financial Statements?" *National Tax Journal,* Vol. LVI, No. 4, December 2003. Copyright © 2003 Michelle Hanlon. Used with permission.

| 2006 Income taxes currently payable | = | 2006 Taxable income per tax return | × | 2006 Statutory tax rate |
|---|---|---|---|---|

Substituting the two pieces of data from Merck's tax footnote, we get:

| 2006 Income taxes currently payable | = | 2006 Taxable income per tax return | × | 2006 Statutory tax rate |
|---|---|---|---|---|
| $2,317.8 million | = | ? | × | 0.35 |

Rearranging to isolate the unknown taxable income per tax return on the left side, we get:

| 2006 Taxable income | = | $2,317.8 million/0.35 = $6,622.3 million |
|---|---|---|

Thus, $EC_{06}$ for Merck is ($ in millions):

$$EC_{06} = \frac{2006 \text{ Pre-tax book income (adjusted)}}{2006 \text{ Taxable income}}$$

$$EC_{06} = \frac{\$5,107.4}{\$6,622.3}$$

$$EC_{06} = 0.77$$

In general, an EC ratio below 1.0 indicates relatively conservative financial reporting choices. (Remember that companies have an incentive to minimize the denominator, Taxable income per tax return.) In Merck's case, book income is estimated to be roughly 23% lower than taxable income in 2006.

Analysts can also compare EC ratios for a single company over time to monitor overall earnings conservatism. For example, using Exhibit 13.12, we can compute Merck's 2005 taxable income—the denominator of its $EC_{05}$ ratio—as follows:

The $443.4 million before-tax amount of permanent difference is computed as follows:

| | |
|---|---|
| Pre-tax book income | $7,363.9 |
| Statutory tax rate | 35% |
| Tax based on all pre-tax book income | $2,577.4 |
| 2005 Tax provision (see panel [a] of Exhibit 13.12) | (2,732.6) |
| Tax effects of net permanent difference items | $ (155.2) |
| Before-tax amount of permanent difference items ($155.2/0.35) | $ (443.4) |

$$\frac{2005}{\text{Taxable}} = \frac{2005 \text{ Income}}{\text{taxes currently}} \bigg/ \frac{2005}{\text{Statutory}}$$
$$\text{income} \qquad \text{payable} \qquad \text{tax rate}$$

$$\frac{2005}{\text{Taxable}} = \$2,723.6 \text{ million}/0.35$$
$$\text{income}$$

$$\frac{2005}{\text{Taxable}} = \$7,781.7 \text{ million}$$
$$\text{income}$$

Merck's 2005 pre-tax book income was $7,363.9 million. After increasing its pre-tax book income for $443.4 million of before-tax amount of permanent difference items, Merck's $EC_{05}$ is computed as follows:

$$EC_{05} = \frac{2005 \text{ pre-tax book income (adjusted)}}{2005 \text{ Taxable income}}$$

$$EC_{05} = \frac{\$7,363.9 + \$443.4}{\$7,781.7} = \frac{\$7,807.3}{\$7,781.7}$$

$$EC_{05} = 1.00$$

The relative decline in $EC_{05}$ (1.00) compared to $EC_{06}$ (0.77) suggests that Merck may have been somewhat more conservative in its financial reporting choices for 2006 relative to 2005. However, year-to-year comparisons in EC ratios must be interpreted with caution when dramatic changes in economic conditions or the tax law occur.

The earnings conservatism ratio can also be used to compare reporting choices across companies. For example, Merck's $EC_{06}$ might be compared with the $EC_{06}$ ratio of a competitor, such as Pfizer, to assess whether each has similar earnings conservatism.

Having introduced the EC ratio, we now need to emphasize its three primary limitations.

1. EC ratio comparisons for a single company over time (for example, $EC_{06}$ versus $EC_{05}$) can be misleading if the tax law has changed over the comparison period. For example, if the U.S. Congress allows more accelerated tax depreciation schedules, this will cause the EC ratio to rise (that is, showing *lower* earnings conservatism) even though the firm's real earnings conservatism has remained constant.

2. Comparisons across companies in different industries should be made cautiously. Specifically, tax burdens can vary because of differences in capital intensity or specific tax rules (such as the oil depletion allowance), which affect only certain industries.

3. The EC ratio does not capture one type of deterioration in earnings conservatism. Whenever companies dip into old LIFO layers, the impact of the earnings increase affects both the numerator and the denominator of the ratio because of the LIFO conformity rule discussed in Chapter 9. That's why earnings conservatism deterioration arising from LIFO dipping is not reliably captured in EC.

RE CAP

Tax footnotes provide information that allows the analyst to estimate firms' taxable income. By comparing pre-tax accounting income with the estimate of taxable income, analysts can develop a rough index (subject to the limitations noted) of the overall degree of conservatism in a firm's set of **GAAP** accounting choices. The degree of conservatism in a firm's set of accounting choices is an important part of assessing that company's earnings quality.

## SUMMARY

- The rules for computing income for financial reporting purposes—book income—differ from the rules for computing income for tax purposes.

- The differences between book income and taxable income are caused by both permanent and temporary (timing) differences in the revenue and expense items reported on a company's books versus its tax return.

- Temporary differences give rise to both deferred tax assets and deferred tax liabilities.

- Deferred tax accounting generally allows firms to report tax costs or benefits on the income statement in the period in which the related revenue and expense items are recognized for book purposes regardless of when these amounts are recorded on the tax return.

- The income tax footnote provides useful information for understanding how much of the current period's tax provision (expense) is actually payable to the federal and state governments, and how much is deferred. Tax footnotes also allow users to understand why firms' effective tax rates may differ from the statutory rate.

- *FIN48* disclosures are useful in assessing a firm's uncertain tax positions and whether the firm is aggressive or conservative in recognizing the benefits associated with these positions.

- Finally, tax footnotes provide a wealth of information that can be exploited to improve interfirm comparability and evaluate firms' earnings quality.

## APPENDIX

# COMPREHENSIVE INTERPERIOD TAX ALLOCATION PROBLEM

The following example for Hawkeye Corporation combines the various aspects of accounting for income taxes discussed in this chapter to demonstrate the interrelation between pre-tax accounting income, taxable income, taxes payable, deferred taxes, and tax expense. Working through this example will demonstrate the following points:

1. How to convert a pre-tax accounting income number to a taxable income number.

2. How to determine taxes payable.

3. How to determine the change in deferred tax assets and deferred tax liabilities.

4. How to determine tax expense.

5. How to reconcile the total tax costs (benefits) reported in the income statement with the total taxes payable according to the tax return for the period.

Before working through the Hawkeye Corporation example, look at Figure 13.7, which provides a road map for understanding how the various book and taxable income numbers and tax amounts relate to one another.

## Figure 13.7

OVERVIEW OF
INTERPERIOD TAX
ALLOCATION

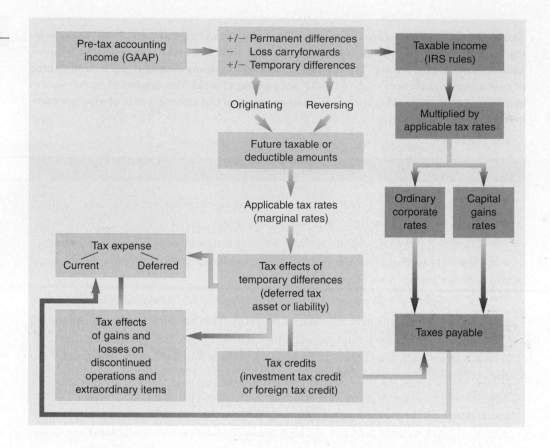

## Computation of Taxable Income and Taxes Payable

Reading from left to right across the top of Figure 13.7, we see three categories of items that cause differences between pre-tax book income and taxable income on the tax return:

1. Permanent differences.
2. Operating loss carryforwards.
3. Temporary differences.

Technically, operating loss carryforwards are treated as a temporary difference under *SFAS No. 109*. Although a deferred tax asset will be reported on the company's books, the operating losses themselves are not carried over from previous periods and, thus, are not included as part of the current period's book income computation. Therefore, to reconcile pre-tax book income to taxable income requires an adjustment for the dollar amount of the loss carryforward. We have chosen to discuss the loss carryforward separately from the other temporary differences, which are discussed later.

Taxable income is determined by making adjustments to the reported pre-tax book income numbers for each of these items.

The first category of reconciling items is permanent differences. We know these are revenue or expense items that the tax rules treat differently—on a permanent basis—than the GAAP (book) rules treat them for income determination purposes. As shown in Schedule 13.1 (p. 779), Hawkeye Corporation has two permanent difference items—Item ①, Interest on municipal bonds and Item ⑥, Premium on executive life insurance.

To arrive at taxable income, the municipal bond interest must be *subtracted* from the reported pre-tax book income number because it is not taxable but has been included in book income. In addition, the executive life insurance premiums that were subtracted in arriving at pre-tax book income must be *added back* because they are not deductible for tax purposes when the company is the named beneficiary.

## EXAMPLE: INTERPERIOD TAX ALLOCATION

Hawkeye Corporation starts the current year, 2008, with a deferred tax asset balance of $20,000 and a deferred tax liability balance of $30,000. The current tax rate is 40% and is projected to be in effect when all temporary differences reverse. The reported pre-tax accounting income is $500,000. Analyze the following items to determine taxable income, the *change* in deferred taxes payable (future taxable and deductible amounts), and the tax expense to be reported on the income statement for 2008. Assume that there is no need for a valuation allowance provision for deferred tax assets.

### ITEM DESCRIPTION

① Book income includes $12,000 of interest revenue from municipal bonds.

② Straight-line depreciation for book purposes is $100,000 in the current year, and $140,000 is deductible for tax purposes under the Modified Accelerated Cost Recovery System (MACRS).

③ Hawkeye collected $60,000 of rent for a warehouse it leases to a local manufacturer. Of this amount, $40,000 is deferred for accounting purposes and will be recognized in 2009 when it is earned.

④ Hawkeye accrued $50,000 for estimated future warranty costs in 2008 and paid $35,000 in warranty expenses in the current period.

⑤ Bad debts written off in the current period totaled $20,000, and the provision for bad debts under the allowance method amounted to $15,000. Hawkeye uses the direct write-off method for tax purposes and the allowance method for book purposes.

⑥ Book income includes an $18,000 deduction for premiums paid on executive life insurance in which the company is the named beneficiary.

⑦ In 2008, Hawkeye collected $15,000 on an installment land sale made several years earlier. The profit on the sale, all of which was recorded at the time of sale for book purposes, amounted to 30% of the selling price. The installment method of recognizing profit is being used for tax purposes. Ignore any imputed interest on the deferred payments.

⑧ Hawkeye has $35,000 of operating loss carryforward at the beginning of 2008.

---

| SCHEDULE 13.1 | Hawkeye Corporation |
|---|---|

### Calculation of Taxable Income and Taxes Payable

| Computation of taxable income | |
|---|---|
| Pre-tax accounting income (given) | $500,000 |
| | |
| Adjustments for permanent differences | |
| — Interest on municipal bonds (Item ①) | (12,000) |
| + Premium on executive life insurance (Item ⑥) | 18,000 |
| Income before adjustment for temporary differences | $506,000 |
| | |
| Adjustment for operating loss carryforward (Item ⑧) | (35,000) |
| | |
| Adjustments for temporary differences | |
| — Excess of accelerated over straight-line depreciation (Item ②) | |
| ($140,000 − $100,000) | (40,000) |
| + Rent received in excess of rent earned (Item ③) | |
| ($60,000 − $20,000) | 40,000 |
| + Excess of accrued warranty costs over actual costs incurred | |
| on warranties (Item ④) | |
| ($50,000 − $35,000) | 15,000 |

*(continued)*

## SCHEDULE 13.1    Hawkeye Corporation *(continued)*

| | |
|---|---:|
| −Excess of accounts written off over current provision | |
|     for bad debts (Item ⑤) | |
|     ($20,000 − $15,000) | (5,000) |
| +Installment profit recognized for tax purposes in 2008 but | |
|     recognized in earlier periods for book purposes (Item ⑦) | |
|     (30% × $15,000) | 4,500 |
| Taxable income | $485,500 |
| Tax rate | × 40% |
| Taxes payable for 2008 | $194,200 |

The second general category of reconciling items is operating loss carryforwards. As shown in Item ⑧, Hawkeye has a $35,000 operating loss carryforward. This represents losses reported on previous years' tax returns (that is, tax deductible expenses and losses exceeded taxable income and gains) that can be offset against the 2008 taxable income. Thus, this amount is subtracted from pre-tax book income to arrive at taxable income in 2008.

The last category of reconciling items involves temporary differences. These are revenue and expense items that enter into the determination of book income in one period and taxable income in a different period. Hawkeye has several temporary differences:

- Item ②: *Depreciation expense.* Hawkeye's pre-tax book income includes a deduction for $100,000 of straight-line depreciation expense. But for tax purposes, Hawkeye is using an accelerated depreciation method, which produces a $140,000 deduction in the current period. To arrive at taxable income, this $40,000 originating timing difference must be subtracted from pre-tax book income because it represents an additional amount that is deductible on the 2008 tax return that was not deducted in arriving at pre-tax book income.

- Item ③: *Rent collections.* In 2008, Hawkeye collected $60,000 of lease rent, and all of this amount is taxable when received. However, for book purposes, $40,000 of this amount is deferred and will be recognized in future periods when it is earned. This leaves $20,000 that was included in the $500,000 of pre-tax book income. Therefore, this $40,000 originating timing difference must be added to the pre-tax income number to arrive at 2008 taxable income.

- Item ④: *Warranty expenses.* Hawkeye accrued $50,000 for estimated warranty costs that were subtracted in arriving at the pre-tax book income number. For tax purposes, Hawkeye is allowed to deduct only the $35,000 of warranty costs that were actually paid. The $15,000 difference represents an originating timing difference that must be added back to the pre-tax book income number to yield taxable income.

- Item ⑤: *Bad debt provisions.* For book income purposes, Hawkeye uses the allowance method (described in Chapter 8) to determine the $15,000 bad debts deduction in 2008. For tax purposes, Hawkeye is allowed to take a deduction only when accounts are actually written off; this is the direct write-off method. As shown, Hawkeye wrote off $20,000 of accounts receivable in 2008. Note that all or a portion of the accounts written off in 2008 would have been deducted as an expense to arrive at GAAP/book income in prior accounting periods. Accordingly, the additional $5,000 deductible for tax purposes, an amount that represents a reversing timing difference, must be subtracted from pre-tax book income to arrive at taxable income for 2008.

- Item ⑦: *Profit on installment sale.* Hawkeye is using the installment method for tax purposes (Chapter 3) to record profit on a land sale made in a previous period. All of this profit was recorded in a previous period's book income number. Thus, the gross profit on the amounts collected in 2008 (30% × $15,000 collected = $4,500) represents a reversing timing difference that must be added to the pre-tax book income number to arrive at taxable income.

After adjustments for the operating loss carryforward and the temporary difference items, Hawkeye's taxable income for 2008 is determined to be $485,500 (see Schedule 13.1). To arrive at taxes payable, the taxable income number must be multiplied by the applicable tax rates, as illustrated in the right-hand column of Figure 13.7. If some of the components of taxable income are subject to special tax rates (for example, capital gains rates), these amounts would need to be isolated and multiplied by the appropriate special rates. For simplicity, we have assumed that a flat tax rate of 40% applies to all components of taxable income, yielding taxes payable to the IRS in 2008 of $194,200 (Schedule 13.1).

## Calculation of Change in Deferred Tax Asset and Liability Accounts

The next step in determining the tax provision (expense) to report on Hawkeye's GAAP (book) income statement for 2008 is to determine the *change* in the deferred tax asset and deferred tax liability accounts. These calculations are represented in the center column of Figure 13.7 and the details are provided in Schedule 13.2. For each temporary difference (including operating loss carryforwards), we must determine three things:

**SCHEDULE 13.2**    **Hawkeye Corporation**

**Calculation of Changes in Deferred Tax Accounts**

| | Deferred Tax Asset | Deferred Tax Liability |
|---|---|---|
| Operating loss carryforward (Item ⑧) | | |
| *Realization of Future Deductible Amount* | | |
| 40% × $35,000 | $(14,000) **CR** | |
| Depreciation (Item ②) | | |
| *Future Taxable Amount* | | |
| ($140,000 − $100,000 = $40,000) × 40% | | $(16,000) **CR** |
| Rent received in advance of rent earned (Item ③) | | |
| *Future Deductible Amount* | | |
| ($60,000 − $20,000 = $40,000) × 40% | 16,000 **DR** | |
| Excess of accrued warranty costs over cash warranty expenses (Item ④) | | |
| *Future Deductible Amount* | | |
| ($50,000 − $35,000 = $15,000) × 40% | 6,000 **DR** | |
| Bad debts written off (Item ⑤) | | |
| *Realization of Future Deductible Amount* | | |
| $20,000 × 40% | (8,000) **CR** | |
| New bad debt provisions in 2008 (Item ⑤) | | |
| *Future Deductible Amount* | | |
| $15,000 × 40% | 6,000 **DR** | |
| Installment profit recognized for tax (Item ⑦) | | |
| *Realization of Future Taxable Amount* | | |
| (30% × $15,000 = $4,500) × 40% | | 1,800 **DR** |
| Gross profit rate    Tax rate | | |
| Change in Deferred Tax Asset/Liability | 6,000 **DR** | (14,200) **CR** |
| Beginning balance | 20,000 **DR** | (30,000) **CR** |
| Ending balance | $ 26,000 **DR** | $(44,200) **CR** |

1. Whether an item is an originating or reversing temporary difference.
2. Whether it affects a deferred tax asset or a deferred tax liability balance.
3. What the applicable tax rate is for determining the tax effect of the temporary difference.

Originating temporary differences are "new" differences between book and taxable income that cause *increases* in either the deferred tax asset or the deferred tax liability balance. Reversing temporary differences are realizations or reversals of "old" temporary differences that gave rise to deferred tax assets or liabilities in previous accounting periods. Because they represent reversals of previously recorded temporary differences, reversing temporary differences are recorded as *decreases* in either the deferred tax asset or the deferred tax liability accounts.

Determining whether a particular temporary difference affects a deferred tax asset or liability balance hinges on whether the item causes taxable income to be higher or lower than book income in the current period and whether it is an originating or reversing temporary difference.

Hawkeye has one originating temporary difference that causes taxable income to be *lower* than book income in the *current* period:

- Item ②. Accelerated depreciation expense deductions for tax purposes ($140,000) exceed the straight-line depreciation deductions for book purposes ($100,000). This temporary difference gives rise to a future taxable amount—that is, taxable income will be *higher* than book income in future periods when this temporary difference reverses. Therefore, this temporary difference causes an increase (credit) to deferred tax liabilities of $16,000, as shown in Schedule 13.2.

Hawkeye has two reversing temporary differences that cause taxable income to be *lower* than book income in the *current* period:

- Item ⑧. The operating loss carryforward is $35,000.
- Item ⑤. The bad debts write-off is $20,000.

Both of these items represent realizations of future deductible amounts and result in a decrease (credit) to the deferred tax asset account, as we see in Schedule 13.2.

Hawkeye has three originating temporary differences that cause taxable income to be *higher* than book income in the *current* period:

- Item ③. Rent received ($60,000) is in excess of rent earned for book purposes ($20,000).
- Item ④. Accrued warranty expenses for book purposes ($50,000) is in excess of warranty expenditures for tax purposes ($35,000).
- Item ⑤. Bad debts expense of $15,000 that is accrued under the allowance method for book purposes will not be deductible for tax purposes until specific accounts are written off in future periods.

Each of these items gives rise to a future deductible amount and accordingly causes increases (debits) to the Deferred tax asset account, as shown in Schedule 13.2.

The one remaining temporary difference for Hawkeye is the profit on the land sale that is recognized under the installment method for tax purposes.

- Item ⑦. This $4,500 amount represents a reversing temporary difference that causes taxable income to be higher than book income in 2008. Because a deferred tax liability would have been set up in a previous period (when the land was sold and the entire profit was recognized for book purposes), the Deferred tax liability account is being reduced (debited) now because the tax will be paid in the current period.

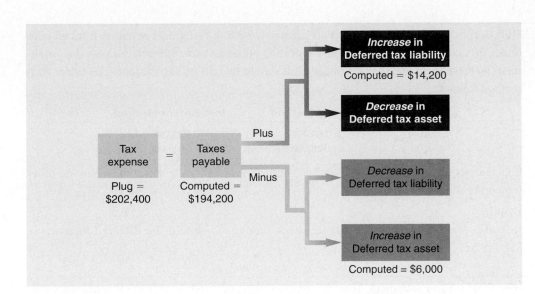

**Figure 13.8**

CALCULATION OF TAX
EXPENSE: INDIRECT
APPROACH

The assumed marginal corporate tax rate of 40% is applied to all temporary differences to determine the dollar amount of the change in the Deferred tax asset or liability account. This is appropriate when no enacted changes in the tax rates are scheduled to go into effect in future periods. Using the 40% rate, the net effect of the temporary differences for Hawkeye is to increase deferred tax assets by $6,000 and increase deferred tax liabilities by $14,200 as in Schedule 13.2.

## Calculation of Tax Expense

The calculation of tax expense that Hawkeye will report on its 2008 GAAP income statement (assuming a 40% tax rate for all periods) follows the formulas presented in Figure 13.5 and is reproduced in Figure 13.8. The numbers appearing below the appropriate boxes are taken from Schedules 13.1 and 13.2.

When tax rates are *not* scheduled to change in the future, the tax expense reported for book purposes can be computed directly by multiplying the pre-tax book income number that is adjusted for permanent difference items by the current tax rate. The pre-tax book income number of Hawkeye adjusted for permanent differences is $506,000 (Schedule 13.1); and the current tax rate is 40%, thus yielding a tax expense of $202,400, which is the same number determined under the indirect approach in Figure 13.8. When tax rates are scheduled to change, tax expense must be determined using the indirect approach, which adjusts taxes payable for changes in the deferred tax asset and liability accounts as in Figure 13.8.

## EXERCISES

On January 2, 2007, Allen Company purchased a machine for $70,000. This machine has a five-year useful life, a residual value of $10,000, and it is depreciated using the straight-line method for financial statement purposes. For tax purposes, depreciation expense was $25,000 for 2007 and $20,000 for 2008. Allen's 2008 book income, before income taxes and depreciation expense, was $100,000, and its tax rate was 30%.

**Required:**

If Allen had made *no* estimated tax payments during 2008, what amount of current income tax liability would it report in its December 31, 2008 balance sheet?

**E13-1**

Determining current
taxes payable

**AICPA**
ADAPTED

E I 3 - 2

**Determining deferred tax liability**

**AICPA**
ADAPTED

Huff Corporation began operations on January 1, 2008. It recognizes revenues from all sales under the accrual method for financial reporting purposes and appropriately uses the install-ment method for income tax purposes. Huff's gross margin on installment sales under each method follows:

| Year | Accrual Method | Installment Method |
|------|----------------|--------------------|
| 2008 | $ 800,000 | $300,000 |
| 2009 | 1,300,000 | 700,000 |

Enacted income tax rates are 30% for 2008 and 2009 and 25% thereafter. There are no other temporary differences.

**Required:**

In Huff's December 31, 2009 balance sheet, how much should the deferred income tax liability be?

E I 3 - 3

**Determining deferred tax liability**

**AICPA**
ADAPTED

In its 2008 income statement, Tow, Inc. reported proceeds from an officer's life insurance pol-icy of $90,000 and depreciation of $250,000. Tow was the owner and beneficiary of the life in-surance on its officer. Tow deducted depreciation of $370,000 in its 2008 income tax return when the tax rate was 30%. Data related to the reversal of the excess tax deduction for depreci-ation follow:

| Year | Reversal of Excess Tax Deduction for Depreciation | Enacted Tax Rates |
|------|---------------------------------------------------|-------------------|
| 2009 | $50,000 | 35% |
| 2010 | 40,000 | 35 |
| 2011 | 20,000 | 25 |
| 2012 | 10,000 | 25 |

Tow has no other temporary differences.

**Required:**

In its December 31, 2008 balance sheet, what amount should Tow report as a deferred income tax liability?

E I 3 - 4

**Determining deferred tax effects on balance sheet**

**AICPA**
ADAPTED

As a result of differences between depreciation for financial reporting purposes and tax pur-poses, the financial reporting basis of Noor Company's sole depreciable asset, acquired in 2008, exceeded its tax basis by $250,000 at December 31, 2008. This difference will reverse in future years. The enacted tax rate is 30% for 2008, and 40% for future years. Noor has no other temporary differences.

**Required:**

In its December 31, 2008, balance sheet, how much should Noor report as the deferred tax ef-fect of this difference? Indicate the amount and whether it is an asset or a liability.

E I 3 - 5

**Determining deferred tax effects on long-term contracts**

**AICPA**
ADAPTED

Mill Company began operations on January 1, 2008 and recognized income from construction-type contracts under the percentage-of-completion method for tax purposes and the completed-contract method for financial reporting purposes. Information concerning income recognition under each method is as follows:

| Year | Percentage of Completion (Tax Purposes) | Completed Contract (Book Purposes) |
|------|------------------------------------------|-------------------------------------|
| 2008 | $400,000 | $  –0– |
| 2009 | 625,000 | 375,000 |
| 2010 | 750,000 | 850,000 |

**Required:**

For all years, assume that the income tax rate is 40% and that Mill has no other timing differences. In its December 31, 2010 balance sheet, Mill should report deferred income taxes of how much? Indicate whether the amount is an asset or a liability.

---

For the year ended December 31, 2008, Tyre Company reported pre-tax financial statement income of $750,000. Its taxable income was $650,000. The difference is due to accelerated depreciation for income tax purposes. Tyre's income tax rate is 30%, and it made estimated tax payments of $90,000 during 2008.

**Required:**

1. What amount should Tyre report as the current portion of income tax expense for 2008?

2. What amount should Tyre report as the deferred portion of income tax expense for 2008?

3. Give the journal entry Tyre would make to record 2008 taxes.

**E13-6**

Determining current portion of tax expense

**AICPA**
ADAPTED

---

Dunn Company's 2008 income statement reported $90,000 income before provision for income taxes. To aid in the computation of the provision for federal income taxes, the following 2008 data are provided:

| | |
|---|---|
| Rent received in advance | $16,000 |
| Income from exempt municipal bonds | 20,000 |
| Depreciation deducted for income tax purposes in excess of depreciation reported for financial statement purposes | 10,000 |
| Enacted corporate income tax rate | 35% |

**Required:**

What amount of current federal income tax liability should Dunn report in its December 31, 2008 balance sheet?

**E13-7**

Determining current taxes payable

**AICPA**
ADAPTED

---

Kent, Inc.'s reconciliation between financial statement and taxable income for 2008 follows:

| | |
|---|---|
| Pre-tax financial income | $150,000 |
| Permanent difference | (12,000) |
| | 138,000 |
| Temporary difference—depreciation | (9,000) |
| Taxable income | $129,000 |

**Additional Information:**

| | At December 31 | |
|---|---|---|
| | **2007** | **2008** |
| Cumulative temporary difference (future taxable amounts) | $11,000 | $20,000 |

The enacted tax rate was 35% for 2007 and 40% for 2008 and years thereafter.

**Required:**

1. In its December 31, 2008 balance sheet, what amount should Kent report as its deferred income tax liability?

2. In its 2008 income statement, what amount should Kent report as the current portion of income tax expense?

**E13-8**

Determining deferred tax liability and current portion of tax expense

**AICPA**
ADAPTED

---

West Corporation leased a building and received the $36,000 annual rental payment on June 15, 2008. The beginning of the lease was July 1, 2008. Rental income is taxable when received. Its tax rates are 30% for 2008 and 40% thereafter. West had no other permanent or temporary differences. It determined that no valuation allowance was needed.

**Required:**

What amount of deferred tax asset should West report in its December 31, 2008 balance sheet?

**E13-9**

Determining deferred tax asset amounts

**AICPA**
ADAPTED

| | |
|---|---|
| **E13-10**<br><br>Determining deferred tax asset amounts<br><br>**AICPA**<br>ADAPTED | Black Company, organized on January 2, 2008, had pre-tax accounting income of $500,000 and taxable income of $800,000 for the year ended December 31, 2008. The only temporary difference is accrued product warranty costs, which are expected to be paid as follows:<br><br>2009      $100,000<br>2010      50,000<br>2011      50,000<br>2012      100,000<br><br>Circumstances indicate that it is highly likely that Black will have taxable income in the future. It had no temporary differences in prior years. The enacted income tax rates are 35% for 2008, 30% for 2009 through 2011, and 25% for 2012.<br><br>**Required:**<br>In Black's December 31, 2008 balance sheet, how much should the deferred income tax asset be? |

Black Company, organized on January 2, 2008, had pre-tax accounting income of $500,000 and taxable income of $800,000 for the year ended December 31, 2008. The only temporary difference is accrued product warranty costs, which are expected to be paid as follows:

| | |
|---|---|
| 2009 | $100,000 |
| 2010 | 50,000 |
| 2011 | 50,000 |
| 2012 | 100,000 |

Circumstances indicate that it is highly likely that Black will have taxable income in the future. It had no temporary differences in prior years. The enacted income tax rates are 35% for 2008, 30% for 2009 through 2011, and 25% for 2012.

**Required:**
In Black's December 31, 2008 balance sheet, how much should the deferred income tax asset be?

---

**E13-11**

Reporting deferred portion of tax expense

**AICPA**
ADAPTED

Quinn Company reported a net deferred tax asset of $9,000 in its December 31, 2008 balance sheet. For 2009 Quinn reported pre-tax financial statement income of $300,000. Temporary differences of $100,000 resulted in taxable income of $200,000 for 2009. At December 31, 2009, Quinn had cumulative taxable differences of $70,000. The income tax rate is 30%.

**Required:**
In its December 31, 2009 income statement, what should Quinn report as the deferred portion of income tax expense?

---

**E13-12**

Assessing temporary and permanent differences

**AICPA**
ADAPTED

(*Note:* Students may want to review the material on the equity method of accounting in Chapter 16 before beginning work on this exercise.) Tara Corporation uses the equity method of accounting for its 40% investment in Flax's common stock. During 2008, Flax reported earnings of $750,000 and paid dividends of $250,000. Assume that:

- All undistributed earnings of Flax will be distributed as dividends in future periods.
- The dividends received from Flax are eligible for the 80% dividends received deduction.
- No other temporary differences exist.
- Tara's 2008 income tax rate is 30%.
- Enacted income tax rates after 2008 are 25%.

**Required:**
In Tara's December 31, 2008 balance sheet, what would be the increase in the deferred income tax liability from the preceding transactions?

---

**E13-13**

Calculating loss carryback and carryforward benefits

**AICPA**
ADAPTED

Town, a calendar-year corporation that was incorporated in January 2007, experienced a $600,000 net operating loss (NOL) in 2009. For the years 2007 and 2008, Town reported taxable income in each year and a total of $450,000 for the two years combined. Assume that (1) there are no differences between pre-tax book income and taxable income for all years, (2) the income tax rate is 40% for all years, (3) the NOL will be carried back to the profit years (2007–2008) to the extent of $450,000, and $150,000 will be carried forward to future periods, and (4) Town expects to report taxable income for the foreseeable future.

**Required:**
1. What amounts should Town report as "Tax benefit due to NOL carryback and carryforward" in its 2009 income statement?
2. How much will Town report as a deferred tax asset on its December 31, 2009 balance sheet?

Dix Company reported operating income/loss before income tax in its first three years of operations as follows:

| | |
|---|---|
| 2007 | $ 100,000 |
| 2008 | (200,000) |
| 2009 | 400,000 |

**E13-14**

Determining tax effects of loss carryback and carryforward

**AICPA**
ADAPTED

Dix had no permanent or temporary differences between book income and taxable income in these years. Dix elected to use the loss carryback in 2008 and to apply unused losses against future taxable income. Assume a 40% tax rate for all years.

**Required:**

1. What amount should Dix report as a tax benefit on its 2008 income statement?

2. What amount of deferred tax asset should Dix report on its December 31, 2008 balance sheet?

3. What amount should Dix report as current taxes payable on December 31, 2009 (the year after the loss)?

---

For the year ended December 31, 2008, Colt Corporation had a loss carryforward of $180,000 available to offset future taxable income. At December 31, 2008, the company believes that realization of the tax benefit related to the loss carryforward is probable. The tax rate is 30%.

**E13-15**

Accounting for loss carryforwards

**AICPA**
ADAPTED

**Required:**

1. What amount of the tax benefit should be reported in Colt's 2008 income statement?

2. What additional account(s) would be affected when the loss carryforward is recognized?

---

Operating income in Mobe's first three years of operations was as follows:

| | |
|---|---|
| 2007 | $ 300,000 |
| 2008 | (700,000) |
| 2009 | 1,200,000 |

**E13-16**

Accounting for loss carrybacks and carryforwards

**AICPA**
ADAPTED

Mobe had no other deferred income taxes in any year, and its income tax rate is 30%. In 2008, Mobe elected to carry back the maximum amount of loss possible and expected to have sufficient taxable income in future years to take full advantage of the loss carryforward tax benefits.

**Required:**

1. What amount of tax benefit would be reported in Mobe's 2008 income statement? Give the entry to record this tax benefit.

2. In 2009, what amount should Mobe report as its current income tax liability after considering the loss carryforward?

---

In Figland Company's first year of operations (2008), the company had pre-tax book income of $500,000 and taxable income of $800,000 at the December year-end. Figland expected to maintain this level of taxable income in future years. Figland's only temporary difference is for accrued product warranty costs, which are expected to be paid as follows:

**E13-17**

Computing deferred tax asset and valuation allowance

**AICPA**
ADAPTED

| | |
|---|---|
| 2009 | $100,000 |
| 2010 | $200,000 |

The enacted income tax rate for these years is 30%. Figland believes there is a high likelihood that one-third of the tax benefit associated with this future deductible amount will not be realized.

**Required:**

Compute the amount of deferred tax asset and related valuation allowance that would be reported in Figland's 2008 tax footnote.

| E13-18 |
|---|

**Reporting deferred tax asset and valuation allowance**

**AICPA**
ADAPTED

(*Note:* Students may want to review the material on the equity method of accounting in Chapter 16 before beginning work on this exercise.) Taft Corporation uses the equity method to account for its 25% investment in Flame, Inc. During 2008, Taft received dividends of $30,000 from Flame and recorded $180,000 as its equity in Flame's earnings. Additional information follows:

- All Flame's undistributed earnings will be distributed as dividends in future periods.
- The dividends received from Flame are eligible for the 80% dividends received deduction.
- Flame has no other temporary differences.
- Enacted income tax rates are 30% for 2008 and thereafter.

**Required:**

In its December 31, 2008 balance sheet, what amount should Taft report for deferred income tax liability?

| E13-19 |
|---|

**Determining tax expense, taxes payable, and deferred taxes**

**CMA**
ADAPTED

The following information is provided for Lally Corporation for 2008 and 2009:

|  | 2008 | 2009 |
|---|---|---|
| Book income before income taxes | $4,000,000 | $5,000,000 |
| Interest income included above that was not subject to income taxes | 100,000 | 100,000 |

- Income before income taxes in 2008 included accrued rent revenue of $80,000 that was not subject to income taxes until its receipt in 2009.
- Lally was subject to an income tax rate of 40% in 2008 and 2009.

**Required:**

1. What was Lally's taxable income for 2008?
2. How much was Lally Corporation's taxes payable for 2008?
3. What was the change in Lally's deferred tax asset (liability) balance for 2008?
4. What amount of income tax expense would Lally report on its 2008 income statement?
5. Repeat requirements 1 through 4 for 2009.

| E13-20 |
|---|

**Computing tax payable, deferred taxes, and tax expense**

Millie Co. completed its first year of operations on December 31, 2008 with pre-tax financial income of $400,000. Millie accrued a contingent liability of $900,000 for financial reporting purposes; however, the $900,000 will be paid and therefore is deductible for tax purposes in 2009. Millie also has gross profit from installment sales of $800,000 recognized currently for financial reporting purposes but will be taxable in 2009 and 2010 when the cash is received ($400,000 each year). Millie's pre-tax financial income includes $38,000 interest earned on its holdings of the bonds of the State of Montana. The tax rate is 30% for all years.

**Required:**

1. Determine Millie's taxable income and taxes payable for 2008.
2. Determine the changes in Millie's deferred tax amounts for 2008.
3. Calculate tax expense for Millie for 2008.

| E13-21 |
|---|

**Determining tax benefit for uncertain tax position**

Collins Company incurs a $1,000 book expense that it deducts on its tax return. The tax law is unclear whether this expense is deductible, so the deduction leads to an uncertain tax position. Assuming a 35% tax rate, the deduction results in a $350 tax benefit.

**Required:**

Consider the following three separate cases and determine how much of the tax benefit associated with the uncertain tax position Collins can recognize and how much of a tax contingency reserve for uncertain tax benefits Collins needs to record.

|  | Case 1 | Case 2 | Case 3 |
|---|---|---|---|
| Management's assessment of the likelihood of the uncertain tax position being sustained based on technical merits | 65% | 40% | 80% |
| Likelihood of realizing $350 | 10 | 5 | 55 |
| Likelihood of realizing $250 | 30 | 5 | 25 |
| Likelihood of realizing $100 | 20 | 35 | 15 |
| Likelihood of realizing $0 | 40 | 55 | 5 |

# PROBLEMS / DISCUSSION QUESTIONS

Moss, Inc. uses the accrual method of accounting for financial reporting purposes and appropriately uses the installment method of accounting for income tax purposes. It will collect $250,000 of installment income in the following years when the enacted tax rates are as indicated.

| | Collection of Income | Enacted Tax Rates |
|---|---|---|
| 2007 | $ 25,000 | 35% |
| 2008 | 50,000 | 30 |
| 2009 | 75,000 | 30 |
| 2010 | 100,000 | 25 |

The installment income is the firm's only temporary difference.

**Required:**

What amount should be included as the deferred income tax liability in Moss's December 31, 2007 balance sheet?

**P13-1**

Calculating deferred tax amounts with different tax rates

**AICPA**
ADAPTED

The following information pertains to Ramesh Company for the current year:

| | |
|---|---|
| Book income before income taxes | $106,000 |
| Income tax expense | 52,000 |
| Income taxes payable for this year | 32,000 |
| Statutory income tax rate | 40% |

The company has both a permanent and a temporary difference between book and taxable income. The permanent difference relates to goodwill (that is, assume that amortization of goodwill is not allowed as an expense for tax purposes), and the temporary difference relates to depreciation expense.

**Required:**

1. Calculate the amount of temporary difference for the year and indicate whether it causes the book income to be more or less than the taxable income.

2. Calculate the amount of permanent difference for the year and indicate whether it causes the book income to be more or less than the taxable income.

3. Provide the journal entry to record the income tax expense for the year.

4. Compute the effective tax rate (that is, income tax expense divided by book income before taxes). Explain why this rate is different from the statutory tax rate of 40%.

**P13-2**

Calculating the amount of temporary and permanent differences and tax entry

---

**P 1 3 - 3**

Reporting deferred tax amount on income statement

**AICPA**
ADAPTED

For financial statement reporting, Lexington Corporation recognizes royalty income in the period earned. For income tax reporting, royalties are taxed when collected. At December 31, 2007, unearned royalties of $400,000 were included in Lexington's balance sheet. All of these royalties had been collected in 2007. During 2008, royalties of $600,000 were collected. Unearned royalties in Lexington's December 31, 2008 balance sheet amounted to $350,000. Assume that the income tax rate was 50%.

**Required:**

What amount should be reported as the provision for deferred income taxes in Lexington's income statement for the year ended December 31, 2008?

---

**P 1 3 - 4**

Reporting current and deferred portion of tax expense

**AICPA**
ADAPTED

Joy Corporation prepared the following reconciliation of income per books with income per tax return for the year ended December 31, 2008:

| | |
|---|---:|
| Book income before income taxes | $750,000 |
| Add temporary difference: Construction contract | |
|    revenue that will reverse in 2009 | 100,000 |
| Deduct temporary difference: Depreciation expense that will | |
|    reverse in equal amounts in each of the next four years | (400,000) |
| Taxable income | $450,000 |

Joy's income tax rate is 35% for 2008.

**Required:**

1. What amount should Joy report in its 2008 income statement as the current provision for income taxes?

2. How much should Joy report as deferred income taxes on the income statement in 2008?

---

**P 1 3 - 5**

Computing tax expense and making deferred tax calculations

Nelson Inc. purchased machinery at the beginning of 2008 for $90,000. Management used the straight-line method to depreciate the cost for financial reporting purposes and the sum-of-the-years'-digits method to depreciate the cost for tax purposes. The life of the machinery was estimated to be two years, and the salvage value was estimated at zero. Revenues less expenses other than depreciation expense and goodwill impairment equaled $500,000 for 2008 and 2009. Nelson pays income tax at the rate of 20% of taxable income. The goodwill impairment equaled $50,000 for 2008 and 2009.

**Required:**

1. Compute the taxable income and the financial reporting income (before tax) for the years 2008 and 2009.

2. What are the permanent and timing differences? Give an example of each for Nelson.

3. Complete the following table on your answer to requirement 1.

| Year | Ending Balance in Tax Liability | Tax Expense | Ending Balance in Deferred Income Taxes |
|---|---|---|---|
| 2008 | | | |
| 2009 | | | |

(*Note:* Be sure to identify whether it is a debit or credit balance for deferred income taxes.)

4. Assume that the federal government changes the tax rate to 30% at the beginning of 2009. Compute the following:

    Increase/decrease in deferred income taxes
    Income tax liability for 2009
    Income tax expense for 2009

Metge Corporation's worksheet for calculating taxable income for 2008 follows:

| ($ in thousands) | 2008 |
|---|---|
| Pre-tax income | $1,000 |
| Permanent differences | |
| Goodwill impairment | 400 |
| Interest on municipal bonds | (200) |
| Temporary differences | |
| Depreciation | (800) |
| Warranty costs | 400 |
| Rent received in advance | 600 |
| Taxable income | $1,400 |

**P13-6**

Determining current and deferred portion of tax expense and reconciling statutory and effective tax rates

The enacted tax rate for 2008 is 35%, but it is scheduled to increase to 40% in 2009 and subsequent years. All temporary differences are originating differences.

**Required:**

1. Determine Metge's 2008 taxes payable.

2. What is the change in deferred tax assets (liabilities) for 2008?

3. Determine tax expense for 2008.

4. Provide a schedule that reconciles Metge's statutory and effective tax rates (in both percentages and dollar amounts).

Smith Corporation started doing business in 2007. The following table summarizes the company's taxable income (loss) over the 2007–2019 period and the statutory tax rate effective in each year:

**P13-7**

Recording entries for loss carrybacks and carryforwards

| Year | Taxable Income (Loss) | Enacted Tax Rate |
|---|---|---|
| 2007 | $ 100,000 | 40% |
| 2008 | 200,000 | 40 |
| 2009 | 250,000 | 35 |
| 2010 | 400,000 | 32 |
| 2011 | (350,000) | 30 |
| 2012 | (275,000) | 30 |
| 2013 | 125,000 | 30 |
| 2014 | 175,000 | 30 |
| 2015 | 275,000 | 30 |
| 2016 | 300,000 | 35 |
| 2017 | (800,000) | 35 |
| 2018 | (250,000) | 35 |
| 2019 | 150,000 | 35 |

Because Smith had no permanent or timing differences during this period, its pre-tax financial reporting income was identical to its taxable income in each year. During the 2016–2019 period, Smith expected the current and future tax rates to be 35%. When possible, the company took advantage of the loss carryback provision of the tax law. When recording the tax benefits of the loss carryforward provision, management believed it was more likely than not that the tax benefits would be fully realized.

**Required:**

1. Provide journal entries to record income tax expense for the years 2011, 2012, 2017, 2018 and 2019.

2. In answering this requirement, make the following assumptions. During 2017 and 2018, Smith management believed it was more likely than not that only 40% of the tax benefits would be realized through a loss carryforward. However, during 2019, the company

revised its expectation, believing that it was more likely than not that 100% of the tax benefits would be fully realized through a loss carryforward. Provide journal entries to record income tax expense for the years 2017, 2018, and 2019. Also show how to report the deferred tax asset as of the end of 2017, 2018, and 2019.

**P13-8**

Making entries for loss carrybacks and carryforwards

Barron Corporation started doing business in 2007. The following table summarizes the company's taxable income (loss) over the period 2007–2015.

| Year | Taxable Income (Loss) |
|------|-----------------------|
| 2007 | $ 200,000 |
| 2008 | 150,000 |
| 2009 | 125,000 |
| 2010 | 90,000 |
| 2011 | 200,000 |
| 2012 | (150,000) |
| 2013 | (180,000) |
| 2014 | 125,000 |
| 2015 | (120,000) |

Because Barron had no permanent or timing differences during this period, its pre-tax financial reporting income was identical to its taxable income in each of the preceding years. During the entire period, Barron's current as well as its expected future tax rate was 40%. Whenever possible, the company took advantage of the loss carryback provision of the tax law. When recording the tax benefits of the loss carryforward provision, management believed it was more likely than not that the tax benefits would be fully realized.

**Required:**

Provide journal entries to record income tax expense for the years 2012–2015.

**P13-9**

Reconciling statutory and effective tax rates

The following information pertains to Enis Corporation for the year ended December 31, 2008. The company reported a $1,500,000 loss before taxes in its GAAP income statement, which included the effects of the following items:

- On January 1, 2008, Enis acquired Hansen Technology Group for $5,000,000 in cash. The breakdown for the acquisition cost is:

| | |
|---|---|
| Marketable securities | $1,800,000 |
| Other current assets | 200,000 |
| Value of in-process technology | 2,000,000 |
| Goodwill | 1,000,000 |
| | $5,000,000 |

Under GAAP, if a portion of the acquisition price can be allocated to the value of "in-process technology" (that is, technology under development), that portion should be expensed as a part of the R&D expense of the acquiring company (that is, Enis) in the year of the acquisition. However, the value of the in-process technology is not considered as an expense for tax purposes.

In its 2008 GAAP income statement, Enis wrote off $50,000 of the goodwill acquired in the Hansen Technology acquisition because it was determined to be impaired. However, none of the goodwill write-off qualifies for a deduction in Enis's tax statement.

- The bad debts written off during the year were $75,000 more than the provision for uncollectibles (or bad debt expense) recorded during the year.

- Enis Corporation earned $80,000 during 2008 from income on municipal bonds. The company has hired an investment management company to manage its portfolio of municipal bonds. Enis paid a $10,000 fee to the management company during 2008. This fee is nondeductible for tax purposes because the income is nontaxable.

- Enis recorded a straight-line depreciation expense of $140,000 in its GAAP income statement. The corresponding accelerated tax depreciation was $210,000.
- Enis incurred an insurance expense of $15,000 during 2008 for the premium on the life insurance policies of its senior executives. Enis is the beneficiary on these policies. During 2008, one of the senior executives died, and Enis received $250,000 from the insurance company as death benefits.

**Required:**

1. Determine the taxable income and taxes payable for Enis in 2008. Assume a 35% statutory tax rate.
2. Determine the change in deferred tax assets (liabilities) for 2008.
3. Calculate Enis's income tax expense for the year 2008.
4. Determine the effective book tax rate for Enis in 2008, and prepare a schedule to explain why the effective tax rate is different from the statutory tax rate.
5. Provide the journal entry to record the income tax expense, taxes payable, and deferred taxes for the year 2008.

---

Weber Manufacturing Company started doing business on January 1, 2008. Its current business plan predicts significant growth in sales over the next several years. To respond to this predicted growth, Weber is planning to buy each year new factory equipment at a $60,000 cost during the first six years of its operations (2008–2013). It purchased the first piece of equipment on January 1, 2008. The company plans to use the straight-line method to depreciate the equipment cost for financial reporting purposes and the sum-of-the-years'-digits method for tax purposes. The equipment's useful life was estimated to be three years with no salvage value for both tax and financial reporting purposes. Weber expects to pay taxes at the rate of 35% of its taxable income and except for the depreciation expense, expects no other temporary or timing differences.

**P13-10**

Obtaining analytical insights from deferred tax account

mhhe.com/revsine4e

**Required:**

1. Calculate the balance in the Deferred income tax liability account as of the end of years 2008–2013.
2. In answering this requirement, assume that Weber purchased the factory equipment at the beginning of each year (starting from 2008) for six years. However, the equipment costs $60,000 in 2008, which is expected to increase by $6,000 each year over the following five years ($66,000 in 2009, $72,000 in 2010, and so on). Calculate the balance in the Deferred income tax liability account as of the end of 2008 through 2013.
3. Consider the facts given in requirement 2. Due to expected changes in business technology, the company expects the demand for its current products to start falling in 2014. Consequently, it plans to reduce its production substantially after 2014. In fact, Weber expects to purchase no more machinery after 2013. With this new information, compute the balance in the Deferred income tax liability account for 2014 and 2015.
4. Based both on your answers to requirements 1 through 3 and on changes in its Deferred income tax liability account, what conclusions might you draw about Weber's financial condition?

---

(*Note:* Students may want to review the material on accounting for trading securities in Chapter 16 before beginning this problem.)

Over the past two years, Madison Corporation has accumulated operating loss carryforwards of $66,000. This year, 2008, Madison's pre-tax book income is $101,500. The company is

**P13-11**

Converting book income to taxable income and computation of taxes payable subject to a 40% corporate tax rate. The following items are relevant to Madison's deferred tax computations for 2008.

1. Equipment purchased in 2005 is depreciated on a straight-line basis for financial reporting purposes and using an accelerated method for tax purposes as follows:

| | Book | Tax |
| --- | --- | --- |
| 2005 | $100,000 | $200,000 |
| 2006 | 100,000 | 150,000 |
| 2007 | 100,000 | 100,000 |
| 2008 | 100,000 | 50,000 |
| 2009 | 100,000 | –0– |

2. Madison's trading securities portfolio generated a $13,000 unrealized gain that is not recognized for tax purposes until the securities are sold.

3. Madison has not yet paid its rent for November and December of 2008, a total of $25,000. The expense was accrued for book purposes and is included in pre-tax book income.

4. During 2008, Madison paid a $6,500 fine to its state corporation commission for allegedly violating state security laws. Madison neither denied nor admitted guilt related to the charges. The expense is not deductible for tax purposes but has been included in computing pre-tax book income.

**Required:**

1. Determine Madison Corporation's taxable income for 2008.

2. Calculate the amount of tax payable for Madison Corporation for 2008.

---

**P13-12**

Calculating taxes payable, deferred taxes and tax expense

(*Note:* Students may want to review the material on accounting for trading securities in Chapter 16 before beginning this problem.)

At the end of its third year of operations, December 31, 2008, Delilah Corp. is reporting pre-tax book income of $223,000. The following items are relevant to Delilah's deferred tax computations:

1. A $55,000 unrealized holding gain on its trading securities that is not recognized for tax purposes until it sells the securities.

2. Bad debt expense of $24,000 was recorded on its accounts receivable, although during 2008 no actual write-offs took place.

3. During 2008, Delilah received $19,000 cash from one of its customers. The payment received relates to a product that will be completed and delivered to the customer in late January 2009.

Delilah is subject to a 40% corporate tax rate.

**Required:**

1. Determine Delilah Corp.'s taxable income and taxes payable for 2008.

2. Determine the changes in Delilah Corp.'s deferred tax amounts for 2008.

3. Calculate tax expense for Delilah Corp. for 2008.

---

**P13-13**

Converting from taxable income to book income

Mozart Inc.'s $98,000 taxable income for 2008 will be taxed at the 40% corporate tax rate. For tax purposes, its depreciation expense exceeded the depreciation used for financial reporting purposes by $27,000. Mozart has $45,000 of purchased goodwill on its books; during 2008, the company determined that the goodwill had suffered a $3,000 impairment of value for financial reporting purposes. None of the goodwill impairment is deductible for tax purposes. Mozart purchased a three-year corporate liability insurance policy on July 1, 2008 for $36,000 cash. The entire premium was deducted for tax purposes in 2008.

**Required:**

1. Determine Mozart's pre-tax book income for 2008.

2. Determine the changes in Mozart's deferred tax amounts for 2008.

3. Calculate tax expense for Mozart Inc. for 2008.

---

In Year 1, Phillips Company reported $10,000 net income for both book and tax purposes. It incurred a $1,000 book expense that it deducted on its tax return. Assuming a 35% tax rate, this deduction results in a $350 tax benefit. The tax law was unclear at that time whether this expense was deductible, so it led to an uncertain tax position.

In Year 1, this uncertain tax position had a 60% likelihood of being sustained based on technical merits, $150 of the benefit was recognized, and a tax contingency reserve of $200 was created for this position.

A court decision in Year 2 lowered the likelihood that this uncertain tax position could be sustained on technical merits to 40% and led to the following amounts and related individual probabilities of possible outcomes:

> 10% likelihood of realizing $350
> 15% likelihood of realizing $250
> 30% likelihood of realizing $50
> 45% likelihood of realizing $0

**P13-14**

Making entries for uncertain tax positions

**Required:**

1. Based on these facts, provide the journal entry that Phillips would make in Year 1 to record tax expense, taxes payable, and the tax contingency for unrecognized tax benefits.

2. Provide the entry Phillips would make in Year 2 to record any change in the status of the tax contingency reserve.

---

In Year 1, MB, Inc. is subject to a 40% tax rate. For book purposes, it expenses $1,500 of expenditures. MB intends to deduct these expenditures on its Year 1 tax return despite tax law precedent that makes it less than 50% probable that the deduction will be sustained on its technical merits. Instead, the best estimate is that the IRS will allow these expenses to be amortized straight line over a 15-year period. In Year 1 and each of the subsequent 14 years, $100 of amortization would be allowed.

**P13-15**

Making entries for uncertain tax positions

**Required:**

1. In Year 1, determine which accounts MB would debit and credit and for how much in properly accounting for this uncertain tax position.

2. Determine the entries that MB would make in Year 2 related to this uncertain tax position.

---

Flower Company started doing business on January 1, 2007. For the year ended December 31, 2008, it reported $450,000 pre-tax book income on its income statement. Flower is subject to a 40% corporate tax rate for this year and the foreseeable future. Additionally, it has the following issues that impact its tax situation:

**P13-16**

Comprehensive tax allocation problem

1. During 2008, Flower acquired $600,000 of specialized productive machinery that it depreciates using the straight-line method over five years with no salvage value for accounting purposes. For tax purposes, this specialized equipment is being depreciated $200,000 per year for the first three years of its productive life.

2. During 2008, the federal government fined Flower $100,000 for violating environmental laws. The amount was paid on November 15, 2008 and was deducted in determining this year's book income.

3. Flower received $40,000 of interest revenue as a result of its investment in the bonds issued by the State of Arizona.

4. On January 2, 2008, Flower leased warehouse space for $2,000 per month for a three-year period. On January 2, 2008, as a condition of the lease, Flower paid $30,000 to the lessor to cover the first 15 months of rent. Because Flower leased space in excess of its needs, it immediately (January 2, 2008) subleased part of the warehouse to a small, local company. The sublease was also for a period of three years and required the tenant to make $800 monthly rent payments to Flower. During 2008, Flower received $8,800 in monthly rental payments from the sublessee. Pre-tax book income includes an accrual for rent revenue earned but not yet received in cash.

5. During the year, Flower's CEO was killed in an automobile accident. The company had a $200,000 life insurance policy on the CEO and collected the proceeds of the policy during October 2008.

6. During 2008, Flower sold a parcel of land held for speculative purposes. The historical cost of the land was $320,000, and it was sold for $680,000. The cash will be collected from the purchaser in 10 monthly installments of $68,000 each. During 2008, Flower collected five of these $68,000 payments; the remaining payments are assumed to be fully collectible during 2009.

7. During 2007, Flower accumulated $22,000 operating loss carryforward it can use to offset 2008 taxable income.

8. The beginning balance in the Deferred income tax asset account is $8,800 and there was no beginning balance in the Deferred income tax liability account.

**Required:**

1. Beginning with pre-tax accounting income, compute taxable income and taxes payable for 2008. Clearly label all amounts used in arriving at taxable income.

2. Using the following schedule, compute the change in the Deferred tax asset and Deferred tax liability accounts for 2008. The depreciation temporary difference has been completed as an example.

| Temporary Difference | Deferred Tax Asset | Deferred Tax Liability |
|---|---|---|
| Depreciation ($200,000 − $120,000) × 40% | | $32,000 **CR** |

3. Determine tax expense for 2008.

---

**P13-17**

Determining taxes payable, deferred taxes, and tax expense

mhhe.com/revsine4e

(*Note:* Students may want to review the material on the equity method of accounting in Chapter 16 before beginning work on this problem.)

In the current year, 2008, Reality Corporation reported $200,000 of pre-tax earnings on its income statement. The corporate tax rate is 40% in the current year and next year, and it is scheduled to remain at this level for the foreseeable future. Additional information relevant to figuring taxes is as follows:

1. Reality acquired $500,000 of machinery in 2007. The machinery is being depreciated on a straight-line basis over five years (zero salvage) for accounting purposes and MACRS for tax purposes. A comparison of depreciation charges under these two methods is as follows:

| | 2007 | 2008 | 2009 | 2010 | 2011 |
|---|---|---|---|---|---|
| Straight line | $100,000 | $100,000 | $100,000 | $100,000 | $100,000 |
| MACRS | 165,000 | 225,000 | 75,000 | 35,000 | –0– |

2. Investment income from a 30% ownership of an investee company carried under the equity method is shown on the income statement as $80,000. The investee paid $30,000 in dividends to Reality in the current year. The remaining undistributed earnings total for 2008 is expected to be received in equal amounts over the next two years in the form of dividends. All dividends are subject to the 80% dividend exclusion rule.

3. During the year, Reality recognized $4,000 of rental income that had been collected and taxed in 2007. In addition, $10,000 of rent revenue was received in advance in the current year. This amount was deferred for accounting purposes and will be recognized as income in 2009.

4. Reality received $5,000 of interest on State of North Carolina bonds in the current year that is included in pre-tax income.

5. Reality sold land in the current year for $50,000 that had a $20,000 book value and tax basis. The entire gain (*not* considered extraordinary) was recognized for accounting purposes in 2008. However, because collections are to be received in three equal installments, Reality elected to use the installment sales method for tax purposes and picked up one-third of the gain on its tax return in 2008. The remaining amount of the gain will be recognized equally in 2009 and 2010.

6. Reality provided for future product warranty costs in the amount of $50,000 in the current year for book purposes. For tax purposes, such costs are deductible when paid. Actual warranty costs paid in 2008 were $15,000. It is expected that the remainder of the accrued warranty costs will be paid in 2009.

7. Included in pre-tax accounting income is a deduction for $3,000 for insurance premiums paid on Mr. Reality's life.

8. Reality made charges to bad debts expense in the current year of $15,000. The beginning balance in the Allowance for bad debts account was $12,000, and $6,000 of accounts was written off in the current year. It is expected that the 2008 year-end balance in the allowance account will be written off in 2009.

9. Reality has a $10,000 operating loss carryforward that can be used to offset the current period's taxable income.

10. The balance in the deferred tax asset (liability) account was $40,000 ($50,000) at the beginning of 2008.

11. It is estimated to be more likely than not that 20% of the deferred tax asset at the end of 2008 will not be realized.

**Required:**

1. Starting with pre-tax accounting income, compute taxable income and taxes payable for 2008. Clearly label all amounts used in arriving at taxable income.

2. Using the following schedule, compute the change in the deferred tax asset (liability) account for 2008. The depreciation temporary difference has been completed as an example.

| Temporary Difference Item | Deferred Tax Asset | Deferred Tax Liability |
|---|---|---|
| Depreciation ($225,000 − $100,000) × 40% | | $50,000   **CR** |

3. Determine the tax expense for 2008.

## CASES

**C13-1**

Mandalay Resort Group
and Subsidiaries: Analyzing
tax footnote

The following is adapted from the 2003 financial statements of the Mandalay Resort Group, one of the largest hotel/casino operators in the United States. The components of the provision for income taxes in fiscal years ended January 31, 2003, 2002, and 2001 were as follows:

| | Years Ended January 31 | | |
| ($ in thousands) | 2003 | 2002 | 2001 |
|---|---|---|---|
| Current income tax expense (benefit): | | | |
| Federal | $46,446 | $39,147 | $53,716 |
| State | 1,504 | 1,438 | 1,417 |
| Current income tax expense | 47,950 | 40,585 | 55,133 |
| | | | |
| Deferred income tax expense (benefit): | | | |
| Federal | 29,919 | (623) | 19,559 |
| Income tax expense | $77,869 | $39,962 | $74,692 |

The income tax effects of temporary differences between financial and income tax reporting that gave rise to deferred income tax assets and liabilities at January 31, 2003 and 2002 follow:

| | January 31 | |
| ($ in thousands) | 2003 | 2002 |
|---|---|---|
| **Deferred tax liabilities** | | |
| Property and equipment | $221,662 | $205,434 |
| Investments in unconsolidated affiliates | 14,205 | 10,671 |
| Other | 12,982 | 1,061 |
| Gross deferred tax liabilities | 248,849 | 217,166 |
| | | |
| **Deferred tax assets** | | |
| Accrued vacation benefits | 8,137 | 9,232 |
| Bad debt reserve | 9,159 | 3,510 |
| Preopening expenses | 4,875 | 9,762 |
| Pension plan | 8,122 | 5,176 |
| Other | 7,427 | 7,784 |
| Gross deferred tax assets | 37,720 | 35,464 |
| **Net Deferred tax liabilities** | $211,129 | $181,702 |
| Comprehensive income | | |

Other comprehensive income for the Company includes adjustments for minimum pension liability and adjustments to interest rate swaps, net of tax. The accumulated other comprehensive loss reflected on the balance sheet consisted of the following:

| | January 31, | |
| ($ in thousands) | 2003 | 2002 |
|---|---|---|
| Minimum pension liability adjustment | $11,370 | $ 5,799 |
| Adjustment to interest rate swaps | 5,550 | 16,103 |
| Accumulated other comprehensive loss | $16,920 | $21,902 |

(*Note:* Mandalay reports its swap-related assets and liabilities on a net basis in the Other long-term liabilities account.)

**Required:**

1. Provide journal entries to record the income tax expense for fiscal years 2001 through 2003. You may indicate the sum of the changes in the various deferred tax assets/liabilities by a single debit or credit to the Net deferred tax asset/liability account.

2. Refer to the deferred income tax asset and liability items reported by Mandalay at December 31, 2003 and 2002. For each item (except Other), determine whether the balance changed because of a net originating or net reversing timing difference. Provide a likely explanation for each of the timing differences and clearly discuss whether it indicates a higher or lower financial reporting revenue or expense relative to the amount reported on the fiscal 2003 tax return.

3. Mandalay's reported deferred tax expense in 2003 ($29,919) does not equal the reported increase in net deferred tax liability ($211,129 − $181,702 = $29,427) over the course of fiscal 2003. Is this difference explained by Mandalay's comprehensive income disclosure? Provide calculations to support your answer.

---

Edited excerpts from Sara Lee Corporation's Year 2 tax footnote follow:

### Excerpts from Tax Footnote

| ($ in millions) | Year 2 | Year 1 |
|---|---|---|
| **Effective Income Tax Rates** | | |
| Tax expense at U.S. statutory rate* | $415 | $ 648 |
| State taxes, net of federal benefit | 5 | 9 |
| Difference between U.S. and foreign rates | (144) | (169) |
| Gain on disposal of Coach business | | (338) |
| Exit activities and business dispositions | (10) | 140 |
| Nondeductible amortization | | 50 |
| Benefit of foreign tax credits | (69) | (38) |
| Other, net | (22) | (54) |
| **Taxes at effective worldwide tax rates** | $175 | $ 248 |

\* Assume a statutory rate of 35%.

C13-2

Sara Lee Corporation: Analyzing tax footnotes

Current and deferred tax provisions (benefits) were:

| | Year 2 | | Year 1 | |
|---|---|---|---|---|
| | Current | Deferred | Current | Deferred |
| United States | $ 27 | $(95) | $ (12) | $29 |
| Foreign | 105 | 130 | 169 | 48 |
| State | 22 | (14) | 3 | 11 |
| | $154 | $ 21 | $160 | $88 |

The following are components of the deferred tax (benefit) provisions occurring as a result of transactions being reported in different years for financial and tax reporting:

| ($ in millions) | Year 2 | Year 1 |
|---|---|---|
| Depreciation | $(27) | $ 11 |
| Inventory valuation methods | 7 | 22 |
| Nondeductible reserves | 7 | 31 |
| Other, net | 34 | 24 |
| Net deferred tax provision | $ 21 | $ 88 |
| Cash payments for income taxes | $266 | $259 |

### Required:

1. Prepare the book journal entry for income tax expense for Year 2 (combine U.S., foreign, and state income taxes). Clearly indicate both the account title and whether the account is being debited or credited.

2. Using information given in the segment Effective Income Tax Rates regarding the statutory marginal tax rate for Year 2, estimate Sara Lee Corporation's pre-tax book income for Year 2. Show your work.

3. What was the Year 2 effective overall tax rate for Sara Lee after considering differences arising from state and foreign income taxes, nondeductible amortization, and so on? Show your work.

4. Estimate Sara Lee's taxable income. (*Note:* You do not have enough information to do this by category; therefore, combine U.S., foreign, and state taxes.) Show and clearly label all work.

5. Using information found in the tax footnote, determine whether depreciation expense was higher for book or tax purposes in Year 2 and by how much.

6. Using information found in the tax footnote, determine whether expenses related to Nondeductible reserves were higher for book or tax purposes in Year 2 and by how much.

---

**C13-3**

**Motorola vs. Intel: Adjusting for depreciation differences**

Motorola and Intel are both in the semiconductor industry and compete in many of the same product sectors. But each uses a different depreciation method. Motorola's Year 2 10-K states the following:

Depreciation is recorded principally using the declining-balance method based on the estimated useful lives of the assets (buildings and building equipment, 5–50 years; machinery and equipment, 2–12 years).

So, Motorola is using accelerated depreciation for most of its assets. By contrast, Intel's Year 2 report says:

Depreciation is computed for financial reporting purposes principally by use of the straight-line method over the following estimated useful lives: machinery and equipment, 2 to 4 years; land and buildings, 4 to 45 years.

The following table gives several key financial statement figures for each company from its respective Year 2 10-K and excerpts from its income tax footnote:

### From the Year 2 10-Ks of Motorola and Intel

**Selected, Edited Financial Statement Disclosures**

**Motorola**

| ($ in millions) | Year 2 | Year 1 |
|---|---|---|
| Book depreciation | $2,308 | $1,919 |
| Income before income taxes | 1,775 | 3,225 |
| Property, plant and equipment, net of accumulated depreciation (at year-end) | 9,768 | 9,356 |

| | December 31 | |
|---|---|---|
| **Significant Deferred Tax Assets (Liabilities)** | Year 2 | Year 1 |
| Inventory reserves | $440 | $345 |
| Contract accounting methods | 231 | 157 |
| Employee benefits | 291 | 286 |
| Capitalized items | 138 | 89 |
| Tax basis differences on investments | (199) | (176) |
| Depreciation | (213) | (197) |
| Deferred taxes on non-U.S. earnings | (545) | (382) |
| Other deferred income taxes | 329 | 132 |
| Net deferred tax asset | $472 | $254 |

*(continued)*

## From the Year 2 10-Ks of Motorola and Intel (*continued*)

**Intel**

| ($ in millions) | Year 2 | Year 1 |
| --- | --- | --- |
| Book depreciation | $1,888 | $1,371 |
| Income before income taxes | 7,934 | 5,638 |
| Property, plant and equipment, | | |
| less accumulated depreciation (at year-end) | 8,487 | 7,471 |

| | December 31 | |
| --- | --- | --- |
| **Significant Deferred Tax Assets (Liabilities)** | **Year 2** | **Year 1** |
| **Deferred tax assets** | | |
| Accrued compensation and benefits | $ 71 | $ 61 |
| Deferred income | 147 | 127 |
| Inventory valuation and related reserves | 187 | 104 |
| Interest and taxes | 54 | 61 |
| Other, net | 111 | 55 |
| | $ 570 | $ 408 |
| **Deferred tax liabilities** | | |
| Depreciation | (573) | (475) |
| Unremited earnings of certain subsidiaries | (359) | (116) |
| Other, net | (65) | (29) |
| | $(997) | $(620) |

Assume a statutory tax rate of 35% for all years.

**Required:**

1. Using the information provided and the analytical techniques illustrated in the chapter, determine the tax depreciation for Motorola and Intel for Year 2.

2. Adjust each firm's pre-tax income to reflect the same depreciation method and useful lives used for tax purposes.

3. Explain why the adjusted numbers provide a better basis for comparing the operating performance of the two companies.

---

ABC Inc. is in the business of airframe maintenance, modification and retrofit services, avionics and aircraft interior installations, the overhaul and repair of aircraft engines, and other related services.

The following are excerpted from its income statement for the year ended December 31, 2008.

| ($ in thousands) | 2008 |
| --- | --- |
| Earnings (loss) before income taxes | $10,891 |
| Income tax benefit (provision) | (3,267) |
| Net earnings (loss) | $ 7,624 |

The details for the income tax expense or provision follow.

| Income Tax Expense | 2008 |
| --- | --- |
| Current | $1,756 |
| Deferred | 1,511 |
| Income tax expense | $3,267 |

Due to the nondeductibility of amortization of goodwill, the company's tax expense was higher by $1,076 than would be expected based on the statutory tax rate of 35%. State taxes further

**C13-4**

ABC Inc.: Interpreting tax footnotes and reconciling statutory and effective rates added another $927 to the tax expense. However, the reduction in the valuation allowance decreased the accounting income tax expense. In addition, several other items caused the tax expense to deviate from the tax liability. Since these items by themselves are immaterial, no separate breakdowns are available.

The following breakdowns are available for the balance sheet values of deferred tax assets and liabilities:

| | December 31 | |
|---|---|---|
| ($ in thousands) | 2008 | 2007 |
| **Deferred Tax Assets** | | |
| Accounts receivable | $ 977 | $ 1,070 |
| Inventories, principally due to additional costs inventoried for tax purposes and financial statement allowances | 3,523 | 1,679 |
| Employee benefits, principally due to accrual for financial reporting purposes | 9,814 | 13,510 |
| Accrual for costs of restructuring | 5,392 | 8,750 |
| Accrual for disposal of discontinued operations | 4,312 | 5,020 |
| Others | 23,634 | 19,257 |
| Gross deferred tax assets | $47,652 | $49,286 |
| Less: Valuation allowance | (13,588) | (15,710) |
| Total deferred tax asset | $34,064 | $33,576 |
| **Deferred Tax Liability** | | |
| Plant and equipment | $(7,770) | $(8,993) |
| Others | (5,187) | (1,964) |
| Total deferred tax liability | (12,957) | (10,957) |
| **Net deferred tax asset** | $21,107 | $22,619 |

The book value of the company's inventories increased from $91,130 at the end of 2007 to $127,777 at the end of 2008.

**Required:**

1. Prepare a schedule reconciling the statutory and effective tax rates of ABC Inc. for the year ended 2008.

2. Provide the journal entry to record the income tax expense for 2008, showing separately the effects on deferred tax asset, valuation allowance, and deferred tax liability.

3. For each component of deferred tax asset/liability, provide possible reasons for the change in its values from 2007 to 2008.

---

**C13-5**

Understanding tax footnote disclosures

Excerpts from Wrigley Company's Year 2 tax footnote follow.

### Year 2 Annual Report Footnote on Income Taxes

| | Years Ended December 31 | | |
|---|---|---|---|
| ($ in thousands) | Year 2 | Year 1 | Year 0 |
| **Current provision** | | | |
| Federal | $ 21,401 | $ 30,142 | $ 30,704 |
| Foreign | 135,901 | 121,137 | 109,184 |
| State | 6,786 | 6,770 | 7,954 |
| | 164,088 | 158,049 | 147,842 |
| **Deferred provision** | | | |
| Federal | 16,113 | 2,384 | 961 |
| Foreign | 908 | 2,704 | 2,170 |
| State | 787 | 1,243 | (603) |
| | 17,808 | 6,331 | 2,528 |
| Total | $181,896 | $164,380 | $150,370 |

Reconciliation of the provision for income taxes computed at the U.S. federal statutory rate of 35% for Years 2, 1, and 0 to the reported provision for income taxes follows:

| ($ in thousands) | Year 2 | Year 1 | Year 0 |
|---|---|---|---|
| Provision at U.S. federal statutory rate | $204,197 | $184,578 | $167,759 |
| State taxes—net | 4,922 | 4,401 | 5,351 |
| Foreign tax rates | (27,045) | (23,832) | (19,546) |
| Tax credits (principally foreign) | (2,438) | (1,400) | (1,675) |
| Other—net | 2,260 | 633 | (1,519) |
| Reported tax expense | $181,896 | $164,380 | $150,370 |

Components of net deferred tax balances follow:

| ($ in thousands) | Year 2 | Year 1 |
|---|---|---|
| Accrued compensation, pension, and post-retirement benefits | $ 15,493 | $ 26,419 |
| Depreciation | (28,888) | (21,898) |
| Unrealized holding gains | (5,488) | (7,638) |
| All other—net | (2,361) | (317) |
| Net deferred tax liability | $(21,244) | $ (3,434) |

Balance sheet classifications of deferred taxes follow:

| ($ in thousands) | Year 2 | Year 1 |
|---|---|---|
| Deferred tax asset | | |
| Current | $ 19,560 | $ 14,846 |
| Noncurrent | 33,000 | 29,605 |
| Deferred tax liability | | |
| Current | (3,215) | (1,455) |
| Noncurrent | (70,589) | (46,430) |
| Net deferred tax liability | $(21,244) | $ (3,434) |

**Required:**

1. Provide a journal entry to record the aggregate income tax expense for Year 2.

2. What amount of Wrigley's Year 2 tax expense was deferred? Did this deferral result in an increase in deferred tax liabilities or a decrease in deferred tax assets?

3. Determine Wrigley's effective tax rate for Year 2.

4. What tax policy or operating decision accounts for the majority of the divergence between Wrigley's statutory tax rate and effective tax rate?

5. Did Wrigley report any deferred tax assets in Year 2? If so, what temporary differences between the carrying amounts of assets and liabilities for financial reporting purposes and the amounts used for income tax purposes gave rise to these assets?

6. Did Wrigley have any significant changes in its net deferred tax liability during Year 2 related to nonoperating items? Explain.

# COLLABORATIVE LEARNING CASE

Following is the 2007 first quarter *FIN48* footnote disclosure for Under Armour, a maker of athletic sportswear. All amounts are in thousands of dollars.

**C13-6**

Interpreting *FIN48* disclosures

**Provision for Income Taxes**

The Company adopted the provisions of FIN 48 on January 1, 2007. As a result of the implementation of FIN 48, the Company recorded an additional $1,597 liability for unrecognized tax benefits, of which $1,152 was accounted for as a reduction to the January 1, 2007 balance of retained earnings with the remainder recorded within deferred tax assets. After recognizing these impacts upon adoption of FIN 48, the total unrecognized tax benefits were approximately $2,054. Of this amount, approximately $1,609 would impact our effective tax rate if recognized. The Company does not expect that the total amounts of unrecognized tax benefits will significantly increase or decrease within the next twelve months.

The Company recognizes accrued interest and penalties related to unrecognized tax benefits in the provision for income taxes on the consolidated statements of income. The unrecognized tax benefits liability recorded on January 1, 2007 included $512 for the accrual of interest and penalties.

The Company files income tax returns in the U.S. federal jurisdiction and various state and foreign jurisdictions. The majority of the Company's returns are no longer subject to U.S. federal, state and local or foreign income tax examinations by tax authorities for years before 2003.

## Required:

1. Give the journal entry that Under Armour made on January 1, 2007 to reflect the adoption of *FIN48*.

2. What amount of contingent liability had Under Armour recorded on its books for uncertain tax benefits prior to adoption of *FIN48*?

3. Do you think Under Armour was taking a conservative or aggressive approach to recognizing tax benefits on uncertain tax positions prior to adoption of *FIN48*? How can you tell?

4. What was the total amount in the Tax contingency reserve account for Under Armour on January 1, 2007 after adoption of *FIN48*?

5. Of the total Tax contingency reserve amount on January 1, 2007, what amount represents interest and penalties?

6. What amount of the Tax contingency reserve account on January 1, 2007 after adoption of *FIN48* represents permanent difference benefits that have yet to be recognized?

7. What amount of the January 1, 2007 Tax contingency reserve account represents temporary differences?

8. What amount of temporary difference benefits had Under Armour recognized prior to adoption of *FIN48*?

**www** **.mhhe.com/revsine4e**

**Remember to check the book's companion Web site
for additional study material.**

# Pensions and Postretirement Benefits | 14

E mployer-provided pension and retiree health benefits represent valuable income security to the elderly during retirement. These benefits can also represent substantial liabilities and cash outflows for employers. Because the workers earn the benefits over their work lives and receive the benefits during retirement, employer accounting for some types of plans must use numerous assumptions regarding return on plan assets, life expectancy, salary at retirement, and so on. Actual experience can deviate substantially from these assumptions. Most of the accounting challenges revolve around these estimation issues.

## RIGHTS AND OBLIGATIONS IN PENSION CONTRACTS

A **pension plan** is an agreement by an organization (**sponsor**) to provide payments—called a **pension**—to employees when they retire, either in a series of payments (an **annuity**) or as a one-time "lump-sum" distribution. In the United States, the plan sponsor makes contributions to a **pension trust**—a legal entity that invests and holds the assets for the employee's benefit—over the employee's career. The retiree then receives pension payments from the trust during retirement. In most instances, these company pension payments supplement payments from government-sponsored pension plans—such as Social Security in the United States. A pension plan represents a valuable benefit to employees. Employers create these plans as a way to attract and retain a qualified workforce. Because pensions benefit firms in the form of higher productivity from employees, the cost of a worker's pension plan is treated as an expense over that worker's period of employment.

Pension plans can be divided into two categories—*defined contribution plans* and *defined benefit plans*—based on the nature of the plan promise.

**Defined contribution plans** specify the amount of cash that the employer puts *into* the plan trust. No explicit promise is made about the size of the periodic benefits the employee will receive during retirement. Rather, the promise is the amount of contributions the employer will make periodically. The employee exchanges service for this promise. The employee is generally given a variety of alternative investment funds (broad stock funds, growth stock funds, bond funds, etc.), and the ultimate size of the payments the employee will receive depends on the success of these investments. The employer receives a tax deduction for amounts contributed to the pension plan trust, and subsequent investment returns do not generate tax for the

employer or the employee until the employee retires. The retiree is taxed on the amount of annual withdrawals at ordinary income tax rates. The amount that will ultimately be paid to the employee is determined by the accumulated value at retirement of the amounts contributed to the plan over the period of employment. In defined contribution plans, the *employee* bears the risk that the ultimate pension payments will be large enough to sustain a comfortable retirement income.

The common types of defined contribution plans are money purchase, profit sharing, and 401(k). In a **money purchase plan,** the employer contributes a fixed percentage of an employee's salary to the pension plan. The employer must make this contribution whether it is having a good year or a bad year. In a **profit-sharing plan,** the employer contributes to the plan only when profits exceed a predetermined threshold. The contribution may then be allocated to participants on the basis of salary or seniority. In a **401(k) plan,** the employer makes a contribution only if the employee voluntarily contributes to a pension plan. The terms of the plan specify the matching percentage (often 50%) and the maximum annual employer contribution or the maximum percentage of salary eligible for matching. Some 401(k) plans have very generous terms; others are somewhat miserly. Because of the fixed commitments associated with money purchase plans, they consistently result in cash outflows for the firm whereas the cash outflows for the other types of defined contribution plans vary from year to year.

> The employer's contributing of assets to the plan trust is termed **funding.** Employees may also be required to contribute to the plan. For example, a plan might specify that the employer is to contribute 10% of the employee's salary to the plan and that the employee is to contribute 5%, for a total of 15%. The employees' 5% contributions are typically deducted from their paychecks and directly transferred to the plan trust.

A **defined benefit plan** is quite different. These agreements specify the formula that determines the annual benefit amount (lifetime annuity) to be *paid out* to the employee during retirement rather than the annual amount that will be *contributed* to the plan. The annual pension benefit typically depends on each employee's years of service and salary. For example, a defined benefit plan may specify that an employee will receive an annual pension equal to 3% (called a *generosity factor*) of his or her salary at retirement for each year of service. An employee with 25 years of service and an annual salary at retirement of $60,000 would receive an annual pension benefit of $45,000 (25 years of service × 3% for each year × the ending salary of $60,000). Because the pension payout formula is specified in advance in a defined benefit plan, the *employer* bears the investment risk instead of the *employee.* However, the employee bears the risk that the firm will go bankrupt and default on unfunded pension liabilities. Determining how much cash must be contributed to the fund to provide the annual pension benefit of $45,000 is complex and may be expensive to compute. These amounts must be computed using assumptions and procedures described later in the chapter.[1] The tax treatment for defined benefit plans is similar to that for defined contribution plans. The employer receives tax deductions for amounts contributed to the pension trust, and the employee does not pay tax until pension payments are received during retirement. Also, the parties involved in a defined benefit plan are the same as those in a defined contribution plan. However, under a defined benefit plan, employees receive in exchange for service the promise of a lifetime annuity instead of the promise of contributions to a trust.

> A plan is **fully funded** if its assets equal its liabilities. If assets exceed liabilities, the plan is said to be **overfunded;** if liabilities exceed assets, it is said to be **underfunded.**

The relationships among the plan sponsor, the plan trust, and the plan beneficiaries (the eventual retirees) for both types of plans are shown in Figure 14.1.

Refer to Figure 14.2 for the total dollar amount of assets in each of the two types of pension plans over the years from 1988 to 2005. The proportion of assets in defined benefit plans as a percent of total pension assets declined over

---

[1] **Actuaries** use statistical methods to estimate the defined benefit plan obligation and annual funding. Assumptions must be made about length of service, return on assets, life expectancy, and salaries at retirement. These assumptions are called **actuarial assumptions.** When actual experience is different from assumptions, **actuarial gains or losses** arise.

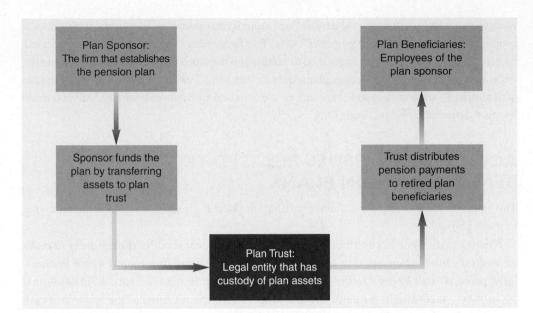

**Figure 14.1**

PENSION PLAN ENTITIES
AND RELATIONSHIPS

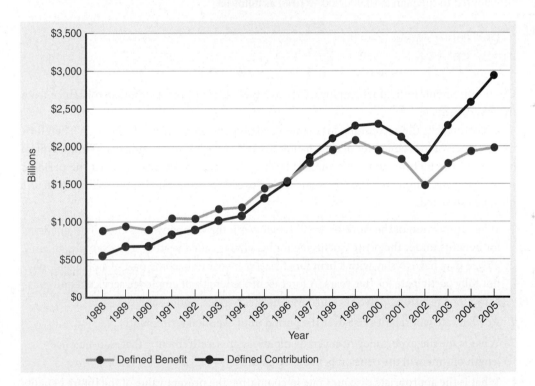

**Figure 14.2**

ASSETS BY PLAN TYPE

*SOURCE:* Employee Benefit Research
Institute, Washington, D.C., www.ebri.
org/publications/books/index.cfm?fa=
databook. *EBRI Databook on Employee
Benefits,* Chapter 11, "Retirement Plan
Finance: Defined Benefit and Defined
Contribution, Public and Private Plans,"
Table 11.3a–c. Updated August 2007.

this period. Defined benefit plans, which have been in existence since the late 19th century, grew rapidly in the manufacturing, telecommunication, airline, and utility industries in the first half of the 20th century. These plans still exist, but young firms in growth industries tend to have defined contribution plans because they are less costly to manage, less risky for the employer, improve job mobility for the employee, and may not be at risk if the employer declares bankruptcy.[2] In 1988, the value of defined contribution plan assets in the United States

---

[2] A defined contribution plan may be an **employee stock ownership plan (ESOP)** whose primary asset is employer stock. For example, Procter & Gamble Co. sponsors a profit-sharing plan that also is an ESOP. If an employee has invested 100% of his or her account in employer stock, the pension is essentially worthless in the event of employer bankruptcy, which is what occurred with Enron in 2001.

was approximately 62% of the value of defined benefit plan assets. By the end of 2005, the percentage had increased to approximately 148%. The figure also shows that both plan types experienced asset value declines from 2000 to 2002 when the stock market was weak. Despite the trend toward defined contribution plans, data in Figure 14.2 show that defined benefit plans held almost $2 trillion in assets at the end of 2005. In addition, the majority of S&P 500 firms sponsor defined benefit pension plans.

## ACCOUNTING ISSUES RELATED TO DEFINED BENEFIT PENSION PLANS

The employer accounting for defined contribution plans is straightforward, as the following example shows.

Assume that a defined contribution pension plan agreement requires *the company to make an annual contribution equal to 10% of each employee's salary into a fund whose accumulated proceeds will be paid to the employee at retirement.* Employees' salaries in 2008 total $10 million. Accordingly, the company records pension expense equal to the amount of cash contributed to the plan ($10,000,000 × 10%) as follows:

| | | | |
|---|---|---|---|
| **DR** | Pension expense | $1,000,000 | |
| | **CR** Cash | | $1,000,000 |

Upon retirement, individual employees receive their share of the accumulated balance from the investments.

Unfortunately, the accounting for defined benefit pension plans is not this easy. Therefore, we use much of the remainder of this chapter to explain it. The accounting complications arise because of the lifetime annuity promised by the employer. To determine what the periodic pension expense should be over the span of employees' working careers, the following factors must be estimated:

1. What proportion of the workforce will remain with the company long enough to qualify for benefits under the plan? Qualifying for benefits is called **vesting.** For example, an employee may have to stay with a firm for at least one year to become part of a plan and may not fully participate for five years. A forecast of the length of employee service requires assumptions regarding personnel turnover, mortality rates, and disability.

2. At what rate will salaries rise over the period until eventual retirement?

3. What is the life expectancy of covered employees after retirement—that is, over what length of time will the pension benefits be paid?[3]

4. What is the appropriate discount rate in computing the present value of the future benefits earned by employees in the current period?

5. What do firms do when actual experience differs from expectations? It's impossible to predict exactly how long someone will work for a company, what she or he will be earning at retirement, and how long she or he will live after retiring. Consequently, the accounting must address the differences between actual and expected experience.

The accounting problem is further complicated by the presence of the pension trust assets. In a defined contribution plan the *employee* bears the risk associated with pension investments.

---

[3] Upon a retired worker's death, plans often pay pension benefits (at a reduced amount) to a surviving spouse. Consequently, actuaries must estimate for these plans the life of the spouse in addition to that of the employee.

However, in a defined benefit plan the *employer* bears the risk. Just as pension liabilities can change over time because actual experience differs from expectations, pension asset returns can vary greatly from year to year. Consequently, the accounting must incorporate asset returns and expected fluctuations in returns.

*Statement of Financial Accounting Standards (SFAS) No. 87* issued in December 1985 specified measurement and disclosure requirements for defined benefit pension plans.[4] The disclosure aspects of *SFAS No. 87* were amended by *SFAS No. 132* in 1998 and by *SFAS No. 132* (revised 2003) in 2003.[5] In 2006, the Financial Accounting Standards Board (FASB) revised both recognition and disclosure requirements by issuing *SFAS No. 158*, "Employers' Accounting for Defined Benefit Pension and Other Postretirement Plans."[6] *SFAS No. 87* includes several smoothing features to make annual pension expense less volatile. These smoothing features were included in response to corporate lobbying and because short-term gains and losses on pension assets and obligations may not result in cash inflows or outflows. Until the issuance of *SFAS No. 158*, the gains and losses omitted from pension expense also were excluded from the balance sheet and were merely disclosed in footnotes. Under *SFAS No. 158*, the gains and losses are recognized in **accumulated other comprehensive income (AOCI)**[7] with a corresponding offset to a balance sheet pension asset or liability account. The FASB views *SFAS No. 158* as an interim measure while it continues to consider pension presentation and measurement issues.

The smoothing techniques and recognition rules that govern pension accounting can make it very difficult for accountants, analysts, and other external users to understand how pensions affect financial statements. We try to clarify the topic by providing an intuitive overview of the financial reporting rules for defined benefit pension plans.

## FINANCIAL REPORTING FOR DEFINED BENEFIT PENSION PLANS

Under current GAAP, pension expense comprises five separate components[8] (a + indicates increase in expense, and a − indicates decrease in expense):

1. Service cost (+).
2. Interest cost (+).
3. Expected return on the market-related value of pension plan assets (−).
4. Recognized gains or losses (− or +).
5. Recognized prior service cost (− or +).

> In *SFAS No. 87*, **market-related value** of pension plan assets is a technical term. It can be either (1) the fair value of the assets or (2) a smoothed value that recognizes gains and losses more slowly (over not more than five years).

---

[4] Entitled "Employers' Accounting for Pensions," *SFAS No. 87* replaced both *Accounting Principles Board (APB) Opinion No. 8*, "Accounting for the Cost of Pension Plans," 1966, and *SFAS No. 36*, "Disclosure of Pension Information," 1980, which previously governed pension accounting and disclosure.

[5] "Employers' Disclosures about Pensions and Other Postretirement Benefits," *SFAS No. 132* (Norwalk, CT: FASB, 1998), and *SFAS No. 132* (revised 2003). The revised version of *SFAS No. 132* has the same title as the 1998 version. For simplicity, citations throughout the chapter simply refers to *SFAS No. 132*. When warranted, we refer to significant revisions mandated in the December 2003 revision of *SFAS No. 132*.

[6] "Employers' Accounting for Defined Benefit Pension and Other Postretirement Plans," *SFAS No. 158* (Norwalk, CT: FASB, 2006).

[7] This chapter assumes a thorough knowledge of **other comprehensive income (OCI)** and AOCI. Please review Chapter 2 if you have questions on these concepts.

[8] *SFAS No. 87* also included amortization of the off-balance sheet transition asset or liability existing at the adoption of *SFAS No. 87*. Because *SFAS No. 87* was issued in 1987, the transition asset or liability is now fully amortized for most firms. Consequently, we do not include it in our primary discussions of pension accounting. Also, if a company either (1) curtails a plan or (2) settles a plan's liabilities by purchasing an annuity contract and generates a gain or loss from either event, that gain or loss would also be included in pension expense as another element. Measuring the gain or loss on plan settlements or curtailments is outlined in "Employers' Accounting for Settlements and Curtailments of Defined Benefit Pension Plans and for Termination Benefits," *SFAS No. 88* (Stamford, CT: FASB, 1985).

We use a simple example to illustrate how to compute pension expense Components 1 through 3 under the *SFAS Nos. 87* and *158* rules.[9] The example assumes an environment characterized by *complete certainty*. This assumption simplifies the setting and clarifies the relationship between the various pension expense components. The complete certainty assumption shows that Components 4 and 5 would not be needed in an environment with no surprises. We also use the example to introduce institutional features of defined benefit plans and employer balance sheet recognition. In subsequent examples, we show how Components 4 and 5 come into play in a world of *uncertainty* in which expectations are often not realized and changes in assumptions occur frequently.

## A Simple Example: A World of Complete Certainty

Consider the following example[10] of a hypothetical company with a defined benefit retirement plan:

---

On January 1, 2008, Wildcat Corporation decides to provide a lump-sum pension payment equal to $10,000 for each year of service to its newly hired and sole employee, Ed Cate. No previous pension plan existed. Wildcat expects Cate to retire on December 31, 2009 and desires to pay him the pension in one lump sum on December 31, 2010.

Further assume that Wildcat operates in an environment of complete certainty in which the interest rate and the rate of return on investments are equal, known, and constant. Furthermore, the length of Cate's life and the duration of his employment service are also known in advance. Wildcat uses a 7% **discount rate,** which is **the interest rate used to compute the present value of pension benefits and interest cost** (*SFAS No. 87,* para. 39).[11] In addition, the pension trust will earn exactly 7%. Contributions equal to the present value of new benefits earned are made at the end of each year to the pension fund.

---

We now show how to compute Components 1 through 3 for this simple example.

Usually, pension plans provide survivor benefits and pay benefits monthly. To make calculations easier to follow, we exclude survivor benefits and use lump-sum or annual pension payments in our hypothetical examples. This chapter's self-study problem includes calculations for a retirement annuity.

**Component 1—Service Cost** In a typical defined benefit pension plan, the pension payout increases for each additional year of service. The present value of this increase is **service cost.** Stated more rigorously, *service cost is the increase in the discounted present value of the pension benefits ultimately payable that is attributable to an additional year's employment.*

In the simplified example, Cate worked throughout 2008 and, according to the terms of the pension benefit formula, became eligible for a $10,000 pension payable on December 31, 2010. The discounted present value of this obligation on December 31, 2008 (at a 7% annual discount rate) is $8,734 ($10,000 $\times$ 1/[1.07]$^2$). Because no obligation existed at the start of 2008, the *increase* in the obligation's discounted present value during the year is $8,734—this is the service cost element of pension expense on Wildcat's books for 2008 as well

---

[9] The discussion of the first three components of pension expense is adapted from L. Revsine, "Understanding Financial Accounting Standard 87," *Financial Analysts Journal*, January–February 1989, pp. 61–68, and is presented here with the publisher's permission.

[10] This example is adapted from a pre-*SFAS No. 87* illustration prepared by Professor Norman Bartczak of Columbia University.

[11] Pension computations rely on the present value techniques discussed in the Chapter 8 appendix. Present value tables appear in Appendix I on page 1109.

as the pension obligation at year-end. A pension liability that is computed using **future** salaries is called the **projected benefit obligation (PBO)**. Because Wildcat fully funds the pension expense, the pension plan's economic status at December 31, 2008 is:

**Wildcat Corporation**

$$\text{Pension expense} = \text{Pension obligation} = \frac{\$10,000}{(1.07)^2} = \$8,734 = \text{Service cost}$$

Pension funding $\qquad\qquad\qquad\qquad\quad \$8,734 = $ Cash transferred to trust

**Wildcat Employees' Pension Trust**

Pension fund assets and obligation $\quad = \quad \$8,734 = $ Cash received from
$\qquad\qquad\qquad\qquad\qquad\qquad\qquad\qquad\qquad\qquad\qquad\qquad$ Wildcat Corporation

Wildcat makes the following journal entry on December 31, 2008 to record pension expense and its contribution to the plan:

| | | | |
|---|---|---|---|
| **DR** | Pension expense | $8,734 | |
| **CR** | Cash | | $8,734 |

Wildcat Corporation does not recognize on its balance sheet either the *gross* pension assets or PBO. ***The gross assets and liabilities are reflected only on the statements of the plan trust.*** However, *SFAS No. 158* requires Wildcat to recognize the **funded status,** the net difference between the fair value of plan assets and the PBO. In this simple example, the funded status is zero, so no asset or liability is recognized on the balance sheet. Balance sheet recognition is discussed in detail in subsequent examples.

Ed Cate's continued employment throughout 2009 qualifies him for a $20,000 pension payable on December 31, 2010. The service cost element of pension expense for the year 2009 is the increase in the present value of the amount ultimately payable that is attributable to an additional year's employment. Exhibit 14.1 shows the computation.

The ultimate pension payout has increased by $10,000 because Cate earned additional benefits by working in 2009. As shown in Exhibit 14.1, the discounted present value of this increase is $9,346 ($10,000 × .9346). By definition, this is service cost.

In addition to service cost, the 2009 *total* pension expense for Wildcat Corporation includes two other items—interest cost and return on plan assets.

| EXHIBIT 14.1 | Wildcat Corporation |
|---|---|

**Computation of Service Cost for 2009**

| | | |
|---|---|---:|
| Pension payout to Cate with two years of service (2008 and 2009) | | $20,000 |
| Less: Pension payout to Cate with one year of service (2008) | | −10,000 |
| *Undiscounted* increase attributable to 2009 service | = | 10,000 |
| Discount factor at 7% for one year (from Appendix I, Table 1) | | |
| | × | .9346 |
| Service cost for 2009 | = | $ 9,346 |

### Component 2—Interest Cost

Service cost for 2008 was initially recorded at $8,734, the discounted present value of the pension payment due on December 31, 2010. Because the payment of this liability drew one year closer by the end of 2009, its present value increased by $611 ($8,734 × 0.07). Another way to view the interest cost component is that the employer incurs interest on any unpaid pension obligations. Therefore, in addition to service cost, there is interest cost in 2009. The **interest cost** component of pension expense (and the increase in the liability) arises from the passage of time. *Interest cost is computed by taking the pension liability at the beginning of the period (here, $8,734) and multiplying it by the annual interest rate factor (here, 7%).*

### Component 3—Expected Return on Plan Assets

Plan assets are invested in stocks and bonds that pay dividends and interest. Furthermore, the stocks and bonds could appreciate in value. The dividends, interest, and appreciation comprise the return on plan assets. At December 31, 2008, the pension fund assets (held by the trust) had a balance of $8,734. During 2009, these assets earned a return of $611 ($8,734 × 0.07). *This return reduces pension expense.* As a consequence of all of these events, total pension expense for 2009 is $9,346 ($9,346 + $611 − $611). See Exhibit 14.2 for the 2009 pension expense components and pension fund asset balance at December 31, 2009.

The journal entry for the 2009 pension expense and contribution is:

| | | |
|---|---|---|
| **DR** Pension expense . . . . . . . . . . . . . . . . . . . . . . . . . . . . . . . . . . . . . . . . . . . . . . | $9,346 | |
| **CR** Cash . . . . . . . . . . . . . . . . . . . . . . . . . . . . . . . . . . . . . . . . . . . . | | $9,346 |

If Cate retires at the end of 2009, there will be no service cost component of pension expense in 2010 because he didn't work during 2010. However, there will be interest cost of $1,308 ($18,692 × 7%) because the present value of the amount owed at the pension payout date increases as time passes. There will also be a return on plan assets in 2010. *Exhibit 14.3 shows that the $1,308 interest cost and the $1,308 return on plan assets offset each other, so*

> In this example, no pension benefits are paid during the year, and plan contributions are received at year-end. In practice, interest cost reflects the timing of any changes (e.g., benefit payments) to the amount of the PBO during the year. Similarly, the expected return reflects the timing of both the employer contributions and benefit payments. For example, if Wildcat had not funded its 2008 pension cost until April 1, 2009, the expected return would have been $459 ($8,734 × 0.07 × 9/12) instead of $611.
>
> *Source:* "A Guide to Implementation of Statement 87 on Employers' Accounting for Pensions—Questions and Answers" (Norwalk, CT: FASB, 1986), para. 24.

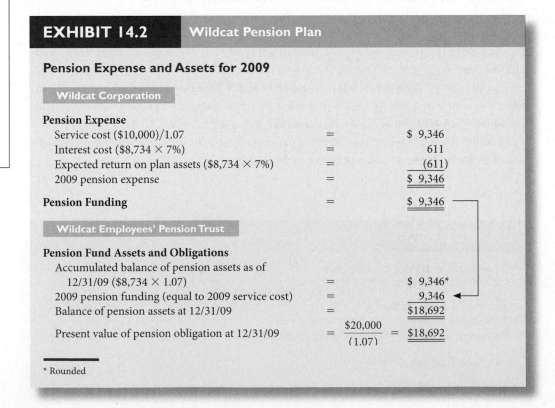

**EXHIBIT 14.2** **Wildcat Pension Plan**

**Pension Expense and Assets for 2009**

**Wildcat Corporation**

**Pension Expense**

| | | |
|---|---|---|
| Service cost ($10,000)/1.07 | = | $ 9,346 |
| Interest cost ($8,734 × 7%) | = | 611 |
| Expected return on plan assets ($8,734 × 7%) | = | (611) |
| 2009 pension expense | = | $ 9,346 |

| | | |
|---|---|---|
| **Pension Funding** | = | $ 9,346 |

**Wildcat Employees' Pension Trust**

**Pension Fund Assets and Obligations**

| | | |
|---|---|---|
| Accumulated balance of pension assets as of 12/31/09 ($8,734 × 1.07) | = | $ 9,346* |
| 2009 pension funding (equal to 2009 service cost) | = | 9,346 |
| Balance of pension assets at 12/31/09 | = | $18,692 |
| Present value of pension obligation at 12/31/09 | = $\dfrac{\$20,000}{(1.07)}$ = | $18,692 |

\* Rounded

---

**EXHIBIT 14.3**    Wildcat Pension Plan

### Pension Expense and Assets for 2010

**Wildcat Corporation**

**Pension Expense**

| | | |
|---|---|---|
| Interest cost (that is, present value of pension obligation at 12/31/09 × discount rate: $18,692 × 7%) | = | $ 1,308 |
| Expected return on plan assets ($18,692 × 7%) | = | (1,308) |
| 2010 pension expense | = | –0– |
| **Pension Funding** | = | –0– |

**Wildcat Employees' Pension Trust**

**Pension Fund Assets and Obligations**

| | | |
|---|---|---|
| Accumulated balance of pension assets as of 12/31/10: ($18,692 × 1.07) | = | $20,000 |
| Less: 12/31/10 payment to Cate | = | (20,000) |
| Balance of pension assets at 12/31/10 | = | –0– |
| Present value of pension obligation as of 12/31/10 | = | $20,000 |
| Less: 12/31/10 payment to Cate | = | (20,000) |
| Balance of pension obligation at 12/31/10 | = | –0– |

---

*2010 pension expense is zero.* Notice that the December 31, 2010 accumulated asset balance of $20,000 exactly equals the required pension payment.

To recap, *perfect certainty* in this example meant:

1. The exact *date of retirement was known* at the time the plan was initiated. In technical terms, the precise service life of employees was known with certainty.

2. The ultimate *amount of the pension was also known in advance.* No unexpected salary increases raised the amount of the final payment, nor were there unforeseen actuarial events such as turnover or death.

3. *Discount rates and earnings rates were equal and could be perfectly forecast over the entire period.*

Pension expense equals service cost in our "perfect world" example because interest cost is exactly offset by the return on plan assets. In these simple (but unrealistic) circumstances, pension expense equals service cost in every period over which the pension plan is in effect:

| Year | Service Cost | Total Pension Expense |
|---|---|---|
| 2008 | $8,734 | $8,734 |
| 2009 | 9,346 | 9,346 |
| 2010 | –0– | –0– |

When cash funding equals service cost, the accumulated amount of pension assets is exactly sufficient to pay the liability (see Exhibit 14.3).

We use perfect certainty in this example to help you see the relationship among the components comprising pension expense. Of course, no perfect certainty exists in the real pension world. On the contrary, unforeseen pension events arise continuously. Examples include the following:

1. Employee turnover may be higher or lower than anticipated.

2. Preretirement mortality may be unusually high or low (vis à vis actuarial estimates).

3. The return earned on pension plan assets could differ significantly from expectations.

4. Interest rates will change, thereby causing changes in discount rate assumptions.

5. Changes in social and economic conditions may prompt companies to retroactively alter the level of benefits.

All of these factors explain why, in the real world, no simple equality exists between pension plan assets and pension plan liabilities and why pension expense does not equal service cost. Depending on the age distribution of the workforce, interest cost instead of service cost could be the dominant part of pension expense.

**If the future were known with certainty, pension expense for defined benefit plans would always equal service cost, and pension plan assets would always equal pension plan liabilities. Starting with this simple setting will help you understand the complications that uncertainty introduces.**

## The Real World: Uncertainty Introduces Gains and Losses

Uncertainty requires estimates of discount rates, expected return on plan assets, and numerous other future events such as employee turnover and mortality. *SFAS No. 87* requires that the same interest rate be used for computing both the service cost *and* the interest cost components of pension expense. However, companies are free to choose some other rate for computing the *expected* rate of return on pension plan assets, and most do so.

The simplified complete certainty example shows that the higher the interest rate initially chosen for computing service cost, the lower is the reported service cost component of pension expense (see Exhibit 14.4). This reduction in service cost is offset by an increase in the interest cost component of pension expense, which is due to the higher interest rate. In our Wildcat Corporation example, if the same higher rate is *also* used for computing the expected return on plan assets, pension expense is reduced. The data in Exhibit 14.4 illustrate the decrease in pension expense that results from using an 8% interest rate rather than 7% in the Wildcat Corporation example. Given that the expected return offsets exactly the interest cost, the entire decrease results from the decrease in service cost.

| EXHIBIT 14.4 | Wildcat Corporation | | | |
|---|---|---|---|---|

**Pension Expense at Two Different Interest Rates**

| | | | Interest Rate | |
|---|---|---|---|---|
| | | | **8%** | **7%** |
| **2008 Pension Expense** | | | | |
| 2008 Service cost | $10,000/(1.08)^2 | = | $8,573 | |
| | $10,000/(1.07)^2 | = | | $8,734 |
| **2009 Pension Expense** | | | | |
| 2009 Service cost | ($20,000 − $10,000)/1.08 | = | $9,259 | |
| | ($20,000 − $10,000)/1.07 | = | | $9,346 |
| Interest cost | $8,573 × 8% | = | 686 | |
| | $8,734 × 7% | = | | 611 |
| Return on plan assets | $8,573 × 8% | = | (686) | |
| | $8,734 × 7% | = | | (611) |
| | | | $9,259 | $9,346 |

If the assumed 8% rate of return is not *actually earned* on plan assets, the accumulated pension fund assets will be too small to fund Cate's pension, and pension expense will have been *understated*. But by generalizing from Exhibit 14.4 data, you can see that companies can temporarily alter pension expense (either up or down) by choosing a higher or lower discount rate and by choosing a higher or lower expected rate of return on plan assets.

*SFAS No. 87* provides explicit criteria for estimating discount rates. It states that "assumed discount rates shall reflect the rates at which the pension benefits could effectively be settled"(para. 44). *SFAS No. 87* paras. 44 and 44a (as amended by *SFAS No. 158*) suggest that employers look to prevailing rates of return on high-quality debt instruments with maturities that match expected payouts to retirees. Because average time to retirement and average life expectancy can differ across firms, assumed discount rates also can differ. The *SFAS No. 87* (as amended by *SFAS No. 158*) guidance reduces managers' ability to manipulate its pension expense and its projected benefit obligation but does not eliminate it.

See Figure 14.3 for a graphic comparison of discount rates and rate of return assumptions for plan assets used by a sample of Compustat firms from 2001 to 2006.[12] The top and bottom of each bar represent the rates in the 99th and 1st percentiles, respectively; the line crossing each bar represents the median rate. As you can see, there is considerable variation in both the discount rate and the expected long-term rate of return across firms within a given year. For example, the discount rates in 2002 range from 5.0% to 7.5% with a median of 6.8%; the expected long-term rate

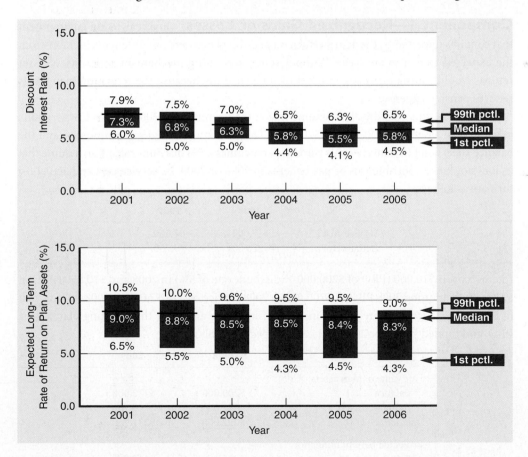

## Figure 14.3

PENSION DISCOUNT RATE AND EXPECTED LONG-TERM RATE OF RETURN ON PLAN ASSETS 2001–2006

Sample consists of all U.S. AMEX and NYSE firms with defined benefit plans and necessary data.

*Source:* Standard & Poor's Compustat® as data source; methodology not verified or controlled by Standard & Poor's.

---

[12] Compustat® is a computerized financial database for more than 10,000 active firms listed on the New York Stock Exchange (NYSE), American Stock Exchange (AMEX), and National Association of Securities Dealers Automated Quotations (NASDAQ) exchanges which is developed and distributed by Standard & Poor's Corporation. The samples for Figure 14.3 and subsequent figures exclude non-U.S. corporations (corporations with American depositary receipts [ADRs] or incorporated outside the United States). The sample for Figure 14.3 includes all U.S. AMEX and NYSE firms with available data for expected long-run rate of return and discount rates. The sample size ranges from a low of 773 firms in 2001 to a high of 890 firms in 2005.

of return on plan assets ranges from 5.5% to 10%, with a median of 8.8%. The median discount rate was 7.3% in 2001 and fell each year until hitting a low of 5.5% in 2005. In 2001, the median expected rate of return on plan assets was 9% but dropped to 8.5% by 2003 and stayed close to that rate through 2006. Note that the assumed rate of return at the 99th percentile is only 0.7% above the median whereas the assumed rate of return at the 1st percentile is 4% less than the median. We see a similar but less extreme pattern for the discount rate assumption.

> One explanation for these patterns is that the SEC has questioned discount rate or rate of return assumptions that appear to be unusually high. As discussed earlier, increases to rate of return or discount rate assumptions reduce pension expense. The discount rate assumption can have an even greater effect on plan liabilities as we discuss later in the chapter.
>
> *Source:* E. Schultz, "Ford and GM Get SEC Request on Pension Accounting Practices," *The Wall Street Journal*, October 20, 2004, p. A1.

Uncertainty not only complicates the measurement of service cost and interest cost but also means that actual outcomes will likely differ from expectations. For example, the **actual return** (the interest, dividends, and appreciation obtained during the year) on pension plan assets differs from the expected return, and actual turnover and pay increases differ from actuarial assumptions. As we are about to show, *these deviations between expected and actual events—if recognized immediately—would inject volatility into the periodic measure of pension expense.* Managers abhor earnings volatility because of its potential negative effects on stock valuations and accounting-based contracts (see Chapters 6 and 7) and, not surprisingly, strong sentiments for reducing this volatility emerged early in the exposure draft stage of *SFAS No. 87.* Components 4 and 5 of the annual pension expense calculation are designed to smooth this volatility. Our discussion now turns to each of these smoothing components of pension expense.

### Component 4—Recognized Gains or Losses

In a real-world environment that contains uncertainty, the actual return on pension plan assets can differ considerably from the expected return in any year. Without some smoothing mechanism, volatility in asset returns would translate directly into net income volatility because the return on plan assets reduces pension expense.

To illustrate this volatility, let's assume that at the beginning of 2008, Roger Corporation's pension plan assets and PBO equal $200,000. There are no deferred gains or losses, and the balance sheet asset (liability) equals zero. Roger assumes a 5% discount rate. Also assume that it does not make contributions or pay benefits in 2008 or 2009. Its service cost and actual return are as follows:

|                | 2008     | 2009    |
|----------------|----------|---------|
| Service cost   | $ 7,000  | $7,550  |
| Actual return  | 22,000   | 9,750   |

Interest cost is $10,000 (PBO of $200,000 × discount rate of 5%) in 2008 and $10,850 (PBO of $217,000 [beginning 2008 PBO of $200,000 + 2008 service cost of $7,000 + 2008 interest cost of $10,000] × discount rate of 5%) in 2009. Using these amounts, the resulting plan assets, PBO, and funded status for 2008 and 2009, respectively follow:

|                                | 2008      | 2009      |
|--------------------------------|-----------|-----------|
| Fair value of plan assets      |           |           |
|   Balance at 1/1     | $200,000  | $222,000  |
|   Actual return      | 22,000    | 9,760     |
| Balance at 12/31               | $222,000  | $231,760  |
|                                |           |           |
| Projected benefit obligation   |           |           |
|   Balance at 1/1     | $200,000  | $217,000  |
|   Service cost       | 7,000     | 7,500     |
|   Interest cost      | 10,000    | 10,850    |
| Balance at 12/31               | $217,000  | $235,350  |
| Funded status                  | $ 5,000   | $ (3,590) |

If no smoothing were permitted, Roger's pension expense in the two years would be:

|  | 2008 | 2009 |
|---|---|---|
| Service cost | $ 7,000 | $ 7,500 |
| Interest cost | 10,000 | 10,850 |
| Less: Actual return on plan assets | (22,000) | (9,760) |
| Pension expense (income) | $ (5,000) | $ 8,590 |

This accounting would result in recognition of the funded status on Roger's balance sheet. In 2008, to offset the pension income, a pension asset equal to $5,000 would be created. In 2009, this asset would be reduced by the pension expense of $8,590, resulting in a pension liability of $3,590.

Although the funded status would be on the balance sheet, the extreme change in year-to-year pension expense (income)—$5,000 income versus $8,590 expense—would cause year-to-year volatility in the firm's operating income. *SFAS No. 158* makes it possible to avert this volatility in pension expense by allowing firms to reduce pension expense by the *expected* return on plan assets rather than by the *actual* return. This result is accomplished in two steps:

- First, firms make an assumption about the expected long-term rate of return on plan assets (**rate of return assumption**). This rate should reflect the average long-term returns on the types of investments held in the pension trust (*SFAS No. 87*, para. 45). For example, long-term returns for stock investments would be expected to be higher than long-term returns for U.S. Treasury bonds. The dollar amount of the expected return is computed by multiplying this rate by the market-related value of plan assets.

> Recall from Chapter 2 that AOCI is the cumulative gain and that **OCI** is the change in AOCI for the year. OCI is the net of new gains and losses and reclassifications of prior gains and losses into net income.

- Second, any difference between the dollar amount of the expected return and the actual return that is earned in a given year is recognized in OCI instead of pension expense.

If the cumulative balance of these gains (losses) becomes large relative to the pension plan assets and liabilities, some of the cumulative amount is shifted from AOCI to pension expense. The specific details of this shifting process are discussed in a later example.

To show how the initial smoothing works, assume that Roger expects to earn an 8% return. Under the *SFAS No. 87* smoothing approach, Roger's pension expense would be reduced by the *expected* return in each year—$16,000 in 2008 (plan assets of $200,000 × 8%) and $17,760 in 2009 ([beginning 2008 plan assets of $200,000 + 2008 actual return of 22,000] × 8%). This expected return is pension expense Component 3 discussed earlier. The difference between the expected and actual return in each year is deferred using AOCI. Specifically:

|  | 2008 | | 2009 | |
|---|---|---|---|---|
| Service cost |  | $ 7,000 |  | $ 7,500 |
| Interest cost |  | 10,000 |  | 10,850 |
| Less: |  |  |  |  |
|   Actual return on plan assets | $(22,000) |  | $(9,760) |  |
|   Unrecognized gain (loss) | 6,000 |  | (8,000) |  |
| Expected return on plan assets |  | (16,000) |  | (17,760) |
|   Pension expense |  | $ 1,000 |  | $ 590 |

In years such as 2008 when the actual return ($22,000) exceeds the expected return ($16,000), an unrecognized gain of $6,000 (see highlight) occurs. By *unrecognized,* we mean that it is *not recognized in pension expense.* However, as mentioned earlier, the gain is recognized in OCI. In our example, there is an unrecognized loss of $8,000 for 2009 because the actual return ($9,760) is less than the expected return ($17,760). By using the *expected* return to compute pension expense, the year-to-year *decrease* in Roger Corporation's pension expense was only $410 ($1,000 − $590). In contrast, pension expense would have *increased* by $13,590 if *actual* return on plan assets had been used (negative $5,000 − positive $8,590).

The pre-tax effects on OCI and AOCI follow:

|  | 2008 | 2009 |
| --- | --- | --- |
| AOCI (loss) – 1/1 | $ 0 | $ 6,000 |
| OCI (loss) | 6,000 | (8,000) |
| AOCI (loss) – 12/31 | $6,000 | $(2,000) |

From these effects, we can see that OCI reflects the volatility removed from pension expense. By recognizing the gain and loss in AOCI, Roger will still recognize a balance sheet pension asset (liability) equal to the funded status—just as it would have if actual return had been used to compute pension expense. The details of the journal entries to obtain the asset (liability) amount are discussed later in the chapter.

See Figure 14.4 for a graphic presentation of how large the differences between the actual return and expected return can be. The data in Figure 14.4 come from the pension footnotes for General Electric Company (GE) for the years 1998–2006, excerpts of which are given in Exhibit 14.5. While GE's expected return as a percentage of beginning plan assets remained stable during the period, the actual rate of return ranged from a high of 21.7% in 2003 to a low of −11.7% in 2002. For the years 2002–2003, the actual dollar return on GE's plan assets went from negative $5.251 billion to a positive $8.203 billion. GE's earnings before taxes and accounting changes for the 2001–2003 period were (in billions) $19.701, $18.891, and $19.904, respectively. Clearly, without some mechanism to smooth out the big swings in the yearly actual returns on pension assets, considerable volatility would be introduced into GE's pension expense and net income.

The data highlighted in the middle row of Exhibit 14.5 represent the deferred portion of each year's actual return. This is the unrecognized gain or loss, and it is represented by the vertical distance between the actual return line and expected return line in Figure 14.4. Note that in six of the years (1998, 1999, 2003, 2004, 2005, and 2006), this deferral increases

### Figure 14.4

GENERAL ELECTRIC COMPANY

Comparison of Actual and Expected Return on Pension Plan Assets (1998–2006)

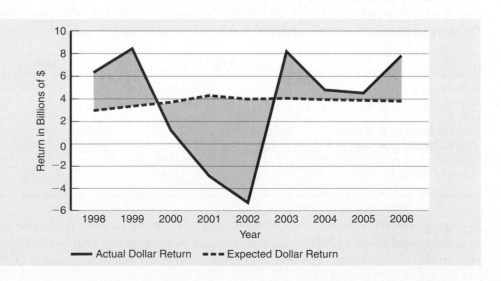

| **EXHIBIT 14.5** | **Excerpts from General Electric Company Footnotes Underlying Figure 14.4 Data** | | | | | | | | |
|---|---|---|---|---|---|---|---|---|---|
| ($ in billions) | 1998 | 1999 | 2000 | 2001 | 2002 | 2003 | 2004 | 2005 | 2006 |
| Fair value of plan assets* | $38.742 | $43.447 | $50.243 | $49.757 | $45.006 | $37.811 | $43.879 | $46.665 | $49.096 |
| Actual dollar return | 6.363 | 8.472 | 1.287 | (2.876) | (5.251) | 8.203 | 4.888 | 4.558 | 7.851 |
| Expected dollar return | 3.024 | 3.407 | 3.754 | 4.327 | 4.084 | 4.072 | 3.958 | 3.885 | 3.811 |
| Unrecognized gains or losses (actual minus expected return)† | 3.339 | 5.065 | (2.467) | (7.203) | (9.335) | 4.131 | 0.930 | 0.673 | 4.040 |
| Actual return as a % of plan assets | 16.4% | 19.5% | 2.6% | (5.8%) | (11.7%) | 21.7% | 11.1% | 9.8% | 16.0% |
| Expected return as a % of plan assets | 7.8% | 7.8% | 7.5% | 8.7% | 9.1% | 10.8% | 9.0% | 8.3% | 7.8% |

\* This is the value of the plan assets at the *start* of each year.

† These gains and losses were off-balance sheet through 2005. In 2006, they appeared as part of AOCI.

*Source:* General Electric Company annual reports, 1998–2006.

pension expense. In 2000 to 2002, the deferral adjustments reduce pension expense. The deferred gains and losses were off-balance sheet prior to 2006. Upon adoption of *SFAS No. 158,* the cumulative gains and losses became part of AOCI.

**How Component 4 is Measured**   Because pension accounting requires numerous estimates of future events, differences between forecasted amounts and subsequent occurrences should be expected. Cumulative deferred net gains or losses can arise from three causes:

1. Cumulative differences between actual and expected returns on pension plan assets as illustrated in Exhibit 14.5 and Figure 14.4.
2. Cumulative differences between actuarial assumptions and actual experience (e.g., employee turnover, pay increases, and longevity beyond retirement).
3. Changes in assumptions (e.g., a change in the discount rate used for computing service cost and interest cost).

As discussed, smoothing adjustments allow the cumulative amount of the deferred gains and losses to be recorded in AOCI. *SFAS No. 87* does not require each year's pension expense to reflect actual returns on plan assets or observed actuarial outcomes. However, if the smoothing adjustments do not offset one another over time, the periodic differences will ultimately accumulate and exceed a materiality threshold (called the **"corridor"** in *SFAS No. 87*). The FASB believes that some of the excess gains or losses should be recognized once the corridor has been exceeded. This is the role of Component 4—recognized gains or losses.

Here's how the component 4 adjustment mechanism works.[13] First, the corridor is computed. It is defined as 10% of the *higher* of the following two numbers:

1. The PBO.
2. The market-related value (MRV) of the pension plan assets.

---

[13] This approach results in the *minimum* amortization required by *SFAS No. 87*. A systematic method consistently applied to both gains and losses that results in a larger amount is permissible (*SFAS No. 87*, para. 33).

Second, the corridor is compared to the beginning balance of net actuarial loss (gain) in AOCI to determine whether it exceeds the corridor. If it does, then, third, the excess AOCI loss (gain) above the 10% corridor is amortized straight-line over the estimated **average remaining service period** (*an actuarial computation of the average number of years over which existing employees are expected to continue on the job*). We'll now illustrate the corridor method step-by-step:

On January 1, 2008, Dore Corporation has ($1,600,000) in AOCI — actuarial (gain) loss. The MRV of pension plan assets on that date is $10,000,000, and the PBO is $8,500,000. The estimated average remaining service period of active employees is 15 years.

Figure 14.5 shows the steps in computing Component 4—recognized gains or losses. The 10% corridor is computed by first comparing the size of the MRV ($10,000,000) with the PBO ($8,500,000) and choosing the higher—the $10,000,000 MRV in this instance. This $10,000,000 is then multiplied by 10% to arrive at the corridor of $1,000,000 (see Step 1 in Figure 14.5). Because the gain of $(1,600,000) is more than the $1,000,000 corridor, the recognition mechanism is triggered (see Step 2). ***This means that component 4—recognized gains or losses—will be included in computing pension expense for the year.*** The $(600,000) amount in excess of the threshold will be amortized over 15 years. This amortization means that pension expense component 4 will be *reduced* for $40,000 ($[600,000]/15), thereby *reducing* pension expense (see Step 3). AOCI—actuarial (gain) loss also will be reduced by $40,000, thereby decreasing it to $(1,560,000).

If there were no future actuarial gains or losses and the MRV remained constant, the $560,000 unamortized excess ($600,000 − $40,000) would be fully amortized into income over the ensuing 14 years. Realistically, however, pension accounting requires many estimates of uncertain future events, and uncertainty means that further adjustments are likely.

## Figure 14.5

COMPUTING COMPONENT 4—RECOGNIZED GAINS OR LOSSES

**Step 1. Compute the 10% corridor.**
   **a.** Compare beginning-of-year amounts of market-related value (MRV) of pension plan assets and projected benefit obligation (PBO).

   **b.** Select the larger one, that is, MRV of $10,000,000.
   **c.** Multiply the larger one by 10%; so, $10,000,000 × 10% = $1,000,000.
   *This is the 10% corridor.*

**Step 2. Determine whether the corridor is exceeded.**
   **a.** Compare beginning-of-year AOCI—(gain) loss to the corridor computed in Step 1c.

   **b.** Recognition is required because AOCI—(G)L—a cumulative gain in this example—exceeds the corridor by $600,000.
   **c.** So, Component 4—recognized gains or losses—will appear in pension expense for the current year.

**Step 3. Compute the current year's Component 4 amortization.**
   **a.** Obtain the average remaining service period (ARSP) figure from the actuary. Here, ARSP equals 15 years.
   **b.** Divide the amount by which AOCI—(G)L exceeds the corridor (Step 2.b) by ARSP.

   **c.** *The quotient from Step 3b, $(40,000) (that is, $[600,000]/15) is the Component 4 amount for the current year. Pension expense will be reduced by $40,000 in the current year.*

Consequently, **SFAS No. 87** *requires that the computation illustrated in the example be re-done at the start of each subsequent year to determine that year's pension expense Component 4.* Nonetheless, just because Component 4 was required in 2008 doesn't necessarily mean it will be required again in 2009.

To illustrate, let's assume that one year later—on January 1, 2009—Dore Corporation's AOCI—actuarial (gain) loss has fallen to $(250,000), plan assets are $11,000,000, and the PBO is $9,000,000. The 10% corridor is now $1,100,000 (that is, $11,000,000 × 0.10). This is higher (in terms of absolute value) than the $(250,000). Thus, the corridor is not exceeded, and no amortization would be required in 2009.

Why did the FASB choose the PBO and the MRV of pension plan assets as the two benchmarks that potentially trigger the Component 4 amortization? Measures of projected benefit obligations and plan assets constitute the "critical 10% corridor" because the factors giving rise to the cumulative gain or loss represent misestimates of the "real" pension plan obligations and assets. In other words, gains and losses occur because the expected return on plan assets included in pension expense understated or overstated the actual return on pension assets. Similarly, gains or losses related to service cost and interest cost included in pension expense understated or overstated the actual increase in pension obligations. Thus, obligations and assets constitute the appropriate benchmarks for assessing when the cumulative error is "excessive." The 10% corridor is simply an arbitrary measure of this "excessiveness."

### Component 5—Recognized Prior Service Cost

Pension plans may be amended to increase or decrease benefits to employees. Firms may enhance—or "sweeten"—pension plans for various reasons. One is to generate employee goodwill and loyalty to the organization, thereby retaining a quality workforce. Another reason for pension enhancement—particularly retroactive enhancement—is a result of union demands in labor negotiations. However, if a company suffers financial difficulties, as have many airlines in recent years, it may amend the plan to *reduce* benefits. When a firm *retroactively* enhances (reduces) the benefits provided by its pension plan, past pension expense and pension funding—which were both based on the "old" pension plan terms—were too low (high). This also means that when a firm enhances (reduces) its pension plan benefits, it immediately increases (decreases) its projected benefit obligation under the plan. The dollar amount of the increase (decrease) in the projected benefit obligation due to plan enhancements (reductions) is called **prior service cost (credit),** and adjusting for this expense is the role of Component 5. Here's an example that illustrates how prior service cost arises:

---

Schiller Corporation's pension plan contract grants employees a pension of 2% of ending salary at retirement for each year of service to a maximum of 30 years. Therefore, an employee with 30 years of service at Schiller could retire with a pension equal to 60% of her or his salary at retirement.

Schiller's management now believes that the 60% pension maximum is inadequate given existing general economic conditions. The pension plan is retroactively changed on January 1, 2008. Under the revised plan, employees qualify for a pension of 2.25% of ending salary at retirement for each year of service, again to a maximum of 30 years. Under the revised plan, the maximum pension is 67.5% of the employee's salary at retirement (2.25% × 30 years).

Based on Schiller's employee demographics and expected salaries, the plan enhancement increases the projected benefit obligation by $14,000,000. The average remaining service period of employees expected to receive benefits under the plan is 10 years.

Although the plan enhancements are computed on the basis of services rendered in prior periods, the benefits to the firm will be realized in future periods. The firm realizes the benefits of retroactive plan enhancements in future periods because of decreased employee turnover or better labor relations. Accordingly, *SFAS No. 87* allows this $14,000,000 amount of prior service costs to be amortized into pension expense on a straight-line basis over the expected remaining 10-year service lives of employees who are expected to receive benefits under the plan. So, $1,400,000 would be added to pension expense over each of the next 10 years (that is, $14,000,000/10). This is the role of Component 5.

Similar to net actuarial losses, unrecognized prior service costs reduce AOCI. In the Schiller example, when pension expense is *increased* for $1,400,000, AOCI–prior service cost is *reduced* for the same amount.

## RECAP

**Estimates pervade pension accounting. When these estimates need to be adjusted, the adjustment could conceivably be recorded all at once. Doing this would make pension expense volatile from year to year. Under *SFAS No. 158*, the gains and losses are initially recognized in AOCI. If the cumulative net gains or losses exceed a materiality threshold called the *corridor*, a portion of the excess is recognized as pension expense Component 4. Firms may amend pension plan agreements to improve or reduce pension benefits as market conditions change. When an amendment is made, the effect is initially recognized in AOCI and amortized to pension expense Component 5 over future years.**

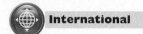
**International**

International Financial Reporting Standards (IFRS) for pensions are specified by *IAS 19*, "Employee Benefits," International Accounting Standards Board (London, UK, 1998, amended through 2002). The expense recognition provisions roughly parallel the provisions in *SFAS No. 87*. However, *IAS 19* doesn't include the AOCI balance sheet recognition provisions contained in *SFAS No. 158*, and the unrecognized prior service costs and net actuarial (gain) loss remain off-balance sheet. Additionally, the balance sheet pension asset can't exceed the sum of (1) the net plan assets available from refunds or reduced plan contributions, (2) the unrecognized prior service costs, and (3) the unrecognized net actuarial losses (*IAS 19*, para. 58).

## Journal Entries for Changes in Funded Status

To illustrate the journal entry for pension expense, let's assume that Adess Corporation disclosed the following components in its pension footnote at December 31, 2008:

| | |
|---|---:|
| Service cost (Component 1) | $23,000 |
| Interest cost (Component 2) | 42,500 |
| Expected return on plan assets (Component 3) | (38,250) |
| Amortization of actuarial loss (Component 4) | 10,000 |
| Amortization of prior service cost (Component 5) | 12,750 |
| 2008 Pension expense | $50,000 |

Service cost (Component 1) and interest cost (Component 2) increase PBO, and expected return (Component 3) increases plan assets. Consequently, the excess of service cost and interest cost over the expected return decreases funded status by $27,250. This decrease to funded status is reflected on the balance sheet through the following entry:

| Journal Entry 1: Pension expense Components 1–3 | | |
|---|---|---|
| **DR** Pension expense ........................................... | $27,250 | |
| **CR** Pension asset (liability) ............................... | | $27,250 |

If the net balance in the Pension asset (liability) is a debit, it would be classified as an *asset*. If the net balance is a credit, it would appear on the balance sheet as a *liability*. Components 4 and 5 are transfers from AOCI and do not affect funded status. Consequently, we make the following entry to record their effects on pension expense:

| Journal Entry 2: Pension expense Components 4 and 5 | | |
|---|---|---|
| **DR**  Pension expense | $22,750 | |
| **CR**  AOCI—net actuarial loss | | $10,000 |
| **CR**  AOCI—prior service cost | | 12,750 |

These two entries may be combined into one entry, but we use two entries to make it easier to trace the balance sheet effects.

In addition to service cost and interest cost, plan amendments also can change PBO. If the amendment increases pension benefits, the PBO increases, thereby decreasing funded status. Decreases in benefits would have the opposite effects on PBO and funded status. Amendments are recognized in the Pension asset (liability) account, but the offset is recorded in AOCI—prior service cost instead of Pension expense. To illustrate, assume that Adess adopted an amendment that increased PBO by $7,700. To record the effect of the amendment, Adess makes the following entry:

> In the journal entries involving AOCI and OCI, we make entries directly to AOCI to avoid having to close OCI to AOCI. New gains or losses and reclassifications included in OCI for the year must be disclosed in the notes related to comprehensive income or the statement of shareholders' equity. We discuss this issue in more depth at the end of the General Electric pension example.

| Journal Entry 3: Plan amendment | | |
|---|---|---|
| **DR**  AOCI—prior service cost | $7,700 | |
| **CR**  Pension asset (liability) | | $7,700 |

We now turn to events that affect plan assets. Entry 1 was based on expected return. If the actual return differs from expected return, then an additional entry must be made to reflect funded status on the balance sheet. As stated earlier, the difference between actual and expected return must be recognized in AOCI with the offsetting debit or credit to the Pension asset (liability) account. To illustrate, assume that Adess Corporation's expected return exceeds its actual return by $5,000. To record this difference, Adess makes the following entry:

| Journal Entry 4: Difference between actual and expected return | | |
|---|---|---|
| **DR**  AOCI—net actuarial loss | $5,000 | |
| **CR**  Pension asset (liability) | | $5,000 |

An entry identical to Entry 4 would be made for increases or decreases to PBO caused by changes in assumptions or experience losses or gains.

A firm typically funds an amount different than pension expense. (Factors that affect firms' funding policies are discussed in the next section.) Also, the timing of pension plan contributions does not usually match the timing of expense recognition. As contributions increase plan assets, the Pension asset (liability) account is *debited* for the amount of the contribution. Assuming that Adess Corporation chooses to fund $53,000 in 2008, the entry is:

| Journal Entry 5: Plan contribution | | |
|---|---|---|
| **DR**  Pension asset (liability) | $53,000 | |
| **CR**  Cash | | $53,000 |

After making these entries, Adess Corporation's balance sheet Pension asset (liability) account will equal its funded status. Note that we did not make any entries for benefits paid to retirees. Because both plan assets and PBO are typically reduced by the same amount for benefits paid to retirees, there is no effect on funded status, and consequently, no journal entry is required.

## Pension Funding Decision

Labor law, income tax rules, and varying cash flow needs strongly impact a firm's pension plan funding. Let's first consider the role of labor law.

The U.S. Congress enacted legislation to regulate private U.S. *defined benefit* pension plans in 1974. The **Employees Retirement Income Security Act (ERISA)** was designed to protect workers covered by company- or industry-sponsored pension plans. This law was deemed necessary because some companies with underfunded pension plans went out of business and defaulted on their obligations to pay benefits to employees. When Studebaker Corporation—once a major automobile manufacturer headquartered in South Bend, Indiana—experienced severe economic hardship and declared bankruptcy in 1964, its pension liabilities greatly exceeded its plan assets. Studebaker retirees were unprotected and consequently lost most of their promised pensions. Such hardships ultimately motivated legislation designed to prevent recurrences.

ERISA introduced minimum funding requirements, limited investments in employer stock to 10% of plan assets, and created the **Pension Benefit Guaranty Corporation (PBGC)** to assume pension obligations when sponsors are bankrupt and plan assets are inadequate.[14] The PBGC receives its funds from defined benefit plan sponsors.[15] In 2000, the PBGC had a surplus of $9.7 billion. However, low stock returns and low discount rates (previously mentioned) led to a $23.3 billion deficit by the end of 2004.[16] The bankruptcies of large airlines and manufacturers with billions of unfunded pension liabilities worsened the deficit. To provide additional protection to plan participants and to improve PBGC's health, **The Pension Protection Act of 2006 (PL 109-280)** amended ERISA. Most of its provisions began in 2008 and will be phased in through 2011. The law requires firms to reduce the amount of underfunding more quickly than they would have under prior law. Additionally, the law creates an "at-risk" category for severely underfunded plans and requires them to reduce the underfunding faster. The Pension Protection Act of 2006 includes guidelines for determining whether a plan is overfunded or underfunded, and the PBGC has issued regulations for interpreting these guidelines.[17] These guidelines differ from those in *SFAS No. 87* as to how liabilities are defined and what assumptions are to be used. As of September 30, 2007, the PBGC's deficit had fallen to $14.1 billion as a result of higher interest rates, strong investment returns, and employer premiums.[18]

---

[14] The PBGC only partially guarantees benefits. The maximum annual pension benefit it guaranteed in 2007 was $49,500. This amount is adjusted for changes to the Social Security wage base. See Pension Benefit Guaranty Corporation, *Pension Insurance Data Book 2006*, Number 11, Fall 2007, www.pbgc.gov/publications/databook, p. 102. This limitation affected high-wage employees, such as pilots in the airline industry.

[15] The payment formula has been amended several times since 1974. Sponsors now pay a $30 flat fee per participant plus a variable premium of $9 per $1,000 of underfunding.

[16] See J. VanDerhei, "Retirement Income Adequacy after PPA and FAS 158: Part One—Plan Sponsors' Reactions," *EBRI Issue Brief no. 307*, n.d., www.ebri.org, July 2007, p. 4.

[17] See Pension Benefit Guaranty Corporation, *Federal Register* 72, no. 104 (May 31, 2007).

[18] See Pension Benefit Guaranty Corporation, *Annual Management Report—Fiscal 2007*, November 14, 2007, www.pbgc.gov/about/annreports.html, p. 4.

The U.S. income tax law also influences pension plan funding. Because plan contributions are tax deductible and plan earnings are nontaxable to the plan sponsor, there is a tax incentive to overfund pension plans. Because of this incentive, the tax law limits the deductibility of contributions to already overfunded pension plans. Consequently, a firm with an overfunded plan limits its funding to an amount that is deductible for tax purposes.

Finally, firms with pension plans have a wide range of other uses for cash flows generated by operating activities. Examples include plant expansion, corporate acquisitions, debt retirement, and dividend increases. So, firms sometimes reduce or even forgo funding of the current period's pension expense—provided minimum ERISA funding guidelines are satisfied—to meet competing investment or financing cash needs.

The longer term pension funding strategy that a firm chooses to follow is determined not only by its internal cash flow needs but also by many complex economic forces. Two studies sought to explain firms' funding strategies by examining the relationship between **funding ratios**—plan assets divided by pension obligations—and a variety of variables that represent the economic incentives (and costs) associated with pension funding.[19] These economic incentives can be broadly classified as (1) tax incentives, (2) finance incentives, (3) labor incentives, and (4) contracting/political cost incentives.

The findings of this research follow:

- Firms with high marginal tax rates tend to have higher funding ratios—higher marginal tax rates provide an incentive to overfund.

- Firms with less stringent capital constraints and larger union membership tend to have higher funding ratios.

- Firms with more "precarious" debt/equity ratios (that is, firms close to violating debt covenant restrictions) tend to fund a lower proportion of their pension obligations.

In general, variables designed to measure political costs were not found to be significant determinants of pension funding ratios.

---

**Tax and labor laws govern pension funding. While economic incentives appear to influence long-term corporate pension funding strategies, our understanding of this multidimensional decision is far from complete.**

RECAP

---

## CASE STUDY OF PENSION RECOGNITION AND DISCLOSURE—GENERAL ELECTRIC

To understand how pension plan assets and liabilities change during the year and how these changes affect the financial statements, analysts must understand the pension footnote disclosures required under *SFAS No. 132* and *SFAS No. 158*. We build on prior examples by analyzing excerpts of General Electric's 2006 pension footnote (see Exhibit 14.6). We have numbered the schedules to make it easier to follow our explanations.

Schedule 1 gives the components of pension cost. Note that they mirror the components described in prior examples. Expected return, service cost, and interest cost are relatively stable for the three-year period. Service cost is less in absolute magnitude than

> The total is called "cost," not "expense," because some of the pension costs go into inventory before they are expensed in cost of sales.

---

[19] See J. R. Francis and S. A. Reiter, "Determinants of Corporate Pension Funding Strategy," *Journal of Accounting and Economics,* April 1987, pp. 35–60; and J. K. Thomas, "Corporate Taxes and Defined Benefit Pension Plans," *Journal of Accounting and Economics,* July 1988, pp. 199–238.

| EXHIBIT 14.6 | General Electric Company |
|---|---|

### Edited, Condensed 2006 Pension Benefits Footnote

**PRINCIPAL PENSION PLANS** are the GE Pension Plan and the GE Supplementary Pension Plan.*

The GE Pension Plan provides benefits to certain U.S. employees based on the greater of a formula recognizing career earnings or a formula recognizing length of service and final average earnings. Certain benefit provisions are subject to collective bargaining.

The GE Supplementary Pension Plan is an unfunded plan providing supplementary retirement benefits primarily to higher-level, longer-service U.S. employees. . . .

**Schedule 1: Cost of Pension Plans**

| ($ in millions) | | 2006 | 2005 | 2004 |
|---|---|---|---|---|
| Expected return on plan assets | ① | $(3,811) | $(3,885) | $(3,958) |
| Service cost for benefits earned | ② | 1,402 | 1,359 | 1,178 |
| Interest cost on benefit obligation | ③ | 2,304 | 2,248 | 2,199 |
| Prior service cost | ④ | 253 | 256 | 311 |
| Net actuarial loss recognized | ⑤ | 729 | 351 | 146 |
| Total cost (income) | | $ 877 | $ 329 | $ (124) |

**Schedule 2: Actuarial Assumptions**

The discount rates at December 31 were used to measure the year-end benefit obligations and the earnings effects for the subsequent year.

| | December 31 | | | |
|---|---|---|---|---|
| | 2006 | 2005 | 2004 | 2003 |
| Discount rate | 5.75% | 5.50% | 5.75% | 6.00% |
| Compensation increases | 5.00 | 5.00 | 5.00 | 5.00 |
| Expected return on assets | 8.50 | 8.50 | 8.50 | 8.50 |

**Schedule 3: Accumulated Benefit Obligation**

| | December 31 | |
|---|---|---|
| ($ in millions) | 2006 | 2005 |
| GE Pension Plan | $ 38,137 | $ 38,044 |
| GE Supplementary Pension Plan | 2,314 | 2,178 |

**Schedule 4: Projected Benefit Obligation**

| ($ in millions) | | 2006 | 2005 |
|---|---|---|---|
| Balance at January 1 | | $43,331 | $39,969 |
| Service cost for benefits earned | | 1,402 | 1,359 |
| Interest cost on benefit obligation | | 2,304 | 2,248 |
| Plan amendments | ⑥ | 80 | — |
| Participant contributions | | 162 | 174 |
| Actuarial (gain) loss[a] | ⑦ | (1,514) | 1,988 |
| Benefits paid | | (2,472) | (2,407) |
| Balance at December 31[b] | | $43,293 | $43,331 |

---

[a] Principally associated with discount rate changes.

[b] The PBO for the GE Supplementary Pension Plan was $3,554 million and $3,534 million at year-end 2006 and 2005, respectively.

*(continued)*

EXHIBIT 14.6    General Electric Company (*continued*)

### Schedule 5: Fair Value of Plan Assets

| ($ in millions) | | 2006 | 2005 |
|---|---|---|---|
| Balance at January 1 | | $49,096 | $46,665 |
| Actual gain on plan assets | ⑧ | 7,851 | 4,558 |
| Employer contributions | ⑨ | 121 | 106 |
| Participant contributions | ⑩ | 162 | 174 |
| Benefits paid | ⑪ | (2,472) | (2,407) |
| Balance at December 31 | | $54,758 | $49,096 |

### Schedule 6: Prepaid Pension Asset (Liability)

| ($ in millions) | December 31 | |
|---|---|---|
| | 2006 | 2005 (authors' pro forma)† |
| Funded status(c) | $11,465 | $ 5,765 |
| Pension asset (liability) recorded in the Statement of Financial Position | | |
| Prepaid pension asset | $15,019 | $ 8,404 |
| Unfunded liabilities | | |
| Due within one year | (106) | (90) |
| Due after one year | (3,448) | (2,549) |
| Net amount recognized | $11,465 | $ 5,765 |
| Amounts recorded in shareowners' equity | | |
| Prior service cost | $    831 | $ 1,004 |
| Net actuarial loss | 2,162 | 8,445 |
| Total | $ 2,993 | $ 9,449 |

(c) Fair value of assets less PBO, as shown in the preceding tables.

The estimated prior service cost and net actuarial loss for the principal pension plans that will be amortized from shareowners' equity into pension cost in 2007 are $200 million and $700 million, respectively.

### Schedule 7: Estimated Future Benefit Payments

| ($ in millions) | 2007 | 2008 | 2009 | 2010 | 2011 | 2012–2016 |
|---|---|---|---|---|---|---|
| Principal pension plans | $2,500 | $2,500 | $2,550 | $2,600 | $2,600 | $14,500 |

**FUNDING POLICY** for the GE Pension Plan is to contribute amounts sufficient to meet minimum funding requirements as set forth in employee benefit and tax laws plus such additional amounts as we may determine to be appropriate. We have not made contributions to the GE Pension Plan since 1987. We will not make any contributions to the GE Pension Plan in 2007. In 2007, we expect to pay approximately $140 million for benefit payments under our GE Supplementary Pension Plan and administrative expenses of our principal pension plans ($121 million in 2006). . . .

* *Author note:* The 2006 GE footnote includes additional sets of columns for other pension plans. These columns have been omitted to facilitate our discussion. We also have numbered the schedules to make it easier for the reader to follow our discussions.

† GE adopted *SFAS No. 158* in 2006. Under its transition provisions, GE did not have to recognize the unrecognized prior service cost and the unrecognized actuarial losses as of December 31, 2005. Instead, the amounts were determined and recognized in AOCI as of December 31, 2006, *after* applying the provisions of *SFAS No. 87*. To make it easier to understand financial statements issued after the *SFAS No. 158* transition year, we have recast the GE footnote as if it had made the following pre-tax journal entry at December 31, 2005:

| | | | |
|---|---|---|---|
| **DR** | AOCI—prior service cost............................ | $1,004 | |
| **DR** | AOCI— net actuarial loss ........................... | 8,445 | |
| | **CR** | Prepaid pension asset.......................... | $9,449 |

The actual 2006 pension note shows a Prepaid pension asset of $15,214 as of December 31, 2005.

expected return and interest cost, which is typical of mature plans. Service cost is approximately 60% of interest cost and 35% of expected return. In younger plans, service cost would be a higher percentage. GE reports a declining amount of prior service cost amortization (Component 5), which suggests that some of the plan amendments have been fully amortized. The amount of net actuarial loss recognition increased substantially from 2004 to 2006, largely due to reductions in discount rate assumptions that increased PBO.

Schedule 2 gives the actuarial and accounting assumptions. The 5.5% discount rate for 2005 is used to compute the PBO at December 31, 2005 and the service cost and interest cost for 2006. The 5.0% assumed compensation increase is also used to compute the December 31, 2005 PBO and 2006 service cost. This rate is compounded annually to estimate the average salary at retirement. The 8.5% expected return assumption is used for accounting purposes to compute the expected return component of pension cost.[20] Changes in various pension rate assumptions affect reported pension amounts. An increase in the discount rate lowers service cost and PBO. If the assumed rate of compensation increase used in determining the PBO is lowered, service cost is reduced too. Also an increase (decrease) in the *spread* between the discount rate and the assumed rate of compensation increase lowers (raises) service cost. Finally, an increase (decrease) in the expected return on plan assets decreases (increases) pension expense.

Schedule 3 provides an alternative measure of the pension liability, the **accumulated benefit obligation** (**ABO**). The ABO differs from the PBO because the ABO does not include projected salary increases between the statement date and the employee's expected retirement date. Note that GE's reported ABO in Schedule 3 is less than its reported PBO in Schedule 4. If GE terminated its pension plan (i.e., prevented employees from earning additional pension benefits) as of December 31, 2006, it would have to pay only the ABO of $40,451 million ($38,137 million + $2,314 million) instead of the PBO of $43,293 million. This difference also represents the losses workers would suffer if they leave GE prior to retirement. Under *SFAS No. 87,* firms were required to record a net pension liability based on the difference between plan assets and *ABO if ABO exceeded plan assets.* In contrast, **SFAS No. 158 *uses PBO and requires balance sheet recognition for both underfunded and overfunded plans.***

Schedule 6 provides the funded status of GE's pension plans. GE's funded status of $11,465 million for 2006 is computed as the difference between the fair value of plan assets of $54,758 million (Schedule 5) and the PBO of $43,293 million (Schedule 4). As mentioned earlier in the chapter, when the fair value of pension assets exceeds plan liabilities, a plan is **overfunded.** If pension liabilities exceed the fair value of plan assets, a plan is **underfunded.** This funded status disclosure is important to statement readers because the plan sponsor—the reporting entity—is ultimately responsible for underfunded pension plans. Moreover, sometimes the reporting entity can reclaim a portion of the excess in overfunded plans. So, information about the funded status helps analysts assess the sponsor's financial condition.

See Figure 14.6 for the causes for increases and decreases in plan assets.[21] Using GEs fair value of assets disclosures in Exhibit 14.6, Schedule 5, we discuss the separate elements of Figure 14.6:

- Item A represents the beginning-of-period fair value of the pension plan assets. For GE, the January 1, 2006 amount totaled $49,096 million.

---

[20] To help analysts assess the reasonableness of this assumption, *SFAS No. 132* requires that firms describe their approach to establishing the assumption, the target and actual asset allocation, and investment guidelines. These disclosures have been omitted from the GE excerpts to facilitate discussion. In addition, a proposed FASB Staff Position (FSP) issued in March 2008 would require new pension asset disclosures regarding investment categories, concentration of risk, and fair value measurement methods.

[21] In addition to the items shown in Figure 14.6, *SFAS No. 132* (para. 5) requires—if applicable—disclosure of (1) changes in plan assets arising from exchange rate changes for pension plans of certain foreign subsidiaries and (2) changes in plan assets arising from business combinations, divestitures, and plan settlements.

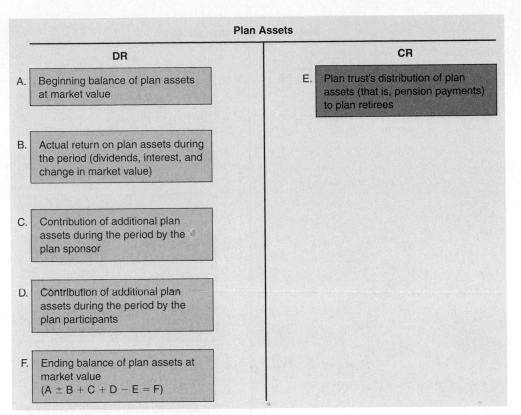

**Figure 14.6**

CAUSES OF INCREASES AND DECREASES IN PLAN ASSETS

Compare with Schedule 5 of Exhibit 14.6

- Item B, the actual return on plan assets, increased the dollar value of plan assets. Generally, the amount is positive, but in very bad investment years, Item B can be negative. GE's 2006 actual return on plan assets was a positive $7,851 million.

- Item C, the amount that the plan sponsor funds during the period, further increased plan assets. GE's 2006 contribution was $121 million.[22]

- Item D, contributions by plan participants, also increased plan assets. During 2006, contributions by GE plan participants totaled $162 million.

- Retirees receive benefits during the period; these benefits are disbursed by the plan trust and reduce plan assets, as indicated by Item E. Benefits paid to participants by the plan trust in 2006 were $2,472 million.

- The end-of-period market value of plan assets is Item F. This amount totaled $54,758 million for the GE plans.

See Figure 14.7 for the general reasons for increases and decreases to the PBO.[23] We use GE's projected benefit obligation disclosures in Exhibit 14.6, Schedule 4 to explain the elements in Figure 14.7:

- Item G is the start-of-period present value of expected future benefits that will ultimately be paid both to currently active and already retired employees. The 2006 GE beginning amount is $43,331 million.

---

[22] The contributions were made to the GE Supplementary Pension Plan, which is a pay-as-you-go plan. The other plan—the GE Pension Plan—is overfunded. According to information in Exhibit 14.6, GE has not contributed to this plan since 1987.

[23] In addition to the items shown in Figure 14.7, *SFAS No. 132* (para. 5) requires—if applicable—disclosure of (1) changes in the PBO arising from exchange rate changes for pension plans of certain foreign subsidiaries and (2) changes in the PBO arising from business combinations, divestitures, curtailments, plan settlements, and special termination benefits.

## Figure 14.7

CAUSES OF INCREASES
AND DECREASES IN PBO

Compare with Schedule 4 of
Exhibit 14.6

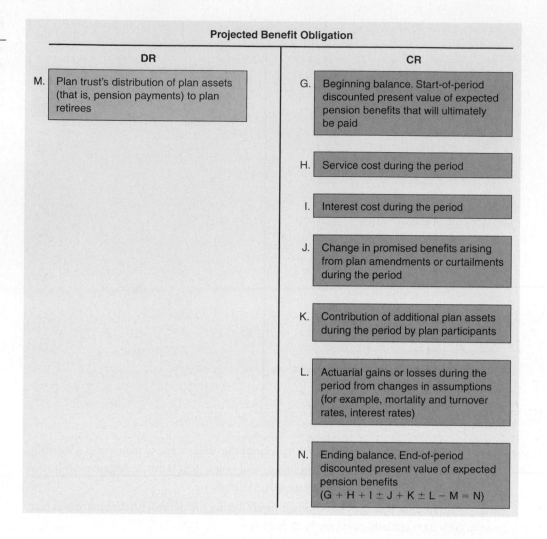

- Item H represents the increase in benefits that active employees continue to earn from additional years of work. This increase in the PBO is service cost. GE's service cost in 2006 was $1,402 million.

- As time passes, the present value of future pension benefit payouts increases because the number of discount periods decreases as employees approach retirement. This increase in the discounted present value of the liability represents interest cost, which increases the PBO (as shown in Item I). GE's 2006 interest cost was $2,304 million.

- Changes in economic and other social conditions cause firms to adjust promised benefits, as Item J indicates. These prior service cost adjustments either increase the PBO (when the plan is sweetened) or decrease it (when benefits are reduced). GE increased benefits by $80 million in 2006.

- Item K, contributions by plan participants, also increased the PBO. During 2006, such contributions totaled $162 million, which matches the employer contribution in the plan assets analysis (Schedule 5).

- The assumptions used in estimating the pension liability lead to gains or losses due to changing medical, lifestyle, and economic conditions. Denoted by Item L, these increases (or decreases) in the PBO can also arise from revised interest rate assumptions. Recall from earlier discussions that an *increase* in the discount rate assumption results in a *decrease* to the PBO. In 2006, GE increased its discount rate assumption from 5.50% to 5.75%, thereby decreasing its PBO by $1,514 million in 2006.

- Item M represents the payout of retirement benefits to participants. This is the offsetting debit to the Item E credit in Figure 14.6. GE's 2006 amount was $2,472 million.
- Finally, the ending PBO balance (Item N) is the net result of each of the preceding items. This amount totaled $43,293 million for the GE plans.

Often Exhibit 14.6 Schedules 4 (PBO) and 5 (plan assets) are shown in the same schedule, and the ending balances are netted to obtain the funded status (see the funded status schedule in the earlier Roger example). In GE's case, funded status is shown in Schedule 6—Prepaid Pension Asset (Liability). The 2006 reported $11,465 funded status is obtained by subtracting the ending PBO of $43,293 million (Schedule 4) from $54,758 million of plan assets (Schedule 5).

The purpose of Schedule 6 is to show how the funded status is reflected on the balance sheet. In 2006, the $11,465 million in net pension assets is recognized across three accounts: Prepaid pension asset of $15,019 million, Unfunded liabilities—due within one year of $(106 million), and Unfunded liabilities—due after one year of $(3,448 million). In the previous illustrative examples, each firm had only one pension plan. However, it is common for large public companies such as GE to have multiple pension plans. Companies may wish to have different plan formulas for salaried versus nonsalaried workers or union versus nonunion workers. In addition, firms may have obtained a variety of plans by acquiring other companies. *SFAS No. 158,* para. 4.b requires firms to group plans according to whether they are overfunded or under-

**International**

funded. The net asset for overfunded plans is classified as a long-term asset. For underfunded plans, the portion of the PBO due in the next 12 months that exceeds plan assets must be classified as a current liability. For GE, the current liability probably relates to the GE Supplementary Pension Plan because it is unfunded.

> The disclosures required under *IAS 19* are similar to the ones shown for GE. Because the funded status generally differs from the amount recognized on the balance sheet under *IAS 19*, the standard requires a reconciliation of funded status to the balance sheet amount. The main reconciling items are unrecognized prior service costs and unrecognized net actuarial (gain) loss.

Schedule 6 also shows the portion of the balance sheet pension assets and liabilities that have not yet been recognized in pension expense. As mentioned previously, these amounts are in AOCI. In GE's case, at the end of 2006, AOCI includes reductions for prior service cost of $831 million and net actuarial losses of $2,162 million. Later we will discuss how these balances changed during 2006 and how the accounts relate to pension expense, plan assets, and PBO.

To understand how pension accounting affected GE's 2006 financial statements, we use Schedules 1, 4, 5, and 6 to reconstruct the journal entries. In discussing them, we follow the order of the GE schedules and use the circled numbers. The entries are very similar to the ones we made in the Adess example earlier in the chapter. Some of these entries could be combined, but we are trying to make it easier to link the amounts in the footnote with the amounts in the journal entries.

We begin with the first three components of pension cost (Schedule 1). The service cost and interest cost components of pension cost decrease funded status and the pension asset on the balance sheet. The *expected* return increases funded status and the balance sheet pension asset.[24] To record these components of pension cost, we make the following journal entry:

| Journal Entry 1 | | ($ in millions) |
|---|---|---|
| **DR**   Prepaid pension asset...................................... | | $105 |
| **CR**   Pension cost ........................................ | ①+②+③ | $105 |

The prior service cost and actuarial loss components of pension expense do not impact funded status. Instead they represent transfers from AOCI. Consequently, the credits for these items go to AOCI, not to the prepaid pension asset. Therefore, we make the following entry:

| Journal Entry 2 | | ($ in millions) |
|---|---|---|
| **DR**   Pension cost............................................. | | $982 |
| **CR**   AOCI—prior service cost............................ | ④ | $253 |
| **CR**   AOCI—net actuarial loss ............................ | ⑤ | 729 |

The net effect of these two entries on pension cost is $877 million ($982 million from Journal Entry 2 less $105 million from Journal Entry 1), the total pension cost shown in Schedule 1.

We now turn to the PBO reconciliation (Schedule 4). We have already made a journal entry for service cost and interest cost. The next row in the reconciliation shows that GE had plan amendments of $80 million. These amendments increase PBO, and consequently decrease funded status and the prepaid pension asset. Under *SFAS No. 158*, the amendment affects AOCI, not pension expense. Consequently, we make the following entry:

| Journal Entry 3 | | (in millions) |
|---|---|---|
| **DR**   AOCI—prior service cost ................................ | ⑥ | $80 |
| **CR**   Prepaid pension asset ............................... | | $80 |

The next row in the reconciliation is "participant contributions." We do not make an entry for this row because it is offset by an increase in plan assets (see Schedule 5). We use a similar rationale for Benefits paid. The decrease of $2,472 million in the PBO reconciliation (Schedule 4) is offset in the plan asset reconciliation (Schedule 5).

The remaining row in the PBO reconciliation is an actuarial gain of $1,514 million (Schedule 4 ⑦). In the Adess Corporation example, the only new actuarial gain was caused by the difference between the expected and the actual return. In most cases, we also would expect to see gains or losses for changes in estimates of PBO. As shown in Figure 14.7, these gains decrease PBO and consequently increase the funded status and prepaid pension asset.

---

[24] Journal Entry 5 increases the balance sheet asset for the difference between actual return and expected return that is recognized in AOCI.

We reduce the deferred net actuarial loss existing at the beginning of the year with the following entry:

| **Journal Entry 4** | | |
|---|---|---|
| | | (in millions) |
| **DR** Prepaid pension asset........................................ | $1,514 | |
| **CR** AOCI—net actuarial loss .............................. | | ⑦ $1,514 |

We now turn to the reconciliation of plan assets (Schedule 5). Journal entry 1 increased the Prepaid pension asset for *expected* return, but plan assets and consequently the funded status and the Prepaid pension asset must reflect *actual* return. Therefore, we must adjust the Prepaid pension asset for the difference between the actual $7,851 return (Schedule 5, ⑧) and the expected $3,811 return (Schedule 1, ①). In this case, the actual return exceeds the expected return by $4,040, so we reduce the deferred actuarial loss existing at the beginning of the year with the following entry:

| **Journal Entry 5** | | |
|---|---|---|
| | | (in millions) |
| **DR** Prepaid pension asset....................................... | $4,040 | |
| **CR** AOCI—net actuarial loss ............................ | | ⑧−① $4,040 |

The next row in Schedule 5 is the employer contribution of $121 million ⑨, which increases funded status and the balance sheet pension asset. Consequently, we make the sixth journal entry:

| **Journal Entry 6** | | |
|---|---|---|
| | | (in millions) |
| **DR** Prepaid pension asset....................................... | $121 | |
| **CR** Cash................................................. | | ⑨ $121 |

For many companies, this series of entries would result in the ending pension asset or liability recorded on the balance sheet. However, because GE has multiple pension plans, some of the Prepaid pension asset must be *reclassified* to unfunded liability accounts. Additionally, as mentioned in our earlier discussion of Schedule 6, the unfunded liabilities must be split between long-term and current accounts. To obtain this entry, we compute the difference between the beginning and ending unfunded liability accounts shown in Schedule 6. The difference for the Unfunded liabilities—due within one year account is $16 million (the ending balance of $106 million less the beginning balance of $90 million), and the difference for the Unfunded liabilities—due after one year account is $899 million (the ending balance of $3,448 million − the beginning balance of $2,549 million). To accomplish the reclassification, we make the following entry:

| **Journal Entry 7** | | |
|---|---|---|
| | | (in millions) |
| **DR** Prepaid pension asset ..................................... | $915 | |
| **CR** Unfunded liabilities—due within one year .............. | | $ 16 |
| **CR** Unfunded liabilities—due after one year ................ | | 899 |

| Journal Entry | | (in millions) Prepaid pension asset | |
|---|---|---|---|
| | **January 1, 2006** | $ 8,404 | |
| 1 | Pension cost | 105 | |
| 3 | Plan amendment | | $80 |
| 4 | PBO actuarial gain | 1,514 | |
| 5 | Actual return less expected return | 4,040 | |
| 6 | Employer contribution | 121 | |
| | | $14,104 | |
| 7 | Reclassification | 915 | |
| | **December 31, 2006** | $15,019 | |

| Journal Entry | | (in millions) AOCI— prior service cost | |
|---|---|---|---|
| | **January 1, 2006** | $1,004 | |
| 2 | Amortization | | $253 |
| 3 | Plan amendment | 80 | |
| | **December 31, 2006** | $ 831 | |

| Journal Entry | | Unfunded liabilities— due within one year | |
|---|---|---|---|
| | **January 1, 2006** | $ 90 | |
| 7 | Reclassification | 16 | |
| | **December 31, 2006** | $106 | |

| Journal Entry | | AOCI— net actuarial loss | |
|---|---|---|---|
| | **January 1, 2006** | $8,445 | |
| 2 | Amortization | | $ 729 |
| 4 | PBO actuarial gain | | 1,514 |
| 5 | Actual return less expected return | | 4,040 |
| | **December 31, 2006** | $2,162 | |

| Journal Entry | | Unfunded liabilities— due after one year | |
|---|---|---|---|
| | **January 1, 2006** | $2,549 | |
| 7 | Reclassification | 899 | |
| | **December 31, 2006** | $3,448 | |

**Figure 14.8** ANALYSIS OF BALANCE SHEET ASSET, LIABILITY, AND AOCI ACCOUNTS

See Figure 14.8 for the cumulative effects of the journal entries on the Prepaid pension asset, Unfunded liabilities, and AOCI accounts. Note that the Prepaid Pension asset, Unfunded liabilities—due within one year, and Unfunded liabilities—due after one year accounts have ending balances of $15,019 million, $(106 million), and $(3,448 million), respectively, which sum to the funded status of $11,465 million.

## Accumulated Other Comprehensive Income Disclosure and Deferred Income Taxes

**Analysis**

Thus far, we have ignored the effects of income taxes. As you learned in Chapter 2, all AOCI items must be shown net of tax. Additionally, the OCI components related to new plan amendments or new actuarial (gains) losses must be distinguished from the components related to amortization. The reason for distinguishing the sources of (gain) loss is so that investors can separate new changes in firm wealth from transfers of prior (gains) losses to pension expense and net income. See Exhibit 14.7 for the required disclosure for the GE pension plan. This type of disclosure is usually found in the statement of shareholders' equity or a note related to the statement.

The Pre-Tax column in Exhibit 14.7 corresponds to the T-account analysis presented in Figure 14.8. In most cases, each amount can be traced directly to the AOCI—prior service cost or the AOCI—net actuarial loss T-accounts. However, a few numbers from Figure 14.8 have been combined. First, the $9,449 million of AOCI at January 31, 2006 is the sum of the beginning balance in AOCI—prior service cost of $1,004 million and the beginning balance in AOCI—net actuarial loss of $8,445 million. The ending balances for these accounts have been combined in the same manner. This type of aggregation is common. In fact, the beginning and ending balances often contain gains and losses related to marketable securities, derivatives, and foreign currency (the other components of AOCI). A second difference is that

| EXHIBIT 14.7 | General Electric Company |
|---|---|

**Impact of Pensions on 2006 OCI and AOCI (Author Calculations)**

| ($ in millions) | Pre-Tax | Tax Effect | After-Tax |
|---|---|---|---|
| AOCI—January 1, 2006 | $9,449* | $3,950† | $5,499‡ |
| Prior service cost from plan amendment | 80 | 33 | 47 |
| Less: Amortization of prior service cost included in net pension cost | (253) | (106) | (147) |
| Net prior service cost arising during period | (173) | (73) | (100) |
| New actuarial (gain) loss arising during period | (5,554)§ | (2,322) | (3,232) |
| Less: Amortization of net actuarial loss | (729) | (305) | (424) |
| Net actuarial (gain) loss arising during period | (6,283) | (2,627) | (3,656) |
| OCI | (6,456) | (2,700) | (3,756) |
| AOCI—December 31, 2006 | $2,993 | $1,250 | $1,743 |

---

\* Beginning AOCI—prior service cost of $1,004 million + AOCI—net actuarial loss of $8,445 million from Figure 14.8.

† Tax effects are computed using a 41.8% tax rate imputed from Note 23—Shareowners' Equity of GE's 2006 annual report.

‡ The after-tax amount equals the difference between the pre-tax and tax effect amounts.

§ PBO actuarial gain of $1,514 million + Difference between the actual return and the expected return of $4,040 million from Figure 14.8.

the PBO gain of $1,514 million in Figure 14.8 has been combined with the difference between the actual return and the expected return of $4,040 million to obtain the New actuarial gain (loss) of $5,554 million shown in Exhibit 14.7. Third, we have added a row for OCI. This row combines the $173 million net gain from prior service cost with the $6,283 million net actuarial gain arising during the period.

The Tax Effect column in Exhibit 14.7 gives the tax effect of the amounts presented in the first column. We obtain the tax effects by multiplying the 41.8% tax rate (based on information in GE's Note 23—Shareowners' Equity) by each amount in the first column. For example, the $33 million plan amendment tax amount is computed by multiplying $80 million by 41.8%. The resulting after-tax amounts for 2006 would be included in GE's shareowners' equity through the following entry:

| | | ($ in millions) | |
|---|---|---|---|
| **DR** | AOCI—prior service cost **tax effect** | $ 73 | |
| **DR** | AOCI—net actuarial loss **tax effect** | 2,627 | |
| **CR** | Deferred income tax asset | | $2,700 |

This entry uses "tax-effect" contra accounts to offset the pre-tax amounts in the Figure 14.8 T-accounts. These accounts and the tax-effect accounts are netted to obtain after-tax amounts on the balance sheet. The entry presumes that the January 1, 2006 AOCI—prior service cost tax effect and AOCI—net actuarial loss tax effect balances are $420 million ($1,004 million × 41.8%) and $3,530 million ($8,445 million × 41.8%), respectively. These balances sum to the $3,950 tax effect shown for the AOCI—January 1, 2006 row in Exhibit 14.7. Because gains were recorded in both the AOCI—prior service cost and AOCI—net actuarial loss accounts in 2006, the journal entry debits the tax-effect accounts. The journal entry credit goes to a *deferred* income tax account because GE does not have to pay tax on these gains in 2006. Recall from our earlier discussions that GE receives a tax deduction when contributions are made and does not obtain tax deductions or report taxable income for pension expense or OCI amounts recognized for Generally Accepted Accounting Principles (GAAP) purposes. We credit a deferred income tax *asset* account because the beginning and ending *balances* in the AOCI—prior service cost and AOCI—net actuarial loss accounts represent losses that have been recognized for GAAP purposes but not for tax purposes.

The After-Tax column in Exhibit 14.7 represents the actual effects on AOCI income and OCI. Recall from Chapter 2 that OCI is added to net income to obtain comprehensive income. Because pension notes are usually shown before tax and shareholders' equity notes use aggregate amounts that are shown after tax, it is often difficult for the financial statement reader to link the two footnotes. We hope that this detailed analysis will help you to understand better the ultimate after-tax effects of pensions on AOCI and OCI.

## Additional Issues in Computing Expected Return

The GE example illustrates other complications that arise in calculating the expected return component of pension expense. Refer to Exhibit 14.6, Schedule 1. If we divide the 2006 $3,811 expected return by the assumed rate of return of 8.5%, we obtain $44,835. Why doesn't this amount equal the beginning $49,096 fair value of plan assets? Two factors contribute to the difference. First, recall from our initial discussion of expected return calculations that firms may define the MRV as fair value at a point in time or a smoothed fair value measured over several years. GE uses a smoothed fair value. Some of the asset gains arising from the higher returns from 2003 to 2005 (see Figure 14.4) have not been included in the smoothed asset value.

Second, the expected return is to be computed using the beginning fair value of plan assets *after* adjusting for the timing of contributions and benefit payments made during the year. If GE had used the fair value of plan assets (as opposed to a smoothed value), the approximate value used to compute the expected return would have been $48,001 (computed as $49,096 Beginning fair value + 0.5 × [Employer contributions of $121 ⑨ + Participant contributions of $162 ⑩ − Benefits paid of $2,472 ⑪]). Multiplying the payments and contributions by 0.5 assumes that they were made evenly throughout the year. Note that the $48,002 is still considerably higher than the asset value obtained by dividing the expected return by 8.5%. In the prior examples, we did not have to make this adjustment because contributions were made at the end of each year, thereby receiving zero weight in the expected return calculation.

The use of smoothed values also affects the amount of actuarial (gains) losses to be amortized. *SFAS No. 87* (para. 32) states that the minimum amortization method should exclude gains and losses not yet included in the MRV. Furthermore, as mentioned earlier, the corridor is based on the higher of the MRV or the PBO. The effects of these rules on GE's 2006 calculations are shown as follows:

*($ in millions)*

| | |
|---|---:|
| Unrecognized loss (gain) at January 1 | $ 8,445 |
| Difference between MRV and fair value | |
| ($48,001 fair value − $44,835 MRV as computed earlier) | 3,166 |
| Amount subject to amortization | $11,611 |
| Corridor — 10% of beginning MRV | |
| 10% × ($44,835 + benefits of $2,472 − contributions of $283) | 4,702 |
| Amount outside corridor | $ 6,908 |

> *IAS 19* doesn't allow the use of smoothed asset values. Instead, expected return and corridor calculations are based on pension asset fair values.

**International**

If the $49,096 beginning fair value had been used with the $8,445 beginning unrecognized loss, only $3,535 would have been outside of the corridor. The $6,908 in the table is more consistent with the large $893 amortization component of 2006 pension expense.

Unfortunately, the use of smoothed values is not clearly disclosed in financial statement footnotes. Most firms do not disclose that they are using a smoothed MRV to compute expected return. Most firms that do disclose the use of smoothed values do not state the smoothing techniques they are using. Firms may average gains and losses for both investment in equity and fixed income securities or limit smoothing to gains and losses on equity investments only. Furthermore, some firms may smooth gains and losses over three years while other firms smooth them over five years. A recent study of approximately 200 U.S. firms with large pension plans suggests that two-thirds of them are using some form of smoothing.[25] During the bull market of the late 1990s, fair values exceeded smoothed values by 15% to 20% for firms using the most extreme forms of smoothing. When interpreting financial statements, readers must assume that the expected return has been computed correctly. Because of the use of smoothed values, financial statement readers are not usually able to verify the expected return dollar amount by multiplying the stated rate of return by the beginning fair value of plan assets (adjusted for contributions and benefits). Because of the use of MRV, estimating the next year's amortization component also is difficult. This problem is mitigated by the *SFAS No. 158* requirement to disclose the actuarial (gain) loss to be amortized to pension expense in the subsequent year. GE's note states that it expects to amortize $700 million of actuarial losses from AOCI to pension expense in 2007 (see the paragraph following Schedule 6).

## Extraction of Additional Analytic Insights from Footnote Disclosures

The funded status in Exhibit 14.6 provides insights regarding expected *future* pension-related cash flows. Firms with greatly overfunded pension plans have been tempting takeover targets in the past.[26] After such takeovers, acquirers could terminate the overfunded plan, set up a new plan whose funding just equaled the liability, and use the excess funds from the terminated plan to help finance the takeover. To prevent this from happening, many potential takeover targets voluntarily terminated their the overfunded plans themselves and redeployed the excess cash proceeds. Some firms used the cash proceeds to pay dividends to shareholders; others increased capital expenditures or otherwise spent the funds. After doing this, they were no longer a tempting target. However, the **Tax Reform Act of 1986** increased the tax on the gains from plan termination; consequently, terminations of overfunded plans are somewhat less attractive to both acquirers and targets, but they still constitute a potential source of cash.[27]

By scrutinizing the causes for increases and decreases in plan assets in the pension footnote (see Figure 14.5), analysts can often make more refined estimates of future cash flows. For example, let's assume that the plan assets disclosure shows that a firm did not contribute additional funding during the reporting period. Also assume that the note shows that the market value of plan assets barely exceeds the PBO at year-end. Because the plan was overfunded, the firm could *temporarily* suspend funding. But can it continue not to fund? Depending on the extent of the overfunding and future asset returns, the answer may be no. *If its funded status were to change in future periods, the firm would be compelled to fund the plan in future years, thereby decreasing future net*

---

[25] See P. Davis-Friday, J. Miller, and H. F. Mittelstaedt, "Market-Related Values and Pension Accounting," Working Paper, Mendoza College of Business, University of Notre Dame, 2007. The authors determine the extent of smoothing using an approach similar to the one used here in the analysis of General Electric's expected return calculation.

[26] L. Asinof, "Excess Pension Assets Lure Corporate Raiders," *The Wall Street Journal*, September 11, 1985.

[27] Empirical studies investigate what factors underlie firms' decisions to remove excess pension assets from overfunded pension plans. See J. K. Thomas, "Why Do Firms Terminate Their Overfunded Pension Plans?" *Journal of Accounting and Economics*, November 1989, pp. 361–98; and H. F. Mittelstaedt, "An Empirical Analysis of the Factors Underlying the Decision to Remove Excess Assets from Overfunded Pension Plans," *Journal of Accounting and Economics*, November 1989, pp. 399–418.

*operating cash flows.* Lenders and others who forecast future cash flows to estimate "safety cushions" must consider these factors when preparing their forecasts. Merely extrapolating the most recent net operating cash flow into future years would overlook the possibly unsustainable "boost" provided by the absence of current pension funding. Thus, while companies with greatly overfunded plans can suspend funding for long periods and use the cash for other operating purposes, underfunded plans may reflect past and continuing cash flow difficulties. Recall from earlier discussions that severely underfunded plans will be put into an at-risk category and be required to increase cash contributions. *SFAS No. 132* (revised 2003) requires firms to provide their best estimate of the amount of funding expected to be paid into the plan in the ensuing year. This disclosure will help analysts forecast firms' future funding requirements. In the discussion of its funding policy, GE states that it expects to contribute $140 million to its Supplementary Pension Plan (see the discussion below Schedule 7 in Exhibit 14.6).

To help analysts determine whether fund assets are large enough to satisfy currently anticipated pension benefit payouts, *SFAS No. 132* (revised 2003) requires firms to provide a table that lists the dollar benefits expected to be paid in each of the ensuing five years and in the aggregate for the five years thereafter. GE's information is shown in Schedule 7. For the next five years, annual payments increase from $2,500 million in 2007 to $2,600 million in 2011. The total amount expected to be paid from 2007 to 2016 is $27,250 million, or approximately one-half of the fair value of plan assets. Consequently, we would conclude that GE's pension plans will not be a drain on cash.

As stated earlier in the chapter, the PBGC will take over an underfunded plan when a firm sponsor is in bankruptcy. But the PBGC tries to recover the pension payments from the pension plan sponsor. The PBGC claim ranks on an equal footing with those of unsecured creditors; accordingly, the funded status reconciliation could serve as an early warning device for signaling other cash demands on the firm.

As part of its bankruptcy reorganization in 2006, Delta Air Lines, Inc. terminated its pilots' pension plan and reached an agreement with the PBGC to assume responsibility of the plan in exchange for unsecured notes and claims totaling $2.425 billion. At the time of the agreement, the estimated underfunding in the pension plan was $3 billion. When Delta emerged from bankruptcy in April 2007, the PBGC converted $800 million of the claims into Delta common stock and continued to attempt to collect its remaining claims.[28]

Because pension funding status is important for assessing a firm's current and future cash flows, it is important to understand how sensitive the asset and liability measures are to changes in interest rates. For firms with a young workforce whose pension commitments will be paid 20 to 30 years in the future, small changes in discount rate assumptions can cause large increases in the present value of these estimated obligations. This large multiplier effect is due to the impact of duration—the further into the future the cash flows are to be paid out, the greater the impact of a change in interest rates on the present value of those cash flows. A common rule of thumb is that a 1% decrease in discount rate would *increase* PBO by 17.0% whereas a 1% increase would *decrease* it by 14.5%.[29] Again, the specific effect depends on the workforce demographics.

The effect of a 1% change in interest rates on the asset side is typically much smaller because fixed income investments generally represent only 30% to 40% of the pension asset portfolio and the maturity of those investments is often shorter than the duration of the pension liability. *Therefore, even modest declines in interest rates can easily shift the funded status of pension plans from year to year.*

---

[28] See R. Grantham, "Delta Air Lines: Pensions Fatter for Some Pilots: Guarantor Cites Stock, Assets," *The Atlanta Journal-Constitution,* August 21, 2007, p. C1; and "Business Brief—Delta Air Lines Inc.: Deal Is Reached with PBGC to End Pilots' Pension Plan, *The Wall Street Journal,* December 5, 2006, p. B10.

[29] See H. E. Winklevoss, *Pension Mathematics with Numerical Illustrations,* 2nd ed. (Philadelphia: University of Pennsylvania Press, 1993), pp. 213–14. The specific rule of thumb is that for each 0.25% change in discount rate, the liability will be altered by 4%. For a 1% change, there are four 0.25% changes. Using the Winklevoss method, we compute the effect of a 1% decrease as $1.04^4 - 1 = 17.0\%$ and the effect of a 1% increase as $1.04^{-4} - 1 = -14.5\%$.

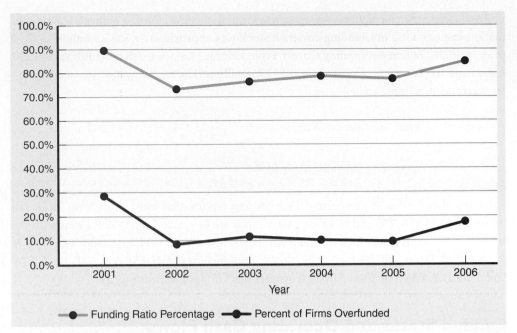

**Figure 14.9**

FUNDING RATIOS AND
PERCENT OF FIRMS
OVERFUNDED (2001–2006)

*SOURCE:* Standard & Poor's Compustat®
as data source; methodology not verified
or controlled by Standard & Poor's.

Refer to Figure 14.9 for data on the median funding ratio—fair value of plan assets (FVPA) divided by PBO and the percentage of firms that are overfunded (funding ratio > 1) for the 2001–2006 period.[30] During the six-year period, the median *funding ratio* fell from a high of 89.7% in 2001 to a low of 73.5% in 2002 and climbed to 85.1% in 2006. The *percentage of overfunded firms* follows a similar pattern. In 2001, 28.5% of the firms were overfunded, but from 2002 to 2005, less than 12% were. In 2006, the number increased to 17.6%. ***In 1999 (not shown in Figure 14.9), 69.1% of the firms were overfunded.*** The plunge in the proportion of firms with overfunded plans at the turn of the century resulted from two factors: (1) the sharp drop in equity market prices (see GE's actual returns during this period in Figure 14.4) and (2) the decline in discount rate assumptions (see Figure 14.3). As the data show, the actual return performance of pension assets from year to year and changes in discount rates can quickly—and materially—alter funded status.

The preceding analysis shows how both equity returns and interest rates can have dramatic effects on a firm's funded status. Bear Stearns & Co., Inc., an investment banking firm, suggests that this uncertainty makes pension debt riskier than traditional debt.[31] Consequently, Bear Stearns analysts have developed metrics to assess short-term and long-term pension risk. Short-term risks include liquidity problems, debt downgrades, union negotiations, and possibility of bankruptcy.[32] Long-term risks address the possibility that declines in interest rates or equity values could force firms to make additional cash outflows. Specifically, the two pension-related risk ratios are defined as follows:

$$\text{Short-term pension risk ratio} = \frac{\text{PBO } - \text{ Pension assets}}{\text{Market value of common stock}}$$

$$\text{Long-term pension risk ratio} = \frac{\text{PBO}}{\text{Market value of common stock}}$$

[30] The sample for Figure 14.9 includes all U.S. AMEX and NYSE firms with available data for the fair value of plan assets and PBO. The sample size ranges from a low of 915 firms in 2006 to a high of 997 firms in 2003.

[31] Bear Stearns & Co. Inc., "Pension Tension: When the Benefits Tail Wags the Dog Quantifying Pension and Other Postretirement Benefit Risk," *Accounting Issues,* New York, NY, June 2007.

[32] Ibid., p. 8.

To illustrate the calculations, we again use GE's disclosures. On December 31, 2006, the market value of GE's outstanding common stock was approximately $385.4 billion ($37.50 price × 10.277 billion outstanding shares). From Exhibit 14.6, we see that the PBO is $43.293 billion and the fair value of plan assets is $54.758 billion. The resulting short-term and long-term ratios (in billions) are:

$$\text{Short-term pension risk ratio} = \frac{\$43.295 - \$54.758}{\$385.4} = -0.03$$

$$\text{Long-term pension risk ratio} = \frac{\$43.295}{\$385.4} = 0.11$$

To put these ratios in perspective, Bear Stearns reports that most short-term ratios fall between −0.03 and 0.06 and most long-term ratios are between 0 and 0.25.[33] Firms with the highest short-term ratios include Delta Air Lines, 0.67; Ford, 0.49; and Goodyear Tire & Rubber, 0.34. Firms with the highest long-term ratios include General Motors, 5.56; Ford, 4.74; and AMR, 1.8. Based on this analysis, it appears that GE has low pension risk.

## Funded Status and Operating Cash Flows

The funded status of a pension plan appears to be an indicator of potential cash flow problems. Figure 14.10 provides evidence that firms with underfunded plans are not only experiencing lower *current* cash flows but are also likely to experience lower *future* cash flows than firms with overfunded plans. To demonstrate this, we form two portfolios based on firms' funded status at the end of 2001: (1) firms in an overfunded position (FVPA > PBO) and (2) firms in an underfunded position (PBO > FVPA).[34] The 2001 sample contains 242 overfunded firms and 637 underfunded firms. The bar graph in Figure 14.10 displays the median cash flow from operations (on a per share basis) for the year of the portfolio formation (2001) and for the subsequent five years.

Firms whose pension plans were underfunded in 2001 experienced lower operating cash flows in that year ($2.85 per share) in comparison to firms with overfunded plans ($3.01 per share). Moreover, the operating cash flows of the underfunded firms continued to lag behind those of the overfunded firms in the subsequent three years. In 2005 and 2006, the cash flows for the two groups are approximately even, but this may be due to weaker firms being acquired, declaring bankruptcy, or taking actions to improve cash flow. By 2006, 208 overfunded firms (86.0% of the 2001 overfunded sample) remain, and 514 of the underfunded firms (80.7% of the underfunded sample) remain. Overall the results suggest that pension funded status is a potentially useful indicator of the level of future cash flows.

 RECAP

A company's pension footnote provides information about the current economic status of its pension plan. This provides insight regarding expected future pension-related cash flows and their potential effect on firm cash flows. The funded status and the PBO can be used to assess defined benefit pension risk for the firm. Underfunded pension plans represent a potential drain on future cash flows and should be viewed as unsecured debt. The funded status of pension plans may also help predict operating cash flows for the firm as a whole.

---

[33] Ibid., p. 20.

[34] The sample for Figure 14.10 includes all U.S. AMEX and NYSE firms with available data for the fair value of plan assets, PBO, operating cash flows, and common shares. Because the sample is based on funding status as of the end of 2001, the sample size is highest in 2001 at 879 firms. The sample size is lowest in 2006 at 722.

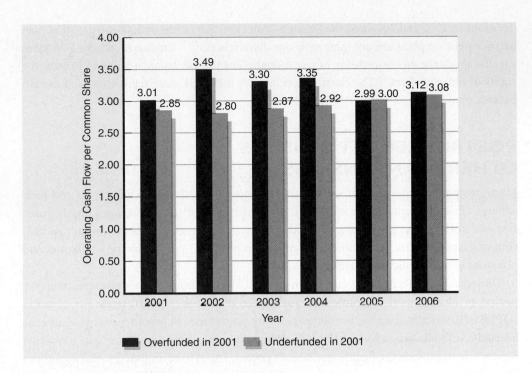

**Figure 14.10**

OPERATING CASH FLOWS
BY FUNDED STATUS
GROUP 2001–2006

*SOURCE:* Standard & Poor's Compustat®
as data source; methodology not verified
or controlled by Standard & Poor's.

## Cash Balance Plans

Toward the end of the 1990s, more than 400 U.S. companies with defined benefit pension plans modified their existing plan and adopted a new method for determining the rate at which pension benefits accumulate. These modified or **hybrid plans** are called **cash balance plans.** With them, employers contribute a fixed amount per year (say, 5% of annual pay) to the account of individual employees. The employer also guarantees a minimum rate of return on the pension assets (e.g., the rate on long-term U.S. Treasury bonds). Cash balance plans are defined benefit plans "because the employer [still ultimately] bears the investment risks and rewards and the mortality risk if the employee elects to receive benefits in the form of an annuity."[35] However, should employees leave the firm prior to retirement, the accumulated vested balance belongs to them and can be rolled over into another pension plan. *SFAS No. 158* treats these plans as defined benefit plans. However, the FASB is continuing to study appropriate accounting for these types of plans.[36]

Cash balance pension plans are attractive to firms because after they switch, firms with older employees usually experience decreases in service cost. Here's why: In traditional defined benefit pension plans, the largest benefits accrue in the later years of employment. But when older workers are switched to a cash balance plan, they usually receive the same benefit accumulation percent as do younger workers.

While popular with firms, these plans have been challenged as discriminating against older employees. Until recently, conflicting court decisions, IRS positions, and competing proposed regulations raised a number of questions regarding the legality of cash balance plans. Consequently, adoption of these plans stalled in the early 2000s. However, court

[35] A. T. Arcady and F. Mellors, "Cash Balance Conversions," *Journal of Accountancy,* February 2000, pp. 22–28. **Mortality risk** is the risk of misestimating life expectancy when calculating PBO, service cost, and funding. For example, if a firm promises to pay an annuity for life and a retiree lives to be 92 instead of the expected age of 78, the firm experiences a mortality loss because it has to pay benefits for 14 years more than expected.

[36] *SFAS No. 158,* para. B28.

decisions in 2006 and 2007 and the Pension Protection Act (PPA) of 2006 suggest that cash balance pension plans are not inherently age discriminatory.[37] Furthermore, the PPA gives specific guidance on conversions of traditional plans to cash balance plans to protect the rights of older workers.[38] The clarification in rules may lead more firms to switch to cash balance plans.

# POSTRETIREMENT BENEFITS OTHER THAN PENSIONS

Many companies promise to provide health care and life insurance to employees and their spouses during retirement. The intent of these benefits is to attract and retain a highly qualified workforce just as pensions are intended to do. Also, the employment contract and accounting issues are similar to those encountered for pensions. We discuss the similarities and point out important differences in these benefits.

Under accrual accounting, an expense and liability should be recognized over the period of employment as employees qualify for these **other postretirement benefits (OPEB)**. Historically, however, few companies with postretirement benefit plans made expense accruals. Instead, "pay-as-you-go" accounting was employed—that is, as cash payments were made to provide the health care benefit coverage to retired employees, the amount of the cash outflow was charged to expense. No liability appeared on the books. Worse yet, few companies funded these OPEB plans as benefits were earned. Two reasons for this lack of funding were:

- First, in contrast to pension plans, no ERISA rules required that the benefits be funded.
- Second, even if firms did consider voluntarily funding their plans, the payments would not have been deductible for U.S. income tax purposes, thus creating a disincentive to fund.[39]

 **Contracting**

As a result of both of these circumstances, enormous unrecorded (off-balance sheet) liabilities for postretirement benefits existed by the mid-1980s, but neither periodic debits to expense nor credits to a liability account were made to reflect the continued growth of these obligations. To correct for the lack of transparency with respect to OPEB benefits, the FASB issued *SFAS No. 106* in December 1990.[40] To give some idea of the size of these previously unrecorded postretirement benefit liabilities, when General Motors (GM) adopted *SFAS No. 106* in 1992, its liability totaled $33.1 billion, and its after-tax charge to the income statement was $20.8 billion. In 1992, GM's pre-tax loss *before* the cumulative effect of the change in accounting principle was $3.3 billion.

> Near the time that the FASB issued *SFAS No. 106*, many firms reduced retiree health benefit coverage by limiting which employees could qualify for benefits, shifting costs to retirees, or in some cases, ending benefits entirely. One study suggests that firms with high *SFAS No. 106* liabilities and high debt-to-asset ratios prior to the adoption of *SFAS No. 106* were more likely to reduce retiree benefits.[41] The authors argue that potential debt covenant violations may have motivated the firms to reduce plan benefits and that employment contracts would have been written differently if *SFAS No. 106* had always been in effect.

---

[37] A. D. Lurie, "Cash Balance Decisions Busting Out All Over," n.d., *CCH Pensions and Benefits*, February 7, 2008, http://hr.cch.com/news/pension/092607a.asp., September 26, 2007.

[38] Watson Wyatt Worldwide, *The Long and Short of the Pension Protection Act of 2006—Long-Term Implications and Short-Term Actions for Plan Sponsors*, 2006, watsonwyatt.com, February 7, 2008.

[39] Employers can achieve limited tax benefits by making contributions to a **Voluntary Employees Beneficiary Association (VEBA) trust.**

[40] "Employers' Accounting for Postretirement Benefits Other Than Pensions," *SFAS No. 106* (Norwalk, CT: FASB, 1990).

[41] See H. F. Mittelstaedt, W. Nichols, and P. Regier, "SFAS No. 106 and Benefit Reductions in Employer-Sponsored Retiree Health Care Plans," *The Accounting Review*, October 1995, pp. 535–56.

As with pensions, *SFAS No. 132* and *SFAS No. 158* subsequently amended the disclosure and accounting. Consequently, the accounting recognition and disclosure requirements are nearly identical to the ones that we discussed for pensions earlier in this chapter.

See Exhibit 14.8 for excerpts from the postretirement benefit plans footnote in General Electric Company's 2006 annual report.

The computations for postretirement benefits expense and measures of the liability generally parallel the format for pension expense and liability. Notice in Exhibit 14.8 that GE maintains both retiree health and life insurance benefit plans. Similar to the pension components of the

> By the end of 2005, GM's net postretirement benefit liabilities had increased to $64.7 billion, but only $34.0 billion was on the balance sheet, primarily because of unrecognized actuarial losses. As discussed earlier, *SFAS No. 158* requires unrecognized actuarial losses and prior service costs to be recognized in AOCI. Consequently, at the end of 2006, GM had a balance sheet postretirement liability of $50.4 billion.

---

| **EXHIBIT 14.8** | **General Electric Company** |
| --- | --- |

### Edited, Condensed 2006 Annual Report Retiree Health and Life Benefits Footnote

We sponsor a number of retiree health and life insurance benefit plans (retiree benefit plans). Principal retiree benefit plans are discussed below; other such plans are not significant individually or in the aggregate. We use a December 31 measurement date for our plans.

   **PRINCIPAL RETIREE BENEFIT PLANS** provide health and life insurance benefits to employees who retire under the GE Pension Plan with 10 or more years of service. Eligible retirees share in the cost of healthcare benefits. Effective January 1, 2005, we amended our principal retiree benefit plans to provide that, upon retirement of salaried employees who commenced service after that date, such retirees will pay in full for their participation in the GE retiree health benefit plans. These plans cover approximately 240,000 retirees and dependents. . . .

   The effect on operations of principal retiree benefit plans is shown in the following table.

#### Schedule 1: Cost of Principal Retiree Benefit Plans

| ($ in millions) | 2006 | 2005 | 2004 |
| --- | --- | --- | --- |
| Expected return on plan assets | $(127) | $ (138) | $(149) |
| Service cost for benefits earned | 229 | 243 | 210 |
| Interest cost on benefit obligation | 455 | 507 | 518 |
| Prior service cost | 363 | 326 | 298 |
| Net actuarial loss recognized | 64 | 70 | 60 |
| Retiree benefit plans cost | $ 984 | $1,008 | $ 937 |

#### Schedule 2: Actuarial Assumptions

The discount rates at December 31 were used to measure the year-end benefit obligations and the earnings effects for the subsequent year. Actuarial assumptions used to determine benefit obligations and earnings effects for principal retiree benefit plans follow.

| | December 31 | | | |
| --- | --- | --- | --- | --- |
| | 2006 | 2005 | 2004 | 2003 |
| Discount rate[a] | 5.75% | 5.25% | 5.75% | 6.00% |
| Compensation increases | 5.00 | 5.00 | 5.00 | 5.00 |
| Expected return on assets | 8.50 | 8.50 | 8.50 | 8.50 |
| Initial healthcare trend rate[b] | 9.20 | 10.00 | 10.30 | 10.50 |

---

[a] Weighted average discount rates of 5.90% and 6.40% were used for determination of costs in 2004 and 2003, respectively.

[b] For 2006, gradually declining to 5% for 2013 and thereafter.

*(continued)*

**EXHIBIT 14.8** General Electric Company (*continued*)

### Schedule 3: Accumulated Postretirement Benefit Obligation (APBO)

| ($ in millions) | 2006 | 2005 |
|---|---|---|
| Balance at January 1 | $9,084 | $9,250 |
| Service cost for benefits earned | 229 | 243 |
| Interest cost on benefit obligation | 455 | 507 |
| Participant contributions | 43 | 41 |
| Actuarial gain | (707) | (55) |
| Benefits paid[(c)] | (810) | (856) |
| Other | (32) | (46) |
| Balance at December 31[(d)] | $8,262 | $9,084 |

[(c)] Net of Medicare Part D subsidy of $75 million in 2006.

[(d)] The APBO for the retiree health plans was $6,001 million and $6,713 million at year-end 2006 and 2005, respectively.

Increasing or decreasing the healthcare cost trend rates by one percentage point would have had an insignificant effect on the December 31, 2006, accumulated postretirement benefit obligation and the annual cost of retiree health plans. Our principal retiree benefit plans are collectively bargained and have provisions that limit our per capita costs.

### Schedule 4: Fair Value of Plan Assets

| ($ in millions) | 2006 | 2005 |
|---|---|---|
| Balance at January 1 | $1,619 | $1,652 |
| Actual gain on plan assets | 222 | 107 |
| Employer contributions | 636 | 675 |
| Participant contributions | 43 | 41 |
| Benefits paid[(e)] | (810) | (856) |
| Balance at December 31 | $1,710 | $1,619 |

[(e)] Net of Medicare Part D subsidy of $75 million in 2006.

### Schedule 5: Retiree Benefit Asset (Liability)

| | December 31 | |
|---|---|---|
| ($ in millions) | 2006 | 2005 (authors' pro forma)* |
| Funded status[(f)] | $(6,552) | $(7,465) |
| Liability recorded in the Statement of Financial Position | | |
| Retiree health plans | | |
| Due within one year | $ (681) | $ (740) |
| Due after one year | (5,320) | (5,973) |
| Retiree life plans | (551) | (752) |
| Net liability recognized | $(6,552) | $(7,465) |
| Amounts recorded in shareowners' equity | | |
| Prior service cost | $ 2,046 | $ 2,409 |
| Net actuarial loss | 4 | 902 |
| Total | $ 2,050 | $ 3,311 |

[(f)] Fair value of assets less APBO, as shown in the preceding tables.

(*continued*)

| EXHIBIT 14.8 | General Electric Company (*continued*) |
|---|---|

The estimated prior service cost and net actuarial loss for our retiree benefit plans that will be amortized from shareowners' equity into retiree benefit plans cost in 2007 are $290 million and $10 million, respectively. Comparable amortized amounts in 2006 were $363 million and $64 million, respectively.

Our estimated future benefit payments are as follows:

**Schedule 6: Estimated Future Benefit Payments**

| ($ in millions) | 2007 | 2008 | 2009 | 2010 | 2011 | 2012–2016 |
|---|---|---|---|---|---|---|
| Gross | $935 | $920 | $880 | $860 | $840 | $3,760 |
| Expected Medicare Part D subsidy | 85 | 95 | 105 | 110 | 115 | 660 |
| Net | $850 | $825 | $775 | $750 | $725 | $3,100 |

**FUNDING POLICY.** We fund retiree health benefits on a pay-as-you-go basis. We expect to contribute approximately $700 million in 2007 to fund such benefits. We fund retiree life insurance benefits at our discretion.

---

\* *Author note:* GE adopted *SFAS No. 158* in 2006. As we saw with its pension plans, GE did not have to recognize the unrecognized prior service cost and the unrecognized actuarial losses as of December 31, 2005. Instead, the amounts were determined and recognized in AOCI as of December 31, 2006, *after* applying the provisions of *SFAS No. 106*. To make it easier to understand financial statements issued after the *SFAS No. 158* transition year, we have recast the GE footnote as if it had made the following pre-tax journal entry at December 31, 2005 ($ in millions):

| | | | |
|---|---|---|---|
| **DR** | AOCI—Prior service cost | $2,409 | |
| **DR** | AOCI—Net actuarial loss | 902 | |
| | **CR** Unfunded liabilities—Retiree health plans, due after one year | | $2,578 |
| | **CR** Unfunded liabilities—Retiree life plans | | 733 |

The actual 2006 pension note shows a net liability recognized of $4,154 as of December 31, 2005.

---

pension cost discussed earlier, the net postretirement benefit cost of $984 million for 2006 (as shown in Exhibit 14.8, Schedule 1) includes expected return, service cost, interest cost, prior service cost, and recognized actuarial loss components.[42]

Further scrutiny of this section shows that *SFAS No. 106* also incorporates smoothing devices that are virtually identical to Components 4 and 5 in pension accounting. Specifically, when OPEB plans are funded and thus have plan assets, postretirement benefit expense is reduced by the *expected* return on plan assets. To accomplish this smoothing, asset gains or losses are excluded from pension expense but recognized as a component of AOCI. Similarly, these gains and losses are accumulated and amortized as Component 4 if they exceed a 10% corridor. OPEB Component 5—amortization of prior service cost—exists as well in instances in which firms enhance or reduce the level of postretirement benefits subsequent to adopting *SFAS No. 106*.

GE's other OPEB schedules are similar to its pension schedules. Schedule 2 gives the assumptions for its OPEB plans. Note that instead of a salary growth assumption, the schedule contains an assumption for health care cost trend rates. The cost trend includes projected costs

---

[42] Similar to pension accounting, postretirement cost may include amortization of a transition liability. The FASB permitted companies to adopt the provisions of *SFAS No. 106* in one of two ways:

1. Recognize the transition obligation or transition asset (the difference between the accumulated postretirement benefit obligation and the fair value of plan assets) immediately in net income of the period in which *SFAS No. 106* is adopted (immediate recognition).
2. Amortize the transition obligation or transition asset as a component of OPEB expense on a straight-line basis over the *longer* of (a) the average remaining service period of active plan participants or (b) 20 years (deferred recognition).

Most companies recognized the liability immediately to avoid a drag on future earnings. However, a few companies are still amortizing a transition liability, which has the same effect on expense as prior service cost amortization.

related to physician care, hospital care, prescription drugs, medical equipment, and so on. Health care liabilities are rarely tied to salary at retirement. The typical postretirement benefit plan promises employees full coverage (for example, comprehensive postretirement health insurance) after a certain period of employment—say, 10 years. In such circumstances, the actuarially determined service cost of the plan is accrued over the first 10 years of the employee's service. The liability attributed to service to date is the **accumulated postretirement benefit obligation** (**APBO**). The health care cost trend rate can have a dramatic effect on the estimated APBO. Consequently, firms are required to make sensitivity disclosures regarding the effect of a 1% increase or decrease in the health care trend rate assumption. In the paragraph following Schedule 3, GE states that the effects are insignificant because its plans limit the company's share of per capita costs.

Schedules 3 and 4 relate to the APBO and plan assets, respectively, and are nearly identical in form to the ones presented for pensions. Schedule 5, the funded status and balance sheet accounts, is also very similar except that the balance sheet titles differ. The journal entries could be reconstructed in the same manner as we reconstructed the pension journal entries.

Schedule 6 gives the estimated future payments. Note that the amounts are reduced for Expected Medicare Part D subsidy. Also, the APBO and plan assets schedules (Schedules 3 and 4, respectively) state that the benefits paid are net of the **Medicare Part D subsidy.** What is this subsidy? The Medicare Prescription Drug, Improvement and Modernization Act of 2003 introduced a drug benefit for Medicare. The law also provided plan sponsors with a subsidy that is based on 28 percent of the participants' drug costs when the sponsor plan is actuarially equivalent to the Medicare Part D benefit. The *FASB Staff Position FAS 106–2,* "Accounting and Disclosure Requirements Related to the Medicare Prescription Drug, Improvement and Modernization Act of 2003" (FSP 106-2) states that the subsidy created by the act represents an actuarial gain in APBO (para. 14). The subsidy will also reduce the service cost in subsequent years (para. 15). Consistent with FSP 106-2, GE reduced its APBO for an actuarial gain of $583 million in 2004.

> Case 14-1 requires the reconstruction of GE's OPEB journal entries.

## Analytical Insights: Assessing OPEB Liability

Similar to pensions, the OPEB liability is riskier than many traditional forms of debt. To assess the magnitude of this risk, Bear Stearns & Co., Inc. has developed risk measures for OPEBs similar to the ones discussed earlier for pensions. The specific ratios are defined as follows:

$$\text{Short-term OPEB risk ratio (quick version)} = \frac{\text{APBO} - \text{Plan assets}^{43}}{\text{Market value of common stock}}$$

$$\text{Short-term OPEB risk ratio (extended version)} = \frac{\text{5 years of expected benifit payment} - \text{Plan assets}}{\text{Market value of common stock}}$$

$$\text{Long-term OPEB risk ratio} = \frac{\text{APBO}}{\text{Market value of common stock}}$$

To illustrate the calculations, we again use GE's disclosures. On December 31, 2006, the market value of GE's outstanding common stock was approximately $385.4 billion ($37.5 price $\times$ 10.277 billion outstanding shares). From Exhibit 14.8, we see that the APBO is $8.262 billion

---

[43] If VEBA trust assets are not included in plan assets (i.e., they are included elsewhere on the balance sheet), then they would also be deducted in the numerator in both short-term OPEB risk ratios.

and the fair value of plan assets is $1.710 billion. The sum of the net estimated future benefit payments for the next 5 years is $3.925 billion (Schedule 6). The resulting short-term and long-term ratios ($ in billions) are:

$$\text{Short-term OPEB risk ratio (quick version)} = \frac{\$8.262 - \$1.710}{\$385.4} = 0.017$$

$$\text{Short-term OPEB risk ratio (extended version)} = \frac{\$3.925 - \$1.710}{\$385.4} = 0.006$$

$$\text{Long-term OPEB risk ratio} = \frac{\$8.262}{\$385.4} = 0.021$$

To put these ratios in perspective, Bear Stearns reports that most short-term quick version ratios fall between 0.00 and 0.03[44] and most long-term ratios are between 0 and 0.04. Firms with some of the highest short-term quick version ratios include GM, 2.63; Ford, 1.56; and AMR Corp., 0.50. Firms with the highest long-term ratios include GM, 3.50; Ford, 1.85; and Delta Air Lines Inc., 0.76. Given the magnitude of GM's ratios, it is clear why GM wanted the United Auto Workers (UAW) to take over responsibility for the OPEB liabilities during its 2007 negotiations.[45]

> Case 14-2 deals with GM and the effects of the 2007 labor agreement.

**RECAP**

**The accounting and disclosures for postretirement benefit plans are similar to pension accounting and disclosures. However, most postretirement benefit plans are poorly funded. Additionally, firm sponsors bear the risk of future medical inflation unless they have capped their share of the expected cost. Consequently, statement readers must be mindful that the future cash outflows associated with these plans could be much higher than the current cash outflows.**

## Evaluation of Pension and Postretirement Benefit Financial Reporting

Although *SFAS No. 87* was passed more than 20 years ago, it remains controversial. Calculations are extremely complex, and net income does not reflect immediately actual asset returns or PBO actuarial (gains) losses as they arise. However, after *SFAS No. 158*, the funded status of pension and postretirement plans is recognized as a liability or an asset on a firm's balance sheet. Management has discretion in choosing the rate of return assumption and the measurement method for the market-related value. Allowing actual return to come through net income instead of showing the unexpected portion in OCI would eliminate the discretionary expected rate of return, but it would make net income more volatile. Most managers and many accountants argue that such a move could reduce the predictive power and representational faithfulness of net income.

In addition, some analysts and financial writers argue that deducting pension expense or adding pension income in the operating section of the income statement misstates operating income. They maintain that only service cost is a true current period operating item because service cost represents the present value of the increased pension payout arising from current

---

[44] Bear Stearns, op. cit., p. 25.
[45] See J. White, J. Stoll, and J. McCracken, "GM Labor Deal Ushers in New Era for Auto Industry," *The Wall Street Journal*, September 27, 2007, p. A1.

services. They believe interest cost (Component 2 of pension expense) is a financing cost, not an element of operating income. Similarly, these critics believe that the expected return on plan assets (Component 3) should be shown in other income just like the return on investment securities firms may hold.[46]

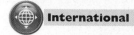

Both the FASB and the International Accounting Standards Board (IASB) have ongoing projects on pensions and other retiree benefits. The FASB's project focuses on the financial statement presentation of postretirement assets, liabilities, and expense. Consistent with the discussion in the prior paragraph, the primary issue related to expense is how the various components of pension expense should be classified within the various components of comprehensive income. The IASB project also concentrates on balance sheet and income statement presentation. Additionally, it addresses measurement issues associated with cash balance plans. After the completion of their studies, which is not expected until 2011, the FASB and IASB plan to address any remaining issues and achieve convergence for postretirement accounting.[47]

Despite concerns about prior accounting, studies provide evidence that pension and OPEB expense components found in footnotes are priced by the market.[48] Additionally, other studies suggest a positive relationship between stock prices and the funded status of pension and OPEB plans disclosed in the footnotes (and not recognized on the balance sheet prior to 2006). These studies also show that the perceived reliability of the pension and OPEB amounts affects their relation with stock prices.[49] Although the studies suggest that the market finds the pension and OPEB information useful, the results are not always consistent across years, and some results suggest that investors may not *fully* price the impact of the pension disclosures.[50] Regulators, analysts, preparers, and researchers will continue to debate the appropriate recognition, disclosure, and valuation techniques for pensions and OPEBs.

## SUMMARY

- Pension plan contracts allow employees to exchange current service for payments to be received during retirement.

- Defined contribution pension plans specify amounts to be invested for the employee during the employee's career, and the employee's pension will be based on the value of those investments at retirement.

- In the United States, most new pension plans are defined contribution plans. Consequently, defined contribution pension plans now hold 48% more assets than do defined benefit plans. Still, U.S. defined benefit pension plans hold approximately $2 trillion in assets.

[46] For example, see R. McGough and E. E. Schultz, "How Pension Surpluses Lift Profits," *The Wall Street Journal,* September 20, 1999; G. Morgenson, "What's Hiding in Big Blue's Small Print," *The New York Times,* June 4, 2000; and Bear Stearns, "Retirement Benefits Impact Operating Income," *Accounting Issues* (New York: Bear Stearns & Co. Inc., September 17, 1999).

[47] See www.fasb.org/project/postretirement_benefits_phase2.shtml for more information on this project.

[48] See, for example, M. E. Barth, W. H. Beaver, and W. R. Landsman, "The Market Valuation Implications of Net Periodic Pension Cost Components," *Journal of Accounting and Economics,* March 1992, pp. 27–62; and E. Amir, "The Effect of Accounting Aggregation on the Value-Relevance of Financial Disclosures: The Case of SFAS No. 106," *The Accounting Review,* October 1996, pp. 573–90.

[49] See M. E. Barth, "Relative Measurement Errors among Alternative Pension Asset and Liability Measures," *The Accounting Review,* July 1991, pp. 443–63; B. Choi, D. Collins, and W. Johnson. "Valuation of Reliability Differences: The Case of Nonpension Postretirement Obligations," *The Accounting Review,* July 1997, pp. 351–83; P. Y. Davis-Friday, L. B. Folami, C. Liu, and H. F. Mittelstaedt, "The Value Relevance of Financial Statement Recognition versus Disclosure: Evidence from SFAS No. 106," *The Accounting Review,* October 1999, pp. 403–23; P. Y. Davis-Friday, C. Liu, and H. F. Mittelstaedt, "Recognition and Disclosure Reliability: Evidence from SFAS No. 106," *Contemporary Accounting Research,* Summer 2004, pp. 399–427.

[50] See, for example, M. Picconi, "The Perils of Pensions: Does Pension Accounting Lead Investors and Analysts Astray?" *The Accounting Review,* July 2006, pp. 925–55.

- The accounting for defined contribution plans is straightforward. Defined benefit pension plans specify amounts to be received during retirement, thereby complicating the underlying economics of the exchange and the accounting.

- Under *SFAS Nos. 87* and *158,* pension expense for defined benefit pension plans consists of service cost, interest cost, expected return on plan assets, and two other "smoothing" components.

- The two smoothing mechanisms avoid year-to-year volatility in pension expense but make pension accounting exceedingly complex because many pension-related items are presented in AOCI.

- Under *SFAS No. 87,* the balance sheet asset (liability) on the balance sheet differed from the plan's actual funded status. *SFAS No. 158,* passed in 2006, requires that the balance sheet asset (liability) equal the plan's funded status.

- Employer funding of defined benefit pension plans is influenced by tax law, labor law, union membership, and the employer's financial needs.

- The reporting rules for other postretirement benefits (OPEB) closely parallel the pension accounting rules.

- *SFAS No. 132 (revised 2003)* and *SFAS No. 158* require information about expected future cash flows, future amortization amounts, and major classes of investments so that investors can make cash flow projections, assess risk, and evaluate rate of return assumptions.

- Academic research suggests that stock prices reflect pension and OPEB disclosures but their impact may not be fully valued.

- Statement readers should view the following circumstances as potential warning signals or indicators of earnings management:

  - A significant disagreement between any of the various pension and OPEB rates selected by a firm (that is, the discount rate, the expected rate of return on plan assets, or the rate of increase in future compensation levels or health care costs) and the rates chosen by other firms in its industry.

  - A very large difference between the chosen expected rate of return on plan assets and the discount rate used.

  - An increase in the year-to-year expected rate of return on plan assets that seems unrelated to changes in market conditions.

  - A decrease in the assumed rate of increase in future compensation levels (or, for OPEB, future health cost trends) that cannot be explained by changing industry or labor market conditions.

  - Rate of return assumptions that are inconsistent with prior investment experience or mix of equity and debt investments.

## SELF-STUDY PROBLEM

## ILLUSTRATION OF PENSION COMPUTATIONS

Hayes Corporation's pension benefit formula provides a $400 pension benefit per year for each year of service to the company plus 40% of the employee's salary at the expected time of retirement, which is age 68. Payments begin one year after retirement and are paid annually thereafter. The actuarially determined life expectancy of employees is 78 years.

Hayes adopts the pension plan on January 1, 2008. One of its employees, Scott Schaefer, is granted credit for 10 years of prior service. He is exactly 48 years old on the date the plan is adopted. His salary on January 1, 2008 is $75,000; his salary at retirement in 20 years is expected to be $130,000.

Hayes uses 7% for both the discount rate and the expected rate of return on plan assets.

1. **Compute the PBO related to Schaefer's benefits as of January 1, 2008.** Schaefer will retire on his 68th birthday, which is January 1, 2028. His first pension benefit will be paid one year later, and he expects additional benefits to continue to January 1, 2038 for a total of 10 payments.

   To compute the PBO, first determine the undiscounted annual expected pension benefits as of January 1, 2028, the retirement date:

   | | | |
   |---|---|---|
   | Years of service credit as of 1/1/08: 10 years × $400 per year | = | $ 4,000 |
   | Benefits tied to expected salary at retirement: 0.40 × $130,000 | = | 52,000 |
   | Total annual pension benefit based on service credit as of 1/1/08 | | $56,000 |

   This $56,000 annual pension benefit will be paid for 10 years beginning on January 1, 2029. The present value of an ordinary annuity of $56,000 per period for 10 periods at 7% (Appendix I, Table 2) is:

   $$\$56,000 \times 7.02358 = \$393,320.48$$

   So, $393,320.48 is the present value of the annuity at the retirement date, January 1, 2028. To determine the PBO, we must compute the present value of this annuity as of January 1, 2008—that is, discount the still distant annuity back to the present. To do this, we take the present value factor for a payment to be received in 20 periods at 7%, which Appendix I, Table 1 indicates is 0.25842:

   $$\$393,320.48 \times 0.25842 = \$101,641.87$$

   The PBO related to Schaefer's benefits as of January 1, 2008 is $101,641.87.

2. **Compute the ABO related to Schaefer's benefits as of January 1, 2008.** This computation is similar to the PBO computation *except* that the annual pension benefit is based on Schaefer's current salary of $75,000, not on his expected salary at retirement. The computation is:

   | | | |
   |---|---|---|
   | Years of service credit as of 1/1/08: 10 years × $400 per year | = | $ 4,000 |
   | Benefits tied to current salary: 0.40 × $75,000 | = | 30,000 |
   | Total annual pension benefit based on service credit as of 1/1/08 | | $34,000 |

   This is the annual pension benefit that Schaefer would receive if his salary at retirement equals his current salary. As of January 1, 2028, the present value at 7% of a 10-year annuity of $34,000 per year with the first payment on January 1, 2029 is:

   $$\$34,000 \times 7.02358 = \$238,801.72$$

   Because $238,801.72 is the present value 20 years in the future, we must now determine the present value at January 1, 2008. To do this, we multiply $238,801.72 by the 7% present value factor for a flow 20 years distant:

   $$\$238,801.72 \times 0.25842 = \$61,711.14$$

   So, the ABO related to Schaefer's benefits as of January 1, 2008 is $61,711.14.

3. **Compute the PBO related to Schaefer's benefits as of January 1, 2009.** The January 1, 2009 PBO will exceed the January 1, 2008 figure because (a) Schaefer's additional year of

service adds $400 to his annual pension benefit and (b) the present value of the pension stream has increased because one year has elapsed.

a. Increase in annual pension benefit:

| | | |
|---|---|---|
| Years of service credit as of 1/1/06: 11 years × $400 per year | = | $ 4,400 |
| Benefits tied to expected salary at retirement: 0.40 × $130,000 | = | 52,000 |
| Total annual pension benefit based on service credit as of 1/1/06 | | $56,400 |

b. Increase in present value:

The present value of the 10-year annuity at January 1, 2028 is simply:

$$\$56,400 \times 7.02358 = \$396,129.91$$

But this annuity is now only 19 years away, not 20. So, its present value at January 1, 2009 is:

$$\$396,129.91 \times 0.27651 = \$109,533.88$$

Note that the present value factor is from the 19-period row of the 7% column from Appendix I, Table 1. During 2008, the PBO increased to $109,533.88.

4. **Compute pension expense for 2008 attributable to Schaefer's employment. Show the components of pension expense.**

a. *Service cost* is defined as the increase in the discounted present value of the pension benefit ultimately payable (PBO) attributable to an additional year's employment.

In our example, Schaefer's annual pension benefit increased by $400 (that is, $56,400 − $56,000) by virtue of his having accrued an additional year of service credit in 2008. The present value of this increase in the 10 expected pension benefit payments as of January 1, 2028 is:

$$\$400 \times 7.02358 = \$2,809.43$$

This $2,809.43 is the increase in the present value as measured 19 periods in the future—that is, at January 1, 2028. The increase in the present value during 2008 measured as of January 1, 2009 is:

$$\$2,809.43 \times 0.27651 = \$776.84$$

So, service cost for 2008 is $776.84.

b. *Interest cost* is determined by multiplying the start of the period PBO by the discount rate. The PBO at January 1, 2008 was $101,641.87 (see example 1). So, interest cost for 2008 is:[51]

$$\$101,641.87 \times .07 = \$7,114.93$$

c. *Recognized prior service cost*: Because the plan was adopted on January 1, 2008 and because Schaefer was given credit for prior service, the entirety of the PBO at January 1, 2008 is composed of prior service cost. Because his expected remaining service period is 20 years (January 1, 2008 through January 1, 2028), the prior service cost recognized in pension expense for 2008 is:

$$\$101,641.87/20 \text{ years} = \$5,082.09$$

---

[51] Notice that the change in the PBO during 2008 was $7,892.01 ($109,533.88 − $101,641.87). Because there were no changes in actuarial assumptions, plan benefits, or discount rates, the PBO change is totally attributable to 2008 service cost plus interest cost. As computed here, service cost plus interest cost totals $7,891.77, which differs from $7,892.01 only because of rounding error.

d. *Other pension expense elements for 2008:* Because there were no plan assets at the start of 2008 and there were no actuarial gains or losses, there are no other pension expense elements for 2008. *So, total pension expense for 2008 attributable to Schaefer's employment is:*

$$\$776.84 + \$7,114,93 + \$5,082.09 = \$12,973.86$$

## EXERCISES

### E14-1

**Determining projected benefit obligation**

**AICPA**
ADAPTED

The following information pertains to Seda Company's pension plan:

| | |
|---|---|
| Actuarial estimate of projected benefit obligation at 1/1/08 | $72,000 |
| Service cost for 2008 | 18,000 |
| Pension benefits paid on 12/31/08 | 15,000 |
| Assumed discount rate | 10% |

**Required:**

If no change in actuarial estimates occurred during 2008, how much would Seda's projected benefit obligation be at December 31, 2008?

### E14-2

**Determining balance sheet pension asset (liability)**

**AICPA**
ADAPTED

At December 31, 2008, Kerr Corporation's pension plan administrator provided the following information:

| | |
|---|---|
| Fair value of plan assets | $3,450,000 |
| Accumulated benefit obligation | 4,300,000 |
| Projected benefit obligation | 5,700,000 |

**Required:**

What amount of the pension liability should be shown on Kerr's December 31, 2008 balance sheet?

### E14-3

**Determining balance sheet pension asset (liability)**

**AICPA**
ADAPTED

On January 2, 2008, Loch Company established a defined benefit plan covering all employees and contributed $1,000,000 to the plan. At December 31, 2008, Loch determined that the 2008 service and interest costs totaled $620,000. The expected and the actual rate of return on plan assets for 2008 was 10%. Loch's pension expense has no other components.

**Required:**

What amount should Loch report in its December 31, 2008 balance sheet as a pension asset (liability)?

### E14-4

**Determining PBO and ABO**

**AICPA**
ADAPTED

Mary Abbott is a long-time employee of Love Enterprises, a manufacturer and distributor of farm implements. Abbott plans to retire on her 65th birthday (January 1, 2013) five years from today. Her current salary is $48,000 per year, and her projected salary for her last year of employment is $60,000.

Love Enterprises sponsors a defined benefit pension plan. It provides for an annual pension benefit equal to 60% of the employee's annual salary at retirement. Payments commence on the employee's 66th birthday or one year after the anniversary date of his or her retirement. The discount and earnings rate on plan assets is 8%. The average life expectancy for male and female employees is 76 and 80, respectively.

**Required:**

1. Compute the PBO related to Abbott's pension benefits as of January 1, 2008.

2. Compute ABO for the year ended December 31, 2008.

Use the facts given in E14-4. Repeat the requirements assuming that the discount and earnings rate is 11% instead of 8%.

**E14-5**

Determining PBO and ABO

**AICPA**
ADAPTED

---

The following information pertains to Gali Company's defined benefit pension plan for 2008:

| | |
|---|---:|
| Fair value of plan assets, beginning of year | $350,000 |
| Fair value of plan assets, end of year | 525,000 |
| Employer contributions | 110,000 |
| Benefits paid | 85,000 |

**Required:**
What was the dollar amount of actual return on Gali Company's plan assets in 2008?

**E14-6**

Determining actual return on plan assets

**AICPA**
ADAPTED

---

The following information pertains to Kane Company's defined benefit pension plan:

| | |
|---|---:|
| Balance sheet asset, 1/1/08 | $ 2,000 |
| AOCI—prior service cost, 1/1/08 | 24,000 |
| Service cost | 19,000 |
| Interest cost | 38,000 |
| Expected return on plan assets | 22,000 |
| Prior service cost amortization | 6,000 |
| Employer contributions | 40,000 |

Kane has no net actuarial gains or losses in AOCI.

**Required:**
In its December 31, 2008 balance sheet, what amount should Kane report as a pension asset (liability)?

**E14-7**

Determining balance sheet pension asset (liability)

**AICPA**
ADAPTED

---

Dell Company adopted a defined benefit pension plan on January 1, 2008. Dell amortizes the initial prior service cost of $1,334,400 over 16 years. It assumes a 7% discount rate and an 8% expected rate of return. The following additional data are available for 2008:

| | |
|---|---:|
| Service cost for 2008 | $320,000 |
| Prior service cost amortization | 83,400 |
| Employer contribution made at 12/31/08 | 335,000 |

**Required:**
Compute the pension asset (liability) to be reported on Dell's December 31, 2008 balance sheet.

**E14-8**

Determining balance sheet pension asset (liability)

**AICPA**
ADAPTED

---

On January 1, 2008, East Corporation adopted a defined benefit pension plan. At plan inception, the prior service cost was $60,000. In 2008, East incurred service cost of $150,000 and amortized $12,000 of prior service cost. On December 31, 2008, East contributed $160,000 to the pension plan. East assumes a 6% discount rate and 5% expected rate of return.

**Required:**
At December 31, 2008, what amounts should East report as a pension asset (liability) and AOCI on its balance sheet?

**E14-9**

Determining balance sheet pension asset (liability)

**AICPA**
ADAPTED

---

Nome Company sponsors a defined benefit plan covering all employees. Benefits are based on years of service and compensation levels at the time of retirement. Nome has a September 30 fiscal year-end. It determined that as of September 30, 2008, its ABO was $320,000, its PBO was $380,000, and its plan assets had a $290,000 fair value. Nome's September 30, 2008 trial balance showed a balance sheet asset of $20,000.

**E14-10**

Adjusting balance sheet pension asset (liability)

**AICPA**
ADAPTED

**Required:**

What adjustment should Nome make to report the appropriate pension asset (liability) on its September 30, 2008 balance sheet?

---

**E14-11**

Determining postretirement expense

**AICPA**
ADAPTED

Hukle Company has provided the following information pertaining to its postretirement plan for 2008:

| | |
|---|---|
| Service cost | $240,000 |
| Benefit payment made at 12/31/08 | 110,000 |
| Interest on accumulated postretirement benefit obligation | 40,000 |
| Prior service cost amortization | 10,000 |

**Required:**

Calculate Hukle Company's 2008 net postretirement benefit cost.

---

**E14-12**

Determining pension expense

**AICPA**
ADAPTED

The following information pertains to Lee Corporation's defined benefit pension plan for 2008:

| | |
|---|---|
| Service cost | $160,000 |
| Actual and expected return on plan assets | 35,000 |
| Amortization of prior service costs | 5,000 |
| Interest on pension obligation | 50,000 |

**Required:**

Determine the pension expense that Lee Corporation would include in its 2008 net income.

---

**E14-13**

Determining pension expense, fair value of plan assets, and deferred return on plan assets

Bostonian Company provided the following information related to its defined benefit pension plan for 2008:

| | |
|---|---|
| PBO on 1/1/08 | $2,500,000 |
| Fair value of plan assets on 1/1/08 | 2,000,000 |
| Service cost | 120,000 |
| Actual return on plan assets | 320,000 |
| Payments made to retirees on 12/31/08 | 100,000 |
| Amortization of prior service cost | 40,000 |
| Recognized actuarial losses | 50,000 |
| Contributions made to plan during 2008 | 80,000 |
| Interest rate for discounting pension obligations | 6% |
| Expected return on plan assets | 8% |

**Required:**

1. What amount of pension expense should Bostonian report for 2008?

2. What is the fair value of plan assets at December 31, 2008?

3. What dollar amount of return on plan assets was deferred in 2008?

---

**E14-14**

Determining pension expense and AOCI balances

Cummings, Inc. had the following reconciliation at *December 31, 2008*:

| | |
|---|---|
| Fair value of plan assets | $5,000 |
| PBO | 4,200 |
| Funded status | $ 800 |
| AOCI—prior service cost | $ 300 |
| AOCI—net actuarial (gain) loss | 700 |
| Total | $1,000 |

The following assumptions are being used for the pension plan in *2009*:

| | |
|---|---|
| Discount rate | 5% |
| Expected rate of return on assets | 8% |
| Average remaining worklife | 10 years |
| Remaining amortization period for prior services costs | 6 years |

**Additional *2009* Information:**

| | |
|---|---|
| Service cost | $442 |
| Cash contributed to the plan (year-end) | 250 |
| Pension benefits paid by the plan (year-end) | 465 |
| Actual return on plan assets | 650 |
| New actuarial (gain) loss on the PBO | 64 |

**Required:**

1. Compute pension expense for 2009.

2. Compute the fair value of plan assets at *December 31, 2009.*

3. Compute the PBO at *December 31, 2009.*

4. Compute AOCI—net actuarial (gain) loss as of *December 31, 2009.*

---

Jones Company has a postretirement benefit (health care) plan for its employees. On January 1, 2008, the balance in the Accumulated postretirement benefit obligation account was $300 million. The assumed discount rate—for purposes of determining postretirement obligations and expenses—is 8%. Jones does not prefund postretirement benefits, so there are no plan assets. It created a $45 million prior service cost *credit* at the end of 2007 when the company modified the health care plan to reduce the maximum benefits paid to each employee. This amount is being amortized over 15 years. The service cost component of postretirement benefits for 2008 is $35 million.

**E14-15**

Determining postretirement (health care) benefits expense and obligation

**Required:**

1. Determine the amount of postretirement benefits cost for 2008.

2. If benefits paid to retirees totaled $64 million in 2008, determine the balance in the Accumulated postretirement benefit obligation account on December 31, 2008.

---

Zeff Manufacturing provides the following information about its postretirement health care plan for 2008:

**E14-16**

Determining postretirement health care expenses and plan assets and liabilities balances

| | |
|---|---|
| Accumulated postretirement benefit obligation on 1/1/08 | $300,000 |
| Fair value of plan assets on 1/1/08 | 30,000 |
| Benefits paid to retirees at 12/31/08 | 6,500 |
| Service cost for 2008 | 20,000 |
| Recognized prior service cost | 10,000 |
| Recognized actuarial loss | 7,000 |
| Actual return on plan assets | 4,500 |
| Contributions to the plan at 12/31/08 | 12,000 |
| Discount rate | 8% |
| Expected long-run rate of return on plan assets | 10% |

**Required:**

1. Determine Zeff's postretirement health care expense in 2008.

2. Determine the fair value of plan assets at December 31, 2008.

3. Determine the APBO amount at December 31, 2008.

| E14-17 |
|---|
| Determining plan assets, PBO, and AOCI |

Bonny Corp. has a defined benefit pension plan for its employees who have an average remaining service life of 10 years. The following information is available for 2008 and 2009 related to the pension plan:

|  | 2009 | 2008 |
|---|---|---|
| Projected benefit obligation, 1/1 | ? | $750,000 |
| Service cost | $ 70,000 | 60,000 |
| Actual return on plan assets | 66,400 | 72,000 |
| Bonny Corp. contributions for year ended 12/31 | 74,000 | 68,000 |
| Benefits paid during year | 67,000 | 60,000 |
| Fair value of plan assets, 1/1 | ? | 600,000 |
| Actuarial (gain) loss on PBO during year | (13,000) | 4,400 |
| Expected return on plan assets | 7% | 7% |
| Discount rate | 6% | 6% |

Bonny Corp. had no beginning balance in its AOCI—net actuarial (gain) loss on January 1, 2008. The actuarial (gains) losses on PBO arose due to changes in assumptions made by the actuaries regarding salary increases (2008) and mortality estimates (2009).

**Required:**

1. Compute Bonny's PBO at December 31, 2008 and December 31, 2009.

2. Compute the fair value of plan assets at December 31, 2008 and December 31, 2009.

3. Compute the year-end balance in AOCI—net actuarial loss (gain) for Bonny Corp. for 2008 and 2009.

4. Compute OCI for the years ended December 31, 2008 and December 31, 2009.

| E14-18 |
|---|
| Determining amount of recognized net gain or loss using the corridor approach |

At January 1, 2008, Milo Co.'s projected benefit obligation is $300,000, and the fair value of its pension plan assets is $340,000. The average remaining service period of Milo's employees is 10 years. The following additional information is available for Milo's net actuarial gains and losses:

|  | 2008 | 2009 | 2010 |
|---|---|---|---|
| AOCI—net actuarial (gain) loss at 1/1 | $ 40,000 | $ 28,000 | $ 53,000 |
| PBO at 12/31 | 341,000 | 402,000 | 416,000 |
| Fair value of plan assets at 12/31 | 323,000 | 419,000 | 438,000 |

**Required:**

Compute the amount of recognized gain or loss to be included in pension expense for each year, 2008 through 2010. Indicate whether the recognized amount increases or decreases pension expense.

| E14-19 |
|---|
| Determining amount of recognized net gain or loss using the corridor approach |

At January 1, 2008, Archer Co.'s PBO is $500,000 and the fair value of its pension plan assets is $630,000. The average remaining service period of Archer's employees is 12 years. The AOCI—net actuarial loss (gain) at January 1, 2008 is $(70,000). The following additional information is available related to Archer's actuarial gains and losses:

|  | 2008 | 2009 | 2010 |
|---|---|---|---|
| New actuarial loss (gain) on PBO | $(30,000) | $ 65,000 | $(63,000) |
| New deferred loss (gain) on plan assets | 60,000 | 55,000 | (32,000) |
| PBO at 12/31 | 560,000 | 675,000 | 628,000 |
| Fair value of plan assets at 12/31 | 575,000 | 530,000 | 650,000 |

**Required:**

For each year, 2008 through 2010, compute

1. The amount of recognized loss (gain) to be included in pension expense. Be sure to indicate whether the recognized amount increases or decreases pension expense.

2. The ending balance of AOCI—net actuarial (gain) loss.

3. OCI—net actuarial (gain) loss.

---

George Corporation has a defined benefit pension plan for its employees. The following information is available for 2008:

E14-20

Determining pension elements

| | |
|---|---:|
| PBO at 1/1 | $ 930,000 |
| Payments made to retirees at 12/31/08 | 204,000 |
| Service cost | 196,000 |
| Actual return on plan assets | 30,000 |
| Plan contributions at 12/31/08 | 130,000 |
| Fair value of plan assets at 12/31/08 | 880,000 |
| Amortization of prior service cost | 76,000 |
| Discount rate | 10% |
| Expected rate of return on plan assets | 6% |

**Required:**

1. What was the January 1, 2008 fair value of the plan assets?

2. What is the expected dollar return on plan assets for 2008?

3. What amount of pension expense should George report for the year ended December 31, 2008?

4. What was the dollar amount of return (loss) on plan assets that was deferred during 2008?

5. Make the journal entries to record pension expense, the contribution, and the deferred return (loss).

---

On January 1, 2008, Cello Co. established a defined benefit pension plan for its employees. At January 1, 2008, Cello estimated the service cost for 2008 to be $45,000. At January 1, 2009, it estimated 2009 service cost to be $49,000. On the plan inception date, prior service credit was granted to employees for five years, the period of time between the company's formation and plan inception. The prior service cost was estimated to be $650,000 at January 1, 2008. Cello uses a 10% discount rate and assumes a return on plan assets of 9%. The average remaining service life of employees is 20 years, and the company will fund at the end of each year an amount equal to service cost plus interest cost for 2008 and 2009.

E14-21

Determining pension elements

| | December 31 | |
|---|:---:|:---:|
| | **2009** | **2008** |
| PBO | ? | ? |
| Benefits paid at 12/31 | 2,000 | –0– |
| Fair value of plan assets | ? | –0– |
| Contributions at 12/31 | ? | ? |
| Actual return on plan assets | 3,200 | –0– |

**Required:**

1. Compute the amount of prior service cost to be included as a component of pension expense for 2008.

2. Compute pension expense for 2008.

3. Compute the fair value of plan assets at December 31, 2008.

4. Compute the PBO balance at December 31, 2008.

5. Prepare the company's required journal entries to record the effects of its pension plan in 2008.

6. Repeat requirements 1 through 5 for 2009.

7. Prepare T-accounts for Pension asset (liability), AOCI—prior service cost, and AOCI—net actuarial (gain) loss to show the effects of the entries made in requirements 5 and 6. Label the effects.

## PROBLEMS / DISCUSSION QUESTIONS

**P14-1**

Determining components of pension expense

The following information pertains to Sparta Company's defined benefit pension plan:

| | |
|---|---|
| Discount rate | 8% |
| Expected rate of return on plan assets | 10% |
| Average service life | 12 years |
| At 1/1/08 | |
| PBO | $600,000 |
| Fair value of pension plan assets | 720,000 |
| AOCI—prior service cost | 240,000 |
| AOCI—net actuarial (gain) loss | (96,000) |
| At 12/31/08 | |
| PBO | 910,000 |
| Fair value of pension plan assets | 825,000 |

Service cost for 2008 was $90,000. No contributions were made or benefits paid during the year. Sparta's Accrued pension liability was $8,000 at January 1, 2008. Sparta uses the straight-line method of amortization over the maximum period permitted.

**Required:**

Determine the amount for each of the following items:

1. Interest cost.

2. Expected dollar return on plan assets.

3. Actual return on plan assets.

4. Recognized actuarial gain (minimum amortization).

5. Recognized prior service costs.

6. Balance in the AOCI—net actuarial (gain) loss account on December 31, 2008.

---

**P14-2**

Determining expense and balance sheet amounts (journal entries)

Turner, Inc. provides a defined benefit pension plan to its employees. The company has 150 employees. The average remaining service life of employees is 10 years. The AOCI—net actuarial (gain) loss was zero at December 31, 2008. Turner uses a market-related (smoothed) value to compute expected return.

**Additional Information:**

| | December 31 | |
|---|---|---|
| **Description** | **2009** | **2008** |
| PBO | $1,450,000 | $1,377,000 |
| ABO | 1,425,000 | 1,350,000 |
| Fair value of plan assets | 1,395,000 | 1,085,000 |
| Market-related value of plan assets | 1,369,000 | 1,085,000 |
| AOCI—prior service cost | ? | 292,000 |
| Balance sheet pension asset (liability) | ? | (292,000) |
| Service cost | 117,400 | |
| Contribution | 169,000 | |
| PBO actuarial gain | 182,100 | |
| Benefit payments made | None | None |
| Discount rate | 10% | 10% |
| Expected rate of return | 10% | 10% |

**Required:**
Round all amounts to nearest dollar:

1. Compute the amount of prior service cost that would be amortized as a component of pension expense for 2009 and 2010.

2. Compute the actual return on plan assets for 2009.

3. Compute the unexpected net gain or loss on plan assets for 2009.

4. Compute pension expense for 2009.

5. Prepare the company's required pension journal entries for 2009.

6. Compute the 2009 increase/decrease in AOCI—net actuarial (gain) loss and the amount to be amortized in 2009 and 2010.

7. Confirm that the pension asset (liability) on the balance sheet equals the funded status as of December 31, 2009.

---

Puhlman Inc. provides a defined benefit pension plan to its employees. It uses a market-related (smoothed) value to compute its expected return. Additional information follows:

**P14-3**

Determining expense and balance sheet amounts (journal entries)

| Description | December 31 | |
| --- | --- | --- |
| | **2008** | **2007** |
| PBO | ? | $2,500,000 |
| ABO | $2,335,000 | 2,150,000 |
| Fair value of plan assets | ? | 2,100,000 |
| Market-related value of plan assets | 2,342,800 | 2,100,000 |
| Benefit payments made | 272,000 | 231,000 |
| AOCI—net actuarial (gain) loss | 114,000 | –0– |
| AOCI—prior service cost | ? | 400,000 |
| Balance sheet pension asset (liability) | ? | (400,000) |
| Service cost | 214,000 | |
| Contribution | 321,000 | |
| Actual return | 129,000 | |
| Discount rate for PBO | 9% | 10% |
| Expected rate of return | 10% | 10% |
| Average remaining service life of employees | 15 years | 15 years |

During 2008, the PBO increased by $33,000 due to a decrease in the discount rate from the previous year. The 2007 discount rate assumption was used to compute 2008 service cost and interest cost.

**Required:**
Round all amounts to nearest dollar:

1. Compute the fair value of plan assets at December 31, 2008.

2. Compute the prior service cost that would be amortized as a component of pension expense for 2008 and 2009.

3. Compute the PBO at December 31, 2008.

4. Compute pension expense for 2008.

5. Prepare the company's required pension journal entries for 2008.

6. Compute the 2008 increase/decrease in AOCI—net actuarial (gains) or losses and the amount to be amortized in 2008 and 2009.

7. Confirm that the pension asset (liability) on the balance sheet equals the funded status as of December 31, 2008.

**P14-4**

Relating pension concepts to
*SFAS No. 87* and *SFAS No. 158*

You have the following information related to Chalmers Corporation's pension plan:

1. Defined benefit, noncontributory pension plan.
2. Plan initiation, January 1, 2008 (no credit given for prior service).
3. Retirement benefits paid at year-end with the first payment one year after retirement.
4. Assumed discount rate of 7%.
5. Assumed expected rate of return on plan assets of 9%.
6. Annual retirement benefit equals years of credited service × 0.02 × highest salary.

You have the following information for Frank Bullitt, the firm's only employee:

| | |
|---|---|
| Start date | January 1, 2005 |
| Expected retirement date | December 31, 2022 |
| Expected number of payments during retirement | 20 |

Selected actual and expected salary levels:

| Date | Salary Level |
|---|---|
| January 1, 2005 | $22,000 |
| January 1, 2008 | 27,000 |
| January 1, 2009 | 30,000 |
| January 1, 2022 | 75,000 |

**Required:**

1. Calculate the service cost and the interest cost components of pension cost for 2008 and 2009.
2. Calculate the PBO at the end of 2008 and 2009.
3. Compute the fair value of plan assets for 2008 and 2009, assuming that $1,200 in contributions is made to the pension fund at the end of each year.
4. Calculate pension expense for 2008 and 2009. There were no actuarial gains or losses during 2008 or 2009.
5. Make the required journal entries for 2008 and 2009.
6. Show how your answer for 2008 would change if the plan had granted credit for prior service.

**P14-5**

Calculating PBO, ABO, and
pension expense

Assume that the pension benefit formula of ABC Corporation calls for paying a pension benefit of $250 per year for each year of service with the company plus 50% of the projected last year's salary at retirement. Payments begin one year after the employee attains the age of 65 and are paid annually thereafter. The average life expectancy of employees is 76.

The pension plan is adopted on January 1, 2008. One of the company's employees, I.M. Workaholic, is granted credit for 10 years of prior service. He is 50 years old at the date the plan is adopted. His current annual salary is $20,000, but his salary level when he retires in 15 years is expected to be $30,000.

Assume a 10% rate of interest for both the discount rate and the expected rate of return on plan assets.

**Required:**

1. Determine the PBO and ABO related to Workaholic's pension benefits as of January 1, 2008.
2. What would the projected benefit obligation be on December 31, 2008?
3. How much pension expense should ABC Corporation recognize in 2008 for Workaholic? Show the components of pension expense.

Assume the same facts for ABC Corporation as in P14-5 with the following exceptions:

**P14-6**

Determining PBO, ABO, and pension expense

- Assume both that ABC fully funds the estimated PBO on January 1, 2008 and that invested funds earn an actual return of 12% in 2008.

- Suppose that in addition to funding the estimated PBO on January 1, 2008, ABC follows a policy of contributing to the pension fund (at the end of each year) an amount equal to the estimated pension expense less the prior service cost component, which was prefunded. On January 1, 2009, the discount rate drops from 10% to 9% while the expected return on plan assets remains at 10% for 2009.

**Required:**

1. How much pension expense should ABC recognize in 2008? Show the components of pension expense. Explain how this differs from your answer in requirement 3 of P14-5.

2. Compute the pension expense and amount funded in 2009. (Assume that the actual return on plan assets was 10% in 2009.) Compare the funded status of the plans at the end of 2009 and 2008. Explain the change.

On January 1, 2008, Magee Corporation started doing business by hiring R. Walker as an employee at an annual salary of $50,000, with an annual salary increment of $10,000. Based on his current age and the company's retirement program, Walker is required to retire at the end of the year in 2011. However, at his option, he could retire any time after completing one full year of service. Regardless of when he retires, the company will pay a lump-sum pension at the end of 2012. The lump-sum payment is calculated to be 25% of the cumulative lifetime salary Walker earned. Magee's annual discount rate is 10%. Assume that Walker retires at the end of 2011.

**P14-7**

Identifying effect of funding and discount rate assumption on pension expense

**Required:**

1. Assuming that Magee Corporation does not fund its pension expense, calculate this expense for 2008–2011. Clearly identify the service and interest cost components. Based on your calculations, provide journal entries to record the effects of pensions during 2008–2012.

2. Assume that Magee fully funds its pension cost as soon as it vests and that the contributions to the pension fund earn exactly a 10% rate of return annually. Based on these revised assumptions, redo requirement 1.

3. Explain why the total pension expense in requirement 1 and in requirement 2 differ.

4. Assume that Magee does not fund its pension expense. Discuss how different assumptions regarding the discount rate affect the pension expense. Compare the pension expense with discount rates of 5%, 10%, and 15%.

Use the same set of facts as in P14-7. In addition, assume that based on ERISA rules, Magee Corporation must contribute the following amounts to the pension fund:

**P14-8**

Determining effect of discount rate assumption on pension expense and PBO

mhhe.com/revsine4e

|  | 2008 | 2009 | 2010 | 2011 |
|---|---|---|---|---|
| Contributions | $8,475 | $11,000 | $15,000 | $18,000 |

Magee intends to fund the pension plan only to extent required by ERISA rules. Assume that the contributions to the pension fund earn exactly a 10% rate of return annually.

**Required:**

1. The CEO of the company, Reece Magee, is considering three possible discount rates (8%, 10%, and 12%) for calculating the annual pension expense. Provide schedules showing how much pension expense will be reported under each of the three scenarios during the 2008–2012 period.

2. Provide schedules showing the funded status of the pension plan during the 2008–2011 period.

3. Magee is wondering which of the three discount rate assumptions would be considered the most and least conservative for the purposes of determining net income. Prepare a schedule that shows how total pension expense compares across the three discount rate assumptions. Explain your results.

---

**P14-9**

Interpreting OPEB disclosures and making journal entries

The following information is based on an actual annual report. Different names and years are being used.

Bond and some of Green's subsidiaries provide certain postretirement medical, dental, and vision care and life insurance for retirees and their dependents and for the surviving dependents of eligible employees and retirees. Generally, the employees become eligible for postretirement benefits if they retire no earlier than age 55 with 10 years of service. The liability for postretirement benefits is funded through trust funds based on actuarially determined contributions that consider the amount deductible for income tax purposes. The health care plans are contributory, funded jointly by the companies and the participating retirees. The December 31, 2009 and 2008 postretirement benefit liabilities and related data were determined using the January 1, 2009 actuarial valuations.

Information related to the accumulated postretirement benefit obligation plan for the years 2009 and 2008 follows:

| | Years Ended December 31 | |
|---|---|---|
| ($ in thousands) | 2009 | 2008 |
| **Change in benefit obligation** | | |
| Benefit obligation at beginning of period | $1,236,000 | $1,139,000 |
| Service cost | 41,000 | 38,000 |
| Interest cost | 82,000 | 78,000 |
| Plan participants' contributions | 4,000 | 3,000 |
| Actuarial loss (gain) | (188,000) | 25,000 |
| Benefits paid | (51,000) | (47,000) |
| Special termination benefits | 27,000 | — |
| Benefit obligation at end of period | 1,151,000 | 1,236,000 |
| **Change in plan assets** | | |
| Fair value of plan assets at beginning of period | 865,000 | 767,000 |
| Actual return on plan assets | 105,000 | 122,000 |
| Employer contributions | 24,000 | 20,000 |
| Plan participants' contributions | 4,000 | 3,000 |
| Benefits paid | (51,000) | (47,000) |
| Fair value of plan assets at period-end | 947,000 | 865,000 |
| Plan assets less than benefit obligations | (204,000) | (371,000) |
| AOCI—net actuarial (gain) loss | (555,000) | (352,000) |
| AOCI—prior service cost | 41,000 | 48,000 |

The assumed discount rates used to determine the benefit obligation as of December 31, 2009 and 2008 were 7.75% and 6.75%, respectively. The fair value of plan assets excludes $9 million and $7 million held in a grantor trust as of December 31, 2009 and 2008, respectively, for the payment of postretirement medical benefits.

The components of other postretirement benefit costs, portions of which were recorded as components of construction costs for the years 2009, 2008, and 2007 follow:

| ($ in thousands) | 2009 | 2008 | 2007 |
|---|---|---|---|
| Service cost | $    ? | $    ? | $ 34,000 |
| Interest cost on APBO | ? | ? | 76,000 |
| Expected return on plan assets | ? | ? | (61,000) |
| Amortization of prior service costs | 4,000 | 4,000 | 4,000 |
| Recognized gain | (14,000) | (14,000) | (13,000) |
| Curtailment loss | 30,000 | –0– | –0– |
| Net periodic benefit cost | $    ? | $    ? | $ 40,000 |

The other postretirement benefit curtailment losses in December 2009 represent the recognition of $3,000 of additional prior service costs and a $27,000 increase in the benefit obligations resulting from special termination benefits.

The health care cost trend rates used to measure the expected cost of the postretirement medical benefits are assumed to be 8.0% for pre-Medicare recipients and 6.0% for Medicare recipients for 2009. Those rates are assumed to decrease in 0.5% annual increments to 5% for the years 2018 and 2011, respectively, and to remain level thereafter. The health care cost trend rates, used to measure the expected cost of postretirement dental and vision benefits, are a level 3.5% and 2.0% per year, respectively. Assumed health care cost trend rates have a significant effect on the amounts reported for the health care plans. A percentage change of one point in the assumed health care cost trend rates would have the following effects:

| | I Percentage Point | |
|---|---|---|
| ($ in thousands) | Increase | Decrease |
| Effect on total 2009 service and interest cost components | $ 26,000 | $ (20,000) |
| Effect on APBO as of 12/31/2009 | 190,000 | 151,000 |

**Required:**

1. Assuming an expected rate of return on plan assets for 2009 and 2008 of 8.8% and 9%, respectively, compute the missing amounts in the first table and determine the Net periodic benefit cost for years 2009 and 2008. (Round amounts to nearest million.)

2. Assuming that the employer submitted the $4,000,000 of participant contributions directly to the trust, show the journal entry that Bond would make to record its 2009 company (employer) contribution, Net periodic benefit cost, and AOCI effects.

3. Show that the 2009 journal entries result in a balance sheet pension asset (liability) equal to the funded status. Assume that the beginning 2009 balance equals the ending 2008 funded status.

The following information pertains to the pension plan of Beatty Business Group:

**P14-10**

Amortizing actuarial gains (losses)

mhhe.com/revsine4e

| | | Beginning of the Year | |
|---|---|---|---|
| Year<br>(1) | PBO<br>(2) | Fair Value of<br>Pension Plan Assets<br>(3) | (Gain ) Loss<br>for the Year<br>(4) |
| 2008 | $   400,000 | $   390,000 | |
| 2009 | 450,000 | 410,000 | $ (60,000) |
| 2010 | 570,000 | 500,000 | (120,000) |
| 2011 | 840,000 | 800,000 | 120,000 |
| 2012 | 1,000,000 | 1,100,000 | 175,000 |
| 2013 | 1,200,000 | 1,280,000 | 250,000 |
| 2014 | 1,450,000 | 1,310,000 | 80,000 |

Note that the information in Columns (2) and (3) are as of the beginning of the year, whereas the information in Column (4) is measured *over* the year.

The AOCI—net actuarial (gain) loss at the end of 2008 was $(70,000). The Gain (loss) for the year account represents the excess of the realized return on pension plan assets over the expected return for the specific year. When a (gain) loss was reported, the realized return was (higher) lower than the expected return during that year. The estimated remaining service period of active employees is five years for each of the calendar years.

**Required:**

Provide a schedule showing how the (gain) loss is amortized over the 2009–2014 period. Clearly indicate whether the amortization increases or decreases the pension expense in each year.

---

**P14-11**

Determining pension expense and funded status

The following is the funded status of the pension plan of McKeown Consulting Company at December 31, 2007:

| | |
|---|---:|
| PBO | $ (900,000) |
| FVPA | 1,000,000 |
| Fair value in excess of PBO | $ 100,000 |
| AOCI—prior service cost | –0– |
| AOCI—net actuarial (gain) loss | –0– |
| Pension asset (liability) | $ 100,000 |

The following information is available for the years 2008 and 2009:

| | Years Ended December 31 | |
|---|:---:|:---:|
| | **2008** | **2009** |
| Discount rate | 10% | 10% |
| Expected rate of return on plan assets | 9 | 11 |

The service costs for 2008 and 2009 were $125,000 and $145,000, respectively. During the years 2008 and 2009, the pension fund's actual earnings were $100,000 and $64,740, respectively.

At the end of 2008, McKeown retroactively enhanced the benefits provided under its pension plan, and this increased the PBO by $110,000. The average remaining service period of employees expected to receive these retroactive benefits under the plan was 10 years.

During 2008 and 2009, the company contributed $99,000 and $123,000, respectively, to the pension fund. In turn, the pension fund paid $120,000 and $85,000, respectively to the retired employees during the same periods.

**Required:**

1. Compute pension expense for the years 2008 and 2009.

2. Calculate the ending balances for PBO, fair value of plan assets, funded status, AOCI—prior service costs, and AOCI—net actuarial (gain) loss at the end of 2008 and 2009.

3. Provide necessary journal entries in McKeown's books for the years 2008 and 2009 to record all transactions and events relating to its pension plan.

4. Show that the journal entries result in a balance sheet pension asset (liability) equal to the funded status.

---

**P14-12**

Determining APBO and preparing journal entries

The following information on postretirement benefit obligations is excerpted from Ordonez Corporation's Form 10-K for the fiscal year ending June 30, 2008. (This is a real company whose name has been disguised.)

| | As of June 30 | |
|---|---|---|
| | **2008** | **2007** |
| APBO | $(21,743,000) | $(20,494,000) |
| AOCI—net actuarial (gain) loss | (699,000) | (1,192,000) |
| OPEB asset (liability) | $(21,743,000) | $(20,494,000) |

| Assumptions | 2008 | 2007 |
|---|---|---|
| Discount rate used to determine APBO | 7.00% | 7.25% |

| | Year Ended June 30, 2008 |
|---|---|
| Service cost | $ 467,000 |
| Interest cost | 1,444,000 |
| Amortization of unrecognized net gain | –0– |
| Net periodic benefit (OPEB) cost | $1,911,000 |

Benefit payments in 2008 totaled $1,155,000.

**Required:**

1. Provide the journal entry to record all transactions pertaining to the OPEB liability during fiscal 2008.

2. Prepare a schedule showing the changes in the APBO from 2007 to 2008.

3. What would have been the OPEB expense had the company used the cash basis approach?

4. Show that the journal entries result in a balance sheet pension asset (liability) equal to the funded status.

## CASES

Refer to the 2006 General Electric Retiree Health and Life Benefits Footnote appearing in Exhibit 14.8.

**C14-1**

Interpreting OPEB disclosures

**Required:**

1. Reconstruct the journal entries that GE would have made in 2006 to record the effects of its pensions. Assume that the "authors' pro forma" amounts were on its balance sheet in 2005. Also, assume that the "other" decrease in PBO of $(32) is treated as an actuarial gain.

2. Explain how GE's health and life benefit plans affected its OCI account for 2006.

GM first provided retiree health care benefits to UAW employees in 1961. In the fall of 2007, after a short strike, the UAW and GM reached an agreement to end that coverage. The key terms and effects of the agreement are as follows:

**C14-2**

Interpreting OPEB footnote disclosures

1. The agreement relates to approximately $46.7 billion of the $64.3 billion OPEB liability reported in its 2006 annual report.

2. GM would continue to take responsibility for retiree health benefits through 2010.

3. Between January 1, 2008 and January 1, 2010, GM will make $13.5 billion in cash payments to the UAW portion of GM's existing VEBA trust (the UAW portion of trust assets was approximately $16 billion at the time of the agreement).

4. GM will issue to the VEBA trust a convertible note for $4.327 billion (approximate maturity date, January 1, 2013).

5. GM will have a two-tier wage structure.

6. Pension benefits will be improved, thereby resulting in an increase of $4.3 billion in GM's pension PBO.

7. On January 1, 2010, GM will transfer the UAW portion of its VEBA trust to a new UAW–controlled VEBA trust, and *the UAW will assume responsibility for UAW–related retiree health benefits.*

8. GM may be required to make up to $1.575 billion in additional payments if the VEBA trust experiences significant shortfalls.

9. The UAW *may not negotiate further for retiree health care benefits.*

10. Upon the transfer of its UAW–related retiree health benefits, GM plans to recognize a negative plan amendment of approximately $22 billion.

11. Other key elements relate to cost-of-living adjustments, outsourcing, and job security.

Information related to its 2006 annual report includes the following:

| | |
|---|---|
| Total debt | $191,633 million |
| Total shareholders' equity | (5,441 million) |
| 2006 net loss | (1,978 million) |
| Outstanding common shares | 756.64 million |
| Stock price per share | $30 per share |

The 2006 annual report also provides the following information related to GM's OPEB plans.

GM also provides post-employment extended disability benefits comprised of income security, health care, and life insurance to U.S. and Canadian employees who become disabled and can no longer actively work. The cost of such benefits is recognized during the period employees provide service. . . .

GM contributes to its U.S. hourly and salaried Voluntary Employees Beneficiary Association (VEBA) trusts for OPEB plans. There were no contributions made by GM to the VEBA trust during 2006 and 2005. Contributions by participants to the other OPEB plans were $129 million, $89 million, and $87 million for 2006, 2005, and 2004, respectively. GM withdrew a total of $4.1 billion and $3.2 billion from plan assets of its VEBA trusts for OPEB plans in 2006 and 2005, respectively. GM uses a December 31 measurement date for the majority of its U.S. pension plans and a September 30 measurement date for U.S. OPEB plans.

| | U.S. Other Benefits | |
|---|---|---|
| | **2006** | **2005** |
| **Change in benefit obligations** | | |
| Benefit obligation at beginning of year | $ 81,181 | $ 73,772 |
| Service cost | 551 | 702 |
| Interest cost | 3,929 | 4,107 |
| Plan participants' contributions | 129 | 88 |
| Amendments | (15,091) | — |
| Actuarial (gains) losses | (6,468) | 6,720 |
| Benefits paid | (3,945) | (4,208) |
| Curtailments, settlements, and other | 4,012 | — |
| Benefit obligation at end of year | $ 64,298 | $ 81,181 |
| **Change in plan assets** | | |
| Fair value of plan assets at beginning of year | $ 20,282 | $ 16,016 |
| Actual return on plan assets | 1,834 | 2,258 |
| Employer contributions | (5,177) | 2,008 |
| Fair value of plan assets at end of year | $ 16,939 | $ 20,282 |
| Funded status | $(47,359) | $(60,899) |
| Unrecognized actuarial loss | — | $ 30,592 |
| Unrecognized prior service cost (credit) | — | (714) |
| Employer contributions/withdrawals in fourth quarter | (60) | (1,176) |
| Benefits paid in fourth quarter | 765 | 846 |
| Net amount recognized | $(46,654) | $(31,351) |

*(continued)*

| | U.S. Other Benefits | |
|---|---|---|
| | **2006** | **2005** |
| Amounts recognized in the consolidated balance sheet consist of: | | |
| Current liability | $ (134) | |
| Noncurrent liability | (46,520) | $(31,351) |
| Net amount recognized | $(46,654) | $(31,351) |
| Amounts recognized in accumulated other comprehensive income consist of: | | |
| Net actuarial loss | $ 21,957 | |
| Net prior service cost (credit) | (12,450) | |
| | $ 9,507 | |

The components of pension and OPEB expense along with the assumptions used to determine benefit obligations are as follows:

| | U.S. Other Benefits | | |
|---|---|---|---|
| | **2006** | **2005** | **2004** |
| Components of expense | | | |
| Service cost | $ 551 | $ 702 | $ 566 |
| Interest cost | 3,929 | 4,107 | 3,726 |
| Expected return on plan assets | (1,593) | (1,684) | (1,095) |
| Amortization of prior service cost (credit) | (1,071) | (70) | (87) |
| Recognized net actuarial loss | 1,986 | 2,250 | 1,138 |
| Curtailments, settlements, and other | (505) | — | — |
| Net expense | $3,297 | $5,305 | $4,248 |
| Weighted average assumptions used to determine benefit obligations at December 31[†] | | | |
| Discount rate | 5.90% | 5.45% | 5.75% |
| Rate of compensation increase | 4.60 | 4.20 | 3.90 |
| Weighted average assumptions used to determine net expense for years ended December 31[‡] | | | |
| Discount rate | 5.45 | 5.75 | 6.25 |
| Expected return on plan assets | 8.80 | 8.80 | 8.00 |
| Rate of compensation increase | 4.20 | 3.90 | 4.20 |

[†] Determined as of end of year.

[‡] Determined as of beginning of year. Appropriate discount rates were used during 2006 to measure the effects of curtailments and plan amendments on various plans.

The following are estimated amounts to be amortized from AOCI into net periodic benefit cost during 2007 based on December 31, 2006 and January 1, 2007 plan measurements (dollars in millions):

| | U.S. Other Benefits |
|---|---|
| Amortization of prior service cost (credit) | $(1,845) |
| Recognized net actuarial loss (gain) | 1,357 |
| | $ (488) |

On February 7, 2006, GM announced it would increase the U.S. salaried workforce's participation in the cost of health care, capping GM's contributions to salaried retiree health care at the level of 2006 expenditures. The remeasurement of the U.S. salaried OPEB plans as of February 9, 2006 as a result of these benefit modifications generated a $0.5 billion reduction in OPEB expense for 2006 and is reflected in the components of expense table above. This remeasurement reduced the U.S. accumulated postretirement benefit obligation (APBO) by $4.7 billion.

Effective March 31, 2006, the U.S. District Court for the Eastern District of Michigan approved the tentative settlement agreement with the UAW (UAW Settlement Agreement) related to reductions in hourly retiree health care; this approval is now under appeal. . . . GM accounted for the reduced health care coverage provisions of the UAW Settlement Agreement as an amendment of GM's Health Care Program for Hourly Employees (Modified Plan). . . . The Modified Plan APBO reduction of $17.4 billion is being amortized on a straight-line basis over the remaining service lives of active UAW hourly employees (7.4 years) as a reduction of OPEB expense.

The following benefit payments, which include assumptions related to estimated future employee service, as appropriate, are expected to be paid in the future:

| | **Other Benefits** | | |
| ($ in millions) | **Gross Benefit Payments** | **Gross Medicare Part D Receipts** | **Net** |
|---|---|---|---|
| 2007 | $ 3,994 | $ 243 | $ 3,751 |
| 2008 | 4,163 | 268 | 3,895 |
| 2009 | 4,327 | 292 | 4,035 |
| 2010 | 4,475 | 314 | 4,161 |
| 2011 | 4,589 | 335 | 4,254 |
| 2012–2016 | $24,050 | $1,966 | 22,084 |

**Required:**

1. Compute the following OPEB ratios for GM as of December 31, 2006:

    a. Short-term OPEB risk ratio (quick).

    b. Short-term OPEB risk ratio (extended).

    c. Long-term OPEB risk ratio.

2. Explain how the increase in pension benefits of $4.3 billion and the decrease to OPEB benefits of $22 billion resulting from the 2007 UAW contract will affect GM's future balance sheets and income statements.

3. Give possible reasons for GM to enter into the 2007 contract with the UAW.

4. Give possible reasons for the UAW to enter into the 2007 contract with GM.

## COLLABORATIVE LEARNING CASE

**C14-3**

AMR Corporation:
Interpreting pension and
OPEB footnote disclosures

Selected pension information extracted from AMR's 2006 annual report follows. Author modifications have been made to reflect amounts as if *SFAS No. 158* had been adopted as of December 31, 2005.

### 10. Retirement Benefits

All employees of the Company may participate in pension plans if they meet the plans' eligibility requirements. The defined benefit plans provide benefits for participating employees based on years of service and average compensation for a specified period of time before retirement. The Company uses a December 31 measurement date for all of its defined benefit plans. American's pilots also participate in a defined contribution plan for which Company contributions are determined as a percentage (11 percent) of participant compensation. Certain non-contract employees (including all new non-contract employees) participate in a defined contribution plan in which the Company will match the employees' before-tax contribution on a dollar-for-dollar basis, up to 5.5 percent of their pensionable pay.

In addition to pension benefits, other postretirement benefits, including certain health care and life insurance benefits (which provide secondary coverage to Medicare), are provided to retired employees. The amount of health care benefits is limited to lifetime maximums as outlined in the plan. Substantially all regular employees of American and employees of certain other subsidiaries may become eligible for these benefits if they satisfy eligibility requirements during their working lives.

Certain employee groups make contributions toward funding a portion of their retiree health care benefits during their working lives. The Company funds benefits as incurred and makes contributions to match employee prefunding.

The following table provides a reconciliation of the changes in the pension and other benefit obligations and fair value of assets for the years ended December 31, 2006 and 2005, and a statement of funded status as of December 31, 2006 and 2005 (in millions):

| | Pension Benefits | | Other Benefits | |
|---|---|---|---|---|
| | **2006** | **2005** | **2006** | **2005** |
| Reconciliation of benefit obligation | | | | |
| Obligation at January 1 | $11,003 | $10,022 | $ 3,384 | $ 3,303 |
| Service cost | 399 | 372 | 78 | 75 |
| Interest cost | 641 | 611 | 194 | 197 |
| Actuarial (gain) loss | (390) | 649 | (212) | (12) |
| Plan amendments | — | — | (27) | — |
| Benefit payments | (605) | (651) | (161) | (179) |
| Obligation at December 31 | $11,048 | $11,003 | $ 3,256 | $ 3,384 |
| | | | | |
| Reconciliation of fair value of plan assets | | | | |
| Fair value of plan assets at January 1 | $ 7,778 | $ 7,335 | $ 161 | $ 151 |
| Actual return on plan assets | 1,063 | 779 | 31 | 11 |
| Employer contributions | 329 | 315 | 171 | 178 |
| Benefit payments | (605) | (651) | (161) | (179) |
| Fair value of plan assets at December 31 | $ 8,565 | $ 7,778 | $ 202 | $ 161 |
| Funded status at December 31 | $(2,483) | $(3,225) | $(3,054) | $(3,223) |
| | | | | |
| Amounts recognized in the consolidated balance sheets | | | | |
| Current liability | $ 8 | $ 251 | $ 187 | — |
| Noncurrent liability | 2,475 | 2,974 | 2,867 | $ 3,223 |
| | $ 2,483 | $ 3,225 | $ 3,054 | $ 3,223 |
| | | | | |
| Amounts recognized in accumulated other comprehensive loss | | | | |
| Net actuarial loss (gain) | $ 1,310 | $ 2,175 | $ 70 | $ 300 |
| Prior service cost (credit) | 153 | 168 | (77) | (61) |
| | $ 1,463 | $ 2,343 | $ (7) | $ 239 |

The following tables provide the components of net periodic benefit cost for the years ended December 31, 2006, 2005 and 2004 (in millions):

| | Pension Benefits | | |
|---|---|---|---|
| | **2006** | **2005** | **2004** |
| Components of net periodic benefit cost | | | |
| Defined benefit plans: | | | |
| Service cost | $399 | $372 | $358 |
| Interest cost | 641 | 611 | 567 |
| Expected return on assets | (669) | (658) | (569) |
| Amortization of: | | | |
| Prior service cost | 15 | 15 | 13 |
| Unrecognized net loss | 81 | 52 | 58 |
| Net periodic benefit cost for defined benefit plans | 467 | 392 | 427 |
| Defined contribution plans | 150 | 154 | 156 |
| | $617 | $546 | $583 |

| | Other Benefits | | |
|---|---|---|---|
| | **2006** | **2005** | **2004** |
| Components of net periodic benefit cost | | | |
| Service cost | $ 78 | $ 75 | $ 75 |
| Interest cost | 194 | 197 | 202 |
| Expected return on assets | (15) | (14) | (11) |
| Amortization of: | | | |
| Prior service cost | (10) | (10) | (10) |
| Unrecognized net loss | 1 | 2 | 8 |
| Net periodic benefit cost | $248 | $250 | $264 |

The estimated net loss and prior service cost for the defined benefit pension plans that will be amortized from accumulated other comprehensive income into net periodic benefit cost over the next fiscal year are $25 million and $16 million, respectively. The estimated net gain and prior service credit for the other postretirement plans that will be amortized from accumulated other comprehensive income into net periodic benefit cost over the next fiscal year are $7 million and $13 million, respectively.

| | Pension Benefits | | Other Benefits | |
|---|---|---|---|---|
| | **2006** | **2005** | **2006** | **2005** |
| Weighted-average assumptions used to determine benefit obligations as of December 31 | | | | |
| Discount rate | 6.00% | 5.75% | 6.00% | 5.75% |
| Salary scale (ultimate) | 3.78 | 3.78 | — | — |

| | Pension Benefits | | Other Benefits | |
|---|---|---|---|---|
| | **2006** | **2005** | **2006** | **2005** |
| Weighted-average assumptions used to determine net periodic benefit cost for the years ended December 31 | | | | |
| Discount rate | 5.75% | 6.00% | 5.75% | 6.00% |
| Salary scale (ultimate) | 3.78 | 3.78 | — | — |
| Expected return on plan assets | 8.75 | 9.00 | 8.75 | 9.00 |

| | Pre-65 Individuals | | Post-65 Individuals | |
|---|---|---|---|---|
| | **2006** | **2005** | **2006** | **2005** |
| Assumed health care trend rates at December 31 | | | | |
| Health care cost trend rate assumed for next year | 9% | 4.5% | 9.0% | 9.0% |
| Rate to which the cost trend rate is assumed to decline (the ultimate trend rate) | 4.5% | 4.5% | 4.5% | 4.5% |
| Year that the rate reaches the ultimate trend rate | 2010 | — | 2010 | 2010 |

The Company expects to contribute approximately $364 million to its defined benefit pension plans and $13 million to its postretirement benefit plan in 2007. In addition to making contributions to its postretirement benefit plan, the Company funds the majority of the benefit payments under this plan. This estimate reflects the provisions of the Pension Funding Equity Act of 2004 and the Pension Protection Act of 2006.

The following benefit payments, which reflect expected future service as appropriate, are expected to be paid:

|  | Pension | Other |
|---|---|---|
| 2007 | $ 543 | $ 187 |
| 2008 | 584 | 196 |
| 2009 | 689 | 204 |
| 2010 | 681 | 214 |
| 2011 | 662 | 223 |
| 2012–2016 | 3,843 | 1,163 |

### Additional AMR Corporation Information:

| | |
|---|---|
| Total assets (in millions) | $29,145 |
| Total debt (in millions) | 29,751 |
| Shares outstanding (in millions) | 228 |
| Price per share | $30 |

### Required:

1. Pension plans

   a. Reconstruct the journal entries that AMR would have made for its pension plan in 2006.

   b. Compute the Bear Stearns short-term and long-term pension risk ratios as of December 31, 2006.

   c. Based on your answer to requirement 1(b), does AMR have low or high pension risk?

2. Other benefit plans

   a. Explain what probably caused the $(212) in the actuarial (gain) loss in the benefit obligation.

   b. The reconciliation of the benefit obligation indicates that the Plan amendments decreased the obligation by $27. Explain why a plan amendment would decrease the obligation.

   c. Compute the pre-tax effect of other benefits on AMR's OCI.

   d. Compute the Bear Stearns short-term and long-term OPEB risk ratios as of December 31, 2006.

   e. Based on your answer to requirement 2(d), does AMR have low or high OPEB risk?

**Remember to check the book's companion Web site
for additional study material.**

# Financial Reporting for Owners' Equity | 15

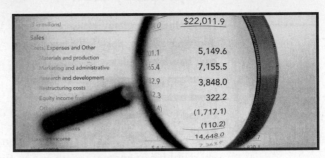

| ($ in millions) | | $22,011.9 |
|---|---|---|
| Sales | | |
| Costs, Expenses and Other | 01.1 | 5,149.6 |
| Materials and production | 65.4 | 7,155.5 |
| Marketing and administrative | 2.9 | 3,848.0 |
| Research and development | 2.3 | 322.2 |
| Restructuring costs | 4) | (1,717.1) |
| Equity income fr | | (110.2) |
| income | | 14,648.0 |

S tatement readers must understand the accounting procedures and reporting conventions for owners' equity for these reasons:

1. *Appropriate income measurement.* Differentiating between owners' equity changes that increase income or decrease income and changes that don't increase or decrease income will help answer these questions: Why are bond interest payments an expense that reduces income while dividend payments on common and preferred stock are not an expense that reduces income? Why do certain financing transactions—such as early debt retirements—generate accounting gains and losses while others—such as stock repurchases—do not generate accounting gains and losses?

2. *Compliance with contract terms and restrictions.* Many "exotic" securities having characteristics of both debt and equity have been developed over the years by investment bankers. How should these hybrid securities be classified for monitoring compliance with contractual restrictions such as maximum allowable debt-to-equity ratios?

3. *Legality of corporate distributions to owners.* Owners' equity is generally regarded as a financial "cushion" protecting corporate creditors. Cash distributions to shareholders—dividends and stock repurchases—reduce this cushion. How much of this cushion can legally be distributed as dividends? When a company liquidates, in what order of priority can cash payouts be made to its various claimants?

4. *Linkage to equity valuation.* Analyzing the true worth of equity shares requires an understanding of the amount of earnings that accrue to each share. Equity valuation thus depends on how a company's options, warrants, and convertible instruments affect its earnings per share.

After discussing each of these issues, we will look at existing GAAP for employee stock options and the controversy surrounding current reporting practice.

## LEARNING OBJECTIVES

**After studying this chapter, you will understand:**

1. Why some financing transactions—such as debt repurchases—produce reported gains and losses while others—such as stock repurchases—do not.

2. Why companies buy back their stock, and how they do it.

3. Why some preferred stock resembles debt, and how preferred stock is reported on financial statements.

4. How and when retained earnings limits a company's distributions to common stockholders.

5. How to calculate basic earnings per share (EPS) and diluted EPS, and whether EPS is a meaningful number.

6. What generally accepted accounting principles (GAAP) says about employee stock options, and why the accounting treatment has been controversial.

7. How and why GAAP understates the true cost of convertible debt, and what to do about this understatement.

8. Why employee stock ownership plans (ESOPs) have become popular, and what they mean for statement readers.

## APPROPRIATE INCOME MEASUREMENT

*Chapter*

Some increases (decreases) in owners' equity are considered to be income (loss), while other increases (decreases) are not income (loss). To know why, you must understand the modern GAAP definition of the "firm."

# What Constitutes the "Firm"? Entity View versus Proprietary View

Recall the basic accounting equation; it depicts the resources available to management as the sum total of all assets in the firm:

Entity view of the firm:

$$\underbrace{\text{Assets}}_{\text{Capital Deployed}} = \underbrace{\text{Liabilities} + \text{Owners' Equity}}_{\text{Capital Sources}}$$

This **entity view** of the firm focuses on the firm's *assets*. It lumps capital sources (debt and shareholder financing) together. The firm's assets are considered to drive economic performance, so the *firm* is considered to be the capital deployed—the assets themselves. Who provided those assets (whether creditors or shareholders) is of secondary importance.

Prevailing GAAP is based on a different perspective—called the **proprietary view** of the firm—that transforms the basic accounting equation to focus on the net resources (assets *minus* liabilities) available to management and the capital provided by owners of the firm. The proprietary view sharply differentiates between capital provided by owners and capital provided by creditors.

Proprietary view of the firm:

$$\underbrace{\text{Assets} - \text{Liabilities}}_{\text{Net Capital Deployed}} = \underbrace{\text{Owners' Equity}}_{\text{Owners' Capital}}$$

The proprietary view isolates the capital provided by owners. In this perspective, the firm and its owners are inseparable—the *firm* is considered to be the owners' equity investment or net assets.

The prevalence of the proprietary view in GAAP greatly influences income measurement. To see why and how it influences the way income is measured, consider the basic accounting principle that income can be earned (or expenses incurred) *only* through transactions between the firm and "outsiders." But who is "inside" the firm, and who are the outsiders? *Under the proprietary view, the firm and its owners are one and the same.* The firm is the net capital deployed (net assets), and owners are the "insiders" who provided that net capital. Consequently, no income or loss can arise from transactions between the firm and its owners because owners are *not* outsiders. This perspective explains why interest payments to banks or bondholders are expenses that reduce income while dividend payments to common and preferred shareholders are *not* expenses that reduce income.

- Banks and bondholders are outsiders—hence, interest costs are expenses.
- Shareholders are not outsiders—thus, dividends are a *distribution of earnings* to owners, not an expense of the company.

The proprietary view helps us understand why certain financing transactions generate income or losses while other transactions do not.

**Financing Transactions**    One way corporations raise capital is by selling equity shares to investors. Called **common stock,** equity shares provide the opportunity for purchasers to participate in the company's future profitability.[1] In addition to conveying ownership

---

[1] Investors who buy **preferred stock** (discussed later in the chapter) also participate in the company's future profitability. However, investors who buy debt instruments do not participate in the company's future profitability. Instead, debtholders gain only a specified (fixed or variable) rate of return—for example, "7% interest per annum," or in the case of variable rate debt, "prime plus ½%."

rights, common stock has **limited liability.** As long as each share is initially sold for more than the per share dollar amount—called **par value**—printed on each share, the shareholder's potential loss is limited to the original purchase price of the common share. Limited liability makes investing in common stock attractive because although potential gains from ownership are unlimited, the risk of loss is limited to the share purchase price.

> The term *par value* refers to the **nominal** value or **face value** of a security—a dollar amount printed on the face of each stock certificate. With common stock, par value is set by the company issuing the stock. At one time, par value represented the original investment in cash, goods, or services behind each share of stock. Today, par value is an assigned amount (such as $1 per share) used to compute the dollar accounting value of the common shares on the company's balance sheet. ***Par value has no relation to market value.***

To see how the accounting for common stock works, assume that at its creation, Nahigian Corporation issues (meaning "sells to investors") 5,000 shares of common stock at $50 per share and that the shares have a par value of $1 each. Nahigian records the stock issuance as:

| | | | |
|---|---|---|---|
| **DR** | Cash ................................................. | $250,000 | |
| | **CR** Common stock—$1 par value ....................... | | $ 5,000 |
| | **CR** Paid-in capital in excess of par ....................... | | 245,000 |

The $1 par value per share bears no necessary relationship to the *market value* of the shares. (Remember that par value is just the dollar amount printed on each stock certificate.) The difference between the $50 issue price and the $1 par value is credited to the separate owners' equity account Paid-in capital in excess of par—sometimes called Additional paid-in capital.

> What if rather than being held in treasury for later use, Nahigian is to permanently retire the repurchased shares? When shares are retired, the Common stock account is reduced for the par value of shares retired ($200 in our example) and the Paid-in capital account is reduced for the "excess" purchase price ($9,600 − $200 = $9,400). The share certificates are then canceled, thus reducing the total number of shares issued.

Suppose that several years later, Nahigian Corporation reacquires 200 of these shares at a cost of $48 each. When a corporation buys back its own shares, the repurchased shares are called **treasury stock** because the shares are held in the corporate treasury for later use. The accounting entry is:

| | | | |
|---|---|---|---|
| **DR** | Treasury stock ........................................... | $9,600 | |
| | **CR** Cash ........................................... | | $9,600 |

Notice that no gain or loss is recorded for the difference between the $50 per share price at which the shares were first issued and the $48 repurchase price. ***The reason stock repurchases do not involve accounting gains and losses is that they are transactions between the company and its owners.***

When treasury stock is acquired, it is not considered a corporate asset. Instead, treasury stock is treated as a reduction in owners' equity. Treasury stock is debited, as shown earlier, and it then appears on the balance sheet as a **contra-equity** account. Here's how the owners' equity section of Nahigian's balance sheet looks after the company repurchased 200 shares of common stock for $9,600:

## Nahigian Corporation

### Owners' Equity

| | |
|---|---|
| Common stock, $1 par value, 5,000 shares issued | $ 5,000 |
| Paid-in capital in excess of par | 245,000 |
| Retained earnings (assumed for illustration) | 700,000 |
| Total paid-in capital and retained earnings | $950,000 |
| Less: Treasury stock (at cost) | (9,600) |
| Total owners' equity | $940,400 |

Now assume that Nahigian decides to raise more equity capital by reselling all 200 treasury shares several months later at $53 per share. The entry would be:

| | | |
|---|---|---|
| **DR** Cash ........................................................ | $10,600 | |
| **CR** Treasury stock .......................................... | | $9,600 |
| **CR** Paid-in capital in excess of par............................ | | 1,000 |

This entry eliminates the contra-equity account Treasury stock. The $53 per share selling price is $5 per share higher than the $48 paid to reacquire the shares. Despite this "excess," *no income is recognized on the transaction.* This is because GAAP adopts the proprietary view of the firm; thus, no income or loss can arise from transactions between the firm and its owners. Instead, the difference of $1,000 (or 200 shares × [$53 − $48]) is added to the Paid-in capital in excess of par account.

But if Nahigian had reacquired outstanding *debt* at a price lower than its book value, a gain *would* be recorded, as described in Chapter 11. Debt repurchases generate accounting gains (and losses) while stock repurchases do not because debtholders are outsiders under the GAAP proprietary view while shareholders are insiders.

**RECAP**  No income (or loss) arises from treasury stock transactions—in the proprietary view, which equates the firm with its owners. Because treasury stock transactions are between the company and its shareholders (owners) and not outsiders, no income is recognized— even when the successive stock transactions are favorable such as those in the Nahigian Corporation illustration.

## Why Companies Repurchase Their Stock

Firms reacquire their own common stock for many reasons. Sometimes a company needs shares for employee stock options. Sometimes management may conclude that the company's shares are undervalued at the prevailing market price and that the best use of corporate funds is to invest in those shares by buying some of them back from stockholders. At other times, perhaps management just wants to distribute surplus cash to shareholders rather than to keep it inside the company.

A company's *surplus* cash—the amount over and above the cash needed for day-to-day operating activities—can be a problem for management and for shareholders. Management worries that another company or investor group might launch a hostile takeover of the business, using the company's own cash surplus to partially finance the takeover. If a hostile takeover is successful, some managers will inevitably lose their jobs. Shareholders, on the other hand, worry that management might spend the company's surplus cash on unprofitable— negative net present value—projects and on lavish "perks" such as corporate speedboats or race cars. So, it is better to give the money to shareholders—after all, it is their money.

Stock repurchases have one other advantage: Shareholders who take the cash are taxed at capital gain rates. If the cash is paid out as dividends, shareholders would be taxed at ordinary income rates, which are often higher than capital gain tax rates.

The popularity of stock repurchases has varied over time as a result of changes in the economic climate, stock market price levels, and the availability of surplus corporate cash. Only 87 U.S. companies

Suppose that Raider Company intends to acquire Target Company for $150 million in cash. Raider already has $30 million cash set aside for the takeover and has lined up another $100 million bank loan. But that still leaves Raider $20 million short. Where can it find the money it needs to complete the takeover? One possibility is to tap into Target's surplus cash. In other words, the more surplus cash that Target has, the easier it becomes for Raider to use the money to help pay for the takeover.

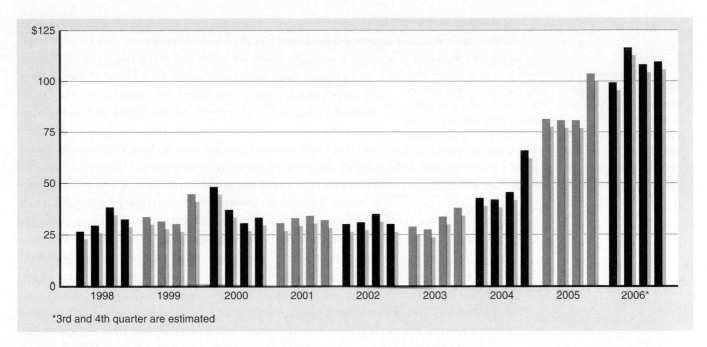

**Figure 15.1** THE DOLLAR VALUE OF STOCK REPURCHASED EACH QUARTER 1998–2006 BY U.S. COMPANIES IN THE STANDARD & POOR'S 500 INDEX (IN $ BILLIONS)

The Standard & Poor's 500 Index (S&P 500) is one of the most commonly used benchmarks for the overall U.S. stock market. A team of analysts and economists at Standard & Poor's chooses 500 stocks for the index for market size, liquidity and industry grouping, among other factors.

*SOURCE:* G. Morgenson, "Why Buybacks Aren't Always Good News," *The New York Times,* November 12, 2006.

announced stock buyback plans in 1980, with the dollar value totaling $1.4 billion. In 1998, 1,570 U.S. companies announced stock repurchases that totaled $222.0 billion.[2] Figure 15.1 shows the total dollar value of the buybacks for each quarter from 1998 through 2006 for Standard & Poor's 500 companies. These large U.S. firms repurchased more than $435 billion worth of their shares in 2006, or more than triple the $128 billions in shares that were bought in 1998.

A company can repurchase its shares in a number of ways. The most common is an **open market repurchase**—the company buys back its stock a little at a time over a period, sometimes two to three years. Company boards approve open market repurchase programs and disclose them to the public. However, companies do not disclose each and every stock repurchase transaction, so it is difficult for analysts and investors to track the completion of the open market buyback.

Another common way a company repurchases its own stock is the **fixed-price tender offer**—the company announces both the number of shares it wants to repurchase and the price it will pay for those shares. The offer is typically valid for a limited time and may be withdrawn if not enough shares are tendered. If the offer is oversubscribed—meaning too many shares are tendered—management has the option to increase the number of shares comprising the repurchase.

In the 1980s, the **Dutch auction** became a popular way for firms to repurchase their own stock. In a Dutch auction, the company announces the total number of shares it will repurchase and sets a range of prices within which it is willing to buy back its stock. Shareholders

---

[2] G. Grullon and D. Ikenberry, "What Do We Know About Stock Repurchases?" *Journal of Applied Corporate Finance,* Spring 2000, pp. 31–51.

responding to the offer must specify how many shares they are willing to sell and at what price within the range. The company then determines the lowest offered price that allows it to re-purchase the number of shares it seeks. All shares are purchased at this single price.[3]

The typical share repurchase is at a price about 23% more than the stock's market value just before the repurchase offer is an-nounced.[4] Those shareholders who sell their stock back to the com-pany capture this price premium. But what about the shareholders who don't sell? According to perhaps the best-known study on the subject, the stock of the average corporation that repurchases its shares outperforms the rest of the market by 12% over the four years following the announcement of the repurchase program. Even bet-ter, high book-to-market price stocks that are repurchased beat the market by 45% over the next four years.[5] So, it seems that everybody wins when shares are repurchased. Those who sell shares back to the company capture a price premium for doing so, and those who don't sell but instead continue to own the shares capture an above market return on their invest-ment over the next four years.

> The Dutch auction appears to be the most satisfactory way to treat shareholders fairly. A shareholder who names too high a price may have no shares accepted. Naming too low a price simply increases the likelihood that the price paid will be low. Consequently, the Dutch auction approach en-courages shareholders to be truthful and to name a price that reflects their personal valuation of the stock.

But not all buybacks are created equal.[6] While share repurchases as a whole help to boost investor returns, not all companies use repurchases to demonstrate that their stock is under-valued or to distribute excess cash to shareholders, skeptics say. Instead, share repurchases are sometimes used for other purposes. For example, here's what Microsoft said in 1997 about its stock repurchase program:

 **Analysis**

> Management believes existing cash and short-term investments together with funds generated from operations will be sufficient to meet operating requirements for the next twelve months. Microsoft's cash and short-term investments are available for strategic investments, mergers and acquisitions, other potential large-scale cash needs that may arise, and to fund an increased stock buyback program over historical levels to reduce the dilutive impact of the Company's employee stock option and purchase programs. *Despite recent increases in stock repurchases, the buyback program has not kept pace with employee stock option grants or exercises.* Beginning in fiscal 1990, Microsoft has repurchased 134 million common shares for $4.2 billion while 336 million shares were issued under the Company's employee stock option and purchase plans.[7] [Emphasis added.]

Microsoft's buyback program partially offsets **share dilution**[8] caused by the company's stock option and repurchase plans. But what does a company gain from buying back its shares with one hand while issuing shares through options with the other hand? Some analysts an-swer not much. While an employee usually buys shares for less than the market price under option programs, the company pays the market price to buy them back. In dollar terms, the number of shares outstanding may seem to be shrinking because the company has spent more

---

[3] See D. B. Hausch, D. E. Logue, and J. K. Seward, "Dutch Auction Share Repurchases: Theory and Evidence," *Journal of Applied Corporate Finance,* Spring 1992, pp. 44–49.

[4] D. Ikenberry, J. Lakonishok, and T. Vermaelen, "Market Underreaction to Open Market Share Repurchases," *Journal of Financial Economics,* October 1995, pp. 181–208.

[5] Ibid.

[6] G. Morgenson, "Why Buybacks Aren't Always Good News," *The Wall Street Journal,* November 12, 2006.

[7] Microsoft Corporation, Quarterly Report to Shareholders [10-Q filing], March 31, 1997.

[8] Share dilution is akin to taking an apple pie that is already cut into six large pieces and then slicing each piece in half again so that the pie ends up divided into 12 much smaller pieces. Consider a simplified example of share dilution. Suppose that a company is worth $60 million, and 6 million shares of stock are in the hands of investors. Each share is then worth $10. Next suppose that management gives stock options for 6 million shares to employees, who then exercise their options and receive the new shares. If the company's value is unchanged, each outstanding share is now worth only $5 because the same $60 mil-lion pie (that is, the company) is now divided into twice as many slices (the 12 million shares outstanding). That's share dilu-tion in a nutshell.

to buy back shares than employees have spent to acquire them. But in fact, the number of shares could remain unchanged or even increase.

Another concern for analysts is that many companies are now borrowing to finance their stock repurchase programs. While such moves might have tax or other advantages, these companies simply replace equity with debt, so shareholders get the buyback's benefits only at the expense of owning a more leveraged company—one with more debt and less equity than before the repurchase. Also, these companies face the risk that an economic downturn could make it more difficult to service debt.

Even more worrisome is that *some stock buybacks are motivated solely by a desire to boost EPS.* Consider Rocket Software, which completed a successful third quarter with earnings of $220,000 and EPS of $1.00. This was the ninth consecutive quarter that Rocket Software's EPS increased by 10% or more. But it appears that this string of EPS increases would be broken—fourth quarter earnings were projected to be only $220,000, unchanged from the third quarter.

How can the company keep its EPS record intact? Management could increase earnings (as well as EPS) by finding ways to grow sales revenues or reduce expenses. Or Rocket Software could buy back some of its common stock:

> Intel's experience highlights the issue. Every year since 1992, this semiconductor manufacturer has bought back stock. But in 1999, for example, while it issued only $543 million of stock and bought back a whopping $4.6 billion of stock under its share repurchase plan, its common shares outstanding actually increased to 3,334 million from 3,315 million. What is the reason for this growth in shares? The company paid $64.95 a share for the stock it repurchased—but it received only $9.70 for each share issued through options. More shares were issued than were repurchased. (Intel also issued some shares in connection with an acquisition.)

> Microsoft terminated its stock buyback program in January 2000. Before doing so, the company sold "put" warrants for 157 million shares. The warrants—an off-balance-sheet liability—entitle the holders to sell shares of Microsoft back to the company at a price of about $74 per share. If Microsoft shares are trading at $54 when the warrants are exercised and the average purchase price is $74, the company will have to come up with $20 a share—or $3.14 billion—to settle the warrants. That's a lot of cash!

|  | Without Buyback | With Buyback |
|---|---|---|
| Projected fourth quarter earnings/Common shares outstanding | $220,000 | $220,000 |
|  | 220,000 | 200,000 |
| Projected EPS | $ 1.00 | $ 1.10 |

If the buyback should reduce total shares outstanding from 220,000 to 200,000, fourth quarter EPS will be $1.10, and the company can claim another quarter of 10% EPS growth.

Sounds simple? It's not! There is a hidden assumption. Stock buybacks consume cash. Where did Rocket Software get the cash needed for its buyback? Suppose that the company had to borrow the cash. Then the (after-tax) interest expense on the loan—let's say it's $5,500—would have reduced projected fourth quarter earnings to $214,500. The company would then have to buy back 25,000 shares—or 5,000 more than originally anticipated—to reach its $1.10 EPS goal ($1.10 EPS = $214,500/195,000 shares outstanding after the expanded buyback). Instead of borrowing the cash, Rocket Software could sell some of its marketable securities, investments, or other productive assets. But asset sales may also have a dampening effect on future earnings.

As long as earnings fall by less (in percentage terms) than the buyback percentage reduction in shares outstanding, EPS will indeed go up! But this EPS increase may actually mask deteriorating business fundamentals. One recent example involved AutoNation. In July 2003, it reported record second quarter EPS of $0.37, a 16% increase from its quarterly EPS one year earlier. But the company's second quarter net income was up only a paltry 2.4% from the previous year's figure. AutoNation achieved the added jump in EPS by repurchasing 47.8 million of its shares over the year—shrinking its outstanding shares by nearly 14%, thus boosting its EPS.

By artificially inflating a company's reported EPS, stock buybacks can be used to camouflage business slowdowns. Research evidence confirms that firms sometimes use stock buybacks to boost EPS and thereby meet (or beat) the quarterly earnings targets set by Wall Street analysts.[9] Buybacks can also wind up bolstering top executives' pay when short-term or long-term incentive compensation is tied to EPS performance.

When it comes to stock buybacks and EPS growth, it pays to look behind the numbers. That is why it has become increasingly important for prudent investors and analysts to sort through the individual share repurchase plans and to determine the reasons behind each buyback. Only then can investors and analysts figure out whether a repurchase plan is a sign to buy—or not to buy—the stock.

**Stock repurchases don't produce accounting gains or losses, but they can produce above market returns for investors. Still, it's important to look behind the numbers and determine why and how a company is buying back its stock.**

## COMPLIANCE WITH CONTRACT TERMS

Owners' equity is one of the accounting numbers used in many contracts with lenders, suppliers, and others (Chapter 7). For example, lending agreements usually include covenants that restrict maximum allowable debt-to-equity levels, where equity refers to the book value amount disclosed on the company's balance sheet. Firms have incentives to use their financial reporting latitude to circumvent these contractual restrictions. Consequently, financial statement analysts must understand how owners' equity is reported to determine whether a company they are evaluating is in compliance with its contract terms.

For example, the annual report of Sears Roebuck and Company contained the following statement:

**Contracting**

> The Illinois Insurance Holding Company Systems Act permits Allstate Insurance Company to pay, without regulatory approval, dividends to Sears Roebuck and Co. during any 12-month period in an amount up to the greater of 10% of surplus (as regards policyholders) or its net income (as defined) as of the preceding Dec. 31. Approximately $477 million of Allstate's **retained income** at Dec. 31, 1992 had no restriction relating to distribution during 1993 which would require prior approval. As of Dec. 31, 1992, subsidiary companies could remit to Sears Roebuck and Co. in the form of dividends approximately $5.6 billion, after payment of all related taxes, without prior approval of regulatory bodies or violation of contractual restrictions. [Emphasis added.][10]

In this case, insurance regulators are using policyholder surplus (as defined by state insurance regulators), net income, and an owners' equity item—retained earnings—to restrict Allstate's ability to distribute cash to stockholders (in this case, the only stockholder is Sears Roebuck and Company).

> Preferred stock does not ordinarily carry voting rights. *Participating* preferred stock entitles its holders to share in profits above the declared dividend along with common shareholders. Most preferred stock is *nonparticipating*, meaning that holders are entitled to receive only the stipulated dividends.

This restriction was intended to ensure that Allstate maintain a cash cushion for payment of insurance claims. Monitoring compliance with the form and substance of this regulation requires an understanding of accounting for owners' equity.

Some financial experts suggest that certain equity instruments, such as **preferred stock,** are popular because they can be used to avoid various contractual restrictions. Preferred stock gets its name because relative to common stock, it confers on investors certain *preferences* to dividend payments and the distribution of corporate assets. Preferred shareholders must be paid their dividends in full before *any* cash distribution can be made to common shareholders; if the

---

[9] P. Hribar, N. Thorne-Jenkins, and W. B. Johnson, "Stock Repurchases as an Earnings Management Device," *Journal of Accounting and Economics*, April 2006, pp. 3–28.

[10] Sears Roebuck and Company, 1992 annual report. Allstate was a wholly owned subsidiary of Sears in 1992, but the company sold it in 1995.

company is liquidated, preferred stockholders must receive cash or other assets at least equal to the **stated (par) value** of their shares before any assets are distributed to common shareholders.

> An alternative to the 8% fixed-rate preferred stock is an **adjustable-rate preferred,** which pays a dividend that is adjusted, usually quarterly, based on changes in the Treasury bill rate or other money market rates.

The stated value of preferred stock is typically $100 per share. The dividend is often expressed as a percentage of the stated value. A typical 8% preferred issue would promise a dividend of $8 per share ($100 stated value $\times$ 8%). Unlike bond interest expense, however, preferred stock dividends are not contractual obligations that, if unpaid, could precipitate steps toward bankruptcy. Instead, the company's board of directors must declare each quarterly preferred dividend and can omit them even in profitable years. Bank loans do not provide the flexibility to omit payments when cash flows are tight.

However, preferred shares are usually *cumulative.* This means that if for any reason a particular quarter's preferred dividend is not paid, no dividends on common shares can be paid until all unpaid past and current preferred dividends are paid. This feature protects purchasers of preferred shares from excessive cash distributions to common stockholders. Also because it's okay to occasionally "skip" a preferred dividend, preferred shares are less risky to issuing corporations than is debt.

Figure 15.2 shows the dollar value of preferred stock issued by U.S. companies each year from 1990 through 2001. Eighty-eight companies issued $4.0 billion of preferred stock in 1990, compared to $39.5 billion issued by 202 companies in 2001.

Companies' widespread use of preferred stock is a curious phenomenon. Preferred dividends—unlike bond interest expense—are not a deductible corporate expense for tax purposes. Why do companies choose to raise capital through preferred stock rather than through debt where tax-deductible interest payments reduce financing costs relative to preferred stock?

One reason preferred stock is attractive to *corporate investors* is that 70% to 80% of the dividends that corporations receive from their stock investments can be tax free (Chapter 13) whereas the interest income corporations receive from debt investments is fully taxable. But what about the companies that issue preferred stock?

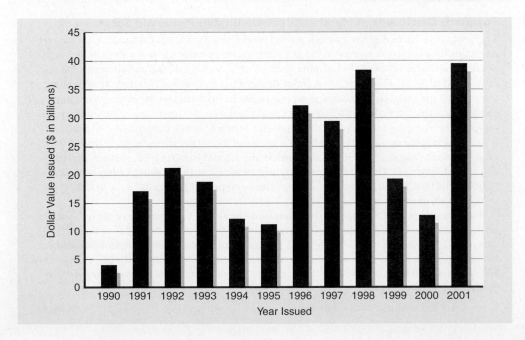

## Figure 15.2

DOLLAR VALUE OF PREFERRED STOCK ISSUED BY U.S. COMPANIES 1990–2001

*Source:* U.S. Census Bureau, *Statistical Abstract of the United States* for 2000 and 2002. This statistical series was discontinued in 2003.

Corporations that *issue* preferred stock do so because:

1. Preferred stock is less risky than debt because missing a preferred dividend payment, unlike missing an interest payment, will not trigger bankruptcy. This feature of preferred stock appeals to financially weak companies.

2. Companies with a history of operating losses usually don't pay income taxes because of their operating loss carryforwards. For these companies, debt no longer has a tax advantage, and thus preferred stock becomes more attractive as a source of new money.

3. Preferred stock is treated as equity rather than debt on financial statements. Companies precluded from issuing more debt because of covenant restrictions can sometimes issue preferred stock instead and sidestep these restrictions.

The distinction between preferred stock and debt can be murky because preferred stock (like debt) usually does not grant its holders voting rights, and preferred shareholders have no direct control over the company's affairs.

The distinction between debt and preferred stock has been further blurred recently as companies began issuing **mandatorily redeemable preferred stock.** Although called preferred *stock,* mandatorily redeemable preferred stock *requires* the issuing company to retire it (as with debt) at some future date—usually in 5 or 10 years. This type of preferred stock represents what many consider to be debt "disguised" as equity.

Exhibit 15.1 shows excerpts from Sealed Air's footnote disclosure for mandatorily redeemable preferred stock. Notice that the preferred shares (a) are convertible into common stock, (b) carry voting rights as if they had already been converted, and (c) have a mandatory redemption price of $50 per share, meaning that Sealed Air is obligated to buy back the preferred shares at this fixed price and at a specific future date (March 31, 2018).

Mandatorily redeemable preferred stock has been around since the 1940s, but its use increased substantially during the late 1970s and 1980s. At first, the accounting approach used for this new form of preferred stock was identical to that for traditional (nonredeemable) preferred

---

**EXHIBIT 15.1**     **Sealed Air Corporation**

**Footnote Disclosure of Mandatorily Redeemable Preferred Stock**

The Company's Series A preferred stock is listed on the New York Stock Exchange and is convertible at any time into approximately 0.885 of a share of common stock for each share of preferred stock. These shares vote with the common stock on an as-converted basis and are entitled to receive cumulative cash dividends, when and as declared by the Board of Directors, at an annual rate of $2.00 per share, payable quarterly in arrears on the first business day of the succeeding calendar quarter. The Series A preferred stock ranks senior to the Company's common stock and junior to the Company's indebtedness. On and after March 31, 2003, the Series A preferred stock is redeemable at the option of the Company at a price of $51.00 per share declining ratably on each March 31 thereafter to $50.00 per share on and after March 31, 2008, plus any accrued and unpaid dividends. The Series A preferred stock is subject to **mandatory redemption** on March 31, 2018 at $50.00 per share, plus any accrued and unpaid dividends, to the extent these shares remain outstanding.

 **Because it is subject to mandatory redemption, the Series A convertible preferred stock is classified outside of the shareholders' equity section of the consolidated balance sheets.** At its date of issuance, the fair value of the Series A preferred stock exceeded its mandatory redemption amount primarily due to the common stock conversion feature. Accordingly, the book value of the Series A preferred stock is reflected in the consolidated balance sheets at its mandatory redemption value. [Emphasis added.]

*Source*: Sealed Air Corporation 2002 annual report.

---

**EXHIBIT 15.2**     Sealed Air Corporation

### Balance Sheet Excerpts

| ($ in thousands) | 2002 | 2001 |
|---|---|---|
| Current liabilities: | | |
|   Short-term borrowings | $ 53,355 | $ 135,548 |
|   Current portion of long-term debt | 2,049 | 1,943 |
|   Accounts payable | 167,039 | 135,533 |
|   Deferred income taxes | 4,239 | 5,097 |
|   Asbestos settlement liability | 512,500 | — |
|   Other current liabilities | 413,572 | 348,859 |
| Total current liabilities | 1,152,754 | 626,980 |
| Long-term debt, less current portion | 868,030 | 788,111 |
| Deferred income taxes | 31,037 | 210,830 |
| Other liabilities | 68,980 | 65,682 |
|   Total Liabilities | 2,120,801 | 1,691,603 |
| | | |
| Series A convertible preferred stock | | |
|   mandatory redemption in 2018 | 1,327,005 | 1,366,154 |
| | | |
| Shareholders' equity: | | |
|   Common stock, $.10 par value per share | 8,476 | 8,449 |
|   Treasury common stock at cost | (31,139) | (31,133) |
|   Common stock reserved for issuance | | |
|     related to asbestos settlement | 900 | — |
|   Additional paid-in capital | 1,037,150 | 699,088 |
|   Retained earnings | 31,885 | 394,799 |
|   Deferred compensation | (9,853) | (10,973) |
| | 1,037,419 | 1,060,230 |
|   Accumulated other comprehensive loss | (224,459) | (210,078) |
|   Total Shareholders' Equity | 812,960 | 850,152 |
| Total Liabilities, Preferred Stock | | |
|   and Shareholders' Equity | $4,260,766 | $3,907,909 |

shares; namely, the proceeds obtained from issuing the stock were shown as part of owners' equity and any periodic cash distributions to preferred shareholders were recorded as dividends. Things changed in 1979 when the Securities and Exchange Commission (SEC) prohibited firms issuing such securities from including them under the balance sheet caption Owners' Equity.[11] This prohibition means that amounts for redeemable preferred stock cannot be combined with true owners' equity items such as nonredeemable preferred stock and common stock in financial statements that are filed with the SEC. Exhibit 15.2 illustrates the required SEC treatment in Sealed Air's condensed balance sheet. Notice that the $1.327 billion of mandatorily redeemable preferred stock is shown on a separate line *between* liabilities and shareholders' equity. The company's preferred shares are more than half as large as its total liabilities.

In May 2003, the Financial Accounting Standards Board (FASB) went one step further by requiring "liability" treatment for most mandatorily redeemable preferred stock.[12] The FASB concluded that, even though the securities are called "preferred stock," they meet the definition of a balance sheet liability and should be classified as such. In other words, if it looks like a duck and quacks like a duck, it must indeed be a duck!

---

[11] *Accounting Series Release No. 268* (Washington, DC: Securities and Exchange Commission [SEC], 1979).

[12] "Accounting for Certain Financial Instruments with Characteristics of Both Liabilities and Equity," *Statement of Financial Accounting Standards (SFAS) No. 150* (Stamford, CT: FASB, 2003).

In July 2003, two months after *SFAS No. 150* was issued, Sealed Air bought back all of the outstanding shares of its mandatorily redeemable preferred stock using borrowed cash. The company paid a $25.1 million early redemption premium to preferred stock owners.

What does this mean for Sealed Air and its $1.327 billion of mandatorily redeemable preferred stock? The answer is quite simple. Beginning in 2003, these securities could no longer be shown on the balance sheet in the "mezzanine" between liabilities and owners' equity (as illustrated in Exhibit 15.2). Instead, mandatorily redeemable preferred stock would now be shown as a balance sheet liability and included beside long-term debt. Had this been the case in 2002, Sealed Air would have reported total liabilities of $3.448 billion ($1.327 billion plus $2.121 billion) rather than the $2.121 billion shown in Exhibit 15.2. The FASB's "liability" treatment for mandatorily redeemable preferred stock also required Sealed Air and other companies to record as interest expense any dividends on the preferred stock.[13]

SEC rules require companies to differentiate clearly between common stock and any type of preferred stock, whether redeemable or not. This means that preferred stock must always be shown separately from common stock on the balance sheet. Finally, *SFAS No. 47* requires companies to disclose the dollar amount of preferred stock redemption requirements for each of the five years following the balance sheet date.[14] Accordingly, future cash flow commitments for redeemable preferred stock are clearly highlighted for statement users.

Here's what Samsonite Corporation said about its preferred stock redemption schedule:

> The Company is required to redeem all of the Senior Redeemable preferred Stock outstanding on June 15, 2010, at a redemption price equal to 100% of the liquidation preference thereof, plus, without duplication, all accumulated and unpaid dividends to the redemption date. The Senior Redeemable Preferred Stock is redeemable at the option of the Company in whole or in part, at any time and from time to time on or after June 15, 2001, at redemption prices ranging from 110% of the liquidation preference to 100% of the liquidation preference depending on the redemption date.[15]

Samsonite had about $286 million of mandatorily redeemable preferred stock outstanding. The redemption provision requires Samsonite to redeem all of the outstanding shares on June 15, 2010 at 100% of the liquidation preference ($286 million). Samsonite had the option to redeem shares as early as 2001, but it must pay a higher price for the shares (up to 110%).

The SEC and the FASB exclude mandatorily redeemable preferred stock from the owners' equity section of the balance sheet. However, this classification exclusion may not capture the real economic characteristics of these securities because many companies—including Sealed Air—have issued mandatorily redeemable preferred shares that are convertible into common stock. It's possible that the company may never redeem preferred shares with this convertibility feature for cash. If instead it retires the preferred shares by converting them into common shares, then they truly represent equity, not debt—and thus their SEC and FASB status as nonequity may be arguable.[16]

---

[13] Buried in the details of *SFAS No. 150* is an exception to the required liability treatment, and the exception applies to Sealed Air. Recall that the preferred shares can be converted into common stock. The conversion option makes the preferred stock **conditionally** (not mandatorily) redeemable in the FASB's eyes—the stock must be redeemed only if stockholders do not exercise their option to convert the preferred into common shares. Because the company's ultimate obligation to redeem the preferred shares is uncertain, *SFAS No. 150* does not require immediate "liability" treatment for conditionally redeemable preferred stock. This means that Sealed Air can continue to classify its redeemable preferred stock in the balance sheet mezzanine between liabilities and owners' equity and that preferred dividends need not be reflected as interest expense. "Liability" treatment is required, however, once the conversion privilege expires and the preferred stock becomes mandatorily redeemable.

[14] "Disclosure of Long-Term Obligations," *SFAS No. 47* (Stamford, CT: FASB, 1981).

[15] Samsonite Corporation 2003 annual report.

[16] See P. Kimmel and T. D. Warfield, "Variation in Attributes of Redeemable Preferred Stock: Implications for Accounting Standards," *Accounting Horizons*, June 1993, pp. 30–40. These authors report that almost 69% of the mandatorily redeemable preferred stock issued in 1989 and included in their sample was convertible into common stock.

Investors seem to be aware of the possibility that some redeemable preferred shares are a lot like debt while other redeemable preferred shares are a lot like equity. One study confirmed that the stock price behavior of companies whose redeemable preferred shares had clear debt-like characteristics was different from the behavior of companies whose shares had equitylike characteristics.[17] Investors apparently use disclosures about redeemable preferred shares to assess whether a particular issue should be regarded as debt or equity for valuation purposes.

A new form of mandatorily redeemable preferred stock, called a **trust preferred security,** has become popular in recent years. The company first creates a special purpose entity—the trust—that then sells redeemable preferred stock to outside investors. The company then borrows money from the trust with repayment terms identical to those of the preferred stock issued by the trust. Outside investors own "trust preferred" stock, but the company itself has issued debt—not preferred stock—and thus gains the tax advantages associated with debt.

Here's what Motorola said about its newly issued trust preferred securities:

> In February 1999, Motorola Capital Trust I, a . . . wholly-owned subsidiary of Motorola, sold 20 million Trust Originated Preferred Securities ("TOPrS") to the public at an aggregate offering price of $500 million. The Trust used the proceeds from this sale . . . to buy . . . Subordinated Debentures from Motorola with the same payment terms as the TOPrS. Motorola, in turn, used the $484 million of net proceeds from the sale of the Subordinated Debentures to reduce short-term indebtedness.[18]

Motorola formed a wholly owned subsidiary—Motorola Capital Trust—that sold $500 million of trust preferred stock to the public. Motorola then borrowed $484 million of cash ($500 million of proceeds minus $16 million in investment banking fees and other transaction costs) from the Trust in exchange for Motorola's subordinated debentures. Motorola has the cash and debt, its wholly owned subsidiary has the debentures receivable, and outside investors have trust preferred stock. It sounds complicated, but it's really simple. And here's the final piece of the puzzle: The interest and principal payments on the loan are matched to the dividend and mandatory redemption payments on the preferred stock. So, when Motorola makes an interest (or principal) payment to the trust, the trust then makes a dividend (or redemption) payment to outside investors.[19]

The benefit to Motorola should now be clear—interest expense is tax deductible but preferred dividends are not. By issuing trust preferred securities instead of traditional preferred stock, Motorola transformed what would otherwise be a nondeductible preferred dividend payment into an interest expense tax deduction.

How are trust preferred securities shown on the balance sheet? Despite having the characteristics of debt—a required payment each period (called a *dividend* instead of *interest*) and a final payment at the end (called a *mandatory redemption payment* instead of a *principal payment*)—these hybrid securities have *not* always been classified as debt on the balance sheet. Instead, they have often been listed in the "mezzanine" section of the balance sheet between debt and equity along with all other mandatorily redeemable preferred stock. Beginning in 2003, however, most trust preferred securities— as well as most mandatorily redeemable preferred stock—must be shown as balance sheet liabilities.[20]

> Motorola's debt held by the wholly owned trust is eliminated when the company prepares its consolidated financial statements (Chapter 16 tells you why this occurs when the trust—a subsidiary—is wholly owned by Motorola—the parent company). That leaves only the redeemable preferred stock sold to outside investors on the consolidated balance sheet.

---

[17] P. Kimmel and T. D. Warfield, "The Usefulness of Hybrid Security Classifications: Evidence from Redeemable Preferred Stock," *The Accounting Review,* January 1995, pp. 151–67.

[18] Motorola. Inc. 2000 annual report.

[19] The key features of trust preferred securities are described in P. J. Frischmann, P. D. Kimmel, and T. D. Warfield, "Innovation in Preferred Stock: Current Developments and Implications for Financial Reporting," *Accounting Horizons,* September 1999, pp. 201–18.

[20] *SFAS No. 150,* op. cit.

**RECAP**

**Equity or debt?** When it comes to mandatorily redeemable preferred stock, the answer isn't obvious. That's why preferred stock with a mandatory redemption feature was shown on a separate balance sheet line between liabilities and owners' equity. The FASB now requires redeemable preferred stock to be classified as a balance sheet liability as long as the obligation to redeem is unconditional. When redemption is conditional—for example, because the preferred can be converted into common shares—liability treatment is not required.

## LEGALITY OF CORPORATE DIVIDEND DISTRIBUTIONS

State laws govern corporate dividend distributions to shareholders, and these laws vary from state to state. The intent of these laws is to prohibit companies from distributing "excessive" assets to owners and thereby making themselves insolvent—that is, incapable of paying creditor claims. Some states limit dividend distributions to owners to the amount of retained earnings; in other states, the limit is retained earnings plus paid-in capital in excess of par. These laws protect creditors by ensuring that only solvent companies distribute cash to owners. (Stock repurchases, another way companies can distribute cash to owners, are not subject to these dividend distribution limitations.)

> Remember the repayment problem described in Chapter 7? Managers have incentives to borrow money and then pay all of the cash to shareholders, leaving the company insolvent and the bank with a loan receivable that will never be repaid!

Assume that the Owners' Equity section on Delores Corporation's balance sheet appears on December 31, 2008 as:

| | |
|---|---|
| Common stock, $1 par value | $20,000,000 |
| Paid-in capital in excess of par | 35,000,000 |
| Retained earnings | 43,000,000 |
| Owners' equity | $98,000,000 |

> If the distribution involves inventory, equipment, or land, it's called a **property dividend**.

In some states, Delores Corporation could distribute only up to $43,000,000 of assets—the retained earnings amount—as dividends to owners. The dividend distribution could be in the form of cash or other assets such as inventory, equipment, or even land. In other states, the maximum might be $78,000,000—retained earnings ($35,000,000) plus paid-in capital ($43,000,000). Many states would require corporations to give public notice if their dividends were "paid" from paid-in capital.

Existing GAAP disclosures focus on the *source* of owners' equity—*contributed* capital (par plus capital in excess of par) versus *earned* capital (retained earnings, from which GAAP deducts dividends)—under the often erroneous presumption that this distinction informs analysts about legally permitted asset distributions. But many states have now adopted the **1984 Revised Model Business Corporation Act** as a guide to the legality of dividend distributions. This act redefined solvency. Under this act, as long as the *fair value of assets* exceeds the *fair value of liabilities* after the distribution, the company is considered to be solvent. In extreme cases, this means that an asset distribution would be legal even if the *book value* of net assets is *negative* after the distribution. If Delores Corporation's fair value of assets minus fair value of liabilities totaled $200 million, then $200 million (rather than $43 million or $78 million) would be the maximum legal asset distribution. Notice that a $200 million distribution would result in negative owners' equity of $102 million. *The point is that the book value of owners' equity may not give an accurate picture of potentially legal distributions in states that have adopted the 1984 Act.*

**EXHIBIT 15.3**   Holiday Corporation and Consolidated Subsidiaries

**Balance Sheet Excerpts**

| ($ in thousands, except share amounts) | January 1, 1988 | January 2, 1987 |
|---|---|---|
| **Stockholders' equity** | | |
| Preferred stock, $100.00 par value, authorized—150,000 shares, none issued | | |
| Special stock, authorized—5,000,000 shares | — | — |
| Series A—$1.125 par value, redeemable at $105.00, convertible into | | |
| 1.5 shares of common stock, outstanding—none and 170,171 shares | | |
| (excluding none and 98,072 shares held in treasury) | — | $    191 |
| Series B—$1.25 par value, none issued | — | — |
| Common stock, $1.50 par value, authorized—120,000,000 shares, | | |
| outstanding—26,225,980 and 23,592,569 shares (excluding 14,613,417 | | |
| and 17,246,828 shares held in treasury) | $  39,339 | 35,389 |
| Capital surplus | 12,625 | 205,717 |
| Retained earnings (deficit) | (791,021) | 404,655 |
| Cumulative foreign currency translation adjustment | 7,972 | (63) |
| Restricted stock | (38,861) | (7,156) |
| Total stockholders' equity | $(769,946) | $638,733 |

The potential irrelevance of traditional equity disclosures is forcefully demonstrated in an article by Michael Roberts, William Samson, and Michael Dugan.

> As an example of the inadequacies of existing accounting disclosures, consider the 1987 and 1988 stockholders' equity balance sheet sections of Holiday Corporation, the parent corporation of Holiday Inns of America [see Exhibit 15.3]. The January 2, 1987 stockholders' equity section reports the traditional segregation of stockholders' equity items: par value of common stock, additional paid-in capital, and retained earnings, less treasury stock at cost, and foreign currency adjustments. Total stockholders' equity is $639 million. However, the January 1, 1988 stockholders' equity section reveals a $770 million deficit in Holiday's total stockholders' equity. How did this deficit occur? The explanation lies in the $65 per share dividend that Holiday distributed in 1987 to prevent a hostile takeover. This aggregate $1.55 billion dividend, financed with borrowed funds, not only exceeded the corporation's retained earnings but total stockholders' equity as well by more than three quarters of a billion dollars.
>
> Holiday was able to borrow a large portion of the amount required for the dividend by using the fair value (that is, appraised value) of its real estate assets as collateral. Holiday was able to distribute the dividend (legally, according to Delaware law) because the fair value of its assets exceeded its liabilities after the distribution, and therefore it has positive equity on a fair value basis. *However, the traditional accounting disclosures of par value, additional paid-in capital, and retained earnings do not contain any information (either before or after the dividend distribution) enabling financial statement users to assess the corporation's capacity for making such distributions.* While stockholders and other interested parties may have had notice of Holiday's intent to leverage its assets to make the massive dividend, only Holiday's management had information about the fair values of the assets involved.
>
> The point of the Holiday example is that state laws governing a corporation's ability to make distributions to stockholders have continued to evolve from the time when minimum legal capital was considered to be equivalent to the par value of the corporation's stock. Thus, the traditional stockholders' equity presentation of par value, additional paid-in capital, and retained earnings is obsolete because it implies that some amount, represented by a portion of stockholders' equity, exists to protect creditors. [Emphasis added.][21]

---

[21] M. L. Roberts, W. D. Samson, and M. T. Dugan, "The Stockholders' Equity Section: Form Without Substance?" *Accounting Horizons,* December 1990, pp. 36–37.

As the Holiday Corporation example illustrates, existing disclosure rules for owners' equity *". . . focus attention on the source of capital, but ignore the capacity of the corporation for making distributions to stockholders."*[22] To ascertain the amount of potential distributions, statement analysts would need to know two things: (1) the distribution law in the state where the firm is incorporated and (2) fair value information if state law permits distributions based on the excess fair value of net assets. Unfortunately, this fair value information may be difficult to obtain because GAAP does not yet require that information to be disclosed except for marketable securities and certain investments (Chapter 16) and limited other items.

Certain limited disclosures regarding potential distributions are required by GAAP. When mandatorily redeemable preferred stock has been issued, the dollar amount of the redemption requirement for each of the ensuing five years after the balance sheet date must be disclosed. Similarly, preferred stock dividend and liquidation preferences must be disclosed along with significant differences between the liquidation amount and the par or stated value of the underlying shares.[23] Nevertheless, these disclosures still do not allow interested readers to compute the *total* potential distribution to owners.

Holiday Corporation paid a cash dividend to owners, but what happens when companies distribute stock instead of cash? Under current U.S. GAAP, stock *dividends* reduce retained earnings, but stock *splits* may not. Small stock distributions (less than 25% of shares outstanding) are required to be recorded as stock dividends: The market value of the distributed shares is transferred from retained earnings to the par value and paid-in capital account. Distributions that equal or exceed 25% of shares outstanding—commonly called *stock splits*—can be treated in either of two ways: (1) like a true split, which reduces the per share par value and increases the number of shares proportionately or (2) like a stock dividend. Consequently, stock dividends—and stock splits recorded as stock dividends—reduce the company's future cash dividend paying ability in states where cash dividends are limited by retained earnings. Peterson, Millar, and Rimbey (1996) report that 83% of the 285 "stock split" companies in their study actually accounted for the distribution as stock dividends.* They also found that the stock market does indeed recognize that retained earnings reductions may restrict future dividends in some states but *not* in others.

The United States is the only country that records stock dividends at market value. All other countries record the "dividend"—a distribution in name only—at a nominal amount, either par value or book value.

* C. A. Peterson, J. A. Millar, and J. N. Rimbey, "The Economic Consequences of Accounting for Stock Splits and Large Stock Dividends," *The Accounting Review,* April 1996, pp. 241–53.

---

**GAAP reporting rules usually may not be sufficient to allow analysts to ascertain the maximum legal dividend distribution available to common stockholders. Analysts must be aware that other data may have to be gathered to ascertain the dollar amount that can be distributed.**

## EARNINGS PER SHARE

The amount of future income and cash flow that a company is expected to generate is a major determinant of that company's value (Chapter 6). Valuing the firm *as a whole* is crucial during merger negotiations, corporate takeovers, and buyouts—relatively rare events in the ongoing life of a firm. For day-to-day valuations, many analysts prefer to focus on the value of *individual* common shares. For this purpose, knowing how much of the company's total earnings accrue to each share is helpful. This is why **earnings per share (EPS)** is computed.

Computing EPS is straightforward when the company has a simple capital structure. We'll first describe the procedures for computing EPS for a simple capital structure, and then we'll extend those procedures to situations involving more complicated capital structures.

---

[22] Ibid., p. 35. According to Standard and Poor's Compustat database, 49 publicly traded U.S. companies—including Ford and Western Union—paid cash dividends in 2006 despite having negative stockholders' equity.

[23] "Disclosure of Information about Capital Structure," *SFAS No. 129* (Norwalk, CT: FASB, 1997).

# Simple Capital Structure

A simple capital structure exists when a company has no convertible securities (neither convertible debt nor convertible preferred stock) and no stock options nor warrants outstanding. In these circumstances, a straightforward formula is used to compute **basic earnings per common share:**[24]

$$\text{Basic EPS} = \frac{\text{Net income} - \text{Preferred dividends}}{\text{Weighted average number of common shares outstanding}}$$

To illustrate, assume that Solomon Corporation had the following capital structure in 2008:

|  | January 1 | December 31 |
|---|---|---|
| Preferred stock, $100 par value, 7%, | | |
| 10,000 shares issued and outstanding | $ 1,000,000 | $ 1,000,000 |
| Common stock, $1 par value | | |
| 160,000 shares issued and outstanding | 160,000 | |
| 200,000 shares issued and outstanding | | 200,000 |
| Paid-in capital in excess of par | 12,000,000 | 16,000,000 |
| Retained earnings | 1,100,000 | 1,800,000 |
| Total stockholders' equity | $14,260,000 | $19,000,000 |

The 40,000 additional common shares were issued on September 1 and thus were outstanding for the last third of the year. The change in Retained earnings during 2008 is:

| | |
|---|---|
| Retained earnings, January 1 | $1,100,000 |
| Net income for the year | 1,257,331 |
| Preferred stock dividends | (70,000) |
| Common stock dividends | (487,331) |
| Retained earnings, December 31 | $1,800,000 |

The denominator of the basic EPS formula uses the **weighted average** number of common shares outstanding. Because additional shares were issued in September, this weighted average number of outstanding shares is computed as follows:

| Time Span | (a)<br>Shares<br>Outstanding | (b)<br>Portion<br>of Year | (c)<br>Weighted Shares<br>([a] × [b]) |
|---|---|---|---|
| January 1–August 31 | 160,000 | ⅔ | 106,667 |
| September 1–December 31 | 200,000 | ⅓ | 66,667 |
| | | | 173,334 |

Solomon Corporation's basic EPS for the year 2008 is:

$$\text{Basic EPS} = \frac{\text{Net income} - \text{Preferred dividends}}{\text{Weighted average number of common shares outstanding}}$$

$$= \frac{\$1,257,331 - \$70,000}{173,334 \text{ shares}} = \$6.85 \text{ per share}$$

---

[24] The guidelines for computing EPS are contained in "Earnings per Share," *SFAS No. 128* (Norwalk, CT: FASB, 1997).

You should know about a new wrinkle in the computation of basic EPS. As you saw in the previous section, sometimes companies issue securities—most commonly it's preferred stock—that *must* be converted into common shares. The FASB and the International Accounting Standards Board (IASB) recently agreed that these **mandatorily convertible securities** should also be included in the computation of basic EPS as soon as conversion becomes mandatory.[25] The rationale for doing so is that mandatorily convertible securities will eventually be included in the basic EPS computation anyway once they are converted into common stock. But why wait until the conversion actually occurs because conversion is mandatory and thus inevitable? It makes more sense to include them in the weighted average common shares outstanding as if they had already been converted.

To see how mandatorily convertible securities alter the computation of basic EPS, suppose that Solomon Corporation's 10,000 shares of preferred stock mandatorily convert into 20,000 shares of common stock on January 1, 2010. (Notice that preferred stockholders have no say in the matter—the preferred shares will automatically convert into common stock in 2013.) Two adjustments to our basic EPS computation are required to accommodate the mandatorily convertible preferred:

1. Increase the weighted average common shares outstanding by 20,000 shares to reflect the "as if" conversion of preferred into common as of the first day of the reporting period (here, January 1, 2008) because the preferred shares were outstanding for the entire period.
2. Eliminate the preferred dividend adjustment to net income because preferred stockholders are now viewed as though they are common stockholders.

Solomon Corporation's basic EPS for the year 2008 now becomes:

$$\text{Basic EPS} = \frac{\text{Net income} - \text{Preferred dividends}}{\text{Weighted average number of common shares outstanding}}$$

$$= \frac{\$1,257,331 - \$0}{173,334 \text{ shares} + 20,000 \text{ "as if" shares}} = \$6.50 \text{ per share}$$

## Complex Capital Structure

A firm has a **complex capital structure** when its financing includes either securities that are convertible into common stock or options and warrants that entitle holders to obtain common stock under specified conditions. These financial instruments increase the likelihood that additional common shares will be issued in the future. This possible increase in the number of shares is called **potential dilution** because, once the additional common shares are issued, current shareholders—those who did not receive any of the new shares—will then own a smaller slice of the company.

To illustrate the EPS calculation for a complex capital structure, suppose that Jackson Products

**Convertibles** are corporate securities—usually preferred shares or bonds—that are exchangeable for a set number of other securities—usually common shares—at a prestated price and at the option of the security holder. Convertibility "sweetens" the marketability of the bond or preferred stock. A **call option** gives the holder the right to buy shares (typically 100) of the underlying stock at a fixed price before a specified date in the future—usually three, six, or nine months. **Employee stock options** are often of three to five years in duration. If the stock option is not exercised, the right to buy common shares expires. A **subscription warrant** is a security usually issued with a bond or preferred stock that entitles the holder to buy a proportionate amount of common stock at a specified price—usually higher than market price at the time of issuance—for a period of years or in perpetuity.

---

[25] As this book goes to press, the FASB and IASB have yet to formally ratify this change to the computation of basic EPS, but it is expected to become effective in 2008. For more information on this issue and other proposed changes to the guidelines for calculating EPS, see "Participating Securities and the Two-Class Method under FASB No. 128," *Emerging Issues Task Force (EITF) Abstract No. 03-6* (Norwalk, CT: FASB, 2003); "Computational Guidance for Computing Diluted EPS under the Two-Class Method," *FASB Staff Position FAS No. 128a* (Norwalk, CT: FASB, 2007); and "Short-Term International Convergence," *Project Updates* (Norwalk, CT: FASB, 2007). As you are about to discover, convertible securities have always been considered in the computation of diluted EPS.

has 20,000 shares of common stock outstanding and $100,000 of convertible debentures—that is bonds that can be converted into common stock at a specified price (say, $5 per share of common stock) at anytime at the bondholder's option. According to the terms of the debenture agreement, each $1,000 face value bond can be exchanged for 200 shares of common stock (200 shares = $1,000 bond/$5 per share conversion price). If all debentures were exchanged, bondholders would receive 20,000 new shares of common stock. The effect on current common shareholders would be to *dilute* their claim to earnings from 100% (when they own all of the common shares outstanding) to 50% (when they own only half of the common shares outstanding).

Computed basic EPS overlooks this potential dilution of current shareholders' ownership interest in the company. To recognize the increase in outstanding shares that would ensue from conversion or options exercise, *SFAS No. 128* requires companies with complex capital structures to compute another measure called **diluted EPS.**

The diluted EPS figure is a conservative measure of the earnings flow to each share of stock. It's conservative because the diluted EPS measure presumes the *maximum* possible new share creation—and thus the *minimum* earnings flow to each share. The computation of diluted EPS also requires that certain reasonable assumptions be made. For example, consider the potential conversion of convertible debentures into common shares. Once the bonds are converted to common stock, the company no longer needs to make further debt principal and interest payments. Consequently, the diluted EPS computation recognizes that:

1. New shares are issued upon conversion (a denominator effect).
2. After-tax net income increases when the debt interest payments are eliminated after conversion (a numerator effect).

Assumptions must also be made for employee stock options or warrants when computing diluted EPS. When holders of options or warrants exercise them, they receive common shares; but at the same time, the company receives cash in an amount representing the exercise price of the options or warrants. In the computation of diluted EPS, this cash is assumed to be used to acquire already outstanding common shares in the market. Because of adjustments for assumptions such as these, the diluted EPS formula is slightly more complicated:

$$\text{Diluted EPS} = \frac{\text{Net income} - \text{Preferred dividends} + \begin{array}{c}\text{Income adjustments due to}\\ \text{dilutive financial instruments}\end{array}}{\begin{array}{c}\text{Weighted average number of}\\ \text{common shares outstanding}\end{array} + \begin{array}{c}\text{Newly issuable shares due to}\\ \text{dilutive financial instruments}\end{array}}$$

To illustrate how the diluted EPS computation works, we extend the Solomon Corporation example. Assume that as of January 1, 2008, Solomon also had the following financial instruments outstanding:

- $1,000,000 of 5% convertible debenture bonds due in 15 years, which were sold at par ($1,000 per bond). Each $1,000 bond pays interest of $50 per year and is convertible into 10 shares of common stock.
- Options to buy 20,000 shares of common stock at $100 per share. These options were issued on February 9, 2006 and expire on February 9, 2009.

Assume that the tax rate is 35% and Solomon stock sold for an average $114 market price during 2008. Each of these two financial instruments is potentially dilutive and must be incorporated into the diluted EPS computation as shown in the following equations. (To keep things simple, assume also that Solomon's preferred stock does not have a mandatory conversion feature so that basic EPS is still $6.85.)

There are 1,000 bond certificates outstanding ($1,000,000/$1,000 par value = 1,000 certificates), each convertible into 10 shares of common stock. Conversion of all bond certificates results in 10,000 new shares (or 1,000 certificates × 10 shares per certificate).

The convertible debentures are included in diluted EPS by assuming conversion on the first day of the reporting period (here, January 1, 2008). The after-tax effect of interest payments on the debt is *added back* in the EPS numerator, and the additional shares that would be issued on conversion are added to the denominator. *SFAS No. 128* calls this the **"if-converted" method.** We now illustrate the computation of diluted EPS in the presence of convertible debt.

The convertible debentures are presumed to have been converted into 10,000 additional shares of stock at the beginning of the year (January 1, 2008). Accordingly, 10,000 new common shares are added to the diluted EPS denominator. Under the if-converted method, no interest would have been paid on the debentures this year because all bonds are assumed to be converted as of January 1. This means that interest of $50,000 would not have been paid on the presumptively converted bonds. With a 35% tax rate, net income would increase by $32,500 ($50,000 × [1 − 0.35]), and this amount is added to the diluted EPS numerator.

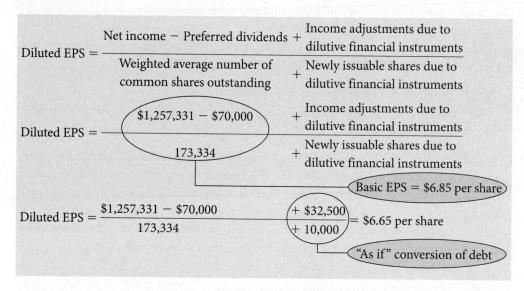

The outstanding stock options in our example will affect only the denominator of the diluted EPS computation. This denominator adjustment reflects the difference between the option **exercise price** ($100 per common share) and the **average market price** ($114 per common share) during the period. *SFAS No. 128* assumes that any proceeds received on exercise of the options ($100 per share) are used to buy back already outstanding common shares at the average market price for the period. This is called the **treasury stock method.**

We next illustrate the adjustment to compute diluted EPS under the treasury stock method.

Stock options are dilutive when they are "in the money"—that is, when the average market price (here, $114) exceeds the option exercise price ($100). Using the treasury stock method, we assume that the $2,000,000 proceeds to the company from presumptive exercise of the options (that is, 20,000 shares at $100 per share) are used to repurchase previously issued common shares at the $114 average market price. The cash from the options is sufficient to acquire 17,544 shares (that is, $2,000,000/$114 per share = 17,544 shares). Because 20,000 shares are presumed issued and

In-the-money options are dilutive because the number of shares that can be repurchased with the proceeds from the options is smaller than the number of new shares issued on exercise of the options. To see this dilution, suppose that employees exercise options for 1,000 shares of common stock at a $10 per share exercise price when the stock is trading at $20 per share. The company will receive proceeds of $10,000 cash from employees ($10 per share exercise price × 1,000 options) and issue 1,000 new shares of stock. The company can then use the cash proceeds to buy back at most 500 shares ($10,000/$20 market price per share) from other investors. The net result is dilution because 500 additional shares of common stock are now outstanding.

17,544 are presumed acquired, the difference (2,456 net new common shares) is added to the diluted EPS denominator:

$$\text{Diluted EPS} = \frac{\$1,257,331 - \$70,000 + \$32,500}{173,334 + 10,000 + \underbrace{2,456}_{\substack{\text{Treasury stock} \\ \text{conversion of options}}}} = \$6.57 \text{ per share}$$

Notice that diluted EPS equals $6.57, which is lower than the basic EPS number $6.85. This potential decrease in the computed earnings flow to each common share motivates the diluted EPS computation. Diluted EPS allows current stockholders to see how small their slice of earnings will be when the potential dilution from convertible securities, options, and warrants is considered.[26]

## Analytical Insights

**Analysis**

Now that you understand the guidelines in *SFAS No. 128* for computing diluted EPS, let's revisit our earlier claim that the diluted EPS figure is a conservative measure of the potential dilution from convertible securities. To see why this is so, consider how the if-converted method is applied in computing diluted EPS for Jackson Products. Recall that the company issued its convertible bonds with a conversion price of $100 per share of common stock, meaning that the bondholder can exchange each $1,000 bond certificate for 10 shares of common stock at any time. Remember too that the if-converted method assumes that all of the bonds are exchanged for common shares at the beginning of the reporting period (January 1, 2008).

But what if Jackson Products' common stock is worth only $75 per share on January 1, 2008? Are bondholders willing to exchange their certificates for common shares under these conditions?

Probably not. If bondholders surrender their certificates, they will receive 10 shares of stock for each certificate. Each share of stock is worth only $75, so the total value of shares received is just $750 per certificate. That's what bondholders get when they elect to convert a certificate into common shares, but what do they give up? By surrendering the certificate, bondholders forgo the right to collect $1,000 in cash later when the bonds mature. Unless the risk of nonpayment is extremely high, bondholders will hold on to their certificates rather than exchange them for common shares.

The message here is that conversion—and thus EPS dilution—is unlikely when a company's stock price ($75 in our example) is substantially below the conversion price ($100). Conversion becomes much more attractive to bondholders once the underlying stock price rises above the conversion price. For example, if Jackson Products' common stock was trading at $150 per share, bondholders would then receive $1,500 worth of stock for each $1,000 bond certificate surrendered.

The if-converted method for computing EPS dilution ignores the fact that bondholders are unwilling to convert their debt certificates into shares of common stock when the share price is below the conversion price. Instead, the if-converted method presumes that all convertible debt certificates are exchanged for common shares at the beginning of the reporting period regardless of the prevailing share price. This approach yields a diluted EPS figure that is conservative because it reflects the maximum potential new common shares from conversion. The

---

[26] One study suggests that *SFAS No. 128* systematically underestimates the economic dilution from stock options. See J. Core, W. Guay and S. P. Kothari, "The Economic Dilution of Employee Stock Options: Diluted EPS for Valuation and Financial Reporting," *The Accounting Review,* July 2002, pp. 627–52.

resulting EPS figure overstates earnings dilution—and understates diluted earnings per share—when a company's share price is substantially below the conversion price of the debt.

The treasury stock method suffers from the opposite problem. The treasury stock method tends to understate potential earnings dilution—and overstate diluted EPS—from employee stock options in some situations. To see why, recall from the Solomon Corporation example that the treasury stock method for computing diluted EPS involves a denominator adjustment that reflects the difference between the option exercise price ($100 per common share) and the average market price ($114 per common share) during the period. *SFAS No. 128* assumes that any proceeds received on exercise of the options ($100 per share) are used to buy back already outstanding common shares at the average market price for the period.

But what if the average market price of Solomon shares is slightly *below* the exercise price, say $99.95 per share? According to the treasury stock method, employee stock options are no longer dilutive when the average share price during the period falls below the exercise price. So, no adjustment at all is made to the denominator in computing diluted EPS. This approach ignores the possibility that Solomon's share price may rise above the exercise price ($100) sometime in the near future. As a result, the treasury stock method understates potential earnings dilution—and overstates diluted EPS—from employee stock options when the average share price for the period is slightly below the exercise price.

## Is Earnings per Share a Meaningful Number?

**Analysis**

EPS data are reported in the financial news and are prominent in corporate financial reports even though EPS can be a misleading financial performance measure. One reason for this is that managers can use their accounting discretion to distort reported earnings, the EPS numerator. These potential threats to earnings quality are described throughout this book. A second reason is that stock repurchases can be used to distort the EPS denominator, as previously mentioned in this chapter. But there is still another reason that EPS can be a misleading financial performance measure.

EPS ignores the amount of *capital* required to generate the reported earnings. This is easy to show. Consider the 2008 financial performance of two companies:

|  | Company A | Company B |
|---|---|---|
| Net income available to common shareholders | $ 1,000,000 | $ 1,000,000 |
| Weighted average common shares outstanding | 100,000 | 100,000 |
| Basic earnings per share | $10 | $10 |
| Gross assets | $20,000,000 | $30,000,000 |
| Liabilities | 10,000,000 | 10,000,000 |
| Equity capital (Assets − Liabilities) | 10,000,000 | 20,000,000 |
| Return on equity (ROE) | 10% | 5% |

Company A and Company B report identical basic EPS of $10, but Company B needed twice as much equity capital and 50% more gross assets to attain the $1,000,000 net income. Even though both A and B report the same *level* of net income and EPS, B has a return on equity of only 5%, while A's figure is 10%. Company A generates more earnings from existing resources—that is, from its equity capital.

Because EPS ignores capital commitments, problems can arise when trying to interpret EPS. The narrow focus of the EPS ratio clouds comparisons between companies as well as year-to-year EPS changes for a single company. For example, even if year-to-year earnings' levels are the same, a company can "improve" its reported EPS by simply repurchasing some previously outstanding common shares.

**EPS is a popular and useful summary measure of a company's profit performance. If tells you how much profit (or loss) each share of common stock has earned after adjustments for potential dilution from employee stock options, warrants, and convertible securities are factored in to the calculation. But as discussed, EPS has its limitations.**

# ACCOUNTING FOR STOCK-BASED COMPENSATION

Many U.S. companies compensate managers and other salaried employees with a combination of cash and stock options—that is, options to purchase equity shares in the company. A typical employee stock option gives the employee the right to purchase a specified number of common shares at a specified price within some specified time period. The specified price—called the **exercise price**—usually equals or is higher than the market price of the company's shares at the time the options are issued. An option to buy 100 shares at $50 per share at any time within the next five years might be issued when the shares themselves are selling for $30. When the exercise price exceeds the current share price, the stock option is "out of the money." Nevertheless, an option to purchase common shares at $50 is valuable even though the shares are currently selling for only $30 because there's a chance the stock price will climb above $50 sometime during the ensuing five years.

> In 2002, Microsoft gave its employees stock options that can be converted into 41 million shares of the company's common stock at $62.50 per share. Employees have until 2012 to decide whether they will exercise the options. Microsoft scrapped its employee stock option program in 2003 in favor of direct stock grants.

The number of U.S. employees holding stock options has risen dramatically, as shown in Figure 15.3. In 1975, only about 250,000 employees held stock options. Five years later, stock options were an important part of the compensation paid to roughly 3.1 million employees, and by 2002, this number had increased to 9.3 million employees. According to one estimate, companies in the Standard & Poor's 500 stock index awarded $126 billion in employee stock options in 2002 alone, more than the 2002 gross domestic product of Ireland.[27] Senior executives in these companies are not the only ones who receive part of their pay in the form of stock options. In 2002, almost all of Amazon.com's 7,700 full- and part-time employees and a "very large percentage" of Microsoft's 50,500 employees had been granted stock options. In

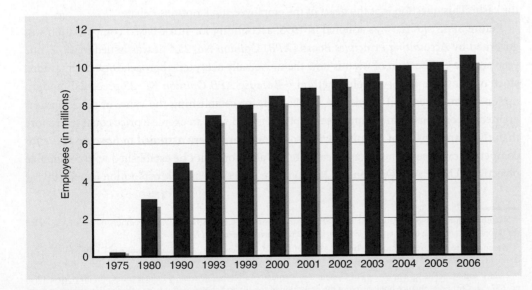

**Figure 15.3**

NUMBER OF U.S. EMPLOYEES HOLDING STOCK OPTIONS

*Source:* National Center for Employee Ownership.

---

[27] L. Lavelle, A. Borrus, R. D. Hof, and J. Weber, "Options Grow Onerous," *BusinessWeek*, December 1, 2003.

most companies, however, only between 10% and 20% of options go to nonmanagement employees.

Companies use stock options to augment cash compensation for several reasons:

- Options help align employees' interests with the interests of owners (stockholders). Employees with stock options have an incentive to make decisions that ultimately cause the share price to exceed the option exercise price.

- Many "start-up" high-growth companies are "cash starved" and cannot afford to pay competitive cash salaries. Stock options provide a way for them to attract talented employees while conserving cash.

- As long as the exercise price is equal to or more than the market price of the underlying stock when the option is issued, this compensation is not taxable to the employee until the option is exercised. This is an attractive feature because it allows employees to accumulate wealth while postponing taxes.

Granting employee stock options with an exercise price *less than* the current market price of the firm's common stock—for instance, an exercise price of $10 per share when the grant date market price is $15 per share—imposes a tax cost on employees. This is because the excess of market price over exercise price ($5 in our example) must be included in employees' taxable income when the options are granted.

Until 2005, *SFAS No. 123* and the GAAP guidelines that preceded it governed financial reporting for employee stock options granted as compensation.[28] The controversy over stock options reporting that raged during the evolution of this FASB rule was unprecedented in the history of U.S. accounting standard setting. Companies that issued employee stock options, their auditors, the SEC, and ultimately, the U.S. Senate lobbied the FASB to influence the final reporting rules. The intense debate over stock options presents an opportunity to discuss financial reporting incentives (Chapters 1 and 7) in a concrete setting and to illustrate how politics often enters the standard-setting process.

## Historical Perspective

Suppose an employee agrees to work this year in exchange for a small current salary and the promise of additional cash compensation to be paid in five years. No one disputes the notion that the employee's salary should be recorded on the company's books as an expense of the current year. But what about promised compensation? Should it be recorded as a current year's expense, or should the expense be postponed five years until the employee actually receives the cash? This question is at the heart of the employee stock options debate.

Before *SFAS No. 123* was adopted in 1995, accounting for stock-based compensation was governed by *Accounting Principles Board (APB) Opinion No. 25.*[29] It was issued in 1972, one year prior to publication of what is now the universally accepted approach for valuing traded stock options: the Black–Scholes method.[30] Because *APB Opinion No. 25* preceded modern option pricing theory, it offered no mechanism for establishing the value of stock options granted as compensation to employees. Options issued with an exercise price equal to or more than the market price of the underlying common shares **were assumed to have no value** for compensation expense purposes because their value could not be established with reasonable objectivity. Under *APB Opinion No. 25*, if on June 28, 1972, Ramos Corporation issued 10-year

---

[28] "Accounting for Stock-Based Compensation," *SFAS No. 123* (Norwalk, CT: FASB, 1995). In December 2004, the FASB ended the favorable accounting treatment employee stock options received under *SFAS No. 123*.

[29] "Accounting for Stock Issued to Employees," *APB Opinion No. 25* (New York: American Institute of Certified Public Accountants [AICPA], 1972).

[30] F. Black and M. Scholes, "The Pricing of Options and Corporate Liabilities," *Journal of Political Economy*, May–June, 1973, pp. 637–54. Corporate finance books explore the derivation of the Black–Scholes method and other option valuation techniques in detail; for example, see R. A. Brealey, S. C. Meyers, and F. Allen, *Principles of Corporate Finance*, 8th ed. (New York: McGraw-Hill, 2005).

options to employees that entitled each to buy 100 shares at $10 per share when the existing share price was also $10, *no compensation expense would be recognized because the value of these options could not be established reliably.*

Obviously, options with terms such as those in the Ramos Corporation example are valuable; the price of the company's common stock could easily rise above the $10 exercise price sometime during the option's 10-year life. Over the 1970s and early 1980s, option pricing *theory* evolved into option pricing *practice* using the Black–Scholes model as the standard for valuing traded options. Despite this post-*APB Opinion No. 25* breakthrough, options issued as compensation were generally treated as being valueless at the grant date for accounting purposes. Compensation expense *was* recognized in rare instances.

During the 1980s, U.S. companies increasingly adopted employee compensation packages designed to link employee pay to company performance. Stock option plans proliferated as an element of employee compensation. Many auditors and other financial experts considered the *APB Opinion No. 25* presumption that options were valueless to be simply incorrect. Because these beliefs were widespread, the FASB began reconsidering the accounting for stock options in 1984.

> An expense would be recorded under *APB Opinion No. 25* if the option exercise price is *below* the market price of the shares at the grant date. For example, Ramos would record $200 of compensation expense (and a corresponding increase to owners' equity) if the option exercise price was $8 per share and the grant-date market price was $10 per share. This pattern of exercise price and market price rarely occurs, so most companies do not record an expense under *APB Opinion No. 25*. This feature of *APB Opinion No. 25* was retained in *SFAS No. 123*.

Strong and widespread opposition to the FASB's stock options initiative surfaced quickly as it became clear to the business community that the new proposal would result in expenses being recognized on the income statement when stock options were granted. Those opposed to the FASB's proposal raised arguments against expense recognition that roughly parallel the four themes of this chapter:

1. Appropriate income measurement.
2. Compliance with contract terms and restrictions.
3. Legality of corporate distributions to owners.
4. Linkage to equity valuation.

Objections to the FASB's stock option approach reflected each of these themes. Next, we survey those objections.

## Opposition to the FASB

Some opponents of the FASB's proposal questioned whether providing stock options to employees constituted an accounting expense. These opponents said that treating stock options as an expense would violate *appropriate income measurement* because stock options do not involve a cash outflow. On the contrary, they argued, when—and if—the options were eventually exercised, cash would flow *into* the company, not *out*.[31] FASB supporters counterargued that cash was not the issue. Expenses often arise independently of cash outflows. One prominent advocate of this position was Warren Buffett, chairman of Berkshire Hathaway, Inc., who said:

> [Some contend] that options should not be viewed as a cost because they "aren't dollars out of a company's coffers." I see this line of reasoning as offering exciting possibilities to American corporations for instantly improving their reported profits. For example, they could eliminate the cost of insurance by paying for it with options. So if you're a CEO and subscribe to this "no cash–no

---

[31] To illustrate the point, there is no cash outflow or inflow to the company when Ramos Corporation first grants 100 options with a $10 exercise price to an employee. But there may be a cash inflow to Ramos at some later date if (and when) the employee exercises the options. At the exercise date, Ramos will receive $1,000 cash ($10 per option × 100 options) from the employee if all of the options are exercised.

cost" theory of accounting, I'll make you an offer you can't refuse: Give us a call at Berkshire and we will happily sell you insurance in exchange for a bundle of long-term options on your company's stock.

Shareholders should understand that companies incur costs when they deliver something of value to another party and not just when cash changes hands.[32]

Buffett's position that expenses arise when stock options are issued is consistent with how we account for issued stock. When stock is issued, shareholders give up something of value—a portion of their ownership interest—in exchange for something else of value, usually cash from new investors. Both the value given up and the value received are recorded. Buffett argues that the same accounting rules should apply for employee stock options. Shareholders are giving up a portion of their ownership interest by having the company issue additional stock—or options for stock—to employees. In exchange, shareholders receive valuable services from the employees—that are paid for in stock options rather than in cash. From this perspective, issuing stock options to employees represents an expense to the company.

 **Contracting**

Another argument raised by opponents to the FASB's proposal was that treating employee stock options as an expense could jeopardize *compliance with contract terms and conditions.* Companies with large employee stock option awards might, under the FASB's proposal, violate loan covenants tied to reported earnings. For example, the times-interest-earned ratio would deteriorate if option grants were expensed because the recorded expense would reduce the earnings number used in this ratio.

Impartial observers who understand contracting incentives can see why companies with significant employee options would raise this objection. Their interests would be harmed by the FASB proposal, and economic intuition tells us that companies would resist such initiatives. But you can appreciate the FASB's mission to "do the right thing"—to draft rules that closely mirror underlying economic circumstances. If a particular accounting approach correctly captures these economic effects, it presumably should be used even though some companies may be harmed. Furthermore, many of the FASB's most vocal opponents were companies whose employee stock options—if expensed—would have decreased earnings by a trivial amount. Because the potential impact of the FASB proposal on these firms' covenants was insignificant, what was really motivating their opposition? Perhaps the answer lies in how (and how much) corporate executives are paid.

The compensation paid to top corporate executives was under intense scrutiny in the early 1990s. Corporate restructurings and layoffs were widespread, a recession was in progress, and many companies demonstrated lackluster financial performance. In this climate, some critics questioned whether top corporate executives should continue to enjoy increasingly large salaries and bonuses while their employees were experiencing financial hardship. The issue quickly became political.

In 1993, the U.S. Congress limited the tax deductibility of executive compensation to $1,000,000 per employee—any excess over that amount could not be claimed as a deduction on the corporate tax return except when compensation was tied to the achievement of explicit and preset performance goals. The passage of this law clearly illustrates public sentiment on this issue. Corporate leaders, sensitive to the increasing scrutiny of executive compensation levels, may have felt that the FASB's plan to expense stock options would draw unwanted attention to executive pay.

The *legality of corporate distributions to owners* was never at issue regarding executive compensation. Political considerations aside, companies are free under the law to pay corporate executives whatever amounts their boards of directors deem appropriate. However, an issue

---

[32] Warren Buffett, Letter to Shareholders, Berkshire Hathaway, Inc., 1992 annual report.

of whether large executive salaries were *proper* did arise. Some companies were perceived to oppose the FASB's stock options expense proposal because it would add the value of options to cash compensation and thus make it easier for critics of "excessive" pay to spotlight certain companies and executives.

Opponents to the FASB's proposal also invoked an argument based on **equity valuation.** They believed that a simple "price–earnings multiple" relationship exists between reported earnings and common stock values. Under the FASB's plan, they argued, employee stock option grants would increase compensation expense and lower earnings—and thus lower stock price. (Our discussion of equity valuation in Chapter 6 suggests that the relationship between earnings and share price is more complicated than this.) Opponents of the FASB's plan argued that as stock prices fell, small companies who were heavy users of stock options would have difficulty raising new equity capital. This position was voiced by Senator Dianne Feinstein (Democrat, California) when she introduced legislation designed to block the FASB. She said:

> [The Bill] will also require the Financial Accounting Standards Board (FASB) to reexamine [its] recent decision to impose huge new accounting charges on the use of employee stock options. I am seriously concerned that if FASB's rule is adopted, tens of thousands of desperately needed jobs in California and the Nation will never be created.[33]

Senator Feinstein believed that the FASB's proposed stock options expense rule would make it more difficult for high-technology companies to raise new equity capital, thereby inhibiting expansion and job creation.

Despite growing business opposition, the FASB persisted and continued to move toward expense treatment of stock-based compensation. In response to intense business lobbying, Congress later initiated legislation which would have eliminated the FASB's independence by requiring the SEC to approve all new FASB standards.[34] Faced with this threat, the FASB was compelled to abandon its proposal and implement a compromise treatment.

## The Compromise—*SFAS No. 123*

The widespread, powerful opposition to recognizing stock-based compensation as an expense caused the FASB to allow a choice of accounting methods:

1. Companies could choose to continue using the *APB Opinion No. 25* approach under which compensation expense was rarely recognized.

2. Alternatively, companies could measure the **fair value** of the stock option at the grant date and charge this amount to expense.[35]

A stock option's fair value is measured using standard option-pricing models with adjustments for factors unique to employee stock options. The FASB encouraged companies to adopt the fair value approach rather than to continue using *APB Opinion No. 25* because it considered the fair value approach to be preferable. Companies that chose to continue using *APB Opinion No. 25* accounting were also required to disclose in a footnote what net income would have been had compensation expense been recognized under the fair value

> Suppose that Ramos Corporation used the fair value approach for its employee stock options. Recall that Ramos granted 100 options with a $10 exercise price to an employee. Let's assume that these options vest immediately—meaning the employees can exercise them at any time after the grant date—and have a fair value of $1.50 each (or $150 in total), as determined by an appropriate options-pricing model. Under the fair value approach, Ramos would record $150 of compensation expense on the date the options were granted. Ramos would also record a corresponding increase to owners' equity.

---

[33] *Congressional Record—Senate*, June 29, 1993, S8252.

[34] Called the *Accounting Standards Reform Act of 1994*, this bill was introduced by Senator Joe Lieberman (Democrat, Connecticut). *Congressional Record—Senate*, October 6, 1994, S14510.

[35] *SFAS No. 123*, para. 11.

## Figure 15.4

EMPLOYEE STOCK OPTION
REPORTING ALTERNATIVES
UNDER *SFAS NO. 123*

*SFAS No. 123* was revised in June 2005
to prohibit continued use of the *APB
Opinion No. 25* approach (Method 1).
Now firms must use the fair value
approach (Method 2).

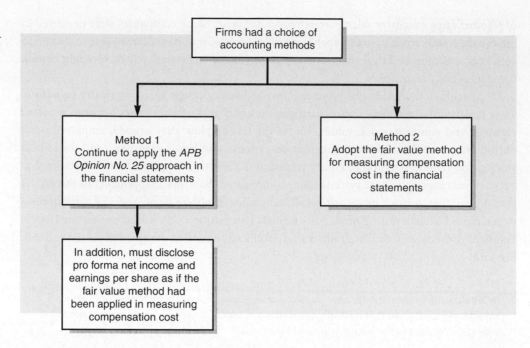

For most companies today,
the expected life of employee
stock options is somewhere
between 3 and 10 years.

approach. See Figure 15.4 for a graphic presentation of the stock option reporting
alternatives.

Implementing *SFAS No. 123*'s fair value approach is not difficult. However, the standard
contains many detailed guidelines for measuring compensation expense. We describe these
procedures tersely using a "big-picture" approach—that's all you need to grasp the overall impact of the fair value approach on financial numbers.

Assume that Guyton Corporation grants 100 common stock options to each of its top
300 managers on January 1, 2008. At that date, both the exercise price of the options and the
market price of Guyton's stock is $30. To provide managers an incentive to remain at Guyton,
the options cannot be exercised before January 1, 2011. This time span between the grant date
and the first available exercise date is called the **vesting period.** Guyton's options do not expire
until January 1, 2018, giving the options a 10-year legal life. But *SFAS No. 123* required that we
estimate the **expected life of the options**—meaning we must forecast when the employees
are likely to exercise the options. Factors to consider in estimating the expected life include the
average length of time similar grants have remained outstanding in the past and the expected
volatility of the company's common stock price. Let's assume that Guyton's options have an
expected life of five years.

*SFAS No. 123* specified that the fair value of stock options is to be measured at the **grant
date**—the date when both the grant's terms are set and the stock options are awarded to individual employees. Here's how the fair value of a stock option should be determined:

> The fair value of a stock option . . . shall be estimated using an option-pricing model (for example,
> the Black–Scholes or a binomial model) that takes into account as of the grant date the exercise
> price and expected life of the option, the current price of the underlying stock and its expected
> volatility, expected dividends on the stock . . . and the risk-free interest rate for the expected term
> of the option.[36]

It is not necessary to understand the theory behind option pricing models to understand the
financial reporting for employee stock options. As the preceding excerpt indicates, measuring

---

[36] *SFAS No. 123,* para. 19.

| EXHIBIT 15.4 | Guyton Corporation |
| --- | --- |

**Variables Used to Estimate the Value of Employee Stock Options**

| | |
| --- | --- |
| Options granted (100 shares × 300 employees) | 30,000 |
| Exercise price | $30 |
| Stock price at grant date | $30 |
| Expected life of options | 5 years |
| Risk-free interest rate | 6.75% |
| Expected volatility of common stock | 20% |
| Expected dividends on common stock | –0– |

Using the Black–Scholes Option Valuation formula, the fair market value of each Guyton option is estimated to be $10.05 at the grant date.

fair value requires estimating several other variables that we have not yet specified in the Guyton example. We will assume that the risk-free interest rate is 6.75%, no dividends are forecasted for the company's common stock, and the expected volatility of Guyton's common stock is 20%. See Exhibit 15.4 for a summary of these facts.

Inserting the numbers from the top at Exhibit 15.4 into the Black–Scholes option pricing model indicates that each option has a fair value of $10.05 at the grant date.[37] The total compensation cost of all employee stock option awards is $301,500 ($10.05 × 30,000 options). Let's assume that all 300 managers will meet the vesting requirements and ultimately exercise all 30,000 options.

> **Volatility** in option pricing models is measured using a benchmark of 1 standard deviation of a stock's return over a specified time period. Assume that Guyton stock has experienced an average annual historical return of 10%, higher in some years and lower in others. Because 1 standard deviation is roughly 66% of a normal distribution, the 20% expected volatility means there is a 66% probability that the return on Guyton's stock will be 10% ± 20% in any one year—that is, there is a two-thirds chance that the return in any one year will range between a low of −10% to a high of +30%.

> *SFAS No. 123* (para. 28) requires firms to estimate what proportion of the options originally granted will never vest due to employee turnover. Compensation expense includes only those options that are not forfeited. For example, if Guyton Corporation estimated that only 29,000 options would ultimately vest, total compensation cost would be $291,450.00 (that is, $10.05 × 29,000) rather than $301,500.00.

Stock-based compensation is intended to increase the employees' stake in the firm, creating an incentive for them to work in the best interests of all owners. The vesting requirements provide an extra incentive to stay with the company long enough to benefit from the anticipated value of the options. For these reasons, *SFAS No. 123* charged total compensation cost of $301,500 to expense on a **straight-line basis over the vesting period.** Guyton Corporation would recognize $100,500 ($301,500/3 years) as compensation expense in each of the years 2008 through 2010:

| | | | |
| --- | --- | --- | --- |
| **DR** | Compensation expense ................................... | $100,500 | |
| | **CR** Paid-in capital—stock options ........................ | | $100,500 |

> For income tax purposes, employers can deduct the *tax cost* of options—calculated as the difference between the exercise price and the stock price on the day the employee exercises the options—from taxable income. This means that companies using the *APB Opinion No. 25* intrinsic value approach for employee stock options almost never recognize any compensation expense for financial reporting purposes, but they do capture a tax benefit when the options are exercised.

[37] Designed for valuing options traded in open stock exchanges, the standard Black–Scholes formula doesn't consider the added restrictions of employee options, such as vesting and lack of transferability. Those limits make employee options worth much less than exchange-traded options. So, companies that use the standard Black–Scholes formula to determine options expense would take a much larger charge to earnings than is necessary. Another way to calculate option expense is called the *binomial* (or *lattice*) *model*. This approach uses a different mathematical formula and requires more assumptions including those that explicitly address vesting and other features unique to employee stock options. A key advantage of the binomial model is that it considers the possibility that changes in the stock price may influence the timing of when employees exercise options.

This same entry is made each year although the market value of the company's stock—and therefore the fair value of outstanding employee stock options—will undoubtedly change over time. **SFAS No. 123** *specified that compensation cost—option fair value—is measured only once, at the grant date.*

Let's say that Guyton's share price rises above the $30 exercise price after the vesting period and managers exercise all 30,000 options on the same day. The entry to record the exercise of employee stock options (assuming $20 par value stock) is:

| | | | |
|---|---|---|---|
| **DR** | Cash (30,000 × $30) | $900,000 | |
| **DR** | Paid-in capital—stock options ($100,500 × 3 years) | 301,500 | |
| **CR** | Common stock—par ($20 × 30,000) | | $600,000 |
| **CR** | Paid-in capital in excess of par | | 601,500 |

Notice that (1) compensation expense is recognized in the same amount each year over the vesting period and (2) if the options are exercised, the total amount added to the common stock and capital in excess of par is $1,201,500—the sum of the cash received when the options are exercised plus the calculated fair value of the options at the grant date.

If we assume that Guyton's share price never rises above the exercise price, the options will never be exercised. No cash will flow in. The offset to cumulative three-year compensation expense ($301,500) will remain in the Paid-in capital—stock options account. This dollar figure represents the estimated value of employee productivity (measured at the option grant date) that in effect was "donated" to the company without any corresponding ownership claim being given up to Guyton's employees.

*SFAS No. 123* was a political compromise. FASB members were unanimous in the belief that companies incur expenses when they grant stock options to employees as part of a compensation

| EXHIBIT 15.5 | Earnings per Share Impact of Expensing the Value of Employee Stock Option Grants for Selected Companies in 2002 |
|---|---|

| | EPS as Reported | EPS Adjusted for Compensation Expense | EPS Decrease in $ | Percent Decrease |
|---|---|---|---|---|
| Adaptec | $ (1.92) | $ (2.68) | $0.76 | 40% |
| AOL Time Warner | (22.15) | (22.39) | 0.24 | 1 |
| Autodesk | 0.28 | 0.13 | 0.15 | 54 |
| Biogen | 1.33 | 1.00 | 0.33 | 25 |
| Bristol-Myers Squibb | 1.07 | 0.94 | 0.13 | 12 |
| Cisco Systems | 0.26 | 0.05 | 0.21 | 81 |
| Citrix Systems | 0.53 | (0.35) | 0.88 | 166 |
| First Data | 1.63 | 1.49 | 0.14 | 9 |
| Fluor | 2.06 | 1.99 | 0.07 | 3 |
| Hewlett-Packard | (0.37) | (0.68) | 0.31 | 84 |
| Intel | 0.47 | 0.29 | 0.18 | 38 |
| Kroger | 1.65 | 1.49 | 0.16 | 10 |
| Lucent Technologies | (3.49) | (4.22) | 0.73 | 21 |
| Microsoft | 1.81 | 1.57 | 0.24 | 13 |
| PepsiCo | 1.89 | 1.68 | 0.21 | 11 |
| Schering Plough | 1.35 | 1.29 | 0.06 | 4 |
| Texas Instruments | (0.20) | (0.43) | 0.23 | 115 |
| United Technologies | 4.67 | 4.42 | 0.25 | 5 |
| Verizon Communications | 1.49 | 1.32 | 0.17 | 11 |

*Source:* Company annual reports.

package, yet *SFAS No. 123* allowed companies to avoid doing so by continuing their use of the *APB Opinion No. 25* "intrinsic value" method. Most companies opted to account for employee stock options as they had in the past. This meant that they recorded no compensation expense except in those rare cases where the option exercise price was below the stock price on the grant date.

Because two methods were allowed, *SFAS No. 123* required companies not using the fair value approach to provide **pro forma**—"as-if"—disclosures of net income and EPS calculated with a charge to compensation expense for options granted. Refer to Exhibit 15.5 for the impact on 2002 EPS for a representative sample of companies. Citrix Systems, for example, would have reported a $0.35 per share loss that year under the fair value method instead of a $0.53 profit.

*The dollar impact of stock compensation expense for some companies was staggering.* Cisco Systems' net income for 2002 was $1.893 billion, but this figure did not include compensation expense for employee stock options because the company still used the intrinsic value method allowed by *SFAS No. 123*. If it had included compensation expense, Cisco Systems' 2002 EPS would have been reduced from $0.26 to just $0.05 (the *pro forma* amount in Exhibit 15.5), a decrease of $0.21 per share. This 81% decline represents $1.520 billion of the company's 2002 earnings. Of course, for many companies, the dollar impact was much smaller.

## Stock Options Debate Rekindled

*"It's going to happen, and quite appropriately so."*

—Alan Greenspan, referring to the growing momentum for
counting stock options as an expense, in testimony before
the Senate Banking Committee July 16, 2002

In early March 2003, the FASB renewed its deliberation of stock-option compensation accounting. It reached a tentative decision in April 2003 to require all companies to expense the fair value of employee stock options at the grant date. This decision eliminated further use of the "intrinsic value" approach first introduced in *APB Opinion No. 25* and later incorporated in *SFAS No. 123* as a compromise. For most U.S. companies, the FASB's decision meant that they would have to abandon the intrinsic value method and begin using the fair value method. The dollar impact of this required accounting change would be substantial. For example, the composite 2001 earnings per share of firms in the Standard & Poors' 500 Index would have been reduced by 24.5% (representing about $45 billion in composite earnings) if the fair value of options granted that year had been expensed.

Congress reacted swiftly to forestall the FASB's move. In late March 2003, Representatives David Dreier (Republican, California) and Anna Eshoo (Democrat, California) introduced legislation entitled the "Broad-Based Stock Option Plan Transparency Act of 2003" (H.R. 1372). If enacted, the bill would direct the SEC to require enhanced reporting disclosures for employee stock options. It would also prevent the SEC from recognizing any new stock option accounting standard until the SEC submitted a report to Congress on the effectiveness of the new disclosures *following a three-year period of study.*

The IASB opposed the bill and expressed concern about the impact it could have on accounting standards in general: "If the U.S. Congress or political authorities in other countries seek to override the decisions of the competent professional standard setters . . . accounting standards will inevitably lose consistency, coherence, and credibility."[38] In testimony before a house committee, FASB chairman Robert Herz warned in June 2003 that the bill to delay new

---

[38] Paul A. Volcker, former Federal Reserve Board chairman and chairman of the foundation that oversees the IASB, in written testimony to Congress, as quoted in C. Schneider, "Who Rules Accounting," *CFO Magazine,* August 2003.

rules on stock options would set a "dangerous precedent" of congressional interference in accounting standard setting.[39]

What sparked renewed debate over stock option accounting? Two factors brought the issue back into the political and regulatory arena:

1. The explosive increase in stock option grants during the late 1990s.
2. Public outrage over the accounting abuses uncovered subsequently at many companies.

Stock option "overload" was widely regarded as one—perhaps the most important—factor contributing to the accounting fiascoes at companies such as Enron and WorldCom. The prevailing view was that managers who were eager to cash in their options resorted to questionable accounting practices designed to inflate revenues and earnings, and boost share prices. Rather than align the interests of shareholders and managers, options were thought to have done the opposite: transferring vast amounts of wealth to executives even as outside shareholders suffered. These concerns spawned a reform movement aimed at curbing the use of options by forcing companies to count them as an expense.

But not everyone agreed! The battle between those who favored and those who opposed stock options expensing involved familiar arguments:

# NEWS CLIP

## WHY CRITICS SAID OPTIONS SHOULD BE EXPENSED

- Some 75% to 80% of executive pay now comes in the form of options. Because all other forms of compensation must be deducted from earnings, options should be treated the same.

- Deducting the cost of options will yield more accurate earnings numbers, which should help restore investor confidence.

- Because options are now all but free to companies, excessive grants to top execs have been encouraged. But options do have costs: They dilute shareholders' stakes and deprive companies of the funds they would otherwise get by selling those shares in the open market. Such costs should be reflected in earnings.

- Bringing more discipline to options grants will also reduce the incentives top execs now have to pump their stocks through short-term earnings maneuvers in hope of cashing in big option gains.

## WHY OPTIONS EXPENSING DEFENDERS DISAGREED

- Unlike salaries or other perks, granting options requires no cash outlay from companies. Because there is no real (cash) cost to the company to deduct, doing so will unjustly penalize earnings.

- There are no universal standards for expensing options; all valuation methods require big assumptions and estimates. So, expensing them will reduce the accuracy of income statements and leave them open to manipulation.

- Deducting the cost of options will reduce earnings, which is likely to drive down share prices.

- Rather than take the hit to earnings, companies can issue far fewer options. That would hurt morale, limit a key tool used to lure talent, and inhibit companies from aligning employee and shareholder interests.

- Tech firms argue that generous option grants have spurred the risk taking and entrepreneurship so crucial to innovation. Expensing options risks damaging that benefit.

*Source:* A. Borrus, P. Dwyer, D. Foust, and L. Lavelle, "To Expense or Not to Expense," *BusinessWeek,* July 29, 2002.

---

[39] A companion bill was introduced in the Senate in May 2003. A third bill, introduced in November 2003 by Senator Michael Enzi (Republican, Wyoming) would limit expensing to options granted to a company's five highest paid executives. In response to this proposal, one financial commentator quipped: "While Congress is at it, why not make only the salaries of the top dogs expenses, while the lower rungs of employees get to be free for a company. Think how many employees a company could hire if it didn't cost them anything. Why, if Congress could outlaw all expenses, the economy would really boom." See J. Eisinger, "Microsoft Can Count, Intel Can't," *The Wall Street Journal,* July 21, 2004.

As the options reform movement gained steam in 2003, nearly 500 U.S. companies—including Amazon.com, Bank One, Coca-Cola, Computer Associates, and Procter & Gamble—said that they would soon begin expensing stock options voluntarily using the fair value method in *SFAS No. 123*. (Boeing and Winn Dixie had been doing so already for several years.) Other companies such as General Electric and Microsoft curtailed their employee stock options programs in favor of outright stock grants.[40] Still others, most notably Intel and Sun Microsystems, remained steadfast in their opposition to counting stock options as an expense.

By February 2004, Canadian accounting regulators and the IASB had issued new standards mandating the use of fair value approaches to employee stock option accounting.[41] Then in December 2004, the FASB released a revised version of *SFAS No. 123* (known as *SFAS No. 123R*) that affirmed its earlier tentative decision to prohibit the use of *APB Opinion No. 25*'s intrinsic value method of stock option compensation accounting.[42] *SFAS No. 123R* thus required all U.S. firms to use the fair value method. Several days later, the Economic Union advisory panel approved the new IASB stock option accounting rules. By then, more than 800 U.S. firms had announced their intent to voluntarily adopt the fair value method in *SFAS No. 123*. Companies that expensed their employee stock options voluntarily tended to experience a positive or neutral share price reaction when the decision to expense was announced.[43]

## Current GAAP Requirements

The key provisions of *SFAS No. 123R* are:

1. Companies must record the cost of employee services received in exchange for a stock option award (limited exceptions exist).

2. This compensation cost is determined by the awards' grant-date fair value measured using option-pricing models adjusted for the unique characteristics of employee stock options (unless observable market prices are available).[44]

3. This grant-date compensation cost is recognized as an expense on a straight-line basis over the vesting period (recall the Guyton Corporation example).

4. Incremental compensation cost arising from modifications to the original award terms is also recognized during the vesting period; however, changes in the fair value of the original options award itself are not recognized.

> "It's an accounting issue that shouldn't be resolved by our yelling, that shouldn't be political, that shouldn't be settled in op-ed columns—it should [be] settled by [the] FASB going away on a deserted island and thinking about it. A lot of emotion has blocked this rational accounting issue. A lot of what people are pissed about is executive compensation. The distinction between executive compensation and option expensing kind of gets lost."
>
> *Source:* Andy Grove, CEO of Intel Corporation, as quoted in *Fortune,* September 16, 2002.

---

[40] Under a stock grant program, employees receive shares of common stock as part of their compensation packages. The employer (say, Microsoft) must record as compensation expense the fair value of the shares granted.

[41] "Share-Based Payment," *International Financial Reporting Standard [IFRS] No. 2* (London: IASB, 2004).

[42] "Share-Based Payment," *SFAS No. 123* (revised 2004) (Norwalk CT: FASB 2004), referred to as *SFAS No. 123R.* Although it focuses primarily on stock option compensation and other equity payments for employee services, it also establishes guidelines for a much broader class of transactions in which a company either (1) exchanges equity instruments for any goods or services or (2) incurs a liability in exchange for goods and services, and that liability's settlement amount is linked to the fair value of the company's equity instruments.

[43] See D. Aboody, M. Barth, and D. Kasnik, "Firms' Voluntary Recognition of Stock-Based Compensation Expense," *Journal of Accounting Research,* May 2004, pp. 123–50; F. Elayan, K. Pukthuanthong, and R. Roll, "Investors Like Firms That Expense Employee Stock Options and They Dislike Firms That Fail to Expense," *Journal of Investment Management,* 2005; and N. Bastian, S. Rajgopal, and M. Venkatachalam, "Recognition versus Disclosure: Evidence from Voluntary Recognition of Stock Option Compensation," Working Paper, Stanford University and Duke University, 2003.

[44] For a detailed comparison of the option prices obtained by using different valuation models, see M. Amman and R. Seiz, "Valuing Employee Stock Options: Does the Model Matter?" *Financial Analysts Journal,* September/October 2004, pp. 21–37. Recent research on the use of the modified Black–Scholes–Merton model for valuing employee options includes J. Carpenter, "The Exercise and Valuation of Executive Stock Options," *Journal of Financial Economics,* May 1998, pp. 127–58; C. Marquardt, "The Cost of Employee Stock Option Grants: An Empirical Analysis," *Journal of Accounting Research,* September 2002, pp. 1191–1217; and C. Bettis, J. Bizjak, and M. Lemmon, "Exercise Behavior, Valuation, and the Incentive Effects of Employee Stock Options," *Journal of Financial Economics,* May 2005, pp. 445–70.

These key provisions of *SFAS No. 123R* do not alter how Guyton Corporation, our earlier illustration, records its stock option compensation under the fair value method. Under current GAAP, Guyton would still use the grant-date fair value ($301,500) as the measured cost of stock option compensation. Guyton would then recognize one-third of that amount, or $100,500, as compensation expense in each of the three years of the vesting period. *SFAS No. 123R* retains the original provision that compensation cost is measured only once, at the grant date (unless the original award is later modified by, for example, resetting the exercise price). This provision ignores the inevitable—that both the market value of the company's stock and the fair value of any outstanding employee stock options will change during the vesting period. Guyton's entry to record the exercise of employee stock options illustrated earlier is also unchanged.

*SFAS No. 123R* has also changed the way companies must report on cash flow statements the tax benefits they obtain from employee stock option compensation. The income tax and accounting details are somewhat complex, but we can use the Guyton Corporation example to illustrate the major points. Recall that Guyton issued options for 30,000 shares with an exercise price of $30 per share. Suppose the stock's market value is $50 per share when the options are later exercised. Under current U.S. tax law, Guyton is allowed a tax deduction for the intrinsic value of the options ($50 share price − the $30 option exercise price, or $20 per share) in the exercise year. (Employees who exercise stock options must pay ordinary income taxes that same year on the $20 per share intrinsic value.) Guyton's tax deduction ($600,000, assuming that all 30,000 options are exercised) exceeds the total compensation expense ($301,500) the company has recorded. Because Guyton pays out less cash in taxes, this $104,475 excess tax benefit—or ($600,000 − $301,500) × 0.35 if Guyton's marginal income tax rate equals 35%—is recognized on the cash flow statement.

**Analysis**

Prior to *SFAS No. 123R*, most firms listed their excess tax benefits as part of operating cash flow, which is where tax-related items typically are shown. Analysts and investors closely watch operating cash flow. They see it as perhaps the purest measure of company performance because it is immune to accrual accounting gimmicks that can distort reported earnings. Firms now must shift the excess tax benefit to financing cash flow, a less important part of the cash flow statement that measures cash flowing in and out of the company for things such as stock and debt offerings, dividend payments, and share repurchases (see Chapter 17). The classification shift required by *SFAS No. 123R* slashed millions of dollars off operating cash flow at some companies—$260 million at Cisco Systems and $77.3 million at Google—but left total company cash flow unchanged.

> The accounting for restricted stock is simple enough. Suppose that Guyton grants 10,000 shares of restricted stock to its employees when the stock is trading at $30 per share. Employees can't sell any shares for three years (the vesting period). The shares' value at the grant date ($300,000) increases owners' equity, and an equal amount representing deferred compensation is recorded as an offsetting contra-equity account. The net effect on owners' equity at the grant date is zero. Guyton then recognizes one-third of the grant-date fair value (or $100,000) as compensation expense each year during the service (vesting) period and records a corresponding reduction to the deferred compensation contra-equity account.

Fewer companies today than in the past use employee stock options as a form of compensation.[45] One popular alternative to stock options is **restricted stock,** which are shares issued to employees that can be sold only in the future (say three years) after the stock vests. Employees forfeit their shares if they leave the company during the vesting period. Other companies have abandoned stock options in favor of larger annual performance-based cash bonuses. Among companies that still use stock options, many have cut back the size of their awards, shortened the exercise life, or reduced the number of employees covered by the options plan.

---

[45] R. Simon, "With Options on the Outs, Alternatives Get a Look," *The Wall Street Journal*, April 28, 2004.

# Options Backdating Scandal

On a summer day in 2002, shares of Affiliated Computer Services Inc. sank to their lowest level in a year. Oddly, that was good news for Chief Executive Jeffrey Rich. His annual grant of stock options was dated that day, entitling him to buy stock at that price for years. Had they been dated a week later, when the stock was 27% higher, they'd have been far less rewarding. It was the same through much of Mr. Rich's tenure: In a striking pattern, all six of his stock-option grants from 1995 to 2002 were dated just before a rise in the stock price, often at the bottom of a steep drop.[46]

In March 2006, *Wall Street Journal* reporters Charles Forelle and James Bandler published a story alleging that top executives at six companies repeatedly received stock option grants on days when share prices hit lows. Was this pattern just blind luck? In Jeffrey Rich's case, the likelihood is extraordinarily remote according to the reporters: "around one in 300 billion. The odds of winning the multistate Powerball lottery with a $1 ticket are one in 146 million."[47] If not just luck, then why were such favorable grant dates chosen? One possibility is that the effective dates on some of those options were deliberately and improperly changed—a practice known as **backdating**—thus conferring extra pay to executives regardless of company stock performance.

Forelle and Bandler's *Wall Street Journal* article was the tipping point in the options backdating scandal. One week after the allegations first surfaced, federal or state officials were investigating more than 20 companies for backdating options grants, and 10 executives or directors at those companies had resigned. Over the next 12 months, more than 260 companies launched internal reviews of their options grants. Criminal investigations by the Department of Justice were under way at 54 companies, and many others were targets of SEC inquiries. Shareholders at 158 companies brought suit against officers and directors seeking monetary damages.

How did the two *Wall Street Journal* reporters spot questionable options timing? They enlisted the help of Erik Lie, a University of Iowa finance professor, whose results of a 2005 study of nearly 6,000 option grants between 1992 and 2002 strongly suggested that some option awards had grant dates retroactively set to an earlier date when the stock price was lower.[48] Backdating can be detected by carefully analyzing stock prices before and after the grant date. While companies can (and do) time their option awards to coincide with stock price downturns, they cannot predict with certainty when prices will rebound upward. Thus, it would be highly unlikely for option grants to routinely be awarded on dates just ahead of sharp stock price gains. Statistical procedures estimate just how unlikely are the option grant dates. Utilizing Lie's data, the two *Wall Street Journal* reporters identified a number of suspicious option grants including those at Affiliated Computer Services (Figure 15.5).

Backdating stock option awards can violate accounting rules and SEC disclosure regulations and, depending on how it is done, may constitute fraud. The practice also can violate federal income tax rules. To understand how the accounting and tax rules are violated, let's first consider an award that is not backdated. Suppose that Streit Corporation grants stock options to employees on August 4 when the stock is trading at $30 per share but sets the strike price at only $22. (Firms are free to set strike prices at whatever level they deem appropriate.) Using the intrinsic value method in *SFAS No. 123*, as did most firms at the time, Streit immediately recognizes compensation expense equal to the $8 per share difference between the grant date share price ($30) and the strike price ($22). Employees who receive the option awards also have

> The exercise (or "strike") price on employee stock options typically equals whatever the market price of the stock happens to be on the day the options are granted. The lower the strike price, the better the employee's chance for future profit when later exercising the options. For example, an options grant made on August 4 when the stock is trading at $30 per share becomes more valuable to the employee if it is backdated to July 8 when the market value of the stock was only $22.

> Of course, firms using the fair value method of *SFAS No. 123* immediately recognized an even larger compensation expense.

---

[46] C. Forelle and J. Bandler, "The Perfect Payday," *The Wall Street Journal,* March 18, 2006.

[47] Ibid.

[48] E. Lie, "On the Timing of CEO Stock Option Awards," *Management Science,* May 2005, pp. 802–12.

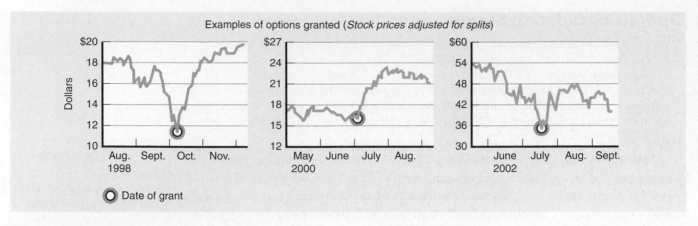

Examples of options granted (*Stock prices adjusted for splits*)

 Date of grant

**Figure 15.5** SUSPICIOUS STOCK OPTION AWARD GRANT DATES

Three especially favorable stock grants to Jeffrey Rich, former CEO at Affiliated Computer Services, and what the stock price did two months before and after each grant date.

*Source:* Graph from C. Forelle and J. Bandler, "Perfect Payday: Options Scorecard," *The Wall Street Journal,* March 18, 2006. Copyright © 2006 Dow Jones & Company, Inc. All rights reserved worldwide. Reprinted with permission.

to pay ordinary income taxes that year on the $8 per share. Backdating the award to, say, July 8 when the stock's market price was also $22 meant that Streit and unscrupulous managers at other firms could claim that the grant date intrinsic value was zero for both accounting and tax purposes. This result misstates GAAP compensation expense and employees' taxable income.

To rectify the GAAP violation, backdating firms must restate previously issued financial reports. That's what happened at Affiliated Computer Services. An internal investigation unearthed a handwritten note in which the company's chairman discussed the practice of always picking the lowest price "so far" in the quarter to award stock options.[49] The company later acknowledged that it had issued backdated stock options to top executives, including former CEO Jeffrey Rich. Compensation expense in earlier years was understated and pre-tax income overstated by $51 million. Several top executives resigned in the wake of the scandal.

*The Wall Street Journal* won a Pulitzer Prize, journalism's highest honor, for exposing the widespread practice of backdating stock option awards, and *Time* magazine recognized Erik Lie as among the 100 most influential people in the world.

## RECAP

**Stock options are an important part of employee pay at many corporations—today—and for good reason. They save cash and motivate employees, and companies previously could avoid recording compensation expense for options grants. That changed with *SFAS No. 123R:* Firms must now record as compensation expense the grant-date fair value of any option awards.**

## CONVERTIBLE DEBT

In late 1999, VerticalNet offered investors the opportunity to purchase up to $100 million of convertible bonds. These bonds paid a stated interest rate of 5.25% annually, matured in five years, and could be exchanged at any time for VerticalNet stock at a conversion price of $20 per

---

[49] J. Bandler and C. Forelle, "Note Raises Pressure on ACS," *The Wall Street Journal,* March 22, 2007. Prior to enactment of the Sarbanes-Oxley Act in August 2002, firms reported their stock option grants to the SEC on a monthly basis with a window of 10 days after the close of each calendar month—conceivably, a 40-day window. Now companies have only 2 days after the grant date to report awards.

common share. Because the bonds were issued in units of $1,000 face value, the conversion price meant investors could exchange each bond for 50 shares of stock ($1,000 face value/$20 per share conversion price = 50 shares). Investors snapped up the entire $100 million of the convertible bonds.

What price do you suppose VerticalNet received for each $1,000 face value bond?

To put this question in context, the average yield to maturity—that's the effective interest rate—on newly issued high-grade industrial debt in late 1999 was about 8% per year. Given the economic climate of the time, it may surprise you to learn that VerticalNet was able to sell its 5.25% bonds at par, receiving $1,000 in cash for each $1,000 face value issued. By contrast, the promised cash flows associated with each bond—$52.50 each year plus another $1,000 at maturity in the year 2004—have a discounted present value at 8% of only $890.20. ***Investors were willing to pay $109.80 more than the present value of each VerticalNet bond because of the conversion feature attached to the debt.***

We now explain the financial reporting for convertible debt and its implications for those who use financial statements.

## Background

Convertible bonds give investors the opportunity—but not the obligation—to exchange a company's debt for common stock in accordance with terms in the bond indenture. The **conversion price**—the dollar value at which the debt can be converted into common stock—is typically higher than the prevailing market price of the company's common shares when the debt is issued. The option to convert is solely at the investor's discretion and it will be exercised only when and if the investor finds the exchange financially desirable. Shares of VerticalNet were trading around $16 in September 1999—or about $4 less than the conversion price. Investors had little incentive to exchange their bonds for stock immediately. The conversion feature's real value to investors was the possibility that the stock price might climb higher than $20 sometime over the next five years.

Figure 15.6 reports the dollar value of new convertible debt issues in the United States between 2000 and 2006. Industrial corporations were the primary issuers of convertible debt.

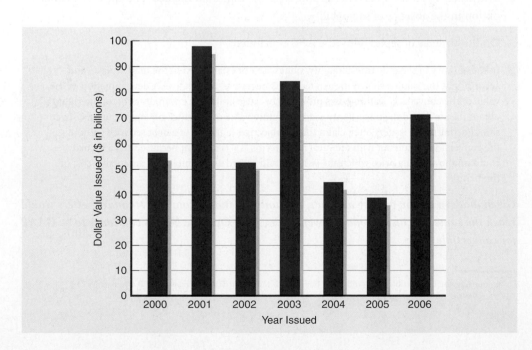

## Figure 15.6

DOLLAR VALUE OF CONVERTIBLE DEBT ISSUED BY U.S. COMPANIES 2000–2006

*Source:* Dealogic as cited in R. Sidel, K. Richardson, and D. Enrich, "Financial Firms, Capital Depleted, Hunt for Cash," *The Wall Street Journal,* November 28, 2007. Copyright © 2007 Dow Jones & Company, Inc. All rights reserved worldwide. Reprinted with permission.

Convertible debt offerings increase during periods of rising stock prices or turmoil in debt markets, which explains much of the year-to-year variation in Figure 15.6. The opportunity to share in future stock price increases is more attractive during a period of bullish market expectations for common stocks. This sentiment is what enables companies to issue convertibles on favorable terms.

Convertible bonds are also usually **callable,** or redeemable, by the issuer at a specified price before maturity. When convertible bonds are called, investors must either convert or have the debt redeemed for a cash price that is generally less than the value of the common stock into which the debt can be converted. Call provisions protect the company against extreme price increases by forcing investor action. Otherwise, investors would simply continue holding the debt in anticipation of further share price increases.

> To illustrate, suppose that VerticalNet's stock price reached $25 per share in 2000. Each $1,000 par value convertible bond would then represent a claim to $1,250 in common stock (50 shares × $25 per share). Suppose that VerticalNet's bonds were callable at a redemption price of $1,027.50 each. VerticalNet could force conversion by "calling" the debt and investors would then take the more valuable common stock ($1,250) rather than the less valuable redemption cash payment ($1,027.50).

## Financial Reporting Issues

Convertible debt poses this financial reporting dilemma: Should a value be assigned to the debt's conversion feature? Clearly, conversion features are valuable to both the issuing company and investors. The conversion option enabled VerticalNet to borrow $100 million at 5.25% annual interest when other more established companies were paying 8% annual interest. Moreover, the availability of Black–Scholes and other option pricing models means that we now have well-established methods for assigning values to option features—like the VerticalNet conversion privilege. However, GAAP for convertible debt is outlined in *APB Opinion No. 14,* which predates the development of modern option pricing theory.[50]

*APB Opinion No. 14* specifies that convertible bonds must be recorded as *debt only,* with no value assigned to the conversion privilege. Two reasons for not assigning a value to the conversion privilege are cited:

1. The inseparability of the conversion feature from the debt component of the convertible security.
2. The practical problems of determining separate values for the debt and the conversion option in the absence of separability.

On the absence of separability, the APB concluded:

> In the absence of separate transferability, values are not established in the marketplace, and accordingly, the value assigned to each feature is necessarily subjective. A determination of the value of the conversion feature poses problems because of the uncertain duration of the right to obtain the stock and the uncertainty as to the future value of the stock obtainable upon conversion. Furthermore, issuers often claim that a subjective valuation of a debt security without the conversion option but with identical other terms . . . is difficult because such a security could not be sold at a price which the issuer would regard as producing an acceptable cost of financing.[51]

***Given modern option pricing methods, it is unlikely that accounting standard setters would reach the same conclusion today. Nevertheless,*** APB Opinion No. 14 ***continues to be GAAP for convertible debt.***

---

[50] "Accounting for Convertible Debt and Debt Issued with Stock Purchase Warrants," *APB Opinion No. 14* (New York: AICPA, 1969).

[51] Ibid., para. 8.

Here's how VerticalNet records the issuance of all $100 million of its convertible subordinated debentures at par value:

| | | |
|---|---|---|
| **DR** | Cash .............................................. | $100,000,000 |
| | **CR** Convertible subordinated debentures ............. | $100,000,000 |

This entry assigns the entire $100 million to the convertible debt liability. One year later, VerticalNet records interest expense of $5,250,000 (or 0.0525 × $100 million) and the cash interest payment, which also occurs that day:

| | | |
|---|---|---|
| **DR** | Interest expense ...................................... | $5,250,000 |
| | **CR** Cash ........................................... | $5,250,000 |

(This entry ignores the real-world complication that arises when companies accrue interest throughout the year.)

Thus far, the accounting for convertible debt parallels the accounting for the straight-debt securities described in Chapter 11. VerticalNet will continue to record interest expense at the rate of 5.25% annually until the debt is retired or converted. Let's move several years forward to see what happens at conversion.

Suppose that some (but not all) investors have now chosen to exercise their conversion privilege by exchanging $50 million of the debentures. Furthermore, the company's stock has a current market value of $30 per share, which is above the $20 conversion price. This means that investors will surrender bonds with a face value (and book value) of $50 million in exchange for common stock with a market value of $75 million. *APB Opinion No. 14* permits companies to record debt conversion in either of two ways:

> At the stated conversion price, investors will receive 2,500,000 common shares for their $50 million of debentures ($50 million/$20 conversion price per share). Because each share has a $30 market value, investors receive stock worth $75 million.

1. The **book value method** records the newly issued stock at the book value of debt retired.

| | | |
|---|---|---|
| **DR** | Convertible subordinated debentures .................. | $50,000,000 |
| | **CR** Common stock ($1 par) ........................ | $ 2,500,000 |
| | **CR** Paid-in capital in excess of par ................... | 47,500,000 |

2. The **market value method** records the newly issued shares at their current market value. Any difference between that $30 market value and the $20 conversion price is recognized as a loss (or gain) on conversion.

| | | |
|---|---|---|
| **DR** | Convertible subordinated debentures ................. | $50,000,000 |
| **DR** | Loss on debt conversion ............................ | 25,000,000 |
| | **CR** Common stock ($1 par) ........................ | $ 2,500,000 |
| | **CR** Paid-in capital in excess of par ................... | 72,500,000 |

The conversion loss is not classified as an extraordinary item because it is neither *unusual in nature* nor *infrequent in occurrence.*[52] Of course, VerticalNet would continue to record interest expense on the remaining $50 million of convertible debentures outstanding.

---

[52] From Chapter 2, remember that to qualify as an extraordinary item under GAAP, the event must be both unusual *and* infrequent.

The book value approach recognizes no accounting gain or loss at retirement because the debt book value is just transferred to the common stock accounts. The market value approach, however, credits common stock at full market value *as if* the shares issued were sold for cash on the conversion date. It's easy to see why the book value method is more popular. Almost all debt conversions occur when the company's stock price is above the conversion price, and this situation triggers recognition of an accounting loss under the market value method. Managers can avoid recording this loss by instead selecting the book value approach.

## Analytical Insights

This discussion of convertible debt has two messages for financial statement readers.

One message: ***Estimating the future cash flow implications of convertible debt is difficult.*** This is because it is necessary to consider both the scheduled interest and principal payments for the debt as well as the likelihood of conversion prior to maturity. Option pricing methods can be used to evaluate the probability of conversion over long time intervals. For near-term projections, however, a simple comparison of the conversion price with the current market price of common stock can prove informative—that is, if the exercise price is more than the current share price and the options are close to expiration, they are unlikely to be exercised. The bond indenture agreement should also be examined for call provision details.

The other message: ***Recorded interest expense may seriously understate the true cost of debt financing for companies that issue convertible bonds or notes.*** Few people would argue that VerticalNet is more creditworthy than the U.S. government. Yet the company borrowed money at 5.25% annually when investors were charging the federal government 5.9% annual interest for loans of similar duration. By ignoring the value of conversion features, current GAAP understates interest expense.

The recent appearance of "zero-coupon, zero-yield" convertible debt issued by U.S. companies has served only to underscore the inherent deficiencies of *APB Opinion No. 14* when it comes to interest expense.[53] To see why, consider this example. In April 2008, Skagit Inc. sold $750 million of "zero-coupon" convertible notes and received proceeds equal to the notes' $750 million face value. The notes mature in 2013 and can be converted into shares of Skagit common stock at the note holder's option.

Recall from Chapter 11, that "zero-coupon" notes do not require the borrower (in this case, Skagit) to make periodic interest payments over the life of the loan. And, because the notes were issued at par—meaning that Skagit received cash equal to the $750 million face value— there is no discount to amortize over the life of the loan. No periodic coupon interest and no discount amortization together mean no interest expense under *APB Opinion No. 14*. In short, Skagit will not recognize any interest expense on the loan even though the notes may never be converted into shares of common stock.

The lesson for corporate managers is clear: Current GAAP allows you to avoid interest expense as long as you issue zero-coupon convertible debt and structure the conversion features so that the debt sells for par (face) value. The lesson for analysts is equally clear: Interest expense computed under *APB Opinion No. 14* can seriously understate a company's true cost of debt.

U.S. GAAP for convertible debt securities may soon change. The FASB has proposed that a convertible debt instrument should be separated into both its debt and equity components.[54] In Skagit's case, for example, this would mean assigning a portion of the $750 million proceeds

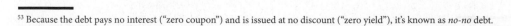

[53] Because the debt pays no interest ("zero coupon") and is issued at no discount ("zero yield"), it's known as *no-no* debt.

[54] "Accounting for Financial Instruments with Characteristics of Liabilities, Equity or Both," *Exposure Draft* (Stamford, CT: FASB 2000). The issues raised in 2002 are yet to be resolved. See "Financial Instruments with Characteristics of Equity," *Exposure Draft* (Stamford, CT: FASB 2007).

to debt (say, $600 million for the "zero-coupon" loan) and the remainder to equity ($150 million for the conversion option) based on the relative fair value of each component. It would then classify the separated debt as a liability and the conversion option (or "warrant") as equity. Under the FASB's proposal, Skagit would record periodic interest expense on the discounted "zero-coupon" loan even though no cash interest payment is required.[55] This approach overcomes the deficiencies of *APB Opinion No. 14.*

One of the reasons the FASB proposed separating convertible debt into its debt and equity components was to bring U.S. GAAP in line with IFRS. Those standards have required the separation of convertible securities into debt and equity components since 1996.[56] Canadian GAAP also requires a similar treatment. As this book goes to press, the FASB has not reached a conclusion on the matter.[57]

**Convertible debt gives investors the upside potential of common stock and the safety net of debt. That's why the interest rate on convertible debt is so low—the option value of the conversion feature compensates for the lower interest paid to investors. Because GAAP ignores the conversion option, interest expense may be understated and cash flow forecasting may be impeded.**

## SUMMARY

- Many aspects of financial reporting for owners' equity transactions are built on technical rules and procedures that have evolved over time.
- Other aspects of owners' equity accounting have not changed despite changing economic and legal environments.
- Still other aspects of owners' equity accounting involve complicated pronouncements that reflect political compromises.
- Financial statement readers must recognize these influences and avoid unwarranted inferences based on the reported figures.
- Stock buybacks don't produce accounting gains and losses, but they can be used to artificially inflate a company's reported EPS.
- Preferred stock that has a mandatory redemption feature looks a lot like debt, so GAAP now requires it to be classified as debt in most cases.
- Some companies can pay dividends in excess of their retained earnings balance, but their ability to do so depends on state law.
- EPS numbers are adjusted for potential dilution from stock options, warrants, and convertible securities.
- GAAP now requires companies to record compensation expense when stock options are given to employees, but GAAP ignores the option value in convertible debt.

[55] The periodic interest expense that Skagit would record is the discount amortization amount computed using the effective interest method described in Chapter 11.

[56] "Financial Instruments: Disclosure and Presentation," *International Accounting Standard No. 32* (London: International Accounting Standards Committee, 1996). International Accounting Standards are now known as *International Financial Reporting Standards,* and the International Accounting Standards Committee (IASC) is now the IASB.

[57] In 2003, the FASB issued the final version of "Accounting for Financial Instruments with Characteristics of Both Liabilities and Equities," *SFAS No. 150* (Norwalk, CT: FASB 2003), but this pronouncement did not address so-called compound financial instruments such as convertible debt.

- GAAP can understate interest expense when companies issue convertible debt, but new GAAP rules may soon correct this problem.
- While some rules for owners' equity accounting may seem arbitrary—and therefore insignificant—these financial statement items have a profound impact on lending agreements, regulation, and the cost of equity capital.

## APPENDIX

# EMPLOYEE STOCK OWNERSHIP PLANS

An **employee stock ownership plan** (**ESOP**) is an employee pension plan that invests primarily in the common stock of the employer company. To establish an ESOP, the company first sets up a trust to hold the ESOP assets and makes contributions of up to 25% of payroll for employees in the plan. Stock contributed to (or purchased by) the trust is allocated to the accounts of employees who have met certain eligibility requirements, such as having worked at the company for at least three years. ESOPs are subject to vesting like other pensions. Plan enrollees are not taxed on the income earned by the plan, on contributions to the plan, or on other amounts added to their accounts until distribution. So, ESOPs enable employees to gain a tax-free ownership stake in their company. Figure 15.7 illustrates the relationships among the ESOP, employer company, employees, and external funding sources like banks.

ESOPs are attractive to employer companies for three reasons:

1. ESOPs have considerable tax advantages.
2. ESOPs can provide a source of low-cost debt financing for firms.
3. ESOPs have been used to finance management buyouts and as part of a takeover defense.

In a **leveraged ESOP,** the trust borrows money from a bank or other financial institution to purchase shares of the employer company's stock. As an example, suppose that Buchner Manufacturing sets up an ESOP trust that then obtains a $20 million bank loan to purchase shares of Buchner stock. Next, the trust hands the cash over to Buchner in exchange for the stock. Buchner then makes annual or quarterly tax-deductible cash contributions to the trust, and the trust uses the cash to make the interest and principal payments on the bank loan. In other words, loan proceeds flow directly to the company as it purchases ESOP shares, and loan

### Figure 15.7

RELATIONSHIP BETWEEN THE ESOP, EMPLOYER COMPANY, EMPLOYEES, AND EXTERNAL FUNDING SOURCES

Cash contributions and dividends paid by employer company to trust are deductible for income tax purposes within certain limits. Hence, the sponsoring company can lower the cost of debt financing when compared to direct borrowing by the company.

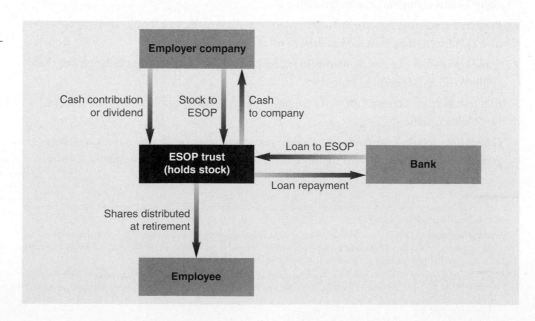

repayment occurs over time with the ESOP shares serving as collateral for the loan. Employee ownership of the shares accrues according to the rate at which the loan principal is repaid.

Notice the ESOP tax advantage to Buchner Manufacturing—all payments to the ESOP trust become tax deductible so long as the cash is then used to pay down the ESOP borrowing. In effect, Buchner obtains a tax deduction for ESOP-debt principal *and* interest payments. Without the leveraged ESOP structure, only debt interest payments are tax deductible.

> Company payments to the ESOP trust are tax deductible (within certain limits) even when there is no bank borrowing. If Buchner contributes stock to the ESOP it can take a tax deduction for the fair value of the contributed shares.

In addition to their tax advantages, ESOPs have been used to take companies private, to acquire divested subsidiaries or divisions, to provide takeover defenses, and to save failed companies. ESOPs were widely used as takeover defenses because ESOP shares are relatively impervious to buyout by a hostile acquirer. Thus, a corporate raider who wants to accumulate a controlling interest in Buchner Manufacturing—for example, by owning 51% of the company's common stock—will find this difficult when Buchner's ESOP trust already owns 60% of the company's shares. The raider's only hope is to convince the ESOP to sell its shares—an unlikely event because the decision to sell shares rests with the ESOP trustees including typically one or more of the company's top executives (in our example, that's Buchner Manufacturing).

See Exhibit 15.6 for a description of a footnote from Maytag Company's 2002 annual report, which illustrates the financial statement implications of ESOPs.

The top portion of Maytag's footnote describes the company's ESOP, who participates in the plan, and how cash and Maytag shares flow between the company and the ESOP trust. Panel (a) tracks the year-to-year change in Maytag shares held by the trust. Here you learn that the trust held roughly 2.9 million shares of Maytag common stock at the end of 2002 and that the company contributed nearly 1.2 million shares to the trust that year. Panels (a) and (b) provide information about ESOP–related cash flow and expense components. Maytag made a $2.969 million cash contribution to the trust in 2002 as well as an $8.194 million stock contribution, for a total contribution of $11.163 million. Maytag also recorded a corresponding $11.163 million ESOP expense comprised of $0.453 million classified as interest expense and the remaining $10.710 million classified as compensation expense.

In addition to this footnote, Maytag Company's 2002 balance sheet included $14.1 million of ESOP debt as part of long-term liabilities and a corresponding $14.1 million owners' equity *reduction* labeled Employee stock plans.

The following example illustrates how these two balance sheet items—ESOP debt as part of long-term liabilities and the owners' equity reduction from employee stock plans—arise and how employers account for ESOPs.[58]

Assume that Wulff Manufacturing established an ESOP for hourly employees on January 1, 2008. The following transactions summarize the activities of the ESOP over its first year:

1. On January 1, the ESOP borrowed $20 million from a large regional bank by signing a 10-year installment note with annual interest payments equal to 9% of the outstanding balance. The company guaranteed the note.
2. That same day, the ESOP purchased 400,000 unissued shares of $10 par common stock from Wulff at the current $50 per share market price. These stock shares are collateral for the bank loan.

---

[58] The accounting standards for ESOPs are described in "Accounting Practices for Certain Employee Stock Ownership Plans," *Statement of Position No. 76–3* (New York: AICPA, 1976).

## EXHIBIT 15.6   Maytag Company

### Footnote Disclosure for Employee Stock Ownership Plan (ESOP)

The Company established an Employee Stock Option Plan (ESOP), and a related trust issued debt and used the proceeds to acquire shares of the Company's stock for future allocation to ESOP participants. ESOP participants generally consist of all U.S. employees except certain groups covered by a collective bargaining agreement. The Company guarantees the ESOP debt and reflects it in the Consolidated Balance Sheets as Long-term debt with a related amount shown in the Shareowners' equity section as part of Employee stock plans. Dividends earned on the allocated and unallocated ESOP shares are used to service the debt. The Company is obligated to make annual contributions to the ESOP trust to the extent the dividends earned on the shares are less than the debt service requirements. As the debt is repaid, shares are released and allocated to plan participants based on the ratio of the current year debt service payment to the total debt service payments over the life of the loan. If the shares released are less than the shares earned by the employees, the Company contributes additional shares to the ESOP trust to meet the shortfall. All shares held by the ESOP trust are considered outstanding for earnings per share computations and dividends earned on the shares are recorded as a reduction of retained earnings.

The ESOP shares held in trust consisted of the following:

**Panel (a)**

| | December 31 | |
|---|---|---|
| | **2002** | **2001** |
| Original shares held in trust: | | |
| Released and allocated | 2,469,377 | 2,366,589 |
| Unreleased shares (fair value; 2002—$11,051,331; | | |
| 2001—$15,221,891) | 387,766 | 490,554 |
| | 2,857,143 | 2,857,143 |
| Additional shares contributed and allocated | 1,172,471 | 895,144 |
| Shares withdrawn | (1,085,719) | (861,564) |
| Total shares held in trust | 2,943,895 | 2,890,723 |

The components of the total contribution to the ESOP trust consisted of the following:

**Panel (b)**

| | Years Ended December 31 | | |
|---|---|---|---|
| *($ in thousands)* | **2002** | **2001** | **2000** |
| Debt service requirement | $ 3,983 | $ 8,238 | $8,600 |
| Dividends earned on ESOP shares | (1,014) | (2,042) | (2,086) |
| Cash contribution to ESOP trust | 2,969 | 6,196 | 6,514 |
| Fair market value of additional shares contributed | 8,194 | 4,257 | 3,133 |
| Total contribution to ESOP trust | $11,163 | $10,453 | $9,647 |

The components of expense recognized by the Company for the ESOP contribution consisted of the following:

**Panel (c)**

| | Years Ended December 31 | | |
|---|---|---|---|
| *($ in thousands)* | **2002** | **2001** | **2000** |
| Contribution classified as interest expense | $    453 | $ 1,178 | $1,540 |
| Contribution classified as compensation expense | 10,710 | 9,275 | 8,107 |
| Total expense for the ESOP contribution | $11,163 | $10,453 | $9,647 |

*Source:* Maytag Company 2002 annual report.

3. During 2008, Wulff declared and paid common dividends of $3 per share. The company also contributed $2.6 million in cash to the ESOP.

4. At the end of 2008, the ESOP "released and allocated" 40,000 shares to company employees.

These shares actually remain in the ESOP trust until distributed to employees at retirement or when they leave the company.

Keep in mind that the following accounting entries are made on the books of Wulff Manufacturing; they are not the accounting entries made by the ESOP trust itself.

Wulff records the first two transactions as:

| | | |
|---|---|---|
| 1. **DR** Employee stock plan ............................. | $20,000,000 | |
|     **CR** ESOP note payable .......................... | | $20,000,000 |
| 2. **DR** Cash ........................................... | $20,000,000 | |
|     **CR** Common stock—$10 par ...................... | | $ 4,000,000 |
|     **CR** Paid-in capital in excess of par ................ | | 16,000,000 |

Entry 1 records the ESOP borrowing. The debit is to the balance sheet contra-equity account Employee stock plan (the same account title Maytag uses). It tracks the cost ($50 per share × 400,000 common shares) of unreleased ESOP shares, as you will see. Entry 2 records the sale of 400,000 shares of common stock to the ESOP.

Wulff declared and paid cash dividends of $3 per share during the year. Entry 3 that follows reflects this transfer of $1.2 million ($3 per share × 400,000 ESOP shares) to the ESOP trust. However, the trust is required to make a $2.0 million principal payment on the note ($20 million/10 years) and to pay $1.8 million in interest ($20 million outstanding × 9%) at year-end. Consequently, the company must contribute $2.6 million in cash to the ESOP in addition to the $1.2 million in cash already in the trust. Entry 4 records this $2,600,000 contribution by the company to the ESOP.

| | | |
|---|---|---|
| 3. **DR** Dividends .......................................... | $1,200,000 | |
|     **CR** Cash (to ESOP trust) .......................... | | $1,200,000 |
| 4. **DR** Interest expense .................................... | $1,800,000 | |
|     **DR** Compensation expense ........................... | 800,000 | |
|     **CR** Cash (to ESOP trust) ......................... | | $2,600,000 |

When the trust makes the $3.8 million payment to the bank and allocates shares to employees, Wulff reduces the carrying value of the ESOP debt and the contra-equity account by the amount of the loan *principal* payment and shares allocated:

| | | |
|---|---|---|
| **DR** ESOP Note payable .................................... | $2,000,000 | |
|     **CR** Employee stock plan ............................ | | $2,000,000 |

At this point, Wulff's balance sheet shows an $18 million liability for the unpaid ESOP note and a corresponding $18 million contra-equity item Employee stock plan. The income statement shows $800,000 of compensation expense and $1.8 million of interest expense, but the other $1.2 million paid by Wulff is shown as a dividend distribution.

Financial statement readers must keep three points in mind when examining ESOPs.

1. ***ESOP debt is not hidden in financial statement footnotes as an off-balance sheet item.*** Instead, the employer carries the debt on its books like any other long-term liability. Consequently, the future cash flow implications of ESOP debt are no more difficult to assess than the company's other long-term debt obligations.

2. **ESOP accounting produces an unusual balance sheet item, Employee stock plan, in our example.** This account tracks the cost of ESOP shares not yet allocated to employees but still held by the trust. All common shares purchased by the ESOP—whether allocated to employees or not—are included in the Common stock par and Paid-in capital in excess of par accounts as outstanding stock.

3. **Some analysts argue that ESOP accounting understates the company's true cost of employee compensation.** To see why they argue there is understatement, notice that Wulff's employees "earned"—that is, were allocated—40,000 ESOP shares during 2008 for a total cost of $2 million at $50 per share. This $2 million equals the ESOP debt principal repayment made during the year. Because the only source of ESOP cash is the employer company, Wulff effectively made the $2 million debt payment using $1.2 million of cash labeled Dividends and another $800,000 labeled Compensation expense. Wulff's total cash outlay for stock-based compensation was $2 million—excluding ESOP debt interest— even though only $800,000 is recorded as an expense. This treatment *understates* employee compensation expense by $1.2 million, and so it *overstates* the company's gross margin and net income for the year. Analysts must be aware of this possibility when evaluating companies that have large ESOPs.

## EXERCISES

### E15-1
Issuing common stock

Spridget Company has 1 million shares of common stock authorized with a par value of $3 per share, of which 600,000 shares are outstanding. The company received $7 per share when it issued shares to the public.

**Required:**

What is the book value of the Common stock par account and the Additional paid-in capital account?

### E15-2
Retiring common stock

**AICPA**
ADAPTED

The stockholders' equity section of Peter Corporation's balance sheet at December 31, 2008 follows:

| | |
|---|---|
| Common stock ($10 par value); authorized 1,000,000 | |
| shares, issued and outstanding 900,000 shares | $ 9,000,000 |
| Additional paid-in capital | 2,700,000 |
| Retained earnings | 1,300,000 |
| Total stockholders' equity | $13,000,000 |

On January 2, 2009, Peter purchased and retired 100,000 shares of its stock for $1,800,000.

**Required:**

What is the balance in the Additional paid-in capital *and* Retained earnings accounts immediately after the shares were retired?

### E15-3
Analyzing debt and redeemable preferred stock

ForeEver Yours, Inc., a manufacturer of wedding rings, issued two financial instruments at the beginning of 2008: a $10 million, 40-year bond that pays interest at the rate of 11% annually and 10,000 shares of $100 preferred stock that pays a dividend of 7.5% annually. The preferred stock has a mandatory redemption feature that requires the company to repurchase all outstanding shares at par ($100 per share) in 40 years.

**Required:**

Describe how each financial instrument will affect the company's balance sheet and income statement in 2008.

Warren Corporation was organized on January 1, 2008 with an authorization of 500,000 shares of common stock ($5 par value per share). During 2008, the company had the following capital transactions:

| | |
|---|---|
| January 5 | Issued 100,000 shares at $5 per share |
| April 6 | Issued 50,000 shares at $7 per share |
| June 8 | Issued 15,000 shares at $10 per share |
| July 28 | Purchased 25,000 shares at $4 per share |
| December 31 | Sold 25,000 shares held in treasury at $8 per share |

**Required:**
What should be the balance in the Additional paid-in capital account at December 31, 2008?

**E15-4**

Analyzing various stock transactions

**AICPA**
ADAPTED

Selected information for Irvington Company follows:

| | December 31 | |
|---|---|---|
| | **2007** | **2008** |
| Preferred stock, 8%, per $100 | $125,000 | $125,000 |
| Common stock | 300,000 | 400,000 |
| Retained earnings | 75,000 | 185,000 |
| Dividends paid on preferred stock | 10,000 | 10,000 |
| Net income | 60,000 | 120,000 |

**Required:**
What is Irvington's return on common stockholders' equity (ROCE) for 2008, rounded to the nearest percentage point?

**E15-5**

Calculating return on common equity

**AICPA**
ADAPTED

Munn Corporation's records included the following stockholders' equity accounts:

| | |
|---|---|
| Preferred stock, par value $15, authorized 20,000 shares | $255,000 |
| Additional paid-in capital—preferred stock | 15,000 |
| Common stock, no par, $5 stated value, 100,000 shares authorized | 300,000 |

**Required:**
How many shares of preferred stock and how many shares of common stock have been issued?

**E15-6**

Determining how many shares

**AICPA**
ADAPTED

Newton Corporation was organized on January 1, 2008, On that date, it issued 200,000 shares of its $10 par-value common stock at $15 per share (400,000 shares were authorized). During the period from January 1, 2008 through December 31, 2010, Newton reported net income of $750,000 and paid cash dividends of $380,000. On January 5, 2010 Newton purchased 12,000 shares of its common stock at $12 per share. On December 31, 2010 the company sold 8,000 treasury shares at $8 per share.

**Required:**
What is the book value of total shareholders' equity as of December 31, 2010?

**E15-7**

Determining stockholders' equity after a stock repurchase

**AICPA**
ADAPTED

On December 31, 2008 the Stockholders' Equity section of Mercedes Corporation was as follows:

| | |
|---|---|
| Common stock, par value $5; authorized 30,000 shares; | |
| issued and outstanding, 9,000 shares | $ 45,000 |
| Additional paid-in capital | 58,000 |
| Retained earnings | 73,000 |
| Total stockholders' equity | $176,000 |

**E15-8**

Stock dividends and retained earnings

**AICPA**
ADAPTED

On March 1, 2009, the board of directors declared a 10% stock dividend and accordingly issued 900 additional shares. The stock's fair value at that time was $8 per share. For the three months ended March 31, 2009, Mercedes sustained a net loss of $16,000.

**Required:**

What amount should the company report as retained earnings on its quarterly financial statement dated March 31, 2009?

---

**E15-9**

Stock dividends and market prices

AICPA
ADAPTED

On June 30, 2008, the Stockholders' Equity section of Comet Corporation's balance sheet was as follows:

| | |
|---|---|
| Common stock, par value $25; authorized 500,000 shares; | |
| issued and outstanding 300,000 shares | $7,500,000 |
| Additional paid-in capital | 1,400,000 |
| Retained earnings | 1,890,000 |

On July 1, 2008, Comet's board of directors declared a 5% stock dividend on common stock to be distributed on August 10, 2008 to shareholders of record on July 31, 2008. The market price of Comet's common stock on each of these dates was as follows:

| | |
|---|---|
| July 1 | $30 per share |
| July 31 | $31 per share |
| August 10 | $32 per share |

**Required:**

Prepare the general journal entry to record the stock dividend on Comet's books.

---

**E15-10**

Determining stockholders' equity after a stock split

AICPA
ADAPTED

Effective April 27, 2008, Dorr Corporation's stockholders approved a two-for-one split of the company's common stock and an increase in authorized common shares from 100,000 shares (par value of $20 per share) to 200,000 shares (par value of $10 per share). The stock split shares were issued on June 30, 2008. Dorr's stockholders' equity accounts immediately before issuance of the stock split shares were:

| | |
|---|---|
| Common stock, par value $20; 100,000 shares authorized; | |
| 50,000 shares outstanding | $1,000,000 |
| Additional paid-in capital | 150,000 |
| Retained earnings | 1,350,000 |

**Required:**

After issuing the stock split shares, what are the balances of the Additional paid-in capital and Retained earnings accounts in Dorr's June 30, 2008 statement of stockholders' equity?

---

**E15-11**

Recognizing employee stock options

AICPA
ADAPTED

On July 1, 2004, Austin Company granted Harry Ross, an employee, an option to buy 500 shares of Austin common stock at $30 per share. The option was exercisable for five years from the date of the grant. Ross exercised his option on October 1, 2004 and sold his shares on December 2, 2004. The quoted market prices for Austin common stock during the year were:

| | |
|---|---|
| July 1 | $30 per share |
| October 1 | 35 per share |
| December 2 | 37 per share |

**Required:**

1. How much compensation expense should Austin recognize in 2004 as a result of the option granted to Ross if it follows *APB Opinion No. 25*?

2. How much compensation expense should Austin have recognized in 2004 if it follows the fair value method in *SFAS No. 123* and the options were worth $2 each on the grant date?

Tam Company's net income for the year ending December 31, 2008 was $10,000. During the year, Tam declared and paid $1,000 cash dividends on preferred stock and $1,750 cash dividends on common stock. At December 31, 2008, the company had 12,000 shares of common stock issued and outstanding—10,000 had been issued and outstanding throughout the year and 2,000 were issued on July 1, 2008. No other common stock transactions occurred during the year, and the 5,000 shares of preferred stock are not convertible into common shares.

**Required:**

What should be the 2008 earnings per common share of Tam Company, rounded to the nearest penny?

| E15-12 |
| --- |

Computing basic EPS

**AICPA**
ADAPTED

---

Fountain Inc. has 5,000,000 shares of common stock outstanding on January 1, 2008. It issued an additional 1,000,000 shares of common stock on April 1, 2008 and 500,000 more on July 1, 2008. On October 1, 2008 Fountain issued 10,000 convertible bonds; each one had a $1,000 face value and paid 7% interest. Each bond is convertible into 40 shares of common stock. No bonds were converted during 2008.

**Required:**

What number of shares should be used in computing basic EPS and diluted EPS, respectively?

| E15-13 |
| --- |

Finding the number of shares for EPS

**AICPA**
ADAPTED

---

Information concerning the capital structure of the Petrock Corporation is as follows:

| | December 31 | |
| --- | --- | --- |
| | **2007** | **2008** |
| Common stock | 90,000 shares | 90,000 shares |
| Convertible preferred stock | 10,000 shares | 10,000 shares |
| 8% convertible bonds | $1,000,000 | $1,000,000 |

During 2008, Petrock paid dividends of $1 per share on its common stock and $2.40 per share on its preferred stock. The preferred stock is convertible into 20,000 shares of common stock. The 8% convertible bonds are convertible into 30,000 shares of common stock. The net income for the year ending December 31, 2008 was $285,000, and the company's income tax rate was 40%.

**Required:**

1. What was basic EPS for 2008, rounded to the nearest penny?
2. What was diluted EPS for 2008, rounded to the nearest penny?

| E15-14 |
| --- |

Calculating earnings per share

**AICPA**
ADAPTED

---

On July 18, 2003, Amos Corporation granted nontransferable options to certain key employees as additional compensation. The options permit the purchase of 20,000 shares of Amos's common stock at a price of $30 per share. On the grant date, the stock's market value was $42 per share. The options were exercisable beginning January 1, 2004 and expire on December 31, 2012. On February 3, 2004 when the stock was selling for $45 per share, all options were exercised.

**Required:**

1. How much compensation expense should Amos record from the issuance of these options in 2003 and in 2004 if Amos follows *APB Opinion No. 25?*
2. How much compensation expense should Amos have recorded in 2003 and 2004 if it follows the fair value method in *SFAS No. 123* and the options are worth $17 per share on the grant date?

| E15-15 |
| --- |

Employee stock options

**AICPA**
ADAPTED

---

**E15-16**

Identifying incentives for stock repurchases

Keystone Enterprises just announced record 2008 EPS of $5.00, up $0.25 from last year. This is the 10th consecutive year that the company has increased its EPS, an enviable record. Unfortunately, management fears that this string of EPS increases is about to be broken. Keystone is forecasting net income for 2009 and 2010 at $10 million each year, the same level earned in 2008. The company has 2,000,000 shares of common stock outstanding, no preferred stock, and no convertible debt.

**Required:**

1. How many common shares does Keystone need to buy back at the beginning of 2009 *and* 2010 to maintain EPS growth of $0.25 per share each year? (*Note:* Keystone will use excess cash from operations to pay for the stock.)

2. Explain why your answer to requirement 1 would change if the buybacks were to occur in the middle of each year.

3. Why do you think Keystone's management would be concerned about maintaining the company's record of EPS growth?

---

**E15-17**

Understanding ESOPs

The 2002 annual report of Procter & Gamble Company contained the following information:

> The ESOP borrowed $1,000 in 1989, which has been guaranteed by the Company. The proceeds were used to purchase Series A ESOP Convertible Class A Preferred Stock.... Principal and interest requirements are $117 per year, paid by the trust from dividends on the preferred shares and from cash contributions by the Company.... In 1991 the ESOP borrowed an additional $1,000 also guaranteed by the Company. The proceeds were used to purchase Series B ESOP Convertible Class A Preferred Stock.... Debt service requirements are $94 per year, funded by preferred stock dividends and cash contributions from the Company.

**Required:**

1. What journal entry is made on Procter & Gamble's books when its ESOP trust borrows money?

2. How will the ESOP affect Procter & Gamble's cash flows?

3. How will the ESOP affect Procter & Gamble's income statement?

---

# PROBLEMS / DISCUSSION QUESTIONS

**P15-1**

Recording cash and stock dividends

The stockholders' equity section of Warm Ways Inc.'s balance sheet at January 1, 2008 shows:

| | |
|---|---:|
| Preferred stock, $100 par value, 10% dividend, 50,000 shares issued and outstanding | $ 5,000,000 |
| Common stock, $6 par value, 1 million shares issued and outstanding | 6,000,000 |
| Paid-in capital in excess of par | 119,000,000 |
| Retained earnings | 50,000,000 |
| Total stockholders' equity | $180,000,000 |

Warm Ways reported net income of $9,250,000 for 2008, declared and paid the preferred stock cash dividend, and declared and paid a $0.25 per share cash dividend on 1 million shares of common stock. The company also declared and paid a 10% stock dividend on its common shares. When the stock dividend was declared, 1 million common shares were outstanding, and the market price of common stock was $135 per share.

**Required:**

1. Prepare journal entries to record the three dividend "events" that took place during 2008.

2. If the company's common stock was valued at $135 per share when the stock dividend was declared, what would the stock price be just after the dividend shares were distributed?

It's July 1, 2009, and the market price of Warm Ways' common stock (Problem P15-1) is $175 per share. There are 1.1 million common shares outstanding, and the Retained earnings account shows a balance of $45,000,000. Management wants to declare and pay a 20% common stock dividend, but this would mean halting the company's cash dividend payments because a 20% stock dividend would cause retained earnings to fall by $38,500,000 (that is, 20% × 1.1 million shares × $175 per share). This would leave a balance of only $6,500,000, far below the $25,000,000 minimum required for cash dividends as specified in the company's loan agreement. It would take several years to build up retained earnings so that Warm Ways could again pay cash dividends.

**P15-2**

Determining effect of splits and dividends on retained earnings

The chief financial officer of the company has proposed two ways it could distribute common shares and still manage to pay cash dividends:

- Option A: Split the stock 12 for 10.
- Option B: Increase the size of the stock dividend from 20% to 30%, and record the share distribution as a stock split.

**Required:**

1. How will these two approaches affect the company's retained earnings?
2. As a common stockholder, would you prefer a 20% stock dividend, a 12-for-10 stock split, or a 30% stock dividend? Why?

On January 1, 2006 when its $30 par-value common stock was selling for $80 per share, Gierach Corporation issued $10 million of 4% convertible debentures due in 10 years. The conversion option allowed the holder of each $1,000 bond to convert the bond into five shares of the company's $30 par-value common stock. The debentures were issued for $10 million. Without the conversion feature, the bonds would have been issued for $8.5 million.

**P15-3**

Analyzing convertible debt

**AICPA**
ADAPTED

On January 1, 2008, the company's $30 par-value common stock was split three for one. On January 1, 2009 when the company's $10 par-value common stock was selling for $90 per share, holders of 40% of the convertible debentures exercised their conversion options.

**Required:**

1. Prepare a journal entry to record the original issuance of the convertible debentures.
2. How much interest expense would the company recognize on the convertible debentures in 2006?
3. Prepare a journal entry to record the exercise of the conversion option.
4. Why do many companies use the book value method to record debt conversions?

The Shareholders' Equity section of Holiday Roads Company's balance sheet shows:

**P15-4**

Computing EPS

|  | December 31 2007 | December 31 2008 |
|---|---|---|
| Preferred stock, $200 par value, 5% dividend, 20,000 shares issued and outstanding | $ 4,000,000 | $ 4,000,000 |
| Common stock, $2 par value | 400,000 | 520,000 |
| Paid-in capital in excess of par | 19,600,000 | 26,800,000 |
| Retained earnings | 3,000,000 | 4,000,000 |
| Total stockholders' equity | $27,000,000 | $35,320,000 |

Net income for 2008 was $1,700,000, preferred stock dividends were $200,000, and common stock dividends were $500,000. The company issued 60,000 shares of common stock on July 1, 2008.

**Required:**

1. What is the company's basic EPS for 2008?

2. Suppose that Holiday Roads also had $500,000 of 10% convertible subordinated debentures outstanding at the beginning and end of 2008. Each $1,000 bond is convertible into 100 shares of common stock, and the company's income tax rate is 34%. What is the company's diluted EPS for 2008?

3. What other types of securities in addition to convertible debt can affect the calculation of diluted EPS?

---

**P15-5**

Setting limits on dividends

Tredegar Industries Inc. makes plastic films and molded plastic products and soft alloy aluminum extrusions, distributes business applications software, and provides proprietary chemistry services. A footnote to the company's annual report states.

While certain of the Company's subsidiaries' debt facilities are outstanding, the Company's subsidiaries must meet specific financial tests on an ongoing basis, which are customary for these types of facilities. Except as provided by applicable corporate law, there are no restrictions on the Company's ability to pay dividends from retained earnings. However, the payment of cash dividends by the Company's subsidiaries to the Company are subject to certain restrictions under the terms of various agreements covering the Company's subsidiaries' long-term debt. Toledo, PDI, and Bal Crank [three of Tredegar's subsidiaries] are not permitted under each subsidiary's respective debt agreements to pay cash dividends. Assuming certain financial covenants are met, General Chemical [another subsidiary] is permitted to pay cash dividends of up to 50 percent of the net income (subject to certain adjustments) of General Chemical for the applicable period. Consequently, the Company's ability to pay cash dividends on Common Stock may effectively be limited by such agreements. At [year end] approximately $51,000 was available for dividend payments in accordance with these covenants.

The company's financial statements showed net income of $45,035, dividends of $3,176, and year-end retained earnings of $99,027. (All dollar amounts here and in the footnote are in thousands.)

**Required:**

1. Explain why and how lenders restrict a subsidiary's ability to pay dividends to the parent corporation.

2. What was Tredegar's dividend payout ratio?

3. What is the maximum amount of dividends the company could have paid to common stockholders in the year without violating the terms of its lending agreements?

4. Suppose that Tredegar's loan agreements contained no restrictions on dividend payments by subsidiaries or the parent company. What is the maximum legal amount of dividends the company could have paid to common stockholders?

5. Do contractual or legal restrictions on dividend payments seem to be influencing the company's dividend policy?

---

**P15-6**

Granting and recording stock options

Schlumberger Ltd. provides exploration and production services to the petroleum industry. The following footnote appeared in the company's 2002 annual report:

As of December 31, 2002, the Company has two types of stock-based compensation plans. . . . Schlumberger applies APB Opinion 25 and related Interpretations in accounting for its plans. Accordingly, no compensation cost has been recognized for its stock option plans and its stock purchase plan. Had compensation cost for Schlumberger's stock-based plans been determined based on the fair value at the grant dates for awards under those plans, consistent with the method of FASB Statement 123, Schlumberger's net income and earnings per share would have been the pro forma amounts indicated below:

| ($ in millions except per share amounts) | 2002 | 2001 |
|---|---|---|
| Net income (loss) | | |
| As reported | $(2,320) | $522 |
| Pro forma | (2,476) | 386 |
| Basic earnings (loss) per share | | |
| As reported | (4.01) | 0.91 |
| Pro forma | (4.28) | 0.67 |

## Stock Option Plans

During 2002, 2001, and in prior years, officers and key employees were granted stock options under Schlumberger stock option plans. For all of the stock options granted, the exercise price of each option equals the market price of the Schlumberger stock on the date of grant, an option's maximum life is ten years, and options generally vest in 20% increments over five years. . . . As required by FASB Statement 123, the fair value of each grant is estimated on the date of grant using the multiple option Black–Scholes option-pricing model. A summary of the status of the Schlumberger stock option plans [follows]:

| | Number of Shares | Weighted Average Exercise Price |
|---|---|---|
| Outstanding 12/31/2001 | 32,836,340 | $55.80 |
| Granted | 7,314,617 | 55.14 |
| Exercised | (2,296,593) | 30.02 |
| Forfeited | (984,680) | 66.69 |
| Outstanding 12/31/2002 | 36,869,684 | $57.03 |

Elsewhere in the footnote, the company says that options for 21,142,473 shares were exercisable at year-end, and that the weighted average fair value of options granted during the year was $20.22.

**Required:**

1. Why doesn't Schlumberger grant stock options with a shorter term (say, three years) and vesting period (say, one year)?

2. How much compensation expense would the company have recorded in 2002 under *APB No. 25* if the stock options granted that year had an exercise price $2 below the market price at the grant date?

3. What costs would Schlumberger employees have incurred if stock options granted in 2002 had an exercise price $2 below the grant date market price?

4. What journal entry would the company have made to record compensation expense for options granted in 2002 if it had used the fair value method of *FASB No. 123?*

5. Based on the footnote information, why were some options exercised in 2002 while others were forfeited?

---

Abbott Stores must raise $100 million on January 1, 2009 to finance its expansion into the lucrative Boston metropolitan market. It will use the money to finance construction of five retail stores and a distribution center. The stores are expected to open later this year. Three alternatives for raising the money are being considered:

1. Issue $100 million of 8% nonconvertible debt due in 20 years.

2. Issue $100 million of 6% nonconvertible preferred stock (100,000 shares).

3. Issue $100 million of common stock (1 million shares).

**P15-7**

Managing equity

The company's internal forecasts indicate the following 2009 year-end amounts (before the impact of the $100 million of new financing is considered):

| ($ in millions) | |
| --- | --- |
| Total debt | $425 |
| Total shareholders' equity | 250 |
| Net income for the year | 10 |

Abbott has no preferred stock outstanding but has 10 million shares of common stock outstanding. EPS has been declining for the past several years. Earnings in 2008 were $1 per share, down from $1.10 the year before, and management wants to avoid another decline this year. One of the company's existing loan agreements requires its debt-to-equity ratio to be less than 2. Abbott pays taxes at a 40% rate.

**Required:**

1. Assess the impact of each financing alternative on 2009 EPS and the year-end debt-to-equity ratio.

2. Which financing alternative would you recommend?

---

**P15-8**

Repurchasing stock and calculating EPS

Central Sprinkler Corporation manufactures and sells automatic fire sprinkler heads and valves, and it distributes components for automatic sprinkler systems. Selected information from the company's 2008 financial statements show:

| | Years Ended October 31 | | | |
| --- | --- | --- | --- | --- |
| ($ in thousands except per share amounts) | 2005 | 2006 | 2007 | 2008 |
| Earnings available to common | $2,376 | $4,018 | $8,458 | $3,763 |
| Average common shares outstanding | 4,752 | 5,023 | 3,383 | 3,330 |
| EPS | $ 0.50 | $ 0.80 | $ 2.50 | $ 1.13 |

In late December 2006, Central Sprinkler bought back 1,237,000 shares of common stock for $11,750,000.

**Required:**

1. What would EPS have been in 2007 and 2008 had the company not repurchased its common shares? Assume the stock buyback occurred on December 31, 2006, and notice that the company has an October 31 fiscal year-end.

2. Compare the company's profit performance in 2008 to earlier years, and comment on this comparison.

3. The stock buyback isn't the only reason that average common shares declined from 2006 to 2007. What else do you think could have contributed to this decline in average common shares?

---

**P15-9**

Managing earnings

mhhe.com/revsine4e

General Electric (GE) Company has two major parts: an industrial conglomerate and a financial services conglomerate. In the past decade, GE's EPS have risen almost every year. How does GE do it? One reason is the real growth in earnings of its business units. But another way is what *The Wall Street Journal* calls "earnings management, the orchestrated timing of gains and losses to smooth out bumps." Following is information taken from the company's annual reports to shareholders.

| ($ in millions except per share amounts) | 1999 | 1998 | 1997 | 1996 | 1995 | 1994 | 1993 |
| --- | --- | --- | --- | --- | --- | --- | --- |
| Earnings available for common shares | $10,717 | $9,296 | $8,203 | $7,280 | $6,573 | $5,905 | $4,424 |
| Restructuring charges | (265) | –0– | (2,322) | –0– | –0– | (1,189) | (1,101) |
| Special gains | 653 | –0– | 1,538 | –0– | –0– | –0– | 1,430 |
| Average common shares outstanding | 9,834 | 9,807 | 9,824 | 9,922 | 10,102 | 10,252 | 10,240 |
| Earnings per share | $ 1.07 | $ 0.93 | $ 0.82 | $ 0.72 | $ 0.64 | $ 0.57 | $ 0.42 |

*(continued)*

| ($ in millions except per share amounts) | 1992 | 1991 | 1990 | 1989 | 1988 | 1987 | 1986 |
|---|---|---|---|---|---|---|---|
| Earnings available for common shares | $ 4,305 | $4,435 | $4,303 | $3,939 | $3,386 | $2,119 | $2,492 |
| Restructuring charges | –0– | –0– | –0– | –0– | –0– | (1,027) | (311) |
| Special gains | –0– | –0– | –0– | –0– | –0– | 850 | 50 |
| Average common shares outstanding | 10,282 | 10,426 | 10,659 | 10,833 | 10,797 | 10,953 | 10,905 |
| Earnings per share | $ 0.41 | $ 0.42 | $ 0.40 | $ 0.36 | $ 0.31 | $ 0.19 | $ 0.22 |

Restructuring charges include such items as the costs of employee severance packages and plant closings, as well as losses sustained on shuttered business units. Special gains include profits from the sale of business units, properties, or investments. Restructuring charges and special gains are both included in earnings available for common shares.

**Required:**

1. What would its EPS have been each year if GE had not recorded any of the special gains shown in the table?

2. What would its EPS have been each year if GE had not recorded any of the restructuring charges shown in the table?

3. How do the EPS amounts from requirements 1 and 2 compare to the company's reported EPS amounts? Why might an analyst conclude that GE has engaged in earnings management?

4. Companies can smooth their reported EPS in several ways. One approach is to orchestrate the timing of gains and losses. What other ways can EPS be managed?

---

Hershey Foods Corporation manufactures and sells consumer food products including chocolate bars, chocolate drink mixes, refrigerated puddings, beverages, pasta, cough drops, and jelly beans. In August 1995, the company repurchased 9,049,773 shares of common stock from a single stockholder—Milton Hershey School Trust—for $500 million. This stock buyback plus other repurchases that year reduced shareholders' equity by 25%.

Excerpts from Hershey Foods' 1995 annual report follow:

**P15-10**

Identifying stock buyback incentives

As of December 31, 1995, the Corporation had 530,000,000 authorized shares of capital stock. Of this total, 450,000,000 shares were designated as Common Stock, 75,000,000 shares as Class B Common Stock (Class B Stock), and 5,000,000 shares as Preferred Stock, each class having a par value of one dollar per share. As of December 31, 1995, a combined total of 89,975,436 shares of both classes of common stock had been issued, of which 77,265,883 shares were outstanding. No shares of the Preferred Stock were issued or outstanding during the three-year period ended December 31, 1995.

Holders of the Common Stock and the Class B Stock generally vote together without regard to class on matters submitted to stockholders, including the election of directors, with the Common Stock having one vote per share and the Class B stock having ten votes per share. However, the Common Stock, voting separately as a class, is entitled to elect one-sixth of the Board of Directors. With respect to dividend rights, the Common Stock is entitled to cash dividends 10% higher than those declared and paid on the Class B Stock . . . Class B Stock can be converted into Common Stock on a share-for-share basis at any time.

Hershey Trust Company, as Trustee for the benefit of Milton Hershey School . . . and as direct owner of investment shares . . . was entitled to cast approximately 76% of the total votes of both classes of the Corporation's common stock [as of December 31, 1995]. The Milton Hershey School Trust must approve the issuance of shares of Common Stock or any other action which would result in the Milton Hershey School Trust not continuing to have voting control of the Corporation.

In August 1995, the Corporation purchased an additional 9,049,773 shares of its Common Stock to be held as Treasury Stock from the Milton Hershey School Trust for $500.0 million. In connection with the share repurchase program begun in 1993, a total of 2,000,000 shares were also acquired from the Milton Hershey School Trust in 1993 for approximately $103.1 million.

| | Years Ended December 31 | |
|---|---|---|
| ($ in thousands) | 1995 | 1994 |
| Cash flows from operating activities | $494,929 | $337,306 |
| Common stock book value | $137,707 | $139,802 |
| Treasury stock book value | $685,076 | $158,711 |
| Common shares outstanding | 74,733.9 | 74,679.4 |
| Class B shares outstanding | 15,241.4 | 15,242.9 |
| | 89,975.3 | 89,922.3 |
| Treasury shares held | 12,709.5 | 3,187.1 |

**Required:**

1. Why did Hershey issue two classes of common stock? Both types have a $1 par value. Do they have the same market price?

2. On the basis of the 1995 year-end balance sheet amounts, compute the average price per share that Hershey received for its common and Class B shares.

3. Compute the average price Hershey paid for treasury stock held at the end of 1994. How does this price compare to the average price paid for treasury shares held at the end of 1995?

4. What per share price did Hershey pay for the shares it bought back from Milton Hershey School Trust in 1995 and in 1993?

5. Why did the company buy back its shares? What are some other reasons companies repurchase their common stock?

6. As a credit analyst, how would you react to the company's announcement of its 1995 stock buyback?

---

**P15-11**

Preferred stock and credit analysis

AT&T Wireless Services was once one of the largest wireless communication—think "cell phones"—service providers in the United States. Information from its 2002 annual report to shareholders follows:

| | December 31 | |
|---|---|---|
| ($ in millions) | 2002 | 2001 |
| Long-term debt | $ 6,705 | $ 2,547 |
| Preferred stock | 7,644 | 3,000 |
| Common stockholders' equity | 19,281 | 21,887 |
| Total stockholders' equity | $26,925 | $24,887 |
| Net income before interest and taxes | $972 | $771 |
| Interest expense | $386 | $ 85 |
| Long-term debt/total equity | 0.25 | 0.10 |
| Times interest earned | 2.52 | 9.07 |

The company's preferred stock pays dividends at the rate of 8% annually.

**Required:**

1. Suppose that the increase in the preferred stock account was due to the issuance of new preferred shares at par on January 1, 2002. What journal entry would the company make on the date to record the new preferred stock?

2. What journal entry would the company make to record preferred dividends for 2002 and for 2001?

3. Suppose that AT&T Wireless had issued 8% debt (at par) rather than *any* preferred stock. What general journal entry would the company make to record interest on the debt for 2002 and for 2001?

4. Compute the company's long-term debt-to-total-equity ratio and its interest coverage ratio for 2002 and 2001 *as if* AT&T Wireless had issued 8% debt rather than preferred stock.

5. Lenders generally do not restrict a company's ability to raise more equity capital. That's because the dollars raised from selling stock provide a cash cushion that protects the lender's debt claim. Under what conditions might lenders want to limit a company's ability to issue preferred stock?

6. How would the preferred stock be shown on the company's balance sheet if the shares contained a mandatory redemption feature?

Kadri Corporation reported basic EPS of $3.00 and diluted EPS of $2.40 for 2008. Its EPS calculations follow:

**P15-12**

Calculating comprehensive EPS

| | EPS Calculation for 2008 | |
| --- | --- | --- |
| | **Numerator** | **Denominator** |
| Net income | $3,500,000 | |
| Less dividend on 10% convertible preferred stock | (500,000) | |
| Weighted-average common shares outstanding | | 1,000,000 |
| **Basic EPS = $3.00** | $3,000,000 | 1,000,000 |
| Stock option dilution | — | 33,334 |
| Series A convertible debt dilution | 240,000 | 250,000 |
| Series B convertible debt dilution | 300,000 | 200,000 |
| 10% Convertible preferred stock dilution | 500,000 | 200,000 |
| **Diluted EPS = $2.40** | $4,040,000 | 1,683,334 |

It issued the convertible preferred stock at the beginning of 2008 and the Series A and Series B convertible debt at par in late 2007. No stock options were granted or exercised in 2008.

**Required:**

1. The convertible preferred stock has a $100 par value per share. How many preferred shares were issued, and what was the common stock conversion rate for each preferred share?

2. The Series B convertible debt pays interest at 10% annually, and Kadri's marginal income tax rate for 2008 was 40%. How much Series B debt was outstanding, and what is the common stock conversion rate for each $1,000 face Series B bond?

3. What are the interest rate and common stock conversion rate for the $5 million par of Series A debt?

4. During the year, 50,000 shares were under option, and the average exercise price was $20 per share. What was the average market price of the company's common stock during 2008?

5. Explain why Series A debt carries a lower interest rate than Series B debt although both were issued at par on the same day in 2007.

Trask Corporation, a public company whose shares are traded in the over-the-counter market, had the following stockholders' equity account balances at December 31, 2007:

**P15-13**

Analyzing stockholders' equity

**AICPA**
ADAPTED

| | |
| --- | --- |
| Common stock | $ 7,875,000 |
| Additional paid-in capital | 15,750,000 |
| Retained earnings | 16,445,000 |
| Treasury common stock | 750,000 |

Transactions during 2008 and other information relating to the stockholders' equity accounts follow:

- As of January 1, 2008, Trask had 4,000,000 authorized shares of $5 par-value common stock; it had issued 1,575,000 shares of which 75,000 were held in treasury.

- On January 21, 2008, Trask issued 50,000 shares of $100 par value, 6% cumulative preferred stock at par in exchange for all of Rover Company's assets and liabilities. On that date, the net carrying amount of Rover's assets and liabilities equaled their fair values. On January 22, 2008, Rover distributed the Trask shares to its stockholders in a complete liquidation and dissolution of Rover. Trask had 150,000 authorized shares of preferred stock.

- On February 17, 2008, Trask formally retired 25,000 of 75,000 treasury common stock shares. The shares were originally issued at $15 per share and had been acquired on September 25, 2007 for $10 per share.

- Trask owned 15,000 shares of Harbor, Inc. common stock purchased in 2007 for $600,000. The Harbor stock shares were trading securities. On March 5, 2008, Trask declared a property dividend of one share of Harbor common stock for every 100 shares of Trask common stock held by a stockholder of record on April 16, 2008. Harbor stock's market price on March 5, 2008 was $60 per share. The property dividend was distributed on April 29, 2008.

- On January 2, 2006, Trask granted stock options to employees to purchase 200,000 shares of the company's common stock at $12 per share, which was also the market price on that date. The options had a grant date fair value of $1.50 per share and are exercisable within a three-year period, beginning January 2, 2008. On June 1, 2008, employees exercised 150,000 options when the stock's market value was $25 per share. Trask issued new shares to settle the transaction.

- On October 27, 2008, Trask declared a two-for-one stock split on its common stock and reduced the per share par value accordingly. Trask stockholders of record on August 2, 2008 received one additional share of Trask common stock for each share of Trask common stock held. The laws of Trask's state of incorporation protect treasury stock from dilution.

- On December 12, 2008, Trask declared the yearly cash dividend on preferred stock, payable on January 11, 2009 to stockholders of record on December 31, 2008.

- On January 16, 2009 before the accounting records were closed for 2008, Trask learned that depreciation expense had been understated by $350,000 for the year ended December 31, 2007. The after-tax effect on 2007 net income was $245,000. The appropriate correcting entry was recorded on the same day.

  Net income for 2008 was $2,400,000.

**Required:**

1. Prepare Trask's statement of retained earnings for the year ended December 31, 2008.

2. Prepare the stockholders' equity section of Trask's balance sheet at December 31, 2008.

3. Compute the book value per share of common stock at December 31, 2008.

---

**P15-14**

Stockholders' equity

Nike Inc. is one of the world's largest sellers of athletic footwear and athletic apparel. The following information is from Nike's annual report for the year ended May 31, 2002.

### Note 7: Redeemable Preferred Stock

NIAC is the sole owner of the Company's authorized Redeemable Preferred Stock, $1 par value, which is redeemable at the option of NIAC or the Company at par value aggregating $0.3 million.

### Note 8: Common Stock

The authorized number of shares of Class A Common Stock, no par value, and Class B Common Stock, no par value, are 110 million and 350 million, respectively. Each share of Class A Common Stock is convertible into one share of Class B Common Stock. Voting rights of Class B Common Stock are limited in certain circumstances with respect to the election of directors.

## From the Balance Sheet

Class A Convertible Common Stock—98.1 and 99.1 million shares outstanding at May 31, 2002 and 2001, respectively. Class B Common Stock—168.0 and 169.5 million shares outstanding at May 31, 2002 and 2001, respectively.

## From the Statement of Cash Flow

|  | Years Ended May 31 | | |
| --- | --- | --- | --- |
| ($ in millions) | 2002 | 2001 | 2000 |
| **Cash provided by operations:** | | | |
| Net earnings | $ 663.3 | $ 589.7 | $ 579.1 |
| Adjustments | 417.2 | 66.8 | 120.5 |
| Net cash provided by operating activities | $1,080.5 | $ 656.5 | $ 699.6 |
| **Cash provided (used) by investing activities:** | $ (302.8) | $(342.3) | $(440.0) |
| **Cash used by financing activities:** | | | |
| Proceeds from long-term debt issuance | $ 329.9 | $  0.0 | $ 505.1 |
| Reductions in long-term debt | (511.8) | (119.2) | (1.7) |
| Proceeds from exercise of stock options | 59.5 | 56.0 | 23.9 |
| Repurchase of stock | (226.9) | (157.0) | (646.3) |
| Dividends—common and preferred | (128.9) | (129.7) | (133.1) |
| Net cash provided (used) by financing activities | $ (478.2) | $(349.9) | $(252.1) |

### Required: Part A

1. How many shares of redeemable preferred stock were outstanding on May 31, 2002? What is the par value of each share of preferred stock?

2. Suppose that Nike had sold 10,000 shares of preferred stock for $25 per share on June 1, 2002. Prepare the journal entry to record this sale of preferred stock.

3. Assume the preferred stock described in requirement 2 pays a $0.10 per share annual dividend on May 15 each year. Prepare the journal entry to record the dividend payment on May 15, 2002.

4. How many shares of common stock were outstanding on May 31, 2002?

5. Explain why the number of shares outstanding might differ from the number of shares authorized or the number issued.

6. Why do some companies issue two classes of common stock?

7. Did Nike issue any common stock in the year ended May 31, 2002? Why?

### Required: Part B

Ignore your answers to all of Part A; instead assume the following hypothetical situation:

- Nike had 14,750,000 shares outstanding at the end of May 2002. On this date, the balance in (a) the Common stock account was $147,500, (b) the Additional-paid-in capital account was $2,282,000, and (c) the Retained earnings account was $226,069,000.

- All cash dividends are paid in the year they are declared. Cash dividends in millions were $14.080, $240.830, and $0 in 2005, 2004, and 2003, respectively.

- Net income in millions was $50.059, $49.589, and $45.080 for 2005, 2004, and 2003, respectively.

- During the year ended May 31, 2004, the company issued 17,250,000 common shares to the public as a stock dividend.

Determine the balances of Common stock, Additional paid-in capital, and Retained earnings accounts for the years ended May 31, 2003, 2004, and 2005, respectively.

**P15-15**

Adopting *SFAS No. 123R*

The following excerpt is from Ball Corporation's 2006 annual report.

Effective January 1, 2006, the company adopted SFAS No. 123 (revised 2004), "Share-Based Payment," and elected to use the . . . Black–Scholes valuation model. Tax benefits associated with option exercises are reported in financing activities in the consolidated statements of cash flows beginning in 2006. Prior to January 1, 2006, expense related to stock options was calculated using the intrinsic value method under the guidelines of Accounting Principles Board (APB) Opinion No. 25, and has therefore not been included in the consolidated statements of earnings in 2005 and 2004. Ball's earnings as reported included after-tax stock-based compensation of $6.6 million and $12.5 million for the years ended December 31, 2005 and 2004, respectively. If the fair value based method had been used, after-tax stock-based compensation would have been $8.7 million in 2005 and $9.3 million in 2004. . . . The adoption of SFAS No. 123 (revised 2004) resulted in higher stock-based compensation in 2006 of $6.3 million compared to 2005.

**Required:**

1. Explain why Ball recorded $6.6 million of stock-based compensation expense in 2005 although the company was using the intrinsic value method.

2. What was the approximate fair value of the 2005 and 2004 stock option awards?

3. Some firms reduced the value of their 2006 stock option awards compared to earlier years or curtailed their use of stock options entirely. What is the accounting reason for these actions?

4. Does it appear that Ball reduced the value of its 2006 stock option awards?

5. Explain where Ball reported the "tax benefits associated with option exercises" prior to the beginning of 2006.

**P15-16**

Adopting *SFAS No. 150*

The following excerpts are taken from the 2006 annual report of J. Crew Group, Inc.

At January 29, 2005 and January 28, 2006, 92,800 shares of Series A preferred stock and 32,500 shares of Series B preferred stock were issued and outstanding. Dividends compound to the extent not paid in cash. . . . On October 17, 2009, Group is required to redeem the Series B preferred stock and to pay all accumulated but unpaid dividends on the Series A preferred stock.

Effective at the beginning of the third quarter of 2003, the Company adopted SFAS No. 150, "Accounting for Certain Financial Instruments with Characteristics of Both Liabilities and Equity." This pronouncement required the reclassification to long-term debt of the liquidation value of Group Series B preferred stock and the related accumulated and unpaid dividends and the accumulated and unpaid dividends related to the Series A preferred stock since these amounts are required to be redeemed in October 2009. The preferred dividends related to . . . the Series B preferred stock and to the accumulated and unpaid dividends of the Series A and Series B preferred stock . . . are included in interest expense. The Series A preferred stock is only redeemable in certain circumstances (including a change in control at Group) and does not qualify for reclassification under SFAS No. 150. Accordingly, the dividends related to the Series A preferred stock are deducted from stockholders' deficit.

**Required:**

1. Explain why it makes sense that J. Crew Group is required to include its Series B preferred stock among long-term debt on the balance sheet.

2. Where on J. Crew's balance sheet was this debt shown prior to the company's adoption of *SFAS No. 150?*

3. Explain why it makes sense to include the dividends paid on Series B preferred stock as part of interest expense.

4. Where is the Series A preferred stock shown on the company's balance sheet?

5. Why does J. Crew use a different accounting treatment for Series A preferred stock and Series B preferred?

6. What impact (if any) has *SFAS No. 150* had on the popularity of mandatorily redeemable preferred stock as a corporate financing device?

---

Amazon.com, Inc. is the world's leading online retailer selling books, music, DVDs, videos, toys, electronics, software, video games, and home improvement products. The following footnote appeared in the company's 1999 annual report:

The company follows the intrinsic value method in accounting for its stock options. Had compensation cost been recognized based on the fair value at the date of grant for options granted in 1999, 1998 and 1997, the pro forma amounts of the Company's net loss and net loss per share for the years ended December 31, 1999, 1998 and 1997 would have been as follows:

| | For the Years Ended December 31 | | |
|---|---|---|---|
| ($ in thousands, except per share data) | 1999 | 1998 | 1997 |
| Net loss—as reported | $ (719,968) | $(124,546) | $(31,020) |
| Net loss—pro forma | (1,031,925) | (194,269) | (35,983) |
| Basic and diluted loss per share—as reported | $ (2.20) | $ (0.84) | $ (0.24) |
| Basic and diluted loss per share—pro forma | (3.16) | (1.31) | (0.28) |

The fair value for each option granted was estimated at the date of grant using a Black–Scholes option pricing model, assuming no expected dividends and the following weighted average assumptions:

| | For the Year Ended December 31 | | |
|---|---|---|---|
| | 1999 | 1998 | 1997 |
| Average risk-free interest rates | 5.5% | 4.7% | 6.3% |
| Average expected life (in years) | 3.5% | 3.0% | 3.0% |
| Volatility | 84.9% | 81.6% | 50.0% |

The weighted average fair value of options granted during 1999, 1998 and 1997 was $43.36, $19.07 and $2.07, respectively, for options granted with exercise prices at the current fair value of the underlying stock. During 1998 and 1997, some options were granted with exercise prices that were below the current fair value of the underlying stock. The weighted average fair value of options granted with exercise prices below the current fair value of the underlying stock during 1998 and 1997 was $4.61 and $0.55, respectively. Compensation expense that is recognized in providing pro forma disclosures might not be representative of the effects on pro forma earnings for future years because *SFAS No. 123* does not apply to stock option grants made prior to 1995.

**Required:**

1. Why do you think Amazon.com uses the intrinsic value *(APB Opinion No. 25)* method of accounting for employee stock options rather than the fair value method allowed in *SFAS No. 123?*

2. The footnote states that, during 1998 and 1997, some options were granted with exercise prices below the grant-date market price of Amazon.com stock. What impact (if any) did these awards have on compensation expense?

3. The average exercise price for employee stock options granted in 1999 was $63.60. Suppose that Amazon.com's stock now trades at only $30 per share. Are the options worthless?

4. Some companies "reprice" their stock options when the exercise price gets too high. As a shareholder, do you favor repricing the Amazon.com options so that the exercise price is $30? Why or why not?

## C15-2

Accounting Rule *SFAS No. 150*:
Tripping Up X-Rite

### STANDARD LEADS TO CHARGES, END OF RETIRED FOUNDERS' SHARE-REPURCHASE PLAN

The octogenarian founders of X-Rite Inc. spend less time these days on the golf course and more with estate planners, thanks to an accounting standard introduced last year.

This same accounting standard also led to charges against earnings, investor confusion and, ultimately, the scrapping of a share-repurchase plan for those retired founders of the company, which makes hardware and software that allows paint manufacturers, the dental industry and other customers to match colors.

At issue is a perhaps unintended consequence of the Financial Accounting Standards Board's FAS 150, a guideline introduced by the accounting rule maker in May 2003.

The idea behind FAS 150 was to make sure companies properly account for certain types of preferred securities whose popularity has soared in recent years, in part because they allow companies to raise money without having to show more debt on their books.

Historically these securities were placed on corporate balance sheets in a kind of no-man's land between liabilities and equity. Under FAS 150, companies classify them as liabilities and account for dividend payments and changes in their value in the income statement—as part of profit or loss—under "interest expense."

Here's how FAS 150 tripped up X-Rite: In 1998, the company agreed it would repurchase 4.5 million shares owned by its six aging founders after they and their spouses die. Management's intent was to protect the illiquid stock from plummeting as a result of large share sales in the future by heirs cashing in to cover hefty estate taxes.

At the same time, X-Rite management took out insurance policies to cover the cost of buying back the shares, at prices that were capped and floored in the agreements. X-Rite paid monthly premiums on policies that would fund the future repurchases under the agreement plus extra repurchases should the heirs require.

Prior to FAS 150, X-Rite classified the value of the founders' shares on its balance sheet as a separate line-item titled "temporary shareholders' investment"—an equity instrument, in other words. The company "marked to market" those shares under that heading. The insurance policies were classified under "other assets" and reflected the accumulation of cash from X-Rite's premium payments. Neither entry had any impact on the income statement.

Starting in the third quarter of 2003, however, a new X-Rite management team started classifying the shares as long-term liabilities to comply with FAS 150. Changes in the value of the shares flowed through as interest expense.

But as X-Rite's share price started to rise under new management and better earnings, so too did the value of its founders' shares—and the company's interest expense.

In the fourth quarter of 2003, X-Rite took an interest-expense charge of $657,000 directly related to a rise in the value of the founders' shares from the start of the year. In the first quarter of 2004, the charge climbed another $4.77 million; in the second quarter, another $3.64 million hit.

In just three quarters, X-Rite took charges of more than $9 million in interest expense on the founders' shares, and the company posted net losses in two of those quarters. While these charges hit its bottom line as required by FAS 150, the fact that X-Rite had ample insurance to cover the liabilities was only evident on the balance sheet, not on the income statement, where most investors' eyes are glued.

"This made it look like we don't have a hedged transaction, but we did because we had an insurance policy out there," says Mary Chowning, X-Rite's chief financial officer. "If you're going to move toward fair-value accounting, you have to do it for everything."

By the third quarter of this year, Ms. Chowning says, she was spending more than one-third of her time trying to explain the founders' agreements to shareholders. She worried the "hairy problem" would keep X-Rite from attracting more institutional investors. The company's share price began to sag.

Finally, this month Ms. Chowning persuaded X-Rite's founders to unwind the agreements, and to improve their estate planning. While the company now has an overhang of founders' shares, "we traded one problem for a lesser problem," she says.

FAS 150 is another step in FASB's march toward fair-value accounting, which values companies' financial assets at current market prices rather than their original cost. While FASB deliberates over future fair-value standards, companies like X-Rite can find themselves trapped between a mix of valuations—some at fair value, some at historical cost, and some in-between—as balance sheets evolve.

"That's the balance sheet we're currently living with," says David Zion, an accounting analyst at CSFB in New York. "FASB is moving more of that balance sheet to fair value, but in the meantime, that's what we deal with every single day."

*(continued)*

**Required:**

1. Explain why *SFAS No. 150* requires X-Rite to classify its founders' shares as part of long-term debt rather than stockholders' equity.

2. How did the company "hedge" its financial obligation to buy back shares from its founders? (You may want to consult Chapter 11.) Based on the information provided in the news clip, was the hedge fully effective?

3. Why does it make sense that X-Rite was required to use mark-to-market accounting for its stock repurchase financial obligation?

4. Assuming that the hedge was fully effective, explain how mark-to-market accounting produced so much earnings volatility at X-Rite.

5. How has GAAP changed since 2004 in ways that would have allowed X-Rite to avoid the earnings volatility created by *SFAS No. 150?*

---

Several years ago, RJR Nabisco Holdings Corporation (Holdings) offered for sale 93 million shares of its subsidiary RN-Nabisco Group. According to the prospectus, the estimated initial public offering price for RN-Nabisco common stock would be in the range of $17 to $19 per share. Holdings hoped to raise about $1.7 billion from the stock offering and to use the proceeds to reduce its debt burden. But investors weren't buying—at least not at the prospectus price—and Holdings scuttled the stock offer 23 days after it was first announced.

At the time, the Nabisco Group was one of the world's leading packaged foods businesses with sales of more than $6.7 billion. The Group's Nabisco Biscuit Division was the largest cookie and cracker manufacturer and marketer in the United States with eight of the nine top-selling brands.

Holdings was comprised of the Nabisco Group and the Reynolds Group, which included the R.J. Reynolds Tobacco Company, the second largest manufacturer of cigarettes. The Reynolds Group's net sales as a percentage of Holdings' total consolidated net sales were 57%. Holdings was formed in 1989 when its predecessor company—RJR Nabisco, Inc. (RJRN)—was taken private in a leveraged buyout transaction. Holdings was taken public again in 1991 with the buyout group retaining 49% of Holdings' stock.

The plan at the time was to split off Nabisco Group from Reynolds Group and thereby improve the company's share price. Holdings had seen its stock price fall 36% that year for two reasons: R.J. Reynolds' earnings had been hurt by a brutal cigarette price war that began in early April, and investors had become increasingly concerned about the uncertainty over tobacco liability.

**The Proposal**

The Nabisco stock offered to the public would initially represent 25% of the equity of the Nabisco Group. The Reynolds Group would retain the balance of Nabisco's equity. Each outstanding share of common stock of Holdings would be redesignated into a common share of Reynolds stock, which was intended to reflect separately the performance of the Reynolds Group as well as the retained interest of the Reynolds Group in the Nabisco Group.

**C15-3**

**RN Nabisco Group: Calculating dividends and agency costs**

The offering prospectus described the company's dividend policy as:

The Board of Directors of Holdings currently intends to pay regular quarterly dividends on the Nabisco Stock in an aggregate annual amount equal to approximately 45% of the prior year's earnings of Holdings attributable to the outstanding Nabisco Stock. Consistent with this policy, Holdings currently intends to pay in the fourth quarter of 1993 an initial regular quarterly dividend of $0.13 per share of Nabisco Stock. While the Board of Directors does not currently intend to change such initial quarterly dividend rate or dividend policy, it reserves the right to do so at any time and from time to time. Under the Certificate of Incorporation and Delaware law, the Board of Directors is not required to pay dividends in accordance with such policy.

Dividends on the Nabisco Stock are limited by the Certificate of Incorporation and will be payable when, as and if declared by the Board of Directors out of the lessor of (i) the Available Nabisco Dividend Amount and (ii) funds of Holdings legally available therefore. Payment of dividends on the Nabisco Stock is also subject to the prior payment of dividends on the outstanding shares of Preferred Stock of Holdings (and any new class or series of capital stock of Holdings with similar preferential dividend provisions) and to restrictions contained in the Credit Agreements and certain other debt instruments of RJRN. . . . The "Available Nabisco Dividend Amount" is similar to that amount that would be legally available for the payment of dividends on Nabisco Stock under Delaware law if the Nabisco Group were a separate company, and will be increased or decreased as appropriate by, among other things, Holdings Earnings Attributable to the Nabisco Group. "Holdings Earnings Attributable to the Nabisco Group," for any period, means the net income or loss of the Nabisco Group during such period determined in accordance with generally accepted accounting principles (including income and expenses of Holdings allocated to the Nabisco Group on a substantially consistent basis). . . .

Holdings has never paid any cash dividends on shares of Common Stock. . . . The Board of Directors currently intends to pay future quarterly "pass-through" dividends on the Reynolds Stock with respect to the Reynolds Group's Retained Interest in the Nabisco Group. Holdings currently intends to pay in the fourth quarter of 1993 an initial quarterly pass-through dividend of approximately $0.03 per share of Reynolds Stock. . . . Subject to [certain limitations], the Board of Directors would be able, in its sole discretion, to declare and pay dividends exclusively on the Nabisco Stock or exclusively on the Reynolds Stock, or on both, in equal or unequal amounts, notwithstanding the respective amount of funds available for dividends on each series, the amount of prior dividends declared on each series or any other factor.

**Required:**
As a potential investor in Nabisco Group stock, what agency problems do you face that are not present when you buy common stock in most other companies?

## COLLABORATIVE LEARNING CASE

### C15-4

Classifying as equity or debt

**Collaborative**

**[A] Aon Corporation's Mezzanine Preferred Stock**
In its 2002 annual report to shareholders, Aon Corporation described its mandatorily redeemable preferred stock as follows:

In January 1997, Aon created Aon Capital A, a wholly-owned statutory business trust, for the purpose of issuing mandatorily redeemable preferred capital securities (Capital Securities). The sole asset of Aon Capital A is $726 million aggregate principal amount of Aon's 8.205% Junior Subordinated Deferrable Interest Debentures due January 1, 2027.

Aon Capital A issued $800 million of 8.205% Capital Securities in January 1997. The Capital Securities are subject to mandatory redemption on January 1, 2027 or are redeemable in whole, but not in part, at the option of Aon upon the occurrence of certain events. . . . During 2002, approximately $98 million of the Capital Securities were repurchased on the open market for $87 million, excluding accrued interest. . . .

Aon's 2002 balance sheet showed the following amounts:

| ($ *millions*) **Liabilities and Stockholders' Equity** | **2002** | **2001** |
|---|---|---|
| Insurance premiums payable | $9,904 | $8,233 |
| Insurance policy liabilities | 5,310 | 4,990 |
| General liabilities | | |
| General expenses | 2,012 | 1,770 |
| Short-term borrowings | 117 | 257 |
| Notes payable | 1,671 | 1,694 |
| Other liabilities | 1,673 | 1,071 |
| **Total Liabilities** | 20,687 | 18,015 |
| Redeemable Preferred Stock | 50 | 50 |
| Mandatorily Redeemable Preferred Capital Securities | 702 | 800 |
| **Total Common Stockholders' Equity** | 3,895 | 3,465 |

**Required:**

1. Aon's capital securities are forms of preferred stock. Assume that Aon Capital A (the trustee) issued the securities on January 1, 1997 for $800 million cash, the same day that Aon Corporation issued $800 million of its junior debentures to the trust. Describe the cash flows associated with these two transactions—that is, explain who received cash and who gave up cash in each case.

2. One year later (on December 31, 1997), Aon Corporation must pay 8.205% interest to debt holders, and Aon Capital A must pay an 8.205% dividend to preferred stockholders. Describe the cash flows associated with each of these payments—that is, explain who received cash, who gave up cash, and how much cash was exchanged.

3. For financial reporting purposes, how will Aon Corporation show its cash interest payment on December 31, 1997?

4. Why did Aon Corporation create Aon Capital A?

5. Why does Aon Corporation's 2002 balance sheet show the capital securities in the "mezzanine" section between total liabilities and stockholders' equity?

6. Aon Corporation is an insurance company, so most of its liabilities relate to insurance policy premiums and policy liabilities. The company's debt includes Short-term borrowings and Notes payable. Compute Aon's debt-to-equity ratio for 2002 assuming that the capital securities are treated as part of equity. Repeat the calculation, this time assuming that the capital securities are part of debt. Which debt-to-equity ratio provides the most accurate measure of the company's true debt and equity position? Why?

## [B] Cephalon Inc.'s Zero-Coupon, Zero Yield-to-Maturity Convertible Notes

In June 2003, Cephalon Inc. issued $750 million of zero-coupon convertible notes. Because the notes were issued at par, meaning that Cephalon received $750 million cash for the notes, they have a zero yield-to-maturity. Here is what Cephalon said about the notes:

On June 11, 2003, we issued and sold in a private placement $750.0 million of Zero Coupon Convertible Subordinated Notes (the "Notes"). The interest rate on the Notes is zero and the Notes will not accrete interest. . . . The Notes are subordinate to our existing and future senior indebtedness. The Notes were issued in two tranches and have the following salient terms:

- $375.0 million of Zero Coupon Convertible Subordinated Notes due June 15, 2023 . . . are convertible prior to maturity, subject to certain conditions described below, into shares of our common stock at a conversion price of $59.50 per share (a conversion rate of approximately 16.8067 shares per $1,000 principal amount of notes). . . .

- $375.0 million of Zero Coupon Convertible Subordinated Notes due June 15, 2023 . . . are convertible prior to maturity, subject to certain conditions described below, into shares of our common stock at a conversion price of $56.50 per share (a conversion rate of approximately 17.6691 shares per $1,000 principal amount of notes). . . .

The Notes also contain a restricted convertibility feature that does not affect the conversion price of the notes but, instead, places restrictions on a holder's ability to convert their notes into shares of our common stock ("conversion shares"). A holder may convert the notes if one or more of the following conditions is satisfied:

- if, on the trading day prior to the date of surrender, the closing sale price of our common stock is more than 120% of the applicable conversion price per share (the "conversion price premium");
- if we have called the notes for redemption;
- if the average trading prices of the notes for a specified period is less than 100% of the average of the conversion values of the notes during that period . . . ;
- if we make certain significant distributions to our holders of common stock or we enter into specified corporate transactions.

Because of the inclusion of the restricted convertibility feature of the Notes, our diluted income per common share calculation does not give effect to the dilution from the conversion of the Notes until our share price exceeds the 20% conversion price premium or one of the other conditions above is satisfied.

*Source:* 10-Q filing for Cephalon Inc., June 2003.

**Required:**

1. What accounting entry did Cephalon make to record the proceeds received from issuing the notes on June 11, 2003? Over the next year, what other accounting entries (if any) related to these notes did the company make?

2. The notes mature in 2023, approximately 20 years from the date they were issued. At a 6% rate of annual interest, the present value of $1,000 to be received 20 years from today is only $311.805. (You might want to verify this conclusion.) Suppose that Cephalon's true cost of borrowing money is 6% per year. How much did note holders pay for Cephalon debt, and how much did they pay for the option to convert the notes into shares of common stock?

3. Suppose that Cephalon separated the notes into debt and equity components and then recorded each component separately. What accounting entry would the company make to record the proceeds received from issuing the notes on June 11, 2003? Over the next year, what other accounting entries (if any) related to these notes would the company make?

4. Describe Cephalon's financial reporting advantages of issuing zero-coupon, zero yield-to-maturity notes rather than a more traditional debt instrument. Why aren't the notes included in the company's computation of diluted earnings per share?

5. If Cephalon were to issue those same notes today, would it still be able to use the accounting entries outlined in your answer to requirement 1?

**.mhhe.com/revsine4e**

**Remember to check the book's companion Web site for additional study material.**

# Intercorporate Equity Investments | 16

One company buys equity shares in another company to earn an investment return or to improve its competitive position. When a company buys equity shares for investment purposes, its return comes from share price increases and dividends. But when a company buys shares to improve its competitive position, its return comes from increased operating profits and growth. A company that owns shares in another company that is a supplier or customer gains influence over that company as well as access to new markets or increased production capacity.

Under existing GAAP, the method of accounting for intercorporate investments depends on the size of the ownership share of the investor corporation. Does the investor own a controlling financial interest in the other company? As we will see, the ownership proportion is used to infer the purpose of the investment.

We first discuss noncontrolling (minority) ownership cases in which the corporate investor owns less than 50% of the voting shares of another company. Then we analyze controlling financial ownership (more than 50%), and we look at the special reporting problems created by subsidiaries in foreign countries. See Figure 16.1 for a depiction of the financial reporting methods used under different percentage ownership conditions.

## NONCONTROLLING (MINORITY) OWNERSHIP

Share ownership usually entitles the shareholder (corporate investor) to vote at the company's shareholder meetings. Shareholders vote to elect company directors and approve or reject proposals put forth by management or shareholders. Management asks shareholders to approve the company's outside auditor, proposed mergers and buyouts, compensation plan changes, and corporate charter amendments. Shareholder proposals often address environmental, social, and political issues such as prohibiting the company from doing business in unfavored countries.

Each share of **common stock** usually entitles the owner to one vote, but those who own **preferred stock** usually have no voting rights. There are exceptions. Some companies issue dual-class common stock (often denoted Common A and Common B) in which one class has voting rights and the other does not. In addition, some companies do issue voting preferred stock.

A "one share, one vote" rule governs shareholder voting procedures in most companies. This means that each shareholder's influence over the company is proportional to the shares (votes) owned. A shareholder who owns **controlling financial interest**—one who owns more than 50% of the

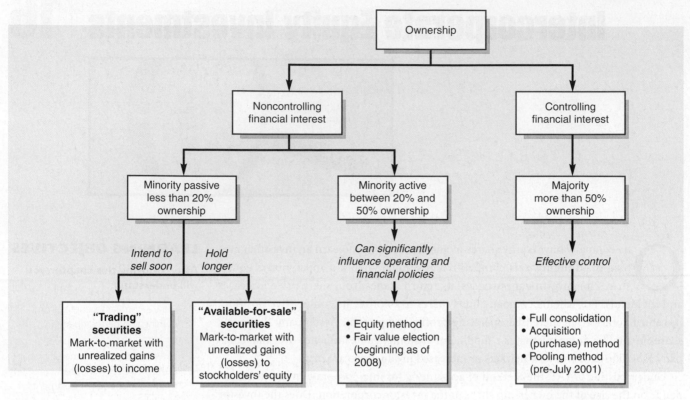

**Figure 16.1** FINANCIAL REPORTING ALTERNATIVES FOR INTERCORPORATE EQUITY INVESTMENTS

voting stock—can often dictate the company's business strategy and its major operating, investment, and financing decisions. A **noncontrolling (minority)** investor—one who owns less than 50% of the voting stock—has less influence over the company but still may be able to elect a corporate director or gain management's ear.

For financial reporting purposes, **noncontrolling financial interests** fall into one of two categories: **minority passive** investments—those in which the shareholder has no ability to influence the acquired company's operating and financial policies; or **minority active** investments—those in which the ownership percentage is large enough for the acquiring shareholder to influence the acquired company's operating and financing decisions. Consider these examples: Owning a single share of stock is a minority passive investment, but owning 40% of the company's voting shares is a minority active investment. Deciding where to draw the line between passive and active minority investments can be difficult, as we shall see.

## Minority Passive Investments: Mark-to-Market Accounting

When one company owns a small proportion of another company's voting shares, it's safe to presume that the investment is made for speculation—that is, the investor hopes to earn a return from dividends and share price increases. We may presume this because owning a small proportion of a public company does not convey the power to elect directors or influence the company's operating policies. The investor company hopes to earn a return on cash not currently needed in its own business. Existing GAAP presumes that ownership of less than 20% of another company's voting shares constitutes a passive investment because owning less than 20%

of a company seldom provides the investor with an opportunity to significantly influence its activities. As in Figure 16.1, minority passive investments are classified on the investor's books in one of two ways, depending on the expected duration of the investment.[1]

Equity or debt securities that the investor intends to hold for a short time are classified as **trading securities.** They are typically purchased to generate profits on short-term differences in price and are generally actively managed to achieve trading gains.[2] All trading securities are shown on the balance sheet as current assets. Equity investments of less than 20% that are not trading securities are called **available-for-sale securities.** These securities are usually shown as noncurrent on the balance sheet. Both trading securities and available-for-sale securities are reported at fair value—current market price—not at historical cost on the balance sheet. The process of adjusting the carrying value of these securities to their market values is called **mark-to-market.**

> This category of securities can also include debt securities that the firm does not intend to hold to maturity. Appendix A to this chapter describes the procedures that firms follow to account for held-to-maturity debt securities.

### Trading Securities

Market price increases of trading securities are debited to a **market adjustment account** that is *added* to the trading securities asset account (reported at original cost). Market price decreases are credited to the same market adjustment account and *deducted* from the trading securities asset account. The offsetting credit for market price increases is made to the unrealized gain on trading securities account on the income statement; market price decreases are offset as a debit to the unrealized loss on trading securities account. An example of mark-to-market accounting for securities that Principal Financial Corporation purchased for **short-term speculation** follows:

> Mark-to-market accounting is a *requirement* for marketable securities under *SAFS No. 115*, but is an *option* that a firm may elect for minority active (equity) investments and certain other types of assets and liabilities under *SFAS No. 159*. For further discussion of fair value measurement, see Chapters 6 and 11.

## Purchases and Sales of Trading Securities by Principal Financial Corporation

| Security | Date Acquired | Acquisition Cost | Market Value December 31 | | | |
| --- | --- | --- | --- | --- | --- | --- |
| | | | 2008 | 2009 | 2010 | 2011 |
| A Company common | 1/1/08 | $10,000 | $11,000 | $13,000 | $ 14,000 | $12,000 |
| B Company preferred | 1/1/08 | 20,000 | 18,000 | 17,000 | 18,000 | * |
| C Company bonds | 7/1/09 | 30,000 | — | 26,000 | 33,000 | 34,000 |
| D Company options | 7/1/09 | 40,000 | — | 41,000 | 37,000 | 30,000 |
| | | | $29,000 | $97,000 | $102,000 | $76,000 |

\* B Company preferred stock was sold on January 1, 2011 for $18,500.

Let's first consider the entry to record the purchase of Company A common shares and Company B preferred shares on January 1, 2008:

| | | | |
| --- | --- | --- | --- |
| **DR** | Trading securities—A Company common...................... | $10,000 | |
| **DR** | Trading securities—B Company preferred...................... | 20,000 | |
| | **CR**   Cash.............................................. | | $30,000 |

---

[1] The reporting rules for minority passive investments are contained in "Accounting for Certain Investments in Debt and Equity Securities," *Statement of Financial Accounting Standards (SFAS) No. 115* (Norwalk, CT: Financial Accounting Standards Board [FASB], 1993).

[2] *SFAS No. 115*, para. 12.

Dividends on these securities are recorded as income when they are declared—if Company A declared dividends of $1,000 on December 15, 2008, the entry would be:

| **DR** | Dividends receivable . . . . . . . . . . . . . . . . . . . . . . . . . . . . . . . . . . . . . . . . . . | $1,000 | |
|---|---|---|---|
| | **CR** Dividend income . . . . . . . . . . . . . . . . . . . . . . . . . . . . . . . . . . . . . . . . . | | $1,000 |

When Principal Financial receives the cash dividend in January 2009, it will debit Cash for $1,000 and credit the Dividends receivable account for $1,000.

The 2008 year-end mark-to-market adjustment entry requires two steps:

**Step 1:** The total market value of all trading securities is compared to the total cost of the securities. Any difference becomes the **target balance** for the market adjustment account.

**Step 2:** The market adjustment account must be increased (or decreased) to equal its target balance, and then an unrealized gain (or loss) for the same amount must be recorded.

Principal Financial's 2008 year-end adjustment would be:

| Step 1 Trading Securities Portfolio | | | Step 2 Market Adjustment Account | |
|---|---|---|---|---|
| Total market value | $ 29,000 | $(1,000) | Target balance (CR) | |
| − Total cost | (30,000) | -0- | Current balance | |
| = Difference | $ (1,000) | $(1,000) | Adjustment needed (CR) | |

| **DR** | Unrealized holding loss on trading securities (income statement) . . . . . . . . . . . . . . . . . . . . . . . . . . . . . . . . . . . . . . . | $1,000 | |
|---|---|---|---|
| | **CR** Market adjustment—trading securities . . . . . . . . . . . . . . . . . . | | $1,000 |

After this entry is recorded, the balance sheet section for trading securities appears as:

| Trading securities (at cost) | $30,000 |
|---|---|
| Less: Market adjustment—trading securities | (1,000) |
| Trading securities at market | $29,000 |

Now let's look at the entry to record the purchase of Company C bonds and Company D stock options on July 1, 2009:

| **DR** | Trading securities—Company C bonds . . . . . . . . . . . . . . . . . . . . . . . | $30,000 | |
|---|---|---|---|
| **DR** | Trading securities—Company D stock options . . . . . . . . . . . . . . . . . | 40,000 | |
| | **CR** Cash . . . . . . . . . . . . . . . . . . . . . . . . . . . . . . . . . . . . . . . . . . . . . . . . | | $70,000 |

Following the two-step process, Principal Financial's 2009 year-end mark-to-market adjustment is:

| Step 1 Trading Securities Portfolio | | | Step 2 Market Adjustment Account | |
|---|---|---|---|---|
| Total market value | $ 97,000 | $(3,000) | Target balance (CR) | |
| − Total cost | (100,000) | − (1,000) | Current balance (CR) | |
| = Difference | $ (3,000) | $(2,000) | Adjustment needed (CR) | |

| **DR** | Unrealized holding loss on trading securities (income statement) . . . . . . . . . . . . . . . . . . . . . . . . . . . . . . . . . . . . . . . | $2,000 | |
|---|---|---|---|
| | **CR** Market adjustment—trading securities . . . . . . . . . . . . . . . . . . | | $2,000 |

This entry highlights why it is necessary to use the two-step procedure. Comparing the portfolio market value to the *cost* of the underlying investments at each valuation date (as shown in Step 1), rather than comparing the total portfolio market value at two successive dates, corrects for changes in the portfolio's composition at successive valuation dates.

The mark-to-market adjustment for 2010 is:

| | Step 1 Trading Securities Portfolio | | Step 2 Market Adjustment Account | |
|---|---|---|---|---|
| Total market value | $ 102,000 | $ 2,000 | Target balance (DR) |
| − Total cost | (100,000) | − (3,000) | Current balance (CR) |
| = Difference | $ 2,000 | $ 5,000 | Adjustment needed (DR) |

| | | | |
|---|---|---|---|
| **DR** | Market adjustment—trading securities......................... | $5,000 | |
| | **CR** Unrealized holding gain on trading securities— (income statement) ................................ | | $5,000 |

When trading securities are sold, the *realized* gain or loss is recorded. The amount of the realized gain or loss is the sale price of the securities *minus* the most recent mark-to-market price. The original cost of the securities sold and the related portion of the market adjustment account are removed from the accounts. This is illustrated for the sale of Company B preferred stock on January 1, 2011 as follows:

> Using the most recent mark-to-market price in computing the realized gain or loss avoids double counting any unrealized gain or loss recorded in previous periods' income statements.

### COMPUTATION OF REALIZED GAIN OR LOSS

| | |
|---|---|
| Sale price of Company B preferred stock | $18,500 |
| Mark-to-market value at 12/31/10 balance sheet data | (18,000) |
| Realized gain | $ 500 |

### ENTRY TO RECORD THE SALE OF COMPANY B COMMON STOCK

| | | | |
|---|---|---|---|
| **DR** | Cash ............................................................ | $18,500 | |
| **DR** | Market adjustment—trading securities ...................... | 2,000* | |
| | **CR** Realized gain on sale of trading securities ............... | | $ 500 |
| | **CR** Trading securities—Company B preferred ............... | | 20,000 |

----

\* $20,000 cost − $18,000 market value at 12/31/10 = $2,000.

After this entry is recorded, the balances in the Trading securities account and the Market adjustment account are:

| | |
|---|---|
| Trading securities account at cost ($100,000 − $20,000) | $80,000 |
| Market adjustment account ($2,000 **DR** balance on 12/31/10 + $2,000 **DR** from sale) | 4,000 |
| Trading securities at market | $84,000 |

The mark-to-market adjustment entry at the end of 2011 compares the target balance for the market adjustment account to the balance that will appear in this account after the sale of the Company B preferred stock, as in the following computation:

| | Step 1 Trading Securities Portfolio | | Step 2 Market Adjustment Account | |
|---|---|---|---|---|
| Total market value | $ 76,000 | $(4,000) | Target balance (CR) |
| − Total cost | (80,000) | − 4,000 | Current balance (DR) |
| = Difference | $ (4,000) | $(8,000) | Adjustment needed (CR) |

| | | | |
|---|---|---|---|
| **DR** | Unrealized holding loss on trading securities (income statement) ....................................... | $8,000 | |
| | **CR** Market adjustment—trading securities ................... | | $8,000 |

After this entry is recorded, the trading securities section of Principal Financial's balance sheet on December 31, 2011 would show:

| | |
|---|---:|
| Trading securities (at cost) | $80,000 |
| Less: Market adjustment—trading securities | (4,000) |
| Trading securities (at market) | $76,000 |

### Available-for-Sale Securities

Now assume that Principal Financial bought the securities described earlier because of their perceived **longer-term investment potential**—not for short-term speculation purposes. In this case, the securities would be classified as "available for sale" and shown (usually) as noncurrent investments on the balance sheet. The entries to record the purchase, dividend, and mark-to-market adjustment for available-for-sale securities are very similar to the entries for trading securities.

The only significant difference between treating investment securities as "available for sale" rather than "trading" is that the *mark-to-market adjustment is not included in income. Instead, the upward or downward adjustment to reflect fair value for available-for-sale securities is a direct (net of tax) credit or debit to a special owners' equity account.* These unrealized gains or losses on available-for-sale securities are one of the other comprehensive income components described in Chapter 2.

Returning to our example, the 2008 year-end downward market adjustment for Principal Financial's available-for-sale portfolio is:

| | | | |
|---|---|---|---:|
| **DR** | Unrealized change in value of available-for-sale securities | | |
| | (owners' equity) ............................................. | $650 | |
| **DR** | Deferred income taxes (assumed 35% tax rate × $1,000) ........... | 350 | |
| | **CR** Market adjustment—available-for-sale securities............. | | $1,000 |

As before, a credit balance in the Market adjustment account is treated as a contra-asset so that the net book value of the available-for-sale portfolio on the December 31, 2008 balance sheet is $29,000 ($30,000 cost − the $1,000 market adjustment).

If market prices rise as they did in 2010, the upward adjustment at December 31, 2010 would be:

| | | | |
|---|---|---|---:|
| **DR** | Market adjustment—available-for-sale securities ................ | $5,000 | |
| | **CR** Unrealized change in value of available-for-sale | | |
| | securities (owners' equity)............................ | | $3,250 |
| | **CR** Deferred income taxes (assumed 35% tax rate × $5,000).... | | 1,750 |

The FASB excluded unrealized gains and losses on available-for-sale securities from earnings because the securities are not held for active trading. Recording the debit or credit directly into owners' equity—rather than through income—alleviates the potential for earnings volatility unrelated to eventual investment performance. When available-for-sale securities are later sold, the cumulative unrealized gain or loss is realized and included in income. The realized loss on sale of Company B preferred that would be recorded in 2011 would be $1,500, which is the difference between the selling price ($18,500) and the *original cost* of these shares ($20,000).

 **RECAP**

**Trading securities and available-for-sale securities—the two types of minority passive investments—are carried at fair value on the balance sheet. The unrealized holding gain or loss on trading securities is run through income in the period of the security price change. Unrealized gains and losses on available-for-sale securities do not affect income in the period of the price change; instead these gains and losses go directly to a special owners' equity account and are reported as a component of other comprehensive income.**

## Minority Active Investments: Equity Method

## NEWS CLIP

### GM AGREES TO BUY 20% OF FUJI HEAVY INDUSTRIES

—General Motors Corp. was to announce today in Japan the signing of an agreement to acquire a 20% stake in Japan's Fuji Heavy Industries Ltd. for $1.4 billion.

The transaction, which was expected, includes plans to form a broad strategic alliance. This would allow GM to tap certain small-vehicle technologies in which Fuji is a leader and will help GM to quickly add a new small sport-utility vehicle for Europe, officials said. Fuji, which makes Subaru cars, will get access to GM's global marketing reach and to expensive propulsion technologies that GM is developing.

GM's alliance with Fuji nails down another plank in the No. 1 auto maker's platform for expanding in Asia. GM has linkups with Japan's Isuzu Motors Ltd., in which it holds a 49% stake, and Suzuki Motor Corp., in which it holds a 10% stake. . . .

Fuji brings experience in building small cars with all-wheel-drive—such as its popular Forester and outback models. In addition, GM wants to use Fuji's advanced continuously variable transmissions and ability to integrate controls for all of a modern vehicle's elements into a single system. . . .

The first fruit of this technology sharing is expected to be the development of a small SUV GM would aim mainly at Europe, although it may appear in North America. . . . [T]he alliance is expected to significantly speed GM's ability to develop vehicles that combine car and truck features for the U.S.

Fuji Heavy is expected to use the partnership to expand its lineup of Subaru vehicles. The company sells 550,000 to 600,000 vehicles a year world-wide and has a limited presence in Europe and South America.

When the ownership percentage equals or exceeds 20%, GAAP presumes two things:

1. A significant ownership position such as 20% implies that the investor has the capability to exert influence over the company. This influence could encompass operating decisions, such as which research and development projects should be undertaken, and financing decisions, such as dividend payouts.

2. A substantial ownership percentage also implies a continuing relationship between the two companies, because investments of this magnitude are usually entered into to achieve some long-run strategic objective.

> The 20% threshold is only a guideline. It is possible that ownership of less than 20% would, under certain circumstances, allow the investor to influence the company's activities. This could happen when share ownership is widely distributed across a large number of individual investors. An investor who owns, say, 18% of a widely held company could still influence management's decisions. Accordingly, judgment must be used to categorize minority investments between passive and active in certain situations.

Both elements are present in GM's ownership stake in Fuji Heavy Industries (hereafter Fuji).

When the ownership percentage becomes large enough for investor influence, the simple accounting approach introduced for passive investments is no longer suitable. To see why, recall that the entry made on a minority passive investor's books when dividends are declared is:

| **DR** Dividends receivable | $1,000 | |
|---|---|---|
|     **CR** Dividend income | | $1,000 |

When the investor can influence the company's dividend policy, the minority passive accounting treatment would allow the investor to augment its own reported income whenever it chose to. Suppose GM wants to increase its reported earnings during the period. It owns enough Fuji stock to influence the company's dividend policy, and it uses that influence to raise Fuji's dividend. This higher dividend would immediately run through GM's income statement.

To preclude this avenue for income distortion, minority active investments are accounted for through the **equity method** as indicated in Figure 16.1. Under the equity method, GM records its initial investment in Fuji at cost. Subsequently, however, the investment account is increased for the pro rata share of Fuji's income, and there is a corresponding credit to the investment income account—or, in the case of a loss, GM's investment account decreases and there's a corresponding debit to the investment loss account.

Because GM's earnings are increased for its share of Fuji's earnings each period, it would be inappropriate to record dividend distributions received from Fuji as income too. This would "double-count" Fuji's earnings on GM's books. Under the equity method, dividends from Fuji are recorded as an increase (debit) to cash—or dividends receivable—and a decrease (credit) to the investment account. ***Thus, the investment account is increased for GM's share of Fuji's earnings and decreased when those earnings are received in the form of dividends.***

The following example illustrates the entries under the equity method.

---

On January 1, 2008, Willis Company purchases 30% of the outstanding common shares of Planet Burbank, Inc. for $9,000,000. The book value and market value of Planet Burbank's net assets (assets minus liabilities) is $30,000,000. Thus, Willis pays book value for its investment in Planet Burbank (30% × $30 million = $9 million). During 2008, Planet Burbank earns a $10,000,000 net profit, and the company declares a $500,000 dividend on December 15, 2008. Using the equity method, Willis makes these entries:

---

### JANUARY 1, 2008

| | | | |
|---|---|---|---|
| **DR** | Investment in Planet Burbank ............................. | $9,000,000 | |
| **CR** | Cash............................................... | | $9,000,000 |

### DECEMBER 15, 2008

| | | | |
|---|---|---|---|
| **DR** | Dividend receivable from affiliate ......................... | $150,000 | |
| **CR** | Investment in Planet Burbank......................... | | $150,000 |

(To reduce the investment account for dividends declared—30% of $500,000)

### DECEMBER 31, 2008

| | | | |
|---|---|---|---|
| **DR** | Investment in Planet Burbank ............................. | $3,000,000 | |
| **CR** | Income from affiliate................................. | | $3,000,000 |

(To recognize 30% of Planet Burbank's total reported income of $10,000,000)

---

The example shows how the equity method reduces possibilities for income distortion. Willis Company's income statement is affected by only its pro rata share of Planet Burbank's income. ***Planet Burbank's dividend declaration—and subsequent payment—has no effect on Willis' income.*** Thus, while Willis could conceivably use the influence arising from its 30% ownership share to increase Planet Burbank's dividend declaration, doing so *would leave its income unchanged* **when the equity method is used.** Under the equity method, the carrying amount in the investment account at any point in time is comprised of the following items:

| | |
|---|---|
| Initial investment amount | $ 9,000,000 |
| Plus: Willis' cumulative pro rata share of | |
| Planet Burbank's income | 3,000,000 |
| Minus: Willis' cumulative pro rata share of | |
| dividends declared by Planet Burbank | (150,000) |
| Investment account carrying amount | $11,850,000 |

## When Cost and Book Value Differ

In contrast to our Planet Burbank example, investors rarely buy shares at a price exactly equal to the book value of those shares. When the investor's cost differs from book value, a new issue surfaces.

To illustrate, let's return to Willis Company's purchase of Planet Burbank stock. The total book value of Planet Burbank's stockholders' equity is $30,000,000, but let's say that Willis paid $24,000,000 for its 30% stake. Why would Willis pay $24,000,000 when the book value of the shares purchased is only $9,000,000 (30% of $30,000,000)? Why would an informed buyer pay $15,000,000 more than book value?

There are two reasons. First, Planet Burbank's books are prepared using GAAP, which reflect most balance sheet items at historical cost rather than at current value. As shown in Exhibit 16.1(a), the fair value of Planet Burbank's *net* assets is $70,000,000, or $40,000,000 more than the $30,000,000 book value (see the highlighted area). Sellers of Planet Burbank stock presumably know that the company's *net* assets are worth $70,000,000 rather than the lower $30,000,000 book value. On the basis of this knowledge, the asking price for the shares acquired by Willis Company will be higher than book value. But how much higher?

Willis decided to pay $24,000,000, or $15,000,000 more than book value. Exhibit 16.1(b) shows that $12,000,000 of the $15,000,000 excess of cost over book value is explained by the

---

| **EXHIBIT 16.1** | **Willis Company** |
| --- | --- |

### Investment with Goodwill

**Panel (a)**

On January 1, 2008, Willis Company purchases 30% of the outstanding shares of common stock of Planet Burbank for $24,000,000. The book value and fair value of Planet Burbank's net assets on this date are as follows:

| ($ in millions) | Book Value | Fair Value | Difference | Investor's Share (30%) |
| --- | --- | --- | --- | --- |
| Cash and receivables | $10 | $10 | $ 0 | $ 0 |
| Inventories (FIFO cost flow) | 15 | 25 | 10 | 3 |
| Depreciable assets (net of depreciation)* | 25 | 55 | 30 | 9 |
| Total assets | 50 | 90 | 40 | 12 |
| Minus liabilities | (20) | (20) | 0 | 0 |
| Net assets | $30 | $70 | $40 | $12 |

* Average remaining useful life of 10 years.

During 2008, Planet Burbank reported a $10,000,000 net profit, and the company declared a $500,000 dividend on December 31, 2008.

**Panel (b)**

($ in millions)

| | |
| --- | --- |
| Analysis of Willis' investment cost over book value | |
| Cost of 30% investment | $24 |
| 30% of Planet Burbank's net asset book value (30% × $30) | (9) |
| Excess of cost over book value of Willis' shares | $15 |
| | |
| Amount of excess attributable to | |
| Inventories—30% × ($25 − $15) | $ 3 |
| Depreciable assets—30% × ($55 − $25) | 9 |
| Remainder attributable to implicit goodwill (plug figure) | 3 |
| | $15 |

difference between fair value and book value of inventories and fixed assets (see highlighted area). This still leaves $3,000,000 of the disparity unexplained. The remaining difference brings us to the second reason why an informed buyer would knowingly pay a premium to acquire influence over another company.

This second potential explanation relates to **goodwill.** Goodwill exists because thriving, successful companies are frequently worth more than the sum of their individual net assets. Planet Burbank has developed a reputation for product quality, prompt service, and fair treatment of both employees and customers. Consequently, employees like to work for the company, and customers actively seek its products. The result is that Planet Burbank is exceptionally profitable—it earns a very large return on its investment base. The capitalized value of this earning potential is what gives rise to the remaining $3,000,000 difference. This "extraordinary" earnings potential is called *goodwill.*

A summary of the factors comprising the $24,000,000 purchase price for 30% of Planet Burbank follows ($ in millions):

| | |
|---|---:|
| Recorded historical book value of the company's net assets ($50 − $20) × 30% | $ 9 |
| Difference between fair value and cost of net assets ($40 × 30%) | 12 |
| Amount attributable to goodwill (plug figure) | 3 |
| Purchase price | $24 |

When the cost of the shares exceeds the underlying book value at the acquisition date, as it does in this case, the investor is required to amortize any excess that is attributable to (1) inventory and (2) depreciable assets.[3] Amortization is recorded as a reduction (debit) to investment income and a reduction (credit) to the investment account. The rationale for amortizing the excess of the investor's cost over book value is based on the matching principle. Because Willis is picking up its share of Planet Burbank's reported earnings each period as investment income, it follows that Willis should write off any amount paid in excess of Planet Burbank's book value as a cost of gaining access to those earnings.

Using the equity method, the entries based on the preceding set of facts are:

**January 1, 2008: Initial Investment in Planet Burbank**

| | | | |
|---|---|---:|---:|
| **DR** | Investment in Planet Burbank | $24,000,000 | |
| | **CR** Cash | | $24,000,000 |

**December 15, 2008: Investor's Share of Dividends Declared**

| | | | |
|---|---|---:|---:|
| **DR** | Dividend receivable from Planet Burbank | $150,000 | |
| | **CR** Investment in Planet Burbank | | $150,000 |

(To reduce the investment account for dividend declared—30% of $500,000)

**December 31, 2008: Investor's Share of Earnings**

| | | | |
|---|---|---:|---:|
| **DR** | Investment in Planet Burbank | $3,000,000 | |
| | **CR** Income from affiliate | | $3,000,000 |

(To recognize 30% of Planet Burbank's total reported income of $10,000,000)

---

[3] Under *SFAS No. 142,* any excess attributable to implicit goodwill is not amortized, nor is it subject to an annual impairment test. For further details see paras. 40 and 59, "Goodwill and Other Intangible Assets," *SFAS No. 142* (Norwalk, CT: FASB, 2001).

| December 31, 2008: Amortization of Excess Cost over Book Value Attributable to Inventory and Depreciable Assets | | |
|---|---|---|
| **DR** Income from affiliate . . . . . . . . . . . . . . . . . . . . . . . . . . . . . . . . . | $3,900,000 | |
| **CR** Investment in Planet Burbank . . . . . . . . . . . . . . . . . . . . . . . . . . . . . | | $3,900,000 |

| | Amount | Amortization |
|---|---|---|
| Amortization is computed as | | |
| Attributed to inventory (all sold during the year) | $3,000,000 | $3,000,000 |
| Attributed to depreciable assets (over 10 years) | 9,000,000 | 900,000 |
| | | $3,900,000 |

The excess investment cost over book value attributable to inventory is assigned to inventory items on hand on January 1, 2008, when Willis purchased Planet Burbank's stock. This inventory is presumed to have been sold during 2008 under the FIFO cost flow assumption (see Chapter 9). The amount attributed to depreciable assets is amortized over the average remaining 10-year life of those assets. The amount attributed to goodwill is no longer amortized under *SFAS No. 142*.

The December 31, 2008 balance in the investment in Planet Burbank's account is $22,950,000 ($24,000,000 + $3,000,000 − $150,000 − $3,900,000).

## Fair Value Option for Equity Method Investments

Firms that use the equity method for their minority active investments may instead elect to use the fair value option allowed under *SFAS No. 159*.[4] This option became effective in 2008 because, according to the FASB:

> . . . fair values for financial assets and financial liabilities provide more relevant and understandable information than cost or cost-based measures. . . . with the passage of time, historical prices become irrelevant in assessing an entity's financial position. (*SFAS No. 159*, para. A3, part d)

Once selected, the fair value option is irrevocable. Firms are not allowed to switch back to the equity method. Firms are allowed to elect the fair value option on **election dates,** which, for equity investments, include dates when one of the following events occurs: (1) the firm first acquires an investment that is eligible for equity method treatment; (2) the investment becomes subject to the equity method of accounting (e.g., investment goes from below 20% of the outstanding voting common stock to more than 20%); or (3) an investor ceases to consolidate a subsidiary (e.g., because the investor no longer holds majority voting interest) but continues to hold sufficient common stock to qualify for equity method treatment.

Under the fair value option, unrealized gains and losses arising from changes in the investment's fair value are reported in the investor's income statement. Once the fair value option has been selected, the investor firm ceases to report its proportionate share of the investee profits

> *International Accounting Standard (IAS) 39*, "Financial Instruments: Recognition and Measurement," provides a fair value option for equity investments. Similar to the provisions of *SFAS No. 159*, *IAS 39* requires that (1) the fair value election be made at initial recognition of the financial asset or financial liability, (2) the election be irrevocable, and (3) changes in fair value be recognized in earnings as those changes occur. The major differences between *SFAS No. 159* and *IAS 39* involve required disclosures, scope exceptions, and whether certain eligibility criteria must be met.*
>
> * *SFAS No. 159*, paras. A51–A52.

---

[4] "The Fair Value Option for Financial Assets and Financial Liabilities," *SFAS No. 159* (Norwalk, CT: FASB, 2007).

and losses in earnings and as an adjustment to the investment account. Dividends received after the fair value election flow directly to earnings rather than as a reduction of the investment account as is done under the equity method. Dividend distributions typically reduce the fair value of the investee's stock. So, increases in investor earnings from investee dividend distributions are likely to be offset by an earnings decrease due to investment fair value declines.

*SFAS No. 159* requires that assets and liabilities measured at fair value be reported on the balance sheet separately from other investments not reported at fair value. This can be accomplished by separate line-item disclosure or by presenting the investment amounts in aggregate with parenthetical disclosure of the fair value amounts included in that line item.

To illustrate the fair value option, recall Willis Company's acquisition of 30% of Planet Burbank's common stock on January 1, 2008 (see Exhibit 16.1). Suppose Willis elects the fair value option for this investment at the acquisition date and that the $24 million that Willis paid reflects that investment's fair value. At December 31, 2008, the fair value of Willis' investment in Planet Burbank stock increases to $30 million. On its 2008 income statement, Willis would report an unrealized gain from equity investment of $6 million ($30 million − $24 million) and as investment income its share of Planet Burbank's declared dividend ($150,000). Willis' income statement would show no equity in Planet Burbank earnings, and no reduction in earnings for amortization of excess investment cost over Planet Burbank book values attributable to inventory or depreciable assets. Willis Company's December 31, 2008 balance sheet would show the Investment in Burbank stock at the $30 million fair value amount.

## RECAP

A majority-owned company may *not* be consolidated if effective control does not rest with the majority owner (parent). For example, if the majority-owned entity is in legal reorganization or in bankruptcy or operates under foreign exchange restrictions, controls, or faces other governmentally imposed uncertainties that cast significant doubt on the parent's ability to control the entity, consolidation is not deemed appropriate.*

* *ARB No. 51*, para. 2, as amended by *SFAS No. 160*.

Under existing financial reporting practice, the general guidelines for intercorporate investments with less than majority ownership are:

1. **Less than 20% ownership requires the use of either the trading securities method or the available-for-sale method. Both methods use mark-to-market accounting.**

2. **Ownership between 20% and 50% requires use of the equity method—not the mark-to-market approach.**

3. **Under the equity method, the excess cost of purchased shares over their book value is amortized as a charge to income and a reduction to the investment account.**

4. **Firms can elect to use the fair value option for equity method investments. Under this option, changes in fair value flow to the income statement as unrealized gains (losses).**

## CONTROLLING FINANCIAL INTEREST (MAJORITY OWNERSHIP)

An entity that gains a **controlling financial interest** in another entity is referred to as the **acquirer** or **parent** company. Controlling financial interest is generally deemed to occur when one entity, directly or indirectly, owns more than 50 percent of the outstanding voting shares of another entity (**subsidiary**).[5] Under these circumstances, the subsidiary's financial statements are combined—line by line—with those of the parent using a process called **consolidation**.

---

[5] "Consolidated Financial Statements," *Accounting Research Bulletin No. 51* (amended by *SFAS No. 160*, "Noncontrolling Interests in Consolidated Financial Statements—An Amendment of ARB No. 51") (Norwalk, CT: FASB, 2007).

**Consolidated financial statements** are designed to cut across artificial corporate boundaries to portray the economic activities of the parent and the subsidiary as if they were one entity.

The procedures for recognizing and measuring the subsidiary's assets and liabilities at acquisition date and reporting **noncontrolling (minority) interest** in the subsidiary on consolidated financial statements have recently undergone major changes. Prior to being amended, *SFAS No. 141*, "Business Combinations," required the use of the **purchase method** to account for business combinations.[6] In December 2007, the FASB issued *SFAS No. 141R*, which requires the use of the **acquisition method** to account for business combinations.[7] The key difference between these two methods is the way the subsidiary's net assets are valued at acquisition date. Under the purchase method, subsidiary assets and liabilities are measured and reported on the consolidated balance sheet partially at fair value and partially at the subsidiary's carryover book value at the acquisition date. In contrast, the acquisition method requires that the acquirer (parent) measure individual assets and liabilities of the acquiree (subsidiary) at their *full* fair values determined as of the acquisition date.

*SFAS No. 160* significantly changes the accounting and reporting for noncontrolling (minority) interests in consolidated financial statements.[8] The provisions of *SFAS No. 141R* and *SFAS No. 160* are to be applied prospectively for business combinations occuring on or after December 15, 2008. Thus, for most firms, the effects of these new standards will be seen for the first time in fiscal 2009 consolidated financial statements. Because the new standards will be applied prospectively, business combinations entered into before 2009 will continue to be reported under the purchase method. So, it is important for you to understand how the purchase method works, how the acquisition method differs, and how the reporting of noncontrolling (minority) interest differs under the two approaches.

The following sections describe the purchase method and the basics of how to prepare consolidated statements, first for a 100% acquisition and then for an acquisition with a minority (noncontrolling) interest (i.e., where the parent acquires less than a 100% of the subsidiary's voting stock). We then highlight the key differences under the acquisition method and describe how noncontrolling (minority) interests are measured and reported on consolidated financial statements under *SFAS No. 160*.

> When two companies form a **joint venture** and each company owns exactly 50% of the joint venture, neither of the "parent" companies consolidates the joint venture. Rather, each accounts for its investment under the equity method. Chapter 11 describes how this allows the joint venture entity to incur debt—usually guaranteed by the "parent" companies—but the debt does not appear on either parent's balance sheet because consolidation is not required. Intercorporate investment rules can be skillfully used to create off-balance sheet assets and liabilities that impede accurate financial analysis.

> A noncontrolling interest is the equity interest in a subsidiary not attributable, directly or indirectly, to the parent. Prior to the issuance of *SFAS No. 141R* and *SFAS No. 160*, noncontrolling interests were referred to as *minority interests*. We use the terms interchangeably in the following discussion.

# Purchase Method and Preparation of Consolidated Statements

Before December 2007, business combinations were accounted for under the purchase method, which follows the cost principle in recording a business combination. Purchase accounting assigns the fair value of the consideration

> Prior to July 2001, business combinations could also be accounted for under the pooling-of-interests method if certain conditions were met. See Appendix B for further discussion of the pooling method.

---

[6] "Business Combinations," *SFAS No. 141* (Norwalk, CT: FASB, 2001).

[7] "Business Combinations," *SFAS No. 141R* (revised) (Norwalk, CT: FASB, 2007).

[8] "Noncontrolling Interests in Consolidated Financial Statements—An Amendment of ARB No. 51," *SFAS No. 160* (Norwalk, CT: FASB, 2007).

given to the acquired entity's identifiable net assets (assets minus liabilities) at acquisition date. If the value of consideration given exceeds the acquired entity's fair value of identifiable net assets, goodwill is recorded. We use the following simple example to illustrate.

Assume that on December 31, 2007, the balance sheet of Alphonse Corporation (the acquirer or parent company) appears as follows:

## Assets

| | |
|---|---|
| Current assets | $ 5,000,000 |
| Fixed assets minus accumulated depreciation | 20,000,000 |
| Total assets | $25,000,000 |

## Liabilities and Stockholders' Equity

| | |
|---|---|
| Current liabilities | $ 1,000,000 |
| Common stock ($1 par) | 20,000,000 |
| Retained earnings | 4,000,000 |
| Total liabilities and equity | $25,000,000 |

On January 1, 2008, Alphonse issues 8,000,000 additional shares of its stock to new outside investors for $10,000,000 cash. Immediately after the stock issue, Alphonse's balance sheet is:

## Assets

| | |
|---|---|
| Current assets | $15,000,000 |
| Fixed assets minus accumulated depreciation | 20,000,000 |
| Total assets | $35,000,000 |

## Liabilities and Stockholders' Equity

| | |
|---|---|
| Current liabilities | $ 1,000,000 |
| Common stock ($1 par) | 28,000,000 |
| Capital in excess of par | 2,000,000 |
| Retained earnings | 4,000,000 |
| Total liabilities and equity | $35,000,000 |

Alphonse immediately uses the cash to buy all of the outstanding shares of Gaston Corporation for $10,000,000. Because Alphonse has used its cash to make an investment, after buying Gaston's shares, Alphonse's current assets will be $10,000,000 less than before and an investment account of $10,000,000 will exist. See Exhibit 16.2 for Alphonse's balance sheet after the stock purchase, as well as Gaston's.

The following steps describe the procedures for preparing the consolidated balance sheet for Alphonse and Gaston in Exhibit 16.2. The individual balance sheets of the two companies are *not* simply added together; doing that would result in double-counting, as we'll see.

## Adjustments to the Consolidated Balance Sheet

### Step 1: **Analysis of the Investment in Gaston Account** Alphonse paid $10,000,000 for Gaston, a company whose *net* assets total only $8,000,000 (assets of $8,500,000 minus $500,000 of liabilities). Why did Alphonse pay more than $8,000,000? An informed buyer would pay more than book value for two reasons (1) the fair value of Gaston's individual assets is more than their combined book value (we assume this excess is $1,500,000 here and is attributable to the fixed assets) and (2) goodwill, which is the remaining $500,000.

**EXHIBIT 16.2**     **Alphonse Company and Gaston Company**

**Preparation of Consolidated Balance Sheet**
**(Purchase Method—100% acquisition)**

| | After the Acquisition | | Adjustments and Eliminations | | Consolidated |
| | Alphonse | Gaston | Dr. | Cr. | Balance Sheet |
|---|---|---|---|---|---|
| **Assets** | | | | | |
| Current assets | $ 5,000,000 | $2,000,000 | | | $ 7,000,000 |
| Fixed assets, net | 20,000,000 | 6,500,000 | $ 1,500,000 (B) | | 28,000,000 |
| Investment in Gaston | 10,000,000 | — | | $ 2,000,000 (B) / 8,000,000 (A) | — |
| Goodwill | | | 500,000 (B) | | 500,000 |
| | $35,000,000 | $8,500,000 | | | $35,500,000 |
| **Liabilities** | | | | | |
| Current liabilities | $ 1,000,000 | $ 500,000 | | | $ 1,500,000 |
| **Stockholders' equity** | | | | | |
| Common stock | 28,000,000 | 6,000,000 | 6,000,000 (A) | | 28,000,000 |
| Capital in excess of par | 2,000,000 | — | | | 2,000,000 |
| Retained earnings | 4,000,000 | 2,000,000 | 2,000,000 (A) | | 4,000,000 |
| | $35,000,000 | $8,500,000 | $10,000,000 | $10,000,000 | $35,500,000 |

The factors comprising the $10,000,000 purchase price for Gaston are:

| | |
|---|---|
| Recorded book value of Gaston's *net* assets | $ 8,000,000 |
| Unrecorded difference between fair value and book value of Gaston's fixed assets ($8,000,000 − $6,500,000) | 1,500,000 |
| Unrecorded value of Gaston's goodwill | 500,000 |
| Purchase price | $10,000,000 |

This purchase price breakdown explains why we do not add the two balance sheets to-gether to get the consolidated balance sheet. Adding the two balance sheets together would double count the $8,000,000 book value of Gaston's net assets. To see why, notice that the $10,000,000 full purchase price is already on Alphonse's balance sheet (under In-vestment in Gaston in Exhibit 16.2); but as we have just seen, $8,000,000 of this purchase price represents the book value of Gaston's net assets. Because this $8,000,000 already appears on Gaston's balance sheet (assets of $8,500,000 − $500,000 of liabilities), simply adding the two balance sheets together would double count the $8,000,000. To avoid do-ing this, we must remove $8,000,000 from Alphonse's Investment in Gaston account, leav-ing a $2,000,000 balance. Notice that this is done in Exhibit 16.2 in the Adjustments and Eliminations column (next to notations A).

**Step 2: Elimination of the Investment in Gaston Account** The remaining balance in the Investment in Gaston account represents the amount of the purchase price that is *not* reflected in Gaston's balance sheet book values. As the purchase price breakdown shows, this $2,000,000 remaining balance represents unrecorded fixed asset appreciation of $1,500,000 and goodwill of $500,000. These amounts must stay on the consolidated bal-ance sheet because Alphonse paid for them. However, they must be assigned to the items they actually represent: (1) an increase to fixed assets and (2) the acquisition of goodwill. This is done in Exhibit 16.2 in the Adjustments and Eliminations column (next to the notations B). After these adjustments are made, notice that the Investment in Gaston account has been eliminated and thus does not appear in the consolidated column of Exhibit 16.2. Also, consolidated fixed assets have been increased by $1,500,000, and goodwill of $500,000 is separately reported.

**Step 3:** **Analysis of Stockholders' Equity Accounts** To consolidate both companies' balance sheets, we need to eliminate one or more elements of potential double counting. Consider the stockholders' equity accounts of Alphonse comprised of $28,000,000 (Common stock), $2,000,000 (Capital in excess of par), and $4,000,000 (Retained earnings). Because it owns Gaston, the stockholders' equity accounts of Alphonse represent the ownership interest of *both* companies.

Now consider the stockholders' equity accounts of Gaston comprised of $6,000,000 (Common stock) and $2,000,000 (Retained earnings). These two accounts represent Gaston's ownership interest. **If the stockholders' equity accounts of the two companies were simply added together, ownership of Gaston would be counted twice**—once as part of the $34,000,000 of Alphonse's stockholders' equity accounts and again in the $8,000,000 of Gaston's stockholders' equity accounts.

To avoid this double counting, Gaston's stockholders' equity accounts are eliminated against Alphonse's Investment in Gaston account when the consolidated balance sheet is prepared. This is done opposite notation (A) in the Adjustment and Eliminations column in the consolidated worksheet in Exhibit 16.2. After this elimination, consolidated owners' equity is comprised of only Alphonse's stockholders' equity accounts because these alone represent the consolidated entity's ownership.

The adjustment process described here can also be expressed in journal entry form. For example, the entry to avoid double counting both the book value of Gaston's net assets and its owners' equity is:

| | | | |
|---|---|---|---|
| **DR** | Common stock | $6,000,000 | |
| **DR** | Retained earnings | 2,000,000 | |
| | **CR**   Investment in Gaston | | $8,000,000 |

To avoid double counting Gaston's net assets and its owners' equity (adjustment notation [A] in Exhibit 16.2).

Similarly, reclassification of the remaining $2,000,000 in the Investment in Gaston account to reflect the fair value of Gaston's fixed assets and purchased goodwill can also be expressed in journal entry form:

| | | | |
|---|---|---|---|
| **DR** | Fixed assets | $1,500,000 | |
| **DR** | Goodwill | 500,000 | |
| | **CR**   Investment in Gaston | | $2,000,000 |

To eliminate the remaining investment account balance and record the write-up of Gaston's Fixed assets, net to fair value, and record purchased goodwill (adjustment notation [B]).

After these adjustments, the last column of Exhibit 16.2 reflects the amounts reported on the consolidated balance sheet. Note that in this case of a 100% acquisition under the purchase method, a new basis of accounting is established for the subsidiary net assets (including goodwill)—they are reported at full fair value as of the acquisition date.

## Other Consolidation Adjustments— Intercompany Transactions

Suppose that several months prior to the Gaston acquisition, Alphonse had borrowed $300,000 from Gaston that had not been repaid at the acquisition on January 1, 2008. Under these circumstances, another adjustment is needed to consolidate the financial statements. ***This adjustment is necessary because Alphonse and Gaston are now part of the same economic unit.*** The ***Alphonse loan receivable*** on Gaston's books and the ***Gaston loan payable*** on Alphonse's books are not owed to outsiders. To include the intercompany receivable and payable in the consolidated balance sheet would overstate assets and overstate liabilities, each by $300,000. That's why the following adjustment is made in preparing the consolidated statements:

| | | |
|---|---|---|
| **DR** Loan payable—Gaston (on Alphonse's books) ................ | $300,000 | |
| **CR** Loan receivable—Alphonse (on Gaston's books) .......... | | $300,000 |

To eliminate the intercompany loan from Gaston to Alphonse.

Another frequently encountered consolidation adjustment arises when Gaston and Alphonse make sales to one another. Suppose that Alphonse sold goods to Gaston on March 15, 2008 after the January 1, 2008 acquisition, and then Gaston resold all of these goods to outside customers. The facts follow:

### INTERCOMPANY SALE

| | Alphonse's Sale to Gaston | Gaston's Resale to "Outsiders" | Total |
|---|---|---|---|
| Selling price | $25,000 | $34,000 | $59,000 |
| Cost of goods sold | 20,000 | 25,000 | 45,000 |
| Profit | $ 5,000 | $ 9,000 | $14,000 |

Merely adding together the income statements of Alphonse and Gaston to form the consolidated income statement would result in double counting. This would happen because neither Alphonse's $25,000 sale to Gaston nor the $25,000 of cost of goods sold on Gaston's income statement represents a transaction with outsiders. This means that the intercompany sales transaction must be eliminated in preparing the consolidated income statement, as follows:

### ELIMINATION OF $25,000 INTERCOMPANY SALE

| | Income Statement Totals | | Sale Elimination | Consolidated |
|---|---|---|---|---|
| | Alphonse | Gaston | | |
| Sales | $250,000,000 | $150,000,000 | $(25,000) | $399,975,000 |
| Cost of goods sold | (200,000,000) | (109,000,000) | 25,000 | (308,975,000) |
| Gross margin | $ 50,000,000 | $ 41,000,000 | — | $ 91,000,000 |

After this elimination, the only remaining aspect of the intercompany sale and Gaston's subsequent resale of the goods to outsiders follows:

| | Alphonse's Sale to Gaston | Gaston's Resale to "Outsiders" | Sale Elimination | Net |
|---|---|---|---|---|
| Selling price | $ 25,000 | $ 34,000 | $(25,000) | $ 34,000 |
| Cost of goods sold | (20,000) | (25,000) | 25,000 | (20,000) |
| Profit | $ 5,000 | $ 9,000 | — | $ 14,000 |

Notice that the consolidated income statement now reflects only revenues realized from outsiders ($34,000) and cost paid to outsiders ($20,000). The double counting of the intercompany sales and cost of goods sold has been eliminated.

## Noncontrolling (Minority) Interest under the Purchase Method

The previous example illustrates the consolidation entries for Alphonse's acquisition of a 100% interest in Gaston's outstanding common shares. But what happens if Alphonse owns less than 100% of Gaston's shares? If ownership exceeds 50%, it must still consolidate, but now there are other shareholders called *noncontrolling* or *minority* shareholders to consider. These shareholders' claim to the subsidiary's net assets and income is referred to as *noncontrolling* or *minority interest*. Because Gaston's *total* assets, liabilities, and income are included in the consolidated statements, the minority shareholders' interest in these amounts must also be reported in the consolidated statements. The portion of Gaston's earnings assigned to minority shareholders is normally deducted from the total combined earnings of Alphonse and Gaston to arrive at consolidated net income. Likewise, the minority shareholders' claim in Gaston's net assets is subtracted from the total combined net assets of Alphonse and Gaston to arrive at consolidated shareholders' equity. For years prior to 2009, this minority interest claim on the consolidated net assets is shown either between the liabilities and stockholders' equity section (sometimes referred to as the *mezzanine* section) or in the stockholders' equity section on the consolidated balance sheet.

> Beginning in 2009, non-controlling (minority) interests are reported as part of consolidated stockholders' equity as we describe in greater detail below. (See SFAS No. 160.)

The following example illustrates how to compute and report minority interests on the consolidated balance sheet under the purchase method prior to *SFAS No. 160*. Referring to the data underlying Exhibit 16.2 on page 953, assume that after selling 8,000,000 additional shares of its own stock on January 1, 2008 for $10,000,000, Alphonse immediately uses $8,000,000 of this amount to acquire 80% of Gaston's outstanding shares whose book value of total net assets totals $8,000,000 ($8,500,000 of assets − $500,000 of liabilities). The difference between the amount ($8,000,000) paid by Alphonse and its equity in the book value of Gaston's net assets (80% × $8,000,000 = $6,400,000) is $1,600,000. If we assume that the excess of fair value over book value of *all* of Gaston's depreciable fixed assets is $1,500,000 as in Exhibit 16.2, the $1,600,000 difference is apportioned as follows:

| | |
|---|---|
| Price paid by Alphonse for 80% interest in Gaston | $8,000,000 |
| Book value of 80% of Gaston's net assets at acquisition (80% × $8,000,000) | 6,400,000 |
| Difference | 1,600,000 |
| Excess attributed to difference between fair value and book value of Gaston's fixed assets 80% × $1,500,000 | (1,200,000) |
| Amount attributed to Gaston's unreported goodwill | $ 400,000 |

| EXHIBIT 16.3 | Alphonse and Gaston Company |
| --- | --- |

**Preparation of Consolidated Balance Sheet**
**(Purchase Method—80% acquistion)**

| | After the Acquisition | | Adjustments and Eliminations | | Consolidated Balance Sheet |
| --- | --- | --- | --- | --- | --- |
| | Alphonse | Gaston | Dr. | Cr. | |
| **Assets** | | | | | |
| Current assets | $ 7,000,000 | $ 2,000,000 | | | $ 9,000,000 |
| Fixed assets, net | 20,000,000 | 6,500,000 | $1,200,000 (B) | | 27,700,000 |
| Investment in Gaston | 8,000,000 | — | | $1,600,000 (B) 6,400,000 (A) | — |
| Goodwill | | | 400,000 (B) | | 400,000 |
| | $ 35,000,000 | $ 8,500,000 | | | $37,100,000 |
| **Liabilities** | | | | | |
| Current liabilities | $ 1,000,000 | $ 500,000 | | | $ 1,500,000 |
| **Minority interest in Gaston** | | | | 1,600,000 (A) | 1,600,000 |
| **Stockholders' equity** | | | | | |
| Common stock | 28,000,000 | 6,000,000 | 6,000,000 (A) | | 28,000,000 |
| Capital in excess of par | 2,000,000 | — | | | 2,000,000 |
| Retained earnings | 4,000,000 | 2,000,000 | 2,000,000 (A) | | 4,000,000 |
| | $35,000,000 | $ 8,500,000 | $9,600,000 | $9,600,000 | $37,100,000 |

Immediately after this acquisition, the worksheet to prepare the consolidated balance sheet of Alphonse and its 80%-owned interest in Gaston appears as in Exhibit 16.3. The two adjustment and elimination entries reflected in the consolidated worksheet in Exhibit 16.3 are shown in journal entry form with brief explanations.

### ADJUSTMENT AND ELIMINATION ENTRY (A)

| | | | |
| --- | --- | --- | --- |
| **DR** | Common stock | $6,000,000 | |
| **DR** | Retained earnings | 2,000,000 | |
| | **CR** Investment in Gaston | | $6,400,000 |
| | **CR** Minority Interest in Gaston* | | 1,600,000 |

To eliminate 100% of Gaston's stockholders' equity accounts against Alphonse's proportionate investment (80%) in Gaston's net assets and to set up the 20% minority interest in Gaston shown on the consolidated balance sheet under the purchase method.

---

\* 20% minority interest × $8,000,000 book value of Gaston's net assets.

### ADJUSTMENT AND ELIMINATION ENTRY (B)

| | | | |
| --- | --- | --- | --- |
| **DR** | Fixed assets | $1,200,000 | |
| **DR** | Goodwill | 400,000 | |
| | **CR** Investment in Gaston | | $1,600,000 |

To allocate the excess of the price paid for Gaston's shares ($8,000,000) over Alphonse's proportionate interest in the book value of Gaston's net assets (80% × $8,000,000 = $6,400,000) to revalue 80% of Gaston's fixed assets and to set up the Goodwill account on the consolidated balance sheet under the purchase method.

Under the purchase method of accounting, when a parent company acquires 100% of a subsidiary's common stock and pays more than book value for the subsidiary's net assets, the excess is allocated in the consolidated worksheet so that *all* of the subsidiary's assets and liabilities are reflected at their fair values on the consolidated balance sheet at the acquisition date (see Exhibit 16.2, adjusting entry [B]). If, however, the parent acquires less than 100% of the subsidiary's stock and pays more than the book value for its *proportionate interest* in the subsidiary's net assets, the subsidiary's assets and liabilities are shown on the consolidated balance sheet at their book values (on the subsidiary's books) plus the parent's proportionate share of the difference between the fair values and book values (see Exhibit 16.3). Thus, under the purchase method, the subsidiary's assets and liabilities are not valued at their full fair values on the consolidated balance sheet when minority interests are present. In essence, the subsidiary's net assets are valued at the parent's proportional interest in the fair values plus the minority interest proportion of the *book value* of the subsidiary's net assets at the acquisition date.

## Acquisition Method

*SFAS No. 141R* and *SFAS No. 160,* effective for 2009 fiscal years, embrace the economic unit concept for consolidation—a concept founded on the principle that the subsidiary's individual accounts should not be divided and measured differently along ownership lines. According to this view, a controlled company must be consolidated as a whole regardless of the parent's level of ownership. *SFAS No. 141R* says that the parent must measure and recognize the subsidiary as a *whole* at **business fair value.** This means that under the acquisition method, the parent company includes in its consolidated statements 100% of the subsidiary's individual assets acquired and liabilities assumed at their *full fair values* determined as of the acquisition date even when the parent owns less than 100% of the controlled subsidiary. This requirement stands in stark contrast to the purchase method (Exhibit 16.3) under which the parent's acquisition cost is allocated only to the *acquired percentage* of the subsidiary asset and liability accounts.

The FASB offers the following justification for reporting subsidiary net assets at full fair value even when there is a noncontrolling (minority) interest:

> The Board concluded that no useful purpose is served by reporting the assets and liabilities of a newly acquired business using a mixture of their fair values at the date acquired and the acquiree's historical costs or carrying amounts. Amounts that relate to transactions and events occurring before the business is included in the acquirer's financial statements are not relevant to users of those [consolidated] financial statements.[9]

How is business fair value determined in the presence of a partial acquisition? *SFAS No. 141R* says business fair value is the sum of (1) the controlling interest fair value and (2) the noncontrolling interest fair value. Measurement of the controlling interest fair value is relatively straightforward—for the vast majority of cases, the value of the consideration transferred provides the best evidence of the controlling interest fair value. Measurement of noncontrolling interest fair value is more difficult. One approach is to use the consideration paid by the parent for the controlling interest to impute a fair value for the acquired firm as a whole and then use the noncontrolling percentage of this imputed total acquired

---

[9] *SFAS No. 141R,* para. B200.

firm fair value to measure the noncontrolling interest fair value. For example, if the fair value of a 75% controlling interest is $240 million, then the imputed total business fair value would be $320 million ($240 million/0.75). The estimated noncontrolling interest fair value would be $80 million ($320 million × 25%).

### Acquisition Method with Noncontrolling Interest

To illustrate the acquisition method, let's return to the Alphonse and Gaston business combination described on page 956. As in that example, Alphonse buys 80% of Gaston, but we now assume that the acquisition occurs on January 1, 2009 after the effective date for *SFAS No. 141R* and *SFAS No. 160* implementation. Recall that Alphonse paid $8,000,000 to acquire 80% of Gaston's outstanding shares. If the price paid reflects the fair value of the controlling interest (i.e., no premium was paid to gain control), Gaston's imputed total business fair value is $10,000,000 ($8,000,000/0.80). Therefore, the fair value of the noncontrolling interest is $2,000,000 (20% × $10,000,000). The worksheet to prepare the consolidated balance sheet of Alphonse and its 80%-owned subsidiary, Gaston, under the acquisition method is shown in Exhibit 16.4.

Note that elimination and adjusting entries A and B in this worksheet are essentially the same entries that were made under the purchase method (Exhibit 16.3). Entry (A) eliminates Alphonse's Investment in Gaston account against the stockholders' equity accounts of Gaston and sets up noncontrolling interest in Gaston for the book value of its shares. Entry (B) writes up Alphonse's share (80%) of Gaston's net assets to fair value and records the

> This approach for estimating the noncontrolling interest's fair value would not be appropriate if the parent pays a premium to secure sufficient acquiree shares to gain financial control. This can sometimes occur when the shares are being acquired from a single party that owns a large block of the acquiree's shares (e.g., 90%). In this case, the noncontrolling interest fair value is independently computed without regard to the consideration paid by the parent (e.g., by using the traded price of the shares not held by the major blockholder).

---

### EXHIBIT 16.4 — Alphonse and Gaston

**Worksheet for Preparing Consolidated Balance Sheet (Acquisition Method—80% acquisition)**

| | After the Acquisition | | Eliminations | | Consolidated |
| --- | --- | --- | --- | --- | --- |
| | Alphonse | Gaston | Dr. | Cr. | Balance Sheet |
| **Assets** | | | | | |
| Current assets | $ 7,000,000 | $2,000,000 | | | $ 9,000,000 |
| Fixed assets, net | 20,000,000 | 6,500,000 | $ 1,200,000 (B) | | 28,000,000 |
| | | | 300,000 (C) | | |
| Investment in Gaston | 8,000,000 | — | | $ 1,600,000 (B) | — |
| | | | | 6,400,000 (A) | |
| Goodwill—controlling interest | | | 400,000 (B) | | 400,000 |
| Goodwill—noncontrolling interest | | | 100,000 (C) | | 100,000 |
| | $35,000,000 | $8,500,000 | | | $37,500,000 |
| **Liabilities** | | | | | |
| Current liabilities | $ 1,000,000 | $ 500,000 | | | $ 1,500,000 |
| **Stockholders' equity** | | | | | |
| Common stock | 28,000,000 | 6,000,000 | 6,000,000 (A) | | 28,000,000 |
| Capital in excess of par | 2,000,000 | — | | | 2,000,000 |
| Retained earnings | 4,000,000 | 2,000,000 | 2,000,000 (A) | | 4,000,000 |
| Noncontrolling Interest in Gaston | | | | 1,600,000 (A) | 2,000,000 |
| | | | | 400,000 (C) | |
| Total Stockholders' Equity | 34,000,000 | 8,000,000 | | | 36,500,000 |
| **Total liabilities and stockholders' equity** | $35,000,000 | $8,500,000 | $10,000,000 | $10,000,000 | $37,500,000 |

goodwill attributable to Alphonse's controlling interest. Entry (C), however, is unique to the acquisition method:

### ADJUSTMENT AND ELIMINATION ENTRY (C)

| | | | |
|---|---|---|---|
| **DR** | Fixed assets ............................................... | $300,000 | |
| **DR** | Goodwill—Noncontrolling interest ......................... | 100,000 | |
| | **CR** Noncontrolling interest in Gaston ...................... | | $400,000 |

To adjust Gaston's net assets to reflect the full fair value—including goodwill attributed to the noncontrolling interest—on the consolidated balance sheet under the acquisition method.

After this adjustment, the net assets of the subsidiary (Gaston) are reported at acquisition date full fair value on the consolidated balance sheet. All of the acquired entity's goodwill is recognized rather than only Alphonse's share as was the case under the purchase method. Moreover, the noncontrolling interest is reported at fair value rather than book value as under the purchase method. Finally, *SFAS No. 160* requires that the noncontrolling interest be shown in the stockholder's equity section of the consolidated balance sheet rather than in a separate mezzanine section between liabilities and stockholders' equity as was typically done under the purchase method.

### Purchase versus Acquisition Method: Some Other Differences

Four items are treated differently under the acquisition method (*SFAS No. 141R*) compared to the purchase method (*SFAS No. 141*). These differences are briefly described below.

- **Direct combination costs.** Business combinations require several types of costly professional services. Examples include investment banking services, preparation of legal documents, and tax planning and accounting services. *SFAS No. 141* (purchase method) capitalized these costs on the consolidated balance sheet. *SFAS No. 141R* (acquisition method) treats these costs as payments for services received that are expensed as incurred and reported on the consolidated income statement.

- **Contingent consideration.** Some business acquisitions provide for contingent consideration to be given to the acquired firm's shareholders if some future performance measures are met. For example, additional payments by the parent may be required if the subsidiary's profits reach a certain threshold within a short time following the acquisition. Under the purchase method, such contingent payments were accounted for as *postcombination adjustments* to the purchase price. The acquisition method treats contingent consideration as a negotiated component of the purchase price and, therefore, is treated as part of the fair value of consideration transferred at acquisition. This means that the estimated value of the contingent consideration is reported as part of the business fair value at the acquisition date and is included in the net asset values reported on the consolidated balance sheet at the acquisition date.

- **Bargain purchases.** When the fair value of the consideration paid by the acquiring firm is less than the fair values of the separately identified assets acquired and liabilities assumed in a business combination, a bargain purchase is deemed to occur. This situation can occur in a forced sale in which the seller is acting under compulsion or financial distress. *SFAS No. 141* (purchase method) recognized **negative goodwill** and reported the subsidiary's assets below their estimated fair values. *SFAS No. 141R* (acquisition method) records no assets at amounts below their assessed fair values and, therefore, recognizes a gain on bargain purchase at the acquisition date.

- **Acquired in-process research and development.** SFAS No. 141 (purchase method) allocated the purchase price (fair value of consideration given) to the tangible and intangible assets acquired and liabilities assumed. For many firms, especially those in high-tech industries, a significant portion of the purchase price was allocated to in-process research and development (IPR&D). *FASB Interpretation No. 4* immediately wrote off amounts allocated to IPR&D on the consolidated income statement unless those assets had an alternative future use.[10] Because of the ambiguity in determining whether IPR&D had alternative future use, firms often abused this discretionary accounting treatment by aggressive allocations that created large write-offs. This paved the way for reporting higher postacquisition earnings when the R&D projects turned out to be viable (see Chapter 3 for further discussion of this earnings management device). *SFAS No. 141R* closes this loophole by requiring that tangible and intangible R&D assets acquired in a business combination, including those that may have no alternative future use, be measured at fair value and recognized in the consolidated balance sheet at the acquisition date. These capitalized R&D costs are reported as intangible assets with indefinite lives subject to periodic impairment reviews under *SFAS No. 144* (see Chapter 10).

---

**RECAP**

**Consolidated financial statements portray the parent company and its majority-owned subsidiaries as a single economic unit. But the individual balance sheets (and income statements) of each subsidiary and the parent are not simply added together. Instead, consolidated adjustments are made to avoid double counting internal business transactions as well as various balance sheet items. When the parent company acquires less than 100% interest in a subsidiary, a noncontrolling or minority interest in the subsidiary's net assets and income is created. Because the consolidated statements include the subsidiary's total assets, liabilities and income, the noncontrolling shareholders' interest in these amounts must be recorded in the consolidated statements. The noncontrolling interests are reported at subsidiary book values under the purchase method but at fair value under the acquisition method.**

## Accounting for Goodwill

As illustrated in the previous examples, purchase and acquisition methods of accounting typically result in recognizing goodwill on the consolidated financial statements. Prior to 2002, goodwill acquired in a purchase transaction was amortized (charged to income) over a period not exceeding 40 years.[11] *SFAS No. 142*, "Goodwill and Other Intangible Assets," which became effective on January 1, 2002, dramatically changed the accounting for purchased goodwill. *SFAS No. 142* no longer permits amortization of goodwill for purchase transactions.[12] Instead, goodwill must be tested for impairment at least annually or when there is reason to suspect that its value has diminished. Goodwill is then expensed only when it is deemed to be impaired. To implement the new

Examples of circumstances that would trigger impairment testing include:

- A significant adverse change in legal factors or in the business climate.
- A regulator's adverse action or assessment.
- Unanticipated competition.
- A loss of key personnel.
- A likelihood that a reporting unit or a significant portion of a reporting unit will be sold or disposed of.
- A significant asset group is being tested for recoverability under *SFAS No. 121*.
- Recognition of a goodwill impairment loss in the financial statements of a subsidiary that is a component of a reporting unit.

---

[10] "Applicability of Statement No. 2 to Business Combinations Accounted for by the Purchase Method—An Interpretation of FASB Statement No. 2," *FASB Interpretation No. 4* (Norwalk, CT: FASB, 1975).

[11] "Intangible Assets," *APB Opinion No. 17*, para. 9 (New York: Accounting Principles Board, 1970).

[12] "Goodwill and Other Intangible Assets," *Statement of Financial Accounting Standards No. 142*, para. 18 (Norwalk, CT: FASB, 2001).

## Figure 16.2

SFAS NO. 142 Goodwill Impairment Test

Source: SFAS No. 142, "Goodwill and Other Intangible Assets" (Norwalk, CT: FASB, 2001).

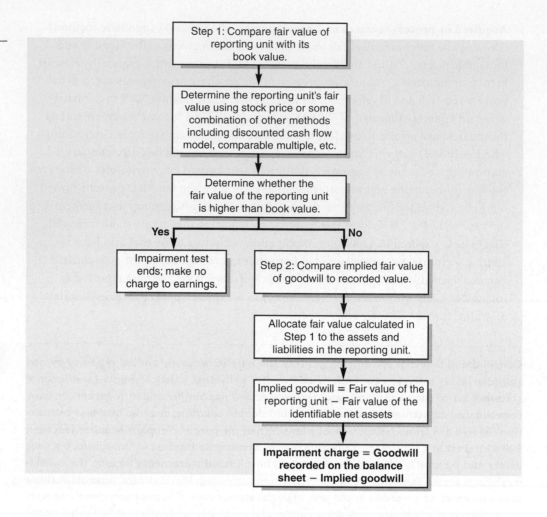

Fair value of a reporting unit "refers to the amount at which the unit could be bought or sold in a current transaction between willing parties."* If the reporting unit is publicly traded, the stock price provides the best evidence of fair value. If stock prices are not available, fair values are determined using one or more other methods including discounted cash flow analysis or a multiple of earnings or some other performance measure such as revenues or earnings before interest, taxes, depreciation, and amortization.

* *SFAS No. 142*, para. 23.

impairment test, firms must first allocate goodwill arising from an acquisition to one or more reporting units (firm segments) at the acquisition date. Once allocated, the two-step impairment test outlined in Figure 16.2 is applied at the reporting unit level.

The first step determines whether goodwill has been impaired, and the second step establishes the amount of the impairment charge. In the first step, goodwill is considered impaired if the book value of the reporting unit's net assets (including allocated goodwill) exceed their fair value. To determine the amount of the impairment charge, the recorded goodwill for each reporting unit is compared to its implied fair value. The implied fair value of goodwill— called **implied goodwill**—is the difference between the fair value of the reporting unit as a whole (established in Step 1) minus the fair value of the identifiable tangible and intangible assets (exclusive of goodwill) assigned to that reporting unit. The impairment charge is the difference between the goodwill recorded on the balance sheet and the implied goodwill. The following numerical example illustrates how to determine goodwill impairment under *SFAS No. 142*:

Assume that Aggressive Company acquires all of Slow Growth Company's outstanding voting stock early in 2008 for $100 million. On that date, Slow Growth's identifiable tangible and intangible net assets had a fair value of $80 million resulting in recorded goodwill of $20 million. Aggressive assigned $15 million of the goodwill to reporting unit A and $5 million to

*(continued)*

reporting unit B. On December 31, 2008, Aggressive performs an impairment test and determines the following:

| ($ in millions) | Unit A | Unit B |
|---|---|---|
| (a) Fair value of reporting unit (including goodwill) | $60 | $45 |
| (b) Book value of reporting unit | 75 | 35 |
| (c) Is goodwill impaired? | Yes | No |
| (d) Sum of fair values of identifiable net assets of unit A, exclusive of goodwill | 50 | — |
| (e) Implied fair value of goodwill (a)–(d) | 10 | — |
| (f) Book value of goodwill | 15 | — |
| (g) Impairment charge (f)–(e) | $ 5 | — |

The *SFAS No. 142* rules for determining goodwill impairment coupled with the rather dramatic downturn in the stock market in 2002 resulted in a significant number of firms reporting goodwill impairments totaling hundreds of billions of dollars in their 2002 annual reports.

The following excerpt taken from a special equity research report prepared by Bear Stearns, an investment banking and brokerage firm, discusses the possible valuation implications of such write-downs:

> The facts and circumstances surrounding each goodwill impairment charge will need to be evaluated for their investment significance. The new FASB rule will require information about goodwill to be provided at the segment level, increasing the likelihood that the market will be cognizant of potential changes in fundamentals diminishing the value of goodwill. If the market is aware of this deterioration from other information, the impairment charge is unlikely to affect the company's stock price. However, if there is an impairment in a reporting unit that previously had been thought to have good fundamentals, it will be news to the market and could have a negative impact on stock price.[13]

 **Valuation**

**RECAP**

**Under *SFAS No. 142*, periodic amortization of goodwill is no longer allowed. Instead, goodwill is subject to an impairment test at least annually. As a result, goodwill impairment charges are likely to occur more frequently under *SFAS No. 142* reporting rules than was the case in the past. Statement users need to carefully assess whether the charge is a sign of a bad acquisition, a miscalculation of the value of the target (that is, the acquirer overpaid), or the result of an unexpected deterioration in the fundamentals of the business acquired.**

## Purchase Method versus Pooling-of-Interests Method

The examples illustrated to this point in the chapter show how business combinations are accounted for under the **purchase and acquisition methods** of accounting. The central idea underlying these methods is that there is a change in ownership when one entity (parent) acquires all, or substantially all, of the ownership interests and net assets of another company (subsidiary). Like any other purchase of an asset—such as inventory or machinery—the parent records the investment in the subsidiary's common stock at the fair value of the consideration given. As shown in the consolidation worksheets in Exhibits 16.2 to 16.4, if the purchase price exceeds the book value of the net assets acquired, this excess is allocated to the identifiable assets and liabilities of the acquired entity: That's the role of the adjustment and elimination entries. What results is that the identifiable net assets of the acquired entity are revalued

---

[13] "Goodbye, Goodwill," *Equity Research Special Report* (New York: Bear Stearns & Company, Inc., 2001).

> A write-up of the acquired company's assets is called a *step up in basis* of those assets.

to their fair values at the acquisition date.[14] Any remaining excess is allocated to goodwill.[15] Postconsolidation earnings is often lower than the combined earnings of the preconsolidated entities under the purchase method of accounting for two reasons:

1. Various assets of the acquired company (for example, inventory and depreciable assets) are frequently written up on the date of acquisition from their carrying value to their fair value—so subsequent cost of goods sold and depreciation is higher.

2. Goodwill may subsequently become impaired and need to be written off.

Prior to the issuance of *SFAS No. 141* in June 2001, GAAP allowed a second method of accounting for business combinations, called the **pooling-of-interests method.** It was allowed when the acquisition was achieved through an exchange of shares and certain other stringent criteria were met. The basic idea underlying pooling accounting is that the ownership interests of the two combining firms are united, and both sets of stockholders therefore share jointly in the rewards and risks of ownership of the new combined entity. Because no new assets are invested, nor do owners in the precombination entities withdraw assets or give up their ownership

> For instance, the combining entities could not dispose of significant operations shortly before or after the combination, and there could be no additional issuances, exchanges, or retirements of securities in contemplation of effecting the combination. Additional criteria that need to be satisfied to use the pooling-of-interests method of accounting are set forth in paras. 46–48 of *APB Opinion No. 16,* "Business Combinations" (New York: Accounting Principles Board, 1970).

rights, **there is no transfer or sale of ownership.** *Consequently, no grounds exist for establishing a new basis of accounting for the net assets of the consolidated entity.* This means that the book values of the net assets of the combining entities are carried forward on the consolidated entity's books and no goodwill is recorded. Because there is no increase in the basis of the combined entity's net assets and no goodwill to be written off, the consolidated entity's postconsolidated earnings would be higher than they would otherwise be under the purchase method.

Although the pooling-of-interests method is no longer allowed, we discuss and illustrate its application in Appendix B to this chapter because a significant number of combinations (particularly the larger mergers) were accounted for as poolings prior to the issuance of *SFAS No. 141.* Because the effects of this treatment will be found in financial statements for years to come, it is important for you to understand the impact of this method and how it complicates comparisons with consolidated statements accounted for under the purchase method.

 **Analysis**

 RE**CAP**

**Under the purchase method of accounting, a change in ownership occurs when the parent acquires all, or substantially all, of the subsidiary's ownership interests and net assets. The investment in the subsidiary's common stock is recorded at the fair value of the consideration given. Through the adjustment and elimination entries on the consolidated worksheet, the excess of the purchase price over the book value of the subsidiary's net assets is allocated to its identifiable assets and liabilities. This results in the subsidiary's identifiable net assets being recorded at their fair values at acquisition date on the consolidated balance sheet. Under the pooling-of-interest method of accounting (which is no longer allowed pursuant to SFAS No. 141), equity interests are exchanged and the shareholders of the two previously separate companies become shareholders of the combined entity. No buyout occurs and, therefore, no new accounting basis—no asset write-up to fair value—is recognized in the consolidated statements. Instead, the book values of the previously separate companies are carried forward on the consolidated financial statements.**

---

[14] If the acquisition is less than 100%, thus creating a minority interest in the consolidated net assets, the revaluation of the subsidiary's net assets reflects only the parent's percentage interest in the fair values of the subsidiary's net assets under the purchase method. The minority interest portion of the subsidiary's net assets is recorded at their book values at acquisition date under the purchase method as illustrated in Exhibit 16.3 on page 957. Under the acquisition method, the subsidiary's net assets are recorded at full fair value and the noncontrolling (minority) interest is also recorded at fair value on the acquisition date.

[15] This goodwill is subject to an annual impairment test and, if met, results in a charge to consolidated earnings. See "Goodwill and Other Intangible Assets," *SFAS No. 142* (Norwalk, CT: FASB, 2001).

## Purchase and Acquisition Methods Complicate Financial Analysis

The disclosure rules for business combinations accounted for as purchases complicate financial analysis. Trend analysis becomes difficult. Why? Because under U.S. GAAP, comparative financial statements are not retroactively adjusted to include data for the acquired company for periods prior to the acquisition. To illustrate, Exhibit 16.5(a) on the following page presents comparative income statements from the 2007 annual report of Lincoln National Corporation, a holding company that operates multiple insurance, investment management, broadcasting, and sports programming businesses through subsidiaries. In April 2006, Lincoln National acquired a 100% interest in Jefferson-Pilot Corporation, a financial services and broadcasting holding company in an acquisition accounted for using the purchase method. Accordingly, Lincoln National's 2006 consolidated income statement includes the revenues and expenses of Jefferson-Pilot from the acquisition date (April 3) through December 31, 2006, Lincoln National's fiscal year-end. Under the rules of purchase accounting,[16] the 2005 numbers reported in Lincoln National's 2007 consolidated comparative income statement do not include any of Jefferson-Pilot's results for that year. However, Jefferson-Pilot's *full-year* revenues and expenses are included in Lincoln National's 2007 consolidated income statement numbers. ***Thus, the income statements over the three years are noncomparable—Lincoln National's 2007 statements include Jefferson-Pilot's results for 12 months, the 2006 statement reflects Jefferson-Pilot's performance for 9 months, and the 2005 statement excludes Jefferson-Pilot's results for the entire year!***

> Because the acquisition method also includes the operating results of the acquired subsidiary in consolidated income only from the date of acquisition, the same distortions in year-to-year growth rates described here for the purchase method also apply to the acquisition method.

To aid interperiod comparisons, existing disclosure rules require a **pro forma** (meaning *as if*) footnote that gives information for key income statement items as if the acquisition had taken place on the first day of the *previous* fiscal year, in this case January 1, 2005. These pro forma footnote numbers for Lincoln National (shown in Exhibit 16.5[c]) reflect full-year results for Jefferson-Pilot in both 2006 and 2005. Notice, however, that these pro forma data do *not* encompass all income statement items and do not include periods prior to 2005. Consequently, even with the footnote disclosure, it is usually not possible for analysts to make comparisons of *complete* income statements adjusted for the acquisition. This is a serious deficiency that destroys the comparability of the time-series financial statement data used by lenders and other financial analysts. Indeed, if the acquired company is large in relation to the size of the acquirer, the consolidated financial statements seriously distort trends and other comparative data.

To illustrate the problem of trying to perform time-series comparisons for a business combination accounted for as a purchase, we concentrate on the operating revenue disclosures in Exhibit 16.5(a). The three-year operating revenue data from Lincoln National's consolidated statement of income, along with a computation of year-to-year growth in this measure is:

| ($ in millions) | 2007 | 2006 | 2005 |
|---|---|---|---|
| Operating revenue as reported in consolidated financial statements | $10,594 | $8,962 | $5,475 |
| Rate of growth in operating revenue compared to prior year | 18.2% | 63.7% | 2.3%* |

* Based on 2004 operating revenue of $5,351.

---

[16] *SFAS No. 141*, para. 49.

**EXHIBIT 16.5**   **Lincoln National Corporation and Subsidiaries**

### Disclosures Subsequent to a Business Combination: Purchase Accounting

**Panel (a)**

**Consolidated Statement of Earnings**
($ in millions)

| | 2007 | 2006 | 2005 |
|---|---|---|---|
| **Revenue** | | | |
| Insurance premiums | $ 1,945 | $ 1,406 | $ 308 |
| Insurance fees | 3,254 | 2,604 | 1,752 |
| Investment advisory fees | 360 | 328 | 256 |
| Net investment income | 4,384 | 3,981 | 2,702 |
| Realized gain (loss) | (118) | (3) | (3) |
| Amortization of deferred gain on indemnity reinsurance | 83 | 76 | 77 |
| Other revenue and fees | 686 | 570 | 383 |
| Total revenues | 10,594 | 8,962 | 5,475 |
| **Expenses** | | | |
| Benefits and interest credited | 5,152 | 4,170 | 2,332 |
| Underwriting, acquisition, insurance and other expenses | 3,284 | 2,790 | 1,981 |
| Interest and debt expense | 284 | 224 | 87 |
| Total benefits and expenses | 8,720 | 7,184 | 4,400 |
| Income before federal income taxes | 1,874 | 1,778 | 1,075 |
| Federal income taxes | 553 | 483 | 244 |
| Income before cumulative effect of accounting changes | 1,321 | 1,295 | 831 |
| Income (loss) from discontinued operation, net of federal income taxes | (106) | 21 | — |
| Net income | $ 1,215 | $ 1,316 | $ 831 |

**Panel (b)**

**Excerpts from Annual Report Footnote**

On April 3, 2006, we completed our merger with Jefferson-Pilot by acquiring 100% of the outstanding shares of Jefferson-Pilot in a transaction accounted for under the purchase method of accounting prescribed by SFAS No. 141, "Business Combinations" ("SFAS 141"). Jefferson-Pilot's results of operations are included in our results of operations beginning April 3, 2006. As a result of the merger, our product portfolio was expanded, and we now offer fixed and variable universal life, fixed annuities, including indexed annuities, variable annuities, mutual funds and institutional accounts, 401(k) and 403(b) offerings, and group life, disability, and dental insurance products. We also own and operate television and radio stations in selected markets in the Southeastern and Western United States and produce and distribute sports programming.

**Panel (c)**

| | | **Year Ended** | |
|---|---|---|---|
| (in millions) | **2007** | **2006** | **2005** |
| Revenue | $10,594 | $10,134 | $9,559 |
| | └── 4.54% ──┘ | └── 6.00% ──┘ | |
| Net Income | 1,215 | 1,430 | 1,352 |
| | └── −15.03% ──┘ | └── 5.80% ──┘ | |

The computed growth rates in operating revenues for 2007 and 2006 are misleading because the basic operating revenue data—and all other items in the income statement—are noncomparable. Again, the reason is that Lincoln National's 2007 data include Jefferson-Pilot's results for the full year, the 2006 figures incorporate Jefferson-Pilot's results for nine months, and the 2005 data exclude it altogether. To perform a valid comparison of operating revenue growth, the 2006 and 2005 numbers must be restated "as if" the combination had occurred at the beginning of each of these two fiscal years. These pro forma numbers are reported in Exhibit 16.5(c) and are reproduced here:

| ($ in millions) | 2007 | 2006 | 2005 |
| --- | --- | --- | --- |
| Total revenue from consolidated statements | $10,594 | — | — |
| Total revenue from pro forma disclosure | — | $10,134 | $9,559 |
| Rate of growth in total revenue compared to prior year | 4.5% | 6.0% | * |

\* Cannot be calculated because 2004 pro forma data are not required to be reported.

The actual rate of operating revenue growth for 2006 and 2007 was 6.0% and 4.5% respectively—assuming that the combination occurred at the beginning of 2005. This is much lower than the rate computed from the operating revenue numbers actually reported in the financial statements—63.7% and 18.2%. Also notice in Exhibit 16.5(c) how the sparseness of pro forma disclosures makes it possible to compare only one other income statement line item in addition to operating revenue: bottom-line net income. The only way to overcome this problem is to gather past financial statement data for Jefferson-Pilot and consolidate its past results with those of Lincoln National (using appropriate assumptions about intercompany sales and loans, of course). It's easy to obtain these data when the acquired company is publicly held. However, if it is not publicly held, these data may be difficult or even impossible to obtain.

For business combinations accounted for as a pooling of interests (allowed until July 1, 2001), this comparability problem did not occur. That's because under pooling, all past financial statement data were retroactively consolidated to include both parties to the combination. Keep in mind, however, that while the pooling-of-interests approach overcomes some income statement comparability problems, the reported financial data using this approach are still fraught with the deficiencies that we describe in Appendix B to this chapter.

RECAP

**Trend analysis under purchase and acquisition method accounting becomes difficult because U.S. GAAP comparative financial statements are not retroactively adjusted to include data for the acquired company for periods prior to the acquisition. In the year of the acquisition, the consolidated income statement includes the parent company results for the full year and the results of the subsidiary from the time the acquisition took place to the end of the year (that is, for the fraction of a year the parent owned the subsidiary). In the year following acquisition, the consolidated income statement includes the full year results for both the parent and the subsidiary. In the year prior to the acquisition, the income statement includes the results of the parent company only and does not include any of the subsidiary's results. This can lead to distortions in year-to-year growth rates in revenues and profits that statement users need to be aware of. Supplemental disclosures allow analysts to make adjustments to the reported numbers to make more valid comparisons but only for selected statement items.**

## Consolidation of Variable Interest Entities

Enron's collapse in 2001 created a demand for increased disclosure and transparency about companies' interests in *special-purpose entities (SPE)* or *variable interest entities (VIE)*. A VIE is a corporation, partnership, trust, or any other legal structure used for business purposes that either (a) does not have equity investors with voting rights or (b) has equity investors that do

Enron, with the help of its chief financial officer, Andrew Fastow, set up a number of limited partnerships through which it engaged in billions of dollars of complex transactions to hedge fluctuating values in some of Enron's broadband telecommunications and other technology investments. Under existing reporting rules at the time, Enron was able to avoid consolidation of these SPEs, thereby keeping hundreds of millions of dollars of debt and losses off of their financial statements.

> For example, a company building a factory can borrow money based on the worth of the factory or on expectations of its future revenue.

not provide sufficient financial resources for the entity to support its activities. VIEs are typically formed to engage in what is called *structured financing arrangements,* which offer a company an opportunity to borrow money based on the value of a specific project or asset rather than on its own credit rating. Major uses of VIEs include synthetic leasing (see Chapter 12), securitizing loans and mortgages (see Chapter 8), selling receivables (see Chapter 8), and setting up **take-or-pay contracts** or **throughput arrangements.**

A *take-or-pay contract* is an "agreement between a purchaser and a seller that provides for the purchaser to pay specified amounts periodically in return for products or services. The purchaser must make specified minimum payments even if it does not take delivery of the contracted products or services."*

For example, two companies may form an SPE with a nominal investment to build an oil refinery that both companies will use. The SPE borrows money to build the refinery with the note being guaranteed by one or both companies. Both companies agree to make minimum payments to the SPE each quarter in exchange for a specified number of barrels of refined oil on which they may or may not take delivery.

A *throughput agreement* is an "agreement between a shipper (processor) and the owner of a transportation facility (such as an oil or natural gas pipeline or a ship) or a manufacturing facility that provides for the shipper (processor) to pay specified amounts periodically in return for the transportation (processing) of the product. The shipper (processor) is obligated to provide specified minimum quantities to be transported (processed) in each period and is required to make cash payments even if it does not provide the contracted quantities."†

* "Disclosure of Long-Term Obligations," *SFAS No. 47,* para. 23(c) (Stamford, CT: FASB, 1981).
† Ibid., para. 23(d).

The accounting for VIEs is difficult because the rules are complex and cover a variety of transactions. Therefore, we do not go into details here. *The critical issue is determining when VIEs have to be consolidated into the financial statements of the sponsoring entity. FASB Interpretation No. 46* requires a company to consolidate a VIE if that company is subject to a majority of the risk of loss from the VIE's activities, is entitled to receive a majority of the entity's residual returns, or both.[17] Generally, a third party has to maintain at least a 10% equity interest in the market value of the VIE's assets for the sponsoring entity to *avoid* consolidation. A company that consolidates a VIE is called that entity's *primary beneficiary.*

The FASB believes that requiring the primary beneficiary of the assets, liabilities, and operating results of VIEs to consolidate them provides financial statement users more complete information about the resources, obligations, risks, and opportunities facing the firm. Time will tell whether the disclosures will provide the benefits hoped for by the FASB.

## ACCOUNTING FOR FOREIGN SUBSIDIARIES

All majority-owned subsidiaries—foreign and domestic—must be consolidated using the methods we've just described. Regrettably, there's an additional complication when consolidating foreign subsidiaries—that is, the subsidiary's financial records will be expressed in foreign currency units. The subsidiary's numbers must first be *transformed* into the parent's currency units—into dollars for a U.S. parent—before the consolidation process begins.

The transformation under U.S. GAAP (*SFAS No. 52*) specifies one of two procedures, depending on the foreign subsidiary's operating characteristics:[18]

1. Foreign subsidiaries that are mere extensions of the parent with no self-sufficiency are **remeasured** using the **temporal method.** For example, in the case of a European sales subsidiary of a U.S. seed company, the subsidiary sells seed produced by the U.S. parent to European farmers and sends the sale proceeds back to the United States. In other words, the subsidiary remits the revenue it collects to the parent company.

---

[17] "Consolidation of Variable Interest Entities: An interpretation of ARB No. 51," *FASB Interpretation No. 46* (revised December 2003) (Norwalk, CT: FASB, December, 2003).

[18] "Foreign Currency Translation," *SFAS No. 52* (Stamford, CT: FASB, 1981). Although our discussion centers on *consolidation* of a foreign subsidiary, the rules described here must also be used in conjunction with the *equity method* when the parent owns between 20% and 50% of a foreign company.

2. Foreign subsidiaries that are essentially freestanding units with self-contained foreign operations are **translated** using the **current rate method.** For example, in the case of a European manufacturing and sales subsidiary of a U.S. computer company, the subsidiary buys parts in Europe, assembles the final product, and sells it to European businesses, retaining the cash proceeds for growth and expansion locally.

The procedure selected to transform subsidiary statements expressed in foreign currency units into the parent's currency units is called the **functional currency choice.** What guides this choice is subtle;[19] foreign subsidiaries whose operations are not self-sufficient are considered to be engaging in a continuing series of **foreign currency transactions.** The consolidation process accordingly treats the financial results of these subsidiaries in the same way foreign currency transactions are treated. To illustrate, we must digress briefly to explain the accounting for foreign currency transactions.

## Foreign Currency Transactions

Foreign currency transactions are simply business transactions denominated in units of a foreign currency. Examples include a U.S. company taking out a bank loan denominated in Norwegian kroner or purchasing inventory in the Netherlands on credit for a price expressed in euros. The accounting for foreign currency transactions depends on the type of asset acquired or liability incurred. Let's consider a foreign currency transaction that involves the acquisition of a **monetary asset**—that is, an asset such as cash or accounts receivable whose value is derived from the number of monetary units into which it is convertible.

Assume that on January 1, 2008 Yankee Corporation (a U.S. company) sells 100 units of its product to a U.K. customer. The selling price is £10 per unit, or £1,000 total. Payment is due on April 1, 2008. On January 1, 2008, assume that £1 is worth $2 U.S. and that the per unit production cost incurred by Yankee is $8. Given this information, Yankee records the foreign currency transaction on its books in this way:

| | | |
|---|---|---|
| **DR** Accounts receivable | $2,000 | |
| **CR** Sales revenue | | $2,000 |
| To record the receivable of £1,000 at its 1/1/08 U.S. dollar equivalent of $2,000. | | |

| | | |
|---|---|---|
| **DR** Cost of goods sold | $800 | |
| **CR** Inventory | | $800 |
| To record 100 units @ $8. | | |

The receivable is denominated in pounds—which makes this a foreign currency transaction. Because Yankee keeps its books in dollars, the receivable must be reexpressed in home-currency units when preparing financial statements. This is done using the exchange rate in effect at the transaction date—£1 = $2 U.S. It is important to understand that while the receivable is initially reflected on the books at $2,000, in reality what the customer owes is £1,000.

By the end of the quarter, the pound has fallen relative to the dollar, so that on March 31, 2008, the exchange rate is £1 = $1.80 U.S. This means that at current exchange rates, the receivable is worth only $1,800, so Yankee books the following entry when preparing its quarterly statements:

| | | |
|---|---|---|
| **DR** Foreign currency transaction loss | $200 | |
| **CR** Accounts receivable | | $200 |
| To reflect the £1,000 receivable at its end-of-quarter dollar equivalent of $1,800. | | |

---

[19] See L. Revsine, "The Rationale Underlying the Functional Currency Choice," *The Accounting Review,* July 1984, pp. 504–14.

Yankee has a loss because it was owed pounds but the pound has fallen in value. This loss is reflected in the income statement of the period in which the loss occurs. Monetary assets (such as accounts receivable) that arise from foreign currency transactions are shown in the financial statements at their dollar equivalent using **the exchange rate in effect at the financial statement date.** Monetary liabilities (such as accounts or bonds payable) are similarly translated using the exchange rate in effect at the statement date. The statement date exchange rate is referred to as the **current rate.**

Suppose that the exchange rate on April 1, 2008 when the receivable is paid, is still £1 = $1.80 U.S. The customer remits £1,000, which Yankee then converts into dollars. The entry on Yankee's books is:

> Most liabilities are monetary because they are expressed in units of currency (for example, a Japanese yen account payable of ¥9,000,000) and will be settled using foreign currency monetary assets. However, a few liabilities are settled by using *nonmonetary* assets; this small class of liabilities is considered to be nonmonetary. Examples include estimated product warranty liabilities and customer deposits for products to be produced and delivered in future periods.

| | | |
|---|---|---|
| **DR** Cash | $1,800 | |
| **CR** Accounts receivable | | $1,800 |

To remove the receivable from the books. The initial $2,000 minus the 3/31/08 write-down of $200 equals the carrying amount of $1,800.

We next illustrate the accounting for a foreign currency transaction that involves a non-monetary asset. Nonmonetary assets are items such as inventory, equipment, land, buildings, and trucks whose value is determined by supply and demand.

Suppose that because of Yankee's growing volume of sales to U.K. customers it decides to purchase a warehouse in London to store inventory awaiting shipment to customers. It purchases a building on June 30, 2008 for £300,000; on that date, the exchange rate is £1 = $1.75 U.S. The building is recorded on Yankee's books at the U.S. dollar equivalent of the foreign currency transaction price at the purchase date:

| | | |
|---|---|---|
| **DR** Warehouse building | $525,000 | |
| **CR** Cash | | $525,000 |

To record the acquisition of the London warehouse at the U.S. dollar equivalent of the foreign currency transaction price: £300,000 × 1.75 = $525,000.

The subsequent accounting for nonmonetary assets acquired in a foreign currency transaction is identical to the accounting for nonmonetary assets acquired in the domestic currency. Specifically, the fixed asset's historical cost in dollars is used as the measurement basis in subsequent financial statements throughout the asset's life. Even if the pound's value falls to £1 = $1.60 U.S. by year-end 2008, the London warehouse is still shown on Yankee's books at $525,000—that is, at its acquisition cost in dollars (minus depreciation, of course). Thus, to reflect the gross carrying amount of nonmonetary assets acquired in a foreign currency transaction, Yankee uses the exchange rate in effect at the time of the transaction. This rate is called the **historical exchange rate.**

## RECAP

**The accounting for assets and liabilities arising from foreign currency transactions depends on the nature of the item—that is,**

1. **Foreign currency monetary assets and liabilities are remeasured using the current rate of exchange in effect at the balance sheet date.**

2. **Foreign currency nonmonetary assets (and liabilities) are remeasured using the historical exchange rate in effect when the item was acquired or incurred.**

# Accounting for Nonfreestanding Foreign Subsidiaries

Now that we've outlined the accounting for foreign currency transactions, we can return to our main theme—that is, accounting for foreign subsidiaries. When we introduced this topic, we said the method used to transform the foreign currency accounts of foreign subsidiaries depends on the nature of the subsidiary's operations. Subsidiaries that are not freestanding—that is, whose operations are simply an extension of the parent—are remeasured using the temporal method. We now explain why.

To see what it means when we say that a foreign subsidiary is not freestanding, let's consider a U.S. company, Doodle Corporation, with a U.K. subsidiary called Dandy Ltd. Dandy's role is to serve as Doodle's U.K. marketing arm. Doodle manufactures a product in the United States using U.S. sourced materials and labor. Some of the production is shipped from the United States to the United Kingdom where it is sold to U.K. customers at a price denominated in pounds sterling. Product distribution and the collection of the receivables are coordinated by two U.K. employees of Dandy Ltd. Upon collection of the receivables, the pounds are remitted to the United States. This cycle is repeated as the pounds are converted into dollars, the dollars are used in the United States to manufacture more inventory, and some portion of the inventory is again shipped to the United Kingdom for sale to customers there. Dandy's only U.K. assets are (1) a small amount of cash to pay expenses, (2) inventory from Doodle that has not yet been shipped to customers, and (3) a building that serves as both a warehouse and an office for the two employees.

The situation described here is a classic illustration of a foreign subsidiary that is merely an extension of the parent. Dandy Ltd. is a marketing arm of Doodle rather than a viable, freestanding company. It is a conduit for administering foreign sales and has no independent life of its own.

Under *SFAS No. 52,* subsidiaries like Dandy Ltd. are treated as if they were created for the sole purpose of facilitating foreign currency transactions. Because such subsidiaries are a conduit for foreign transactions, upon consolidation they are treated as if the parent company had engaged in the foreign transactions directly. That is, ***the numbers included when consolidating a nonfreestanding subsidiary are identical to the numbers that would have been included had the subsidiary not existed and instead the parent had engaged in the foreign currency transactions directly.***

To achieve this effect in the financial statements, the temporal method is used to translate the subsidiary's foreign currency statements into dollars.[20] The exchange rates for translating various accounts under the temporal method are shown in Exhibit 16.6.

| EXHIBIT 16.6 | Translation Exchange Rates under the Temporal Method |
| --- | --- |
| **Account Category** | **Rate Used** |
| Balance Sheet | |
|    Monetary assets and liabilities | Current rate |
|    Nonmonetary assets and liabilities | Historical rate |
| Income Statement | |
|    All revenue and expense accounts except those listed below | Rate at time of transaction |
| Cost of goods sold and depreciation | Historical rate |

---

[20] *SFAS No. 52* uses the term **remeasure** when describing the conversion from foreign currency units to home currency units under the temporal method. For simplicity, we ignore this nuance and refer to the process as *translation.*

To illustrate the temporal method, consider the following transactions for Dandy Ltd. during 2008.

1. On January 1, 2008, it received inventory costing $800 from Doodle when £1 = $2 U.S, and sold these goods on credit for £1,000.

2. The pound falls to £1 = $1.80 U.S. on March 31, 2008. Dandy collects receivables of £1,000 on April 1, 2008, when £1 = $1.80 U.S.

3. Dandy purchases a building in London for £300,000 on June 30, 2008 when £1 = $1.75 U.S.

These transactions are identical to the foreign currency transactions entered into by Yankee Corporation earlier in this section. In Exhibit 16.7, we show the result of using the temporal method to translate Dandy Ltd.'s statements. The results under GAAP for Yankee's foreign currency transactions are displayed in the shaded column for comparison.

Comparing the Dandy statement numbers with those of Yankee in Exhibit 16.7 demonstrates the point of the example. Using the temporal method results in Dandy's statements being denominated in dollar figures that equal those of Yankee. This is no coincidence. **Both Dandy and Yankee are considered to have engaged in identical foreign currency transactions, so the two sets of results should be equal.** Notice how the translation rules under the temporal method help achieve this result.

## Accounting for Self-Contained Foreign Subsidiaries

When the majority-owned foreign subsidiary and its parent operate independently, the translation of the subsidiary's financial statements into dollars uses the current rate method.

| **EXHIBIT 16.7** | **Comparison of Temporal Method Results with Accounting for Foreign Currency Transactions** | | | |
|---|---|---|---|---|
| | **Temporal Method Translation** | | | **Foreign Currency Transactions** |
| | Dandy Ltd. in £s | Exchange Rate | Dandy Ltd. in $s | Yankee Corporation |
| Income Statement | | | | |
| Sales | £ 1,000 | 1£ = $2 | $ 2,000 | $ 2,000 |
| Cost of sales | 400 | 1£ = $2 | 800 | 800 |
| Gross margin | £ 600 | | $ 1,200 | $ 1,200 |
| Loss on receivables* | — | | 200 | 200 |
| Gross income | £ 600 | | $ 1,000 | $ 1,000 |
| | | | | |
| Selected Balance Sheet accounts | | | | |
| At 3/31/08 | | | | |
| Account receivable | £ 1,000 | 1£ = $1.80 | $ 1,800 | $ 1,800 |
| At 4/1/08 | | | | |
| Cash | £ 1,000 | 1£ = $1.80 | $ 1,800 | $ 1,800 |
| At 6/30/08 | | | | |
| Building | £300,000 | 1£ = $1.75 | $525,000 | $525,000 |

* Computed as:

| | | |
|---|---|---|
| Monetary asset on acquisition | £1,000 when 1£ = $2.00 = | $2,000 |
| Monetary asset at March 31, 2008 | £1,000 when 1£ = $1.80 = | 1,800 |
| Loss on receivables | | $ 200 |

To understand why, let's consider a self-contained subsidiary whose operations do not rely extensively on the parent.

A U.S. food company has a Swiss subsidiary formed by a capital infusion from the U.S. parent. Once the equity cushion was in place, the remainder of the Swiss subsidiary's long-term capital was raised using Swiss franc borrowing. The subsidiary engages in no transactions with the parent. Operations are entirely contained in Switzerland where the company hires employees, buys inventory, manufactures its product line, and sells to Swiss and other European customers. The Swiss operation plows back operating profits to expand into new product lines and to increase production capacity. While the parent may periodically receive dividends from the subsidiary, its investment remains until it either sells or liquidates the subsidiary.

For self-contained foreign subsidiaries, the effect of changes in exchange rates on future dollar cash flows is uncertain. Consider a rise in the Swiss franc. One possible effect of the rise is that it will make the subsidiary's products more expensive to foreign purchasers and could adversely affect profits. The rise in the Swiss franc also means that input purchases in other currencies are less expensive, so a favorable profit effect could ensue. The possibilities are many and depend on the subsidiary's individual characteristics and on those of the markets in which it operates. These possibilities include:

1. Does the subsidiary price its product sales in countries outside Switzerland in Swiss francs or in units of the foreign currencies?
2. Does the subsidiary adjust its Swiss franc selling price when the value of the franc rises or falls?
3. What proportion of the product input does the subsidiary purchase in Switzerland in francs?
4. Does the Swiss franc borrowing have a floating rate of interest that would be sensitive to exchange rate changes?

These are only a few of the many possibilities that could influence the magnitude and direction of the effect of the exchange rate change on ultimate dollar cash flows from the subsidiary. ***Because the ultimate exchange rate effects on U.S. dollar cash flows are uncertain, the FASB decided that such subsidiaries should be translated using the current rate method and that any debit or credit arising from translation "gains" or "losses" should be put directly into Other comprehensive income in stockholders' equity, not run through the income statement.*** Under the current rate method, *all* balance sheet accounts are translated at the current exchange rate in effect at the balance sheet date and *all* income statement accounts are translated at the weighted average rate of exchange that was in effect over the period covered by the statement.

> See Chapter 2 for further discussion of Other comprehensive income components.

If *all* accounts in a statement are translated at the *same* rate—which is what happens under the current rate method—the translated statements have the same proportionality as the untranslated statements expressed in foreign currency units. In other words, the Swiss subsidiary's quick ratio derived from its pre-translated Swiss franc statements will be identical to the quick ratio once the statements are translated into dollars using the current rate method. The current rate method provides a practical way to go from foreign currency units to dollars while still maintaining or very closely approximating the subsidiary's financial ratios. ***Furthermore, by denying income***

> Ratio proportionality between foreign currency and translated dollar numbers is maintained *precisely* for any ratio for which the numerator and denominator are confined to a single statement. Examples include the current ratio—both balance sheet accounts—and gross margin ratio—both income statement accounts. This is true because the current rate method translates all accounts within a single statement at the same rate—weighted average rate for income statement items and end-of-year rate for balance sheet items. For ratios that use numbers from both statements—for example, rate of return on assets—the current rate method does not maintain perfect proportionality. However, the difference between the "mixed-statement ratio" expressed in foreign currency and the translated ratio expressed in U.S. dollars is usually very small.

**Figure 16.3**

TRANSLATION APPROACH
USED IN *SFAS NO. 52*

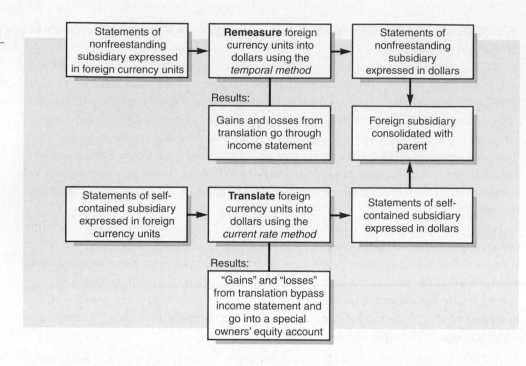

*statement recognition to the balancing debit or credit that arises from translation, the uncertain ultimate effect of exchange rate changes is explicitly carried forward.* Figure 16.3 is a diagram of the *SFAS No. 52* translation approach.

The figure shows that *SFAS No. 52* requires firms to categorize their foreign subsidiaries into one of two groups: (1) *nonfreestanding subsidiaries,* whose activities are so closely integrated with the parent that they are considered to be engaging in foreign currency transactions on behalf of the parent or (2) *self-contained subsidiaries* with an independent or virtually independent operating existence of their own. For subsidiaries in the first group, exchange rate movements have an immediately determinable effect on dollar cash flows; for this reason, translation gains or losses are run through the income statement. By contrast, subsidiaries in the second group are put into an income "holding pattern" because exchange rate movements have an indeterminate impact on the parent's ultimate dollar cash flows. Consequently, a *neutral* translation mechanism—the current rate method—is used for these subsidiaries, and the resulting equity debits or credits are simply treated as balancing items rather than as elements of income.

**Illustrative Disclosure**    Exhibit 16.8 contains excerpts from the Pfizer Inc. 2006 annual report. Exhibit 16.8(a) shows a portion of the footnote disclosure regarding foreign subsidiaries. Most of Pfizer's foreign subsidiaries are translated using the current rate method, which means that translation adjustments go to a currency translation adjustment account in the Other Comprehensive Income section of Pfizer's Shareholders' equity reproduced in Exhibit 16.8(b).

Note that the highlighted currency translation adjustments are quite volatile going from a $2,013 million gain in 2004 to a $1,476 loss in 2005 back to a $1,157 gain in 2006. Clearly, these gains and losses are material and highly transitory in nature, which no doubt is one reason the FASB elected to have these gains and losses reported as a component of stockholders' equity rather than in earnings.

## EXHIBIT 16.8    Pfizer Inc.

### Panel (a): Foreign Currency Translation Footnote

For most international operations, local currencies have been determined to be the functional currencies. The effects of converting non-functional currency assets and liabilities into the functional currency are recorded in *Other (income)/deductions—net*. We translate functional currency assets and liabilities to their U.S. dollar equivalents at rates in effect at the balance sheet date and record these translation adjustments in *Shareholders' equity—Accumulated other comprehensive income/(expense)*. We translate functional currency statement of income amounts at average rates for the period.

For operations in highly inflationary economies, we translate monetary items at rates in effect at the balance sheet date, with translation adjustments recorded in *Other (income)/deductions—net*, and nonmonetary items at historical rates.

### Panel (b): Other Comprehensive Income/(Expense)

Changes, net of tax, in accumulated other comprehensive income/(expense) follow:

| (millions of dollars) | Net Unrealized Gains/(Losses) | | | Benefit Plans | | | Accumulated Other Comprehensive Income/ (Expense) |
|---|---|---|---|---|---|---|---|
| | Currency Translation Adjustment and Other | Derivative Financial Instruments | Available-For-Sale Securities | Actuarial Losses | Prior Service Costs and Other | Minimum Pension Liability | |
| Balance, January 1, 2004 | $ 580 | $ 52 | $138 | $ — | $ — | $(575) | $ 195 |
| Foreign currency translation adjustments | 2,013 | — | — | — | — | — | 2,013 |
| Unrealized holding gains/(losses) | — | (60) | 168 | — | — | — | 108 |
| Reclassification adjustments to income | — | — | (24) | — | — | — | (24) |
| Minimum pension liability adjustment | — | — | — | — | — | (19) | (19) |
| Other | 1 | — | — | — | — | — | 1 |
| Income taxes | — | 7 | (16) | — | — | 13 | 4 |
| Other comprehensive income | 2,014 | (53) | 128 | — | — | (6) | 2,083 |
| Balance, December 31, 2004 | 2,594 | (1) | 266 | — | — | (581) | 2,278 |
| Foreign currency translation adjustments | (1,476) | — | — | — | — | — | (1,476) |
| Unrealized holding losses | — | (148) | (68) | — | — | — | (216) |
| Reclassification adjustments to income | — | (11) | (157) | — | — | — | (168) |
| Minimum pension liability adjustment | — | — | — | — | — | (33) | (33) |
| Other | (5) | — | — | — | — | — | (5) |
| Income taxes | — | 53 | 42 | — | — | 4 | 99 |
| Other comprehensive expense | (1,481) | (106) | (183) | — | — | (29) | (1,799) |
| Balance, December 31, 2005 | 1,113 | (107) | 83 | — | — | (610) | 479 |
| Foreign currency translation adjustments | 1,157 | — | — | — | — | — | 1,157 |
| Unrealized holding gains | — | 126 | 63 | — | — | — | 189 |
| Reclassification adjustments to income | (40) | 5 | (64) | — | — | — | (99) |
| Minimum pension liability adjustment | — | — | — | — | — | (16) | (16) |
| Other | (3) | — | — | — | — | — | (3) |
| Income taxes | — | (50) | 14 | — | — | — | (36) |
| Other comprehensive income | 1,114 | 81 | 13 | — | — | (16) | 1,192 |
| Adoption of new accounting standard, net of tax | — | — | — | (2,739) | (27) | 626 | (2,140) |
| **Balance, December 31, 2006** | $ 2,227 | $ (26) | $ 96 | $(2,739) | $ (27) | $ — | $ (469) |

- Financial reporting for intercorporate equity investments depends on the size of the parent company's ownership share. Proportionate share size is used to infer the investment's purpose.

- When the ownership share is less than 20%, it is presumed that the investor cannot exert influence on the investee's decisions. These *minority passive investments* are shown at market value on the balance sheet. Unrealized gains or losses on the trading portfolio are recorded on the income statement, and unrealized gains and losses on the available-for-sale portfolio are recorded in a special owners' equity account as part of comprehensive income.

- *Minority active investments* involve between 20% and 50% ownership and are presumed to give the investor the ability to influence investee's operating decisions. The equity method is used to account for such investments whereby the investor records its proportionate share of the investee's profits and losses each period with a corresponding adjustment to the investment account.

- *SFAS No. 159* allows firms to elect the fair value option for equity investments. Unrealized gains and losses resulting from market value changes are reported on the investor's income statement.

- Consolidated financial statements are required when one entity (parent) gains a controlling financial interest (more than 50% interest in voting common stock) in another entity (subsidiary). Prior to 2002, the purchase and pooling-of-interests methods were used to account for business combinations. From 2002 through 2008, purchase was the only method allowed, and beginning in 2009, the acquisition method must be used to account for all business combinations. The key differences between these three methods are: (1) how to measure the subsidiary's net assets (assets minus liabilities) at the acquisition date, (2) the amount of goodwill recognized, and (3) how the noncontrolling (minority) interests are measured and reported on the consolidated balance sheet.

- Goodwill is typically recorded in business combinations accounted for under the purchase or acquisition method. Goodwill is no longer amortized but is subject to an annual impairment test. If goodwill is determined to be impaired, it is written down with an offsetting charge to consolidated earnings.

- The purchase and acquisition methods of accounting complicate financial analysis because none of the subsidiary's profit is included in consolidated earnings in the year prior to acquisition, a partial year's profit is included from the date of acquisition through the end of the year in the acquisition year, and 100% of the subsidiary's profits are included in the years following the year of acquisition. This can distort year-to-year growth rates in sales and profits.

- Enron's collapse brought about a demand for increased disclosure and transparency regarding companies' interests in *special purpose entities (SPE)* or *variable interest entities (VIE)*. A VIE is a corporation, partnership, trust, or any other legal structure used for business purposes that either (1) does not have equity investors with voting rights or (2) has equity investors that do not provide sufficient financial resources for the entity to support its own activities. *FASB Interpretation No. 46* requires a company to consolidate a VIE if that company is subject to a majority of the risk of loss from the VIE's activities and is entitled to receive a majority of the entity's residual returns or both. A company that consolidates a VIE is called that entity's *primary beneficiary.*

- Majority-owned foreign subsidiaries also must be consolidated. This requires foreign currency amounts to be re-expressed in dollars. Foreign subsidiaries that are mere extensions

of the U.S. parent and have no self-sufficiency are remeasured using the *temporal method.*
The temporal method treats the subsidiaries' business transactions as if they had been undertaken by the parent—but in the foreign currency.

- Foreign subsidiaries that are freestanding economic units are remeasured using the *current
  rate method.* This method provides an easy way to re-express foreign currency amounts in
  dollars while maintaining the subsidiary's financial ratios.

**APPENDIX A**

# ACCOUNTING FOR HELD-TO-MATURITY DEBT INVESTMENTS

*SFAS No. 115* requires that debt securities (e.g., bonds and notes) that a firm intends to hold to
maturity be accounted for at amortized cost. Interest income is recognized following the effective interest method (see Chapter 11), and the investment account is adjusted for the amortization of premium or discount in each period. No adjustments are made for changes in the
market value of debt securities in the held-to-maturity portfolio.

We illustrate the accounting for held-to-maturity debt investments with the following example. Assume that Principal Financial purchases a five-year $100,000 bond from Baker Com-
pany with a 7% coupon interest rate for $108,660 on January 1, 2008. The effective or yield rate
on this bond investment is 5% percent. Also assume that the bond matures on December 31,
2012 with the $7,000 interest payment due at the end of each year. The following amortization
table reflects interest income, amortization of bond premium, and amortized cost of the bond
at year-end.

| Year-End | Interest | Premium Amortization | Amortized Cost |
|----------|----------|----------------------|----------------|
| Jan. 1   | —        | —                    | $108,660       |
| 2008     | $5,433   | $(1,567)             | 107,093        |
| 2009     | 5,354    | (1,646)              | 105,447        |
| 2010     | 5,272    | (1,728)              | 103,719        |
| 2011     | 5,186    | (1,814)              | 101,905        |
| 2012     | 5,095    | (1,905)              | 100,000        |

The following entry would be made on January 1, 2008 to record the acquisition of the bond.

| **DR** | Investment in Bonds ..................................... | $108,660 |          |
|--------|-----------------------------------------------------------|----------|----------|
| **CR** | Cash ............................................           |          | $108,660 |

Principal makes the following entry on December 31, 2008 to record interest revenue and
amortization of the premium on the bond.

| **DR** | Cash ................................................. | $7,000* |          |
|--------|-------------------------------------------------------|---------|----------|
| **CR** | Interest Revenue ..................................    |         | $5,433[†] |
| **CR** | Investment in Bonds ..............................     |         | 1,567[‡]  |

\* $100,000 × 7%
[†] $108,660 × 5%
[‡] $7,000 − $5,433

Transfers from the held-to-maturity portfolio to the trading (available-for-sale) portfolio
are transferred at fair value on date of transfer with an offsetting unrealized gain or loss

recorded on the income statement (Other comprehensive income component of stockholders' equity). Firms may elect to value debt securities in the held-to-maturity portfolio at fair value under the rules set forth in *SFAS No. 159*.[21] The cumulative unrealized gains and losses as of the date of fair value election are included as a cumulative effect adjustment to retained earnings under the rules for changes in accounting principles (*SFAS No. 154*; see Chapter 2).

## APPENDIX B

# Pooling-of-Interests Accounting

To see how pooling works and its financial statement effects relative to the purchase method, let's return to the Alphonse and Gaston example from earlier in the chapter. Instead of acquiring a 100% ownership in Gaston with cash, assume that Alphonse exchanges 8,000,000 shares of its own stock with a fair value of $10,000,000 for all of Gaston's outstanding stock.

In a stock-for-stock exchange, the owners of *both* Alphonse and Gaston continue as equity investors in the newly merged corporation. This continuation of ownership interests in poolings contrasts sharply with what happens in a cash buyout. After a cash buyout, the acquired company's former shareholders have no further equity interest in the combined enterprise.

The entry to record the acquisition on Alphonse's books would use the *book value* of Gaston's net assets ($2,000,000 + $6,500,000 − $500,000) as the carrying amount in the investment account—that is,

| | | | |
|---|---|---|---|
| **DR** | Investment in Gaston | $8,000,000 | |
| | **CR** Common Stock | | $8,000,000 |

Pooling-of-interests reporting rules treat the two formerly independent companies as though they have decided to join resources and "keep house together." Because both original ownership interests survive, *no buyout is considered to have taken place.* The consolidation of Alphonse's and Gaston's financial statements combines the *book values* of the two entities. As in purchase accounting, however, intercompany transactions and double counted items must be eliminated as in Exhibit 16.9.

## EXHIBIT 16.9   Alphonse and Gaston Company

### Preparation of Consolidated Balance Sheet (Pooling Method—100% acquisition)

| | After the Acquisition | | Adjustments and Eliminations | | Consolidated |
|---|---|---|---|---|---|
| | **Alphonse** | **Gaston** | **Dr.** | **Cr.** | **Balance Sheet** |
| **Assets** | | | | | |
| Current assets | $ 5,000,000 | $2,000,000 | | | $ 7,000,000 |
| Fixed assets, net | 20,000,000 | 6,500,000 | | | 26,500,000 |
| Investment in Gaston | 8,000,000 | — | | $8,000,000 (A) | — |
| | $33,000,000 | $8,500,000 | | | $33,500,000 |
| **Liabilities** | | | | | |
| Current liabilities | $ 1,000,000 | $ 500,000 | | | $ 1,500,000 |
| **Stockholders' equity** | | | | | |
| Common stock | 28,000,000 | 6,000,000 | $6,000,000 (A) | | 28,000,000 |
| Retained earnings | 4,000,000 | 2,000,000 | 2,000,000 (A) | | 4,000,000 |
| | $33,000,000 | $8,500,000 | $8,000,000 | $8,000,000 | $33,500,000 |

[21] "Fair Value Option for Financial Assets and Liabilities," *SFAS No. 159*, para. 28.

The only adjustment needed here is the elimination of the potential double counting of Gaston's net assets and equity. This entry is identical to the purchase accounting (or cash buy-out) adjustment illustrated in Exhibit 16.2 (see notations A and B). No other adjustments or reclassifications are needed because Alphonse's Investment in Gaston account equals the net book value shown on Gaston's books. This means that under a pooling of interests a write-up of assets to a new, higher carrying value will never occur. Similarly, no goodwill will ever be recognized.

## Purchase, Pooling, and Financial Analysis

The pooling-of-interests method has been widely criticized. To help understand why, consider Exhibit 16.10, which highlights the differences in consolidated balance sheets that would result for Alphonse & Gaston Company, the combined organization, under purchase versus pooling-of-interests accounting.

This comparison makes the financial statement differences under purchase versus pooling-of-interests accounting easy to see. Prior to the acquisition, Gaston had a fair value of $10,000,000—the amount of cash Alphonse was willing to pay to gain control. Purchase accounting brings Gaston into the consolidated statement at its fair value of $10,000,000. Under pooling-of-interests accounting, Gaston is shown in the consolidated statement at its net book value of $8,000,000. The $2,000,000 difference is shown in the "Difference" column in Exhibit 16.10.

Critics argue that pooling permits acquiring companies to record acquisitions at artificially low amounts. In our example, Gaston is *worth* $10,000,000, and this is presumably the value that the sellers demanded. Therefore, the value of Alphonse stock that Gaston's shareholders received must have been close to $10,000,000. **Despite this economic reality, the transaction is booked at $8,000,000 under the pooling-of-interests method.** Critics charge that this understatement distorts the balance sheet as well as subsequent income statements. The income in future years is affected because fixed assets are $1,500,000 lower—the unrecorded difference between fair value and book value—under pooling than under purchase accounting, thereby lowering future depreciation

| **EXHIBIT 16.10** | Alphonse and Gaston Company |
|---|---|

**Purchase versus Pooling-of-Interest Method**
**Comparative Consolidated Balance Sheets**

| | Purchase Method | Pooling-of-Interests Method | Difference |
|---|---|---|---|
| **Assets** | | | |
| Current assets | $ 7,000,000 | $ 7,000,000 | — |
| Fixed assets, net | 28,000,000 | 26,500,000 | $1,500,000 |
| Goodwill | 500,000 | — | 500,000 |
| | $35,500,000 | $33,500,000 | $2,000,000 |
| **Liabilities** | | | |
| Current liabilities | $ 1,500,000 | $1,500,000 | — |
| **Stockholders' equity** | | | |
| Common stock | 28,000,000 | 28,000,000 | — |
| Capital in excess of par | 2,000,000 | — | $2,000,000 |
| Retained earnings | 4,000,000 | 4,000,000 | — |
| | $35,500,000 | $33,500,000 | $2,000,000 |

expense. Similarly, because no goodwill exists under pooling, there is no goodwill write-off to reduce future earnings. Both of these effects make income under pooling higher.

Critics further charge that the lower pooling balance sheet numbers for gross assets and equity make rate-of-return ratios appear higher. That's because, under pooling, the denominator of both the return on assets and return-on-equity ratios is lower. Some critics suggest that these distortions are not accidental. They argue that the *cosmetic* statement effects of pooling explain its popularity among takeover-minded executives prior to 2002, when *SFAS No. 141* went into effect. Pooling provided an opportunity to buy companies and then record the acquisition on the books at artificially low numbers, thereby improving the appearance of subsequent financial statements.

Figure 16.4 demonstrates that companies clearly preferred to use pooling rather than the purchase method for large deals before pooling was banned. For deals larger than $100 million,

> By contrast, under purchase accounting, goodwill is subject to an annual impairment test. If impaired, goodwill is written down with an offsetting charge to the consolidated entity's earnings.

## Figure 16.4

LARGE U.S. ACQUISITIONS ACCOUNTED FOR AS PURCHASE VERSUS POOLING OF INTERESTS

Panel (a) Dollar Value of Large U.S. Acquisitions (Deal Size > $100 Million) Using Purchase versus Pooling-of-Interests Accounting
Panel (b) Number of Large U.S. Acquisitions (Deal Size > $100 Million) Using Purchase versus Pooling-of-Interests Accounting

*SOURCE:* Securities Data Corporation.

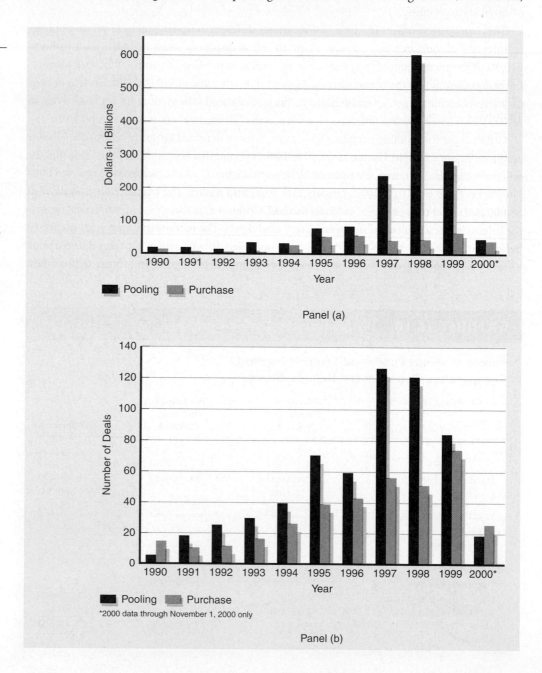

Panel (a)

Panel (b)

*2000 data through November 1, 2000 only

both the dollar value (Panel [a]) and the number of deals (Panel [b]) were much more for transactions accounted for as poolings rather than purchases throughout most of the 1990–2000 period. The reason that pooling was so popular for high dollar-value deals is obvious—pooling avoids the drain on the postcombination earnings that would otherwise result under purchase accounting. As noted previously, however, many believe that pooling artificially inflates the combined entity's postcombination earnings and understates the asset base used to generate those earnings. As a statement user, you need to be aware of these potential distortions because financial statements continue to be impacted by poolings consummated prior to July 2001 when *SFAS No. 141* went into effect.

## EXERCISES

The following data pertain to Tyne Company's investments in marketable equity securities. (Assume that all securities were held throughout 2008 and 2009.)

|  | | Market Value | |
| --- | --- | --- | --- |
|  | Cost | 12/31/09 | 12/31/08 |
| Trading | $150,000 | $155,000 | $100,000 |
| Available for sale | 150,000 | 130,000 | 120,000 |

**E16-1**

Mark-to-market accounting for trading and available-for-sale securities

**AICPA**
ADAPTED

**Required:**

1. What amount should Tyne report as unrealized holding gain (loss) in its 2009 income statement?

2. What amount should Tyne report as net unrealized gain (loss) on available-for-sale securities at December 31, 2009 in its statement of stockholders' equity? Ignore tax effects.

During 2008, Rex Company purchased marketable equity securities as a short-term investment. These securities are classified as available for sale. The cost and market values at December 31, 2008 follow:

| Security | Cost | Market Value |
| --- | --- | --- |
| Company A—100 shares | $ 2,800 | $ 3,400 |
| Company B—1,000 shares | 17,000 | 15,300 |
| Company C—2,000 shares | 31,500 | 29,500 |
|  | $51,300 | $48,200 |

**E16-2**

Mark-to-market accounting for available-for-sale securities

**AICPA**
ADAPTED

Rex sold 1,000 shares of Company B stock on January 31, 2009 for $15 per share, incurring $1,500 in brokerage commission and taxes.

**Required:**

1. Ignoring taxes, how much should Rex report as unrealized gain or loss on its available-for-sale securities at December 31, 2008 in the statement of stockholders' equity?

2. On the sale, Rex should report a realized loss of how much?

Information related to Jones Company's portfolio of trading securities for December 31, 2008 follows:

| | |
| --- | --- |
| Aggregate cost of securities | $340,000 |
| Gross unrealized gains | 8,000 |
| Gross unrealized losses | 52,000 |

**E16-3**

Mark-to-market accounting for trading securities

Jones reported a $10,000 credit balance in its Market adjustment—Trading securities account in its December 31, 2007 (prior year) balance sheet. Assume that it sold no trading securities during 2007 or 2008.

**Required:**

1. How much should Jones report as unrealized gain or loss on its 2008 income statement?

2. Give the journal entry that Jones would make to record the mark-to-market adjustment to its trading portfolio.

---

**E16-4**

Using the equity method

AICPA
ADAPTED

In January 2008, Harold Corporation acquired 20% of Otis Company's outstanding common stock for $400,000. This investment gave Harold the ability to exercise significant influence over Otis. The book value of these shares was $300,000. The excess of cost over book value was attributed to an identifiable intangible asset, a patent, which was undervalued on Otis' balance sheet and had a remaining 10-year useful life.

For the year ended December 31, 2008 Otis reported net income of $90,000 and paid cash dividends of $20,000 on its common stock.

**Required:**

1. How much would Harold Corporation's income increase in 2008 as a result of its investment in Otis?

2. What is the carrying value of Harold's investment in Otis Company at December 31, 2008?

---

**E16-5**

Using the equity method and fair value option

AICPA
ADAPTED

Sage, Inc. bought 40% of Adams Corporation's outstanding common stock on January 2, 2008 for $400,000. The carrying amount of Adams' net assets at the purchase date totaled $900,000. Fair values and carrying amounts were the same for all items except for plant and inventory, for which fair values exceeded the carrying amounts by $90,000 and $10,000, respectively. The plant has an 18-year life. All inventory was sold during 2008. During 2008, Adams reported $120,000 net income and paid a $20,000 cash dividend.

**Required:**

1. What amount should Sage report in its income statement from its investment in Adams for the year ended December 31, 2008?

2. What is the December 31, 2008 balance in the Investment in Adams account?

3. Assume that on January 2, 2008 when Sage acquired a 40% interest in Adams, it elected to account for this investment at fair value. If the fair value of Sage's investment in Adams is $470,000 on December 31, 2008, what amount should Sage report in its 2008 income statement for this investment under the fair value option?

---

**E16-6**

Using equity versus cost method for long-term investments

CMA
ADAPTED

On January 1, 2008, Boggs, Inc. paid $700,000 for 100,000 shares of Mattly Corporation, which represented 30% of Mattly's outstanding common stock. Boggs made the following computation:

| | |
|---|---|
| Purchase price | $700,000 |
| 30% equity in book value of Mattly's net assets | 500,000 |
| Excess of cost over book value | $200,000 |

The excess cost over book value was attributed to undervalued depreciable assets with a remaining life of 20 years (zero salvage). Mattly reported net income for the year ended December 31, 2008 of $300,000. Mattly paid cash dividends of $100,000 on July 1, 2008.

**Required:**

1. If Boggs exercised significant influence over Mattly and properly accounted for the long-term investment under the equity method, what amount of net investment revenue should Boggs report from its investment in Mattly for 2008?

2. If Boggs did not exercise significant influence over Mattly and properly accounted for the long-term investment under the cost method, what amount of net investment revenue should Boggs report from its investment in Mattly?

On April 30, 2008, Pound Corp. purchased for cash all 200,000 shares of the outstanding common stock of Shake Corp. for $20 per share. At April 30, 2008, Shake's balance sheet showed net assets with a $3,000,000 book value. On that date, the fair value of Shake's property, plant and equipment exceeded book value by $300,000.

**E16-7**

Determining the value of goodwill

**Required:**
What amount should Pound report as goodwill on its April 30, 2008 consolidated balance sheet?

---

On April 1, 2008, Dart Company paid $620,000 for all issued and outstanding common stock of Wall Corporation in a transaction properly accounted for as a purchase. Wall's recorded assets and liabilities on April 1, 2008 follow:

**E16-8**

Goodwill—purchase method

**AICPA**
ADAPTED

| | |
|---|---:|
| Cash | $ 60,000 |
| Inventory | 180,000 |
| Property and equipment (net of accumulated depreciation of $220,000) | 320,000 |
| Goodwill (net of accumulated write-downs of $50,000) | 100,000 |
| Liabilities | (120,000) |
| Net assets | $540,000 |

On April 1, 2008, Wall's inventory had a $150,000 fair value, and its property and equipment (net) had a $380,000 fair value.

**Required:**
What is the amount of goodwill resulting from the business combination?

---

On January 1, 2008, Pitt Company purchased an 80% investment in Saxe Company. The acquisition cost was equal to Pitt's equity in Saxe's net assets at that date. On January 1, 2008, Pitt and Saxe had retained earnings of $500,000 and $100,000, respectively. During 2008, Pitt had net income of $200,000, which included its equity in Saxe's earnings, and declared dividends of $50,000. Saxe had net income of $40,000 and declared dividends of $20,000. No other intercompany transactions between the parent and subsidiary occurred.

**E16-9**

Preparing consolidated financial statements

**AICPA**
ADAPTED

**Required:**
What should the consolidated retained earnings be on December 31, 2008?

---

On January 1, 2008, Pack Corp. purchased all of Slam Corp.'s common stock for $500,000. On that date, the fair values of Slam's net assets equaled their book values of $400,000. During 2008, Slam paid cash dividends of $8,000. The following balance sheet and income statement accounts are reported on Pack and Slam's separate financial statements at December 31, 2008:

**E16-10**

Determining consolidated retained earnings

| | Pack | Slam |
|---|---:|---:|
| **Balance sheet accounts** | | |
| Investment in Slam | $552,000 | $ 0 |
| Retained earnings | 780,000 | 250,000 |
| **Income statement accounts** | | |
| Equity in earnings of Slam | 60,000 | 0 |
| Net income | 150,000 | 60,000 |

**Required:**
What amount of retained earnings will Pack report in its December 31, 2008 consolidated balance sheet?

| **E16-11**

Preparing consolidated
balance sheet

CMA
ADAPTED

Immediately after Sea Company purchased 60% ownership of Island Company, the separate condensed balance sheets of the two companies are as follows:

|                             | **Sea Company** | **Island Company** |
| --------------------------- | --------------: | -----------------: |
| Other assets                |        $750,000 |           $320,000 |
| Investment in Island Company |         187,500 |                  — |
|                             |        $937,500 |           $320,000 |
| Liabilities                 |        $250,000 |           $ 70,000 |
| Common stock                |         450,000 |            200,000 |
| Retained earnings           |         237,500 |             50,000 |
|                             |        $937,500 |           $320,000 |

**Required:**

What is the dollar amount of the total assets in the consolidated balance sheet immediately after the acquisition under the purchase method?

| **E16-12**

Recording transaction foreign
exchange gain/loss

AICPA
ADAPTED

On September 1, 2008, Cano & Company, a U.S. corporation, sold merchandise to a foreign firm for 250,000 euros. Terms of the sale require payment in euros on February 1, 2009. On September 1, 2008, the spot exchange rate was $0.20 per euro. At Cano's year-end on December 31, 2008, the spot rate was $0.19, but the rate increased to $0.22 by February 1, 2009, when payment was received.

**Required:**

1. What foreign currency transaction gain or loss should be recorded in 2008?

2. What foreign currency transaction gain or loss should be recorded in 2009?

| **E16-13**

Mark-to-market accounting
for available-for-sale securities

AICPA
ADAPTED

Stone has provided the following information on its available-for-sale securities:

| | |
| --- | ---: |
| Aggregate cost as of 12/31/08 | $170,000 |
| Unrealized gain as of 12/31/08 | 4,000 |
| Unrealized losses as of 12/31/08 | 26,000 |
| Net realized gains during 2008 | 30,000 |

It reported $1,500 in the contra-asset valuation account to reduce these securities to their market value at December 31, 2007.

**Required:**

What amount should be debited as an unrealized loss to the stockholders' equity section of Stone's December 31, 2008 balance sheet as a result of 2008 market value changes related to its available-for-sale securities? (Ignore taxes.)

| **E16-14**

Mark-to-market accounting
for trading securities

Founded on January 1, 2008, Gehl Company had the following short-term investments in securities at the end of 2008 and 2009 (all were held in the "trading" portfolio):

| **Equity Security** | **Cost** | **2009 Market Value** |
| :---: | ---: | ---: |
| A | $ 96,000 | $ 94,000 |
| B | 184,000 | 162,000 |
| C | 126,000 | 136,000 |

**Required:**

If the company recorded a $4,000 debit to its Market adjustment—Trading securities account at the end of 2009 as its mark-to-market adjustment, what must have been the unrealized gain or loss recorded at the end of 2008?

**Required:**

1. An entity is generally considered to be a variable interest entity (VIE) subject to consolidation by the sponsoring entity if outside third-party equity is less than what percentage of the market value of the VIE's assets?

2. When two or more corporations establish an entity deemed to be a VIE subject to consolidation, what is the guiding principle used to determine which corporation should consolidate the VIE?

**E16-15**

Consolidating variable interest entities

---

Pinto, Inc. owns 100% of Scale Inc. The following information is from the 2008 income statements of Pinto and Scale:

**E16-16**

Eliminating intercompany profit

|  | Pinto | Scale |
|---|---|---|
| Sales | $1,000,000 | $600,000 |
| Cost of goods sold | 600,000 | 540,000 |
| Gross profit | 400,000 | 60,000 |
| Depreciation expense | 60,000 | 15,000 |
| Other expenses | 130,000 | 30,000 |
| Income from operations | 210,000 | 15,000 |
| Gain on sale of equipment to Scale | 16,000 | 0 |
| Income before income taxes | $ 226,000 | $ 15,000 |

**Additional Information:**

1. Pinto's reported sales revenue includes $200,000 of intercompany sales to Scale. Scale sold three-fourths of this inventory to outside customers by the end of 2008. Pinto sells to Scale on terms similar those available to its outside customers.

2. Scale purchased equipment from Pinto for $60,000 on January 1, 2008. The equipment is depreciated using the straight-line method over eight years and no residual value is assumed.

**Required:**

1. How much intercompany profit should be eliminated from Scale's inventory when preparing 2008 consolidated financial statements?

2. What amount of depreciation expense should be reported in the 2008 consolidated income statement?

---

Crest Corp. recorded the following transactions with its investees during 2008.

**E16-17**

Eliminating intercompany inventory transactions

1. It sold inventory to Drape Inc. for $75,000. The inventory had originally cost Crest $65,000. Drape had one-fourth of this inventory on hand at year-end. Crest owns 15% of Drape's common stock and does not exert significant influence over Drape's operations.

2. It purchased $200,000 of inventory from Stream Corp., a wholly owned subsidiary. Stream's gross profit on the sale was $40,000. Crest had $20,000 of this inventory remaining on December 31, 2008.

**Required:**

What amount of inventory will be eliminated when preparing Crest's December 31, 2008 consolidated balance sheet?

---

Pate Corp. owns 80% of Strange Inc.'s common stock. During 2008, Pate sold inventory to Strange for $600,000 on the same terms as sales made to outside customers. Strange sold the entire inventory purchased from Pate by the end of 2008. Pate and Strange report the following for 2008.

**E16-18**

Consolidating sales and cost of goods sold with intercompany transactions

|  | Pate | Strange |
|---|---|---|
| Sales | $2,700,000 | $1,600,000 |
| Cost of sales | 1,800,000 | 900,000 |
| Gross profit | $ 900,000 | $ 700,000 |

**Required:**

1. What amount should Pate report as sales revenue in its 2008 consolidated income statement?

2. What amount should Pate report as cost of sales in its 2008 consolidated income statement?

---

**E16-19**

Using purchase versus pooling methods

**CMA**
ADAPTED

On July 1, 2000, Pushway Corporation issued 200,000 shares of $5 par value common stock in exchange for all of Stroker Company's common stock. This stock had a fair value that was $200,000 in excess of Stroker's stockholders' equity on the date of exchange. This difference was attributed to the fact that the fair value of Stroker's equipment was higher than book value. The equipment has an estimated remaining life of 10 years. Pushway and Stroker reported depreciation expense in 2000 of $400,000 and $100,000, respectively, before consolidation and before any adjustment for the exchange. For financial reporting purposes, both companies use a calendar year and the straight-line depreciation method with depreciation calculated on a monthly basis beginning with the month of acquisition.

**Required:**

1. Assume that the business combination is appropriately accounted for as a purchase. How much consolidated depreciation expense would be reported in 2000?

2. Assume that the business combination is appropriately accounted for as a pooling of interests. How much consolidated depreciation expense would be reported in 2000?

---

**E16-20**

Translating foreign currency

**AICPA**
ADAPTED

A wholly owned subsidiary of Ward, Inc. has certain expense accounts for the year ended December 31, 2008, stated in local currency units (LCU) as follows:

|  | **LCU** |
|---|---|
| Depreciation of equipment (related assets were purchased January 1, 2006) | 120,000 |
| Provision for doubtful accounts | 80,000 |
| Rent | 200,000 |

The exchange rates at various dates are as follows:

|  | **Dollar Equivalent of LCU** |
|---|---|
| 12/31/08 | $0.40 |
| Average for year ended 12/31/08 | 0.44 |
| 1/1/06 | 0.50 |

Assume that the LCU is the subsidiary's functional currency and that the charges to the expense accounts occurred approximately evenly during the year.

**Required:**

What total dollar amount should be included in Ward's 2008 consolidated income statement to reflect these expenses?

---

**E16-21**

Reporting transaction foreign exchange gain/loss

**AICPA**
ADAPTED

Lindy, a calendar-year U.S. corporation, bought inventory items from a supplier in Germany on November 5, 2008 for 100,000 euros, when the spot rate was $0.4295. At Lindy's December 31, 2008, year-end, the spot rate was $0.4245. On January 15, 2009 Lindy bought 100,000 euros at the spot rate of $0.4345 and paid the invoice.

**Required:**

How much foreign exchange gain or (loss) should Lindy report in its income statements for 2008 and 2009?

On January 5, 2009, Alpha Inc. acquired 80% of the outstanding voting shares of Beta Inc. for $2,000,000 cash. Following are the separate balance sheets for the two companies immediately after the stock purchase, as well as fair market value information regarding Beta Inc.:

**E16-22**

Adjustments and eliminations for consolidation under acquisition method

| | Alpha | Beta Book Value | Beta Fair Value |
|---|---|---|---|
| **Assets** | | | |
| Current assets | $1,750,000 | $ 500,000 | $ 500,000 |
| Fixed assets, net | 5,000,000 | 1,625,000 | 2,000,000 |
| Investment in Beta | 2,000,000 | — | — |
| **Total Assets** | $8,750,000 | $2,125,000 | $2,500,000 |
| **Liabilities** | | | |
| Current Liabilities | $ 250,000 | $ 125,000 | $ 125,000 |
| **Stockholders' Equity** | | | |
| Common Stock | 7,000,000 | 1,500,000 | |
| Capital in excess of par | 500,000 | — | |
| Retained earnings | 1,000,000 | 500,000 | |
| Total Stockholders' Equity | 8,500,000 | 2,000,000 | |
| **Total Liabilities and Stockholders' Equity** | $8,750,000 | $2,125,000 | |

**Required:**

1. Give the journal entries for adjustments and eliminations required to prepare the consolidated balance sheet immediately after acquisition under the acquisition method.

2. Prepare the consolidated balance sheet immediately after acquisition.

## PROBLEMS / DISCUSSION QUESTIONS

Balance sheet data for Herb Corporation and Aside Chemical Company at December 31, 2007 follow:

**P16-1**

Reporting intercorporate investments—Balance sheet preparation

| ($ in thousands) | Herb | Aside |
|---|---|---|
| Assets | $850 | $400 |
| Liabilities | $275 | $100 |
| Common stock (par value, $1) | 200 | 100 |
| Other equity (paid-in capital plus retained earnings) | 375 | 200 |
| | $850 | $400 |

**Required:**

1. Assume that on January 1, 2008, Herb sold an additional 100,000 shares of its stock to its existing shareholders for $425,000. It then used the stock issue's entire proceeds to buy all of Aside's shares. Prepare a consolidated balance sheet after the acquisition using the purchase method.

2. Assume the preceding facts except that Herb acquired only 80% of the stock for a cash payment of $425,000. How would the consolidated balance sheet differ from that in requirement 1?

3. Now assume a slightly altered set of initial conditions. While the respective December 31, 2007 balance sheet data for the two companies were identical to those shown, the 100,000 shares of Herb stock were not sold to existing Herb Corporation shareholders. Assume instead that these 100,000 shares (which had a January 1, 2008 market value of $425,000) were issued to Aside's shareholders in exchange for all 100,000 shares of Aside's stock. Prepare a consolidated balance sheet after the acquisition under the pooling method. (*Note to student:* Ignore the fact that the dates in this problem are after *SFAS No. 141* that eliminated the pooling method.)

**P16-2**

**Equity method accounting**

On January 1, 2008, Figland Company purchased for cash 40% of Irene Company's 300,000 shares of voting common stock for $1,800,000. At the time, 40% of the book value of the underlying equity in Irene's net assets was $1,400,000; $50,000 of the excess was attributed to the excess of fair value over book value of inventory, which Irene accounts for using the first-in, first-out (FIFO) inventory method; and $150,000 is attributed to undervaluation of depreciable assets with an average remaining life of 10 years. The remainder is attributed to implicit goodwill.

As a result of this transaction, Figland can exercise significant influence over Irene's operating and financial policies. Irene's net income for the year ended December 31, 2008 was $600,000. During 2008, Irene paid $325,000 in dividends to its stockholders.

**Required:**
1. How much income would Figland report on its 2008 income statement for its investment in Irene?
2. What would be the balance in the Investment in Irene Company account on December 31, 2008?

**P16-3**

**Mark-to-market accounting**

Consider the following information:

1. Giant Motors purchases 5% of Crane Tire Company's common stock (one of its suppliers) for $30 million on January 1, 2008.
2. Crane earned $25 million in net income for 2008.
3. Crane pays total dividends of $15 million during 2008.
4. The market value of Giant's 5% investment in Crane is $25 million on December 31, 2008.

**Required:**
1. Assume that Giant's management considers its investment in Crane as a trading security. At what amount should Giant report its investment in Crane in its 2008 balance sheet?
2. How would Giant's investment in Crane affect its 2008 income statement?
3. In contrast to requirement 1, assume that Giant's management considers its investment as an available-for-sale security. At what amount should Giant report its investment in Crane in its 2008 balance sheet?
4. Using the facts presented in requirement 3, determine how, if at all, Giant's investment in Crane would affect its 2008 income statement.

**P16-4**

**Recording mark-to-market accounting for trading securities**

Second National Insurance Company provided this information for its trading securities portfolio:

| Security | Date | Acquisition Cost | Market Values 12/31/07 | Market Values 12/31/08 | Market Values 12/31/09 |
|---|---|---|---|---|---|
| Company A Common | 1/15/07 | $50,000 | $60,000 | $55,000 | $58,000 |
| Company B Common | 6/30/07 | 30,000 | 25,000 | 13,000* | 10,000 |
| Company C Preferred | 2/1/08 | 20,000 | — | 25,000 | 18,000 |
| Company D Warrants | 5/1/09 | 10,000 | — | — | 12,000 |

* Second National sold 50% of the Company B common shares for $14,000 on July 1, 2008. Market values for December 31, 2008 and December 31, 2009 are for the Company B shares remaining in the trading portfolio.

**Required:**
1. Provide the journal entries to record the mark-to-market adjustment on December 31, 2007. Assume that Second National uses an account entitled Market adjustment—trading

securities to adjust the cost of the trading portfolio to year-end market values. Show supporting calculations in good form.

2. Provide the entry to record the sale of Company B's common shares on July 1, 2008. Assume that the last market adjustment for these shares was on December 31, 2007.

3. Provide the journal entry and supporting calculations for the mark-to-market adjustment on December 31, 2008.

4. Provide the journal entry and mark-to-market adjustment on December 31, 2009.

5. What would the entry to record the sale of Company B common shares on July 1, 2008 have been if this security had been considered an available-for-sale security? Ignore tax effects.

---

At December 31, 2007, Poe Corporation properly reported the following available-for-sale securities. All were acquired in 2007.

**P16-5**

Comprehensive intercorporate investments problem

**AICPA**
ADAPTED

| | Cost | Fair Value |
|---|---|---|
| Axe Corporation, 1,000 shares, $2.40 convertible preferred stock | $ 40,000 | $ 42,000 |
| Purl, Inc., 6,000 shares of common stock | 60,000 | 66,000 |
| Day Company, 2,000 shares of common stock | 55,000 | 40,000 |
| Total available-for-sale securities | $155,000 | $148,000 |

On January 2, 2008, Poe purchased 100,000 shares of Scott Corporation common stock for $1,700,000, representing 30% of Scott's outstanding common stock and an underlying equity of $1,400,000 in Scott's net assets on that date. The excess of cost over Poe's equity in the book value of Scott's net assets at acquisition is attributed to fixed assets to be depreciated over a 40-year period with zero salvage value. As a result of Poe's 30% ownership of Scott, Poe has the ability to exercise significant influence over Scott's financial and operating policies.

During 2008 Poe disposed of the following securities:

- January 18—sold 2,500 shares of Purl for $13 per share.
- June 1—sold 500 shares of Day for $21 per share.

The following 2008 dividend information pertains to stock owned by Poe:

- April 5 and October 5—Axe paid dividends of $1.20 per share on its $2.40 preferred stock to stockholders of record on March 9 and September 9, respectively.
- June 30—Purl paid a $1.00 per share dividend on its common stock.
- March 1, June 1, September 1, and December 1—Scott paid quarterly dividends of $0.50 per share on each of these dates. Scott's net income for the year ended December 31, 2008 was $1,200,000.

At December 31, 2008, Poe's management intended to hold Scott's stock on a long-term basis with the remaining investments considered available-for-sale securities. Market prices per share of these securities were as follows:

| | Market Value at December 31, 2008 |
|---|---|
| Axe Corporation—preferred | $56 |
| Purl, Inc.—common | 11 |
| Day Company—common | 22 |
| Scott Corporation—common | 16 |

**Required:**

1. Determine the unrealized gain or loss on Poe's available-for-sale securities for 2007, and provide the journal entry to record the mark-to-market adjustment on December 31, 2007. Ignore tax effects.

2. Prepare the journal entries to record the realized gains or losses on Poe's sales of securities for 2008.

3. Prepare the entries to record Poe's receipt of dividends on all securities in 2008 and all entries related to Poe's equity investment in Scott Corporation.

4. Determine the unrealized gain or loss on Poe's available-for-sale securities for 2008, and provide the journal entry to record the mark-to-market adjustment on December 31, 2008. Ignore tax effects.

---

**P16-6**

Reporting intercorporate investments—Equity method

Consider the following sequence of events:

- On January 1, 2008, Big Time Motors purchased 25% of Cooper Tire Company's common stock (one of its suppliers) for $150 million. The book value of Cooper's net assets on this date was $400 million.*

- Cooper earned $25 million in net income for 2008.

- Cooper declared and paid total dividends of $15 million during 2008.

- On January 1, 2009, Big Time purchased an additional 15% of Cooper common stock for $100 million.*

- Cooper had a net loss of $40 million for 2009.

- Cooper paid total dividends of $18 million during 2009.

---

*Assume that cost in excess of book value is attributable to goodwill.

**Required:**

1. What amount of investment income should Big Time report on its 2008 income statement as a result of its investment in Cooper? At what amount would Big Time Motors report its investment in Cooper in its December 31, 2008 balance sheet?

2. At what amount should Big Time report its investment in Cooper in its December 31, 2009 balance sheet?

---

**P16-7**

Fair value option for equity method of recording investments

On January 5, 2008, Newyork Capital Corporation purchased 30% of the outstanding common shares of Delta Crating Corp. for $250 million and accounts for this investment under the equity method. The following information is available regarding Delta Crating Corp.

|  | $ in millions |
|---|---|
| Net assets at acquisition: |  |
| Fair value | 700 |
| Book value | 500 |
| 2008 net income | 100 |
| 2008 dividends declared and paid | 24 |

Two-thirds of the difference between the book value and fair value of Delta's net assets at acquisition is attributable to depreciable assets having fair value greater than their undepreciated cost and the remaining one-third is attributable to land having fair value in excess of its cost. The depreciable assets have an average remaining useful life of 10 years and are being depreciated by the straight-line method with zero salvage value.

**Required:**

1. Provide the journal entries that Newyork Capital would make in 2008 to account for its investment in Delta Crating under the equity method. Provide supporting details for all calculations needed.

2. Determine the carrying value of Newyork's Investment in Delta Crating account on December 31, 2008 under the equity method?

3. On January 1, 2009 the fair value of Delta's stock is $1,000 million. On this date Newyork Capital decides to change the method of recording its investment in Delta to the fair value option. Prepare the entry that Newyork Capital would make at this time to record the election of the fair value option.

4. Assume Delta reports net income of $80 million and pays $20 million in dividends in 2009. The fair value of Delta's stock is $1,200 million on December 31, 2009. Provide the entries that Newyork Capital would make for its investment in Delta Crating in 2009 under the fair value option.

5. How much would Newyork's Income be affected in 2009 as a result of accounting for its investment in Delta under the fair value option?

---

On January 1, 2008, Delta Inc. acquired 80% of Sigma Company's outstanding stock for $80,000 cash. Following are the balance sheets for Delta and Sigma immediately before the acquisition, as well as fair value information regarding Sigma:

**P16-8**

Using purchase versus acquisition methods with goodwill

|  | Delta Inc. | Sigma Company Book Value | Sigma Company Fair Value |
|---|---|---|---|
| **Assets** |  |  |  |
| Cash | $ 91,000 | $ 8,000 | $ 8,000 |
| Accounts receivable | 19,000 | 15,000 | 9,000 |
| Inventory | 47,000 | 31,000 | 43,000 |
| Land | 12,000 | 5,000 | 12,000 |
| Plant and equipment, net | 66,000 | 35,000 | 51,000 |
| Total | $235,000 | $94,000 | $123,000 |
| **Liabilities and shareholders' equity** |  |  |  |
| Accounts payable | $ 52,000 | $35,000 | $ 35,000 |
| Long-term debt | 66,000 | 15,000 | 15,000 |
| Common stock |  |  |  |
| Delta—5,000 shares, $1.00 par | 5,000 | — |  |
| Sigma—4,000 shares, $0.50 par | — | 2,000 |  |
| Additional paid-in capital | 30,000 | 12,000 |  |
| Retained earnings | 82,000 | 30,000 |  |
| Total | $235,000 | $94,000 |  |

**Required:**

1. Give the journal entry Delta would make to record the acquisition of Sigma under the purchase method.

2. Calculate the amount of goodwill that Delta will record as a result of acquiring Sigma.

3. Provide the adjustment and elimination entries Delta would make to prepare the consolidated balance sheet immediately after the acquisition.

4. Prepare the consolidated balance sheet for Delta immediately after its acquisition of Sigma Company.

5. Repeat requirements 1–4 under the acquisition method. Use the amount paid by Delta for its 80% interest to impute the total fair value of Sigma at acquisition.

P16-9

Using the purchase method versus pooling and determining the effect on ratios

On January 1, 2000, DGA, Inc. acquired all of CLH Systems' outstanding stock in exchange for DGA's common stock, which had a $100,000 market value. The acquisition is accounted for as a purchase. Following are the balance sheets for DGA and CLH Systems immediately before the acquisition, as well as fair value information regarding CLH Systems:

| | | CLH Systems | |
| | DGA Inc. | Book Value | Fair Value |
| --- | --- | --- | --- |
| **Assets** | | | |
| Cash | $166,000 | $ — | $ — |
| Account receivable | 25,000 | 15,000 | 15,000 |
| Inventory | 49,500 | 13,000 | 13,000 |
| Land | 12,000 | 7,000 | 7,000 |
| Plant and equipment, net | 76,000 | 25,000 | 36,000 |
| Patents | 2,500 | 6,500 | 10,500 |
| Total | $331,000 | $66,500 | $81,500 |
| | | | |
| **Liabilities and shareholders' equity** | | | |
| Accounts payable | $ 64,000 | $29,000 | $29,000 |
| Other liabilities | 35,000 | — | |
| Common stock, no par | 80,000 | 5,000 | |
| Retained earnings | 152,000 | 32,500 | |
| Total | $331,000 | $66,500 | |

**Required:**

(*Student Note:* This problem was set in 2000 when goodwill was still amortized under *APB Opinion 17* and pooling-of-interest accounting was still permitted.)

1. Give the journal entry that DGA would make to record the acquisition of CLH.

2. Calculate the amount of goodwill that DGA would record as a result of acquiring CLH.

3. Provide the elimination entry that DGA would make to prepare the consolidated balance sheet immediately after the acquisition.

4. Prepare DGA's balance sheet immediately after its acquisition of CLH.

5. Assume that DGA and CLH reported net income of $145,000 (before equity in CLH earnings) and $25,000, respectively, in 2000. Also, consolidated total assets (before adjustments for goodwill amortization and stepped-up-basis depreciation) at December 31, 2000 were identical to the consolidated total assets at acquisition (determined in requirement 4).

    Goodwill is being amortized over 40 years in accordance with *APB 17*. Assume that the remaining useful life for the plant and equipment and the patents is five years. Determine the following (ignore income taxes):

    • Consolidated net income for the year ended December 31, 2000.

    • ROA at December 31, 2000 (Net Income/Total assets).

6. Under *SFAS No. 142,* purchased goodwill is no longer amortized but is carried on the balance sheet at its historical value unless impaired. How would your answer to requirement 5 change under the following conditions:

    • No impairment of goodwill.

    • Goodwill impairment of 90%.

7. Repeat requirements 1, 2, 3, 4, and 5, assuming all of the preceding facts except that DGA acquired CLH by issuing 2,000 shares of its no par common stock and accounted for the transaction as a pooling of interests. At that time, DGA's shares were trading for $50.00 per share.

Prince Corp. and Sprite Corp. reported the following balance sheets at January 1, 2008:

**P16-10**

Consolidating at acquisition: Purchase vs. acquisition method

| | Prince | Sprite |
|---|---|---|
| Current assets | $30,000 | $15,000 |
| Noncurrent assets | 55,000 | 25,000 |
| Total assets | $85,000 | $40,000 |
| Current liabilities | $20,000 | $10,000 |
| Long-term debt | 20,000 | 5,000 |
| Stockholders' equity | 45,000 | 25,000 |
| Total liabilities and stockholders' equity | $85,000 | $40,000 |

On January 2, 2008, Prince issued $36,000 of stock and used the proceeds to purchase 90% of Sprite's common stock. The excess of the purchase price over Sprite's book value of net assets was allocated 60% to inventory and 40% to goodwill.

**Required:**

Show the amounts that Prince will report on its January 2, 2008 consolidated balance sheet for the following items under the (a) purchase method and (b) acquisition method.

1. Current assets.
2. Noncurrent assets.
3. Goodwill.
4. Current liabilities.
5. Noncurrent liabilities (include minority interests).
6. Stockholders' equity (controlling interest).
7. Stockholders' equity (noncontrolling or minority interest).

The following information is reported in the separate and consolidated balance sheets and income statements of Palace Corp. and its subsidiary, Show Corp., at December 31, 2008:

**P16-11**

Consolidating account balances with intercompany transactions

| | Palace | Show | Consolidated (after eliminations) |
|---|---|---|---|
| **Balance sheet accounts** | | | |
| Accounts receivable | $ 58,000 | $ 36,000 | $ 80,000 |
| Inventory | 52,000 | 40,000 | 80,000 |
| Investment in Show | 120,000 | — | — |
| Goodwill | — | — | 30,000 |
| Minority interest | — | — | 5,000 |
| Stockholders' equity | 308,000 | 100,000 | 308,000 |
| **Income statement accounts** | | | |
| Revenues | $350,000 | $240,000 | $510,000 |
| Cost of goods sold | 245,000 | 200,000 | 377,000 |
| Gross profit | 105,000 | 40,000 | 133,000 |
| Equity in earnings of Show | 16,000 | — | — |
| Net income | 70,000 | 20,000 | 80,000 |

**Additional Information:**

During 2008, Palace sold goods to Show at the same markup on cost it uses for all sales. At December 31, 2008, Show had not paid for all of these goods and still held 50% of them in inventory.

**Required:**

1. What was the amount of intercompany sales from Palace to Show during 2008?
2. What was the carrying amount of the inventory that Show purchased from Palace on the December 31, 2008 consolidated balance sheet?

3. How much did Show owe to Palace for intercompany sales at December 31, 2008?

4. What percent of Show's stock does Palace own?

---

**P16-12**

Consolidating intercompany sales

On October 1, 2008, Pacer Corp. acquired all of Sunny Corp.'s outstanding stock for cash. The fair value of Sunny's net assets was less than the purchase price but more than the net carrying amount. During October 2008, Pacer sold goods to Sunny at a profit. At December 31, 2008, 40% of these goods remained in Sunny's inventory.

**Required:**

1. Specify reasons for preparing consolidated financial statements that present operating results, cash flows, and financial position as if a parent company and its subsidiaries were a single entity.

2. How will the acquisition affect Pacer's consolidated balance sheet at October 1, 2008?

3. What eliminations are required for the intercompany sales when preparing consolidated financial statements at December 31, 2008?

4. What is the effect on Pacer's separate balance sheet immediately after the October 1, 2008 acquisition?

---

**P16-13**

Elimination entries and consolidated balance sheet

The following are the balance sheets for Plate and Salad immediately prior to Plate's September 1, 2008 acquisition of Salad:

|  | Plate | Salad |
|---|---|---|
| **Assets** | | |
| Cash | $500,000 | $100,000 |
| Accounts receivable | 50,000 | 20,000 |
| Inventory | 100,000 | 30,000 |
| Land | 50,000 | 10,000 |
| Bldg. & equip. net | 200,000 | 100,000 |
| Total | $900,000 | $260,000 |
| | | |
| **Liabilities & equity** | | |
| Accounts payable | $ 40,000 | $ 80,000 |
| Bonds payable | 200,000 | –0– |
| Common stock & PIC | 300,000 | 100,000 |
| Retained earnings | 360,000 | 80,000 |
| Total | $900,000 | $260,000 |

Consider the following cases:

**Case 1**

Plate buys 100% of Salad's common stock for $180,000 cash. The fair value of Salad's assets and liabilities equal their book value.

**Case 2**

Plate buys 100% of Salad's common stock for $210,000 cash. The fair value of Salad's land is $20,000 and of its buildings and equipment is $110,000. All other fair values equal book values.

**Required:**

1. Prepare the September 1, 2008 journal entry on Plate's books to record the acquisition of Salad.

2. Prepare the elimination entries needed to prepare a consolidated balance sheet immediately after the acquisition.

3. Prepare the consolidated balance sheet immediately after the acquisition.

Refer to the balance sheets of Plate and Salad in P16-13. Assume that Plate buys 80% of Salad's common stock for $180,000 cash. The fair value of Salad's land is $20,000, the fair value of Salad's buildings and equipment is $110,000 and all other fair values equal book values.

**P16-14**

Elimination entries and consolidated balance sheet under purchase versus acquisition method

**Required:**

Give answers to the following under (a) purchase method and (b) acquisition method.

1. Give the journal entry on Plate's books to record the acquisition of Salad.
2. Prepare the elimination entries needed to prepare a consolidated balance sheet immediately after the acquisition.
3. Prepare the consolidated balance sheet immediately after the acquisition.

On January 1, 2008, Pluto Company purchased all of Saturn Company's common stock for $1,000,000 cash. On that date, Saturn had retained earnings of $200,000 and common stock of $600,000. The book values of Saturn's assets and liabilities were equal to fair values except for the following:

**P16-15**

Eliminating entries and accounting for goodwill

|  | Book Value | Fair Value |
|---|---|---|
| Equipment (net) | $200,000 | $220,000 |
| Land | 250,000 | 300,000 |

**Additional Information:**

1. The equipment had an estimated remaining useful life of five years at acquisition.
2. Goodwill was not impaired in 2008 but was impaired by $25,000 in 2009.
3. Reported income for Pluto (excluding equity income from Saturn's earnings) and Saturn follows:

|  | Pluto | Saturn |
|---|---|---|
| Year 2008 | $500,000 | $200,000 |
| Year 2009 | $350,000 | $100,000 |

**Required:**

1. Prepare the January 1, 2008 journal entry on Pluto's books to record the acquisition of Saturn.
2. Prepare the elimination entries needed to prepare a consolidated balance sheet immediately after acquisition.
3. Calculate consolidated income for 2008 and 2009.
4. How would your answers to requirement 3 change under pre-*SFAS No. 142* amortization rules for goodwill? (Assume a 40-year amortization period.)

Company B, an auto parts company, made several acquisitions with newly issued stock over the past five years using the purchase method of accounting. In each case, the purchase price exceeded the fair value of the acquired company's net assets. AutoParts Heaven, a competitor, made no acquisitions. Wholesale prices of auto parts have been rising over the last five years. Both Company B and AutoParts Heaven account for inventories using the FIFO method.

**P16-16**

Business acquisitions and ratio analysis

CFA
ADAPTED

**Required:**

1. Briefly explain why Company B's acquisition history makes it difficult to analyze the *trend* of its financial data and ratios.
2. Briefly explain why Company B's acquisition history makes it difficult to compare its *ratios* with those for AutoParts Heaven.

3. For each of the following financial measures, compare the effect (higher, lower, or no effect) of the purchase method on the financial measure of Company B to the effect of the pooling-of-interests method. Briefly explain why each effect occurs:

   a. Gross profit margin percentage.

   b. Long-term debt-to-equity ratio.

   c. Pre-tax earnings.

---

**P16-17**

Comparing translation effect on ratios

**CFA**
ADAPTED

AutoParts Heaven is a U.S. company whose operations include a large, 100% owned foreign subsidiary. The subsidiary's functional currency is the dollar. The local currency in the country where the foreign subsidiary operates is appreciating against the U.S. dollar. The subsidiary accounts for inventories using the FIFO method.

**Required:**

Compare each of the following ratios for the foreign subsidiary *in its functional currency after translation* to the same ratios *in the local currency before translation*. Briefly explain why each ratio differs.

1. Gross profit margin percentage.

2. Operating profit margin.

3. Net profit margin.

---

## CASES

---

**C16-1**

Shopko: Business acquisitions and analysis of sales growth

The disclosure rules for business combinations complicate financial analysis. Trend analysis becomes difficult because comparative financial statements are not retroactively adjusted to include data for the acquired company for periods prior to the acquisition.

For example, consider Shopko's acquisition of Pamida on July 6, 1999. Excerpts from Shopko's 1999 annual report highlight the revenue and earnings growth achieved in that year. In the president's letter, William Podany noted the following:

For more than ten consecutive years we have achieved new records for revenues and this year we are pleased to report another year of record earnings.

The management's discussion and analysis (MD&A) section began with the following statement:

Consolidated net sales for fiscal 1999 (52 weeks) increased $939.5 million or 31.8% over fiscal 1998 weeks (52 weeks) to $3,898.1 million.

The details of the acquisition were disclosed in the following note in Shopko's 1999 annual report:

On July 6, 1999, the Company acquired all of the outstanding voting and nonvoting common stock of Pamida for $94.0 million in cash, $285.8 million in assumed debt and $138.6 million in assumed trade and other accrued liabilities. Pamida is a retail chain headquartered in Omaha, Nebraska, operating Pamida retail stores in 15 Midwest, North Central and Rocky Mountain states. In connection with the Pamida acquisition, the Company incurred special charges of $8.1 million for employee retention programs, elimination of administrative functions and various integration initiatives. The allocation of the purchase price of Pamida was based on estimated fair values at the date of acquisition.

This acquisition was accounted for under the purchase method of accounting and the allocation of the purchase price was based on fair values at the date of acquisition. Goodwill associated with the Pamida acquisition of approximately $186.6 million is being amortized on a straight-line basis over 40 years. The results of operations since the dates of acquisition have been included in the consolidated statements of earnings.

The following presents selected unaudited pro forma consolidated statement of earnings information that has been prepared assuming the Pamida acquisition occurred on January 31, 1999 and February 1, 1998, respectively:

| | Fiscal Years Ended | |
| --- | --- | --- |
| ($ in thousands, except per share data—unaudited) | January 29 2000 | January 30 1999 |
| Net sales | $4,181,567 | $3,630,951 |
| Earnings before extraordinary item | 101,190 | 56,678 |
| Diluted earnings per share before extraordinary item | 3.54 | 2.14 |

Shopko's consolidated statements of earnings for the years ended January 29, 2000 and January 30, 1999 follow:

## Consolidated Statement of Earnings

| | Fiscal Years Ended | |
| --- | --- | --- |
| ($ in thousands) | January 29 2000 | January 30 1999 |
| Revenues: | | |
| Net sales | $3,898,090 | $2,958,557 |
| Licensed department rentals and other income | 13,856 | 12,325 |
| | 3,911,946 | 2,970,882 |
| Costs and Expenses: | | |
| Cost of sales | 3,047,930 | 2,296,085 |
| Selling, general and administrative expenses | 601,157 | 471,546 |
| Special charges | 8,068 | 5,723 |
| Depreciation and amortization expenses | 84,438 | 67,590 |
| | 3,741,593 | 2,840,944 |
| Income from operations | 170,353 | 129,938 |
| Interest expense—net | (46,894) | (38,311) |
| Gain on sale of ProVantage stock | 56,760 | — |
| Earnings before income taxes, minority interest and extraordinary item | 180,219 | 91,627 |
| Provision for income taxes | 71,800 | 35,991 |
| Earnings before minority interest and extraordinary item | 108,419 | 55,636 |
| Minority interest | (2,463) | — |
| Earnings before extraordinary item | 105,956 | 55,636 |
| Extraordinary (loss) on retirement of debt, net of income taxes of $2,443 | (3,776) | — |
| Net earnings | $ 102,180 | $ 55,636 |

**Required:**

1. How should a financial statement user interpret the reference to 31.8% sales growth in the MD&A section?

2. Suppose you are asked to prepare a sales forecast for the year ended February 3, 2001. Based on the information shown here, what is the best estimate of Shopko's sustainable growth in sales between the years ended January 30, 1999 and January 29, 2000? Explain your answer.

---

City Holding Company is a multibank holding company headquartered in West Virginia. The Company is comprised of multiple facilities located in West Virginia, Ohio, and California. The banking subsidiaries provide a full range of banking services and make investments in debt and equity securities under limitations and restrictions imposed by regulations of the Comptroller of the Currency.

Appearing on the following pages are City Holding Company's consolidated balance sheet and cash flow statement as well as selected footnote information pertaining to the available-for-sale securities for Year 2 and Year 1.

**C16-2**

City Holding Company: Using mark-to-market accounting for available-for-sale securities

Using the information provided, determine responses to the questions that follow. Provide detailed support where appropriate.

(*Note:* Unrealized gains [losses] on available-for-sale securities are not recognized for tax purposes until the securities are sold. Accordingly, the tax effects of these unrealized gains [losses] are recognized as adjustments to the deferred tax liability [asset] accounts. Unrealized gains [losses] on available-for-sale securities are shown net of related tax effects as an adjustment to stockholders' equity. Assume that the all realized gains and losses reported in the footnote on page 1001 relate to available-for-sale securities. Transfers of securities from the held-to-maturity to available-for-sale category are recorded at fair value with the unrealized gain [loss] recorded in stockholders' equity.)

**STRETCH**

**Required:**

1. Determine the net before-tax unrealized holding gain (loss) on available-for-sale securities that City Holding recognized in Year 2. Assume no adjustments are made to the unrealized holding gain (loss) account when securities are sold.

2. Assuming a 35% tax rate, determine the deferred tax amounts related to the net unrealized holding gains (losses) that were recorded in Year 2. Indicate whether the deferred tax amounts were a liability or an asset.

3. Give the entry that City Holding made at December 31, Year 2 to record the unrealized gain (loss) on available-for-sale securities and to adjust the related stockholders' equity account.

4. Give the entry that City Holding made to record sales and calls on available-for-sale securities in Year 2.

5. To the extent possible, explain the year-to-year change in the cost basis of the available-for-sale securities (from $377,013,000 on December 31, Year 1 to $436,070,000 on December 31, Year 2).

## City Holding Company and Subsidiaries

### Consolidated Balance Sheets

| ($ in thousands) | December 31 | |
| --- | --- | --- |
| | **Year 2** | **Year 1** |
| **Assets** | | |
| Cash and due from banks | $ 109,318 | $ 81,827 |
| Federal funds sold | 20,000 | 88,500 |
| Cash and cash equivalents | 129,318 | 170,327 |
| Investment securities available for sale, at fair value | 445,384 | 383,552 |
| Investment securities held-to-maturity, at amortized cost | | |
| (approximate fair value at December 31 Year 2—$74,415) | 72,410 | — |
| Total investment securities | 517,794 | 383,552 |
| Securities purchased under agreement to resell | 27,202 | — |
| Loans | | |
| Gross loans | 1,204,391 | 1,390,255 |
| Allowance for loan losses | (28,504) | (48,635) |
| Net loans | 1,175,887 | 1,341,620 |
| Retained interests | 80,923 | 71,271 |
| Premises and equipment | 37,802 | 43,178 |
| Accrued interest receivable | 11,265 | 12,422 |
| Net deferred tax assets | 35,895 | 47,443 |
| Other assets | 31,825 | 46,482 |
| Total assets | $2,047,911 | $2,116,295 |

*(continued)*

## City Holding Company and Subsidiaries *(continued)*

## Consolidated Balance Sheets

| | December 31 | |
| --- | --- | --- |
| ($ in thousands) | Year 2 | Year 1 |
| **Liabilities** | | |
| Deposits | | |
| Noninterest-bearing | $ 281,290 | $ 284,649 |
| Interest-bearing | 1,283,290 | 1,406,646 |
| Total deposits | 1,564,580 | 1,691,295 |
| Federal funds purchased and securities sold under agreement to repurchase | 146,937 | 127,204 |
| Securities sold, not yet purchased | 26,284 | — |
| Long-term debt | 25,000 | 29,328 |
| Corporation-obligated mandatorily redeemable capital securities of subsidiary trusts holding solely subordinated debentures of City Holding Company | 87,500 | 87,500 |
| Other liabilities | 32,217 | 34,619 |
| Total liabilities | 1,882,518 | 1,969,946 |
| Preferred stock, par value $25 per share: 500,000 shares authorized; none issued | — | — |
| Common stock, par value $2.50 per share: authorized— 50,000,000 shares authorized; 16,919,248 and 16,892,913 shares issued and outstanding at December 31, Year 2 and Year 1, respectively, including 261,563 and 4,979 shares in treasury | 42,298 | 42,232 |
| Capital surplus | 59,029 | 59,174 |
| Retained earnings | 66,076 | 41,152 |
| Cost of common stock in treasury | (6,426) | (136) |
| Accumulated other comprehensive income | 4,416 | 3,927 |
| Total stockholders' equity | 165,393 | 146,349 |
| Total liabilities and stockholders' equity | $2,047,911 | $2,116,295 |

## Consolidated Statements of Cash Flows

| | Years Ended December 31 | | |
| --- | --- | --- | --- |
| ($ in thousands) | Year 2 | Year 1 | Year 0 |
| **Operating Activities** | | | |
| Net income | $ 32,459 | $ (26,000) | $(38,373) |
| Cumulative effect of accounting change, net of tax | — | 17,985 | — |
| Net income (loss) before cumulative effect | 32,459 | (8,015) | (38,373) |
| Adjustments to reconcile net income (loss) to net cash provided by operating activities: | | | |
| Amortization and accretion, including write-off of goodwill | 1,621 | 1,014 | 40,837 |
| Loss on fixed asset disposals | — | 3,951 | 4,805 |
| Provision for depreciation | 5,749 | 8,777 | 12,291 |
| Provision for loan losses | 1,800 | 32,178 | 25,480 |
| Deferred income tax expense (benefit) | 11,214 | (8,463) | (22,802) |
| Net periodic pension benefit | (322) | (273) | (285) |
| Loans originated for sale | — | (93,875) | (219,748) |
| Purchases of loans held for sale | — | — | (16,065) |
| Proceeds from loans sold | 2,929 | 112,146 | 324,354 |
| Realized (gains) losses on loans sold | (445) | (3,039) | 1,596 |
| (Increase) decrease in retained interests | (9,652) | 2,435 | — |
| Realized investment securities (gains) losses | (1,459) | (2,382) | 5,015 |

*(continued)*

## Consolidated Statements of Cash Flows

| ($ in thousands) | Years Ended December 31 | | |
| --- | --- | --- | --- |
| | Year 2 | Year 1 | Year 0 |
| Decrease (increase) in accrued interest receivable | 1,157 | 4,821 | (93) |
| Decrease in other assets | 4,111 | 5,785 | 25,572 |
| Increase (decrease) in other liabilities | 2,901 | (12,661) | 5,045 |
| Net cash provided by (used in) operating activities | 52,063 | 42,399 | 147,629 |
| **Investing Activities** | | | |
| Proceeds from maturities and calls of securities held-to-maturity | 4,994 | — | — |
| Purchases of securities held-to-maturity | (40,783) | — | — |
| Proceeds from sales of securities available-for-sale | 348,052 | 262,241 | 51,606 |
| Proceeds from maturities and calls of securities available for sale | 165,014 | 171,546 | 32,417 |
| Purchases of securities available for sale | (608,709) | (431,113) | (80,640) |
| Net decrease (increase) in loans | 147,121 | 400,832 | (64,191) |
| Net cash paid in sales of subsidiaries, divisions, and branches | — | (37,869) | — |
| Realized gain on sales of subsidiaries, divisions, and branches | — | (8,036) | — |
| Purchases of premises and equipment | (373) | (3,511) | (97) |
| Net cash provided by (used in) investing activities | 15,316 | 354,090 | (60,905) |
| **Financing Activities** | | | |
| Net (decrease) increase in noninterest-bearing deposits | (3,359) | 16,280 | 24,803 |
| Net (decrease) increase in interest-bearing deposits | (123,356) | (234,508) | 103,368 |
| Net increase in short-term borrowings | 19,733 | (98,562) | (153,953) |
| Proceeds from long-term debt | 10,000 | — | — |
| Repayment of long-term debt | — | — | (85,000) |
| Purchases of treasury stock | (7,473) | — | — |
| Exercise of stock options | 1,104 | — | — |
| Cash dividends paid | (5,037) | — | (7,426) |
| Net cash provided by financing activities | (108,388) | (316,790) | (118,208) |
| Increase (decrease) in cash and cash equivalents | (41,009) | 79,699 | (31,484) |
| Cash and cash equivalents at beginning of year | 170,327 | 90,628 | 122,112 |
| Cash and cash equivalents at end of year | $129,318 | $170,327 | $ 90,628 |

## Notes to Consolidated Financial Statements
## City Holding Company and Subsidiaries

### Note Four: Investments

During Year 2, the Company initiated an investment strategy to invest in trust preferred securities issued by other financial institutions. Only those securities issued by financial institutions that satisfy various asset size, profitability, equity-to-asset ratio, and certain other criteria, as pre-established by management, are evaluated for potential investment. Securities acquired were predominantly investment grade or were reviewed and approved for investment by the Company's executive loans committee. As of December 31, Year 2, the Company had invested $40.75 million, classified as held-to-maturity, and $17.43 million, classified as available-for-sale, pursuant to this strategy.

Also during Year 2, the Company transferred debt securities debt securities with an estimated fair value of $37.14 million and an amortized cost basis of $36.03 million from the available-for-sale classification to the held-to-maturity category. Transfers of debt securities into the held-to-maturity category from the available-for-sale classification are made at fair value at the date of transfer. The unrealized holding gain of $1.11 million at the date of transfer is retained in the other comprehensive income section of stockholders' equity and in the carrying value of the held-to-maturity securities. Such amount are amortized over the remaining life of the security.

The aggregate carrying and approximate market values of securities follow. Fair values are based on quoted market prices, where available. If quoted market prices are not available, fair values are based on quoted market prices of comparable financial instruments.

## Available-for-Sale Securities

| ($ in thousands) | | December 31, Year 2 | | |
| --- | --- | --- | --- | --- |
| | Cost | Gross Unrealized Gains | Gross Unrealized Losses | Estimated Fair Value |
| U.S. Treasury securities and obligations of U.S. government corporations and agencies | $107,108 | $5,607 | $— | $112,715 |
| Obligations of states and political subdivisions | 22,687 | 804 | — | 23,491 |
| Mortgage-backed securities | 130,739 | 2,819 | — | 133,558 |
| Other debt securities | 51,591 | 101 | (76) | 51,616 |
| Total debt securities | 312,125 | 9,331 | (76) | 321,380 |
| Equity securities | 123,945 | 59 | — | 124,004 |
| | $436,070 | $9,390 | $(76) | $445,384 |

## Available-for-Sale Securities

| ($ in thousands) | | December 31, Year 1 | | |
| --- | --- | --- | --- | --- |
| | Cost | Gross Unrealized Gains | Gross Unrealized Losses | Estimated Fair Value |
| U.S. Treasury securities and obligations of U.S. government corporations and agencies | $202,422 | $6,751 | $ (318) | $208,855 |
| Obligations of states and political subdivisions | 64,609 | 1,426 | (135) | 65,900 |
| Mortgage-backed securities | 90,969 | 90 | (1,519) | 89,540 |
| Other debt securities | 6,089 | 161 | — | 6,250 |
| Total debt securities | 364,089 | 8,428 | (1,972) | 370,545 |
| Equity securities | 12,924 | 83 | — | 13,007 |
| | $377,013 | $8,511 | $(1,972) | $383,552 |

Gross gains of $1.46 million were realized during Year 2 on sales and calls of securities. There were no gross losses realized during Year 2. Gross gains of $2.67 million and $105,000 and gross losses of $290,000 and $5.12 million were realized on sales and calls of securities during Year 1 and Year 0, respectively. Of the gross gains reported in Year 2, $1.35 million was directly attributable to two interest rate risk management processes utilized during the year. First, the Company reported $0.62 million in gains realized from the Company's investment in a mutual fund that generates capital gains, as opposed to interest income. Second, as further discussed in Note Five, the Company reported $0.73 million in gains realized from an investment transaction that entailed the short-sale of a high-coupon U.S. Treasury bond. Gross gains of $2.67 million in Year 1 include $1.62 million of gains realized from the Company's investment in a mutual fund during Year 1. The Company maintained an average balance of $46.25 million invested in the mutual fund during Year 1. This mutual fund generated capital gains, as opposed to interest income, which utilized capital loss carryforwards available to the Company for income tax purposes. The capital loss carryforwards were primarily generated by the gross securities losses recognized in Year 0. Gross losses of $5.12 million in Year 0 are comprised of losses the Company recognized on its investments in small business investment corporations.

The book value of securities pledged to secure public deposits and for other purposes as required or permitted by law approximated $158.11 million and $260 million at December 31, Year 2 and Year 1, respectively.

---

**C16-3**

Sears' Acquisition of Lands' End

On June 17, Year 2, Sears, Roebuck, and Company acquired Lands' End. Sears' income statements and balance sheets have been condensed from the Year 2 annual report. Sears disclosed the acquisition in Note 2, and disclosed the effect of implementing *SFAS No. 142* in Note 17.

## Consolidated Statements of Income

| ($ in millions) | Year 2 | Year 1 | Year 0 |
|---|---|---|---|
| **Revenues** | | | |
| Total revenues | $41,366 | $40,990 | $40,848 |
| **Costs and Expenses** | | | |
| Cost of sales, buying and occupancy | 25,646 | 26,234 | 26,632 |
| Selling and administrative | 9,249 | 8,892 | 8,807 |
| Provision for uncollectible accounts | 2,261 | 1,866 | 884 |
| Depreciation and amortization | 875 | 863 | 839 |
| Interest | 1,143 | 1,415 | 1,248 |
| Special charges and impairments | 111 | 542 | 251 |
| Total costs and expenses | 39,285 | 39,812 | 38,661 |
| Operating income | 2,081 | 1,178 | 2,187 |
| Other income, net | 372 | 45 | 36 |
| Income before income taxes, minority interest, and cumulative effect of change in accounting principle | 2,453 | 1,223 | 2,223 |
| Income taxes | 858 | 467 | 831 |
| Minority interest | 11 | 21 | 49 |
| Income before cumulative effect of change in accounting principle | 1,584 | 735 | 1,343 |
| Cumulative effect of a change in accounting for goodwill | (208) | — | — |
| Net Income | $ 1,376 | $ 735 | $ 1,343 |

## Consolidated Balance Sheets (Condensed)

| ($ in millions) | Year 2 | Year 1 |
|---|---|---|
| **Assets** | | |
| Total current assets | $39,983 | $36,105 |
| Total property and equipment, net | 6,910 | 6,824 |
| Goodwill | 944 | 294 |
| Tradenames and other intangible assets | 704 | — |
| Other assets | 1,868 | 1,094 |
| Total Assets | $50,409 | $44,317 |
| **Liabilities** | | |
| Total current liabilities | 18,597 | 15,584 |
| Long-term debt and capitalized lease obligations | 21,304 | 18,921 |
| Pension and postretirement benefits | 2,491 | 2,417 |
| Minority interest and other liabilities | 1,264 | 1,276 |
| Total Liabilities | 43,656 | 38,198 |
| Total Shareholders' Equity | 6,753 | 6,119 |
| Total Liabilities and Shareholders' Equity | $50,409 | $44,317 |

## Note 2—Acquisition

On June 17, Year 2, the Company acquired 100 percent of the outstanding common shares of Lands' End. The results of Lands' End's operations have been included in the consolidated financial statements since that date. Headquartered in Dodgeville, Wisconsin, Lands' End is a leading direct merchant of traditionally styled, casual clothing for men, women and children, accessories, footwear, home products and soft luggage.

The Company acquired Lands' End for $1.8 billion in cash. The acquisition has been accounted for using the purchase method in accordance with *SFAS No. 141,* "Business Combinations." Accordingly, the total purchase price has preliminarily been allocated to the assets acquired and liabilities assumed based on their estimated fair values at acquisition as follows (amounts in millions):

| | |
|---|---:|
| Merchandise inventories | $ 238 |
| Property and equipment | 185 |
| Intangible assets (primarily indefinite lived tradenames) | 704 |
| Goodwill | 834 |
| Other assets | 48 |
| Accounts payable and other liabilities | (169) |
| Total | $1,840 |

Of the $704 million acquired intangibles, $700 million was assigned to registered tradenames that are not subject to amortization and $4 million was assigned to customer lists with an estimated useful life of three years.

The amount allocated to goodwill is reflective of the benefit the Company expects to realize from leveraging the Lands' End brand name across its retail business. The goodwill related to the Lands' End acquisition is not deductible for tax purposes.

## Note 17—Implementation of New Accounting Standard

Effective at the beginning of Year 2, the Company adopted *SFAS No. 142,* "Goodwill and Other Intangible Assets." Upon adoption of *SFAS No. 142,* goodwill amortization ceased. Goodwill is now subject to fair-value based impairment tests performed, at a minimum, on an annual basis. In addition, a transitional goodwill impairment test is required as of the adoption date. These impairment tests are conducted on each business of the Company where goodwill is recorded, and may require two steps. The initial step is designed to identify potential goodwill impairment by comparing an estimate of fair value for each applicable business to its respective carrying value. For those businesses where the carrying value exceed fair value, a second step is performed to measure the amount of goodwill impairment in existence, if any.

The Company had approximately $371 million in positive goodwill and $77 million in negative goodwill recorded in its consolidated balance sheet at the beginning of Year 2 as well as approximately $104 million in positive goodwill related to an equity method investment which is not subject to *SFAS No. 142* impairment tests. The $77 million in negative goodwill was required to be recognized into income upon adoption of the Statement. The Company completed the required transitional goodwill impairment test in the first quarter of Year 2 and determined that $261 million of goodwill recorded within the Company's Retail and Related Services segment, primarily related to NTB and Orchard Supply Hardware, was impaired under the fair value impairment test approach required by *SFAS No. 142.*

The fair value of these reporting units was estimated using the expected present value of associated future cash flows and market values of comparable businesses where available. Upon adoption of the Statement, a $208 million charge, net of tax and minority interest, was recognized in the first quarter of Year 2 to record this impairment as well as the recognition of negative goodwill and was classified as a cumulative effect of a change in accounting principle.

The following table presents the pro forma effect of the adoption of *SFAS No. 142* on recent fiscal periods as if the change was applied at the beginning of the respective fiscal year:

| ($ in millions) | Year 1 | Year 0 |
|---|---|---|
| Reported net income | $735 | $1,343 |
| Add back: | | |
| Negative goodwill amortization | (14) | (15) |
| Positive goodwill amortization | 20 | 24 |
| Pro forma net income | $741 | $1,352 |

The Company's policy is to test the realizability of goodwill as of the end of the fiscal year. The Company tested the realizability of the $944 million of goodwill as of December 28, Year 2 resulting in no additional impairment being recorded.

**Required:**

1. What amount did Sears allocate to goodwill in the Lands' End acquisition? Provide possible reasons that Sears paid this premium to purchase Lands' End.

2. How does Sears account for this goodwill under *SFAS No. 142*? How would Sears have accounted for this goodwill under pre-*SFAS No. 142* rules?

3. How will the change in goodwill accounting affect Sears' income in future years?

4. Based on the disclosures, explain the change in Sears' reported goodwill on its balance sheet from Year 1 and Year 2.

5. Note 2 states that the acquired tradenames are not subject to amortization, but the acquired customer lists are amortized over three years. Explain the different accounting treatments for these two acquired intangible assets.

---

**C16-4**

**Air Products: Joint ventures and off-balance sheet effects**

Excerpts from the Year 2 annual report of Air Products and Chemicals, Inc. follow. The income statement and balance sheet are condensed but the footnote entitled "Summarized Financial Information of Equity Affiliates" is shown in its entirety.

The footnote provides information on several joint ventures that Air Products has entered into—primarily to incinerate municipal solid waste and generate electricity.

## Air Products and Chemicals, Inc. and Subsidiaries

### Consolidated Income Statement (Modified)

| | Years Ended September 30 | |
|---|---|---|
| ($ in millions) | Year 2 | Year 1 |
| Sales and other income | $5,401.2 | $5,857.8 |
| Costs and expenses | | |
| Cost of sales | 3,827.7 | 4,243.3 |
| Selling and administrative | 715.1 | 752.1 |
| Research and development | 120.6 | 122.5 |
| Other (income) expense, net | (37.1) | (5.5) |
| Operating income | 774.9 | 745.4 |
| Income from equity affiliates, net of related expenses | 76.2 | 81.2 |
| Gain on sale of U.S. packaged gas business | 55.7 | — |
| Gain on divestiture of interest in cogeneration facilities | — | 101.6 |
| Loss on early retirement of debt | — | (75.8) |
| Interest expense | 122.3 | 191.2 |
| Income before taxes and minority interest | 784.5 | 661.2 |
| Income taxes provision (benefit) | 240.8 | 190.5 |
| Minority interest in earnings of subsidiary companies | 18.3 | 5.1 |
| Net income | $ 525.4 | $ 465.6 |

*(continued)*

## Consolidated Balance Sheets (Modified)

| | September 30 | |
|---|---|---|
| ($ in millions) | **Year 2** | **Year 1** |
| **Assets** | | |
| Total current assets | $ 1,909.3 | $ 1,684.8 |
| Investment in net assets of and advances to equity affiliates | 484.2 | 499.5 |
| Plant and equipment, at cost | 10,879.8 | 10,226.5 |
| Less accumulated depreciation | (5,502.0) | (5,108.0) |
| Plant and equipment, net | 5,377.8 | 5,118.5 |
| Goodwill | 431.1 | 384.7 |
| Other noncurrent assets | 292.6 | 396.6 |
| Total assets | $ 8,495.0 | $ 8,084.1 |
| **Liabilities and shareholders' equity** | | |
| Total current liabilities | $ 1,256.2 | $ 1,352.4 |
| Long-term debt | 2,041.0 | 2,027.5 |
| Deferred income and other noncurrent liabilities | 827.4 | 702.0 |
| Deferred income taxes | 725.6 | 778.4 |
| Total liabilities | 4,850.2 | 4,860.3 |
| Minority interest in subsidiary companies | 184.4 | 118.0 |
| Total shareholders' equity | 3,460.4 | 3,105.8 |
| Total liabilities and shareholders' equity | $ 8,495.0 | $ 8,084.1 |

## Summarized Financial Information of Equity Affiliates

The following table presents summarized financial information on a combined 100% basis of the principal companies accounted for by the equity method. Amounts presented include the accounts of the following equity affiliates: Stockton CoGen Company (50%); Pure Air on the Lake, L.P. (50%); Bangkok Cogeneration Company Limited (48.8%); Daido Air Products Electronics, Inc. (49%); Sapio Produzione Idrogeno Ossigeno S.r.L. (49%); INFRA Group (40%); Air Products South Africa (50%); Bangkok Industrial Gases Company Ltd. (50.6%); INOX Air Products Limited (INOX) (49.4%); APP GmbH in WPS GmbH & CoKG (20%); DuPont Air Products Nanomaterials, LLC (50%); Island Pipeline Gas (33%); Tyczka Industrie-Gases GmbH (50%); and principally other industrial gas producers. In the fourth quarter of Year 2, the company obtained control of San Fu after increasing its ownership interest from 48% to 70%. In the fourth quarter of Year 1, the company sold its 50% interest in Cambria CoGen Company and Orlando CoGen Limited. Amounts presented reflect the accounts of these companies for the periods during which the equity method was applied.

| ($ in millions) | **Year 2** | **Year 1** |
|---|---|---|
| Current assets | $ 732.6 | $ 833.9 |
| Noncurrent assets | 1,148.7 | 1,391.0 |
| Current liabilities | 572.5 | 605.1 |
| Noncurrent liabilities | 452.2 | 620.3 |
| Net sales | 1,608.8 | 1,690.2 |
| Sales less cost of sales | 543.0 | 611.5 |
| Net income | 196.3 | 219.4 |

The company's share of income of all equity affiliates for Year 2, Year 1 and Year 0 was $88.7, $91.1 and $99.6, respectively. These amounts exclude $12.5, $9.9 and $12.0 of related net expenses incurred by the company. Dividends received from equity affiliates were $42.0, $44.9 and $49.7 in Year 2, Year 1 and Year 0, respectively.

The investment in net assets of and advances to equity affiliates at 30 September Year 2 and Year 1 included investment in foreign affiliates of $449.5 and $465.9, respectively.

As of 30 September Year 2 and Year 1, the amount of investment in companies accounted for by the equity method included goodwill in the amount of $69.6 and $77.2, respectively. Goodwill is no longer amortized, as discussed in Note 1.

**Required:**

1. What are some reasons companies give to justify entering into joint ventures?

2. Using the information provided, estimate what the effect on Air Products' return on assets ratio and debt-to-equity ratio would have been if its proportionate share of the joint ventures had been included as individual assets and liabilities on the consolidated balance sheet. For this purpose, use a 35% tax rate, and assume that Air Products' proportionate ownership in these equity affiliates averaged 45%.

**Remember to check the book's companion Web site for additional study material.**

# Statement of Cash Flows | 17

| ($ in millions) | | $22,011.9 |
| --- | --- | --- |
| Sales | | |
| Costs, Expenses and Other | | |
| Materials and production | 01.1 | 5,149.6 |
| Marketing and administrative | 65.4 | 7,155.5 |
| Research and development | 82.9 | 3,848.0 |
| Restructuring costs | | |
| Equity income from | 2.3 | 322.2 |
| | 4) | (1,717.1) |
| | | (110.2) |
| | | 14,648.0 |

*Ode to Cash Flow*

*Though my bottom line is black, I am flat upon my back,*
*My cash flows out and my customers pay slow,*
*The growth of my receivables is almost unbelievable;*
*The result is certain—unremitting woe!*
*And I hear the banker utter an ominous low mutter,*
*"Watch cash flow!"*[1]

A s this poem suggests, accrual earnings may not always provide a reliable measure of enterprise performance and financial health. There are several reasons for this. Accrual accounting is often based on subjective judgments that can introduce measurement error and uncertainty into reported earnings. Examples include estimates of uncollectible receivables, useful lives of assets, and future pension and health care benefits. One-time write-offs and restructuring charges require subjective judgments that can adversely affect the quality of the reported earnings number as a reliable indicator of a company's long-run performance. Moreover, managers can readily manipulate accrual income by postponing discretionary expenditures for research and development or advertising or by purposeful last-in, first-out (LIFO) dipping.

For these reasons, analysts must scrutinize a firm's cash flows—not just its accrual earnings—to evaluate its performance and creditworthiness. A significant difference between accrual earnings and operating cash flow may be a "red flag" that signals distortions of reported profits or impending financial difficulties.

Equity analysts are interested in operating cash flows because a firm's value ultimately depends on the discounted present value of its expected future cash flows. Recent operating cash flows are sometimes used in conjunction with current earnings as a jumping-off point for generating forecasts of expected future operating cash flows. Thus, cash flows can provide useful information for assessing equity values.[2]

## LEARNING OBJECTIVES

**After studying this chapter, you will understand:**

1. The major sources and uses of cash reported in the operating, investing, and financing sections of the statement of cash flows.

2. Why accrual net income and operating cash flow differ and the factors that explain this difference.

3. The difference between the direct and indirect methods of determining cash flow from operations.

4. How to prepare a statement of cash flows from comparative balance sheet data, an income statement, and other financial information.

5. Why changes in balance sheet accounts over a year may not reconcile to the corresponding account changes included in the statement of cash flows.

6. How operating cash flows can be distorted.

---

[1] H. S. Bailey, Jr., cited in R. Green, "Are More Chryslers in the Offing?" *Forbes,* February 2, 1981, p. 69.

[2] Research evidence that supports this assertion includes J. Rayburn, "The Association of Operating Cash Flow and Accruals with Security Returns," *Journal of Accounting Research,* Supplement 1986, pp. 112–33; P. Wilson, "The Relative Information Content of Accruals and Cash Flows: Combined Evidence at the Earnings Announcement and Annual Report Release Date," *Journal of Accounting Research,* Supplement 1986, pp. 165–200; P. Wilson, "The Relative Information Content of Accrual and Funds Components of Earnings after Controlling for Earnings," *The Accounting Review,* April 1987, pp. 293–322; M. Johnson and D. Lee, "Financing Constraints and the Role of Cash Flow from Operations in the Prediction of Future Profitability," *Journal of Accounting, Auditing and Finance,* Fall 1994, pp. 619–52.

International

*Chapter*

Commercial lenders monitor a firm's operating cash flows because such cash flows provide the resources for periodic interest payments and the eventual repayment of principal. Low or negative operating cash flows signal poor credit risks.

Investment bankers scrutinize operating cash flows before deciding whether to underwrite a debt or equity issue. They know that the ultimate purchasers of the securities will assess the attractiveness of the securities based, in part, on the firms' expected operating cash flows.

## STATEMENT FORMAT

Generally accepted accounting principles (GAAP) has required some form of **funds flow statement** since the early 1970s.[3] The purpose of this statement is to provide users a clear explanation of what caused the company's liquid assets to increase or decrease during the reporting period. The format of this statement was originally designed to explain changes in **working capital**—current assets minus current liabilities. But since 1988, the Financial Accounting Standards Board (FASB) has mandated that firms provide a **cash flow statement** that explains the sources and uses of cash.[4] Firms are required to disclose cash flows generated (or used) from three distinct types of activities:

> *Funds* is a generic term used to describe liquid assets—those readily convertible into cash or cash equivalents. The two most common definitions of funds are *working capital* and *cash*. A funds flow statement shows the inflows and outflows of funds as defined for that statement.

1. **Operating cash flows** result from events or transactions that enter into the determination of net income—that is, transactions related to the production and delivery of goods and services to customers. In effect, operating cash flows are a company's cash-basis revenues and expenses.

2. **Investing cash flows** result from the purchase or sale of productive assets such as plant and equipment, from the purchase or sale of marketable securities (government bonds or stocks and bonds issued by other companies), and from the acquisitions of other companies or divestitures.

3. **Financing cash flows** result when a company sells its own stocks or bonds, pays dividends or buys back its own shares (treasury stock), or borrows money and repays the amounts borrowed.

*SFAS No. 95* allows firms the option of choosing between two alternative formats for presenting cash flows from *operating* activities: (1) the **direct approach** and (2) the **indirect approach.** Each of these alternative formats is illustrated on the following pages.

> The International Financial Reporting Standards (IFRS) format for cash flow statements is similar to the U.S. GAAP format. See "Cash Flow Statements," *IAS No. 7* (London: International Accounting Standards Committee, revised 1992). Cash flows are classified by operating, investing, and financing activities. Operating cash flows can be reported using either the direct method or the indirect method, but the direct method is preferred (paras. 18–20). One difference in the IAS approach is that firms have latitude in classifying cash flows from interest and dividends received or paid. Interest paid can be classified either as operating or financing cash flows; interest and dividends received can be classified either as operating or investing cash flows (para. 33).

## The Direct Approach

Exhibit 17.1 presents the fiscal 2007 (and comparative 2006) statement of cash flows for Golden Enterprises whose fiscal year ends June 1, 2007. The statement shows the cash flows separated into operating, investing, and financing activities. Operating activities generated positive cash flows of $4.622 million. Investing activities resulted in net cash outflows of $1.100 million. The major outflow was to purchase property and equipment. The company

---

[3] "Reporting Changes in Financial Position," *Accounting Principles Board (APB) Opinion No. 19* (New York: American Institute of Certified Public Accountants [AICPA], 1971).

[4] "Statement of Cash Flows," *Statement of Financial Accounting Standards (SFAS) No. 95* (Stamford, CT: Financial Accounting Standards Board [FASB], 1987).

## EXHIBIT 17.1 Golden Enterprises, Inc. and Subsidiary

**Consolidated Statements of Cash Flows**
**For the Fiscal Years Ended June 1, 2007, and June 2, 2006**

|  | Fiscal* | |
| --- | --- | --- |
|  | 2007 | 2006 |
| **Cash Flows from Operating Activities** | | |
| Cash received from customers | $110,731,854 | $105,874,804 |
| Interest income | 144,687 | 146,072 |
| Rental income | 31,974 | 36,469 |
| Other operating cash payments/receipts | 255,423 | 300,940 |
| Cash paid to suppliers & employees for cost of goods sold | (54,923,539) | (55,762,586) |
| Cash paid for suppliers & employees for selling, general & administrative | (50,336,873) | (47,888,447) |
| Income taxes | (1,007,958) | 231,982 |
| Interest expense | (273,209) | (294,549) |
| Net cash provided by operating activities | $ 4,622,359 | $ 2,644,685 |
| **Cash Flows from Investing Activities** | | |
| Purchase of property, plant and equipment | (1,731,230) | (1,670,021) |
| Proceeds from sale of property, plant and equipment | 577,355 | 188,221 |
| Collection of notes receivable | 53,672 | 49,558 |
| Net cash used in investing activities | $ (1,100,203) | $ (1,432,242) |
| **Cash Flows from Financing Activities** | | |
| Debt proceeds | 23,163,475 | 21,525,001 |
| Debt repayments | (23,587,618) | (22,433,469) |
| Decrease in checks outstanding in excess of bank balances | (1,233,363) | 1,125,873 |
| Cash dividends paid | (1,479,425) | (1,479,425) |
| Net cash used in financing activities | $ (3,136,931) | $ (1,262,020) |
| Net Increase in Cash and Cash Equivalents | 385,225 | (49,577) |
| Cash and Cash Equivalents at Beginning of Year | 321,627 | 371,204 |
| Cash and Cash Equivalents at End of Year | $ 706,852 | $ 321,627 |

*Author note: Golden's 2007 fiscal year runs from June 3, 2006 to June 1, 2007.

paid out $3.137 million of cash for financing activities, principally for debt repayment and payment of dividends. As a result of its operating, investing, and financing activities, Golden Enterprises generated a net increase in cash of slightly over $385 thousand highlighted in Exhibit 17.1.

Golden Enterprises follows the direct approach to presenting cash flows from operations. The direct approach requires that firms report major classes of gross cash receipts (cash revenues) and gross cash payments (cash expenses). Note that Interest income and Interest

The specific categories included by the FASB in para. 27 of *SFAS No. 95* are:

(a) Cash collected from customers (including lessees and licensees).
(b) Interest and dividends received.
(c) Other operating cash receipts.
(d) Cash paid to employees and other suppliers of goods and services.
(e) Interest paid.
(f) Income taxes paid.
(g) Other operating cash payments.

| EXHIBIT 17.2 | Golden Enterprises, Inc. and Subsidiary |
| --- | --- |

**Consolidated Statements of Operations**
**For the Fiscal Years Ended June 1, 2007, and June 2, 2006**

| | Fiscal* | |
| --- | --- | --- |
| | **2007** | **2006** |
| Net sales | $110,826,925 | $106,546,696 |
| Cost of sales | 57,977,398 | 57,018,901 |
| Gross margin | 52,849,527 | 49,527,795 |
| Selling, general and administrative expenses | 51,481,437 | 49,168,289 |
| Operating income | $    1,368,090 | $      359,506 |
| | | |
| Other income (expenses): | | |
| Gain on sale of assets | 488,174 | 138,884 |
| Interest expense | (273,209) | (294,549) |
| Other income | 432,084 | 483,481 |
| Total other income (expenses) | 647,049 | 327,816 |
| Income before income tax | 2,015,139 | 687,322 |
| Provision for income taxes | 801,905 | 398,386 |
| Net income | $    1,213,234 | $      288,936 |

* *Author note:* Golden's 2007 fiscal year runs from June 3, 2006 to June 1, 2007.

expense are shown as components of cash flows from operating activities. This treatment is in accordance with *SFAS No. 95*. However, many financial analysts and other statement users believe that interest paid (expense) should be included as part of cash flows from financing activities while interest received (income) should be included with cash flows from investing activities. Nevertheless, the FASB classifies these two items as elements of cash flows from operating activities because "in general, cash flows from operating activities should reflect the cash effects of transactions and other events that enter into the determination of net income."[5]

Golden Enterprises discloses Cash received from customers of $110.732 million on its fiscal 2007 cash flow statement (year ended June 1, 2007). This number differs from the accrual accounting revenue number of $110.827 million, which is reported on Golden's 2007 income statement shown in Exhibit 17.2. There are several reasons for this difference:

1. Some 2007 credit sales made late in the year had not been collected in cash by year-end.
2. Some 2007 credit sales were made to customers who ultimately were unable to pay their balance due.
3. During 2007, cash was received for payment on accounts receivable generated from sales in prior years.

The "Cash paid to suppliers & employees for cost of goods sold" of $54.924 million on Golden's 2007 cash flow statement (Exhibit 17.1) differs from the $57.977 million reported for Cost of sales on Golden's accrual-basis income statement (Exhibit 17.2). Similarly, "Cash paid for suppliers & employees for selling, general & administrative" of $50.337 million and the $1.008 million of cash paid for Income taxes on the cash flow statement differs from the $51.481 million of Selling, general & administrative expenses and the Provision for income taxes of $802 thousand reported on Golden's income statement.

[5] *SFAS No. 95*, para 88.

**EXHIBIT 17.3**     Golden Enterprises, Inc. and Subsidiary

Consolidated Statements of Cash Flows
For the Fiscal Years Ended June 1, 2007, and June 2, 2006

| | Fiscal* | |
| --- | --- | --- |
| | 2007 | 2006 |
| **Cash Flows from Operating Activities** | | |
| Net income | $1,213,234 | $ 288,936 |
| Adjustment to reconcile net income to net | | |
| cash provided by operating activities: | | |
| ① Depreciation | 2,268,468 | 2,284,669 |
| ② Deferred income taxes | (14,933) | (190,049) |
| ③ Gain on sale of property and equipment | (488,174) | (138,884) |
| ④ Change in receivables—net | (95,071) | (671,892) |
| ⑤ Change in inventories | (99,603) | (306,004) |
| ⑥ Change in prepaid expenses | (14,441) | 828,289 |
| ⑦ Change in cash surrender value of insurance | 178,214 | 149,732 |
| ⑧ Change in other assets | 51,892 | (9,550) |
| ⑨ Change in accounts payable | 1,550,473 | (60,009) |
| ⑩ Change in accrued expenses | 333,005 | 26,027 |
| ⑪ Change in salary continuation plan | (69,585) | (65,898) |
| ⑫ Change in accrued income taxes | (191,120) | 509,318 |
| Net cash provided by operating activities | $4,622,359 | $2,644,685 |

* *Author note:* Golden's 2007 fiscal year runs from June 3, 2006 to June 1, 2007.

Overall, Exhibits 17.1 and 17.2 show that Golden Enterprises generated positive operating cash flows of $4.622 million in fiscal 2007 while its accrual-basis net income was only $1.213 million. Why is there such a large discrepancy between Golden's net income and operating cash flows? The answer is found in the reconciliation of net income to cash from operations, the alternative indirect approach allowed by *SFAS No. 95* for presenting cash flows from operating activities. This other statement format from Golden Enterprises 2007 cash flow statement is shown in Exhibit 17.3.[6]

## The Indirect Approach

The indirect approach begins with the accrual-basis net income and adjusts for the following:

- Items *included* in accrual-basis net income that *did not* affect cash in the current period, such as

  1. Noncash revenues or gains (such as revenues earned but not received in cash and gains on the disposal of fixed assets).

  2. Noncash expenses or losses (such as depreciation and amortization, provision for bad debt expense, and expenses accrued but not paid in cash).

---

[6] This reconciliation schedule is required of all firms that use the direct method of presenting operating cash flows. See *SFAS No. 95*, para. 28.

- Items *excluded* from accrual-basis income that *did* affect operating cash flows in the current period, such as
  3. Cash inflows (revenues) received but not recognized as earned in the current period (such as rent received in advance and collections on account).
  4. Cash outflows (expenses) paid but not recognized for accrual accounting purposes in the current period (such as prepaid insurance and payments on account).

The overwhelming majority of public companies use the indirect approach. Of the 600 companies included in the AICPA's annual financial reporting survey, 592—or 98.7%—used the indirect approach for reporting cash generated by operating activities in 2005.[7] Firms favor the indirect approach for two reasons:

1. The indirect approach is easier for firms to implement because it relies exclusively on data already available in the accrual accounts.
2. The indirect approach is more familiar to many accountants because this format was widely used in the changes in working capital statement that preceded *SFAS No. 95*.

We'll use Exhibit 17.3 to show how the indirect approach reconciles accrual accounting net income ($1,213,234 in Exhibit 17.2) with cash flow from operations ($4,622,359 in Exhibit 17.1). Each of the reconciling items is discussed individually.

Items ① through ③ in Exhibit 17.3 represent amounts included in the accrual-basis net income figure *that did not have a cash flow effect*—that is, they did not cause cash to increase or decrease during the year. Because they did not have a cash flow effect, the accrual-basis net income must be adjusted for these items to arrive at cash flows from operations.

### ① Depreciation
This is the most common example of an indirect method adjustment. During 2007, Golden Enterprises made the following entry for depreciation:

| | | |
|---|---|---|
| **DR** | Depreciation and amortization . . . . . . . . . . . . . . . . . . . . . . . . . . . . | $2,268,468 |
| | **CR** Accumulated depreciation and amortization . . . . . . . . . . | $2,268,468 |

The entry to record Golden's taxes for 2007 follows. Adjustment ⑫ (discussed below) corrects for the current portion of tax expense not paid in cash and for the previous year's taxes paid in the current year.

| | | |
|---|---|---|
| **DR** | Tax expense . . . . . . . . . . . . . . . . . . . . . . . . . . . . | $801,905 |
| **DR** | Deferred tax asset . . . . . . . . . . . . . . . . . . . . . . | 14,933 |
| | **CR** Cash or taxes payable . . . . . . . . . . . . . . | $816,838 |

While the debit reduced income, the credit did not represent a cash outflow. Hence, this typical noncash expense causes Net income to diverge from Cash provided by operating activities. That's why depreciation expense must be added back to net income as a reconciling item under the indirect method.

### ② Deferred Income Taxes
Golden showed an increase in its net deferred tax assets (or a decrease in deferred tax liabilities) for 2007 of $14,933. Thus, Golden's taxable income exceeded its book income in 2007 due to a variety of temporary differences we discussed in Chapter 13. When this happens, the debit to income tax expense falls below the taxes owed and paid in the current period. This increase in net deferred tax assets must be subtracted from accrual-basis net income because the tax expense *understates* the cash outflow for taxes.

---

[7] Y. Lofe and A. Mrakovcic (eds.), *Accounting Trends and Techniques* (New York: AICPA, 2006).

③ **Gain on Sale of Property and Equipment**    This represents the difference between the selling price and book value of assets sold during the period. For 2007, Golden sold assets for a gain of $488,174. The proceeds from the asset sales shown in the Investing Activities section of Golden's cash flow statement totaled $577,355. Thus, the gain of $488,174 that increased accrual income does *not* reflect the increase in cash related to this transaction. Because the gain is a noncash addition to accrual income, it must be subtracted from this amount to arrive at cash flows from operations.

> We can infer that the assets sold had a net book value of $89,181 by subtracting the gain of $488,174 from the cash proceeds received from the sale of $577,355. So, the entry to record the sale of assets was:
>
> | **DR** | Cash ................................. | $577,355 | |
> |---|---|---|---|
> | **CR** | Assets (net of accumulated depreciation) .................... | | $ 89,181 |
> | **CR** | Gain on sale ...................... | | 488,174 |

Items ④ through ⑫ represent amounts that were included in the $1,213,234 net income for which the income effect either exceeds or falls below the cash flow effect. Because the income effect and the cash flow effect differ, the following adjustments must appear in the reconciliation.

④ **Change in Receivables—Net**    During 2007, the amount in Golden's Accounts receivable (net of Allowance for uncollectibles) account increased by $95,071. This means that sales on account (accrual-basis revenue) totaled more than cash collections on account (cash-basis revenue) in 2007. Accordingly, a subtraction must be made from the accrual-basis income to arrive at cash provided by operating activities.

⑤ **Change in Inventories**    During 2007, the amounts in Golden's inventory accounts (Raw materials and Finished goods) increased by $99,603. So, ending inventory was higher than beginning inventory, which means that inventory purchased was greater than the cost of inventory sold during the year. Let's temporarily assume that all inventory purchases were paid for in cash. (Adjustment ⑨ discusses changes in the Accounts payable account that corrects for noncash inventory purchases.) The inventory buildup means that cash outflow for inventory exceeded the accrual-basis Cost of goods sold on Golden's income statement. Thus, the increase in inventories must be subtracted from accrual-basis income to obtain cash flows from operations because the cash outflow for inventory exceeded the amount charged to expense under accrual accounting.

⑥ **Change in Prepaid Expenses**    Golden's Prepaid expenses increased in fiscal 2007 by $14,441. This increase represents cash payments for items such as insurance and rent that were in excess of the amounts expensed on Golden's accrual-basis income statement. Because cash payments exceeded the accrual-basis expenses, Golden subtracts this increase from accrual earnings to obtain cash flows from operations.

⑦ **Change in Cash Surrender Value of Insurance**    Golden carries life insurance policies on certain key executives in the firm. When it pays the premiums, part of the payment increases the cash surrender value of those policies. When policies are terminated, the company receives cash from the insurance company. During the year, Golden's balance sheet (not shown) shows a decrease in the Cash surrender value of life insurance of $178,214, which indicates that cash was received from termination of one or more of these policies. Golden treats this as an operating source of cash.

> An alternative and perhaps preferable method is to treat this as an investing source of cash inflows because the cash surrender value of life insurance policies could be viewed as a noncurrent investment.

⑧ **Change in Other Assets**   Golden's balance sheet shows a $51,892 decrease in the Other asset account. This decrease likely resulted in a charge (debit) to one or more expense accounts on Golden's income statement. Because these expenses do not reflect cash outflows, this amount is added to Golden's accrual-basis earnings to arrive at the operating cash flows for the period.

⑨ **Change in Accounts Payable**   Golden's Accounts payable account increased by $1,550,473 during the year. Thus, credit purchases on account exceeded cash payments on account by this amount. Because credit purchases are included as part of the Cost of goods sold on Golden's income statement, this amount represents an accrual-basis expense in excess of cash outflows for inventory during the period. Hence, this amount is shown as an addition to accrual-basis earnings to arrive at cash flows from operations.

⑩ **Change in Accrued Expenses**   Accrued expenses payable represent expenses for items such as salaries, wages, and interest incurred in the current period but not paid. Golden's Accrued expenses payable (liability account on its balance sheet) increased by $333,005 during fiscal 2007. Because this increase in expense accruals, which resulted in an offsetting debit to expense accounts on Golden's income statement, did not require an outflow of cash, this amount is shown as an add-back to the accrual earnings to arrive at cash flows from operations for the year.

⑪ **Change in Salary Continuation Plan**   Golden has a salary continuation (pension) plan for certain key executives. This long-term liability account is increased each year for the present value of increased retirement benefits earned during the year (which are reported as an expense on the accrual-basis income statement) and is decreased for the cash payments made to retired executives during the year. Golden's balance sheet shows a $69,585 decrease in this account for fiscal 2007, which implies that the cash payments for retirement benefits exceeded the amount recognized as expense on the accrual-basis income statement. Therefore, this amount is deducted from the accrual-basis income to arrive at cash flows from operations for the period.

⑫ **Change in Accrued Income Taxes**   This current liability account is increased for income taxes that are due for the period (with an offsetting debit to Tax expense on the accrual-basis income statement) and is reduced for cash payments made to the government for taxes in the current period. Golden's Accrued income taxes payable account decreased by $191,120 in 2007. This implies that Golden's cash outflow for income taxes exceeded the tax expense recorded on the accrual-basis income statement. Thus, this amount is subtracted from accrual income to arrive at cash flows from operations for the year.

*Both the direct and indirect approaches for computing net cash provided by operating activities will obviously report the same number—$4,622,359 in Golden's 2007 annual report.* Those who prefer the direct approach justify their preference by claiming that this method discloses operating cash flows by category—inflows from customers, outflows to suppliers, and so on. They contend that this categorization facilitates cash flow predictions. For example, assume that an analyst expects product selling prices to increase by 6% in the ensuing year. The direct method's disclosure of cash received from customers could then be multiplied by 106% to construct next year's cash forecast. (There is no similarly easy way to incorporate the expectation of a 6% price increase in the indirect method approach.)

Analysts who prefer the indirect approach do so because the size and direction of the items reconciling income to operating cash flow provide a rough yardstick for evaluating the quality of earnings. When a company reports high accounting income but simultaneously has low or negative cash flow from operations, this situation is considered a sign of low-quality earnings that are not sustainable. For example, if the excess of income over cash flow is accompanied by a large buildup in accounts receivable, this increase could indicate that the company is aggressively recognizing revenue (see Chapters 3 and 8). The receivables buildup may have occurred, for example, if a company shipped unwanted merchandise to distributors in an effort to inflate sales. Or the buildup could result from sales to customers with marginal creditworthiness that may never be collected.

Although the FASB allowed a choice between the direct and indirect approaches when it formulated *SFAS No. 95,* it anticipated that the vast majority of firms would use the indirect approach. Because few firms were expected to use the direct approach, the FASB feared that users might find it difficult to compare the operating cash flows of firms using the direct approach to that of firms using the indirect approach. To address this comparability concern, the FASB requires firms using the direct approach to *also* provide a reconciliation between accrual earnings and operating cash flows such as the one that is presented by those firms using the indirect approach. Golden Enterprises' choice of the direct approach explains why we have operating cash flow information for them under both methods.

*Additionally, firms using the indirect approach are required to separately disclose the amount of interest paid.* Consequently, those who believe interest expense represents a cash flow from financing activities will always have sufficient information available to reclassify this item out of cash flows from operating activities for firms using the indirect approach. However, the FASB does *not* require a separate disclosure of dividends and interest income *received.* Therefore, analysts who believe that these items should be classified as cash flows from investing activities will not have sufficient information to make this reclassification for firms that opt for the indirect approach.

> *SFAS No. 95* also requires firms using the indirect approach to separately disclose income taxes paid.

One additional difficulty confronting analysts using *SFAS No. 95* disclosures relates to the treatment of income taxes. Recall from Chapter 2 that intraperiod income tax allocation is followed in constructing the income statement—that is, the income tax expense associated with income from continuing operations is separately disclosed. Items not included in the computation of income from continuing operations (such as gains and losses from discontinued operations and extraordinary items) are reflected *net* of their associated income tax effects. This is done to facilitate predictions by statement users. The tax expense associated with the presumably recurring income from continuing operations is reported separately from the tax expense associated with items appearing below income from continuing operations. Regrettably, *SFAS No. 95* does not treat *cash* outflows for income taxes in the same way. The entire amount of taxes paid in cash is included in the Cash Flows from Operating Activities section even though some of the taxes relate, for example, to gains on sales of assets whose gross cash flows are included in the Cash Flows from Investing Activities section of the statement. The failure to differentiate tax cash flows by type (those pertaining to income from continuing operations versus other items) complicates forecasts of future cash flows. The FASB justifies this treatment as follows:

> The Board decided that allocation of income taxes paid to operating, investing, and financing activities would be so complex and arbitrary that the benefits, if any, would not justify the costs involved.[8]

---

[8] *SFAS No. 95,* para. 92.

While this cost-benefit justification may be correct, *SFAS No. 95* provides no evidence to support this assertion.

 RECAP

The statement of cash flows provides a summary of a firm's operating, investing, and financing activities that explains its change in cash position for the period. Operating cash flows can be presented using either the direct or indirect approach. The direct approach details major sources of cash receipts and major categories of cash expenditures. The indirect approach begins with accrual earnings and adjusts for (1) items included in accrual-basis income that did not affect cash and (2) items excluded from accrual earnings that did affect operating cash flows.

## Other Elements of the Cash Flow Statement

Let's return to Exhibit 17.1. Golden Enterprises' cash flow statement illustrates the typical range of items included in the Investing Activities and Financing Activities sections of the statement. The items included are relatively straightforward, and there should be no difficulties in interpreting these disclosures. For example, Golden shows investing cash outflows in 2007 for purchases of property, plant and equipment ($1,731,230). Direct cash inflows from investing activities resulted from the sale of property, plant and equipment ($577,355) and collection of note receivable ($53,672).

Financing cash inflows resulted from the issuance of debt ($23,163,475); financing cash outflows were for debt repayment ($23,587,618), a reduction in bank overdrafts ($1,233,363), and cash dividends paid ($1,479,425).

The net result of Golden's operating, investing, and financing activities for the year was an increase in cash and cash equivalents of $385,225.

## PREPARING THE CASH FLOW STATEMENT

This section illustrates the procedures used to prepare a cash flow statement. Exhibits 17.4(a) and (b) provide comparative 2007–2008 balance sheet data, a 2008 income statement, and selected additional information for Burris Products Corporation.

Reviewing the comparative balance sheets in Exhibit 17.4(a) shows that the cash balance decreased by $8,000 during 2008. The purpose of a cash flow statement is to explain the underlying *causes* for this $8,000 change in the cash balance. Recall that the causes for change arise from operating, investing, and financing activities.

Constructing a cash flow statement requires the preparer to gather information like that in Exhibit 17.4. The three-step process that follows is then used to build the components of the statement.

**Step 1:** Identify the journal entry or entries that led to the reported change in each noncash balance sheet account.

**Step 2:** Determine the net cash flow effect of the journal entry (or entries) identified in Step 1.

**Step 3:** Compare the financial statement effect of the entry (Step 1) with its cash flow effect (Step 2) to determine what cash flow statement treatment is necessary for each item.

This three-step approach is used to develop Burris's cash flow statement in Exhibit 17.5 on page 1018 using the indirect method of determining cash flow from operations.

## EXHIBIT 17.4 Burris Products Corporation

### Comparative Balance Sheets, 2008 Income Statement, and Additional Information

**Panel (a)**

| Comparative Balance Sheets | December 31 2008 | December 31 2007 | Increase or Decrease |
|---|---|---|---|
| Cash | $ 25,000 | $ 33,000 | $ 8,000 Decrease |
| Accounts receivable | 171,000 | 180,000 | 9,000 Decrease |
| Inventory | 307,000 | 295,000 | 12,000 Increase |
| Land | 336,000 | 250,000 | 86,000 Increase |
| Buildings and equipment | 1,628,000 | 1,430,000 | 198,000 Increase |
| Accumulated depreciation | (653,000) | (518,000) | 135,000 Increase |
| | $1,814,000 | $1,670,000 | |
| | | | |
| Accounts payable | $ 163,000 | $ 160,000 | $ 3,000 Increase |
| Customer advance deposits | 99,000 | 110,000 | 11,000 Decrease |
| Bonds payable | 500,000 | 500,000 | –0– — |
| Discount on bonds payable | (66,000) | (70,000) | 4,000 Decrease |
| Deferred income tax payable | 100,000 | 94,000 | 6,000 Increase |
| Common stock | 850,000 | 800,000 | 50,000 Increase |
| Retained earnings | 168,000 | 76,000 | 92,000 Increase |
| | $1,814,000 | $1,670,000 | |

**Panel (b)**

#### 2008 Income Statement

| | |
|---|---|
| Sales revenues | $ 3,030,000 |
| Cost of goods sold | (2,526,625) |
| Depreciation expense | (158,000) |
| Sales commissions (all cash) | (34,000) |
| Interest expense | (44,000) |
| Gain on sale of equipment | 17,000 |
| Income before taxes | $ 284,375 |
| Income tax expense | (102,375) |
| Net income | $ 182,000 |

**Additional Information**

1. Equipment with a cost of $63,000 and a book value of $40,000 was sold for $57,000.
2. Cash dividends of $90,000 were paid in 2008.

## Cash Flows from Operations

The Operating Activities section of the statement in Exhibit 17.5 begins with net income of $182,000. Under the indirect approach, net income represents an initial rough approximation of the cash generated by operations. Starting the statement with net income presumes that revenues are ultimately collected in cash and that expenses represent cash outflows. In the long run, this approximation is basically correct. In any single period, however, accrual accounting net income will not equal that same period's cash flow from operations. The reason is that cash flows for some revenue and expense items occur either before or after accrual

| EXHIBIT 17.5 | Burris Products Corporation | |
|---|---|---|

**2008 Statement of Cash Flows**

**Operating Activities**

| | | |
|---|---|---|
| Net income | | $ 182,000 |
|   Adjustments to reconcile net income to cash | | |
|     provided by operating activities | | |
|     ① Depreciation | $158,000 | |
|     ② Gain on equipment sale | (17,000) | |
|     ③ Amortization of bond discount | 4,000 | |
|     ④ Deferred income taxes increase | 6,000 | |
|     ⑤ Accounts receivable decrease | 9,000 | |
|     ⑥ Customer advance deposits decrease | (11,000) | |
|     ⑦ Inventory increase | (12,000) | |
|     ⑧ Accounts payable increase | 3,000 | |
| | | 140,000 |
| Cash provided by operating activities | | $ 322,000 |
| | | |
| **Investing Activities** | | |
|   ② Equipment sale | | $ 57,000 |
|   ⑨ Land purchase | | (86,000) |
|   ⑩ Buildings and equipment purchase | | (261,000) |
| Cash used for investing activities | | $(290,000) |
| | | |
| **Financing Activities** | | |
|   ⑪ Common stock issued | | $ 50,000 |
|   ⑫ Dividend paid | | (90,000) |
| **Cash used for financing activities** | | (40,000) |
|   Net decrease in cash during 2008 | | $ (8,000) |

accounting revenue and expenses are recognized. The adjustment for these differences between the timing of revenue and expense recognition and cash flow impact appear as the eight numbered items following the net income figure in Exhibit 17.5. We now explain each of these items.

① **Depreciation** The income statement in Exhibit 17.4(b) indicates that depreciation expense recognized during 2008 was $158,000. We use the three-step analytic approach, as follows:

**Step 1:** The journal entry that generated the account change was:

| | | | |
|---|---|---|---|
| **DR** | Depreciation expense | $158,000 | |
| | **CR**   Accumulated depreciation | | $158,000 |

**Step 2:** Neither of the two accounts that appear in the Step 1 journal entry involves cash. Indeed, depreciation is unlike most other expenses because cash outflow often occurs *before* the expense recognition—that is, when the asset is initially purchased.

**Step 3:** Depreciation expense was included as an element in the determination of net income (Step 1) as if it were a cash outflow. But depreciation expense does not represent a cash outflow (Step 2). Consequently, depreciation expense must be added back to net income.

In short, depreciation expense is added back to accrual-basis income to obtain operating cash flows because it was included in the determination of net income even though—unlike most other expenses—it doesn't represent a cash outflow of the current period.

## ② Gain on Equipment Sale

The net income number includes a gain on equipment sale of $17,000, as shown in Exhibit 17.4(b). Using the same three-step approach, we arrive at the following:

**Step 1:** With the additional information disclosed below the income statement in Exhibit 17.4(b), we can develop the following journal entry for the gain:

| | | |
|---|---|---|
| **DR** Accumulated depreciation | $23,000 | |
| **DR** Cash | 57,000 | |
| **CR** Equipment | | $63,000 |
| **CR** Gain on sale | | 17,000 |

**Step 2:** Scrutiny of the journal entry reveals that the sale resulted in a cash inflow of $57,000. This cash inflow is the result of investment activities.

**Step 3:** Comparing the accrual accounting effect (Step 1) to the cash flow effect (Step 2) reveals three problems: (1) the recognized accrual gain ($17,000) does not correspond to the cash inflow ($57,000), (2) the $17,000 gain is included in income and thus would be categorized as an operating cash inflow unless adjustments are made, and (3) the $57,000 cash inflow from investing activities must be separately reflected in the statement.

> Notice that if the equipment originally cost $63,000 and its book value was $40,000, the accumulated depreciation must have been $23,000.

The cash flow statement in Exhibit 17.5 reflects the information uncovered in Step 3. The $17,000 gain is subtracted from net income to arrive at cash flow from operations, and the $57,000 total cash received is correctly categorized and shown as a cash inflow from investing activities.

## ③ Amortization of Bond Discount

Exhibit 17.4(a) discloses that the Discount on bonds payable account decreased by $4,000 during 2008. The three-step approach shows the following:

**Step 1:** Because the income statement reports interest expense as $44,000, the journal entry that led to the balance sheet change for discount on bonds payable was:

| | | |
|---|---|---|
| **DR** Interest expense | $44,000 | |
| **CR** Discount on bonds payable | | $ 4,000 |
| **CR** Cash | | 40,000 |

**Step 2:** An examination of the journal entry reveals that interest expense of $44,000 was deducted in computing net income, although the cash outflow for the payment of interest in 2008 was only $40,000.

**Step 3:** Because the accrual accounting income statement charge for interest expense ($44,000) exceeds the cash outflow ($40,000), the $4,000 difference must be added back to net income in the operating section of the cash flow statement.

④ **Deferred Income Taxes Increase** Deferred income taxes payable increased by $6,000, as shown in Exhibit 17.4(a). The three-step approach shows the following:

Step 1: Because income tax expense for 2008 was $102,375, the journal entry for taxes in 2008 was:

| | | |
|---|---|---|
| **DR** Income tax expense ........................................ | $102,375 | |
| **CR** Deferred income taxes payable ...................... | | $ 6,000 |
| **CR** Cash .............................................. | | 96,375 |

Step 2: Again, there is a disparity between the amount of the expense included in the determination of net income ($102,375) and the cash outflow to pay taxes ($96,375).

Step 3: Because the income statement expense charge is more than the cash outflow by $6,000, this $6,000 must be added back in the Operating Activities section of the cash flow statement in Exhibit 17.5.

⑤ **Accounts Receivable Decrease** During 2008, Exhibit 17.4(a) shows that the Accounts receivable account decreased by $9,000. Following the three-step approach we obtain:

Step 1: If we assume that all 2008 sales were initially credit sales, the aggregate entry to record these sales would be:

| | | |
|---|---|---|
| **DR** Accounts receivable ..................................... | $3,030,000 | |
| **CR** Sales revenue ...................................... | | $3,030,000 |

If we assume that the only transaction causing a decrease in the Accounts receivable account is for collections on account, the $9,000 decrease during 2008 implies the following entry for cash collections:

| | | |
|---|---|---|
| **DR** Cash ................................................ | $3,039,000 | |
| **CR** Accounts receivable................................. | | $3,039,000 |

Step 2: Examination of the entries in Step 1 reveals that when the total in Accounts receivable decreased, the amount of cash collections during the year ($3,039,000) exceeded the amount of accrual revenues included in income ($3,030,000).

Step 3: The $9,000 excess of cash collections over accrual revenues must be added back to net income in Exhibit 17.5 to obtain cash from operations.

⑥ **Customer Advance Deposits Decrease** Burris Products Corporation requires cash payments from customers prior to the sale of special order custom merchandise. This advance payment represents a liability on the balance sheet. As the custom products are delivered to customers, the liability is reduced and revenue is recognized. During 2008, the amount of the liability decreased by $11,000, as shown in Exhibit 17.4(a).

Step 1: The accounting entry that reflects the reduction in the advance payment liability during 2008 was:

| | | |
|---|---|---|
| **DR** Customer advance deposits .............................. | $11,000 | |
| **CR** Sales revenues....................................... | | $11,000 |

**Step 2:** Scrutinizing the entry in Step 1 indicates that accrual-basis sales revenues increased by $11,000. However, there was no corresponding cash flow effect this year because the cash flow originated in 2007 when the special products were ordered and paid for and the liability was initially recorded.

**Step 3:** Because revenues included in the computation of 2008 net income exceeded 2008 cash inflows by $11,000, this amount must be deducted in the operating section of the cash flow statement.

⑦ **Increase in Inventory** When inventory increases during a period, the dollar amount of new inventory purchases exceeds the cost of goods that were sold.

**Step 1:** If we initially assume that all inventory is purchased for cash (we will relax this assumption in adjustment ⑧ discussed next), the two accounting entries giving rise to a $12,000 increase in inventory (see Exhibit 17.4[a]) are:

| | | | |
|---|---|---|---|
| **DR** | Inventory | $2,538,625 | |
| | **CR** Cash | | $2,538,625 |

[$2,526,625 Cost of goods sold + $307,000 Ending inventory − $295,000 Beginning inventory]

and

| | | | |
|---|---|---|---|
| **DR** | Cost of goods sold | $2,526,625 | |
| | **CR** Inventory | | $2,526,625 |

Notice that the combined result of these two entries increases inventory by $12,000.

**Step 2:** Comparing the two journal entries in Step 1 indicates that the cost of goods sold number that is deducted in the computation of net income ($2,526,625) is $12,000 *lower* than the cash outflow to buy inventory.

**Step 3:** Because net income understates the cash outflow to acquire inventory, $12,000 must be deducted from income in Exhibit 17.5.

⑧ **Increase in Accounts Payable** Adjustment ⑦ for the increase in inventory was computed under the assumption that all inventory was purchased for cash. We assumed this because it makes it easier to see why an increase in inventory must be adjusted for when preparing a cash flow statement. We now relax this assumption because scrutiny of Exhibit 17.4(a) shows that the Accounts payable account increased by $3,000 during 2008. A $3,000 increase in Accounts payable means that $3,000 of the $12,000 inventory increase during the year was not paid for in cash. Therefore, $3,000 is added to net income in the cash flow statement.

There is another way to look at adjustments ⑦ and ⑧ that may make it easier for you to understand the accrual-to-cash adjustment. Together, adjustments ⑦ and ⑧ are designed to isolate the difference between accrual accounting's cost of goods sold measure and cash inventory purchases. Specifically:

| | |
|---|---|
| Accrual accounting cost of goods sold deduction included in determining income | $2,526,625 |
| Add: Adjustment ⑦ (inventory increase) | 12,000 |
| Equals: 2008 *total* inventory purchases | $2,538,625 |
| Subtract: Adjustment ⑧ (payables increase) | (3,000) |
| Equals: 2008 *cash* inventory purchases | $2,535,625 |

In combination, adjustments ⑦ and ⑧ subtract $9,000 from income, an amount equal to the difference between cost of goods sold ($2,526,625) and cash inventory purchases ($2,535,625).

# Cash Flows from Investing Activities

Turning to the investing activities section of Burris's cash flow statement (Exhibit 17.5), we see three transactions affected cash—one that resulted in a cash inflow and two that reduced cash.

② **Equipment Sale**    This transaction was analyzed earlier when we adjusted accrual net income for the gain on sale of equipment. The $57,000 cash received when this equipment was sold represents an investing source of cash.

⑨ **Land**    Exhibit 17.4(a) indicates that the Land account increased by $86,000. The analysis here is straightforward.

**Step 1:** The journal entry that reflects this increase is

| | | |
|---|---|---|
| **DR**  Land ................................................. | $86,000 | |
| **CR**  Cash ............................................. | | $86,000 |

**Step 2:** This transaction represents an outflow of cash of $86,000.

**Step 3:** The cash outflow is categorized as an $86,000 investment outflow.

⑩ **Buildings and Equipment Purchase**    The Buildings and equipment account increased by $198,000 during 2008 (see Exhibit 17.4[a]). However, in computing the cash outflow that was incurred to acquire these fixed assets, we cannot simply use the $198,000 net account change. The reason is that some equipment was also sold during 2008 (see preceding Item ②). It is therefore necessary to adjust the change in the Buildings and equipment account for the cost of the equipment sold to deduce the amount of the buildings and equipment purchased.

**Step 1:** When several items affect a particular account, it is useful to begin by reconstructing the account over the period being analyzed.

### Buildings and Equipment

| 12/31/07 Balance | $1,430,000 | | |
|---|---|---|---|
| "Plug" figure necessary to balance the account | 261,000 | Reduction in account arising from sale of equipment (see discussion of Item ②) | $63,000 |
| 12/31/08 balance | $1,628,000 | | |

The analysis reveals that the gross increase in the Buildings and equipment account was $261,000 and resulted in the following journal entry:

| | | |
|---|---|---|
| **DR**  Buildings and equipment ................................... | $261,000 | |
| **CR**  Cash ............................................. | | $261,000 |

**Step 2:** This transaction represents a cash outflow of $261,000.

**Step 3:** The outflow is categorized as a $261,000 investment cash outflow.

*This adjustment illustrates that when constructing a cash flow statement, the analyst must be careful to look beyond just the net change in the account*—he or she must also consider other known items that were added to or subtracted from the account during the period.

## Cash Flows from Financing Activities

The financing section of Burris's cash flow statement in Exhibit 17.5 shows two other account changes during the period that had cash flow implications.

⑪ **and** ⑫ **Stock Sale and Dividend Paid** The increase in the Common stock account indicates that additional capital was raised when new shares were sold. Furthermore, the additional information lists a $90,000 cash dividend (see Exhibit 17.5). The analysis of these items is straightforward:

Step 1: The stock sale journal entry was:

| | | | |
|---|---|---|---|
| **DR** | Cash ........................................................ | $50,000 | |
| | **CR** Common stock ........................................ | | $50,000 |

The dividend generated the following entry:

| | | | |
|---|---|---|---|
| **DR** | Retained earnings ........................................... | $90,000 | |
| | **CR** Cash ................................................ | | $90,000 |

Step 2: The cash effects of these items are unambiguously indicated in the entries—that is, a $50,000 inflow for the new financing and a $90,000 dividend outflow.

Step 3: Both the $50,000 cash inflow and the $90,000 cash outflow should be categorized as cash flows from financing activities.

---

RE|CAP

To prepare a cash flow statement, (1) re-create the accounting entries that explain the changes in all noncash balance sheet accounts, (2) determine the net cash flow effect of the entry and the type of activity that generated or used the cash, and (3) compare the accrual accounting effect of the entry with the cash flow effect to determine what adjustments, if any, are needed to convert accrual earnings to cash flow from operations.

# RECONCILIATION BETWEEN STATEMENTS: SOME COMPLEXITIES

Users of financial statements frequently encounter situations in which changes in balance sheet accounts over the year do *not* reconcile to the corresponding account changes in the statement of cash flows. We'll demonstrate this discrepancy and explain why it happens using data from the H.J. Heinz Company's 2006 10-K report. The fundamental point of our analysis is this: *While all accruals cause changes in balance sheet accounts, not all changes in operating balance sheet accounts (for example, receivables, inventory, and payables) result in accruals that are recognized on the income statement.* Therefore, trying to infer accruals that affect income from analyzing changes in balance sheet accounts can be, and often is, misleading.

Exhibit 17.6 shows Heinz's statement of cash flows for the fiscal year ended May 3, 2006 and the previous fiscal year. Exhibit 17.7 shows data from Heinz's 2006 comparative balance sheet for two selected accounts—Inventory and Property, plant and equipment. The operating section of Heinz's cash flow statement is prepared using the indirect approach, and starts with fiscal 2006 accrual-basis net income of $645,603,000. Adjustments to reconcile net income to cash provided by operations are presented next. Notice that on the cash flow statement, the $47,401,000 change in inventory is

> The term *accruals* is used in a generic sense to include not only accrued revenues and accrued expenses but also deferred revenues and deferred expenses. So, *accrual adjustments* include situations in which the revenue or expense recognition under accrual accounting occurs both before and after the cash flow.

| EXHIBIT 17.6 | H. J. Heinz Company and Subsidiaries |
| --- | --- |

## Consolidated Statements of Cash Flows

| ($ in thousands) | May 3, 2006 (53 Weeks) | April 27, 2005 (52 Weeks) |
| --- | --- | --- |
| **Operating activities:** | | |
| Net income | $ 645,603 | $ 752,699 |
| Adjustments to reconcile net income to cash provided by operating activities: | | |
| Depreciation | 227,454 | 227,187 |
| Amortization | 36,384 | 25,265 |
| Deferred tax (benefit)/provision | (57,693) | 53,857 |
| ① Impairment charges and losses on disposals | 188,772 | 100,818 |
| Gains on disposals | (140,749) | — |
| ② Other items, net | 39,066 | 43,989 |
| Changes in current assets and liabilities, excluding effects of acquisitions and divestitures: | | |
| Receivables | 115,583 | 45,851 |
| ③ Inventories | (47,401) | (25,315) |
| Prepaid expenses and other current assets | 13,555 | 2,633 |
| Accounts payable | 56,545 | 8,140 |
| Accrued liabilities | 57,353 | 25,077 |
| Income taxes | (59,511) | (99,408) |
| Cash provided by operating activities | 1,074,961 | 1,160,793 |
| **Investing activities:** | | |
| ④ Capital expenditures | (230,577) | (240,671) |
| Proceeds from disposals of property, plant and equipment | 19,373 | 22,252 |
| ⑤ Acquisitions, net of cash acquired | (1,100,436) | (126,549) |
| ⑥ Proceeds from divestitures | 856,729 | 51,150 |
| Purchases of short-term investments | — | (293,475) |
| Sales of short-term investments | — | 333,475 |
| Other items, net | 3,094 | (10,236) |
| Cash used for investing activities | (451,817) | (264,054) |
| **Financing activities:** | | |
| Payments on long-term debt | (727,772) | (480,471) |
| Proceeds from long-term debt | 230,790 | — |
| Proceeds from/(payments on) commercial paper and short-term debt, net | 298,525 | 26,468 |
| Dividends | (408,151) | (398,869) |
| Purchase of treasury stock | (823,370) | (291,348) |
| Exercise of stock options | 142,046 | 79,383 |
| Other items, net | 18,507 | 13,952 |
| Cash used for financing activities | (1,269,425) | (1,050,885) |
| Cash provided by operating activities of discontinued operations spun-off to Del Monte | 13,312 | 28,196 |
| Effect of exchange rate changes on cash and cash equivalents | (5,353) | 69,660 |
| Net (decrease)/increase in cash and cash equivalents | (638,322) | (56,290) |
| Cash and cash equivalents at beginning of year | 1,083,749 | 1,140,039 |
| Cash and cash equivalents at end of year | $ 445,427 | $ 1,083,749 |

To understand why, review discussion on p. 1021 for Item ⑦ in Exhibit 17.5 for Burris Products.

*subtracted* from accrual-basis income, implying that inventory *increased* by this amount. However, the change in Inventory on Heinz's comparative balance sheet (Exhibit 17.7) shows a $183,094,000 *decrease*—a discrepancy of nearly $230.5 million.

A similar discrepancy exists when trying to reconcile changes in Heinz's "Property, plant and equipment" balance sheet account with information presented on its cash flow statement. Heinz's

| EXHIBIT 17.7 | H.J. Heinz Company and Subsidiaries |
| --- | --- |

**Selected Accounts from Comparative Balance Sheets**

| ($ in thousands) | 3-May-06 | 27-Apr-05 | Changes in Account Balances* |
| --- | --- | --- | --- |
| **Inventories:** | | | |
| Finished goods and work-in-process | $ 817,037 | $ 974,974 | |
| Packaging material and ingredients | 256,645 | 281,802 | |
| Total inventories | 1,073,682 | 1,256,776 | $ (183,094) |
| | | | |
| **Property, Plant and Equipment Accounts:** | | | |
| Land | 55,167 | 67,000 | (11,833) |
| Buildings and leasehold improvements | 762,735 | 844,056 | (81,321) |
| Equipment, furniture and other | 2,946,574 | 3,111,663 | (165,089) |
| | 3,764,476 | 4,022,719 | (258,243) |
| Less: Accumulated depreciation | −1,863,919 | −1,858,781 | −5,138 |
| Total property, plant and equipment, net | $ 1,900,557 | $ 2,163,938 | $ (263,381) |

\* Amounts without parentheses represent increases in accounts from 2005 to 2006, while amounts with parentheses represent decreases in accounts.

comparative balance sheets show a year-to-year *decrease* in the Property, plant and equipment account (before accumulated depreciation) of $258,243,000 (Exhibit 17.7). However, the "Investing activities" section of Heinz's statement of cash flows (Exhibit 17.6) shows fiscal year 2006 capital expenditures (implying an *increase* in Property, plant and equipment) of $230,577,000—a difference of nearly $490 million.

Why don't the changes in working capital accounts like Inventory and fixed asset accounts like Property, plant and equipment shown on Heinz's balance sheet correspond with the changes in these accounts shown on its statement of cash flows? There are at least four reasons for these differences:

1. Asset write-offs due to impairment, corporate restructuring, or retirement,

2. Translation adjustments on assets and liabilities held by foreign subsidiaries,

3. Acquisitions and divestitures of other companies, and

4. Simultaneous investing and financing activities not directly affecting cash.

## Discrepancies in Current Accruals

We'll use Heinz's inventory account to illustrate reasons for the discrepancy between working capital components of net accrual adjustments on the cash flow statement and changes in these accounts on the balance sheet. From Exhibit 17.7, the change inventories from Heinz's comparative balance sheet is a decrease of $183,094,000 while the inventory increase implied by the accrual adjustment on Heinz's cash flow statement (Exhibit 17.6) is $47,401,000. Although a precise reconciliation is not possible, the primary factors causing the $230,495,000 difference arise for the reasons explained next.

**Write-Offs Due to Asset Impairments and Restructuring**    The following excerpt from Heinz's footnote 4 "Transformation Costs" describing its "strategic transformation" (reorganization and restructuring) program reveals that a portion of the charges shown on its 2006 cash flow statement (Item ① in Exhibit 17.6) relates to inventory and property, plant and equipment write-downs:

An excerpt from footnote 4 from H.J. Heinz 2006 10-K report follows:

As a result of the finalization of the strategic reviews related to the portfolio realignment, the following non-core businesses and product lines were sold in Fiscal 2006 or are anticipated to be sold in Fiscal 2007, and, accordingly, the following gains/(losses) or non-cash asset impairment charges have been recorded in continuing operations during Fiscal 2006:

| Business or product line ($ in millions) | Pre-Tax | After-Tax |
|---|---|---|
| Loss on sale of Seafood business in Israel | $ (15.9) | $ (15.9) |
| Impairment charge on Portion Pac Bulk product line | (21.5) | (13.3) |
| Impairment charge on U.K. Frozen and Chilled product lines | (15.2) | (15.2) |
| Impairment charge on European production assets | (18.7) | (18.7) |
| Impairment charge on Noodle product line in Indonesia | (15.8) | (8.5) |
| Impairment charge on investment in Zimbabwe business | (111.0) | (105.6) |
| Other | (1.5) | 0.5 |
| **Total** | $ (199.6) | $ (176.7) |

Of the above pre-tax amounts, $74.1 million was recorded in cost of products sold, $15.5 million in SG&A, $111.0 million in asset impairment charges for cost and equity investments, and $(1.0) million in other expense.

The $199.6 million pre-tax charge shown in the schedule from Heinz's footnote 4 is the major source of the $188.8 million adjustment shown in the Operating Activities section of Heinz's cash flow statement labeled Impairment charges and losses on disposals (Item ① in Exhibit 17.6). The explanation following the schedule in footnote 4 indicates that $74.1 million pre-tax was recorded in cost of products sold. This amount most likely reflects inventory write-downs that are not part of the $47.4 million inventory accrual adjustment shown in the cash flow statement (Item ③ Heinz's cash flow statement).

## Translation Adjustments

Heinz has numerous foreign subsidiaries whose statements are translated using the current rate approach described in Chapter 16. This method of measuring the increase or decrease in inventories of foreign subsidiaries generates a potential discrepancy between the balance sheet inventory change figure and the statement of cash flows inventory change figure. Here's why. On the cash flow statement, inventory change is computed by comparing purchases with cost of goods sold. If purchases exceed cost of goods sold, an inventory increase is indicated. To determine the direction of the inventory change for *foreign* subsidiaries, *translated* purchases and cost of goods sold are compared. Inventory purchases and cost of goods sold are translated into dollars using the exchange rate in effect at the time of the transaction. In contrast, the inventory change on the balance sheet is computed differently. Foreign subsidiaries' beginning inventories are translated at the beginning-of-period rate of exchange while ending inventories are translated at the end-of-period rate of exchange. The difference corresponds to the different nature of the two statements: The balance sheet reflects an *instant in time* (and thus uses the *exchange rate at that instant*); the cash flow statement uses a *series of exchange rates*. It should not be surprising therefore that the measures of inventory change on the two statements will differ. The foreign currency translation adjustment gains and losses are likely shown as part of the Other items, net adjustment on Heinz's cash flow statement (Item ② in Exhibit 17.6).

> For simplicity, the translation may also be done using the weighted average rate of exchange in effect over the period.

> This difference usually does not arise when *all* foreign subsidiaries are accounted for using the temporal method (Chapter 16). The reason is that the method for computing inventory change for temporal method subsidiaries on the cash flow statement translates both beginning and ending inventory at the *historical* rate of exchange. The historical rate is also used on the balance sheet. For firms whose subsidiaries all utilize the temporal approach, inventory change differences between the two statements usually do not arise.

**Acquisitions and Divestitures**    Another reason why the inventory change on the two statements differs is because of acquisitions and divestitures. Companies bought and sold usually possess inventories. The ending inventory number reported on the consolidated balance sheet includes the inventory of subsidiary companies purchased and excludes the inventories of subsidiaries or divisions sold during the year. Heinz had both acquisitions and divestitures during fiscal 2006. On the statement of cash flows, the inventory of companies acquired is reported as a component of Acquisitions, net of cash acquired and the inventory of companies sold is part of the Proceeds from divestitures reported in the Investing Activities section of Exhibit 17.6. ***Therefore, the inventory change figure in the Operating Activities section of Heinz's cash flow statement is limited to inventory changes for those segments of the firm that were owned at both the start and end of the reporting period.***

> Changes in inventories due to acquisitions or divestitures do not create a corresponding accrual adjustment to cost of goods sold on the income statement. Therefore, changes due to these events would *not* be included as part of the inventory adjustment to accrual-basis income (Item ③ in Exhibit 17.6) to arrive at operating cash flows.

The same factors explain discrepancies between changes in other working capital accounts on the balance sheet and accrual adjustments shown on the statement of cash flows.

## Discrepancies Related to Property, Plant and Equipment

A portion of the discrepancy between the change in Property, plant and equipment on the balance sheet (a decrease of $258.2 million before accumulated depreciation shown in Exhibit 17.7) and Capital expenditures on the cash flow statement ($230.6 million in Exhibit 17.6, Item ④) can be explained by asset write-downs taken in conjunction with Heinz's strategic transformation (reorganization and restructuring) program described earlier. As shown in the schedule of footnote 4 of its 2006 10-K report, Heinz took an $18.7 million pre-tax impairment charge on European production assets, which explains some of the decline in the Property, plant and equipment account on the balance sheet.

Three additional events are likely to have contributed to the reported balance sheet change:

**Retirements**    During the year, Heinz may have retired fixed assets (not related to the restructuring) that were not fully depreciated. Recall from Chapter 10 that the entry to record the retirement would take the following form:

| | | | |
|---|---|---|---|
| **DR** | Accumulated depreciation—plant and equipment ................ | $XXX | |
| **DR** | Loss on retirement .......................................... | XXX | |
| | **CR** | Plant and equipment (for cost of assets retired) ............. | $XXX |

Prior to 1995, it was possible to determine the cost of assets retired from Schedule V, Property, Plant and Equipment—a required schedule in firms' 10-K reports filed with the SEC—that reconciled the beginning and ending balances of the Property, plant and equipment account reported in firms' balance sheets. Unfortunately, this schedule is no longer required. Therefore, it is generally not possible for external users to determine the exact dollar amount of the year-to-year change in fixed asset accounts due to retirements.

**Foreign Currency Translation Adjustment**    As noted already, Heinz translates the accounts of most of its foreign subsidiaries using the current rate approach. Accordingly, the Property, plant and equipment accounts of these subsidiaries are translated using the current rate of exchange—at the balance sheet date—between the dollar and the foreign currency.

The fall (rise) of the dollar in relation to the functional currencies of these subsidiaries would result in an increase (decrease) in the balance of the Property, plant and equipment account that would not be reflected on the cash flow statement. Again, these adjustments were recorded in Schedule V of the 10-K report prior to 1995 but are no longer disclosed, making it difficult to ascertain the impact of translation adjustments on individual changes in balance sheet accounts.

### Acquisitions and Divestitures

Heinz acquired and sold companies during the year. These companies all owned property, plant and equipment. This immediately raised a classification dilemma in preparing Heinz's statement of cash flows: Should that portion of cash flow related to the cost of properties acquired be classified as Capital expenditures, or should it be included as a part of Acquisitions, net of cash acquired? Under *SFAS No. 95* classification criteria, Capital expenditures contain only cash outflows made to acquire property directly. Cash outflows for property acquired as part of a business acquisition are classified under Acquisitions following *SFAS No. 95* guidelines. You can see from examining the Investing Activities section of the statement of cash flow in Exhibit 17.6 that Heinz paid $1,100.4 million for acquisitions, net of cash acquired (Item ⑤). Part of this purchase price would contribute to an increase in the Property, plant and equipment account because the acquired firms' assets are included in Heinz's consolidated reports if Heinz's ownership gives it control over the acquired company.

The Investing Activities section of Exhibit 17.6 also shows cash proceeds from divestitures of $856,729,000 (Item ⑥). When business units included as part of a consolidated entity are sold, the Property, plant and equipment account is reduced by the book value—cost minus accumulated depreciation—of the fixed assets in the business unit sold. Before it was eliminated by the SEC, Schedule V of the 10-K report provided detailed information on increases and decreases in the Property, plant and equipment account due to acquisitions and divestitures. Now that this schedule is no longer required, analysts and other statement users must rely on fragmented and somewhat incomplete information provided elsewhere in the statements to deduce the book value of assets sold.

## Simultaneous Noncash Financing and Investing Activities

Occasionally firms engage in investing and financing activities that cause changes in balance sheet asset and liability accounts even though they do not affect cash receipts or cash payments. Examples include (1) purchasing a building by incurring a mortgage to the seller, (2) acquiring an asset by entering into a capital lease, or (3) issuing stock for noncash assets in connection with a business acquisition. *SFAS No. 95* requires firms to disclose these noncash simultaneous financing and investing activities either in a narrative or in a schedule, which is sometimes included as a separate section of the statement of cash flows. Although there is no evidence in Heinz's 2006 10-K report that any of the balance sheet changes in property, plant and equipment were acquired with noncash consideration, this is fairly common, especially for Internet and start-up companies that are typically short on cash.

See Exhibit 17.8 for Amazon.com's 2006 cash flow statement. The supplemental cash flow information (at the bottom of this statement) summarizes simultaneous financing and investing activities (highlighted) totaling $69 million that increased fixed asset accounts on Amazon's balance sheet but did not have a direct effect on cash flows.

| EXHIBIT 17.8 | Amazon.Com, Inc. |
| --- | --- |

## Consolidated Statements of Cash Flows

| | Year Ended December 31, | |
| --- | --- | --- |
| ($ in millions) | 2006 | 2005 |
| Cash and Cash Equivalents, Beginning of Period | $ 1,013 | $ 1,303 |
| **Operating Activities:** | | |
| Net income | 190 | 359 |
| Adjustments to reconcile net income to net cash from operating activities: | | |
| Depreciation of fixed assets, including internal-use software and website development, and other amortization | 205 | 121 |
| Stock-based compensation | 101 | 87 |
| Other operating expense (income) | 10 | 7 |
| Gains on sales of marketable securities, net | (2) | (1) |
| Remeasurements and other | (6) | (37) |
| Deferred income taxes | 22 | 70 |
| Excess tax benefit on stock awards | (102) | (7) |
| Cumulative effect of change in accounting principle | — | (26) |
| **Changes in operating assets and liabilities:** | | |
| Inventories | (282) | (104) |
| Accounts receivable, net and other current assets | (103) | (84) |
| Accounts payable | 402 | 274 |
| Accrued expenses and other liabilities | 241 | 67 |
| Additions to unearned revenue | 206 | 156 |
| Amortization of previously unearned revenue | (180) | (149) |
| Net cash provided by operating activities | 702 | 733 |
| **Investing Activities:** | | |
| Purchases of fixed assets, including internal-use software and website development | (216) | (204) |
| Acquisitions, net of cash acquired | (32) | (24) |
| Sales and maturities of marketable securities and other investments | 1,845 | 836 |
| Purchases of marketable securities and other investments | (1,930) | (1,386) |
| Net cash used in investing activities | (333) | (778) |
| **Financing Activities:** | | |
| Proceeds from exercises of stock options | 35 | 59 |
| Excess tax benefit on stock awards | 102 | 7 |
| Common stock repurchased | (252) | — |
| Proceeds from long-term debt and other | 98 | 11 |
| Repayments of long-term debt and capital lease obligations | (383) | (270) |
| Net cash used in financing activities | (400) | (193) |
| Foreign-currency effect on cash and cash equivalents | 40 | (52) |
| Net increase (decrease) in cash and cash equivalents | 9 | (290) |
| Cash and cash equivalents, end of period | $ 1,022 | $ 1,013 |
| **Supplemental cash flow information:** | | |
| Cash paid for interest | $ 86 | $ 105 |
| Cash paid for income taxes | 15 | 12 |
| Fixed assets acquired under capital leases and other financing arrangements | 69 | 6 |

The year-to-year changes in comparative balance sheet accounts may not coincide with the changes implied from amounts reported on the statement of cash flows. The factors contributing to these differences include (1) asset write-downs due to impairment or restructuring, (2) the translation of foreign subsidiary accounts using the year-end current exchange rate between the dollar and the foreign currency, (3) acquisitions and divestitures of other companies, and (4) simultaneous noncash financing and investing transactions. Footnote disclosures, along with information in the income statement and in the operating section of the cash flow statement, are often helpful in reconciling some of these differences.

## ANALYTICAL INSIGHTS: WAYS OPERATING CASH FLOWS CAN BE DISTORTED OR MANIPULATED

Healthy firms generate cash from their day-to-day operating activities. Firms that can't generate cash internally jeopardize their operations and risk loan default or bankruptcy. That is why an understanding of operating cash flows is so critical to assessing a company's financial health. Analysts watch operating cash flow for another reason—major discrepancies between accrual earnings and operating cash flows sometimes can be used to indentify instances in which earnings have been managed upward. Because cash flow from operations is such a carefully monitored number, firms have incentives to make this number look as strong as possible. Therefore, it is important for you to understand the ways in which operating cash flows can be distorted or managed. In this section, we briefly review and illustrate some of the ways this can happen.

### Changes in Working Capital Accounts

Changes in working capital accounts are the major sources and uses of operating cash flows. For example, collections on accounts receivable *increase* operating cash flows while payments on accounts payable or accrued expenses *decrease* operating cash flows. Two ways management can improve the short-run appearance of a firm's operating cash flows are to (1) accelerate the collection of receivables in the current period or (2) delay the payment of accrued expenses and accounts payable until after period-end. For example, receivables collection can be accelerated by offering special cash discounts or incentive programs to encourage customers to pay early. Payment of accounts payable can be extended beyond the normal collection period, but the firm may incur late payment fees by doing so. Thus, these improvements in operating cash flows are only temporary. So, large decreases in accounts receivable or large increases in accounts payable and accrued expenses should be viewed with a healthy level of skepticism because the impact on operating cash flows is not sustainable. As demonstrated in Chapters 5 and 8, quarter-to-quarter changes in the number of days accounts receivable outstanding and of days accounts payable outstanding can be monitored to spot shifts in collection or payment policies that contribute to operating cash flow distortions.

> Days accounts receivable outstanding = 365/Accounts receivable turnover where
> Accounts receivable turnover = Net credit sales/Average accounts receivable;
> Days accounts payable outstanding = 365/Accounts payable turnover where
> Accounts payable turnover = Inventory purchases/Average accounts payable.

### Accounts Receivable Sale (Securitization) versus Collateralized Borrowing

As you recall from Chapter 8, firms can accelerate the conversion of receivables into cash by selling (factoring) the receivables, securitizing the receivables, or borrowing against receivables pledged as collateral on the loan. You should be aware of how the cash flow statement reflects each transaction and you should monitor whether a firm has increased its use of one or more of these ways of accelerating the collection of cash from receivables during the period.

The accounting treatment for an accounts receivable sale either through factoring or securitization is determined by the criteria in *SFAS No. 140*.[9] If the receivables transfer fails to qualify as a sale under *SFAS No. 140*, it is treated as a secured (collateralized) borrowing. The outstanding receivables stay on the company's balance sheet, and the loan proceeds received are shown as a *financing* cash inflow. Thus, receivable transfers that are secured borrowings have no effect on operating cash flows.

> *SFAS No. 140* states that the transferor surrenders control over the receivables and the transfer can be treated as a sale of receivables when *all* of the following conditions are met: (1) The transferred assets are beyond the reach of the transferor and its creditors, that is, the transferor and its creditors have no legal claim on the assets, (2) the transferee has the right to dispose of the assets, (3) no agreement obligates the transferor to repurchase or redeem the transferred assets in the future, nor can the transferor unilaterally force the holder to return the assets (see para. 9 and paras. 27–28).

On the other hand, two things happen when the transfer qualifies as a true sale under *SFAS No. 140*: (1) The accounts receivable are removed from the company's balance sheet and (2) the decrease in receivables is shown as an operating cash inflow on the cash flow statement.[10] Some analysts believe that classifying receivables sales as operating cash inflows provides a potentially misleading picture of sustainable cash flows from current operations.[11] The reason is that the outright sale or securitization of accounts receivable transfers what would be future operating cash flows into the current period. Accounts receivable that normally would be collected in the subsequent period and be recorded as operating cash inflow in that period are instead collected and reported as cash flows from operations in the current period. Although new receivables may be sold or securitized in the future period, these new receivables would serve only to replace those sold in the previous period. Only by increasing the amount of receivables sold or securitized in the subsequent period can the firm increase operating cash flows in the subsequent period. Clearly, statement users should monitor major changes in firms' use of receivable sales and securitized transactions and be aware of how it can temporarily distort operating cash flows.

## Capitalizing versus Expensing

Many recent accounting frauds involved improper capitalization of costs that instead should have been expensed. The poster child for this accounting abuse was WorldCom's improper capitalization of line costs from 2001 to 2002 that resulted in an earnings overstatement of nearly $4 billion. WorldCom's operating cash flows over this time frame were also overstated because the improperly capitalized costs were treated as investing cash outflows on its cash flow statement. This type of distortion permanently boosts operating cash flow because amounts capitalized are later expensed as depreciation or amortization, which are noncash income statement deductions that do not reduce cash flow from operations. Identifying improper capitalization of operating costs is difficult to spot. But one should be suspicious of significant increases in capital expenditures reported in the investing section of the cash flow statement that coincide with significant

> Costs expensed on the income statement are treated as operating cash outflows to the extent that they are paid in cash.

---

[9] "Accounting for Transfers and Servicing of Financial Assets and Extinguishment of Liabilities," *SFAS No. 140* (Norwalk, CT: FASB, 2000).

[10] *SFAS No. 95*, para. 22, and *SFAS No. 102*, para. 9, provide guidance on the cash flow statement reporting of receivable sales. "Statement of Cash Flows—Exemption of Certain Enterprises and Classification of Cash Flows from Certain Securities Acquired for Resale, and amendment of FASB Statement No. 95," *SFAS No. 102* (Norwalk, CT: FASB, 1989).

[11] See "Cash Flow Metrics and Cash Flow Statement Navigation Guide," *Accounting Issues* (New York: Bear Stearns, June 2006); and C. W. Mulford and K. Shkonda, "The Impact of Securitizations of Customer-Related Receivables on Cash Flows and Leverage: Implications for Financial Analysis," College of Management, Georgia Institute of Technology, no date, www.mgt.gatech.edu/finlab, June 2006.

decreases in operating expenses as a percentage of sales (typically shown in the Selling, general, and administrative expenses account).

## Software Development Costs

Computer software companies must expense all software development costs as incurred until the software reaches **"technological feasibility."** These costs are also treated as components of operating cash outflows on the cash flow statement.[12] When technological feasibility is achieved, software development costs are capitalized, and the corresponding cash flows are shown as investing activity outflows on the cash flow statement.[13] There are no bright-line GAAP criteria for determining when technological feasibility is achieved. So, firms can use their discretion to determine technological feasibility in ways that can distort operating cash flows. By selecting a low threshold for technological feasibility, firms can move software development costs out of the operating section and into the investing section of the cash flow statement, thereby improving their operating cash flows.

> Technological feasibility is established when the company has completed a detailed program design or a working model (*SFAS No. 86*, para. 4).

Because the technological feasibility thresholds are likely to vary considerably across firms, some analysts believe that the amount of capitalized software development costs should be deducted from operating cash flows to improve interfirm comparability of that number.[14] We believe this to be a prudent adjustment to make when comparing the operating cash flow results of software development companies. If material, the amount of software development costs is typically disclosed as a line item in the investing section of firms' cash flow statement as illustrated by the excerpt from BMC Software's 2005 cash flow statement in Exhibit 17.9. Moving the amount of capitalized software development costs from

| EXHIBIT 17.9 | Capitalization of Software Development Costs | | |
|---|---|---|---|

**BMC Software**

| | Fiscal Year Ended March 31, | | |
|---|---|---|---|
| *($ in millions)* | **2003** | **2004** | **2005** |
| Cash flow from operations (as reported): | $ 606 | $ 499 | $ 502 |
| Adjustment for capitalized software development costs | (88) | (53) | (62) |
| Revised cash flow from operations | 518 | 446 | 440 |
| | | | |
| Cash flows from investing: | | | |
| Purchases of property and equipment | (24) | (50) | (58) |
| Cash paid for technology acquisitions & other investments | (408) | (54) | (266) |
| Purchases of marketable securities | (134) | (322) | (191) |
| Proceeds from maturities/sales of marketable securities | 404 | 229 | 331 |
| Capitalization of software development costs | (88) | (53) | (62) |
| Other investing activities | 1 | 2 | 11 |
| Net cash used by investing activities: | $(250) | $(248) | $(235) |

*Source:* BMC Software 10-K report.

---

[12] "Accounting for the Cost of Computer Software to Be Sold, Leased, or Otherwise Marketed," *SFAS No. 86* (Stamford, CT: FASB, 1985).

[13] Ibid., para. 5.

[14] Bear Stearns, op. cit., p. 21.

the investing to the operating section of the cash flow statement not only improves interfirm comparability of operating cash flows but also corrects for a firm's attempt to improve operating cash flows by lowering the technological feasibility threshold in the current period relative to prior periods.

## Capital versus Operating Leases

The accounting treatment for leased assets is another area that hinders interfirm comparability of operating cash flows. Recall from Chapter 12 the two ways to account for leased assets—the capital lease approach and the operating lease approach. These two alternative accounting methods have quite different effects on firms' cash flow statements. Under a capital lease, an asset and a liability equal to the present value of the minimum lease payments are recorded on the lessee's balance sheet at the inception of the lease. This has no immediate cash flow impact because the asset acquisition and capital lease obligation are considered to be a single simultaneous financing and investing transaction. Thus, the lease liability increase is not shown as a financing source of cash, nor is the leased asset increase recorded as an investing use of cash.

> If material, these simultaneous financing and investing transactions are required to be disclosed in the Supplemental Cash Flow Information section of the cash flow statement as shown in Exhibit 17.8 for Amazon.com.

Under capital lease treatment, each lease payment comprises two elements: (1) an interest element and (2) a loan principal paydown amount as reflected in the following entry.

| Capital lease entry for lease payment | | |
|---|---|---|
| **DR**  Interest expense | $60,000 | ◄——— Operating cash outflow |
| **DR**  Lease payable | 40,000 | ◄——— Financing cash outflow |
| **CR**  Cash | | $100,000 |

To record a $100,000 lease payment of which $60,000 is interest and the remainder is a principal payment on the lease obligation.

The interest expense amount reduces earnings and operating cash flows. The principal repayment amount ($40,000) is a financing cash outflow (debt repayment). Therefore, only the interest expense component of the capital lease payment reduces operating cash flows.

For an operating lease, the lessee records no asset or liability on its balance sheet at the inception of the lease. It records the entire amount of each lease payment as rent expense and as an operating cash outflow as reflected in the following entry.

| Operating lease entry for lease payment | | |
|---|---|---|
| **DR**  Rent expense | $100,000 | ◄——— Operating cash outflow |
| **CR**  Cash | | $100,000 |

To record an operating lease payment of $100,000.

Thus, a firm using operating lease treatment reports lower operating cash flows in every year of the lease term relative to a firm that uses capital lease treatment for a lease with an identical payment schedule. The difference in operating cash flows in any given year is the lease principal repayment under the capital lease treatment ($40,000 in the capital lease entry for lease payment). Over the life of the lease, the total difference in operating cash flows under capital versus operating lease treatment is the present value of the minimum lease payments—firms using capital lease treatment record higher operating cash flows equal to this amount.

> For a firm with a 10-year lease requiring a payment of $100,000 at the end of each year and using a 10% discount rate, the present value of the lease payments and the total difference in operating cash flows under capital versus operating lease treatment is $614,457.

The proportion of leases treated as capital versus operating leases varies greatly across firms, even for firms within the same industry (see Exhibit 12.4 in Chapter 12). Firms' operating cash flows therefore also vary greatly, complicating comparison of firms' operating cash flows. One approach to make the financial statement effects (including the operating cash flow effects) more comparable across firms that use varying amounts of operating versus capital leases is to use the data disclosed in lease footnotes to prepare a pro forma capitalization of operating leases. Following the procedures outlined in the appendix to Chapter 12, the present value of operating leases can be estimated as of the end of the current report year (Year $t$). Multiplying this amount by the interest rate used in computing the present value of the operating leases gives the portion of the next year's (Year $t + 1$) scheduled operating lease payment that would be considered interest under capital lease treatment. To adjust the reported operating cash flows in Year $t + 1$ for differences between operating and capital lease treatment, one adds back the total operating lease payments for that year (shown in the lease footnote) and deducts the amount of pro forma interest on the capitalized operating leases as just described. By making this adjustment, the operating cash flows of firms with varying proportions of operating to capital leases are made more comparable.

We use the data from the Safeway example in the appendix to Chapter 12 to illustrate this adjustment. The present value of Safeway's operating leases as of December 31, 2005 was $2.527 billion. Using a 10% discount rate, the amount of the 2006 scheduled operating lease payment of $426 million (see Exhibit 12.11) that would be considered pro forma interest under capital lease treatment is $252.7 million ($10\% \times \$2.527$ billion). The adjustment to Safeway's reported operating cash flows for 2006 for capital versus operating lease treatment is as follows ($ in millions).

| | |
|---|---|
| Safeway's reported operating cash flow for 2006 | $2,175 |
| Add: Operating lease payment in 2006 (in 2005 lease footnote) | 426 |
| Subtract: Pro forma interest in 2006 if operating leases capitalized | (253) |
| Operating cash flow adjusted for capital lease treatment of operating leases | $2,348 |

## Cash Flow Impact of Stock Option Expensing[15]

*SFAS No. 123(R),* "Share-Based Payment," effective January 1, 2006 for calendar year-end companies, significantly changes the accounting for stock option grants and the reporting of the cash flow tax benefits that firms receive from these grants. Prior to the adoption of *SFAS No. 123(R),* most firms did not expense stock option grants for GAAP purposes. However, firms do receive a tax deduction on their tax return for the intrinsic value of nonqualified stock options in the year the employees *exercise* the options. The intrinsic value is calculated as the difference between the market price of the firm's stock on the date of exercise and the option's exercise price. The tax benefit is obtained by multiplying this amount by the statutory U.S. corporate tax rate, currently equal to 35%. So, if an employee exercised 1,000 options at an option price of $40 per share when the stock was selling for $100, the company would receive a tax benefit in the year of *exercise* of $21,000 ($35\% \times 1,000 \times [\$100 - \$40]$).

Prior to *SFAS No. 123(R),* these tax benefits were not reflected as a reduction to the company's GAAP tax expense on the income statement but were shown as an increase to Additional paid-in capital in the equity section of the balance sheet. Because the options exercised resulted in real cash savings by reducing the taxes otherwise payable to the government, the tax benefit realized by the company was shown on the cash flow statement as an operating cash

---

[15] This discussion and the example draw heavily from "Stock Options: Clarity on Cash Flow," *Accounting Issues* (New York: Bear Stearns & Co., May 2007). We thank Bear Stearns for allowing us to use excerpts from its report.

| EXHIBIT 17.10 | Cash Flow Statement Presentation of Stock Option Benefits Prior to Adoption of *SFAS No. 123(R)* Year of Option *Exercise* |
|---|---|

| Cash Flows from Operating Activities | |
|---|---|
| Net income | $50,000 |
| Change in deferred taxes | –0– |
| Tax benefit from exercised employee stock options | 21,000* |
| Change in income taxes payable | –0– |
| = Operating cash flows | $71,000 |

* $1000 \times (\$100 - \$40) \times 35\% = \$21,000$

inflow. This adjustment resulted in operating cash flow reflecting the amount of taxes actually paid in cash in the year that options were exercised.

Exhibit 17.10 reflects how the stock option tax benefits were reported on the cash flow statement prior to adoption of *SFAS No. 123(R)* for the exercise of 1,000 options when the market price of the stock at date of exercise is $100, the exercise price is $40, and the tax rate is 35%. The firm reports $50,000 of income for GAAP and for tax purposes.

Before we present the cash flow statement impact of stock option *exercises* following the adoption of *SFAS No. 123(R),* let's quickly review the measurement and reporting of stock option *grants* under this standard (see Chapter 15 for details). *SFAS No. 123(R)* requires companies to (1) measure the cost of employee services received in exchange for an award of equity instruments (such as stock options) based on the award's grant date fair value and (2) recognize this cost as compensation expense over the period during which an employee is required to provide services in exchange for the award, which is typically the vesting period of three to five years. The fair value at grant date is determined using an option pricing model such as the Black–Scholes or binomial models.

To illustrate the measurement and reporting of option expense under *SFAS No. 123(R),* assume that an employee is granted 1,000 nonqualified stock options with an exercise price of $40 and a Black–Scholes fair value of $15 on the *grant* date. The options vest over three years, which is equal to the employee's service period. Also assume that during these three years, the company has income *before* employee option expense of $100,000 for both book and tax purposes. We assume a 35% tax rate throughout.

The option expense that the company would report in Years 1–3 is $5,000 ([1000 × $15]/3). Because nonqualified stock options are not deductible on the tax return until exercised, a deferred tax asset is created in Years 1–3 for the tax benefit related to the $5,000 compensation expense recorded on the company's GAAP financial statements (see Chapter 13 for discussion of temporary differences). The amount of the deferred tax asset recorded in each year is $1,750 ($5,000 × 35%). See Exhibit 17.11 for the cash flow statement presentation in Years 1–3.

When the employee *exercises* the option (assumed to be in Year 4), the tax benefit that the company receives as a reduction on the taxes paid to the government in that year is $21,000 (1,000 × [$100 − $40] × 35%). Under the reporting rules of *SFAS No. 123(R),* a tax benefit equal to the amount of the previously recognized deferred tax asset is reported in the *operating* section of the cash flow statement (3 × $1,750 = $5,250). On exercise of the option, the amount of tax benefit received that exceeds the deferred tax asset previously reported is considered an "excess benefit." This excess tax benefit ($21,000 − $5,250 = $15,750) is shown as a *financing* cash inflow on the company's cash flow statement rather than as an operating cash flow as was reported prior to *SFAS No. 123(R)* (see Exhibit 17.10).

**EXHIBIT 17.11** **Cash Flow Statement Presentation of Stock Option Benefits Following Adoption of *SFAS No. 123(R)* Years 1–3 (*before exercise*)**

| Cash Flows from Operating Activities | |
|---|---|
| Net income | $ 96,750* |
| Add: Stock option expense (noncash expense) | 5,000 |
| Subtract: Increase in deferred tax asset (noncash reduction of tax expense) | (1,750) |
| Tax benefit from exercised employee stock options | –0– |
| Change in income taxes payable | –0– |
| = Operating cash flows | $100,000 |

* $100,000 Income before option compensation expense
  −5,000 Option compensation expense ($15,000/3 yrs.)
  +1,750 Deferred portion of current period's tax provision (35% × $5,000)
  $ 96,750 Reported GAAP income

**EXHIBIT 17.12** **Cash Flow Statement Presentation of Stock Option Benefits Following Adoption of *SFAS No. 123(R)* Year of *Exercise***

| Cash Flows from Operating Activities | |
|---|---|
| Net income | $ 50,000 |
| Add: Tax benefit from exercised employee stock options | 21,000* |
| Deduct: Excess tax benefit from exercised employee stock options ($21,000 − $5,250) | (15,750)† |
| Change in income taxes payable | –0– |
| = Operating cash flows | $ 55,250 |
| Cash Flows from Financing Activities | |
| Excess tax benefit from exercised employee stock options | $ 15,750 |

* 1000 × ($100 − $40) × 0.35 = $21,000

† $21,000 − (3 × $1,750) = $15,750

Note that the tax benefit recognized in the operating section of the cash flow statement is $21,000 − $15,750 = $5,250, which is the amount of the previously recorded deferred tax asset related to the option awards recognized in Years 1–3 (3 × $1,750). This is the reduction in deferred tax asset that occurs in the year of exercise.

The cash flow statement presentation of the company's tax benefits in the year of option *exercise* under *SFAS No. 123(R)* is shown in Exhibit 17.12. To provide comparability with Exhibit 17.10, we assume that the company reports income of $50,000 for GAAP and tax purposes and recognizes no stock option expense in the year.

Comparing Exhibit 17.12 and Exhibit 17.10 demonstrates the rather dramatic negative effect that *SFAS No. 123(R)* has had on the reported operating cash flows of firms with significant option grants and exercises. Exhibit 17.13 lists some companies with relatively large reclassifications of tax benefits from operating to financing cash flow as a result of adopting *SFAS No. 123(R).* Some analysts recommend, and we concur, that the operating cash flows of companies such as these need to be adjusted by adding back the "excess tax benefits" to make valid year-to-year comparisons.[16]

---

[16] Ibid.

| **EXHIBIT 17.13** | Selected Companies Impacted by Stock Option Tax Benefit Cash Flow Statement Reclassifications in 2006 | | |
|---|---|---|---|
| **Company Name** *($ in millions)* | **Excess Tax Benefit Reported in Financing Cash Flow Section** | **Reported 2006 Operating Cash Flow** | **Excess Tax Benefit as % of Operating Cash Flow** |
| Allegany Technologies | $ 81 | $ 309 | 26% |
| Akamai Technologies | 33 | 132 | 25 |
| Analog Devices | 181 | 621 | 29 |
| Apple Computer | 361 | 2,220 | 16 |
| Citrix Systems | 58 | 323 | 18 |
| Corporate Executive Board | 41 | 136 | 30 |
| F5 Networks | 21 | 125 | 17 |
| Starwood Hotels | 87 | 500 | 17 |
| Tibco Software | 21 | 106 | 20 |
| Yahoo! | 597 | 1,372 | 44 |

*Source:* "Stock Options: Clarity on Cash Flow," *Accounting Issues* (New York: Bear Stearns & Co., May 2007).

In this section, we describe ways that operating cash flows can be distorted or managed and how accounting alternatives can hinder interfirm comparisons of this number. Analysts and other statement users should be aware of the techniques for enhancing the comparability of operating cash flows both across firms and over time.

RECAP

## SUMMARY

- The statement of cash flows provides information for assessing a firm's ability to generate sufficient cash to pay for operating expenses, capital improvements, and currently maturing obligations.

- Firms able to generate consistently strong positive cash flows from operations are considered better credit risks and benefit from a lower cost of capital.

- The two alternative methods for presenting the operating section of a cash flow statement are the direct and indirect approaches.

- Most firms use the indirect approach that begins with accrual-basis earnings and adjusts for depreciation, amortization, noncash gains and losses, and changes in noncash working capital accounts—for example, inventories, receivables, and payables—that cause earnings to differ from operating cash flows for the period.

- You will frequently encounter situations in which the changes in noncash accounts shown on comparative balance sheets will not reconcile with the adjustments shown on the cash flow statement. These discrepancies are due to one or more of the following causes: (1) asset write-offs due to impairment, corporate restructuring, or retirement, (2) translation adjustments on assets and liabilities held by foreign subsidiaries, (3) acquisitions and divestitures of other companies or operating units, and (4) simultaneous investing and financing activities not directly affecting cash. Failure to understand how these events cause balance sheet account changes to differ from changes in account balances shown on the cash flow statement can lead to incorrect interpretation of both statements.

- Operating cash flows can sometimes be distorted or manipulated. You should be aware of the ways this can occur and how to adjust reported operating cash flows to enhance the comparability of this important number across firms and over time.

## EXERCISES

**E17-1**

Determining cash flow from operations

Information for ABC Company is as follows ($ in thousands):

| | |
|---|---:|
| Net income | $280 |
| Equity in investee loss | 20 |
| Decrease in prepaid expenses | 7 |
| Cash paid for new plant equipment | 30 |
| Amortization of premium on bonds payable | 10 |
| Decrease in accounts payable | 2 |
| Increase in inventory | 21 |
| Depreciation expense | 13 |
| Increase in salaries payable | 8 |
| Increase in accounts receivable | 15 |
| Dividends paid to stockholders | 5 |

**Required:**

What is the net cash provided by operating activities?

---

**E17-2**

Determining cash flow from operations

**AICPA**
ADAPTED

Lino Company's worksheet for the preparation of its 2008 statement of cash flows included the following information:

| | December 31 | January 1 |
|---|---:|---:|
| Accounts receivable | $29,000 | $23,000 |
| Allowance for uncollectible accounts | 1,000 | 800 |
| Prepaid rent expense | 8,200 | 12,400 |
| Accounts payable | 22,400 | 19,400 |

Lino's 2008 net income is $150,000.

**Required:**

What amount should Lino include as net cash that is provided by operating activities in the statement of cash flows?

---

**E17-3**

Determining cash flow from operations

**AICPA**
ADAPTED

Patsy Corporation has estimated its activity for December 2008. Selected data from these estimated amounts are as follows:

| | |
|---|---:|
| Sales | $350,000 |
| Gross profit (based on sales) | 30% |
| Increase in gross trade accounts receivable during month | 10,500 |
| Change in accounts payable during month | –0– |
| Increase in inventory during month | 5,000 |
| Variable selling, general, and administrative (SG&A) | |
|    expenses include a charge for uncollectible accounts | |
|    of 1% of sales; accounts receivable write-offs were $3,000 | |
| Total SG&A expenses are $35,000 per month plus 15% of sales | |
| Depreciation expense of $20,000 per month is included in fixed SG&A | |

**Required:**

1. Calculate accrual-basis net income for December.

2. On the basis of the preceding data, what is the net cash flow provided from operating activities for December?

Roe Company is preparing a statement of cash flows for the year ended December 31, 2008. It has the following account balances:

| | December 31 | |
| --- | --- | --- |
| | 2007 | 2008 |
| Machinery | $250,000 | $320,000 |
| Accumulated depreciation—machinery | 102,000 | 120,000 |
| Loss on sale of machinery | | 4,000 |

During 2008, Roe sold for $26,000 a machine that cost $40,000, and purchased several other items of machinery.

**Required:**

1. How much depreciation expense was recorded on machinery for 2008?

2. What was the amount of machinery purchased in 2008?

Karr, Inc. reported net income of $300,000 for 2008. Changes occurred in several balance sheet accounts as follows:

| | |
| --- | --- |
| Equipment | $25,000 increase |
| Accumulated depreciation | 40,000 increase |
| Note payable | 30,000 increase |

**Additional Information:**

1. During 2008, Karr sold equipment that cost $25,000 and had accumulated depreciation of $12,000, for a gain of $5,000.

2. In December 2008, Karr purchased equipment costing $50,000 with $20,000 cash and a 12% note payable of $30,000.

3. Depreciation expense for the year was $52,000.

**Required:**

1. In Karr's 2008 statement of cash flows, what should be the net cash from operating activities?

2. In Karr's 2008 statement of cash flows, what should be the net cash used in investing activities?

In preparing its cash flow statement for the year ended December 31, 2008, Reve Company collected the following data:

| | |
| --- | --- |
| Gain on sale of equipment | $ 6,000 |
| Proceeds from sale of equipment | 10,000 |
| Purchase of A.S., Inc. bonds (par value $200,000) | 180,000 |
| Amortization of bond discount | 2,000 |
| Dividends declared | 45,000 |
| Dividends paid | 38,000 |
| Proceeds form the sale of treasury stock (carrying amount $65,000) | 75,000 |

**Required:**

Determine the following amounts that should be reported in Reve's 2008 statement of cash flows.

1. What amount should Reve report as net cash used in investing activities?

2. What amount should Reve report as net cash provided by financing activities?

Alp, Inc. had the following activities during 2008:

- Acquired 2,000 shares of stock in Maybel, Inc. for $26,000.

- Sold an investment in Rate Motors for $35,000 when the carrying value was $33,000.

- Acquired a $50,000, four-year certificate of deposit from a bank. (During the year, interest of $3,750 was paid to Alp.)

- Collected dividends of $1,200 on stock investments.

**Required:**

In Alp's 2008 statement of cash flows, what amount would be shown for net cash used in investing activities?

---

**E17-8**

Calculating cash flows from investing and financing activities

**AICPA**
ADAPTED

Kollar Corporation's transactions for the year ended December 31, 2008 included the following:

1. Purchased real estate for $550,000 using cash borrowed from a bank.
2. Sold investment securities for $500,000.
3. Paid dividends of $600,000.
4. Issued 500 shares of common stock for $250,000.
5. Purchased machinery and equipment for $125,000 cash.
6. Paid $450,000 toward a bank loan.
7. Reduced accounts receivable by $100,000.
8. Increased accounts payable by $200,000.

**Required:**

1. Determine Kollar's net cash used in investing activities for 2008.
2. Determine Kollar's net cash used in financing activities for 2008.

---

**E17-9**

Determining operating cash flow

**AICPA**
ADAPTED

Metro, Inc. reported net income of $150,000 for 2008. Changes occurred in several balance sheet accounts during 2008 as follows:

| | |
|---|---|
| Investment in Videogold, Inc. stock, carried on the equity basis | $5,500 increase |
| Accumulated depreciation caused by major repair to projection equipment | 2,100 decrease |
| Premium on bonds payable | 1,400 decrease |
| Deferred income tax liability (long term) | 1,800 increase |

**Required:**

Determine the reported net cash provided by operating activities for Metro in 2008.

---

**E17-10**

Determining operating, investing, and financing cash flows

**AICPA**
ADAPTED

The differences in Beal Inc.'s balance sheet accounts at December 31, 2008 and 2007 are presented next:

| | Increase (Decrease) |
|---|---|
| **Assets** | |
| Cash and cash equivalents | $  120,000 |
| Short-term investments | 300,000 |
| Accounts receivable, net | –0– |
| Inventory | 80,000 |
| Long-term investments | (100,000) |
| Plant assets | 700,000 |
| Accumulated depreciation | –0– |
| | $1,100,000 |
| | |
| **Liabilities and Stockholders' Equity** | |
| Accounts payable and accrued liabilities | $   (5,000) |
| Dividends payable | 160,000 |
| Short-term bank debt | 325,000 |
| Long-term debt | 110,000 |
| Common stock, $10 par | 100,000 |
| Additional paid-in capital | 120,000 |
| Retained earnings | 290,000 |
| | $1,100,000 |

The following information is related to 2008:

- Net income of $790,000.
- Declared cash dividends of $500,000.
- Sold a building costing $600,000 and having a carrying amount of $350,000 for $350,000.
- Acquired equipment costing $110,000 through the issuance of long-term debt.
- Sold a long-term investment for $135,000. There were no other transactions affecting long-term investments.
- Issued 10,000 shares of common stock for $22 a share.

**Required:**

In Beal's 2008 statement of cash flows, determine:

1. Net cash provided by operating activities.
2. Net cash used in investing activities.
3. Net cash provided by financing activities.

---

During 2008, Xan, Inc. had the following activities related to its financial operations:

| | |
|---|---|
| Payment for the early retirement of long-term bonds payable (carrying value $370,000) | $375,000 |
| Distribution in 2008 of cash dividend declared in 2007 to preferred shareholders | $ 31,000 |
| Carrying value of convertible preferred stock in Xan converted into common shares | $ 60,000 |
| Proceeds from sale of treasury stock (carrying value at cost, $43,000) | $ 50,000 |

**E17-11**

Determining cash used in financing activities

**AICPA**
ADAPTED

**Required:**

In Xan's 2008 statement of cash flows, how much should net cash used in financing activities be?

---

## PROBLEMS / DISCUSSION QUESTIONS

The following condensed trial balance of Probe Co., a publicly held company, has been adjusted except for income tax expense.

**P17-1**

Indirect approach, classification of cash flows, and disclosure

**AICPA**
ADAPTED

### Condensed Trial Balance

| | 12/31/08 Balance Dr. (Cr.) | 12/31/07 Balance Dr. (Cr.) | Net Change Dr. (Cr.) |
|---|---|---|---|
| Cash | $ 473,000 | $ 817,000 | $(344,000) |
| Accounts receivable, net | 670,000 | 610,000 | 60,000 |
| Property, plant and equipment | 1,070,000 | 995,000 | 75,000 |
| Accumulated depreciation | (345,000) | (280,000) | (65,000) |
| Dividends payable | (25,000) | (10,000) | (15,000) |
| Income tax payable | 35,000 | (150,000) | 185,000 |
| Deferred income tax liability | (42,000) | (42,000) | — |
| Bonds payable | (500,000) | (1,000,000) | 500,000 |
| Unamortized premium on bonds | (71,000) | (150,000) | 79,000 |

*(continued)*

| | 12/31/08 Balance Dr. (Cr.) | 12/31/07 Balance Dr. (Cr.) | Net Change Dr. (Cr.) |
|---|---|---|---|
| Common stock | (350,000) | (150,000) | (200,000) |
| Additional paid-in-capital | (430,000) | (375,000) | (55,000) |
| Retained earnings | (185,000) | (265,000) | 80,000 |
| Sales | (2,420,000) | | |
| Cost of goods sold | 1,863,000 | | |
| Selling and administrative expenses | 220,000 | | |
| Interest income | (14,000) | | |
| Interest expense | 46,000 | | |
| Depreciation | 88,000 | | |
| Loss on sale of equipment | 7,000 | | |
| Gain on extinguishment of bonds | (90,000) | | |
| | $ –0– | $ –0– | $ 300,000 |

## Additional Information:

- During 2008, sold equipment with an original cost of $50,000 for cash and purchased equipment costing $125,000.

- On January 1, 2008, redeemed bonds with a par value of $500,000 and related premium of $75,000. The $1,000 face value, 10% par bonds had been issued on January 1, 1998, to yield 8%. Interest is payable annually every December 31 through 2017.

- Probe's tax payments during 2008 were debited to Income taxes payable. Probe's recorded Deferred income tax liability of $42,000 at December 31, 2008 is based on cumulative net taxable temporary differences of $120,000 and an enacted tax rate of 35%. Probe's 2008 financial statement income before income taxes was higher than its 2008 taxable income, due entirely to temporary differences of $60,000.

- On December 31, 2007, Probe had 60,000 shares of common stock, $2.50 par value, out-standing. Probe issued an additional 80,000 shares on April 1, 2008.

- There were no changes in Retained earnings other than dividends declared.

## Required:

For each transaction in items 1 through 6, choose where to report those activities from list A and the dollar amount from list B.

1. Cash paid for income taxes

2. Cash paid for interest

3. Redemption of bonds payable

4. Issuance of common stock

5. Cash dividends paid

6. Proceeds from sale of equipment

- **List A**

  a. Operating activities on Probe's statement of cash flows

  b. Investing activities on Probe's statement of cash flows

  c. Financing activities on Probe's statement of cash flows

  d. Supplementary information to Probe's statement of cash flows

  e. Not reported on Probe's statement of cash flows

- **List B**

  f. $20,000    h. $42,000    j. $50,000

  g. $23,000    i. $46,000    k. $55,000

l. $65,000    o. $200,000    r. $410,000

m. $80,000    p. $255,000    s. $485,000

n. $185,000    q. $265,000    t. $575,000

---

Dice Corporation's balance sheet accounts as of December 31, 2008 and 2007 and information relating to 2008 activities follow.

**P17-2**

Determining cash provided (used) by operating, investing, and financing activities

**AICPA**
ADAPTED

## Balance Sheet

|  | 2008 | 2007 |
|---|---|---|
| **Assets** | | |
| Cash | $ 230,000 | $ 100,000 |
| Short-term investments | 300,000 | –0– |
| Accounts receivable—net | 510,000 | 510,000 |
| Inventory | 680,000 | 600,000 |
| Long-term investments | 200,000 | 300,000 |
| Plant assets | 1,700,000 | 1,000,000 |
| Accumulated depreciation | (450,000) | (450,000) |
| Goodwill | 90,000 | 100,000 |
| Total assets | $3,260,000 | $2,160,000 |
| | | |
| **Liabilities and Stockholders' Equity** | | |
| Accounts payable and accrued liabilities | $ 825,000 | $ 720,000 |
| Short-term debt | 325,000 | –0– |
| Common stock ($10 par) | 800,000 | 700,000 |
| Additional paid-in capital | 370,000 | 250,000 |
| Retained earnings | 940,000 | 490,000 |
| Total liabilities and stockholders' equity | $3,260,000 | $2,160,000 |

Information relating to 2008 activities follows:

- Net income for 2008 was $690,000.
- Declared and paid cash dividends of $240,000 in 2008.
- Sold equipment costing $400,000 and having a carrying value of $150,000 in 2008 for $150,000.
- Sold a long-term investment in 2008 for $135,000. There were no other transactions affecting long-term investments in that year.
- Issued 10,000 shares of common stock in 2008 for $22 per share.
- Had short-term investments consisting of Treasury bills maturing on June 30, 2009.

**Required:**

1. What was the amount of net cash provided by Dice's 2008 operating activities?
2. What was the amount of net cash used in Dice's 2008 investing activities?
3. What was the amount of net cash provided by Dice's 2008 financing activities?

---

Spoke Company, a major retailer of bicycles and accessories, operates several stores and is a publicly traded company. The comparative statement of financial position and income statement for Spoke as of May 31, 2008 follows. The company is preparing its statement of cash flows to comply with *SFAS No. 95*.

**P17-3**

Comparing direct and indirect methods of determining cash flows from operations

**CMA**
ADAPTED

## Comparative Statement of Financial Position as of May 31, 2008 and May 31, 2007

|  | May 31 | |
|---|---|---|
|  | **2008** | **2007** |
| **Assets** | | |
| Cash | $ 43,250 | $ 20,000 |
| Accounts receivable | 70,000 | 50,000 |
| Merchandise inventory | 210,000 | 250,000 |
| Prepaid expenses | 9,000 | 7,000 |
| Total current assets | 332,250 | 327,000 |
| Plant assets | 600,000 | 510,000 |
| Less: Accumulated depreciation | (150,000) | (125,000) |
| Net plant assets | 450,000 | 385,000 |
| **Total assets** | $782,250 | $712,000 |
| **Liabilities and Shareholders' Equity** | | |
| Accounts payable | $123,000 | $115,000 |
| Salaries payable | 47,250 | 72,000 |
| Interest payable | 27,000 | 25,000 |
| Total current liabilities | 197,250 | 212,000 |
| Long-term debt | | |
| Bonds payable | 70,000 | 100,000 |
| Total liabilities | 267,250 | 312,000 |
| **Shareholders' Equity** | | |
| Common stock, $10 par | 370,000 | 280,000 |
| Retained earnings | 145,000 | 120,000 |
| Total shareholders' equity | 515,000 | 400,000 |
| **Total liabilities and shareholders' equity** | $782,250 | $712,000 |

## Income Statement for the Year Ended May 31, 2008

| | |
|---|---|
| Sales | $1,255,250 |
| Cost of merchandise sold | 712,000 |
| Gross margin | 543,250 |
| Expenses | |
| Salary expense | 252,100 |
| Interest expense | 75,000 |
| Other expenses | 8,150 |
| Depreciation expense | 25,000 |
| Total expenses | 360,250 |
| Operating income | 183,000 |
| Income tax expense | 43,000 |
| Net income | $ 140,000 |

The following is additional information concerning Spoke's transactions during the year ended May 31, 2008:

- All sales during the year were made on account.
- All merchandise was purchased on account, comprising the total Accounts payable account.
- Plant assets costing $90,000 were purchased by paying $40,000 in cash and by issuing 5,000 shares of stock.
- The Other expenses account is related to prepaid items.
- All income taxes incurred during the year were paid during the year.

- To supplement its cash, Spoke issued 4,000 shares of common stock at par value.
- There were no penalties assessed for the retirement of bonds.
- Cash dividends of $115,000 were declared and paid at the end of the fiscal year.

**Required:**

1. Prepare Spoke Company's statement of cash flows for the year ended May 31, 2008 using the direct method. Be sure to support the statement with appropriate calculations. (A reconciliation of net income to net cash is not required.)

2. Using the indirect method, calculate only Spoke Company's net cash flow from operating activities for the year ended May 31, 2008.

3. Compare and contrast the direct method and the indirect method for reporting cash flows from operating activities as prescribed by *SFAS No. 95*. What are the advantages and limitations of each approach?

---

The following are selected balance sheet accounts of Zach Corporation at December 31, 2008 and 2007, as well as the increases or decreases in each account from 2007 to 2008. Also presented is selected income statement information for the year ended December 31, 2008, as well as additional information.

**P17-4**

Determining amounts reported on statement of cash flows

**AICPA**
ADAPTED

### Selected Balance Sheet Accounts

|  | 2008 | 2007 | Increase (Decrease) |
|---|---|---|---|
| **Assets** | | | |
| Accounts receivable | $ 34,000 | $ 24,000 | $10,000 |
| Property, plant and equipment | 277,000 | 247,000 | 30,000 |
| Accumulated depreciation | (178,000) | (167,000) | 11,000 |
| **Liabilities and Stockholders' Equity** | | | |
| Bonds payable | 49,000 | 46,000 | 3,000 |
| Dividends payable | 8,000 | 5,000 | 3,000 |
| Common stock, $1 par | 22,000 | 19,000 | 3,000 |
| Additional paid-in capital | 9,000 | 3,000 | 6,000 |
| Retained earnings | 104,000 | 91,000 | 13,000 |

### Selected Income Statement Information for the Year Ended December 31, 2008

| | |
|---|---|
| Sales revenue | $155,000 |
| Depreciation | 33,000 |
| Gain on sale of equipment | 13,000 |
| Net income | 28,000 |

**Additional Information:**

- Accounts receivable relate to sales of merchandise.
- During 2008, equipment that cost $40,000 was sold for cash.
- During 2008, $20,000 of bonds payable were issued in exchange for property, plant and equipment. There was no amortization of bond discount or premium.

**Required:**

Items 1 through 5, which follow, represent activities that will be reported in Zach's statement of cash flows for the year ended December 31, 2008. For each item, determine both the amount that should be reported in Zach's 2008 statement of cash flows and the section (operating, investing, or financing) in which the item should appear.

1. Cash collections from customers (direct method)
2. Payments for the purchase of property, plant and equipment
3. Proceeds from the sale of equipment
4. Cash dividends paid
5. Redemption of bonds payable

| | | |
|---|---|---|
| **P17-5** | | |
| Determining amounts reported on statement of cash flows | | |
| AICPA ADAPTED | | |

Flax Corporation uses the direct method to prepare its statement of cash flows. Flax's trial balances at December 31, 2008 and 2007 follow:

| | December 31 | |
|---|---|---|
| | **2008** | **2007** |
| **Debits** | | |
| Cash | $ 35,000 | $ 32,000 |
| Accounts receivable | 33,000 | 30,000 |
| Inventory | 31,000 | 47,000 |
| Property, plant and equipment | 100,000 | 95,000 |
| Unamortized bond discount | 4,500 | 5,000 |
| Cost of goods sold | 250,000 | 380,000 |
| Selling expenses | 141,500 | 172,000 |
| General and administrative expenses | 137,000 | 151,300 |
| Interest expense | 4,300 | 2,600 |
| Income tax expense | 20,400 | 61,200 |
| | $756,700 | $976,100 |
| | | |
| **Credits** | | |
| Allowance for uncollectible accounts | $ 1,300 | $ 1,100 |
| Accumulated depreciation | 16,500 | 15,000 |
| Trade accounts payable | 25,000 | 17,500 |
| Income taxes payable | 21,000 | 27,100 |
| Deferred income taxes | 5,300 | 4,600 |
| 8% callable bonds payable | 45,000 | 20,000 |
| Common stock | 50,000 | 40,000 |
| Additional paid-in capital | 9,100 | 7,500 |
| Retained earnings | 44,700 | 64,600 |
| Sales | 538,800 | 778,700 |
| | $756,700 | $976,100 |

**Additional Information:**

- Flax purchased $5,000 in equipment during 2008.
- Flax allocated one-third of its depreciation expense to selling expenses and the remainder to general and administrative expenses.

*Show your work* for all answers to the following questions:

**Required:**

What amount should Flax report in its statement of cash flows for the year ended December 31, 2008 for the following:

1. Cash collected from customers?
2. Cash paid for goods sold?
3. Cash paid for interest?
4. Cash paid for income taxes?
5. Cash paid for selling expenses?

The balance sheets of Global Trading Company follow:

## Balance Sheets as of December 31

P17-6

Preparing and analyzing cash flow statement

| | 2008 | 2007 |
|---|---|---|
| **Assets** | | |
| Cash | $120,000 | $108,000 |
| Accounts receivable | 50,000 | 300,000 |
| Less: Allowance for doubtful accounts | (20,000) | (30,000) |
| Inventory | 80,000 | 250,000 |
| Prepaid insurance | –0– | 20,000 |
| Property, plant and equipment | 500,000 | 500,000 |
| Less: Accumulated depreciation | (450,000) | (400,000) |
| Goodwill | –0– | 70,000 |
| Total assets | $280,000 | $818,000 |
| **Liabilities and Owners' Equity** | | |
| Accounts payable | $100,000 | $ 22,000 |
| Salaries payable | 17,000 | 11,000 |
| Bank loan | 82,500 | 390,000 |
| Capital stock | 75,000 | 75,000 |
| Retained earnings | 5,500 | 320,000 |
| Total liabilities and owners' equity | $280,000 | $818,000 |

### Additional Information:

- The company reported a net loss of $279,500 during the year 2008.
- There are no income taxes.
- Goodwill as of December 31, 2007 was part of an acquisition made during 2007.
- The company's bank provides a working capital loan to a maximum of 75% of net accounts receivable and inventory.

### Required:

1. Prepare a statement of cash flows using the indirect method for the year ended December 31, 2008.

2. On the basis of available information, assess the financial performance of the company during 2008. In answering this part, consider both the net income and cash flows of the company. Also evaluate the future prospects of the company.

3. Assuming that the bad debt expense during 2008 was $55,000, calculate the amount of bad debts written off during the year. Further assume that the company collected $1,250,000 cash from its customers during 2008, and then compute the sales revenue for the year. You may assume that all sales are credit sales.

4. In answering this part, assume that Global uses the first-in, first-out (FIFO) inventory method. On December 31, 2008, the company purchased $35,000 worth of inventory on credit from a supplier. The transaction was inadvertently not recorded because physical possession was not obtained as of December 31, 2008. Discuss the effect of this omission on Global Trading Company's financial statements.

The following is the cash account of JKI Advertising Agencies for the year ended December 31, 2008:

P17-7

Preparing the cash flow statement and balance sheet

### Cash Account

| | DR | CR |
|---|---|---|
| Beginning balance as of 1/1/08 | $ 30,000 | |
| Cash collected from clients | 215,000 | |
| Cash received from sale of land at book value | 150,000 | |
| Rent collected | 50,000 | |
| Capital contributions | 35,000 | |
| Line of credit borrowing from Town Bank | 50,000 | |
| Salaries paid | | $130,000 |
| Purchase of office equipment | | 20,000 |
| Cash paid for insurance | | 12,000 |
| Building loan repaid | | 85,000 |
| Cash paid for interest | | 9,000 |
| Dividends declared and paid | | 18,000 |
| Cash paid for customer lawsuit | | 32,000 |
| Cash paid for taxes | | 31,000 |
| | $530,000 | $337,000 |
| Ending balance as of 12/31/08 | $193,000 | |

Provided next are the income statement for the year ended December 31, 2008 and the balance sheet as of December 31, 2008 for JKI Advertising Agencies.

Assume there are no bad debts and no deferred taxes.

### Income Statement for the Year Ended December 31, 2008

| | |
|---|---|
| Advertising revenue | $ 250,000 |
| Rent revenue | 36,000 |
| Salaries expense | (126,000) |
| Employee incentive bonus | (25,200) |
| Depreciation expense—building | (20,000) |
| Depreciation expense—office equipment | (8,000) |
| Insurance expense | (12,000) |
| Interest expense | (10,000) |
| Income before taxes | 84,800 |
| Income tax expense | (33,920) |
| Net income | $ 50,880 |

### Balance Sheet as of December 31, 2008

| | |
|---|---|
| Cash | $193,000 |
| Accounts receivable | 80,000 |
| Prepaid insurance | 3,000 |
| Building | 600,000 |
| Less: Accumulated depreciation | (380,000) |
| Office equipment | 80,000 |
| Less: Accumulated depreciation | (39,000) |
| Total assets | $537,000 |
| Salaries payable | $ 7,000 |
| Interest payable | 3,500 |
| Rent received in advance | 14,000 |
| Bonus payable | 25,200 |
| Taxes payable | 2,920 |
| Borrowing from Town Bank | 50,000 |
| Building loan | 35,000 |
| Capital stock | 135,000 |
| Retained earnings | 264,380 |
| Total liabilities and equities | $537,000 |

**Required:**

1. Based on the Cash account, prepare a statement of cash flows using the direct approach.

2. Prepare the balance sheet as of December 31, 2007.

3. Prepare the operating section of the cash flow statement for the year ended December 31, 2008 under the indirect approach.

4. Evaluate the following statements:

   a. Because depreciation is added to net income when calculating cash flow from operations, depreciation is a direct source of operating cash flow.

   b. Over the entire life of a company, its cash flow from operations will equal its net income.

5. JKI has the policy to accrue an employee's incentive bonus at 20% of salary. Instead, if JKI had calculated the bonus at 25% of salary, what would be the revised figure for cash flow from operations under the indirect approach?

---

Excerpts from the financial statements of Briggs & Stratton Corporation and Ramsay Health Care, Inc. are provided next. (*Note:* Year 1 is previous year and Year 2 is current year.)

**P17-8**

Reconciling changes in balance sheet accounts with amounts reported in the cash flow statement

### Briggs and Stratton Corporation

## Excerpts from Consolidated Balance Sheets as of July 3, Year 2 and June 27, Year 1

|  | Year 2 | Year 1 |
|---|---|---|
| **Assets** |  |  |
| Current assets |  |  |
| Cash and cash equivalents | $221,101,000 | $ 39,501,000 |
| Short-term investments | –0– | 70,422,000 |
| Receivables, less reserves of $1,678,000 |  |  |
| and $754,000, respectively | 122,597,000 | 124,981,000 |

## Consolidated Statements of Cash Flows for the Years Ended July 3, Year 2 and June 27, Year 1

|  | Year 2 | Year 1 |
|---|---|---|
| Cash Flows from Operating Activities |  |  |
| Net income | $ 69,923,000 | $ 70,345,000 |
| Adjustments to reconcile net income to net cash provided by operating activities: |  |  |
| Cumulative effect of accounting changes, net of income taxes | 32,558,000 | –0– |
| Depreciation | 42,950,000 | 47,222,000 |
| (Gain) loss on disposition of plant and equipment | (96,000) | 4,027,000 |
| Loss on foreign subsidiary | –0– | 3,500,000 |
| Change in operating assets and liabilities: |  |  |
| (Increase) decrease in receivables | 2,384,000 | (21,366,000) |
| (Increase) in inventories | (11,605,000) | (1,576,000) |
| (Increase) in other current assets | (10,593,000) | (1,893,000) |
| Increase in accounts payable, accrued liabilities and income taxes | 38,132,000 | 13,731,000 |
| Other, net | 1,420,000 | (3,699,000) |
| Net cash provided by operating activities | $165,073,000 | $110,291,000 |

## Ramsay Health Care, Inc. and Subsidiaries

### Consolidated Statements of Cash Flows
### Year Ended June 30

| | Year 2 | Year 1 |
|---|---|---|
| **Cash Flows from Operating Activities** | | |
| Net income (loss) | $ 1,322,000 | $ (1,560,000) |
| Adjustments to reconcile net income (loss) to | | |
| net cash provided by operating activities: | | |
| Cumulative effect of change in accounting | | |
| for income taxes | –0– | (2,353,000) |
| Depreciation and amortization | 7,638,000 | 7,173,000 |
| Loss on early extinguishment of debt | 258,000 | 1,580,000 |
| Write-off of development and other costs | –0– | 1,367,000 |
| (Gain) loss on disposal of assets | 722,000 | (121,000) |
| Provision for deferred income taxes | (1,188,000) | (696,000) |
| Provision for doubtful accounts | 5,846,000 | 8,148,000 |
| Provision for loss on sales and closure of facilities | –0– | 6,415,000 |
| Minority interests | 4,824,000 | 1,126,000 |
| Adjustments for (increase) decrease in | | |
| operating assets: | | |
| Patient accounts receivable | (2,169,000) | (8,833,000) |
| Other current assets | (2,071,000) | 1,233,000 |
| Other noncurrent assets | (554,000) | 164,000 |
| Adjustments for increase (decrease) in | | |
| operating liabilities: | | |
| Accounts payable | (2,484,000) | 940,000 |
| Accrued salaries, wages and other liabilities | 3,150,000 | (674,000) |
| Unpaid self-insurance claims | (1,078,000) | (456,000) |
| Amounts due to third-party contractual agencies | (1,385,000) | 724,000 |
| Total adjustments | $11,509,000 | $15,737,000 |
| Net cash provided by operating activities | $12,831,000 | $14,177,000 |

### Excerpts from Consolidated Balance Sheets

| | June 30 | |
|---|---|---|
| | Year 2 | Year 1 |
| Current Assets | | |
| Patient accounts receivable, less allowances for | | |
| doubtful accounts of $3,925,000 and $4,955,000 | | |
| at June 30, Year 2 and Year 1, respectively | $23,019,000 | $26,696,000 |

### Required:

1. Reconcile the difference, if any, between the change in Patient accounts receivable as reported in the statement of cash flows and the change in receivables based on the balance sheet values for each company.

2. Explain the different reporting practices adopted by the two companies with respect to adjustments made in the statement of cash flows for changes in accounts receivable.

Presented next are the balance sheet accounts of Bergen Corporation as of December 31, 2008 and 2007.

**PI7-9**

Preparing cash flow statement—Indirect method

AICPA
ADAPTED

| | 2008 | 2007 | Increase (Decrease) |
|---|---|---|---|
| **Assets** | | | |
| Current Assets: | | | |
| Cash | $ 541,000 | $ 308,000 | $233,000 |
| Accounts receivable, net | 585,000 | 495,000 | 90,000 |
| Inventories | 895,000 | 780,000 | 115,000 |
| Total current assets | 2,021,000 | 1,583,000 | 438,000 |
| Land | 350,000 | 250,000 | 100,000 |
| Plant and equipment | 1,060,000 | 720,000 | 340,000 |
| Accumulated depreciation | (295,000) | (170,000) | (125,000) |
| Leased equipment under capital lease | 158,000 | -0- | 158,000 |
| Marketable investment securities, at cost | -0- | 75,000 | (75,000) |
| Investment in Mason, Inc. at cost | 180,000 | 180,000 | -0- |
| Total assets | $3,474,000 | $2,638,000 | $836,000 |
| **Liabilities and Stockholders' Equity** | | | |
| Current liabilities: | | | |
| Current portion of long-term debt | $ 159,000 | $ -0- | $159,000 |
| Accounts payable and accrued expenses | 760,000 | 823,000 | (63,000) |
| Total current liabilities | 919,000 | 823,000 | 96,000 |
| Note payable, long-term | 300,000 | -0- | 300,000 |
| Liability under capital lease | 124,000 | -0- | 124,000 |
| Bonds payable | 500,000 | 500,000 | -0- |
| Unamortized bond premium | 16,000 | 18,000 | (2,000) |
| Deferred income taxes | 60,000 | 45,000 | 15,000 |
| Common stock, par-value $20 | 640,000 | 600,000 | 40,000 |
| Additional paid-in capital | 304,000 | 244,000 | 60,000 |
| Retained earnings | 611,000 | 408,000 | 203,000 |
| Total liabilities and stockholders' equity | $3,474,000 | $2,638,000 | $836,000 |

**Additional Information:**

- On January 2, 2008, Bergen sold all of its marketable investment securities for $95,000 cash.

- On March 10, 2008, Bergen paid a cash dividend of $30,000 on its common stock. No other dividends were paid or declared during 2008.

- On April 15, 2008, Bergen issued 2,000 shares of its common stock for land having a fair value of $100,000.

- On May 25, 2008, Bergen borrowed $450,000 from an insurance company. The underlying promissory note bears interest at 15% and is payable in three equal annual installments of $150,000. The first payment is due on May 25, 2009.

- On June 15, 2008, Bergen purchased equipment for $392,000 cash.

- On July 1, 2008, Bergen sold equipment costing $52,000, with a book value of $28,000 for $33,000 cash.

- On September 1, 2008, Bergen paid a $20,000 additional tax assessment for 2007 due to an error in tax calculation discovered by the Internal Revenue Service. Bergen appropriately recorded this payment as a prior period adjustment.

- On December 31, 2008, Bergen leased equipment from Tilden Company for a 10-year period. Equal payments under the lease are $25,000 due on December 31 each year. The first payment was made on December 31, 2008. The present value at December 31, 2008 of the 10 lease payments is $158,000. Bergen appropriately recorded the lease as a capital lease.

The $25,000 lease payment due on December 31, 2009 will consist of $9,000 principal and $16,000 interest.

- Bergen's net income for 2008 is $253,000.
- Bergen owns a 10% interest in the voting common stock of Mason, Inc. Mason reported net income of $120,000 for the year ended December 31, 2008 and paid a common stock dividend of $55,000 during 2008.

**Required:**

Prepare a cash flow statement for Bergen using the indirect method for 2008.

---

**P17-10**

Preparing an income statement from statement of cash flows and comparative balance sheets

The following are balance sheets of Kang-Iyer Financial Consultants:

## Balance Sheet December 31, 2008

| | December 31 | |
| --- | --- | --- |
| | **2008** | **2007** |
| Cash | $ 30,000 | $ 70,000 |
| Accounts receivable | 80,000 | 15,000 |
| Less: Allowance for doubtful accounts | (8,000) | (1,500) |
| Prepaid rent | –0– | 30,000 |
| Land | 600,000 | 400,000 |
| Building | 500,000 | –0– |
| Less: Accumulated depreciation | (10,000) | –0– |
| Total assets | $1,192,000 | $513,500 |
| | | |
| Salaries payable | 100,000 | 20,000 |
| Interest payable | 20,000 | 5,000 |
| Loan from Village Bank | 700,000 | 200,000 |
| Contributed capital | 75,000 | 30,000 |
| Retained earnings | 297,000 | 258,500 |
| Total liabilities and owners' equity | $1,192,000 | $513,500 |

The bad debts total written off during the year 2008 totaled $41,500.

## Statement of Cash Flows for the Year Ended December 31, 2008

| | |
| --- | --- |
| **Cash Flow from Operating Activities** | |
| Cash collected from customers | $250,000 |
| Cash paid to employees | (70,000) |
| Cash paid for interest | (50,000) |
| Cash flow from operations | 130,000 |
| | |
| **Cash Flow from Investing Activities** | ? |
| | |
| **Cash Flow from Financing Activities** | |
| Dividends paid | (15,000) |
| Change in cash | (40,000) |
| Beginning cash balance | 70,000 |
| Ending cash balance | $ 30,000 |

**Required:**

Complete the following cash flow statement and prepare an income statement for the year ended December 31, 2008. (*Hint:* To prepare the income statement, use the information in the balance sheets and the cash flow statement to "solve" for the income statement items. For example, by preparing a T-account for Salaries payable and then incorporating in this account the information on cash paid to employees, you can solve for Salaries expense.)

The financial statements of Cavalier Toy Stores (a fictitious merchandising company) follow:

**P17-11**

Analyzing statement of cash flows

## Income Statements for the Year Ended December 31, 2008

| | | |
|---|---|---|
| Sales revenue | | $ 1,500,000 |
| Cost of goods sold | | (1,200,000) |
| Gross margin | | 300,000 |
| Other expenses: | | |
| Salaries expense | $200,000 | |
| Bad debt expense | 100,000 | |
| Insurance expense | 30,000 | |
| Office supplies expense | 55,000 | |
| Depreciation expense—office building | 30,000 | |
| Depreciation expense—office equipment | 45,000 | |
| Interest expense | 90,000 | 550,000 |
| Net loss | | $ (250,000) |

## Statement of Retained Earnings for the Year Ended December 31, 2008

| | |
|---|---|
| Retained earnings 1/1/08 | $ 600,000 |
| Net loss for the year | (250,000) |
| Dividends paid | (300,000) |
| Retained earnings 12/31/08 | $ 50,000 |

## Balance Sheets

| | December 31 | |
|---|---|---|
| | **2008** | **2007** |
| **Assets** | | |
| Current assets: | | |
| Cash | $ 30,000 | $ 180,000 |
| Accounts receivable | 100,000 | 525,000 |
| Less: Allowance for doubtful accounts | (10,000) | (30,000) |
| Prepaid insurance | 5,000 | 35,000 |
| Inventory | 50,000 | 550,000 |
| Noncurrent assets: | | |
| Office building | 900,000 | –0– |
| Less: Accumulated depreciation | (30,000) | –0– |
| Office equipment | 200,000 | 200,000 |
| Less: Accumulated depreciation | (85,000) | (40,000) |
| **Total assets** | $1,160,000 | $1,420,000 |
| **Liabilities and Owners' Equity** | | |
| Current liabilities: | | |
| Salaries payable | $ 100,000 | $ 80,000 |
| Interest payable | 8,000 | 16,000 |
| Accounts payable for inventory purchases | 252,000 | 64,000 |
| Dividends payable | –0– | 50,000 |
| Noncurrent liabilities: | | |
| Loan from Thrifty Bank | 700,000 | 560,000 |
| Owners' Equity: | | |
| Contributed capital | 50,000 | 50,000 |
| Retained earnings | 50,000 | 600,000 |
| **Total liabilities and owners' equity** | $1,160,000 | $1,420,000 |

## Required:

1. Prepare a statement of cash flows using the indirect method.

2. Compute the following for the year ended December 31, 2008:

   a. Bad debts written off during the year.

   b. Cash collected from customers.

c. Purchases of inventory made during the year.

d. Cash paid to suppliers for inventory purchases.

e. Cash paid for insurance.

3. The following is an excerpt from the chief executive officer's letter to the stockholders included in the annual reports of Cavalier Toy Stores:

It feels real good to finish 2008 and be thankful that your company achieved its best year ever. I am sure that you are all puzzled by my statement given the net loss we have reported in the income statement. Let me explain. Although our gross margin has declined from last year's because of competitive pressures, we have set a company record in terms of sales revenue. You know quite well how accounting income can be manipulated. We don't play that game. We let cash flows tell our success story. Also, we have very efficiently managed our receivables and inventory and, at the same time, taken advantage of all available credit from our suppliers. More importantly, I am sure all of you are very pleased with the dividends that you have received this year. Let me end this letter by proudly inviting you to visit our new executive office building. While touring the luxurious executive suites, please remember that your top management team did not burden you with one dollar of debt to buy this building.

Assume that you are a commercial lending officer at Thrifty Bank. The working capital loan given to Cavalier Toy Stores has a balance outstanding as of December 31, 2008 of $700,000 and is repayable by April 1, 2009. The CEO has sent a loan proposal to Thrifty Bank requesting renewal of the loan for one more year and an increase in the credit limit to $1,000,000. Your job is to write a report to your boss with a specific recommendation on whether to accept or reject the proposal. Base your recommendation on the information available to you. In your report, please consider all of the CEO's claims in the letter to stockholders.

---

**P17-12**

Preparing a statement of cash flows—Indirect approach

AICPA
ADAPTED

Omega Corporation's comparative balance sheet accounts worksheet at December 31, 2008 and 2007 follow with a column showing the increase (decrease) from 2007 to 2008.

**Comparative Balance Sheet Worksheet**

| | 2008 | 2007 | Increase (Decrease) |
|---|---|---|---|
| Cash | $ 800,000 | $ 700,000 | $100,000 |
| Accounts receivable | 1,128,000 | 1,168,000 | (40,000) |
| Inventories | 1,850,000 | 1,715,000 | 135,000 |
| Property, plant and equipment | 3,307,000 | 2,967,000 | 340,000 |
| Accumulated depreciation | (1,165,000) | (1,040,000) | (125,000) |
| Investment in Belle Company | 305,000 | 275,000 | 30,000 |
| Loan receivable | 270,000 | –0– | 270,000 |
| Total assets | $6,495,000 | $5,785,000 | $710,000 |
| Accounts payable | $1,015,000 | $ 955,000 | $ 60,000 |
| Income taxes payable | 30,000 | 50,000 | (20,000) |
| Dividends payable | 80,000 | 90,000 | (10,000) |
| Capital lease obligation | 400,000 | –0– | 400,000 |
| Capital stock, common, $1 par | 500,000 | 500,000 | –0– |
| Additional paid-in capital | 1,500,000 | 1,500,000 | –0– |
| Retained earnings | 2,970,000 | 2,690,000 | 280,000 |
| Total liabilities and stockholders' equity | $6,495,000 | $5,785,000 | $710,000 |

**Additional Information:**

- On December 31, 2007, Omega acquired 25% of Belle Company's common stock for $275,000. On that date, the carrying value of Belle's assets and liabilities, which approximated their fair values, was $1,100,000. Belle reported income of $120,000 for the year ended December 31, 2008. No dividend was paid on Belle's common stock during the year.

- During 2008, Omega loaned $300,000 to Chase Company, an unrelated company. Chase made the first semiannual principal repayment of $30,000 plus interest at 10%, on October 1, 2008.

- On January 2, 2008, Omega sold equipment for $40,000 cash that cost $60,000 and had a carrying amount of $35,000.

- On December 31, 2008, Omega entered into a capital lease for an office building. The present value of the annual rental payments is $400,000, which equals the building's fair value. Omega made the first rental payment of $60,000, when due, on January 2, 2009.

- Net income for 2008 was $360,000.

- Omega declared and paid cash dividends for 2008 and 2007 as follows:

|          | 2008      | 2007      |
|----------|-----------|-----------|
| Declared | 12/15/08  | 12/15/07  |
| Paid     | 2/28/09   | 2/28/08   |
| Amount   | $80,000   | $90,000   |

**Required:**
Prepare a statement of cash flows for Omega Corporation for the year ended December 31, 2008 using the indirect approach.

---

Rite Aid Corporation operates retail drugstores in the United States. It is one of the country's largest retail drugstore chains with 3,333 stores in operation as of March 3, 2007. The company's drugstores' primary business is pharmacy services. The company also sells a full selection of health and beauty aids and personal care products, seasonal merchandise, and a large private brand product line.

**P17-13**

Operating cash flow impact of securitization

The following condensed information was extracted from Rite Aid's Form 10-K for the fiscal year that ended March 3, 2007 (all dollars in thousands).

### Consolidated Statements of Cash Flows

|                                                      | Year Ended |           |           |
|------------------------------------------------------|-----------|-----------|-----------|
|                                                      | 3/3/2007  | 3/4/2006  | 2/26/2005 |
| Net Income                                           | $ 26,826  | $1,273,006 | $302,478 |
| Total noncash charges (credits)                      | 379,715   | (810,731) | 129,729   |
| Changes in operating assets and liabilities:         |           |           |           |
|   Net proceeds from accounts receivable securitization | 20,000    | 180,000   | 150,000   |
|   Accounts receivable                      | (39,543)  | (51,494)  | 36,549    |
|   Net changes in other operating assets and liabilities | (77,853)  | (173,616) | (100,310) |
| Net cash provided by operating activities            | $309,145  | $ 417,165 | $518,446  |

### Consolidated Statements of Operations

|                                                      | Year Ended |           |           |
|------------------------------------------------------|-----------|-----------|-----------|
|                                                      | 3/3/2007  | 3/4/2006  | 2/26/2005 |
| Revenues                                             | $17,507,719 | $17,270,968 | $16,816,439 |
| Costs and expenses:                                  |           |           |           |
|   Cost of goods sold                       | 12,791,597 | 12,571,860 | 12,202,894 |
|   Selling, general and administrative expenses | 4,370,481 | 4,307,421 | 4,127,536 |
|   Store closing and impairment charges     | 49,317    | 68,692    | 35,655    |
|   Interest expense                         | 275,219   | 277,017   | 294,871   |
|   Loss on debt modifications and retirements, net | 18,662 | 9,186 | 19,229 |
|   (Gain) loss on sale of assets, net       | (11,139)  | (6,462)   | 2,247     |
|                                                      | 17,494,137 | 17,227,714 | 16,682,432 |
| Income before income taxes                           | 13,582    | 43,254    | 134,007   |
| Income tax benefit                                   | (13,244)  | (1,229,752) | (168,471) |
|   Net income                               | $ 26,826  | $ 1,273,006 | $ 302,478 |

## Selected Data Pertaining to Accounts Receivable

| | Year Ended | | |
| --- | --- | --- | --- |
| | **3/3/2007** | **3/4/2006** | **2/26/2005** |
| Year-end Accounts receivable, net | $374,493 | $354,949 | $483,455 |
| Allowance for uncollectible accounts at year-end | 30,246 | 32,336 | 31,216 |
| Additions to uncollectible accounts charged to costs and expenses | 26,603 | 34,702 | 47,291 |

## Accounts Receivable

The Company maintains an allowance for doubtful accounts receivable based upon the expected collectibility of accounts receivable. The allowance for uncollectible accounts at March 3, 2007 and March 4, 2006 was $30,246 and $32,336, respectively. The Company's accounts receivable are due primarily from third-party payors (e.g., pharmacy benefit management companies, insurance companies or governmental agencies) and are recorded net of any allowances provided for under the respective plans. Since payments due from third-party payors are sensitive to payment criteria changes and legislative actions, the allowance is reviewed continually, and adjusted for accounts deemed uncollectible by management.

The Company maintains securitization agreements with several multi-seller asset-backed commercial paper vehicles ("CPVs"). Under the terms of the securitization agreements, the Company sells substantially all of its eligible third party pharmaceutical receivables to a bankruptcy remote Special Purpose Entity (SPE) and retains servicing responsibility. The assets of the SPE are not available to satisfy the creditors of any other person, including any of the Company's affiliates. These agreements provide for the Company to sell, and for the SPE to purchase these receivables. The SPE then transfers an interest in these receivables to various CPVs. Transferred outstanding receivables cannot exceed $400,000. The amount of transferred receivables outstanding at any one time is dependent upon a formula that takes into account such factors as default history, obligor concentrations and potential dilution ("Securitization Formula"). Adjustments to this amount can occur on a weekly basis. At March 3, 2007 and March 4, 2006, the total of outstanding receivables that have been transferred to the CPVs were $350,000 and $330,000, respectively. The Company has determined that the transactions meet the criteria for sales treatment in accordance with SFAS No. 140 "Accounting for Transfers and Servicing of Financial Assets and Extinguishment of Liabilities."

**Required:**

1. Calculate cash collected from customers during fiscal 2007.

2. Had Rite Aid *not* securitized receivables during 2007, 2006, and 2005, what would its operating cash flows have been in each of these years? Do you believe that Rite Aid's operating cash flows were materially affected by its receivables securitization practices?

3. Calculate pre-tax operating income for 2007, 2006, and 2005, and compare it to operating cash flows as originally reported and to operating cash flows assuming that Rite Aid did not securitize receivables. Compare both results and comment on the impact of Rite Aid's practice of securitizing receivables. (*Hint:* When calculating pre-tax operating income, include only items that relate to core business operations.)

Vulcan Corporation (a real company whose name has been disguised) is a leading worldwide manufacturer and distributor of uncoated and coated rubberlike fiberboard products. Vulcan's products are marketed to various industries, including companies in the following businesses: footwear, headwear, luggage, leather goods, belt backing, furniture, electronic integrated component packaging, and automotive supplies.

Information developed using Vulcan Corporation's financial statements for the year ended October 31, 2008 appears below.

**C17-1**

Vulcan Corporation: Understanding cash flow statements

## Vulcan Corporation

### Cash Flow from Operating Activities

| ($ in thousands) | Year Ended October 31, 2008 |
|---|---|
| Cash received from customers | $37,378 |
| Cash paid to suppliers | (26,884) |
| Cash paid for general and administrative expenses | (8,002) |
| Cash paid for interest | (810) |
| Cash paid for income taxes | (74) |
| Net cash provided by operating activities | $ 1,608 |

### Selected Balance Sheet Information

| | October 31 | |
|---|---|---|
| ($ in thousands) | 2008 | 2007 |
| Accounts receivable, net | $14,120 | $11,043 |
| Inventories | 5,465 | 5,798 |
| Property, plant and equipment, net | 10,707 | 11,523 |
| Accounts payable | 7,756 | 6,375 |
| Accrued general and administrative expenses | 2,559 | 1,871 |
| Interest payable | 130 | 52 |
| Deferred taxes payable | 936 | 675 |

**Additional Information:**

- Total comprehensive income for the year ended October 31, 2008 was $336,000.
- Other comprehensive loss (net of applicable income taxes) consisted of unrealized loss on investments classified as available-for-sale securities of $286,000.
- Equipment purchased during the year totaled $854,000.
- The book value of equipment retired during the year totaled $348,000.

**Required:**

1. Compute Vulcan Corporation's net income loss for the year ended October 31, 2008. (*Hint*: All components of other comprehensive income or loss have been provided.)

2. Prepare Vulcan Corporation's combined statement of income (loss) and comprehensive income (loss) for the year ended October 31, 2008.

3. Determine Vulcan Corporation's net cash provided by operating activities using the indirect method.

| | |
|---|---|
| **C17-2**<br><br>Lucky Lady, Inc.: Preparing comprehensive statement of cash flows | The income statement for the year ended December 31, 2008 as well as the balance sheets as of December 31, 2008 and December 31, 2007 for Lucky Lady, Inc. follow. This information is taken from the financial statements of a real company whose name has been disguised. |

## Income Statement

| ($ in thousands) | For the Year Ended December 31, 2008 |
|---|---|
| **Revenues** | |
| Casino | $ 26,702 |
| Rooms | 2,897 |
| Food and beverage | 2,351 |
| Other hotel/casino | 5,066 |
| Airline | 20,784 |
| Total revenues | 57,800 |
| **Operating Expenses** | |
| Casino | 9,341 |
| Rooms | 1,016 |
| Food and beverage | 2,529 |
| Other hotel/casino | 5,777 |
| Airline | 20,599 |
| Selling, general, and administrative (including bad debt expense of $3,855) | 19,679 |
| Depreciation expense | 8,018 |
| Hotel preopening expenses | 45,130 |
| Aircraft carrying value adjustment | 68,948 |
| Total operating expenses | 181,037 |
| Operating income | (123,237) |
| Nonoperating items: | |
| Interest income | 12,231 |
| Interest expense | (6,596) |
| Other, net | 16 |
| Income before taxes | (117,586) |
| Provision for income taxes | –0– |
| Net income (loss) | $(117,586) |

## Balance Sheets

| | December 31 | |
|---|---|---|
| ($ in thousands) | 2008 | 2007 |
| **Assets** | | |
| Cash | $ 211,305 | $ 579,963 |
| Gross accounts receivable | 35,249 | 2,178 |
| Less: Allowance for doubtful accounts | (4,733) | (1,531) |
| Prepaid expenses | 11,755 | 1,219 |
| Inventories | 12,662 | 154 |
| Total current assets | 266,238 | 581,983 |
| Gross property, plant and equipment | 953,796 | 471,506 |
| Less: Accumulated depreciation | (86,512) | (21,796) |
| Pre-opening expenses | –0– | 10,677 |
| Other operating assets | 26,601 | 21,116 |
| Total assets | $1,160,123 | $1,063,486 |
| **Liabilities and Stockholders' Equity** | | |
| Accounts payable | $ 14,181 | $ 4,322 |
| Accrued salaries and wages | 8,194 | 945 |
| Accrued interest on long-term debt | 9,472 | 9,429 |

*(continued)*

| ($ in thousands) | December 31 | |
| --- | --- | --- |
| | **2008** | **2007** |
| Other accrued liabilities | 33,502 | 9,744 |
| Construction payables | 96,844 | 32,296 |
| Current maturities, capital leases | 1,830 | 289 |
| Current maturities, long-term debt | 1,573 | –0– |
| Total current liabilities | 165,596 | 57,025 |
| Deferred revenues | 10,784 | –0– |
| Deferred income taxes | 6,517 | 6,517 |
| Long-term obligation, capital leases | 14,044 | 162 |
| Long-term debt | 481,427 | 473,000 |
| Total liabilities | 678,368 | 536,704 |
| Common stock | 506 | 485 |
| Capital in excess of par value | 662,365 | 589,827 |
| Common stock in treasury | (29,490) | (29,490) |
| Retained earnings (deficit) | (151,626) | (34,040) |
| Total stockholders' equity | 481,755 | 526,782 |
| Total liabilities and equity | $1,160,123 | $1,063,486 |

## Additional Information and Author Notes:

- *Aircraft valuation adjustment:* The company reduced the book value of its aircraft and related equipment to their expected recoverable values and recognized an aircraft carrying value adjustment in the 2008 income statement. [*Author Note:* You may treat this item as "extra" depreciation recorded during the year due to abnormal decline in the asset value.]

- *Property, plant and equipment:* Includes land, buildings, aircraft equipment, furniture and fixture, equipment under capital lease, and so on. During 2008, the company acquired equipment under capital leases for $16,987,000. The company also sold equipment with a net book value of $2,501,000 for $684,000 cash. [*Author Note:* The gain or loss on this sale is combined with some other item in the income statement. Any other change in the gross book value of Property, plant and equipment may be attributed to outright purchase of other equipment and building construction costs.]

- *Capital lease and long-term liabilities:* [*Author Note:* When preparing the cash flow statement, you may find it convenient to combine the current and long-term portions of each of these liabilities.]

- *Pre-opening expenses:* Pre-opening expenses include direct project salaries, advertising, and other pre-opening services incurred during the pre-opening period of the Lucky Lady Hotel. Such expenses were expensed upon opening the facility.

- *Stock offering:* The increases in Common stock and Capital in excess of par accounts are due to a common stock offering completed on August 17, 2008.

- *Laundry loan:* On June 16, 2008, the company obtained a $10,000,000 loan from a financial institution for a laundry facility in North Las Vegas, Nevada. As of December 31, 2008, $10,000,000 has been drawn down under the loan. Construction of the facility was completed in December 2008. The laundry provides the laundry and dry cleaning services for the Lucky Lady Hotel.

## Required:

1. Using the indirect method, prepare the statement of cash flows for the year ended December 31, 2008 in as much detail as possible. For example, borrowing and repayment, if any, should be shown separately as financing inflow and outflow, respectively. Similarly, to the extent that information is available, separately disclose and explain the changes to each asset and each liability account that affected Lucky Lady's cash flows during 2008.

2. Redo the operating section of the cash flow statement using the direct method.

The following information is based on the 2008 annual report of Opus One, Inc. (a real company whose name has been disguised). Opus One operates in a single business segment, the retailing and servicing of home audio, car audio, and video equipment. Its operations are conducted in Texas through 20 stores and two service centers. The information provided in the annual report has been combined and abbreviated.

**Additional Information Regarding Year Ended June 30, 2008:**

- The company did not declare or pay any cash or stock dividends during the year.
- The company reported a $7,377 loss from scrapping equipment with a book value of the same amount.
- The depreciation expense for the year was $2,265,735.
- The following breakdown is provided for the long-term debt:

| | June 30 | |
| --- | --- | --- |
| ($ in thousands) | 2008 | 2007 |
| **Long-Term Debt** | | |
| Term loan | $3,420,000 | $ –0– |
| Mortgage note | 534,475 | 555,455 |
| Total | 3,954,475 | 555,455 |
| Less: Current installments | (681,716) | (21,348) |
| Long-term debt—current installments | $3,272,759 | $534,107 |

## Opus One, Inc.

## Balance Sheet June 30, 2008 and 2007

| | June 30 | |
| --- | --- | --- |
| ($ in thousands) | 2008 | 2007 |
| **Current Assets** | | |
| Cash | $ 50,885 | $ 19,481 |
| Receivables | 4,625,920 | 6,963,195 |
| Less: Allowance for bad debts | (403,000) | (1,200,000) |
| Inventories | 25,986,364 | 26,801,526 |
| Prepaid expenses | 455,875 | 710,058 |
| Income taxes receivable | 1,573,055 | 3,073,537 |
| **Noncurrent Assets** | | |
| Property and equipment | 22,182,371 | 20,637,912 |
| Less: Accumulated depreciation | (9,031,181) | (6,822,553) |
| Deferred tax asset, net | 1,043,403 | 531,803 |
| Pre-opening costs | 370,458 | 877,179 |
| Goodwill | 366,750 | 366,750 |
| Less: Accumulated amortization | (122,509) | (98,059) |
| Total assets | $47,098,391 | $51,860,829 |
| **Current Liabilities** | | |
| Revolving credit agreements | $ 4,810,398 | $18,743,407 |
| Accounts payable | 11,054,418 | 7,951,545 |
| Accrued liabilities | 4,025,816 | 3,257,672 |
| Current installments of long-term debt | 681,716 | 21,348 |

*(continued)*

|  | June 30 | |
| --- | --- | --- |
| ($ in thousands) | **2008** | **2007** |
| **Long-Term Liabilities** | | |
| Long-term debt minus current installments | 3,272,759 | 534,107 |
| Other liabilities and deferred credits | 4,072,586 | 3,308,714 |
| Total liabilities | 27,917,693 | 33,816,793 |
| **Shareholders' Equity** | | |
| Common stock and additional paid-in capital | 10,126,944 | 10,117,946 |
| Retained earnings | 9,053,754 | 7,926,090 |
| Total shareholders' equity | 19,180,698 | 18,044,036 |
| Total liabilities and shareholders' equity | $47,098,391 | $51,860,829 |

On February 26, 2008, the company obtained a $3,600,000 term loan from a bank due February 28, 2012.

**Required:**

1. Prepare a statement of cash flows for the year ended June 30, 2008 using the indirect approach.

2. On the basis of the cash flow statement, analyze Opus One's financial performance during the fiscal year 2008.

---

Cardinal Health, Inc., an Ohio corporation formed in 1979, is a leading provider of products and services that improve health care safety and productivity. The following edited balance sheet and cash flow statement are from the company's fiscal 2007 annual report.

**C17-4**

Cardinal Health, Inc.: Reconciling balance sheet and cash flow statements

## Consolidated Balance Sheet (Condensed)

|  | June 30, | |
| --- | --- | --- |
| ($ in millions) | **2007** | **2006** |
| **Assets** | | |
| Current assets | | |
| Cash and equivalents | $ 1,308.8 | $ 1,187.3 |
| Short-term investments available for sale | 132.0 | 498.4 |
| Trade receivables, net | 4,714.4 | 3,808.8 |
| Current portion of net investment in sales-type leases | 354.8 | 290.1 |
| Inventories | 7,383.2 | 7,493.0 |
| Prepaid expenses and other | 651.3 | 558.8 |
| Assets held for sale and discontinued operations | — | 2,739.5 |
| Total current assets | $14,544.5 | $16,575.9 |
| Property and equipment, at cost | | |
| Land, buildings and improvements | 1,694.0 | 1,837.2 |
| Machinery and equipment | 1,657.4 | 1,278.1 |
| Furniture and fixtures | 185.8 | 167.7 |
| Total property and equipment, at cost | 3,537.2 | 3,283.0 |
| Accumulated depreciation and amortization | (1,890.2) | (1,778.0) |
| Property and equipment, net | $ 1,647.0 | $ 1,505.0 |
| Other assets | | |
| Net investment in sales-type leases, less current portion | 820.7 | 754.7 |
| Goodwill and other intangibles, net | 5,860.9 | 4,283.4 |
| Other | 280.7 | 314.3 |
| Total assets | $23,153.8 | $23,433.3 |

*(continued)*

| ($ in millions) | June 30, 2007 | 2006 |
|---|---:|---:|
| **Liabilities and Shareholders' Equity** | | |
| Current liabilities | | |
| Current portion of long-term obligations | | |
|   and other short-term borrowings | $    16.0 | $   199.0 |
| Accounts payable | 9,162.2 | 8,907.8 |
| Other accrued liabilities | 2,247.3 | 1,941.1 |
| Liabilities from businesses held for sale and | | |
|   discontinued operations | 34.2 | 534.2 |
|     Total current liabilities | $11,459.7 | $11,582.1 |
| Long-term obligations, less current portion | | |
|   and other short-term debt | 3,457.3 | 2,588.6 |
| Deferred income taxes and other liabilities | 859.9 | 771.9 |
|     Total shareholders' equity | 7,376.9 | 8,490.7 |
| Total liabilities and shareholders' equity | $23,153.8 | $23,433.3 |

## Consolidated Cash Flow Statement (Condensed)

| | FY 2007 |
|---|---:|
| **Cash Flows from Operating Activities** | |
| Net earnings | $ 1,931.1 |
| Earnings from discontinued operations | (1,091.4) |
|   Earnings from continuing operations | $    839.7 |
| Adjustments to reconcile earnings to net cash from operations | |
|   Depreciation and amortization | 322.1 |
|   Asset impairments | 19.2 |
|   Acquired in-process research and development | 84.5 |
|   Equity compensation | 138.1 |
|   Provision for deferred income taxes | 11.7 |
|   Provision for bad debts | 24.0 |
| Change in operating assets and liabilities, net of effects from acquisitions | |
|   Increase in trade receivables | (783.1) |
|   Decrease in inventories | 217.4 |
|   Increase in net investment in sales-type leases | (130.8) |
|   Increase in accounts payable | 224.4 |
|   Other accrued liabilities and operating items, net | 35.8 |
|   Net cash provided by operating activities—continuing operations | $ 1,003.0 |
| Net cash provided by operating activities—discontinued operations | 220.1 |
|   Net cash provided by operating activities | $ 1,223.1 |
| **Cash Flows from Investing Activities** | |
| Acquisition of subsidiaries, net of divestitures and cash acquired | (1,629.8) |
|   Proceeds from sale of property and equipment | 9.2 |
|   Additions to property and equipment | (357.4) |
|   Sale of investment securities available for sale | 366.5 |
|   Net cash used in investing activities—continuing operations | $(1,611.5) |
| Net cash provided by investing activities—discontinued operations | 3,148.7 |
|   Net cash provided by investing activities | $ 1,537.2 |
| **Cash Flows from Financing Activities** | |
| Net change in commercial paper and short-term borrowings | (38.9) |
| Reduction of long-term obligations | (784.0) |
| Proceeds from long-term obligations, net of issuance costs | 1,453.4 |
| Proceeds from issuance of common shares | 552.6 |
| Tax benefits from exercises of stock options | 29.9 |
| Dividends on common shares | (144.4) |

*(continued)*

|  | **FY 2007** |
|---|---|
| Purchase of treasury shares | (3,662.0) |
| Net cash used in financing activities—continuing operations | $(2,593.4) |
| Net cash used in financing activities—discontinued operations | (45.4) |
| Net cash used in financing activities | $(2,638.8) |
| **Net increase in cash and equivalents** | 121.5 |
| **Cash and equivalents at beginning of year** | 1,187.3 |
| Cash and equivalents at end of year | $ 1,308.8 |

**Required:**

1. For the following working capital accounts, calculate the changes that occurred during fiscal 2007:

   - Short-term investments available for sale.

   - Trade receivables.

   - Inventories.

   - Prepaid expenses and other.

   - Current portion of long-term obligations and other short-term borrowings.

   - Accounts payable.

   - Other accrued liabilities.

   Compare these changes to the accrual adjustments and other information found on Cardinal's cash flow statement and note any differences. Reconcile these differences if possible. (*Hint*: Retrieve Cardinal's fiscal 2007 Form 10-K from the SEC's Web site; information in the financial statement footnotes may help identify reconciling differences.) http://www.sec.gov/Archives/edgar/data/721371/000095015207007107/l27624ae10vk.htm.

2. Investments in sales-type leases are listed among both the Current Assets and Other Assets sections. Calculate the changes that occurred in these line items during 2007, and reconcile these changes to the related item on the cash flow statement.

3. Calculate the changes in the property and equipment accounts and compare them to the related items in the Investing Activities section of the cash flow statement. (*Hint*: Perform a T-account analysis of Property and equipment and Accumulated depreciation, beginning with the latter.) To the extent possible, recreate the summary journal entries that Cardinal made to record asset retirements and acquisitions. Note any changes in Property and equipment that remain unexplained.

4. Refer to footnote 2 in Cardinal's 2007 financial statements. Recreate the journal entry to record the acquisitions that took place during 2007 taking into consideration the Acquisition of subsidiaries item that appears in cash flows from investing activities. Assume that any previously unidentified additions to property and equipment and the unexplained changes in operating assets and liabilities (from requirements 1 and 3, respectively)—which appear on the cash flow statement net of effects from acquisitions—relate to the acquisitions referred to in footnote 2.

5. Refer to footnote 8 in Cardinal's 2007 financial statements. To reconcile the changes in balance sheet line items related to Held for sale and Discontinued operations with the corresponding items on the cash flow statement, recreate Cardinal's summary journal entry to record the disposal of these assets and liabilities.

6. Suggest possible reasons for (a) the differences between changes in balance sheet accounts over the course of a fiscal year and related items on the cash flow statement and (b) any of these differences that could not be reconciled. Support your answers.

## COLLABORATIVE LEARNING CASES

**C17-5**

Best Buy Company, Inc.:
Analyzing financial performance from the cash flow statement and other information

 **Collaborative**

What follows are the consolidated statements of cash flows of Best Buy Company, Inc. The information provided in the annual report has been combined and abbreviated.

### Consolidated Statements of Cash Flows

| ($ in thousands) | For the Fiscal Years Ended | | |
| --- | --- | --- | --- |
| | **February 26 Year 3** | **February 27 Year 2** | **February 28 Year 1** |
| **Operating Activities** | | | |
| Net earnings | $347,070 | $216,282 | $ 81,938 |
| Depreciation, amortization and | | | |
| other noncash charges | 109,541 | 78,367 | 71,584 |
| | 456,611 | 294,649 | 153,522 |
| Changes in operating assets and liabilities: | | | |
| Receivables | (56,900) | (36,699) | (16,121) |
| Merchandise inventories | (137,315) | 14,422 | 71,271 |
| Other assets | (11,005) | (4,251) | (3,278) |
| Accounts payable | 302,194 | 249,094 | 147,340 |
| Other liabilities | 108,829 | 82,544 | 63,950 |
| Accrued income taxes | 97,814 | 62,672 | 33,759 |
| Total cash provided by operating activities | 760,228 | 662,431 | 450,443 |
| **Investing Activities** | | | |
| Additions to property and equipment | (361,024) | (165,698) | (72,063) |
| (Increase) decrease in recoverable | | | |
| costs from developed properties | (21,009) | (65,741) | 45,270 |
| (Increase) decrease in other assets | (18,081) | (18,128) | 4,494 |
| Total cash used in investing activities | (400,114) | (249,567) | (22,299) |
| **Financing Activities** | | | |
| Long-term debt payments | (29,946) | (165,396) | (22,694) |
| Long-term debt borrowings | –0– | –0– | 10,000 |
| Issuance of common stock | 32,229 | 20,644 | 14,869 |
| Repurchase of common stock | (397,451) | (2,462) | –0– |
| Total cash (used in) provided by financing activities | (395,168) | (147,214) | 2,175 |
| **Increase (Decrease) in Cash and Cash Equivalents** | $(35,054) | $265,650 | $430,319 |

The following data are based on information provided by the company in its SEC filings:

Best Buy Co., Inc. is the nation's largest volume specialty retailer of name-brand consumer electronic, home office equipment, entertainment software, and appliances. Part of the Company's strategy is to provide a selection of brand name products comparable to retailers that specialize in the Company's principal product categories and seeks to ensure a high level of product availability for customers. The number of stores operated by the company increased from 272 at the end of Year 0, to 284, 311, and 357 at the end of Year 1, Year 2, and Year 3, respectively. When entering a major metropolitan market, the Company establishes a district office, service center, and major appliance warehouse. Each new store requires working capital of approximately $4 million for merchandise inventory (net of vendor financing), leasehold improvements, fixtures, and equipment. Preopening costs of approximately $600,000 per store are incurred through hiring, relocating and training new employees, and in merchandising the store. These costs are expensed as incurred.

**Required:**

1. Using information provided in the cash flow statement, compare Best Buy's earnings and cash flows from operations for the last three years and provide an explanation for the differences between these two numbers within each year and from year to year. Explain whether earning or operating cash flows provide a better indication of Best Buy's performance.

2. How have new store openings affected Best Buy's working capital needs over the last three years? Compare the company's actual changes in working capital to the working capital needed to support new store openings and comment on any differences.

3. Comment on the year-to-year changes in inventories for the last three years and how these changes have been financed.

4. Comment on any insights gained from an analysis of the Investing and Financing section of Best Buy's cash flow statement.

---

ESCO Technologies Inc. and Take-Two Interactive Software, Inc. both capitalize software development costs in accordance with their respective policies as summarized here. The condensed financial information that follows was extracted from each company's fiscal 2007 Form 10-K (all dollars are in thousands). Full financial statements for each company may be accessed at www.sec.gov.

**C17-6**

Capitalizing software development costs

## ESCO Technologies Inc.

ESCO Technologies Inc. and its wholly owned subsidiaries are organized into three reporting units: Communications, Filtration/Fluid Flow, and RF Shielding and Test. The Communications unit is a proven supplier of special purpose fixed network communications systems for electric, gas, and water utilities, including hardware and software to support advanced metering applications. The Filtration unit develops, manufactures, and markets a broad range of filtration products used in the purification and processing of liquids. The Test unit provides its customers with the ability to identify, measure, and contain magnetic, electromagnetic, and acoustic energy.

### Statement of Cash Flow Data Affected by Software Capitalization Policies

| | Years Ended September 30, | | |
|---|---|---|---|
| | **2007** | **2006** | **2005** |
| Net cash provided by operating activities | $ 45,263 | $ 58,626 | $ 68,556 |
| Cash flows from investing activities: | | | |
| Acquisition of businesses, net of cash acquired | (8,250) | (91,968) | — |
| Capital expenditures | (19,503) | (9,117) | (8,848) |
| Additions to capitalized software | (30,094) | (27,977) | (8,342) |
| Net cash used by investing activities | $(57,847) | $(129,062) | $(17,190) |

### Selected Other Financial Statement Items

| | Years Ended September 30, | | |
|---|---|---|---|
| | **2007** | **2006** | **2005** |
| Total current assets | $260,350 | $207,257 | |
| Net property, plant, and equipment | 78,277 | 68,754 | |
| Goodwill | 149,466 | 143,450 | |
| Capitalized software, net | 65,700 | 45,200 | |
| Other intangible assets, net | 11,542 | 14,002 | |
| Other assets | 10,772 | 10,031 | |
| Total assets | $576,107 | $488,694 | |
| | | | |
| Amortization of capitalized software | 7,700 | 3,300 | |
| Net earnings | $ 33,713 | $ 31,280 | $43,544 |

## Condensed Footnote: Capitalized Software

The costs incurred for the development of computer software that will be sold, leased, or otherwise marketed are charged to expense when incurred as research and development until technological feasibility has been established for the product. Technological feasibility is typically established upon completion of a detailed program design. Costs incurred after this point are capitalized on a project-by-project basis in accordance with SFAS No. 86. Costs that are capitalized primarily consist of external development costs. Upon general release of the product to customers, the Company ceases capitalization and . . . amortizes the software development costs over a three- to seven-year period based upon the estimated future economic life of the product.

## Take-Two Interactive Software, Inc.

Take-Two Interactive Software, Inc. is a global publisher, developer, and distributor of interactive entertainment software, hardware, and accessories. Its publishing segment develops, markets, and publishes software titles for leading gaming and entertainment hardware platforms.

## Statement of Cash Flow Data Affected by Software Capitalization Policies

| | Years Ended October 31, | | |
| --- | --- | --- | --- |
| | 2007 | 2006 | 2005 |
| Operating activites: | | | |
| Net Income (loss) | $ (138,406) | $ (184,889) | $ 35,314 |
| Adjustments to reconcile net income (loss) to net cash provided by (used for) operating activities: | | | |
| Amortization and write-off of software development costs and licenses | 109,891 | 147,832 | 81,959 |
| Other adjustments, net | 54,499 | 89,728 | 43,573 |
| Changes in assets and liabilities, net of effect from purchases and disposal of businesses: | | | |
| Software development costs and licenses | (163,859) | (143,248) | (138,609) |
| Other changes in assets and liabilities, net | 73,830 | 133,939 | 17,743 |
| Net cash (used for) provided by operating activities | $ (64,045) | $ 43,362 | $ 39,980 |
| Investing activities: | | | |
| Payments for purchases of businesses, net of cash acquired | (5,795) | (191) | (37,753) |

## Selected Other Financial Statement Items

| | Years Ended October 31, | | |
| --- | --- | --- | --- |
| | 2007 | 2006 | 2005 |
| Current assets: | | | |
| Software development costs and licenses | 141,441 | 85,207 | |
| Other current assets | 357,082 | 459,666 | |
| Total current assets | 498,523 | 544,873 | |
| Software development costs and licenses, net of current portion | 34,465 | 31,354 | |
| Other non-current assets | 298,155 | 292,579 | |
| Total assets | $ 831,143 | $ 868,806 | |
| Net income (loss) | $(138,406) | $(184,889) | $35,314 |

## Condensed Footnote: Software Development Costs

We utilize both internal development teams and third party software developers to develop the titles we publish.

We capitalize internal software development costs (including stock-based compensation, specifically identifiable employee payroll expense, and incentive compensation costs related to the completion and release of titles), third party production and other content costs, subsequent to establishing technological feasibility of a software title. Technological feasibility of a product includes the completion of both technical design documentation and game design documentation. Amortization of such capitalized costs is recorded on a title-by-title basis in cost of goods sold (software development costs) using (1) the proportion of current year revenues to the total revenues expected to be recorded over the life of the title or (2) the straight-line method over the remaining estimated useful life of the title, whichever is greater.

We frequently enter into agreements with third party developers that require us to make advance payments for game development and production services . . . . We capitalize all advance payments to developers as software development. On a product-by-product basis, we reduce software development costs and record a corresponding amount of research and development expense for any costs incurred by third party developers prior to establishing technological feasibility of a product. We typically enter into agreements with third party developers after completing the technical design documentation for our products and therefore record the design costs leading up to a signed developer contract as research and development expense. We also generally contract with third party developers that have proven technology and experience in the genre of the software being developed, which often allows for the establishment of technological feasibility early in the development cycle. In instances where the documentation of the design and technology are not in place prior to an executed contract, we monitor the software development process and require our third party developers to adhere to the same technological feasibility standards that apply to our internally developed products.

Prior to establishing technological feasibility, we expense research and development costs as incurred.

### Required:

1. Make any needed adjustment to Take-Two's statement of cash flows to improve interfirm comparability of its operating cash flows.

2. Make any needed adjustment to ESCO Technologies' statement of cash flows to improve interfirm comparability of its operating cash flows.

3. What is the likely impact of any adjustment(s) you made in requirements 1 and 2 on an analysis of operating cash flows?

4. What impact do ESCO's software capitalization policies have on the company's net income as reported for fiscal 2007? (*Hint:* Compare to income assuming that ESCO expenses all software development costs when incurred. Ignore income taxes.)

5. Compare Take-Two's and ESCO Technologies' policies with respect to establishing technological feasibility and comment on the impact of these policies on reported net income.

6. Re-create summary journal entries for the fiscal 2007 activity in Take-Two's Software development costs and licenses account. Do your entries reconcile with the information reported on Take-Two's cash flow statement? If not, offer a plausible explanation for any discrepancy. (*Hint:* Combine both current and noncurrent balance sheet items related to software development costs and licenses.)

 **.mhhe.com/revsine4e**

**Remember to check the book's companion Web site for additional study material.**

# Overview of International Financial Reporting Differences and Inflation | 18

Cross-border holdings of long-term debt and equity securities have increased substantially in the last few years. U.S. holdings of foreign equity securities at the end of 2005 increased to $3,000 billion—five times the $600 billion held at the end of 1994 (Figure 18.1). U.S. holdings of $350 billion foreign long-term debt almost tripled from the end of 1994 to $1,000 billion at the end of 2005. The growth in foreign holdings of U.S. securities has outpaced the growth of U.S.–owned securities. At the end of 2005, the $2,300 billion of foreign holdings of U.S. equity securities were 5.50 times the amount held at the end of 1994. The $4,400 billion in foreign holdings of U.S. long-term debt at the end of 2005 were 5.18 times the $850 billion of long-term debt holdings at the end of 1994. During this time period, the foreign-owned share of long-term U.S. securities doubled from 8% to 16%.[1]

Other evidence of the growth in cross-border investment exists. Stock exchanges across the world now list significant numbers of foreign companies. For example, Exhibit 18.1 shows that foreign firms comprise 18.5% of the listings on the New York Stock Exchange (423/2,291) and 21.5% of the listings on the London exchange (709/3,297). And the number of these foreign listings continues to grow.

This unprecedented access to global capital as well as to global consumer markets has allowed companies from many countries to grow large. See Exhibit 18.2 for the home country of the five largest firms in eight selected industries for 2006. Clearly, investors who choose to concentrate on a specific industrial or commercial sector are compelled to think globally these days.

Several factors have fueled the increased global investing. For example, many major industrial countries have relaxed their security market regulatory rules, thus making it easier for foreign firms to meet listing requirements. Another factor relates to improvements in telecommunications and computer technology. Finally, investors understand that portfolios based on a global investment strategy are less risky than portfolios composed exclusively of domestic securities. That's because foreign issuers of securities are often subject to economic conditions that differ from those of domestic companies, thereby creating more portfolio diversification.

## LEARNING OBJECTIVES

**After studying this chapter, you will understand:**

1. Why financial reporting philosophies and detailed generally accepted accounting principles (GAAP) procedures differed across countries.

2. How globalization has relaxed cross-border barriers and prompted convergence of reporting standards across countries.

3. The reasons for the increased importance of the International Accounting Standards Board (IASB).

4. Efforts by the Financial Accounting Standards Board (FASB) and the IASB to converge their respective standards and facilitate cross-border financial transactions.

5. Mechanisms for coping with reporting differences that persist.

6. Actions of the Securities and Exchange Commission (SEC) to ease rules for foreign registrants using International Financial Reporting Standards (IFRS).

7. That companies in foreign countries with high inflation rates depart from the historical cost reporting model.

8. The two major approaches for adjusting financial reports for changing prices—current cost accounting and general price-level accounting.

*Chapter*

---

[1] See C. C. Bertaut, W. L. Griever, and R. W. Tryon, "Understanding U.S. Cross-Border Securities Data," *Federal Reserve Bulletin*, May 4, 2006, www.federalreserve.gov/pubs/bulletin/2006/cross_border_securities.pdf, January 28, 2008, p. A60.

## Figure 18.1

FOREIGN HOLDINGS
OF U.S. LONG-TERM
SECURITIES AND U.S.
HOLDINGS OF FOREIGN
LONG-TERM SECURITIES
BY SECURITY TYPE,
1994–2005

SOURCE: C. C. Bertaut, W. L. Griever, and
R. W. Tryon, "Understanding U.S. Cross-
Border Securities Data," *Federal Reserve
Bulletin*, May 4, 2006, p. A59.

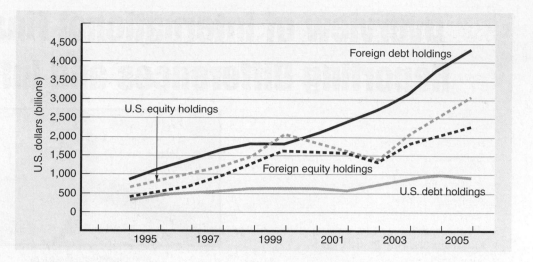

| | | | |
|---|---|---|---|
| **EXHIBIT 18.1** | **Foreign Listings on Selected Stock Exchanges, 2007** | | |

| Stock Exchange | Total Number of Companies Listed | Number of Domestic Companies Listed | Number of Foreign Companies Listed |
|---|---|---|---|
| Australian SE | 1,958 | 1,876 | 82 |
| Deutsche Börse | 866 | 761 | 105 |
| Euronext | 1,164 | 937 | 227 |
| London SE | 3,297 | 2,588 | 709 |
| Nasdaq | 3,067 | 2,757 | 310 |
| NYSE Group | 2,291 | 1,868 | 423 |
| Singapore Exchange | 752 | 467 | 285 |
| Tokyo SE Group | 2,409 | 2,383 | 26 |
| TSX Group | 3,942 | 3,871 | 71 |

*Source:* World Federation of Exchanges Web site, www.world-exchanges.org. Data as of 2007.

# INTERNATIONAL FINANCIAL REPORTING
## Earlier Impediments to Foreign Securities Transactions

This reporting approach originated and evolved in both the United Kingdom and the United States. In turn, this Anglo-American accounting perspective had an important influence on financial reporting in most British Commonwealth countries and numerous others. The phrase **true and fair view** is central to this financial reporting approach because it expresses the notion that financial statements must reflect the underlying economic conditions experienced by the reporting firm.

Before the early 1990s—that is, before cross-border investment began to soar—the diversity of financial reporting measurement and disclosure rules used in different countries complicated global investment decisions. Even the philosophy and objective of financial reporting differed considerably between nations. Two widely divergent financial reporting approaches existed. First was a group of countries whose financial statements were intended (at least in principle) to capture and reflect the underlying economic performance of the reporting entity. Financial reporting rules in those countries were designed and selected to achieve this objective and thereby help external users make informed investment decisions. We'll call this reporting philosophy the **economic performance approach.**

Second, a large group of countries had financial rules that did not necessarily try to capture "economic reality." Instead, accounting reports in these countries simply conformed to mandated laws or detailed tax rules designed to achieve purposes such as raising tax revenues to fund government activities or stimulating capital investment. We'll call this financial reporting

**EXHIBIT 18.2**  Largest Companies in Eight Selected Industries Ranked by 2006 Revenues

| ($ in billions) | 2006 Revenues | ($ in billions) | 2006 Revenues |
|---|---|---|---|
| **Banks: Commercial and Savings** | | **Insurance: Life, Health (Stock)** | |
| 1. Citigroup, U.S. | $146.8 | 1. ING Group, Netherlands | $158.3 |
| 2. Crédit Agricole, France | 128.5 | 2. AXA, France | 139.7 |
| 3. Fortis, Belgium/Netherlands | 121.2 | 3. Assicurazioni Generali, Italy | 101.8 |
| 4. Bank of America Corp., U.S. | 117.0 | 4. Aviva, U.K. | 83.5 |
| 5. HSBC Holdings, U.K. | 115.4 | 5. Prudential, Britain | 66.1 |
| **Electronics, Electrical Equipment** | | **Motor Vehicles and Parts** | |
| 1. Siemens, Germany | 107.3 | 1. General Motors, U.S. | 207.3 |
| 2. Samsung Electronics, South Korea | 89.5 | 2. Toyota Motor, Japan | 204.7 |
| 3. Hitachi, Japan | 87.6 | 3. DaimlerChrysler, Germany | 190.2 |
| 4. Matsushita Electric Industrial, Japan | 77.9 | 4. Ford Motor, U.S. | 160.1 |
| 5. Sony, Japan | 70.9 | 5. Volkswagen, Germany | 132.3 |
| **Food and Drug Stores** | | **Petroleum Refining** | |
| 1. Carrefour, France | 99.0 | 1. Exxon Mobil, U.S. | 347.3 |
| 2. Tesco, U.K. | 80.0 | 2. Royal Dutch Shell, Netherlands | 318.8 |
| 3. Metro, Switzerland | 75.1 | 3. BP, U.K. | 274.3 |
| 4. Kroger, U.S. | 66.1 | 4. Chevron, U.S. | 200.6 |
| 5. Royal Ahold, Netherlands | 56.9 | 5. ConocoPhillips, U.S. | 172.5 |
| **Food Consumer Products** | | **Telecommunications** | |
| 1. Nestlé, Switzerland | 79.9 | 1. Verizon Communications, U.S. | 93.2 |
| 2. Unilever, U.K./Netherlands | 51.0 | 2. Nippon Telegraph & Telephone, Japan | 92.0 |
| 3. PepsiCo, U.S. | 35.1 | 3. Deutsche Telekom, Germany | 77.0 |
| 4. Sara Lee, U.S. | 18.5 | 4. Telefónica, Spain | 66.4 |
| 5. Groupe Danone, France | 17.7 | 5. France Télécom, France | 65.9 |

Source: *Fortune 2007 Global 500*, http://money.cnn.com/maganzines/fortune/global500/2007/industries, January 15, 2008. Reprinted with permission of *Fortune*.

grouping the **commercial and tax law approach.** Because this latter approach was widespread, investors reading foreign financial statements were frequently confronted with unfamiliar reporting rules, unique tax-driven financial statement items, and country-specific nuances. Happily, this confusing array of cross-border financial reporting options has been greatly simplified in recent years. Indeed, this simplification continues at a rapid rate as the economic performance approach becomes widespread. In the next section, we outline this important transformation and explain why it happened.

## Increased Predominance of the Economic Performance Approach

The difference in financial reporting standards between various foreign countries has been greatly reduced in recent years. This is remarkable because the growing complexity of societal and scientific advances often leads in the exact opposite direction—more complicated, not less complicated, decision models. So, it is important to understand the factors driving the convergence of international reporting standards and the resulting decrease in financial reporting differences across countries. To understand this convergence, it is first necessary to understand the causes for the diversity that previously prevailed in worldwide financial reporting.

Examples include France, Italy, and Belgium, where national tax laws heavily influence financial statements prepared for domestic distribution. In Germany, Japan, and Switzerland, both commercial and tax laws influence the standards. For example, to qualify for tax benefits in many countries, a company that claims expense deductions on its tax return must also include these same expenses in its published financial statements. Specifically, to obtain the extra depreciation allowed by the German tax law, a company's financial statement depreciation expense must reflect the same depreciation charges shown on the tax return. This effectively requires conformity between tax and book amounts and greatly restricts the ability of financial statements to reflect economic performance. Even as many of these countries have required IFRS, they often still require a second set of financial statements prepared under the original local rules.

## Why Do Reporting Philosophies Differ across Countries?

What factors give rise to differences among countries' financial reporting concepts and rules? Why do certain countries' statements adopt an economic performance approach while the statements in other countries merely conform to arbitrary legal formats using a commercial or tax law approach?

A country's financial reporting philosophy does not exist in a vacuum. Instead, it is designed to achieve certain goals. The objective of financial reporting evolves from the specific legal, political, and financial institutions within a country, as well as from its social customs and systems. As one example, German workers have been entitled to representation on governing boards of German firms since the early 1950s. Understandably, these labor representatives championed accounting practices that would ensure firm continuity—and thus future employment opportunities. Partially as a consequence of labor's active board participation, Germany developed ultraconservative accounting rules and dividend guidelines designed to protect companies' survival prospects and workers' jobs. So, financial reporting differences across countries often mirror societal differences.

One critically important reason for cross-country differences in financial reporting arises from differences in how companies obtain financing. In countries where the bulk of the investment capital is attracted from a broad base of external investors, these investors understandably want comprehensive data to help them select appropriate securities. So, external investors who provide capital demand a reporting system that clearly reflects the past economic performance and future prospects of potential investment opportunities. The United States, United Kingdom, and Canada are examples of this type of broad-based ownership because an exceedingly large portion of firms' capital requirements in these countries are provided by individual debt and equity investors—either through direct investments in companies or indirectly through pension plans and mutual funds. *The financial reporting environment in these countries has evolved to meet this demand for information.* The economic performance approach flourished and guided policymakers such as the SEC and FASB as they addressed new reporting issues.

By contrast, in countries such as Japan and Germany, only a small amount of firms' financing had been historically provided by individual investors. The primary capital providers in Germany were several large banks—and the government itself. The German stock market was small. Similarly, six or eight large banks provide much of the financing in Japan; in addition, firms there also raise capital from members of their associated corporate group. As a consequence, external equity financing from individual investors was also relatively unimportant in Japan. Countries such as Japan and Germany historically had just a few important capital providers who had great power—such as the ability to acquire information directly from the firm seeking capital. *Because of this concentrated power and the insignificance of the public market, the demand for economically realistic reporting standards was low.* Instead, financial reporting standards conformed to income tax rules or other commercial laws.

But sources of financing do shift over time. When this happens in a country, changes in the financial reporting environment occur as well, as we discuss in the next section.

> These loosely interconnected corporate associations are called **keiretsu.** Keiretsu members typically own shares of other members of the keiretsu; this arrangement provides a source of financing and further aligns the group's incentives toward mutual benefits. Cross-ownerships in the 20% to 30% range are not unusual in these situations.

> Traditionally, Japanese companies have been managed on behalf of their employees, not shareholders. The majority of a company's shares are likely to be held by banks and other companies for the purpose of maintaining a relationship, so there was little concern about shareholder returns and little fear of hostile takeovers. . . . [A]ccounting rules now under consideration would compel greater disclosure, making it harder for companies to sweep problems under the rug.
>
> *Source:* A. Pollack, "Japan Considers Opening the Veiled Corporate Ledger," *The New York Times,* August 5, 1997.

## Convergence of Reporting Standards across Countries

Earlier in this chapter, Figure 18.1 and Exhibit 18.1 presented data showing the surge in certain cross-border financial transactions. These data represent one facet of a phenomenon called *globalization.* "The term globalization describes the increased mobility of goods, services, labor, technology and capital throughout the world."[2] Globalization is an ongoing process that accelerated over the 1990s as telecommunications and distribution facilities grew increasingly sophisticated.

This "relaxation" of cross-border barriers in markets for goods, labor, and capital has increased international competitiveness—that is, globalization. Many firms throughout the world have accordingly sought to maintain or strengthen their market position by expanding and investing in new facilities and technologies. This expansion has made it necessary for the firms to access new and ever larger sources of capital to finance these initiatives. But in countries that used the commercial and tax law approach to financial reporting such as France, Germany, and Japan, firms faced a severe disadvantage in raising capital as globalization progressed in the mid-1990s. Foreign investors and other potential capital providers demanded transparent financial reports prepared using familiar reporting standards that reflected underlying firm economic performance. Statements based on narrow, national tax rules, which firms in these countries normally used, were deemed unsuitable. Consequently, many firms in countries whose financial reporting used the commercial and tax law approach felt compelled to provide foreign investors *supplemental* financial statements prepared using either U.S. GAAP or standards issued by the IASB called **IFRS.** The hope was that preparing their financial reports using procedures required by the home countries of potential investors would make their statements more understandable to these foreign investors. Examples include Daimler-Benz, which began issuing U.S. GAAP reports in 1996, and Hoechst, which began using IFRS for financial reporting beginning in 1995. These foreign firms apparently believed that the greater transparency and familiarity of either U.S. GAAP- or IFRS-based financial reports would help attract more capital from investors outside their home country.

> IFRS—like U.S. GAAP—also incorporate the economic performance approach to financial reporting. Statements prepared using IFRS are designed to provide a "true and fair view" of the underlying economic conditions experienced by the reporting firm.

As this trend accelerated, a two-tiered financial reporting system emerged in many countries that previously had used the commercial and tax law approach to financial reporting. In the first financial reporting tier, rigid book/tax conformity is maintained in **parent company** financial statements. The parent is an amalgamation that corresponds to the tax-paying and statutory entities comprising the firm—often (but not always) in the form of a holding company. Because the parent company statements conform to the tax law, they satisfy national legal rules. In the second financial reporting tier, separate statements directed to potential external investors are prepared. They are called **consolidated financial statements** (or **group statements** in foreign accounting terminology). The group statements include all of the firm's various operating subsidiaries. *These statements use either U.S. GAAP or IFRS to report performance. Firms hoped that these group statements—prepared using more investor-friendly and familiar rules—would facilitate access to foreign capital.*

> Consolidated financial statements were described in Chapter 16.

So, during the late 1990s, both U.S. GAAP and IFRS were widely used in an effort to make financial reports more understandable to foreign investors using this two-tiered approach.

**Rise of IFRS**   In 2001 and 2002, accounting scandals at companies such as Enron, WorldCom, HealthSouth, and Global Crossing tarnished U.S. financial reporting and consequently lowered the appeal of U.S. GAAP for some foreign firms. Many believe this tipped the scales in favor of IFRS as firms began to cope with the financial reporting demands of globalization. In June 2002, the Council of the European Union (EU) required all publicly traded EU

---

[2] Government of Canada Web site: www.gc.ca.

companies to adopt IFRS for financial reporting in consolidated statements by January 1, 2005. In the words of the European Commission:

> The Regulation will help eliminate barriers to cross-border trading in securities by ensuring that company accounts throughout the EU are more reliable and transparent and that they can be more easily compared.[3]

The Regulation affected approximately 8000 companies in the EU and dramatically enhanced the visibility of IFRS. For this reason, we describe the IASB in more detail in the next section.

## International Accounting Standards Board

The name of the IASB was the International Accounting Standards Committee (IASC) prior to its restructuring in 2001. It had begun operating on July 1, 1973, following an agreement by professional accounting organizations in Australia, Canada, France, Germany, Japan, Mexico, the Netherlands, Ireland, the United Kingdom, and the United States. The IASB's objectives follow:

> The IASB is committed to developing, in the public interest, a single set of high quality, understandable and enforceable global accounting standards that require transparent and comparable information in general purpose financial statements.
>
> In addition, the IASB cooperates with national accounting standard setters to achieve convergence in accounting standards around the world.[4]

The IASB follows an open process similar to that of the FASB. To issue a new standard, 8 of the IASB's 14 members must approve it. The standards are arranged by topic, and the IASB amends the standards as needed. For example, *International Financial Reporting Standard No. 3—Business Combinations* (*IFRS No. 3*) was originally passed in 2004 and amended in 2007. The IASB's predecessor, the IASC, issued International Accounting Standards (IAS). These standards also are numbered according to topic and can be amended by the IASB. The IASB also maintains an interpretive committee, the Financial Reporting Interpretations Committee (IFRIC), which issues IFRIC Interpretations. These interpretations are similar to Emerging Issues Task Force (EITF) Abstracts in the United States. IFRIC's predecessor under the IASC was the Standing Interpretations Committee (SIC). The predecessor standards (as amended) are still in effect, so you may see references to IAS, IFRS, SICs, and IFRICs when IASB accounting rules are discussed.

Guidelines for selecting IASB members state that the Board should not be dominated by any particular constituency or regional interest. As of December 2007, nine different countries were represented on the board. Compared to U.S. GAAP, existing IASB standards allow firms more latitude. IFRS often permit different accounting treatments for similar economic events. One of these treatments is the **benchmark treatment,** and other reporting approaches are the **allowed alternative treatment.** Use of *either* treatment complies with IFRS. Some critics contend that this latitude is a natural result of the diversity of IASB's board members and constituencies. However, efforts to converge IFRS and U.S. GAAP (to be discussed) have reduced much of this latitude.

IFRS differ from U.S. GAAP in another important way—the level of detail they encompass. IFRS frequently follow a more generalized overview approach than do U.S. GAAP counterpart standards. This difference in the level of standard-setting detail has generated a strong debate

---

[3] European Commission Press Release, June 7, 2002.

[4] International Accounting Standards Board Web site, www.iasb.org/About + Us/About + IASB.

about which of the two approaches is preferable. Critics of the IASB approach contend that IFRS are so general and their guidance is so ambiguous that firm managers have excessive latitude in choosing reporting methods. This latitude makes it easier for them to evade debt covenant restrictions, realize bonus targets, reach earnings goals, and/or achieve other contracting incentives. Critics of IFRS contend that because U.S. GAAP contains more detailed rules and implementation guidance, similar transactions tend to result in more similar accounting treatments. Some accountants view IFRS standards as less mature and therefore have allowed less opportunity for interpretive guidance.

Supporters of the IASB approach counter that IFRS are built on broad principles and are not narrowly defined, detailed rules such as those of U.S. GAAP. They further assert that under a broad principles approach, the standard's financial reporting objective is made clear. This leads to closer conformity between the financial statement numbers and the underlying economic performance. By contrast, they argue that narrow U.S. GAAP rules allow managers to invent "loopholes" that conform to the letter of the standard but simultaneously violate its spirit. These critics point to examples like Enron's use of off-balance sheet special purpose entities (SPEs) to hide corporate liabilities. Provided that certain narrow guidelines were satisfied, U.S. GAAP did not require consolidation of SPEs, thereby allowing Enron to keep real corporate liabilities off the consolidated balance sheet.[5] The numerous other financial reporting irregularities and abuses in the United States during 2001–2002 added credibility to this argument.

> Chapters 8 and 16 discuss SPEs.

In response to concerns about U.S. GAAP being too rules driven, both the SEC and FASB issued reports on *principles-based* (or *objectives-oriented*) standards in the United States.[6] The reports suggested that most existing U.S. GAAP pronouncements are based on principles but that the principles being followed are not always clear. In addition, the reports suggested that pronouncements (and subsequent interpretations from numerous organizations) provide too much detailed guidance and too many scope exceptions. Following the recommendations in these reports, new FASB pronouncements attempt to:

> An IASB interpretation succinctly outlines conditions that identify when SPEs are controlled by the parent and thus require consolidation. Following this IASB guideline would have precluded Enron from keeping these liabilities off-balance sheet.
>
> See SIC-12, "Consolidation—Special Purpose Entities," IASB, June 1998.

1. Clearly identify the accounting objective.

2. Give the scope of the pronouncement.

3. Highlight and explain important terminology.

4. Explain the accounting principle(s) being applied.

5. Avoid bright-line rules.

6. Provide enough implementation guidance for consistent application.[7]

In addition, the FASB and IASB have undertaken a series of activities designed to "further the goal of convergence of U.S. GAAP with International Financial Reporting Standards." In 2002, the FASB and the IASB reached an agreement to strive for high-quality "compatible" standards.[8] They agreed to undertake short-term projects to eliminate minor differences and to conduct long-term coordinated or joint projects to address major accounting issues. As part

---

[5] This loophole is now mostly closed in U.S. GAAP. See "Consolidation of Variable Interest Entities," *FASB Interpretation No. 46* (Norwalk, CT: FASB, 2003).)

[6] See FASB, "Proposal: Principles-Based Approach to U.S. Standard Setting," October 21, 2002; and Securities Exchange Commission, "Study Pursuant to Section 108(d) of the Sarbanes-Oxley Act of 2002 on the Adoption by the United States Financial Reporting System of a Principles-Based Accounting System," July 2003.

[7] See FASB, "On the Road to an Objectives-Oriented Accounting System," *The FASB Report*, August 31, 2004, http://72.3.243.42/articles&reports/on_the_road_article_tfr_aug_2004.pdf, January 16, 2008.

[8] See FASB, "Memorandum of Understanding—The Norwalk Agreement," September 2002, http://www.fasb.org/news/memorandum.pdf.

of short-term convergence, the FASB made changes to the accounting for inventory, asset exchanges, and accounting changes.[9] After conducting a long-term joint project, in 2007, each Board issued a standard on business combinations.[10] Interestingly, the standards are not identical, and the accounting differs in a few areas. Therefore, we should not interpret "compatible" as "identical." In 2006, the Boards extended their agreement and outlined plans through 2008.[11] Short-term coordinated and joint projects include impairment, investment properties, and segment reporting. Long-term projects include revenue recognition, postretirement benefits, financial instruments, derecognition, and leases. We expect that these convergence efforts will continue to narrow the differences between IFRS and U.S. GAAP.

## Some Differences between U.S. GAAP and IFRS

As the previous section indicated, both the FASB and IASB are engaged in efforts to converge U.S. GAAP and IFRS. But as this book goes to press, numerous differences still exist. Several examples follow.

- *Long-lived asset revaluations.* U.S. GAAP specifies that long-lived assets be measured at original cost minus both accumulated depreciation and impairment loss (if any). Under IFRS, an allowed alternative treatment permits firms to revalue property, plant and equipment upward if its replacement cost has increased above original cost.[12]

- *Reversal of impairment losses.* Under U.S. GAAP, once an impairment loss has been recognized on either long-lived tangible assets, intangible assets, or goodwill, subsequent reversal of the previously recognized impairment loss is prohibited, as discussed in Chapters 10 and 16. IFRS permits reversals of impairment losses.[13]

- *Joint ventures.* Under U.S. GAAP, if a joint venturer does not own more than 50% of a venture, it accounts for its investment using the equity method, as discussed in Chapters 11 and 16. Under IFRS, the benchmark treatment requires a venturer to report its interest in a jointly controlled entity using proportionate consolidation.[14] This means that if the venturer owns a 50% interest in the entity, the venturer's balance sheet and income statement should include 50% of the entity's assets, liabilities, revenues, and expenses. But an allowed alternative treatment under *IAS 31* is to use the equity method—as in U.S. GAAP.[15]

- *Research and development (R&D).* Under U.S. GAAP, R&D expenditures are charged to expense in the period they are made. Under IFRS, separate rules apply to the "research phase" and the "development phase." *IAS 38* expenses research as incurred, just as U.S.

[9] See "Inventory Costs—An Amendment of *ARB No. 43, Chapter 4,*" *Statement of Financial Accounting Standards (SFAS) No. 151* (Norwalk, CT: FASB, 2004); "Exchanges of Productive Assets—An Amendment of *APB Opinion No. 29,*" *SFAS No. 153* (Norwalk, CT: FASB, 2004); and "Accounting Changes and Error Corrections—A Replacement of *APB Opinion No. 20* and *FASB Statement No. 3,*" *SFAS No. 154* (Norwalk, CT: FASB, 2005).

[10] See "Business Combinations," *SFAS No. 141 (revised 2007)* (Norwalk, CT: FASB, 2007) and "Business Combinations," *IFRS 3 (revised 2007)* (London: IASB, 2007). *SFAS No. 141* also is a good example of how the FASB has changed its standards to clearly identify and explain the objective, key terminology, measurement principles, and accounting (see the earlier discussion on principles-based standards).

[11] See Financial Accounting Standards Board, "A Roadmap for Convergence between IFRSs and US GAAP—2006–2008—Memorandum of Understanding between the FASB and the IASB," 2006, http://www.fasb.org/intl/mou_02-27-06.pdf, January 20, 2008.

[12] "Property, Plant and Equipment," *International Accounting Standard (IAS) 16* (revised 2003) (London: IASB, 2003), paras. 29–40.

[13] "Impairment of Assets," *IAS 36* (London: IASB, 2004). paras. 94–112. However, reversals of impairment losses for goodwill are allowed only under exceptional circumstances (para. 109).

[14] "Financial Reporting of Interests in Joint Ventures," *IAS 31* (revised 2003) (London: IASB, 2003), paras. 25–31.

[15] Ibid., paras. 32–33.

GAAP does. However, *IAS 38* allows development phase expenditures to be capitalized if technical feasibility and other criteria demonstrating value creation are attained.[16]

- *Capitalized interest.* U.S. GAAP requires capitalization of interest incurred on borrowed funds during construction of assets for a firm's own use or during construction of assets intended for sale or lease, as described in Chapter 10. Under IFRS, the benchmark treatment is to recognize all interest costs as an expense in the period they are incurred. However, interest capitalization is an allowed alternative treatment for "qualifying assets," similar to the U.S. GAAP rules.[17]

The continuing existence of such differences complicates comparisons between companies using U.S. GAAP and competitors using IFRS.[18]

## Coping with Reporting Differences That Persist

How should regulators such as the Securities and Exchange Commission respond to the remaining diversity in financial reporting requirements that persists across countries? What information requirements should the securities regulatory commission in Country A impose if a firm from Country B wishes to sell securities in Country A?

Regulatory commission(s) in a host country can use at least four different approaches to deal with foreign issuers of securities:

1. Compel foreign issuers to use its reporting rules.
2. Create a bilateral arrangement with a particular foreign country to accept financial statements prepared using that foreign country's financial reporting principles.
3. Allow every foreign issuer to use its own financial reporting rules without a requirement to reconcile to the host's GAAP.
4. Require foreign issuers to use IFRS.

We next examine each of these alternatives.

### Foreign Issuers Use Host Country Financial Reporting Rules

Until 2007, the U.S. SEC required *all* foreign companies that wish to have securities traded on U.S. exchanges to reconcile their own reporting methods to U.S. GAAP. The SEC mandates this reconciliation on Form 20-F. *In 2007, the reconciliation requirement was eliminated for firms using IFRS as issued by the IASB (see below).* Cadbury Schweppes—a large United Kingdom (U.K.)-headquartered producer of beverages and confectionery products—provided the reconciliation in Exhibit 18.3. The disclosure is designed for the convenience of U.S. financial statement readers since it reconciles Cadbury Schweppes' financial results under IFRS to what those numbers would have been under U.S. GAAP. Form 20-F provides U.S. investors with income statement, balance sheet, and other numbers computed using familiar U.S. rules. This allows investors to evaluate the performance of foreign issuers relative to U.S. companies using a common reporting basis—U.S. GAAP. However, this reconciliation is controversial from two perspectives.

---

[16] "Intangible Assets," *IAS 38* (revised 2004) (London: IASB, 2004), paras. 39–52.

[17] "Borrowing Costs," *IAS 23* (revised 1993) (London: IASB, 1993), paras. 7–18.

[18] As part of the convergence project, the IASB has amended rules or issued an exposure draft to eliminate the main differences for two of the above issues. An IASB exposure draft would require the equity method for joint ventures, and a 2007 revision to *IAS 23* requires firms to capitalize interest on qualifying assets. Firms are not required to adopt this change until 2009.

### EXHIBIT 18.3 — Cadbury Schweppes

**Edited Excerpts from the 2006 Form 20-F Reconciliation to U.S. GAAP Summary of Differences between IFRS and U.S. Generally Accepted Accounting Principles**

**Effects on Profit of Differences between IFRS and U.S. GAAP**

| (£ in millions) | 2006 | 2005 | 2004 |
|---|---|---|---|
| Profit for the period (under IFRS) | £1,165 | £776 | £547 |
| Attributable to minority interests | 4 | (11) | (22) |
| Profit for the period attributable to equity holders of the parent | 1,169 | 765 | 525 |
| U.S. GAAP adjustments: | | | |
|   Intangible amortisation | (15) | (22) | (26) |
|   Restructuring | 5 | — | (24) |
|   Interest capitalised | 10 | 8 | 7 |
|   Depreciation of capitalised interest | (4) | (4) | (3) |
|   Depreciation of property, plant and equipment | 1 | — | — |
|   Retirement benefits | (35) | (55) | (19) |
|   Disposal gain adjustments | (82) | (3) | — |
|   Derivatives | (3) | 24 | 15 |
|   Employee share arrangements | (9) | (24) | 18 |
|   Deconsolidation of variable interest entity | — | (9) | 17 |
|   Gain on sale and leaseback of land and building | (15) | — | — |
|   Other | (3) | — | — |
|   Taxation | 15 | (76) | (26) |
| Net income (under U.S. GAAP) before cumulative effect of change in accounting principle | 1,034 | 604 | 484 |
| Cumulative effect of change in accounting principle, net of tax | — | (19) | — |
| Net income (under U.S. GAAP) | £1,034 | £585 | £484 |

One controversy involves competitive disadvantages that the reconciliation may impose on U.S. markets; the second concerns whether the reconciliation really overcomes differences between U.S. and foreign GAAP.

U.S. stock exchanges contend that the Form 20-F reconciliation creates competitive disadvantages because it is costly for foreign firms to reconcile their statements to U.S. GAAP. The result, the exchanges contend, is that burdensome disclosure requirements make foreign issuers reluctant to list their securities on U.S. exchanges. To avoid this burden, some firms simply forgo selling their securities in the United States, the exchanges assert. As a consequence, a dual loss occurs—U.S. exchanges lose the business of listing foreign issues, and the cost of buying foreign securities is higher for U.S. investors because they must buy them abroad.

Some evidence supports the exchanges' position. Prior to October 1983, foreign firms could trade their shares on the National Association of Securities Dealers Automated Quotations (NASDAQ) system without registering with the SEC, nor did they have to reconcile their accounting to U.S. GAAP. After this date, registration became mandatory, and the number of foreign securities traded on NASDAQ declined from 294 to 213 over the ensuing eight years.[19]

---

[19] F. R. Edwards, "Listing of Foreign Securities on U.S. Exchanges," *Journal of Applied Corporate Finance*, Winter 1993, pp. 28–36.

This decline occurred despite the tremendous *increase* in U.S. investors' purchases of foreign securities over these years.

The second problem with the Form 20-F reconciliation is that even after a foreign company reconciles its numbers to U.S. GAAP, the information it provides may still not be truly comparable to the information provided by U.S. firms. The reason is that SEC rules do not require foreign firms to prepare complete financial statements on a U.S. GAAP basis. It requires only that Form 20-F contain a *reconciliation* between the firm's home-country financial statements and U.S. GAAP. This is clear in Exhibit 18.3, Cadbury Schweppes' disclosure of its income statement adjustments necessary to arrive at U.S. GAAP income. Because no "finalized" statement in U.S. GAAP format is provided, it is not straightforward for U.S. investors to reconstruct a multistep income statement that identifies categories such as gross margin that may be useful for financial analysis. Cadbury-Schweppes provided additional footnotes (not shown), but the burden of reconstructing U.S. GAAP format statements falls on the analyst.

## Making Bilateral Multijurisdictional Agreements

Another method for dealing with international financial reporting diversity is "multijurisdictional disclosure," a procedure followed to an extent between Canada and the United States. Under this procedure, the U.S. SEC accepts for registration purposes the Canadian GAAP statements of a Canadian firm seeking to issue debt or preferred stock. The agreement does not cover other equity issues such as common stock.

The firm issuing financial statements benefits because it avoids the cost of reformulating its statements into another country's GAAP, but statement users must be knowledgeable about the financial reporting standards of *both* Canada and the United States. This cost is tempered by the fact that reporting methods in Canada and the United States are somewhat similar. Indeed, the multijurisdictional disclosure approach seems feasible only between countries with broadly similar accounting measurement and disclosure standards.

## Allowing Foreign Issuer's Reporting Standards to Be Used

The third approach for coping with international reporting diversity is for a host country to allow foreign firms to use the financial reporting rules of their own country. The host country could allow Mexican firms to report their results using Mexican accounting principles, Indian firms could report their results using Indian accounting principles, and so on. This approach imposes no costs on the reporting firm; however, it does place tremendous burdens on analysts in the host country who need to be knowledgeable about a wide range of foreign financial reporting practices.

## Using IFRS

The International Organization of Securities Commissions (IOSCO) is an association of 188 national securities regulators from throughout the world based in Madrid, Spain. One of the organization's objectives is "to promote high standards of regulation in order to maintain just, efficient and sound markets."[20] In the 1990s, IOSCO stated that it would consider recognizing IASB standards for cross-border registrations if IASB developed a set of acceptable fundamental, or core, financial reporting standards. These core standards were completed in 1998. IOSCO then evaluated their suitability and issued a press release on May 17, 2000. The release recommended that IOSCO members permit use of the core standards "as supplemented by reconciliation, disclosure and interpretation where necessary...."

---

[20] IOSCO Web site, www.iosco.org.

This qualified acceptance gives individual countries' securities commissions the following choices in cross-border registrations:

1. The statements prepared using IFRS can be accepted without adjustment.
2. The IFRS must be reconciled to local GAAP.
3. Supplemental disclosures that contain more information than IFRS must be provided.
4. Certain accounting treatments may be disallowed.

While the IOSCO endorsement of IFRS left considerable discretion regarding their utilization in cross-country filings, it did stimulate further efforts toward international convergence of financial reporting standards.

As stated earlier, the EU began requiring the use of IFRS in 2005. At the end of 2007, approximately 100 countries around the world required or allowed IFRS.[21] Australia has taken actions to make its national standards the same as IFRS. Canada and Korea expect to adopt IFRS in 2011. Other countries, such as Japan and India, expect to converge their national standards to IFRS by 2011.[22]

In 2005, the SEC outlined a "roadmap" for eliminating the reconciliation requirement for foreign registrants using IFRS.[23] The roadmap suggested that the following conditions had to be present for the elimination:

1. An independent IASB.
2. High-quality IFRS.
3. Appropriate education and training in IFRS.
4. Support of IFRS by preparers, auditors, and investors.
5. Appropriate internal controls to ensure proper application of IFRS.
6. High-quality auditing.
7. Active regulatory oversight.

After reviewing IFRS–based filings (with Form 20-F reconciliations) for 2005 and 2006, the SEC issued a proposal to eliminate Form 20-F.[24] Proponents of the proposal argued that the roadmap conditions had been met and that Form 20-F did not serve a useful purpose for IFRS-based financial statements.[25] However, opponents held that convergence between U.S. GAAP and IFRS is insufficient, regulatory oversight is not effective, and Form 20-F provides useful information. Some opponents also believe that the SEC acceptance of the current IASB standards could stall convergence efforts. After considering the arguments for and against the proposal, the SEC dropped the reconciliation requirement for financial years ending after November 15, 2007 for financial statements prepared using IFRS *as issued by the IASB*.[26]

---

[21] See SEC, "Acceptance from Foreign Private Issuers of Financial Statements Prepared in Accordance with International Financial Reporting Standards without Reconciliation to U.S. GAAP," *Release No. 33-8879,* December 21, 2007, p. 6. http://www.sec.gov/rules/final/2008/33-8879fr.pdf.

[22] See Deloitte, "IFRSs in Your Pocket 2007" (Deloitte, 2007), www.iasplus.com, p. 22; and KPMG, "IFRS Baseline—Participant Material" (KPMG, 2008), p. 174.

[23] See D. Nicolaisen, "Statement by SEC Staff: A Securities Regulator Looks at Convergence," 2005, http://www.sec.gov/news/speech/spch040605dtn.htm, January 22, 2008.

[24] See SEC, "Acceptance from Foreign Private Issuers of Financial Statements Prepared in Accordance with International Financial Reporting Standards without Reconciliation to U.S. GAAP—Proposed Rule," *Release No. 33-8818,* July 11, 2007. http://www.sec.gov/rules/proposed/2007/33-8818.pdf.

[25] See SEC, *Release No. 33-8879,* p. 8.

[26] Ibid., p. 2.

The phrase "as issued by the IASB" is important. Some countries may not adopt all provisions of IASB standards. For example, the EU did not adopt certain provisions related to hedge accounting in *IAS 39*, "Financial Instruments: Recognition and Measurement."[27] These "carve-outs" have primarily affected financial institutions in Europe. In future cases, such an exception would require firms to file Form 20-F. However, the rule granted temporary relief for the first two years of filings for EU firms using this carve-out.[28]

As noted, one condition for eliminating Form 20-F is active regulatory oversight of IFRS application. The SEC believes that an adequate infrastructure exists to ensure consistent and accurate applications of IFRS around the world.[29] IOSCO, of which the SEC is a member, has established a database for sharing regulator issues regarding the application of IFRS. In addition, the SEC and the Committee of European Securities Regulators (CESR), which is responsible for monitoring the application of IFRS in the EU, consult with one another to achieve consistent enforcement. We will have to wait over the next few years to see whether the SEC's contention of an adequate infrastructure is warranted.

Soon after the SEC released its proposal to eliminate Form 20-F, it issued a Concept Release to allow U.S. firms the option of using IFRS.[30] The Concept Release suggested that some U.S. firms may wish to use IFRS when many firms in their industry are doing so or if they are preparing IFRS statements for the majority of its subsidiaries to comply with local regulations.[31] As this book goes to press, we do not know the outcome of the SEC's deliberations on this issue. However, the FASB and many of the large CPA firms have expressed concerns about allowing an IFRS option for U.S. issuers. Instead, many comment letters suggest that the SEC establish a timeline for moving to an improved version of IFRS, which is similar to the approach used in Canada.[32] A timeline would provide goals and benchmarks for educators, licensing boards, the U.S. Congress, auditors, preparers, and investors.

**Several methods exist for coping with diverse international financial reporting standards. Existing U.S. rules require foreign registrants to reconcile their accounting to U.S. GAAP. But the emerging "front-runner" approach for overcoming reporting differences is a movement to an internationally consistent set of reporting principles developed by the IASB. In 2007, the SEC began accepting financial statements prepared using IFRS as issued by the IASB. Also, the SEC has issued a Concept Release that would allow *U.S. issuers* to use IFRS.**

## INFLATION ACCOUNTING

Inflation—a decline in the purchasing power of a country's currency—complicates analyzing international financial reports. When inflation is high, historical cost-based financial statements are misleading or totally irrelevant. Financial reporting standards in countries with high rates of inflation, for example, Mexico, mandate some form of **inflation accounting** for both tax and financial statement reporting. Mexican GAAP requires two forms of inflation accounting: (1) specific price-change adjustments, and (2) general price-level adjustment. This section explains and illustrates each of these inflation accounting approaches.

---

[27] EU approval of IASB standards is not automatic. Several EU committees, the European Commission, and a Committee of the European Parliament must endorse the standards. See Deloitte, p. 18 for more detail on the process.

[28] See SEC, *Release No. 33-8879*, p. 36.

[29] Ibid., p. 26.

[30] See SEC, "Concept Release on Allowing U.S. Issuers to Prepare Financial Statements in Accordance with International Financial Reporting Standards (Corrected)," *Release No. 33-8831* (Washington, DC: SEC, August 7, 2007).

[31] Ibid., p. 12.

[32] See, for example, FASB, "Comment Letter on File Number S7-20-07," November 7, 2007; and KPMG, "Comment Letter on File Number S7-20-07," November 9, 2007.

Not all prices change at the same rate. During periods of inflation, it is not unusual for the prices of some goods and services to actually fall and move in the opposite direction of prices in general. Let's illustrate using U.S. data. Between 2001 and 2006, the general level of prices as measured by the gross domestic product (GDP) implicit price deflator *increased* by 14%. Over this same period, the average price level for computers *fell* by 56%. This illustrates that the *direction* of price change sometimes differs among economic sectors. Furthermore, the *rate* of price change can also differ across items. For example, the producer price index (PPI) for commodities rose from a 2001 level of 134.2 to 164.7 in 2006, an increase of 23%; over the same period, the PPI for natural gas went from 171.8 to 280.3, an increase of 63%. Thus, the rate of increase for the natural gas sector was 2.7 times the rate of increase for all commodities.

These examples illustrate that significant differences are likely to arise between *average* rates of inflation for the economy as a whole and *specific* rates of price change for a given firm. Diversity in rates of price changes generates controversy regarding the appropriate method for reflecting economic activity in these circumstances. Some believe that adjustments for changing prices should be based on the specific level of costs and prices experienced by each individual firm. This approach is called **current cost accounting.** The rationale for the current cost approach is that because each firm is unique, its own unique level of costs and prices should be reflected in its accounts.

Others believe that adjustments for changing prices should be based on the general rate of inflation experienced in the economy as a whole. According to those who hold this view, inflation adjustments would be derived from broad indices of overall price changes, such as the consumer price index (CPI). This method of adjusting for inflation is called **general price-level accounting.**

We'll first explain and illustrate current cost accounting and then do the same for general price-level accounting.

## Current Cost Accounting

*Current cost* refers to the market price that an individual firm would have to pay to replace the specific assets it owns. Current cost accounting (discussed briefly in Chapter 9, which contrasted last-in, first-out [LIFO] and first-in, first-out [FIFO]) is designed to accomplish the following two objectives: (1) to reflect all nonmonetary assets such as inventory, buildings, and equipment at their current replacement cost as of the balance sheet date and (2) to differentiate between (a) current cost income from continuing operations and (b) increases or decreases in current cost amounts (also called *holding gains* or *inventory profits*).

> Remember that current cost accounting for inventories and long-lived assets is a departure from historical cost and is not allowed under U.S. GAAP.

These objectives are accomplished by first periodically increasing or decreasing the balance sheet asset carrying amount as current cost changes. Then, as the asset is sold or used up, this current cost carrying amount is written off the books and matched against the revenues from sales. These steps are illustrated in simplified form by the following example.

---

A firm purchases a unit of inventory for $100 at the beginning of 2008. The asset's current cost increases by $15 in 2008, and it is sold for $180 on January 1, 2009.

---

Exhibit 18.4 illustrates income statements and inventory carrying amounts for this example.

The way to treat increases in current cost such as the $15 is controversial. Are the increases to be included in net income? Alternatively, are they a direct (nonincome) equity increase?

---

**EXHIBIT 18.4**   **Current Cost Versus Historical Cost**

**Income Statements and Inventory Carrying Amounts**

|  | 2008 | 2009 | Total |
|---|---|---|---|
| **Current Cost** |  |  |  |
| Sales revenues | — | $180 | $180 |
| Current cost of goods sold | — | 115* | 115 |
| Current cost income from continuing operations | — | 65 | 65 |
| Unrealized increase in current cost amount (or holding gain) | $ 15 | — | 15 |
| Change in owners' equity | $ 15 | $ 65 | $ 80 |
| Inventory carrying amount (end of year) | $115* | — |  |
| **Historical Cost** |  |  |  |
| Sales revenues | — | $180 | $180 |
| Historical cost of goods sold | — | 100 | 100 |
| Total historical cost income | — | $ 80 | $ 80 |
| Inventory carrying amount (end of year) | $100 | — | — |

---

\* ($100 + $15)

If the firm wishes to maintain start-of-period equity capital expressed in nominal dollars, the increase is included in net income. However, if the firm wants to maintain start-of-period equity expressed in dollars of physical productive capacity, the $15 increase in current cost is not income—that is, it is a direct credit to owners' equity.[33]

Regardless of whether increases in current cost are part of net income or as a (nonincome) direct credit to owners' equity, the cumulative change in owners' equity under the current cost approach for the two years combined—$80 in this case—equals the *cumulative* equity change under the historical cost approach. However, although the total equity change is the same, the *timing* of equity change recognition and the *classification* of the equity change by causes differ for the current and historical cost approaches.

Current cost income differentiates between operating profits and holding gains. In the example, $15 of the total $80 change in equity is attributable to increases in current cost amounts; these increases are recognized as they occur by increasing the inventory carrying amount. Assuming that the increase is considered to be a direct credit to owners' equity, the accounting entry to recognize the inventory carrying amount change is:

In its 2006 annual report, Teléfonos de México S.A. (Telmex) describes its current cost adjustment process for domestic origin nonmonetary assets as follows:

> The appraised value of land, buildings and other fixed assets of Mexican origin at December 31, 1996, and the cost of subsequent additions to such assets are restated based on the NCPI.

Prior to 1997, Mexican accounting required appraisals of nonmonetary assets. But since January 1, 1997, the previous appraised values can be updated by applying the Mexican national consumer price index (NCPI) to the December 31, 1996 appraisal amounts. *In accordance with Mexican FRS, the restatement debit or credit offset is included in Other accumulated comprehensive income, a component of stockholders' equity.*

| | | |
|---|---|---|
| **DR** Inventory ................................................. | $15 | |
|     **CR** Owners' equity—Unrealized increase in current cost amount ..................................... | | $15 |

---

[33] For a simple overview of different capital maintenance concepts, see L. Revsine, "A Capital Maintenance Approach to Income Measurement," *The Accounting Review,* April 1981, pp. 383–89. Current cost is not GAAP in the United States. If it were, the direct credit to owners' equity would be a part of accumulated other comprehensive income, which was discussed in Chapter 2.

When the sale is made in 2009, the new inventory carrying amount ($115) is matched against the $180 selling price to yield the $65 current cost income from continuing operations shown in Exhibit 18.4. By contrast, historical cost procedures recognize no equity change as input costs increase. Instead, equity increases are deferred until the sale occurs in 2009. At that time, historical cost accounting reports the equity change as one lump-sum number ($80) and does not break this number into separate operating profit and holding gain components.

The failure of historical cost accounting to differentiate between operating profits and holding gains is a serious limitation of traditional accounting. Proponents of current cost accounting argue that the $80 profit number reported under historical cost accounting provides a misleading picture of current operating efficiency because it seems to imply that the spread between sales price and cost is $80. Statement readers might infer that each *future* sale would also generate an $80 margin, but this is incorrect. Because the current spread between selling price and replacement cost is only $65 ($180 − $115), current cost advocates contend that the $65 figure provides the better measure of existing *operating* efficiency and is also the proper starting point for analysts to use in developing estimates of future per unit net operating cash inflows. Furthermore, the $15 difference between the $65 current cost operating profit and $80 total historical cost income is attributable to cost increases over the period that the inventory was held. These holding gains, it is argued, may or may not be sustainable, so they should be disclosed as a separate item to avoid unwarranted inferences. ***Because historical cost does not separately disclose operating profits and holding gains, critics claim that it obscures different elements of total profitability that may have different patterns of sustainability.***

LIFO inventory accounting represents an attempt to separate operating profits from holding gains within the framework of the historical cost model. As discussed in Chapter 9, this separation is not achieved when LIFO dipping occurs because reported LIFO profit includes both current cost operating profits *and* realized holding gains. Furthermore, during periods of rising input costs, the LIFO inventory carrying amount can be far below the current economic cost of the assets that are tied up in inventory. Consequently, traditionally computed ratios (e.g., return on assets) will tend to be overstated because of the understatement of the denominator. A further distortion of return ratios exists when LIFO dipping occurs because the numerator—income—is inflated by the realized holding gains. So, in summary, LIFO doesn't reliably approximate current cost accounting numbers.

Over the 1979–1985 period, U.S. companies with inventories plus property, plant and equipment totaling more than $125 million were required to disclose certain supplementary information prepared on a current cost basis.[34] Exhibit 18.5 presents a representative current cost disclosure based on an actual annual report. For most companies, 1985 represents the latest disclosure because these disclosures were made voluntary in 1986.[35]

Under the *SFAS No. 33* current cost rules, the only balance sheet accounts adjusted were nonmonetary assets such as inventory, buildings, and equipment. (Monetary and nonmonetary

---

[34] "Financial Reporting and Changing Prices," *SFAS No. 33* (Stamford, CT: FASB, 1979).

[35] See "Financial Reporting and Changing Prices," *SFAS No. 89* (Stamford, CT: FASB, 1986). The ostensible reason for altering the disclosure requirement was that because inflation rates had abated, the disclosures were no longer essential. An unexpressed—but more plausible—explanation was that managers of capital-intensive firms opposed the disclosures because they generated adverse reactions directed against managers by shareholders. For example, it is difficult to justify managerial bonuses tied to reported income when the supplemental disclosure indicated that losses were being incurred on a current cost basis. The simplest financial reporting remedy for avoiding this conflict is to dispense with the disclosure altogether. Managers of firms aggressively lobbied the FASB to rescind *SFAS No. 33*. One explanation for the FASB's acquiescence to such efforts is developed in L. Revsine, "The Selective Financial Misrepresentation Hypothesis," *Accounting Horizons*, December 1991, pp. 16–27.

## EXHIBIT 18.5 Crews Manufacturing (CM)

**2008 Annual Report Supplemental Disclosure Year Ended December 31, 2008 Data on Changing Prices**

| ($ in millions) | At Historical Cost— Nominal Dollars | Adjusted for Changes in Specific Prices Current Cost— Nominal Dollars |
|---|---|---|
| **Summary statement of income adjusted for changing prices** | | |
| Net sales | $9,003 | $9,003 |
| Cost of sales | 6,252 ① | 6,281 ② |
| Depreciation | 596 ③ | 711 ④ |
| Other operating expense—net | 1,708 | 1,708 |
| Interest expense | 292 | 292 |
| Provision for income taxes | 53 | 53 |
| Minority share of income | 27 ⑤ | 29 ⑥ |
| **Net income before unusual charges and extraordinary item** | $ 75 ⑦ | $ (71) ⑧ |
| Per share | $ 0.36 | $ (0.34) |
| **Summary balance sheet data adjusted for changing prices** | | |
| Inventories | $1,422 | $2,259 |
| Property, plant, and equipment, net of accumulated depreciation | 5,780 | 7,453 |
| CM stockholders' equity | 4,019 | 6,529 |

items are defined in more detail later in this chapter on p. 1091.) Actual market replacement costs were used wherever such data were available. When actual market replacement costs were not available, *specific price indices* that reflected cost changes for the specific asset categories being measured were employed. All monetary assets and liabilities (such as cash, receivables, and accounts payable) were reported at their face value without adjustment. In Exhibit 18.5, Crews Manufacturing (CM) displays the current cost amounts for these balance sheet categories as well as their income statement effects on cost of sales and depreciation side-by-side with the historical cost amounts. CM's historical cost income ($75 million) becomes a current cost loss ($71 million).

The CM stockholders' equity amount in Exhibit 18.5 is increased as a balancing item that results after the inventory and other assets are written up. Specifically,

| | | |
|---|---|---|
| **DR** Inventories ($2,259 − $1,422) | $ 837 | |
| **DR** Property, etc. ($7,453 − $5,780) | 1,673 | |
| **CR** Stockholders' equity ($6,529 − $4,019) | | $2,510 |

In countries such as Mexico where inflation is a continuing problem, current cost data for inventories can be determined from invoices received near the balance sheet date, suppliers' end-of-period price lists, or recently updated standard cost amounts. In all cases, the objective is to estimate the current cost that would be incurred to *replace* the actual asset in use. **Input costs that would be paid by the firm are used, not the selling prices that would be charged to customers.**

To illustrate the procedure, let's assume that a building constructed in 1993 has the following book value at December 31, 2008:

| | |
|---|---|
| Historical cost of building | $100,000,000 |
| Accumulated depreciation | 30,000,000 |
| Net book value | $ 70,000,000 |

Also assume that a construction cost index (base period 1980 = 100.0) for this type of building is available and has the following index values:*

| | |
|---|---|
| Average index value for 1993 | 246 |
| Index value for December 31, 2008 | 396 |

The estimated replacement cost of the building at December 31, 2008 would be:

| | Historical Cost Amounts | | Index Adjustment | | Estimated Current Cost Amounts |
|---|---|---|---|---|---|
| Cost of building | $100,000,000 | × | $\dfrac{396}{246}$ | = | $160,975,610 |
| Accumulated depreciation | 30,000,000 | × | $\dfrac{396}{246}$ | = | 48,292,683 |
| Net book value | $ 70,000,000 | | | | $112,682,927 |

* The measurement and use of price indices is discussed on pp. 1089–1091.

Because inventories are purchased virtually continuously, actual market prices are usually available at any date, making index adjustments rarely necessary for inventory. Land, buildings, and equipment are purchased sporadically, so actual current market costs are not always available for these items. When fixed asset market costs *are* available—for example, from used equipment dealers' price lists—these market costs are used to determine current cost balance sheet amounts. For custom-designed buildings and special purpose equipment, actual market replacement costs seldom are determinable. In these cases, **market value estimation techniques** must be used.

Market value estimation techniques may take several forms. For example, construction cost price indices by geographical area are widely available. The construction cost index value would be applied to the historical book value of buildings to yield an estimated replacement cost. Special purpose price indices for equipment are also available. These price indices are reported on both an industry basis (for example, an index specific to equipment used in the automotive industry) and by type of equipment (for example, an index for general purpose electronics equipment). Again, the index value would be multiplied by the historical book value of the equipment to obtain an estimated replacement cost. Market value estimation techniques can also be used to estimate land values. For example, real estate tax assessment data can form the basis for estimating the current cost of land.

Under *SFAS No. 33,* current cost adjustments on the income statement were usually limited to cost of goods sold and to depreciation expense. The current cost expense on the income statement was defined as the cost that prevailed at the time an asset was sold or used up in operations. These amounts were often approximated by the average change in specific prices for the year. *If current costs changed after assets were sold or used up, no retroactive adjustment was made to reflect end-of-year current costs in the income statement.*

Here's an example. Sallas Company had the following sales transactions and associated costs during 2008:

| | |
|---|---|
| Sales during the year | $3,300,000 |
| Current cost of inventory sold using current cost *at the time of sale* | 2,700,000 |
| Current cost of inventory sold using current cost *at year-end* | 2,950,000 |

The reported gross margin using current cost accounting would be:

| | |
|---|---|
| Sales revenues | $3,300,000 |
| Current cost of goods sold | 2,700,000 |
| Current cost gross margin | $ 600,000 |

The $2,950,000 *year-end* current cost of inventory sold is ignored because the objective of current costing is to reflect the margin that existed using costs and selling prices that prevailed *at the time of each sale.* Such items as sales revenues, salaries, and miscellaneous expenses are presumed to be stated at or near prevailing prices at the time that they appear on the income statement, and therefore they do not require adjustment. **Thus, the current cost income statement results in a matching of actual sales revenues with the current costs that were in effect at the time of each sale.**

By capturing the margin that was in effect at the time of each sale, current costing provides a basis for forecasting future margins and therefore future cash flows. The reasoning is based on the premise that today's *real* margin provides the best basis for estimating tomorrow's margin. The desire to capture the contemporaneous margin—or spread—between selling price and replacement cost explains why the Cost of goods sold account is not adjusted "after-the-fact" to year-end replacement cost. If an "after-the-fact" adjustment were made, actual sales prices would be "matched" with subsequent costs that were not even known when sales prices were set.

Exhibit 18.5 shows a $146 million difference ($75 million ⑦ − [$71 million ⑧]) between historical and current cost net income in 2008 for CM. Recall that conventional historical cost income has two components: (1) current cost income from continuing operations and (2) realized holding gains. So, the $71 million current cost loss means that much more than 100% of CM's 2008 historical cost income ($75 million) consisted of realized holding gains. Examining the Exhibit 18.5 income statement disclosure reveals that CM's realized holding gains (in millions) arose from three sources:

> This is easily seen by returning to Exhibit 18.4. Conventional historical cost income ($80) can be decomposed as follows:
>
> | | |
> |---|---:|
> | Current cost income from continuing operations | $65 |
> | Plus: Realized holding gains | 15 |
> | Equals: Historical cost income | $80 |

| | | |
|---|---:|---|
| Cost of goods sold difference | $ 29 | ($6,281 ② − $6,252 ①) |
| Depreciation difference | 115 | ($711 ④ − $596 ③) |
| Minority share difference* | 2 | ($29 ⑥ − $27 ⑤) |
| Realized holding gains in 1985 | $146 | |

---

\* The minority share difference arises because the current cost income from those subsidiaries with minority shareholders was apparently *higher* than the historical cost income.

---

Computing realized holding gains allows us to see the various components of CM's historical cost income number (in millions):

| | | |
|---|---:|---|
| Reported current cost loss from continuing operations | $(71) | ⑧ |
| Realized holding gains | 146 | **(Computed above)** |
| Historical cost income | $ 75 | ⑦ |

---

Over the period that the *SFAS No. 33* disclosures were required, it was not unusual for capital-intensive companies such as CM to report historical cost income while simultaneously revealing losses on a current cost basis. The frequency of these disparities fueled the criticisms directed against the traditional income determination approach of historical cost. To give some idea about the relative size of adjusted current cost earnings in relation to reported historical cost earnings, consider the Exhibit 18.6 data from the 1983 *SFAS No. 33* disclosures.

We deliberately focus on 1983 because this was a year of relatively low inflation—3.2% as measured by the CPI. Nevertheless, as noted in Exhibit 18.6, the ratio of current cost profit as a percentage of historical cost profit was only 43% across all industries. That meant that for every dollar of historical cost profit reported during 1983, 57% (1.00 − 0.43) was attributable to realized holding gains. The eight "worst off" industries (airlines, etc.) reported *losses* on a current cost basis. Consequently, no meaningful ratio value could be computed for these firms in Exhibit 18.6 because the numerator was negative.

| EXHIBIT 18.6 | Summary of SFAS No. 33 Disclosures for 1983 |
|---|---|

### Ratio of Current Cost to Historical Cost Income

| The Best Off | Current-Cost Profits as Percentage of Historical Cost | The Worst Off | Current-Cost Profits as Percentage of Historical Cost |
|---|---|---|---|
| 1. Publishing/TV | 86% | 1. Airline | Loss |
| 2. Office equipment | 85 | 2. General machinery | Loss |
| 3. Aerospace | 84 | 3. Metal and mining | Loss |
| 4. Drugs | 84 | 4. Paper | Loss |
| 5. Retailing (nonfood) | 80 | 5. Rails and trucking | Loss |
| 6. Tobacco | 77 | 6. Special machinery | Loss |
| 7. Services | 76 | 7. Steel | Loss |
| 8. Instruments | 76 | 8. Tire and rubber | Loss |
| 9. Electrical | 75 | 9. Natural resources | 38% |
| 10. Textiles | 72 | 10. Building materials | 42 |
| 11. Appliances | 72 | 11. Real estate | 47 |

**All-industry average   43%**

*Source:* Reprinted from April 30, 1984 issue of *Business Week* by special permission, Copyright © 1984 by The McGraw-Hill Companies, Inc.

Even modest rates of increase in input cost can lead to significant differences between historical cost financial statement numbers and their inflation-adjusted equivalents. The reason is that the effect of changing prices on balance sheet numbers is cumulative. An example is plant and equipment. If equipment prices are increasing at a rate of 6% per year, a piece of equipment purchased six years ago for $100,000 would have a replacement cost today of $141,852. Furthermore, this cumulative balance sheet effect ultimately affects the income statement because the "misstated" assets are depreciated or charged to cost of goods sold at their original historical cost. The following excerpt from the 2006 20-F filing of Telmex illustrates the materiality of cumulative price-change adjustments:

The Company's consolidated financial statements are prepared in accordance with Mexican financial reporting standards (Mexican FRS), which differ in certain significant respects from accounting principles generally accepted in the United States ("U.S. GAAP"). . . .

The reconciliation to U.S. GAAP does *not* include the reversal of the adjustments to the financial statements for the effects of inflation required under Mexican FRS (Bulletin B-10), because the *application of Bulletin B-10 represents a comprehensive measure of the effects of price level changes in the Mexican economy* as permitted by the SEC. [Emphasis added.]

Telmex states that its 20-F reconciliation between Mexican FRS and U.S. GAAP does not reverse the inflation adjustments required by Mexican FRS. The reason is that the inflation-adjusted numbers are deemed to be "a comprehensive measure of the effects of price level changes." In its 2006 annual report, Telmex uses inflation adjustments of 6.5% and 10.0%, respectively, for its 2005 and 2004 comparative financial information. So, even relatively modest input cost increases can—in the opinion of Telmex's management—lead to significant statement effects.

### Current Cost Disclosures and Monetary Items
During the 1970s and 1980s, current cost disclosures centered on nonmonetary assets such as inventory and equipment.

When the rate of U.S. inflation abated in the 1980s, the perceived importance of the effort to adjust nonmonetary assets diminished. With the collapse of the U.S. savings and loan industry in the mid-1980s and the difficulties experienced by many commercial banks, the focus of market value disclosures began to shift to certain types of monetary assets and liabilities. The reason for this shift is that financial institutions are regulated using accounting numbers, particularly owners' equity. These institutions are required to have a certain minimum proportion of equity, which is called **regulatory capital.** Financial assets and liabilities—loans to borrowers, customer deposits, etc.—comprise the bulk of these financial intermediaries' balance sheet amounts. Because savings and loans (S&Ls) and banks used historical cost accounting, the measure of capital used for regulatory purposes was insensitive to changes in the underlying value of these financial institutions' assets and liabilities. Consequently, it was widely believed that inadequate accounting rules were a factor in many of the S&L and bank failures.

In an effort to provide more complete information to the financial community and regulators, the FASB has required footnote disclosure of the fair value of financial institutions' items such as loans and deposits.[36] The FASB also introduced disclosure requirements for financial instruments such as long-term investments and long-term debt obligations.[37] These fair value disclosures are in the footnotes rather than in the body of the financial statements themselves. In addition, fair value data for certain investments in debt and equity securities now appear on the balance sheet itself as illustrated in Chapter 16.[38] The FASB has also issued three statements that require fair value measurements on the balance sheet for derivative instruments as discussed in Chapter 11.[39] So, there is a clear trend toward including more fair value data in U.S. GAAP financial statements.

## General Price-Level Accounting

A currency unit such as the U.S. dollar possesses value because of the goods and services that it will buy. The real amount of goods and services that can be acquired at any moment is what determines a currency's **purchasing power.**

Current costing, as we just discussed, is one way to measure purchasing power. It measures changes in the prices of the firm's specific assets and liabilities. Current costing thus captures changes in *specific purchasing power.*

**General price-level accounting,** another way to measure purchasing power, makes no attempt to measure changes in specific prices. Instead, it focuses on changes in *general purchasing power.*

The general purchasing power approach uses a **price index.** All indices are intended to price a market basket of goods and services at various points of time to determine how the price of the market basket has changed.

### Overview of Adjustment Mechanics

U.S. GAAP financial statements record the dollar amount expended or incurred at the date of the original transaction. However, because the purchasing power of these dollars changes over time, the amounts stated in original (or "nominal") dollars are not comparable. In other words, historical cost statements ignore changes in the currency's purchasing power. ***The objective of general price-level accounting is***

---

[36] "Disclosures about Fair Value of Financial Instruments," *SFAS No. 107* (Norwalk, CT: FASB, 1991).

[37] "Disclosure of Information about Financial Instruments with Off-Balance Sheet Risk and Financial Instruments with Concentrations of Credit Risk," *SFAS No. 105* (Norwalk, CT: FASB, 1990); and "Disclosure about Derivative Financial Instruments and Fair Value of Financial Instruments," *SFAS No. 119* (Norwalk, CT: FASB, 1994).

[38] "Accounting for Certain Investments in Debt and Equity Securities," *SFAS No. 115* (Norwalk, CT: FASB, 1993).

[39] "Accounting for Derivative Instruments and Hedging Activities," *SFAS No. 133;* "Accounting for Certain Derivative Instruments and Certain Hedging Activities," *SFAS No. 138;* and "Amendment of Statement 133 on Derivative Instruments and Hedging Activities," *SFAS No. 149* (Norwalk, CT: FASB, 1998, 2000, and 2003, respectively).

*to adjust all historical amounts into common purchasing power units using a broad purchasing-power index.* Here's an example. Adess Corporation owns two assets. One was acquired on January 1, 1991 and the other on January 1, 2006:

| Date | Original Transaction Amount | General Purchasing Power Index as of January 1 |
|---|---|---|
| 1991 (Asset 1) | $200,000 | 76 |
| 2006 (Asset 2) | 200,000 | 193 |
| 2008 | — | 207 |
| | $400,000 | |

The $200,000 gross book value for each asset using historical cost doesn't reflect the difference in the purchasing power of the *nominal* dollars invested in each asset. That is, the $200,000 of 1991 dollars that were expended on Asset 1 did not have the same purchasing power as the $200,000 of 2006 dollars that were expended on Asset 2, nor does the sum of these amounts have the same purchasing power as $400,000 of January 1, 2008 dollars. *To reflect changes in the purchasing power of the measuring unit between 1991 and 2008, all amounts must be restated into dollars of uniform purchasing power.* If all amounts were restated to reflect the purchasing power of the January 1, 2008 dollar, the adjustment would be:

| Asset Acquired in | Amount | | Restatement Factor | | Restated into 2008 Dollars |
|---|---|---|---|---|---|
| 1991 | $200,000 | × | $\dfrac{207}{76}$ | = | $544,737 |
| 2006 | 200,000 | × | $\dfrac{207}{193}$ | = | 214,508 |
| | | | | | $759,245 |

To understand these restated numbers, let's consider the $544,737 amount in 2008 dollars for the asset acquired in 1991. This number indicates that it would take $544,737 dollars on January 1, 2008 to have the same purchasing power that $200,000 had on January 1, 1991. Similarly, the $200,000 invested on January 1, 2006 has a purchasing-power equivalent in January 1, 2008 dollars of $214,508.

Generalizing from the example, to restate historical amounts into current purchasing power units, the nominal dollar amount is multiplied by a **restatement factor,** which is a ratio of price indices. The numerator of the ratio is the price index level of the current period, and the denominator of the ratio is the price index relating to the period of the original transaction amount. To restate 1991 dollars into what those dollars are equivalent to in 2008 purchasing power, we calculate:

$$\text{1991 Transaction amount to be restated} \times \frac{\text{2008 General purchasing power index}}{\text{1991 General purchasing power index}} = \text{2008 Purchasing power equivalent}$$

In our example, the 2008 index value is 207 and the 1991 index value is 76, so the restatement factor is 207/76 as shown.

General price-level accounting is not intended to reflect current market values of assets and liabilities. This is not surprising because the restatement factor relates to overall average purchasing power changes rather than to changes in the prices of the specific items being adjusted. The intent of general price-level accounting is simply to make historical currency amounts that are expended in different time periods comparable by adjusting all amounts to current purchasing-power dollar equivalents. In this sense, general price-level accounting does not abandon the historical cost principle. Instead, nominal dollar historical costs are simply restated into dollars of constant purchasing power.

To apply constant dollar accounting in practice, *SFAS No. 33* required firms to measure purchasing power changes by using the CPI for all urban consumers.[40] This index was selected because it is published monthly, and, unlike most other broad purchasing power indices, it is not retroactively adjusted after initial publication. This meant that the "final" CPI value was always available promptly for use in preparing annual constant dollar financial statements. Some critics argued, however, that this practical advantage of using the CPI was negated by the fact that a price index such as the CPI, which is based only on consumer purchases, doesn't necessarily measure the purchasing power changes experienced by industrial firms.

After restating financial statements to a current cost basis, Telmex then applies a general price-level (constant peso) adjustment described as follows:

> The effects of inflation on financial information are recognized in the financial statements, consequently, the amounts shown in the accompanying financial statements and in these notes are expressed in thousands of Mexican pesos with purchasing power at December 31, 2006. The December 31, 2006 weighted restatement factors applied to the financial statements for the years ended December 31, 2005 and 2004 as originally issued were 1.0648 and 1.1003. The weighted average factors considered the inflation rate and the changes in the exchange rate for each of the countries in which the Company operates. The weighted average of inflation rates and exchange rate changes was made based on the revenues obtained from each country in 2005.

This puts all years' comparative statements in pesos of constant purchasing power. Year-to-year comparisons devoid of inflation illusion can then be made.

**Overview of the Concepts**    General price-level accounting requires a clear delineation between monetary items and nonmonetary items because purchasing power changes affect each category differently. A **monetary item** is money, or a claim to receive or to pay a sum of money, which is fixed in amount. Examples include cash, accounts receivable, accounts payable, and bonds payable. What you should understand about these items is that they are stated in monetary units and that the claim or amount remains fixed even if the price level changes. By contrast, a **nonmonetary item** is not fixed in amount, and its price will likely change as the general level of prices changes. Examples of nonmonetary items include inventories, buildings, manufacturing equipment, and obligations under product warranties.

To illustrate the general concepts of constant dollar accounting, let's consider a firm that is financed entirely with equity. Suppose that its only asset is land (a nonmonetary asset), which was purchased for $1,000 on January 1, 2008. Using the basic accounting equation, the firm would appear as follows on this date:

| A | = | L | + | E |
|---|---|---|---|---|
| Land $1,000 | | | | Owners' equity $1,000 |

If we assume that the general level of prices rose by 4% during 2008 and that no transactions occurred during the year, the constant dollar basic accounting equation at the end of 2008 would reflect:

| A | = | L | + | E |
|---|---|---|---|---|
| Land $1,040 | | | | Owners' equity $1,040 |

Notice that both amounts have been restated by the ratio 104/100 to reflect December 31, 2008 general purchasing power. This means that it takes $1,040 on December 31, 2008 to have the same general purchasing power that $1,000 had on January 1, 2008. All other nonmonetary items would be adjusted similarly in preparing general price-level financial statements.

Under constant dollar accounting, the upward restatement of owners' equity is *not* considered to be income. An analogy makes it easy to understand why. Whether you express a

---

[40] *SFAS No. 33*, para. 39.

temperature at 12° Celsius or at its equivalent of 54° Fahrenheit does not change the underlying real level of the temperature. So too with the purchasing power adjustment from $1,000 January 1, 2008 dollars to $1,040 December 31, 2008 dollars. The only thing that has happened is that the measurement unit has been changed. There is no income or loss.

By contrast, when the assets held are monetary, rather than non-monetary, a gain or loss *does* occur. Let's illustrate this by assuming that the asset held on January 1, 2008 was cash rather than land. Cash, of course, is a monetary item. Because prices, on average, rose by 4% during 2008 to be in the same general purchasing-power position at the end of 2008 as it was at the beginning of 2008, the firm would have to possess a cash balance of $1,040. The reasoning is simple—it takes $1,040 end-of-year dollars to buy what $1,000 bought at the start of the year. If, however, no transactions accurred during 2008 and if the ending cash balance is still $1,000, the firm has suffered a real loss of $40 during 2008 because the purchasing power of its cash has declined. This would be reflected in the end-of-period general price-level accounting equation as:

> Net monetary assets are the difference between gross monetary assets and gross monetary liabilities. So, if a firm's only monetary items are cash of $35,000 and accounts payable of $15,000, its net monetary assets balance is $20,000. Notice that monetary liabilities generate a *gain* when price levels rise. The reason is that, by definition, the liability's dollar amount is fixed and can be paid off with dollars possessing diminished purchasing power. So, it is the *net* monetary asset or liability position of the firm that determines whether purchasing power changes result in a loss or a gain. That is, firms with a net monetary liability position (that is, an excess of gross monetary liabilities over gross monetary assets) experience purchasing-power gains from inflation.

| A | = | L | + | E | |
|---|---|---|---|---|---|
| Cash $1,000 | | | | Owners' equity | 1,040 |
| | | | | Purchasing-power loss | (40) |

When a firm holds *net* monetary assets during a period of inflation, a loss occurs because the purchasing power of the net monetary assets declines. Put somewhat differently, because monetary items are automatically expressed in end-of-period dollars, no adjustment of these items is necessary in constant dollar balance sheets; however, the implicit gain or loss that results from holding monetary items during a period of general inflation must be recognized. The Purchasing-power gain or loss account appears on the income statement and is ultimately closed to Owners' equity.[41]

> Telmex described the gain or loss from holding monetary items as follows in its 2006 annual report:
>
> The net monetary position gain included in the statements of income as part of the caption "comprehensive financing cost" represents the effect of inflation on monetary assets and liabilities.

---

[41] A loss on monetary items that is recognized while the asset carrying value is not changed might cause you to question how the balance sheet can still balance under such circumstances. The issue is best understood by considering the gain or loss on monetary items as a two-step computational process. First, when 4% inflation occurs during 2008 for the all-cash firm in the example, the following entry might be made to put all amounts into end-of-period dollars:

| **DR** | Cash .................................................... | $40 | |
|---|---|---|---|
| | **CR**   Owners' equity ...................................... | | $40 |

After this entry is made, the end-of-period general price-level accounting equation is:

| A | | = | L | + | E | |
|---|---|---|---|---|---|---|
| Cash | $1,040 | | | | Owners' equity | $1,040 |

Cash is now shown as $1,040 when, in reality, the December 31, 2008 balance is only $1,000. The difference, of course, is the purchasing-power loss. To adjust cash to the proper year-end balance, the following entry must be made:

| **DR** | Owners' equity (purchasing-power loss)....................... | $40 | |
|---|---|---|---|
| | **CR**   Cash............................................... | | $40 |

After this entry is made, the basic accounting equation shows:

| A | | = | L | + | E | |
|---|---|---|---|---|---|---|
| Cash | $1,040 | | | | Owners' equity | $1,040 |
| | | | | | Purchasing-power loss | (40) |

Although formal journal entries are seldom employed when historical cost statements are adjusted to a general price-level basis, an understanding of the hypothetical journal entries described here makes it easier to grasp the mechanics of the purchasing-power gain or loss on monetary items.

- Cross-border investing in debt and equity securities grew at a phenomenal rate in the last decade.

- Initially, the diversity of financial reporting measurement and disclosure rules required in various countries impeded the ease of engaging in international securities transactions.

- Reporting rules in some countries such as the United States, Canada, and the United Kingdom strived to reflect firms' underlying economic performance.

- But reporting rules in many other countries—Germany, France, and Japan, for example—merely complied with taxation or other statutory requirements.

- Investors in countries such as the United States were uneasy about providing capital to foreign firms whose financial statements were often difficult for them to understand.

- Globalization forced many firms in countries using a commercial or tax law approach to seek foreign capital. In turn, this has led many countries—particularly in the EU—to move to IFRS, making it easier for firms in their country to raise investment capital from abroad.

- Various mechanisms for coping with cross-country reporting diversity have evolved. In the United States, foreign issuers not using IFRS are required to reconcile their home country reporting rules to U.S. GAAP. In 2007, the SEC agreed to accept from foreign registrants financial statements prepared using IFRS as issued by the IASB.

- The FASB and the IASB are working together to converge U.S. GAAP and IFRS.

- Inflation is a serious problem in certain countries. Where this is the case, historical cost reporting becomes less meaningful, so inflation accounting is often used.

- Two methods for reflecting changing prices are current cost accounting and general price-level accounting.

- Current cost accounting measures changes in the specific purchasing power of the company for which the financial statements are being prepared.

- By contrast, general price-level accounting strives to reflect overall, average changes in purchasing power.

Allocating resources in the most efficient manner maximizes the wealth of any country. It is generally acknowledged that financial information plays an important role in efficient resource allocation.

**E18-1**

Determining why financial reporting rules differ

**Required:**

Given that both of the preceding statements are correct, why are the financial reporting rules in some countries designed to be very helpful to external individual investors (for example, in the United States and Canada) whereas in other countries (for example, in Japan and Germany), they are less helpful?

---

**E18-2**

Overcoming reporting diversity

Some analysts contend that a single, standardized set of uniform financial reporting rules that would be required for all companies in all countries would improve interfirm comparisons and enhance financial analysis.

**Required:**

Do you agree that uniform reporting across many countries would always enhance the comparability of financial data and analyses? Why or why not?

---

**E18-3**

Predicting attitude of U.S. companies toward IFRS

As the text described, IFRS allow firms to exercise more latitude than exists in U.S. GAAP.

**Required:**

1. Considering this latitude difference, what will happen when the SEC allows foreign issuers of securities in the United States to use IFRS in lieu of U.S. GAAP? What problems do you anticipate? Will there be a "level playing field" for both foreign and U.S. companies when they seek investment capital?

2. How do you think top management of U.S. companies will react to the SEC decision to allow foreign issuers to use IFRS?

---

**E18-4**

Applying current cost accounting

Highrate Company's 2008 historical cost income statement is as follows:

| | |
|---|---:|
| Sales | $20,000 |
| Cost of sales | 8,000 |
| Gross margin | 12,000 |
| Depreciation | 2,000 |
| Other operating expenses | 8,000 |
| Net income | $ 2,000 |

Highrate's management is concerned about the increase in inventory costs as well as the increasing costs of property, plant and equipment. Management believes that the current cost of inventory sold is 25% higher than its historical cost at the time of sale. In addition, if property, plant and equipment were valued at current costs, an additional $1,000 of depreciation would be recorded.

**Required:**

1. Prepare a current cost income statement for Highrate Company.

2. Assume that you are a Highrate Company shareholder. Which net income figure do you think is more useful? Why?

---

**E18-5**

Using general price-level accounting

**AICPA**
ADAPTED

The following schedule shows the average general purchasing-power index of the indicated years:

| | |
|---|---|
| 2006 | 100 |
| 2007 | 125 |
| 2008 | 150 |

Carl Corporation's plant and equipment consisted of the following totals at December 31, 2008:

| Date Acquired | Percentage Depreciated | Historical Cost |
|---|---|---|
| 2006 | 30% | $30,000 |
| 2007 | 20 | 20,000 |
| 2008 | 10 | 10,000 |
| | | $60,000 |

Depreciation is calculated at 10% per annum on a straight-line basis. A full year's depreciation is charged in the year of acquisition. There were no disposals in 2008.

**Required:**

What amount of depreciation expense should be included in a general price-level accounting income statement?

---

**Required:**

When computing purchasing-power gain or loss on net monetary items, which of the following accounts are classified as nonmonetary?

1. Receivables under capitalized leases.

2. Obligations under capitalized leases.

3. Minority interest.

4. Unamortized discount on bonds payable.

5. Long-term receivables.

6. Equity investment in unconsolidated subsidiaries.

7. Obligations under warranties.

8. Accumulated depreciation of equipment.

9. Advances to unconsolidated subsidiaries.

10. Allowance for uncollectible accounts.

11. Unamortized premium on bonds payable.

> **E18-6**
>
> Distinguishing between monetary and nonmonetary items
>
> **AICPA**
> ADAPTED

---

Lewis Company was formed on January 1, 2007. Selected balances from the historical cost balance sheet at December 31, 2007 follow:

| | |
|---|---|
| Land (purchased in 2007) | $120,000 |
| Investment in nonconvertible bonds (purchased in 2007 and expected to be held to maturity) | 60,000 |
| Long-term debt | 80,000 |

The general purchasing-power index was 100 when the debt was issued and the land and bonds were purchased: it was 110 at December 31, 2008.

**Required:**

In a general price-level accounting balance sheet at December 31, 2008, at what amounts should the land, investment, and long-term debt be shown?

> **E18-7**
>
> Applying general price-level accounting
>
> **AICPA**
> ADAPTED

---

## PROBLEMS / DISCUSSION QUESTIONS

Accounting standards vary across national boundaries. As the chapter stated, a specific country's financial reporting standards are a function of its legal environment, customs, and social objectives. In addition, the primary source of capital for companies within a country influences the country's financial reporting standards.

**Required:**

Assume that there are two countries in the world. In the first country, Equityland, companies acquire capital through individual investors, who purchase equity shares on public stock exchanges. Companies in the second country, Debtland, acquire their capital from a few large banks. Answer the following questions on the basis of your understanding of the differences in the financial reporting incentives of firms domiciled in Equityland versus Debtland.

> **P18-1**
>
> Identifying capital sources and disclosure differences

1. Who are the primary users of companies' financial reports?

2. What are the users concerned about when they assess companies' financial reports?

3. What financial ratios might financial statement users in the two countries employ when examining companies' economic performances?

4. How do the disclosure demands of Equityland financial statement users differ from those of Debtland users?

---

**P18-2**

Overcoming reporting diversity: Extraordinary items

The 2002 income statement of Portugal Telecom (PT) was prepared in accordance with Portuguese GAAP and reported the following amounts for extraordinary items and net income:

| (€ in thousands) | 2002 | 2001 | 2000 |
|---|---|---|---|
| Extraordinary items | (15,620) | 218,916 | 496,406 |
| Net income | 316,435 | (35,259) | 498,058 |

During this three-year period, some of the extraordinary items included the following:

| | |
|---|---|
| Provisions to adjust the assets and liabilities of TMN subsidiary (2002) | (50,915) |
| Gains on disposals of shares of Telefónica, the Spanish telecom company (2000, 2001, 2002) | 185,840 |
| Gain on disposal of PT Multimedia shares (2000) | 483,063 |
| Gains on disposal of PT M.com shares (2000, 2001) | 375,979 |
| Issuance of additional common stock by subsidiaries (2000, 2001) | (171,303) |
| Loss on transfer of the investment in Zip.net between two subsidiaries of Portugal Telecom (2000) | (336,097) |

**Required:**

1. Discuss whether each of the following would be reported as extraordinary under U.S. GAAP:

   a. Provisions to adjust the assets and liabilities of a subsidiary.

   b. Gains on disposal of shares of an investee.

   c. Gains or losses resulting from the issuance of additional common stock by an investee.

2. Assume that you subscribe to a global data service providing only summary financial information limited to net income, total assets, and total stockholders' equity. How does this limit your analysis of international companies?

3. The loss resulting from the transfer of one subsidiary's investment in Zip.net to another would not have been recognized under U.S. GAAP because both subsidiaries are under the common control of Portugal Telecom. However, U.S. GAAP would have required the recognition of an impairment charge of similar magnitude because the fair value of Zip.net had declined. Would this impairment loss have been extraordinary? Explain.

---

**P18-3**

Overcoming reporting diversity: Proportional consolidation

At the end of 2002, Portugal Telecom (PT) and Telefónica, the Spanish telecom company, formed Brasilcel, a 50:50 joint venture that provides mobile phone service to the Brazilian market. Under Portuguese GAAP, PT must account for this joint venture using the proportional consolidation method. Proportional consolidation requires PT to include 50% of Brasilcel's assets and liabilities in its balance sheet. Under U.S. GAAP, PT would have accounted for its investment in Brasilcel using the equity method.

PT is listed on the New York Stock Exchange, so the company files a Form 20-F with the U.S. SEC. The 2002 20-F provided a comparison of PT's actual balance sheet showing the Brasilcel joint venture under the proportional consolidation method with a pro forma balance sheet accounting for Brasilcel using the equity method. Both balance sheets, which follow, were prepared using identical accounting principles except for the treatment of the joint venture.

| (€ in millions) | December 31, 2002 | |
| --- | --- | --- |
| | **Proportional Consolidation** | **Equity Method** |
| Other assets | €13,350 | €10,646 |
| Investments | 376 | 2,277 |
| Total assets | €13,726 | €12,923 |
| Liabilities | €10,615 | € 9,812 |
| Shareholders' equity | 3,111 | 3,111 |
| Total liabilities and shareholders' equity | €13,726 | €12,923 |

**Required:**

1. Why is shareholders' equity equal under the two methods while assets and liabilities are larger under the proportional consolidation method?

2. Using PT as an example, discuss how the application of proportional consolidation might affect an investor's perceptions of a company's financial leverage and return on assets. For simplicity, assume that PT's net income plus after-tax interest was €695 in 2002 under both methods.

---

China Petroleum and Chemical Corporation (Sinopec) is a large integrated Chinese petroleum and petrochemical company. Its shares are listed on the Shanghai Stock Exchange as well as exchanges in Hong Kong, New York, and London. The company prepares two full sets of financial statements using China's accounting rules and IFRS, as well as a reconciliation of its IFRS accounts to U.S. GAAP.

A summary of the reconciliation between IFRS and U.S. GAAP follows in renminbi (RMB) currency.

**P18-4**

**Revaluing fixed assets**

| (RMB in millions) | 2002 | 2001 |
| --- | --- | --- |
| Shareholders' equity under IFRS | 154,485 | 147,669 |
| Revaluation of property, plant and equipment* | (12,699) | (16,528) |
| Reversal of impairment of long-lived assets | (608) | (667) |
| Other | (349) | (103) |
| Shareholders' equity under U.S. GAAP | 140,829 | 130,371 |
| | | |
| Net income under IFRS | 16,080 | |
| Revaluation of property, plant and equipment† | 3,236 | |
| Reversal of impairment of long-lived assets | 59 | |
| Other | 140 | |
| Net income under U.S. GAAP | 19,515 | |

---

\* The revaluation amount was credited directly to shareholders' equity, not in income.

† Adjusted for approximated tax effects.

**Required:**

1. Identify various approaches that companies can use to make their financial statements more understandable to foreign investors. What approaches has Sinopec used?

2. IFRS permits the revaluation of property, plant and equipment and reversals of impairment charges on long-lived fixed assets. These accounting differences cause IFRS shareholders' equity to be overstated relative to U.S. GAAP. However, as indicated in the income reconciliation, they also cause IFRS net income to be *understated* relative to U.S. GAAP. Explain why IFRS standards in this case cause opposite directional adjustments to the balance sheet (decreasing U.S. GAAP equity) and the income statement (increasing U.S. GAAP income).

3. What is Sinopec's return on equity (ROE) when it reports under IFRS? What is the company's ROE under U.S. GAAP? Which measure do you prefer? Explain.

Slough Estates is a U.K.-based property developer with holdings of investment properties in the United Kingdom, France, Germany, United States, and Canada. The company prepares its financial statements based on annual revaluations of its property portfolio, which are allowed under IFRS.

Information from Slough Estates' balance sheets for 2002 and 2001 include the following data:

| (£ in millions) | 2002 | 2001 |
|---|---|---|
| Investment properties (at valuation) | £3,632.6 | £3,514.2 |
| Other assets (at cost or valuation) | 598.5 | 651.2 |
| Total assets | 4,231.1 | 4,165.4 |
| | | |
| Liabilities | 1,986.0 | 1,928.8 |
| Unrealized revaluation reserves | 1,481.6 | 1,502.0 |
| Other shareholders' equity | 763.5 | 734.6 |
| Total liabilities and shareholders' equity | £4,231.1 | £4,165.4 |

Net income plus after-tax interest was approximately £136.7 million in 2002. The company also disclosed that the historical cost basis of the investment properties portfolio was £2,141.6 million and £1,999.5 million in 2002 and 2001, respectively. Despite this large difference, historical cost net income would have been essentially the same as the amount reported in the table, which was computed on a current cost basis.

**Required:**

1. Calculate Slough Estates' 2002 return on assets based on the company's published profit and loss statement and balance sheets.

2. Recalculate this ratio assuming that Slough Estates had used historical cost accounting. Which ratio would you prefer to use when analyzing the company?

3. Real estate companies commonly use revaluation accounting for their property portfolios when accounting standards permit this treatment. Speculate on reasons for this behavior.

As noted in P18–5, Slough Estates is a U.K.-based property developer that prepares its profit and loss statement and balance sheet using current cost accounting. Slough Estates' senior executive compensation is governed by the remuneration committee made up of nonexecutive directors of the company. This committee is charged with establishing performance criteria under which executives are awarded bonuses and stock options. The annual report discloses that the two performance criteria selected by committee are diluted earnings per share and net assets per share.

**Required:**

1. Describe the role that property revaluations play in setting executive compensation at Slough Estates.

2. Assume that Slough's compensation committee has assigned you to design an executive bonus scheme based on asset revaluations. What factors would you consider in setting your policy? (*Hint:* You should certainly consider who would perform the revaluations, what assets would be included, and who would control the timing of such revaluations.)

Stork N.V., domiciled in Amsterdam, The Netherlands, is an industrial company with worldwide operations. It applies IFRS in its financial statements. In a footnote to its Year 2 financial report, Stork disclosed the following current value information:

| (€ in thousands) | Year 2 | Year 1 |
|---|---|---|
| Fixed assets | 858,000 | 825,000 |
| Additional depreciation to be recorded under current value accounting | 12,106 | 12,066 |

Information from Stork's profit and loss statement and balance sheet includes the following:

| | | |
|---|---|---|
| Net income | 81,257 | 55,906 |
| Fixed assets | 692,913 | 657,315 |
| Shareholders' equity | 778,364 | 749,093 |

**Required:**

1. Using the data on Stork's profit and loss statement and balance sheet, what is its Year 2 ROE?

2. If Stork N.V. were to book the revaluation of its fixed assets, what is its Year 2 ROE?

3. Which ROE is more relevant when comparing Stork's performance to the performance of an industrial firm domiciled in the United States? Explain.

---

A recent income statement of ENH, a Swedish company that manufactures appliances, reports the following (in millions of euros):

**P18-8**

Overcoming reporting diversity

| | |
|---|---|
| Sales | 100,121 |
| Operating expense | (92,594) |
| Share of income in associated companies | (10) |
| Operating income before depreciation | 7,517 |

A footnote discloses that operating expense included the following items:

| | |
|---|---|
| Capital gains on sales of real estate | 114 |
| Losses on sales of operations | (325) |
| Capital gains on sale of shares in Email Ltd. | 204 |
| Total included in operating expense | (7) |

**Required:**

Describe how each of the items disclosed in the footnote would be reported if ENH prepared its financial statements in accordance with U.S. GAAP.

---

Both Canadian GAAP and IFRS currently allow companies the choice of expensing or capitalizing interest incurred on construction-related borrowings. Canadian Pacific Railway expenses all such interest. As discussed in Chapter 10, U.S. GAAP requires companies to capitalize "avoidable" construction-related borrowing costs.

**P18-9**

Capitalizing interest

**Required:**

1. Assume that Canadian Pacific's construction-related spending and borrowings are smoothly increasing over time. How would you expect the company's policy of expensing all construction-related interest to affect the time series of the company's reported income and owners' equity?

2. Assume that Canadian Pacific undertakes a very large bridge and tunnel construction project and incurs substantial borrowing costs during 2008. What effect would the company's policy of expensing rather than capitalizing borrowing costs have on the following for 2008?

   a. Net income

   b. Fixed asset turnover (that is, sales divided by fixed assets)

   c. Operating cash flow

   d. Return on assets

---

SABMiller was formed in 2002 when South African Breweries acquired Miller Brewing Company, thereby creating one of the world's largest brewers. The company's shares are listed in London and Johannesburg, and it prepares its accounts using IFRS.

**P18-10**

Reversing impairment losses

SABMiller's accounting policy on fixed asset impairment states,

When the [historical cost] carrying values of fixed assets are written down by any impairment amount, the loss is recognized in the profit and loss account in the period in which incurred. Should circumstances or events change and give rise to a reversal of the previous impairment loss, the reversal is recognized in the profit and loss account in the period in which it occurs and the carrying value of the asset is increased. The increase in the carrying value of the asset will only be up to the amount that it would have been had the original impairment not occurred.

In conformity with this policy, SABMiller's 2002 income statement contained the following items (in millions of U.S. dollars):

| | |
|---|---|
| Brewery closure costs in Pitesti, Romania | $ 9 |
| Asset impairment provision in Ursus, Romania | 10 |
| Reversal of asset impairment provision in Velke Popovice, Czech Republic | (11) |

**Required:**

1. How does SABMiller's accounting for fixed asset impairment differ from that prescribed by U.S. GAAP?

2. Should investors be concerned that a company's management might time the reversal of impairment provisions to smooth income or achieve other financial reporting goals? What factors would a company's auditors consider when scrutinizing such reversals?

---

**P18-11**

Capitalizing product development costs

As this chapter described, *IAS 38* permits firms to capitalize "development phase" costs incurred on internal projects once technical feasibility and other criteria demonstrating the existence of an asset are met.

Nokia, the Finnish telecommunications giant, prepares its financial statements using IFRS and, consistent with the *IAS 38* standard, capitalizes a range of product development costs.

Nokia lists its shares on the New York Stock Exchange and discloses the impact of capitalizing its various product development costs in the following U.S. GAAP reconciliation included with its Form 20-F filing. The reconciling item includes only nonsoftware development costs. Software development costs are capitalized under Nokia's application of both IFRS and U.S. GAAP.

| (€ in millions) | 2002 | 2001 | 2000 |
|---|---|---|---|
| Net income reported under IFRS | €3,381 | €2,200 | €3,938 |
| Development costs | (66) | (104) | (65) |
| Other adjustments | 288 | (193) | (26) |
| Net income under U.S. GAAP | €3,603 | €1,903 | €3,847 |

| | 2002 | 2001 |
|---|---|---|
| Shareholders' equity reported under IFRS | €14,281 | €12,205 |
| Development costs | (421) | (355) |
| Other adjustments | 290 | 171 |
| Shareholders' equity under U.S. GAAP | €14,150 | €12,021 |

**Required:**

1. Did Nokia's capitalization of development costs increase or decrease IFRS net income relative to U.S. GAAP income during 2000 to 2002? Explain. Can you expect this relationship always to hold?

2. Did Nokia's capitalization of development costs increase or decrease IFRS shareholders' equity relative to U.S. GAAP equity during 2001 and 2002? Explain. Can you expect this relationship always to hold?

3. List some reasons why a company's management might capitalize development costs.

LM Ericsson is one of the world's largest suppliers of mobile and fixed-line telecommunications products. The company is headquartered in Stockholm, with shares listed in Sweden and other European exchanges, as well as American depository receipts (ADRs) listed on the NASDAQ market in the United States. Until 2002, the company expensed all software development expenditures in conformity with Swedish GAAP. In 2002, Ericsson adopted *SFAS No. 86,* the U.S. accounting standard under which software development expenditures are capitalized when technical feasibility for that product is established. The company now amortizes software development assets over three to five years in addition to testing them for impairment annually.

In the notes to its 2002 annual report, Ericsson disclosed that its expenditures on software development totaled 3,442, 8,084, and 11,339 in 2002, 2001, and 2000, respectively. (All data in this problem are stated in millions of Swedish kronor—SEK.) The notes also disclosed that intangible assets on the balance sheet contained the newly created software development asset. This asset's value was SEK3,200 million, which was net of accumulated amortization and impairment write-downs of 242 million.

The company's 20-F filing with the U.S. SEC contained the following reconciliation to U.S. GAAP shareholders' equity and net income:

| *(SEK in millions)* | **2002** | **2001** | **2000** |
|---|---|---|---|
| Shareholders' equity under Swedish GAAP | 73,607 | 68,587 | 91,686 |
|   Capitalization of software development costs | 11,562 | 16,502 | 18,637 |
|   Other | (1,966) | (7,288) | (1,106) |
| Shareholders' equity under U.S. GAAP | 83,203 | 77,801 | 109,217 |
| | | | |
| Net income (loss) under Swedish GAAP | (19,013) | (21,264) | 21,018 |
|   Capitalization of software development costs | (4,940) | (2,135) | 4,133 |
|   Other | 4,035 | (1,004) | (1,758) |
| Net income (loss) under U.S. GAAP | (19,918) | (24,403) | 23,393 |

**Required:**

1. Would Ericsson's net income have been higher or lower than that actually reported in 2000, 2001, and 2002 had the company always capitalized its software development expenditures? Explain.

2. Assuming that the company had always capitalized its software development expenditures, what would the value of the software development asset have been in the 2000, 2001, and 2002 balance sheets?

3. What was the impact of the company's accounting change on the reported pre-tax loss for 2002?

**P18-12**

Capitalizing software development costs

---

Infosys, an Indian software company, prepares its Indian GAAP financial statements primarily using the historical cost convention. However, the company also provides supplemental balance sheets in which it books and annually revalues two self-developed intangible assets, brand equity and human resources. The disparity between these balance sheets as of March 31, 2003 can be seen in the following table:

| *(in millions of Indian rupees)* | **Indian GAAP Balance Sheet** | **Supplemental Balance Sheet** |
|---|---|---|
| Brand equity | — | 74,880.0 |
| Human resources | — | 104,170.3 |
| Other assets | 36,143.0 | 35,638.8 |
|   Total assets | 36,143.0 | 214,689.1 |
| | | |
| Liabilities | 7,078.1 | 7,032.3 |
| Shareholders' equity | 29,064.9 | 207,656.8 |
|   Total liabilities and shareholders' equity | 36,143.0 | 214,689.1 |

**P18-13**

Recording self-developed intangible assets

The pro forma entry that Infosys uses to construct its supplemental balance sheet is approximately as follows:

| | | | |
|---|---|---|---|
| **DR** | Brand equity | 74.9 | |
| **DR** | Human resources | 104.2 | |
| | **CR** Other assets | | .5 |
| | **DR** Shareholders' equity | | 178.6 |

**Required:**

1. How does Infosys's supplemental balance sheet depart from standard accounting practices used in the United States?

2. Infosys justifies recording intangibles in supplemental disclosures in its 2003 annual report by noting that "intangible assets have a significant role in defining the growth of a hi-tech company." What arguments might Infosys use to support this statement?

3. The supplemental balance sheet reports that the company's largest economic asset is "human resources." What factors would an appraiser consider when assigning a valuation to this asset?

---

**P18-14**

Providing group and parent-level financial statements

In its 2002 annual report, Nokia provides consolidated financial statements for the Nokia Group prepared under IFRS. These statements combine the annual report of the Nokia parent company, based in Finland, with those of its many subsidiaries around the world. Nokia also provides parent-level statements prepared under Finnish Accounting Standards. A summary of the 2002 group and parent-level balance sheets follows.

| (€ in millions) | IFRS Group | Finnish Parent Level |
|---|---|---|
| Property, plant and equipment | € 1,874 | € –0– |
| Investments in subsidiaries | –0– | 3,519 |
| Loans to group companies (including receivables) | –0– | 10,023 |
| Deferred tax assets | 731 | –0– |
| Other assets | 20,722 | 4,715 |
| Total assets | €23,327 | €18,257 |
| | | |
| Liabilities from group companies | € –0– | € 3,738 |
| Other liabilities | 9,046 | 2,649 |
| Shareholders' equity | 14,281 | 11,870 |
| Total liabilities and shareholders' equity | €23,327 | €18,257 |

**Required:**

Refer to Chapter 16 on consolidated financial statements for these questions.

1. Why might a parent company report no holdings of property, plant and equipment on its balance sheet?

2. Why might a parent company report no significant deferred tax items?

3. Why does the Nokia Group report no loans to or liabilities from group companies?

---

**P18-15**

Assessing inflation and monetary gains/losses

Cemex is one of the world's largest cement companies. Based in Monterrey, Mexico, the company has significant operations in such diverse economies as those of the United States, Spain, Venezuela, Colombia, Thailand, and Egypt. Some of these countries have recently experienced substantial inflation.

The following table summarizes the consolidated income statements presented in Cemex's 2002 annual report. As the chapter discussed, Mexican FRS requires companies to make various adjustments for the effects of inflation. One adjustment is to present comparative income statements and balance sheets in units of constant purchasing power. Another is to recognize a gain or loss from holding monetary items. Cemex refers to its net gain from holding monetary items as its "monetary position result."

| (in millions of constant Mexican pesos as of December 31, 2002) | 2000 | 2001 | 2002 |
|---|---|---|---|
| Operating income | 17,193.5 | 16,549.9 | 13,602.0 |
| Comprehensive financing result | | | |
| Financial expense | (4,853.6) | (4,121.6) | (3,451.6) |
| Financial income | 255.7 | 407.7 | 463.0 |
| Results from valuation and liquidation of financial instruments | (80.0) | 1,999.2 | (3,285.1) |
| Foreign exchange result | (312.9) | 1,539.6 | (800.3) |
| Monetary position result | 3,183.9 | 2,824.5 | 3,655.2 |
| Net comprehensive financing result | (1,806.9) | 2,649.4 | (3,418.8) |
| Other (including taxes) | (4,187.0) | (5,874.8) | (4,398.1) |
| Consolidated net income | 11,199.6 | 13,324.5 | 5,785.1 |

In its **2002 report,** Cemex disclosed that domestic Mexican inflation rates were 9.03%, 4.56%, and 5.53% in 2000, 2001, and 2002, respectively. These rates were substantially below those that generally prevailed in the 1990s. Cemex also provided a weighted average inflation rate computed across all the economies in which the company operates. In 2002, this multicountry rate grew from comparatively low levels to 9.16%, substantially above the domestic Mexican rate of inflation. Cemex specifically cited hyperinflation in Venezuela of 31.2% as having affected its performance in 2002.

**Required:**

1. Does holding a monetary asset exposed to the effects of inflation result in a monetary gain or monetary loss? What about a monetary liability? Explain.

2. Cemex consistently reports gains classified as "monetary position results." Is the company in a net monetary asset or liability position; that is, does the company have a higher amount of monetary assets or liabilities? Explain.

3. Why might the monetary position result for 2002 be higher than for 2000 despite the fact that Mexican inflation was substantially lower?

4. Cemex's **2001 annual report** calculates consolidated net income for 2000 and 2001 as 10,259.8 and 12,206.4 million pesos, respectively. These figures differ from the numbers for 2000 and 2001 consolidated net income as presented. Can you explain the discrepancy?

## CASES

### C18-1

Robinson Company: Making general price level and current cost adjustments

Robinson Company's statement of financial position on January 1, 2008, follows:

**Statement of Financial Position**
**January 1, 2008**

| Assets | | | Equities | |
|---|---|---|---|---|
| Cash | | $ 5,000 | | |
| Inventory | | 8,000 | | |
| Fixed asset—cost | $10,000 | | | |
| Less: Accumulated depreciation | 5,000 | | | |
| | | 5,000 | Common stock | $18,000 |
| | | $18,000 | | $18,000 |

The inventory consisted of 10 units acquired at an original cost of $800 per unit on November 1, 2007. Robinson owns only a single fixed asset that it purchased new on January 1, 2003 for $10,000. The asset has a 10-year life, no salvage value, and experiences a straight-line decline in service potential.

On June 30, 2008, 5 of the 10 inventory units were sold for $8,600 cash. Robinson's pricing strategy was based on a target return of 20% on the original cost of the assets sold and/or utilized in operations. Dividends equal to total reported historical cost income were also declared and paid on June 30. No other transactions occurred during 2008. Assume, for simplicity, that the only costs incurred were depreciation and cost of goods sold. Robinson's historical cost financial results for 2008 follow:

### Statement of Income and Retained Earnings
### Year Ended December 31, 2008

| | | |
|---|---:|---:|
| Sales revenues | | $8,600 |
| Cost of goods sold | $4,000 | |
| Depreciation | 1,000 | |
| | | 5,000 |
| Operating income | | 3,600 |
| Plus: Retained earnings, 1/1/08 | | –0– |
| Less: Dividend | | 3,600 |
| Retained earnings, 12/31/08 | | –0– |

### Balance Sheet
### December 31, 2008

| Assets | | | Equities | |
|---|---:|---:|---|---:|
| Cash | | $10,000 | | |
| Inventory | | 4,000 | | |
| Fixed asset—cost | $10,000 | | | |
| Less: Accumulated depreciation | 6,000 | | | |
| | | 4,000 | Common stock | $18,000 |
| | | $18,000 | | $18,000 |

Overall inflation as measured by the CPI was

| | | |
|---|---|---|
| Index value on | 1/1/03 | 100 |
| Index value on | 11/1/07 | 178 |
| Index value on | 1/1/08 | 180 |
| Index value on | 6/30/08 | 190 |
| Index value on | 12/31/08 | 200 |

At January 1, 2008, the replacement cost of a five-year-old fixed asset that was identical in all respects to the asset owned by Robinson was $7,000. A newer, more efficient model of this machine was introduced in early February 2003; the estimated replacement cost of the improved model in a condition equivalent to that of Robinson's asset was $8,000 on January 1, 2008. Both used asset prices remained in effect throughout 2008.

The replacement cost of the inventory on January 1, 2008 was $810 per unit. The replacement cost at the date of sale (June 30) was $875. At year-end, the per unit inventory replacement cost was $890.

**Required:**

1. Using the preceding data, compute Robinson Company's historical cost/constant dollar income for 2008 (in year-end dollars) and the December 31, 2008 historical cost/constant dollar balance sheet.

To answer this part, you must compute the gain or loss on net monetary items for 2008. This computation was not illustrated in the chapter but is straightforward. First, the net change in monetary items *in nominal dollars* as well as the causes for the change must be computed. These are:

| | |
|---|---:|
| Net monetary assets, 1/1/08 | $ 5,000 |
| Increase in net monetary assets | |
| From sales revenues | 8,600 |
| Decrease in net monetary assets | |
| To pay dividends | (3,600) |
| Net monetary assets in historical dollars, 12/31/08 | $10,000 |

Next, the timing of the increases and decreases must be established. Each took place on June 30. The beginning balance as well as the increases or decreases must be restated to their December 31, 2008 purchasing-power equivalent. For example, the January 1 balance would be adjusted by a ratio of 200/180 while sales and dividends would be adjusted by a factor of 200/190. The sum of these three adjusted figures indicates what the net monetary asset balance would have been had all monetary flows been "indexed." Comparing this number to the actual $10,000 amount in nominal dollars results in the gain or loss on monetary items.

Adjusting the income statement also requires you to carefully assess the timing of the income statement flow and to apply the appropriate index adjustment factor.

2. Based on these data, determine current cost income on a physical capital maintenance basis for 2008—that is, treat holdings gains as a direct owners' equity adjustment (other comprehensive income) rather than as an element of net income. Also prepare the December 31, 2008 current cost balance sheet. Does the current cost income number you derive provide a valid measure of the dividend that can be paid without endangering future productive capacity? Discuss.

---

**C18-2**

Comparing differences in reporting philosophies

**TOKYO, WEDNESDAY, AUGUST 19, 1992**

With another steep drop in share prices deepening the sense of crisis in Japan's financial system, the Finance Minister announced a series of measures Tuesday aimed at halting the two-and-a-half-year stock market slide. . . .

In his package . . . the Finance Minister, Tsutomu Hata, sought to put pressure on big investors not to sell shares and said financial institutions would be permitted to withhold negative financial data from the public in the hope of easing worries about the system's fundamental health. He also said steps would be taken to encourage Japanese banks to make more loans. . . .

"This was perhaps the first real admission from the Finance Minister that the situation is severe and that they have to do something," said Richard Koo, a senior economist at the Nomura Research Institute. "But as far as the content goes, I'm not impressed. . . ."

*Source:* J. Sterngold, "Japan Announces Series of Steps to Try to Halt Stock Market Slide," *The New York Times,* August 19, 1992.

**Required:**

1. Evaluate the financial reporting philosophy inherent in the Finance Ministry announcement and compare it to what you understand to be the objective of financial reporting that is designed to enhance efficient investment decisions. What are the differences? What do you think motivated the announcement?

2. What is your conjecture about the nature of the *specific* "negative financial data" that financial institutions would be permitted to withhold?

3. Do you think that the announcement achieved its intended objective?

## COLLABORATIVE LEARNING CASE

**C18-3**

Understanding non-U.S. financial statements

 **Collaborative**

LVMH Group is a French company that specializes in luxury brands in 5 industry segments. The Wine and Spirits segment includes Hennessy, Château d'Yquem, Veuve Clicquot, Moët & Chandon, Dom Pérignon, and Mercier. The Fashion and Leather Goods segment includes such companies as Louis Vuitton, Fendi, Celine, Givenchy, and Thomas Pink. The Perfumes and Cosmetics segment includes Parfums Christian Dior, Guerlain, Parfums Givenchy, and Kenso. TAG Heuer, Zenith, and Fred are part of its Watches and Jewelry segment. Its final segment, Selective Retailing, contains DFS, Sephora, and Le Bon Marché.

LVMH Group uses IFRS. The purpose of this case is to provide you with an opportunity to use your understanding of U.S. GAAP and IFRS along with logic and intuition to familiarize yourself with some of the differences between these two sets of standards. The income statement, balance sheet, and statement of changes in equity of LVMH Group follow on the next two pages.

**Required:**

1. Some of LVMH Group's terminology and account titles differ from U.S. usage. Under U.S. GAAP, what would the following LVMH Group balance sheet accounts be called? You may also wish to refer to the statement of changes in equity.

    a. Share capital

    b. Share premium account

    c. Revaluation reserves

    d. Group share of net profits

    e. Provisions (long term and short term)

2. Explain how the format of the balance sheet differs from that of U.S. balance sheets.

3. Both the income statement and balance sheet contain amounts related to "Investments in associates." Explain the nature of these investments and which accounting method is being used to account for them.

4. Refer to the statement of changes in equity. For 2006, the statement shows a decrease to "Cumulative translation adjustment" of € (411) million and an increase to "Revaluation reserves" of €259 million. What are the changes in and cumulative amounts of these accounts called under U.S. GAAP?

5. Based on your review of the balance sheet and the statement of changes in equity, what items might be expected to affect the "Revaluation reserves"? Consider the nature of LVMH Group's main subsidiaries.

6. Explain whether all of the items identified as affecting LVMH Group's "Revaluation reserves" in question 5 would be allowed under U.S. GAAP.

## Consolidated Balance Sheet

| *(in millions €)* | 2006 | 2005 | 2004[1] |
|---|---|---|---|
| **Assets** | | | |
| Brands and other intangible assets—net | 8,227 | 8,530 | 7,838 |
| Goodwill—net | 4,537 | 4,479 | 4,048 |
| Property, plant and equipment—net | 5,173 | 4,983 | 4,541 |
| Investments in associates | 126 | 128 | 115 |
| Non-current available for sale financial assets | 504 | 451 | 718 |
| Other non-current assets | 658 | 660 | 628 |
| Deferred tax | 395 | 306 | 217 |
| **Non-current assets** | **19,620** | **19,537** | **18,105** |
| Inventories and work in progress | 4,383 | 4,134 | 3,598 |
| Trade accounts receivable | 1,461 | 1,370 | 1,364 |
| Income taxes | 512 | 317 | 113 |
| Other current assets | 1,587 | 1,225 | 1,302 |
| Cash and cash equivalents | 1,222 | 1,470 | 1,035 |
| **Current assets** | **9,165** | **8,516** | **7,412** |
| **Total assets** | **28,785** | **28,053** | **25,517** |
| **Liabilities and Equity** | | | |
| Share capital | 147 | 147 | 147 |
| Share premium account | 1,736 | 1,736 | 1,736 |
| LVMH treasury shares | (1,019) | (972) | (1,006) |
| Revaluation reserves | 917 | 658 | 521 |
| Other reserves | 7,062 | 6,158 | 5,390 |
| Cumulative translation adjustment | (119) | 292 | (200) |
| Group share of net profit | 1,879 | 1,440 | 1,194 |
| Equity-Group share | 10,603 | 9,459 | 7,782 |
| Minority interests | 991 | 1,025 | 893 |
| **Total equity** | **11,594** | **10,484** | **8,675** |
| Long term borrowings | 3,235 | 3,747 | 4,188 |
| Provisions | 983 | 949 | 883 |
| Deferred tax | 2,862 | 2,925 | 2,458 |
| Other non-current liabilities | 3,755 | 3,357 | 3,237 |
| **Non-current liabilities** | **10,835** | **10,978** | **10,766** |
| Short term borrowings | 2,100 | 2,642 | 2,529 |
| Trade accounts payable | 1,899 | 1,732 | 1,581 |
| Income taxes | 692 | 373 | 201 |
| Provisions | 255 | 305 | 259 |
| Other current liabilities | 1,410 | 1,539 | 1,506 |
| **Current liabilities** | **6,356** | **6,591** | **6,076** |
| **Total liabilities and equity** | **28,785** | **28,053** | **25,517** |

[1] Data published previously under French accounting standards has been restated under IFRS.

## Consolidated Income Statement

| *(in millions € except for earnings per share)* | 2006 | 2005 | 2004[1] |
|---|---|---|---|
| **Revenue** | **15,306** | **13,910** | **12,481** |
| Cost of sales | (5,481) | (5,001) | (4,373) |
| **Gross margin** | **9,825** | **8,909** | **8,108** |
| Marketing and selling expenses | (5,364) | (4,892) | (4,512) |
| General and administrative expenses | (1,289) | (1,274) | (1,224) |
| **Profit from recurring operations** | **3,172** | **2,743** | **2,372** |
| Other operating income and expenses | (120) | (221) | (199) |

*(continued)*

| (in millions € except for earnings per share) | 2006 | 2005 | 2004[1] |
|---|---|---|---|
| **Operating profit** | 3,052 | 2,522 | 2,173 |
| Cost of net financial debt | (173) | (188) | (214) |
| Other financial income and expenses | 120 | 45 | (6) |
| **Net financial income (expense)** | (53) | (143) | (220) |
| Income taxes | (847) | (718) | (537) |
| Income (loss) from investments in associates | 8 | 7 | (14) |
| **Net profit** | 2,160 | 1,668 | 1,402 |
| of which: minority interests | 2,81 | 228 | 208 |
| Group share | 1,879 | 1,440 | 1,194 |
| **Basic Group share of net earnings per share** | 3.98 | 3.06 | 2.55 |
| Number of shares on which the calculation is based | 471,901,820 | 470,206,389 | 468,953,254 |
| **Diluted Group share of net earnings per share** | 3.94 | 3.04 | 2.53 |
| Number of shares on which the calculation is based | 477,471,955 | 474,047,257 | 472,601,925 |

[1] Data published previously under French accounting standards has been restated under IFRS.

## Consolidated Statement of Changes in Equity

| (EUR millions) | Number of Shares | Share Capital | Share Premium Account | LVMH Treasury Shares and Related Derivatives | Revaluation Reserves | Cumulative Translation Adjustment | Net Profit and Other Reserves | Total Equity Group Share | Total Equity Minority Interests | Total Equity Total |
|---|---|---|---|---|---|---|---|---|---|---|
| Notes | | 14.1 | | 14.2 | 14.4 | 14.5 | | | 16 | |
| **As of December 31, 2005** | 489,937,410 | 147 | 1,736 | (972) | 658 | 292 | 7,598 | 9,459 | 1,025 | 10,484 |
| Translation adjustment | | | | | | (411) | | (411) | (90) | (501) |
| Income and expenses recognized directly in equity | | | | | 259 | | | 259 | 29 | 288 |
| Net profit | | | | | | | 1,879 | 1,879 | 281 | 2,160 |
| **Total recognized income and expenses** | — | — | — | — | 259 | (411) | 1,879 | 1,727 | 220 | 1,947 |
| Stock option plan expenses | | | | | | | 32 | 32 | 3 | 35 |
| (Acquisition)/disposal of LVMH treasury shares | | | | (47) | | | (2) | (49) | — | (49) |
| Capital increase in subsidiaries | | | | | | | | — | 6 | 6 |
| Interim and final dividends paid | | | | | | | (566) | (566) | (120) | (686) |
| Changes in consolidation scope | | | | | | | | — | (6) | (6) |
| Effects of purchase commitments for minority interests | | | | | | | | — | (137) | (137) |
| **As of December 31, 2006** | 489,937,410 | 147 | 1,736 | (1,019) | 917 | (119) | 8,941 | 10,603 | 991 | 11,594 |

# Appendix I

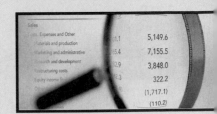

Please visit our Internet site (**www.mhhe.com/revsine4e**) for a spreadsheet template that can be used to find present value factors for interest rates not shown in this appendix.

| TABLE I | Present Value of $1 |
|---|---|

$$P = \frac{1}{(1+r)^n} = (1+r)^{-n}$$

| (n) Periods | 2% | 3% | 4% | 5% | 6% | 7% | 8% | 9% | 10% | 11% | 12% | 15% | 16% | 17% |
|---|---|---|---|---|---|---|---|---|---|---|---|---|---|---|
| 1 | 0.98039 | 0.97087 | 0.96154 | 0.95238 | 0.94340 | 0.93458 | 0.92593 | 0.91743 | 0.90909 | 0.90090 | 0.89286 | 0.86957 | 0.86207 | 0.85470 |
| 2 | 0.96117 | 0.94260 | 0.92456 | 0.90703 | 0.89000 | 0.87344 | 0.85734 | 0.84168 | 0.82645 | 0.81162 | 0.79719 | 0.75614 | 0.74316 | 0.73051 |
| 3 | 0.94232 | 0.91514 | 0.88900 | 0.86384 | 0.83962 | 0.81630 | 0.79383 | 0.77218 | 0.75132 | 0.73119 | 0.71178 | 0.65752 | 0.64066 | 0.62437 |
| 4 | 0.92385 | 0.88849 | 0.85480 | 0.82270 | 0.79209 | 0.76290 | 0.73503 | 0.70843 | 0.68301 | 0.65873 | 0.63552 | 0.57175 | 0.55229 | 0.53365 |
| 5 | 0.90573 | 0.86261 | 0.82193 | 0.78353 | 0.74726 | 0.71299 | 0.68058 | 0.64993 | 0.62092 | 0.59345 | 0.56743 | 0.49718 | 0.47611 | 0.45611 |
| 6 | 0.88797 | 0.83748 | 0.79031 | 0.74622 | 0.70496 | 0.66634 | 0.63017 | 0.59627 | 0.56447 | 0.53464 | 0.50663 | 0.43233 | 0.41044 | 0.38984 |
| 7 | 0.87056 | 0.81309 | 0.75992 | 0.71068 | 0.66506 | 0.62275 | 0.58349 | 0.54703 | 0.51316 | 0.48166 | 0.45235 | 0.37594 | 0.35383 | 0.33320 |
| 8 | 0.85349 | 0.78941 | 0.73069 | 0.67684 | 0.62741 | 0.58201 | 0.54027 | 0.50187 | 0.46651 | 0.43393 | 0.40388 | 0.32690 | 0.30503 | 0.28478 |
| 9 | 0.83676 | 0.76642 | 0.70259 | 0.64461 | 0.59190 | 0.54393 | 0.50025 | 0.46043 | 0.42410 | 0.39092 | 0.36061 | 0.28426 | 0.26295 | 0.24340 |
| 10 | 0.82035 | 0.74409 | 0.67556 | 0.61391 | 0.55839 | 0.50835 | 0.46319 | 0.42241 | 0.38554 | 0.35218 | 0.32197 | 0.24718 | 0.22668 | 0.20804 |
| 11 | 0.80426 | 0.72242 | 0.64958 | 0.58468 | 0.52679 | 0.47509 | 0.42888 | 0.38753 | 0.35049 | 0.31728 | 0.28748 | 0.21494 | 0.19542 | 0.17781 |
| 12 | 0.78849 | 0.70138 | 0.62460 | 0.55684 | 0.49697 | 0.44401 | 0.39711 | 0.35553 | 0.31863 | 0.28584 | 0.25668 | 0.18691 | 0.16846 | 0.15197 |
| 13 | 0.77303 | 0.68095 | 0.60057 | 0.53032 | 0.46884 | 0.41496 | 0.36770 | 0.32618 | 0.28966 | 0.25751 | 0.22917 | 0.16253 | 0.14523 | 0.12989 |
| 14 | 0.75788 | 0.66112 | 0.57748 | 0.50507 | 0.44230 | 0.38782 | 0.34046 | 0.29925 | 0.26333 | 0.23199 | 0.20462 | 0.14133 | 0.12520 | 0.11102 |
| 15 | 0.74301 | 0.64186 | 0.55526 | 0.48102 | 0.41727 | 0.36245 | 0.31524 | 0.27454 | 0.23939 | 0.20900 | 0.18270 | 0.12289 | 0.10793 | 0.09489 |
| 16 | 0.72845 | 0.62317 | 0.53391 | 0.45811 | 0.39365 | 0.33873 | 0.29189 | 0.25187 | 0.21763 | 0.18829 | 0.16312 | 0.10686 | 0.09304 | 0.08110 |
| 17 | 0.71416 | 0.60502 | 0.51337 | 0.43630 | 0.37136 | 0.31657 | 0.27027 | 0.23107 | 0.19784 | 0.16963 | 0.14564 | 0.09293 | 0.08021 | 0.06932 |
| 18 | 0.70016 | 0.58739 | 0.49363 | 0.41552 | 0.35034 | 0.29586 | 0.25025 | 0.21199 | 0.17986 | 0.15282 | 0.13004 | 0.08081 | 0.06914 | 0.05925 |
| 19 | 0.68643 | 0.57029 | 0.47464 | 0.39573 | 0.33051 | 0.27651 | 0.23171 | 0.19449 | 0.16351 | 0.13768 | 0.11611 | 0.07027 | 0.05961 | 0.05064 |
| 20 | 0.67297 | 0.55368 | 0.45639 | 0.37689 | 0.31180 | 0.25842 | 0.21455 | 0.17843 | 0.14864 | 0.12403 | 0.10367 | 0.06110 | 0.05139 | 0.04328 |
| 25 | 0.60953 | 0.47761 | 0.37512 | 0.29530 | 0.23300 | 0.18425 | 0.14602 | 0.11597 | 0.09230 | 0.07361 | 0.05882 | 0.03038 | 0.02447 | 0.01974 |
| 30 | 0.55207 | 0.41199 | 0.30832 | 0.23138 | 0.17411 | 0.13137 | 0.09938 | 0.07537 | 0.05731 | 0.04368 | 0.03338 | 0.01510 | 0.01165 | 0.00900 |
| 35 | 0.50003 | 0.35538 | 0.25342 | 0.18129 | 0.13011 | 0.09366 | 0.06763 | 0.04899 | 0.03558 | 0.02592 | 0.01894 | 0.00751 | 0.00555 | 0.00411 |
| 40 | 0.45289 | 0.30656 | 0.20829 | 0.14205 | 0.09722 | 0.06678 | 0.04603 | 0.03184 | 0.02209 | 0.01538 | 0.01075 | 0.00373 | 0.00264 | 0.00187 |

## TABLE 2 — Present Value of an Ordinary Annuity of $1

$$P_{OA} 5 \left(1 - \frac{1}{(1+r)^n}\right)/r$$

| (n) Periods | 2% | 3% | 4% | 5% | 6% | 7% | 8% | 9% | 10% | 11% | 12% | 15% | 16% | 17% |
|---|---|---|---|---|---|---|---|---|---|---|---|---|---|---|
| 1 | 0.98039 | 0.97087 | 0.96154 | 0.95238 | 0.94340 | 0.93458 | 0.92593 | 0.91743 | 0.90909 | 0.90090 | 0.89286 | 0.86957 | 0.86207 | 0.85470 |
| 2 | 1.94156 | 1.91347 | 1.88609 | 1.85941 | 1.83339 | 1.80802 | 1.78326 | 1.75911 | 1.73554 | 1.71252 | 1.69005 | 1.62571 | 1.60523 | 1.58521 |
| 3 | 2.88388 | 2.82861 | 2.77509 | 2.72325 | 2.67301 | 2.62432 | 2.57710 | 2.53129 | 2.48685 | 2.44371 | 2.40183 | 2.28323 | 2.24589 | 2.20958 |
| 4 | 3.80773 | 3.71710 | 3.62990 | 3.54595 | 3.46511 | 3.38721 | 3.31213 | 3.23972 | 3.16987 | 3.10245 | 3.03735 | 2.85498 | 2.79818 | 2.74324 |
| 5 | 4.71346 | 4.57971 | 4.45182 | 4.32948 | 4.21236 | 4.10020 | 3.99271 | 3.88965 | 3.79079 | 3.69590 | 3.60478 | 3.35216 | 3.27429 | 3.19935 |
| 6 | 5.60143 | 5.41719 | 5.24214 | 5.07569 | 4.91732 | 4.76654 | 4.62288 | 4.48592 | 4.35526 | 4.23054 | 4.11141 | 3.78448 | 3.68474 | 3.58918 |
| 7 | 6.47199 | 6.23028 | 6.00205 | 5.78637 | 5.58238 | 5.38929 | 5.20637 | 5.03295 | 4.86842 | 4.71220 | 4.56376 | 4.16042 | 4.03857 | 3.92238 |
| 8 | 7.32548 | 7.01969 | 6.73274 | 6.46321 | 6.20979 | 5.97130 | 5.74664 | 5.53482 | 5.33493 | 5.14612 | 4.96764 | 4.48732 | 4.34359 | 4.20716 |
| 9 | 8.16224 | 7.78611 | 7.43533 | 7.10782 | 6.80169 | 6.51523 | 6.24689 | 5.99525 | 5.75902 | 5.53705 | 5.32825 | 4.77158 | 4.60654 | 4.45057 |
| 10 | 8.98259 | 8.53020 | 8.11090 | 7.72173 | 7.36009 | 7.02358 | 6.71008 | 6.41766 | 6.14457 | 5.88923 | 5.65022 | 5.01877 | 4.83323 | 4.65860 |
| 11 | 9.78685 | 9.25262 | 8.76048 | 8.30641 | 7.88687 | 7.49867 | 7.13896 | 6.80519 | 6.49506 | 6.20652 | 5.93770 | 5.23371 | 5.02864 | 4.83641 |
| 12 | 10.57534 | 9.95400 | 9.38507 | 8.86325 | 8.38384 | 7.94269 | 7.53608 | 7.16073 | 6.81369 | 6.49236 | 6.19437 | 5.42062 | 5.19711 | 4.98839 |
| 13 | 11.34837 | 10.63496 | 9.98565 | 9.39357 | 8.85268 | 8.35765 | 7.90378 | 7.48690 | 7.10336 | 6.74987 | 6.42355 | 5.58315 | 5.34233 | 5.11828 |
| 14 | 12.10625 | 11.29607 | 10.56312 | 9.89864 | 9.29498 | 8.74547 | 8.24424 | 7.78615 | 7.36669 | 6.98187 | 6.62817 | 5.72448 | 5.46753 | 5.22930 |
| 15 | 12.84926 | 11.93794 | 11.11839 | 10.37966 | 9.71225 | 9.10791 | 8.55948 | 8.06069 | 7.60608 | 7.19087 | 6.81086 | 5.84737 | 5.57546 | 5.32419 |
| 16 | 13.57771 | 12.56110 | 11.65230 | 10.83777 | 10.10590 | 9.44665 | 8.85137 | 8.31256 | 7.82371 | 7.37916 | 6.97399 | 5.95423 | 5.66850 | 5.40529 |
| 17 | 14.29187 | 13.16612 | 12.16567 | 11.27407 | 10.47726 | 9.76322 | 9.12164 | 8.54363 | 8.02155 | 7.54879 | 7.11963 | 6.04716 | 5.74870 | 5.47461 |
| 18 | 14.99203 | 13.75351 | 12.65930 | 11.68959 | 10.82760 | 10.05909 | 9.37189 | 8.75563 | 8.20141 | 7.70162 | 7.24967 | 6.12797 | 5.81785 | 5.53385 |
| 19 | 15.67846 | 14.32380 | 13.13394 | 12.08532 | 11.15812 | 10.33560 | 9.60360 | 8.95011 | 8.36492 | 7.83929 | 7.36578 | 6.19823 | 5.87746 | 5.58449 |
| 20 | 16.35143 | 14.87747 | 13.59033 | 12.46221 | 11.46992 | 10.59401 | 9.81815 | 9.12855 | 8.51356 | 7.96333 | 7.46944 | 6.25933 | 5.92884 | 5.62777 |
| 25 | 19.52346 | 17.41315 | 15.62208 | 14.09394 | 12.78336 | 11.65358 | 10.67478 | 9.82258 | 9.07704 | 8.42174 | 7.84314 | 6.46415 | 6.09709 | 5.76623 |
| 30 | 22.39646 | 19.60044 | 17.29203 | 15.37245 | 13.76483 | 12.40904 | 11.25778 | 10.27365 | 9.42691 | 8.69379 | 8.05518 | 6.56598 | 6.17720 | 5.82939 |
| 35 | 24.99862 | 21.48722 | 18.66461 | 16.37419 | 14.49825 | 12.94767 | 11.65457 | 10.56682 | 9.64416 | 8.85524 | 8.17550 | 6.61661 | 6.21534 | 5.85820 |
| 40 | 27.35548 | 23.11477 | 19.79277 | 17.15909 | 15.04630 | 13.33171 | 11.92461 | 10.75736 | 9.77905 | 8.95105 | 8.24378 | 6.64178 | 6.23350 | 5.87133 |

## TABLE 3    Present Value of an Annuity Due of $1

$$P_{AD} \; 5 \; 1 + \left(1 - \frac{1}{(1+r)^{n-1}}\right)/r$$

| (n) Periods | 2% | 3% | 4% | 5% | 6% | 7% | 8% | 9% | 10% | 11% | 12% | 15% | 16% | 17% |
|---|---|---|---|---|---|---|---|---|---|---|---|---|---|---|
| 1 | 1.00000 | 1.00000 | 1.00000 | 1.00000 | 1.00000 | 1.00000 | 1.00000 | 1.00000 | 1.00000 | 1.00000 | 1.00000 | 1.00000 | 1.00000 | 1.00000 |
| 2 | 1.98039 | 1.97087 | 1.96154 | 1.95238 | 1.94340 | 1.93458 | 1.92593 | 1.91743 | 1.90909 | 1.90090 | 1.89286 | 1.86957 | 1.86207 | 1.85470 |
| 3 | 2.94156 | 2.91347 | 2.88609 | 2.85941 | 2.83339 | 2.80802 | 2.78326 | 2.75911 | 2.73554 | 2.71252 | 2.69005 | 2.62571 | 2.60523 | 2.58521 |
| 4 | 3.88388 | 3.82861 | 3.77509 | 3.72325 | 3.67301 | 3.62432 | 3.57710 | 3.53129 | 3.48685 | 3.44371 | 3.40183 | 3.28323 | 3.24589 | 3.20958 |
| 5 | 4.80773 | 4.71710 | 4.62990 | 4.54595 | 4.46511 | 4.38721 | 4.31213 | 4.23972 | 4.16987 | 4.10245 | 4.03735 | 3.85498 | 3.79818 | 3.74324 |
| 6 | 5.71346 | 5.57971 | 5.45182 | 5.32948 | 5.21236 | 5.10020 | 4.99271 | 4.88965 | 4.79079 | 4.69590 | 4.60478 | 4.35216 | 4.27429 | 4.19935 |
| 7 | 6.60143 | 6.41719 | 6.24214 | 6.07569 | 5.91732 | 5.76654 | 5.62288 | 5.48592 | 5.35526 | 5.23054 | 5.11141 | 4.78448 | 4.68474 | 4.58918 |
| 8 | 7.47199 | 7.23028 | 7.00205 | 6.78637 | 6.58238 | 6.38929 | 6.20637 | 6.03295 | 5.86842 | 5.71220 | 5.56376 | 5.16042 | 5.03857 | 4.92238 |
| 9 | 8.32548 | 8.01969 | 7.73274 | 7.46321 | 7.20979 | 6.97130 | 6.74664 | 6.53482 | 6.33493 | 6.14612 | 5.96764 | 5.48732 | 5.34359 | 5.20716 |
| 10 | 9.16224 | 8.78611 | 8.43533 | 8.10782 | 7.80169 | 7.51523 | 7.24689 | 6.99525 | 6.75902 | 6.53705 | 6.32825 | 5.77158 | 5.60654 | 5.45057 |
| 11 | 9.98259 | 9.53020 | 9.11090 | 8.72173 | 8.36009 | 8.02358 | 7.71008 | 7.41766 | 7.14457 | 6.88923 | 6.65022 | 6.01877 | 5.83323 | 5.65860 |
| 12 | 10.78685 | 10.25262 | 9.76048 | 9.30641 | 8.88687 | 8.49867 | 8.13896 | 7.80519 | 7.49506 | 7.20652 | 6.93770 | 6.23371 | 6.02864 | 5.83641 |
| 13 | 11.57534 | 10.95400 | 10.38507 | 9.86325 | 9.38384 | 8.94269 | 8.53608 | 8.16073 | 7.81369 | 7.49236 | 7.19437 | 6.42062 | 6.19711 | 5.98839 |
| 14 | 12.34837 | 11.63496 | 10.98565 | 10.39357 | 9.85268 | 9.35765 | 8.90378 | 8.48690 | 8.10336 | 7.74987 | 7.42355 | 6.58315 | 6.34233 | 6.11828 |
| 15 | 13.10625 | 12.29607 | 11.56312 | 10.89864 | 10.29498 | 9.74547 | 9.24424 | 8.78615 | 8.36669 | 7.98187 | 7.62817 | 6.72448 | 6.46753 | 6.22930 |
| 16 | 13.84926 | 12.93794 | 12.11839 | 11.37966 | 10.71225 | 10.10791 | 9.55948 | 9.06069 | 8.60608 | 8.19087 | 7.81086 | 6.84737 | 6.57546 | 6.32419 |
| 17 | 14.57771 | 13.56110 | 12.65230 | 11.83777 | 11.10590 | 10.44665 | 9.85137 | 9.31256 | 8.82371 | 8.37916 | 7.97399 | 6.95423 | 6.66850 | 6.40529 |
| 18 | 15.29187 | 14.16612 | 13.16567 | 12.27407 | 11.47726 | 10.76322 | 10.12164 | 9.54363 | 9.02155 | 8.54879 | 8.11963 | 7.04716 | 6.74870 | 6.47461 |
| 19 | 15.99203 | 14.75351 | 13.65930 | 12.68959 | 11.82760 | 11.05909 | 10.37189 | 9.75563 | 9.20141 | 8.70162 | 8.24967 | 7.12797 | 6.81785 | 6.53385 |
| 20 | 16.67846 | 15.32380 | 14.13394 | 13.08532 | 12.15812 | 11.33560 | 10.60360 | 9.95011 | 9.36492 | 8.83929 | 8.36578 | 7.19823 | 6.87746 | 6.58449 |
| 25 | 19.91393 | 17.93554 | 16.24696 | 14.79864 | 13.55036 | 12.46933 | 11.52876 | 10.70661 | 9.98474 | 9.34814 | 8.78432 | 7.43377 | 7.07263 | 6.74649 |
| 30 | 22.84438 | 20.18845 | 17.98371 | 16.14107 | 14.59072 | 13.27767 | 12.15841 | 11.19828 | 10.36961 | 9.65011 | 9.02181 | 7.55088 | 7.16555 | 6.82039 |
| 35 | 25.49859 | 22.13184 | 19.41120 | 17.19290 | 15.36814 | 13.85401 | 12.58693 | 11.51784 | 10.60857 | 9.82932 | 9.15656 | 7.60910 | 7.20979 | 6.85409 |
| 40 | 27.90259 | 23.80822 | 20.58448 | 18.01704 | 15.94907 | 14.26493 | 12.87858 | 11.72552 | 10.75696 | 9.93567 | 9.23303 | 7.63805 | 7.23086 | 6.86946 |

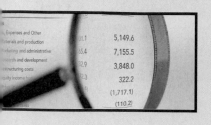

# Appendix II

## WWW/ELECTRONIC RESOURCES FOR FINANCIAL INFORMATION

*This appendix describes some of the many www/electronic resources currently available for gathering industry-level and company-specific financial information to support the text and your ongoing financial information needs. Some of these resources are free, others are available only on a "subscription" basis, and still others charge a fee per unit of time or information.*

## INTERNET RESOURCES
## WWW.MMHE.COM/REVSINE4E

**For students,** www.mmhe.com/revsine4e provides study aids, a online quizzes tied chapter-by-chapter to the text, Internet exercises, and more.

**For faculty,** Instructor's Resource Center located at www.mmhe.com/revsine4e provides access to all faculty supplements—all in one place.

## Accounting Organizations

**American Institute of Certified Public Accountants:** The AICPA is the national professional organization for all U.S. certified public accountants. This site describes the organization and answers frequently asked questions about becoming a CPA. Member resources and information about the profession are also provided. **www.aicpa.org**

**Financial Accounting Standards Board:** The FASB sets the standards for financial accounting and reporting in the United States. Its Internet site provides information about the organization's structure and workings, current standards, and emerging issues. **www.fasb.org**

**International Accounting Standards Board:** The IASB sets global financial accounting and reporting standards, promotes the rigorous use of those standards, and works toward the convergence of national accounting standards and International Accounting Standards. This site will help you stay abreast of financial accounting and reporting practices worldwide. **www.iasb.org**

**Public Companies Accounting Oversight Board:** The PCAOB is a private sector, nonprofit corporation created by the Sarbanes-Oxley Act of 2002 to oversee the audits of public companies. The PCAOB has broad authority to investigate and discipline public accounting forms and auditors. **www.pcaobus.org**

## Government Agencies

**Department of Commerce:** This site provides links to other sites, many of which have important information for businesspeople. **www.doc.gov**

**Federal Trade Commission:** This site contains a large amount of information about the Commission itself as well as the laws and regulations it administers. It also contains good links to other business-oriented sites. **www.ftc.gov**

**Internal Revenue Service:** This is a surprisingly flashy site, full of free information about the IRS and tax-related issues. **www.irs.ustreas.gov**

**Securities and Exchange Commission:** This site can be helpful for researching specific industries and companies (see also the next site). **www.sec.gov**

**SEC EDGAR Database:** This site contains electronic copies of SEC filings by publicly traded companies. The EDGAR project was launched several years ago on a voluntary basis, so not all public companies have been participating since inception. It is a valuable source for full text 10-K (annual) and 10-Q (quarterly) financial information as well as corporate proxy statements. **www.sec.gov/edgar.shtml** and **www.10kwizard.com**

## Securities Exchanges

**American Stock Exchange:** As the nation's second largest floor-based exchange, the AMEX has a significant presence in common stocks, index shares, and equity derivative securities. **www.amex.com**

**Chicago Board of Trade:** One of Chicago's two major futures and options exchanges, the Board of Trade deals in agricultural products such as corn and soybeans and in financial instruments such as U.S. Treasury bonds. **www.cbot.com**

**Chicago Mercantile Exchange:** Chicago's other futures and options exchange, the Merc has plenty of information about futures and options investing, including online courses. This site also has information on prices and the products that are traded from pork bellies to eurodollars. **www.cme.com**

**NASDAQ:** The exchange Web site of the National Association of Securities Dealers Automated Quotation (NASDAQ) has tools that help you track the market, search for stock quotes, research company information, and keep abreast of financial news. **www.nasdaq.com**

**New York Stock Exchange:** The site of the world's most famous stock exchange provides a history of the exchange and details on the companies that are added each week. You can track the movement of the entire market and find links to every listed company that has a Web site. **www.nyse.com**

## General Business News

**Newspapers:** For up-to-the-minute business news from around the world and a wealth of information about the economy and specific companies and industries, try the *Financial Times* (**www.ft.com**), *Investors Business Daily* (**www.investors.com**), *The New York Times* (**www.nyt.com**), and *The Wall Street Journal* (**www.wsj.com**).

**Financial Magazines:** *BusinessWeek* (**www.businessweek.com**), *The Economist* (**www. economist.com**), and *Fortune* (**www.fortune.com**) are just three of the many financial magazines that provide business news and analysis on the Internet.

**Financial Portals:** These sites have financial news, stock quotes, earnings projections, and information about companies and industries plus links to other useful sites. Try Microsoft's MoneyCentral (**www.moneycentral.msn.com**), The Street.com (**www.thestreet.com**), SmartMoney's Map of the Market (**www.smartmoney.com**), or the granddaddy of financial portals, Yahoo! (**finance.yahoo.com**).

# Industry and Company Information

**BestCalls.com:** Listen in via phone or Webcast to the CEO of your favorite company explaining recent performance of the business and its future prospects. The site has live broadcasts and recordings of quarterly earnings announcements and management interviews for nearly 2,600 companies. **www.bestcalls.com**

**Bloomberg Personal Online:** This is the most recent addition to the Bloomberg media family. It provides the interactive investor with data and analysis previously available only on the Bloomberg Terminal, as well as industry and company data (some at a fee) with links to other sources. **www.bloomberg.com**

**Businesswire:** This site contains information about U.S. companies both large and small, primarily in the form of press releases. **www.businesswire.com**

**Dun & Bradstreet:** This site has tips about a variety of business-related topics, as well as marketplace information. You can purchase D&B services here, too. **www.dnb.com**

**Hoover's Online:** This massive site provides information, some of which you must pay for, about thousands of companies. **www.hoovers.com**

**PR Newswire:** This is an excellent source of current news about companies. Hundreds of companies post their press releases here. **www.prnewswire.com**

# Commercial Vendors and Databases

**Factiva:** A joint venture between Dow Jones and Reuters, this service provides current and archival information about companies, industries, and important business events worldwide. The service is available by subscription and provides electronic access to business news wires, financial and trade publications, and company financial reports.

**Global Access:** This subscription service of Disclosure Incorporated offers a comprehensive searchable financial database of U.S. and international companies. It includes real-time and historical SEC filings, scanned images of annual reports, full-text articles and summaries from the financial and business press, earnings estimates and stock quotes, insider information, and investment research reports. Financial reports are downloadable to Excel or other spreadsheet formats.

**Lexis-Nexis:** This service is available by subscription. The Accounting Information Library (NAARS) includes the complete financial statement portion of annual reports for more than 4,000 publicly traded companies plus a vast collection of professional accounting literature.

**Standard & Poor's:** This service is available by subscription. The COMPUSTAT database consists of fundamental financial and market information on U.S. traded companies with hundreds of financial data items collected from a wide variety of sources including news wire services, news releases, shareholder reports, direct company contacts, and quarterly and annual documents filed with the SEC. The GLOBAL Vantage database contains detailed information on 11,000 companies from 70 countries.

# Index

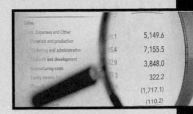

Page numbers followed by n indicate material found in notes.